ISBN 978-1-5285-3540-3
PIBN 10916791

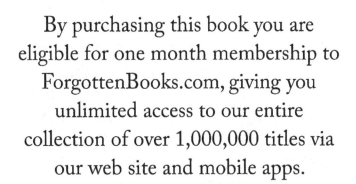

National
Municipal Revie

CONTENTS

EDITORIAL COMMENT . . . . *H. W. Dodds*
THE HOLLAND TUNNEL — AN ENGINEERING ACHIEVEMENT
THIRTY-THIRD ANNUAL MEETING OF THE NATIONAL MUNICIPAL
   LEAGUE . . . . *Russell Ramsey*
THE DEFEAT OF THE WESTCHESTER COUNTY CHARTER   *Laurence Arnold Tanzer*
FOOTNOTES AND FIELDNOTES IN OLD-ENGLAND . . . . . *Luther Gulick*
BUFFALO ADOPTS A NEW CHARTER — ABANDONS COMMISSION
   GOVERNMENT . . . . *Harry Freeman*
THE HAMBURG ELECTION . . . . *Roger H. Wells*
HOW CITY MANAGER PERSONALITIES FIGURED IN TWO ELECTIONS:
   I. CLEVELAND MANAGER PLAYS ACTIVE PART IN NOVEMBER
     ELECTION . . . . *Randolph O. Huus*
   II. CINCINNATI MANAGER LESS CONSPICUOUS BUT STILL
     INVOLVED . . . . *Alfred Henderson*
POLITICS IN CIRCLE CITY, OKLAHOMA . . . . *Harry Barth*
OUR AMERICAN MAYORS:
   VIII. MAYOR GEORGE E. CRYER OF LOS ANGELES . . *John T. Morgan*
A MUNICIPAL PROGRAM FOR COMBATING CRIME . . . . . *Bruce Smith*
RECENT BOOKS REVIEWED
JUDICIAL DECISIONS . . . . *C. W. Tooke*
PUBLIC UTILITIES . . . . *John Bauer*
GOVERNMENTAL RESEARCH CONFERENCE NOTES . . . . . *Russell Forbes*
NOTES AND EVENTS . . . . *H. W. Dodds*

PUBLISHED BY THE

NATIONAL MUNICIPAL LEAGUE

RUMFORD BUILDING, CONCORD, N. H.

EDITORIAL OFFICE, 261 BROADWAY, NEW YORK, N. Y.

THE NATIONAL MUNICIPAL REVIEW covers the field of government by means of articles, comment and news notes. It is sent to all members of the National Municipal League. Those who do not desire to become members of the League may subscribe to the REVIEW by paying five dollars a year in advance. Canada subscription rates $5.25 in advance; foreign $5.50. Single copies of the REVIEW 50 cents. Checks should be made payable to the National Municipal League and mailed to 261 Broadway, New York, N. Y.

Entered as second-class matter April 15, 1914, at the post-office at Concord, New Hampshire, under the Act of August 24, 1912. Acceptance for mailing at special rate of postage provided for in Section 1103, Act of October 3, 1917 authorized December 4, 1920.

NATIONAL
MUNICIPAL REVIEW

.

1928

VOLUME XVII

January	1 – 62		July	387 – 446
February	63 – 132		August	447 – 492
March	133 – 194		September	493 – 564
April	195 – 250		October	565 – 660
May	251 – 312		November	661 – 718
June	313 – 386		December	719 – 788

NATIONAL MUNICIPAL REVIEW
261 BROADWAY
NEW YORK

NATIONAL

MUNICIPAL REVIEW

PUBLISHED MONTHLY BY THE

National Municipal League

VOL. XVII, No. 1   JANUARY, 1928   TOTAL No. 139

CONTENTS

EDITORIAL COMMENT..........................*H. W. Dodds*.........   1
THE HOLLAND TUNNEL — AN ENGINEERING ACHIEVEMENT.............   5
THIRTY-THIRD ANNUAL MEETING OF THE NA-
    TIONAL MUNICIPAL LEAGUE...............*Russell Ramsey*........   7
THE DEFEAT OF THE WESTCHESTER COUNTY
    CHARTER.............................*Laurence Arnold Tanzer*   9
FOOTNOTES AND FIELDNOTES IN OLD ENGLAND...*Luther Gulick*.........   12
BUFFALO ADOPTS A NEW CHARTER — ABANDONS
    COMMISSION GOVERNMENT................*Harry Freeman*   13
THE HAMBURG ELECTION.....................*Roger H. Wells*........   15
HOW CITY MANAGER PERSONALITIES FIGURED IN TWO ELECTIONS:
    I. CLEVELAND MANAGER PLAYS ACTIVE
    PART IN NOVEMBER ELECTION...........*Randolph O. Huus*.....   18
    II. CINCINNATI MANAGER LESS CONSPICUOUS
    BUT STILL INVOLVED...................*Alfred Henderson*......   20
POLITICS IN CIRCLE CITY, OKLAHOMA..........*Harry Barth*   22
OUR AMERICAN MAYORS:
    VIII. MAYOR GEORGE E. CRYER OF LOS
    ANGELES..............................*John T. Morgan*.......   27
A MUNICIPAL PROGRAM FOR COMBATING CRIME..*Bruce Smith*.........   33

DEPARTMENTS

I. Recent Books Reviewed..   40
II. Judicial Decisions...*Edited by C. W. Tooke*   46
III. Public Utilities...*Edited by John Bauer*   50
IV. Governmental Research Conference Notes...................*Edited by Russell Forbes*   54
V. Notes and Events..*Edited by H. W. Dodds*   59

THE LEAGUE'S BUSINESS

Portland Prize Award for 1927.—The Portland Prize, awarded annually to a student in Reed College for the best essay in municipal government, has been granted to Wayne Woodmansee for his paper upon "The Longview Bridge Controversy." The amount of the prize is twenty-five dollars. The judges were D. W. G. Eliot, Jr. William L. Brewster and C. C. Ludwig.

❧

Proceedings of Annual Meeting Now Ready.—The Governmental Research Conference has published in mimeographed form the Proceedings of the Thirty-third Annual Meeting of the National Municipal League held in New York City on November 10 and 11 in coöperation with the Governmental Research Conference and the National Association of Civic Secretaries. The proceedings also include a full report of the separate sessions of the Conference held on November 9. This is the only complete report of the meeting which will be issued. Copies may be secured from the secretary of the Governmental Research Conference, 261 Broadway, New York, at $2.00 each.

❧

Research Conference Members Become Members of League.—The Executive Committee of the Governmental Research Conference has voted to take out individual memberships in the League for all conference members in good standing during 1928. This arrangement involves a subscription to the NATIONAL MUNICIPAL REVIEW. According to present plans the arrangement will begin with the March number of the REVIEW.

❧

The Municipal Administration Service, operating under the joint auspices of the League and the Governmental Research Conference, has issued two additional numbers in its pamphlet series on public administration. The first, entitled "The Codification of Ordinances," is from the pen of E. D. Greenman, and the other, "The Administration of Gasoline Taxes in the United States," was prepared by Professor Finla G. Crawford. Copies may be secured for 25 cents each.

❧

New League Publications.—The revised edition of the Model Charter, representing two years' work on the part of the Committee on New Municipal Program, is now ready for distribution. It makes a sizeable booklet of eighty pages and is being sold for 50 cents per copy. There will also come from the press this month the third number of the League's series of monographs. It is entitled "The President's Power of Removal," and is from the pen of Professor Edward S. Corwin of Princeton University. It is a criticism of the opinion of the Supreme Court in the recent case of *Meyers* v. *United States* which established the absolute power of the president to remove all persons in the executive service of the government. It is a matter which will be of increasing importance in years to come as public administration increases in scope and contact with the daily lives of the people. The price of the monograph, bound in boards, is $1.50.

The fourth edition of "Administrative Consolidation in State Governments" by A. E. Buck will be ready for distribution on January 15. The present edition represents a thorough rewriting and contains the latest developments as well as the valuable material of earlier editions. The price of the sixty-page pamphlet is 35 cents per copy. Reduced prices are allowed on orders in quantity.

NATIONAL
MUNICIPAL REVIEW

Vol. XVII, No. 1   JANUARY, 1928   Total No. 139

EDITORIAL COMMENT

Consolidation of the tax assessment and collection department of the city of Sacramento with that of the county is being discussed as a method of economy by the new municipal council which assumed control this month. The new council was elected last November under a pledge to appoint a new city manager to succeed Manager H. C. Bottorff at a reduced salary. The Civic League opposed the reduction of salary and the change in the manager's office, but were out-voted by those who supported the People's Ticket.

✢

Samuel S. Wyer, in a report on the Fundamentals of Our Fertilizer Problem, discovers that 165,000 tons of nitrogen could have been saved and the unnecessary smoke nuisance eliminated by substituting entirely by-product coke for raw bituminous coal used in homes in the year 1926. The unorganic nitrogen consumed in the United States during that year totalled 324,000 tons. As is well known, nitrogen convertible into fertilizer is derived from coal distilled in making the coal-gas or by-product coke. In 1926, 150,000 tons were recovered in this manner.

✢

It is with sorrow that we are compelled to announce the death of Nathan Matthews, four times mayor of Boston, who died on December 11 in the seventy-fourth year of his age. Mr. Matthews was known nationally, not only for his service as mayor of Boston but for his work on the Boston Finance Commission and his service on many public boards and commissions. He was the author of "The City Government of Boston" and "Municipal Charters," as well as of many magazine articles on political and legal subjects. He contributed from time to time to the NATIONAL MUNICIPAL REVIEW, and whatever he said was always important and helpful.

✢

The problem of the government of metropolitan areas presses more and more for consideration and calls for the highest inventive genius. After several unsuccessful attempts at annexation, the municipalities of Greater Cleveland are now discussing a borough plan of government for the area. Extensive studies are now being prosecuted to determine how this may best be secured.

Montreal also seems to be making headway towards the adoption of a common government for the Montreal region. At present the trend is towards the borough plan. J. A. A. Leclair, ex-mayor of Verdun, has proposed that the area be organized into ten or twelve boroughs each with a council and mayor of its own for the administration of local affairs. Over the entire area there would be a metropolitan council chosen by the component boroughs with a lord mayor elected by the members of the borough councils. Mayor Leclair praises the London system and terms the New York City government too autocratic. Curiously enough, these kind words for the London plan come at a time when it is under serious attack from English observers.

✦

On December 6 Tampa, Florida, voted to abandon city manager government in favor of the aldermanic form. This makes the sixth city to discard a manager charter drafted and adopted by the people under home rule powers.

Although not at this moment in possession of all the details, it appears that the effort to change the charter has been going on for some time. Last May a bill was hastily passed through the legislature providing commission government for the city and making it optional for the commission to hire a manager if they desired. The manager plan if continued at all, would thus have become merely a matter of ordinance. This charter, however, had a referendum provision attached, and it was voted down by the citizens on July 12. Subsequently a new charter commission prepared a "representative government plan" (more properly the aldermanic-mayor plan) which was accepted by the people.

The effect of the new charter is to concentrate considerable power in the hands of a mayor, elected at large at a salary of $10,000 per year. Twelve councilmen elected from districts are to receive $600 per year.

✦

Federal Investigation of Electric Power — Among the several investigations which will probably be ordered by the United States Senate, is an inquiry proposed by Senator Thomas J. Walsh of Montana into the organi-

zation, financing, production and distribution of electric power, especially in so far as these matters come within the field of interstate commerce.

The chief purpose of the resolution is to show not only the tremendous scope of holding company organization in the electric business, but its effect upon valuation, service and rates. It would establish the fact concretely,—if it is a fact,—that the methods of financing the successive consolidations which have brought a large proportion of the electric properties under the control of a few huge holding company groups have prevented, to a large extent, the passing of the economies realized on to the consumers. The claim has often been made that the prices paid for old properties have been excessive and that the reorganizations have been predicated in most instances upon high reproduction cost, so that the savings effected through the consolidations and the efficiency of centralized management are absorbed by the fixed charges imposed upon the system, with little or no benefit to the consumers. No concrete investigation of the facts has ever been made, and Senator Walsh's inquiry would greatly illuminate a situation which may not be so dark as commonly supposed.

The investigation will have importance also in bringing out the essential facts relative to the best policy to be pursued in the Muscle Shoals and Boulder Dam projects. That these properties must be developed and the benefits made available to the public at large is assumed by everybody. Whether they should be turned over to private capital under public contracts and control, or whether they should be developed directly under public ownership and operation is a question of policy which requires the consideration of many facts lightly passed over by the proponents of both sides. It is certain, however, that all essential facts and conditions will be rigorously gone into by Senator Walsh without regard to the policy which the results may tend to support. We shall follow the inquiry with unusual interest and report developments in later numbers of the REVIEW.

J. B.

*

Strikes in Public Utilities. One of the moot questions repeatedly before the public is how to deal properly with public utility strikes and lock-outs. During the past summer a tie-up of the Interborough Rapid Transit system in New York City was narrowly averted by the intervention of Mayor James J. Walker, but at the moment of writing it is again a lively possibility for the near future. How can such a situation be reasonably treated?

Such interruptions of utilities are sufficiently frequent as to constitute a major problem. Unfortunately little has been done to develop far-reaching policies. What is the best public course in dealing with labor conditions in all such fundamental industries? How can strikes and lock-outs be prevented? What machinery is necessary for adjustment of disputes? What legislative regulation should be provided to maintain proper standards of wages, hours and conditions of labor? A recent study by the Russell Sage Foundation prepared by Mr. Ben M. Selekman throws considerable light upon considerations of policy. It is entitled, Postponing Strikes: A Study of the Industrial Disputes Investigation Act of Canada. This law, enacted in 1907 and modified but slightly since, has been tested by the experience of twenty years, and should, therefore, furnish much data upon the prevention and adjustment of industrial disputes. It is primarily an act for mediation, and applies particularly to public utilities, railroads, coal and all such industries as are closely identified with public utilities. It provides for a suspension of strikes or lock-outs during a period of investigation conducted under the department of labor. The investigation is made by a "mediation board" consisting of a representative appointed by labor, one by the employers, and the third by the two or by the department of labor. The board investigates the facts in an informal way, and prepares a report with recommendations. These findings, however, have no compulsory force. After the report is made, either side is free to proceed as it pleases.

Mr. Selekman's study presents an analysis of the act, describes the administrative machinery, and analyzes the disputes that have arisen since the provisions have been in force. The act has by no means succeeded in preventing strikes, but it has brought about mediation in a large number of cases which otherwise would doubtless have resulted in costly disputes. Nevertheless, there have been many strikes in which the act and its machinery were disregarded altogether.

The Canadian act has undoubtedly provided very useful industrial machinery for mediation and in many instances has brought contending groups together in successful termination of disputes. Whether it furnishes a model for American action is, of course, difficult to state. The prevention of strikes ultimately depends upon the establishment of proper standards of employment. The act makes no direct provision for formulating and establishing better standards of labor, or for providing a constant adjustment in the industries so that labor will have little cause for strikes. This is the preventive aspect which needs particular consideration.

J. B.

The City Manager in Election Campaigns As Dr. White points out in his book, *The City Manager*, the consensus of opinion of those in the profession is that the manager should remain behind the political scene. True, not all managers have accepted this theory of exclusion, and still others have demonstrated in practice a belief that the manager belongs out in front, prompting the political actors who forget or stammer their lines and occasionally taking part in the dialogue with all the eloquence he may possess.

Nevertheless, the pure theory of the plan condemns the manager to be content with his "administrative functions"; because he is a professional, non-political official, he is to renounce any inclination to political leadership. Otherwise he becomes identified with policies and politics to which it is the peculiar duty of the council to attend, and when the people turn against a council whose policies are no longer approved, the manager falls with the politicians.

The pure theory of the manager's office thus renders him less a crusader and more a workaday chief of operations. Yet many managers have felt it their mission to bring about radical improvements in the city government, an attitude naturally encouraged by the deplorable state of affairs often encountered by the new manager of a city which has just adopted the plan. Sometimes they conceive themselves as possessed of many of the duties and obligations of a strong mayor. No permanent official in an English municipality feels such an onus of responsibility; his post is much more prosaic and, it may be added, more secure. But with us, most managers find themselves occupying the center of the stage even if they are not strong evangelical natures.

Has this position of the manager been of his own making? Perhaps the manager, irrespective of his wishes, must "get out in front" because he can't help himself. Perhaps the people, conscious of his broad powers under the charter, demand that he be a Napoleon. Perhaps it is a sound instinct which guides them to go directly to the man who controls the administration and manages the council.

The situation is well illustrated in the last elections in Cleveland and Cincinnati, described in this issue by Mr. Huus and Mr. Henderson. In Cleveland, where a proposal to abolish the manager plan was before the voters, the slogan was "Keep Hopkins." During the campaign Manager Hopkins was a familiar figure on political platforms. More than any other manager in the country, he has grasped the rôle of civic leader. He is what optimists used to hope for in the elected mayor.

But in Colonel Sherrill, Cincinnati has a manager of another type, a man who by his own profession desires to remain an operating head and the agent, not the master, of the council. In Mayor Seasongood, Cincinnati possesses a leader sufficiently strong and competent to supply the political guidance necessary in a large city, and the combination of Seasongood and Sherrill has been considered as ideal for the success of manager government in accordance with specifications. Yet in the recent councilmanic election all candidates, charter and organization alike, ran on a platform of "Support Sherrill." The very importance of his job and the success which has attended it irresistibly injected his personality into the campaign.

The above considerations will have a strong bearing upon the evolution of city managership as a profession.

THE HOLLAND TUNNEL—AN ENGINEER-
ING ACHIEVEMENT

A NEW BOND UNITING THE NEW YORK REGION

THE Holland Tunnel, officially opened on November 12 and providing
vehicular communication under the
Hudson River between New York and
Jersey City, is a small promise of what
we may expect in the future to expedite
us in getting from where we are to
where we want to go. It consists of
two tubes, the north to accommodate
west-bound traffic from the New York

20 feet in width, permitting two lanes
of traffic. Maximum speed is 30 miles
per hour, and vehicles must keep 75
feet apart. Almost 2,000 vehicles an
hour can pass through each tube. In
the first twenty-four hours of its operation, 51,748 vehicles made use of the
tunnel.

Among the novel engineering problems involved in the construction and

FULL-SIZED SECTION VEHICULAR TUNNEL COMPARED WITH HUDSON & MANHATTAN R. R.
TUNNEL

entrance plaza and the south tube
serving east-bound traffic from the
western entrance plaza in New Jersey.
On each side of the river the entrance
and the exit are located two blocks
apart, to prevent traffic congestion in
the city streets.

The roadway in each tube averages

operation of this underground passage
were those of ventilation and lighting.
Extensive experiments were performed
to determine the amount and composition of the exhaust gases from automobiles and their effect upon human
beings. As a consequence a ventilation system has been established by

which the air in the entire tunnel can be changed in a little less than one and one-half minutes. Fresh air is supplied along the roadway and the foul air is carried off through the ceiling. It is believed that failure of the air supply is impossible under any conceivable condition.

From the first it was recognized that successful operation would depend upon lighting the interior to approximate daylight. There must be no sudden strain upon the eyes of the driver coming suddenly from full daylight into the subterranean passage, no glare upon leaving it. Sharp shadows must be eliminated and the eye of the driver protected against bright lights when in transit. Artificial daylight has been attained by lights that will not go out. An essential part of the scheme are the white tiles that line the tunnel walls. As one enthusiastic visitor exclaimed, "This does not seem like a tunnel; it looks like a Childs' restaurant."

The total cost of construction was $48,000,000, to be amortized by fees received from vehicles passing through.

INTERIOR OF TUNNEL SHOWING TILE WALLS

THIRTY-THIRD ANNUAL MEETING OF THE NATIONAL MUNICIPAL LEAGUE

BY RUSSELL RAMSEY

Director, Taxpayers' Research League of Delaware

The spirit of the occasion described for those who did not attend.

It would be a doubtful compliment —and one of questionable veracity— to call the Thirty-Third Annual Meeting of the National Municipal League unusual. That it was entirely satisfactory in all its features, and that it measured up to the high standard set by the League in previous gatherings of the kind, is sufficient commendation, and is quite in accord with the truth. The coöperation of the Governmental Research Conference and the National Association of Civic Secretaries, which met in individual sessions on Wednesday, November 9, but joined with the League on November 10 and 11, contributed materially to the success of the occasion.

Were it not that Francis Oakey says that questionnaires are seldom understood, that the answers are not always given correctly, and that correct answers are sometimes misunderstood by the man who receives them, it might be interesting to attempt to ascertain by questionnaire what benefits those who attend the annual meetings of the League feel they receive beyond those that might be derived from reading the papers afterwards in the REVIEW. On second thought, the answer is so obvious that a questionnaire is quite unnecessary.

The coveted privilege of meeting old friends and acquiring new ones, the spontaneous uprising of many incidental questions and discussions, the occasion to exchange experiences with those engaged professionally or other-wise in civic work, and the opportunity for informal round-table discussion of the papers on the program—these are some of the satisfactions and stimuli that make the League's annual gatherings an oasis for those who are striving for the fulfillment of democracy.

A THREE-RING SHOW

If any one feature of the recent meeting is outstanding, perhaps it is the round-table method of discussion already referred to—a method that was used consistently and most successfully throughout the program. The papers, sometimes brilliant and always highly informative, provided a rich intellectual pasture in which to feed. The round-table discussions which followed the reading of the papers (usually one paper at each session) furnished a much needed and satisfying opportunity, venturing a homely parallel, to "chew our cud."

For historical purposes, it may as well be recorded at this point that the meeting of the League was held on November 10 and 11, 1927, in the beautiful and ample building which houses The Association of the Bar, at 42 West Forty-Fourth Street, New York, except for the luncheon session on Friday, the 11th, which filled to overflowing the Library of the New York City Club across the street.

So generous were the builders of the program, that it had to follow literally the mechanics of a three-ring circus. That is to say, at each morning and afternoon session on each day there were in simultaneous session in different rooms three round tables considering different subjects. I had occasion four times in the two days to wish that I were triplets. Some ingenious persons announced the intention of moving from one round table to another during the sessions, in order to obtain a general benefit from each. Usually they found the one they started with so interesting that they remained in it to the end.

Having confessed my lack of omnipresence, I realize I have admitted my inability to tell adequately the story of those round tables which I had not the pleasure of attending. I do not know which were the most popular, but that probably makes no difference. Nor should I venture to estimate their relative importance; that presumably is a matter of individual opinion and interest. I am impressed with the fact, however, that four of the twelve round tables were devoted to budget questions, and two to other financial subjects, so that half the time of the meeting was occupied with problems of public finance. Probably no one would criticize this distribution as being disproportionate, for after all the matter of finance permeates all public activities. Two other round tables were devoted to crime (readers of the NATIONAL MUNICIPAL REVIEW are intelligent enough not to misunderstand the meaning of this statement), two to college training, one to the molding of public opinion, and one to non-voting.

SUBJECTS OF PAPERS

At Thursday morning's opening round table on budget procedure three papers were presented—Transfers of Itemized Items, by George M. Link, secretary of the Board of Estimate and Taxation, of Minneapolis; Preventing

Over-Expenditure of Appropriations, by Joseph O'C. McCusker, budget accountant for the state of Maryland; Control of Salaries Where Standardization Is Lacking, by Charles J. Fox, budget commissioner of the city of Boston.

At the two other round tables on Thursday morning, papers were read on Special Assessments, by Philip H. Cornick, of the New York Bureau of Municipal Research, and on Popular Misconceptions Regarding Crime, by Raymond Moley, of Columbia University.

At the afternoon session on Thursday, the three round tables were occupied by the presentation and discussion of papers on The Scope and Form of the Budget Document, by H. P. Seidemann, of the Institute for Government Research, Washington, D. C.; State Supervision of Local Finances, by Philip Zoercher, of the Indiana State Board of Tax Commissioners; and What Makes Public Opinion? by Harry A. Overstreet.

On Friday morning the budget round table continued with a presentation of the tentative provisions of the proposed Model Budget Law of the National Municipal League. These provisions were explained by C. E. Rightor, of the Detroit Bureau of Governmental Research.

The second round table on Friday morning considered a paper by Bruce Smith, of the National Institute of Public Administration, on A Municipal Program for Combating Crime, while at the third were presented papers on The Case Method of Instruction in Municipal Government, by A. C. Hanford, of Harvard University, and Utilizing the City for Laboratory Work in College Classes, by O. Garfield Jones, of Toledo University.

The final series of round tables on Friday afternoon offered papers on

Executive Allotments as a Means of Budget Control, by Henry Burke, assistant budget director of North Carolina; Is the Large Slacker Vote a Menace? by Prof. W. B. Munro, of Harvard University; and University Training for Public Service, by Samuel C. May, of the University of California.

THE BUSINESS MEETING AND AFTERWARDS

The one exception to the round-table rule was the luncheon session on Friday, which constituted the annual business meeting of the League, where the table was more in the fashion of a horseshoe, bringing us by way of good luck the opportunity, in small groups, to pursue discussions unfinished at round-table sessions, and to venture into many and intimate subjects unassigned on the program. The business events of the session have, I believe, been already reported. The outstanding event of this session was the presentation of brief reports from members of those round tables which had concluded their sessions.

This bare recital of the titles and authors of the various papers must be most unsatisfactory. Even a close reading of the Proceedings as published by the Governmental Research Conference will not reproduce the atmosphere of discussion which,—in the give-and-take of question, answer, and comment, usually penetrated to the heart of the subject in hand,— must be stored up only in the memories of the participants.

If I may be permitted to modify my opening statement, perhaps the consistent use of the round-table method did mark the Thirty-Third Annual Meeting of the League as unique. It so thoroughly justified itself that it will create in those fortunate enough to have been present a keen anticipation of the Thirty-Fourth. If to others it brings a realization of having missed something worth while, they may be consoled with the prospect of another year.

THE DEFEAT OF THE WESTCHESTER COUNTY CHARTER

BY LAURENCE ARNOLD TANZER

For a second time the voters refused to desert their ancient form of county government. :: :: :: :: ::´ :: :: ::

THE proposed new charter for Westchester County, New York, defeated at the election on November 8, 1927, was the third charter proposal to be submitted.

The first draft, prepared by a nonpartisan commission, was defeated in the referendum vote at the election of 1925 by a majority of 5,000. It proposed to substitute for the present form of government a board of supervisors of forty-one members and an executive consisting of a county president, a county vice-president, and a commissioner of finance, who together were to constitute the board of estimate and apportionment, leaving the board of supervisors vested with legislative, but not executive powers. Another bill, passed by the legislature in the following year, was vetoed by Governor Smith because of its failure to provide flexibility of administration, its failure to give any protection against changes by the legislature in the charter after its adoption by the voters, and because it provided for the election of the first county officers at the time of the presidential election of 1928.

The third proposal represented an effort on the part of the Republican organization in control of the county to remove some of the grounds of objection to the former drafts. It gave the board of supervisors power to create new departments and to consolidate departments. It also restored the power of the board of supervisors over salary items in the budget to the extent of empowering the board of supervisors to reject or diminish the total amount asked for salaries for any office, board or department, without, however, dictating the amount of individual salaries. It required all elections of county officials to be held in odd-numbered years, when there would be no state or presidential elections. And finally, the charter was supplemented by an amendment to the constitution, passed for the first time by the 1927 legislature, requiring a referendum vote on any changes of a fundamental character, or which failed to meet with the approval of the board of supervisors or elicited a protest by 5 per cent of the voters.

The principal features of the charter as submitted were the transfer of the executive powers of the county from the board of supervisors to the executive officials and the board of estimate and apportionment mentioned above, with the change that in the latest 1927 proposal the board of estimate and apportionment, instead of being composed solely of the three elected officials, had added to its membership the county attorney and the county en-

gineer, appointed by the county president, thus giving him virtual control of the board; an executive budget in substantially the form adopted for the state by the constitutional amendment approved by the voters at the same election, with the qualification above mentioned as to salaries, and the greater protection from charter tinkering by the legislature which would be afforded upon the final adoption in 1929 of the constitutional amendment referred to above.

The Westchester County Civic Association, which had opposed the 1926 draft, supported the 1927 proposal as a substantial improvement, obviating the chief defects of the former draft. The Home Rule Association continued its former opposition, and attacked the charter on various grounds, some of them inconsistent with each other, and some having little relation to the merits of the proposal, and calculated to appeal to the fears of the uninformed. Officeholders were told that their offices would be interfered with, while independent voters were warned that the charter represented an attempt of the Republican machine to establish political control. It was stated to the friends of local government that the cities, villages and towns would be deprived of their local functions, which would be transferred to the county; while it was stated to the advocates of a centralized government that the charter failed to clothe the county with any new functions which would justify its adoption. Great stress was laid upon the danger of giving substantial powers to an executive head, and fears were expressed lest a possible failure to repass the constitutional amendment, to which both parties had been committed, might leave the county unprotected against future changes by the legislature. The charter was attacked in the same breath, and by the same people, for changing an existing government that was represented as having worked with reasonable satisfaction, and for not effecting a sufficiently radical improvement in the government of the county. These conflicting arguments appear to have worked on the fears of the voters much as did the similar line of attack resulting in the defeat of the proposed new state constitution of 1915, the major proposals of which have since been individually adopted.

Going deeper, the real cause of the defeat of the charter may be found in the failure to arouse and rally public interest in its support. While the question of a new charter for the county has been under discussion for some years, no single proposal has been before the public long enough for thorough public discussion. In each year a draft has been completed while the legislature was in session, has been passed through the legislature without any great amount of public discussion, and has been carried into the ensuing campaign, where the entire public consideration of the proposal was limited to the two or three weeks' period of active campaigning, in which the charter was merely one of a number of issues. The absence of any extended educational campaign, and the conse-

quent lack of public understanding of and support for the proposal, are reflected in the vote. The charter was defeated by a majority of about 12,000 out of a total vote of about 80,000. At the same election there were cast for the office of commissioner of public welfare, the only county officer voted for, 119,000 votes. Of the votes cast for this county officer, some 39,000, or one third of the total number, failed to vote on the charter at all. In other words, voters equal in number to 50 per cent of those voting for and against the charter failed to record themselves either for or against it. In view of the aggressive campaign that was waged against the charter, it may be assumed that all who were actively opposed to it, out of interest or fears, registered their negative vote, and that the 39,000 voters who failed to vote either were not interested in the proposition at all, or were not convinced of the necessity or of the merits of the proposal. The vote evidences a lack of understanding and interest in the proposal rather than any overwhelming opposition to it. The result would appear to indicate the need of a more extensive campaign of education if any reform is to be effected in the government of the county.

FOOTNOTES AND FIELDNOTES IN OLD ENGLAND

BY LUTHER GULICK

Old Sarum's decline and fall in terms of modern city planning.

THE town of Old Sarum in the Salisbury Plain is only a footnote in the histories of electoral reform. Until the Reform Act of 1832, it was the rottenest rotten borough of England, with two parliamentary representatives and no true population. For over a hundred years, the Pitts owned the manor and solemnly elected themselves, including the great William, to Parliament. The electors met in an open field under an old oak tree. But now even the oak tree is gone. It, too, was rotted through and fell some years ago.

The editor of the REVIEW and I strolled across the stretch of rolling meadow and climbed up the steep grass-covered hill to see Old Sarum. Though it was a holiday and the thoroughfares were busy with motorists and sightseers on their way to Stonehenge and Salisbury, we seemed to be the only pilgrims who had turned aside here.

Old Sarum should be of interest to the city planners. It is a city which evaporated because of bad planning. It was originally a Saxon and then a Roman citadel. Parliament met here in 960. And here, in 1070, William the Conqueror assembled and paid off his victorious army. So it was once quite a city, with its conical hill, well defended with earthworks, moats, and drawbridges, and crowned with a castle with twelve-foot stone walls and a great tower. Within the outer walls was the cathedral which was finished by Bishop Osmond in 1092. The houses of the soldiers, the priests, and the townsmen were huddled about the cathedral, though part of the population spilled out through the eastern and western gates into the plains. This was the city that gradually but completely moved away, carrying with it almost every hewn stone, to build a new town with new walls and a new cathedral a few miles away in Salisbury. You can detect many of these Norman-worked stones today in the precinct wall of Salisbury Cathedral.

The reasons for the abandonment of the old town were, in modern terms: the housing problem, a limited water supply, the inadequate health program, the traffic problem, and friction due to the division of authority. Probably peace, or at least a change in the technique of warfare, finally robbed the fortress of its value, but this was long after the town had been abandoned. Evidence of the difficulties of the town is found in a petition to move the religious establishment which was addressed to Pope Honorious III in 1217. It was as follows:

They state that the Cathedral Church, being within the line of defence, is subject to so many inconveniences that the Canons cannot live there without danger to life.

Being in a raised place the continued gusts of wind make such a noise that the clerks can hardly hear one another sing, and the place is so rheumatic by reason of the wind that they often suffer in health.

The Church they say is so shaken by wind and storm that it daily needs repair, and the site is without trees and grass, and being of chalk has such a glare that many of the clerks have lost their sight.

Water, they say, is only to be got from a distance and often at a price that elsewhere would buy enough for the whole district.

If the clerks have occasion to go in and out on business, they cannot do so without leave of the Castellan; so that on Ash Wednesday, Holy Thursday, and on Synodal and Ordination and other solemn days, the faithful who wish to visit the Church cannot do so, the keepers of the Castle declaring that the defences would be endangered.

Moreover, as many of the clerks have no dwellings there, they have to hire them from the soldiers, so that few are found willing or able to reside on the spot.

This complaint was investigated and the petition granted. The new cathedral was built in the plains and the population followed to the new town. The old town became little more than a quarry, and many years later even the cathedral, the bishop's house, and the homes of the canons were carried away

to the new town and built into its cathedral and walls. The castle was used as late as 1360, when there was a French scare, but even then it must have been a pitiful spectacle. Except for recent excavations, not a stone would be visible now above the surface of the ground and its heavy turf of wild grass.

For the city planner, this whole episode would have been much more valuable if all the mistakes of Old Sarum had been intelligently avoided in the new town. The churchmen did learn, and laid out their cathedral with what is now one of the finest church enclosures in all England, but the townsmen did not do quite so well, though even here the streets may not be quite so narrow or crooked as in some of the other old towns.

BUFFALO ADOPTS A NEW CHARTER— ABANDONS COMMISSION GOVERNMENT

BY HARRY H. FREEMAN
Director, Buffalo Municipal Research Bureau

Buffalo has returned to mayor-council government on a partisan basis after twelve years of commission government and the non-partisan ballot. :: :: :: :: :: :: :: :: :: ::

AFTER twelve years' experience, Buffalo has definitely given up commission government. A new charter, approved by the electors in August, 1927, became effective January 1, 1928, and Buffalo passed from "the largest city under commission government" to a less conspicuous standing in the list of mayor-and-council communities. Many Buffalonians will waste no tears over this apparent loss of caste.

The charter campaign, during August, was a spirited contest. Defenders of the commission government

charter pointed what they claimed to be a wonderful record of achievement during the past twelve years in schools, parks, playgrounds, harbor development and water supply, and insisted that any worthwhile features could be added to the existing charter by amendment.

On the other hand, advocates of the proposed charter called attention to the trebled city budget and assessments under commission government, pointed out that there have already been over 180 amendments made to the existing charter without much improvement being seen and stressed the many fine administrative provisions of the new document.

The vote on the new charter was 53,041 divided as follows: For, 32,079; against, 20,962.

THE NEW CHARTER

The charter commission, in its address to the electors, stated that it carried on its work with two thoughts constantly in mind, *i.e.*, to rid the city of what they considered was "an automatic form of city government" and to bring about "a separation of the taxing power from the spending power."

To entrust to any five men, the power to expend each year the sum of $58,000,000 and, at the same time, almost unlimited power to tax citizens annually $47,000,000 of this amount seems to us a gross misconception of the American ideals of government.

The new charter provides for:

A mayor, elected for a four-year term and ineligible to succeed himself. An annual salary of $12,000 is provided, but not effective until January 1, 1930.

A comptroller, elected for a four-year term. His salary is fixed at $8,000 per year, and he is not limited as to the terms he may serve.

A council of fifteen members, five of whom, with the president, are elected at large, and nine from nine newly created council districts. The terms of councilmen-at-large and president are four years and they are ineligible for the next succeeding term. District councilmen are elected for two-year terms and are ineligible to serve more than two succeeding terms. The salary of a councilman was fixed at $2,500 a year and the salary of the president at $6,000 a year.

The administrative service is divided into eleven departments, viz., the executive, audit and control, treasury, assessment, public works, police, fire, health, social welfare and law, paralleling in all but the executive existing departments or branches of the city government. The executive department was given four main divisions of budget, purchase, license and markets, each to be headed by a director to be appointed by the mayor without confirmation by the council.

The mayor is given power of appointment, subject to confirmation by the council, of important administrative officers such as the commissioner of public works, corporation counsel, director of parks, police, fire, etc. The mayor's power of appointment, however, does not become effective until January 1, 1930. Until that date such appointments are to be made by a board of three composed of the mayor, comptroller and president of the council. This restriction was made because the present mayor holds over for two more years, the unexpired balance of his present term of office.

The new charter contains many provisions of merit governing the city's business and administrative methods, such as an executive budget, centralized purchasing, better control over expenditures, expediting public work, cleaning up deficiency bonds, opening the "closed door" on paving, etc.

THE NEW GOVERNMENT

At the recent November election, the new councilmen, president of the council and comptroller were elected. As the new charter provides for partisan nomination and election, the political parties came back into municipal affairs for the first time in more than twelve years. Both the Republican and Democrat parties were torn by internal dissensions and each had regular and insurgent tickets in the September primaries. This proved costly to the regular organizations, especially the Republican, for, while the organization and "re-organization" candidates for council president were cutting each other's throat, an outsider, who is credited with being an Independent and sometimes accused of being a Socialist, captured the Republican nomination. He won an easy victory at the polls. The Republicans also elected the comptroller, the five councilmen-at-large, and filled eight of the nine district council seats. As the hold-over mayor is also Republican, responsibility of municipal affairs in Buffalo, for the next few years, has been definitely placed upon the Republican party.

Local sentiment over the results of the election was admirably summed up in an editorial in the Buffalo *Courier-Express*, issue of November 9:

For several years past, Buffalonians have wagged their heads at the actions of the council and said that things would not be so if there had been party nominations instead of the non-partisan system. With the sweeping win of the Republican party yesterday, this theory can be demonstrated most effectively. The new council is composed of excellent timber. It has the brains, ability, and power and with proper leadership should do much to regain the respect due to those who administer municipal affairs.

THE HAMBURG ELECTION

BY ROGER H. WELLS
Bryn Mawr College

Politics, campaign methods, and election procedure in Germany's second largest city.   ::   ::   ::   ::   ::   ::   ::   ::

1927 was an "off year" in German politics, with no national elections and relatively few state and local elections taking place. Of the latter, the election on October 9, 1927 of the house of burgesses (Bürgerschaft) of the city-state of Hamburg was probably the most interesting and most significant. The importance of the Bürgerschaftswahl arose not only from the fact that Hamburg is the second largest city in Germany and a great trade and commercial center, but also from the fact that the national parties are already preparing for the choice of a new Reichstag in 1928.

SPIRITED PARTISAN CAMPAIGN

"As goes Maine, so goes the Union," is an old adage in the United States, and while Hamburg is perhaps not to be regarded as a similar political barometer, nevertheless, the election in that state was viewed with interest in all parts of Germany. This was especially true of the national party organizations which supplied "heavy artillery" for the campaign in the form of speeches by prominent party leaders imported from other states. National, state, and local politics are inextricably mixed in Germany—more so than in the United States—and this fact was obvious in the propaganda and political rallies in Hamburg. At one Democratic mass meeting which the writer attended, national issues were chiefly discussed and aroused such heckling and disorder from Communist and Nationalist hearers that the presiding officer sarcastically reminded the audience that they were not called upon to elect the president of the Reich on October 9.

As for the campaign in general, it was spirited and spectacular, even when measured by American standards. While no professional gunmen were employed, as sometimes happens in cities of the United States, still there were broken heads on various occasions when extremist elements met. Several hundred political rallies were held by the various parties, to say nothing of the picturesque torchlight parades of the Communists and Socialists. Posters, newspaper articles, advertisements, and handbills were widely used, particularly the latter. The Social Democrats estimated that they alone distributed about three million "Wahlzeitungen" and "Flugblätter." Hence, it was not surprising that the usually clean streets were littered with thousands of handbills. Although not as untidy as American city streets on Armistice Day, 1918, yet one could at least say that "the street cleaning department reaped a magnificent paper harvest."

As usual, the election was held on Sunday. While the church bells rang out to summon the citizen to his Sabbath devotions, numerous auto-truck loads of noisy partisans with fife, drum, and bugle, reminded him of his civic duty. Just one thing was lacking in the whole picture, namely, the use of the radio for political propaganda. Unfortunately (or fortunately; it depends upon the point of view), this is forbidden in Germany.

LIST SYSTEM EMPLOYED

The Hamburg house of burgesses is composed of one hundred and sixty members, elected for a three-year term, according to the list system of proportional representation.[1] In this con-

nection, it may be recalled that Hamburg was one of the first German states to introduce proportional representation.[2] That step was taken in 1906, but the existing system is very different from the one provided in the original law of that year. At present, the voter votes for the party and only for the party; he cannot "split" his ticket, express any preference for particular candidates, or change the order of the candidates' names as determined by the party.[3] Moreover, the parties themselves may not combine to form a united "Bürger" List or "Left" Ticket. The only combination that is permissible is that between lists of the same party in the two electoral areas (Wahlkreise) into which the state is divided. The first of these areas comprises the city proper and elects one hundred and fifty members; the second is the surrounding rural area which chooses ten members. The seats are allotted to the parties according to the d'Hondt quota method, but any remaining votes in the rural Wahlkreis are transferred to the credit of the same party in the urban Wahlkreis.

At the 1927 election, a total of nine parties placed 572 candidates in the field. In the 1924 Bürgerschaftswahl, there had been fifteen tickets, five of which secured no representatives whatever, and five more of which had only eleven seats combined. In order to prevent such "Splittergruppen,"

---

[1] Arthur Obst, ed., *Die Verfassung der Freien und Hansestadt Hamburg* (2nd ed., Hamburg, 1926). This work also contains the present law governing the election of the house of burgesses.

[2] Proportional representation was also introduced in Württemberg in 1906. See C. G. Hoag and G. H. Hallett, *Proportional Representation* (New York, 1926), pp. 282–283. See also Carl Albrecht, *Das Hamburger Bürgerschafts-Wahlgesetz* (Hamburg, 1906).

[3] The ballot contains the names of the parties numbered in consecutive order as determined by lot with a party circle after each name. Underneath the party title are the names of the four leading candidates (Spitzkandidaten) in fine print.

the Hamburg election law was amended on June 27, 1927, so as to provide:

1. That the number of voters' signatures required for candidates' nominating petitions be increased from 30 to 3,000 (1,000 for the rural Wahlkreis), but this provision does not apply to any party which already has one-sixteenth of the total number of representatives in the Bürgerschaft or Reichstag. For such parties, thirty signatures are enough.

2. For each ticket placed on the ballot (official ballots have been used since 1924, but the official envelopes are also still employed), a deposit of 3,000 marks is required which is forfeited to the state if no candidate from the ticket is elected.

This second provision is, of course, similar to the English rule for parliamentary elections and is likewise found in one other German state, Saxony, where it was adopted in 1926.[1] At the recent election, only one deposit was forfeited, that of the Catholic Center Party in the rural Wahlkreis.

A SWING TO THE LEFT

The results of the polling indicated a swing toward the Left, a drift which was likewise apparent in the recent city elections in Königsberg and Altona and in the state election in Mecklenburg last summer. This is clearly shown by the following comparative table of the Hamburg Bürgerschaft elections of 1924 and 1927.

Although the Middle and Right parties have been weakened, it is not yet certain that the present party composition of the senate (i.e., the cabinet) will be greatly changed.[2] The Social Democrat-Democrat-People's Party coalition may continue as heretofore but with the Social Democrats holding a larger proportion of the cabinet seats; or the Socialists and Communists may join forces, and forget the bitter warfare which has previously divided those parties in Hamburg and elsewhere. At the present writing, this issue is not yet settled.

During the campaign, extraordinary efforts were made to arouse the non-voters and overcome their lack of interest and "Wahlmüdigkeit." It was thought that the non-voters chiefly belonged to the "Bürger" or Middle

---

[1] Filing fees for nominating petitions are required in Brunswick and in Lippe, but these are not returnable. See Walter Jellinek, *Die deutschen Landtagswahlgesetze* (Berlin, 1926) *passim*.

[2] Although Hamburg is primarily a city, it has the legal status of a state and, as such, is required by the constitution of the Reich to have a parliamentary form of government. The term "senate" instead of "cabinet" is very misleading to an American.

Name of party	Number of representatives	
	1924	1927
Kommunistische Partei	24	27
Sozialdemokratische Partei	53	63
Deutsche Demokratische Partei	21	16
Deutsche Volkspartei	23	18
Zentrumspartei	2	2
Mittelstandspartei	2	6
Volksrechtpartei	..	1
Deutschnationale Volkspartei	28	25
Nationalsozialistische Deutsche Arbeiterpartei (Hitler's party)	4	2
Other parties (in 1924 only)	3	..
	160	160

and Right parties, as the Socialist and
Communist machines have something
of Tammany's efficiency in "delivering
the vote." The election returns
showed an improvement over the 1924
Bürgerschaftswahl but were still rather
disappointing in view of the great
exertion put forth and the exception-

ally favorable weather conditions. In
this connection, it may be of interest
to note the following comparative
table which shows Hamburg's voting
record since 1919:[1]

[1] *Statistisches Jahrbuch für die Freie und Hansestadt Hamburg, 1926–1927* (Hamburg, 1927), p.
404.

Year	Election	Percentage of qualified voters voting
January, 1919	National constitutional convention	90.41
March, 1919	Bürgerschaft	80.55
June, 1920	Reichstag	74.53
February, 1921	Bürgerschaft	70.90
May, 1924	Reichstag	78.42
October, 1924	Bürgerschaft	66.06
December, 1924	Reichstag	76.20
March, 1925	Reichs President	70.27
April, 1925	Reichs President	78.23
June, · 1926	Volksentscheid (Initiative over princes' property)	57.48
October, 1927	Bürgerschaft	74.24

HOW CITY MANAGER PERSONALITIES FIGURED IN TWO ELECTIONS

RECENT HISTORY IN CLEVELAND AND CINCINNATI

I. CLEVELAND MANAGER PLAYS ACTIVE PART IN NOVEMBER ELECTION

BY RANDOLPH O. HUUS

Western Reserve University

AFTER having been in operation for
three years and ten months the council-
manager plan in Cleveland met its
first direct test at the polls on November 8, when the voters defeated three
charter amendments and a proposal for
a commission to revise the present
charter. The effect of the vote was to
keep the present plan in operation
without change. Two of the amendments were in reality new charters,
both providing for a return to the dis-

carded mayor-council form. The only
change proposed by the third amendment was the abolition of proportional
representation and a return to the
ward system and the preferential ballot
for councilmanic elections.

The only amendment to receive serious consideration was the one sponsored by Harry L. Davis, ex-mayor of
Cleveland and former governor of
Ohio. By the close vote of 80,148 to
73,732 this amendment was rejected.

It provided not only for the mayor-council form but the ward system and plurality elections for councilmen.

The Davis forces contended early in the campaign that the only real issue was the relative merits of the two forms of government. For obvious reasons such a campaign was out of the question. On the one side was the strong personal following of Davis and his recent political activities in and out of public office. Add to this the resentment of members of the Cleveland Federation of Labor against City Manager W. R. Hopkins for alleged unfriendly acts. On the other side was the outstanding place of Mr. Hopkins in the city's government and the record achieved under the council-manager plan. Under such circumstances a discussion of personalities, records and motives was inevitable.

In short order the Davis forces centered their attack, not so much on the iniquities of the council-manager plan and proportional representation, as on the policies of Maurice Maschke and Burr Gongwer (respectively the local Republican and Democratic party leaders) and on Mr. Hopkins and his official record. And the anti-Davis forces (some favoring the council-manager plan as such and many not, but all against the Davis amendment) attacked the past record of Mr. Davis in public office and questioned the sincerity of his expressed desire to "return the government to the people" in view of provisions in his charter favorable if adopted to his possible candidacy for mayor. Quickly and decisively the political speeches, the propaganda, the newspaper write-ups and the editorials became concerned primarily with the personalities and records of W. R. Hopkins, city manager, and Harry L. Davis, ex-mayor. Billboards and placards urged the voter to "Keep Hopkins." Newspaper headlines featured Hopkins and Davis rather than either form of government, e.g., "Calls Women to Support Hopkins," "Stand by Hopkins, Maschke Advises," "Labor Fights for Davis to Get Hopkins." And it was apparent that at the political meetings W. R. Hopkins and Harry L. Davis were the centers of interest. An outsider might easily have thought that the two men were the rival candidates for mayor. In the nature of the case the personality and record of the city manager became directly involved in the campaign.

MANAGER HOPKINS' CAMPAIGN ACTIVITIES

With this in mind let us consider the campaign activities of City Manager Hopkins. During the three weeks of active campaigning Mr. Hopkins was a familiar figure on political platforms. He spoke in every section of Cleveland and frequently a number of times during an evening. But his talks were not like those of the average mayor seeking reëlection,—they differed both in substance and in presentation. The customary political fireworks were not lacking, however, being supplied by a corps of speakers representing all of the factions opposing the Davis charter amendment. Often sitting on the same platform with Mr. Hopkins these speakers vigorously attacked the past record of Mr. Davis, his present political motives, his labor group support and particulars in the amendment. They stressed the accomplishments of City Manager Hopkins and party allegiance as well, but said little or nothing about the city manager plan and proportional representation as such. One reason for this is that many of the selected speakers represented the viewpoint of the leaders of the party organizations who are unfavorable to the new form of government.

The city manager's talks were in contrast to those described above. On the whole he was successful in limiting them to two subjects,—an endorsement and explanation of the city manager plan and a review and defense of the accomplishments under the city manager plan. He carefully avoided the personal or partizan approach. However, during the latter part of the campaign he tended to become more directly and personally involved. This resulted from his direct replies (without mentioning any names) to attacks made by Davis speakers on his administrative record. City Manager Hopkins has none of the mannerisms of the political stump speaker—rather he gives the impression while talking of an able executive presenting a report to his board of directors. His speeches are factual, lucid and interesting and his presentation direct and conversational in tone.

Was City Manager Hopkins justified in taking the active part in the campaign that he did? The writer believes that under the circumstances he was. The particular task Mr. Hopkins performed in the campaign was to acquaint the voter with the record of the present administration. It may be objected that the public defense of the conduct of the government under the council-manager form is the responsibility of the mayor or other leaders of the dominant faction in the council. It is doubtful if any of the other leaders of the dominant faction (the Republican) had the willingness or the peculiar qualities of leadership necessary. Mayor John Marshall did take an effective and active part in the campaign, but in no sense did he supplant City Manager Hopkins in this respect. Certain obvious reasons suggest themselves:

1. There is no clear mandate in the city charter to the mayor to assume such responsibility.

2. The mayor is also a councilman and must concern himself with his own reëlection in his particular district.

3. The council-manager mayor does not represent the voters at large since he is elected from one of the four districts, as the other councilmen.

4. The outstanding position of Mr. Hopkins in the city government.

In conclusion it is worth noting that the candidates for the council stressed primarily their records, platforms or party allegiance rather than their relation to the present administration—probably due to their fear of losing votes among the many supporters of the Davis charter amendment.

II. CINCINNATI MANAGER LESS CONSPICUOUS BUT STILL INVOLVED

BY ALFRED HENDERSON

Cincinnati "Times-Star"

City Manager Clarence O. Sherrill, although not an "issue" in the recent Cincinnati municipal election campaign, received a splendid endorsement not only because all candidates elected to the city council were pledged to him and his work but by reason of approval by the voters of a series of bond issues by unprecedented majorities.

Colonel Sherrill was the instigator and inspiration of a capital improvement program providing for bond issues aggregating nearly $9,000,000, a very large amount in Cincinnati except for such self-sustaining purposes as the Cincinnati Southern Railway, the rapid transit system and the new water works.

Many of the bond issues at the recent election were approved by so much as three to one majorities and none received less than a two to one favorable vote. This is all the more convincing because for years under previous administrations bond issues were uniformly voted down. A year ago, after ten months of the Sherrill administration a large bond issue was approved, yet it was predicted this year the people would reverse their verdict and vote down the bond issues.

This prediction was the more confidently made because of the increase in expenditures under the Sherrill administration and a higher tax levy. So when Sherrill came forward early in the fall this year with even a larger bond program some of the reputed wise while admiring his temerity were sure he would meet the fate of the rash and reckless.

Yet in spite of these prophets of evil and the misgivings of not a few doubting Thomases among his closest friends, Colonel Sherrill, right on the eve of the election, issued a signed statement in favor of all the bond issues to go to a referendum of the voters. Thus the die was cast, the hazard was taken by a man who could well have remained silent and content with the declarations of loyalty of all councilmanic candidates having a shadow of chance of election.

SHERRILL BACKS BOND ISSUES

Colonel Sherrill in his statement definitely identified the fate of the bond issues with his own fortunes, and he and his friends are justified in accounting the result of the bond ballot as a vote of confidence in his administration.

During the campaign there was not a little open criticism of specific incidents of the administration and particularly of the increase in taxes as compared with the previous city administration, but on the stump and in the press the fault was ascribed not to Sherrill but to his "wicked" advisers, much like the practice in the days when monarchy was in flower and the doctrine obtained that the "king can do no wrong."

Yet Colonel Sherrill has never essayed the rôle of a king nor has he ever sought to influence the action of the legislative branch of the Cincinnati city government, thereby making himself a contrast to some other city managers. At the same time Sherrill has not hesitated to make unprompted suggestions to the city council and even to the so-called independent boards and commissions. But he has, many think, leaned backwards, in avoiding even a suspicion of invading a coördinate branch of the municipal government.

The political complexion of the new city council will remain the same as the present, except that the regular Republican organization will have two of the nine members instead of three, the third having been defeated at the polls and an independent elected along with six accredited Citizen Charter Committee candidates. The six are the same men as before, save that Julius Luchsinger declined to run again and is succeeded by Charles Eisen.

Mayor Murray Seasongood was re-elected councilman with an increased vote under proportional representation. Under the Cincinnati charter the mayor is elected by the council.

The independent elected is Municipal Court Judge W. Meredith Yeatman, a Republican in national politics.

POLITICS IN CIRCLE CITY, OKLAHOMA

BY HARRY BARTH

University of Oklahoma

The fate of a good city manager in a town that knows its politics. Of course the names are fictitious. :: :: :: :: ::

CIRCLE CITY is a quiet town of eight thousand people, and twenty miles of concrete pavement, in no way distinguished from the other communities which dot the Oklahoma plains. Yet an election was held last spring which is worth describing. The affair arose over the city manager who was turned out of office as the result. Its interest, however, lies not so much in the fact that one manager was superseded by another, as in the light which the incident can throw upon the operation and theory of the managerial plan, and the picture which it presents of small town politics.

DRAMATIS PERSONÆ

The two leading characters were Pat McQuillan, city manager, and Elmer Bristow, mayor. Today Pat is in the surveying business in Circle City. Elmer runs the leading dry goods store, and is one of the city's big business men. Pat is quiet, unassuming, conscientious. Elmer is ambitious and forward, a glad hander. Pat, on the other hand, is afraid of people and would never rate as a good fellow. Elmer is genial and comradely. There is more to Elmer than the typical Rotarian, for under cover he gives the impression of calculating chances and weighing proposed roads to political eminence with a canny shrewdness. Also, he seems to have a certain ruthless quality which causes him to keep his eye on the main chance, and to go rough-shod over those who stand in his way. He should go far in Oklahoma

politics, although of course you cannot be sure. Frequently a man who seems to have all the qualities for success in politics will carry along a weakness which will wreck his career. Elmer may have trouble in convincing the tenant farmers of Oklahoma of his sincerity, and it is these who wield a potent influence in politics in our state. His calculating is a trifle too obvious, and this hurt him even among Circle City's business men who worship the self-centered man at their noonday luncheon clubs.

The facts are complicated and involved, and it is hard to be sure of them. Yet one stands out clearly, and that is that Pat was an efficient city manager. When Pat took office four years ago the city was operating at a loss. An earlier manager, brought in from outside Circle City, had proved an unmitigated crook. He let paving contracts at five dollars a square yard for concrete, and mulcted the water revenues. After he had left town hurriedly, the people decided that thereafter they would have local men, with whose background they were familiar. Their next manager was honest, but he did not stand as well as he might have with certain fraternal organizations. Pat followed. In two years he cleaned up a deficit of four years' standing, and finally made sizable cuts in the tax rates. During his last year he reduced the rate for city purposes from fourteen to eight mills, and this included the sinking fund levy.

His chief achievements centered

around the water works, just as they must with any city manager who is to be a success in the plains country. Water is scarce where the West begins and ability to secure a usable supply is the best criterion of good government. Pat found that it was costing around a thousand dollars a month to pump water from Circle City's deep wells. He called in experts, substituted oil-burning Diesel engines for the old coal-burning steam outfit on their advice, and now in spite of an increased consumption, Circle City pumps the water for two hundred and fifty dollars per month.

It was necessary to make extensions to the water mains and the sewer system. Bids were asked, and the lowest was for twelve thousand dollars for the work, the city to furnish the material. Pat thought this was a hold-up, and considered doing the work by direct labor. He found that by purchasing a ditch-digging machine and hiring labor, he could do the work for seven thousand. The books, which have been checked by a certified public accountant, indicate that his savings were about one half of the contract price, even writing off one-third the cost of the ditch digger against this one job. The savings paid for the machine and left a surplus of three thousand.

The streets were kept clean, the fire department was efficient, the police were far less listless than in the average town. Police court fines were unusually high, thanks to the stop lines and traffic frogs which were placed at bad crossings. In the other fields, the administration of the manager was equally successful.

The efficiency of the manager was not an issue in the campaign. The only changes made by the manager who followed Pat were to use yellow paint to mark stop lines instead of white paint, to make the police buy new uniforms and to dismiss some policemen and firemen to make room for friends. The new manager consults the old constantly. There have been no modifications of policy.

MANAGER'S ACHIEVEMENTS USED AGAINST HIM

If one is to look for the causes of Pat's defeat one must seek elsewhere than in the operation of the city government. Surprising enough, the chief cause was the ditch digger. There is no question as to its value. It snorts down the streets and literally rips a lane in the ground at a much faster clip than manual labor. Its only fault is that it puts men out of work. Circle City has a laborer's ward and this was strong on the side of the mayor. You cannot fool these Oklahoma laborers. They know their interests when they see them, and, in the words of a local politician, they turned out "strong as horse radish" against Pat on election day, and the candidates favoring Pat were beaten by two hundred votes, a comparatively small number. The ditch digger must probably assume responsibility.

There was another side. Ed Hunter is in the plumbing business. As soon as the old city manager decided on digging his ditches and laying his pipes directly, he antagonized every contractor who might have gotten the job. Ed ran for commissioner on a platform of honesty and efficiency and he said that if he were elected, the ditch digger would never be used again. Ed won, though in fairness to the other commissioners and the new manager it must be said that the ditch digger is still being used. However, had it not been for the city going directly into the contracting business, Pat would have been spared a number of enemies.

If one analyzes the situation further, he will find that another money-saving measure played a part in the manager's downfall. This was the adoption of the Diesel engines. On the face of things one would imagine the use of these engines a feather in the manager's bonnet. Unfortunately there was an alternative to the engines, and this was electric current. Why not pump the water with electricity, purchased from the Circle City' Power Company, asked the mayor when the matter of the engines came up. There was much bitter strife and many heated meetings. The Diesel engines won out on the advice of engineers, but the battle left scars. This particular utility is notorious for its interference in local politics. The old manager says he has no evidence that the Power Company tried to affect the results of this election, but here again was a source of irritation.

THE MAYOR HAD AMBITIONS

One further element entered into the situation, and this was the ambitions of the mayor. There seems little doubt but that in a few years he plans to run for state office. He is generally credited with this objective by the business men of Circle City, while every move he makes seems directed toward this end. The city manager appointed to take Pat's place is a state house politician with wide connections over the state. In time of elections he makes an excellent campaign manager. He has run for state office several times and knows his political wires. Elmer, the mayor, has also consistently played the rôle of defender of the utility companies. These are powerful in Oklahoma. Their public relations counsels are many and their lobbyists able. One cannot trace any direct connection between utilities and politics, and yet there is much circumstantial evidence. At any rate Elmer has always fought for them. His attitude when the issue

of the Diesel engines came up is illustrative.

The mayor wanted control of the city government of Circle City, and the manager stood in his way. The men are temperamentally antipathetic. The election was a battle to the death.

THE ELECTION

Circle City has a commission of five members. The terms of office overlap,—three commissioners are chosen every other year. Four of them hold office for four-year terms, the fifth for two years. The commissioner chosen every two years has the title of mayor and is the presiding officer. When the spring of 1927 came around, as usual the mayor and two commissioners were up for election. Elmer ran for mayor and chose the plumbing contractor and a local celebrity as his running mates. Pat put a ticket in the field. His candidate for mayor was a physician with a wide acquaintance. His candidates for commissioner were both young men of untried caliber.

Mud flew thick as Oklahoma hail, and anyone who stuck his head above the parapets stood a fair chance of being plastered. The only real question, theoretically, at least, should have been the competence of the manager, but, of course, this was never considered. Popular interest was great. It was not the interest which comes when real issues are at stake, but rather the attention which is aroused by a sporting event.

Each side probably spent over a thousand dollars in the primary. Most of this went to buy advertising in the local paper, whose owner sat in his swivel chair and beamingly raked in the cash in advance. There were other expenses. Elmer sent a personal letter to each voter in town and also got out handbills. Dr. Jones distributed posters broadcast. There was abundant "literature."

Elmer began almost all of his advertisements with "Dear Folks," a salutation calculated to rouse a warm feeling of comradeship. He then went ahead and told how much he had lowered taxes and how excellent had been the administration of the water works. He cheerfully claimed credit for every accomplishment which the manager had achieved. Meanwhile Pat sat in his office and swore.

PAT A POOR POLITICIAN

Pat's campaign was singularly mismanaged. All his friends could say was, "Look at the efficiency of our city government." They could not find a single issue to arouse emotions. They were just ordinary matter-of-fact men, while Elmer is a political artist of some ability. Then there was the feeling abroad that after all Pat had been drawing a good salary (two hundred, later three hundred dollars per month) for four years. Was not that long enough?

Elmer played his trump card when he brought in the hospital issue. Some years ago the citizens built a hospital by private subscription. This has never done very well, and is always more or less financially embarrassed. On two occasions the physicians in town have tried to get the people to take it over as a municipal hospital, and on both occasions without success. The citizens are opposed to the idea, for it means higher taxes, besides endless litigation, as Oklahoma cities are held liable for negligence in hospital operation. Elmer accused the opposition of planning to saddle the hospital on the city. The fact that the candidate of the manager was a physician lent color to the charge. The manager's group answered by saying that they could not take over the hospital without a direct vote of the people even if they wanted

to. The mayor's charge, however, was a shrewd political move, and there may have been some basis for it.

At this point the leader of the hospital crowd became excited. On the afternoon before the election the *Democrat*, a local paper, carried a large advertisement stating that Elmer some weeks back had asked the leader of the hospital group not to put a candidate in the field against him and had stated that he would back the hospital in exchange for support at the election. The same evening Elmer had handbills over the city accusing the signer of the ad of lying. "Dear Folks," he said, "the doctor who published the malicious and scurrilous ad in this evening's paper is a liar. Dear Folks, do you want liars to run your city?" There is still speculation among Circle City's people as to who the liar was, though evidence points strongly in one direction.

By this time the election was far away from anything remotely concerning the real issues. In good old American fashion, red pepper had been sprinkled over every significant trail, and emotions had been roused to supercede whatever of reason the average man possesses. The citizens, prepared by the diverting spectacle of a row between toreadors, went forth to decide a question whose real merits they cared not a rap about. The votes were counted and the only apparent result was that a competent city manager went down to defeat.

He probably deserved what happened to him. How can a man stay in office, if he cannot make a speech? What right has a man who is not a good mixer to hope for preference? Furthermore, he bungled in his selection of candidates. If he had not picked a physician as his candidate, the hospital issue could never have been raised. That he was a good manager was, of course, irrelevant.

POLITICS AND THE MANAGER PLAN

Can any lessons for the managerial plan be drawn from this election? We must recognize the fact that a single election is not conclusive; but this affair illustrates one point, and this is that the efficiency of a manager is no guarantee that he will hold his office. In fact, efficiency may, as in this instance, be a handicap. If the manager had done things in the good old way, he might still be in office. Hylan's defeat of John Purroy Mitchell in 1916 in New York was wondered at, for it substituted one of New York's sorriest mayors for one of her best. This sort of situation seems more widespread than is usually believed. Here in Oklahoma is another instance of a man being turned out of office for doing his job too well.

The manager is often in a position where he is up for election every time his commission is elected, and must go into the political arena every time the voters go forth to cast their ballots. Here is the chief weakness of the managerial plan. The managerial plan, as it worked out in Circle City, is in no essential different from the mayor-council plan. Just as the mayor comes up for reëlection under the mayor plan, so the manager. The only difference is that the manager does not have as good a chance as the mayor, for he must stand or fall partly on the merits of the men he selects as his candidates for commissioner, while the mayor is voted on directly. This analysis may not hold generally. Possibly Circle City is in a class by itself. There is no point in being didactic, and we trust that we are mistaken.

Even though our conclusion is correct, and even though the manager cannot be taken out of politics, still there is reason for the adoption of this plan in preference to the mayor-council system. After all, the managerial plan does contain the idea that an expert should run the city's affairs rather than a politician. In course of time, this idea may bear fruit.

Certainly Circle City gives a good picture of a manager caught in the maw of local politics, and illustrates the vicissitudes liable to befall him. Personal enemies, ambitious politicians, disgruntled office seekers, antagonistic laborers, dissatisfied contractors all unite to make a manager's tenure insecure. While the good people of the town who are benefited by efficiency, and theoretically, at least, demand it, seldom rush to his defence. No one ever had the cockles of his heart warmed by the slogan of economy.

One point more. The eastern cities rather pride themselves on the politics which goes on in their borders. After talking to a Chicagoan about Big Bill Thompson or to a New Yorker about Hylan, one feels that he takes a certain pride in the magnitude and finesse of the game these politicians play. But the western cities can give a good account of themselves also. No one can live through elections in Circle City without feeling that out in the wide-open spaces we know our politics too.

OUR AMERICAN MAYORS

VIII. MAYOR GEORGE E. CRYER OF LOS ANGELES

BY JOHN T. MORGAN

*Mr. Cryer has thrice been elected mayor of Los Angeles. Each
reëlection was in spite of the opposition of the leaders who first gave
him to the city. Hydro-electric power is practically the only issue.*

To know George E. Cryer, mayor of
Los Angeles, it is first necessary to
know and understand Los Angeles
itself, for it is hardly probable that Mr.
Cryer would be chosen the mayor of a
large eastern city, and it is beyond
possibility that Los Angeles would
select as its mayor, the type of official
eastern cities ordinarily place in office.

Drawing its new citizens from the
Middle West in the main, and from the
state of Iowa in such numbers that the
fact is made the subject of numerous
witticisms, Los Angeles has doubled its
population within the period of a few
years and continues to grow rapidly.
Still feeling old home ties, these newcomers take but a passing interest in
Los Angeles political affairs. They
apparently care little who heads the
city government so long as the Southern California sun continues to shine
and their real estate investments prove
profitable. They decline to become excited over municipal elections.

POLITICAL LINES LOOSELY DRAWN

The resulting situation is that the
Los Angeles lines of political demarcation are loosely and indistinctly drawn.
There is but one permanent political
issue, municipal ownership. Other
issues come and go, but they are always
minor and never lasting. With 90 per
cent of its population native-born
Americans and the greater proportion
of these coming from stock of several
generations of residence in this country,

there is no racial issue. The only large
colony of foreign-born is the Mexican,
and it displays no interest in civic
affairs. Elections are conducted without red fire, shootings or stolen ballot
box scandals. The question of religion,
a paramount issue in many other cities,
seldom makes its appearance in a
campaign and, when it does, only in the
form of whisperings which receive little
attention and are of no effect.

Between elections, the city goes
about its business, giving little thought
to affairs at the city hall beyond the
universal grumbling over tax bills.
During campaigns it listens somewhat
impatiently to the usual declamations
of the out's who desire to become in's
and the in's who desire with equal
fervor to remain such, gives a snap
decision and returns to work. Those
citizens whose interests are directly or
indirectly affected by the conduct of
the municipal government of course
pay strict attention the year round.
They are many in number but few in
comparison to the bulk of the city's
population.

Los Angeles has six metropolitan
daily newspapers. At times one or
more of these publications become vo-
ciferous in denouncing this or that in
connection with the administration in
power. Laying the groundwork for
the next municipal campaign, two of
these papers representing the out's are
busily engaged at present in criticising
Mr. Cryer, his policies and his political

friends. The amusing feature of their attacks is that one of them, the *Los Angeles Times*, was responsible for Mr. Cryer's first election to the mayor's chair, and the other, the *Evening Ex-*

MAYOR CRYER DISPENSING CALIFORNIA'S FAVORITE FRUIT

press, aided and abetted its contemporary.

MAYOR CRYER DISCOVERED

M. P. Snyder was mayor of Los Angeles from 1919 to 1921. He is one of the city's well-known business men and had been mayor twice before, once for a two-year term beginning in 1897 and again in 1903. During his first two terms, Mr. Snyder, known as "Pinky," was credited with being a "silk stocking" mayor. He was friendly with the conservative elements of the city. Then, elected for a third term, he was charged, rightly or wrongly, with being too close to elements which had a great deal to gain from police leniency. These elements distrusted him because of his previous record in office, and the conservatives turned against him because of his reputed new alliances.

With the cards thus stacked against Mr. Snyder, *The Times*, to the utter surprise of the wise ones, brought forth George E. Cryer as a candidate for mayor. Mr. Cryer is an attorney. For several years he was chief deputy district attorney for Los Angeles county. Previous to this, he was an assistant United States district attorney, and a deputy city attorney. His name was well known to news readers, incidental to his labors as a responsible yet minor official. Otherwise, he had registered very lightly on the public mind previous to his becoming a mayoralty candidate. Few knew where he stood on public questions, and included among the many who apparently lacked such knowledge was Mr. Harry Chandler, wealthy publisher of *The Times*, one of the large figures in the political and business life of California, implacable enemy of municipal ownership and sponsor of Mr. Cryer.

With the conservative forces of the city, *The Times*, the Southern California Edison Company and the old guard Republicans supporting him, Mr. Cryer defeated Mr. Snyder by a narrow margin in the final election. In the primary Mr. Snyder was given a larger vote than Mr. Cryer but, with the elimination of minor candidates,

Mr. Cryer won in the general election. Mr. Chandler and his corporation friends were very happy over the result. They imagined they had a man in the mayor's office who would be tractable and amenable to reason. Shortly they were completely disillusioned.

SURPRISES BACKERS BY FAVORING MUNICIPAL OWNERSHIP

Almost before he had accustomed himself to the furniture in the mayor's office, Mr. Cryer began this process of disillusionment. He announced himself to be a firm friend of the municipal department of water and power, competitor to the powerful Edison Company and extremely distasteful to Mr. Chandler, especially the power division of the department. He became the political friend and ally of Senator Hiram W. Johnson. Mr. Chandler and Senator Johnson hate each other with a hatred so bitter and consuming that it has become a tradition in the political life of California. Senator Johnson denounces the Edison Company as being a large and vicious tentacle of the power octopus.

Mayor Cryer has become a leader in the movement for the Boulder Canyon project for the building of a great dam on the Colorado River. Mr. Chandler and the Edison Company lead the Southern California opposition to the plan. The mayor was the Southern California chairman for the campaign committee of Governor C. C. Young, a Johnsonite who defeated former Governor Friend W. Richardson, Mr. Chandler's personal possession, at the last state election in 1926.

Mr. Chandler and his friends started Mr. Cryer on the political highway, but at the first crossroads he took the wrong turn as far as they were concerned and never has looked back. That Mr. Cryer failed to follow the course marked out for him on the municipal ownership issue has been painful to his original backers, for it is this issue, with its many ramifications, local, state-wide and national, in which Mr. Chandler and the Edison company are especially interested. It is probable that outside the municipal ownership question they care but little who runs the city's business so long as they are in a position to obtain desired street improvements and other minor favors. But when it comes to the city entering the power business, or making a bid for electricity from the proposed Boulder dam, they shudder with horror.

This shuddering began when Los Angeles built the Owens Valley aqueduct, going 250 miles north into the snow-capped High Sierras to obtain a water supply sufficient to keep pace with its astonishing growth. Immediately it was found that in its course from the mountains to the city, the aqueduct has a 3000-foot fall, thereby creating opportunity for the generation of hydro-electric power. When a plan for the construction of power generating plants to take advantage of this opportunity was announced, the Southern California power corporations, of which the largest was and still is the Southern California Edison Company, marshalled their forces in opposition. Mr. Chandler supported the aqueduct, but looked with disfavor on the power phase of the project. Municipal ownership advocates won their fight, and five such municipally-owned plants have been built.

THE FIGHT WITH THE EDISON COMPANY

This opposition has continued throughout the years and has resulted in many bitter and spectacular political battles. Time and again the people of Los Angeles, voting on bond issues or other propositions in which the municipal ownership issue was involved, overwhelmingly have indicated their approval of the city's course, but the Edison Company and Mr. Chandler never have given an inch except when forced. In 1922, the municipal ownership forces won a major battle to have the city purchase and take over the Edison Company's Los Angeles distributing system, thus making the city a real factor in the power field. Forcing the Edison Company beyond the Los Angeles boundaries, the municipal bureau of power and light lowered rates to its customers and caused its one remaining competitor, the Los Angeles Gas and Electric Corporation, close ally of the Edison Company, to do likewise.

Today the battle has extended to the Boulder dam project and has become nation-wide in its scope. The Los Angeles power corporations, closely related to the National Association of Public Utility Corporations, have called on that powerful body for aid in preventing passage by congress of the Swing-Johnson bill for the development of the water and power resources of the Colorado River. This bill provides that the government shall construct a high dam at Boulder Canyon, thus providing not only vitally needed flood protection for the fertile Imperial Valley, but hydro-power available for purchase by Los Angeles and all other sections of the Southwest.

It is readily understandable, then, how Mr. Chandler is so strenuously opposed to the Swing-Johnson bill and to Mr. Cryer. The mayor has come to be one of the forceful leaders in the campaign for the bill, and Mr. Chandler has at least two moving reasons for wishing it to be defeated. One reason is the All-American Canal provision in the bill which, if enacted, will have the effect of safeguarding the domestic and irrigation water supply of American citizens in Imperial Valley, California. The All-American Canal project, Mr.

Chandler fears, may interfere with his plan of developing, with cheap Mexican peon and Chinese coolie labor and in competition to the American farmers, some 800,000 acres of Mexican land just below the border now possessing a decided advantage over the American ranches in the matter of a water supply from the Colorado River.

The second reason is that of Mr. Chandler's business associates, the private power corporation men. The power corporation operators naturally realize the tremendous hydro-electric possibilities of the Colorado River. Consequently, they desire to monopolize the dam building and operating business on the river, and bitterly oppose the suggestion that this work be carried forward by the government. Mr. Cryer is the mayor of Los Angeles and as such his leadership in the Boulder dam fight has helped materially to advance the campaign for this project. This fact has caused Mr. Chandler and the Edison Company much grief and, undoubtedly, they look back to 1921 and wish they had picked another man to run for mayor— any other man.

In no other large American city could such a political accident have happened. Mr. Chandler and his friends, and the public as well, would have known to which "gang" he belonged, where he stood and where he was going to remain to stand. It is not likely that Mr. Chandler will make this same mistake again, but the voters, having placed their hands in the grab bag and, luckily, drawn something to their liking, as has been evidenced by their twice returning Mr. Cryer to office, will, in all probability, blithely repeat the performance at first opportunity.

EFFORTS TO DEFEAT CRYER

That Los Angeles really likes George Cryer, despite mistakes of his administration, was thoroughly demonstrated when he was reëlected for the second time. His first reëlection was practically by default, Mr. Chandler and his friends apparently not having recovered from the shock of their candidates' "desertion"; but in 1925 they made a heroic effort to displace Mr. Cryer.

Inducing Federal District Judge Benjamin F. Bledsoe to resign, they pitted him against the mayor and spent much time and money in a vain attempt to gain control of the city hall. Their choice was an unfortunate one, for Judge Bledsoe, dictatorial on the bench and possessed of a Wilsonian belief in his own destiny, campaigned in such a way that he lost supporters more rapidly than *The Times* and its allies could manufacture them. The judge was president of the Los Angeles Grand Opera Association, held teas for women campaigners, permitted sewing thimbles to be given away as gifts to feminine voters and equivocated at length on the Boulder dam issue. Cryer supporters plastered the city with posters caricaturing Chandler and Bledsoe and captioned "Harry calls him Ben." Again Mr. Cryer was reëlected at the primary despite the fact that there were three other candidates in the contest. The conclusion may be drawn that Los Angeles likes its mayors plain, not fancy. Mayor Cryer's elections in 1921 and 1923 were for two-year terms; his 1925 election, in accordance with a change in the city charter, carried with it a four-year term.

THE MAYOR ANALYZED

George Cryer is plain, in the best sense of the word. He appears to be unassuming to the point of bashfulness. He is accused of lack of decision, but his friends say that there is no foundation for the charge, that he merely declines to take snap judgment and

that, judicially rather than executive-minded, he demands of himself that his conclusions be certain and well supported before he acts. Personally he is well liked even by those who attack his administration most vigorously. He is a Presbyterian, went to church regularly before he became a candidate for office and still goes. He plays golf and likes it. During the Spanish War he enlisted and was the first sergeant of a company of California volunteers. "Top kickers" usually have minds of their own. Mr. Cryer makes mistakes, but seldom makes the same one twice.

When he first took office he was a halting and hesitant public speaker, but, while he will never be an orator, he soon developed into a pleasing and facile talker. He has come to realize the vital necessity of publicity for political success but, nevertheless, appears inwardly embarrassed when called upon to participate in some publicity "stunt." His appointments to Los Angeles municipal offices have not always resulted fortunately, but when analyzed have revealed good and practical reasons. At one time he was called upon to fill a vacancy in the presidency of the board of harbor commissioners. He sought a business man of real qualifications for the position, but could find no one of sufficient size who would accept the appointment.

One, Edgar McKee, a real estate dealer, appeared at the mayor's office, armed with a sheaf of recommendations a foot thick and containing endorsements from scores of the most responsible bankers and business men of the city. Not impressed with McKee, the mayor continued a diligent search for a man fully qualified for the post, but without success. Finally he appointed McKee. Later it became necessary to remove McKee, it having been found he had accepted a suit of clothes from persons seeking favors of the board.

Mr. Cryer was strenuously attacked, but barely mentioned the fact that the position had gone begging for weeks.

The Los Angeles mayor was born in Nebraska and was brought to California by his parents when a child. He was graduated from the University of Michigan Law School. Forty-six years of age when first elected mayor and fifty-two now, Mr. Cryer makes no secret of the fact that he is ready and willing to step down from his executive position. His ambition is to become a member of the supreme court of the state. With the Johnson-Young administration in power the ambition may be gratified. In any event, it is practically certain that the mayor, in 1929, will decline to be a candidate to succeed himself.

In making up his mind that he is through in so far as municipal politics are concerned, Mr. Cryer very likely was influenced by a natural desire for promotion in the public service, but the character of the recent attacks upon his administration by *The Times* and its little brother, *The Express*, has convinced him that public officials whether they be good or bad, right or wrong, lead miserable lives. Los Angeles has the largest area of any city in the world. It is a community composed of small communities. Within its boundaries are Hollywood, where motion pictures are made and where the residents find it difficult even to remember the name of the city's mayor, and San Pedro, the city's port, twenty miles away.

Like a ten-year-old boy still clothed in rompers, Los Angeles needs boulevards and highways, street lights and other improvements. The city must dress itself as becomes its size. Residents of one neighborhood petition for paving or ornamental lights. Residents of another neighborhood want additional police protection. They are unanimous and persistent in these desires. All these things cost money, and when the tax bills are sent out there is a wail which makes a calliope sound like a whisper.

To point out that the taxpayers themselves gave the order and that they must pay the bill avails nothing. To cite the fact that Los Angeles has the third lowest tax rate of any of the twelve largest cities of the nation, merely brings upbraidings.[1]

Mr. Cryer has said that he wishes to resign his office because of the illness of Mrs. Cryer, but the continual pounding of the hammer wielders, the out's who want in for their own purposes, undoubtedly has brought the mayor to the point where he is anxious to relinquish the job of being a target in an exhibition where he has no more chance than the colored boy sticking his head out of a hole in the canvas at an amusement park sideshow. The boys heave tomatoes at him and he cannot dodge.

[1] EDITOR'S NOTE. — C. E. Rightor's adjusted comparative tax rates published in the December REVIEW do not give Los Angeles quite so favorable a position.

A MUNICIPAL PROGRAM FOR COMBATING CRIME

BY BRUCE SMITH

National Institute of Public Administration

The city's part in the fight against crime.

THE objection may be raised that there is very little that the municipality, of its own motion, can do to reduce the number of serious law infractions within its borders; that prosecutors, courts, sheriffs, coroners, and jailers are for the most part under state or county control; that the penal law and code of criminal procedure are state-wide in their effect, and may be revised only through action by the state legislature. These things are true and, so far as is known, there is nowhere a serious intention to bring any of such matters within the exclusive sphere of municipal authorities.

There are two fields, however, over which the municipal government may exercise a considerable influence. The causes which underlie the commission of criminal acts, if they once can be identified, may be profoundly influenced by city departments without too much dependence upon other administrative agencies; and the local police forces are now almost everywhere under direct municipal control.

As between the elimination of crime causes and improvement in police administration, it is probable that the latter offers the greater immediate opportunity. The things which make for crime are deeply imbedded in what we loosely term "human nature," and run through the whole warp and woof of our social institutions. There is scarcely an unwholesome external influence which, at some time or other, has not been identified as a cause of criminality. While it is clearly the task of the municipality to attack these matters with vigor, it is just as clear that positive and substantial results can only be secured after years of unremitting effort.

It is otherwise with the police. They are more readily affected by administrative action. In fact, they are highly responsive to all of the many influences which are brought to bear upon them, both official and unofficial. If the unofficial influences have sometimes become so strong as virtually to control the functioning of the police force, the municipalities have themselves to blame. With a few partial exceptions, they have provided neither a sound organization nor a sound discipline.

It therefore would appear that the police provide the natural focus for municipal efforts directed at combating crime. What, then, is the present status of police administration in the cities of this country? What has been accomplished and what things have been left undone? One might well hesitate to commit oneself to generalizations in such a broad and varied field, but it is believed that the statements of fact which follow are at least substantially true.

POLICE CONTROL

We find that police boards as devices for multiple control are slowly

33

but surely disappearing, particularly in the larger cities. In their stead, however, is a marked disposition to combine police, fire, health, weights and measures, and sometimes building inspection service, under a single administrative agency, bearing the engaging title of "department of public safety." This, of course, is a necessary expedient under commission government charters, but it is also becoming fairly common under mayor and council charters, and occasionally under the commission-manager plan as well. As a result, the old problem of securing continuity of administrative control remains with us, as well as the question of how to distinguish between the proper fields of the civilian and technical heads of the force. Multiple police control has reappeared in a different guise.

It must be conceded that there is a certain theoretical justification for vesting control of the entire public safety function in a single commissioner. There is, without question, a certain degree of coöperation required between a police and fire department, or between a police and health department. But a scheme for coöperation which depends upon continuous amicable relations between independent authorities is clearly faulty. The consolidation of these various services under a single commissioner may be viewed as an attempt to meet the situation. Beyond this point, the disadvantages of this system heavily outweigh its single theoretical advantage. The difficulty involved in trying to differentiate between the proper fields of the public safety commissioner and the police chief is generally recognized. Another objection arises from the fact that the commissioner of public safety is usually an official bird of passage, while the police chief customarily enjoys a much more extended tenure

of office. Changes of administration bring new commissioners into the picture, men who are unfamiliar with police administration, but who proceed to impose their views upon police headquarters. Under these circumstances, conflicts are natural and almost inevitable. They finally become the outstanding feature of police administration in the cities where this plan is followed.

Where the commission form of government has been adopted, it is difficult to see how anything can be done to cure this police problem without changing the entire scheme of government under which the city operates. Elsewhere, however, a vigorous and courageous handling of the matter will satisfy practical police needs without extensive charter revision. If the cities which have consolidated their public safety services, as well as those which have set up civilian and technical heads of their police departments, will meet the issue squarely and provide a single responsible administrator with complete powers and sufficient guarantees of official tenure to protect him against removal with each change of administration, a very substantial advance will have been made.

There is great concern in some quarters as to what official qualifications should be demanded of such a police executive. There are those who believe that he should be recruited directly from the police force. To these, it should be sufficient to answer that the job of the police administrator is after all rather remote from that of the professional policeman. Others maintain that the administrative head should be drawn from outside the force, from groups which are alien to the deadening effects of police routine. These seek their administrators among certain professional groups, such as the law and the military, without any great confidence that they are on the right track.

It is submitted that the key to the situation is to be found in establishing security of tenure for the administrative head. That obtained, the official himself may be recruited from a considerable number of callings. The essential things are that he shall be vigorous and resourceful in thought and action, of unblemished integrity, and possess marked capacity for handling men, because the essence of police administration consists in the intelligent direction of personnel. As time goes on, the administrator will acquire and develop a technique of police administration. When that time comes, the police department will be on a sound basis so far as overhead control is concerned, and a beginning will have been made towards a solution of the municipality's police problem.

THE CIVIL SERVICE QUESTION

It must be admitted that a complicating factor appears at this point. We have been contemplating a police system which commits itself to direct and single responsibility for police management. In the vast majority of those cities having civil service commissions, responsibility for the selection, promotion, and discipline of police personnel is divided between the police authorities on the one hand, and the civil service commission on the other. And in a practical sense, the civil service commission possesses the larger half. Here is a problem which must be faced squarely. It is submitted that if there is any solution short of complete exclusion of civil service control from police affairs, it will be found in confining the civil service commission to the duty of eliminating, by competitive examination, those police applicants who are palpably unfit. To concede to them the power virtually of

selecting individual recruits or officers is to trim down the powers of the administrative head to a point where the office will no longer attract men of marked capacity. Thus the vicious circle is completed.

For many years we have been concerned with problems of civil service reform. The time seems to have come for a reform of civil service.

UNIFORMED PATROL

Turning now to the major aspects of police service, we are confronted with the fact that continuous and systematic patrol threatens to become a vanishing institution. The addition of new and burdensome police activities, of which traffic control is a striking example, has withdrawn large numbers of men from patrol duty. Establishment of district stations without regard for modern facilities of transportation and communication has had the same effect. Every police station requires from ten to fifteen officers and men to operate it during a given 24-hour period. These are necessarily drawn from the patrol force. Special details, public office assignments, replacements for those on sick leave, rest days, and vacations are drawn from the same source. The patrol force has come to be viewed as a vast reservoir of manpower. Special and temporary duties almost necessarily take precedence over routine patrol.

Here is a serious condition. We are in danger of losing sight of the fact that crime repression, through continuous patrols, is fundamental to all police work. Yet there are now large cities in which less than half of the patrol posts are covered. In some cases, the men on station duty actually outnumber those who are patrolling beats. Foot patrol beats embracing two square miles and twenty miles of streets are not uncommon. In short, the patrol force has been progressively diluted and dispersed until those who remain are unable either to familiarize themselves with their beats or to apply that continuous pressure which serves so effectively as a deterrent to certain types of criminal acts. It is suggested (though the fact clearly cannot be proved) that here may lie one of the causes of our so-called crime waves.

These facts and these conditions are not unrecognized. There has been insistent demand in police circles for material additions to the police quota. But if additional manpower was not forthcoming, the matter usually has been allowed to rest there. It is a fact, however, that the effect of a substantial increase of patrol personnel may be secured by a vigorous pruning of special details, the consolidation of patrol districts, and a close adaptation of patrol methods to local requirements. Practical adaptation of fixed post duty and of circular and straightaway beats, the uses of foot and motor patrols, and of patrol booths, modern means of communicating with patrols, maintenance of reserves, redistribution of the patrol force throughout the 24 hours of the day, in accordance with proved need,— all these may be studied and reviewed with profit. They constitute the very bone and sinew of the police organism.

CRIMINAL INVESTIGATION

The detective bureau is coördinate with the patrol force only in an administrative sense. Actually it supplements the latter. With certain notable exceptions, the detective bureau does not function unless and until there has been a failure by the patrol force to repress crime. Because criminal investigation captivates the fancy and is relieved of the routine features of patrol work, the detective bureau is likely to be far more completely manned than is the patrol force. It is generally

assumed that criminal investigation requires greater intelligence than patrol. This may be a debatable question. But it is certain that it requires a different type of individual. Here again, however, the cut and dried methods of civil service control have failed to operate with any selective effect. The nature of detective service demands certain qualities which, in the present state of our knowledge, can best be tested in the actual performance of detective duty. To select detective personnel by means of a set examination and then make it difficult or impossible for superior officers to return them to patrol, represents the last word in futility.

Some of the considerations entering into the distribution of uniformed patrols apply with almost equal force to criminal investigations. The hard and fast system of district detectives is seriously weakened when these are evenly distributed over the police districts of the city. Under this plan, certain district detectives may daily be assigned as many as ten or a dozen complaints for investigation. Successful investigations are clearly impossible. It may fairly be questioned, however, whether any serious attempt to this end is made in the majority of cities. The information available indicates that close supervision of detective work by qualified superiors is the exception rather than the rule. Assignment records are rarely maintained. Chiefs of detectives often are merely superior operatives who attach themselves to the investigation of especially important cases or to cases which bulk large in the public eye. Bureau clerks sometimes succeed in partially filling the gap. They assume the prerogative of assigning cases and keeping personal memoranda concerning them. By such expedients, many detective bureaus are saved from chaos.

It is clear that in the cities where these conditions prevail, an effort should be made to systematize detective operations from top to bottom. There will be nothing superhuman about the task. Probably no other sphere of police administration has received more intensive study. Record forms covering the assignment of cases, daily reports, and progress reports exist in wide variety and nearly all are adequate. Nothing is needed but a directing intelligence.

CRIME PREVENTION

As already indicated, the matter of crime prevention merits the closest attention from municipal authorities, since it is one of a very few of the really constructive features of criminal justice administration. No program for combating crime which does not include it can be considered complete. Crime may be prevented, however, only to the extent that the actual and underlying causes are removed. Some of these, such as the suppression of the liquor and narcotic traffic, are matters which primarily concern the police. There are other features, however, which appear clearly beyond the sphere of the police, but which are nevertheless well within the scope of municipal jurisdiction. The prompt and efficient relief of actual distress, the gradual elimination of degrading conditions of housing, provision of facilities for juvenile recreation by means of strategically located playgrounds,—to these matters the municipalities may apply themselves in the confident belief that they will eventually be influential in reducing crime.

There is emphatic demand in some quarters that the whole concept of police service be revised so that the rank and file of the force may devote their efforts to prevention rather than to repression or apprehension. This view overlooks the fact that social welfare agencies exist in great number and variety. To project the police into their field would serve further to complicate a situation which is already complex. Furthermore, it might fairly be doubted whether a police force consisting largely of social workers armed with police powers would possess the stern qualities required to deal effectively with certain types of offenses and offenders.

It therefore seems reasonable to conclude that the police may best serve the ends of crime prevention by familiarizing themselves with the type of work performed by all of the social welfare agencies of the community, both public and private. With this accomplished, the usefulness of the patrolman on his beat will be greatly increased. As the eyes and ears of the city government, he will serve as a highly useful reporting agency, and many conditions which now receive no attention will be brought to the notice of competent authority. But because social welfare agencies operate only during the hours of the business day, the police should also be prepared to relieve certain cases of acute distress of their own motion and on their own responsibility. The police department, which operates at all hours, is in a position occasionally to render real constructive service in this manner.

The creation of women's bureaus in police departments in recent years has resulted in a few substantial contributions to police technique. That such bodies of women police officers do not constitute a complete solution of the crime prevention problem is, however, abundantly clear. The extension of women's bureaus to all but the very smallest police departments should be actively encouraged. But the point cannot be stressed too strongly that from the necessities of the situation police forces must continue to be stern guardians of law and order, and recruited, organized, trained, and equipped accordingly.

POLICE TRAINING

Finally, the attention of American cities might well be directed to the matter of police training. The rise and development of police schools probably constitute the greatest achievements of police administration in the past twenty years. A generation ago, it would have been necessary to argue the advisability of formal instruction for police recruits. It is not necessary to do so today. The early opposition of police administrators has almost disappeared. A number of admirable police training schools have been established not only by some of the larger cities, but also by several of the states maintaining police forces. So far as is known, all of these are open to the members of other police departments. Moderate advantage has been taken of the opportunity thus offered.

It still remains true, however, that the promising extension of police schools has been somewhat retarded in recent years. There appear to be two reasons for this condition. In the first place, the smaller police forces naturally find it difficult or impossible or organize, man, and operate their own training units. In other cities, where by reason of larger police quotas these considerations do not apply, the difficulty lies in the fact that police administrators are likely to be unfamiliar with pedagogical methods and procedure. One is likely to find the liveliest appreciation of the value of police training as an abstract proposition, but little or no grasp or comprehension of the actual course to be followed in order to secure it. There are instances of otherwise imposing police schools which employ the catechism method of instruction. There are other cases where the training period has been so frequently interrupted by demands upon the recruits' time that the schools themselves have virtually suspended operation. The widest variety of curricula still prevails. Time devoted to instruction ranges from one week to three months. The idea that a police training program consists largely of setting-up exercises, the simpler forms of military drill, and memorizing the location of police telegraph boxes, proves most persistent.

There are, then, two problems presented. The difficulty of establishing training units in the smaller police departments is clearly insuperable. If the members of these police forces are to receive systematic instruction in the policeman's art, it must be at other hands than those of their immediate administrative superiors. Cities which fall into this category can best meet the situation by requiring their police recruits to attend a police school operated by another municipality or by the state.

The problem of raising the standard and improving the curriculum of police schools operated by the larger cities is one requiring more extended consideration. It is submitted that the proposal made a few months ago by the New York State Crime Commission may offer a possible solution. The commission recommended that the board of regents be given the power and the duty of licensing and supervising police training schools throughout the state; that the board engage the services of an inspector who should give his assistance to any police department desiring to establish a police school or to improve one already in existence, and who should periodically inspect all police schools and certify those which maintain satisfactory standards. The commission further recommended that no member of a police force in the larger cities should be promoted to the rank of lieutenant, captain, inspector, or to equivalent grades, unless he should have completed a course of instruction in an approved school for police.

In making these proposals, the New York State Crime Commission intended that the larger cities of the state should be offered two alternatives; either to establish a satisfactory training unit of their own, or to turn their police recruits over to competent hands. It is not intended, of course, that such training should be required of a policeman prior to every promotion to which he might aspire, but merely to close the doors leading to the higher ranks and grades to those policemen who joined the force subsequent to the establishment of the plan and who had not at some time satisfactorily completed an approved course of police instruction. By these means, the commission hoped that the whole standard of police service might eventually be raised. It is certain that no program for the improvment of police administration can be complete without serious regard being given to the matter of police training.

CONCLUSION

The foregoing matters represent a few of the salient features of police administration to which municipalities may apply themselves in their efforts to combat crime. They all have an important, and some have an intimate bearing upon the question. It is probable that in many jurisdictions, state legislative action may be necessary in order to clear the decks for such a program. With one or two exceptions, however, the cities should experience little difficulty in securing the necessary charter revisions.

The fact that the suggestions here presented are rather numerous should not be allowed to obscure the fact that in the last analysis success in police administration depends upon sound organization and competent direction of personnel. For these two there is no satisfactory substitute. The methods employed in the selection, training, advancement, and discipline of the rank and file actually condition the kind of police service that is rendered, day and night, year in and year out.

The police stand in the first line of defense against crime. If that line holds, some of the pressure upon all of the other agencies of criminal justice will be relaxed, and the way will be open for thoughtful and orderly improvement in the entire process, from apprehension to punishment.

RECENT BOOKS REVIEWED

THE CALIFORNIA PLANNING ACT OF 1927. With Notes and References by Charles Henry Cheney, Secretary, California Conference on City Planning, Member American City Planning Institute. Pp. 67.

The enactment of the California Planning Act of 1927 is a long step forward in the city planning legislation of this country. Most of our laws with regard to city planning commissions, the city plan and platting are crude and chaotic, as recently they were with relation to zoning. First in zoning and now in this branch of planning law, the department of commerce at Washington has begun the work of standardization, to the end that each state may evolve the law on this subject in the light of the best general practice in this country. Perhaps the greatest service which California has done the law of this country on this subject is in the intelligent use it has made of the standard act. It has by no means slavishly followed the form prepared in Washington more as a summary of the best thought on this subject than as an actual standard even for today, and much less for the indefinite future. On a few doubtful points it has adopted its own methods. In some ways it has conformed to Pacific coast ideas. To some extent it has followed the recent 'legislation of the state of New York, drafted with the aid of the Regional Plan of New York and Its Environs. Hereafter with the example of California before it there will be no excuse in any state for the crudities which so far have been the rule. The act is issued by the California Conference on City Planning in book form with helpful notes and references.

A few comments on the features of the California act in which it departs from the standard act may not be out of place. The "master plan," as framed by the commission, cannot in either act be varied contrary to the advice of the commission, except by a two-thirds vote of the local legislature; but it does not, in the California law, go into effect as soon as adopted by the commission; it must be passed by the local legislature. In this the California law would seem to the writer to be an improvement on the standard act. It is the modern practice, founded on experience and sound reasoning, to center power and responsibility. The old division of government among boards and commissions is, happily, obsolete. Even the requirement of a two-thirds vote by the council to overrule the commission is criticised by some. Any further step in this direction seems to the writer to be unwise and unnecessary. The council, holding the purse, has the real power in any event.

The commission has the right of approving plats, and may by its rules require the subdivider to leave areas unoccupied not only for streets but for other open spaces. He is not required to dedicate these spaces, however, but may make a notation on his plat that he has not done so. In this attempt to obtain small parks without infringing constitutional limitations the California act follows the New York laws; the standard act does not have this feature. To the writer the California adaptation of the New York law would seem to be inferior to it. The effect of the New York legislation is to give the commission a freedom of bargaining with the subdivider which the mere making of rules cannot do; and in the undeveloped areas adaptability is of great value, as the success of English methods in this field seems to show.

The California law adopts both the Standard and (to a considerable extent) the New York method of keeping buildings off mapped streets. It seems obvious, however, that some buildings will be constructed which do not need street connections, and no provision for such cases is made in California as it is in New York. Here again, in its anxiety to lay down fixed rules, this legislation seems to have sacrificed flexibility. Let us hope that developing practice on the Pacific coast will find some method of securing this most-essential attribute.

FRANK B. WILLIAMS.

✣

THE MECHANISM OF THE MODERN STATE. A Treatise on the Science and Art of Government. By Sir John A. R. Marriott. Oxford: Clarendon Press, 1927. 2 vols. Pp. xxiii, 596; xii, 595.

This extensive treatise deals primarily with the government of Great Britain and the British self-governing dominions; but also includes some discussion of general problems of political organization, and of governments in other countries, notably the ancient city-state of Greece, the Swiss federation and the United States. On some subjects, such as federalism, second chambers, financial procedure and the judiciary, there are comparisons with conditions in still other countries; but there is no attempt at an all-embracing survey of governments throughout the world.

The author has been for many years fellow, lecturer and tutor in modern history and political science at Worcester College, Oxford, and is well known as the author of numerous articles on political subjects in the English quarterly and monthly journals and also of previous books on *Second Chambers* and *English Political Institutions*. In recent years he has been a member of Parliament from Oxford and York, and has served as a member of the Bryce Committee (Second Chamber Conference), the Committee on National Expenditures (1918), the Committee on Public Accounts and the Estimates Committees of the House of Commons. The work thus combines the training and methods of the academic student and teacher with considerable practical experience in political life.

In its general tone, the study is distinctly academic; and the author's attitude is in the main conservative, in a non-partisan sense, though he is at the same time a member of the Conservative party. Much of the contents are familiar to students of the subject, but important contributions are made on the subjects of composite governments, second chambers and financial procedure and methods. The final chapter is an interesting sketch of previous works on British government, by both domestic and foreign authors; and the appendix presents a number of typical documents and forms used in public business, with a selected bibliography of books and of articles by the author.

The one chapter on Political Parties is inevitably less thorough than Lowell's extended treatment of that topic. There are only brief references to Scotland and Ireland. And the discussion of financial procedure in the United States is based on Bryce's *American Commonwealth*, and shows no knowledge of the important changes made by the Budget and Accounting Act of 1921.

Two chapters on local government (in which readers of the NATIONAL MUNICIPAL REVIEW will be interested) give a useful general survey of developments, but add little or nothing to the information in other works, and reflect no special study of this field. JOHN A. FAIRLIE.

THE GOVERNMENT OF EUROPEAN CITIES (Revised Edition). By William Bennett Munro, Ph.D., LL.B. New York: The Macmillan Co., 1927. Pp. 432.

Professor Munro, in the numerous texts on various aspects of government which have come from his pen, has shown himself to be master of a fluent, readable, interesting, one might almost say, popular style. This characteristic lifts his texts above the usual classroom book and makes them available in no small degree to the general reader. *The Government of European Cities*, a revised edition of an earlier treatise on the same subject, is of the same general type as these other volumes. It deals with the complex details of the government of overseas municipalities in such a manner as to rob the subject of many of its terrors for the general reader. In a clear, lucid, racy style the book covers the cities of England and France in detail, while enough is presented as to the German and Italian cities to give the reader a general idea of their organization. The first edition was published eighteen years ago. In the meantime great changes have taken place both in the form and spirit of the European city, more particularly since the close of the war. The significance of these changes is very great. The revised edition carries the subject into the present and makes clear the extent of and the reasons for the recent changes.

Over three-fourths of the text is given over to a detailed treatment of British and French municipal history and institutions. Emphasis is placed, in addition to the historical developments of these cities, on their legal status and powers, central control, party systems, governing organization, permanent officials and municipal services. Individual chapters are devoted to London, Paris, and the Scottish and Irish cities. Professor Munro adds greatly to the interest of the American reader through a running comparison of English and French institutions and practices with those of the United States. This makes the volume understandable in a most worthwhile manner. Throughout the text the reader is constantly required to check and balance his American experiences against those of France and England. This is very helpful for classroom purposes.

One is slightly disappointed not to find a more adequate treatment of the German city. Only two chapters are allotted to this important experimental country in the field of municipal institutions; one chapter is devoted to German cities before the war, another to German government today. This scanty treatment is in contrast to ten chapters devoted to England and eight to France. The book, the reviewer believes, would have been better balanced, at least for classroom purposes, if more attention had been devoted to the German city, a country so important in the field of municipal institutions. One chapter is devoted to the Italian city.

A final chapter, of much value to the student, covers the available source material and literature on the subject. This has been very carefully prepared according to countries and covers such subjects as bibliography, official publications, statistics, municipal corporation acts, periodicals, history, special studies and descriptions of present day governments. The instructor will find this indispensable.

The Government of European Cities in its revised form is a welcome addition to the general books on the subject. To the instructor of government interested in an elementary text in this field, or for supplementary reading in municipal or co-operative government, this volume meets the need.

RUFUS SMITH.

✣

PERSONNEL. By George R. Hulverson. New York: Ronald Press Company, 1927. Pp. 400.

This volume is intended as an elementary manual for business executives generally, and it is, therefore, a summary of the best known methods of personnel administration rather than an attempt to advance the cause of scientific personnel management. In fact, Mr. Hulverson writes in considerable sympathy with the viewpoint of the ordinary man of business, who feels that after all the selection of employees is largely a question of common sense and good judgment, rather than of the use of instruments which measure ability and aptitude accurately.

As a rule he avoids expressing an opinion on controversial matters and endeavors to present to the reader the relative merits of the different methods which he describes. He recognizes personnel management as a major function and also the desirability of centralizing all employment activities, but concludes that as a practical matter, many such activities and much of the administration of personnel work must be left in the hands of departmental executives. He points out that in any case the personnel department must be placed so that it will be supported by some officer having real authority, preferably the chief executive, as any effort to centralize control of personnel results in a degree of restriction in the authority of departmental executives, and is doomed to failure unless sufficient authority lies behind it.

As is natural in a volume of this scope, some important topics are treated sketchily, as, for example, Methods of Judging and Testing Applicants, and the subjects treated in the chapter on Personal Service Work.

Job analysis procedure and the use of data obtained thereby are discussed in considerable detail. Other subjects covered include Building Up a Labor Supply, Employee Training, Training Supervisors and Salesmen, Transfer, Promotion, Separation, and Personnel Records. Seventy pages are devoted to wage rate determination and control, of which Mr. Hulverson writes with an appreciation of the employee's viewpoint, although he still clings to the ancient notion that women are merely a casual excrescence on the industrial body.

Discussion of matters which, according to the author, have not crystallized into a "definite and reasonably premanent form" has been excluded. Among these apparently are the matter of employee representation and the effect of trade unionism on wage rates, to which no reference is made.

A considerable amount of methods material, as charts, forms, and scales, based on those used by the four large commercial corporations which were studied by Mr. Hulverson, is included.

Executives who desire a broad survey of general personnel procedure will find this a useful book.

ELDRED JOHNSTONE.

✣

THE INITIATIVE AND REFERENDUM ELECTIONS OF 1926. Bulletin No. 107 of the National Popular Government League. By Judson King, Director. Washington, D. C., February, 1927. Pp. 14 (mimeographed).

This bulletin is generally similar to its two predecessors which reviewed the 1922 and 1924 elections. Its content is broader than the title indicates inasmuch as it deals with all the measures submitted to popular vote in the I. and R. states. It is a valuable summary and discussion of this material. The author's count, however, is not quite the same as the reviewer's. He omits two proposals of amendment and one initiated measure voted upon in North Dakota, and attributes three other amendments to the initiative which the latter credits to the legislatures. But for such inaccuracies in handling this subject-matter, let him that is without error cast the first stone; the reviewer will not do it, for fear that the walls of his house are glass.

Some of the comments offered by Mr. King upon the circumstances and significance of the elections deserve attention. He believes the chief cause of the several recent overwhelming popular rejections of proposals for constitutional conventions is the fear of the people that the convention movements were backed by the opponents of direct nomination and legislation, and fear of the power of special interests through the use of money and publicity. But a good many people believe almost the direct contrary. The people of Iowa voted in favor of a convention a few years ago and the legislature refused to call it. In so far as Mr. King's contention applies to that situation, it would almost seem that the legislature saved the people from the possible bad outcome of a mistake by gallantly violating the terms of the Iowa constitution. Defeat of the convention proposal in Pennsylvania is not laid at the door of the friends of progressive measures. These are not I. and R. states, it is true.

Mr. King sees the emergence of a new kind of leadership on the part of citizens not engaged in ordinary politics through the use of the initiative in the fields of education, road building, public health, and reforestation, when the legislature has been lethargic.

On these matters Mr. King speaks from an acquaintance due to almost continuous study and no little personal investigation on the ground. That he is an ardent friend of the I. and R. goes without saying. He condemns outright no popular judgment. But he does not seem to do violence to the facts; it is only his interpretation which is eminently sympathetic toward what is sometimes called direct democracy.

RALPH S. BOOTS.

✤

REPORT OF THE DEPARTMENT OF THE ASSESSOR OF THE CITY OF ST. PAUL AND THE COUNTY OF RAMSEY, 1926. Pp. 32.

This is a biennial report which is intended primarily to analyze for the benefit of the taxpayers of St. Paul and Ramsey County the methods used by the assessor in making real estate,

personal property, and money and credits assessments. The report aims to show that the department in appraising property follows improved and scientific methods. The samples of office records in the form of cards and maps included enhance considerably the value of the report as a manual on assessment practice and procedure. In the opinion of the assessor, the determination of land values by the application of the market value theory is an absurdity. With the assistance of real estate experts the department worked out an adjustment of land values by establishing proper unit values in the several districts throughout the city. But the assessor does not present information as to the nature of the data used by these experts in determining the unit values. Corner influence, evaluating lots of varying depths, and the valuation of buildings are explained in detail. The report criticizes the method of handling complaints. The practice of the taxpayers appealing to the district court results in unfair advantages to individual taxpayers and frequently upsets many values. The assessor believes that the reëxamination of assessments by the State Tax Commission should precede such appeals to the district court.

MARTIN L. FAUST.

✤

CHICAGO CIVIC AGENCIES. Union League Club, Chicago. 1927. Pp. 315.

This "directory of associations of citizens of Chicago interested in civic welfare" has been compiled jointly by the Public Affairs Committee of the Union League Club and the Committee on Local Community Research of the University of Chicago. It describes the census methods followed, which will be helpful to other cities undertaking a similar or comparable task. The agencies are classified by membership, governmental interests, civic interests, and localities. Other valuable features are lists of public officers of Chicago and Cook County, and a taxpayers' calendar.

RUSSELL FORBES.

✤

CURRENT REPORTS

The Directory of American Municipalities for 1927 is useful as a directory to those interested in the names, titles and addresses of officials in the larger cities. This information is furnished by chambers of commerce and local officials and is revised by the publishers each year.

For some cities additional facts are given, such as population, date of next election, general historical data and other miscellaneous information. These facts cover, in one city or another, almost every conceivable item in any way connected with a municipality. This general information is, however, fragmentary, and it would be purely accidental if a particular item desired for a particular city were to be found. Thus, it cannot be depended upon for special information.

✸

Municipal Insurance, by O. F. Nolting, secretary of the Municipal Reference Bureau of the University of Kansas, is "a survey of the practices of cities in insuring their property and liability risks." The problem of insuring city-owned property is now receiving special consideration in many localities. Mr. Nolting's pamphlet, aside from dealing with a statement of the problem as such, presents methods of insuring and costs, losses and amounts. The last chapter is devoted to brief treatment of other kinds of municipal insurance.

The appendices contain an ordinance providing for the creation of insurance funds, the insurance funds for public buildings, data on municipal insurance for eighty-one cities, a table giving a comparison of workmen's compensation laws in thirty-nine states and in thirty-four cities, and a bibliography on municipal insurance. To anyone interested in the particular problem, the facts here set forth will be useful.

✸

Instructions for Municipal Accounting in Local Improvements and Special Assessments, by J. O. Cederberg, reprinted from *Minnesota Municipalities*, is publication No. 18 of the Minnesota League. The complete system to be employed by any municipality in Minnesota is explained and simple forms are given in detail. The information presented is of a practical nature and will be an important aid to municipalities in Minnesota. It will also offer suggestions to cities throughout the country.

✸

The Proposed Traffic Ordinance for Municipalities in Minnesota was drafted by a committee of the League of Minnesota Municipalities as a suggestive ordinance to be modified to meet varying local conditions. As differences between municipalities require only minor changes, the committee hoped to secure the uni-

formity necessary for safety on the highways. The pamphlet has been given wide circulation throughout the state in order that the general public may be informed of the rules and regulations most effective in securing a reduction in traffic accidents.

✸

A Report of the Minnesota Crime Commission is the result of the work of a committee appointed by the governor of Minnesota in January, 1926, to investigate existing conditions in crime, procedure and punishment and to make suggestions of ways in which existing evils may be corrected. The report contains the results of the investigation together with forty-four recommendations for improving the method of dealing with criminals.

✸

The Law of Special Assessments in Minnesota, by Harold F. Kumm, is a recent publication of the League of Minnesota Municipalities. The law as it is interpreted by the courts constitutes Part I and a summary of the statutory provisions, Part II. As the title indicates, the study is limited to Minnesota, but constitutes a complete and accurate account of the law of special assessments for all cities and villages in Minnesota with the exception of the four largest: Minneapolis, St. Paul, Duluth and Winona. The question of special assessments is so important, however, and information so scattered that any treatise on the subject, although limited in scope, should be of widespread interest.

✸

The Water Debt, a report on a liquidation of the bonded debt of the bureau of water in the city of Buffalo, N. Y., was submitted as a memorandum to that department by the Buffalo Research Bureau, and is one of the steps in its survey of the financial practices of the city government. Constructive suggestions of procedure are contained in the report, and six tables give a record of conditions as they exist.

✸

The Report on a Survey of the Rochester Public Market and Marketing Problem was presented to the commissioner of public works through the Rochester Bureau of Municipal Research. A brief introduction is followed by a history of marketing experience of Rochester. Division V contains a detailed survey of the present public market and is accompanied by a map of its vicinity. Interesting tables show the financial status of the market since its establishment. A comparison with other cities completes the chapter. The appendix contains a proposed plan of operation for the Rochester Market Bureau and the market ordinance adopted by the city council on June 8, 1926. In parallel columns are shown the conclusions of the survey and recommendations on each.

※

Tax Rates, Assessed Valuations, and Exempt Property in Minnesota for 1927 is the third similar tabulation published by the League of Minnesota Municipalities. It is by far the most complete of the three, however. The state tax rate, tax rates in cities and villages, county tax rates and assessed valuations, exempt real property in Minnesota—all this information is taken from the records of the Minnesota Tax Commission and the state auditor, and is presented in detail.

※

A Second Analysis of the Detroit Special Assessment Sinking Fund was prepared by the Detroit Bureau of Governmental Research at the request of the city controller and submitted in June, 1927. The report sets forth the condition of the sinking fund as of December 31, 1926. An interesting fact mentioned was a ruling of the attorney general that special assessment bonds come under the provision of the state bond law which forbids an issue of bonds of over $25,000 to be sold except at public sale. Thus the city of Detroit has not been complying with the law in selling its bonds. It has also failed to notify the state controller before the sale of special assessment bonds.

※

The Milwaukee Health Department is a forty-four-page pamphlet describing the work and organization of the city health department. It was published with the hope that it would not only be of assistance to various organizations studying city government, but also that it would explain to the Milwaukee public just what services the health department is in a position to offer.

※

Traffic Accidents and Their Causes is an annual report for 1926 by the Milwaukee Safety Commission. The statistics show a steady increase in the number of accidents in that city.

The problem of accident prevention is found in every locality, and such suggestions as are contained in this report should be welcomed as a possible help in solving that problem whether in Milwaukee or elsewhere.

※

Indebtedness of Counties and Municipalities of the State of New Jersey, 1926, published by the Municipal Service Bureau, Plainfield, N. J., presents a table showing the debt situation in the political subdivisions of that state. The department of municipal accounts furnished the records from which the information was obtained and, although the figures are not guaranteed, they were taken from official statements submitted by local finance officers.

The headings of the different columns, which are clearly defined, are as follows: gross debt, school debt, total debt, assessed valuation, percentage of gross debt to assessed valuation, deductions allowed by statute, net debt under statutes, percentage net debt to three years' average, water debt and sinking funds or funds in hand.

The pamphlet should be of interest not only to those interested in the purchase of municipal bonds in New Jersey, but also to general students of municipal finance.

※

Public Accident Reporting is a recent pamphlet published by the National Safety Council and is a revision of Public Accidents Statistics issued in 1926. The purpose is set forth on the title page: "To present a standard accident reporting system for use by police, motor vehicles, and highway departments."

The system of reporting was started in 1925 and at the present time, fifty-nine cities and counties and one state have adopted it. A list of these is given on pages 25 and 26.

During 1925, about 90,000 people were killed by accidents in the United States. In 1926, there were nearly 23,000 deaths from automobile accidents alone. These figures with many others of a similar nature are used to prove the vital need for the adoption of measures to prevent as many of these accidents as possible. As the quotation on the cover states: "Accident reporting is the foundation of accident preventing." Therefore, it is felt that the facts presented by adequate reports will form the basis for the prevention of many similar accidents in the future.

ESTHER CRANDALL.

JUDICIAL DECISIONS

EDITED BY C. W. TOOKE

Professor of Law, Georgetown University

Municipal Functions—Sale of Gasoline.— On December 5, the Supreme Court handed down a decision in the case of the *Standard Oil Co.* v. *City of Lincoln,* affirming the right of a municipality under legislative authority engaging in the business of selling gasoline. The *per curiam* opinion bases the decision upon the prior decisions of *Jones* v. *Portland* (1917), 245 U. S. 217, which affirmed the right of the municipality expressly authorized by statute to maintain a public yard for the sale of wood, and of *Green* v. *Frazier* (1920), 253 U. S. 233, which sustained legislation of North Dakota, which provided for the state engaging in the business of manufacturing farm products, providing homes for the people and creating a state bank. Thus in the instant case the court accepts the judgment of the legislature as interpreted by the state courts upon the question whether a given use is public in its nature, so as to justify the exercise of the power of taxation or of eminent domain. In *Mutual Oil Co.* v. *Zehrung,* 11 Fed. (2nd) 887, decided in 1925, the district federal court held that the city of Lincoln under its home-rule charter had power to determine the expediency of engaging in the sale of gasoline without any express delegation of authority from the state legislature. [1]

❖

Eminent Domain—Attempt to Limit by Contract.— It is a fundamental principle that a city may not contract away any of the governmental powers delegated to it. In *City of Maberly* v. *Hogan* (298 S. W. 327), the city brought a proceeding to condemn certain lands for street purposes, and the defendant set up a contract executed in 1908 by which he conveyed a part of the tract to the city upon its agreement to use and improve the lands so conveyed as a street and its covenant that the city would never take any more of the tract by condemnation proceedings. In holding that the covenant was void, and of no binding force whatsoever, the Supreme Court of Missouri especially relies upon the

[1] See note on Extension of Municipal Functions in the August, 1926, issue at page 491.

authority of the Supreme Court of the United States in *Pennsylvania Hospital* v. *Philadelphia* (245 U. S. 20, affirming 254 Pa. 392, 98 Atl. 1077) in which that court said: " There can be now, in view of the many decisions of this court on the subject, no room for challenging the general proposition that the states cannot by virtue of the contract clause be held to have divested themselves by contract of the right to exert their governmental authority in matters which from their very nature so concern that authority that to restrain its exercise by contract would be a renunciation of power to legislate for the preservation of society or to secure the performance of essential governmental duties."

This doctrine applies, of course, to the maintenance and control as well as to the opening of streets. (*Penley* v. *Auburn,* 85 Me. 278, 27 Atl. 158; *Chicago* v. *Union Traction Co.,* 199 Ill. 259, 65 N. E. 243.)

❖

Home Rule—No Power to Authorize Discharge of Tax Liens.— In *Hauke* v. *Ten Brook,* 259 Pac. 908, the Supreme Court of Oregon reversed a decree of the circuit court denying an injunction against the cancellation by the city of Astoria of certain special assessments liens levied against a private corporation. The city council, under a charter amendment purporting to authorize the act, passed an ordinance releasing the Astoria Box and Paper Company from existing liens against its property up to the amount of $150,-000, for the purpose of assisting the corporation in its plans to build a large paper manufacturing plant. In holding that the amendment and ordinance were void, the court points out that the home-rule powers of the city are subject to the rule that all taxation must be equal and uniform and to the express constitutional provision against a municipality loaning its credit or giving aid to a private corporation.

The limitation upon the power of a state legislature to authorize a tax for the purpose of private interest instead of a public use has been settled since the decision of the Supreme Court in *Loan Association* v. *Topeka,* 20 Wall. 655. And no distinction can be drawn between direct pecuniary aid and aid by means of a release from a pecuniary burden. (*Jersey City* v. *N. Jersey City Ry. Co.*, 78 N. J. L. 72, 73 Atl. 609.) It may be noted that while these salutary principles are of uniform application in this country, Canadian municipalities may be given legislative authorization to make exemptions from taxation, or to give a bonus to manufacturing corporations located within their limits, no question of constitutional limitations being involved. (*Halifax* v. *Nova Scotia Car Works, Ltd.*, A. C. 992, 8 Brit. Rul. Cas. 171.)

✤

Police Power—Limitation of Rates of Public Utilities by Contract.—Under an application for a declaratory judgment, the Supreme Court of Connecticut in *New Haven Water Co.* v. *New Haven*, 139 Atl. 99, was called upon to construe a franchise contract in which as to the water company the rates were fixed for an indefinite term. In declaring that the company had a right to prosecute its claim for an increase of rates before the public utilities commission, the court held that the clause fixing the rates for an indefinite term was not a contract obligation even though authorized by statute, as the legislature may not directly or indirectly surrender the governmental powers of the state by contract.

The principle that the legislature may not contract away its control over rates of public service corporations is qualified by the federal doctrine that contract rates may be protected when the term is definite and not unreasonable in point of time. This temporary surrender of a portion of its police power is a very grave act; the authority must be plain and the intention to do so unmistakable. (*Paducah* v. *Paducah Ry.*, 261 U. S. 264.) Subject to the same qualifications, the state may likewise expressly authorize one of its municipalities to establish by inviolable contract rates to be charged by a public service corporation. But for the very reason that such a contract will result in extinguishing *pro tanto* a governmental power, both its existence and the power to make it must clearly appear and all doubts will be resolved in favor of the continuance of the power. (*Home Tel. Co.* v. *Los Angeles*, 211 U. S. 265.) As to the protection of the city's right to the maintenance of the contract rates, the state authority which confers the power may withdraw or modify its exercise. (*New Orleans* v. *N. O. Waterworks Co.*, 142

U. S. 79.) Outside of the home-rule cities the legislature may directly or through a public utility commission control the rates of municipally owned public utilities, and this principle applies to rates fixed by home-rule cities for services rendered beyond their boundaries. (*Hillsboro* v. *Public Service Commission*, 97 Ore. 321, 187 Pac. 617; *City of Lamar* v. *Town of Wiley* (Colo. 1926), 248 Pac. 1009.)

✤

Streets and Highways—Regulation of Vehicles for Hire.—The wide extent of the power of cities to make all reasonable regulations for the operation of vehicles for hire on the public streets is illustrated in several recent cases. That such carriers may be classified and each class made subject to special rules was held by the Supreme Court of West Virginia in *Charleston-Ripley Bus Co.* v. *Shaffer* (137 S. E. 360). That bus lines may be restricted to the use of certain thoroughfares so as to prevent competition with established transportation lines was sustained by the Federal Circuit Court of Appeals, Eighth Circuit, in passing upon the validity of an ordinance of Oklahoma City in the case of *People's Transit Co.* v. *Henshaw* (20 Fed. (2nd) 87).

That taxicabs, like the earlier hackney coaches, may be placed in a class by themselves and subjected to special regulations is supported by the uniform weight of authority. The recent spread of the movement to require the owners of taxicabs to take out indemnity insurance has resulted in numerous test cases, two of which deserve passing notice. In *State* v. *Deckebach*, 157 N. E. 758, the Supreme Court of Ohio affirmed the denial of a writ of mandamus to compel the auditor of Cincinnati to issue a permit to a taxicab owner who had failed to comply with the ordinance requiring an insurance policy or bond of indemnity as a condition precedent to the grant of a license to operate his car for hire. The court sustained the power of the city to pass the ordinance on the general grant to municipalities by the state constitution of "authority to exercise all forms of local self-government and to adopt and enforce within their limits such local police, sanitary and other similar regulations as are not in conflict with the general laws." As the use of the highways for commercial purposes is not a right but a privilege, the grant of the general power to regulate traffic carries with it the plenary power to impose the conditions under which such use shall be exercised. In fact no vested right to the commercial use of the highways can be acquired which will not be subject to the exercise of the police power, a power that the municipality cannot contract away.[1]

That the nature of the security to be given is solely within the discretion of the authority which enacts the ordinance is held by the Supreme Court of California in *Kruger* v. *California Highway Indemnity Exchange* (258 Pac. 602), decided July 27, rehearing denied August 25, 1927. The ordinance of the city and county of San Francisco in question provided that the policy of insurance or bond should guarantee the payment of any judgment obtained against the owner, irrespective of his financial responsibility or any act or omission on his part. The owner in question took out a bond with the defendant, one of the terms of which obligated him to give timely notice of the accident, pendency of action, etc. The facts showed that the plaintiff had received a judgment against the owner without the knowledge of the defendant, owing to the failure of the owner to give the agreed notice. In affirming the right of the plaintiff to payment of his judgment by the surety company, the court held that while the lack of notice might have been a defense if the owner had brought an action on his bond to compel the defendant to reimburse him, it could be no defense in the present action by the judgment creditor, as its contract so far as the plaintiff was concerned was to pay the judgment. The police power extends to the control of the right of freedom of contract in cases of this kind; the city has a right to prescribe that an acceptable bond shall be given only by approved sureties and may reasonably fix the terms which such sureties must include in the bonds they execute to comply with the requirements of the ordinance.

✤

Torts—Liability for Nuisance Existing in Street.—Among the recent cases affirming the positive duty of a city to keep its streets in a condition safe for travel and its consequent liability to one injured through its failure to perform such obligation, the most important is

[1] *In re Cardinal*, 170 Cal. 519, 150 Pac. 348; *Huston* v. *Des Moines*, 176 Ia. 455, 156 N. W. 883; *West* v. *Asbury Park*, 89 N. J. L. 402, 99 Atl. 190; *Commonwealth* v. *Thebarge*, 231 Mass 386, 121 N. E. 30; *Lutz* v. *New Orleans*, 235 Fed. 978; *Northern Pac. R. R. Co.* v. *Duluth*, 208 U. S. 583; *Packard* v. *Banton*, 264 U. S. 140.

that of *Klepper* v. *Seymour House Corporation and the City of Ogdensburg*, 158 N. E. 29. In this case the New York Court of Appeals sustained a judgment of $37,500 in favor of the plaintiff who was injured by snow and ice sliding from the projecting roof of the hotel upon her as she was passing on the sidewalk. The decision is supported by a long line of precedents in New York beginning with *Weet* v. *Brockport* (15 N. Y. 161) in 1856. In *Cohen* v. *New York City* (113 N. Y. 532, 21 N. E. 700), decided in 1889, the storage of a wagon in the street by license of the city was held to be a nuisance and the city held liable for injuries occasioned to a pedestrian who was struck by the falling of the thills. In *Spier* v. *City of Brooklyn* (139 N. Y. 6, 34 N. E. 727), decided in 1893, the city was held liable for injuries inflicted upon the plaintiff's property by the explosion of a rocket, which was fired from a public street under a permit granted for such an exhibition. This New York doctrine of the absolute liability of the city for failure to use due care by permitting a nuisance in its streets has been generally followed, except in a few states which were influenced by the New England doctrine of immunity for defects in streets except so far as imposed by statute.

In contrast to this decision may be noted a recent case in the Court of Appeals of Ohio, *Kreiger* v. *Village of Doylestown* (158 N. E. 197), in which the municipality was held not liable for an injury to a pedestrian who was shot by some patron of a shooting gallery operated in the public street under permit of the authorities. The Ohio Court seems to have lost sight of the nuisance doctrine and to have based its finding upon the immunity of a municipal corporation for failure to enforce its police powers. While the theory of the plaintiff's case was predicated upon negligence, the allegations of the complaints were sufficient to sustain a liability for breach of a positive duty in any jurisdiction where the system of common law pleading still prevails, but under the so-called liberal code system of Ohio the court held that the plaintiff must fail because he alleged the negligence of the village. In the Klepper case, also under a system of code pleading which applies the principles of the theory of the case, the highest court sustained the judgment although the plaintiff's case was based upon the theory of negligence and was thus submitted to the jury by the trial judge. "Nuisance and negligence," says the New York Court of Appeals, "at times so nearly merge into each other that it is difficult to separate them. A cornice, such as that in this case, may be a nuisance by means of its danger to passers-by on the street, and at the same time the owner may be guilty of negligence in permitting snow and ice to accumulate upon it and fall in heavy mass upon the heads of people below. The existence of a nuisance in many, if not in most instances, presupposes negligence. These torts may be, and frequently are, coexisting and practically inseparable, as when the same acts constituting negligence give rise to a nuisance." It is to be hoped that the Supreme Court of Ohio will reverse the lower court and hold the village of Doylestown liable upon the clear and logical principles set forth by the New York Court of Appeals.

✱

Zoning—Effect of Application for Permit Prior to Enactment of Ordinance.—In *State* v. *Christopher* (298 S. W. 720) the Supreme Court of Missouri declared constitutional the 1925 zoning ordinance of St. Louis and reversed the lower court which had issued a peremptory writ of mandamus to the defendant, the building commissioner of the city, to grant a permit to the Oliver Cadillac Company to erect in a residence and apartment district a building for use as an automobile salesroom. The allegations, admitted for the purpose of the decision, showed that land in the area had largely lost its value as residence property and had become more valuable for business; that the proposed structure complied with all the other building regulations, and that the application for the permit was made

shortly before the ordinance went into effect. Under the facts of the case, it is not strange that the decision was by a bare majority of the court, three of the judges dissenting. Justice Graves wrote an able dissenting opinion, in which he caustically comments on the acceptance of modern theories of the police power by his majority associates. A similar decision, holding that a zoning ordinance may forbid the granting of permits, applications for which have been made prior to its adoption, was handed down recently by the Supreme Court of Louisiana in *State* v. *Harrison* (114 So. 159).

Independently of the constitutionality of these ordinances it seems that the writ of mandamus might have been upheld in both instances if the petitioners were entitled to their permits at the time they filed their applications, and the failure to issue them was arbitrary and unreasonable. In the recent New York case of *Carlton Court* v. *Switzer* (221 N. Y. App. Div. 799), a mandamus issued by the Supreme Court directing the building inspector of New Rochelle to issue a permit under similar circumstances was affirmed. It appeared that the delay of the inspector in this case was for the purpose of giving the council time to amend the ordinance so as to exclude the applicant. But clearly in the absence of bad faith on the part of the city officials, applications made after the ordinance is passed and before it becomes effective, or those filed in contemplation of the imminent enactment of such an ordinance, should not give the petitioner any right to a permit, especially if the reasonable time the administration officials have to act upon them has not yet expired.

PUBLIC UTILITIES

EDITED BY JOHN BAUER

Director, American Public Utilities Bureau

The St. Louis and O'Fallon Recapture Case.— This case has been discussed and its importance emphasized in previous numbers of the REVIEW. It involves the fundamental considerations that enter into valuation for railway rate-making and the recapture of excess earnings under the federal statute. The Interstate Commerce Commission had fixed a valuation of the St. Louis & O'Fallon Railroad Company's properties according to general principles adopted for the administration of the 1920 Transportation Act; primarily upon the prudent investment basis.[1]

The company appealed to the federal courts against the commission's order requiring the payment of excess earnings to the railway reserve fund under the terms of the Transportation Act. It claimed the right to a return upon the reproduction cost of its properties. The matter was argued on October 5, 1927. The commission was sustained in the decision of the court made December 10, 1927. The company lost in its claim for reproduction cost.

The importance of the case can hardly be exaggerated. It is a test case, involving all the railroads in the country, and will determine whether workable and financially sound policies of valuation can be legally established for state public utility regulation in general. As to the immediate financial results, it limits the railroads to the sums determined by the Interstate Commerce Commission; about $10,000,000,000 less than would be the case under reproduction cost. But it involves much more as to future policy and consequences. It permits the establishment of a definite rate base which can be readily administered and which will provide for the financial stability necessary to furnish the returns reasonably expected by investors and to attract the new capital as needed for new railway developments. The reproduction cost basis would be extremely difficult if not impossible of administration; it would require repeated valuations both for rate-making and for the recapture of excess earnings and would thus practically nullify the purposes of the system of regulation as established by Con-

[1] For more detailed analysis of methods see the NATIONAL MUNICIPAL REVIEW, May and July, 1927.

gress. From the financial standpoint the reproduction cost would promote extreme speculation in railway stocks during a period of rising prices and would impair the credit of the companies and create disorganization during falling prices. It would make impossible of realization the far-reaching system of regulation prescribed by Congress.

The case involves also the practicability of public utility regulation in general. If reproduction cost must be used as the rate base for regulation of ordinary utilities, the administration will be almost hopeless and there will be the same financial difficulties as in the case of the railroads. While the O'Fallon case applies only to railroads and is based upon the federal statute, the same questions of practical administration and financial stability are involved in all regulation. The reproduction cost does not permit effective and sound regulation. If a workable policy can be established by legislation for railroads, it can be provided by legislative action for regulation of all utilities.

The case will, of course, be carried to the Supreme Court of the United States. The company will naturally be supported by all the railway and public utility interests of the country. Likewise the Interstate Commerce Commission should be supported by all of the state commissions, municipalities and persons interested in effective and sound methods of regulation. The final decision will be easily the most important one handed down in a generation. It is probably a matter of considerable advantage that the decision by the lower federal court is in favor of the public interest and that the case will reach the Supreme Court through appeal by the company rather than by the Interstate Commerce Commission.

Those who are especially interested in the problems at issue may profitably study the Interstate Commerce Commission's brief submitted to the federal court in this case. It consists of 259 pages of closely printed matter. It covers comprehensively the entire problem of regulation from the economic, administrative and legal standpoints. Its discussion is extremely clear and the arguments forceful. It emphasizes especially the public aspect of transportation; that railroads constitute in reality a public enterprise; that the properties and their uses are public notwithstanding the private interests and titles. This view is supported extensively by quotations from Supreme Court opinions. A differentiation is made between railways and other utilities because of the paramount public character of the railroads, the peculiarity of the problem of regulation, and especially because of the legislative provisions enacted during the long period of our national struggle with railway rate control.

The brief presents also an excellent historical analysis of the various Supreme Court cases dealing in general with valuation and rate-making. It shows that the court has always held to the conception of "fair value" without fixing specific limitations or prescribing specific weight for the various elements. It insists that the fixing of rates is a legislative function, and that the courts are ultimately concerned not with the methods and processes used, but only with the consequences,—whether in fact the rates are confiscatory. With this conception, the commission contends that the rate base can be fixed by legislation and by the commission according to the practical requirements for administration and the financial needs to establish financial stability and to procure the necessary capital for railway developments and improvements. This view was sustained by the decision of the court. If finally upheld by the Supreme Court, it will permit the Interstate Commerce Commission to carry out its responsibility in a sensible way, and will indicate to the states how to put regulation of other utilities upon a workable basis.

✦

New York Law Prohibiting Gas Service Charge Unconstitutional.—The traditional gas rate has been a flat charge per hundred or per thousand cubic feet of gas used. This system has been under discussion for a number of years, and has been often criticized as unjust to large consumers or to users served for special purposes and circumstances. It has been attacked particularly because it causes a loss on very small consumers who do not use sufficient gas at a flat rate to pay the out-of-pocket costs incurred directly for their service.

THE THREE PART RATE

The attack has come mostly from the companies and large consumers. A three-part differential rate has been frequently proposed and has the support of a special committee of the National Association of Railroad and Utilities Commissioners. The essential part includes a threefold separation of the total costs incurred in the manufacture and distribution of gas: (1) consumer costs, (2) demand costs, and (3) commodity costs. The first group consists of the various costs which are practically the same for each consumer no matter whether he uses a large amount of gas or only a few hundred feet; meter reading and repairs, customers' bookkeeping, billing and collecting, all charges directly identified with individual consumers and directly variable with the number of consumers. The second group contains those expenses and fixed costs which vary according to the maximum hourly use of gas; it depends upon the relative demand made upon plant requirement and use. The last group includes the cost of labor and materials directly consumed in connection with the production and distribution of gas.

The first two elements of the three-part rate would be represented as a constant sum for each consumer without regard to the quantity of gas used; the burden per thousand cubic feet becomes less as the quantity consumed increases. The third element, however, would remain as a flat rate per thousand cubic feet without variation as to quantity used, but would be much lower than the level of the single flat rate. The schedule as a whole would present considerable differentiation of rates between groups of consumers. While the three-part rate has made considerable headway in recent years, especially in favorable comment the single flat rate is still the prevailing method of charging for gas used, with some modifications in respect to successive blocks of gas consumed. The first element of the three-part rate, however, has come up for extensive discussion. This appears especially in the so-called service charge. This has been urged by the companies to stop the alleged losses incurred in behalf of small consumers, and has usually been placed at $1.00 per consumer per month. It has been opposed by the large group of small consumers affected as excessive and unwarranted, and has thus incurred strong political opposition in the interest of the small consumers.

SERVICE CHARGE PROHIBITIVE BY STATUTE

In the state of New York, in 1923, the legislature directly prohibited a service charge (Public Service Commissions Law, Section 65, Subdivision 6). The same subdivision, however, provides for a "fair and reasonable price" to be charged for gas; another makes legal a classification of rates according to quantity of use, the time of use, the purpose, duration of use, or "any other reasonable condition." There is thus wide statutory scope for diversification of rates as warranted under various conditions, but there is a prohibition of a special service charge as such.

The prohibition of the service charge was involved in a recent case decided by the United States District Court, Western District of New York. The Niagara Falls Gas and Electric Light Company in 1924 filed a three-part rate with the Public Service Commission, which rejected the schedule because it included a service charge. A large prospective consumer brought action for injunction to restrain the commission from enforcing its order made under the statute prohibiting the service charge. There was also an intervening plaintiff, and the company itself supported the plaintiff.

The decision was rendered on November 4, 1927, and was based upon the report of a special master who had made an extensive investigation of the facts. It granted the injunction and thus rendered invalid the statutory prohibition of the service charge. The court found that without the service charge the company is estopped from allotting the cost of production to the consumer in equal proportion and is prevented from earning a reasonable return upon its property; and that the large consumers are required to pay more than the cost of their service and are thus deprived of their property rights. The statute was found to be arbitrary as applied both to the large consumer and the company, and is thus regarded as causing an impairment of property rights.

The decision apparently applies only to the particular case and does not legalize the service charge in general so far as the New York statute is concerned. The case will be appealed for a final decision to the Supreme Court of the United States. For all practical purposes, unless the decree is reversed, the decision will destroy the statutory prohibition and will make the service charge not only available as a part of the rate structure, but probably compulsory upon the commission whenever proposed by a company.

ENCROACHMENT UPON LEGISLATION

The chief public interest in the decision is its apparent encroachment upon legislation. There had been left wide latitude for adjustment of rates to meet not only the requirements of a fair return to the company, but also differential conditions affecting various classes of consumers. There was only the one thing prohibited, and yet the single prohibition was found to be confiscatory in its consequences. All the other possibilities of rate modification,—according to quantity, time of use, purpose, duration of use, or other grounds except the single basis of service charge,— were found inadequate to overcome the claimed confiscatory effect of the law. It does seem that under the circumstances a clever financial analyst might have found a substantial substitute adjustment for the single prohibited factor. The statute, in fact, seems to invite methods of adjustment or contravention so long as in mere terms no service charge is included in the rate schedule.

A rather unusual aspect of the decision is the outright recognition of a property right on the part of individual consumers,—even a prospective consumer has a right to such rates as not to include any costs properly allocable to other consumers. This in general is reasonable; but to draw the exact limits of such costs is difficult, and to hold that the principle cannot be carried out except through the adoption of a service charge as such, appears to go far along the way of judicial determination of facts.

If the law had fixed a flat rate for gas, and had prohibited any modification whatever, either as to quantity, time of use, etc., then there probably would be force in the contention that a single flat rate would injure the rights of the companies or groups of consumers. But when the statute expressly provides for flexibility in several specific respects, the prohibition of the service charge might well be viewed as a matter of special legislative policy not to be disturbed, even if it is a political foible, except upon very conclusive evidence in a particular case that substantial rights are injured. The decision does seem to place rather strict limits upon legislative discretion.

REASONS FOR SERVICE CHARGE

As to the justification of a service charge, apart from the statute, there is reason for it and there is no substantial ground for the statutory prohibition. Every company does incur certain costs which vary almost directly with the number of consumers and are properly covered by a service charge; so much per consumer per month according to the cost. But when such a charge is expressly forbidden, probably in every instance a rate schedule could be established, nevertheless, to meet substantially a proper allocation of costs between different classes of consumers,—if the quantity of gas, time of use, purpose, duration of use and other conditions as provided by the statute, may be taken into account in fixing the schedule. As a matter of fact, evasion is easy; in a number of instances the schedules provide for $1.00 per month for 200 cubic feet or less of gas used,—which would appear more than an ample substitute for a service charge.

Perhaps the chief reason for the statute was the excessive service charge proposed by most of the companies. The usual amount has been $1.00 per month, which the writer firmly believes is unwarranted in practically all cases. There are probably very few instances in which all the costs properly included in a service charge amount to more than 30 cents per month per consumer. Such a moderate charge would meet little or no objection. Its fairness could not be disputed, and it would not have met legislative opposition. In reality, therefore, we have had first, unwarranted action by the companies; second, unreasonable action by the legislature to stop the unwarranted action by the companies; and, third, unreasonable action by the courts to stop the unreasonable action by the legislature to stop the unwarranted action by the companies, —and thus collapses the house that Jack built.

There appears to be an extensive movement on the part of gas companies to fix a service charge. The Boston Consolidated Gas Company, for example, has announced a service charge of $1.00 per month, effective January 1, 1928, and it will doubtless meet severe opposition. If the companies could be reasonable, they doubtless would succeed in obtaining recognition of the service charge upon a proper basis. There should, of course, be reasonable rate differentiation based upon proper cost allocation and apportionment, but the extent and the basis should be determined by scientific analysis and not upon arbitrary schedules,—nor upon arbitrary legislative prohibition.

NEED OF SCIENTIFIC ANALYSIS

This whole matter needs extensive investigation from a scientific standpoint. Unfortunately very little scientific study has been made. Apart from the general theory of the service charge, no factual analyses have been prepared. Unfortunately, even the commissions have given sanction through loose use of figures to the acceptance of $1.00 per month per consumer. This appears in the illustrations used by the special committee above referred to in discussing the three-part gas rate. While there was no special validity in the illustration, yet it indicates the conception in the commissioners' minds and tends to support the unproved claims oft-repeated by the companies for the particular $1.00 charge. Why deal in generalities? Why not determine the cost according to the facts in each case, and fix the service charge accordingly?

GOVERNMENTAL RESEARCH CONFERENCE NOTES

EDITED BY RUSSELL FORBES
Secretary

Printed Proceedings of Annual Meeting.—The proceedings of the sixteenth meeting of the conference, held in New York City on November 9, 10 and 11, have been mimeographed and are now ready for distribution. The proceedings are given to members, but may be secured by non-members, at the cost price of $2.00 per copy, from the secretary of the conference, 261 Broadway, New York City.

✤

1928 Work Programs.—Next month's issue of the *Notes* will give the 1928 work programs of a number of the research bureaus.

✤

Municipal Research Abandoned in China.—H. C. Tung, director of the Bureau of Municipal Research at Woosungtseng, China, in a recent letter to Lent D. Upson, announces the abandonment of his work on account of political conditions:

Under the changing conditions, no organization can be permanent here. It is therefore with deep regret that I inform you that the National Institute of Political Sciences has been abolished and the Bureau of Municipal Research naturally discontinued. All those municipal pamphlets and bulletins collected by me during the last four years have been taken over by the municipality of Hangchow; but efforts are being made to take them over by the National Municipal League of China because that collection is the only collection we have in China and is of much value to us.

The National Municipal League of China is an association organized by the returned students of municipal government both from the States and Europe, with the object of introducing Western methods to apply to Chinese municipal administration, and of promoting the development of municipal science. This League is modeled after the National Municipal League of the States.

✤

Boston Finance Commission.—The commission has issued the report of L. O. Cummings, assistant professor of the Graduate School of Education, Harvard College, on the objectives of a survey of the educational system of the city of Boston and the probable cost.

✤

California Taxpayers' Association.—The California Taxpayers' Association on November 23 delivered to the Santa Paula City Committee of the Association a research study covering an analysis of past growth and expenditures for a fifteen-year period and a projected ten-year financial program from 1927 to 1937. A study was also included covering the past and present expenditures of the elementary, kindergarten and high schools of the Santa Paula districts. School costs were shown in relation to the ten-year financial program.

The primary object of the survey was to determine how the funds of the city were expended in the past, what the trend of these expenditures had been, and from this past experience the ten-year financial program was projected. Past experience indicated the probable expenditures for the ordinary expense of government. To this was added the amount necessary to take care of the desired improvements. The whole plan was coördinated on a basis of progressive development within the ability of the taxpayers to carry the burden. The Santa Paula report provides another example of the long-term budget for public improvements, coördinated with the necessary expenditures for the ordinary cost of government.

On December 1 Harold A. Stone became staff engineer. Mr. Stone is a graduate of the School of Citizenship and Public Affairs of Syracuse University, and has recently been connected with the Municipal Research Bureau of Cleveland.

✤

Citizens' Research Institute of Canada.—The proceedings of the annual convention of the Canadian Tax Conference were published December 15. Orders for additional copies have been received from all over the Dominion, as well as a considerable number from the United States.

The first of the annual series, " Cost of Govern-

54

ment in Canada" (municipal), has been issued. The second of the series (provincial) is now in course of preparation.

✲

Bureau of Business and Government Research, University of Colorado.—The Colorado Municipal League is conducting a high school essay contest on the topic "Civic Needs of My Town." Cash prizes are to be offered for the winning essay. The contest closes January 15, 1928.

A comparative study of budgets and appropriation ordinances in Colorado cities is being made.

✲

Taxpayers' Research League of Delaware.—The League has continued its preparation of material for the proposed new finance code for the state, on which it is working in coöperation with a committee of the Delaware Bankers' Association. Additional work has also been done for the Delaware Industrial School for Girls on its purchasing, accounting, and budget system.

✲

Des Moines Bureau of Municipal Research.—The Des Moines Bureau of Municipal Research has completed a report comparing various items of expense of the local county hospital system with those of private hospitals in this city. All the public hospital facilities have been consolidated into one county hospital system which embraces the tuberculosis sanitarium, contagious hospital, and general hospital with some outpatient activity.

This report was made at the request of the county. It merely compares costs and not services rendered. It was found that the county hospital payroll expense was higher per patient day than that of the private hospitals by reason of the employment of graduate physicians and nurses, instead of internes and pupil nurses as in the private hospitals, and by reason of a higher salary scale for pupil nurses. The county hospital authorities say that this situation will be adjusted as soon as the nurses' training school has acquired standing and the county hospital system has become firmly established in its accredited rating. On the other hand, the per patient day costs for provisions, medical supplies, and other items, were lower than those in the private hospitals.

Detroit Bureau of Governmental Research.—A philanthropy has recently appropriated $50,000 to the Detroit Bureau which is to be spent on behalf of the committee on standardization of police crime statistics of the International Association of Chiefs of Police. This committee, of which Chief William P. Rutledge of Detroit is chairman, has as its purpose the securing of uniform comparable statistics of major crimes over the United States as a means of measuring the effectiveness of police departments and of indicating possible methods of crime prevention. Bruce Smith of the National Institute of Public Administration has been appointed director of the study. Lent D. Upson of the Detroit Bureau of Governmental Research will serve as chairman of the advisory committee consisting of representatives from the United States Census Bureau, United States Department of Justice, and other organizations interested in the project.

The Bureau has just completed a study of a pay-as-you-go plan for Detroit schools and is discussing the project with school and city authorities. Under the proposal the change could be made over a thirty-year period without increase in the present tax rate for school construction purposes. By adopting pay-as-you-go, there would be a saving to the taxpayers at the end of the thirty-year period of some $93,000, and a yearly saving thereafter of $4,000,000. The change would also permit a gradual increase in the city debt for other than school purposes.

The county authorities recently presented an ordinance to the voters placing the county upon a pay-as-you-go basis. The Bureau directed the attention of numerous civic organizations to certain defects of the ordinance and pointed out that as much as $42,000,000 might be taken from the taxpayers in the ten years. In conference, the county auditors agreed to eliminate a reserve fund of ten million dollars; to submit the capital items in the county budget four months in advance so that they might be reviewed by the civic organizations; and to prepare a ten-year construction program. The project was defeated by a narrow majority, and the Bureau is now taking up with the county authorities a plan for preparing a long-term construction program and embodying the aforementioned safeguards in the ordinance voted by the people rather than in a supplementary resolution by the supervisors.

Recent changes in the state law governing the retirement of teachers have made necessary a revision of the Bureau's report on the teachers' retirement fund. This report showed an existing actuarial deficit of about $8,000,000. Since it is impractical to make up this sum, the Bureau is recommending that money contributed by teachers, and returnable to them upon resignation, be held intact, and that funds be made available to pay present pensioners until their death.

The governmental committee of the Board of Commerce, consisting of some thirty civic organizations, is this year extending their analysis of the Detroit city budget. The requests of each department will be reviewed by a separate committee of citizens, a professional researcher acting as secretary to each committee. A consolidated report to the mayor and city council will be formulated by the secretaries, C. E. Rightor, chief accountant of the Bureau, being chairman of this group.

Recently there has been considerable discussion of the prices paid for private property condemned for public purposes. At the request of a number of civic organizations, the Bureau has undertaken a study of the entire condemnation procedure.

A recent change in personnel in the division of municipal wastes has resulted in the minimizing of labor-saving machinery, notably in the use of street-sweeping machines, catch basin cleaning devices, hauling by street railways instead of by truck, and the salvaging of waste material in lieu of hauling. Since the Bureau has been urging the adoption of modern methods by the department for many years, it is naturally much concerned in this reversal. A study of the situation is being prepared for the incoming administration.

The recent mayoralty campaign was fought out on issues which had little or nothing to do with the administrative character of the local government. In some quarters it is believed that if the choice of mayor is to be thrown definitely into the political arena, with newspaper rivalries playing an important part in the election, administrative continuity should be secured by employing a city manager. At the request of the Board of Commerce, the Bureau has prepared a memorandum indicating the advantages and disadvantages to Detroit of such a change in the charter.

A detailed analysis of over 200,000 arrests made in Detroit over a five-year period is being prepared. This study throws considerable light on the criminal proclivities of various racial groups, the ages at which crime is committed, and the criminal progress of the recidivists. The analysis is expected to be the forerunner of the study of arrest records as a larger source of information in crime prevention.

At the request of the Detroit Real Estate Board, the Bureau has undertaken a study of the tract index department of the county which issues abstracts of titles at cost. Indications are that the budget of this department will be considerably revised, the number of employees reduced, and the charge for abstracts increased.

Recent Bureau publicity covers "The Squeal Book," by Lent D. Upson, in the NATIONAL MUNICIPAL REVIEW; "A Promising Field— Research in Government," in the *Commerce Magazine* of the University of Wisconsin; and "Reports, Memoranda and Publications of the Bureau" and "The Cost of County Government," issued as *Public Business*, numbers 113 and 114.

✠

The Albert Russel Erskine Bureau for Street Traffic Research, Harvard University.—The Bureau, under the direction of Dr. Miller McClintock, is bringing to completion the "Report of the Mayor's Street Traffic Survey of the City of Boston." This survey was started early in 1927 on the initiative of Mayor Malcolm E. Nichols, and is under the general supervision of a traffic advisory committee of 40 prominent citizens.

The expense of the study was provided by a special appropriation of the city council, and the work has been done by the staff of the Erskine Bureau, together with the employees of the various departments of the city government. The Boston Chamber of Commerce has contributed the services of Ellerton J. Brehaut, director of its Civic Bureau. It is estimated that the report will exceed 300 pages in length, and will follow in general the method of presentation used by the Erskine Bureau in its reports upon the cities of Chicago and San Francisco. It is anticipated the report will be published early in the year, and will be available for general distribution.

✠

The Municipal Reference Bureau, University of Kansas.—The Bureau announces the publication of two bulletins in mimeographed form as follows: "Courses in Municipal Government in

Colleges and Universities," and "University Bureaus of Municipal Research." Both bulletins were compiled by O. F. Nolting, former secretary of the Bureau.

✽

National Institute of Public Administration.— The Cincinnati Bureau of Municipal Research has undertaken to outline a program for the revision of the financial procedure of the city administration including budget, special assessments, and accounting. William Watson, Philip Cornick, and A. E. Buck of the National Institute of Public Administration have been retained by the Cincinnati Bureau to assist in this work.

Bruce Smith is making a study of rural justice in Illinois for the Illinois Association for Criminal Justice.

The Institute has just completed a study of public utility taxation in Virginia. Clarence Heer was in charge of the work. The study of county government in Virginia, made by the Institute at the request of Governor Byrd, is shortly to be published. Copies may be obtained from J. H. Bradford, director of the budget, Richmond, Va.

Clarence E. Ridley has recently been added to the staff of the Institute to fill the position of engineer made vacant by the resignation of William A. Bassett, who is now professor of municipal and industrial engineering at the Massachusetts Institute of Technology. Mr. Ridley is a graduate of the Institute, was city manager of Bluefield, W. Va., for four years, and was at one time vice-president of the City Managers' Association.

✽

The Ohio Institute.—In a memorandum submitted to Governor Donahey in November, the Ohio Institute suggested changes in the dates of collection of several state taxes. The object of the proposed changes is to bring the receipts into the state treasury more evenly throughout the year, and thereby have cash on hand, in the general revenue fund at all times, to pay the state's payrolls and bills.

At present during the first half of the calendar year (which will be the fiscal year in 1928) the expenditures are considerably more than twice as great as the receipts. During the first six months of 1926, state general revenue fund expenditures were $11,364,000, while receipts were only $4,826,000. The 1926 receipts did not accumulate

sufficiently to cover 1926 expenditures until December. Such conditions, of course, are unsatisfactory. The present general property tax is only for one year to meet a deficit and therefore does not apply to the situation previously described.

✽

St. Louis Bureau of Municipal Research.—The Bureau recently completed a preliminary report on civil service in St. Louis under the city Efficiency Board. The report was published shortly before a luncheon meeting held by the League of Women Voters, at which the principal speaker was Fred Telford, director of the Bureau of Public Personnel Administration. The meeting was well attended and much interest in personnel matters was manifested by those present. The Bureau's report furnished some of the topics for round table discussion which was participated in by the chairman of the Efficiency Board.

Officials of the Efficiency Board have shown considerable interest in the Bureau's study and have indicated a willingness to coöperate by favorably considering suggestions to improve the service.

The Bureau is preparing a complete tabulation of all pavements in the city, showing the age and area for each type, with a view to determining the average life of various types of pavements and whether the average volume of construction is adequate to replace pavements before the maintenance cost becomes excessive. Studies are being made of the operations of the pavement maintenance sections.

A detailed study of the operations of the bituminous pavement section, which maintains and reconstructs asphalt paving, was recently completed. A preliminary report was prepared in which several suggestions were made to improve operating methods and to develop an effective system of operating and cost records. The preliminary report has been submitted to and discussed with the director of streets and sewers. A final report will be prepared as a result of the discussions.

Following suggestions in the Bureau's reports to the former administration and discussions with the present administration, eight motor flushers have been purchased and put into service by the street cleaning section.

The director of streets and sewers recently requested the Bureau to suggest a system of adequate records for motor flushing. This study is nearly complete. A report of the suggested procedure for maintaining all street cleaning records, including sample record forms, will be submitted in the near future. The Bureau later expects to study the comparative efficiency and economy of various methods of street cleaning now being used in St. Louis.

✦

Toronto Bureau of Municipal Research.—The report dealing with motor accidents has been issued and received considerable comment in the daily press.

Following a report of the city council's special committee on assessment, in which it was recommended that the citizens be asked next election day to vote on whether or not they wished assessment reform, the Bureau issued an open letter in which it respectfully suggested that it was part of the duties of the city council to decide whether or not heads of departments were competent and that this question should not be passed on to the people. A very warm fight ensued in council. The Bureau's attitude was quoted several times. It is interesting to note that the council finally took the stand that they should decide the question, not the people.

Following the request to the city council by the chief of police for 600 extra policemen, and the various reports that the city was greatly under-policed, the Bureau is collecting considerable material dealing with police systems in various Canadian and United States cities, and in some cities in England comparable in size to Toronto.

A bulletin dealing with civic election questions has been prepared and will be issued shortly.

NOTES AND EVENTS

Cincinnati's Second Councilmanic Election under Its City Manager-Proportional Representation Charter.—On November 8, Cincinnati administered a third decisive defeat to the local Republican organization which for so many years controlled her municipal government. The voters not only elected to council six of the nine candidates sponsored by the non-partisan City Charter Committee which had initiated the present city manager government in Cincinnati, but also expressed their confidence in the charter administration by approving bond issues amounting to $8,688,000. Bond issues had been repeatedly voted down under the former so-called "gang" control. The Republican organization elected only two candidates to the city council, the ninth man elected being an Independent. This is the more significant in view of the fact that at the same election the Republican organization candidate for a vacancy in Congress was elected by more than 14,000 votes over the Democratic candidate and more than 19,000 votes over an Independent candidate.

The twenty-four candidates for city council consisted of three groups, nine sponsored and endorsed by the City Charter Committee, nine organization Republican candidates of whom seven were sponsored and named by the organization, the other two being independent Republicans sponsored two years ago and again this year by the charter group. These two charter candidates were endorsed by the Republican organization, though at the last, the rank and file of the Republican organization did not support them. Of the eight independent candidates, two were negroes, two were Republican councilmen in the pre-city manager days, one was a former coroner, one a Democratic politician, and one (the Independent elected) was a well-known municipal court judge, a Republican who was refused the official party endorsement.

Capitalizing the popularity of the present city manager and the city manager plan, the Republican organization pledged allegiance to the manager and the plan of government and promised to continue the undisputed progress of the past two years. They also promised to continue in office and coöperate with the present city manager, C. O. Sherrill, and to exercise individual judgment in municipal legislation instead of subjecting policy questions to party caucus. The Independents likewise pledged themselves to support the plan which is so successfully operating.

The City Charter Committee, which fathered the present house-cleaning régime, based the campaign for its candidates on the plea that the group which initiated the movement, which secured the present city manager and has successfully operated Cincinnati's government for the past two years, should be returned to power. They questioned the sincerity of the sudden conversion of the Republican organization and termed the presence of several high calibre men on the Republican ticket (later defeated) as whitewash merely applied to secure control of the city government again.

The results of the election, which is by proportional representation, gave the City Charter Committee six of the nine councilmen. Mayor Murray Seasongood, the picturesque leader who, as one speaker said, "fired the gun heard round the wards," secured the highest vote, namely, 24,121 votes, the quota being 12,429. The chairman of the Hamilton County Republican Central Committee, who was also a candidate, came second highest with 19,949 votes, but only one other on his ticket, the Republican ticket, was elected despite his large surplus. The Independent Republican elected, though not officially endorsed by any group, secured 6,729 first choice votes, receiving enough votes by transfer to reach the quota.

The proportional representation count of Cincinnati's votes occupied eight days, three days fewer than were required in her first P. R. count two years ago. The votes from the twenty-six wards were brought to a central counting place on the roof garden of a down-town hotel. The tellers were of a distinctly higher grade than those of two years ago. Outstanding features of the count were the tremendous surplus secured by the three leading candidates and the large first-choice vote received by the Independent candidate. The other candidates ran far behind, none being elected until the nineteenth count, when five received their quota through transfers. On the twentieth count the remaining candidate of the nine elected received his quota. Of the victorious nine, seven are in the present council, five charter men and two Republicans. Cincinnati confidently looks torward to two more years of the type of government which has accomplished so much in the past two years.

LEONA KAMM.

✤

Illinois Cities Want More Home Rule.— Students of municipal affairs are familiar with the rising discontent among Illinois municipalities over the Illinois Commerce Commission and its regulation of local utilities. This dissatisfaction has now broadened into a full-fledged demand for constitutional home rule. These matters were made subjects of resolutions passed by the Illinois Municipal League at its recent annual convention. The resolutions were as follows:

That the Illinois Municipal League declares in favor of a constitutional grant of home rule to the municipalities of Illinois, which will enable them to exercise all reasonable powers of local self-government, and permit each municipality to frame and adopt such a plan of government as it may desire, and that to further this object the President of the League is hereby directed to appoint a committee of five to draft such constitutional provisions and promote the coöperation of all the municipalities of the State in presenting such proposals to and securing their approval by the General Assembly of Illinois.

That the Illinois Municipal League reaffirms its position with reference to local control of local public utilities, and declares it to be a settled belief of the League that the Illinois Public Utility Act should be so amended that cities, villages, and incorporated towns shall have power and authority upon a referendum to take over the control of all contracts and relations with local public utilities, including gas, electricity, heat, water, telephone and transportation utilities,—with reference to terms, rates and conditions of service within the corporate limits of such cities, villages and incorporated towns, and in such cases that the Illinois Commerce Commission shall be excluded from jurisdiction over such local public utilities.

✤

Farewell Testimonial to Dr. Hatton.—Dr. A. R. Hatton, who for twenty years held the stage in Cleveland as the college professor in politics, has resigned from the Cleveland city council and Western Reserve University to become professor of political science at Northwestern University. Dr. Hatton is probably best known to the readers of the REVIEW for his work as charter draftsman and his nation-wide advocacy of city manager government and proportional representation.

Last month the City Club of Cleveland gave Dr. Hatton a testimonial and farewell luncheon. The meeting was one of the largest of the year. In his address following the luncheon Dr. Hatton said, "The greatest danger to the continuance of effective city manager government in Cleveland is the unquestioned desire of the political bosses and some misled, but well-intentioned, citizens to kick out proportional representation."

The Cleveland *Plain Dealer* states that Dr. Hatton has served the community long and well in a variety of ways and that his parting advice constitutes another service to Cleveland.

✤

Stephen B. Story First City Manager of Rochester.—It was announced in advance by the councilmen-elect who took office on January 2 under Rochester's new charter that Stephen B. Story, director of the Bureau of Municipal Research of Rochester, would be appointed the first city manager at a salary of $20,000 per year. Mr. Story was the unanimous choice of the nine members of the council and is well known to many readers of the REVIEW by virtue of his position in the municipal research movement. He is exceptionally well fitted by experience and personality for the difficult task of starting Rochester along the right track of city management. Those who know him well feel a personal interest in his success, and those who do not may be assured that the new government will begin under most promising auspices.

✤

A Correction.—On page 740 of the November REVIEW it was stated that the Ohio legislature had passed an act making permanent registration for elections optional for Ohio cities with a population of more than 25,000. We now learn that this is incorrect, and apologize to our readers for the error. The truth is that the bill passed the General Assembly, but was vetoed by the governor after the two houses had adjourned *sine die* and there was no opportunity therefore for passage over his veto. The bill would have provided a new election code for the state.

NOTES ON PUBLIC PERSONNEL MANAGEMENT

BY FRED TELFORD

Director, Bureau of Public Personnel Administration

Personnel Legislation in 1927.—Public personnel administrators in general look upon the establishment of the merit system in Alameda county, California, in which Oakland is located, as the outstanding extension in 1927. The legislation was adopted in 1926, but the system was put into effect in 1927. The Alameda county commission has built up its staff, established records, made some progress toward the development of classification and compensation plans, held tests for a good many classes of positions, and established much of its procedure, though detailed rules have yet to be worked out.

As usual, a good deal of opposition has been encountered from those accustomed to receive patronage. When the tests were given for deputy sheriffs and an employment list established, the sheriff refused to replace twelve deputies who had either not been tested or had not secured places on the employment list high enough to justify their appointment and in the courts tested the right of the civil service commission to force their appointment. The courts upheld the commission and the sheriff finally made his appointments from the employment list, saying at the time that he had no reason to believe that the new employees would not be efficient but deploring his inability to choose deputies in whom he had personal confidence. At various times, too, the disgruntled individuals and groups have publicly found fault with the tests given, though from the point of view of technical soundness the Alameda county civil service commission has done unusually well for a new organization. There have also been more or less unfavorable news stories and editorial comments in some of the newspapers. On the whole, however, the new personnel agency seems to be quite firmly established with the end of the first year of operations.

Legislation has also provided for the establishment of the merit system to be administered through a civil service commission for Wayne county, in which Detroit is located. As yet little work has been done toward getting the new system established.

In most public jurisdictions where there is a central personnel agency there was little legislation of significance in 1927. Attempts to bring about by legislative means the extension of the merit system and improvement of its administration or to remove from the statute books existing legislation were in the main equally futile.

The legislation that probably attracted the most attention was that providing for the selection of prohibition enforcement officers in the federal service of the United States in accordance with the original civil service act of 1883. Though the legislation provides that the work must be done within six months after the passage of the act in March, the United States civil service commission made relatively little progress. The reason alleged was the failure of Congress to provide extra funds for this work; the commission held, despite its annual appropriations of a million dollars to do almost exclusive recruiting work, that it was unable to take on this extra burden. The commission asked for $200,000 additional appropriations to hold tests for filling 2,500 positions which, if allowed, would make these tests the most expensive ever held on a large scale in the United States. The commission did "borrow" $30,000 from its regular funds to use in getting the tests under way and has nearly completed the tests for some of the administrative classes of positions; at the time this is written (December 14) it is all but marking time waiting for the provision of funds through the passage of the deficiency appropriation bill that failed last March. The Better Government League, with headquarters in Washington, is opposing the appropriation on the ground that the commission should have been able to take on this additional work without additional funds, and that in any case $50,000 to $60,000 would be a reasonable amount for holding tests for filling 2,500 positions if special funds were provided.

✱

Classification and Compensation Studies.—Following a long delay, revised classification and compensation plans for some 12,000 positions in the Massachusetts state service have finally been put into effect through action by the governor and council. In the last half of 1926 a detailed study was made by a group of technical experts; their report recommended extensive revisions in the classification in effect and also many increases in the compensation levels. During the 1927 session of the legislature an attempt was made to change the classification and compensation plan in many important respects, but this attempt failed. Finally the plans with some modification were put into effect by the governor and council.

At the November election in Cleveland the voters approved an additional tax levy for the purpose of adjusting and equalizing salaries. A new classification plan was put into effect more than a year ago, but at that time no adjustments in salaries were made. It is expected that police and fire officers will receive the bulk of the additional money provided in the new tax levy, but that equalizations will be made in the salaries for other classes of positions. The city council has appointed a commission to deal with the details of the matter.

In Detroit the classification worked out two years ago has now been made fully effective and the salaries of employees brought into line with the rates provided by the compensation plan. Practically no salaries are now outside the scales, and the practice of making salary adjustments in accordance with the scheme of administration for the compensation plan is becoming established.

In San Francisco neither classification nor compensation matters have as yet been worked out at all satisfactorily. A study was made two years ago, but a great deal of opposition to the original proposal developed and at that time no action was taken. The board of supervisors provided for an additional study which has been carried on by the civil service commission in coöperation with the San Francisco Bureau of Governmental Research. Although the new work was begun almost a year ago, there have been so many delays that the report is not yet ready. At the same time requests for additional salaries increasing payroll costs almost a quarter of a million dollars have been made by employees and individual supervisors. The Bureau of Governmental Research is recommending that no action on these requests be taken until the results of the study under way are made available and that then adjustments be made on the basis of the duties and responsibilities attached to the various positions rather than on the basis of the length of service of the employees holding the positions.

❋

Retirement Legislation.—In several jurisdictions action has been recently initiated intended to establish retirement plans for large and small groups of public employees. In the state of California a commission has been appointed to make a study of the whole situation and propose a plan for the state service. In Seattle facts are being secured and analyzed in an attempt to bring about agreement with regard to a plan to be proposed for legislative action. In New York City an attempt is being made to apply the general retirement plan to additional groups of positions and to bring about other changes. In the federal service of the United States, the question as to whether the federal government should begin providing funds for meeting its accruing obligations and whether the maximum annuity should be increased and a minimum annuity established are receiving attention.

In an executive order dated July 25 and made public August 8 by the department of state, a retirement and disability system for the consular and diplomatic members of the foreign service of the United States was established. The system provides for payments of 5 per cent of the basic salary and annuities on retirement ranging from 30 per cent of the final average salary for those who have served 15 to 18 years up to 60 per cent for those who have served 27 to 30 years. A system entirely separate from the general retirement system for federal employees is set up, adding one more to the number of separate units concerned with personnel matters in the federal service of the United States.

A retirement system for the civil servants of the province of Saskatchewan became effective in March. The system provides for contributions of 4 per cent of their salaries by employees. The retirement age is placed at 65 years for males and 60 years for females who have served continuously for 35 years or more; upon reaching the age of retirement, an employee may be continued a further period not exceeding five years. The amount of the retirement annuity is one-fiftieth of the average salary for the last three years of service multiplied by the number of years of continuous service, with a provision that the yearly allowance shall not in any case be less than $360 nor more than $2,000.

NATIONAL
MUNICIPAL REVIEW

PUBLISHED MONTHLY BY THE

National Municipal League

VOL. XVII, No. 2   FEBRUARY, 1928   TOTAL No. 140

CONTENTS

EDITORIAL COMMENT.........................*H. W. Dodds*.........   63

LABOR PARTY GAINS IN MUNICIPAL ELECTIONS IN
    BRITAIN..............................*James K. Pollock*......   67

THE ATTACK ON CLEVELAND'S COUNCIL-MANAGER
    CHARTER.............................*Randolph O. Huus*.....   69

SAN FRANCISCO PROPOSES A NEW PLAN FOR MU-
    NICIPAL OPERATION.....................*Delos F. Wilcox*.......   74

A PROPOSAL TO CURE VOTE-SHIRKING..........*Victor Rosewater*......   77

IS THE SLACKER VOTE A MENACE?............*William B. Munro*.....   80

N. A. L. G. O..............................*Clinton Rogers Woodruff*   87

STANDARDS OF FINANCIAL ADMINISTRATION —
    A SUPPLEMENT.........................*Lent D. Upson and
                                        C. E. Rightor*......... 117

DEPARTMENTS

  I. Recent Books Reviewed..   93
 II. Judicial Decisions...*Edited by C. W. Tooke*   98
III. Public Utilities...*Edited by John Bauer* 102
 IV. Governmental Research Association Notes...................*Edited by Russell Forbes* 106
  V. Notes and Events...*Edited by H. W. Dodds* 113

THE LEAGUE'S BUSINESS

Geographic Distribution of League Members.—G. R. Howe, assistant secretary, reports that New York leads among the states in the number of members of the National Municipal League. At this writing they number 368. The following states rank in the order named: Pennsylvania 174; Massachusetts 151; California 126; Ohio 124; and Illinois 112.

Among the foreign nations Japan is in the lead with thirty members. In all twenty-four other nations are represented on our roll. In spite of disturbed domestic conditions in China, twelve members of that nation continue their membership in the League. Canada, which we do not reckon as a foreign nation, supplies fifty-two members on our list.

✳

Colonel Waite Leaves New York.—Colonel Henry M. Waite, Dayton's first city manager and former president of the National Municipal League, has moved from New York to Cincinnati to take charge of the building of a new union depot and freight terminal to cost $75,000,000. Seven railroads will share these facilities and construction will be pressed without delay.

Colonel Waite is deeply interested in better government and in the League, and the secretary feels a personal loss in his departure from New York.

✳

The Municipal Administration Service which is operating under the joint auspices of the National Municipal League and the Governmental Research Association has in press two additional pamphlets in its series on municipal administration as follows:

"Street Name Signs," by Adolph J. Post, Assistant Engineer, Public Works Department, City of Boston.

"Reporting Municipal Government," by Professor Wylie Kilpatrick of the University of Virginia.

Copies may be secured for twenty-five cents. These are numbers 8 and 9 in the Municipal Administration Service Series.

✳

Startling Revelation Regarding National Municipal League.—It will come as a surprise to most members of the National Municipal League that we are in reality a syndicate representing the manufacturers of materials commonly used by municipalities and that our real purpose is to place sales representatives in the various cities, who would be known as city managers, but who would secure for the League a monopoly of orders for city supplies. This amusing charge was a part of the under-cover propaganda against the city manager charter for Charleston, S. C. That it was taken seriously by many voters is one example of the mysterious processes of democracy.

NATIONAL
MUNICIPAL REVIEW

Vol. XVII, No. 2   FEBRUARY, 1928   Total No. 140

EDITORIAL COMMENT

The New York City Board of Health has improved the milk standard by reducing the number of bacteria permitted by half. Hereafter Grade B milk after pasteurization must contain not more than 50,000 bacteria per cc. Before pasteurization the maximum number is now 1,500,000 per cc.

❧

On November 8 the citizens of Portsmouth, Ohio, voted in favor of a commission to draft a new charter for the city and elected a charter commission of fifteen members. At the first meeting of the commission Miss Emma Cramer was elected chairman. The organization of a charter league is now under consideration.

❧

Students of city manager government recognize Kansas City as the one conspicuous example of failure to fulfill the implications of the manager plan. Manager H. F. McElroy is a Democrat. The city administration, he says, functions for the entire citizenship but is Democratic in its organization. Each party, he continues, has always made control of the city departments a party affair and the Democratic majority on the council are merely continuing in the footsteps of their predecessors.

Mr. McElroy is a man of integrity and courage, and we regret that he, together with many people in Kansas City, has not caught the spirit of the new charter.

Stephen B. Story has begun his term as city manager of Rochester by ordering all employees who are members of committees of political parties to resign immediately or forfeit their positions. In so doing Mr. Story called attention to Section 59 of the charter which prohibits a city employee from serving on a political committee, being a candidate to a nominating convention or soliciting campaign funds.

❧

According to the Citizens Research Institute of Canada, per capita municipal expenditures in the Dominion for 1926 varied from $62.42 in Edmonton to $13.54 in Charlottetown. In general the per capita expenditures of cities west of Toronto exceed $50 per year, while those east of Toronto are less than this amount.

❧

The New York metropolitan area as defined for the purposes of the 1927 census of manufactures includes 9,500,-000 persons and comprises a district within a forty mile radius of New York City instead of the previous ten mile limits. As pointed out by Mr. Dodge in the Review for last July, the census bureau has adopted a new definition of a metropolitan area on the basis of the economic and social activities centering in the big city. Among the factors considered were commuting distances, range of free delivery services, telephone service, and density of population.

63

Other metropolitan territories are reforming their boundaries in a manner similar to New York and it is believed that this new definition of a metropolitan region will be utilized in the 1930 general census as well as in the 1927 census of manufactures.

✣

Bureaucratic Control Over English Municipalities Increased The English have an officer known as the district auditor who examines accounts of local authorities as the appointed agent of the ministry of health. The audit is annual and the auditor has power to reduce charges and payments, and to disallow illegal expenditure and to surcharge it upon the individual members of the authority which authorized the spending. Some time ago, the broad powers of these district auditors were exemplified in the case of the borough of Poplar. Readers will remember that this labor-controlled borough desired to pay high wages to employees but that such wages were considered unreasonable by the district auditor and were disallowed. The wide discretion of the district auditor in this case was sustained by the House of Lords, and thus the situation was established by which an officer, appointed and removable by the minister of health, could nullify the discretionary action of municipal councils if such action does not conform to the auditor's theories of the social order.

In the face of much expressed doubt as to whether the district auditor should be continued at all, parliament recently passed a measure increasing the penalty which he may inflict. Hereafter every person who has been surcharged to an amount exceeding five hundred pounds shall be disqualified "for being elected or appointed or being a member of any local authority" for a period of five years. Appeal in such cases may be made to the High Court on the ground that the surcharged officer acted reasonably or in the belief that his action was authorized by law.

The *London Municipal Journal* sees in the act a declaration of failure and mistrust of local government and denies that the minister of health through his nominated auditors should be endowed with power to disqualify political opponents "because they hold exceptionally large—or absurdly narrow—views as to the nature and extent of the public services which the rate fund ought to bear."

✣

Dallas Adopts Longterm Financial Program In 1910 the late George E. Kessler prepared a city plan for Dallas, Texas. Since that time railroad passenger terminals have been unified; trunk line tracks have been removed from a principal downtown street, and terminal tracks lifted from other streets; many streets have been widened; new boulevards have been constructed; parks have been promoted; and reclamation of the whole river bottom district has been begun.

The carrying out of the Kessler plan with fidelity has proved expensive. According to John E. Surrat, writing in the January issue of *City Planning*, the cost has averaged about $1,500,000 a year, but the people of Dallas have never faltered. On December 15 the voters again evidenced their confidence in a comprehensive plan by authorizing bond issues totalling $23,900,000, to be expended over a period of nine years in accordance with a plan prepared by a citizens' advisory committee. The bonds will be issued from year to year as the physical work progresses, with a limitation of a maximum issue within any one year of $4,000,000.

Some of the larger items include street openings and widenings to cost $5,500,000; extension of the water system, $4,000,000; a storm drainage system, $3,500,000 for the city's share; public schools, $1,900,000; and parks and boulevards, $1,500,000. Dallas thus affords a commendable example not only of physical planning for the future, but of long time financial planning correlated with her physical development.

George B. Dealey, publisher of the Dallas *Morning News* and for many years an officer of the National Municipal League, has been a prominent leader in the movement. C. E. Ulrickson was chairman of the committee which prepared the present bond program.

✢

N. A. L. G. O., a Trustee for the Merit System in English Local Government N. A. L. G. O., described in this issue by Mr. Woodruff, is much more than a trade union. It is the National Association of Local Government Officers of England, Scotland and Wales, and boasts a membership of 40,000. Like a fully organized trade union, it extends insurance and benevolent facilities to its members and sponsors the interests of local officers before parliament. Comprehensive superannuation schemes have been enacted through its efforts and it is quick to aid individual officers to secure redress for wrongs suffered from local authorities. Like a properly conducted trade union, it is concerned with conditions of entrance and promotion, and its activities along this line supply the chief organized application to English local government of what we in the United States term the merit system.

We do not mean to suggest that English municipal government is honeycombed with the spoils system, although N. A. L. G. O. believes that parochialism and personal favoritism, not necessarily political, do exist as undesirable influences. But, with the exception of the London County Council,

English municipalities do not have organized agencies setting examinations, recommending applicants for appointment, maintaining efficiency ratings and administering classification systems. In the appointment of permanent officers and employees the local authorities are free from any supervisory checking or assisting agency such as our civil service commissions are designed to be.

True, in the professional branches, such as law, public health, finance and engineering, it is generally established that persons holding advanced office must possess adequate professional training and satisfy the requirements of the appropriate professional organization; as for example, the Institute of Civil Engineers and the Institute of Municipal Treasurers and Accountants. Such organizations, therefore, supply for the professional offices a testing machinery enforcing minimum qualifications though the examinations are not competitive for particular posts.

Ninety per cent of English local government officers enter the service at sixteen years of age or less. With the exception of the medical men, who must attend regular medical schools, the majority who go up the professional side take their training under a head of a department while at work. These are the "articled pupils," to whom Mr. Woodruff refers, to whom certificates are issued in due time by the appropriate professional society. Several technical colleges and institutes have been induced to provide instruction in subjects useful to local government officers preparing for professional and technical examinations with a view to promotion. For the benefit of officers who are out of reach of such instruction N. A. L. G. O. has established courses of instruction by correspondence.

But on the lay side no organized

tests have been employed and one of the activities of N. A. L. G. O. is to meet this lack. In response to its efforts, more than one hundred authorities have recognized the school leaving certificate, or its equivalent, as a standard for junior entrants. For those who have not attended school the association itself has prepared a preliminary examination which is considered equivalent to the school leaving certificate, but this will be abolished if and when local authorities take in none but school boys. Several local authorities have gone so far as to recruit juniors by competitive examinations conducted by the association.

For the intermediate and higher grades on the lay side, N. A. L. G. O. has also prepared examinations for the successful passage of which she will issue examination certificates. At present she is seeking to persuade local authorities to require such certificates and, as a basis of administering the plan, proposes joint examination boards on which the local authorities will be represented.

In brief N. A. L. G. O. is struggling for the principle of training for lay workers evidenced by examination as well as for the professional and technical staffs of local governments, and for the doctrine that the professional and technical force as well as the lay side, should have some special instruction in subjects related to public administration. Accordingly she has worked for the establishment of university courses leading to a diploma in public administration, which will be supplementary to all other professional qualifications. In this she had had the coöperation of the Institute for Public Administration. London University is the first to carry out the idea by offering an academic diploma in public administration, commonly known as the D. P. A.

For us, N. A. L. G. O.'s chief interest lies in the fact of an association of municipal employees fighting for the adoption of the merit principle in all its various phases, and from among its own members supplying, in coöperation with existing professional and educational agencies, the very machinery for carrying it into execution in the service of the state.

LABOR PARTY GAINS IN MUNICIPAL ELECTIONS IN BRITAIN

BY JAMES K. POLLOCK, JR.

Continued gains by the Labor party and frank line up under national party standards were the outstanding features.   ::   ::

THE annual municipal elections in Britain are over and for the second year in succession the Socialists have won the largest number of seats. On November 2 polling took place in over 300 towns in England and Wales and in about a hundred Scottish burghs.

LABOR GAINS 100 SEATS

The elections, especially in the north of England and in Wales, were keenly fought, but municipal elections in Britain never have the excitement and enthusiasm of the parliamentary contests. There is a rasp about the parliamentary campaigns which compels even quiet men to join in the struggle. But neither fear of high rates nor any other terror can arouse the citizens at the municipal poll.

Out of several thousand contests, the Socialists have gained in England approximately 100 seats as compared with 140 seats a year ago. In Scotland the elections resulted in a position as between the Moderates and the Socialists of "all square." Labor thus has some ground for rejoicing, although when one looks at the individual councils throughout the country one finds that Labor controls but a few. Nevertheless this year's election places her in the position of the strongest single party in a rather long string of boroughs, although the combined vote of the other two parties in these boroughs can keep Labor from controlling. Both the Conservatives and Liberals lost in number of seats, but the Conservative loss was greater.

On the other hand, there were some surprising Labor upsets in Glasgow and Dundee and some Conservative gains in the Home Counties. Even in boroughs like Nelson the system of coöpting the aldermen is likely to keep the Moderate party in control.

Municipal elections in England, as in America, have not given any important indication of the trend of forces in national politics, because local or personal questions play the chief part and the elections are not managed from the central offices of the parties. In past years, municipal elections in England were largely non-partisan and the candidates who stood for election did not carry the labels of the national parties. But all this has undergone a change and in this year's election the candidates were Liberal, Conservative or Socialist. For several years the Labor party has helped its candidates for municipal office. This year the Conservative party at its annual conference at Cardiff passed a resolution urging the central office of the party to assist Conservative candidates for municipal offices thus introducing a new partisan factor. Although many candidates still stand as independents or camouflaged as "Ratepayers" or "Moderates," the contest in many parts of Britain is becoming an out and out fight among the three national parties. Fortunately for the English ratepayer, whichever party wins, the administration of the city is entrusted to the competent hands of the permanent town officers who know no party and who work only for the good of their municipalities.

LIGHT VOTE IN SPITE OF SHORT BALLOT

To an American observing the mechanics of an English election, nothing is more interesting than the orderliness and the precision of the officials. Selected entirely for their ability, they carry on their job without partisan cares. Not less interesting than the excellence of the election staffs is the simplicity and ease with which an elector votes. In contrast to America, where the average voter is confronted with a large and complicated ballot bearing party designations and scores of names, the English voter is handed a simple ballot paper of small size carrying at most the names of three or four candidates, often only two. In addition to this, the English voter has not had to register himself, this being taken care of by the officials, and when election day comes, all that he has to do is to present himself at the polling place, receive his simple ballot paper, make one mark, and his task is completed. One cannot help wondering how the American voter ever manages his almost overwhelming burden. Englishmen would certainly be flabbergasted if they had to vote in an American city election.

Though the task of the English voter is a simple one, less than 50 per cent of the registered voters went to the polls in the recent municipal elections. In some "safe" wards the percentage dropped as low as 30, and rarely was the percentage as high as 60. The 80 per cent and 90 per cent polls achieved in parliamentary elections come only after hard canvassing and the expenditure of large sums of money. Such expenditures and such canvassing are not present in municipal contests and the result is that half the voters do not vote.

The Socialists realize that their policies cannot be carried out unless they control the local councils and in consequence they have put forth every effort in recent years to capture as many municipal seats as possible. The average Englishman, however, is not a strong believer in a Socialist menace to his local government and a steady Socialist gain is the result. The determined attempt which is being made in England in many quarters to present all political issues as a contest between Socialist and anti-Socialist can scarcely be said to have been accepted by the electorate.

THE ATTACK ON CLEVELAND'S COUNCIL-MANAGER CHARTER

BY RANDOLPH O. HUUS

Western Reserve University

City Manager Hopkins is still on the job and the Cleveland charter still intact as a result of the November election.   ::   ::   ::   ::

THE attack on the manager plan was led by Harry L. Davis, who had thrice been elected mayor of Cleveland by the aid of Morris Maschke, local Republican leader. From 1921 to 1923 Davis served as governor of Ohio although his home county (Cuyahoga) turned against him in the election of 1920, for which defection he blamed Maschke. In 1924 he ran again for governor but was defeated. Since the 1920 election Maschke and Davis have not been on friendly terms. Dissatisfaction with Davis as mayor was evidenced by the Cuyahoga vote for him in in 1920 and by the election of Fred Kohler as mayor in 1921 and the adoption of the city manager plan in the same year. From 1924 to 1927 Davis was out of the public eye.

Davis renewed his activities in the spring of 1927 by filing a petition for a special election on a proposed charter amendment. Legal questions delayed proceedings until the state supreme court finally decided that the petition was filed with the wrong authorities. Davis then revised his amendment and filed a new petition. This amendment was placed on the ballot to be voted on at the regular municipal election in November. Two other charter amendment proposals, sponsored by George B. Harris and Carl D. Friebolin respectively, were also put on the ballot. The Davis and Harris amendments were in reality new charters while the Friebolin amendment made only one important revision. Both the Harris and Davis proposals restored the mayor-council form and the ward system, but the Davis amendment provided for plurality elections while the Harris amendment proposed the preferential system. A striking feature of the Davis proposal was the extraordinary powers given the mayor; for example, the board of control appointed by the mayor was to approve all contracts in excess of $1,000 and to have exclusive power to fix all rates for publicly owned public utility services.

Of these amendments the Davis proposal was the only one to receive serious consideration. The effect of the other two was merely to confuse the voter. This confusion was enhanced by the lack of any distinguishing marks on the Harris and Davis amendments—they were almost identical in form as they appeared on the ballot. In addition the Citizens' League of Cleveland sponsored a charter commission proposal as a counter to the three amendments. Its theory was that the only orderly and sensible method of submitting an entirely new charter to the voters was through a duly elected charter commission.

THE CAMPAIGN AS A STRUGGLE FOR POLITICAL POWER

The foregoing suggests that the real basis for the campaign was the attempt on the part of Davis and the groups supporting him to get political control of Cleveland and Cuyahoga County. The mayor-council and the council-manager forms of government became merely instruments in the contest. For all practical purposes the alignment was pro-Davis and anti-Davis; in the last analysis a struggle of the local party organizations, especially the Republican led by Maurice Maschke, to remain in power. The resulting combinations on both sides produced strange bed-fellows.

THE DAVIS FORCES

Probably the strongest active group supporting Davis was the labor element. The Cleveland Federation of Labor endorsed his amendment and President Harry McLaughlin campaigned actively in its behalf. Labor's chief grievance seemed to be against past activities of City Manager Hopkins and the council, who were considered hostile to union standards. Especial displeasure was voiced over the application of the Sulzmann salary ordinance and particularly as regards the payment of overtime to city employees. As one prominent labor leader said in the campaign, "Hopkins has denied overtime to certain workers of this city while every contractor does grant overtime to those he employs. Hopkins is the leader of the group which means to destroy organized labor in Cleveland. This fight means the life and death struggle to the labor movement. Lose this fight and organized labor is done." Evidently the labor leaders felt that their interests would be given more consideration if Davis would return to power. Opposition to the council-manager plan and proportional representation was also manifest among them. A pamphlet issued by the Cleveland Federation of Labor stated, "The City

Manager Plan is un-American, undemocratic and autocratic and should not be tolerated by anyone who desires to conserve the liberties of the people." Proportional representation was also denounced in this pamphlet. However, most of the time of the labor leaders was spent in attacking the city council, City Manager Hopkins and the leaders of the party organizations.

Some labor support was anti-Davis, a few labor union locals particularly among the railroad groups declaring against the Davis amendment. Thomas S. Farrell, president of the waiters union and former public utilities director under Davis, and Rose Moriarity, appointed to the state industrial commission by Davis, campaigned actively against his amendment.

The defection of the leaders of the Cuyahoga Democratic Club from their party organization deserves mention. This rebellion on the part of a younger group of Democrats was due to dissatisfaction with the leadership of W. Burr Gongwer, chairman of the Democratic County Executive Committee. Thus it happened that a few Democrats prominent in the organization campaigned actively for a charter amendment sponsored by a Republican which the official organization was seeking to defeat.

Davis naturally had a considerable personal following as well and the active campaign support of Walter D. Meals, a former law partner of Maschke. And yet most of the political aides that held office during the Davis administrations took the stump against his amendment in this election.

Cleveland has a serious unemployment problem but conditions are probably no worse than in many other cities. The Davis forces were able to make effective political capital of this in the campaign speeches.

THE ANTI-DAVIS FORCES

There was an amazing diversity in the organizations, groups and individuals uniting to defeat the Davis amendment. In the forefront were the official organizations of the Republican and Democratic parties, which the passage of this amendment would have threatened. In special danger was dominant control of Maschke, the Republican leader. Both party organizations are unfavorable to proportional representation and neither party has shown any enthusiasm for the council-manager plan, as such. However the adoption of the manager charter did not demoralize the existing party organizations; despite the council-manager plan the present municipal government is not insensitive to party influence. But support of the record of the council and the city manager by the campaign speakers representing the official party attitude seemed to imply endorsement of the present council-manager charter—a rather awkward situation. As Professor A. R. Hatton put it in a recent talk, "The Democrats and the Republicans have no use for the present charter but they were driven into the position of defending it to preserve themselves against the threat of Harry Davis." Naturally, the party speakers, when not attacking Davis, placed most of their emphasis on the record of City Manager Hopkins rather than on the merits of the council-manager plan.

Another organization actively concerned with the outcome of the vote was the Citizens League of Cleveland. Being also anti-Davis, the officials of the League found themselves fighting shoulder to shoulder with the leaders of the two parties! The attorney of the League, Francis T. Hayes, took an active part in the campaign speaking against the Davis charter proposal.

The Charter Commission proposal of the Citizens League was endorsed by the two parties—in fact the leaders of three organizations met in conference and selected the fifteen designated candidates on the Charter Commission ballot. The chief interest of the Citizens League in this campaign was to preserve the council-manager plan for Cleveland.

The possibility of the repeal of the council-manager charter and the return of Harry L. Davis as mayor aroused many other groups to action. Numerous church organizations endorsed the present government and opposed Davis and all his political works and ways. Rabbi Abba H. Silver defended the council-manager plan in an able keynote speech made before an audience of 2,500 people. This was the first time, he said, that he had spoken from a political platform during his career in the ministry, but the moral seriousness of the present attack on good government justified his action. The Reverend Joel B. Hayden was also active against the Davis amendment, as well as a number of clergymen prominent in the Catholic Church.

The women seemed especially interested in the retention of the council-manager plan. The Women's City Club and the local branch of the League of Women Voters were both in favor of retaining the present charter. Women industrial leaders in the city organized to combat the Davis amendment, while both parties had women chairmen directing the activities in the wards and precincts.

The Chamber of Commerce in a published statement urged the defeat of all three amendments saying that the time was too short as yet to pass on the merits of the council-manager plan. This public alignment of the Chamber of Commerce was repeatedly called to the attention of the voters in the labor districts by the Davis speakers and with considerable effect. Of the three newspapers in Cleveland the *Press* and the *Plain Dealer* were strongly anti-Davis while the *News* was non-committal.

THE CAMPAIGN AND THE ISSUES

This campaign was no pink tea affair. Political tricks of every description were used to get votes. For the most part the audiences at the meetings were strongly partizan and the few that had the temerity to heckle were ousted with scant ceremony. It developed into a continuous round of charges and counter-charges involving personalities, records and motives. Party loyalty was often stressed by the anti-Davis speakers. The Davis speakers said their cause was that of the people against the big business interests. Davis himself stated that his only interest was that the government should again be returned to the hands of "the people" by allowing them to elect their chief executive. Numerous meetings were held every evening during the three weeks of active campaigning. The voters were given many elementary lessons on how to cast their ballots—especially on the Davis side due to the similarity of the Davis and Harris amendments. There was an excess of dodgers, pamphlets, placards and also considerable bill-board advertizing. Through it all the voters maintained an unusual interest despite the confusion that must have existed in their minds as to what it was all about.

The adoption of the Davis amendment would have eliminated the council-manager plan and restored the mayor-council form. But the speakers, with a few prominent exceptions, showed little inclination to discuss the merits of these issues. The anti-Davis speakers centered their attack on Davis and his proposed charter. The Davis speakers dubbed the council-manager plan as "czaristic" and proportional representation as a "joke," but the argument seldom reached any higher level. One of the significant characteristics of the campaign was the widespread apathy and antagonism exhibited toward proportional representation.

THE ELECTION RESULTS

The election results as they affected the present charter are as follows:

	For	Against
Davis amendment	73,732	80,148
Harris amendment	34,654	113,249
Friebolin amendment	43,910	101,318
Charter commission	53,157	72,215

The Davis amendment was defeated by a majority of only 6,416. The election result is a distinct threat to the political leadership of Maschke in Cleveland and Cuyahoga County. Although the Davis amendment lost, it carried seventeen of the thirty-three wards of the city. Evidence of assistance to the Davis campaign from down state Republican forces shows that the election is of more than local significance since Maurice Maschke is also Republican national committeeman from Ohio.

ELECTION FRAUDS

Immediately after the election, the Davis forces, claiming that they had lost many votes through fraud, secured a temporary injunction from the common pleas court prohibiting the board of elections from certifying to the election results. They also appealed to Governor A. V. Donahey to order a special investigation but he has taken no action. County Prosecutor Edward Stanton requested the Davis forces to present their evidences of fraud to the grand jury for investigation but this was not done. Later Mr.

Stanton filed a demurrer to the temporary injunction alleging that the Davis petitioners should have asked for a recount instead of asking the court for a new election date and that the time for filing a recount petition expired December 1. Final hearings on the fraud charges are set for the early part of January, the temporary injunction still being in effect. Independent election fraud evidence was brought before a local justice of peace court by Councilman W. J. Kennedy but nothing of importance developed as a result of these hearings.

NEW ATTACK PLANNED FOR APRIL

The Davis forces seem determined to continue the fight for their charter proposal. In the early part of December Attorney Richard E. Collins announced in behalf of the Davis organization that the charter amendment had been redrafted with only minor changes. No change was made in some of the provisions severely criticized during the campaign. These included the unusual powers of the mayor, his $25,000 salary and the clause providing that the minimum wage for city employees should be $2.50 per day. It is expected that petitions will be circulated to put the redrafted charter on the ballot at the presidential primary election on April 24. Though the new charter has been ready for a number of weeks petitions have not as yet been circulated.

The party leaders with the present election out of the way are insistent that proportional representation be eliminated from the present charter. Mayor John Marshall has appointed a councilmanic committee to hold public hearings at which proposed changes in the present charter may be presented. No hearings have as yet been held but it is possible that the party leaders will submit an amendment to the present charter eliminating proportional representation, if the Davis amendment is resubmitted.

The most interesting development after the election has been the apparent reconciliation between City Manager Hopkins and the officials of the Cleveland Federation of Labor. There are indications however that the rank and file of labor are still willing to support the Davis charter proposal in another campaign even though the leaders remain neutral. So it may be that the harassed voter will have to pass again on the merits of the present charter at the spring election.

SAN FRANCISCO PROPOSES A NEW PLAN FOR MUNICIPAL OPERATION

BY DELOS F. WILCOX

The board of supervisors have presented a charter amendment to consolidate all her utility enterprises under a single utility commission.

ALONE among the great cities of the country, the city of San Francisco has been committed by its charter for many years to the general policy of municipal ownership. It has been operating a system of municipal railways since 1912, in partial competition with the privately owned systems, and has committed itself politically and otherwise to complete municipal ownership and operation of street railways, water supply, and electric lights and power, at least.

After fifteen years of experience with municipal operation by the board of public works under the more or less minute control of the board of supervisors, the city has become conscious of the need for a more effective plan of municipal operation, and there seems to be practical unanimity in public sentiment for the establishment of a non-political utility commission to administer all the city's utility enterprises. A charter amendment providing for such a commission has been drafted, and has been approved by the board of supervisors to go on the ballot in November, 1928. After being ratified by the people, all city charter amendments in California are subject to approval by the legislature; but thus far, such approval has always been given without question or delay.

THE CHARTER AMENDMENT

The San Francisco plan for the administration of municipal utilities, if adopted, will set a landmark for the entire country. The comprehensive nature of the plan is expressed in the first section of the proposed charter amendment as follows:

The construction, management, supervision, maintenance, extension, operation, and control of all public utilities and other properties, used, owned, acquired, leased or constructed by the City and County of San Francisco, as well as all extensions, additions and betterments thereto, for the purpose of supplying to the said City and County and its residents and inhabitants, and territory outside the limits of said city and county and the residents and inhabitants thereof, with water, light, heat, power or transportation shall be exclusively vested in a utility commission of three members, anything in this Charter to the contrary notwithstanding. The commission shall have power to make all rules and regulations not inconsistent with the provisions of this Article which it deems necessary or proper for the conduct of its business and the regulation of the matters herein committed to its charge.

The commission will consist of three members appointed by the mayor subject to confirmation by the board of supervisors. The terms of office will be six years, except that the first appointees will hold office for two, four, and six years, respectively. Commissioners will be removable in the same way as elective officers.

The commission must appoint, as its chief executive and administrative official, a manager of utilities, who need not be, at the time of his appointment, a resident of the city. The commission may create departments or bureaus, with sub-managers or directors. Neither the manager nor the sub-

74

manager will be subject to civil service rules, and they will hold their positions at the pleasure of the commission. An auditor and all the other employees, subordinates and assistants required for the conduct of its business may be appointed by the commission subject to civil service rules, except that persons employed on construction work outside of the city and one personal secretary or confidential clerk to the manager and each sub-manager will be exempt. Also the civil service rules will not apply to "persons employed for temporary service in positions requiring high techincal skill." The operating employees of any utility taken over by the city will retain their positions and acquire a status in the civil service, if they have been employed for at least a year before the utility is taken over.

POWERS OF THE COMMISSION

Salaries, wages and working conditions are to be fixed by the commission subject to the limitation of the hours of labor prescribed by law and by the charter. The charter contains the following provisions for platform men and bus operators on the Municipal Railway:

The basic hours of labor shall be eight hours, to be completed within ten consecutive hours; there shall be one day of rest in each week of seven days; all labor performed in excess of eight hours in any one day or six days in any one week shall be paid for at the rate of time and one-half.

The manager of utilities will have the power of suspension over the employees of the commission for cause or for disciplinary purposes. The commission may continue a suspension for disciplinary purposes for a time not to exceed thirty days, and may order the manager to prefer charges against a suspended employee. Removals by the commission will be subject to the appeals provided for in the civil service rules.

The commission will have power "to make contracts for work, supplies, materials, or equipment" when the cost can be met out of current revenues or from the funds appropriated for its use or derived from the sale of bonds authorized for the construction or acquisition of public utilities. Construction work is to be done by public contract unless, upon recommendation of the manager, the commission decides that the work can be more advantageously carried on by its own employees. The commission may make its own rules in regard to public letting, but they must provide for at least five days' advertising for bids and award to the lowest responsible bidder, with the right to reject all bids and readvertise, or to reject the proposal of any bidder who in the opinion of the commission is not competent to fulfill the contract.

One of the greatest problems in municipal operation of street railways is the control of extensions. In this matter the commission will be supreme.

Accounts are to be kept separately for each utility in the form prescribed by the railroad commission for utilities of like character, and other necessary accounts, accounting forms, and procedure are to be maintained as prescribed by the utility commission. Monthly reports of receipts and expenditures, for each utility, and annual reports, are to be filed with the board of supervisors and printed for public distribution.

FINANCIAL PROVISIONS

The manager of utilities must prepare a separate annual budget for each utility. After public hearings the commission may adopt this budget, or modify it. Copies of the budget as adopted must be filed with the mayor and with the board of supervisors, and expenditures are not to exceed the appropriations for the respective items in the budget as adopted. Each utility is to be self-sustaining unless funds for its relief are appropriated by the board of supervisors.

The funds of one utility may not be diverted to any other utility, but any surplus accumulated in excess of a maximum fixed by the commission will be automatically transferred to the city's general fund. However, by unanimous vote the commission may adopt "a program for the accumulation of a surplus to cover a period not exceeding ten years, for the purpose of financing extensions and additions to existing utilities out of said accumulation." No funds accumulated from one utility may be used to pay for additions or extensions of another utility, and no surplus accumulated for additions and extensions may be used for any other purpose unless authorized by the board of supervisors by ordinance.

The commission will have authority to capitalize interest during construction, and for a period of not more than six months after the completion of construction.

The receipts from the operation of each utility are to be paid into the city treasury and kept in a separate fund from which the commission may make appropriations for the following purposes in the order named:

(a) For payment of the operating expenses of such utility, including pension charges and compensation insurance;

(b) For repairs and maintenance;

(c) For depreciation and accident reserves;

(d) For payment of interest and sinking funds on the bonds issued for the acquisition or construction of such utility and extensions thereto;

(e) For reserve funds out of which to construct or acquire extensions and betterments to said utility;

(f) For a surplus reserve.

The commission must maintain pension and compensation insurance accounts, with annual estimates of the proper reserves required therefor. The manager must appraise the lines of the several classes of property for each utility and determine the amount of a reasonable reserve for depreciation and obsolescence as they accrue, subject to reappraisal once in five years. Pending such appraisal the monthly appropriations to the reserve are to be on the basis of four per cent per annum on the historical cost of the utility property. Reasonable accident reserves also must be maintained out of revenues subject to a reappraisal every five years.

RATES AND FARES

The commission will have power to fix and adjust rates and fares. Rates may be fixed at varying scales for different classes of service or consumers; and the rates so fixed "must include rates for services rendered any department or other utilities of the City and County." The rates fixed must be such that the aggregate revenue derived from them for each specific utility "shall represent not less than the actual total cost of the service of that utility as determined by the commission; provided further, that when the utility commission on the basis of a financial analysis in writing by the manager of utilities, may recommend to the board of supervisors a scale of rates under which estimated aggregate revenues from a specific utility may represent less than the actual cost of the service rendered by such utility, the board of supervisors, by a two-thirds vote of all members, may authorize such scale of rates, and must, at the same time, specify the manner in which the estimated annual operating deficits will be met. Such rate schedule may then be adopted by the commission."

The commission may provide for the rendition of utility services outside of the city limits at rates which may include proportionate compensation for interest during construction paid out of taxes.

Each utility must pay out of its revenues the cost of services rendered to it by other departments and utilities, and in its use of the streets the commission must obey all ordinances, and regulations of the board of public works in regard to street openings, and must pay the same fees in connection therewith that privately owned utilities would have to pay.

The commission, with the approval of the board of supervisors, will have authority to lease lands under its control for periods of not to exceed ten years, and will have power to acquire by purchase, lease, condemnation, or otherwise, property within or without the city limits which it may deem necessary for the construction, maintenance, extension or operation of the works under its control.

A PROPOSAL TO CURE VOTE-SHIRKING

BY VICTOR ROSEWATER, Ph.D.

Philadelphia

Voting-by-mail will remove the deterrent imposed by involved systems of personal registration and facilitate casting the ballot on election day.

It is undeniable that there has been a deplorable increase in the number of vote-slackers in the United States. Whether the stay-at-homes constitute 52 per cent of the total entitled to vote, or not over 40 per cent, does not invite debate since, either way, the figure is altogether too large and betokens a real menace to democratic self-government. If people possessing the suffrage will not help govern themselves, they will be governed by others, and very likely in a manner neither satisfactory nor creditable.

But how remedy the ominous situation? A variety of ways to solve the problem are being suggested, most of them intended to convert the non-voter by inflicting a penalty that will force him to the polls or to the police court. "Deposit your ballot or deposit your fine," would be the gist of the law with, presumably, a jail sentence in the offing. While some-thing, no doubt, can be said in its favor, compulsory voting has serious limitations. Voting, in its very essence, denotes a choice, and a free choice, between candidates, or for or against measures, and a compelled choice defeats its own object. Obviously, a man compelled to vote as some one else dictates merely enables the boss to vote a second time, or as often as he can enforce his will on others. And a man compelled to vote, yet with no will to vote and no choice to express, is apt to mark his ballot hit or miss, or to become the puppet of another. Threat of a tax or fine for not voting is but the reverse of an offer of a premium for voting. "You will be better off by five dollars or ten dollars (or whatever penalty be fixed) if you vote," is exactly what the vote-buyer tells his prospect—the only difference being the added condition in the latter case that the beneficiary "vote right."

The proposal to tax non-voters assumes that the great body of those who now do not vote abstain deliberately and refuse, through indifference, prejudice, disinclination, or sheer viciousness, to do their plain duty. In point of fact, this is a far-drawn conclusion. Some of the slacker vote probably is explainable on the ground of crass laziness. Again some of it is due to a feeling that the effort is useless or needless, especially where no issue is at stake, where no hot and heavy campaign has been waged to excite popular interest and stir the public to participation. But much of the seeming lethargy, altogether too much, is chargeable to the hurdles which, by our registration and election laws, we put in the way of voting—to absurd laws that make it hard to vote instead of facilitating voting.

In some of our states, for example, a tax is imposed, not on non-voters, but on voters. Pennsylvania, that hobgoblin of gang rule, limits the franchise to taxpayers and makes the exhibit of a tax receipt prerequisite to registration. The "machine" of course sees to it that its cohorts procure the necessary poll tax receipts—but how many independent citizens refuse to step up to the counter and pay for the privilege of voting? It should be understood that, in Pennsylvania, the poll tax is collected right in the registration booth, that no attempt is made to collect it from non-voters, that its payment carries no other connotation. Similar poll taxes, payable far in advance of the election, have long furnished a favorite device in certain southern states for keeping the blacks from the polls, and it is said a high grade of ingenuity has often been developed to lure the receipts away from those who insist on paying.

When it comes to registration as we commonly practise it, let us be honest with ourselves and confess that it would be difficult to produce any more effective vote-deterrent. The man or woman who asks to be registered is regularly treated like a criminal being subjected to a Bertillon measurement. Every voter is presumed to be a colonized crook or an imminent repeater until he proves himself innocent. The answers that must be recorded correspond with those inscribed under the pictures in the rogues' gallery—name, age, birthplace, location and length of residence, height, weight, color of hair and eyes, physical defects, and what not. More sensitive folks, especially women, are frightened into vote-shirking than are brought to the polls by all the pulpit preaching.

Then think of the multiplied demands for sacrifice of time just when time means money, the distances to be traveled, the distasteful polling places, the standing in line, the broken engagements. All this has to be undergone in most of our states not once or twice only, but once every year for registration and again and again for every regular and special election that may be held. Some commonwealths have successfully installed permanent registration which, at least, has the advantage of exacting personal appearance to register only a single time, barring change of residence from one district to another. Let none of us, however, underestimate the obstacles to voting in the necessity of repeated registrations, in the numerous trips to polling places to mark and deposit ballots, in all the annoying loss of time, embarrassing questions, interference with business and social engagements, and the apparent in-effectiveness of the act. Under such circumstances, it too frequently looks easier to "let George do it."

THE VOTE-BY-MAIL PLAN

If we will realize that vote-shirking is ascribable, at least in part, to our over-complicated election machinery, we will approach the problem from a different angle and ask ourselves new questions. Before putting a tax on non-voting, why not take off the tax on voting? Before fining men and women for failing to present themselves to registration and election officers and submit to an inquisition from two to six times a year, why not credit most folks with a desire to do their duty so far as they know how and try to do something to smooth for them the path to the ballot box?

The vote-by-mail plan, inaugurated by certain states a few years ago in the interest of the traveling salesmen and later extended to the soldiers in camp, may point a way. Uncle Sam's post office service has come to cover practically all the inhabited area of the country and can be made to reach every person entitled to vote regardless where he happens to be. If people who are out of town on election day can be provided with ballots, be allowed to mark them at leisure, and have them gathered in by mail and counted for the election, all under proper safe-guards, surely the same privilege could be accorded to people who are not out of town. What logic is there in com-pelling a person to leave his home in order to enjoy the benefit of postal voting? To be able to vote by mail from your own fireside is not an ultra-Utopian idea. Even registration by mail, or through the mail carrier, does not stretch the imagination to the breaking point. Consider for a mo-ment what improvement would be thus brought about. Ballots with full instructions mailed in ample time to you and every person on the officially verified list of voters. Ballots pre-pared by each voter carefully and thoughtfully, no confusion or haste because of the long line waiting im-patiently behind you. Ballots dis-tinctly marked and affirmed under oath to record your uncoerced, un-bought choice, then sealed and called for by the postman on the day set by law. An opening for fraud—possibly, but no more than now and no more difficult to prevent or to detect. No interference of inclement weather, no stay-at-homes on account of bad roads, no necessary abstention because of weddings, religious holidays, accident or sickness that does not impair the faculties. Little or no possibility of detention through over-lapping working hours, not so feasible for the employer to disfranchise em-ployes unsympathic to his preferences. Every qualified elector would have an unimpeded chance to vote and loss of vote would be, in nearly every in-stance, self-inflicted.

It goes without saying that we would be foolhardy to expect such a radical step to be taken over night, or in a short time, or for the whole country at once. All our important electoral reforms have reached us piece-meal after much pioneering and experimentation. Fortunately, our federal system of government, which leaves to the constituent common-wealths the enactment and adminis-tration of election laws, permits and encourages this very thing. We have several states that shine as ground-breakers in reform legislation—legisla-tion which, when shown to be salutary, has been adopted more or less generally. There should be at least a few pro-gressive commonwealths whose people have sufficient confidence in their own

intelligence and integrity to trust themselves. Once set in motion by one or
two of these states, discarding the
inherited straight-jacket election machinery and substituting a well-worked-
out scheme of universal voting by mail,
a complete transformation of our elections would in time be accomplished
whose efficacy would then rest entirely
on the political education of the people.

IS THE SLACKER VOTE A MENACE?

BY WILLIAM B. MUNRO

Vice President, National Municipal League

*Get-out-the-vote propagandists have a mistaken theory of popular
government.*   ::   ::   ::   ::   ::   ::   ::   ::

SURELY it takes some hardihood to
answer this question in the negative.
Everywhere we hear it proclaimed that
voting is a duty imposed on men and
women by the very nature of popular
government; that this duty is being
widely evaded, and that the evasion on
so large a scale constitutes a grave
menace to the very existence of free
institutions. Our newspapers and our
uplift organizations are warning the
people that the situation is fraught
with danger, and telling us that "Rome
fell because her citizens became indifferent to their civic obligations."
Even the President of the United
States has deemed it worth while to
join in the appeal for a better attendance at the polls. This solicitude for
the stay-at-home voter seems, indeed,
to have become a nation-wide obses-
sion, and to protest against it is like the
voice of one crying in the wilderness.

FALLING VOTE DESPITE
BALLYHOO METHODS

The statistics of non-voting, of
course, look formidable. We must
have about sixty million eligible voters
in the United States. But out of this
total it is figured that nearly a third
have never taken the trouble to get

themselves registered as voters. That
leaves something above forty million
registrants. Of these, only 22,000,000
went to the polls in the congressional
election of 1926. True enough, this
was an off-year election; but the total
polled vote at the presidential election
of 1924 did not rise above 30,000,000.
The proportion of stay-at-homes is
often 25 to 30 per cent, even in lively
campaigns; and when there are no
important contests on the ballot it
sometimes runs to 50 per cent, or more.
Taking the average for all our elections,
national, state and local, it can fairly
be said, therefore, that what we really
have in this country is not government
by a majority of the people, but
government by a mere plurality of the
politically-interested.

Nor does the situation seem to be
growing better. The proportion of the
polled vote to the total vote is, on the
whole, smaller than it was twenty-five
years ago. It has been suggested that
the ratio used to be larger because
there was more repeating, personating
and fraudulent registration in the old
days; but that explanation hardly
accounts for the whole discrepancy.
Everywhere there are indications that
electoral apathy is growing, not de-

creasing. And this in spite of the country-wide efforts that are being made by organizations of all sorts to increase the attendance at the polls. A dozen of them are at it—the National Civic Federation, the Daughters of the American Revolution, the National League of Women Voters, and the National Association of Manufacturers (with its slogan of "vote as you please, but vote"), not to speak of chambers of commerce, Rotary and Kiwanis clubs, and various other organizations. Not long ago a National Get-Out-the-Vote Club was formed, with headquarters in Washington and branches all over the country. Large amounts of oratory and effort, along with considerable sums of money, are being expended in bawling at the voters whenever any sort of election is approaching—bombarding them with appeals to vote whether they are interested or not, whether they know anything about the candidates or not, in other words, to vote for the sake of voting.

In a certain western city, at a recent election, the Chamber of Commerce hired a staff of clerks for the day and had them call up every name in the telephone book with the injunction: "Go to the polls and do your duty. Don't be a civic slacker." The cost of doing this was considerable; it demoralized the whole telephone service during the day and the results were negligible so far as increasing the size of the total vote was concerned.

In another city several hundred Boy Scouts were kept at home from school in order that they might stand near the polling booths and hand out buttons inscribed: "I have voted, have You?" Such gestures mean little or nothing in terms of enlightened citizenship.

Worst of all is the insincerity which characterizes much of this endeavor

to inflate the ballot box. Not long ago, one of the candidates for the governorship in a middle-western state bellowed at his people from the stump: "I want your votes, but if you can't vote for me, vote for my opponent. Don't stay at home. Come out and vote for somebody." Of course he didn't mean what he said. It was hillbillie hokum of the first order. No candidate ever honestly desires a bumper vote in the interest of his opponent. It is contrary to human nature.

The whole thing shows how enslaved we have become to impostor pietisms about bad citizenship, and everyone's "sacred duty" to vote. There is nothing in our constitutions, laws, nor civic morality which makes it the duty of any man to vote unless he feels that he can thereby contribute to the greater effectiveness of popular government. To vote unintelligently is a greater disservice to the commonwealth than not to vote at all.

People do not become good citizens by going to the polls. They go to the polls because they are good citizens. They go when and because they are interested. They stay away because they have no interest, or too little interest, in the issues or the candidates. And when one reflects upon the kind of issues and candidates that are so often presented to them, this lack of popular interest is hardly a matter for amazement. Many voters remain befogged, confused, bewildered, because that is what the leaders often intend them to be.

In such cases is there anything to be gained by having them certify their bewilderment and lack of knowledge at the ballot box? It is hard to see what real service can ever be rendered to the cause of enlightened government by the mere expedient of herding to the polls, with some sort of militant propaganda, a larger number of uninterested, uninformed, reluctant people who go because they are shamed into it by clarion calls to the performance of their duty as citizens.

We ought to concentrate our energies upon the task of clarifying the issues, vitalizing the party system, and improving the quality of the candidates as a means of getting the people interested, informed, and aroused between elections. We should do this by making the governmental process simpler, not more complicated. We should try to increase, not simply the total number of voters, but the number of intelligent voters who will go to the polls of their own accord and who will know what they want when they get there. We need more widespread and better-sustained campaigns of civic education the year round, and less of this ballyhoo at the moron vote on the eve of an election day.

ARE THE WELL-TO-DO THE CHRONIC NON-VOTERS?

There is a common impression that chronic non-voters are to be found chiefly in the ranks of well-to-do, educated people who ought to know better. Everywhere you hear it said that the crowded, proletarian precincts always poll the highest percentage of votes in proportion to their population, and that the fine residential wards make the poorest showing. It has become one of the formulas of practical politics, so often repeated that most people believe it to be true. But it has never been proved. On the contrary, every study that has been made of this matter indicates that the best showing at the polls is often made by the best neighborhoods.

Let us look for a moment at the results of these investigations. One of the best and most comprehensive is the one made three years ago in Chicago under the direction of Messrs.

Charles E. Merriam and H. F. Gosnell.[1] This investigation covered many thousand non-voters and clearly indicated that electoral indifference was the chief cause of abstention from the polls and that this indifference was closely associated with political unintelligence.

A less extensive but even more searching study was made by Dr. Ben A. Arneson in the city of Delaware, Ohio, two years ago. This investigation covered the entire voting population in a typical mid-western community of about 9,000 population.[2] Dr. Arneson found that the percentage of non-voters was smallest among public officials and public employees, professional men, teachers, business executives, persons engaged in banking, insurance and real estate, merchants, and men engaged in the skilled mechanical occupations. It proved to be highest among laborers, unskilled mechanics, clerical employees, people engaged in domestic and personal service; and highest of all among persons of "no occupation." The best showing at the polls was made by heads of families, who had lived for more than two years in the community and who owned their own homes. Contrary to the popular impression, moreover, his investigation showed that the percentage of non-voters among college graduates was only about half that found among persons who had merely an elementary school education.

In support of my contention that the poorer neighborhoods do not regularly make the best showing at the polls, as is so commonly believed, let me give a couple of illustrations. I have taken them from Boston and Cambridge, two communities which

[1] It is published in a volume entitled *Non-Voting* (University of Chicago Press, 1925).

[2] The results may be found in the *American Political Science Review* for November, 1925, pp. 816–825.

	East Boston			The Back Bay		
	Ward 1 (Formerly Wards 1 and 2)			Ward 5 (Formerly Ward 8)		
Date	Registered vote	Polled vote	Percentage	Registered vote	Polled vote	Percentage
1916................	8,023	5,827	73%	4,801	3,517	73%
1917................	7,843	5,704	73	4,551	3,398	75
1918................	7,441	2,990	40	4,128	1,775	44
1919................	7,917	2,704	34	4,589	1,882	41
1920................	12,237	3,163	26	10,664	3,564	33
1921................	12,288	9,233	75	10,314	7,913	77
1922................	13,331	4,190	31	10,188	4,027	40
1923................	12,265	4,541	37	9,243	4,499	49
1925................	12,916	10,050	78	10,065	7,661	76
Total............	94,261	48,402	52%	68,543	38,236	55%

are near at hand. Above are the figures for two Boston wards. One of them includes that part of the city known as East Boston, which is largely inhabited by workers. In an economic sense it is clearly one of the poorer sections of Boston. Politically, it is heavily Democratic. The other ward is made up very largely of the Back Bay, the city's best residential district, the habitat of Boston's aristocracy and intelligentsia—at any rate what is left of it.

Here is a condensed table showing the results in two sections of Cambridge, Massachusetts, at the state and national elections of the past decade.[1]

[1] I have not included the municipal elections because some of the councilmen are elected by

Wards 1 and 2 are in East Cambridge, and form a typical working-class, tenement-house, semi-industrial section. Wards 8 and 9 include Harvard Square, the Brattle Street area, and the best residential district of Cambridge. Being adjacent to Harvard University these two wards contain a heavy sprinkling of college professors and instructors. But even the presence of the latter does not appear to have turned the district into a slacker's paradise.

At the meeting of the National Municipal League, when I read this

wards. At these elections there is sometimes a bitter contest in one ward and no contest at all in another. This makes a fair comparison impracticable.

	Ward 1	Ward 2	Ward 8	Ward 9
1918 State election........................	59.4%	57.9%	65.6%	70.0%
1920 Presidential election..................	74.7	71.6	85.6	84.8
1922 State election........................	77.0	76.1	76.4	79.2
1924 Presidential election..................	85.0	87.3	88.7	90.0
1926 State election........................	75.3	70.6	82.3	80.3
Average........................	74.3%	72.7%	79.7%	80.8%

paper, a delegate from one of the Detroit civic organizations interposed to remark that whatever might be the situation in Chicago, Delaware, Boston, Cambridge, or other cities, it was an "obvious fact" that in Detroit the well-to-do neighborhoods regularly failed in their civic duty as compared with the poorer districts. This assertion does not seem to be borne out by the figures. Here is a tabulation showing the polled vote cast at the last Detroit mayoralty election in six districts of each type. They have been selected at random from the poorer sections and the well-to-do districts of Detroit.

The former is a sailor, lodging-house, cheap-tenement area; the latter is an extra high-grade residential section, the locus of Detroit's old aristocracy. The former polled 33.7 per cent of its registered vote, while the other polled 56.9 per cent.

It should be mentioned, however, that Detroit has a system of semi-permanent registration, and hence it is quite possible that the registration figures are higher in the poorer districts than they ought to be, due to the shifting of population there. On the other hand, the wet *versus* dry issue figured rather heavily in the last Detroit election and brought out a larger

POORER SECTIONS

Ward	District	Registered vote	Polled vote
1...	1	970	328
1...	9	831	303
3...	5	1,296	408
3...	7	1,262	528
5...	4	1,684	522
5...	5	1,456	526

Percentage of polled vote, 34.8%

WELL-TO-DO SECTIONS

Ward	District	Registered vote	Polled vote
12...	27	1,047	720
17...	3	1,127	472
17...	6	675	337
17...	10	723	412
21...	54	1,394	1,013
22...	9	706	517

Percentage of polled vote, 45.3%

Now it will be observed that the selected districts from the well-to-do sections made a distinctly better showing, in point of attendance at the polls, than did the selected districts in the poorer sections of the city. Compare, for example, District 1, Ward 1 (the "foist of the foist," as it is locally designated), with District 10, Ward 17.

vote in the poorer districts than is usually polled there.[1]

True enough, these various studies and illustrations cover only a few spots

[1] For these figures and comments I am indebted to Dr. Lent D. Upson, director of the Detroit Bureau of Governmental Research, and to Mr. Oakley E. Distin, secretary of the Detroit Election Commission.

in a vast country. One cannot safely generalize from them. But it is at least a striking coincidence that they all point to the same conclusion, and there is no good reason to believe that a nation-wide survey of non-voting, as related to neighborhoods, occupation, education, and intelligence would warrant an altogether different assertion. Professor Charles H. Titus, for example, in his recent study of California cities, has found that non-voting appears to vary with density of population—the larger and more crowded the community, the higher the percentage of registered voters who stay away from the polls.[1] Dr. Harold F. Gosnell of Chicago, who recently undertook an interesting experiment in the "stimulation" of non-voters, reached the conclusion that "persons with some knowledge of politics and government are much more apt to vote than those with little knowledge of governmental matters." Among the latter he includes persons with little or no schooling such as negroes, foreign-born and foreign-speaking women, and poor native whites who have failed to make proper social and economic adjustments to the complexity of modern city life.[2]

Now if this be true, the so-termed slacker vote can hardly be looked upon as a "menace" to anything except the political machine which depends for success upon herding a high percentage of propertyless, semi-illiterate, uninformed and undiscriminating voters to the ballot box on election day. May it not be that our uplift organizations, in their rabble-rousing campaigns to "harry the slackers to the polls," are merely playing into the hands of the

[1] This study has not yet been published. I am indebted to Dr. Titus for the privilege of examining his conclusions in manuscript form.

[2] See his little volume on *Getting Out the Vote* (University of Chicago Press, 1927), pp. 109–110.

boss and doing some of his work for him? That question is worth more consideration than it has received.

WHAT DOES OUR THEORY OF GOVERNMENT DEMAND?

It is the theory of popular government that every adult citizen shall have the privilege of voting; but I take issue with the doctrine that either the theory or the practice of popular government requires everyone to exercise this privilege whenever his rulers offer him the opportunity to do so. The safeguard of democratic government lies in the preservation of the opportunity, not in the hundred percent exercise of it. The great body of the voters form a reserve which can be mobilized to express the will of the people when momentous issues of principle or of policy are at stake. But it does not follow that we need, or ought to expect, a full mobilization when the issues are of relatively slight consequence.

As a matter of fact, the people as a whole appreciate that differentiation and act upon it. Everywhere their ratio of attendance at the polls is in direct proportion to the intensity of the feeling aroused, and this, again, is proportioned to the gravity of the issues that are before them for decision. The people, in fact, are wiser than those who so vociferously undertake to remind them of their duty.

If we undertook to run corporate business on the principle that every stockholder is in duty bound to come and vote whenever directors are to be elected, or routine questions decided, our whole system of corporate organization would break down. Only when some question of deep and real interest arises do the stockholders muster their full strength in person or by proxy. To the extent that government is business (which it has become to a large extent in the cities) the analogy would seem to hold. It avails nothing, either in business or in government, to make men go through the gesture of displaying an interest which they do not feel. It is easier to get men to vote than to think—and propaganda too often slips into the error of choosing the easiest way.

In this field we can learn something from the experience of Europe. Why do a larger percentage of the people come to the polls there than here. It is not that Europeans are inherently more interested in politics than Americans; and much less is it true that the propaganda for getting out the vote is more active there than here. It is largely because elections do not come so frequently, and when they do come they turn on fundamental issues of policy with a sharp cleavage between the programs of the various political parties. Systems of proportional representation, which are now used in many of the continental European countries, have also had something to do with it. Under such procedure a minority has an opportunity to make its will felt. In the United States, under the straight plurality system, the voter who belongs to a hopeless minority is doing a perfectly futile thing when he goes to the polling booth —and he knows it. To get such voters interested you must give them a fighting chance. In Europe it is the issue that produces the election; in America the election comes on a fixed date and issues must then be dug up for the occasion. It is small wonder that the voter does not let himself get wildly excited about issues which have been produced in that way.

The organizations which are spending so much effort and money in trying to make the country vibrate with this "get-out-the-vote" propaganda, and in promoting a movement for compulsory voting, would therefore do well to ask themselves the question whether an enterprise which confines itself to a mere trumpeting of platitudes about the duty of the sovereign citizen, and the menace of electoral inertia, is likely to contribute anything, in the long run, to a more enlightened expression of the public will. By all the indications it will not. They are applying the stimuli at the wrong spot. What we most need is to make registration less of an irksome task, the ballot simpler (with provision for the representation of minorities), elections less frequent, the issues clearer, party cleavages more distinct and vital, the party programs less evasive, and, above all, to organize our campaigns of civic education so that they will be more comprehensive, more persistent, and more effective in reaching those sections of the electorate which have enough intelligence to understand what it is all about.[1]

One way to bring out the vote is to bring out the issues. "A civic educational program 'for adults, as well as for children," writes Professor Harold F. Gosnell as the result of his experiment in vote-stimulating, "would undoubtedly have an immediate and continuous effect upon the interest shown in elections." We should, therefore, study the processes by which sound ideas and sure information can be most effectively lodged in the public mind. At present we have not got beyond the technique of the circus barker.

[1] It is encouraging to see that the National Civic Federation, one of the most active of the various organizations in the warfare on slacker voting, has adopted this point of view. In a recent announcement this Federation declares that its future program will include three aims, "first, to educate the voter on the questions; second, to get out the vote; and third, to have it counted as cast." In other words, the work of informing the voter concerning the issues is put first in the order of importance.

N. A. L. G. O.

NATIONAL ASSOCIATION OF LOCAL GOVERNMENT OFFICERS

BY CLINTON ROGERS WOODRUFF

An organization of local government employees performing a notable service for its members and for the nation. :: :: :: ::

ENGLISHMEN have a happy faculty of giving short titles to their organizations, which helps in identifying them as well as in giving them a desirable publicity. N. A. L. G. O. is the popular title by which that large and influential body of men and women engaged in the administration of local affairs in Great Britain is known. The official name is National Association of Local Government Officers.

Organized in 1905 it now has 39,875 members according to the report of the president at the meeting in Bournemouth (June, 1927), an increase of 2,756 over the previous year. The beginning was a modest one in London and the date July 29, 1905. Prior to that date a Municipal Officers' Association had been in existence in London, and there were one or two guilds in the provinces. Probably the Liverpool Municipal Officers' Guild was the first organization of this character, in the activities of which, H. E. Blain (now Sir Herbert E. Blain, C.B.E.) had taken considerable interest prior to his transfer to London as the tramways manager of the West Ham Corporation. After his removal to London, Mr. Blain's interest in the organization of local government officers was directed to the London Municipal Officers' Association, and it was due to the threatened disbandment of this Association that he determined that the movement should be placed on a national basis. In this connection he was supported by Sir Homewood

Crawford and a few other active spirits. The result was that the conference was held and the National Association of Local Government Officers was formally organized.

It is also interesting to record that at the third meeting, held in Bradford, in February, 1906, a sub-committee, composed principally of representatives of the Liverpool Guild, was appointed to consider, to draft, and to submit to the council, a bill containing superannuation and security of tenure office clauses.

MEMBERSHIP

At the end of the first year the total membership of the Association, including affiliated professional and sectional organizations, was 8,122 drawn from sixteen local guilds and associations, certainly a most remarkable initial growth showing the need for the organization and the general interest in it.

The president since 1911 has been A. P. Johnson, M.A., town clerk of Hampstead, who has gained a great reputation as a presiding officer. Since 1918 he has also been chairman of the National Executive Council.

Some idea of the methods of increasing the membership may be gathered from a series of resolutions adopted in 1925 and published in the annual report under the head "Peaceful Suasion." These resolutions recited that it is now recognized by most, if not all local authorities that it is desirable for local government officers to be represented, when occasion arises, by an association or union, such as the National Association of Local Government Officers, and that such associations or unions cannot be maintained without the officers contributing to its funds, and that a large number of local government officers benefit through the activities of such associations, without making any financial contribution towards the expenses of such activities; and that membership should be a point of honor on the part of all local government officers and that therefore the Conference requested the National Executive Council:

(1) To ascertain the local authorities, if any, in whose Standing Orders there is incorporated the principle that all officers and servants in their employment should be members of an association or union:

(2) To take steps, if deemed advisable, and with the consent of the branches interested, to secure the recognition of this principle by all local authorities; and

(3) To report the result of its efforts to the Annual Conference in 1926.

Rather a suggestive way to attract members and an effective one, because N. A. L. G. O. has come to be recognized as a potent factor in giving professional standing to those engaged in governmental work and in protecting their rights and promoting their interests.

As indicating the financial strength of the body it is interesting to record that in 1925–1926, new headquarters being necessary, an offer of a freehold building at No. 24 Abingdon Street, Westminister S. W. 1, was received.

The purchase of these premises was authorized and the organization is now housed in a beautiful, commodious and really charmingly remodelled old house, within the shadows of the Houses of Parliament, where N. A. L. G. O. has such close and vital interests.

SUPERANNUATION

Superannuation is one of the big questions now before N. A. L. G. O., and it is receiving that sort of careful, intensive and exhaustive consideration which characterize British government studies. In accordance with the promise made to representatives of the Association in March, 1925, the minister of health established a departmental committee to enquire and to report as to whether any amendments were required in the Local Government and Other Officers Superannuation Act, 1922; and in particular whether it was desirable that the scheme of superannuation established by the act should be made obligatory on all local authorities, and whether that scheme should, with or without modification in respect of particular classes of officers, be made applicable to all persons in the employ of those local authorities other than school teachers and police. The committee decided to commence its deliberations by receiving evidence from the Association in support of amending the act, and in September and October the president of the Association submitted this evidence. There were also in attendance the general secretary, and the Association's parliamentary agent. A summary of the evidence was forwarded to each branch, necessary to recapitulate the arguments in favor of making the adoption of schemes by all local authorities compulsory. A draft bill to amend the act had previously been prepared by the Association, and this was submitted to the committee as a basis for its deliberations.

At the Bournemouth meeting it was reported that the number of local authorities who had adopted the 1922 Superannuation Act had been increased by about 120, a very satisfactory result. They were awaiting with anticipation the report of the Departmental Committee on Superannuation on the question. The decision of the committee would not be known before parliament rose for the autumn recess. Efforts would have to be continued meantime, to induce more and more authorities to adopt the present act. A short time ago the Association was invited by the Royal Commission on Local Government to give evidence on the present position of local government officers. They appeared before the Commission in March and April, and the evidence submitted dealt with practically all the points regarded by the members as essential to service conditions of local government officers and the staffing of local authorities. This was regarded by the president as a distinct recognition of the status and standing of the Association.

One of the speakers at Bournemouth referring to superannuation said that while certain progress had been made with the act of 1922, large areas yet remained uncovered which tended to make for less mobility, less attractiveness and less efficiency. These are three ends which N. A. L. G. O. always has in mind, and to which it persistently directs its attention and efforts.

Other superannuation schemes in which N. A. L. G. O. is interested are the School Teachers Superannuation Act of 1925; the Fire Brigade Officers Pension Act of 1925; the Asylums Officers Superannuation Bill of 1925; the Police Pension Bill of 1926; the Widows, Orphans and Old Age (Contributory) Pensions Act of 1925. From this brief recital it will be seen that the organization is giving that sort of constructive attention to a highly important problem in local administration and it illustrates the scope and thoroughness of the attention given

to such problems. It also affords an example for the consideration and example of American government officials.

COMPENSATION ON ABOLITION OF OFFICE

Compensation for the abolition of offices is another special subject to which constructive attention has been given. Parliamentary bills and orders have been examined, and action has been taken to secure the inclusion of satisfactory provisions for compensation on abolition of office, or on diminution or loss of fees or salary. The Association's solicitors and parliamentary agents have drafted separate sets of model clauses, with precedents and observations, for use in connection with bills and orders to extend borough boundaries; to amalgamate urban districts; and to constitute urban districts. Model clauses, with precedents and observations, have also been submitted to the Privy Council, with a request that they be included in all charters of incorporation of municipal boroughs. Representatives of the Association have attended local enquiries which have been held in connection with Parliamentary Orders and have handed in model compensation clauses for inclusion in them. Similar clauses have also been submitted for approval to the local authorities concerned.

ATTENTION TO INTERESTS OF INDIVIDUALS

Not only is N. A. L. G. O. concerned about the larger problems and policies of local administration but it concerns itself with the problems and troubles of the individual. It is literally the guardian of their rights and privileges. To illustrate: A local newspaper published statements which alleged fraud and improper performance of their duties against the staff of the superintendent assistant overseer of an urban council. On the application of the branch of which the officers concerned were members, the Association's solicitors and parliamentary agents were instructed to communicate with the editor of the newspaper, and the writer of the statements, requesting that the latter should be withdrawn, and equal publicity given to the withdrawal as was given to the statements. As a result, the writer unreservedly withdrew them, and disclaimed any intention to cast any reflection on the staff of the overseer. This withdrawal was published in the newspaper with ample apologies.

Again on the application of a branch, the Association's solicitors and parliamentary agents were instructed to communicate with the editor of a local newspaper, and the writer of an article published therein, requesting that certain statements contained in this article, which were alleged to be defamatory to the office of an urban district council, should be withdrawn; and equal publicity given to the withdrawal as was given to the statements. As a result, the proprietors, the publishers and the editor of the newspaper, published a special edition of their publication, which contained a complete withdrawal of the statements and ample apologies. The writer of the article, however, did not withdraw his statements, although he agreed to amend them so as to make it clear that there was no allegation of a fraudulent connection between the members of the urban district council and the officers concerned; and that his criticism of the administration in the district was directed solely against the council as being responsible for the administration. A further communication was forwarded to him reiterating the request, and in response he complied forthwith.

A telephone operator of a county borough council met with a serious accident while carrying out her duties, and an application was considered from the branch concerned for her interests to be safeguarded in order that she might obtain adequate compensation in the event of her injuries resulting in her being permanently disabled. The branch was authorized to engage a local solicitor to watch the interests of the officer concerned, with the result that the latter obtained the full amount of compensation to which she was entitled under the workmen's compensation acts.

After considering reports by the superintendent of a cleaning department and his assistant on the question of the erection of a large new refuse disposal work, a special sub-committee of the cleansing committee of a borough council decided to recommend that the superintendent should be called upon to resign his position. The sub-committee had not been authorized to consider the question of terminating the appointment of the superintendent of the department, and the latter refused to tender his resignation. A local solicitor was engaged to be in attendance on the occasion of the meeting of the committee at which this recommendation of the special sub-committee was considered, to support the action taken by the superintendent; and as the latter was not called upon to resign by the committee no further action was necessary.

Such instances as these, and they could be multiplied many times, show why N. A. L. G. O. is not only highly and generally respected, but is referred to so affectionately by local government officers throughout the kingdom for its jurisdiction covers and its membership is recruited from Scotland and Wales as well as England.

THE QUESTION OF TRAINING

The "articled pupil," as he is called, is a problem now receiving rather animated attention. *The Municipal Journal* editorially (April 15, 1927) attacked the N. A. L. G. O. position on this question, saying:

Before the Royal Commission on Local Government, as we reported last week, the Association put its view regarding the qualifications of entrants for the local civil service. In the course of evidence it was urged that the system by which pupils are articled should be discontinued, or that town clerks at any rate, should not be allowed to take pupils. In support of that view it was stated it had been found that persons articled to town clerks were provided with an unfair jumping-off ground. In other words, that jobs had been found for them.

Whatever may have happened in the past, not many would subscribe to this allegation as having force so far as present-day appointments are concerned. The Councils are now composed of men and women who give their time for the good of the community, who serve to the best of their ability, whether it be in connection with the appointment of officers, the acceptance of a tender, or in regard to any of the other multitudinous duties imposed on local authorities.

The proposal to debar a person already in the local government service from being articled to another in a superior grade will require a deal of justification. It would mean that a young man, qualified by examination to enter the local government service, after two or three years' work would have to quit his office if he wished to take up serious study and qualify for a legal post with a municipal body. Is it seriously suggested that there are sufficient private firms who could give young men so thorough a training in local government law and practice as those receive who are in constant touch with the subject? The adage that an ounce of practice is worth a pound of theory could not be better applied. If the higher posts in the municipal service are to be filled with skilled men they are more likely to be found among those who were engaged in that service from the commencement of their career, rather than from those who gain a cursory knowledge of the work in an outside office. How many leading town clerks began their legal training elsewhere than in the local government

service? An impediment would be put in the way of the better man who wished to rise in the local government service were he debarred from being articled with his own chief.

The proposition is not consistent with the rest of the N. A. L. G. O.'s work. In the first place it desires that every entrant to the service shall be qualified by examination; it then insists that a section shall not have the opportunity of rising in the profession unless its members leave the service for several years. Trade unions do not as a rule follow this practice. If an official were forced to leave the service to become articled so that he might later secure an executive post, he could hardly be expected to view the Association in any too good a light.

To this the able, highly effective general secretary of N. A. L. G. O., Mr. L. Hill, replied:

The question of articled pupilage bristles with difficulties and possibly the variety of questions and answers before the Royal Commission on Local Government may have given rise to the wrong impression which you have obtained. You will know that a number of officers have a professional right to take pupils and, unless it is made a condition of the employment of the officer at the time of his appointment, nobody has any right to interfere with that privilege.

The National Association is *not* opposed to professional officers having articled pupils, but it does hold the opinion that the present conditions are not altogether satisfactory, especially where professional officers take under their wing fee-paying "outsiders," who may afterwards be placed in a privileged position as regards obtaining appointments in the Local Government Service. What the Association advocated was a system which would encourage professional officers to confer articles upon promising members of their staffs in order to lift young men of ability, probably without private means over the barrier which separates the "lay" side from the "professional" side. Whether the local authority should recompense the professional officer for granting articles to promising members of the staff, is a matter which we did not discuss.

Whereabouts in America do we find city officials training men to succeed themselves and where would we find associations to give consideration to the difficulties involved? Indeed where can we find in the nation and outside of a few states (happily increasing in number) organizations that parallel N. A. L. G. O., or even approach it in the character and extent of its activities?

INSURANCE AND BENEVOLENT ACTIVITIES

Nalgo Provident Society is one of the collateral activities. . In 1914 the idea was conceived that the Association, representing a body of healthy persons, should be successful in launching a scheme, in order to offer sickness and life assurance to its members, at lower rates than those quoted in other directions. Experience had been gained in administering the National Health Insurance Benefits through the Nalgo Approved Society and, although enthusiasm for inauguration of another society was confined to a few, the suggestion was adopted. Sufficient members were obtained to warrant a commencement, but owing to the outbreak of war, the Society did not actually commence operations until January, 1920, and was registered as a friendly society in April, 1921. The position now is that approximately five thousand benefits are being contributed for, and rapid progress is being reported.

Still another collateral activity is the Benevolent and Orphan Fund, now in its seventeenth year. A commencement was made in 1920 to build up a fund which would be worthy of the service and able to meet all claims which might be put forward on behalf of its members who were in needy circumstances. A total sum of £16 was received during the first year. That amount was more than doubled during the next year, and in 1912 claims commenced to be received and three grants were made amounting in total to £23 3s. 0d. For the next two years excellent progress was made, but owing to the outbreak of war, the fund received a set back in 1915. A great increase in income was recorded in 1916, due to the inauguration of a special war relief fund, and the annual amount contributed varied slightly until 1919, when the fund almost touched the £2,000 mark, and nearly £350 was distributed in grants. The phenomenal progress of the Association in 1920 resulted in a tremendously increased income to the fund, and £6,055 3s. 4d. was received. The outstanding feature of the year, however, was the fact that the Glamorgan County Officers Branch contributed the sum of £1,732 9s. 6d., which undoubtedly spurred other branches to increased activity. This progress was not maintained during the two succeeding years, and the income fell to less than £5,000 in 1922, while grants had increased to £1,224. The Fund's own record was broken in 1923, and again the following year.

At Bournemouth the Lady Mayoress received from the various branches purses for the fund amounting to £6,914 as compared with £6,021 contributed a year ago.

There is much, much more that could be said about N. A. L. G. O. and its manifold activities, but sufficient has been said to show how useful and extensive are its activities. Sufficient has been said to prove a stimulant to American local government officials. Perhaps a national society along similar lines is not feasible in the United States at the present time when we consider the forty-eight different standards and forms of local government. Moreover, we do not have the compact, homogeneous territory and population of the United Kingdom. Nevertheless, there are certain problems which officials of all the localities have in common that might be effectively considered in common by a mutual organization.

RECENT BOOKS REVIEWED

BOSS TWEED. By Denis Tilden Lynch. New York: Boni & Liveright, 1927. Illustrated. Pp. 433.

A good antidote for any current pessimism regarding American city government is this volume, packed with picturesque details, and written in a spicy style, regarding the historic Napoleon of political graft and corruption. Whatever evils now exist, our cities, even the big ones, are not so badly off as some of them were in the century made notable by Bryce's American Commonwealth. As Bryce, in his last work, testified to a vast improvement in conditions, so this author remarks, concerning Tweed, "No other country but ours could have produced him, and no other age but his own."

"Simply awful," and other trite characterizations of ultimate intensity are in order, if one tries to describe this pictorial description of Tweed and his reign. Chapter after chapter is filled with facts, piling up the evidence showing how prominent men and women, banks, newspapers, and practically all agencies of public influence, were enmeshed in the Tweed net. Today it is hard to imagine the amounts of money stolen from the public, the ease with which nefarious schemes were brought to success, and the length of time during which the arch-thief was allowed to hold sway with a power which reached out, through government and great corporations, into the state and national fields. Like some of its modern progeny, this octopus was bi-partisan: "Tweed's power could have been destroyed by an honest Republican machine. But one did not exist. What passed as the New York County Republican Committee was owned, lock, stock, and barrel, by Tweed."

From beginning to end, including Tweed's downfall and demise, the book assembles in readable form elaborations of sensational incidents, in a manner which doubtless makes this a volume of importance to students of our political history. Tweed is pictured as neither a drunken Falstaff nor a cheap and vulgar rogue. "He was a rogue, but monumental."

Lest we of today feel complacent, the author thus analyzes the trend and cause of corruption:

"Public thieving did not begin with Tweed. Nor did it die with him. It exists because of the apathy of the mass. Sometimes the mass is roused to a sense of the wrongs inflicted upon it. Invariably, it is immediately blinded by passions of racial, religious, or partizan strife, kindled by politicians. On rare occasions the mass struggles until it has effected a reform. But eventually the politician triumphs and the mass is divided and one side wars upon the other and then succumbs to inertia. The looting is resumed."

We prefer to accept the dictum of Walter Lippmann: "There has come a realization on the part of the leading machine politicians that the old job-grafting type of government was not such very good politics after all."

W. P. LOVETT.

*

LAND VALUES—DISTRIBUTION WITHIN NEW YORK REGION AND RELATION TO VARIOUS FACTORS IN URBAN GROWTH. By Harold M. Lewis, Wayne D. Heydecker, and Raymond A. O'Hara. New York. Plan of New York and Its Environs. (Engineering Series, Monograph Number Three.) 1927. Pp. 72, 4 maps, 14 plates, 12 tables.

A region comprising an area of 5,528 square miles in three states; a population of 10,000,000 living in 425 municipalities; 60,000 factories including the largest of their kind in the country; the financial heart of a great nation; a port from which steamship lines radiate to all parts of the globe, and on which rail lines and inland waterways covering a continent converge; towering office buildings, hotels and apartment houses within sight of farms, woodlands and meadows; skyscraping centers and sub-centers linked to one another, and to the outlying sections of one family homes, by subways and elevated lines, commuting steam railways, and motor highways —that is the background against which Messrs. Lewis, Heydecker and O'Hara sketched their study of land values.

Their estimated total for the value of the land within the region for 1923 is well in excess of nine billion dollars—almost as much as the aggregate assessed values of land and improvements for the same year in the group of eleven states stretching from the eastern slope of the Rocky Mountains to the Pacific Ocean. This value, however, they find to be very unevenly distributed throughout the area. Somewhat more than one-half of it is concentrated in the 22 square miles which make up Manhattan Island. The averages per acre by counties range from $57 in Putnam County, New York, to $460,000 in Manhattan. On the outskirts of the region, entire townships show average values of considerably less than $50 per acre. Whole tax sections in Manhattan average above one million dollars per acre, and smaller areas flanking important streets for a distance of several blocks approximate $10,000,000 per acre.

In their approach to the subject from the standpoint of city planning, the authors outline a dual problem, which may be stated as follows: Why should this enormous concentration of land values have taken place in the New York Region; and why should an acre at the heart of that region be worth 300,000 times as much as another along the edge?

The answer to the first question is sketched in only in barest outline. The usual topography of New York harbor, the far-flung network of foreign and domestic trade routes which center on it, and the "high average of energy and enterprise on the part of its people," are among the outstanding reasons advanced to explain the phenomenon. The analysis is qualitative rather than quantitative, and this section of the report makes no outstanding contribution.

In answer to the second question, definitely quantitative analyses are presented. The authors do not pretend that they are either comprehensive or conclusive. They realize that they had invaded a field in which they were among the pioneers. Like the "forty-niners," they had to clear their own trails; they had to turn over much material before they struck pay dirt; they had to make their own assays as they went along; but after several years of hard work, they came out with some nuggets of real gold.

The effects of density of population on values per acre; of railway terminals; of rapid transit lines; of wide streets in the original city plan; of newly opened and widened streets; of parkways and boulevards; of open spaces; of high buildings; of interest rates and tax rates; and of premature booms—all these factors and others are discussed more or less completely in quantitative form. Even when one regrets the evident condensation which took place when the text was prepared for publication—a condensation so drastic that it results in some cases in incomplete analyses of the material at hand—one marvels at the industry and patience of the authors in compiling the basic data.

Economists, city planners, and real estate men will find the volume one of compelling interest. After they have read it, they will almost certainly join the reviewer in his ardent wish for more studies of the same kind.

PHILIP H. CORNICK.

✣

THE GENERAL ACCOUNTING OFFICE. By Darrell Hevenor Smith. Baltimore: Johns Hopkins Press, 1927. Pp. 215.

This study follows the general plan of the other monographs in the series issued by the Institute of Government Research, presenting a careful descriptive account of the history, activities and organization of the General Accounting Office. It traces the development of the accounting and auditing methods of the national government from the period of the Revolutionary War to the present system established by the Budget and Accounting Act of 1921. The discussion of activities sets forth the changes in methods and expansion of functions under the present law, noting controversies that have arisen with the treasury departments, and conflicts between the rulings of the comptroller-general, the attorney general and the court of claims. The author does not, however, enter into the problem as to the best method of settling these disputes, which has been discussed in Mr. Willoughby's study on the *Legal Status and Functions of the General Accounting Office.*

On this important question, the reviewer disagrees with the theory on which the General Accounting Office is now based. The office is not in fact an agency of congress directly responsible to that body; it is controllable only by the joint action of the president and congress, and is substantially independent of either acting alone. It is the reviewer's opinion that the main work of the Accounting Office should be as an agency of central administrative control, organized as an integral part of the treasury department. The judicial functions might be vested in the court of claims. Congressional control should be exercised by energizing the committees on expenditures, with power to employ technical experts, not to duplicate the detailed work of the Accounting Office, but to examine the methods of administrative control and the results as shown in the financial reports; as is done by the Committee on Public Accounts of the British House of Commons.

JOHN A. FAIRLIE.

PUBLIC SCHOOL FINANCE. By Arthur B. Moehlman. Chicago: Rand McNally & Company, 1927. Pp. xviii, 508.

Professor Moehlman of the University of Michigan has written what appears to be a useful book on public school finance. The text is very well organized and, on the whole, quite readable. The introductory section to each part and the summary at the end of each chapter, however, contribute little, if anything, to the book.

Throughout the text the author is very practical in his approach to the subject, especially on the phase of school budgeting which is treated at length. But he largely disregards the inseparable connection which public school finance has, and will probably long continue to have, with the administration of many local governments. Even where the school administration is organized independently of local governmental authorities, a definite relation or balance ought to be maintained between the fiscal requirements of education and those of other public functions. It does not seem to the reviewer that these facts should be overlooked or lightly passed up in any general discussion of public school finance.

Professor Moehlman's book is divided into three parts, dealing with the problem, the attack, and the application or technique of public school finance. Part I is little more than an introduction and undoubtedly the weakest part of the book. Part II covers general finance policy, finance organization, cost methods, the budget, finance control, financing the school program, and public information. The chapter on cost methods as applied to schools is perhaps the best chapter in the book; it discusses this important subject in a lucid manner, getting at the basic elements and disposing of a lot of misconceptions. The chapter on the school budget is also very good. Part III relates to budget making, accounting, and cost data. The placing of emphasis on school budgeting is a very commendable and up-to-date feature of the book. The author demonstrates the practical aspects of this subject by setting up a complete budget for a local school organization.

A. E. BUCK.

*

MAJOR ISSUES IN SCHOOL FINANCE; PARTS I AND II. National Education Association, Washington, D. C., January, 1927.

The careful reading of these two bulletins should result in the acquisition of a very fair working knowledge in the field of educational economics. Dr. Norton, to whom they may be attributed, has gathered together in brief space a wealth of suggestive material. There is treated, for example, the nation's economic ability to meet school costs, under which there is discussed the ratio of school costs to income and wealth. The question is raised and answered: Has the tendency to increase the percentage of income of the United States devoted to education been accompanied by decreases or increases in the economic power available for other purposes?

A section which should be read by captious critics of educational costs is the one on school costs and economy in public expenditures. It includes a brief but able discussion of the causes of the growth in school costs.

Part II supplies a great many comparisons between the various states with regard to their ability to support education. For example, there are tabulations of savings accounts, expenditures for life insurance, purchases of certain luxuries, and state wealth and income.

After pointing out the weak spots in financing certain state educational systems, certain essentials of a sound plan of state and local taxation are outlined.

Though largely but statistical compilations, the bulletins contain enough descriptive material to make them interesting reading as well as an authentic source for reference.

H. E. AKERLY.

*

PRINCIPLES OF REAL ESTATE APPRAISING (Second Edition). By John A. Zangerle. Cleveland: Stanley McMichael Publishing Organization, 1927. Pp. 443.

"This is the most valuable book on the subject I have ever seen. It is valuable to every appraiser of real estate and invaluable to every assessor. It should be in the library of every assessing department in the United States. The chambers of commerce and boards of trade of the United States should every one of them have a copy and see to it that every assessor has a copy."

So wrote Mr. Lawson Purdy in 1924 in referring to Mr. Zangerle's first edition of this book. These comments are all the more true for the second edition, which has been enriched by the addition of considerable material.

The qualifications and ability of Mr. Zangerle to discuss the subject need no argument. By reason of his position as county auditor of Cuyahoga county (Cleveland) since 1910, he is the assessor of the county. And the position is an elective one,—even his own people know he is good. Much good has come from Mr. Zangerle's works, as reflected in improved assessing methods of our cities. Even Detroit, for example, has copied the major portion of his procedure, and Chicago is giving it consideration.

Readers of the REVIEW probably are more concerned with appraisals for tax purposes than for realty, banking and other objectives, all of which are considered in writing the book. But even for this limited use, the new edition has been improved, the material of the first edition having been reassembled and new chapters added, as well as a more extended discussion of many subjects such as plottage rule, corner influence values, effect of auto transportation, long term leases, etc.

To those who did not act upon Mr. Purdy's suggestion to acquire the volume, now is the time. To those who did act, however, it may be questioned whether the first edition should be replaced by this one. The growing interest in the subject of property assessment has led to the publication of many valuable treatises on various phases of the subject, all of which must be acquired or at least mastered to keep abreast of the field.

As a minor criticism, it is believed that greater definiteness of references, such as to authors and dates of citation, might be had. Some of the statistics could be revised and some be brought up to date. Possibly a bibliography would help the volume.

C. E. RIGHTOR.

✤

COMPARATIVE COST OF LOCAL GOVERNMENT. Statement of Receipts and Disbursements of the Counties of Virginia compiled by William F. Smyth, State Accountant, 1926. Pp. 354.

The state accountant of Virginia by an act of 1924 is required to prepare an annual statement showing in detail comparative and per capita costs of local government as among the counties and cities of the state. While this report indicates a serious attempt to comply with the legislative mandate, the contents, nevertheless, reveal that the efforts of the department have been seriously compromised by the failure of the legislature to supply adequate funds for the work and by the refusal to vest the department with

authority to prescribe for the local governments uniform accounting methods.

Because of the insufficient appropriation, for example, the department was unable to include any statistics on cities, although the law specifically requires it. The absence of uniformity in accounting methods is well illustrated in the wide range of dates marking the end of the county fiscal year. The fiscal periods for the one hundred counties terminate on more than thirty different days. The state accountant also admits that by reason of the varying financial methods it was impossible for him to make a clear-cut division of either receipts or disbursements. Particularly weak are the expenditure classifications. County treasurers do not make any classification of the warrants which they pay other than by funds. Consequently it is impossible to determine amounts paid for salaries, material, labor, etc. Then again there is no division made by treasurers between ordinary expenses of operation and capital expenditures. While the report distinguishes between expenditures made from ordinary revenue and those made from extraordinary receipts, such a classification obviously cannot be used as a reliable criterion of operating expenditures and capital outlays.

In addition to ten summary tables, the report includes detailed data showing receipts, disbursements, per capita expenditures, indebtedness, assessed values, and local tax rates for each one of the one hundred counties of the state of Virginia. While the compilation of these analytical tables is well worth while, it is a matter of regret that the legislature has not made possible a really scientific analysis of comparative local government costs.

MARTIN L. FAUST.

✤

WAYNE COUNTY, MICHIGAN. TWENTY-FIRST ANNUAL REPORT OF THE BOARD OF COUNTY ROAD COMMISSIONERS FROM SEPTEMBER 1, 1926 TO AUGUST 31, 1927. Pp. 175.

This report of the excellent work being done by the Wayne county road commissioners is a very attractive and worth-while piece of work. It perhaps comes closer to meeting more of the accepted standards of good report writing than any recent similar report. For example, its attractiveness, arrangement, type used, grade of paper, clearness, and selection of illustrations are all excellent. It does have, however, some characteristics which will greatly limit its utility. In the first place, it is far too long to secure a general reading. A report of this nature should never exceed fifty, better twenty-five pages, if it is intended to be read throughout by the general public. The public is overwhelmed by a long report and will cast it aside without any definite impression. It contains nearly thirty pages of statistics which have a value but hardly in such a report. A few charts well distributed through the reading material would have served the same purpose in a much clearer and more interesting manner. The plan of placing a picture opposite each page of reading material is one that should be copied by future report writers. All will not agree on the appropriateness of placing the picture of the board and its chief staff members in the front of the report, but there should be quite universal agreement that this report, if any, is justified in including them for it is an excellent report based on work designed and executed consistent with the best engineering and planning practices of the day.

✱

RICHMOND, VIRGINIA. ANNUAL REPORT OF THE DIRECTOR OF PUBLIC WORKS, R. KEITH COMPTON, FOR THE YEAR ENDING DECEMBER 31, 1926. Pp. 169.

The chief fault with this report is common to 90 per cent of all such reports. It is far too long. It could have been shortened considerably by condensing the more significant data of the 43 pages of statistics into a few charts and graphs. Then further, by shortening the 50 pages of unbroken reading material to 12 or 15 pages and making it readable and interesting by emphasizing the more important by heavy type. The clear organization charts, seven exceptionally well prepared maps of past, present, and proposed improvements, and the nearly 20 appropriate pictures, stamp this as one of the best public works reports that has come to the attention of this reviewer in a long time. The charts, graphs, and pictures, however, should have been better distributed throughout the report and placed near the relevant reading material. It is well written on good paper of a clear type and indicates a wise choice and balance of material. The short table of contents is a great aid to the reader who is interested in a particular phase of the work and is a feature too often overlooked in report writing. The comparative data are very illuminating and add an interest that can be

supplied in no other manner. The "volume of traffic map" of Richmond's principal thoroughfares is a clear and convincing method of showing this problem which is so vital to every city. This report is not only of interest to the taxpayers of Richmond, but it has much of value for the directors of public works and city engineers everywhere.

✱

CITY OF ST. PAUL. ANNUAL REPORT OF THE COMMISSIONER OF PUBLIC WORKS FOR THE YEAR ENDING DECEMBER 31, 1926. Pp. 113.

On the front cover of this attractive report, the all important question in report writing is answered above the signature of John H. McDonald, commissioner, to wit, "This report is published for the information of the taxpayer. . . ." If all public report writers would first of all be certain of its purpose and the group they desired to reach, better and more readable reports would result. The present case, however, does not fully justify this conclusion, for the report contains far too many tables of statistics which are very valuable for the office files and perhaps for a limited circulation, but have no place in a report for general reading. The report contains 22 pages of well written and interesting reading material; three excellent maps illustrating present improvements; three well chosen pictures and one clear and complete organization chart. The remaining 84 pages are devoted to statistics that busy taxpayers will hardly look at, much less attempt to understand. Had the statistical material of general interest been separated from the whole, worked into simple charts and graphs, and distributed throughout the reading material, it would have made a much more interesting document for the taxpayer.

A table of contents in the front of the report either to replace or supplement the general index in the back would have increased the ease in locating particular information. A better arrangement of material would also have increased its utility. For example, a very interesting table of general city statistics is all but concealed on page 82. Such data, which are always of primary interest, should have been placed in a more conspicuous place, perhaps on the inside of the front cover. The only serious criticism that can be placed against this report is the fact that the writer overestimated the amount of report material that the average taxpayer is willing to consume.

CLARENCE E. RIDLEY.

JUDICIAL DECISIONS

EDITED BY C. W. TOOKE

Professor of Law, Georgetown University

Constitutional Limitations—Basis of Classification of Cities.—The limitation requiring that statutes relating to municipalities shall be general in character, now included in most of the state constitutions, has always been held to be subject to reasonable classification. That based upon population is the most common method and has been uniformly upheld. In *Doherty* v. *Spitznagle*, 139 Atl. 424, decided by the Supreme Court of New Jersey November 25, 1927, the validity of the classification based upon the form of government of cities was before the court. An amendment to a general act, which was to become operative only upon approval by local referendum, provided that it should be effective in consolidated municipalities without a direct referendum. In holding that the basis of classification was a reasonable one under the constitution, the court follows the precedents of *Van Riper* v. *Parsons*, 40 N. J. L. 1, and *State* v. *Wright*, 54 N. J. L. 130. In the latter case a classification for purposes of authorizing cities located upon the ocean to build drives and construct walks along the beach was upheld. It may be noted, however, that the same court in *State* v. *Philbrick*, 50 N. J. L. 756, refused to uphold a statute imposing a special limitation for general taxation based upon classification of boroughs lying on the ocean which were organized under a commission form of government. It is clear that in this case the contiguity to the sea was not a valid ground for basing a difference in the amount of general taxes to be raised.

In the instant case Justice Black in his opinion says: "It may be this kind of legislation is unwise, as creating a tangled skein of statutes that is difficult and most perplexing to unravel. It certainly is not a desirable method of changing municipal officials. But, as has been said by this court, where that which is directed to be done is within the sphere of legislation, and the terms used clearly express the intent, all reasoning derived from the supposed inconvenience, or even absurdity of the result, is out of place. It is no province of the courts to supervise legislation, and keep it within the bounds of propriety and common sense."

Streets and Highways—Rights of Abutting Owners.—The recognition of the rights of abutting owners to have the street adjoining their property to be kept free from encroachments was exemplified in numerous important decisions the past year, and should result in a marked influence upon the present day tendency of municipal authorities to assume that they may ignore such rights because of the necessity of exercising a more extensive control of the highways for the convenience or protection of the public. In the June issue, several cases bearing upon this point were commented upon and their bearing upon the scope of ordinances regulating traffic suggested.

Of the more recent cases, we may note that of *Jobst* v. *Mayer* 158 N. E. 745, finally decided by the Supreme Court of Illinois December 9th, 1927. In this case an abutting owner on a private alley successfully maintained an action to enjoin the continuance of a fire-escape and awnings projecting over the right of way, which a neighbor proposed to erect. The defendant's contention was that his plans had been approved by the commissioner of buildings and further that the city had assumed control of the alley by virtue of the fact that it had maintained a lighting system therein and regulated the traffic thereon by ordinance for the past twenty years. While the decision was based on the finding that the alley had not been dedicated to the public, there can be no doubt that if the alley had been a public one, the plaintiff's rights would have been similarly protected as the facts showed that the obstructions seriously interfered with the plaintiff's rights of access.

In *Lowell* v. *Pendleton Auto Co.*, 261 Pac. 415, decided by the Supreme Court of Oregon November 22, 1927, the action was brought by neighboring property owners to restrain the defendant from parking cars in the street adjoining his premises for the purpose of testing and repairing them, as was alleged by the petitioners. The defendant pleaded an ordinance of the city designating the street in question as open for all-time parking and also that as abutting owner he had a special right to occupy the portion of

98

the street contiguous to his property. In answer to these pleas, the court points out that a parking ordinance can not enlarge or limit the rights of an abutting owner, that it is merely a police regulation which governs the relation of the city and the owner of the automobile. As to the claim based upon the ownership of the property adjacent to the street, the court says that the rights of the peculiar defendant apart from those of the general public do not warrant him in occupying the street for business purposes and that as a member of the public his right to park cars along the curb, except as directly affecting his ingress and egress, is only the right accorded to any other member of the public as incidental to the use of the highway for travel. His occupancy of the street beyond these limitations therefore constitutes a nuisance which the city should abate and which the adjoining property owners whose own rights in the street are affected thereby may maintain an action to enjoin. In effect, the decision of the court adopts Lord Ellenborough's classic statement in *Rex* v. *Cross* (3 Camp. 224). "No one can make a stable-yard of the king's highway," which the Supreme Court of Iowa paraphrased some years ago in *Pugh* v. *Crawford* (176 Ia. 593) in the words, "No one may make a private garage of a public street."

✢

Police Power—Vested Rights of a Property Owner in a Street Number.—In *Bacon* v. *Miller*, 225 N. Y. S. 99, decided November 4, 1927, the Appellate Division, First Department, of the Supreme Court of New York held that while the board of aldermen of a borough in the city of New York had the implied power to rename and renumber city streets, yet this power cannot be arbitrarily or capriciously exercised. Park Avenue in the borough of Manhattan extended from Thirty-fourth Street to the Harlem River; and the board passed a resolution which ordered that portion of Fourth Avenue between Thirty-second and Thirty-fourth streets to be renamed Park Avenue and renumbered accordingly. The petitioner had, for many years, owned and resided in a house designated as number "1 Park Avenue." The present action was brought to have the ordinance declared invalid and to restrain the borough president from allotting number "1 Park Avenue" to the defendant "Number One Park Avenue Corporation", which had erected a large commercial building on Fourth Avenue near Thirty-second Street.

In granting the relief sought, the court declared that an exercise of police power, such as numbering streets, must be made in good faith and for the apparent benefit of the locality at large. The decision points out that there was no physical or governmental reason for the present change and that the ordinance amounted to an attempt to arbitrarily take away one person's house number and give it to another. The case of *Anderson* v. *Lord Mayor and Corporation of Dublin*, 15 L. R. (Ireland) 410, decided in 1885 on a similar state of facts in accord with the case under discussion is the only precedent cited by the court to sustain its decision.

That the reasonableness of the exercise of the police power by a municipality is subject to the control of the courts is beyond question. This principle, however, finds its application only in the case where by the exercise of the power an individual's personal or property rights are invaded and is the test of the extent to which they may be taken or modified by governmental action. As a city may not contract away its governmental powers, so it is uniformly held that a private individual may not acquire a vested right through the exercise of a power or a privilege for which he has a license under the police power. The naming of streets and the numbering of houses is an exercise of the police power for the convenience of the public, and while a given number is often of value to the owner, it is difficult to see upon what theory he can acquire a property right in a given number not subject to change or revocation by the governmental authority which established it. We shall be interested to note the disposition that may be made of this case by the Court of Appeals.

✢

Officers—Compensation—Constitutional Inhibition against Increase of Compensation During Term Held Not to Apply to Municipal Officers.—Article 5 of the constitution of Montana provides that "No law shall extend the term of any public officer or increase or diminish his salary or emolument after his election or appointment." The statutes of the state dealing with officers and elections in cities and towns provide that "the salary and compensation of an officer must not be increased or diminished during his term of office." The city of Havre after the election of the mayor, but before his term of office commenced, passed a resolution increasing the salary of the office and a taxpayer's action was brought to enjoin the treasurer from paying the mayor in excess of the salary previously authorized. (*Broadwater* v. *Kendig*, 261 Pac. 264, November 18th, 1927.) The Supreme Court held that the term "law" in the constitutional provision cited was restricted to statutes and did not cover ordinances of municipalities. As the ordinance did not contravene the statute, it was upheld and the judgment for an injunction granted by the lower court reversed.

The court based its decision upon the fact that the constitutional provision in question was a section of the article imposing limitation upon the powers of the state legislature and fortified its conclusion by the decision of the Supreme Court of Pennsylvania in *Baldwin* v. *Philadelphia*, 99 Pa. 164, in which a similar clause in the state constitution was given a like construction. It is to be noted that the office in question was not one established by the constitution as in *State* v. *Moores*, 61 Nebr. 9, which held that a similar constitutional provision applied to the increase of the salary of a police judge of the city of Omaha. For a more liberal construction of such a constitutional inhibition so as to include municipal officers, see *Wolf* v. *Hope*, 210 Ill. 50.

✣

Remedies—Waiver of Constitutional Defenses.—In *State* v. *Becker*, 215 N. W. 902, decided by the Supreme Court of Wisconsin November 8, 1927, a mandamus proceeding to compel a town board to apportion to the petitioning school district the amount of money which the town had received from the state treasurer on account of the assessment of a public utility therein as provided by statute, the question arose whether failure to plead the constitutional objections by the city officials amounted to a waiver of these defenses. The court held that the school district might not waive any defenses which the constitution gave it, that such action would be against public policy and that the trial or appellate court should raise the question itself where it appears necessary to a proper disposition of the case. A statute apportioning the distribution of money collected by taxation is clearly within the province of the legislation and does not violate the requirement of uniformity in town government. While, for example, a final judgment that may increase the indebtedness of a municipality beyond the constitutional limitation may not be attacked collaterally (*Edmundson* v. *Independent School District*, 98 Ia. 639), until such final judgment is rendered the constitutional defense may be

raised either by the litigant or by the court. (*Hjelming* v. *La Crosse County*, 188 Wis. 581.)

✣

Police Power—Restriction Excluding Gasoline Stations from Certain Districts.—The Supreme Court of Oklahoma in *City of Muskogee* v. *Morton*, 261 Pac. 183, decided November 8, 1927, upholds the power of the city to declare gasoline filling stations in restricted districts nuisances and to forbid their erection therein. The plaintiff sought a writ of mandamus to compel the building inspector to grant him a permit to erect a gasoline station in a restricted district. In upholding the ordinance against the plaintiff's claim that it violated the state and federal constitutional guaranties the court based its decision on *Reinman* v. *Little Rock*, 237 U. S. 171, which sustained the power of the city to exclude livery stables already established from certain restricted sections.

The plaintiff also attacked the ordinance upon the ground that the provision, that such a permit might be granted in the restricted district if the owners of two-thirds of the property, estimated by the front footage, lying within 300 feet of the proposed station give their consent in writing, was invalid as an unauthorized delegation of the legislative power of the municipality. The court, however, applied the well-known distinction between an ordinance to take effect upon the filing of consents of adjacent property owners and one to whose application an exception may be made by such action. (*Eubank* v. *Richmond*, 226 U. S. 137; *Cusack Co.* v. *Chicago*, 243 U. S. 526.)

✣

Streets and Highways. Abatement of Gasoline Pumps.—The Supreme Court of Ohio in *Rowe* v. *Cincinnati*, decided November 30, 1927, (26 Ohio Law Bulletin 198) upheld an ordinance of the city which in effect provides that all gasoline pumps, filling stations or other automotive services maintained or operated in or upon any sidewalk or sidewalk space of the public streets are obstructions to public travel and public nuisances and directs their abatement by the city officials, and makes their continuance a misdemeanor. Rowe, the plaintiff, had maintained two gasoline pumps on the sidewalks adjoining his premises upwards of seventeen years under a valid permit from the city, which only recently was revoked in compliance with the above ordinance. Claiming that his property rights guaranteed by the state and federal constitutions were invaded, he filed a petition for an injunction to restrain the city officials from enforcing the ordinance against him. In affirming the judgment of the lower court dismissing the petition, the court in an able opinion by Miss Justice Allen holds that a valid permit for the temporary occupancy of any portion of a public street is a mere revocable license and cannot be the basis of any permanent property right to such use. A city cannot contract away its police power and no contract right can arise from a permit to use the streets for private purposes. (*Wood* v. *City of Richmond*, 138 S. E. 500, Va., 1927; *Lacey* v. *Oscaloosa*, 143 Ia. 704, 121 N. W. 544.)

✦

Streets and Highways—Establishment of Taxicab Stands.—In *Commonwealth* v. *Rice*, 158 N. E. 797, decided by the Supreme Judicial Court of Massachusetts November 23rd, 1927, the ordinance of Springfield requiring taxicabs and vehicles used for hire to make use of taxicab-stands established by the city was sustained. The court recites the statutes conferring power upon cities and towns to control traffic which clearly authorize municipalities to regulate the use of public streets and highways by "all vehicles . . . whatsoever." They authorize rules and regulations which shall prescribe the routes, the stands and the movements which shall be observed by vehicles for hire conveying persons or freight. The court holds that the ordinance is not unreasonable as it tends to the control of public traffic, protects persons from annoying solicitation and prevents confusion, disorder and danger in the streets. From other recent cases affirming the power of the city to control the movements of public vehicles even under a general grant of power to regulate traffic, the reader may be referred to *Kinger* v. *California Indemnity Exchange*, 258 Pac. 602; *Peoples Transit Co.* v. *Henshaw*, 20 Fed. (2d) 87; *Charleston-Ripley Bus Co.* v. *Shaffer*, 137 S. E. 360.

✦

Implied Powers—City Held without Power to Lease Rooms in Memorial Building to a Patriotic Society.—The Supreme Court of Kansas in *Darby* v. *Otterman*, 252 Pac. 903, sustained an injunction in a tax-payer's action brought to restrain the trustees of the Kansas City Soldiers and Sailors Memorial Building from leasing several rooms therein to the Veterans of Foreign Wars at a nominal rental. The memorial building costing some six hundred thousand dollars was erected with the proceeds of a municipal bond issue and is operated and maintained at public expense with funds raised by taxation. The ground upon which the court rested its decision is that the trustees and the commissioners of the city in the absence of express legislative authority are without power to lease any of the property to a private corporation, even though organized solely for public purposes.

The expenditure of money for patriotic celebrations is generally held not to be for a municipal purpose, although the power may be granted or the duty imposed by the legislature (*Schieffelin* v. *Hylan*, 236 N. Y. 254). The opinion in the instant case is strangely silent as to the provisions of the statutory authorization to erect and manage the memorial in question. Had a discretionary power as to the means of maintaining the memorial for patriotic purposes been conferred upon the city, there is abundant authority that the purpose might be carried out through the agency of a private corporation as well as by the direct expenditure of the municipal funds. "The test to be applied in determining whether a particular agency may be employed by the state or some particular subdivision thereof by legislative authorization to perform any particular work, is not whether the agency is public, but whether the purpose is public within the legitimate functions of our constitutional government." (*State ex rel. Trustees of La Crosse Public Library* v. *Bantley*, 163 Wis. 632.) It is not essential that the agency be one in which the public are interested and which might be conducted at public expense to warrant the use of the taxing power to aid it *ex donatio;* the taxing power may be used for the purpose of compensating for an equivalent of public service rendered under proper regulations to protect municipal interests unless the particular governmental functions to which it relates are expressly or necessarily limited to governmental agencies. (*Wisconsin Industrial School* v. *Clark County*, 103 Wis. 651.)

PUBLIC UTILITIES

EDITED BY JOHN BAUER

Director, American Public Utilities Bureau

The Appeal of the O'Fallon Case.—Last month we announced the decision by the federal court upholding the interstate commerce commission in its order of recapture as to excess earnings of the St. Louis & O'Fallon Railroad Company, under the 1920 Transportation Act. The company has given notice that it will appeal to the Supreme Court of the United States, and the case will probably be given precedence, so that the earliest possible ruling may be obtained for the interstate commerce commission in administering the provisions of the Transportation Act.

In our statement last month there was—quite unintentionally—a misrepresentation as to what was actually decided by the lower court. The decision was reported in the newspapers on the day when the copy for this department had to go to the printer. Consequently, we were compelled to rely upon the first press statements as to the principal point,—that the commission's methods of valuation had been approved. This, however, was not borne out by the opinions and the decision. The court did uphold the commission in its order requiring the company to pay a certain sum as excess earnings under the Transportation Act. In approving the order, however, the majority did not find it necessary to pass on the question of valuation.

The statute provides that one-half of the excess earnings shall be paid to the interstate commerce commission, and the remaining half shall be reserved by the company. While the commission predicated its order, for the most part, upon the prudent investment, with certain adjustments explained in the previous numbers of the REVIEW the company claimed the reproduction cost of the properties as the proper basis. The court, however, did not meet this issue. It decided that the entire income above the amount recaptured by the commission constituted income of the company. This included not only the 6 per cent upon the value as determined by the commission, but also one-half of the excess retained by the company. The court concluded that this total income constituted a return of over 8 per cent for the greater part of the period in question, even on the reproduction cost valua-

tion claimed by the company. It thus concluded that the return was not confiscatory, and refused to pass upon the methods of valuation employed by the commission. The question considered was only whether the income retained by the company was sufficient to meet the constitutional requirement of a fair return.

✳

Hydro-Electric Power Policies in Ontario and Quebec.—There has been so much controversy over the achievements of the Ontario Hydro-Electric Commission, so much difference in point of view and statement of facts, that a dispassionate and intelligent study is welcome. Professor Harald S. Patten, of the University of Cincinnati, has furnished such a study in the May and August numbers of the *Journal of Land and Public Utility Economics*. In the first article he outlined the development of the Ontario hydro-electric system, setting forth the economic background and the principal steps in the development. In the second he presents the Quebec organization, and compares the accomplishments in the two provinces under the different policies and circumstances.

Mr. Patten had no particular thesis to support. His object was to present the essential facts as to geography, industrial conditions, technological factors and social policies, and he left comparisons mostly to the readers. In Ontario the hydro-electric development has been conducted by a commission; production, transmission, and distribution have been principally under public ownership and operation. In Quebec the organization has been chiefly private. The figures presented and analyzed by Professor Patten indicate that neither province has been particularly injured or benefited by the special policy pursued. It appears that the investment per horsepower developed is considerably higher in Ontario than in Quebec; $275 per h.p. compared with $165, but the conditions are so different that no valid conclusion can be reached as to relative efficiency in capital outlay.

On the side of rates, there is a striking contrast, but this also may be largely due to the difference in conditions in the two provinces. In Ontario the deliberate policy has been to bring electric power as cheaply as possible to ordinary consumers. A special object has been to make life in rural sections more convenient and to promote social improvements. In Quebec the development has centered around the paper and other manufacturing industries. No such broad public policy has been involved. Domestic light and power has been more of an incidental phase of the business. This difference in policy appears also in the relative rate structures. In Quebec there is a greater difference between the manufacturing rates and domestic lighting rates. In Ontario the rate differential has been greatly limited. The domestic rates for ordinary consumers in Ontario municipalities average less than 2 cents per kw.h. for 83 per cent of the sales. In Quebec the average is more than twice as high. Opponents to the Ontario hydro-electric policy have frequently charged that the domestic rates have been made low for political reasons and that they have not covered the cost of service. This position is not sustained by Professor Patten's study. His conclusion is:

While private ownership has conspicuously justified itself in Quebec, there is little doubt that a salutary, if indirect, influence upon the public relations policy of its power corporations has been exercised by the example of Ontario's co-operative hydro-electric enterprise.

✢

What Is a Proper Service Charge?—In the January number, we considered the gas service charge in relation to the New York law, which had been declared unconstitutional by the federal court. The decision, it is reported, will be appealed to the Supreme Court of the United States for final determination of the issue.

The subject of the service charge has rapidly assumed considerable importance as an element in reasonable gas rates during recent months. Reports from a number of states refer to contentions over the matter. Word comes from Boston that a request has been made to the legislature to provide for a thorough investigation of the subject. There are now two cases before the New York public service commission which involve substantially the same issue in New York City, except that the adjustments in the rate schedule take the form of an initial charge for the first 200 cu. ft. or less of gas used, instead of the outright service charge, in order to avoid the statutory prohibition.

The issue in New York City between the consumers and the companies has taken a definitive form, which may be presented briefly because of its general importance. The consumers recognize that there are certain costs which are properly borne by a service charge or the substitute initial charge. They do not agree, however, with the companies as to the scope of those charges and the amounts to be included. For the purpose of clear presentation, they separate all the costs incurred in the manufacture and distribution of gas into three groups:

(1) Costs that depend directly upon the *amount of gas* produced and distributed to consumers;

(2) Costs that depend directly upon the *number of consumers;*

(3) Costs that do not depend directly either upon the quantity of gas or the number of consumers; *non-variable costs*, depending upon the general scope and form of organization.

The consumers contend that only the second group of costs are properly included in the service or initial charge. These are the direct, out-of-pocket costs that are incurred by a company because of particular families attached as consumers. They include the cost of meter reading, billing, consumer accounting, maintenance of meters, repairs on consumers' premises, and return upon meters used. In an ordinary case, these costs would aggregate between 25 to 50 cents per consumer per month.

The companies, however, would include in the service or initial charge also the greater part of Group 3 costs. These are all substantially fixed charges or overheads, which do not vary directly either with the number of consumers or the amount of gas consumed. The apportionment, therefore, is rather arbitrary, and must be determined according to reasonable public policy, and not according to logical identification of the costs either with the number of consumers or the amount of gas used.

These costs include the ordinary administrative overhead, including general office salaries, general office expenses, new business expenses, repairs of mains, and interest or return on all of the investment except the property used directly for the production of gas. The consumers contend that such charges are more reasonably apportioned according to the relative quantity of gas used for domestic purposes, rather than the number of consumers. It is more reasonable, in other words, to distribute these charges in proportion to relative use rather than evenly between the number of consumers. Where the service charges are placed by the companies at $1.00 per month per company, they are predicated usually upon the inclusion of the greater part of the Group 3 costs. Whether this basis of apportionment is justified, is a question that the commissions must face squarely and decide according to reasonable policy. Is the more important consideration, equality on the consumer basis, or on the relative use basis?

✦

The Massachusetts Basis—Prudent Investment or What?—It is commonly assumed that Massachusetts has handled public utility valuation much better than the other states. Many years ago it adopted regulation of security issues, and has limited the bonds and stocks to the actual investment in the properties. The capitalization authorized by the state has thus been considered as substantially equal to the investment in the properties and as the accepted basis of determining the "fair value" for rate-making purposes. The status of valuation in Massachusetts has thus been distinguished from other states in that it has adopted a definite policy of valuation for rate making, while others have not, and consequently, it may escape the force of the Supreme Court's trend toward reproduction cost and preserve the prudent investment basis of rate making.

The accuracy of the above view as to Massachusetts has been called in question by highly competent authority. When, at the recent Dallas meeting of the National Association of Railway and Utility Commissioners Chairman William A. Prendergast, of the New York public service commission, commented on the Massachusetts doctrine, and pointed out that the difficulties encountered appeared to be as great as elsewhere, Commissioner H. G. Wells of the Massachusetts commission protested against Mr. Prendergast's assumption that the Massachusetts commission had adopted prudent investment as against "fair value":

Whatever may be the opinion of different individuals as to whether prudent investment is a proper rate base or not, since the consolidation of the departments in Massachusetts in 1919 the Commission has not considered prudent investment as the Massachusetts theory.

Mr. Wells explained that the prevailing conception grew out of a decision many years ago in a street railway case, where there had been depreciation of the property. The representatives of the public urged the reproduction upon which the rates should be based, which was manifestly less than the actual prudent investment. The decision in that case was based upon the fact that the stockholders had actually invested their money in the property, and, consequently, "the fact that the value of that property was less than the prudent investment was of no moment."

The doctrine of prudent investment as the Massachusetts theory, is quoted as opposed to the reproduction cost theory where the reproduction cost is more than the prudent investment; whereas the only decision in Massachusetts was based on the fact that the prudent investment was more than the reproduction cost.

The substance of Mr. Well's explanation appears to be that the Massachusetts commission accepts generally the "fair value" basis as laid down by the Supreme Court, but that where the amount is plainly less than the prudent investment, it would take the prudent investment as the basis of rate making. In his further discussion, however, he indicates plainly that for all practical purposes, in the ordinary case, the commission does hold closely to the facts of the securities outstanding and reasonable dividends paid, and that the work of rate control is greatly simplified in most cases as compared with commissions in other states. The commission thus really clings to prudent investment, and yet recognizes other considerations that may enter into the determination of "fair value."

Commissioner Wells's explanation as to the old railway decision is, however, pertinent and extremely illuminating as to what will almost inevitably happen if reproduction cost should become firmly established as the measure of "fair value."

✦

Each Utility on Its Own Feet.—When a company furnishes two or more allied services, there is always the difficult question in rate making as to what extent each utility must be financially self-sustaining and in what respects the various joint costs should be apportioned between the services. Must there be a complete separation of operating expenses, including overheads; also of the property and the return required? Can a deficiency in one department be made good to any considerable extent by the excessive earnings of another? In the case of a railroad, may inadequate earnings of the passenger service be counterbalanced by excessive returns from freight? In the case of a gas and electric company, can a deficiency in one division be balanced by the greater earnings of the other? Under what principles must the various joint costs of operation be apportioned between the two?

For the most part, however, the course adopted is that each utility must bear its own burdens; that inadequate returns in the one cannot be justified by excessive returns in the other; that each must bear its own costs and bring a fair return in the property used in its own operation.

This view has recently been emphasized in the case decided on December 6, 1927, by the Georgia commission in the matter of street railway fares in Atlanta. The Georgia Power Company serves the city of Atlanta and other sections of the state, not only with street railway service but also with gas and electricity. The particular case involved an increase in the street railway fares to 10 cents, or 4 tickets or tokens for 30 cents. The opposition to the increase urged that in fixing the street railway fares, the company's entire business should be considered; that the increase should not be allowed because the company was earning a fair return on its entire property. On this point the commission stated that

if the street railway department is not earning a reasonable return on the fair value of its property it would be a discrimination and unfair to the users of gas and electricity to require them to pay excessive rates to make up the loss in the railway department.

The view thus expressed carries out the general policy recognized by the commissions, but not always followed in detail in individual cases.

✤

The Right of Municipalities in Rate Cases.—
On August 4, 1927, the board of public utility commissioners of the state of New Jersey authorized the Public Service Transportation Company to make certain changes in zones on some of the lines operated under permits granted by local municipalities. These permits had been originally granted to private operators, and they fixed the terms of operation, including the routes,

fares and zones. Subsequently, the company purchased the permits and proceeded to operate the bus lines in coördination with the Public Service Railway Company, which practically has a monopoly of street railway operation in northern New Jersey. After acquiring a large proportion of the permits, the Transportation Company took steps to change the fare zones on certain lines and asked the approval of the commission in disregarding the terms fixed by the municipalities.

The municipalities affected appeared in opposition to the company's petition, and attempted to show that the company was already earning an adequate return on the fair value of the bus properties, and that, in any case, the particular lines were arbitrarily selected for the duplication of fares, without regard to the entire bus system. The commission—in respect to some of the municipalities—substantially complied with the petition, and authorized the change in zones.

This action was deemed arbitrary and illegal by the municipalities, which petitioned the supreme court of the state for a writ of certiorari to review and set aside the commission's findings and order as arbitrary and illegal; the writ was granted, and the matter is now before the court.

The chief point of general interest in this proceeding is the fact that the municipalities were recognized as a legal party in this action. While cities throughout the country have been involved in rate litigation, both before commissions and the courts, in almost innumerable cases, their legal status has never been clearly defined and their appearance has been regarded more on sufferance than as a matter of right. While the standing of the municipalities was questioned in the New Jersey case, the writ was, nevertheless, granted to the petitioners, which included also private individuals. It appears, therefore, that the grant of the writ constitutes in New Jersey an outright recognition that the municipalities as such have a legal status in rate and public utility matters, as representing their citizens collectively.

GOVERNMENTAL RESEARCH ASSOCIATION NOTES

EDITED BY RUSSELL FORBES,

Secretary

Change of Name.—By vote of the membership, the name of the Governmental Research Conference has been changed to the Governmental Research *Association.*

1928 WORK PROGRAM OF THE RESEARCH BUREAUS

Bureau of Business and Government Research, University of Colorado.—Our work program for 1928 includes editing *Colorado Municipalities* every other month, arranging for our annual convention in June, compiling a directory of city officials in April and May, and making a comparative study of the efficiency of cities of over 2,000 population, similar in character to the study we made in 1923. In addition, of course, the routine work of the state association will be carried on, such as sending out information upon request, conducting membership drives, and compiling comparative information on various phases of city government, which is usually published in the magazine.

⚜

Dayton Research Association.—Most of the effort of the Bureau will be spent on the study of county government and its various agencies with emphasis on finance, bonds, roads and the children's home. At the same time we will maintain contact with city and school affairs.

⚜

Taxpayers' Research League of Delaware.—The chief item on the program of the League for 1928 is the state finance code, which contemplates a reorganization of the state's accounting, financial reporting, and budget systems; a revision of the revenue and taxation system; and the fixing of definite debt-incurring and sinking-fund policies. The contemplated code is also to cover the same field for county and local finance.

Subject to the exactions of the finance code, the League's program for 1928 also includes the following: a study of methods of legislative procedure; a plan for state administrative reorganization; preparation of a new charter for Wilmington; further study of a system of centralized purchasing.

The whole program of the League is designed with a view to constructive action in the 1929 session of the legislature.

⚜

Des Moines Bureau of Municipal Research.—The Bureau plans to unde take the following projects during the year 1928:

To assist the city plan commission or other citizen's group in the preparation of a ten-year operating and capital outlay budget for all local taxing subdivisions.

To urge the county board of supervisors to purchase photographic equipment for the recorder's office.

To assist the city clerk in putting the new permanent registration law into effect.

To prepare a report on the operation of the municipal airport with suggestions on its future operation.

To prepare laws for introduction in the 1929 session of the legislature.

⚜

The Taxpayers' League of St. Louis County, Inc. (Duluth).—The 1928 program is as follows:

The study of the organization of St. Louis County will be continued and a program launched looking toward complete reorganization. It is intended that the necessary legislation will be presented to the 1929 session of the state legislature.

Work on the preparation of a ten-year budget of permanent improvements will be continued, and as rapidly as the city planning commission's reports are published, definite recommendations will be made of the proper financing methods.

The League will assist the city engineer in the development of plans for reconstructing Duluth's sewer system. The study of special assessment methods and practices in Duluth will be continued, and in all probability certain recommended revisions will be submitted to the city council. A study of Duluth's garbage collection system will be made. A comparative analysis of governmental costs in Fall River, Dayton, Des Moines, New Bedford and Duluth is contemplated. An analysis and digest of expenditures of the school district will be made. Information appropriate for reforestation and development plans of St. Louis County will be produced.

Essential facts on pending projects will be published as bulletins of the League.

The League will consult and advise committees of the Duluth Chamber of Commerce, Civic Council, and other agencies, in matters of legislation and municipal programs and systems.

✳

Bureau of Municipal Research and Information, University of Florida.—During the year our library and other facilities will be increased as rapidly as finances will permit, while graduate students will conduct investigations and surveys of the state penal and charitable institutions, the effect of municipal advertising, the city-manager plan in Florida, and the expense of present county government in the state.

✳

The Albert Russel Erskine Bureau for Street Traffic Research, Harvard University.—The Bureau will continue to act, during the year 1928, as traffic advisor to the cities of Los Angeles, San Francisco, and Chicago.

The Bureau will complete the traffic survey report of the city of Boston early in 1928, and will serve as technical advisor to the administrative officials of the city in the application of the rules and regulations proposed in the report.

The Bureau will complete a traffic survey report on the city of Providence, Rhode Island, early in the year 1928.

The traffic survey of the city of New Orleans, which has recently been started, will be conducted by the Bureau during the year 1928, with plans for completion of the report late in the year.

✳

The Civic Affairs Department, Indianapolis Chamber of Commerce.—The department will carry out the following projects during 1928:

The customary watch over the administration of the annual budget appropriations and investigations concerning the budgets prepared in 1928 for operation in 1929. A survey of municipal employment with a view to determine what, if any, positions of employment may be eliminated or combined in betterment of the public service. The department will continue its efforts to restore the merit system of employment and promotion in police and fire departments, and to obtain its adoption for all other public employes.

The department will study each proposed capital expenditure of all units of local government and submit recommendations to the officials in charge.

It will endeavor to bring about improvement in school-city budget procedure because of the present overlapping of fiscal and tax levying years.

It will make a study of the county road building program.

✳

Kansas City Public Service Institute.—The Kansas City Public Service Institute's program for 1928 is largely a continuance of previous activities extended and expanded to meet new conditions and to include new subjects within the general scope of work previously done. Some principal items have been the subject of extensive study previously; others are almost new. The program, of course, is subject to change as conditions arise which demand immediate attention or which are deemed of particular importance.

City Finance.—Each year analysis of the city budget and coöperation in the improvement of budget methods are a part of the spring activities. This year effort will be made to make the city budget a more complete and informing document and one which will control city finances more effectively. If possible, it is hoped that a study of city purchasing methods and results may be made. As usual, current reports on the condition of city finances and on the cost of local government generally will be made.

Financial Program and Bond Issues.—Efforts will be continued to secure the adoption of a financial program. Aid will be given in the preparation of such a program if one is prepared. Bond issues in accordance with such a program will be analyzed and reported on in accordance with past custom. For all bond issues, all available information on proposals, needs, tax cost, plans, etc., will be presented.

Special Assessments.—Following up the report on special assessment procedure and practices in other cities, made in 1927, further study will be made of the methods of special assessment in Kansas City, including cost, equity of the methods of distribution used, and suggestions on possible improvements. At the same time, it is planned to make reports on large improvement projects to be paid for by special assessment before such projects are approved by the council.

Assessment for Taxation.—Careful study of the results secured by the present method of assessing property for taxation will be made. Previous studies have shown that present assessments are very inequitable in many cases. An effort will be made to determine the extent of the inequity. Methods used in other cities will be studied and presented to determine in what respects improvements can be made in Jackson County and Kansas City, and what steps are necessary to secure them.

County Government.—Further study of the organization of Jackson County government, of its financial methods and financial results, will be made. Based on the studies, changes in state law necessary to make possible a simple, centralized form of county government with financial control through modern accounting and budget systems will be drafted, probably in co-operation with county officials and interested organizations. Steps will be taken also looking toward the adoption of the recommendations made in the report on county welfare activities. Further studies will be made of the possible increase in efficiency and saving in cost from the adoption of the photostatic method in the recorder's office, and support will be enlisted toward securing the adoption of this method.

City Service.—A considerable amount of activity in the various city departments is almost a routine matter with the Institute. Current operations are watched, plans and programs are analyzed, special features are studied carefully, and officials are aided in improving operation. This applies to such departments as the fire department, health department, finance department, etc. The report on the water department will be completed and followed up.

Little progress has yet been made on the adoption of modern personnel methods in selecting, retaining, classifying and paying city employes. It is hoped that some definite results can be reported before the end of the year.

A complete administrative study of the police department is one which the Institute has had on its program for some time; but because of the special nature of the work and the necessity of employing police administration specialists for the study, the Institute has not been able to finance it as yet.

Legislation.—There will be no session of the state legislature until the early months of 1929. The usual investigation of subjects of interest to Kansas City's government will come up, and assistance will be given in drafting the bills, organizing support, etc.

Among the bills which undoubtedly will come up again and in which the Institute will be interested are the permanent registration bill, police home rule bill, pension bills, and bills relating to the organization and operation of the county government.

Publicity and Education.—Publicity and education, and coöperation with other agencies will be continued as in the past, except that effort will be made to extend them and increase their effectiveness. Particular effort will be made to secure the preparation and adoption of a suitable text and course of study on Kansas City and Kansas City's public affairs in the public school system.

✳

Municipal Reference Bureau, University of Minnesota, and League of Minnesota Municipalities.—*Minnesota Municipalities.*—The most important activity carried on by these organizations is the monthly publication of the official magazine of the League of Minnesota Municipalities. This consists of forty-eight pages each month. It contains articles on local and state government. The mailing list now includes about 4,000 state and municipal officials.

Ordinance Drafting and Revision.—The Municipal Reference Bureau maintains a valuable file of ordinances on more than one hundred subjects. As new ordinances are drafted in response to requests from municipal officials, they are added to this collection. In addition to drafting single ordinances, the League, at the request of various municipalities, has undertaken complete surveys of ordinances and has recommended the adoption of complete ordinance codes.

Inquiries.—During the past year, 1,175 inquiries were received at League headquarters by letter, telephone, telegram, or personal request and were answered by the League and Bureau staff.

Conferences and Conventions.—An annual convention of the municipal officials is held in June. The 1928 convention will be held at Brainerd, Minnesota, June 13-15, 1928. Other conferences for the current year include: a half day on the afternoon of February 9 at the Red River Valley Winter Shows Week, Crookston, Minnesota, which has been set aside by the management of the show as Municipalities' Day; the annual Minnesota Tax Conference, which, although a separate organization, is aided in its preparation and is supported in its meeting by the League, Bureau, and University, will meet at the University, February 7 and 8, 1928; plans are now being made to conduct a firemen's school for a week during August, 1928. This school will be conducted under the auspices of the League and University and the city of Minneapolis.

Publications.—The publications now in process of preparation include: an eight-page pamphlet containing the history and services of the League of Minnesota Municipalities; an article and model ordinance on the subject of billboard regulation; salaries of village officers in Minnesota; telephone rates in Minnesota; tax rates in Minnesota; a suggested accounting system for villages; forms to be used in connection with street improvements under chapter 65 of the laws of 1919; indebtedness of municipal subdivisions of Minnesota.

Committee Activities.—The League of Minnesota Municipalities, with the coöperation of the Municipal Reference Bureau, is carrying on through its committees a program of research into problems which are of vital interest to municipalities in this state. The subjects of these inquiries are indicated by the titles of the committees which are as follows: budgets and municipal accounting, bus regulation, elections and salaries, exempt property and delinquent taxes, fire prevention and fire fighting, garbage and refuse disposal, gross earnings, home rule and charters, judicial decisions, legislation, membership, municipal indebtedness, ordinances, planning and zoning, public health, public safety, public utilities, revision of village laws, sewers and sanitation, stream pollution, streets and pavements, swimming pool sanitation, taxation and assessments, townships, and traffic.

Particularly important in the foregoing list are the committee on exempt property and delinquent taxes which is engaged in making a thorough study, which will probably continue over several years, of the causes and effects of tax delinquency in this state; and the committee on the revision of the village law which is engaged in preparing a suggested draft of a new village code to replace all existing laws on the subject and to bring the villages of the state of Minnesota under a single act. They are now operating under three different types of organization.

Essay Contest.—An essay contest among the students of the high schools of the state on the subject "My Home Town" is now being conducted, and prizes are being offered by the League to a total amount of $100. The material secured through this contest will undoubtedly be of value in the files of the League, and the contest itself is designed to stimulate the interest of the high school students in their local governments. More than fifty high schools have already indicated their intention to participate in the contest.

✸

Bureau of Research, Newark, N. J., Chamber of Commerce.—The Bureau will, as in previous years, closely follow the bills proposed in the state legislature. It will also interest itself in all matters pertaining to municipal government in the city of Newark. Specific problems will be a revision of the state highway finance program, and a study of consolidation in this area.

If the opportunity presents itself, reports will be made on both street cleaning and refuse disposal, and on the central market.

✸

Philadelphia Bureau of Municipal Research.—The 1928 program of the Bureau of Municipal Research of Philadelphia may be divided into three general classes: studies of city government, consultation and information service, and public dissemination of information.

Philadelphia's Water Supply Problem.—The particular phase of the water supply problem of Philadelphia to which the Bureau is giving most attention at present is the prevention of water waste and especially the possibility of reducing water waste by the universal installation of meters. Only 30 per cent of Philadelphia's water services are metered now. In coöperation with the receiver of taxes, by whose office water rents are now collected, the Bureau has undertaken to compute from the records of meter readings in that office the actual consumption of water on metered premises. With this information, which has previously not been available, an estimate can be made of the consumption on unmetered premises and of the probable effect of universal metering. The information will also be useful in studies of classes and distribution of consumption and in consideration of meter rates and income from the water works.

The City's Borrowing Policy.—The Bureau is continuing its study of the city's borrowing policy, especially the relative merits of sinking-fund bonds and serial non-sinking-fund bonds.

The City's Sinking Funds.—Closely related to the study of the city's borrowing policy is its study of the city's sinking funds. This study is designed to assist in improving the administration of the city's sinking funds.

Employment Conditions in the City Service.—As a means of stimulating greater public interest in the city's need of a better classification of positions and a standardization of pay, the Bureau is making inquiries into the employment conditions of the city service. At present it is making an analysis of the turnover in the competitive class in recent years.

Methods of Recording Deeds and Other Instruments.—With a view to discovering whether the recording of deeds and other instruments in Philadelphia is being done as cheaply and as expeditiously as possible, and, if not, what improvements could be recommended, the Bureau has undertaken and now has under way a study of these methods. Among other things, the Bureau is giving attention to the feasibility of the use of form books and of the photographic process of recording and copying instruments.

Methods of Registering Voters.—Because of the widespread discussion of permanent registration, the Bureau is studying methods of registering voters and especially of the feasibility of permanent registration in this city.

Survey of the Municipal Court.—The survey of the municipal court, which was begun in 1925 upon invitation of the board of judges of the court, is still under way. A little of the field work and a great deal of editorial work remains to be done. This survey is being made by the Bureau as agent of the Thomas Skelton Harrison Foundation.

Municipal Contracts in Philadelphia.—This is another study which the Bureau is making as agent of the Thomas Skelton Harrison Foundation. At present attention is being given to methods of controlling force account work, and to the problem of bonding contractors and in other ways securing the city against failure on the part of contractors to perform their contracts.

Special-Assessment Methods in Philadelphia.—Partly as a piece of coöperation with other research bureaus who are studying special-assessment methods and partly to assist in improving Philadelphia's methods, the Bureau is making a study of special-assessment methods in this city.

Methods of Assessing Real Estate for Taxation.—In view of the rather widespread dissatisfaction with the city's present methods of assessing real estate for taxation purposes, the Bureau is studying these methods. A general survey of the problem is now being made. Later some specific phase of the problem will be selected for intensive study.

Indexing of City Solicitor's Opinions.—As a supplement to its index of ordinances, the Bureau is now preparing an index of city solicitor's opinions from 1883, the earliest year for which the opinions are printed, to the present time.

Consultation and Information Service.—The Bureau's consultation and information service varies according to the demands made upon the Bureau by city officials, citizens' organizations, and private individuals. It is therefore not possible to plan this phase of the Bureau's work in advance. It consists of consultation service by members of the Bureau's staff to city officials, committees of such organizations as the Chamber of Commerce, the City Club, and the Philadelphia Conference on Government, and to representatives of other civic and social agencies of the city. Much of the time of the Bureau's staff is devoted to supplying information upon request.

Public Dissemination of Information.—Under this heading belong such activities of the Bureau as the publication of its weekly bulletin, *Citizens' Business*, the preparation and issuance of press notices and of open letters to city officials, the preparation of articles for civic and educational periodicals, the delivery of public addresses, and the distribution of Bureau literature. All of these activities will continue in 1928.

✢

The Thomas Skelton Harrison Foundation of Philadelphia.—The work of the Thomas Skelton Harrison Foundation in 1928 will probably consist chiefly of financing civic work done by others. There will be a continuation of the study of the Philadelphia magistrates' courts which is in charge of Spencer Ervin, Esq., of the Philadelphia bar. His report is now being written. Two other pieces of work which the Foundation will continue to finance are a survey of the municipal court of Philadelphia and a study of municipal contracts in Philadelphia. Both these studies are being made by the Philadelphia Bureau of Municipal Research as the Foundation's agent. Further particulars concerning them will be found in the statement of the Bureau's plans for 1928.

✤

Rochester Bureau of Municipal Research.—It has seemed almost impossible for our organization to work out a program for 1928 with any definiteness inasmuch as the transition from the present form of government to the new form will undoubtedly give rise to many important problems, in the solution of which the Bureau will be called upon to help. It seems that one of the greatest services the Bureau will be able to render will be that of aiding in this transitional period. It is impossible to forecast the exact nature of these problems.

One of the biggest undertakings with which the Bureau will be concerned is that of outlining a complete municipal code and that, so far, is the main job projected for 1928.

✤

San Francisco Bureau of Governmental Research.—Subject to unavoidable interruptions, the Bureau's program of major activities is outlined in the following paragraphs.

*Charter Revision.—*The Bureau has done a vast amount of work during the past several years on the analysis of our existing charter, and the formulation and drafting of an extensive charter amendment designed to reorganize the governmental structure, and to revise and modernize municipal procedure along business-like lines.

Further activity under this heading will constitute the most important of the major Bureau operations during the next year, with the hope of bringing such a complete charter revision program before the people at the November, 1928, election.

*Salary Standardization.—*One of the most important Bureau activities for the coming year is involved in the completion of the study of all municipal employments (now about two-thirds finished) for the purpose of properly classifying each position and defining each of the numerous employment classes in the municipal service. Two Bureau staff men are now giving full time to this work.

Upon the completion of the proposed classification, and hearings thereon, this will be proposed for adoption by the civil service commission for examination purposes, and by the board of supervisors for salary standardization purposes.

A second phase of the work will involve a comprehensive study for the determination of proper standards of compensation for each class of employment, and the preparation of a complete schedule of compensations covering the entire city service.

*San Mateo Survey.—*This work is being performed by the Bureau and financed by the San Francisco Chamber of Commerce. Three men have been assigned to this study, working out of a temporary office in Burlingame.

The study will bring together information on finances, governmental functions, organization and many other pertinent factors that should be considered in any proposal for the consolidation of, or coöperative action by, San Francisco and San Mateo counties. It is expected that the study will be completed and the report based thereon issued for public distribution early in 1928.

*Garbage Survey.—*A survey of garbage collection rates and procedure, requested by the Board of Health, and to which the Bureau has assigned an engineer, is in its preliminary stages. Subject to the continuation of coöperation by the two scavengers' associations, this will be carried to completion.

This should result in a complete analysis of the equity of garbage rates now specified by ordinance. It should likewise provide a basis for the establishment of rates for business houses, buildings and hotels for which legal rates are not now specified, and for the improvement in many details of the present collection procedure.

*Fiscal Information.—*The keeping of a system of "skeleton" accounts will be continued for the purpose of maintaining up-to-date Bureau information on the expenditures from and commitments against all city funds, also the revenues received or payable into such funds. This work has proved of great value to the Bureau, and indirectly to city officials, during the past year.

*Accounting Improvements.—*Work is now in progress, and should be completed in the near future, involving analysis of present methods of annually preparing the city's assessment roll and tax bills. It is expected that the use of mechanical office equipment and less complex forms will reduce the present labor cost for this work.

Measures have been proposed looking to a saving of time and cost in two city offices, by the use of mechanical bookkeeping processes to replace the existing detailed hand-posting and balancing methods. It is hoped that these improvements can be effected during the coming year.

Similarly, proposals are being developed for an improved and more economical procedure for the preparation of departmental payrolls. In addition, the Bureau has renewed its previous proposals for the payment of employees on the job, to eliminate the existing losses occasioned by requiring employees to travel to the city hall for their pay checks.

Market Street Railway.—Compilation and mapping has recently been completed and published, showing dates of expiration of all private street-railway franchises, as a basis for public information of the particular services affected.

The Bureau will keep in touch with, and study all proposals for the solution of the street-railway transportation problem, which will become of increasing importance, due to the expiration of important franchises in 1929.

Health Department.—The health officer has requested the Bureau to complete its report, based on a previous survey, and to submit to him proposals designed to improve the organization and procedure of the health department. It is hoped that this can be taken up early in 1928 and pushed to completion.

Street Cleaning.—The superintendent of the bureau of street cleaning has requested the Bureau to make a survey of his department from the standpoint of need for additional men and equipment.

It is hoped, if staff service can be made available, to take this matter up, including also the factors of organization and procedure as applied to street-cleaning operations, and complete the study and report in time for consideration in connection with next year's budget.

Street Reconstruction.—Several requests have come to the Bureau for an analysis of street repair and reconstruction methods and costs. Controversies between the board of supervisors and the board of public works relative to the cost and programming of the work make such a survey highly desirable.

The superintendent of the bureau of street repair has expressed his interest in having such a survey made and has promised complete coöpera-

tion. It is hoped that work on this can be started at an early date and pushed to completion.

Public Information.—As a continuing item on its program, the Bureau serves as a staff agency for each of the five sections of the municipal affairs committee of the Chamber of Commerce, each section having a major work-program.

Staff service is also rendered on request to the Down Town Association, Real Estate Board, San Francisco Center, Commonwealth Club, Building Owners' and Managers' Association, and other civic organizations.

Capital Expenditure Program.—The Bureau recently completed a re-compilation of officially-proposed major and continuing projects, involving a total cost of $335,000,000, together with the Bureau's estimate of from $172,000,000 to $260,700,000 as the extent of the city's resources during the next ten years for the financing of such projects. Efforts will be renewed to secure the formulation of an orderly program.

Police Department.—The chief of police has requested the Bureau to bring its previous police department survey up to date, and to submit to him a report proposing such changes and improvements as the survey and analysis may seem to indicate as desirable. The completion of this work is entirely dependent on the availability of staff service therefor. At the present time, it seems impossible to undertake this work for at least several months.

✤

Taxpayers' Economy League of Spokane.—The work of the Taxpayers' Economy League of Spokane may be divided into two parts: that relating to the government and finance of the local governments, and that relating to state government and finance.

During the coming year we will continue our current work of checking expenditures of the city, county, and school governments, carefully analyze the budgets of each and make investigations on any special matter that may come up in any of the budgets. Special study will be made of city-owned motor vehicles and the matter of a central city garage, the problem of traffic congestion in the city and means for its control, photostatic recording of public documents, and tax contribution to public charity.

Since the legislature meets in January, 1928, we shall be busied with investigations of proposed initiative measures as well as the proposed constitutional amendment relating to classification.

NOTES AND EVENTS

Ashtabula, Ohio, Retains Municipal Ownership of Electric Light Plant.—By the narrow margin of 28 votes, the people of Ashtabula last November decided against the sale of the municipally owned electric plant. The campaign was an extremely bitter one. The proposal was to put the plant up for public sale, but the Cleveland Illuminating Company had indicated that their bid would be at least $2,000,000, and this company is believed by some to have been deeply involved in the campaign. Following the election, the Cleveland Company was given a permit to bring its power into the city to serve the docks and railways, but immediately referendum petitions were circulated against the ordinance, and the newspaper report is that sufficient were filed to carry the matter to the electorate.

✢

Error in Published Tax Rates.—In the " Comparative Tax Rates for 249 Cities," appearing in the REVIEW for December, 1927, the final readjusted rate for Buffalo, the twelfth city in the list, was given as $18.70. This is an unfortunate error. This figure should be $26.50, which is the amount of the total rate of $33.98 reduced to a 78 per cent basis.

✢

City Charter Movement in Milwaukee.—The City Charter League adopted on December 21, 1927, an outline of the principles of a strong-mayor—P. R. form of government.

It is planned that the charter will be voted upon April, 1929, and the work necessary to complete it is now under way. Such subjects as pensions, special assessments, amortization fund, civil service, etc., have still to be covered, but will be finished within two months.

The outstanding item in the new charter is the elimination of the ward system and the adoption of P. R. system of electing the aldermen. The council will be elected from three districts. A variation from the Cleveland system was adopted; instead of deciding the size of the council in advance, the number of votes necessary to elect a candidate was decided, *i.e.*, a uniform quota of 7,000 ballots. Based on the election figures of 1924, the council would contain about nineteen

members. This system of P. R. has not been used in this country, but where a district system is provided it has the following advantages over the usual system:

(1) It automatically re-apportions the members to the three districts each election time to correspond with growth of the city through annexations or otherwise, thus eliminating the inequalities which might otherwise develop between the times fixed for re-apportionment. District lines do not have to be disturbed no matter how large the city may grow.

(2) It tends to bring out a full vote, with increased representation for the district as a reward and decreased representation as a penalty.

(3) It insures approximate equality of voting power in all parts of the city. All voters (except the few who do not vote for any winning candidates) form parts of quotas of approximately equal size, no matter in which district they may live.

(4) Under the uniform quota plan a voter never helps win an extra seat for his district unless he can win the seat for a candidate he is willing to vote for. He can never defeat his own wishes by securing a seat for a candidate he considers worse than no representative at all.

(5) The uniform quota is easier to explain than a quota calculated on the basis of a definite number to be elected.

The city manager plan was carefully considered, but due to strong opposition from the labor and socialist groups the strong-mayor plan with a few variations was adopted. The ballot was shortened by eliminating the election of the city treasurer, controller and city attorney. The veto of the mayor was eliminated, but he has the right to ask for a reconsideration of an ordinance. The mayor appoints his department heads with the confirmation of the council for indefinite terms, but he may discharge them without approval of the common council. This provision will prevent holdover appointees.

The board of estimates is abolished and an executive budget system established. A new department of finance is created consolidating seven separate departments. It will have complete control over the financial affairs of the city including the keeping of accounts, current auditing, custodian of funds, tax assessing, purchasing supplies and real estate.

The council is to appoint an auditor for indefinite term who shall be a certified public accountant. He shall make a continuous audit, make investigation for the council, certify all financial reports, act as secretary of the budget and in general function as a research department of the council.

Ex-officio members are removed from the city planning commission. Five members are to be appointed by the mayor and approved by the council.

Civil service provisions are carried higher, covering all officials including department deputies. But the backdoor is opened, and dismissal of all bureau and division heads may be made without approval of the civil service commission. Clerical employees still retain the right to a trial before the civil service commission in case of dismissal.

Our present charter includes about 800 pages of printed matter. By providing for an administrative code, it is hoped to keep the new document under one hundred pages. The model charter recently revised by a committee of the National Muncipal League was used whenever possible, and in completing the charter will be used to an even greater extent.

HAROLD L. HENDERSON.

Unsuccessful Recall Attempted in Greensboro. —Six years ago Greensboro, North Carolina, adopted the council-city manager type of municipal government, and it has proven very successful. However, a few months ago dissatisfaction arose, due primarily to the fact that the council granted the city manager a leave of absence of four months in order that he might recuperate from a serious illness. He was to receive a little more than half pay for this period and in the meantime the mayor was to take over the office of manager. This decision of the council was made by a three to two vote in the face of active opposition.

When news of the action reached the people, a mass meeting was called by a group of the voters and a movement for the recall of three councilmen and the mayor was started. The charges brought against these men were based on the following:

1. The granting of the taxpayers hard-earned money to the city manager for a vacation.

2. Failure to decrease the number of officeholders or expenses.

3. Failure of the council to keep certain promises made during the last election.

It was a necessary requirement of the charter that one-fourth the number of voters who participated in the last election should sign the petition of recall before the machinery could be put in operation. This number having been secured with considerable difficulty, a day was set for the people to vote whether these men should be removed from office. Four men appeared as opposing candidates and the recall became the chief topic of conversation for the entire town. In the meantime the registration books were opened and nearly three thousand people registered who had not voted in the last city election.

In opposition to the arguments stated in the recall petition, the supporters of the incumbents maintained that the recall could properly be used only in case of malfeasance of office and this had not been proven. This group also maintained that, if men should be recalled on such trivial grounds and without just cause, it would be impossible for Greensboro to secure any self-respecting citizen to serve on the council. Their last point was, if men who labor so hard for the city on a salary of two hundred dollars a year should be recalled, it would reflect upon the good name of Greensboro. Consequently advertisements appeared containing the following statements: "What is the matter with Greensboro?" "Greensboro resents the recall and all that it implies"; "A vote for these men is a vote for Greensboro."

The result of the election on September 26 was an overwhelming vote of confidence in the council; and the four men, whose recall was desired, received over twice as many votes as the men who were running against them. It was not only a vindication of the men but also a vindication of the council-city manager type of government with which they were identified; and it is safe to say that Greensboro will not use the recall for many years to come unless the emergency is very great.

Typical of this attitude is the following statement which appeared in one of the Greensboro papers when the results of the recall became known: "The recall is a powerful weapon which the people saw fit to acquire and preserve in their charter. Many years have passed, and it has not before been resorted to for any purpose. A plain meaning of the election figures this morning is that nothing is more unlikely than it will be invoked under similar conditions, for similar purposes, for a long time to come."

R. S. RANKIN.
Duke University.

✢

Right of a Citizen to Inspect Federal Personnel Records Denied.—The federal courts have defined and finally held that a citizen as such has no right to inspect the personnel records of the United States civil service commission in order to find out who federal officers and employees are and without question the decision applies in full to the records of the score or more of other federal personnel agencies. E. C. Stowell, president of the Better Government League, with headquarters in Washington, requested the civil service commission in his capacity of a citizen of the United States to furnish him with a list of temporary employees in the District of Columbia or to allow him to inspect its records so he could make up such a list himself. When the civil service commission refused to furnish him with the information, Mr. Stowell instituted mandamus proceedings in the supreme court of the District of Columbia. When an adverse decision was made, Mr. Stowell appealed the case to the court of appeals of the District of Columbia, which likewise decided the case adversely. Mr. Stowell then asked the Supreme Court for a writ of certiorari, which was denied.

In opposing the issuance of the writ of mandamus, the civil service commission held that "the law does not impose upon the Commission either the duty of keeping its temporary appointment records in a form available for public distribution or the duty of permitting access to or the obtaining of information from such records." The courts accepted this view of the situation and took occasion to point out that it would not give aid and comfort to "somebody nosing around, who, without stating any interest except that he is a citizen of the United States, demands a long list of officers." This reasoning seems to be based upon the assumption that because "citizens merely" are numerous the interests of any one of them as a citizen are so slight that neither the courts nor administrative officers need take cognizance of them.

The Better Government League, finding that the courts will not give redress in this matter, proposes two measures—the passage of a bill specifically making it the duty of the personnel agencies and departments to make their personnel records accessible to citizens with the exception of law enforcement officers, whose usefulness would be destroyed if their identity were known, and a congressional investigation into the whole situation for the purpose of discovering and proposing remedies. The Better Government League holds that the federal personnel system can hardly be worthy of the name with a score of central administrative agencies engaged in personnel work and that, in fact, the results now obtained are highly unsatisfactory from the point of view both of employees and the public as an employer.

A copy of the Better Government League's publication, "The Public Business," giving details of the suit will be sent free of charge to any interested person on request.

FRED TELFORD.

✢

To Study Classification and Reporting of Crimes.—A gift of $50,000 has been received by the Detroit Bureau of Governmental Research from an unnamed philanthropy to finance a project of the International Association of Chiefs of Police for developing a uniform classification of crimes and the uniform reporting of offenses throughout the country. Police Commissioner William P. Rutledge of Detroit is chairman of the Committee on the Standardization of Police Crime Records which will have charge of the new work. Other members of the committee include Chief Joseph A. Gerk of St. Louis, Chief Jacob Graul of Cleveland, Chief James Higgins of Buffalo, Chief L. V. Jenkins of Portland, Oregon, Chief Thomas Healy of New Orleans, Supt. Michael Hughes of Chicago, and Chief August Vollmer of Berkeley, California.

It is expected that the study will furnish not only a means of measuring the effectiveness of police activity, but more particularly, a basis of diagnosing and attacking at the source the social causes of crime, and will constitute a first step in crime prevention. At present there is no means of telling how extensive the crimes are or how effective are the current remedies.

An advisory committee is to be appointed to coöperate with the police chiefs' committee so that its crime statistical collection work will be correlated with work now being undertaken or proposed with regard to judicial and penal statistics. Dr. Lent D. Upson will be chairman of this committee, which will include representatives of the census bureau, department of justice, the American Institute of Criminal Law and Criminology, and several widely known penologists.

Bruce Smith of the National Institute of Public Administration, who has had more than ten years practical experience with police problems, and who has written extensively on the subject, has been named director of the work.

✤

Alameda County Civil Service Commission Defines Its Functions.—As was pointed out in the last issue of the NATIONAL MUNICIPAL REVIEW, the Alameda County civil service commission in the first year of its existence met with much opposition from various groups of persons unfavorably affected by its operations. This opposition was so strong and so frequently manifested misconceptions as to the fundamental aims of the public as an employer that the commission, early in December, felt called upon to address an open letter to the executive committee of the employees' association. Much of the opposition, it should be pointed out, was based upon the idea that certain individuals and groups should profit from the commission's employment work at the expense of other individuals and groups; this stand was often publicly expressed. The most significant portions of the commission's letter are as follows:

The Commission feels that its duties under the charter are similar to that of the employment agency of any large corporation and that the selection of the highest grade employees is and must be its primary duty. It is not sufficient that a candidate shall be qualified; he must be the *best* qualified.

The Commission is not infallible and it does

not claim, nor even assume, that the methods now in use are above and beyond criticism. The Commission will at all times welcome constructive criticism, but criticism in order to be constructive must view the problem from the standpoint of the best interests of Alameda County, as a whole, and not from the standpoint of any individual or group of individuals.

FRED TELFORD.

✤

Program for Next Meeting of the Assembly of Civil Service Commissions.—Two members of the program planning committee met with the president of the Assembly in Washington early in January and decided to continue section meetings at the convention to be held in Denver, probably early in September, though a number of topics was added. The new sections are to discuss and report upon the functions of the personnel agency in government, the financial requirements of the public personnel agency, the relations of lay members of the public personnel agency to the permanent technical staff, service (efficiency) ratings, and the factors involved in the evaluation of the work of a public personnel agency. The chairmen of the various sections will be appointed immediately, and it is expected that papers which will serve as a basis for the discussion of the various sections will be prepared in advance and distributed among members in order that the discussions may hinge upon moot points and reports be made to the Assembly for action.

In this connection it should be pointed out that the Assembly welcomes individuals and representatives of civic agencies at its meetings and is glad to have them attend section meetings and to participate in the discussions.

FRED TELFORD.

STANDARDS OF FINANCIAL
ADMINISTRATION

By
LENT D. UPSON
AND
C. E. RIGHTOR

Supplement to the
NATIONAL MUNICIPAL REVIEW
February, 1928.   Vol. XVII, No. 2

PUBLISHED BY
NATIONAL MUNICIPAL LEAGUE
261 Broadway, New York, N. Y.

STANDARDS OF FINANCIAL ADMINISTRATION

By LENT D. UPSON, *Director* and C. E. RIGHTOR, *Chief Accountant*

Detroit Bureau of Governmental Research

THE purpose of this chapter is to enumerate some of the more important and generally accepted qualities, both of organization and procedure, that characterize sound financial administration in an urban community. Public finance covers a wide scope of community endeavor, and obviously the criteria of correct practices must be expanded in minute detail if the numerous ramifications of the subject were to be explored to final conclusions. Such minuteness is impractical in any discussion intended for the use of the lay citizen, and this discussion, therefore, is limited to the general divisions of public finance,—particularly to budgeting public needs, financing current activities, financing permanent improvements, collection, custody and disbursement of funds, controlling financial transactions, and purchasing.

I. BUDGETING PUBLIC NEEDS

Every unit of government, regardless of type or location, collects and disburses revenue for presumably public purposes. Usually some more or less regular process is followed in preparing the estimates of expenses and in having these estimates approved by a legislative body. These authorizations are commonly spoken of as the budget, and the process by which the estimated income is correlated with estimated expenses and the latter finally authorized is called the budget procedure. Whether this process of correlation and the resulting budget are good depends upon the amount of care that is given to the procedure.

As almost a first step in the direction of the more efficient expenditure of public funds (excepting, of course, civil service, which had been inaugurated many years previously) the public turned to the introduction of scientific budget measures,—that is, careful planning and control of public expenditures. High hopes, that have been largely justified by experience, were had for the results to come from the introduction of scientific procedure.

What is this procedure from which so much has been realized that it has been adopted by the national government, forty-seven of forty-eight states, every large city, and many counties and smaller units of government? And what tests can be applied by the lay citizen to the appropriating procedure of his own community to determine to what extent it comports with modern practices?

1. *The estimates of expenditures for the fiscal period must be submitted to the legislative body as a carefully prepared program in which the needs of each city activity are correlated with the needs of every other activity, i.e., the budget must comprehend a thoroughgoing work program.*

Early budget requests were merely independent estimates submitted by public departments without regard to the needs of the other departments and of the city as a whole. The legislative body, having no intimate and continuous knowledge of all work done by the city, was scarcely in a position to weigh the merits of each request and correlate them into a well rounded

119

program in which no activity was out of balance. In consequence heavy appropriations were given those departments that had the greatest oratorical or political influence, and less colorful departments, perhaps having even more pressing requirements, were neglected. For example, health and education might be well supported while street cleaning and rubbish removal were neglected, or vice versa.

Such inequalities can be eliminated only when the chief executive,—that is, the mayor, the city manager, or in some few cities the city commission,— having an intimate knowledge of detail, carefully weighs the needs of each public activity and presents to the legislative body—which represents the taxpayers—a program which is susceptible of a minimum of justifiable modification.

2. *The estimated costs of this program should be balanced with available or expected income.*

In financial matters a city is little different from a private citizen, and when either consistently permits outgo to exceed income serious difficulties are ahead.

3. *Every principal activity conducted by a city should stand alone as an appropriation unit, and indicate the department conducting it.*

It is not proper to give a department head a large sum of money to be expended according to his best judgment, for such judgment may not conform to that of the taxpayers who pay the bill. For example, take police. In addition to general administration, the activities include record keeping, criminal identification, foot patrol, traffic control, detection, etc. The superintendent of police may be best qualified to indicate the emphasis that shall be placed on each of these services; presumably the legislative body and the public will

follow his recommendations. However, so long as the theory prevails that the taxpayer is entitled to determine the purposes for which his money shall be spent, the budget should be so arranged that these purposes and the amounts appropriated for them are clearly indicated.

4. *The estimates of both revenues and expenditures should be stated in terms that can be understood by both citizens and the legislative body.*

It is not sufficient that a department should make a request for so much money to conduct a particular activity, —that would result in lump sum appropriations. Those concerned with appropriating public funds and paying the bills are entitled to know the basis of the estimates, *i.e.*, how much is to be spent for personal services, contractual services, supplies, materials, equipment, etc. In turn, each of these principal classifications should be further subdivided as to number of men to be employed, with their salary or wage rate under the heading personal service, what type of contractual service it is proposed to engage, and what kind of supplies, materials or equipment is to be bought. In modern budget practice these classifications are uniform throughout all departments, with the result that the departments speak the same financial language when making requests and permit the responsible authorities to compare detailed budget requests with the expenditures of the previous year and with similar expenditures in other departments.

Such detailed request is not necessarily the unit of appropriation, but rather is used to support the larger unit of appropriation which is ordinarily the activity, except with respect to salaries and wages.

5. *Within reason the budget through the appropriation ordinance should con-*

trol and appropriate all of the 'funds belonging to the city.

Cities have a practice imposed by charter and state law—sometimes with very little reason back of such legislation—of segregating their income into a number of funds, to be devoted to a specific purpose. For example, the revenues from taxation and miscellaneous sources are usually designated as the operating fund and sometimes divided into numerous minor funds, all of which must be spent for current operation or minor permanent improvements, although there is nothing to prevent acquiring major permanent improvements also, and in fact such procedure is to be advocated in some instances. Money from the sale of long term securities is usually segregated for the specific purposes for which the bonds were issued. Money raised by special assessments for benefits assessed must be used to meet the cost of the specific benefits incurred. In addition, frequently there are trust funds, each kept separate, the income of which is to meet the future cost of pensions, gifts for specific purposes, etc. The maintenance of these more important funds is justifiable, but wherever feasible their income and expenditures should be included in the budget procedure and the appropriation ordinance to insure both being under proper control and in order that the budget may be a reasonably complete picture of the city's operations.

6. *There should be an ample time schedule for the budget procedure.*

The estimates should be prepared several months prior to the beginning of the fiscal year, with adequate time for their review and correlation by the executive, and for consideration and adoption by the legislative body. All budget action should be completed before the beginning of the fiscal year. The executive might well have a permanent agency assisting in budget study.

7. *Public hearings should be provided.*

In addition to the executive and legislative bodies affording a hearing to the department heads, the legislative body should provide for one or more public hearings upon the tentative budget, with ample advance notice to the public of the time and place of such hearings. A budget exhibit provided by a city deserves special credit, in judging of the adequacy of budget procedure.

8. *The budget should contain adequate comparative and supplementary data.*

Data relative to appropriations and expenditures for two or more preceding years are invaluable; also supplementary information relative to the city's finances, by funds, etc. A summary should be prepared, and accompanying the transmittal of same by the executive to the legislative body might well be a budget message, concisely setting forth the major facts about the budget for the ensuing year. Provision should be made also for transfers, contingencies, salary schedules, etc. The city should adopt an adequate appropriation ordinance.

9. *After the budget has been enacted as an appropriation ordinance, procedure should be established to insure the 'funds being spent in accordance with the wishes of the appropriating authorities.*

One of the principal weaknesses of present budget procedure is found in an absence of thorough-going control over expenditures. The principal step that can be taken in the direction of budget control is to insure that liabilities are not incurred unless properly authorized. This is a relatively simple procedure if cities will undertake it.

It is customary to provide that no order from a department and upon a vendor is valid unless it is approved by the city controller. The controller, incident to such approval, charges the amount of the order against the appropriation of the department, correcting his books when the actual figure is obtained from the invoice. In the meantime this charge is called an encumbrance. These encumbrances deducted from the actual cash balance in the appropriation give the remaining amount that the department has still to spend. With this control, it is impossible for the department to run up bills in excess of appropriations.

It is equally important that the department does not spend all of its money the first few months of the fiscal year. To control this, a system of allotments is coming into use. Monthly or quarterly each department is required to deposit with the controller for his approval a program for expending the balance of the available appropriation. If the proposed expenditures exceed one-twelfth, or one-quarter, of the total, some explanation must be forthcoming.

There are numerous other elements that go to make up a sound budget procedure and which will eventually be incorporated in the budget procedure of the future. However, it is at present unfair to judge the budget procedure of a city government by improvements that have not yet been generally adopted.

Briefly, among such improvements is the desirability that the budget estimates present a complete picture of what is eventually hoped to be accomplished by any department with some indication as to how far that hope can be realized by the appropriation requested and granted. For example, the public health authorities have a fairly clear idea of the reasonable limits of public health work as measured in the possible reduction of the morbidity and mortality rates. To accomplish these ends, it may be estimated that such a sum of money must be expended. When future health officers present their budget estimates to the chief executive, it may be expected that they will outline what a complete program would cost and what per cent of that program is being met by the appropriations they expect to secure. Thus an important administrative problem will be placed squarely before the public, who can say how much public health they wish to purchase.

Also public officers will submit estimates not only in terms of activities, but in units of work to be done and in unit costs of such work. Many public services are easily measurable in units of service. For example, it will be impossible for a superintendent of street cleaning to request such a sum of money for the hand brooming of streets. He will be compelled to estimate so many thousands of square yards of street to be hand broomed at a given unit cost, showing how the total compares with the units of work of the years previous and the unit cost compares with prior unit costs, and possibly even with such figures of other cities. The budget will then furnish a yardstick by which the effectiveness of a city government can be measured by the public.

Further, possibly inter-departmental services will be charged for. For example, every public water department is furnishing large quantities of water to school buildings, public offices, the fire department, and even to semi-public institutions free of cost. On the other hand, it enjoys a freedom from taxation that would be imposed upon a utility owned by private citizens. Efficient management and accurate costs will require that public utilities owned by the city be put upon a business basis, showing these charges and credits, and operating as nearly as possible like privately owned utilities.

II. FINANCING CURRENT ACTIVITIES

In financing current activities, the city obtains its revenues from many sources,—taxes, licenses, fines, forfeits, subventions or grants from the state and other units, donations and gifts, pension assessments, sale of privileges, etc.

It would be impossible in the scope of this paper to discuss each of these sources of revenue and the criteria of its proper assessment and collection. This discussion is confined entirely to the methods of assessment of property taxes, which usually comprise from 60 per cent to 90 per cent of municipal revenue devoted to the purposes of current operation.

Also, it is necessary to confine the tests to the actual procedure by which taxes are levied, ignoring any question of the justice of the incidence of taxation. The chief elements of a modern assessing system have been set forth so thoroughly in the numerous assessing manuals that it will be sufficient to mention them only briefly.

1. *There should be a single authority imposing the assessments for taxation purposes, having a long term of office and being as completely divorced from politics as possible.*

The difficulty with the prevailing assessment organization as found in most cities is that the assessing authorities, usually a board of some sort, are closely connected with the political life of the community. The public so far has demanded the right either to elect its assessors or to have them appointed for such short terms that they are subject to political influences. Assessments honestly and accurately arrived at can scarcely exist until the assessor fixing them is beholden to no influence for his job, except that which accrues through merit. It is suggested that the selection of the assessor might be left to the merit system, the incumbent holding office as long as the character of the service warrants, or at least for a very long term.

2. *Assessments should be made at the true cash value of both real and personal property.*

Unless property is assessed at its full value as defined by state law or charter, there will always exist loop holes for under- or over-assessment. Occasionally assessors make use of a percentage of the full cash value, but that percentage should be uniform over all parcels of property within the city. It is impossible to compare the relative equity of assessing unless such uniformity is enforced.

3. *There should be separate assessments of land and improvements.*

The relative equity of assessments can never be determined unless lands and buildings appear separately on the assessment rolls. When the two items are combined in one it is impossible to determine the unit foot value that has been placed upon the land, or the cubic or square foot value that has been placed upon the buildings. A procedure that does not separate these items has not yet laid the groundwork of an effective and fair assessing system.

4. *The district, block and lot system should be used for describing property for assessment purposes.*

This method of describing property in its simplest form is not essential to equitable assessment, but is an aid to it. When the block and lot descriptions are used it is relatively easy for any enquirer to locate property in which he is interested and compare the assessment, and the intentional or unintentional omission of properties is made difficult.

5. *Land value maps of the entire city should be prepared and published.*

Land value maps are designed to

show the unit front foot value of the land frontages of every block in the city. The presence of such maps is the greatest assurance against unequal assessment. Any interested citizen can examine the maps on file in the assessor's office and determine the unit foot values that were utilized in the assessment within a block. With very little calculation the total of any land assessment of any parcel of property can be determined and checked against the actual assessment as appearing on the assessment rolls, and be compared with any other property desired. The publication of such land value maps is always highly desirable, since it stimulates a widespread interest in the land values determined upon by the assessing authorities.

6. *Tax maps are an absolute essential to a complete assessing system. They should give the exact dimensions of every parcel of property within the city on such scale as can be readily used.*

These maps naturally serve as the fundamental basis of assessment and from them the assessors can check their assessment rolls to insure that every parcel of property is properly recorded.

7. *Unit foot rules for measuring land values should be adopted and followed.*

In every city many lots correspond to some standard depth, usually 100 or 120 feet. It is therefore customary for assessing authorities to determine upon a standard unit of measurement,—a single inside front foot for the prevailing depth. For the value of property that deviates from the established depth, a depth table is used. For example, let us assume that the assessors establish a 100-foot rule for downtown property, since most real estate is of that depth. Land near the street is of greater value than land at a distance from it and therefore a lot having less depth than 100 feet would be of greater

proportionate value than the actual depth related to 100 feet would indicate, and depths under or over 100 feet would be measured by a standard depth table. Many such rules have been established, but all of them are similar in character. Land value maps always indicate the front foot value at the middle of the block in terms of the adopted depth.

8. *Additional rules covering corner influence, plottage, triangular and irregular shaped lots, alleys, and other minor variations in values should be determined upon.*

The most important of these rules relates to corner influence. It is obvious that many parcels of property located at the junction of two streets are of greater value than property in the middle of the block, but this corner influence, as it is called, is always difficult to determine. If the matter is left to the opinion of the assessor formulated without some rule, one may be sure that values are not equitably determined and comparisons are made impossible. For that reason considerable thought has been given to corner influence rules for business property particularly.

Plottage rules are established to take into consideration the different utility of property because of peculiarities of size. For example, a piece of property located immediately adjacent to a railroad might be used for a coal yard. Its value for that purpose, however, would be greatly reduced if it were so narrow that it did not have adequate space for both storage and roadway.

Certain rules have also been worked out covering triangular and odd shaped parcels, alleys, etc.

9. *There should be a standard classification of buildings with the establishment of unit factors of value for each class.*

The valuation of buildings opens

large avenues for favoritism and in-equality because buildings in the same neighborhood may and will have large variation in cost, although land values may be more or less uniform. The greatest injustice may be done in fixing assessments, yet the aggrieved property owner find himself estopped from redress because of the large element of personal opinion that enters into a building valuation. However, these opportunities will be reduced to a minimum if buildings are classified into large groups according to character, and each such class further subdivided as necessary. For example, it would be relatively simple to throw certain types of residences into a half dozen or more classes. Downtown office buildings, factories, hotels, etc., are similarly susceptible to grouping. The cubic or square foot factor of each group can then be fixed and from it the assessed value of each building determined. There will, of course, be minor deviations from these established classifications and values, but they will be relatively unimportant as compared to the equity that is secured.

10. *Rules of economic and structural depreciation should be adopted and used.*

Structural depreciation is easily understood. It is the reduction in the value of property due to wear and tear, age, and physical decay not made good by maintenance. No matter how well a building is repaired and maintained, it eventually wears out and its value is lessened accordingly. The structural life of buildings has been fairly well established and the value reduced according to age tables.

Of more importance is the matter of economic depreciation, due to inadequacy, obsolescence, or supersession. Probably most buildings find their way to destruction from this cause rather than because of actual physical depreciation. Every large city has many buildings that for the reasons enumerated are not suitable to the land upon which they are placed, and the income of which is not commensurate with the investment involved. Some reduction in assessment must be made because of this economic deterioration, but rules governing it are difficult of formulation and allowances are usually made in the good judgment of the assessors.

11. *Coöperation should be had with property owners in fixing the assessments.*

Probably one of the most important steps the assessing officials can take in their duty of annual assessment of property is to obtain the coöperation of the owners in determining upon relative valuations. Such coöperation may be through real estate boards and dealers, and other citizen agencies.

12. *In assessing personal property, a personal return should be required to be filed by each taxpayer.*

Such return form should be sworn to by the taxpayer, and in event he refuses or fails to file same, the assessor should fix a satisfactory minimum valuation, subject to annual increases until protest is made.

13. *Ample opportunity should be provided for a review of tentative assessments, and the hearing of complaints.*

III. FINANCING PERMANENT IMPROVEMENTS

Permanent improvements are ordinarily financed through the issuance of bonds, or assessment for special benefits conferred. While special assessments may be paid in cash by the property benefited at the time the construction work is done, more frequently they are liquidated in installments, in which case bonds are issued and the proceeds used to pay the contractor. In consequence, it may be said that every city pays for its principal public improvements by the issuance of bonds. The rules governing the issuance of bonds are more or less determined by common sense, and for that reason it is relatively easy to indicate certain fundamental tests that should govern in every instance in which a city incurs funded debt.

1. *Except in unusual emergency, such as flood, fire, etc., debts should be incurred only for a permanent improvement.*

It is hardly necessary to expatiate on this axiom. A city is no more justified in issuing bonds for current expenses than is the private individual.

2. *The term of the bonds should never exceed the life of the improvement for which they are issued.*

It is reasonable to expect taxpayers to pay for improvements during the life of the benefits that they receive. In examining the outstanding bonded indebtedness of cities, it frequently develops that bonds are still unpaid covering schools, bridges, equipment, etc., that have long since been razed, abandoned, replaced, or junked.

3. *If term bonds be issued, a sinking fund or reserve should be maintained for their retirement.*

At least enough money should be deposited in the sinking fund annually so that such installments plus the annual earnings thereon will be sufficient to pay the bond at maturity. Unless such a fund be set up, one of two alternatives is presented,—either to pay the entire debt in one lump sum at maturity, or to refund the issue. The former method would put an undue load on one year's debt charges, and in the case of a large bond issue be practically impossible, and the latter would effectually postpone payment probably past the life of the improvement.

4. *In general, preference should be given to serial bonds over term bonds, except in large cities, where a study of the market should be made as to saleability of each type.*

Many erroneous figures have been circulated with respect to the relative cost of serial and term bonds, always in favor of the former. In actual practice the cost of any bond is determined by the amount of the bond, the rate of interest, and the time elapsing before maturity. These elements all being considered, the cost is precisely the same on a serial and a term bond provided the sinking fund earn at the same rate of interest as the bond carries. Should the sinking fund earn at a higher rate, the term bond is actually cheaper; if at a smaller rate it is more expensive. This last statement is predicated on the assumption that the market at the time of the sale is as equally favorable for one type as for the other. Such equality does not always exist. In some markets one type may be sold at a lower rate of interest than the other type. In the case of large cities, consideration should be given to the favorableness of the market in determining the type of bond to be sold. However, in smaller communities preference should be given to serial bonds to obviate the necessity of maintaining a sinking fund with its attendant bookkeeping and investment of funds.

The term of a bond should not be too long, regardless of the type. In either the serial or sinking fund the difference in annual cost between bonds issued for a period of, say, fifty or sixty years, and those issued for, say, thirty or thirty-five years, is so small that there is no justification for assuming additional interest burdens over a period of years while decreasing annual payments by immaterial amounts.

5. *The rate of interest should be fixed as close to the market as possible.*

It is a generally accepted fact that the larger the premium paid on a bond the larger the base rate of interest which the city must pay. A bond selling, at say 105, must, according to authorities, carry a larger base rate of interest than a bond with the same security behind it selling at par. Sound policy suggests that the buyer should fix the rate.

6. *Provision should be made for proper advertisement, sale and delivery of bonds.*

In order to assure competition and the lowest rate of interest to the city, it is essential that wide publicity be given to each bond sale.

7. *A public improvement program financed by bond issues, should be prepared for a considerable number of years in advance.*

The value of budgeting current income and outgo has been discussed. In recent years, however, equal merit of budgeting public improvements has been brought to the fore.

Naturally, such improvement budgets must be longer than for one year, although they will need periodic revision. If a city insists upon picturing its requirements for public improvements for only a short period in advance, it must necessarily plunge into proposals that cannot be afforded with the result that its improvements are out of balance. Any city, with careful study, can determine the major projects that will be before it in the coming decade. Within reason the cost of these projects can be ascertained. Information is also to be had as to the possible increase in the assessed values of the community and the amount of bonds that may be issued and the current revenues that can be devoted to permanent improvements over that period. Under these circumstances, it is the better part of wisdom carefully to set up a list of these major projects with provision for their gradual financing.

8. *Wherever and to whatever extent possible a city should proceed on a pay-as-you-go basis.*

The purpose of bonds is to meet requirements for improvements that cannot be met from current revenues. However, there is no doubt that cities have overlooked the sensible use of this type of financing and have utilized the incurrence of debt as a means of securing improvements that could and should have been paid for by current revenue. Many public improvements in a city are of a recurring nature, such as schoolhouses, fire and police stations, street repairs, etc., which should be taxed for currently, leaving a future generation to meet new requirements as they come along and leaving the bond margin free to take care of emergencies and projects of unusual magnitude.

9. *In assessing the cost of local improvements the procedure should be based upon definitely established principles that will insure uniformity and equality in spreading the assessment.*

Should the city at large pay a certain percentage of the assessments on certain types of improvements,—as for example, municipalities often assume the cost of intersections in assessing street paving,—this ratio of amount paid by general taxation to the amount paid by special assessment should be maintained generally on all improvements of the same type. Further, prescribed rules should determine how special assessment districts are to be established, and all districts should be laid out in accordance with those principles. This would eliminate the size of districts fluctuating with the whims of the authorities responsible. Finally, in principle, the basis of assessment should be according to measurable benefit, rather than upon some ad valorem, square foot, or other arbitrary rule.

IV. COLLECTION, CUSTODY AND DISBURSEMENT OF FUNDS

Originally, the treasurer of any government was an important officer, since he was both a custodial and accounting officer. In modern governments it is customary to fill these positions separately. With the transfer of the control of public funds to the controller or auditor, the office of treasurer has become purely a custodial position and its importance has decreased accordingly. Today, the treasurer takes in and disburses the money as directed by the control authority, and his office becomes one largely of detailed routine in which defalcations can occur only by actually absconding with funds in his possession.

1. *The first test of sound treasury procedure involves appointment rather than election as a means of filling the office.*

Sound arguments cannot be advanced for the election of a city treasurer. He determines no major policies, and as a purely administrative officer he should be selected for a long term by appointment and solely on the merit of conducting the technical routine of collecting, holding and disbursing funds.

2. *The funds in the treasurer's possession should be consolidated so far as consistent with practical administration.*

In depositing public funds it is entirely proper that separate deposits be made of certain revenues that must be devoted to specific purposes,— particularly cash belonging to the sinking fund, proceeds of the sale of bonds, special assessment receipts, pension and other trust receipts, public utilities revenues, and general receipts. Many cities, however, go far beyond these elementary distinctions in depositing money and make segregations of actual cash in the bank when only a proper accounting control is required. In consequence, when cash is temporarily short in one fund, it is necessary to borrow money at interest although the city may have ample resources in

other funds, which is obviously a needless and expensive procedure.

3. *Cash deposited in banks should earn a maximum interest rate.*

Larger cities so arrange their checking accounts and their deposit of funds that a substantial return is secured from interest. Such, however, is not always the case, and the failure to make the most of this opportunity of supplementing city revenues is a sound criterion of the inefficient conduct of the treasurer's office. Periodically, depositaries should be selected upon the basis of the highest interest rates bid.

4. *The collection of minor revenues should be properly controlled.*

This is a very general test and one difficult of application by citizens examining the character of their government. No treasurer's office is so organized that all public receipts can be paid directly to it. To attempt such consolidation would be to cause undue annoyance to citizens making payments to the city and would serve no practical purpose. Individual departments must continue to collect their revenues for general services, as utilities, and for the numerous small services that may be grouped under the head of departmental charges. Such revenues, however, should be carefully audited by the controlling authorities and assurance had that the receipts are transmitted promptly to the city treasury.

5. *All taxes should be pre-billed, and mailed to the taxpayer.*

No privately owned public utility would be permitted to treat the public with such indifference as attends the assessment and collection of taxes. Often a citizen is compelled to spend hours in line to secure his tax bill and spend a similar length of time in getting to another window to make payment, whereas if payment is not made with exceeding promptness heavy penalties are imposed for a brief period, after which his property may be sold for cumulative charges. Progressive municipalities are remedying this situation by pre-billing all taxes and mailing the bills to the citizens in ample time to make the payment. Payment by check is ordinarily permitted. This procedure is not only a convenience and safeguard to the taxpayer, but speeds up collections and reduces the amount of delinquent taxes.

6. *All taxes and other charges should be collected currently.*

One of the acid tests of efficiency in collection is whether taxes are collected within a reasonable time after they are due. This test may be applied also to such charges as special assessments, permits, and other departmental charges. One reason for the strained financial condition of some cities is the failure to enforce prompt collection, particularly with respect to personal property taxes, and it is obvious that unless such collections are promptly and impartially made, political capital may be the reward for the treasurer at the expense of the long-suffering and honest but uninformed public. The greatest of ignorance usually prevails as to the actual collection of taxes levied.

7. *The sale of property for delinquent taxes should be made a judicial procedure, in which any surplus received over and above taxes and penalty reverts to the property owner.*

The procedure governing the sale of property for delinquent taxes works hardship and injustice to the property owner in many jurisdictions. It is now a generally accepted principle that the delinquent taxpayer should never have to deal with other than the city government during the period available for redeeming his property. When this period has elapsed—which should be much longer than generally prevails,—

the property should be sold only in accordance with a judicial practice similar to that involved in the foreclosure of a mortgage, and the property owner should receive any surplus that remains after the delinquent taxes and imposed penalties have been deducted.

V. Controlling Financial Transactions

In present day government the controller is an important officer. His duties are twofold. First, is that of record keeping which involves the recording of all transactions affecting the municipality. The second is auditing, which involves the use of discretion in insuring a complete record of transactions and the honest and wise expenditure of this money. The first is purely administrative and requires no determination of policy, and as such the position may properly be filled by appointment. The second involves the determination of policy and a control over the acts of other elected and appointed officers. As such, it is entirely proper that the position should be filled by election, or by appointment independently of the officers to be controlled. For that reason, it is impractical to set up any standard of selection as a criterion of organization, such as was done with the office of city treasurer. The discussion of criteria will, therefore, be limited entirely to procedure.

1. *Accounts should be centralized in the controller's office.*

It is a first requisite of efficient accounting that it be maintained under a single jurisdiction. This means that all revenues, both major and minor, should be controlled by the controller's office. It also means that appropriation ledgers will be maintained in the controller's office rather than in the several city departments, so that a complete statement of the financial condition of the city may be taken from the controller's books without recourse to subsidiary records maintained in other places.

2. Municipal accounting should be maintained on an accrual basis.

Many municipalities concern themselves only with cash receipts and cash disbursements, and have little or no control of revenues that will become due in a fiscal period or of obligations incurred which are not yet paid. The greatest forward step that has been made in municipal accounting has been the establishment of such control over revenues accrued but not yet collected and liabilities incurred but not yet paid that a complete statement of the city's financial condition with respect to these items, as well as with respect to cash, can be presented.

Such control contemplates a complete, accurate and current record of the several general classes of financial transactions,—current, capital, special, trust, etc. This includes adequate records of general departments including quasi-independent boards, etc., utilities, bonded debt and debt margin, tax limits, special assessments, pension funds, etc. A corollary of such records is a report to the public setting forth this information in concise and understandable form.

3. Controlled inventories of the city's supplies, materials, equipment and real estate should be maintained.

Most cities take an occasional inventory, sometimes annually, of all physical property owned. Such inventories are often included in the financial statement. However, these inventories can be currently maintained and controlled on the books of record so that the unwarranted loss of any property will be detected. Only with such records can a complete balance sheet of the city's assets and liabilities be prepared.

4. Unit and job costs of city services should be available.

No American city at the present time reports to the public the unit cost of the numerous activities undertaken on behalf of the city. Until such records are available, it will be impossible to check accurately the character of government being rendered. It will be a stimulus to sound administration when the public can compare the amount and cost of work done in a community for any year with the year previous and with similar activities undertaken by other cities.

5. Payrolls should be under complete control.

Such control involves the checking of all payrolls by the civil service authorities to assure that persons being paid by the city are properly employed, and the periodic checking of labor payroll clerks who can assure that the persons employed are actually on the job.

6. All accounts of the city should be audited continuously or periodically by auditing authority independent of the controller's office.

Sometimes such audits are made by state authorities, but more often through the employment of qualified private accountants.

7. Periodic reports to be made to the public to include a complete operating statement and balance sheet.

Only complete records can produce adequate reports, and the existence of a properly prepared operating statement and balance sheet is in itself a criterion of a sound accounting procedure, assuming that the items appearing on each are taken from books of record and not from memoranda documents.

8. An operation audit is fully as important as a cash audit.

A cash audit verifies expenditures as to their legal regularity and correctness of invoices as to additions, extensions, etc. An operation audit reviews expenditures as to the value to the community of the services performed.

VI. CENTRALIZED PURCHASING

In many governmental jurisdictions each department is permitted to purchase supplies, material and equipment on its own initiative. While such procedure is highly satisfactory to such departments, since it allows wide discretion in the type of goods purchased and almost invariably results in expeditious purchasing, numerous abuses abound. Goods are purchased which are of a better quality than the proposed use justifies; goods are purchased from friends instead of in the open market; the prices paid more nearly approximate retail than wholesale prices; the benefits of quantity buying are lost; goods are purchased by trade name rather than under specifications that predetermine the quality; inspection is often poor, etc.

For these reasons and many others, many municipalities are taking a leaf out of the experience of private business and have centralized purchasing. The procedure of centralized purchasing is quite detailed, but some of the more outstanding features that may be used as criteria are as follows:

1. *All purchasing, except possibly highly technical and certain kinds of raw materials for municipal industries, should be centralized in a single authority, appointed upon merit and preferably under civil service.*

This would assure the benefits of central purchasing for all departments of the city government.

2. *Purchases should be made in accordance with standard specifications, both as to use and quality.*

Honest purchasing cannot be made unless every vendor knows exactly the quality of goods on which he is submitting bids. On the other hand, the city cannot be sure that it is obtaining its full value for the price paid unless it understands specifically the qualities of the goods it is buying. Specification for use is less well understood. It simply means that the goods shall be most suitable for the purposes for which they are required.

The specifications themselves should, of course, be open so as to permit competition from all manufacturers.

3. *All purchases should be in as large quantities as consistent with economical use.*

Only in this manner can the advantages of wholesale prices and the interest of a large number of vendors be secured. These advantages can best be secured when the purchasing agent calculates well in advance the total quantities of important articles to be bought by the city and enters into a purchase agreement for such goods, and by collecting the orders of the departments for minor goods and buying them not oftener than once a week for each type of supply involved.

4. *The inspection of goods purchased must be thorough.*

This usually involves the maintenance of a corps of inspectors by the purchasing department to cover large items and the deputization of certain individuals in the departments to check minor items delivered directly from the vendors. Incidentally, facilities should be provided for the scientific testing of goods to insure their compliance with specifications.

5. *The usual legal provision permitting purchases in small amounts without competition should not be abused.*

6. *The amounts of all orders should be immediately entered upon the appropriation ledgers of the finance department as an encumbrance against the proper appropriation, and should be paid promptly when the invoice is finally presented.*

The former assures sound financial control by the city; the latter assures a maximum of economy through the city taking all available discounts, as well as more favorable bids by vendors who are assured of prompt payment.

7. *A central house storeroom should be provided for the distribution and storage of minor articles in current use by departments, and all storage yards of every type should be under the purchasing authority in order that the quantity distribution of supplies may be made in an economical manner.*

The need for a storeroom for articles in current use is obvious. Many small articles are requisitioned in small quantities by departments and it is advantageous to have them on hand for immediate distribution. Also in this way larger quantities can be purchased at reduced prices. The question of the control of storage yards is still a subject of discussion. At the present time in most cities each important department maintains a storage yard in which the usual construction materials will be found. The centralization of these yards under one authority would permit a reduction in inventory and also provide for shorter hauls on materials.

NATIONAL
MUNICIPAL REVIEW

PUBLISHED MONTHLY BY THE

National Municipal League

| VOL. XVII, No. 3 | MARCH, 1928 | TOTAL No. 141 |

CONTENTS

EDITORIAL COMMENT ....*H. W. Dodds*.... 133

INFLUENCING PUBLIC OPINION ....*H. A. Overstreet*.. 135

THE POLICEWOMAN'S SPHERE......................*Louis Brownlow*.. 136

CONVENING THE SPECIAL SESSION — OKLAHOMA'S
    PREDICAMENT............................*Arnold J. Lien*... 139

NEW YORK'S FIRST SATELLITE TOWN
    An Interview with Mr. Alexander M. Bing 142

THE SAN FRANCISCO MUNICIPAL RAILWAY...........*William H. Nanry* 147

APPRAISING PUBLIC REPORTS — SOME ESSENTIALS OF A
    GOOD MUNICIPAL REPORT.....................*Clarence E. Ridley* 150

THE PROGRESS OF PERMANENT REGISTRATION FOR
    ELECTIONS................................*Joseph P. Harris*. 153

CINCINNATI SURVEYS ITS POLICE...................*Donald C. Stone*.. 157

AIRPORTS AS A FACTOR IN CITY PLANNING — A SUP-
    PLEMENT..................................*E. P. Goodrich*... 181

DEPARTMENTS

I. Recent Books Reviewed.. 163

II. Judicial Decisions..*Edited by C. W. Tooke* 167

III. Public Utilities...*Edited by John Bauer* 171

IV. Governmental Research Association Notes.................*Edited by Russell Forbes* 175

V. Notes and Events......................................*Edited by H. W. Dodds* 179

City Manager Plan

CHARTER AND INFORMATION SERVICE

This is a service to local charter committees or organizations interested in the adoption of the city manager plan of municipal government.

1. CHARTER DRAFTSMAN: An expert charter draftsman and consultant will be recommended by the National Municipal League when local committees are making studies preparatory to charter drafting.

2. CONSULTING SERVICE BY MAIL: Whole proposed charter drafts or disputed sections may be sent to the National Municipal League for opinions by experts on different questions of structure, principle, draftsmanship, constitutionality, etc. A fee is necessary in some cases.

3. A MODEL CITY CHARTER with home-rule provisions recommended for state constitutions prepared by the committee on municipal program of the National Municipal League. This is a new edition, 1927, completely revised and reprinted, capitalizing more than fifteen years experience with city manager government. Price $.50. One copy sent on request and without charge to regularly established charter commissions.

4. SPEAKERS: a. The services of W. J. Millard, field agent of the National Municipal League, are available for public addresses on the city manager plan. In cities which take up the Proportional Representation election feature of the Model Charter, Mr. Millard is especially valuable by reason of his experience in expounding this somewhat technical subject to popular audiences for the American Proportional Representation League. Available at a nominal fee.

b. Other Speakers. The office of the National Municipal League maintains a list of persons in various parts of the country known to be prepared and willing to make addresses on the City Manager plan.

5. PAMPHLET BUDGET: A collection of all obtainable pamphlet material from various sources including the texts of several charters, City Managers' Yearbook, Model Charter, etc., etc.

Price $2.00. Sent on a loan basis to members of the National Municipal League.

6. CAMPAIGN STORIES: A collection of typewritten stories of local campaigns written by the directors of city manager campaigns in some twelve important cities, includes method of organizing the community and description of propaganda used in each instance.

This is available on a loan basis only.

7. THE STORY OF THE CITY MANAGER PLAN: This is a popular pocket-size pamphlet, 32 pages, comprising a complete, compact story of the movement, definition of the plan, its merits, how it started in 1913, the experience of numerous cities with it, a list of city manager cities and dates, selected references for further study, etc.

Single copies, 10 cents; 100 copies for $5.00

Send All Inquiries and Requests
For Services Listed
to
NATIONAL MUNICIPAL LEAGUE
261 Broadway, New York

NATIONAL
MUNICIPAL REVIEW

Vol. XVII, No. 3   MARCH, 1928   Total No. 141

EDITORIAL COMMENT

A charter commission has been created in Pasadena, California, for the purpose of revising the present manager charter.

＊

Sixteen boroughs in Pennsylvania, half of which are located in Allegheny County which is now considering city-county consolidation with Pittsburgh, are operating under the borough manager form of government. Under the state law, boroughs are authorized to establish the manager plan by ordinance.

＊

The newly formed Chicago Institute of Local Politics, created under the auspices of a number of civic organizations, Northwestern University, Loyola University and the University of Chicago, has issued a report calling for greater home rule for Chicago. The report points out three possible methods by which home rule may be secured but unqualifiedly prefers the plan of amending the state constitution by which adequate powers of local self-government may be guaranteed the city. The report was drawn by Jerome G. Kerwin, J. L. Jacobs, E. O. Griffenhagen, Leonard D. White, A. R. Hatton, George C. Sikes, Francis X. Busch and Harold L. Ickes.

＊

As a consequence of centralized purchasing introduced by its new charter, the city of Rochester, New York, has been able to conclude a contract for gasoline at slightly less than nine cents per gallon. The price is the lowest which the city has received in years. Inasmuch as it uses nearly 100,000 gallons annually the saving will be marked.

＊

The Detroit Bureau of Governmental Research, which among other activities keeps its eye on Wayne County in which Detroit is located, reports that the budget for the current year will amount to almost $20,000,000, an increase of $4,335,000, approximately 30 per cent over the preceding year.

As a supplement to the report on the cost of the county government the Bureau has published an organization chart of Wayne County.

＊

The London *Municipal Journal* has begun the publication of a little periodical called "Local Government Abroad," which will be of interest to all followers of municipal affairs in the United States. The first issue contains the clearest account of the Fascist changes in local government in Italy which has yet appeared in English. Home rule in local affairs has practically disappeared. Members of the municipal council are now appointed by the prefect and act in an advisory capacity exclusively.

The Citizens' League of Cleveland has filed a protest with the city council, asserting that the so-called Davis petition calling for a second election in April on the proposition to abolish city manager-P. R. government contains thousands of fraudulent names. It supports its charge by the testimony of a handwriting expert who reports that whole petition papers were signed in the same handwriting although crude efforts to disguise the fact were made. In many instances, he declares, one person has signed the names and addresses of several members of the same family. City Clerk Thomas is reported to have stated that 10,000 signatures out of a total of 45,000 are questionable.

A full discussion of the Cleveland charter situation will be found in the Notes and Events Department of this issue.

✤

New York's Five Cent Fare in Jeopardy   As pointed out in this issue by Dr. Bauer and Mr. Nanry, the five-cent fare in New York and San Francisco, about the only cities in which the nickel rate has more than antiquarian interest, is under heavy attack. In the latter the historic rate is resulting in a loss to the municipally operated system. In the former the Interborough Rapid Transit Company, operating a major portion of the city's subways, suddenly filed in February with the transit commission a new seven-cent tariff and petition for permission to put the new rate into effect on five days' notice; and prepared to make the necessary changes in the turnstile slot machines over night.

At this writing the transit commission has denied the petition and the Interborough has begun proceedings in a federal court to declare the five-cent fare confiscatory. This move was promptly countered by the city and the transit commission with an injunction from a state court restraining the Interborough from charging the higher fare. What the outcome will be is still uncertain. As heretofore, the fly in the ointment seems to be the elevated properties leased from the Manhattan Railroad Company and for which the Interborough pays a ruinous rental. The loss, therefore, from the elevated is heavy although, as far as the company is concerned, the operation of the subways is profitable.

Moreover, the Interborough is under contract with the city, which built and owns the subways, to charge no more than a five-cent fare. Whether the courts will break this contract in the interest of a seven-cent fare remains to be seen. The city will insist upon its fulfillment and will assert that the fact that the Interborough also operates the elevated has no bearing upon its contractual relation with respect to the subways.

✤

Meyer Lissner, for many years an officer of the National Municipal League and formerly a member of the United States Shipping Board, has been made a member of the California State Industrial Accident Commission. Our readers, many of whom know Mr. Lissner personally as a man of rare capacity for public service, will be glad to learn of his return to governmental work.

INFLUENCING PUBLIC OPINION

BY H. A. OVERSTREET

College of the City of New York

The gist of Professor Overstreet's stimulating talk before the Round Table on Public Opinion at the Thirty-third Annual Meeting of the National Municipal League. :: :: :: :: :: ::

Most of us who are in public service work become fairly doleful about the possibility of changing public opinion. However, notable changes have occurred in the past, and there is no reason why they should not occur in the future. There was, for example, the change from king-worshipping to democracy, a change from a belief in the inferiority of women to a conviction that women should be the political equals of men. At the present time, public opinion seems to be slowly undergoing a change from the traditional belief in the absoluteness of national sovereignty to a belief in the need for national interdependence. In the region of commerce, to take an apparently trifling instance, public opinion has undergone a change in very recent years from a complete acceptance of a variable-price system of retail buying and selling to a one-price system.

I refer particularly to the last change because it gives a clue to the important question how public opinion can be changed. Mr. Wanamaker changed public opinion, and did so with a fair degree of rapidity. How did he do it? In two ways: by setting the stage, and by appealing to certain fundamental impulses in his public.

He did not scold them. He did not preach to them. He did not send them learned pamphlets, explaining that the one-price system was the only system compatible with human intelligence and honesty. In short, he did not waste his time appealing to their "reasoning power." He let the reasoning power take care of itself—which it proceeded to do.

What he did was, first, to arouse expectation. He was a good dramatist. He announced a great opening, and invited the public. And when the public came, the good dramatist turned into the excellent host. He welcomed his public courteously, let them wander through his building without being urged to buy. He did more. He turned into their friend. He announced to them quite frankly that certain goods were not perfect and that they could be had at cheaper prices in the basement.

He gained the day for the one-price system. Why? Because he appealed to certain basic wishes in his public. His public found it a pleasure to be unmolested, a pleasure not to be hoodwinked into buying damaged goods as if they were perfect, a pleasure to be free of the necessity of quarreling over prices.

MEET BASIC WISHES

I think that tells the essence of the story about the technique to be used for changing public opinion. *One must find the basic wishes of the public and apply oneself to the satisfaction of those wishes.* The so-called "reformer" usually does otherwise. He addresses himself to the intellect of his public, tries to reason with them, sometimes scolds them, and always "admonishes" them. All of which subtly infuriates, because the public, admonished and lectured to, is made to feel inferior.

Human beings are essentially systems of wants. They are not, first and foremost, rational beings. Some of these wants are trivial. Some are foolish and self-destructive. But some are basic and constructive. The person interested in the advance of public welfare will seek to find out what the fine basic wishes of his public are and will address himself to them.

Thus the chief need of the person engaged in the attempt to influence any public—and there are, of course, many kinds of public—is to become psychological-minded. He must see his public not as mere voters nor as mere householders nor even as mere dumbbells, but as human beings with warm desires and with equally warm fears and hatreds. If he can visualize these basic emotions and address himself to them, he will have far the greatest chance both of capturing their attention and of winning their effective assent.

I do not mean that there should never be an appeal to the reasoning power of the public. But back of that appeal and deeper than it, there must always be the appeal to what people basically want. Sometimes they are not themselves aware of what they basically want. The astute psychological analyst of his public will know how to raise a dormant want into consciousness. At any rate, dormant or otherwise, it is the basic want which he will learn to discover and to satisfy.

The intellectualistic approach to the public is always the easiest because it requires no careful study of the psychological make-up of the public. It simply requires some favorite ideas (favorite to the promulgator) and paper on which to print them. The intellectualistic way is the easiest way—but also the most futile. The one who succeeds is the one who puts himself at the emotional point of view of his public.

THE POLICEWOMAN'S SPHERE

BY LOUIS BROWNLOW

Washington, D. C.

In preventive work women police are more successful than men.

THE significance of the recent study[1] of the functions and work of the woman's police bureau made by the Bureau of Public Personnel Administration transcends its subject matter. It tells

[1] *Policewomen.* Functions and Work of the Woman's Bureau of a Police Department and Tests for the Selection of Policewomen. Public Personnel Studies; Vol. 5, No. 12, Serial No. 50, Washington: Bureau of Public Personnel Administration, December, 1927. Pp. 29 (245–274, inc.).

all there is to be told about policewomen and thereby throws a flood of light on some of the things that ought to be done about policemen. It ought to be read and pondered with care (I had almost written "with prayer") by every person who is interested in the improvement of police work in American cities. Explicitly, it presents, first, a comprehensive compendium of the theory and practice of the functions and organization of a police unit doing protective and preventive work with women and children; second, a proposed classification and plan of compensation for the woman's bureau of the metropolitan police department of the District of Columbia; and, third, partially standardized tests for policewomen.

The study summarizes a discussion of police functions with these conclusions: "(1) There is a considerable field in which women can do better police work than men. (2) There is another—and larger—field in which men can do better police work than women. (3) There is a third field in which police work can be done with perhaps equal success by either men or women police officers whose education, special training and social background are approximately the same; whether men or women, or both, should be employed to do this work depends upon a number of local and often extraneous circumstances."

This third field includes most of the preventive phases of police work. It has been explored, but not exploited. The spies have come back and have said it is a land flowing with milk and honey, but the host has not been organized to go over and possess it.

WOMEN POLICE SUCCEED IN PREVENTIVE WORK

We talk more and more about preventive police work, but it is to be doubted if we do so very much more about it than we used to do, so far as the usual run of police departments are concerned. The significant feature of this study is that it shows that through women police officers the police departments are successfully exercising functions in this third field, as well as in the field primarily admitted to be the special preserve of the women officers. That men, given the same training, education and social background, could

do as much, and by sheer addition of numbers, more, is manifest. By "background" in that summation, the study does not appear to mean any particular pattern of history, environment and tradition, but simply the possession of social intelligence, plus the social point of view.

The term "social intelligence" is defined as "the ability to adjust to new situations involving other persons and to adopt an effective course of action." Since nearly all the work of a policewoman involves relations with other persons, to be effective in preventive and constructive measures she must understand the motives and probable conduct of various types of persons and must only as a last resort, when all other means fail, use her police powers.

TESTS FOR SOCIAL INTELLIGENCE

The staff of the Bureau of Public Personnel Administration says that it has found the construction of tests which will measure social intelligence a baffling problem, thus repeating what it has said in previous studies, but being able now to report definite progress toward satisfactorily reliable tests.

In this connection the study says: ". . . much of the experimental evidence indicates that a high, low, or medium degree of social intelligence is an innate trait and the amount possessed, as is the case with abstract or mechanical intelligence, is not markedly affected by education or the accumulated experience of individuals."

Reverting to the definition of "social intelligence" quoted above, it follows that the ability to adjust to situations involving other persons and adopting an effective course of action in the case, means that the effectiveness is measured by the accomplishment of the ends the person making the adjustment has in mind. These ends, from the point of view of society, may be desirable or undesirable, legal or illegal, moral or immoral.

The point is that persons possessing a considerable measure of innate social intelligence have the power of achieving their ends.

Here we have the answer to the riddle of The Boss, the Gang Leader, the Lawyer Criminal, the Jury Fixer. He is a socially intelligent person who by reason of that innate endowment is able to predict with reasonable certainty the behavior of other persons under given circumstances, and thus is able to make adjustments by which he has his own way with men and events.

If the police are to do protective and preventive work they must realize that they will not be permitted to do it in a social vacuum. They will have an enemy to meet. It will be a fight. It will be a social struggle in which the adjustment of personal relations of individuals in the community will be the test and measure of success. The enemy is captained, at least, by leaders having social intelligence. The police will not get anywhere unless they select as their representatives in that fight, both rank and file, men and women who have social intelligence.

SOCIAL POINT OF VIEW ALSO NECESSARY

But that is not enough. Social intelligence, as we have seen, may be used either for or against society. So it is necessary also that the socially intelligent policeman who may be expected to do successful protective and preventive work will also have the social point of view—he will be a partisan of society as against its enemies.

Here do come in education, training, historical and environmental backgrounds, and the traditions. Here, I hope it will be admitted, example and contact will have some influence.

Policewomen, the tests applied seem to show, come from a higher intellectual stratum than the average run of policemen. They have better educational equipment, and more often better technical training. They are of high social intelligence and most of them have the social point of view.

This brings up in my mind the question: May not continued experiment in the field of policewomen's work, where there are fewer traditions to tie the hands of police administrators than in policemen's work, tend to promote the adoption of the social point of view by those men police officers who possess native social intelligence?

I have thought so, for years: This study gives me some scientific basis for my wishful thinking. It is a vitally important contribution to the important problem of standardizing and evaluating the important work of women in police departments. But, to me, at any rate, its significance transcends its subject matter. Explicitly it does what its authors set out to do about policewomen, and does it well. Implicitly, whether they intended it or not, they have thrown a flood of light on the whole problem of preventive police work.

CONVENING THE SPECIAL SESSION—
OKLAHOMA'S PREDICAMENT

BY ARNOLD J. LIEN

Washington University, St. Louis

It is an anomaly that most of our legislatures with power to impeach and try the governor should not have the power to convene for this purpose whenever they see fit. :: :: :: :: :: ::

THE recent embarrassing tangle of controversial instability in Oklahoma has brought freshly to the fore the whole question of legislative sessions. Immediately, the question is one of the special session. But the form of the provisions now in force relating to the special session is determined largely by the popular and constitutional attitude towards sessions in general. The strict limitations on legislative sessions are among the numerous evidences of a lack of confidence in the legislature that verges on actual distrust.

Less than a dozen constitutions—the Constitution of the United States is one of them—provide for a general session of the legislature annually. In Alabama, the general session is convened quadrennially. A sizable majority of the states have a general session of the legislature once in two years. All of the forty-nine legislatures have the power of impeachment and all of them, except Nebraska, have the power of trial as well. In Nebraska, the power of impeachment is vested in a joint session of the legislature where action may be taken by a majority vote. The trial takes place in the supreme court. If a judge of the supreme court has been impeached, the trial is conducted by the judges of the district courts sitting *en banc.* This Nebraska arrangement seems worthy of imitation.

HOW SPECIAL SESSIONS ARE CALLED

In all of the constitutions provision is made for special sessions of the legislature. In all of the states as well as in the United States, the chief executive has authority to convene the legislature in special session. In New Hampshire and Massachusetts, the governor acts with the advice of the council. According to more than thirty of the constitutions, the power to call a special session can be exercised only on "extraordinary occasions." Seven state constitutions use a wording which seems a little less restrictive, but which in practice probably means exactly the same thing. New Hampshire, New Mexico, New York, and Wisconsin confer the authority on the governor (with the council in New Hampshire) without any restrictions.

In about one-half of the states, the legislative work of the special session is limited to the purposes stated by the governor in his proclamation or added by him after the legislature has convened. In eighteen, including the United States, there are no limitations on the subjects that may be considered. In the others, the governor must state the purposes in his proclamation, but it is not clear from the wording whether or not the legislature is limited to the subjects enumerated. In Arkansas, after the work has been completed for which the session was called, the legis-

lature may by a two-thirds majority
decide to continue in session for other
work, but it may not extend the sitting
by more than fifteen days. In Mississippi, impeachment proceedings
and the examination of the state
accounts are in order whether mentioned in the call or not.

In Oklahoma the legislature can be
convened in special session by the
governor. No work can be undertaken
in the special session other than that
which relates to the purposes mentioned in the proclamation or to
purposes indicated by the governor in
later messages. During the prolonged and spirited controversy with
Governor Walton, an amendment to
Article VIII of the constitution was
voted upon in the election of October
2, 1923. This amendment, considered
at the time as adopted, gave authority to any member of the house of
representatives on the petition of a
majority of the members of the house
to issue a call for a special session of
the legislature for the purpose of considering the impeachment and trial of
state officers. The validity of the
amendment was questioned. In connection with the recently attempted
impeachment of Governor Johnston,
this amendment was held unconstitutional by the supreme court of the
state. Consequently, during the last
few years in Oklahoma it has not been
easy to distinguish what is from what
is not. And this is what the loudest
part of the fussy fracas has been about.

THE OKLAHOMA MUDDLE

The muddle in Oklahoma emphasizes the need for a change in the constitutional procedure by which the
legislature can be convened in special
session. So long as the legislature has
the power of impeachment and trial
(or even of impeachment alone as in
Nebraska), it seems to be clearly wise

and sound that the legislature should
have full and independent authority
to convene at any time it sees fit to
exercise these functions. Where the
regular sessions are annual, while in
practice the change would not be very
significant, the principle is as fundamental as in the other states.

In the field of legislation also it
appears reasonably clear that no substantial achievements have come as a
result of the wholly formal and essentially superficial tactics of restricting the freedom of the legislature of
coming into session whenever it sees
fit and of continuing its sittings as it
deems necessary. Whenever the members of congress or of a legislature have
reached a stage in their investigation
and study of a problem at which discussion and collective action are desirable they ought to have the means of
convening a session no matter what the
president or the governor may think
the partisan political effects might be.

On this matter, it is of interest to
note the provision agreed upon by the
National Municipal League in its
Model Constitution. Section 18 of
that constitution stipulates that "Special sessions may be called by the governor or by a majority vote of the
members of the legislative council."
Since the legislative council is to consist of the governor and seven members
elected by the legislature from its own
membership on a basis of proportional
representation, the deduction may
validly be made that a special session
can in effect be convoked by the governor or by a majority of five-sevenths of
the legislature.

Since neither the United States nor
the states have either the unicameral
legislature preferred by the National
Municipal League or the legislative
council proposed by that organization,
a more practical model for a constitutional amendment on the subject of

special sessions must be sought. A search through all the state constitutions and the constitution of the United States for suggestions for such a model has not been fruitless. In three states the legislature has been given some authority in the matter of special sessions. In the constitutions of Virginia and West Virginia are suggestive limitations on the exclusiveness of the governor's power to call special sessions. In West Virginia, it becomes the duty of the governor to call an extra session whenever three-fifths of the members of each chamber of the legislature so request. In Virginia, the application must be made by two-thirds of the members of the legislature if the issuing of a proclamation for a special session is to be obligatory on the governor.

In both of the Virginias, however, the actual call depends upon action by the governor. If the special session was to be convened for the purpose of bringing the governor to trial on impeachment charges, the governor would hardly conform without first exhausting the possibilities of litigation and delay. In this infelicity there is probably nothing peculiar about the governors of Oklahoma.

In the constitution of Louisiana (V-14) is a provision that meets the situation a little more adequately. "He (the governor) shall take care that the laws be faithfully executed, and may, on extraordinary occasions, convene the legislature at the seat of government, or, if that should have become dangerous from an enemy, or epidemic, at a different place. It shall become his duty to convene the legislature in extraordinary session whenever petitioned to do so by two-thirds of the members elected to each house. The petition shall be filed with the secretary of state, who shall immediately deliver a certified copy of it to the governor, and shall mail or deliver a certified copy to the lieutenant governor and to the speaker of the house of representatives, and shall file return of such service with the original petition. If the governor shall fail to issue within five days after a certified copy of the petition is delivered to him, his proclamation convening the legislature in accordance with the petition, then either the lieutenant governor or speaker of the house, or both of them, shall give notice in the official journal, not less than ten days before the day fixed in the petition for the session, that by virtue of the petition signed by two-thirds of the members elected to each house, the legislature shall convene in extraordinary session, at noon, on the day, for the purposes, and for the period of time stated in the petition." In another paragraph it is stipulated that the session may consider only those subjects which relate to the purposes enumerated in the proclamation or the petition and that it "shall be limited to the time named therein, which shall never exceed thirty days." The desirability of these added limitations may well be questioned.

The adoption of such an amendment is much more than an obvious precaution in a routine matter. It involves principles which are fundamental.

NEW YORK'S FIRST SATELLITE TOWN

AN INTERVIEW WITH MR. ALEXANDER M. BING

President, City Housing Corporation

Seventeen and a half miles from New York the City Housing Corporation, a limited dividend company, is beginning work upon America's first garden city. Several hundred houses will be ready in 1929. This is the company responsible for the Sunnyside garden community in Long Island City now nearing completion. On what is now farm land Mr. Bing visions a complete town planned to meet the needs of the motor age. :: :: :: :: :: :: :: :: ::

PURCHASE of 1,005 acres of land in nearby New Jersey on which will be built the first town planned from the beginning for the age of the automobile has been announced by the City Housing Corporation, a limited dividend company.

The new community, which is to be named Radburn, will be situated between Paterson and Hackensack about 17½ miles from New York City along the line of the Erie Railroad at Fair Lawn. On what is now farm and pasture land, it is planned to build a complete town for a population of about 25,000 providing for industry, business, homes and recreation. The land purchase involved an expenditure of more than $2,000,000, and the completed town will ultimately represent a value of between $50,000,000 and $60,000,000, it is estimated.

Radburn will be unique and significant for two important reasons, it is thought, on the basis of the plans now being developed. For the first time, the building of a city or town will be related definitely to the age of the automobile and the way of living which has resulted from its advent. Also it will be an initial step toward a more economic and efficient growth of the New York region by providing adequately for industry and affording workers comfortable, modern homes with gardens and parks without further burdening existing transit and transportation facilities. In other words, it will not be merely another dormitory suburb sending all of its inhabitants into New York every morning and out again every evening. Although there will be some commuters, it is expected that most of the dwellers in Radburn will be employed in the town itself or in neighboring factories and business establishments.

PLANNING FOR SAFETY

Of even greater significance, however, is thought to be the novel street and parkways plan by which it is proposed to fit the town to the needs of the motor age by making it a safe place for children, pedestrians and for automobilists as well. Through motor routes will be provided for fast traffic but not at the expense of the safety and comfort of the families occupying homes in the residential sections. The homes will front on side streets which will not, however, afford through communication. They will be used only for access to houses facing on them.

The most notable innovation in the plan will be a complete system of parkways and garden paths for pedestrians which in a sense will be comple-

142

TENTATIVE GROUND PLAN OF TYPICAL UNIT FOR 600 FAMILIES

mentary to the street system. Children will be able to go a half mile to school along these paths and parkways without crossing a street; they will have playgrounds in the park areas which can be reached by tree-lined paths leading directly from their homes; and neighborhood shopping centers will be equally accessible with the same safety.

Up to this time, cities and towns have been built around a street system planned for horse traffic. Houses were built to front on the street which was a pleasant and comparatively safe place. With the coming of the automobile and the motor truck, however, streets have taken on a different character. They have been preëmpted by the automobile. Much of our present difficulty is due to the conflicting use to which streets must now be put since they are required to accommodate fast through traffic, local traffic, pedestrian use, and in most cases are the only places where children can play.

PLAN STREETS FOR SPECIAL USE

In Radburn it is planned to build highways, streets, paths and parkways each for its special use. The highways will provide for through traffic and give access to the short side streets where most of the houses will be located. On the other side, the houses will face on individual gardens from which will run a path leading directly to a parkway. Homes for six hundred families will be grouped around each of these parkways which will be about a half mile long and the width of a city block and in which will be located a school, playgrounds, tennis courts and community rooms. In this way the cultural and social life of these six hundred families will center about the central park space. The town will be made up of a number of these units with connecting parkways.

Work will begin immediately on the new project. Although no definite schedule has yet been decided on it is likely that several hundred houses will be ready for occupants early in 1929.

The building of Radburn will be the second large housing enterprise which the City Housing Corporation has undertaken. It is now completing the Sunnyside Garden model community for moderate income families in Long Island City which when finished will provide for about 1,500 families and have a value of $10,000,000.

SECOND MODEL HOUSING EFFORT

The work at Sunnyside was begun in 1924 when the pressure of the housing shortage for families of moderate income prompted a group of prominent men and women to organize the City Housing Corporation as a limited dividend company and undertake the building of a model community for families of limited income. Among the directors are Dr. Felix Adler, John G. Agar, William Sloane Coffin, Mrs. Franklin D. Roosevelt, Mrs. Joseph M. Proskauer, Prof. Richard T. Ely, Arthur Lehman and V. Everit Macy. Included among the stockholders are Felix Warburg, Anne Morgan, John D. Rockefeller, Jr., Mrs. George Gordon Battle and Ogden L. Mills.

The company sought by large scale operation, scientific planning and careful experiment to improve house and community planning. Clarence S. Stein, former chairman of the New York State Commission of Housing and Regional Planning, was chief architect for Sunnyside, and associated with him were Frederick L. Ackerman and Henry Wright, chairman of the American Institute of Architects' committee on town planning. Mr. Stein and Mr. Wright have prepared the preliminary studies for Radburn in association with Robert D. Kohn and Mr. Ackerman as consultants.

PROSPECTIVE DRAWING OF A SECTION OF A 600 FAMILY UNIT

Many important aspects of the plans being prepared for Radburn can be traced to what was learned in the building of Sunnyside. One of the primary purposes with which the City Housing Corporation started its work four years ago was to provide much more open space and gardens in housing for families of moderate income, and to give their children adequate, safe places to play.

EXPERIMENTED AT SUNNYSIDE

Sunnyside, however, is within the limits of New York City, and the company had to follow the rectangular or gridiron street plan which is required by the city authorities. After some experimenting a plan was devised which provided large interior garden courts, shared in common by the residents of each block, and these block interiors, offering a pleasant relief from the bustle and noise of city streets and providing safe places for small children to play, now constitute one of the outstanding features of the Sunnyside community.

Another experiment worked out at Sunnyside was the development of the Pomander Walk type of grouping houses in which the buildings are arranged in U-shape around a garden court the open end of which is on the street.

Out of these two experiments has developed the plan for Radburn. The interior garden courts, on a much larger scale and linked together, constitute the parkway system which will make it possible for children to go to and from school and playgrounds without crossing traffic streets. The side streets giving access to houses and garages are the Pomander Walk groups of Sunnyside greatly increased in size and adapted to the new requirements.

The fact that in New Jersey the company will be able to devise its own street system has given the necessary freedom in planning and will make it possible to effect important economies. Since the whole community will be planned from the outset, streets can be built for permanent use. Side streets in the residential sections need be no wider than is necessary to serve the given number of houses to be built on them, and in the same way main thoroughfares can be made adequately wide from the outset to avoid all congestion.

The experience gained at Sunnyside will be valuable in other ways. City Housing Corporation has demonstrated that the economies of large scale production can be applied to the building and sale of moderate price homes just as in other fields, and at Radburn it will be our purpose to operate on even a larger scale than at Sunnyside. The savings effected in this and other ways will make it possible to build a substantially better house than the market affords for moderate income families and still keep the price well within their reach. At Sunnyside the average small, brick one-family house sold for about $8,500. In New Jersey it is the hope to produce good houses for a substantially lower figure.

The importance of Radburn in its relation to the development of the plan for the New York region will be demonstrated more fully in the years to come. Virtually every expert who has studied New York's growth and the resulting congestion and problems of traffic, housing and transportation has agreed that some orderly plan needs to be followed if the Metropolitan district is to function with freedom and efficiency.

THE SAN FRANCISCO MUNICIPAL RAILWAY

BY WILLIAM H. NANRY

Director, San Francisco Bureau of Governmental Research

After an initial period of satisfactory returns the Municipal Railway has experienced a deficit which is expected to continue. The five-cent fare has been retained. :: :: :: :: :: :: ::

THE San Francisco Municipal Railway started operation late in 1912 as a system of 13.18 single-track miles. The initial system was constructed through a built-up district and partly over routes on which franchises, previously operated by private interests, had expired.

For years prior to the city's entry into the transportation field restrictive franchise provisions in the city charter had prevented adequate development of the city's transportation system by private capital. These provisions still form part of the San Francisco charter. Their deterrent effect on privately owned street railway transportation development has persisted from 1899 down to the present time.

These restrictions, expressed as limitations on street railway franchises, have likewise operated as checks on the proper growth and development of San Francisco. They have forced the city government to provide service to districts served by lines on which franchises expired and to the 1915 Exposition site; also to try and provide service to various districts, by extending and expanding the initial Municipal Railway system, although frequently such districts were much closer to existing privately owned lines.

By June 30, 1927, the initial municipal system of 13.18 single-track miles had grown to 74.12 single-track miles; and four bus routes covering 10.4 route miles were in operation. Two privately owned systems operate over 217 single-track miles. Franchises on approximately 58 per cent of these expire late in 1929, according to the city's point of view, although one of the private companies concerned does not agree to this date with respect to many franchises.

Bond issues totaling $5,500,000 have been voted by the people for Municipal Railway development.[1] In addition, the sum of $3,221,000 has been expended for extensions, additions and betterments, out of Muncipal Railway revenues.

FIVE-CENT FARE RETAINED

The Municipal Railway, as well as the two privately owned systems, operates on a five-cent fare. This is unique among American cities. It is stated that, of the large cities in the country, only Los Angeles, San Francisco and New York have been able to maintain the five-cent fare. It has been estimated that the five-cent fare, as contrasted with costs under a six-cent rate, represents a saving to San Francisco car riders of about $2,700,000 a year.

Out of the revenues derived from a

[1] A bond issue of $4,600,000 was voted on at the election last November, but failed to secure the necessary two-thirds vote. A bond issue of $4,700,000 failed to secure the necessary two-thirds vote last June.

five-cent fare, the Municipal Railway has paid all its operating and bond interest and redemption charges, has appropriated $3,221,000 for additions and betterments, and has set up reserves for depreciation, damage claims, etc., amounting to $864,683, unencumbered, as of June 30 last.

The Municipal Railways, unlike a privately owned system, are not subject to city or state taxation or to the federal income tax. "Book charges" for these items amount to $3,237,746 for the whole period of operation. If state and local taxes had to be paid in San Francisco as is required of the Detroit Municipal Railway, the above-mentioned payments out of revenue would have been correspondingly decreased.

The Municipal Railway financial picture is also benefited by the supplying of services by other departments of the city government—engineering, legal, police, fiscal, etc.—without cost to the railway. What these amount to has never been estimated.

The financial status of the municipal system has been benefited, further, by inadequate *net* allowances for depreciation. Gross amounts set aside for depreciation have been adequate, but these have been diverted in large part for operating deficits, and extensions.

The adequacy of, and even the necessity for, depreciation reserves are controversial points, particularly as annual payments for the redemption of serial bonds issued for the original cost of the system are being met out of revenues, and also as part of depreciation reserves have been expended for new assets. From the other point of view, the findings of regulatory bodies have indicated that the early difficulties of many public utilities have been traceable to inadequate provision out of current rates and revenues for cumulative depreciation requirements.

PUBLIC OWNERSHIP MUST MEET
SAME TESTS AS PRIVATE

The point is often made that the financial result of operations is only part of the picture, and that the city, as a railway operator, is justified in taking account of the development of districts and the creation of additional taxable values, as an offset to operating losses. A government, however, in operating a railway or other utility, operates in a proprietary capacity. The results of municipal ownership and operation in such capacity are to be guaged by comparison with costs, rates and efficiency of service under private ownership. If efficiency and economy cannot be demonstrated under municipal ownership, such services may just as well be left to private enterprise, subject to necessary public regulation, and governmental agencies be left with greater freedom to exercise functions that are purely governmental. If municipal ownership is to be considered successful and a proper sphere for the development of governmental service, each utility must stand on its own financial bottom and prove itself by cold comparison with similar private enterprises.

Additional taxable values are created by the development of new districts by privately owned lines, without any expression of public opinion that the private owners thereof should be subsidized by a city government. It would be a complete distortion of the financial picture, therefore, to apply such a theory to municipally owned projects.

Due to wage increases authorized during 1926 despite the knowledge that the increased costs could not be met out of operating revenues, the 1926–27 operating statement shows a deficit of nearly $120,000 after reserves and debt charges have been set up, in relation to the total operating revenue of $3,421,266.

Passenger revenues not only are not growing as in past years, but have begun to fall off and deficit is expected to increase.

POOR ADMINISTRATIVE ORGANIZATION

The primary weakness of the San Francisco Municipal Railway as an operating entity is the lack of provision for businesslike management and control. By charter, the board of public works is charged with management, the board of supervisors with financial control. Railway employees or interested neighborhood groups may appeal to one or all of five officials or official bodies. On particular matters the mayor, the city engineer, the board of public works, the board of supervisors, or the public utilities committee of the latter body have functioned—individually, severally, or collectively.

For the greatest possible degree of success with the Municipal Railway and other municipal ownership proposals, San Francisco requires a charter-created public utilities commission, vested with broad and independent powers similar to those of the Detroit utility commission and the Los Angeles public service department, with appointments thereto based on merit

and free from politics. Such a plan has been unsuccessfully urged since 1921, although the present board of supervisors has ordered that a charter amendment creating such a commission be submitted to the people in 1928.[1]

Summing up, the San Francisco Municipal Railway, despite fundamental defects in the machinery provided for its management and control, and free from the burden of taxation, enjoyed an initial period of high returns and expanded development on a five-cent fare. The voting of measures that have continuously increased its operating expenses and its operating ratio has gradually affected its financial results, but the five-cent fare has been maintained. The railway has contributed to the development of the city.

Whether these results have been as great as or any greater than could be expected under properly regulated private operation—paying a tax to the government but unhampered by the restrictive charter provisions that have bound the private companies and impeded San Francisco's development—is open to question.

[1] The details of this plan were described by Dr. Delos E. Wilcox in the REVIEW for February, p. 74.

APPRAISING PUBLIC REPORTS

SOME ESSENTIALS OF A GOOD MUNICIPAL REPORT

BY CLARENCE E. RIDLEY

National Institute of Public Administration

The author has courageously undertaken to grade the annual reports of twelve municipalities on the basis of specified standards of excellence.

IN June, 1927, the writer was delegated the task of reviewing in these columns some of the typical current municipal reports. Since that time twelve reports have been reviewed. With three exceptions they have been general city reports covering the usual municipal activities. The exceptions were the St. Paul and Richmond reports, which cover only public works activities, and the report of the board of county road commissioners of Wayne County (Detroit, Michigan).

This present article attempts to appraise these twelve reports on the basis of twenty points which the writer considers essential for effective reporting. The purpose of such a hazardous undertaking is twofold: first, to attempt the development of a technique in report writing, and, second, to emphasize the importance of public reporting.

The twenty points on which the reports were judged, briefly stated, were as follows:

I. DATE OF PUBLICATION

1. *Promptness.* The report will have little value unless published soon after

Editorial Note.—Mr. Ridley will continue his appraisal of municipal reports in future issues of the "Review." The "National Municipal Review," therefore, invites all cities, counties and local units to send in duplicate copies of their reports as soon as they are available for distribution.

the end of the period covered,—six weeks as a maximum.

II. PHYSICAL MAKE-UP

2. *Size.* Convenient for reading and filing, preferably 6″ x 9″.

3. *Paper and type.* Paper should be of a grade and the type of such size and character as to be easily read.

4. *Important facts.* The more important facts should be emphasized by the use of different types of artistic presentation.

5. *Attractiveness.* The cover, title, introduction, and general appearance should aim to attract the reader and encourage further examination.

III. CONTENT

A. *Illustrative Material*

6. *Diagrams and charts.* Certain established rules should be followed to insure an accurate and effective presentation.

7. *Maps and pictures.* A few well-chosen maps to indicate certain improvements, and a liberal supply of pictures, pertinent to the report, should be included.

8. *Distribution.* Great care should be exercised in placing the illustrative material contiguous to the relevant reading material.

B. *Composition*

9. *Table of contents.* A short table of contents in the front of the report is a great aid for ready reference.

10. *Organization chart.* An organization chart or table indicating services rendered by each unit, if placed in front of report, will help the reader to a clearer understanding of what follows.

11. *Letter of transmittal.* A short letter of transmittal followed by summary of outstanding accomplishments and recommendations for the future should come early in the report.

12. *Recommendations and accomplishment.* A comparison of past recommendations with the progress toward their execution will serve as an index to the year's accomplishment.

13. *Length.* Fifty pages should be the maximum length.

14. *Literary style.* The text should be clear and concise, reflecting proper attention to grammar, sentence structure, and diction.

15. *Arrangement.* The report of the various governmental units should correlate with the organization structure, or follow some other logical arrangement.

16. *Balanced content.* The material should show a complete picture, and each activity should occupy space in proportion to its relative importance.

17. *Statistics.* Certain statistics must be included, but, wherever appropriate, they should be supplemented by simple diagrams or charts.

18. *Comparative data.* The present year's accomplishments should be compared with those of previous years, but only with full consideration of all factors involved.

19. *Financial statements.* Three or four financial statements should be included showing amount expended and the means of financing each function and organization unit.

20. *Propaganda.* It is unethical and poor taste to include material for departmental or personal aggrandizement. Photographs of officials, especially of administrators, do not belong in a public report.

It is readily admitted that many of the above essentials are purely subjective and therefore the resulting values depend to a large extent upon the judgment of the appraiser. It is also to be noted that no attempt has been made to assign "weights" to the different points to represent their relative importance. The whole reporting process is too embryonic at present to attempt any such refinement. The number "5" denotes approach to an acceptable standard, while "0" indicates the effectiveness of the report as far as that point is concerned to be practically negligible. The intervening numbers denote the degree of variation between these two extremes. The following table furnishes the individual rating for each point for the several cities:

CONCLUSIONS

1. *Promptness.* Only two of the twelve reports were available for distribution within six weeks of the end of the period covered. Five of the twelve reports were not available until six months or more had elapsed. In this rating no credit whatever is given for a report six months or more late, for it is contended that by that time it has lost all of its news value and therefore its usefulness depends alone upon whatever function it may serve as a means of recording financial statistics and historical events,—purposes hardly justified in a report to the taxpayers on the current operation of their municipal government.

2. *Physical make-up.* The physical make-up of the reports, on the whole, were quite gratifying. Most of them conformed to the conventional size of 6″ x 9″. The disappointing feature was the almost complete failure of all the reports to emphasize the important

	Berkeley Calif.	Dayton Ohio	Ft. Worth Texas	Lynchburg Va.	Miami Fla.	Milwaukee Wis.	Pontiac Mich.	Richmond Va.	St. Paul Minn.	Stratford Conn.	Wayne Co. Mich.	Westerville Ohio
I. DATE OF PUBLICATION												
1. Promptness	0	0	2	0	3	0	4	3	0	4	5	5
II. PHYSICAL MAKE-UP												
2. Size	5	5	5	2	5	2	3	5	5	5	5	5
3. Paper and type	5	5	5	5	5	4	5	4	4	4	5	5
4. Important facts	4	2	3	2	2	3	3	2	0	2	2	3
5. Attractiveness	4	4	4	5	5	4	4	2	3	4	5	4
III. CONTENT												
A. Illustrative Material												
6. Diagrams and charts	3	0	1	4	5	0	4	2	0	0	0	2
7. Maps and pictures	4	3	4	5	5	4	4	4	3	3	5	4
8. Distribution	4	1	3	5	4	4	4	3	3	3	5	4
B. Composition												
9. Table of Contents	0	0	0	5	3	5	2	5	2	5	0	0
10. Organization chart	5	0	0	5	5	0	0	5	5	0	0	0
11. Letter of transmittal	5	3	0	4	5	3	5	4	4	4	4	4
12. Recommendations and accomplishments	4	4	5	3	2	3	5	4	3	4	4	2
13. Length	0	5	5	0	0	0	0	0	0	4	0	4
14. Literary style	4	4	4	4	3	5	4	4	4	3	4	4
15. Arrangement	4	4	5	5	4	5	5	4	3	4	5	5
16. Balanced content	1	3	5	3	4	5	4	4	3	3	5	3
17. Statistics	2	1	3	4	4	2	3	2	0	3	3	3
18. Comparative data	3	2	4	4	4	4	2	4	2	3	3	4
19. Financial statements	4	1	4	4	4	4	4	3	1	4	3	4
20. Propaganda	5	5	5	5	1	5	5	5	5	5	1	5
	66	52	67	74	72	62	70	69	50	68	64	70

facts. This is very essential, for few, if any, will read an entire report, so an attempt should be made to emphasize the more important facts, and thus give the hasty reader a definite impression, if possible. The reports were uniformly attractive, varying only in degree.

3. *Illustrative material.* A serious error common practically to all the reports was the failure to tell more of the story by charts, pictures, and other illustrative material. Even the effect of well chosen charts and pictures was greatly lessened in some of the reports by poor distribution. In several cases the illustrations were placed entirely outside the relevant context.

4. *Composition.* On the whole, the reports were uniformly good in arrangement, literary style, balance of material, and freedom from propaganda. The conformity to the other essentials under this heading were, however, not so commendable. Some of the letters of transmittal were too long and indefinite, while two of the reports omitted the letter entirely. Only a few of the reports presented a clear-cut and brief statement of important accomplishments and recommendations for future action. Less than one-half of the reports failed to include an organization chart, thereby hindering a ready understanding of the organization units and their relation one to another. Few reports made satisfactory use of comparative data. The financial statements, on the whole, were very unsatisfactory, being either superficial or far too elaborate and encumbered with technical accounting terms. Far too many statistics unsupplemented by charts characterized most of the reports. A table of contents appeared in but three of the reports, while some of the others attempted to substitute for it an exhaustive index in the back of the report. Exceeding all the other violations of the essentials herein presented was the

length of the reports. Only four of the twelve reports came under fifty pages; five were in excess of 100 pages, and three exceeded 150 pages.

Briefly, the chief defect in public reports, as exemplified by those appraised herein, is an overestimation of the capacity and willingness of the average taxpayer to consume such material. There has been, however, a very marked improvement in public report writing in recent years, and the type of reports now coming to this office augurs well for the future.

THE PROGRESS OF PERMANENT REGISTRATION FOR ELECTIONS

BY JOSEPH P. HARRIS

University of Wisconsin

During the past year permanent registration laws were passed by two states. In two others such measures were passed by the legislature but vetoed by the governor. In three more the bills failed to pass the legislature.   ::   ::   ::   ::   ::   ::   ::   ::   ::

BILLS providing for permanent registration of voters were introduced in seven states at the 1927 sessions, and were enacted into law in two states: Wisconsin and Iowa. In Ohio and Washington permanent registration bills were passed by the legislatures, but were vetoed by the governors. In three other states, Pennsylvania, Missouri and California, the bills failed to pass the legislature, but in two of these states the failure was not due to any substantial opposition to permanent registration, but rather because of other factors. The outlook for the adoption of permanent registration in these latter five states in the near future is particularly bright, and several other states will probably join the movement within a few years. It seems probable that permanent registration will spread as widely and almost as rapidly as did the Australian ballot, and it will be only a matter of time until it will prevail throughout the country.

All of the bills in the various states were in substantial conformance with the National Municipal League Committee report on a Model Registration System, though in one or two states the bills were prepared before the report was published. All of the bills provided for permanent, central registration, with loose-leaf or card records, and with thorough means to keep the lists corrected from time to time.

WISCONSIN

The bill in Wisconsin was sponsored by the state League of Women Voters. The state chairman of its efficiency in government department, Mrs. Frederic A. Ogg, was particularly active in promoting the bill, and was largely responsible for its passage. The measure was well advertised, and the League of Women Voters received many commendations in the press for sponsoring it. The leader of the La Follette forces in the senate introduced the bill, where it passed with no dissenting vote. In the assembly there were only three votes cast against it. When the bill was sent to the governor, he held it until the last day of the period during which he could act upon it, and then asked the attorney general for an opinion as to its constitutionality. At this time the attorney general and most of his staff were away at a state convention, and the opinion which was hurriedly prepared held the bill to be unconstitutional on the ground that it violated the constitutional guarantee of municipal home rule. Upon this basis the bill was vetoed, and apparently was dead. Later the attorney general reversed the previous opinion, and the bill was passed over the veto.

The Wisconsin law applies to all cities with more than 5,000 population except Milwaukee, which has had permanent registration since 1912. The city clerk is made the chief officer of registration. He is given wide powers and discretion in the administration of the law. He may conduct registration at any time and place he may see fit, both at the start of the first registration and afterwards. He has ample powers to put on a registration campaign to get every voter registered, and the method is not prescribed by law. Some of the city clerks have already shown considerable ingenuity in devising ways to get the voters registered, sending deputies to public meetings, luncheon clubs, factories, banks, etc., but other clerks have been reluctant to take registration outside of the city hall, and have not registered many voters so far. In several cities the clerk has put on a "week of registration" with good results. The first election under the law has not been held, however, and most of the actual work of registration is yet to be done.

The records provided are very simple. The name, address, occupation, birthplace and signature under the affidavit is all that is required of native-born citizens. The affidavit covers age and length of residence. The most unusual feature of the Wisconsin law is the requirement that the city clerk shall secure each month from the gas and electric company a list of removals, and upon the basis of this information, make the proper transfers. It is anticipated that most voters will be transferred when they move within the city without bother upon their part. So far as it has come to the attention of the writer, the utility companies are glad to coöperate in order to provide this convenience for their patrons.

The new registration law in Wisconsin will effect a saving of more than the entire previous cost of registration. This remarkable accomplishment is due to the fact that under the new law two clerks are dispensed with in each precinct at each election, which saving will more than cover the entire cost of registration. The city clerk is required to supply the precinct election officers with two typewritten lists of the registered voters, which serve as combined poll and check lists and take the place of the two poll lists previously prepared at the polls.

IOWA

The Iowa law is quite similar to that of Wisconsin. It applies only to the city of Des Moines, but is optional for other cities of 10,000 population or over. It will be interesting to observe how many cities will elect to take advantage of this improved method of registration. The law was patterned particularly after the Minnesota law, which has now been in operation for more than four years. It was drafted by the Des Moines Bureau of Municipal Research, which was naturally instrumental in securing its passage.

The city clerk is made the principal registration officer. Central registration is provided, but at the start of the system, precinct sessions are authorized. Duplicate card records are to be used. Several methods are provided to keep the lists corrected from time to time, including the cancellation of registration for failure to vote within a four-year period (instead of the two-year period which is commonly used). A particularly strong feature of the Iowa law is the signature requirement at the polls. Every voter is required to sign a certificate, and the signature is compared with the signature upon the registration record. The card records readily lend themselves to an actual comparison, which is not always secured where large bound registers are used. It is estimated that the new system will accomplish a saving of $10,-000 annually in Des Moines.

OHIO

An official election commission was created by the 1925 Ohio legislature to investigate various problems in connection with the conduct of elections. This commission prepared a new election code, which was submitted to the 1927 legislative session. The changes in the registration law were minor. Biennial registration was provided for cities of over 100,000 population in the place of annual registration which now prevails. During the session this bill was amended at the intercession of the League of Women Voters, the Citizens Association, the Ohio Institute and other civic organizations. The amended bill was passed on the last day of the legislature, but was vetoed by the governor because of other features of the new code. In connection with registration, the bill provided for quadrennial registration in all cities of over 25,000 population, apparently doing away with registration altogether in cities of less size. Heretofore Ohio has had registration in cities of over 11,800 population. The largest cities were to have quadrennial instead of annual registration as at present. Permanent registration was made optional, but a

procedure much along the line of the committee recommendations was provided for such cities as might adopt it.

MISSOURI

The last two sessions of the Missouri legislature have seen permanent registration bills introduced, but neither bill has advanced far. The Kansas City Public Service Institute and the Chamber of Commerce of that city early in 1926 prepared a permanent registration bill and a report. Owing to a peculiar political situation, sufficient support could not be secured for this bill, and these two organizations joined with the Kansas City Bar Association in 1927 and pushed a bill prepared by the latter organization. This bill provided for permanent registration, but otherwise followed very closely the old procedure used under the present quadrennial system, and was consequently fundamentally defective in several respects. The records and the procedure were poorly designed for permanent operation. The Kansas City Public Service Institute and the Chamber of Commerce will continue the fight for a sound permanent registration law.

CALIFORNIA

For the second time a permanent registration bill was introduced in the California legislature and was defeated. The Bill introduced in 1927 provided permanent registration upon the same procedure and with the same records as at present, which, however, are quite well adapted to permanent operation. Adequate means were provided to keep the lists cleaned. An unusual feature was the provision that cancellation for failure to vote was to be made following each general state election—a rather drastic provision and one designed to place a mild compulsion upon voting. The bill was lost because of the opposition of the county clerks. At the present time they receive a fee for each new registration, which constitutes a considerable item of their salary. Permanent registration would practically do away with this source of salary. Until some other means is found to take care of the county clerks, it is unlikely that any permanent law can be passed. There is considerable support of permanent registration in the state, and it is quite likely that this problem will be ironed out at the next session.

WASHINGTON

A permanent registration bill, prepared by Comptroller Carroll of Seattle, was passed by the legislature, but was vetoed by the governor. The bill conformed in almost every detail with the report of the National Municipal League Committee. It was vetoed by the governor ostensibly on the ground that loose-leaf ledgers were not suitable for public records. A permanent registration bill will be presented also at the next session of the legislature.

OTHER STATES

Movements are under way in several other states for permanent registration. Indiana repealed a defective permanent law at the last legislative session, and at present has no registration whatsoever. It will be interesting to watch the effect of the total lack of registration in the larger cities of the state during the coming elections. It is assumed that the next legislature will tackle the problem. The solution will not be easy because of the rigid uniformity required by the state constitution. The rural sections do not want to bother with any registration at all. The New York State Election Commissioners Association has set up a committeee to work for permanent registration in that state, outside of New York City. It will require a constitutional amendment. For a number of years the Chicago Bureau of Public Efficiency has worked for an improvement in the registration laws of Illinois. The party organizations profit greatly by the rich harvest of precinct jobs under the existing inconvenient, ineffective and obsolete system, and vigorously oppose any change. Kentucky is now having some difficulties with a fundamentally defective permanent registration law. The records are so poorly designed that it would seem to be necessary to throw them out altogether and start a new registration before a suitable system can be secured.

CINCINNATI SURVEYS ITS POLICE

BY DONALD C. STONE

Cincinnati Bureau of Municipal Research

The Cincinnati police survey did not stop with general criticisms and recommendations, but outlined in detail the practical steps to be taken in improving the police force. :: :: :: :: :: ::

SOON after Colonel Sherrill had become firmly established as city manager of Cincinnati, he realized that the police department was not so efficient and up-to-date as it might be. He knew that the department had deteriorated and was undermanned. Financially Cincinnati was unable immediately to augment the force and equipment. Yet Colonel Sherrill firmly believed that the force though undermanned could be made a more effective weapon in its battle against crime. However, the demands of his office prevented him from giving the personal attention which a reorganization would require, and so he turned to the Bureau of Municipal Research, believing that it could bring to the solution of his problem the required technical knowledge.

In his request Colonel Sherrill asked the Bureau to make "its investigation include the entire Police Department— organization, equipment, distribution of duties, districting, and all other pertinent matters relating to the general efficiency and operation of this department." The manager requested that the report indicate simply and fully the practical steps to be taken by him in bettering the caliber of police service in Cincinnati.

Mention should be made of the report on the government of Cincinnati and Hamilton County made in 1924 by Lent D. Upson and staff. The section relating to police still serves as a general indication of the extent to which the Cincinnati department measures up to the most advanced police standards. As a part of the comprehensive report, it proved to be of service in providing ammunition for the City Charter Committee in its campaign to secure the council-manager form of government. But it does not provide a working plan for the city manager in his effort to improve police administration in Cincinnati.

Conforming to Colonel Sherrill's request, the approach of the Bureau of Municipal Research was to take certain of the most significant problems, reduce them to concrete form, and then offer a definite and detailed program for their solution. No effort was made to outline the complete requirements of an ideal police department, but rather so to organize and redirect the present equipment and personnel as to secure increased police service. It must be borne in mind that the report was designed primarily as a working sheet for the city manager.

Realizing the highly technical character of the work to be done, the Bureau sought the highest grade of police consultant service and to this end obtained the services of Mr. Bruce Smith of the New York Bureau of Municipal Research.

A DETAILED STUDY FIRST MADE

As the first step a complete picture of the department was obtained by a detailed study of each of the ten dis-

157

tricts and the police buildings therein. Notations were made as follows:

1. The facilities furnished by the equipment and buildings in each district.
2. The personnel assigned to the district and its distribution.
3. The location and description of each beat.
4. Information relating to the signal system and emergency calls.
5. The character and adequacy of records.
6. The crime conditions, topography, nature of employment, population, racial and national characteristics, and special features which in any way might affect the police problem.

In addition to this, special study was made of the detective and record bureaus, the bureau of criminal identification, and the patrol wagon service. Information relating to personnel, such as hours of work, vacations, days off, sick leave, salaries, pensions, retirement, sick and disability benefits, selection, promotion, and the equipment of the men, was gathered. This mass of information disclosed much in the department that required change.

As the work progressed, it was found advisable to concentrate upon four salient features of police administration. Briefly they were as follows:

1. The system of uniformed patrol of the highways of the city.
2. The organization and control of criminal investigations by the detective bureau.
3. The system of records used in the administration both of the various districts and of the department as a whole.
4. The methods employed in the selection, training, and management of police personnel.

The first division of the study relating to patrol received a more extensive consideration and treatment than the other divisions. The analysis of the distribution of the force, buildings, equipment, the topography, crime conditions, and general methods of administration brought forth rather far-reaching recommendations.

ECONOMIES EFFECTED AT ONCE

Ten of the nineteen buildings used for police service were found to be unnecessary. As their appraised value amounted to $137,430, their sale would enable no insignificant amount to be turned into the fund for general police service. Furthermore, rather high operating expenses as well as the drain on police personnel required for manning this property would be saved.

The closing of some of these buildings required the redistricting of the city. Six of the ten police districts were consolidated into three. Unique topography and crime conditions warranted this consolidation. The boundaries of other districts received minor changes with the aim of making all sections of each district more accessible from the district station and of facilitating a better grade of patrol.

By the closing of these buildings and the elimination of special details, a total of twenty-five officers and men were made available for active police duty. For example, the detail of eleven men to the traffic sign shop for the purpose of painting signs was withdrawn for obvious reasons. These twenty-five men were distributed among the districts according to the relative need. The keeping of reserve men on duty in the "basin," or down town districts, without weakening the present patrolling of that section was made possible.

Perhaps the most distinctive feature of this police study was the manner in which provision was made for policing the rearranged districts. A complete distribution of the force within each relief was made for each district. Proper reserves were assigned for emergency duty and for care of the station houses. Not only this, but a thorough study of the districts enabled the revision of all beats, zones of patrol, and the combination of beats and zones according to the number of men on each relief. The beat boundaries in the "basin" area and the patrol zones in the outlying districts were plotted on maps. The method of patrolling these beats and zones as well as the assignment of patrol supervision zones for sergeants was outlined.

In order to secure an equal distribution of box calls throughout the hour, a time schedule was prepared which synchronized the time when each beat was to "ring in." This enabled the district to maintain a closer degree of supervision over the men on the beat and to make the men more readily available in time of emergency.

By means of a thorough study of the signal system, inexpensive improvements were recommended which would make possible periodic comparisons between the recording tape of box calls and the reports forwarded to headquarters by the districts. In fact a complete system for renumbering all call boxes in the city was provided.

The significant part of this section relating to patrol was the manner in which the recommendations were put into operation. Shortly after the report was formally presented to Colonel Sherrill, orders went out from his office putting into effect, with but one exception, all of these recommendations. To a large degree these orders were sections taken bodily from the report. The value of the report as a "working sheet" for the department was thereby demonstrated.

THE DETECTIVE BUREAU

The second phase of police work undertaken in the survey related to the detective bureau. This section of the report limited its consideration to a few major weaknesses of the bureau.

The primary defect lay in the distribution of the detectives among the several districts. With the exception of seven special details, all of the detectives were assigned on an equal basis, two being detailed to each of the ten districts. This policy had certain inherent weaknesses which undermined the effectiveness of the whole detective bureau.

The remedy for these weaknesses was provided by the recommendation that the chief of detectives should assign all cases, not according to the district in which they arise, but according to the circumstances in each case. If this were done, detective headquarters would no longer be left without reserve, thus making detectives available for emergency cases which need to be handled in an expeditious manner. Cases could be assigned according to the peculiar ability of the individual detective, thus developing in the detectives a skill and technique in important phases of detection. Moreover, a reasonable equality in the number of cases assigned to each detective would be obtained. With the aid of proposed records and reports, a close control by the chief of detectives over all detectives as well as the cases assigned to them is thus insured.

Several changes in the division of criminal identification were found imperative in order that adequate identification services might be furnished to police departments in other cities as well as to criminal justice agencies in Cincinnati. An itemization of needed improvements was made among which were listed new cabinets for the "rogues' gallery," portrait and enlarging cameras, standard identification cards, and when money should be available, a new photographic apparatus.

RECORDS AND REPORTS

The third phase of the survey—that of records and reports—demanded much attention. The whole record system and office administration has long been identified by archaic methods. Owing to the difficulty of describing the installation of a record and report system so that a policeman could install and put it in operation, it would have been much more desirable for the Bureau of Municipal Research to actually install a complete and revised system of records and reports. But as this was impossible at the time, recommendations were made only where a change would aid police administration in a vital manner. Unnecessary duplication of records and reports was discontinued. A number of sample record forms placed in the appendix of the report aimed to eradicate the major defects of the record system and thus enable a more effective police service with a force sensitive to crime conditions.

This section of the report as well as the part relating to the detective bureau has not as yet been adopted by Colonel Sherrill. The recommendations for the detective bureau involved a change in detective records. Appreciating the inherent nature of a policeman, Colonel Sherrill deemed it wise to wait till the Bureau could actively revise and install an entirely new system of records. As the Bureau is now prepared to do this, it may be expected that both the second and third portions of the report will be put into full operation in the near future.

PERSONNEL

The final phase of the report—that of personnel—was given nearly as much attention as the first section on patrol. This section of the report discussed primarily the selection of recruits, promotion, disciplinary action, employment conditions, and police training. Similarly as with the recommendations for patrol, the personnel proposals were adopted by Colonel Sherrill almost exactly as recommended.

The major attempt of this section was to bring the policies of the civil service commission and the police department into harmony and agreement in regard to the essentials of police personnel. That the divorcement of police personnel from police administration has been the bane of American cities is the uniform lesson taught by American police experience. When a civil service commission and the police officials each stand upon their supposed rights without hearty coöperation, police efficiency is irretrievably impaired. The control of police personnel by the police authorities is vital to efficient police administration. The desirability of numerous changes in the part played by the Cincinnati civil service commission was apparent. Happily, the commission not only expressed its willingness to make these changes, but desired to coöperate whole-heartedly so that the police administration might be of the highest order. In a most gratifying manner this expression was carried into practice after the completion of the survey.

The selective process for securing recruits has been revised in accordance with the recommendations made in the report. The character investigation is now being made before the eligible list is finally made out. A complete revision of the examination has been made; spelling, penmanship, and other extraneous matters which have no bearing upon police aptitude and qualification have been abolished. Tests, which have demonstrated their positive correlation with police ability, are offered in their place. After these tests were adopted, the Bureau designed the system of grading. Pertinent revisions were effected by means of subjecting to these tests a group of patrolmen, of whom the relative ability could be obtained. The grades received by these patrolmen showed a comparatively high correlation with their relative ability as policemen. The Bureau is still working with the commission in the effort to determine new types of tests which measure even more accurately the candidate's aptitude for police work. Finally, as the best test of the probationer's capacity is not applied till he goes on patrol, greater latitude is being allowed the chief in passing upon the acceptability of the candidate's performance.

Although no promotions have as yet taken place the civil service commission is considering the Bureau's proposals relating thereto. The net result of these proposals is that both the written examination and the seniority rating will be prescribed only as qualifying or elimination tests. The examination on "conduct and capacity in office" will be conducted by a proposed examining board composed primarily of the city manager and the chief of police. This group of examiners will then make its recommendations to the commission, stating the nature and fact basis of its findings.

Very little attention was given by the Bureau to employment conditions. The suggestions that a change in the policy be adopted, relating to sick leave, rest days, purchase of equipment and indemnity bonds, has been held in abeyance by the city manager till the Bureau fulfills his request to make a detailed and thorough report upon the entire personnel problem, including compensation, employment conditions, hours of work, and pensions.

POLICE SCHOOL

At the present time Cincinnati is maintaining a police school which is thoroughly training recruits for active police work. All probationers are subjected with full pay to an eight-weeks' course of instruction. The major studies include penal law and code of criminal procedure, practical police procedure, departmental rules and regulations, the gathering of evidence and presentation of cases in court, criminal *modus operandi*, target practice, drill, topography, and the relationship which exists between police and the work of other city departments such as the fire, health, buildings, highways, and welfare departments. Specialized work is given, dealing with such questions as criminal identification, first aid and personal hygiene, the meaning and value of discipline, the relation of social welfare agencies to crime prevention, and traffic control. To this end, judges, prosecuting attorneys, directors of civic agencies, professors, and heads of city departments as well as officials within the police department itself, are called upon to act as instructors.

The beneficial results of this training are readily manifest in the high standards of performance by the probationers. In the past the sending of probationers out on police duty has been productive of an endless number of complaints as to their official actions, both from their superiors and from private citizens. Not so today. Although at the time this was written two classes of recruits numbering fifty-three men had been sent out on police duty, not a complaint had been entered against them.

Plans are now complete for training present incumbents in the more advanced phases of police technique and procedure. Judging from the comprehensive manner in which police training is now being given, Cincinnati will soon boast of a police force thoroughly trained and competent to render the highest grade of service to the community.

Let us compare this picture with conditions at the time this survey was made. At that time an officer would take the recruit in hand, impart to him the advice of an elder, and regale him with the distilled knowledge derived from many years of police work. This instruction lasted about one hour. At its conclusion the recruit was to all intents and purposes a policeman. At any rate, he was immediately assigned to police duty. Instruction given subsequently was correspondingly inadequate. Police training was all but submerged by the daily routine of police matters.

This in brief summarizes the report and the extent to which it was adopted. If the usual type of survey had been made, that is one which shows in a very general manner the relative strength and weaknesses of the force, few constructive results would have obtained. There are three outstanding reasons why such results were assured in this case. A detailed and instructional report, a working plan, showing step by step the procedure for putting into operation the major proposals, was placed at Colonel Sherrill's disposal. Then Colonel Sherrill had only one motive in requesting the survey—to give the people of Cincinnati the highest grade of police service. To do this he wanted facts; after the facts were obtained he was ready to make fearlessly such changes as the facts demanded. Finally, the Bureau not only made possible this practical type of survey through a preliminary study, but also it remained on the field after its completion, aiding in the installation of the recommendations, tying up loose ends, and giving further attention to phases of the report which could not be completed at the time of the investigation.

RECENT BOOKS REVIEWED

New Towns for Old. Achievements in Civic Improvement in Some American Small Towns and Neighborhoods. By John Nolen. Introduction by Albert Shaw. Boston: Marshall Jones Company. Pp. xxix, 177.

Dr. Nolen has given us another of the readable, helpful books which are to his credit, rounding out a dozen works on community planning, each altogether worth while.

"The primary purpose of this book is to describe a few representative examples of civic improvement actually carried out." So reads the prefatory statement in the book, which then proceeds to appreciatively look over a number of new American towns either made so from the beginning, as in Kistler, Pennsylvania, or Mariemont, Ohio, or Kingsport, Tennessee, or made new by reshaping, as in Walpole and Cohasset, Massachusetts. There is also consideration of the problem of new residential suburbs, a notable instance of which is projected in the description of Myers Park, adjoining Charlotte, North Carolina.

The general thought in this view of new communities and old communities made new is to bring into America as much of the garden city idea as is possible, and town development as here outlined is according to wholesome ideals which cannot but be advantageous both in respect of the influence on the industrial inhabitants of such towns and in the ultimate prosperity of the industry usually dominating the community.

If one item in this book particularly deserves mention above another it is the account of "An Industrial City Built to Order," which tells about Kingsport, Tennessee. Concerning this example of modern American city planning Dr. Nolen writes:

It began as a new town. Its site, though hardly a wilderness, was an out-of-the-way agricultural region remote from the world's activities. In 1912 the only human habitations there were two farm houses. As late as 1915 . . . it was merely a small agricultural community of about 900 inhabitants. In four years more it had become a flourishing city of more than 10,000 people.

Then the illustrations which follow, both in words and in inserted plates, tell a story which truly, as the author says, "reads like a romance." The basis here was the opportunity given in the

extension of a railroad line through a region in southeastern Tennessee replete with natural wealth in coal, timber, many minerals, and other desirable raw materials.

Of course there is nothing new about making a town grow where none was before, but there is much that is new in the way this town has been caused to grow into comfort, beauty and efficiency.

A large order seems to have been suggested in making over the old Massachusetts seacoast town of Cohasset, which "with narrow, crooked streets, eccentric and radiate, and scenic in their vistas, is a survival of old-time New England community life." The plan for a change of conditions is detailed, and the achievements are mentioned which since 1917 have seemingly fastened this plan on the land so that it cannot otherwise than develop desirably while retaining New England attractiveness.

But it is not in point in this review to analyze the various projects discussed in Dr. Nolen's book. Sufficient has been said, it is hoped, to indicate that the handy little volume of 177 pages is altogether worth while having and reading and referring to. It is simply usual and conventional for Dr. Nolen to add to the value of his own writing by citing, as he has done in an appendix, a comprehensive and important list of reports and instances to help the student of town improvement toward greater knowledge and the towns themselves toward greater usefulness.

J. HORACE MCFARLAND.

✤

A Department of Public Welfare for Cincinnati. By Ellery F. Reed, Ph.D. The Helen S. Trounstine Foundation, June, 1927.

Modern social service, with newer and more intelligent standards of work and a developing technique, is beginning to find its place in public service as well as in private philanthropy.

One of the latest of municipal welfare plans is to be found in this carefully prepared and intelligent study. The report recently issued is called A Program for the Development of a Department of Public Welfare for Cincinnati. Dr. Reed has made a careful study of the improvement in public welfare departments in St. Louis, Kansas City, St. Joseph (Missouri), Denver, Chicago, Grand Rapids, Detroit and Cleveland, as well as of the growing literature on this important subject. The result is a carefully considered, practical plan which if followed in Cincinnati cannot help but serve as a stimulus for constructive governmental social work. The proposals include a reorganized department for case work and relief on the basis of the division of work between the public and private relief and caseworking agencies, the development of an improved city correctional farm for dealing with adult delinquents, the extension of probation and parole, and the reorganization and improvement of the state-city employment service.

A division between the public and private relief and case work is made on the basis that the public department should take over the chronic dependent groups, including families of inmates of public institutions, families of prisoners, old couples, families whose chief wage-earners are chronically incapacitated. In addition the department is to undertake the care of homeless men and of non-resident dependents. It is proposed that the city eventually take over all resident dependent families in which the problem is principally that of relief, and of all other cases in which a definite technique of social work is well established, leaving to the private agencies the experimental and unsolved problems of case work. In general such a division of work should operate successfully. Detroit is a city in the country which is outstanding in having carried out this plan of operation. It is to be questioned, however, whether a reorganized department should at present take over the care of families of patients in the Cincinnati General Hospital inasmuch as the average period of stay in a public hospital is of short duration and many of the families of this group are likely to require little relief but may be in need of continued and intensive case-work service. The proposed public department might take over the care of all of the aged inasmuch as this type is a chronic dependent group and institutional care is inadequate and undesirable.

There are excellent recommendations for the development of a city correctional farm which, if carried out, would bring this department of work up to the standards which have been developed in other cities of the country, notably Detroit and Kansas City. Similarly, the extension of parole probation work will apply case-work methods to the problem of delinquency now lacking in Cincinnati. The recommendations for the state-city employment service are in line with the

development of such service in Cleveland, Akron and other cities.

Dr. Reed makes it clear that the successful accomplishment of the proposed changes depends primarily upon the acquisition and retention of a professional personnel, trained and experienced in social work theory and practice. It is in this respect that many city departments otherwise properly planned appear to be deficient. It is to be hoped that Cincinnati with its improved city government will not repeat the mistakes of other communities and attempt a sound plan of organization with unsuitable personnel.

H. L. LURIE.

✦

MOTOR VEHICLES AND THE HIGHWAY IN NEW YORK: A Study of Social Benefits and Financial Burdens. By F. G. Crawford and H. W. Peck. Syracuse: School of Citizenship and Public Affairs, Syracuse University. 1927. Pp. 92.

Financing of highways in New York state through taxation levied according to the benefit received from the highway seems to the authors of "Motor Vehicles and the Highway in New York," to be the most equitable method. It is recommended that this method of financing be accomplished by means of a tax on gasoline.

The above conclusions are based upon data obtained in a study of five counties of the state. Much of the information was gotten first-hand in conferences with farmers, bankers, assessors, appraisers, and others. A questionnaire sent to members of farm bureaus also yielded part of the material, and reports of other studies were utilized.

The results of the inquiry are discussed under two main headings: the social and economic effects of improved highways, and highway finance. Under the first heading, the effect upon urban dwellers and upon rural dwellers is described. Rural areas are divided into three zones, the first, bordering upon the road; the last, furthest from it. From the study of the effect upon these zones, it is concluded, among other things, that the adjacent zone is most benefited while the improved highway is harmful to remote areas.

In the discussion of highways finance, the financing of highways in New York state prior to 1925 is reviewed and various methods of taxation for highways are described. A tax of two cents per gallon on gasoline is recommended. This tax is to be collected from importers and distributors. To those using gasoline for other than transportation a refund would be made. The proceeds of the tax would be distributed to counties of the state according to the number of registered motor vehicles in each county. Only the cost of administration would be retained by the state. Distribution to cities and townships would be made by the counties on the same basis of motor-vehicle registration and money paid to townships would be available to villages for main roads passing through them.

C. A. HOWLAND.

✥

THE CHURCH IN THE CHANGING CITY. By H. Paul Douglass. New York: George H. Doran Co. 1927. Pp. 453.

After giving us in his "1,000 City Churches" a bird's-eye view of urban religious problems, Mr. Douglass, with characteristic Institute of Social and Religious Research thoroughness, now presents an intensive, close-up, case analysis of sixteen big city churches which have met their special problems with a certain originality and distinction. The flood-tide of business enterprises, lodging-houses, and foreign population sweeps into the suburbs the former constituency of a church, some of which may be later returned in the back-wash of expensive apartments and hotels.

In forced adaptation to such changes the church may desert the locality, or, by energetic and ingenious publicity methods, may continue to attract a desirable constituency from a distance. Else it may split its personality, making a primary selective appeal to a socially and economically desirable class at a distance, while ministering to its immediate run-down environment by subsidiary activities. Where none of these are possible the church must definitely adapt itself to its clearly defined, difficult geographic neighborhood. In such adaptations the church sometimes becomes a mere moral and motivating center smothered in a mass of some 200 or more constructive week-day activities, ranging from day nurseries to legal aid societies. The next logical step passes outside of the church field altogether, and the Christian center or settlement house comes into being.

With this increase of social agencies within the individual church comes the question of whether it is predominantly a denominational or a community enterprise and of its just claim to a share

in the community chest or in other city-wide assistance. The relationship of such churches to other social agencies is one important phase of this study. The church is from time to time a host, a beneficiary, or a supporter of constructive social agencies. It supplies members of the executive boards, exchanges services, shares in the conferences of social agencies, and bears a close relation to the various training schools. It is such "an impressive demonstration of the interrelationship of social forces and movements, both on the side of preventive effort, and on that of alleviation and control of the community's ills" that no one desiring a well-rounded understanding of modern urban problems can afford to overlook this important contribution.

NEWBILL NILES PUCKETT.

✥

Comparative Statistics, Cities of Ohio, 1925.— This report was compiled and issued by the bureau of inspection and supervision of public offices of the auditor of the state of Ohio. The *Financial Statistics of Cities* issued by the federal bureau of the census being limited to cities of over 30,000 population, the Ohio report includes 79 cities that are not in the former. It deals in separate sections with four main subjects of city finance, designated as "taxes," "cost," "debt," and "reference," the last relating to "total salaries, fees, and wages in cities" and "tax levy—city property." The amounts shown for each city are reduced to the per capita basis, and some of the statistical tables contain repetitions of data that are contained in other tables. We understand that the "taxes" and "costs" are based upon cash receipts and disbursements rather than upon revenues actually accrued and expenditures actually incurred.

The tables in the "taxes" section of the report include the proceeds not only of general property taxes, but also of "licenses" and special assessments, separate columns in the table of "taxes" being used for these respective sources. It is stated in the report that "the license column includes automobile licenses, gasoline tax, inheritance tax, and other licenses and permits."

"Costs" of operation and maintenance, the latter being understood to comprehend replacements of property, are shown for each of the various departments, activities, services, and so forth, as the units may be severally called according to the standard classification that is provided. It has been attempted to show the "net expense to the taxpayer" of these different departments or activities. In doing this, the revenues other than from general property taxes, "licenses," and special assessments "are offset against the expenditures in the departments which produce them by their own efforts." Hence we find court fines, fees, and costs credited to the expense of the courts, it being represented that the courts return a "net revenue" to the taxpayers in every city, ranging from 7 cents to $5.59 per capita. The costs of outlays are shown in a consolidated statement where they are distributed between "streets," "sewers," and "other." Expenditures for interest are also shown.

The tables in the "debt" section of the report show the outstanding "total net debt" classified according to "general," "water works, electric light, and gas," and "special assessments"; a comparison of the "general debt" in 1925 with that in 1916; and the proportion in amounts and percentages of general property tax receipts applied to debt and current expenses. There seems to be some ambiguity in the designations of "net debt" and "gross debt" in these tables. Usually the former term denotes total outstanding debt less sinking funds, and the descriptive titles of two of the tables indicate that it is this net debt that is therein referred to. Yet in one of these tables, the columnar caption "general gross debt" is used, and still the total of this column is less instead of more than the total of the column in the other table which appears to represent "general net debt." This is an example of ambiguities that appear elsewhere in the report, or at least as they seem to us.

WILLIAM WATSON.

✤

Accounting for Special Assessment Funds with special reference to the requirements of the Illinois local improvement laws, by Lloyd Morey, statistician for the Illinois Municipal League, is a reprint from the *Illinois Municipal Review*. While these recommendations comply exactly with the Illinois law and are of most direct and practical use in that state, they offer very valuable suggestions and with necessary modifications could be adapted to use in any municipality.

E. C.

✤

Sources of Information on Play and Recreation, by Marguerita P. Williams, has been revised as of 1927 and published by the Russell Sage Foundation. The Foreword explains the guiding principles followed in its compilation. "The aim has been to make it, not an exhaustive bibliography, but a fairly comprehensive, carefully selected list of the more important and readily available books, pamphlets, reports and articles dealing with the many phases of recreation, that it may serve as a practical source book on these topics." There is no doubt but what this excellent bibliography has been much needed by those concerned with the problem of recreation.

E. C.

✤

Public Utility Rates in 561 Kansas Cities includes rates for electric light and power, water and gas. This booklet was compiled by the League of Kansas Municipalities, contains 207 pages and sells at $10 per copy. Mr. John G. Stutz, executive secretary of the League in describing the undertaking, writes: "The League spent $3,000 in compiling and publishing this book. I estimate that the city officials spent a $1,000 worth of time in filling out the questionnaires, and the utility companies spent at least $1,000 in furnishing their rate schedules." These figures are an indication of the care exercised in the collection of data and of the coöperation received from city officials and from utility companies—all of which are obviously necessary in compiling adequate public utility rates. Although these rates cover only cities in the state of Kansas, they should be very useful to city officials and utility companies for comparative purposes.

E. C.

✤

Seventy-Fifth Annual Report of the Board of Water Commissioners, Detroit, Michigan, for the Year Ending June 30, 1927.—The 54-page report of the board of water commissioners of Detroit is a delight to the engineer. It contains a wealth of concise and detailed information upon the activities of the water-supply department and gives much of interest to water-works officials generally.

Perhaps the report could be made even more valuable if the water-supply activities were interpreted and their significance indicated for the general reader. This has been done to some extent, but it would seem that a few more sentences in the letter of transmittal or elsewhere might well be devoted to giving the non-technical taxpayer a clear picture of the undertaking. This could be accomplished without sacrificing the excellent presentation of financial and engineering data or creating too bulky or costly a report.

C. A. H.

JUDICIAL DECISIONS

EDITED BY C. W. TOOKE

Professor of Law, Georgetown University

The Control of Streets in Outlying Districts under the City Plan.—On January 6 the Supreme Court of Michigan in *Ridgefield Land Co.* v. *Detroit*, 217 N. W. 58, handed down one of the most important decisions of recent years bearing upon the control of new streets and highways in outlying districts. The facts as stated in the opinion by Justice McDonald may be briefly summarized as follows: Under the Detroit charter as amended in 1915, the city plan commission of nine members is given power to pass upon the acceptance of all plats of land within and for a distance of three miles beyond the city limits. Under authority of Act 360 of Public Acts of 1925, the city council adopted a master plan proposed by the planning and rapid transit commissions in collaboration with the governing boards of the contiguous counties and municipalities which include lands affected thereby. The plaintiff sought to have recorded a plat of eighty acres, on the north side of which the master plan called for a street of the width of 86 feet, and on the east side one of 120 feet. By plat the plaintiff proposed to dedicate to the use of each of these streets only thirty feet, which apparently had been the amount given by the owners of the opposite lands, whose plats, however, had been accepted prior to 1925. The commission refused to accept registration of this plat unless on the north avenue the plaintiff would adopt a ten-foot building line restriction and on the east side dedicate forty-seven feet. The plaintiff refused to comply with these conditions and, from a denial of a writ of mandamus to compel acceptance of his plat, carried the case to the highest court of the state. In affirming the action of the circuit judge, the supreme court thus disposes of the plaintiff's contentions:

The error in plaintiff's position is the assumption that, in requiring an additional dedication and the establishment of a building line to conform to its general plan, the city is exercising power of eminent domain. Its argument would have merit, and the authorities cited would have application, if this were a case where the plat had been recorded and the city were undertaking to widen the streets or to establish a building line. But this is not such a case. Here the city is not trying to compel a dedication. It cannot compel the plaintiff to subdivide its property or to dedicate any part of it for streets. It can, however, impose any reasonable condition which must be complied with before the subdivision is accepted for record. In theory at least, the owner of a subdivision voluntarily dedicates sufficient land for streets in return for the advantage and privilege of having his plat recorded. Unless he does so, the law gives him no right to have it recorded.

So obviously consonant with fundamental principles is the court's position that it deems it necessary to cite but one precedent, that of *Ross* v. *United States, ex rel. Goodfellow,* 7 App. D. C. 1, upholding the validity of a similar statute applicable to the District of Columbia.[1] From the opinion in this latter case the court quotes the following:

It must be remembered that each owner has the undoubted right to lay off his land in any manner that he pleases, or not to subdivide it at all. He cannot be made to dedicate streets and avenues to the public. If public necessity demands parts of his land for highways, it can be taken only by condemnation and payment of its value. But he has no corresponding right to have his plat of subdivision so made admitted to the records.

In providing for public record Congress can accompany the privilege with conditions and limitations applicable alike to all persons. In providing for such record in the Act of 1888 (25 Stat. 451), Congress sought to subserve the public interest and convenience by requiring practical conformity in all subdivisions of land into squares, streets, and avenues, with the general plan of the city as originally established, and this regardless of the fact that it might, in instances, practically coerce the dedication of streets to public use which would otherwise have to be paid for.

It may be worth while to point out the bearing of the instant case on the much mooted question of the basis of the sanctions to be applied to attain an effective control of outlying lands, which is so essential to the success of the city plan. The preparation of the model Enabling Act by the department of commerce has brought to the front the advocates of two different meth-

---

[1] The constitutionality of this act was unanimously upheld by the Supreme Court in *Bauman* v. *Ross*, 167 U. S. 548.

ods of attaining such control, the one by the exercise of the power of eminent domain, the other by the exercise of the police power, using that term in its narrow modern signification. The first method involves the unique proposal of a present condemnation of any right the landowner might have in the future to have his property condemned if taken for streets designated on the master plan; the second method proposes to take from the landowner by the exercise of the police power any right he would otherwise have to compensation upon later condemnation in so far as the damages might be based upon any improvements made by him in the platted streets after the publication of the master plan.[1] Both methods are admitted to be experimental; against the first may be urged the doubt of its predicability, against the second may be raised the serious question of its constitutionality. But so ably and so persistently were these two methods presented by their advocates that the committee has been driven to incorporate in its tentative draft both as alternative plans and to dismiss without a personal hearing the modest suggestion that a full and adequate method, which has borne the test of long practical application, and has run successfully the gamut of attack before the courts, might be found in the comparatively simple expedient of controlling the owner's privilege of dedicating his lands for street purposes.

It is this last method that is now so fully vindicated by the Michigan courts. The conditions that may be attached as precedent to the right to have a subdivision platted and recorded may include as binding on the property the acceptance of any regulations as to building lines, area or use as have been sustained under the police power by the courts of the given state or by the Supreme Court. There seems to be no question that the state may require a statutory dedication for all subdivisions and may prohibit the sale of lots with reference to "streets" or "avenues" or other terms indicative of a public highway, unless platted and recorded according to the requirements of the city plan. It is submitted that the adoption of a method of control similar to that of Detroit and of the District of Columbia would accomplish every desirable end, would avoid the legal pitfalls of untried legislation and fortify the city plan with a sanction making it completely effective in the outlying districts

[1] See the tentative draft of the proposed act issued February 1927, pp. 418–64.

which will become so important a part of the city of the future. It may be added that neither of the methods proposed by the department of commerce is adapted to the control of outlying lands in states which like Washington have constitutional limitations precluding the municipalities from exercising any governmental powers whatsoever beyond their borders.[2]

✦

Streets and Highways—Abutter's Right to Continuance of Sidewalk.—The recognition of the extent of the rights in streets vested in owners of abutting property has been marked in numerous cases within the past two years. We noted last month that one of the appellate courts of New York recently held that such an owner has a right to the maintenance of a street number assigned to his property by the city. The Supreme Court of Oklahoma in *Tulsa* v. *Hindman*, 261 Pac. 910, sustains an award of damages to the owner of abutting property who has suffered by the cutting down of the width of a sidewalk made necessary by the widening of the pavement for vehicular traffic. So dense had the traffic become that the street in question was ordered paved its entire width of fifty-six feet, which brought it within a foot and a half of one of the plaintiff's buildings.

The court bases its decision partly upon the local constitutional provision for damages for any permanent injury to property, but mainly upon the broad doctrine that the old common law of highways is archaic, being based "upon a European or Asiatic custom." As emphasizing the necessity of sidewalks under the modern conditions, the court says:

According to the actions and proceedings of the various chambers of commerce, civic clubs, safety councils and efforts of the newspapers and metropolitan journals, the thoughts and efforts of serious men are directed at means of providing additional facilities for pedestrian traffic instead of abolishing what the people already have. Sidewalks are not only being retained, but footroads, over and under many streets, are being proposed and established. Several cities have already built many of these footways, primarily for the use of children going to and from school. If we are correctly informed, at least one city in Oklahoma is launching the same enterprise.

Upon this reasoning the court discards the authority of several comparatively recent cases, pointing out that their *rationes decidendi* can be traced back to an ancient North Carolina case (*Hester* v. *Durham Traction Co.*, 170 N. C. 24,

[2] *Brown* v. *City of Cle Elum*, 261 Pac. 112.

86 S. E. 792), decided in 1904, before modern conditions arose. While the opinion, thus, does not fully satisfy the requirement of legal thinking laid down by either the historical or analytical schools of jurisprudence, the broad principle it enunciates was adopted by unanimous court and is now the law of a great state. It is indicative of a palpable effort evinced by some courts to conform the legal structure to new social conditions, which, if it progresses as rapidly as in the past decade, will profoundly modify the present law of municipal corporations.

✸

Streets and Highways—State Control of Traffic Supersedes Local Regulations.—The question of the effect of the enactment of general statutes regulating traffic on all public highways upon the power of municipalities to regulate vehicles on their streets by ordinance is of peculiar difficulty in those states which give to their municipalities by constitutional mandate the power to adopt and amend their own charters. The solution of this question by the courts of California has proven the most practical ever yet worked out, and may well be taken as a model by other states confronted with the same problem. In the leading case of *Ex parte Daniels* (1920), 183 Cal. 636, 142 Pac. 442, in which the opinion was written by Chief Justice Curtis D. Wilbur, the principle was established that so far as the state by general statute assumes to regulate traffic on the public highways, the local power *pro tanto* falls into abeyance, but so far as the entire field is not thus covered, the municipalities may continue to regulate their intramural traffic.

In *Atlas Mixed Mortar Co.* v. *City of Burbank*, 262 Pac. 334, decided by the Supreme Court of California, December 16, the practical value of this rule was again demonstrated. The plaintiff's business required it to carry heavy truck loads of material from its quarries through the streets of the defendant on the way to its market in Los Angeles. The defendant passed an ordinance to limit the weight of loaded trucks using certain designated streets over which the plaintiff had to operate to 6,000 pounds in some instances and to 8,000 pounds in others. In the action to enjoin the enforcement of the ordinance the city attacked the constitutionality of the Motor Vehicle Act, which permits a weight of loads on improved highways up to seventeen tons, on the ground that it attempted to control city streets not recognized as state highways. In granting the plaintiff relief and declaring the ordinance void, the court bases its decision upon the principles of *Ex parte Daniels*, that all public highways are primarily state highways and that home rule cities may regulate their use only to the extent that the state's legislature has failed to cover the subject.[1]

✸

Taxicabs—Extent of Control by City Authorities.—In *Morley* v. *Wilson, Police Commissioner of Boston*, 159 N. E. 41, the Supreme Judicial Court of Massachusetts upholds the plenary power of the city to regulate vehicles plying for hire on the public streets. The action was a bill in equity to restrain the defendant from revoking the petitioners' licenses for their failure to comply with the rules promulgated by the police commissioner upon whom the statute confers the power to establish and enforce all needful regulations. The immediate question arose over the defendant's designation of taxi stands and their allocation. The plaintiffs complained that in assigning them to certain unprofitable stands and revoking their licenses for non-compliance, the commissioner was exceeding his powers and depriving them of their livelihood.

The court in an opinion by Sanderson, J., sustained the demurrer to the petitioners' bill, holding that the use of the public streets for commercial carriage is a privilege and not a right, that its exercise is subject to reasonable control, which includes the power to require licenses of those who wish to engage in such business. The holder of such a license, the court says, cannot complain of limitations attaching to the privilege which he sought and accepted. The designation of stands for traffic not only serves the convenience of the public, but aids in the enforcement of the regulations and the prevention of crime. The refusal of the plaintiffs to occupy the special stands assigned them was reasonable ground for the suspension of their licenses. To the commissioner under the law has been delegated the sole responsibility of deciding what the public interest requires and his conclusion on matters of fact within his jurisdiction cannot be controverted in the absence of bad faith. The legislature having constituted him the tribunal to determine these facts, instead of a court or jury, his decisions on questions of fact relating to

[1] An extended note on this general subject was published in the April, 1926 issue of the REVIEW.

the issuing of licenses and regulations affecting the transportation of passengers for hire upon the public streets must be accepted as final.

*

Zoning—Regulations Prescribing Minimum Height.—In *Brown* v. *Board of Appeals of Springfield*, 159 N. E. 225, the Supreme Court of Illinois held invalid the clause of the general zoning act of the city prescribing a minimum height limitation of forty feet for all buildings to be erected in a district zoned for business purposes. The clause in question limited the height of future buildings to forty feet on the frontage line and for an extent of at least 30 per cent of ground floor area and further provided that no existing building of the prescribed height or higher should thereafter be so altered or repaired as to bring it below the height requirement. The petitioner whose building had been destroyed by fire was refused a permit to erect a one-story building on the lot upon the sole ground that the plan did not conform to the height requirements.

On appeal from a judgment on his application for a writ of certiorari to review the decision of the zoning board of appeals, the court held that the state zoning act did not authorize the minimum height regulation, as it was not based upon the conservation of the public health, safety, comfort, morals or welfare of the community. Upon the point urged by the city that the beauty of the city would be enhanced by compliance with such a requirement, the court merely stated that the promotion or protection of a refined aesthetic taste was not among the purposes enumerated. To the argument that the provision would tend to conserve the taxable value of lands and buildings throughout the city, the answer was given no improvement of property could be held to violate this purpose. For a similar decision, holding that a minimum height provision cannot be sustained in any event unless the authority is specifically delegated to the city, see *Dorison* v. *Saul*, 98 N. J. Law, 112, 118 Atl. 691. It is obvious that the consideration of the promotion of the safety and health of the community which support the imposition of maximum height restrictions, has no application to a minimum height requirement.

Zoning—Exclusion of Industrial Signs in Residence Districts.—In the *Appeal of Liggett*, 189 Atl. 619, the question of the provision of the Pittsburgh zoning ordinance excluding commercial signs from residence districts was before the Supreme Court of Pennsylvania. Under a permit expressly limited to one year, Liggett, the owner of the property in question and his lessee, the Alpha Company, were authorized to erect a large electric sign to advertise a well-known automobile. At the end of the year, in compliance with the ordinance, a renewal of the permit was refused and the sign ordered removed. The enabling statute *inter alia* gives the city the power "to regulate and restrict the location of trades and industries" and under this power the city justified the provision of the ordinance excluding signs of this character from residence districts.

In an able opinion by Moschzisker, C. J., the court sustained the position of the city authorities. Under the facts it appeared that the Alpha Company owned and operated the sign for commercial purposes, clearly a "trade or industry" within the statutory designation. The court distinguishes *Bryan* v. *City of Chester*, 212 Pa. 259, 61 Atl. 894, decided in 1905, in which an ordinance excluding all signs from the city was held beyond the delegated power by reference to the fact that it was based upon purely aesthetic considerations and at a time prior to the enactment of zoning legislation. The court finds the present ordinance well within the police power and not vitiated by the fact that incidentally some consideration of beauty may have prompted its adoption.

*

Police Power—Vested Right of a Property Owner in a Street Number.—On February 14, the Court of Appeals of New York handed down a decision in the case of *Bacon* v. *Miller*, 225 N. Y. S. 99, in which the Appellate Division, First Department, had held that the plaintiff had a vested right in a street number, of which she could not be deprived by the city. The decision is in accord with fundamental principles, which, however, it seems necessary for the higher courts from time to time to affirm.

PUBLIC UTILITIES

EDITED BY JOHN BAUER,

Director, American Public Utilities Bureau

New Transit Complications in New York.— The transit situation in the city of New York has been a thrilling "movie" during the past six months, with unexpected developments in the plot to keep the spectators interested and gasping.

In the December number of the REVIEW we presented in a separate article the situation as it stood at the time of that writing. There were then before the city two alternative general plans. One was sponsored primarily by Mr. Samuel Untermyer, in his report to the Transit Commission, and centered upon the idea that the city will recapture the existing subways under the terms of its contracts with the present lessee companies, with provisions, however, for the purchase of the remaining subway lines, also the elevated lines, if obtainable at a reasonable price. It recommended the institution of a special board to operate the properties under city control, with representation on the part of certain civic organizations.

The second was the so-called Smith plan, presented in a special report to the controller, Hon. Charles E. Berry, who had not been in agreement with the general recapture program. This plan contemplated the consolidation of all the rapid transit as well as surface lines and other forms of transportation. The consolidation would be brought about through negotiations between the companies and the city. It was assumed that there would be no insuperable difficulties in coming to an equitable agreement either as to valuations, return, mode of control, or other matters inevitably encountered.

It had been accepted that the city administration, as represented by the board of estimate and apportionment, was generally in favor of the Untermyer recapture plan, although it did not agree, perhaps, to all his recommendations. It appeared, however, that the controller would be unalterably opposed to this program because it would result, he believed, in the splitting up of the transit facilities into several groups, instead of providing a unified system, with thoroughly coördinated operation. The Untermyer plan definitely proposed the continuance of the five-cent fare, while the controller seemed convinced that a five-cent fare would be inadequate to furnish proper transportation, especially so far as the construction and operation of the much needed new subways are concerned.

The first dramatic development was the capitulation of the controller. After receiving the Smith report, the controller appointed an advisory committee of leading business men, and with their assistance made a further study of the facts and issues. During January he made public his new point of view, virtually repudiating the Smith plan, agreeing to the continuance of the five-cent fare fixed by the city contracts, and practically placing himself in harmony with his colleagues on the board of estimate and apportionment.

The next dramatic occurrence was the wholly unexpected move on the part of the Interborough Rapid Transit Company, which operates a large part of the city subways under the so-called Contract No. 3; it filed a new seven-cent fare tariff applicable both to the subways and to the elevated system, and petitioned the Transit Commission for permission to put the new tariff into effect at five days' notice. Without such permission, the new tariff would go into effect on March 3, 1928, unless suspended by the commission, or the Interborough be prevented, by injunction or otherwise, by the courts from putting into effect the higher fare.

The Interborough has hurled a bold challenge at the city and the Transit Commission. So far as the subways are concerned, the rate of fare is fixed at five cents by Contract No. 3. This covers also all matters of construction, contribution to investment, provisions for operation, and the returns allowed to the company and the city. The five-cent fare is, thus, a part of numerous interrelated financial terms. The subways, themselves, belong outright to the city, and are leased to the Interborough through the instrumentality of the contract, which, with the other conditions, fixes definitely the five-cent fare. The city has the right to recapture certain of the lines operated under the contract, after giving one year's notice, and paying the company for its investment as determined under the provisions of the contract.

At this writing, two court actions have been set in motion: one by the Interborough, the other by the city and the Transit Commission. Without waiting for a decision of the commission, the company asked a federal court to declare the five-cent fare confiscatory. This move was countered by the city and commission by obtaining from a state supreme court judge injunctions restraining the Interborough from charging a higher fare. What the net outcome of this double-header will be, is uncertain.

The city will, of course, stand squarely upon its contractual rights that the company cannot charge more than five cents. So long as the contract continues, the five-cent fare is held to be a positive duty upon the company, and cannot be altered either by the Transit Commission or by the courts. This is viewed not as a matter of ordinary regulation coming within the general provisions of fixing rates under the regulatory statutes, but is solely a matter of contract in respect to the operation of property owned by the city and leased under specific terms to the company, including the five-cent fare. This is wholly a proprietary, and not a regulatory matter coming within jurisdiction of the rate-making authority of the state or within the constitutional provisions under which the company may attempt to get relief.

All this promises a real fight of the first magnitude—one which, with different personalities, might well be staged by "Tex" Rickard at the Yankee Stadium. The Interborough has engaged special counsel, Mr. William L. Ransom, who conducted successfully the fight against the 80 cents and $1.00 gas rates before the Supreme Court of the United States. The company thus appears in earnest, and is doubtless prepared to carry the issue to ultimate conclusion, although there is the belief that it is merely "stalling" for time against recapture and improvements ordered by the commission. On the part of the city, there can be no doubt that the fight will go to the limit. It will never release the company from its contractual obligation, without a final ruling from the highest tribunal of the land.

From a lay standpoint, it is rather difficult to see how the Interborough expects to escape its contractual obligation, but this is the fighting ground for the opposing lawyers, apparently for some time to come. So far as financial facts are concerned, the company is now realizing a surplus

of about $6,000,000 a year above all fixed charges, on the subway operation. This is sufficient to pay 17 per cent in dividends on the $35,000,000 of capital stock. Its financial difficulties are not due to the subways, but to the operation of the elevated system, which is leased, not from the city of New York, but from the Manhattan Railway Co. for 999 years. This lease puts a heavy, fixed burden upon the Interborough, and has caused a huge annual deficit, which has practically consumed the surplus earned on the subways. This is, therefore, one of the fundamental issues—whether a profitable lease from the city may be altered, on any grounds, in order to furnish relief to the company because of its losses on a lease from a private company, with which the city is not concerned.

The practical outcome may very well be that the five-cent fare will be continued on the subways under the city contract, but that a higher fare may be finally authorized on the elevated system, which is not similarly tied down contractually with a five-cent fare, although there are other provisions in the various franchise documents which would seem to make a higher fare of dubious legality even on the elevated lines. But if the seven-cent fare should be allowed on the elevated system, there is the practical difficulty of charging a higher fare on an antiquated mode of transportation, rather than on the subways, which are recognized as the heart of the rapid transit system.

We shall keep closely in touch with the drama, and shall present such reports as can be made monthly.

✷

Buses and Trolleys in Newark.—To those who are interested in the relative place of trolleys and buses in city transportation, especially with a view to probable future developments, the figures supplied us by the Hon. John Howe, director of finance of Newark, are extremely interesting and illuminating. The department of finance receives a tax levied upon the revenue collected from local passengers carried in the city of Newark, under the so-called Kates law, enacted in 1916. In connection with the collection of the taxes, the city keeps statistics of the facilities employed, the number of passengers carried, and the total operating receipts. These figures are stated by years for 1916 to 1927, inclusive.

In 1916 the jitneys were already on the ground with 161 cars operating in the city, carrying a total of 2,661,000 passengers. During the eleven years ending with 1927, the number of cars increased to 458, with a tremendous transformation in the character of the car. The number of passengers increased to 124,248,000 in 1927.

The department has compiled corresponding figures for the street railway traffic within the city. There were a number of changes during the period in rates and methods of fare collection, so that the number of passengers as reported is not strictly comparable throughout the period. The change in fare also affected the volume of traffic. Since 1924, however, there has been a straight five-cent fare, both on the trolleys and on the buses, so that a comparison since that year may be validly made. During this period, moreover, the same company which controls the street railways has acquired substantial control of the buses, for the purpose of eliminating injurious competition with the former. The number of passengers carried each year by each mode of transportation is as follows:

	Trolleys	Buses
1924	164,277,000	93,295,000
1925	163,039,000	103,062,000
1926	161,086,000	112,887,000
1927	151,982,000	124,248,000

During the period there was a decrease each year in the number of street railway passengers. The decrease, moreover, has been at an accumulative rate, and was particularly striking in 1927, when the buses came most completely under the same control as the street railways. In contrast, during the same period there was a rapid increase in bus traffic, equal to over 10,000,000 passengers a year. During the period of three years, the railway traffic decreased 12,295,000, or 8 per cent, while the bus traffic increased 30,952,000, or 33 per cent. In 1924 the bus traffic constituted 27.5 per cent of the total number of passengers carried by the two modes of operation, while in 1927 it constituted 45 per cent; and the greatest change came during 1927, when, presumably, the trolley interests were concerned largely in preserving the street railway business.

What may be reasonably expected for the future, as better and better types of buses become available for general use? In the past, the type of bus equipment used in Newark was not particularly alluring. During 1927, however, a considerable number of new buses were made available, and this may be responsible in part for the large shift of traffic from the street railway. But bus developments are not at an end.

Much superior types are now available than those installed in 1926 and 1927. The prophecy is unavoidable that each year the greater proportion of traffic will be carried by buses, notwithstanding all effort on the part of the companies to "coördinate" or, frankly, to hold back bus developments for the purpose of conserving the street railway investments. This presents an economic situation with which city officials and street railway managements must inevitably cope.

✦

Cleveland Water Supply and Rates.—The director of public utilities of the city of Cleveland, Mr. Howell Wright, under date of January 1, 1928, made a special report to the utilities committee of the city council in regard to the department of water supply. This department constitutes a city-owned and operated utility, and is required to be financially self-sustaining. The city bonds issued for water supply and all waterworks funds may be used only for water-works purposes. The department supplies water not only for the city of Cleveland, but for a large number of suburban municipalities.

The revenues collected under the rates fixed by the city council have not been sufficient to pay all the operating expenses, maintenance, renewals, and to provide adequately for the extension of needed facilities for the future. Mr. Wright places the problem squarely before the council to determine whether a program of expansion shall be adopted to make adequate provisions for the city of Cleveland and the suburban sections, or whether a stationary course shall be pursued. In either case, however, he points out the necessity of revising the business methods and general policies. He shows particularly that the department is required to furnish large amounts of free water to the public, parochial and private schools, hospitals, charitable institutions, public buildings and cemeteries, besides the free water used for street cleaning and fire protection.

Mr. Wright proposes that affirmative measures shall be taken promptly to require these various agencies as well as other city departments to pay for the cost of the water supplied, and thus enable the department better to meet its obligations as a self-sustaining utility. He urges also the modernization in methods of billing, collecting and imposing penalties for delay in paying bills along lines generally adopted by privately-operated utilities. These are immediate measures of relief available, pending the more complete determination and analysis of cost, on the basis of which a new system of rates may be installed. The chief task with which the director has been concerned during the past two years has been to put the department of water supply upon a business basis, to provide for needed expansion and to make the utility self-sustaining through a scientifically fixed system of service and rates.

✤

Consolidations at Reproduction Cost.—The question of "fair value" is important, not only in direct rate cases, but also in the consolidation of properties, especially in the development of the holding company systems. We have before us an illustrative case from one of the leading state commissions that involves the consolidation of several properties. That substantial economies would be achieved and a decrease in the ordinary range of operating expenses realized, there could be no doubt, and the combination was approved by the commission because of the expected economies. On the side of the purchase price, however, the combination provided for the issuance new securities equal to about two and one-half times the amount previously outstanding. This

was based upon the estimated reproduction cost at the time the valuation was made, as compared with prices at the time when the original securities were issued.

While this general basis of consolidation may be justified on the basis of "fair value" as considered by the Supreme Court, one cannot help inquiring what will happen in ten years, or twenty, when another cycle of development has occurred, and when the then-reproduction cost may be much less, or if indeed one would reproduce such properties at all. When the new securities have been issued in the amount of two and one-half to one, and when they have been generally distributed among investors and are identified with the financial stability of the business, how thereafter can the "fair value" ever be reduced without affecting injuriously the business and service? It is this aspect of the reproduction cost valuation which has entered into the numerous consolidations, and which is particularly disconcerting, so far as the future of rate making is concerned. There is also the immediate question, whether the high valuations will not prevent, to a large extent, the realization of the economies of operation by the ordinary consumers through a reduction in rates.

GOVERNMENTAL RESEARCH ASSOCIATION NOTES

EDITED BY RUSSELL FORBES

Secretary

Buffalo Municipal Research Bureau, Inc.— The Bureau is completing two reports in its general survey of Buffalo's financial practices and procedures: one dealing with special assessments and the other with municipal revenues. Other assignments under way at present or contemplated for the near future are a survey of the health department, survey of all salaries and positions, and a report on Buffalo's paving policy.

Buffalo's new charter became effective January 1, and about two weeks prior to that date the trustees of the Bureau entertained members of the new council at a dinner, where the Bureau's aims and purposes were fully explained.

Municipal Research Bulletin, No. 7, on *Concrete Streets* attracted marked attention both locally and nationally. Eighty thousand reprints were ordered by the Portland Cement Association for their own use.

✤

California Taxpayers' Association.—The California Taxpayers' Association, on behalf of and at the request of the Los Angeles city local committee, is doing work in connection with the proposed $25,000,000 San Gabriel dam, which is somewhat different from the usual work of research organizations.

It is in the nature of a follow-up of previous study and recommendations and comes in the form of court action to restrain three members of the county board of supervisors, acting as a county flood control board, from proceeding to construct a flood control dam 425 feet in height, after an impartial board of eminent engineers had recommended that a dam 385 feet in height was as large as was justified economically. The difference in cost between the high dam and the lower dam is estimated to be about $6,000,000 in principal and almost an equal sum in interest.

✤

Municipal Research Bureau of Cleveland.—The Bureau is making a study of the cost of government for the major jurisdictions within Cuyahoga county covering the past five years. The units concerned are the county government, the city of Cleveland, the Cleveland school district, the metropolitan park board and the public library system.

Also—and of more importance—a study is being made of the capital improvement needs of these governments for a future fifteen-year period. This involves a selection of the projects that will be necessary or highly desirable, an estimate of their probable cost, a priority schedule, and a statement of the methods of financing them.

The whole study is sponsored by public officials and by a large group of civic, business and local improvement associations. Among these are such organizations as the Chamber of Commerce, the Chamber of Industry, the Real Estate Board, the Building Owners' and Managers' Association and the Institute of Architects. The Euclid Avenue Association made the original request for the study, and has been highly instrumental in furthering the project.

✤

Citizen Interest in Regional Government.— Recently there has developed in Cleveland and Cuyahoga county a strong and persistent interest in the problem of metropolitan or regional government. The mayor of Cleveland, John D. Marshall, took the initiative in crystallizing his interest by the appointment of a committee of 400 representative citizens of the various governmental units within the country. This is known as the Citizens' Regional Government Committee. This has been divided into several important sub-committees. Among these is a fact-finding and policy committee charged with conducting the necessary research work and evolving a definite course of procedure and governmental plan. Leyton E. Carter, director of the Municipal Research Bureau of Cleveland, has been made secretary of this committee. Also the Bureau has been requested to afford its facilities as far as possible to this committee, which request the Bureau's directors enthusiastically granted. It is confidently hoped that

Cleveland and the large number of neighboring communities are embarked upon a journey which will lead to some form of workable metropolitan or regional government.

❖

Citizens' Research Institute of Canada.—A study has been made of the effect of changes in the Dominion income tax act since 1925. While such changes in rates have in the main been downward, the effect of reductions was complicated to some extent by the fact that "dividends" hitherto exempt from normal taxation were made subject to taxation. The study showed that persons who received a fairly high share of their income from dividends up to $76,000 are really paying a greater income tax under the new and presumably lower rates than they were under the rates existing in 1925. This report in pamphlet form will be issued shortly.

A study is being made of the cost of government in some of the smaller Canadian cities along the lines of the study already completed for larger and representative cities of each province. Such studies are made with the idea of showing the trend of municipal costs and with the ultimate hope of producing some index of proportionate cost of existing services over a period of time.

❖

Taxpayers' Research League of Delaware.— The Taxpayers' Research League of Delaware is continuing its studies of state finances in the preparation of material for a state finance code, which it will formulate in collaboration with a committee of the Delaware Bankers' Association. The work during the past month has dealt particularly with a further analysis of the condition of the state sinking fund and the relative advantages of alternate proposals for absorbing the surplus. The League's actuarial calculations disclosed the fact that at the end of the last fiscal year, June 30, 1927, the surplus in the sinking fund amounted to $1,342,292, and that this, with additional surpluses from the release of reserves for bonds that may be cancelled, will permit the cancellation of $1,404,000 of state highway bonds owned by the sinking funds. The League's calculations show that the cancellation of these bonds will save to the highway fund $3,401,162 in the next 39 years, and that the saving will amount to $94,105 in each of 32 of these years.

The League has also completed an analysis of the operative costs of the Delaware Industrial School for Girls for the first six months of the current fiscal year.

The League has completed a study of the number and salaries of public employes of New Castle county and of the incorporated cities and towns therein.

As the result of agitation among various civic groups for the establishment of public rest rooms in Wilmington and Newark, the League has undertaken, on request, a study of the extent, equipment, financing, and results of public rest rooms in other cities.

The League has been requested by a member of the grand jury to prepare a report on the office of coroner and the progress that has been made elsewhere in the reformation or replacement of this office.

The League has coöperated with the public affairs committee of the Wilmington Kiwanis Club in the preparation and execution of a plan to secure the registration of all potential voters in the immediate families of Kiwanians. When the canvass of the Kiwanis Club has been finished, the public affairs committee, with the coöperation of the League, intends to suggest that all other service and civic clubs in Delaware follow the same plan.

In consequence of the confusion caused by the provisions of the state income tax law in the exemption of certain dividends in order to avoid double taxation, the League has prepared a memorandum on the treatment of this subject in other states imposing income tax.

❖

Des Moines Bureau of Municipal Research.— At the request of the park commissioner and several civic organizations, the Bureau is preparing a report on the future operation and development of the local airport. The city of Des Moines now has 160 acres under a five-year lease, and the United States Government gave the city its air mail lighting equipment. The municipality is faced with the problem of how to finance further development and to lease tracts and concessions to private air operators.

A report is also being prepared relative to the possibility of installing photographic equipment in the county recorder's office. Based on the experience of a number of large local insurance companies which use this equipment, it is estimated that the recorder's office expense can be cut nearly 50 per cent.

Taxpayers' League of St. Louis County, Inc. (Duluth).—The report prepared by C. E. Rightor of the Detroit Bureau of Governmental Research on the water and light department of the city was studied, and, after certain minor changes, the revised draft has been approved by the author. Certain phases of the report are especially important in connection with the controversy relative to gas rates.

A bulletin was prepared relative to the county tax levy; but on the advice of certain county officials it was deemed advisable to postpone the publication pending the county board's action on the proposed reorganization. It has become apparent that the county board is considering a creditable plan of reorganizing, following in many respects the recommendations made in the report of the Taxpayers' League prepared by C. E. Rightor.

Adoption by the county commissioners of a plan for unified administration of county roads, and the installation of an effective accounting procedure for all highway expenditures, marks one of the League's most important achievements. Since early in 1927 the League has continually pointed out the lack of system and the great waste in road administration. It cannot be denied that this criticism is the real reason for the action by the county commissioners. It is quite possible that this new system will result in a greater actual saving to the taxpayers than any other piece of work that the Taxpayers' League has ever performed. It is true that the League evidenced but little concern in the adoption of the final resolution, and that much credit must be given to other forces for securing the necessary number of votes; but all of this would have been impossible had it not been for the early work of the League.

The report on financing the major street improvement program was completed and published. The civic council has given the report considerable study, and the newspapers have given it much space. The report has also been submitted to other civic groups.

The League assisted in the prosecution of the criminal action charged by the grand jury against John Gronros of the sixth commissioner district.

✣

Bureau of Municipal Research and Information, University of Florida.—Dr. W. W. Hollingsworth, director of the Bureau, died on January 2. Angus Laird has been appointed acting director.

Bureau for Research in Government, University of Minnesota.—An outline of county government in Minnesota will be off the press within the next thirty days. This will be a volume of about 175 pages, in which will be considered briefly the historical development, legal position and organization, and major activities of the counties in Minnesota.

The system of classification used jointly by the Bureau for Research in Government and the Municipal Reference Bureau of the University will also be published within the next two months. In addition to the classification there will be a very complete subject index.

The Bureau has recently undertaken a study of the administrative standards of American cities. This is not an attempt to measure *results* of administration, but rather an effort to determine the standards which cities have set for themselves. For example, does the city think public health sufficiently important to provide a full-time trained medical health officer? Has it provided a full-time purchasing officer? Has it established women police? Has it a recreational director devoting full time to the planning and directing of recreation work? Many other similar questions have been framed, and the data are now being collected. Reports upon results will be given at a later date. The results should, among other things, point the way toward a better definition of the needs of the big city as contrasted with the small town. They should also give some indication of the order in which cities tend to make certain administrative provisions.

✣

New Bedford (Mass.) Taxpayers' Association.—The mayor of New Bedford has sixty days after the first of January to submit his budget to the city council. In the past, it has been customary to delay the budget until the end of this sixty-day period. This year the mayor is going to submit his budget earlier. It has been customary in the past for the departments to send their estimates to the mayor in various degrees of details. Some departments would simply ask for a lump sum and others would give considerable detail.

The New Bedford Taxpayers' Association is urging upon the mayor the use of detailed uniform estimate blanks for this purpose, and the mayor is asking his departments to use these new blank forms. It is hoped that all departmental estimates will be in such detail that the mayor, city council and the taxpayer can more completely understand the cost of the various services that the city proposes to render for the coming year.

The Taxpayers' Association is also trying to impress upon the city government that the budget itself should be in detail, but that the appropriations may be made without as much detail as the budget. In the past, the budget and the appropriation bill have been considered as the same document. On account of the established bookkeeping system in the city, it will probably be necessary to continue lump sum departmental appropriations, but these should be based upon the fullest information.

✣

New Mexico Taxpayers' Association.—The Association has started a campaign to secure adoption by the state of the model bond law proposed by the National Municipal League.

✣

St. Louis Bureau of Municipal Research.— Considerable discussion has been given to the need for increasing the tax rate for municipal purposes in St. Louis. For several years expenditures for the maintenance and operation of municipal departments have been lower per capita than in other large cities. A local newspaper, in a series of editorials, asserts that the low per capita tax is an obstacle to the growth of the city and that the city is without financial means to make a modern metropolis what it should be to hold its rank.

The constitution of the state of Missouri provides that the city may levy for municipal purposes, exclusive of schools and debt purposes, a tax rate not to exceed $1.35 on each $100 of assessed valuation. The maximum rate permissible under the constitution has been levied during the past three years.

In 1921 a bill was passed by the state legislature which would further restrict the taxing powers of the city government. That law provides that the board of aldermen shall not have power to levy a tax which will produce more than 10 per cent in excess of the taxes levied for the previous year. The rate of increase in the tax levy during the past eight years has averaged approximately 7 per cent per year. To obtain any further substantial increase in tax revenues it would be necessary to amend the constitution and to repeal the law passed in 1921.

The Bureau of Municipal Research is endeavoring to ascertain whether there is a real need for increasing the tax rate. This involves a study of the purposes for which funds have been expended during a period of years and projecting into the future probable requirements for functions performed in the past as well as the requirements for improvements being provided through the bond issue. Comparisons are being made with other cities as far as possible and due weight is given to the operating efficiency of city departments.

✣

Schenectady Bureau of Municipal Research.— A Bureau of Municipal Research has been established in Schenectady, N. Y. Joseph F. Base, formerly a staff member of the St. Louis County Taxpayers' League, took office as director on March 1.

✣

Toledo Commission of Publicity and Efficiency.—Virgil Sheppard, former secretary of the commission, has resigned to accept a position as secretary to Mayor William T. Jackson.

J. O. Garber, formerly assistant professor of political science at the University of Toledo, was appointed as his successor, and took office February 1, 1928. Mr. Garber is a graduate of Michigan, having received the degree of M.A. in municipal administration.

The commission will probably soon have ready a report on purchasing which was prepared last year. A report on street cleaning is also being considered.

✣

Toronto Bureau of Municipal Research.—The Bureau is continuing its independent study of municipal police service. Information has been collected from various cities in Great Britain, the United States and Canada as to the size of force in its various branches, qualifications for admission to force, training, promotion, hours of work and pension systems. One report dealing with occurrences of a serious nature in Toronto, divided in groups, and the size of the police force from 1913 to 1926 inclusive has been issued, and it is intended to follow this with other reports dealing with certain British, United States and Canadian cities.

The Bureau issued a report which pointed out that some of the election cries which had been raised in recent years by candidates, however important the subjects might be, were really without the scope of municipal government, and that from the standpoint of the saving which could be made for the taxpayer, real municipal business was much more important.

NOTES AND EVENTS

EDITED BY H. W. DODDS

Professor Munro Challenged on Slacker Vote.
To the Editor of the National Municipal Review:
—Discussing in the February REVIEW, the question "Is the Slacker Vote a Menace," Prof. William B. Munro of Cambridge, Mass., mentions "a delegate from one of the Detroit civic organizations," who, at the New York conference of the National Municipal League, interposed objections to Professor Munro's analysis and conclusions.

As the delegate referred to, after reading Professor Munro's article, including the page which he devotes to an attempted reply to my remarks, with a citation from the experience of Detroit, I am compelled to reiterate my objection to Professor Munro's entire treatment of the subject and to repeat what I said in New York: his conclusions are to be respected as the opinions of a competent student in this field, but they are only opinions.

The citations from Detroit unfortunately are taken from figures affecting only one election— that of last November; whereas the experience of the writer in observing Detroit elections, with intimate contacts in all parts of the city, has covered more than eleven years of continuous activity in this area, in addition to previous years of similar local study, though not consecutively made.

If the city of Detroit alone proves anything, it proves that during the past decade the barometer of good government has responded more sensitively to the size of the total vote cast at each primary and election than to any other single factor which may be observed. To develop this thesis with facts and analysis would require several pages of the REVIEW, and I forbear. I am satisfied to call attention again, as I did in New York, to Professor Munro's admission as embodied in the following paragraph of his article:

True enough, these various studies and illustrations cover only a few spots in a vast country. One cannot safely generalize from them.

I am amazed that Professor Munro, or any other similar authority who assumes to use the scientific method, should attempt to answer such a serious question as that concerning non-voting with such a limited "survey" of conditions as he himself admits he has made. In the absence of anything like adequate data from any considerable number of areas on the national map, no doubt many students of the problem besides myself, must refuse to be convinced, even by Professor Munro's confident statement, that the slacker vote is not a menace to America.

W. P. LOVETT.

✦

New Effort to Repeal Cleveland Charter.— Harry L. Davis, who led the attack upon the Cleveland manager-P. R. charter last November, has again filed petitions calling for an election in April on another charter amendment, new in form but substantially the same as the one already voted upon. The new draft calls for a return to the mayor plan, but would postpone the election for mayor until November, 1929. This would give the city manager almost two years more to serve instead of ousting him promptly as provided in the earlier proposal. Other changes over the November measure give the council final control over large contracts and boost the maximum wage clause for city employees from $2.50 to $4.50 per day.

This move on the part of Davis may mean that the Republican organization will not oppose the re-submitted charter in the April election. All the indications at present are that the defence of the present charter will have to be made solely by independent groups. The local Proportional Representation League has already taken steps to organize in opposition to the new Davis amendment, and it is probable that other groups will take the field in the near future. The strength of the Davis forces as shown in the last election, the heavy expense of another campaign and the desire to unite the Republican forces for the national and state campaigns are reasons why the local party leaders are loath to engage in another contest with the Davis followers. After considerable insistence on the part of labor leaders, the present administration is making refunds to employees on back pay for overtime due under the Sulzmann salary ordinance. This may mean that Davis will not get the active support of organized labor as in the last election.

179

There is no longer any indication that any counter amendment will be filed as was thought when the councilmanic committee was appointed to consider proposals to amend the present charter. This committee has been inactive, in itself a commentary on the present attitude of the Republican party leaders.

RANDOLPH O. HUUS.

✦

Relation of Business Frontage to Population.—The Du Page (Illinois) County Real Estate Board has issued a report which will be of interest to all city planners and zoners. The report recommends that a ratio of fifty feet of business frontage to each one hundred population be adopted as a standard for sub-division development throughout the country. A study of forty cities and villages in the region of Chicago was made and the ratio recommended was found to be approximated in all of them. The character of the community (whether industrial or residential) was found to have little effect on the amount of business frontage in use. It was also concluded that the size of the community makes little or no difference in the relation between population and business frontage. Generally, the greater the distance from Chicago in miles and minutes, the greater is the existing amount of business frontage per one hundred people.

✦

The Fourth International Congress of Local Officials to be held in Seville October 5–9 holds out greater promise than any which has heretofore convened. The general subjects to be considered are methods of local financial organization; public services of an industrial character; and the expropriation of land. The leading papers have been prepared in advance and will be distributed to the members of the Congress not later than June. Mr. John G. Stutz, secretary of the City Managers' Association, Law-

rence, Kansas, is organizing a party to attend the Congress and to visit a number of European cities under official patronage. Any of our readers interested in joining Mr. Stutz' party should communicate with him at once.

✦

Philadelphia Conference on City Government.—A three-day conference on city government in which thirty-one organizations are coöperating is to be held in Philadelphia March 15 to 17. A distinguished list of speakers will take part. Assessments, health control, city manager plan, economies in administration, crime prevention and city planning and zoning are among the subjects to be discussed.

The speakers include Lawson Purdy, Dr. A. R. Hatton, Dr. Leonard D. White, Dr. Louis J. Robinson and Mr. William C. Beyer. Sessions will be held at the Bellevue Stratford Hotel.

✦

Renewed Charter Activity in Newport.—The supporters of the manager plan for Newport, R. I., are again making a strenuous effort to secure the passage by the state legislature of the manager charter approved in an advisory referendum of the people by a four to one vote. This charter was rejected by the legislature at its last session and is again experiencing the active hostility of Newport politicians as well as other political leaders throughout the state.

✦

Error in Published Tax Rates.—In the "Comparative Tax Rates for 249 Cities," appearing in the REVIEW for December, 1927, the total rate for Charlotte, N. C., was entered as $11.60, with a final readjusted rate of $8.70. Attention has been called to the fact that this total omitted a county rate of $9.80, which makes the total tax rate $21.40, and the final readjusted rate $16.05.

AIRPORTS AS A FACTOR IN CITY PLANNING

By

E. P. GOODRICH

Consulting Engineer, New York

Supplement to the

NATIONAL MUNICIPAL REVIEW

March, 1928. Vol. XVII, No. 3

PUBLISHED BY

NATIONAL MUNICIPAL LEAGUE

261 Broadway, New York, N. Y.

AIRPORTS AS A FACTOR IN CITY PLANNING

BY E. P. GOODRICH

Consulting Engineer, New York

AIR transportation has become a recognized means of carriage of persons and property. A department of commerce report of July, 1927, records 864 operating air ports and airplane landing fields in the United States with about 3,000 additional unequipped emergency landing fields. Of the 864 fields, 207 are municipally provided, 163 are commercial or private ports, while 124 are department of commerce intermediate landing fields. Eighty-one landing fields are maintained by the Army and the Navy. The characteristics of air ports place them in the same general class with railroads and water carriers in that special terminal arrangement must be provided. Furthermore, air terminals are like railroad and water terminals from the fact that each must be located on favorable topography. Within certain limits, however, an air terminal does not need to be directly connected with the approach facilities. A railroad terminal must have main line tracks leading to it. A water terminal must have a water way to provide access. An air port makes use only of the air for accessibility and consequently is not so tied to topographic approach conditions. However, it must be so situated that the approach routes do not generally lead over cities, and for use by airplanes it should not be surrounded by high hills except at considerable distances with no high trees, chimneys, poles, or other structures in closer range. It is more than possible that the approach routes will some day be fully cleared so that air transport routes will traverse country so prepared that emergency airplane landings will be possible at any

point along the route, instead of only at emergency fields located perhaps five miles apart. An air terminal must usually be placed in the open country. Like terminals of other varieties, however, they should be as close as possible to the business center of the community to be served.

Croydon is about ten miles from Trafalgar Square, London, Le Bourget is seven miles from the center of Paris, while Tempelhof is three miles from the heart of Berlin. The landing fields in New Jersey and on Long Island are so far from the hotels in Manhattan that lately it took as long to motor from one of them to New York as it had taken to fly from Boston. The Cleveland municipal field is nine and a half miles from the public square (air line distance),— about thirty minutes by auto and conceivably about twelve minutes by train. That it is undesirable to locate a field any considerable distance from the business center is indicated from the report that one European city abandoned an outlying air port and created one relatively close to the center by razing several blocks of buildings.

AMPLE MEANS OF ACCESS

Like all other terminals, ample means of access must be provided for conveyances of other types between which and the air carrier transfer of passengers and property must be made. In the early days of the railroad and steamship, large crowds would gather for the arrival and departure of the carriers. In the early days of the automobile, auto race meets would draw large crowds of spectators for which provision had to be made. While air transportation is new, while air circuses are a novelty, and while the exceptional aëronaut is accomplishing unusual feats, extra facilities must be provided at air terminals for spectators, and highways, street railways and even steam railroad connections must be provided to transport the people. When Lindbergh landed at Le Bourget, the roads leading to it from Paris were congested with motors for miles. In other words, the highway approach accommodations were inadequate in that instance. Such thoroughfares should be provided from the field in as many directions as possible and sufficient in capacity to carry away all the automobiles of all the inhabitants of the surrounding territory for a radius of at least fifty miles within a period of perhaps three hours.

With one automobile for each family (there was one car for each five persons on January 1, 1928), and at a running capacity of perhaps 1,000 vehicles per lane per hour under proper policing, after assuming a factor to represent the probable percentage of vehicle owners who would wish to visit an aviation field on some special occasion, a basis is laid for a determination of the highway facilities which should be provided in a given case. (For example, assume that one quarter of Paris had desired to see Lindbergh land at Le Bourget with five persons on the average per automobile and assuming three hours as a legitimate period in which to clear the field, then the following computation gives the number of free lanes of travel which should be provided: 3,000,000 ÷ 4 = 750,000 persons who desired to visit the field; 750,000 ÷ 5 = 150,000 automobiles to be provided for; 150,000 ÷ 3 = 50,000 cars per hour to be handled; 50,000 ÷ 1,000 = 50 lanes of travel required.

Similar methods applied to the trolley transportation, using 100 persons per car and one car per minute would give the required equipment and number of tracks. (For example, assume that one half of the number in the last example had preferred to travel by trolley instead of motor: 750,000 ÷ 2 = 375,000 persons to be accommodated; 375,000 ÷ 3 = 125,000 per hour; 125,000 ÷ 100 = 1,250 car loads of passengers per hour; 1,250 ÷ 60 = 21 single tracks required.)

With steam railroad transportation a ten-car train accommodating 1,000 persons per train can be dispatched every ten minutes. (As a further example assume that one third of the people desired to travel by train: 750,000 ÷ 3 = 250,000 persons to be accommodated; 250,000 ÷ 3 = 83,000 persons per hour; 83,000 ÷ 1,000 = 83 train loads per hour; 83 ÷ 6 = 14 tracks required.)

The problem of parking space for the motors and sidings for the storage of trolley and steam equipment is of importance. An automobile occupies 200 square feet on the average. One hundred per cent must be added for access. This gives 400 square feet per motor car. A trolley car requires 500 square feet, and a ten-car train 10,000 square feet. Something more must be added for switches and leads, loading spaces and safety areas. In each case the figure should be approximately doubled. (In the examples above, had one third of the visitors traveled by each of the three modes, the following parking, standing and loading areas would be required: 750,000 ÷ 3 = 250,000 persons by each type of travel; 250,000 ÷ 5 = 50,000 motors to be parked; 50,000 × 400 = 20,000,000 square feet = 460 acres of parking space required; 250,000 ÷ 100 = 2,500 trolley cars required; 2,500 × 1,000 = 2,500,000 square feet = 58 acres of trolley waiting and loading space needed; 250,000 ÷ 1,000 = 250 trains necessitated; 250 ×

20,000 = 5,000,000 square feet = 116 acres of steam railroad siding and loading space demanded.) Of course, motor buses may replace trolleys in many instances and much express and freight will move by motor truck. In exceptional cases, mail tubes may connect a landing field directly with the post office at the business center of the community.

Incidentally, while transportation accessibility is of great moment in locating an airport, its creation should be such as to hamper transportation as little as possible to points beyond it. The area required for a large flying field will generally overlap one or more major thoroughfares which would consequently have to be closed. Such closings should be obviated if possible. It is sometimes possible to select a site which is adequate for immediate needs and which can be enlarged progressively by being used as the community refuse disposal site. It is hardly to be expected that regular traffic will ever reach such figures as are now being attained while aviation is a novelty. Plans adequate for the present may, therefore, be expected to be ample for the future.

EMERGENCY FIELDS

Pending the future era when a continuous cleared airplane landing strip is provided, numerous emergency landing fields should be arranged, especially in fairly well settled territory like the suburbs of cities. Each of these should have an area of about ten acres and be as strategically located as is possible. They should be located at most not over five miles apart, and around cities should be spaced throughout the whole area, at the corners of five-mile squares, or approximately so.

In addition to air ports, standard practice locates intermediate landing fields at intervals of about thirty miles.

These should have an area of approximately forty acres and be designed as nearly square in shape as is possible. Their placement demands almost as much study with reference to the city plan as is needed with reference to the larger air ports. Since they are for emergency use only, they may be cultivated with any crop which does not grow high.

AREA REQUIREMENTS

The areas required for airplane landing purposes should be clearly differentiated from the area required for the handling and mooring of dirigibles and for the several necessary adjuncts. The department of commerce has tentatively determined the area necessary and advantageous and has proposed a classification of airplane landing fields dependent upon the various facilities available. Fields now actively in use vary all the way from 1,000 acres (Mitchell Field) and 700 acres (Cleveland) down to 40 (Boston and Pittsburg), with 25 acres considered the smallest feasible size for landing except in cases of emergency. Much talk has been heard about roof landing areas, but until new and special designs of planes are common, roofs will not come into general use. Even then, because flying over cities involves extra hazards for both plane and city, roofs are not likely to come into very extensive use for landing purposes.

In rising, an airplane must head into the wind, attain a speed varying from forty to eighty miles an hour on the ground before rising may be attempted. The lighter machines attain this speed rapidly and can, under favorable conditions, leave the ground in from 400 to 800 feet. The heavier planes, those used for freight, mail and passengers, require, under favorable conditions, a distance of from one to two thousand feet before leaving the ground. In addition to the space required on the ground, it frequently happens that the motor stalls immediately after rising, necessitating landing at once. To provide for this emergency, another thousand feet is necessary. A total, therefore, of from 2,700 to 3,000 feet is the minimum length of runway, to accommodate all of the now existing types of planes. In rising or in landing, an airplane makes an angle of approximately eight degrees with the horizontal, or for each foot of rise it moves forward seven feet. If there should be a one-hundred-foot building at the edge of the field, it would render seven hundred feet of the field useless. The minimum distance mentioned (2,700 to 3,000 feet) for a runway must, therefore, be increased by seven times the height of any buildings on the edge of the field.[1]

Several giant planes now under construction are reported to have wing spreads up to 140 feet. This dimension together with an equal side clearance determines the required width of runway. The projected Junkers model J-1000 is to have a wing spread of 220 feet. Detailed specifications for the classification of air ports have been issued by the department of commerce under date of March 13, 1927.

The requirements for air ports for the use of the future mammoth dirigibles, 150 feet in diameter and 750 feet long, have not been as definitely determined. Two such ships moored to towers (with their lofty departure platforms) with space to swing with the change of wind direction would require an area 1,500 feet by 3,000 feet with a border at least 1,000 feet wide entirely around the field and additional area for hangars. The latter must be much larger and differ otherwise from airplane hangars.

While most cities are making efforts to provide one large field as near as possible to the business center, it seems better economics in many instances to provide one or more fields suitable for loading and landing passengers, mail and express, fairly close to the center, with a service field at a more remote and less expensive site.

[1] Quoted from NATIONAL MUNICIPAL REVIEW, February, 1926, p. 106.

FACTORS INFLUENCING AREA NEEDED

The area required for a field will obviously depend largely upon the amount of use to which it will be put. If ten planes arrive and depart each day, a single runway would be sufficient for use by all. If, however, ten planes are to arrive and depart each hour, it may be necessary to use different parts of the field for arrival and departure respectively and to control the arrivals and departures by a signal system operated by a despatcher as is done at Tempelhof (Berlin). The loading and unloading accommodations could then be placed advantageously at the center of a large field, arrivals approaching this center from one direction (against the wind) and departures taking place on the opposite side of the loading and control station (again into the wind). Since the wind may blow from any direction, the central depot would have to be reached on the surface solely by automobile,—the cars approaching in the same direction as the arrival of the airplanes, from a ring drive which entirely encircles the field and outward from which the thoroughfares and transportation lines would extend. In the case of an extensive, intensively used air port, the automobile and other transit lines might advantageously be brought to the central depot under the surface of the field. While expert pilots will doubtless learn to take off irrespective of wind direction (as some do even now in light breezes), there will always be so many who will desire to head into the wind while landing and taking off that it will probably never be possible to ignore the effect of wind in locating and laying out a flying field.

The area required for the air port of the future will depend in a considerable measure upon the development

HELICOPTER CAPABLE OF TAKING OFF AND LANDING PRACTICALLY IN A VERTICAL DIRECTION WHICH IF GENERALLY USED WOULD GREATLY REDUCE THE AREAS NEEDED FOR AIR PORTS

of the air carrier. Several alternatives seem possible: (a) A machine which can ascend vertically or nearly so, by means of (1) the helicopter principle or some related idea, or (2) a new wing design or arrangement, or (3) both combined; and (b) a machine which will fold its wings after it alights, thereby greatly reducing needed storage space and possibly also being able to traverse existing or special new highways. At Teterboro, not long ago, Chamberlain demonstrated a small plane which kept an even keel when flying at only fifteen miles per hour and required only 60 and 75 feet of roll respectively to take off and to land. (Most existing planes will stall and drop into a fatal tail spin at a speed of about fifteen miles or less.)

Devices are sure to be developed to assist in taking off and landing. The compressed air catapult employed for the launching of naval planes, and the decelerating cables which drag bags of sand on the decks of airplane tenders are present-day examples. Perhaps the simplest scheme is to form the surface of the landing field like a flat dome with the depot at the center of the top, —approaching planes landing up the incline and being assisted in stopping by the force of gravity, while departing carriers would leave by sliding down a slope with the assistance of gravity as Lindbergh did (as described in "We"), as Byrd did on his start to the North Pole, and as many others have done from time to time. It is reported that one of the British army air fields used during the war was located on a rounded hill (similar to the scheme here proposed) and that the opinion of the pilots was altogether favorable. Incidentally, the interior of the dome could be used for hangars, for means of access, and for parking of autos, trolleys and other means of land conveyance.

SELECTION OF SITE

From a topographic standpoint, it is now generally felt desirable to secure large level areas for landing fields. (A two per cent grade is considered the maximum.) So as to reduce approach hazards to a minimum, these fields should be chosen as far as possible on hilltops or high ground. This generally reduces ground haze compared with valley sites and the obstructions surrounding the field are not as high as is the case when hills surround the port. Islands, especially artificial ones, if of sufficient size generally possess advantages as to levelness, freedom from approach obstructions, and complete liberty in direction of approach. Accessibility is generally unsatisfactory, however, and they are more apt to be affected by fog. Wherever sea planes can be employed on a route in any direction from a port while land machines operate over other routes, a combined water and land port is considered desirable. However, certain disadvantages inhere in having water ways or water areas as bordering features of a land port because of the incidental hazards to land machines. Larger fields are required under such circumstances. It is believed by many that most planes will eventually be designed so as to alight either on land or water. Obviously, in choosing a site the necessary costs involved in leveling hummocks, doing under-draining, filling ditches, ruts, and sunken roads must be considered, but such work is essential to a successful field. The soil must also be such as to produce a thick tenacious sod and where a practically square or round field cannot be obtained because of topographic difficulty, the greatest length of the area available should extend in the direction of the prevailing winds. In addition to available transportation, electric

light and power, water and sewerage must be available. or obtainable. Where a sod is unobtainable, concrete, asphalt, macadam or cinder surfaces must be provided. It is generally conceded that when an airplane lands it strikes the ground with a blow equal to perhaps five times its dead weight. Consequently, the surface must be very compact. A dusty field is very objectionable, also.

At sea level the length of the field at least in the direction of the prevailing winds should, as has been said, be not less than 2,500 feet plus 7 feet horizontal space for each foot of height of obstructions at and beyond the boundaries of the field at each end. Greater dimensions are considered desirable if they are obtainable. For altitudes above sea level, longer runways are required. An approximate formula for the necessary length of runway for such an air port is as follows:

$$\frac{10}{3}\ \frac{A}{C+10,000} = \log_{10}\left(\frac{15R}{r}-15\right).$$

In this formula

A is the altitude of the air port above sea level,

C is the A.B.S. ceiling of any plane, for which

r is the take-off length of run on a level field at sea level, and

R is the necessary length of runway at altitude A.

The ratio $\frac{1}{7}\frac{R}{r}$ is the angle of clearance of all obstructions which must be maintained beyond the runway. The field arrangement and that of the several accessories,—signals, lighting, hangars, shops, waiting rooms for passengers, pilots and workers, field markings, beacons, foggy weather signals, wind indicators, oil and fuel tanks, radio landing control aids and other items,— is not of moment from a city planning standpoint, and the requirements for each of these matters can be found in department of commerce bulletins and technical publications. The lengths required for taking off by sea planes are longer than for land machines and the water areas should be correspondingly larger. To take off, large sea planes require as much as 3,500 feet clear run unobstructed by such things as bridges, breakwaters, or buoys, with a very flat angle of clearance beyond this take-off stretch. They also require at least six feet of water depth. N. A. C. A. Report No. 249 shows the take-off and landing speeds of nine different makes of plane. They range from 48 to 63 miles per hour at take-off and from 44 to 58 at moment of landing.

A practically smooth surface is thus seen to be necessary. Normally this can be secured by some expenditure, but obviously the site should be selected with this point in mind. The same report gives the take-off and landing rolling distances, which range from 275 to 505 feet for taking off and from 400 to 950 feet for alighting. Unless the surfacing of air ports is such as to minimize the dust, it has been shown that even inside hangars the dust will often be so great as to affect bearings detrimentally. Therefore, the hangars should be placed at the side of the field at right angles to the prevailing winds. With a large field in which the hangars are to be at the center, it is thus seen to be advantageous to have the parked airplanes housed below the surface as would be the case in connection with the dome shaped field elsewhere suggested.

NUMBER AND DISTRIBUTION
OF PORTS

It seems reasonable to expect that eventually air ports will be distributed and be of capacities comparable in those characteristics with existing railroad terminals in the relation of the latter to local population groups. In other words, air ports will be proportional to the population served. Commander Byrd is quoted as saying that "aeroplanes will never be used for popular flying as the automobile is used for traveling." The limiting factor in the development of air carriage will probably be the number of available pilots. Students of the problem suggest that not over 10 per cent of the population possesses the natural capacity to guide safely a vehicle which can move in three dimensions. The licensing of automobile drivers shows that not all persons are capable of operating in two dimensions. Assuming a population of 200,000,000 with 10 per cent capable of operating aeroplanes, there would be a maximum of 20,000,000 possible planes moving around the country simultaneously. Incidentally, the average mileage per year of the present-day motor car is around 600, whereas it would be 60,000 were all cars to be operated at twenty miles per hour for ten hours per day for 300 days per year. The average automobile is thus seen to be moving only one per cent of the time (day time). Or, in another point of view, one per cent of all automobiles are moving at all times. They stop and start at least once every day. In fact, the average trip is probably less than two miles, so that there are twenty stops and twenty starts each day for that one per cent.

As a first approximation, the same ratios may be applied to air carriers. Of the 20,000,000 possible pilots, 200,-000 may be expected to be on the move at all times. With 40 landings and take-offs per day there would be 8,000,-000 per day. Assume one every ten minutes for thirteen hours, or 80 per day. That indicates 100,000 landings or departures each ten minutes throughout the country. While land-

ings can obviously be made at shorter intervals than ten minutes, the time required for the loading and unloading of passengers and freight, the manoeuvering from point of arrival to point of departure, and the signalling to other planes arriving and departing will normally demand approximately ten minutes as the arrival and departure interval on any given runway.

These conditions are strictly comparable with those which hold in connection with passenger and freight railroad terminals. With 200,000,000 population, a landing field or runway is indicated for each 2,000 population. If a factor is introduced to care for a probability concerning air craft like the fact which exists with reference to automobiles, that there are at least 25 per cent less automobiles licensed than actual persons capable of driving them, then the figure 2,000 should be increased to 2,500. If only small planes are to be accommodated, this figure can be multiplied by four. For the smallest present type of plane, such as the one in which Chamberlain lately took off from a city street, this figure can be multiplied by fifteen. Chicago in 1927 had fifteen landing fields,—seven municipal, six commercial, one army, one postal; Los Angeles had eight, seven being commercial. By states, California had 100 fields, Texas 84, Illinois 64, Ohio 50, Oklahoma 40, New York 30, Arizona 29, Colorado 22, Iowa 24. Obviously the figure of 2,000 persons per landing field does not apply to the present. There are not yet 200,000,000 persons in the United States and there are only about 4,000 licensed pilots in the country, with 2,111 planes listed in the 1927 Aircraft Year Book. With New York's prospective 10,000,000 people, 5,000 such landing spaces would have to be provided. Obviously they should be well distributed so as to minimize air traffic accidents, and a signalling system will have to be employed so that planes can land and take off simultaneously, each on its own 300 by 2,500 foot runway. · A circular field with a diameter of 7,500 feet would provide for the simultaneous handling of 44 planes with any direction of the wind. Obviously possibilities exist of reducing the assumed ten-minute landing interval, and of securing a greater use of such a field when a type of plane shall have been developed which will require a shorter runway. In other words, an air port of that size and design would afford the facilities needed by a population of from 220,000 to 450,000, according to whether present-day dimensions or future probable ones are assumed. Using the larger figure, it is seen that New York City should plan to provide thirty-five square miles of landing fields to meet its future requirements. The landing fields in the vicinity of New York City for which the department of commerce had issued aeronautical bulletins up to January 1, 1928, aggregated just over four square miles.

AMPLE SPACE FOR FUTURE
DEVELOPMENT

As to air transportation we are back in the days of the first railroads when cities and citizens fought verbal battles over the location of *the* railroad station. The lesson to be learned from the figures is that ample open spaces available for eventual air fields should be acquired and set aside in each community. Until they are required for aeronautics they can be employed as recreation spaces, either active or passive,—athletic fields, wild life preserves, and formal parks. When they are needed for air use, the radius of travel of the average man by motor, rapid transit, or air will make them relatively unnecessary as open spaces. Meantime, if invention eventually eliminates the necessity of such

long landing and take-off runways, then the open spaces acquired will continue to serve a legitimate purpose to the benefit of the community.

Special purpose flying fields will be developed and must be considered in regional, if not in city planning. Flying schools must have their fields (in 1925 there were twenty-two such schools); special seaside landing areas will be required to serve the planes which bring ashore transatlantic mails and "rush" passengers; special landing fields along mail routes will be created where a mail plane can drop a mail bag and pick up another either without stopping or merely taxying along the ground and taking off without longer pause; a few down-town landing spaces on the tops of buildings will be developed similar in equipment to the airplane tenders in the Navy; special fields will be made available adjacent to large hospitals where ambulance planes can land; of course, the Army and the Navy will require special fields; and other special uses will develop. The parking near a city of planes owned by flying commuters will be another special problem. Aside from the landing runways required, a hundred such planes would require nearly five acres of parking space. Because sea planes are somewhat larger than the average, one hundred such would require approximately seven acres.

. Perhaps inventive genius may some day learn how to dissipate or control fogs, or at least develop neon or other light signals, electric capacity height indicators, radio direction guides and other aids so that landings can be made in spite of this, at present, dangerous meterological handicap. Meantime, that site should be selected which is shown to be naturally freest of foggy weather and ground haze. Factory smoke may be as detrimental as ground haze and a field should not have a large industrial district to windward of it. Certain topographical conditions are known to produce gusty wind conditions and naturally such areas should be shunned. Fields which may experience excessively heavy rainfalls should be so located or so improved with subsurface drains as to provide a quick drying surface. One well known field near New York was put entirely out of commission for about a week by a heavy rainfall which occurred only a few months ago.

Because airplanes are not equipped with mufflers, the noise which is to be expected in the vicinity of a large active field will doubtless be comparable with that incident to a railroad yard so that a field adjacent to a residence district would prove somewhat annoying. The same is true with reference to the location of flashing or rotating airway beacons at points in residence districts. A steady beam of light is less annoying to residents than a flashing or periodically changing light such as flashing electric advertising signs.

Costs of air ports naturally vary widely with variation in area and completeness of improvement. Chicago proposes an expenditure of $2,000,000; Cleveland and Boston, between one and two millions each; Croyden (when completed) about a million; while at the other extreme some small fields have been secured and provided with meager facilities for as little as $50,000. The Assistant Secretary of the Department of Commerce lately stated that "municipalities are building air ports at an average expenditure of $100 per capita."

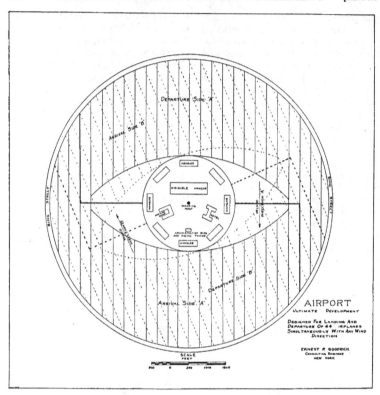

DIAGRAM 1

The parallel solid lines divide the field into 22 departure lanes and 22 arrival lanes, corresponding to wind direction A.   Each of these lanes is 300 feet wide and 2500 feet long.   The dotted lines show the lanes which would be used for wind direction B.   Note that the mooring mast, shops, hangars and other buildings are located around the center of the field, at the point of maximum convenience, but do not in any way obstruct the runways.   The area of this field is approximately 1000 acres.

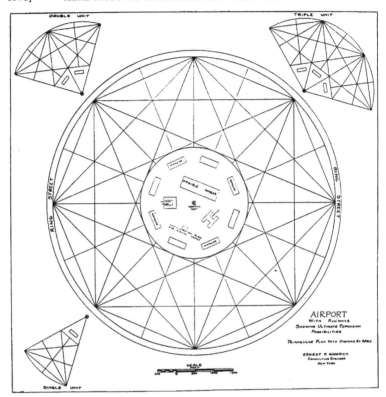

DIAGRAM 2

It is evidently desirable first to construct a small airport and later to expand it gradually to meet future requirements. The single unit, shown in the lower left-hand corner, represents the first construction. The area of this unit is 125 acres. The mooring mast and hangars are at the apex, and eight runways are shown, each 2500 feet long. These runways may or may not be paved, depending on local soil conditions and the amount of use of the airport. These eight runways correspond to eight wind directions varying by about 45°. With an increase in the demand, a second and a third unit may be added, as shown in the upper left and right hand corners respectively. The completed field evidently comprises eight such units.

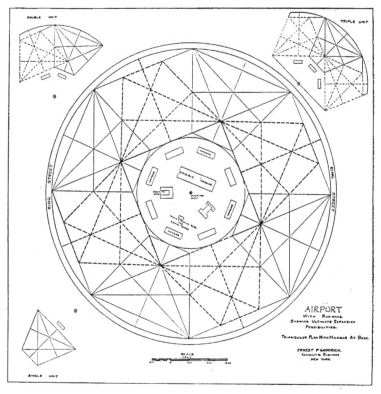

DIAGRAM 3

The principle of building up the complete airport gradually, by adding units, from time to time, may also be carried out with the hangars at the bases of the units as shown in the above illustration. The finished airport will comprise four such units, shown by dotted lines, and spaced between these will be four other units (shown in solid lines) similar to those in Diagram 2. These two types of units will overlap. The double unit developed in this way is somewhat more flexible as concerns the layout of runways than is the double unit of Diagram 2.

NATIONAL
MUNICIPAL REVIEW

PUBLISHED MONTHLY BY THE

National Municipal League

VOL. XVII, No. 4   APRIL, 1928   TOTAL No. 142

CONTENTS

EDITORIAL COMMENT............................*H. W. Dodds*...... 195
MUNICIPALLY OWNED BUS SYSTEM REPLACES STREET
    CARS.......................................*George C. Merkel*.. 199
THE FEE SYSTEM RECEIVES SETBACK IN KENTUCKY..*A. Vanderbosch* ... 200
OUR AMERICAN MAYORS:
    IX. MAYOR LAURENCE C. HODGSON OF ST. PAUL..*George N. Briggs* .. 203
THE RECENT MUNICIPAL ELECTIONS IN ENGLAND....*William A. Robson* 207
DES MOINES TRIES THE CONCILIATION COURT......*Francis R. Aumann* 211
DUBLIN'S PROPOSED MANAGER-COUNCIL PLAN.......*F. H. Boland*...... 214
ADMINISTRATIVE REORGANIZATION ADOPTED IN
    CALIFORNIA................................*John F. Sly* 220
MUNICIPAL LAND POLICIES AND THEIR APPLICATION TO
    CITY PLANNING AND HOUSING.................*Thomas L. Hinckley* 226

DEPARTMENTS

    I. Recent Books Reviewed... 231
    II. Judicial Decisions...*Edited by C. W. Tooke* 236
    III. Public Utilities..*Edited by John Bauer* 240
    IV. Governmental Research Association Notes...................*Edited by Russell Forbes* 244
    V. Notes and Events...*Edited by H. W. Dodds* 248

THE LEAGUE'S BUSINESS

The **Thirty-Fourth Annual Meeting** of the National Municipal League will be held in Cincinnati October 16 and 17 under invitation from Mayor Seasongood, City Manager Sherrill and John B. Blandford, director of the Bureau of Municipal Research. The Governmental Research Association and the National Association of Civic Secretaries will meet on October 15 and will join with the League on the two following days.

It is hoped that the program will permit some round table sessions which proved so popular at the New York meeting last November.

✣

Standards of Financial Administration.—The February supplement bearing this title from the joint pen of Lent D. Upson and C. E. Rightor has been in heavy demand and the supply of extra copies is almost exhausted. An eminent author of two textbooks on public accounting sends in this gratifying note:

> I know of nothing more complete or accurate on this subject. The authors certainly omitted no essential item and have set forth their reasons in a manner thoroughly logical and convincing. I anticipate that this outline will long be referred to as one of the most complete and concise statements of this important subject to be found.

In this connection we are happy to announce the organization of a joint committee to study standards of measurement of municipal services. Delegates from the City Managers Association, the Governmental Research Association and the League compose the committee.

Professor Charles E. Merriam, Louis Brownlow and R. W. Rigsby have been chosen to represent the City Managers Association. The Governmental Research Association has chosen Lent D. Upson, Henry P. Seidemann, and C. E. Ridley; and the president of the League has selected Charles A. Beard, H. M. Waite and A. E. Buck as its representatives. Mr. Ridley will act as secretary of the committee.

✣

Distinguished Service Recognized.—M. N. Baker, associate editor of *Engineering News-Record* and for many years an officer of the League, was the guest of honor at a dinner given recently by about 100 of his associates in the McGraw Hill Co. at the Engineers Club, New York City, in celebration of his fortieth year of continuous editorial service with *Engineering News* and *Engineering News-Record*.

✣

Louis Brownlow, until recently city manager of Knoxville, Tenn., and a member of the editorial council of the REVIEW, has been retained by the City Housing Corporation to act as consultant in connection with the new garden village which the company is building in New Jersey. A full account and description of the plans for the new city of Radburn appeared in the March issue.

NATIONAL
MUNICIPAL REVIEW

| Vol. XVII, No. 4 | APRIL, 1928 | Total No. 142 |

EDITORIAL COMMENT

Detroit is the best governed large city in America, proclaims the Detroit Citizens League. Will any other city dispute her statement? Chambers of commerce and other citizens' associations often assert their city's superiority in industrial or commercial advantages. Now let some step forward with data showing how well governed they are. The REVIEW will be glad to publish communications of this nature. In the meantime we might ask Detroit how does she know that she is the best governed large city in America. What standards of comparison has she used?

*

The Rochester city council by vote of 6 to 2 has enacted a local law providing a non-partisan ballot in municipal elections. It will be recalled that the city manager, home rule charter originally included the non-partisan feature, which was later ruled out by the courts, however, on the technical ground that the sections of the state election law to be superseded were not specified. The new system goes into effect without a referendum of the people, because it was held that the principle of non-partisanship had been approved by the voters when they adopted the charter and the local law was consequently merely a correction in detail of procedure.

Special Assessment Bonds Now General Obligations in Iowa The recent Iowa case, by which street improvement bonds now become general obligation of the city although ostensibly issued against assessed property, is discussed in this issue by Professor Horack in Professor Tooke's Department of Judicial Decisions and will be of interest to many readers. Professor Tooke in a succeeding note points out that the course of law in other jurisdictions has been different. Indeed in a late case, the United States Circuit Court of Appeals relieved the city of Nampa, Idaho of direct liability on the ground that "the bond-holder has a remedy by mandamus to compel the proper officers to make a new or supplementary assessment and collect the necessary funds to liquidate the bonds." In both cases the liability of the city was predicated upon "the negligence of the city in failing to perform its statutory duties to make a valid levy and collect the funds to pay the bonds," but the Circuit Court of Appeals declined to endorse the reasoning so acceptable to the Iowa court.

Precedent, as Professor Tooke points out, lies with the Circuit Court of Appeals. But in our judgment, ethics and sound practice rest with Iowa. To issue a document that looks like a municipal bond and carries words that sound like a municipal bond is misleading. Of course bond dealers and large investors know it isn't a municipal bond; but others may be deceived and innocently purchase the imposing looking evidence of indebtedness, later to learn that they have nothing more than a lien on some private property of questionable value.

In practice the method is socially most expensive. Although it keeps the nominal city debt down, the actual debt of the community is not affected one whit. Generally the assessment bonds are accepted by the contractor who discounts them at the bank. Sometimes the discount is as much as 30 per cent. The city may even decline to act as collecting agent for the bond-holders who are thus left to shift for themselves. In this manner unnecessary risks are introduced through faulty procedure and the cost of improvements rendered unduly high.

The situation in the state of Washington stinks to high heaven. There through collusion, property owners have been able to escape the lien on their property entirely. The device has been to let the county take the property for general taxes, which wipes out the assessment lien, and later to buy it back free of the improvement obligation. But even where collusion has been absent assessments have escaped collection along with other taxes in various cities in which serious real estate deflation has followed the postwar boom. As a consequence many Washington districts are in default with resultant evil effects upon the municipalities in which they lie; and to make matters worse, cities desiring to restore their credit by assuming the district bonds are legally unable to do so.[1]

[1] See NATIONAL MUNICIPAL REVIEW for August, 1927, for article by H. B. Bickner, "Washington's Defaulted Bonds Not To Be Redeemed."

While the Washington predicament is extreme, many other jurisdictions permit the vicious special assessment bond with the attendant actualities and possibilities of evil.

*

Public Works to Check Unemployment
Acute unemployment has developed within the past few months in a number of American cities. Until recently New York seems to have escaped. In February, however, the state labor department reported a decrease during 1927 in the number of factory workers employed, together with an influx of unemployed from other states; and Governor Smith has taken steps to stimulate state and city agencies to quick relief measures.

The present situation has renewed discussion of the possibility of planning public works construction to offset unemployment in private industry. Otto T. Mallery, who has for years been advocating the adoption of such policy, points out that erection of public works represents annually a two billion dollar industry, or more than one-fourth of the construction business of the country. At least twenty-seven lines of manufacture are dependent upon it for a good part of their prosperity, and Mr. Mallery proposes that public building be utilized to stabilize business conditions. This follows the program of the National Committee on Unemployment created by Secretary Hoover in 1921. Under the plan, federal and local governments would set up a sort of "reserve" of construction work for the future which would be known as a "prosperity reserve." When volume of construction shows a marked decline, it is to be incumbent upon the president of the United States to give the signal for local governments to start the work falling within their prosperity reserves. In this manner a smaller percentage of public work would be undertaken when private industry is active and a larger percentage in periods of depression when capital and labor are not fully employed. In 1922 Secretary Hoover committed himself to the scheme and other prominent persons and organizations have since endorsed it.

American cities in the past have generally given little thought to long-time construction programs. In recent years, however, the National Municipal League, in common with the municipal research movement and the city planners, has been impressing upon cities the importance of bond budgets. Only by this means can a sound policy of pay-as-you-go be adjusted to borrowing and the physical growth of the city be rendered harmonious and economic. The adoption of comprehensive city plans, which include schedules of financing, directs attention to long-term fiscal programs and renders bond budgets indispensable.

But if municipal and state governments, which are gradually being brought to a consideration of long-term programs, such as large private businesses have been accustomed to formulate, must now take up the question of adapting their improvements to the employment situation of the country, a new and complicating factor will be introduced; a factor mitigated, however, by the desirability of flexibility in the program to enable the city, within reasonable limits, to take advantage of depressed markets in carrying it out.

When all has been said, the causes of unemployment still lie hidden in the economic cycle, and a governmental "prosperity reserve" is an attack upon symptoms rather than upon the disease itself. Yet if wisely used it may alleviate hardship and thus prove useful. But in applying the remedy, our cities must not lose sight of the social service

to be rendered by the preparation of and adherence to long time improvement and financial programs. We must not sacrifice the proven economies of a well reasoned procedure as opposed to hasty, premature and wasteful use of public funds.

✻

Business Frontage and City Growth Coleman Woodbury, writing in the *Journal of Land and Public Utility Economics*, describes an examination into the size of retail business districts in the Chicago metropolitan region. For all the cities sampled (forty in number) the modal average was 50 feet of retail business frontage for each hundred of population. Residential cities as a class averaged 45 feet per hundred population, and industrial cities 55. As among individual cities, however, wide discrepancies prevailed. In one residential town the retail frontage was 90 feet per hundred while at the other extreme was found one with an average of only 22 feet. In one industrial city the average was 79; in another 45. Nevertheless, fair concentration exists in that 20 cities, or 50 per cent of the total number of all classes, are found in the relatively small range from 45 to 60 feet per hundred population.

In general it was found that the size of the city has no clear effect upon the relative size of the business district. Neither was it possible from the small number of samples to determine whether the general character of the city, i.e., industrial or residential, influenced directly the proportion of business frontage. It was made clear, however, that the size of the business district varies inversely with the distance by express train in minutes from the Chicago shopping center. As a class the cities with the largest ratios are farthest from the central city.

While the above conclusions are of special significance for the city planner and zoner, real estate men and buyers of business or residential lots in new subdivisions should be aided in forming a more accurate estimate of the soundness of their investments viewed in the light of basic economic principles.

The communities studied were distributed among all the main directions of city growth. Although the variation in age and rate of growth was considerable, only cities which were firmly established on a growing basis were included in the sample.

＊

Party Responsibility Under National Party Emblem Alfred Bettman has again placed the people of Cincinnati under obligation by his excellent paper, printed in the February number of *The Bulletin* of the Cincinnati Woman's City Club, surveying the city's future problems and responsibilities. It is a comprehensive report on what is being done under the new charter and what remains to be done. There are many interesting paragraphs, but the section relating to Cincinnati's once popular slogan "party responsibility," is one of the best.

Mr. Bettman points out ')w vague and seductive the slogan i.. As used by the party leaders it was a bid for popular acceptance of partisanship in the administration of the municipal government. Party responsibility, believes Mr. Bettman, can properly be attributed only to parliamentary government where major questions are introduced by responsible party leaders in control of the legislature who risk their fate upon the acceptance of such measures by the legislature. Mr. Bettman recognizes that national parties both in the United States and England do participate in local elections, but correctly asserts that, if our national parties are responsible for anything it is for the policies of the national government. As a matter of fact party responsibility, even in national affairs, is imperfectly understood by Americans. More than once has a skillful organization squared itself with the people by changing its nominal leaders. Under no circumstances does a national party ever identify itself with municipal issues. For this reason the national party can support no true system of party responsibility in city government.

Moreover, the city manager idea is the very negation of party responsibility so far as municipal administration is concerned. Under this form of government the slogan becomes vicious. In any case it is a red herring across the trail.

In Cincinnati the concept was particularly ridiculous because under the old government the party chiefs did not hold public office. Indeed the party leader made his home in New York and rarely honored Cincinnati with his presence.

MUNICIPALLY OWNED BUS SYSTEM REPLACES STREET CARS

BY GEORGE C. MERKEL

Secretary-Manager, Alexandria (Louisiana) Chamber of Commerce

The growing city of Alexandria, La., with a population of 25,000, abandoned its municipally owned street railway in favor of busses, to the profit of everybody. :: :: :: :: :: :: :: ::

FORMERLY when the electrically operated street cars of this metropolis of Central Louisiana made their cumbersome and noisy way down the streets of Alexandria, serving only citizens living within a circumscribed territory, the question was often asked —"What are we going to do about the municipal street railway? How are we going to make it pay?"

Alexandria, like all other progressive communities was stretching out, extending its residential sections, relocating its industrial divisions, and more and more it was realized that it would cost a fortune to extend and reroute the street railway system, buy modern equipment and make improvements commensurate to requirements for years to come.

Other cities throughout the South were junking their street cars, or supplementing their extensions by motor busses. The commission-council of Alexandria studied these changes, obtained data through the Alexandria Chamber of Commerce, through motor bus manufacturers and directly from communities, and decided in favor of the replacement of the entire system by municipally owned motor busses. In this they had the hearty approval of the citizenry.

That was during the latter part of the year 1926. First a trial bus line was operated; then, on January 1, 1927, all of the street cars were taken off and the Municipal Bus Lines began operation along a series of routes worked out according to population growth and to the advantage of persons travelling thereon. Instead of ten cars of the one man type operating over nine miles of single track route, a dozen busses carry passengers over approximately fifteen miles of route, on a closer schedule and to the entire satisfaction of the citizens were provided.

Opponents to the motor busses argued the expense of upkeep of tires, mechanical equipment and depreciation. With an extra bus always in reserve, each bus is given a thorough inspection every twelfth day and such service as may be necessary. A trouble car is ever ready to change a tire or make some adjustment without noticeable delay to the patrons of the route effected.

A seven-cent fare is charged and the system as a whole is a paying institution. Only one of the routes does not pay, and that because it operates beyond the city limits to a railroad terminal with periodically heavy passenger movements and little territory to serve enroute at other times of the day.

The popularity of the busses is indicated by the growing number who utilize their services. In the month of January, 1927, the first month of operation, the busses carried 610 more passengers than the street cars during the previous December, although Christmas is a time of heavy travel. The number of passengers for January, 1927, was 11 per cent greater than for January, 1926, and the number for December, 1927, was 57 per cent greater than for the same month of the preceding year.

One of the interesting features connected with the installation of the municipal bus lines in Alexandria is the fact that the cost, $85,973.25 including garage and repair equipment, was met from the general fund and earnings of the city and not by bond issue or certificates of indebtedness.

The city of Alexandria is under the commission form of government, its council consisting of J. F. Foisy, mayor and commissioner of public health and safety; V. M. Ake, commissioner of finance and public utilities, and R. W. Bringhurst, commissioner of public streets and parks. All public utilities in the city, which include electric light and power, water works, bus lines and gas distribution system are municipally owned and operated.

THE FEE SYSTEM RECEIVES SETBACK IN KENTUCKY

BY A. VANDERBOSCH
University of Kentucky

The $5,000 constitutional limit on officers' salaries held to apply to fees of county officials.   ::   ::   ::   ::   ::   ::   ::   ::

A RECENT series of law suits has forcefully brought home to the people of Kentucky the archaic state of their county government. Incidentally, the decisions in these cases may have destroyed much of the lucrativeness of some of the offices in the more populous counties of the state.

In Kentucky practically all of the county officers are under the fee system, and it was in connection with the sheriff's office that the cases originated. Besides the specified fees which he is allowed for serving as the executive arm of the court, the sheriff, as the collector of the county and state taxes, is allowed 10 per cent commission on the first $5,000 of the taxes he collects, and 4 per cent on the residue.

PERSISTENT TAXPAYER WINS A VICTORY

The sheriffs remained undisturbed in the enjoyment of their ample revenue until a few years ago, when a Fayette county taxpayer brought suit against two ex-sheriffs, their bondsmen, and the members of the fiscal court for fees in excess of a constitutional limitation. Section 246 of the Kentucky constitution provides that "no public officer, except the governor, shall receive more than $5,000 per annum as compensation for official services, independent of the legally authorized deputies and assistants, which shall be fixed and provided for by law." The taxpayer asserted that for one year alone the sheriff has received as fees, per diem salary, and commissions, over $26,000 in excess of the $5,000 he was authorized to receive under the constitution.

Although losing his case before the lower court, the suing taxpayer won a sweeping decision from the court of appeals. The upper court held that the sheriffs' right to retain the commissions and fees was subject to the constitutional limitation of $5,000, independent of the compensation of legally authorized deputies and assistants. This constitutional limitation, the court held, was self-executory, and thus did not require legislative action to bring it into operation.[1]

Upon the return of the case to the circuit court, general demurrers were sustained and the petitions of the taxpayer were again dismissed. The taxpayer again appealed to the court of appeals where the judgments of the court below were affirmed as to the members of the fiscal court, but reversed as to the sheriffs, and the causes were again remanded for trial.[2] The sheriffs thereupon went to the fiscal court and made a settlement of all the claims involved by the payment to the county of $10,000. These settlements they now pleaded as a bar to the further prosecution of the case.

The determined taxpayer, contending that each sheriff had received over $120,000 in excess of the compensation allowed by the constitution, again appealed to the court of appeals. This time he sought contempt of court proceedings on the ground that the settlements by the fiscal court and the sheriffs without his consent was in complete disregard of the orders of the court. The appeal, however, was lost, the court holding that the taxpayer's consent was not necessary to the settlement, and that the compromise settlement was a bar to further action against the ex-sheriffs. Action could be brought by a taxpayer only when the fiscal court refuses to bring such action.[3]

On a petition for a rehearing of the case, the undaunted taxpayer won the right to introduce evidence to show that the settlement was not made in good faith. The court of appeals ruled that the taxpayer's appeal, alleging that the public inspector's report showed the two ex-sheriff defendants were indebted to the county in greater amount than the amount of settlement, and that prior to the compromise agreement an offer had been made to settle for a larger sum, was sufficient pleading of lack of good faith on the part of the fiscal court.[4]

After suits for damages, totaling $300,000, had been brought against the taxpayer by the former county judge and the five magistrates, who were members of his fiscal court, because of alleged libelous statements made about them in connection with the compromise settlement, a final settlement was made. The taxpayer was paid $9,500 in attorney's fees, $1,000 coming from each of the defendant former sheriffs, and $7,500 from the fiscal court. The damage suits were dropped.[5]

As a result of these decisions the last sheriff was made to come to the fiscal court to make a settlement, and the present sheriff is apparently running the office at much less cost than previously. In opposing the compromise settlement of $15,000 with the last sheriff two members of the fiscal court declared that the sums allowed for salaries for deputies were much too large, and over $50,000 more than the present administration is spending for this purpose. Further evidence of the far-reaching effect of these decisions can be gathered from the fact that only recently suit has been brought against a former county attorney of Jefferson county, of which Louisville is the seat, for the recovery of $91,000 in excess fees.[6]

[1] 196 Ky. 523; 245 S. W. 157.

[2] 210 Ky. 51.

[3] 211 Ky. 737.

[4] 219 Ky. 349, 373.

[5] Lexington *Herald*, May 28, 1927.

[6] Louisville *Times*, Oct. 18, 1927.

MAGISTRATES AND CONSTABLES
STILL RECEIVE FEES

Another recent court decision instrumental in arousing general disapprobation of the fee system so prevalent in Kentucky county government, was that of *Tumey* v. *Ohio*,[1] in which the United States Supreme Court declared it a deprivation of due process of law for a defendant in a criminal case to subject his liberty or property to the judgment of a court "the judge of which has a direct, personal, substantial pecuniary interest in reaching a conclusion against him in his case." The Supreme Court pointed out in its decision that Kentucky was one of the states in which the practice which it was declaring illegal was still prevalent. Under an old Kentucky statute magistrates get costs of courts only in cases of conviction and fines, and none in cases of acquittal. So also the constable receives fifty cents for making an arrest and two dollars for his services in summoning a jury, attending the trial, and conducting the defendant to jail, but he receives none of these fees if the party arrested is not fined, for the law provides that the fees are "to be paid by the party convicted." In conformity with this decision of the United States Supreme Court, the unconstitutionality of the magisterial fee system of Kentucky has now been established definitely also by a decision of the Kentucky court of appeals.[2]

As editorially stated by the Lexington *Herald*, this method of paying the magistrates and constables results in "many fines of $1.00 and costs and one cent and costs—things that disgust most citizens with the administration of the law, fines which virtually admit they are not justified and which say to

a defendant, 'You haven't done anything, but I have to get mine.' " In some cases, also, the county judges and justices of the peace are entitled to collect fees for holding alleged law violators for the grand jury. Such a system is an open invitation to extortion. But in spite of the Supreme Court decision in *Tumey* v. *Ohio* and the recent decision of the Kentucky court of appeals, the magistrates' courts of Kentucky are grinding out convictions under the old system.

Another feature of county government in Kentucky that has recently come under fire is the "per diem" under which the members of the fiscal court are paid. Aside from the fees which they receive as justices of the peace in the trial of misdemeanor cases, the only compensation which members of the fiscal court receive is from the "per diem" allowed for the attendance upon committee meetings. A recent investigation in Fayette county disclosed the fact that the magisterial committees met every day not restrained by law, or on an average of about twenty-five days a month. These committee meetings are held for very trivial business transactions. For example, one committee met to authorize the purchase of an ice book at cost of three dollars.[3]

The Fayette county grand jury, unearthing these practices of the fiscal court, recommended the adoption of the commission form of government. However, the commission form of government which the Kentucky constitution allows as an alternate to that of the fiscal court system has very little to recommend it. Under either form one chief defect is apparent— that of a large number of constitutional elective officers. All suggestions offering any promise run into the same

[1] U. S. Supreme Court 71 h. Ed. 508 ff., March 7, 1927.

[2] 222 Ky. 306. Decided Dec. 6, 1927.

[3] Lexington *Herald*, Nov. 7, 1926.

obstacle, the rigid provisions laid down for county government in the constitution. This is quite generally recognized, with the result that a constantly growing opinion is demanding the calling of a constitutional convention for the purpose of drafting an entirely new constitution.

OUR AMERICAN MAYORS

IX. MAYOR LAURENCE C. HODGSON OF ST. PAUL

BY GEORGE N. BRIGGS
St. Paul

The people of St. Paul listened patiently to the heavy debate between Capital and Labor and then elected, by an overwhelming majority, the slender, pale-faced Larry Hodgson who had come out boldly and without reservation for brotherly love.   ::   ::   ::   ::   ::   ::

THAT serious-minded part of the American public which predicts the country will sink unless we have business, more business and yet more business in government should find it difficult to explain what is keeping the city of St. Paul, Minnesota, from going down for the third and last time.

Laurence C. Hodgson, the city's mayor and at this writing a candidate to succeed himself with at least an even chance of doing so, has never claimed to be a business efficiency expert. As a matter of fact he admits something akin to a passion for writing poetry; he would rather talk about brotherly love any time than industrial development, and for this, shortcomings and all, Larry Ho is held in the deepest affection by tens of thousands of people in the Northwest where men are reputed to be men.

Once upon a time Larry Ho lived and labored in Minneapolis. Informed, he explains, that a woman in St. Paul had hit upon the happy scheme of turning her flapjacks by putting popcorn in the batter, he decided that was a pretty good town for a shiftless man to move to, so he came to St. Paul and has been one of its principal points of interest ever since.

"LARRY HO," MAYOR OF ST. PAUL

MORE POET THAN BUSINESS MAN

Two years ago, in opening his campaign, Mr. Hodgson said:

"The charge against me is that if I write poetry, I must, of necessity, know little about business, and perhaps I do."

To which one of the newspaper editors replied:

"There is no 'perhaps' about it. Any man who proposes to let his plant run down, pocket all the profits and leave nothing for reserve, depreciation or future expansion may be a first-class poet, but he certainly is no business man. And there is a great deal more business than poetry in the administration of a corporation such as the city of St. Paul with an annual budget of about $10,000,000."

This dialogue is interesting because it brings out quite clearly what the newspapers think of Larry Ho as a business man, and yet he is so close to newspaper men of the Northwest, having been one of them himself, that no one else may abuse him and go unchallenged.

What Larry thinks of his own poetry may be found summed up in a political speech he made two years ago.

"Inasmuch as my poetry is not very good poetry, I do not think it should be held against me as a major offense."

Larry Hodgson is intimately and affectionately known throughout the Northwest by men, women and children as a poet of no mean attainment, as an orator beyond compare and a man possessed of such endearing qualities that they will gladly forgive his poetry no matter how "bad" it gets. Forgetting for the moment his lack of business sagacity, vision, courage or whatever it is that makes a business leader, we may well inquire into the mystery that has three times returned him St. Paul's mayor and, as we go to press, gives some promise of increasing it to four.

One friend once said of him: "I like to think of Larry as the man he would like to be." Perhaps that feeling is so strong and so general that the mystery of his political success is already solved.

And what Larry thinks of himself generally he expresses in these words:

"I think if you talked to those who have known me intimately all my life you would find that they understand I am something more than a good fellow —that I have a serious purpose in life. I entered the city hall with a very definite purpose in mind. I have seriously given my time to city problems. I have worked hard and achieved some results. I think my administration of the finance department met with considerable approval, both newspapers praising it. The fact that I was the one person to be elected twice to the presidency of the League of Minnesota Municipalities would indicate that I was not regarded as entirely incompetent as an official. And I think the character of some of the intimate friends of my life—men high in business many of them—would indicate that I am not wholly without intellectual quality."

LARRY HODGSON'S ISSUES

It was in 1918 that the writer of this study was assigned by his city editor to campaign with Larry Hodgson in his first bid for the job of mayor. The primary fight had been between a business man, a labor man and Larry, the latter then known, in and out of St. Paul, as a poet, impractical, the victim if possible of too many devoted friends and wholly inexperienced as an executive. The business man, successful in the conduct of his own affairs, forceful and progressive, came in third best, no one knew why.

While the labor candidate harangued the voters with terrifying word pictures of the titanic struggle to the death then ensuing between Capital and Labor: of the palpitating world issues that must and could be settled only by the ballot; of the industrial collapse that would follow failure to vote according to instructions; while the labor candidate was perspiring through a dizzy campaign of intricate issues, Larry Hodgson was talking to the Nature Lovers' Association about the beauties and morals of birdlife; to the Commercial Bowlers' League about strikes and spares and frames; to the Elks, the Moose and the Eagles about the fraternity of men. The result of this heated political discussion was that the nature lovers, bowlers and joiners stepped out and elected Larry Hodgson mayor and the burning problems of industry were put away in moth-balls for another two years.

The campaign of 1918 was repeated in 1920 when the people of St. Paul listened patiently to the heavy debate between Capital and Labor and then elected, by an overwhelming majority, the slender, pale-faced Larry Hodgson who had come out boldly and without reservation for brotherly love.

Of course such a policy had its disadvantages and its enemies. When, after four years of private life during which time he had served as St. Paul's commissioner of finance, Larry came back for a third term, one newspaper editor sized up the situation in the following language: "After standing still for a long time under the Hodgson plan, St. Paul suddenly discovered the necessity for spending a huge amount of money to catch up with the procession. Our school plant had been allowed to run down, our water supply needed elaborate additions, sewers had not been constructed, our park system was a system in name only and our streets required miles and miles of paving. We had to spend nearly $10,000,000 in a lump to bring the city up to date. As a result of the 'standstill' policy, St. Paul was obliged to spend in four years a sum which might have been spread over a decade if there had been any business foresight in the city hall.

"The standstill policy is only justified upon the assumption that St. Paul's growth is at an end—that the city is going to need no more schools, sewers, paving, etc., and that it is to attract no new industries and no new population. This may be Mr. Hodgson's idea, but we doubt very much if the people of St. Paul subscribe to it. New problems connected with the growth of the city constantly are arising, and if St. Paul is to keep up with the procession, it must deal with them as they arise."

So impressed were the voters with the force of this sound business argument, that they rushed out—the nature lovers and the bowlers and the joiners —and elected Larry Hodgson as their mayor for the third time.

CAN HE KEEP IT UP?

Larry is soon again to be opposed by a business man and a labor man. It remains to be seen whether the people of St. Paul are still of the opinion that one who writes pretty good poetry and makes better speeches than any man in the Northwest should be continued as head of a $10,000,000 business corporation in spite of his lack of intensive business training.

"I have never tried to convince myself or others that my election was a public necessity," said Mr. Hodgson two years ago as he mounted the stump. "I hope I have too great a sense of humor to believe that humanity hangs breathless on my political fate. St. Paul is not made by its officials but by the spirit of its citizenship and that citizenship will carry on regardless of what men happen to be in public office. As long as there are horses to be shod, the blacksmith will be at his forge the morning after election and the grocer will open his store as long as people have to eat, whether one man or another is elected mayor of St. Paul.

"The several hundreds of citizens who presented my name for mayor represent every shade of opinion and condition of life. They have asked nothing of me and, I believe, they expect nothing of me except the spirit of service—a willingness to listen to all people who have business with the city, a freedom from prejudice and intolerance in dealing with public questions and the desire to work faithfully in cooperation with all classes for the public welfare."

One may gain from the foregoing statement something of the humility and gentleness that have been outstanding characteristics of Mayor Larry Hodgson since he came upon the horizon as a newspaper man between two and three decades ago. These, and other qualities, have made him unique among public figures in the Northwest.

A POPULAR ORATOR

Several years ago Woodrow Wilson came to St. Paul as President of the United States. He was introduced to an enormous Twin City audience by Mr. Hodgson, at that time mayor and then as always a staunch Democrat in a state where Democrats are scarce —introduced in such brilliant fashion that President Wilson referred to it at some length in his preamble as one of the finest he had ever heard.

Quite a tribute from one who must have known an introduction when he heard it!

About the same time a penniless and friendless wayfarer was mortally stricken on the streets of St. Paul. With the breath that was almost his last he asked that Larry Ho preach his funeral sermon. Never was more tender leave taken of a public benefactor.

On twenty minutes' notice Mr. Hodgson spoke at the bier of one of his best and closest friends—a farewell so touching and beautiful that manly emotions were moved, in spite of all efforts to control them.

Had the business men of New York heard Mr. Hodgson on the occasion of a certain public function in Newark, they would have been tempted to put him at the head of the metropolis and its affairs reaching into the hundreds of millions. His plea for brotherly love would have convinced them that here at last was the man to run their public business.

In competition with all the eulogies that have been delivered in memory of the Unknown Soldier, the Northwest will enter that one spoken by Larry Hodgson a few months ago.

Larry Hodgson is a home product. Hastings, Minnesota, located a few miles distant from St. Paul, prides itself as Larry's birthplace, and Larry will always be Hastings' first citizen. It was there he served the Hastings *Democrat* as reporter, editorial writer, editor and, occasionally, as versifier.

Secretary to two speakers of the Minnesota house of representatives, chief clerk of the state department of public instruction, chief clerk of the census bureau and secretary to two St. Paul mayors, Larry Hodgson learned all he knows of business in these capacities. He had previously written baseball and verse for the old Minneapolis *Times*, and among veteran newspaper men Larry's devotion to the Minneapolis baseball team will long be a tradition. When the team lost Larry recorded the fact with great difficulty and many heart pangs. Once he roamed along the river front until late at night bemoaning the misfortune of a Minneapolis pitcher whose noble efforts had that day been nullified by an unsteady third baseman.

Larry Hodgson reached his greatest political heights when, in 1920, he became the Democratic candidate for governor of Minnesota. But even Larry Hodgson, personally popular as he was, could not overcome the staggering Republican odds. Had it been possible to eliminate the party labels, Larry Hodgson, poetry and all, might easily have been swept into the governor's mahogany chair. Which would have been another triumph for brotherly love over better business methods in government!

Larry Hodgson is a part of every newspaper office in Minnesota; he is in constant demand as a public speaker, and whenever he writes a poem the people read it and applaud. "If he only had a good business manager," is the stock wish of all Larry's friends, who incline to the view that lack of one is all that stands between him and fame and fortune.

And yet, at the age of 53 years, Larry Hodgson has been the mayor of Minnesota's capital city three times, notwithstanding that he never went to business college and may not live to know the difference between administrative and operating cost accounting. But he may be mayor of St. Paul again. Who knows!

THE RECENT MUNICIPAL ELECTIONS IN ENGLAND

BY WILLIAM A. ROBSON

Editor of "Local Government News" published by the Fabian Society in conjunction with the Labor Party

Additional comment[1] on the last municipal election in England from the viewpoint of a member of the Labor Party.   ::   ::

ON November 2 last the election of local councillors took place in all the municipal boroughs of England, Wales and Scotland, with results that are of the utmost importance and significance to the Labor movement and its supporters.

There are no official returns published for British municipal elections, but figures have been compiled for about seventy of the chief cities of the country, and these give the main outlines of what happened last month. In these seventy cities 105 Conservative, 56 Liberal, 50 Labor and 43 Independent candidates were returned unopposed, while 330 Conservative, 184 Labor, 130 Liberal and 104 Independent seats were contested. The

[1] See NATIONAL MUNICIPAL REVIEW for February for article by James K. Pollock, Labor Party Gains in Municipal Elections in Britain.

largest number of candidates was put into the field by the Labor Party (683); the Conservatives came next with 466, the Liberals and Independents presenting 219 and 228 candidates respectively.

The net result of the contested seats in the seventy cities under review was a net gain to Labor of 121, a net loss to the Conservatives of 87, while the Liberals and Independents lost 19 and 15 seats respectively. The dominant feature of the elections was, therefore, a sweeping victory achieved by Labor throughout the country, at the expense, not of one of the other parties, but of them all—in many cases of them all combined. Quite often all the other parties and candidates joined together in a coöperative effort to "Keep out the Socialist," and in more than a few places the differences between Liberal and Conservative candidates appeared to be mere lovers' quarrels. Save for the even more remarkable success of the Labor Party in the municipal elections last year, when 146 seats were gained, this result is far in advance of any previous victory. In 1924, for example, Labor gained only 20 seats, in 1925 less than 50 seats were added to the total. (By "gained" I refer of course to net increases, not to the total aggregate of successful candidates.)

The figures for the total gains do not, however, express the true dimensions of the Labor victory. It is necessary to look at the detailed results for each city before one can comprehend the remarkable evenness with which the Labor successes are spread throughout the electoral field. The 121 additional seats have been achieved, not by a sudden conversion to the Labor point of view of one or two Conservative strongholds, but by a steady advance all along the line—three seats here and four there betoken the rising tide of Socialism. In several towns, indeed, the parties were so evenly balanced before the elections that one or two extra seats have sufficed to place Labor in control of local affairs on the Council. Thus at Birkenhead, Barnsley, Leigh, Nelson, Swansea, Mansfield and Prestonpans, the Labor Party is definitely in control for the first time. In West Ham, Wigan, St. Helens, Merthyr Tydfil, Smethwick, Port Talbot, Cowdenbeath and Lochgelly the preëxisting Labor majority has been maintained. Above all, at Sheffield, which with its population of half a million is easily the largest city under Labor control, the Labor majority has been actually increased despite the most strenuous efforts on the part of its adversaries to regain the control of affairs. Almost everywhere else Labor is strengthening its position by degrees—a form of progress at once both solid and hopeful.

In a large number of the more important cities the Labor Party is the largest party of the council, although it has not an absolute majority over all the other members. At Leeds, for example, Labor now has 33 members, as against 27 Conservatives and 8 Liberals. At Manchester, the new council is composed of 66 Conservatives, 45 Labor, 25 Liberals and 3 Independents, which means that Labor and Liberal can have their own way if they choose to unite on any particular measure before the council.

LOCAL ISSUES MOST PROMINENT

The elections were not fought or won on any single issue, but on a number of different questions. Some of these questions were matters forming part of the general policy of the parties: for example, the continuous and insistent slogan of the Conservatives has been an appeal to keep down the rates (*i.e.*, local taxes) at all events, regardless of local needs, local aspirations and civic duties. The Labor Party stands, in general, for the vigorous and progressive development of municipal activity, and for further enterprise in regard to the social services, such as education, public health and housing. In the main, however, the elections were contested to a large extent on local issues— that is, on the application to particular local problems of these political philosophies. Shall a slum clearing scheme in the city be gone on with? Shall new secondary schools be built? Shall the public utilities, such as gas or water or electricity, be extended? This is the type of question that has interested the local electorate and decided the election.

A NEW CONCEPTION EMERGING

The lesson which emerges from the Labor victory is that the nation is gradually moving towards an entirely different conception of municipal government from that which dominated Britain during the past century. Nearly the whole of the existing structure of local administration was either erected or reformed during the Victorian era. That age was one in which men believed fundamentally in the doctrine of *laissez faire*, and they were unwilling to embark on any form of collective enterprise in the field of government save what was rendered absolutely necessary by the inexorable logic of events. Accordingly, when they were compelled to deal in some way with the problems arising out of the industrial revolution, the municipal bodies which were established to administer public health, education, police, and so forth, bore all the signs of an unwilling parentage. The local councils were to follow the ideal prescribed for good children in the Victorian age: they were to do only what they were expressly told they might do. Apart from that, they were to sit still and be quiet. Hence, no local authority in England may carry out any function of government except those for which it has received express permission in an act of parliament.

The greater part of those acts relate to unavoidable necessities such as drains and sewers, street lighting, gas, water, education, etc. The ideal of civic patriotism which flourished at its greatest height in Elizabethan England, when, despite a deplorable absence of drains and police constables and gasworks, the city was nevertheless regarded by its inhabitants as a great adventure, something to be beautified and made an object of glory—this ideal was utterly forgotten or ignored by the men of business of the nineteenth century. Thus, although English local government is unsurpassed for efficiency and excellence in many fields of utilitarian achievement, such as public health, highways, the police forces, and

so forth, the more cultural elements find no place in municipal life. Our industrial cities are on the whole ugly. We have no municipal theatres, as in Germany, where the city council is often the focus of many of the more spiritual or artistic aspects of town life. We have scarcely any municipal concerts, picture galleries or museums to be proud of as municipal achievements.

There can be little doubt, I think, that the day is passing, and passing rapidly, when the people are content to remain acquiescent with this state of affairs. There is a growing feeling that the cities ought to have a much larger opportunity for the display of spontaneous initiative, that they must be rid of the fetters which compel them to come to parliament, hat in hand, whenever they want some trifling new power. Incidentally, many members of parliament themselves realise that no great progress is possible if everything in the way of new social development has to pass through the bottle-neck at Westminster. The work of the House of Commons suffers from severe congestion as it is, and it would be a tremendous relief of this congestion if local authorities were able to enter on new undertakings without compulsory application to parliament.

LABOR PARTY FOR BROAD HOME RULE

Seen in this background, the Local Authorities (Enabling) Bill, which has been promoted by the Parliamentary Labor Party, is of far-reaching importance. It is a measure designed to give local authorities the same powers as are accorded to ordinary trading and joint-stock corporations. In effect, it would permit them to do everything except undertake certain prohibited activities which would be reserved to the central or national government. In this way, the whole centre of gravity would swing from London to the provinces, so far as local government is concerned, and parliament would have the time it needs to devote to the great national questions of economic and social importance, to foreign affairs and imperial policy.

If the bill were passed, we might reasonably anticipate an immense release of civic energy and municipal activity of a high order, a renaissance of collective effort in the cities of Britain. Whether or not it will pass into law depends, of course, not on the local councils but on parliament itself. No Conservative or Liberal Government would legislate on those lines. Only a Labor Government would pass the bill: but pass it they would, for the principle which it embodies has become official Labor policy. The likelihood of its realization depends, therefore, on the trend of national politics. In order to predict on this matter we must leave the realm of accomplished fact and enter the realm of speculation. Many people are wondering what bearing the recent municipal elections are likely to have upon the next general election—an event which can scarcely be delayed beyond next spring or autumn. It is difficult to prophesy with any certainty. The influence of local elections on parliamentary elections may . be exaggerated: as I have pointed out above, many of the municipal contests are fought on local issues, and when it comes to national affairs the party issues often become more clear-cut, individual prejudices become more marked, apprehension more acute, controversy more embittered, and political intelligence less noticeable. Many electors will vote Labor in the local elections and yet support one of the other parties in the parliamentary elections. Nevertheless, the good work which the Labor town councillors are doing in the localities is helping to convince the nation of the capacity of the Labor Party to govern the country wisely and temperately, and to impress people with the fact that progress and stability can go hand in hand in the political arena. The other parties, particularly the Conservatives, are uneasy at the municipal achievements of the Labor movement, viewed from the standpoint of influencing the trend of national politics, and I think myself that they have reason to be uneasy!

DES MOINES TRIES THE CONCILIATION COURT

BY FRANCIS R. AUMANN

State University of Iowa

Des Moines joins the list of cities which have lifted justice in small matters out of the class of prohibited luxuries available only to the rich.

AFTER much activity on the part of members of the local municipal court a conciliation branch was established at Des Moines on September 1, 1927, under the statute of 1923 providing court rules for the conciliation of small claims. Judge H. H. Sawyer, who had studied the Cleveland and Minneapolis courts, was particularly active; and upon the establishment of the court he was appointed conciliator to serve for the period ending March 31, 1928. He was also authorized to prepare such blanks, books, and dockets as he deemed necessary for the successful transaction of business. Judge Sawyer went about this task with commendable zeal and the court was soon in active operation. From all indications the court is operating with marked success.

At the end of two weeks 75 cases had been filed and the number increased as the public became familiar with the nature of the court. Judge Sawyer felt that it was unfortunate that the court had been called a conciliation court and not a small claims court, because of the confusion resulting to the general public as to its nature. It seems that the public got the impression that because of its name the court was a court of domestic relations.

PROCEDURE IS SIMPLE

The procedure in the new branch of the municipal court is simple. One of the municipal judges is detailed to act as conciliator for the period of one year.

If for any good reason he can not be present any of the other judges may serve in his place. This judge applies the rules of conciliation which have been adopted by the municipal court.

The judge appointed as conciliator receives no increase in pay. One of the deputies of the clerk of the municipal court is made clerk of the conciliation branch at no increase in pay. The state and city incurs no additional expense at all.

Any person who has a claim which is within the jurisdiction of the municipal court may appear before the conciliator and state his claim without formality or written pleadings. The keynote of the new branch is its simplicity and directness of action. Formalism is conspicuously absent. The employee who feels he has been cheated out of $5.00 in salary by his employer may take his grievance before the conciliator without paying an attorney. The conciliator may reach for a telephone, call up the employer and bring him into his office for an informal settlement. There will be no costly notices, no bewildering procedure, no delays, none of the things which in the past stood between justice and the poor man.

If the conciliator finds that it is a proper case for conciliation, the defendant is notified and the conciliator attempts to adjust the claim. On the other hand if he thinks that it is not a proper claim for conciliation, he says so and the claimant is permitted, if he so desires, to file his suit in the municipal court in the usual manner.

FOR SMALL CLAIMS, CONCILIATION MUST FIRST BE ATTEMPTED

The conciliation process is vitalized by the provision that no claim of $100 or less shall be filed in the municipal court until a good-faith effort has been made to settle the claim by conciliation and a certificate to that effect furnished by the conciliator. There are exceptions to this, however, as in cases of suits aided by attachment, or to enforce a lien, or for replevin, or upon written contracts when due, or in cases where the petition states that the defendant is about to change his residence from the county, or where either party to the controversy is a non-resident of the county.

When a claim is filed with the conciliator, he sees to it that the defendant is notified by telephone, or mail, orally, or by service of an original notice. In this notification he must inform the defendant of the amount of the claim, the person making it, the nature of the claim, and the time fixed for the hearing of the matter.

If the defendant has been served with an original notice to appear before the conciliator and he fails to appear, the case may be docketed by the claimant and judgment entered in the usual manner. On the other hand if the defendant has been notified orally, by telephone, or by mail, and he fails to appear, the conciliator may at his discretion, order the case filed in municipal court and an original notice to be served upon the defendant with or without prepayment of costs. Or the conciliator may make any other order in the furtherance of justice.

The parties may appear at the hearing in person and present their respective claims and defenses to the conciliator, or either one of them may be

represented by counsel who is authorized to settle the controversy. The hearing is informal. The conciliator may swear the witnesses and take evidence in such fashion as he deems most conducive to a settlement of the controversy, or he may suspend altogether the rules of evidence and swearing of witnesses. The elasticity and the wide discretion vested in the judge is one of the court's chief merits. Any information obtained at the hearings or during the proceedings is confidential, and may not be used against the one giving it, or in the trial of the case afterwards. The hearings, however, are held in the open court room, the parties sitting with the judge around a table. There is nothing private about the hearings.

If the conciliator is unable to settle the controversy he furnishes a certificate showing that a good-faith effort has been made to conciliate the case. This is made upon the request of either party and permits him to commence his action in the municipal court. An appearance before the conciliator by any party gives the court jurisdiction for the trial of the case, but no case shall be assigned for trial in the municipal court within five days of the hearing by the conciliator, except by the consent of both parties.

When a case has been fully settled by the conciliator, no further record is kept. When the settlement agreed upon is not fully paid or executed, it is reduced to writing, signed by both parties, and filed with the clerk of the municipal court, and afterwards a judgment may be entered on it at the request of either party, or by direction of the conciliator or any judge of the municipal court.

COSTS ARE ONE DOLLAR

In all cases adjusted by the conciliator a fee of $1 is taxed and paid as costs.

This is in lieu of all other costs. This small charge brings the court to the door of any man. If a poor man's court is the ultimate desideratum in the administration of justice, and that is the general contention made by able commentators, then this inexpensive system certainly fulfills the purpose and puts an effective and efficacious agency of settling small disputes close to the people of small means.

The fee is assessed at the direction of the conciliator, and may be required before filing the case if he chooses. When no settlement is made, no fee is taxed, but if a fee has already been paid, it is credited upon the filing fee in the municipal court.

The records show that the cases have continued to increase. In September, the first month of operation, there were 130, in October there were 164, in November the number of cases before the court was still larger, and there is every reason to believe that it will continue to increase as people learn more about it.

The court has not been able to conciliate in every case, but that would be too much to expect. About 254 of the 294 cases heard up until October 1, were disposed of amicably; 18 were still pending on October 31; in 12 cases the service was defective, and 10 were dismissed or dropped. The record shows clearly that the court has made a place for itself.

The forms first devised by Judge Sawyer were used for some time and then discarded in favor of a rubber stamp indicating the disposal of the case. Some of the forms were completely changed, others were permitted to remain intact. The changes effected demonstrate as well as anything the experimental character of the court. It is trying things out and retaining or discarding at the dictate of experience.

Among other changes, Judge Sawyer is of the opinion that there ought to be provision for the service of original notice by registered mail, and that the conciliator ought to have the right, or duty, to enter some kind of judgment after hearing the case when the parties cannot agree on a settlement, and then permit either party to transfer the case to trial before another judge on the payment of a fee of perhaps $2.

It has also been suggested that the conciliator should be appointed, perhaps by the governor, and for a long term, with removal only for cause. Tenure on a classified civil service basis might be the most satisfactory arrangement. At any rate the experience in Des Moines, as well as the experience in Cleveland and Minneapolis, demonstrates that the success or failure of the plan depends very largely on the man who attempts to conciliate. If the right man can be found he should be kept in the place. The great success of the court in Cleveland was largely due to the peculiar talents of the man who founded the court and who acted as Conciliator until his death, a year ago. The whole process is new and in a formative period. Undoubtedly many changes will take place as time passes. The best measure of its success is its continued growth.

DUBLIN'S PROPOSED MANAGER-COUNCIL PLAN

BY F. H. BOLAND

Dublin, Ireland

The Free State is about to confer city manager government upon Greater Dublin. The proposal departs from the American plan in several important features designed to meet conditions peculiar to Ireland. The system of metropolitan government is novel. :: :: :: ::

THE Irish local government system[1] suffered seriously in the revolutionary period from 1918 to 1921. Elected local councils became political storm centers and neglected their duties. Central supervision of local administration became, in the later phases of the struggle, impossible. Many irregularities crept into the conduct of local affairs. The effect of the Criminal Injuries Acts, which made judicial decrees for "malicious injuries" a first charge on the available funds of the local authority within whose area the offence was committed, was to bring the local treasuries to the verge of bankruptcy.

This was the state of affairs which confronted the Free State government when it took office in 1921, and it was enabled to deal with it by the very violent reaction of public opinion which followed the civil disturbances of 1922. Legal proceedings were instituted wholesale against errant local bodies and their officials, while statutory powers were given the minister for local government and public health to dissolve and replace by paid commissioners, appointed by himself, local authorities whose discharge of their duties was found, upon enquiry, to be incompetent or dishonest.

Under these powers, twenty local

[1] See J. J. Horgan, NATIONAL MUNICIPAL REVIEW, XV, 449.

authorities were dissolved and, in all but three cases, their functions were transferred to single commissioners. In every case, the result has been lower taxes and better services. Indeed, so violent is the contrast between the administration of these officials and that of the elected councils that a considerable body of opinion has grown up in favor of the appointed expert, as opposed to the elected body of amateurs, as the model of Irish local government. It is unlikely that reform will go so far as to eliminate the representative element. Drastic modification of the whole local government system is foreshadowed, but the present tendencies are towards such a combination of the expert administrator and elected council as is achieved in the American city manager plan.

DUBLIN NOW GOVERNED BY APPOINTED COMMISSION

Dublin, the capital of the Free State, was governed, from its foundation by charter of Henry II in 1171 until 1924, under a mayor-council form. The government of the city had been, for many years, a byword for corruption and incompetence. On May 20, 1924, the minister dissolved the council and vested the government of the corporation of Dublin in a body of three paid commissioners appointed by himself.

On July 4 of the same year, the minister appointed a commission of enquiry, known as the Greater Dublin Commission, to:

examine the several laws and the practice affecting the administration of local and public utility services, including local representation and taxation, throughout the capital city of Dublin and the county of Dublin and to recommend such changes as may be desirable.

The commission was composed of twelve members, including prominent citizens, labor leaders, university teachers and politicians. It reported on July 7, 1926, and recommended, among other matters, that the manager-representative council plan be adopted in Dublin.

The adoption of the recommendations of the commission lies, not with the citizens of Dublin, but with the national legislature. It is expected that a bill dealing with the report will be introduced in the coming session.

THE METROPOLITAN AREA TO BE CONSOLIDATED

The report deals, at the outset, with the problem created by the agglomeration, immediately outside the existing municipal boundaries, of centers of population and industry enjoying an independent and uncorrelated existence as units of local government. The proposals dealing with this problem exemplify a general tendency in Ireland to enlarge the units of local government, disregarding parochial sentiment in favor of the economies to be derived from the unification of services over the extended areas.

The commission recommends the extension of the boundaries of Dublin to include certain outlying areas. The proposed extension involves an increase in the city's population from 304,802 to 425,692, or 39 per cent; an increase in the valuation from $5,141,-455 to $9,407,400, or 82 per cent, and an increase in area from 13 to 64 square miles, or 392 per cent. The areas which it is proposed to annex are stated to be those which (1) have acquired, or are acquiring, a markedly urban character; or (2) have interests identical to, or indissolubly connected with, those of the existing city; or (3) owe their development to their propinquity to the city.

It will be noticed that the valuation of the incorporated areas is higher *per capita* (but lower per acre) than the valuation of the existing city. The present tax rate in Dublin is considerably in excess of the rates prevailing in the outlying areas.

Over the area to be comprised in the new city, there are at present some nineteen tax-raising and tax-spending bodies maintaining separate establishments of buildings, equipment and personnel. They occupy the time and energy of some 400 elected representatives in the uncoördinated handling of problems which are essentially the same over the entire area. These bodies discharge both policy-making and administrative functions.

In the scheme of government proposed by the commission, all these bodies cease to exist. Greater Dublin will have but one policymaking agency, the great council, and but one administrative agency, the city manager.

THE GREAT COUNCIL ELECTED BY P. R.

All the rights, powers and privileges of the dissolved Dublin council and of the various other local authorities which previously functioned within the area of Greater Dublin will be transferred to one body to be called the great council. Its duties will be to shape the civic policy, to fix the tax rate for all municipal services and to control the administration of the city manager.

The great council will consist of 65

members elected on a system of proportional representation as representatives of areas to be determined by law. Taking as its basis of distribution "population, acreage and extent of common services to be enjoyed," the report recommends an allocation of representatives in the proportion of 35 to the existing city and 30 to the annexed areas. This may justly be considered an over-representation of the wealthy, suburban voter.

Proportional representation is firmly rooted in the political system of the Free State. The "single transferrable vote" principle is the method of calculation invariably employed. The areas of representation in Greater Dublin will probably be small; the legislature is not likely to be led, by the objection that ward-elected councils do not represent the whole city and "at-large" elected councils do not represent the parts, into disregarding the lesson learnt in the attempt to elect a portion of the senate by proportional representation from a nation-wide constituency in 1925.[1]

The great council will hold office for four years. It will appoint a committee of estimates, consisting of nine members, to which the budget prepared by the manager will be submitted and a committee of accounts, of similar though not identical membership, to examine quarterly the manager's expenditure accounts.

No agreement was reached upon the question of the political leadership of the great council. In an obvious compromise, the report recommends the annual election by the great council of one of its own members to be chairman. He will be an ex-officio member of all committees and will be furnished with an office and secretarial staff and with "suitable accommodation for civic re-

[1] See H. F. Gosnell, *Am. Pol. Sci. Rev.*, XX, 118 (1926).

ceptions and similar functions." The question of his remuneration was not decided.

THE DISTRICT COUNCILS—APPOINTMENT OF CHARGES

Annexations of contiguous areas by county boroughs are, in the practice of English local government, usually accompanied by provisions securing the annexed areas a preferential tax rate for a period of years subsequent to their incorporation. No such provisions are made by the report. But the existing localization of certain services —which, however, must be considered temporary—and the desirability of preserving intact the principle "no service, no rate" over the enlarged municipality are provided for in a dubious expedient.

A classification is made of the services to be provided by the new municipality into those of common enjoyment over the entire city and those of limited local user. The former, which include public health and welfare services, main drainage, housing, water and electricity supply, road construction, fire protection and certain services connected with education, elections and the courts, are reserved to the great council. The latter comprise garbage, street cleaning and surfacing, lighting, markets and abattoirs, public baths and rest rooms and recreation facilities.

To provide for the local government of those services designated as being of limited local user, Greater Dublin is divided into two districts—one, called "Dublin," comprising the existing city and contiguous areas, mostly of a markedly urban character, the other, called the "Dublin Coastal Borough," comprising more outlying residential or semi-rural districts. The members elected to the great council as representatives of these two districts will constitute respectively the Dublin Local Council and the Dublin Coastal Borough Council. Each local council, sitting separately, will consider annually the budget for its peculiar local services to be prepared and submitted to it by the city manager.

Although the sole power of levying taxes for all services, common and local, is vested in the great council, the commission seems to recommend that the great council should have no option but to levy the amounts required to finance the budgets passed by the district councils. Moreover, these subsidiary bodies will exercise independent control of the manager's administration of the local services. The proposal thus to subject the manager to the control of a federation or hierarchy of councils would seem to sacrifice a cardinal virtue of the American city manager plan—the simplicity of the relation which the immediate and direct responsibilty of the manager to a single council creates between them

A CONTRAST TO THE AMERICAN PLAN

A brief comparison of the local government *milieu* in Ireland with that in the United States is necessary to explain the proposals of the commission relating to the city manager.

There is no municipal home rule in Ireland. The Irish city (or county borough), the most autonomous of the local government units, is limited as to its powers by statute and, to a great extent, controlled as to the manner of their exercise by the local government and public health department of the national government. The central authority, sharing the responsibility for both the policy and the administration of local affairs, thus enters, as a *tertium quid*, into the ideally simple relations of manager and council, making it impossible to fix upon them

complete responsibility for their respective functions.

Again, Irish local government shows nothing corresponding to the popularly elected or politically appointed, short-term executive of the American city. His place is taken in Ireland by the permanent civil servant. The proposals of the commission relating to the tenure of the Dublin manager reflect the extent to which public confidence in his integrity and ability secures the Irish local official immunity in his dealings with his elected authority.

The condition noted in the last paragraph is likely to have important effects upon the operation of the city manager plan in Dublin. It is probable, for instance, that the ethics of the Dublin manager will be those not of a professional city manager but of a professional civil servant. He will execute unquestioningly the policies of his council, but he will probably exercise a much greater influence on those policies, without appearing to do so, than the school of American managers who act as community leaders and openly advocate political programs.

The reform of American government has proceeded on the principle of fixing political and administrative responsibility. The principle is sometimes lost sight of in the report. In fact, the confusion of responsibility is a formal defect of many governmental institutions in Ireland and England, which, however, owing principally to the character and ability of the civil service, is not apparent in practice.

In general, it may be said that, whereas in the United States the type of municipal life is dynamic and progressive, in Ireland it is static and conservative. A new spirit of enterprise and experimentalism was, indeed, displayed by the Dublin commissioners when they awarded a contract for cleaning the streets of Dublin to a

French firm and by the Free State government when they initiated the $30,000,000 Shannon power project, giving the contract to a German firm. But this spirit is still young in the Free State.

FIRST CITY MANAGER APPOINTED BY CENTRAL GOVERNMENT

The first city manager will be appointed by the minister for local government for a period of three years. Thereafter, the great council will make the appointments for successive renewable periods of seven years. No professional qualifications are required for the position beyond good education and proved capacity in municipal administration. The salary of the manager will be fixed by the minister and the great council may, with the minister's consent, grant a pension to the manager upon cessor of office not due to misconduct or incapacity.

The manager will be assisted in his administration by an advisory board composed of his department heads. They will be known as civic directors and will be responsible solely to the manager though not necessarily appointed or dismissible by him. A departmentalization of the civic administration is proposed under the heads of finance, municipal health, housing, supply and education. The advisory board will meet regularly and function as a coördinating agency. It is an important body in the proposed budgetary procedure, conferring upon the estimates submitted by each director for his department as a preliminary to the preparation of the budget by the manager and its submission to the committee of estimates of the great council. The commission's proposals, that the manager should be civic director of finance and that the minutes of the advisory board should be furnished

regularly to the great council for their determination, must be deemed ill-considered.

The manager will be responsible to the great council for the "due and proper administration of the affairs of the city." But even the mild degree of accountability suggested by the phrase is likely to remain largely theoretical for lack of the machinery to effectuate it in practice. The great council cannot remove the manager. It may suspend him, but then only for "gross dereliction of duty." To remove him finally, written charges must be preferred and established against him at a public sworn enquiry. The immunity which public opinion grants the administrative official in Ireland and the effect of central control on local responsibility are curiously illustrated in the following passage of the report:

Since there is herein recommended duality of function, the general control of administration resting with an elective council and the actual administration carried out by an official responsible to and removable by it, provision must be made both for an appeal on the part of this official against the council—which might properly be made to the minister—and for an appeal to the electorate by the great council, against adverse decision of the minister.[1]

So far as the great council is concerned, the manager will be absolutely independent in his control of the administration. Attempts on the part of the council or its members to interfere with his administrative acts, otherwise than by means of an investigatory procedure outlined in the report, will be punishable as misdemeanors. But in practice the manager will have to share the control of, and consequently the responsibility for, much of the civic administration with the local government department.

[1] Greater Dublin Commission of Enquiry, 1926, Pt. X, Section 57.

In connection with two important matters of administration—purchasing and personnel—the manager's powers will be very limited. Under the system of combined purchasing at present in operation,[1] he will have to purchase jointly with other local authorities from official contractors. As regards personnel, the commission recommends that the great council should fix salaries and make general rules, but that the powers of appointment, dismissal, promotion, etc., should belong to the manager to be exercised subject to the sanction of the minister and in accordance with "any statutory provisions that relate to appointments under local authorities." Under the existing law,[2] the appointment of all executive and professional staffs under local bodies is vested in a state-appointed civil service commission and the minister has a controlling voice in the removal of all officers.

The manager, as director of finance, will prepare the annual budgets for common and local services. The committee of estimates will meet in public session, previously advertised, and the manager will be present to afford all required information to taxpayers and representatives of citizen organizations. He must submit his expenditure accounts quarterly to the committee of civic accounts of the great council and he will also be subject to annual audit by the district auditor of the central department.

[1] Local Authorities (Combined Purchasing) Act, 1925; see Local Government and Public Health Department, Saorstat Eireann, 1st Report, 1922–1925, p. 148.
[2] Local Authorities (Officers and Employees) Act, 1926.

The form of government recommended by the commission is an "adaptation of the city manager idea to the special conditions in Greater Dublin."[3] The great dissimilarity between these conditions and those in, say, Cleveland, Sacramento or Kansas City, particularly with respect to the presence of state administrative control in one case and its absence in the other, has involved wide departures in structure from the model of the American charter. The Greater Dublin Commission may be said to have adopted the *animus*, if not the *corpus*, of the city manager plan. The extent to which the movement initiated by the commission is likely to spread may be estimated from the fact that since the publication of its report the two next largest cities in Ireland, Cork and Belfast, have taken steps to adopt some form of the city manager plan.[4]

To one who knew the intense nationalism of the Sinn Fein movement, the receptivity to outside ideas shown by the report is remarkable. It is avowedly based upon the "best experience of the United States, Germany and . . . Switzerland," but although other, especially German, ideas have influenced its conclusions, it proposes for Dublin the system of government which "has proved in the United States at once the most democratic form of municipal government and the most businesslike form of municipal administration."[5]

[3] Report, p. 2.
[4] *Irish Independent*, Jan. 7, 1928; Jan. 20, 1928.
[5] Report, p. 2.

ADMINISTRATIVE REORGANIZATION ADOPTED IN CALIFORNIA

BY JOHN F. SLY

Harvard University

The successive steps by which consolidation is being accomplished in California. :: :: :: :: :: :: :: :: ::

CALIFORNIA continues to reorganize. The mass of isolated units that served as an administrative structure less than a decade ago has been slowly but methodically refashioned into a carefully integrated system, and recent legislation has capped the structure with a governor's council designed to bring balance and stability to the reformed framework. Even the unadorned record is impressive:

January 1, 1919, one hundred and twelve independent agencies. By July 29, 1927, these had been reduced to fifty-four independent agencies and five departments. Legislation in this year effective July 29, 1927, left but thirty-eight independent agencies and nine departments coördinated by a governor's council. And proposals for 1929 leave but fifteen independent agencies and eleven functionally integrated departments.

For more than a quarter of a century the governors of California have emphasized the need of such a program. In 1899 Governor Gage was condemning "too many state boards and commissions with extensive lists of subordinate employees." Two years later he was warning the legislature against laws "creating unnecessary offices with their incidental charges against the state." In 1907 Governor Gillett complained that California was one of the most expensive states in the Union

"with many commissions to care for, some of which seem . . . to be needless." Governor Johnson was increasingly emphatic. In his inaugural as well as in his first biennial message two years later he not only added his criticism but proposed improvements.

Interest, however, was moderate. The demands were for popularizing the political processes, and direct legislation, the recall, a more effective primary, county home rule, and the short ballot were the panaceas of the moment. But the governor found occasion to urge the appointment of numerous elective officials, to hint at the possibility of "a cabinet like the cabinet of the chief executive of the nation," to recommend a more centralized control of the state's attorneys, and in calling attention to five insane asylums, one home for the feeble-minded, and various reform schools and teachers' colleges, to urge the elimination of local boards controlling each, and the creation "of one centralized body."

Little, however, was done. A state board of control was created with the authority to supervise and in a measure to coördinate the financial affairs of the various administrative units. This was helpful, but inadequate. Overlapping and duplication of functions characterized the leading agencies. On June 30, 1917, there were reported one hundred and twenty-six officers, boards, commissions, and bureaus in the state administrative service. Unofficial interests were aroused. The California Taxpayers' Association devoted numerous issues of its monthly journal to the question, and in January, 1919, prepared a detailed plan for reorganization. It proposed the functional coördination of the various state agencies, and prescribed certain principles to be followed: departments dealing with matters of policy should be controlled by boards; departments dealing with administrative and executive functions should be controlled by a single head; policy-making departments should be divisionally organized; the boards presiding over such departments should consist of the heads of the respective divisions; and all department heads and chiefs of division should be appointed by the governor and be responsible to him. The organization was to consist of twelve departments supervised by some fifty-two officers, in place of one hundred and twenty agencies and four hundred and sixty officers.

EFFICIENCY AND ECONOMY COMMITTEE

But Governor William D. Stephens was moved to official cognizance of conditions. In November, 1918, he appointed a committee on efficiency and economy consisting of eleven members to make a thorough investigation of "the administration of the state's affairs," and the result of its work was given to him the following March. Three recommendations were embodied in the report,—centralization of responsibility, coöperation of the larger organization units, and coördination of the various agencies. These principles were to be given effect through the creation of a governor's cabinet composed of departmental executives, by providing, in addition, an executive council of major administrative officers,

and by placing in departments only those agencies performing similar or allied functions. Some seventy administrative units were grouped into ten departments, and a governor's cabinet provided composed of their respective heads.

The work of the committee was well done,—but fallible. Even the governor gave it only a moderate endorsement. Many services were exempt from the reorganization. Others were retained that seemed needless. Allocation of sensitive agencies caused criticism. And although separate bills urging some of the recommendations were introduced into the legislature (as well as one sponsored by the California Taxpayers' Association) only one,—providing a department of agriculture, —became a law. And the creation of this department was considered and treated largely as an experiment.

But the urgent need of economy was not to be so easily appeased. Early in 1921 Governor Stephens again sent a message to the legislature announcing the introduction of eight bills dealing with matters of governmental efficiency, and during the closing days of the session the measures were passed. These established five departments,— finance, labor and industrial relations, education, public works, and institutions, in addition to reorganizing the newly created department of agriculture. Sixty-three of some one hundred appointive administrative agencies were allocated to appropriate places in the new departments, about seventy-three appointments were eliminated from executive patronage and placed in the hands of administrative officers, and some sixty-one were changed to positions bearing advisory powers only.

But there were those who remained dissatisfied. The legislation was beneficial but still insufficient. In his inaugural address Governor Richardson gave a terse description of what he considered its inadequacies, and, under the authority of the constitutional budget amendment adopted the previous year, expressed vigorous disapproval through drastic cuts in requests for appropriations, even eliminating the funds of some activities altogether. Embarrassed state agencies sought relief in the courts to compel the payment of their bills, while in other instances the state controller enlisted legal aid to obtain sums for the general treasury collected by the agencies themselves. Relying on legislation, predating the budget amendment, providing more or less continuing appropriations, the agencies protested the reduction of these funds through the use of the executive veto. But the court held that while this former legislation was not, in general, affected by the budget amendment, still the governor's action expressed in a budget bill might "impose a limitation upon the amount of money available" to such agencies from such funds. The governor was vindicated, but state reorganization as a scientific problem received little impetus.

GOVERNOR'S COUNCIL CREATED

Such was the heritage of Governor Young. In his inaugural address of January 4, 1927, he reviewed the whole matter and presented his program,—the continuation of the work commenced eight years before. In response to this request the legislature took definite action. Over forty bills were introduced pertaining to various phases of state administrative reorganization, and the close of the session found important enactments among the chaptered laws. Perhaps the most significant was that providing for a governor's council to consist of the directors of the nine departments, which, both as previously existing and

as created and reorganized under the new legislation, are finance, education, public works, public health, institutions, agriculture, industrial relations, social welfare, and natural resources. It is provided that at least once a month this group is to meet in Sacramento at such time and place as the governor may designate. Each member is required to report at the meeting acts pertinent to the administration of his department, and to perform such other duties as may be required from time to time by the governor. "Prior to the organization of this council," said Alexander R. Heron, the new director of finance and sponsor of the recent legislation, "over a period of many years, I doubt whether four or more of the state heads have ever got together round a table to talk over state business. . . . I hope to read in the papers next fall that 'there was a meeting of the directors of the business of the state of California.'" [1] And the project has begun. The council has held (December, 1927) four meetings. They were, indeed, genuine business meetings,—but open to the public. The directors of the various departments reported to the governor upon the public affairs intrusted to them, and conferred with him as well as with one another upon policies, plans for coördination, intelligent economies, and projects for future development. The members have apparently shown every willingness to coöperate in meeting common problems, and the experiment is received as a new departure in effective administration in California.

SUMMARY OF PROGRAM

The general principles that have guided the more strictly administrative

[1] Much of the material recorded here is due to the courtesy of Mr. Heron, who very kindly read the manuscript and made many important suggestions which, it is hoped, are correctly presented.

features of the program may be briefly summarized:

A methodical integration (extending over a period of ten years) of the state's administrative services, within unifunctional departments.

Each department to be in charge of a director appointed by the governor and serving at his pleasure.

Statutory divisions (as well as certain boards and commissions) to be generally provided; but except as otherwise required by law, each division to have only such duties as the director of the department may prescribe.

Additional divisions, bureaus or sections to be established or discontinued by the director with the approval of the governor.

Former boards and commissions abolished in the process of reorganization to have their duties transferred to appropriate departments, but these to be treated as departmental functions and not to be assigned by statute to a division.

The appointment of all division chiefs as well as all subordinate officers, whether serving immediately under the director or under the division, to be vested in the director, —except as otherwise provided by law.

THE STATE BOARD OF CONTROL

Aside from the provisions for a governor's council, the recent legislation has provided for a rearrangement of most of the old departments as well as for the establishment of others. A new state board of control has come into existence. Its personnel is now composed of the director of finance as chairman of the board, the chief of the division of service and supply of the department of finance, and the state controller. Its main duties at present involve the making of rules and regulations governing the presentation and audit of claims against the state for which an appropriation has been made or for which a state fund is available. The department of finance has, indeed, succeeded to most of its former functions,—in a way it is even a superior supervising authority. But the duties of the state board of control are, nevertheless, prescribed by law, and do not depend upon what the director of finance may assign to it.

The department of finance is under the direction of a director of finance, appointed by the governor at a salary of $10,000 a year. He is from time to time to visit and inspect the various state institutions, once a month he is to count the money in the state treasury, title to all real property acquired by the state is taken in his name, the investment of various state funds is under his charge, and he is ex officio member of several important boards. The department is divided into three divisions,—budget and accounts, service and supply, and motor vehicles, while in the manner indicated above, the state board of control forms an additional subordinate unit. It is the duty of the department to approve all contracts made by any state officer or department; to install and supervise a uniform system of accounting for all persons handling public moneys; to furnish the necessary supplies to the various state departments; to superintend the management of the state capitol building as well as other buildings devoted to similar purposes, and to supervise the printing work of the various departments.

The department of public works has likewise been reorganized. It is conducted under the control of a director appointed by the governor at a salary of $10,000 a year. Statutory requirements provide four divisions,—engineering and irrigation, water rights, highways, and architecture; and section three makes provision for the California highway commission (formerly an independent body) to operate within the department. The five members of this commission are, however, appointed by the governor, and the statutes confer certain distinct functions upon it,—principally to budget the state's share of the gasolene tax for the construction and repair of highways. The department of public works has, moreover, had its duties further increased. A separate act transferred to it certain functions with respect to various ports (Eureka, San Diego and San José); and while no separate division to care for this work was specified, it is probable that the director will organize one. At present, however, the new work is simply treated as a separate function of the department.

NEW DEPARTMENTS

There is a new department of natural resources. It is also under the control of a director appointed by the governor at a salary of $6,000 a year. Four divisions are provided,—mines and mining, forestry, parks, and fish and game. The division of mines and mining is in charge of the state mineralogist. The state forester, appointed by the director upon nomination of the state board of forestry, is chief of the division of forestry. The chief of the division of parks is similarly appointed upon nomination of the state park commission. Both the state board of forestry and the state park commission are general policy-determining bodies appointed by the governor for the guidance of their respective divisions. The division of fish and game is administered by a commission of three appointed by the governor. The department succeeds also to the powers and duties of some eleven administra-

tive units formerly operating as more or less independent supervisors, bureaus, boards and commissions.

The department of industrial relations is newly created under the control of an executive officer to be known as director of industrial relations, the position to be held *ex officio* by the chairman of the industrial accident commission, an official designated by the governor at a salary of $6,000 a year from the commission membership. The department is administered through the division of industrial accidents, and safety is to be controlled by the industrial accident commission,— three persons appointed by the governor for four years,—which is continued in existence. Within the division of industrial welfare there is created a commission to be known as the industrial welfare commission to consist of five members (at least one of whom shall be a woman) appointed by the governor for a term of four years, and section five of the act creates a commission of immigration and housing, consisting of five members serving at the pleasure of the governor, the commission to

have power to determine policies for guidance of the department of industrial relations in all matters concerning the functions heretofore vested in the division of immigration and housing of the department of labor and industrial relations.

Two additional departments were established embracing social welfare and public health. The former is under the control of a director of social welfare and six persons appointed by the governor. The director is appointed by and serves at the pleasure of the governor at a salary of $4,000 a year; the others, similarly chosen for four years, serve without compensation. The act does not determine the divisions to be established, but prescribes that the new department shall succeed to all the duties and responsibilities of the state board of charities and corrections, the department of public welfare, the executive board of the department of public welfare and the children's agents of the state board of control. The department of health is similarly organized under a board of health consisting of seven members, one of whom is known as the director of public health and serves as executive officer of the board. He is appointed . by the governor at a salary of $6,000. The remaining members are similarly appointed for terms of four years.

There remain but three other departments,—agriculture, institutions and education. The department of agriculture is headed by the usual director appointed by the governor and serving at his pleasure. His salary is at present $6,000 a year. There is only one division provided by law,— the division of land settlement, but five others have been established,— animal husbandry, markets, weights and measures, agricultural chemistry and plant industry. The department of institutions is similarly directed. There are no statutory divisions, but its work includes the supervision of a dozen state hospitals and welfare institutions. The state superintendent of public instruction (elected by the people for four years with a salary of $5,000) is *ex officio* director of the department of education and a member, therefore, of the governor's council. Statutory provisions require four divisions in this department,—that of libraries, of school planning, of textbooks, certification and trust funds, and of normal and special schools. There is also, at present, a state board of education consisting of ten members appointed by the governor (subject to confirmation by a two-thirds vote of the senate) holding office for four years

and serving without pay. The division of textbooks, certification and trust funds is under its control. In addition it administers the teachers' retirement fund, adopts rules and regulations for the conduct of public schools, and prescribes courses of study for the various state teachers' colleges. A recent constitutional amendment (Senate Constitutional Amendment 26) to be submitted to the voters at the next general election proposes the abolition of the elective superintendent, the appointment of a director of education to hold office at the pleasure of the governor, and a reorganized board of education.

SURVIVING ELECTIVE AND INDEPENDENT AGENCIES

The program is not yet complete. Plans for 1929 provide two additional departments,—professional standards and commerce. The former will consolidate some sixteen boards now operating as independent units, such as the board of accountancy, board of bar examiners, board of barber examiners, board of cosmetology, detective license bureau, etc., and the latter will embrace the various functions of banking, insurance, building and loan supervision, corporations and real estate. If the program succeeds, the administrative services of California will be reduced to eleven elected officials,—governor, lieutenant-governor, secretary of state, four members of the state board of equalization, the controller, treasurer, surveyor-general, and attorney-general; fifteen independent agencies, including a legislative council bureau, civil service commission, advisory pardon board, railroad commission, and veterans' welfare board; eleven departments comprising some ninety subordinate units; and a governor's council of eleven members.

MUNICIPAL LAND POLICIES AND THEIR APPLICATION TO CITY PLANNING AND HOUSING

BY THOMAS L. HINCKLEY

European cities are much advanced in the formulation and execution of land policies. Through ownership of land directly, as well as by regulation of private parcels by means of zoning and planning, future development is controlled. :: :: :: :: :: :: ::

It may as well be admitted at the outset that a definite municipal land policy—meaning by this a plan or program governing the acquisition of land for general municipal purposes— probably does not exist in any American city. School boards, water commissions, park boards, and the like are, it is true, constantly acquiring land for their own specific purposes and are frequently very successful in their efforts; but the purchase of land for general public purposes—which may or may not be defined at the time of purchase—or the coördination of the land policies of the various boards and commissions in a general policy for the entire city—is something of which the writer, after considerable inquiry, has been unable to discover an instance.

Even where city plans have been adopted, and the purchase of land is envisaged as part of the scheme, it cannot be said that land policies exist; for the acquisition of land is in this case incidental to the working out of the plan and does not constitute a major municipal function as should be the case. Zoning, which regulates the use of land, may simplify the problem of what land to purchase for public purposes but is not concerned with any method of procedure in this connection.

There are, of course, obvious reasons

why a definite land policy—"land-planning," to borrow from Miss James [1] —has not become an important factor in American municipal administration. Our city governments have grown up under a system of private initiative which has largely subordinated municipal needs to the requirements of business development. The powers of condemnation which cities possess have been used sparingly and with the utmost consideration for the private owner; and it is quite possible that the conception of urban land as a field for public investment, to be bought with the express purpose of directing or regulating municipal growth, has rarely entered the minds of our municipal authorities.

This absence of a concrete land purchasing program or policy has prevented the accumulation of desirable plots or parcels while prices were cheap, with the result that cities usually pay "through the nose" when the need for land becomes imperative. [2] It has also worked to the disadvantage of cities in

[1] Harlean James, *Land Planning in the United States.*

[2] Every city has had its petty land scandals, and no later than last July the comptroller of New York City was reported to have asserted that the metropolis had paid for school sites and other plots anywhere from three to five times their assessed value!

permitting sporadic developments and encouraging disastrous land booms from the effects of which years are required for recovery.

Foresight and judgment in buying land for ultimate public use will realize economies over a term of years which the most casual citizen can appreciate. Real property values in our cities are almost doubling every ten years, at least one-third of this increase being estimated to be due to land; [1] so that on the average all urban land pays for itself within thirty years. Examples of individual plots which have doubled in value within a year's time are, of course, common.

EUROPEAN THOUGHT SINCE THE WAR

In Europe a proper policy with respect to the acquisition of public land is considered to be most important. The International Union of Cities in 1925 sent a questionnaire on this subject to its membership; and among the conclusions reached were the following: [2]

Every community owes it to itself to adopt a systematic land policy, with the purpose in view of encouraging desirable development, improving the housing situation and bettering means of communication.

The city, in order to pursue a satisfactory land policy, will need to own sufficient public land to control, through its location and amount, the trend of future extensions and at the same time to permit the municipality to exercise its influence on the selling price of building land.

The city should try to secure title to serviceable land in time to avoid paying more than the agricultural price.

The city, through its land policy, should prevent the illicit boosting of land values by offering at any time to dispose of its own land for building purposes.

No student of municipal economy can read these conclusions without realizing how far the exigencies of post-war readjustment have carried the cities of Europe away from the basis of unrestricted private initiative. That this trend towards community control of land within a city's boundaries applies not only to the more "radical" Central European states—whose cities have generally upheld the supremacy of the public welfare—but also to countries conservative in temperament, may be seen in the following quotations from the British reply to the questionnaire of the International Union of Cities. In his reply on behalf of the British municipalities, Dr. I. G. Gibbon, principal assistant secretary of the ministry of health, states: [3]

The general rule has hitherto been that local authorities are authorized to acquire land only if it is needed for the carrying out of their duties or powers. During the past few years there has been a marked change of opinion, and Parliament will now authorize any large town to acquire land for the general good of the community. . . .

This action of Parliament is an index of the change of public opinion. Whereas formerly it was almost taken for granted that land would be developed to the best advantage of the community if it were held in private hands, there is now felt to be a distinct advantage in the ownership of land, in some measure at least, by the local authority, with the consequent control of local development.

This change of view . . . has also been caused in part by the growing demand for communal development in the general interest of the community and the feeling that this control is facilitated if the land is owned by the local authority. [4]

[1] *Cf.* U. S. Census Reports, "Financial Statistics of Cities, 1915 and 1925." The actual reported increase for the period is $24,703,296,-157.

[2] These are conclusions nos. 1, 3, 4 and 6 of the Committees' Report—prepared for the 3rd International Congress of Cities, Paris, 1925.

[3] See pages 30–35 of the Committee's Report.

[4] It is only fair to say that Dr. Gibbon later characterizes this tendency as a swing of the pendulum rather than a permanent factor in English municipal economy; nevertheless, it would appear that the "swing" will be of considerable duration.

Further light on the subject of municipal land policies in European cities is cast by the report of the International Housing and Town Planning Congress held at Vienna last year. In this report Sir Theodore Chambers, chairman of Welwyn Garden City, speaking of planning in built-up urban areas, is quoted as follows: "It is clear that if anything practical is to be done in this generation towards the improvement of congested areas much wider powers should be granted local authorities to acquire the interests that stand in their way."

Gustaf Linden, architect of the Royal Swedish Building Board, after describing how the city of Stockholm acquired a tract of land three times the city's original area in order to make sure of proper future development, stated: "As long as there are possibilities of obtaining land with full (private) ownership, this is considered best. On the other hand, the towns themselves realize more and more the advantages of retaining ownership (in the land) thereby utilizing their right over this land to create adequate and beautiful plans and cheap dwelling houses."

Ernest Hein, chief building inspector of Vienna, after stating that the Austrian capital owns 28 per cent of all land within its borders—exclusive of streets and public plazas—announced that Vienna is fully "sold" on the value of a sane community land policy and will never again relinquish any of its real estate holdings, although it may be willing to use certain parcels as make-weights in negotiating for other property which it may consider more valuable from a public standpoint.

Undeniably, the European demand for the acquisition of excess land by the community and its use in controlling development, combating high prices for real estate and providing housing accommodations for the mass of citizens, is born of a bitter post-war experience which is in no apparent danger of being repeated in this country. Nevertheless, just as city planning—long a "European conceit"—has now achieved a leading place in American municipal economy—so it is well within the bounds of possibility that the necessity to buy up excess land in the public interest, to curb speculation in urban land values—and even to engage in housing—may ultimately come within the purview of our city governments. Indeed, housing is already a municipal issue in New York and is doubtless receiving official attention in many another large city.

WHAT SHOULD BE THE AMERICAN POLICY?

Assuming the possibility of conditions approaching in kind, if not in degree, those which have forced aggressive land policies upon European cities, what should our own cities do to prepare for them?

It would seem that there are at least four essential conditions which must be met before any city can contemplate a definite policy as to the acquisition of land for general municipal purposes; viz:

1. There must be a city plan;

2. The city must have power to acquire not only the land called for by the plan, but other tracts and plots as well, if their ownership by the city can be shown to be in the public interest;

3. In the special contingency of housing, the city must be free to sell or lease its surplus land to licensed housing corporations;

4. There must be provided a definite authority to administer the city's land policy.

The City Plan

First, as to a city plan. It cannot be said that any city which has not at least gone the length of forecasting its future physical needs is in a position to adopt a land policy. The city plan will indicate land which must be acquired to provide schools, parks, airports, playgrounds, parking space, miscellaneous public buildings, etc. It may include the designation of tracts desirable for housing purposes and of central slums which must be abolished and re-planned. It may also point to land outside present boundaries which should be purchased in the public interest. No matter how classified, all land transactions entering into the city plan form at once a basis upon which to formulate the city's land policy.

The financial counterpart of the physical plan must likewise be worked out, otherwise the city may embark upon costly betterment schemes without being properly prepared to finance them. Lack of such a coördination of physical and financial planning has frequently been charged against city plans of otherwise unquestioned merit.

Purchase of Excess Land

If the city is limited to the power of acquiring only such land as its official plan calls for it may handicap itself when conditions change, and revisions are in order. There is also an obvious business advantage to be gained in not specifying in advance all land desired for municipal purchase. Thirdly, as is stated in the general conclusions of the International Union of Cities, the possession of excess land may be necessary in a crisis to combat injurious speculation in land values,—although this will require a greater measure of home rule than most American cities now possess.

Housing

In the matter of housing we are, as already noted, discounting the future. It may be many years before any but our greatest and most congested centers will devote any attention to this problem. When it does come, however, it will conceivably be better to follow along the trail already blazed by the New York state housing law— which provides for licensed, limited-dividend housing corporations—rather than to set up municipal housing departments. Public housing is at best a complicated business and American city governments usually have sufficient troubles of their own without adding to them those of municipal landlord and renting agent!

Organization

The importance of land administration in at least our larger cities would seem to justify a separate controlling body, operating in conjunction with the planning authority, to interpret the city's development in terms of land. When many cities, to judge from some of the replies to the writer's inquiry, do not at present know how much land they own, the need for conserving municipal property is evident, to say nothing of obtaining good counsel in the acquiring of additional real estate.

The men chosen to perform this function will of necessity have to be above suspicion of personal motives— outstanding citizens in every respect. Although payment for expert advice in the selection of land for purchase must doubtless be permitted, the general experience of American cities indicates that the best results will be realized through the appointment of men of such calibre that they will not need to be compensated for their services.

As to the ability (or the desirability, for that matter) of American cities to formulate and pursue a consistent policy in the purchasing of land for general municipal purposes, opinions will naturally differ. To some it will seem an undue extension of municipal powers to let cities "get into the land business" even to the degree intimated, and only when it can be shown to be in the public interest to do so. To others it will seem like locking the barn door after the horse has been stolen to authorize cities to buy excess land when the most desirable plots have all been occupied,—and very likely there are cities where a municipal land policy would be of limited application. Finally, there is always the possibility that those influences which have hampered American civic progress in the past—lack of home rule, changing personnel in the administration, and party politics, to mention but a few—will do so in the future.

On the other hand, the physical, financial and social benefits to be derived from the timely and judicious buying of land—within limits—for ultimate public use—or merely to strengthen the public's bargaining power—are undeniable and have, it is hoped, been clearly outlined here. Municipal land policies are not only practicable but are actually in operation in many important European cities; they are feasible in any city whose citizens will forego a modicum of private gain on behalf of the general welfare.

NOTE.—It had been my hope to present, in connection with this article, a comparative table showing, for the leading cities of this country and Canada, as well as for the more important European cities, the amount of municipally-owned land and the purposes to which it is devoted.. While considerable information was obtained from various sources, some of it direct, the material is, on the whole, so fragmentary that a worth-while comparison of this nature is out of the question. But it must be said that as far as usable data were received the evidence was to the effect that the cities of the Old World own or control a great deal larger percentage of their total area than is the case with us. Eighteen German cities own on an average 27 per cent of their respective areas, while in Finland, due to ancient usage, 36 cities and towns own on an average 88 per cent of their areas! Manchester, Sheffield and Bristol in England own collectively about one-sixth of their combined areas, exclusive of land leased and land outside the city boundaries. The city of Zurich owns considerably more than half of its own area; Budapest owns 15 per cent of its area; The Hague nearly 16 per cent; Utrecht 24 per cent; etc.

RECENT BOOKS REVIEWED

PRINCIPLES OF PUBLIC ADMINISTRATION. By W. F. Willoughby. Washington. Publications of Institute for Government Research, 1927. Pp. xxii, 720.

It is fitting that the series of valuable descriptive monographs issued by the Institute for Government Research, under Mr. Willoughby's direction, should include also a general discussion by him of the principles of administration. The book is divided into four main parts:

General Administration and Organization
Personnel
Matériel, including supplies and their purchase
Finance and Accounting

The first part deals with problems of most general interest and shows at its best the author's broad grasp of scientific realities in administration. He favors the "integrated" basis for administrative departments. This groups together all services whose operations fall in the same general field and must therefore maintain working relations with each other. These services are provided with a single supervision to assure that they work harmoniously towards a common end.

While the national government has generally followed this principle in an approximate way, the states are only recently beginning to do so. The integrated system makes possible greater simplicity and a clear cut program. It is the lack of an administrative program which has weakened most departments.

In adopting the integrated plan, one of two principles may be followed. Services may be grouped together according to their activities (such as statistics, chemistry, photography) or according to the general functions of government activity such as railway regulation, public health, etc. The first of these is scientifically wrong, yet it has been adopted as the basis of many recent proposals for reorganization. The second method involves an analysis of the functions of government activity and a grouping of the services required by each of these functions into separate departments. This does not mean that each department shall duplicate the activities of other departments.

If the Indian service is organized on a functional basis, it will not be under an interior department or a department of public works, yet when it requires the construction of public works, it can call upon that department for the erection of buildings, etc. The facilities for research possessed by a department of education could be utilized by any branch of the government which required work of that special character. The author distinguishes between ordinary administrative services which merely carry out the law and those which are of a quasi legislative, judicial or other special character. The departmental principle should be applied only to the administrative units.

Each department should have one general function, and one only. This will necessarily increase the number of departments which, however, is not an important evil.

For the national government the author endorses the Institute's proposal of departments, as follows:

State	Commerce
National Defense	Labor
Treasury	Public Works and
Justice	Public Domain
Post Office	Education and Science
Agriculture	Public Health.

Inside each department, the author proposes the separate grouping of what might be called the housekeeping or purely institutional activities as contrasted with the functional or primary activities of the department. He favors the establishment of a bureau of general administration to aid the president in acting as general manager.

In considering the bureau type versus the board or commission type of organization, the author points out that if the duties to be performed are not primarily administrative, but rather the exercise of discretion in the formulation of policies, the drafting of rules and regulations, the adjudication of claims, there is ground for a board or commission, but where the work is chiefly administrative, the bureau type, under a single official, is desirable.

Boards and commissions have been more successful in the national government than in the states, because in the former their work has been of the nature of general control and research, while in the state systems, they have been given much administrative work besides. The failure of the states to provide adequate safeguards by civil service rules has also embarrassed and hindered the effective organization of the state boards. The author points out, in an interesting way, the value of advisory councils in keeping the heads of government administrative services in contact with the private interests and organizations concerned. Such councils should be advisory only and should have both government and non-official members, the latter representing outside interests.

Under Personnel, the author discusses various systems—the Bureaucratic, the Aristocratic and the Democratic types.

If the democratic can be so safeguarded as to escape politics and to include technical and efficiency considerations, it is preferable. The aristocratic system assures that all positions of superior importance will be held by men of a broad liberal education. It however closes the door to advancement from the lower ranks and is to that extent weak. There is adequate discussion of the classification of positions, the recruiting of personnel, promotion and dismissal and the organization of a personnel administration together with retirement systems and employees' organizations.

Under Matériel, the author considers specifications and their standardization, purchase and contract forms, organization of the supply division and central purchasing.

The final part on Finance is also extremely valuable and suggestive although the work here has been largely foreshadowed by preceding works. The author discusses the budget, its drafting, form and contents, legislative action upon it and its execution. He points out the administrative authority which is concentrated in the executive by the budget system. He also sketches the systems of collection, custody and disbursement of funds, accounting methods, the data required and expenditures. A final chapter deals with legislative control of finances and their audit. There is an excellent classified bibliography and an inadequate and useless index.

Mr. Willoughby's work will rank as the authoritative American treatment in the theory of administration. It is comprehensive, clear, scientific and based on a broad foundation of data. It is the ripe product of an intelligently

organized and extensive system of research and it places American administrative science on a plane with the great European treatises in this field.

It would be most fortunate if this remarkable work were followed by a series of monographs on special parts of the field, such as regional administration board and commission management, budget administration, advisory councils, etc., and if in each of these, the admirable method set forth by Mr. Willoughby could be followed, viz., a discussion of the types now existing, the scientific principles by which they should be measured and the revision of the present types to conform to these principles.

JAMES T. YOUNG.

*

MUNICIPAL AND RURAL SANITATION. By Victor M. Ehlers and Ernest W. Steel. New York: McGraw Hill Book Company, 1927. Pp. xi, 448.

In this volume, the authors have undertaken to present an outline of principle and practice in municipal and rural sanitation for ready reference purposes. They have succeeded admirably and, although their treatment of many problems of public sanitation is necessarily brief, their work may rightly be regarded as a worthy contribution to the literature on this subject. In fact, its very brevity makes it particularly well adapted to the needs of "the health officers, the sanitary engineers, city managers, and other officials who are frequently called upon to deal with problems and emergencies which require a knowledge of sanitation."

The book is comprehensive in scope, although giving somewhat less space to industrial hygiene, smoke abatement, and public comfort stations than seems desirable, at least to the reviewer. The chapters on excreta disposal, refuse collection and disposal, water supplies, food sanitation, fly and mosquito elimination, plumbing, ventilation and lighting are excellent summaries of present-day knowledge and approved practice. The authors devote considerable attention also to the sanitation of tourists' camps and swimming pool sanitation, neither of which subjects has up to this time received adequate attention by writers of general works on sanitation.

A feature of the book which strikes the reviewer as particularly helpful is the inclusion of chapters on communicable diseases, vital statistics, disinfection, and health organization.

The authors have apparently taken the position, and rightly so, that the reader ought to have clearly in mind the objective of all sanitary work, namely, disease prevention. Accordingly, they have set forth the essential facts about the causes of communicable diseases, the methods of destroying disease producing organisms, the use of vital statistics as a means of measuring sanitary accomplishment, and the type of public health organization best suited to the sanitarian's purpose.

The book is extensively indexed and furnished with a well selected bibliography. As a reference handbook it leaves little to be desired and its use is recommended to all interested in the betterment of environmental conditions in their respective communities.

C. E. McCOMBS, M.D.

✿

LANDSCAPE ARCHITECTURE—A SERIES OF LETTERS. By Stephen Child. Stanford University: Stanford University Press, 1927. Pp. 279.

To the modesty of the author we owe the unusually attractive form of this first adequate presentation of the wide scope and range of problems of the professional landscape architect of today. To quote from his own foreword:

Nearly twenty years' experience in the West, particularly the Southwest, and on the Pacific Coast have but served to emphasize in the author's mind the unrecognized possibilities of the profession and art of landscape architecture, and the genuine need in this great region, perhaps elsewhere, for a clearer interpretation of its ideals and principles. City, suburb, and country-side reveal to the seeing eye not only many unhappy examples of the misdirected zeal of the "improver," the nurseryman, and the amateur—homes robbed of their inherent charm, an appropriate natural beauty—but also, fortunately, countless more opportunities not yet lost. . . .

Current literature on the subject is unfortunately often either a mush of enthusiasm or a kaleidoscopic whirl of half-formed ideas, or perhaps too technical to be readily understood by the average man, and therefore withholds the leaven that should enrich every life and home. The aim of this book is to set forth those principles known to everyone in the profession, so clearly and simply that they may be readily understood, and at the same time to emphasize the art impulse behind it all.

To this end twelve typical problems are discussed in a series of letters. These are the idealized correspondence of a landscape architect

with his client, a representative American, whose successive opportunities are those of a modest home-dweller who at length becomes a city-planning commissioner. At the beginning of each letter the fundamental elements of landscape design applicable to the type problem are set forth in logical order, free from technicalities; these are given authority by quotations from the masters and are then applied to the specific example.

It is realized that conditions, personal, physical and financial, are so varied that one example, however typical, cannot solve even a simple class of problems, such as the suburban home and its garden, for instance. However, it is the purpose of the book neither to instruct the prospective practitioner completely nor to give the reader free rein; but rather to stimulate interest, to check unbridled enthusiasm, directing it into helpful channels, and to impress upon the average intelligence through a clear statement of basic principles the fact that art influences govern; to demonstrate, moreover, that the services of the landscape architect are co-equal with those of the architect, and that true economy for the setting of the simplest home depends upon art principles and is furthered by professional advice.

In all this, Mr. Child is eminently successful. While his examples are drawn largely from California, the application is to American conditions generally. Both the professional landscape architect and the discriminating public are to be congratulated on being brought into closer understanding through the medium of Mr. Child's "Letters."

ARTHUR C. COMEY.

✿

FINANCIAL STATEMENT: Issued to the People of the State of New York, Including a Comparative Statement of Appropriations, 1917–1927. By Governor Alfred E. Smith, August 1, 1927. Pp. 23.

PROGRESS OF PUBLIC IMPROVEMENTS. A Report to the People of the State of New York. By Governor Alfred E. Smith, October, 1927. Pp. 127.

These two statements on the financial operations of the state of New York are presented for the consumption of the man on the street. Governor Smith in clear and forceful language explains in the one instance the operations of the general fund; in the second instance in a profusely illustrated report (80 pages of illustrations) he tells the story of the permanent public improvements of the state in the last four years and the status of these improvements recently completed or still under way. In the first report the governor compares the governmental costs of 1927, first with the governmental costs of 1926, and second with the governmental costs of 1917. In the two cases the governmental costs show a considerable increase for 1927. Increased expenditures for education and highways are the major items that account for the increased costs. The state is to be commended, however, for meeting these costs out of the general fund without resort to any revenues derived from bond issues.

In the second report the governor comments on the state policy as to long term improvements. "I have insisted," he states, "and have so far been successful in securing the adoption of a policy that puts the proceeds of the sale of the state's bonds only into lasting improvements. By that I mean to say that practically all overhead expenditures connected with the work of construction are today paid from current revenue. All equipment for new buildings, whether they be prisons, schools, hospitals or other structures, is paid for from current revenue. Bond money goes into nothing but actual construction and in some instances the purchase of land." The statements of facts and illustrations supplementing the governor's introductory comments make out a convincing case in behalf of the present public improvements policy of the state of New York. It is regrettable that the grade crossing elimination program has been getting under way so slowly, although the governor feels that the progress will be more rapid in the near future. These two reports are intended primarily as an answer to the governor's critics who have been wont to talk glibly about increased costs of state government as resulting from the governor's administrative inefficiency and unwise financial policy.

MARTIN L. FAUST.

✦

INTRODUCTION TO GOVERNMENTAL ACCOUNTING. By Lloyd Morey. New York: John Wiley and Sons, Inc., 1927. Pp. 285.

This book sets forth in clear and logical form the essentials of governmental accounting. It is just what it purports to be, an "Introduction" to the subject and avoids, that which is almost inescapable in this field, the innumerable ex-

ceptions, legal restrictions and impediments which immediately spring to the mind of the practitioner in specific cases, to set at naught sound principles and logical procedure.

There is sufficient explanatory matter to establish the use of the various accounts and statements before taking them up in detail. The budget, with its supporting accounts and statements, the various funds (including working funds), revenues, receipts and disbursements are all logically grouped and separately treated. The final chapters deal with the consolidated balance sheet, classification of expenditures and financial reports. Illustrative journal entries and ledger accounts supplement the text in the most approved manner.

Some fifty forms are interspersed throughout the book, which may be taken as guides or adopted in part or as a whole by the accountant. The text is further supplemented by fifty-three problems. This feature is highly desirable when the book is to be used in the classroom, for which purpose it is excellently adapted.

The author believes, and will find many municipal accountants who will agree with him, that the segregation of funds and proprietary accounts accomplishes no real purpose and, in the interest of simplicity, the distinction between these two groups of accounts should be eliminated in public accounting. His treatment of the affected subjects is guided by this thought.

The principles expounded are not revolutionary but are rather, in concise form, a restatement of those fundamentals which have stood the test of practice.

The book should be welcomed by those seeking a groundwork in governmental accounting fundamentals and may also be studied and used with profit by those engaged in the practice of this special branch of accounting.

A. M. LANDMAN.

✦

OUTLINE OF UNIFORM SYSTEM OF ACCOUNTS FOR MUNICIPALITIES AND HANDBOOK FOR MUNICIPAL OFFICIALS. By Walter R. Darby, Commissioner of Municipal Accounts. Trenton, New Jersey. Pp. 108.

This is a technical treatise in the form of a handbook which outlines for municipal officials and registered accountants dealing with municipal affairs a uniform system of accounts for New Jersey municipalities. The first plan outlined is a plan dealing with the current group of accounts. This plan is based on the use of cash books, journal and ledger, and is the simpler plan for officials familiar with double-entry bookkeeping and the use of a journal. A second plan outlined in the handbook deals with the trust and capital division of municipal accounts. It is the opinion of the commissioner that the procedure presented will meet the requirements of the municipality with 50,000 population just as completely as it will the municipality of 5000, or even 500 population. The explanations which set forth the necessary details for the installation and operation of these two plans should prove useful to municipal officials desirous of improving their bookkeeping and accounting methods. The plans do not seem unduly complicated. An additional feature of the handbook is the inclusion of a model set of working papers for municipal accountants.

MARTIN L. FAUST.

❦

Town Planning is the Technique of Sociology. —This is a quotation from an address by Noulan Cauchon, printed in *La Revue Municipale*, Montreal, for December, 1927,—"Edition Speciale d'Urbanisme"—and typifies the point of view of the City Improvement League of Montreal, under whose direction it was prepared. Throughout this well-illustrated popular report of 140 large pages the strong emphasis is on social welfare, towards which engineering and other sciences and arts and economics itself are properly aimed as means of its attainment and not as ends in themselves.

The bilingual character of the report adds to its interest, particularly as the English and French sections are not translations the one of the other, though broadly traversing similar ground.

To an inhabitant of the United States one phrase, the "homologated line," smacks of strangeness, until he finds that it refers to "a line placed upon certain territory which the city wishes to acquire at a later date. Land affected by this servitude cannot be used for other purposes, except as a temporary measure, as the owner is always liable to expropriation at some future period."

The League hopes, as a result of its endeavors, summarized in this report, that important legislation will be enacted filling out gaps in town planning powers and that official city planning will now take up the burden thus far carried by private initiative. The document is of value to those outside Montreal for its popular presentation and particularly as exemplifying the effective popular appeal of emphasis on social welfare.

ARTHUR C. COMEY.

❦

General Bonded Debt of the city of Buffalo, N. Y., with the plan of liquidation at the least cost to the taxpayer is a report presented to the commissioner of the department of finance and accounts in October, 1927, by the Buffalo Municipal Research Bureau. It includes an analysis of all debts except the water debt which was covered in a separate report issued earlier in the year. A detailed plan for paying for the bonds is recommended accompanied by tables setting forth the facts and recommendations in tabular form.

E. C.

❦

Administration of Private Social Service Agencies, by W. W. Burke of the faculty of the graduate school of Social Service Administration of the University of Chicago, is a topical bibliography prepared for the use of graduate students. It is a reprint from the March and June numbers of the *Social Service Review* of 1927 with a supplement which not only brings it up to date but also adds additional material of an earlier date. It is very complete, and should be useful in its special field.

E. C.

❦

Consolidated Building Code, Greensboro, N. C. —The city of Greensboro, N. C., has issued a consolidated building code containing in one volume the city's building, electrical, plumbing, and zoning ordinances. A handy size, five by seven and one-half inches, has been adopted and the volume is well arranged for easy reference. The zoning map of the city is folded into a pocket inside of the back cover.

C. A. H.

❦

Report of the Geodetic, Topographic and Block Survey, Greensboro, N. C.—In order to obtain information which the city did not have for effective city planning, Greensboro, N. C., had a complete survey made of the city. The several phases of the work are described in the report and the uses of the data are explained. Much of the report consists of survey records but the discussions are of general interest.

C. A. H.

JUDICIAL DECISIONS

EDITED BY C. W. TOOKE

Professor of Law, Georgetown University

The City's Liability on Street Improvement Bonds in Iowa.—A recent decision of the Supreme Court of Iowa, holding a city liable for the issuance of street improvement bonds, will no doubt act as a warning to municipalities in this state in the issuing of such bonds in the future.[1] The Iowa law authorizes cities and towns to assess the cost of street improvements against property subject to assessment therefor, and the council is empowered to issue bonds for the amount of the assessed cost or any part thereof in anticipation of the deferred payment of the assessments. The statute prescribes the form in which such street improvement bonds shall be issued, which among other things must contain the statement:

It is hereby certified and recited that all the acts, conditions, and things required to be done, precedent to and in issuing this series of bonds, have been done, happened, and performed, in regular and due form, as required by law and said resolution, and for the assessment, collection and payment hereon of said special tax, the full faith and diligence of said city (or town) of —— are hereby irrevocably pledged.[2]

It is also provided that

Such certificates, bonds, and coupons shall not make the city liable in any way, except for the proper application of said special taxes.[3]

Many cities have found, for one reason or another, that there was no money in the special fund to pay the principal and interest on the last bonds in the series. Cities have usually contended that they were not liable under the statute for indebtedness incurred in this manner. On December 13, 1927, the Supreme Court of Iowa passed upon this question in a test case which involved four different street improvements' bonds of the city of Des Moines. The court reaffirmed a previous decision that a "city can render itself liable if in breach of the terms of the bond it wrongfully fails to perform its duty and its pledge pertaining to the assessment and collection of the special tax by which the special

fund is to be created,"[4] and the court further held that while these street improvement bonds did not of themselves create an indebtedness of the city, they did, however, create an obligation of the city to perform certain statutory duties in the levy and collection of special taxes for the payment of the bonds. "The liability of the city," said the court, "arises out of the breach of the obligations of the bond. The cause of action of the bondholder is in the nature of damages for such breach. The measure of his damages is necessarily the unpaid amount of the bond which has been rendered uncollectable by the wrongful breach. In view of the fact that the measure of damage is specific and is identical with the amount of the bond, the distinction between an action *on the bond*, and an action for the breach of it, becomes a mere matter of words."

Four different bonds were involved in this case:

1. Payment on the first bond had been refused by the city treasurer on the ground that there was no fund out of which it could be paid. The court held that it was the duty of the city to provide by special assessment a fund sufficient to pay the bonds and the interest on them.

2. In the second bond it appeared that provision had originally been made for special assessments sufficient to pay off all the bonds in the series, but that certain property owners assessed successfully prosecuted appeals in the district court, which materially reduced the anticipated collections for the special assessment fund and thus made the plaintiff's bond uncollectable. The court held the city at fault for not making up the deficiency by reassessing the amount of such depletion against the abutting property. "Its duty at this point," said the court, "was no less than its original duty to make an assessment adequate to the payment of the bonds."

3. In the third case a bond for $200 was rendered uncollectable because certain property owners had failed and refused to pay their

[1] *Hauge v. City of Des Moines*, 216 N. Y. 689.
[2] *Code of Iowa*, 1927, Sec. 6114.
[3] *Ibid.*, Sec. 6123.

[4] *Fort Dodge Electric Co.* v. *City of Fort Dodge*, 115 Iowa 568.

236

assessments and the county treasurer had failed to collect the same by tax sale for want of a bidder. Here the court held that the city had wholly failed to exercise its statutory power in the making of such collections and had breached its pledge of good faith and diligence to that end. The city could have bid in the property and thus enforced its lien.

4. The fourth bond was the last in its series, which could not be paid for lack of funds, because the assessments on certain properties were in excess of 25 per cent of their value. Some of the owners refused to pay the tax, and the county treasurer found no bidders at tax sale, but at an adjourned tax sale the properties were sold for less than the amount of the tax, thus making the deficiency in the fund. The court made quick work of this case, declaring that if the assessment had been confined to 25 per cent of the value of the property, as provided by law, the full amount of the tax could have been collected by tax sale.

In the light of this decision there seems to be nothing for the cities which have defaulted on public improvement bonds to do but to accept their liability. The *American Municipalities* for January, in commenting upon this decision, seems to imply that cities would be better off if they issued "certificates" instead of bonds. In view of another recent decision of the Supreme Court of Iowa in the case of *Western Asphalt Paving Company* v. *City of Marshalltown*,[1] it would seem that there is little opportunity for a city in this state to escape its liability for either bonds or certificates issued in payment of public improvements. This is, no doubt, as it should be, and these decisions should serve as a warning to city councils and the taxpayers alike that when public improvements are undertaken which are payable by special assessments upon the benefited property, the greatest care must be exercised to make sure that the property assessed will be able to pay out. When the city asks the contractor or the public to take these street improvement bonds and certificates, the good name and credit of the city demands that the city make good any deficiencies arising from errors of judgment or negligence on the part of the city authorities. If this were not so, cities might find it difficult to finance such improvements because of lack of confidence on the part of contractors and investors in special assessment securities.

The decision will no doubt work a hardship

[1] 214 N. W. 687 (Iowa, 1927).

upon those cities whose over-optimistic councils have forced street improvements upon their communities in advance of their needs and beyond the ability of the property assessed to meet the payments. But when city councils realize that street improvement bonds will become general obligations of the city, unless properly and legally assessed, they will weigh more carefully the objections of property owners before disregarding them.

FRANK E. HORACK.
The State University of Iowa.

✤

Special Assessments—Direct Liability of City on Bonds Issued.—The interesting note by Professor Horack on the case of *Hauge* v. *Des Moines* suggests a comparison with another recent case involving the same point. In *Moore* v. *City of Nampa*, 18 Fed. (2d) 860, decided by the Circuit Court of Appeals, ninth circuit, in April, 1927, the bonds in question contained recitals similar to those in the Hauge case, and the liability of the city was likewise predicated upon the negligence of the city in failing to perform its statutory duties to make a valid levy and collect the funds to pay the bonds. The Idaho statute provided that the holder of such bonds "shall have no remedy therefor against the municipal corporation by which the same is issued in any event, except for the collection of the special assessment made . . ., but his remedy in case of non-payment shall be confined to the enforcement of such assessment." The court affirmed a judgment of the district court sustaining a demurrer to the complaint.

These two cases illustrate the conflict of decisions that prevails in this class of cases based upon like facts, but the great weight of authority is in support of the view of the Circuit Court of Appeals. If the city is relieved of direct liability, the bondholder has a remedy by mandamus to compel the proper officers to make a new or supplementary assessment and collect the necessary funds to liquidate the bonds. The earlier cases bearing upon the general question of the direct liability of the special assessment district are reviewed in an extensive note to *Capitol Heights* v. *Steiner*, 211 Ala. 640, 101 So. 451, published in 38 A. L. R. 1271 (1925). The Hauge case is supported by a long line of decisions in Iowa (note, 18 Iowa Law Review 81), and evidently the only method left open to avoid the direct liability of municipal corporations on that state is by an amendment to the enabling act further expressly restricting the right of the bondholder against the city to a remedy by mandamus and requiring a recital in the bond itself of such a limitation and that it is payable only out of proceeds of the funds raised by the special assessment. As the constitutional limitations upon municipal indebtedness are uniformly held not to apply to judgments in tort, the evil of excessive direct obligations upon the city, resulting from failure to perform statutory duties of this nature, should be kept within reasonable bounds wherever, as here, it can be done without injustice to anyone.

✣

Municipal Functions—Airports.—The Supreme Court of Kansas in *Wichita* v. *Clapp*, 263 Pac. 12, decided January 7 of this year, holds that a city of the first class under its power to acquire lands within five miles of its limits for park purposes may take land for a park, 70 per cent of which is to be used for an aviation field. The court in its opinion reviews the progress of aviation and cites the statutes of various states expressly conferring the power in question. It also reviews the decisions which show the extension of park functions to include tourist camps and other new social activities. This progressive view of the extension of the implied power of municipalities by the change in social conditions is not followed by some states (*Kennedy* v. *Nevada*, 281 S..W. 56, Mo. 1926), and therefore the express delegation of the power to establish airports is advisable. (See Act No. 328, Pa. Laws of 1925, Ch. 534, Sec. 57, Mass. Laws 1922, Sec. 3667, par. 15, General Code of Ohio.) Upon the general subject of the extension of municipal functions, the reader may be referred to a note published in the August, 1926, number of this REVIEW.

✣

Zoning—Control over Building on Manufacturing Property Included in Residence District.—The Supreme Court of Pennsylvania in *In re Gilfillan's Permit*, 140 Atl. 136, has refused to follow the extremely broad application of the police power which was affirmed by the District Federal Court of Minnesota in *American Woods Product Co.* v. *Minneapolis*, 21 Fed. (2d) 441, which was reported in the December, 1927, issue of the REVIEW. In the instant case the petitioner, who operated a lumber yard in a section that was zoned as a residence district, was refused a permit to erect on his yard a building of concrete blocks to house his lumber and other

supplies. In sustaining the court of common pleas, which directed an issuance of the permit, the supreme court points out that the erection of the building in question would lessen the fire hazard, eliminate the tendency of undesirable persons to gather in the vicinity, conduce to the health of the community and enhance the attractiveness and value of the surrounding property. As the petitioner's business had been long established before the zoning restriction was enacted, the lands were charged with a lawful use which the city was without power to destroy. This is an illustration of the class of cases in which the zoning board of appeals should allow an exception to be made to the strict provisions of the ordinance; otherwise there seems to be no sound reason for its existence. (*Dobbins* v. *Los Angeles*, 195 U. S. 223; *Western Theological Seminary* v. *Evanston*, 156 N. E. 778.)

✣

Police Power—Public Taxicab Stand on Railroad Property.—The Supreme Court of the United States, in a decision handed down February 21, unanimously reversed the decision of the Circuit Court of Appeals, third circuit, in *D. L. & W. R. R. Co.* v. *Morristown*, 14 Fed. (2d) 257, which was commented upon in the April, 1927, issue of this REVIEW. The court holds that the town does not have any right to establish a public hackstand on the driveway upon the plaintiff's premises without just compensation and that the company may grant an exclusive privilege therefor to one operator.

Mr. Justice Butler in his opinion says: "The police power may be and frequently it is exerted to effect a purpose or consummate an enterprise in the public interest that requires the taking of private property; but, whatever the purpose or the means employed to accomplish it, the owner is entitled to compensation for what is taken from him. The railroad grounds, station, platforms, driveways, etc., are used by the petitioner for the purposes of its business as a common carrier and, while the business is subject to regulation in the public interest, the property used belongs to petitioner. The state may not require it to be used in that business, or take it for another public use, without just compensation, for that would contravene the due process clause of the Fourteenth Amendment. (Cases cited.)

"As against those not using it for the purpose of transportation, petitioner's railroad is private property in every legal sense. The driveway in question is owned and held by petitioner in the same right and stands on the same footing as its other facilities. Its primary purpose is to provide means of ingress and egress for patrons and others having business with the petitioner. But, if any part of the land in the driveway is capable of other use that does not interfere with the discharge of its obligations as a carrier, petitioner, as an incident of its ownership and in order to make profit for itself, has a right to use or permit others to use such land for any lawful purpose."

✦

Police Powers—Reasonable Regulation of Business or of Social Activities.—Under a general delegation of the local police power a city may enact regulations which will be in effect local laws, provided they prescribe general rules of conduct fairly definite and are reasonably adapted to protect or insure the safety, health, morals or general welfare of the community. That a city may enact a valid ordinance denouncing as a disorderly person anyone who appears or travels upon the streets masked or disguised so as to conceal his identity was affirmed by the Court of Appeals of Kentucky in *Pineville* v. *Marshall*, 299 S. W. 1072. That an ordinance requiring barber shops to close at 7 p. m. week days except Saturdays at 9 p. m. and prohibiting colored barbers serving white children is unreasonable and void was held by the Supreme Court of Georgia in *Chaires* v. *Atlanta*, 139 S. E. 559.

In *New Castle* v. *Withers*, 139 Atl. 860, the Supreme Court of Pennsylvania held that the city by bill in equity could compel the removal of plumbing installed in the house of the defendant by her husband, a licensed plumber, which was found not to comply with the requirements of the state plumbing code. The judicial control of the courts to set aside such a statute, as distinguished from an ordinance, is limited to those cases where there is a palpable invasion of the fundamental law or where there appears upon its face that it has no real or substantial relation to the public health, safety or morals; in all other cases the legislative determination is held to be conclusive.

Where the ordinance relates directly to the public health, the means adopted to secure its enforcement is most liberally construed. In *State* v. *Spiller*, 262 Pac. 128, an ordinance of the city of Auburn required each home holder to keep a garbage can and deposit all garbage therein and imposed a penalty for noncompliance. It was further provided that the failure to possess such a can and the use of the city water by the home holder should constitute prima facie proof of the violation of the ordinance. The Supreme Court of Washington upheld the ordinance on the authority of *Mobile, etc. R. R.* v. *Turnipseed*, 219 U. S. 35. The extent to which reasonable control over the disposal of garbage by private individuals extends is set forth in *California Reduction Co.* v. *Sanitary Reduction Co.*, 199 U. S. 306.

The extent to which discrimination may be held to be reasonable is illustrated by the decision of the Supreme Court of Washington in *Seattle* v. *Gervasi*, 258 Pac. 328, in which an ordinance excepting from a Sunday closing law the sale of meals served on the premises, prepared tobacco, milk, fruit, confectionery, newspapers, magazines and medical and surgical appliance was sustained. Classification based upon the nature of the business is upheld on the ground that the law operates equally upon all persons similarly situated. A conviction of the defendant, a grocer, for a violation of the ordinance was unanimously affirmed.

PUBLIC UTILITIES

EDITED BY JOHN BAUER

Director, American Public Utilities Bureau

What Price Electricity for Our Homes?—
This is the title of a pamphlet of 49 pages
published by Morris L. Cooke as an open letter
to the electrical industry. It is an interesting
and challenging analysis of electric rates charged
for domestic purposes; it presents the situation,
in our opinion, correctly.

The pamphlet is replete with concrete data as
to power costs, rates, and comparisons. The
general contention is that domestic rates in
American communities are too high; that, with
the present efficiency of production and distribution, there are few places where rates above
five cents per kwh. would be justified. Improvements in production and distribution of
electricity have been going on steadily and rapidly for the past ten years, and have enabled
the companies to compete with increasing effect
for industrial and commercial power, but practically no revisions have been made in domestic
rates. The time has come, Mr. Cooke points
out, for a complete re-determination of the
relative rates for domestic and business uses.

Mr. Cooke shows that, under present conditions, there is little reason for any marked
difference in rates for domestic and other
purposes, so far as direct production is concerned;
but that there are substantial differences in
cost of distribution and commercial expenses.
He finds that domestic rates are commonly
nearly six times as great as power rates, and
sees no reason for such a great differential under
present circumstances. The "load factor" has
improved so greatly during recent years, that
the "peak load," formerly due to domestic
consumption, has largely lost its importance in
the costs and rate structure. For most companies, the average plant utilization per day is
now probably greater than in any other industry,
except in continuous process concerns. Under
the present situation, therefore, he finds no
reason for great rate differentials, so far as
generating costs are concerned, between the
different classes of users.

We have had occasion repeatedly in this
department to refer to the differentials that
commonly exist between domestic and power

rates, and to point out that existing differences
are not justified. We have now under preparation a study which covers a different line of
data than used by Mr. Cook; but our facts
point to exactly the same conclusion. Our
view harmonizes completely with Mr. Cooke's,
that under present conditions domestic rates
above five cents are warranted in very few places.
In most of the larger cities there is no reason why
domestic rates might not be as low as two or three
cents per kwh. Such a radical revision in rates
would reach into the homes of the poorest, and
to the farms; would make available a wide range
of modern conveniences, and would add greatly
to the general standard of living. This would
mean an enormous extension in the utilization
of electric facilities, and would be certain to
broaden the permanent foundation of the prosperity of the electric power industry.

✣

The New York Rapid Transit "Movies."—
The drama of New York rapid transit has been
moving at great speed during the past month,
but with little forward motion. The litigation
described in this department last month, in
respect to the increase in fare to seven cents, has
not advanced in any decisive respect. At this
writing, the question of jurisdiction between the
federal and state courts is still undetermined;
this involves the basic question whether City
Contract No. 3, under which the subways are
operated, is to be regarded legally as a contract,
binding upon the company, or whether the operator, as the company contends, has superior
rights under the general regulatory powers and
duties of the state, notwithstanding the contract.

In the meanwhile, there have been prepared
by both sides legal papers of all sorts enough to
confuse not only the layman who attempts to
understand the situation, but, perhaps, also
the lawyers and judges concerned. It is, however, difficult for a layman to see how the
Interborough Rapid Transit Company, operating
under a contract with the city, can finally free
itself of its obligation of a five-cent fare, when
that contract has been highly profitable to the
company, and when its financial difficulties are

due to another contract—the lease of the elevated lines—with which the city has no contractual concern.

The Interborough management is not content with starting what promises to be the greatest lawsuit that has come out of New York for many years, but has undertaken another enterprise which may prove most costly to the company's ultimate interests.

The company has always opposed the regular unionization of its operating forces, and, largely for that purpose, has organized and developed the Interborough "Brotherhood," a company union. In dealing with its men, it arranged a system of private contracts, under which it had virtually compelled each man to agree not to join a regular union. Notwithstanding these agreements, however, the Amalgamated Association of Street and Electric Railway Employees has succeeded in effecting a regular union organization, apparently including a large proportion of Interborough employees. The company, on the basis of its employment contracts, attempted to enjoin the Amalgamated in its efforts to organize the Interborough and to prevent the men from joining the Amalgamated. It has failed in these legal maneuvers, and apparently has adopted the course of discharging the men who have joined the Amalgamated, although in part, at least, the discharge has been based upon alleged infractions of rules said to endanger the safety and efficiency of operation. This policy seems to be followed with vigor, and has kept the imminence of a strike in the foreground. An actual strike, to date, has been averted by the ability of Mayor James J. Walker in dealing with both sides of the controversy.

This situation points to a moral which the editor cannot evade. Here we have a utility upon which the entire economic life of a vast city depends; for this reason the city of New York has spent hundreds of millions of dollars in subway properties; likewise, for this reason, the state has expended annually millions of dollars in regulation. Yet, the entire business and industrial life of the city and the metropolitan district may be crippled for days and weeks, because of benighted labor policies on the part of the management, and perhaps temperamental qualities on the part of the labor leaders. The time certainly has come when, in respect to public utilities, a positive public labor policy should be adopted: to prevent the conditions that produce strikes, rather than try to cope

with a difficult situation when the crisis has been reached.

✦

Philadelphia Rapid Transit and the New Subways.—Philadelphia has its transit problems, too, but with less dramatic appeal. The city has been engaged in the construction of new subways, and has practically completed the Broad Street line. It is now concerned in making provisions for operation.

In planning and constructing the new subways, the city has intended them to be operated by the Philadelphia Rapid Transit Company in conjunction with the comprehensive and unified system of elevated, subway, and surface lines now operated by that company. No actual agreement for the operation, however, has been entered into. The cost of the Broad Street line, now practically completed, will be about $90,-000,000, and the entire cost of the new subways, including the extension from City Hall to South Street and the Ridge-Eighty Street branch, will come to about $120,000,000. The carrying charges on this new investment will be a heavy burden. For several years there will be deficits, until additional traffic is sufficiently developed. This situation is a drawback to an operating agreement between the city and the company.

The financial status of the Philadelphia subways is somewhat unusual, in that the city pays not only for the construction of the railroad, but also supplies the complete equipment. This differs, materially, for example, from the New York subways, where the operating companies have furnished the equipment. The new Philadelphia subways will be turned over to the operating company as a complete railway ready for operation.

The Market Street and Frankford subway elevated are now operated by the Philadelphia Rapid Transit Company, on the payment of a fixed rental to the city equal to the carrying charges and amortization. Possibly similar terms will be finally adopted for the new subways. A special plan prepared for the city, however, provides for a different type of agreement. While this would combine the operation of the new subways with the other transit facilities, it would, nevertheless, keep the financial results distinct, and would yield the city an undetermined return. There would be a separate accounting as to revenues and expenses, and the city would get whatever net return was actually realized from operation. The company would be paid upon a separate basis for its management, and the same rate of fare would be paid as on the rest of the system.

The type of operating agreement or lease adopted is a matter of first-rate importance for the city, in that it will practically fix its status as to future policy until 1957, when its other agreements with the company terminate. Under the proposed agreement, the city would retain a relatively greater freedom of action during the intervening period, without any "scrambled" finances as in the New York leases. The subway system would not be so tied up financially with the other lines but that it could be extricated, if developments should warrant a separation.

Philadelphia is fortunate beyond most of the large metropolitan centres in having established a thoroughly unified and coördinated system of transportation. The agreement for the operation of the new subways will, doubtless, be in harmony with this situation. The Philadelphia Rapid Transit Company now operates all of the surface lines in the city, the Market Street and Frankford subway elevated lines, all as a single system. The rate of fare is 8 cents, or two tokens for 15 cents. There are free transfers between all parts of the system, except that there are certain "exchange" points in the central delivery district where an additional 3 cents is charged.

The company has acquired also a bus system, which is operated through a subsidiary, the Philadelphia Rural Transit Company. The bus lines charge a 10-cent fare; are coördinated with the street railways, and furnish exchange tickets at 3 cents. The company has purchased also the Yellow Taxicab Company, and is negotiating for the acquisition of other cab companies. One of the objects of this expansion is to remove the "floating" taxi from the streets, and thus to reduce street congestion, which has been one of the factors of interference with street railway operation.

The Mitten management of the Philadelphia Rapid Transit has been one of the outstanding features of urban transportation during the past ten years. It has been singularly successful in dealing both with the public and with labor. It has done more than probably any other group in the country to identify the ordinary rider, as well as the ordinary employee, with the work and success of the company. It has developed an actual good will, the lack of which is one of the real difficulties in the New York situation, as well as in many other cities.

Good will is a fundamental element in successful and efficient operation. This is likely to be more a matter of personal attitude, or psychology, on the part of the management in its dealings with the public and the employees, rather than the actual things that are done. This appears to be particularly true of the Mitten management, but it has an admirable record of achievement to earn the good will. One of the outstanding enterprises of the past year has been the sale of $18,000,000 of 6 per cent preferred stock to the car riders, in maximum sums of $2,000 per rider. Not only the actual sale, but the manner of the sale of the stock has brought the company much closer to its public. Recently an investment corporation was organized, to enable the same public to invest directly in P. R. T. securities.

On the labor side, the management has also been strikingly successful in developing the coöperation and good will of the ordinary conductor, guard, track worker, et al. This, again, is more a matter of attitude than the specific things done. The management has worked out a system of committees with the employees, by which all differences are settled; it has had no strikes, nor has it had regular unions. It has instituted a coöperative wage plan by which the employees share in the economies and surplus of the company. These savings are invested in the company's securities and have made the employees a large factor in the actual ownership of the company. Approximately one-third of the capital stock is now owned by the employees. A recent development has been the purchase and reorganization of a bank to serve the employees in their investment of savings.

*

The Long Island Commutation Case Decided. —On February 25, the Transit Commission of New York disapproved and permanently suspended the proposed 20 per cent increase in commutation rates charged by the Long Island Railroad Company within the city of New York. On February 29, the Public Service Commission likewise rejected the increase, applicable to the traffic between the city and the communities outside.

This is a notable case, because of the long period of time over which it has extended, and because of the strenuous opposition to the increase made by the city of New York and the Long Island Commuters' Association.

In regard to the issues involved, it is worth while to note particularly that both commissions have recognized that, because of the character of the service, and the great difference in density of traffic, an apportionment of costs between commuters and regular passengers must be made with consideration of these differences. The company's position was rejected by both commissions,—that the average cost of carrying a passenger, for the company as a whole, may be used as the measure of the cost of carrying commuters. That there is a large "differential" in the relative costs, was strongly contended by the city, which presented an apportionment upon a basis that seemed correct. While the city's general view was accepted by both commissions, neither of them decided upon what exact basis the "differential" should be determined. The outright recognition of such a difference, however, is a positive step for future treatment of commutation rates.

As to the other important issues, the Transit Commission agreed fully with the city that the "normal" maintenance costs must be used for the determination of rates, and not exceptional expenses due to extraordinary maintenance. Likewise, it agreed that the apportionment of costs and property between the freight and passenger services could not be based upon the rules of expense apportionment issued by the Interstate Commerce Commission in 1920. These rules apply to the conditions of ordinary steam railroads, when both passenger and freight services are operated under substantially similar circumstances. In this case, the passenger service was operated to a large extent by electricity, and the commutation business almost altogether by electricity, while the freight service was operated wholly by steam. Since a large proportion of the common expenses incurred jointly by the two services are divided under the Interstate Commerce Commission's rules on the basis of relative fuel and power costs, the city contended that the rules could not be properly applied to this case, when the two services were operated under such dissimilar conditions. An extensive study was made of the costs and apportionments for all of the railroads of the country; the city's position was borne out statistically, and was sustained by the Transit Commission.

In respect to valuations, the company has used reproduction cost of the physical properties, without any deduction for depreciation; land was appraised on the basis of adjacent and adjoining land values. The methods were subjected to severe criticism by the city and the Long Island Commuters' Association; and the company's figures were rejected by the Transit Commission. The city presented a valuation based upon the methods adopted by the Interstate Commerce Commission in the St. Louis and O'Fallon case,—the amount fixed under the 1913 Federal Valuation Act, plus additions and minus retirements since, and less the further accrued depreciation. Since the legality of this base is now on its way to the Supreme Court of the United States, it was not passed upon by the state commissions in this case.

Although the increase in rates has been denied, there has been no final disposition of any of the issues; nor will there be a final disposition, unless our policies are radically reconstructed through statutory enactment.

The company is very likely to go to the federal court for relief. If so, this will mean a renewed inquiry in great detail, covering the same complicated facts. The decision of the federal court, naturally, would not be acceptable to either side, and the appeal would reach the Supreme Court of the United States. A final decision by that court again would dispose merely of the particular matter, but would settle nothing in regard to the future. At any time thereafter when rate adjustments are attempted, either upward or downward, there will be a repetition of the same costly, tedious and largely futile procedure.

The editor of this department has been retained throughout this extended litigation by the city of New York, for the economic and financial investigations and studies. Through this case he has become all the more convinced that our policies and methods of regulation must be radically reconstructed if regulation is to be effectively and reasonably carried out. If, in fact, the company in this case had needed additional revenues, the protraction of the case over nearly four years would itself constitute real confiscation, and might have caused serious financial difficulties; this, however, does not appear to be the fact in this instance.

In the interest of the public, fortunately the city of New York could almost match the resources of the company in fighting the case. If only small communities had been concerned, an increase in rates would doubtless have gone into effect long ago through default by the opposition. There can be little enthusiasm for a system of regulation which requires almost unlimited municipal funds to defend the public against excessive rates.

GOVERNMENTAL RESEARCH ASSOCIATION NOTES

EDITED BY RUSSELL FORBES
Secretary

Municipal Reference Library Notes.—Many research organizations are already receiving the weekly edition of *Notes*, published by the Municipal Reference Library, 512 Municipal Building, New York City. These *Notes*, list, by subjects, the current literature on municipal government and administration, and are therefore of great help to any individual or organization who wishes to build up a library in this field. The regular subscription price is $2.00 per year. But through arrangements made with the librarian, Miss Rebecca B. Rankin, any municipal research organization, which is a member of this Association, may receive the *Notes* without charge by asking to be placed on the mailing list.

✤

Recent Reports of Research Agencies.—The following reports have been received at the central library of the Association since January 1, 1928:

Municipal Research Bureau of the Akron Chamber of Commerce: *Coöperative Junior High School Study.*

Buffalo Municipal Research Bureau: *The Bureau of Parks,* and *The Natural Science Museum's Proposed Budget.*

California Taxpayers' Association: *Report of Santa Paula County, California;* an analysis of past growth and expenditures and a projected ten-year financial program, 1927–1937.

Chicago Bureau of Public Efficiency: *Chicago School Finances, 1915–1925; How the Chicago School Dollar Is Spent.*

Des Moines Bureau of Municipal Research: *Data on Airports in Cities,* and *Use of Photographic Machine in County Recorder's Office to Replace Typewriter Copying Method.*

Detroit Bureau of Governmental Research: *A Proposal for Financing the Capital Outlay for Detroit Schools, Comparative Bonded Debt of 32 Cities as of January 1, 1928, The Cost of Government City of Detroit,* and *Waste Disposal by Incineration.*

Kansas City Public Service Institute: *Special Assessment Procedure;* report on nature, extent and methods of special assessments for improvements in certain large cities; *A Study of the Water Department of Kansas City, Local Government and Civic Development,* and *Some Facts and Considerations Relative to Kansas City's Bonded Debt, Present and Future.*

Taxpayers' League of St. Louis County (Duluth): *A Preliminary Report on Financing Duluth's Major Street Improvement Program.*

St. Louis Bureau of Municipal Research: *Street Paving* and *Records for Motor Flushers.*

Toledo Commission of Publicity and Efficiency: *Survey of the Purchasing Division of the City of Toledo.*

✤

Boston Finance Commission.—Since February 1, the commission has issued the following: Report to the committee on municipal finance regarding House Bill 509, dealing with the tax limit of the city of Boston for the year 1928, and report to committee on pensions regarding House Bill 102, recommendations of the Finance Commission relative to the permanent school pension fund.

✤

Buffalo Municipal Research Bureau, Inc.— The Buffalo Municipal Research Bureau has been unusually busy during the past three months. One member of the staff has been working with the city purchasing agent in organizing and developing the new centralized purchasing bureau which was provided for in the new city charter effective January 1, 1928.

The Bureau has under way a survey of the police department to determine whether additional men are needed, how well the present force is being used, the possibilities of motor patrol for residence sections, etc.

At the request of the city treasurer, the Bureau is making a study of the various collecting agencies of the city with a view to devising a more simplified and more efficient system with proper and adequate auditing and control. This study will also include the preparation of a procedure for handling claims in arrears.

The Bureau is keeping in close touch with the preparation of the annual budget, and its analysis of the mayor's budget estimates will be issued in pamphlet form on March 15 when the mayor's budget is sent to the council.

A memorandum by the Bureau to the chairman of the finance committee of the city council pointed out that the city auditorium was being operated at an annual cost of $68,700, while the revenues amounted to only $16,000, making a net cost to the city of over $50,000. It pointed out that a permanent force of 35 employees were on the pay rolls and the auditorium was used only 148 times during the past year. A proposal by the council to go thoroughly into the matter has lately taken a sudden turn for a complete investigation, by a councilmanic committee, of all city departments.

The Bureau has also prepared and issued a report on the leasing of office space by various city departments and a memorandum on the proposed budget of the natural science museum.

✦

California Taxpayers' Association.—The Educational Commission of the California Taxpayers' Association is composed of ten outstanding Californians representative of education, agriculture, engineering, business and the California congress of parents and teachers. They were selected for their knowledge of, and sympathy with both the public school system and the taxpayers' problems. The commission forms its opinions and bases its recommendations on painstaking research. It meets quarterly in Los Angeles to review the work of its two full-time secretaries and to direct their research activities.

At present the commission is conducting a study of the county unit system of school control. It has investigated the working of the county unit system in the twelve states where it is used and is seeking information and advice from all the state school superintendents of the United States. Those who were familiar with the county unit recommended it; none opposed it; but a few, mainly in New England, did not consider it feasible in their states. One of the secretaries has just returned from a two-weeks' intensive study of the actual functioning of the county unit in Utah, where it has been in successful operation for thirteen years.

It is felt that California, with its 3,260 elementary school districts, is in dire need of consolidation at once. In 1,795 districts only one-room schools are maintained; and of these, 1,555 have less than 21 children in the entire district. Excellent roads and equable climate make the problem of larger-scale school control relatively easy of solution in this state, but the problem has never been vigorously attacked until the Educational Commission began its studies.

✦

Des Moines Bureau of Municipal Research.— The Bureau is coöperating with the Iowa State Association of Realtors to coördinate state-wide sentiment for tax retrenchment. Effort will be made at the next session of the state legislature to obtain the passage of an economy law and to obstruct passage of bills which would boost public costs. To further this effort, the State Realtors' Association has recommended that each local real estate board appoint a tax retrenchment committee to deal with local problems and to develop sentiment in each locality.

The Bureau suggested to the city council and to the county board of supervisors the possibility of refunding at a lower interest rate several 5 per cent bonds, which are callable before maturity. It also urged the city council to refrain from a small bond issue to purchase a park tract which could be paid for out of current operating revenues.

After an investigation which showed unmistakably that municipal expense increases inordinately in years in which municipal elections are held, the Bureau of Municipal Research strongly urged the present city council to refrain from increasing expenditures this spring prior to the municipal election and thus to set a unique example in the city's financial history.

At the request of the Bureau, the city engineering department has completed a map which shows all the street and sewer improvements made by special assessment in the last five years and the boundaries of each district. This, it is hoped, will guide the council in determining whether or not certain localities can stand further local improvements in the immediate future.

✦

Taxpayers' League of St. Louis County, Inc. (Duluth).—A program for cutting one of Duluth's principal streets through a high rock projection was well on the way to adoption three years ago, involving an outlay of more than two millions of dollars, with some features that would have been more of a detriment than an improvement. The League cited the objections—unbalanced cost, dislocation of the street system, absence of corresponding benefits, and hindrance to the best development of the neighborhood. The city commissioners reconsidered and submitted a proposition to the voters March first, involving an expenditure of $750,000.

Because the proposition proposed by the city commissioners was contrary to the recommendations of the City Planning Commission and for various other reasons, the Taxpayers' League opposed the bond issue submitted by the city commissioners. The position of the League was affirmed by a vote of two to one on March first.

Mr. DeWees of the Bureau staff has been attached to the Chamber of Commerce Gas Committee, and has spent much time in studying the gas problem. In conjunction with Martin Hokanson, an effort has been made to arrive at a scientific allocation of gas costs. The premises of this study are that there are three separate costs accruing to each customer, namely:

1. Customer costs, which are those items of cost that are so much per customer regardless of the quantity of service.

2. Customer demand or readiness-to-serve costs, which are the capital costs necessary to provide sufficient plant to be ready to serve every customer just when he wishes service, and that part of operating expense due to the same necessity of always being ready to serve.

3. Quantity of service costs, or those items of cost that vary with the quantity of output used by each customer.

Seemingly, no effort has been made by the water and light department at such a distribution of costs as is outlined above, and considerable difficulty has been experienced due to lack of detailed information. However, it is believed that reasonably accurate approximations have been made for the missing data, and that fairly accurate figures have resulted for these costs which will be published in the committee report.

A study is also being made of the allocation of the capital costs and the total income as between the gas department and the water department over a period of years. This is an effort to determine whether the interest charges now accruing to gas are properly chargeable thereto.

A tentative report has been prepared on the subject of refuse collection and disposal for a special committee of the Civic Council. This report advocates nothing, but is designed simply to give information to the committee on the various aspects of the refuse problem.

A special effort has been made to work with the county commissioners and to keep close watch of their activities. With the commissioner of the second district serving as chairman of the county unorganized school district, it is believed that considerable economy can be effected in that organization.

All reports and bulletins of the League since its organization in 1921 have been bound in permanent form, and several copies are to be given to libraries where such material is kept on file.

✤

National Institute of Public Administration, New York City.—The 1928 report of the Special Joint Committee on Taxation and Retrenchment of the state of New York has been completed and is in press. The report was prepared by Luther Gulick, C. A. Harrell, and Hubert W. Stone, of the Institute staff. It deals with the fiscal and administrative relations of the city governments and city school systems.

✤

Conference on Public Welfare Statistics.—As the result of an informal conference on public welfare in government held under the auspices of the National Institute of Public Administration in July, 1927, Dr. Carl E. McCombs of the Institute's staff recommended the creation of a special committee of the American Statistical Association to carry out the following program: (1) Prepare a report on the existing status of public welfare statistics; (2) draft a model law for the establishment of central state agencies for the collection and analysis of such statistics; (3) coöperate with the U. S. Bureau of the Census in developing the coöperation of the states for more uniform statistical practice. The American Statistical Association endorsed this recommendation and directed that the matter be referred to its already established committee on institutional statistics of which Dr. H. M. Pollock, statistical director of the New York State Department of Mental Hygiene, is chairman.

On February 10, a joint conference of the committee on institutional statistics and representatives of the national government, several state governments, and interested private agencies was held at the National Institute of Public Administration to consider the program further and to lay out a plan for immediate action. This conference was attended by Dr. H. M. Pollock, director of statistics, New York State Department of Mental Hygiene; Frank Bane, state welfare commissioner of Virginia; Kate H. Claghorn, New York School of Social Work; Neva Deardorf, Welfare Council of New York City; Emil Frankel, director of research, State Department of Institutions and Agencies of New Jersey; Edith M. Furbush, formerly of the National Committee for Mental Hygiene; Dr. Joseph A. Hill, assistant director, U. S. Bureau of the Census; Benjamin Malzberg, statistician, New York State Department of Charities; Dr. Carl E. McCombs, National Institute of Public Administration; Prof. S. P. Breckenridge, department of social economy, University of Chicago; F. W. Brown, National Committee for Mental Hygiene; Richard K. Conant, state commissioner of public welfare of Massachusetts; Katherine F. Lenroot, acting chief, U. S. Children's Bureau; Emma O. Lundberg, Child Welfare League of America; Dr. George K. Pratt, National Committee for Mental Hygiene; Bruce Smith, National Institute of Public Administration; and Sydnor H. Walker, Laura Spelman Rockefeller Memorial.

Discussion of public welfare statistics from the points of view of the federal agencies concerned, state welfare officials, private welfare agencies, and government research agencies by the members of the conference brought out clearly the need for more complete and uniform statistical practice in the various states, and for better coöperative action by all agencies to attain this end. A subcommittee of the committee on institutional statistics was appointed to draw up a plan of action for later consideration. This subcommittee comprises: Dr. H. M. Pollock, *chairman*, Kate H. Claghorn, Edith M. Furbush, Dr. Joseph A. Hill, Benjamin Malzberg and Dr. Carl E. McCombs, *secretary*. A meeting of the subcommittee will be held late in March or early in April to begin the work of preparing uniform statistical schedules for these public welfare services where statistics are as yet un-

standardized and to devise ways and means of securing nation-wide adoption of such schedules, including the drafting of a model law for the registration of public welfare statistics by the various states.

The conference of February 10 was made possible through the generosity of the Laura Spelman Rockefeller Memorial of New York City, which appropriated a sum sufficient to pay the traveling and living expenses of out-of-town members of the conference. The progress of further work by the subcommittee of the committee on institutional statistics of the American Statistical Association, which will have the work of statistical standardization in charge, will depend to a considerable degree upon its success in securing financial support. It is expected that two years or more will be required to carry out the plan.

✣

Sioux City, Iowa, Bureau of Municipal Research.—The latest addition to the fast-growing list of research organizations is the new bureau established at Sioux City, Iowa. The Bureau has not yet employed a research staff, but is now engaged in raising funds to permit the undertaking of a research program. The Bureau's headquarters have been established in the office of the secretary, E. S. Weatherly, 510 Iowa Building.

✣

Toledo Commission of Publicity and Efficiency. —The Commission published on March 3 a survey of the functioning of centralized purchasing in the city of Toledo. During the next month, the Commission plans to publish a survey on street cleaning.

Probably the most important question which is before the city administration at the present time is the subject of fire and police pensions. The Commission of Publicity and Efficiency intends to make a survey of the practice of other cities in this field. At the present time state laws of Ohio do not allow the city to compel firemen and policemen to contribute to the pension fund. The result is that the city pays $75 per month as pension to policemen and $85 per month as pension to firemen, almost entirely out of public funds.

NOTES AND EVENTS

EDITED BY H. W. DODDS

Wichita To Clean House.—Recent events in connection with Wichita's city manager government illustrate the importance of constant vigilance by good citizens and the distance our municipalities have yet to travel before we have finally established an invulnerable tradition of sound administration.

The story is gleaned from the *Wichita Daily Beacon* and begins two years ago with the election of a city councilman through the support of the Ku Klux Klan. Immediately the Klan leader began to interfere in police administration until it was finally discovered that a good many of the policemen looked to him rather than to the chief for orders. Later another klansman was elected, and the two laid down a political barrage against Earle C. Elliott, the city manager. Through control of the police the first klansman was able to extend protection to bootleggers and gamblers under a pay-off system which ran to as much as $3,000 a month.

The *Beacon* criticized the councilman in such definite terms as to incur an action of $500,000 for defamation of character. It countered with an investigation resulting in the confession of several liquor dealers, who declared that they had paid considerable sums of money for the privilege of selling liquor and running resorts. When the findings were placed before the attorney general the councilman was notified that ouster proceedings would be brought against him. Whereupon he resigned from the council and dropped the libel suit against the *Beacon*.

The citizens of Wichita recognize that their experience is not a reflection upon the city manager plan of government. Mr. Elliott is one of the leaders of his profession, having served a term as president of the City Managers Association, and is now an officer of a large corporation at a very satisfactory salary. But the activities of the non-partisan Good Government League, which had exercised an intelligent scrutiny over candidates for office and the affairs of the city, had been allowed to lapse.

That the success of the city manager government, like any other form of public or private organization, depends upon the caliber of its personnel is now recognized in Wichita. Other

cities will do well to profit by her experience before similar afflictions come upon them.

✦

To Reform Philadelphia Magistrates' Courts.—Certain other cities may enjoy as bad magistrates' courts as Philadelphia, but even the casual observer of municipal affairs knows that her minor police and civil courts are a disgrace to her judicial system. They are politics ridden and graft infested. While the matters which come before such courts are small, they concern a larger proportion of the citizens than do the higher courts, and the time is ripe to renovate them. It is gratifying, therefore, to know that some attention is being directed towards cleaning them up. Legislation passed last year providing for a chief magistrate selected by the board of magistrates did not create, in any true sense, a consolidated court. The chief magistrate has few or none of the powers necessary to constitute him the real head of the system.

Former District Attorney Charles Edward Fox, a man who ought to know, charges that the magistrates' courts in Philadelphia are today centers of political activity and even-handed justice is subordinated to oppression, trickery, and extortion. As a means of reform Mr. Fox proposes a reorganization of the whole magisterial system of the city. He would adopt an entirely new code of procedure, require that magistrates be practicing attorneys of at least three years' experience and devote all their time to the work, prohibit any magistrate from active participation in any political organization, and lay down new rules for the acceptance of bail whereby any person appearing as bondsman more than twice in one month could be classed as a professional bondsman and compelled to take out a license. Although these so-called judges receive $5,000 a year, Mr. Fox believes that a great deal of the trouble arises from the low caliber of the personnel selected for the office.

✦

City Manager Sherrill has recommended to the Cincinnati city council that Broadway, a most congested thoroughfare, be widened twenty-five feet from Fifth Street to Reading Road. According to the report of the manager referred to the council, the cost will be $2,100,000, although the actual improvement of the street will cost but $141,000. The official city plan did not contemplate the widening of Broadway for many years, but a proposal to build a million-dollar garage moved the council to favor immediate action in order that the cost of demolishing this building might be avoided. The widened street will give space for two sidewalks twenty-three feet wide and a roadway adequate for six lanes of traffic.

Colonel Sherrill recommends that the device of excess condemnation be used rather than the appropriation of land sufficient only for the physical widening. By the economic assembling of small plots and resale to private owners under the power of excess condemnation it is estimated that approximately $392,000 can be saved.

✦

The Virginia Institute of Public Affairs.—The second session of the Institute of Public Affairs at the University of Virginia which attracted nation-wide and even international attention last year will be held, according to an announcement by Dean Charles G. Maphis, director of the institute, from August 6 to 18, for a continued study and discussion of the outstanding current issues in national, state and local governmental policies and the economic and social problems underlying them.

The program will consist of three features.

For the more serious and consistent study of the questions selected, eight or ten round tables continuing through the entire session of the institute and meeting for about two hours each morning will be organized under the leadership of the best authorities available in their respective fields.

A unique feature and one which should prove intensely instructive and interesting will be an Open Forum, conducted each day from eleven to one o'clock. This forum is the direct result of the memorable McAdoo-Ritchie-Glass debate last year on the Eighteenth Amendment. This year at that hour some timely question will be chosen. Those who participate in the forum discussions will be men and women of national reputations on account of their study of and achievements in politics and public service, but differing in their views on the question under debate.

The third feature of the program will be daily addresses in the evening on public questions by men of national reputation whose opinions are sought and valued by all Americans. Plans are being made to have the presidential candidates of both parties speak, and many others of the nation's leaders have tentatively accepted invitations to attend.

Round table leaders include Dr. John D. Black, Mrs. Aurelia Henry Reinhardt, Dr. John H. Latane, Dr. Thomas H. Reed, Professor Kirk H. Porter, Dr. A. R. Hatton, Mark Graves and Dr. Victor Rosewater.

✦

The Pennsylvania Association of Planning Commissioners held its third annual conference at Altoona, February 16 and 17. This first conference outside of Harrisburg undoubtedly was a distinct advance in the interest of city planning and municipal development in the state.

Mayor McMurray and W. A. Hoyt, chairman of the Altoona city planning commission, welcomed the delegates, and Dr. K. M. J. Klein, president of the Association, responded.

Housing in the city plan was presented by Benjamin H. Ritter, executive secretary, Pennsylvania Housing and Town Planning Association. John Ihlder, manager, Civic Development Department, United States Chamber of Commerce, Washington, D. C., was the dinner speaker. His theme was comprehensive and stressed planning, zoning and traffic.

The forenoon of February 17 was devoted to zoning. Contributions were made by: W. C. Rice, secretary, Pittsburgh Planning Commission; U. N. Arthur, chief engineer, Pittsburgh Department of City Planning, and Frank P. Best of Morris Knowles, Inc., consultants. During the afternoon Russell Van Ness Black, planning engineer for the Regional Planning Federation of Philadelphia Tri-State District, spoke on regional planning. Thomas H. Reed, director, Bureau of Government, University of Michigan, presented his theme on regional government. Francis J. Mulvihill, chief, Division of City Planning and Municipal Engineering, Pennsylvania Bureau of Municipal Affairs, reported on progress of city planning in Pennsylvania during 1927. Leo J. Buettner, secretary, City Planning Commission, Johnstown, in his address on making city planning effective demonstrated his talk with lantern slides.

✦

Detroit Railways Reported Financially Successful.—William H. Hauser, auditor of the Detroit Street Railways, reporting on the result of seven years of municipal ownership and operation, states that in addition to paying off $13,775,656.51 of debt, an accrued depreciation fund to the amount of $4,772,153.32 had been earned and invested in the property. All has come from the pockets of the car riders. In addition to paying operating and maintenance expenses, including paving between the tracks, the system has paid taxes on its physical property the same as if privately owned.

✣

Philadelphia Plans a City Theatre.—A proposal for an elaborate municipal theatre, which would be built on city-owned property, at a cost of $800,000 and dedicated to the "intimate drama," has been laid before Mayor Mackey of Philadelphia by a group represented by Arthur W. Thompson, president of the United Gas Improvement Company, State Senator George Woodward and Samuel P. Wetherill, Jr., president of the Regional Planning Federation of the Philadelphia district.

Senator Woodward at the same time offered to contribute $100,000 to the theatre fund. Bonds would be issued to obtain the rest of the money and a sinking fund set up for the retirement of the securities, under the backers' plan. After the theatre had been freed of all incumbrances it would be deeded over as the city's property.

✣

The University of Cincinnati has reëstablished an office of its Municipal Reference Bureau in the Cincinnati City Hall, under a coöperative arrangement with the city government. The Bureau will serve the city directly in supplying and procuring information on problems of city government, preparing abstracts and reports, and in digesting and making available current municipal literature. The University has appointed Emmett L. Bennett, a graduate of the University of Kansas, to take charge of the Bureau. Some years ago he was in charge of the Municipal Reference Bureau of the University of Minnesota, and recently has been in the service of the Cleveland city council as its legislative aide.

✣

The City Club of New York has announced the appointment of Harry W. Marsh as civic director of the club.

Mr. Marsh has for years been engaged in civic work in connection with the National Civil Service Reform League and the New York Civil Service Reform Association. He was graduated from Columbia University in 1911 and in the following year he entered the offices of the Civil Service Reform organizations as assistant secretary. In 1917 he was commissioned a lieutenant in the Ordnance Corps of the United States Army and saw service with the American Expeditionary Forces in France. Upon leaving the army, he returned to the Civil Service League and was elected secretary in 1920.

His connection with the City Club and his separation from the Civil Service League will be gradual; it being understood that he will not be able to devote his full time to the work of the club until about May 1, 1928.

✣

By-Pass Highways Recommended.—The Regional Planning Federation of the Philadelphia Tri-State District, in a report entitled "By-Pass Highways for Traffic Relief," points out the necessity of by-passing large cities. The report urges the procurement of adequate rights of way at once, as every year adds hundreds of thousands of dollars to the cost. New subdivisions, new industries, new and costly developments of every kind are constantly occurring to obstruct the few remaining practicable locations. In all, the construction of seven trunk highways is recommended, the major portion of which can be built on existing rights of way. Route No. 1, however, which would be a link in the proposed superhighway from Florida to Maine, to be known as the Washington Boulevard, would cut through new territory from Princeton, N. J., and would avoid Philadelphia as well as all other towns of any size.

✣

How a School District Can Obtain a Better Price for Its Bonds is the subject of a little pamphlet written by Tom K. Smith, vice-president of the Investment Bankers Association of America, and published by the Association. The pamphlet contains much helpful information for school boards, and is in conformity with the provisions of the Model Bond Law of the National Municipal League.

✣

The Engineering News-Record reports that the prohibition of automobile parking in the Loop district of Chicago appears to be a success in that "almost at once increased clearness of the streets, rapid and steady traffic movement, and elimination of tangles and congestion became conspicuously evident."

NATIONAL
MUNICIPAL REVIEW

PUBLISHED MONTHLY BY THE

National Municipal League

VOL. XVII, No. 5   MAY, 1928   TOTAL No. 143

CONTENTS

EDITORIAL COMMENT.........................*H. W. Dodds*........ 251

PRAYERS AND PINEAPPLES IN CHICAGO POLITICS...*Edward M. Martin*... 255

WHERE ZONING FAILS........................*R. D. MacLaurin*..... 257

THE NEGRO IN CHICAGO POLITICS..............*Ralph Johnson Bunche* 261

CONNECTICUT CONSOLIDATES STATE FINANCIAL
    CONTROL...............................*Lane W. Lancaster*.... 265

SALARIES OF POLICEMEN AND FIREMEN IN 35 CITIES *E. A. Crandall*....... 268

CENTRALIZATION OF NEW YORK CITY GOVERNMENT *Charles U. Powell*..... 280

COÖPERATION BETWEEN THE FEDERAL AND STATE
    GOVERNMENTS..........................*James D. Barnett*..... 283

A LABORATORY COURSE IN BUDGET MAKING......*Russell Forbes*........ 292

DEPARTMENTS

    I.   Recent Books Reviewed.. 295
    II.   Judicial Decisions.....................................*Edited by C. W. Tooke* 299
    III.   Public Utilities...*Edited by John Bauer* 302
    IV.   Governmental Research Association Notes.................*Edited by Russell Forbes* 305
    V.   Notes and Events.....................................*Edited by H. W. Dodds* 309

THE LEAGUE'S BUSINESS

Model Budget Law in Final Stages.—At a meeting last month of the committee appointed to draft a model municipal budget law the secretary, Mr. C. E. Rightor, was authorized to prepare the final draft for approval by the committee. This has now been completed and awaits final action by the members. It is expected that it will be published as a supplement to the July REVIEW.

The chairman of the committee is Mr. Carl H. Pforzheimer, treasurer of the League. Mr. A. E. Buck and Mr. H. P. Seidemann have assisted the secretary in drafting certain provisions.

*

League's Publications Widely Used by Colleges.—The demand for League publications, including the NATIONAL MUNICIPAL REVIEW, on the part of college classes is increasing, a fact which brightens the outlook for better government in the next twenty-five years.

During the months of January and February the League received orders for material in quantity from the following colleges and universities: Louisiana State University, Washington University, University of California, University of Minnesota, University of South Dakota, Lehigh University, New York University, State Normal School, Princeton University, Western Reserve University, Dartmouth, Oregon State Agricultural College, University of Wyoming, Northwestern University, Alabama College, University of Illinois, De Pauw University, University of Texas, University of Washington, Williamette University, Nebraska Wesleyan University, Stanford University, College of Emporia, Mount Holyoke College, Washington and Lee University, University of Pittsburgh, University of Pennsylvania, University of Southern California, University of Wichita, University of Nebraska, Temple University, Ohio Northern University, Ohio State University, Miami University, Duke University, South West Missouri State Teachers College, West Texas State Teachers College, Nebraska State Normal School and Teachers College, Swarthmore College, Connecticut College, Williams College, Bryn Mawr, Hunter College, University of Cincinnati, and Westhampton College.

NATIONAL
MUNICIPAL REVIEW

VOL. XVII, No. 5   MAY, 1928   TOTAL No. 143

EDITORIAL COMMENT

Well, the Thompson-Crowe forces lost the Chicago crime-ary, but will probably demand that it be shot over, avers Columnist H. I. Phillips in the *New York Sun*.

✲

Apropos of the comment in the April REVIEW on the decision of the Iowa Supreme Court in the case of *Hauge* v. *Des Moines*, Professor Tooke in this issue calls attention to a later decision in the case of *Ballard-Hassett Co.* v. *Des Moines*. In the latter case the supreme court ruled that the recital that "this bond is payable only out of the special assessment fund created by collection of said special tax," which must now appear on special assessment bonds in Iowa, protects the city against personal liability on the bond.

✲

The sudden death of Dr. Delos F. Wilcox, which occurred in New York City on April 4, will come as a sorrowful shock to his numerous friends in the National Municipal League. A heavy cold contracted during a brief business visit in the East developed into pneumonia, to which he succumbed two days after entering the hospital. Although best known in later years for his work in the field of public utilities, he first attained prominence through his writings on municipal government.

He was a frequent contributor to the NATIONAL MUNICIPAL REVIEW and the author of a number of special monographs published by the League. A man of urgent opinion and uncompromising belief when his scientific position was involved, he yet was deeply beloved by all who knew him as a kind and jovial man. The National Municipal League, as well as all other friends of good government, has lost a faithful and courageous friend. Further accounts of his life will be found in other departments in this issue.

✲

We also have to record this month the sad news of the death of Francis T. Hayes, formerly secretary of the Cleveland City Club and at the time of his death attorney for the Citizens' League of Cleveland. "Pat," as he was familiarly known, was deeply interested in civic affairs from high school days. He was one of the best known and best liked young men in Cleveland. Affectionately regarded by all and thoroughly grounded in political theory and in municipal and county affairs in Cleveland, his loss will be felt both by the Citizens' League and his friends in the City Club. Although "Pat" had not been in good health for more than a year his death was sudden, following an operation.

Royal Commission Visitors to London
on London are familiar with the
Squares occasional open
spaces, oases in the wilderness of
bricks and mortar, which have remained unbuilt in certain districts but
which now are in danger of destruction.
There are more than 400 of these
pleasant spots, the majority of them
being held in private ownership as
gardens created for the use of residents
of the surrounding houses. Because
they are in danger of being cut up for
private buildings the London County
Council successfully petitioned for a
Royal Commission on London Squares
to investigate whether they could not
be preserved for the people.

The difficulty turns on whether the
owners of the squares can properly be
prohibited from building on them without being awarded compensation by
the government. On the ground that
private property could only be taken
upon payment of compensation, the
House of Lords more than twenty years
ago rejected a bill to protect a certain square from a speculative builder.
"This decision," states the *Municipal
Journal*, "has served as a barrier to
every subsequent effort to bring these
open spaces within the category of
lands forever dedicated to the public
use."

It is urged by many, however, that
at the time of laying out the estates
on which these squares are found,
there was no intention of building on
them. The houses adjoining them
were not provided with separate gardens and the square was a device which,
by affording a common breathing
space, added to the number of buildings that could be erected in a given
area. Consequently the owners have
secured throughout the years a higher
rental for their properties than otherwise would have been possible. To
prevent their destruction, therefore,

deprives the owners of no profit which
they originally expected to receive.
To compel them to be held in their
present shape causes no loss to the
owners and no compensation is necessary.

In common with other large cities,
London needs more breathing space
rather than less, and it would seem a
pity to permit the destruction of the
squares which, although now held in
private hands, will undoubtedly one
day be dedicated to the public. The
question as to whether they can be
held out of private development without compensation from the government
is one which the Royal Commission
was established to decide. To one
reared in the American doctrine of
police power circumscribed by due
process of law, the contention that the
owners of the squares are not entitled
to damages if prevented from building
thereon appears to be doubtful law.
But many Englishmen who cannot be
classed as socialists do not share this
view.

✣

Civil Service and   "What I want is a
Prohibition   man who can raid a
barroom or knock
off a still. I am not greatly concerned
whether he can spell 'idiosyncrasy.'"
Thus an officer in the bureau of prohibition is reported to have spoken when
he learned that approximately 75 per
cent of the prohibition enforcement
agents failed in the written tests (which
did not involve spelling) recently given
by the United States civil service
commission. Deceptive and exaggerated though his language be, it
fairly represents the attitude of many
politicians as well as honest administrative officials who feel trammeled by
civil service laws. Various persons,
some of them in congress, have accordingly united in accusing the civil service

system, and the federal commission in particular, of practical disruption of the prohibition force through a misguided confidence in written tests and book larnin'. Added to these, has been the criticism of some personnel experts, conspicuous among whom has been the Better Government League through its bi-monthly bulletin, *The Public Business*.[1]

By the Act of March 3, 1927, congress brought all positions, excepting the commissioner of prohibition, into the classified list and required that all present incumbents take tests in competition with outsiders if they wished to hold their places. Unassembled examinations were given for the administrative posts. For the other positions, 2,000 in number, written examinations were given to 15,000 candidates. The mortality rate was extremely high. Only 4,400 attained a grade of 60, the minimum necessary to enable a candidate to proceed to the subsequent oral examination and the character investigation. As already indicated, three-fourths of the present incumbents were "plucked" at the first stage. While the oral and character tests are proceeding for the survivors, incumbents are serving under temporary appointments. Heavy pressure has been brought to bear to hold new examinations but the civil service commission maintains that it has done no wrong and will hold no more examinations except in districts where necessary in order to secure sufficient eligibles for the posts. "A civil service examination," states the commission, "cannot be set aside unless there is irregularity or fraud connected with it."

The critics of the commission speak as follows: The examinations cost too much; a special appropriation of $190,-

[1] *The Public Business,* February–March, 1928. A less severe article covering the same ground appeared in *Public Personnel Studies* for March.

000 was secured when the work could have been done without any extra funds whatever. The mortality rate, especially among present office-holders was too high and should alone have revealed to the commission the error of its ways; and the tests were poorly devised without adequate consultation with the prohibition authorities. According to the latter, the more competent agents failed in about the same proportion as the incompetent. The written tests were of the multiple choice type designed to measure judgment; few items related to the eighteenth amendment, or the Volstead Act. The oral interview and character investigations were inadequately planned and are being poorly executed; oral interviews do not truly reveal character. Indeed its measurement has escaped solution by experienced research workers.

A final criticism relates rather to congress but involves the commission and the National Civil Service Reform League. It is that a grave error was committed in the refusal to "cover in" present incumbents, the incompetent to be weeded out later by administrative action; and that the policy of subjecting old employees to examinations is highly unusual and tends to disrupt the service. To this assault the commission and the Civil Service Reform League reply that prohibition enforcement had become a shameful mockery and the same pressure as was exerted in the original appointment would have been applied to retain the inefficient and dishonest. The service was a sink of corruption which had to be abated.

To the accusation of extravagance the commission responds that the examination procedure in this case can not be compared with that in any other. Because of the certainty that large numbers of persons with heavy sinister backing would continue to try for appointments, it became necessary to go into the life history of every applicant. This involves added expense of travel for investigators, who in some cases have visited as many as five or six places in which a candidate formerly resided. Approximately fifty trained examiners are now conducting such investigations throughout the United States. Furthermore, the small ratio of successful candidates is no reflection on the written tests, but rather an index of the type which is or seeks to become prohibition agents. The questions, which were such as might reasonably confront any enforcement agent, were not intended to test acquired knowledge but rather the intelligence and reasoning power of the applicant. Items on prohibition law were omitted as being easily mastered in the service and as giving a disproportionate advantage to incumbents.

It is beyond the competence of the present writer to determine the guilt or innocence of the civil service commission in the present instance. Written tests for judgment are still in an embryonic stage and the commission did not conduct extensive experiments to develop an approved standardized test, as is claimed it should have done. Time was a limiting factor, denying to the commission much opportunity for experimentation with new tests for new posts. It is questionable, therefore, whether more should be expected than a reasonable utilization of tools readily at hand. Moreover, in spite of the difficulties in appraising integrity and character by oral interview and study of a candidate's record, no other method of measuring such intangibles has yet been invented. Certainly the emphasis by the commission upon this stage of the proceedings is proper in view of the history of prohibition enforcement and blame for the inefficiency of the tools does not lie at their door.

The greatest controversy seems to be raging around the question of "blanketing in" the present employees. The elimination of 1,500, who, to a large extent, owed their appointment to political favoritism, has no doubt brought embarrassment to numerous congressmen. It is not disputed that general practice favors the policy of blanketing in. The question raised is whether special conditions in the prohibition bureau do not render such a policy unwise in this instance.

At this writing the final outcome is somewhat in doubt. Senator Brookhart has introduced a bill to permit incumbents of a year's standing upon recommendation of the commissioner to retain their positions without regard to their success or failure in the civil service examination. According to President McAneny of the Civil Service Reform League the bill is a "specious attempt on the part of various selfish political interests . . . to undo in a serious degree what [has been] done and to open the way widely to the retention of favored persons with continuing disregard of their respective qualifications."

*

A Correction   Mr. Goodrich has called to our attention an error occurring on page 191 of his supplement to the March REVIEW on "Airports as a Factor in City Planning." It is there stated that municipalities are building airports at an average expenditure of $100 per capita. The error is of course obvious. The figure should have been $1.00 per capita.

PRAYERS AND PINEAPPLES IN CHICAGO POLITICS

BY EDWARD M. MARTIN

The story of the Chicago primary of last month.

PRAYERS and "pineapples"[1] have now earned a place on the political menu. The Chicago primary election on April 10 strikingly proved their potency as weapons of political propaganda. They characterize the extremes reached in Illinois' bitterest election contest. They had a definite part in dealing a death blow to the Republican Small-Smith-Thompson-Crowe combination which for many months had brought the state nation-wide notoriety.

The prizes at stake in the election were the delegates to the presidential conventions, party nominations to the seat in the United States senate left vacant by Frank L. Smith's failure to qualify, to the house of representatives, to high state offices, and to various county and city offices, most important of which was the state's attorneyship of Cook County. The election was warmly contested throughout the state, but the greatest activity naturally centered in Chicago and Cook County, for the trend there determines in large part the outcome for the entire state.

THE FACTIONS AND THE ISSUES

The Democrats were united, but on the Republican side two factions fought for supremacy. The combination led by Governor Len Small, Senator-Designate Frank L. Smith, Mayor "Big Bill" Thompson of Chicago and State's Attorney Robert E. Crowe of Cook County paraded under

the banner of "Draft Coolidge" and "America First." This tie-up, with its state, county and city patronage, represented the greatest political machine the state has ever seen.

Opposed to it was the faction led by Senator Charles S. Deneen. This group sought to commit the party to Frank O. Lowden for president, Otis F. Glenn for senator, Louis Lincoln Emmerson for governor, Oscar E. Carlstrom for attorney-general and Circuit Judge John A. Swanson for state's attorney of Cook County. Emmerson is completing three terms as secretary of state and Carlstrom seeks reëlection.

The contests for state offices centered on the issues of the Small interest suits and the Smith campaign contributions. The all-absorbing issue in Cook County was the state's attorneyship. As the chief of the local law enforcement machinery the state's attorney is the most powerful office in the local situation. Robert E. Crowe, who sought renomination to a third four-year term, greatly enhanced the power and authority of the position by political tie-ups. Crowe was aligned with "Big Bill" Thompson, Chicago's circus-minded mayor. Together they bossed the "America First" faction, although Big Bill's flair for the spectacular set the pace for the combination.

In addition to party patronage possibilities, Big Bill's interest in the election centered in thirty-one local bond issues, totalling $77,959,500 for public improvements. Through his

[1] Gangsterese for bomb.

efforts the legislature at its session a year ago automatically doubled the city's debt limit by increasing assessed value from 50 to 100 per cent of fair cash value. Approval of the proposition would have doubled the city's bonded debt.

VIOLENCE RE-ACTS AGAINST THOMPSON

The campaign of the Crowe-Thompson forces appeared headed for a complete clean-up. An organization, well-manned and well-heeled, appeared to assure them success at the polls. Crowe's candidacy had been carefully groomed and had several attributes of respectability. Efforts by the opposition and by the good government forces to unseat him appeared doomed to failure until the last two weeks of the campaign. Here's where the "pineapples" and related tactics come in.

On March 21 Joseph Esposito, a West Side Deneen leader, who opposed a Crowe-Thompson stalwart for ward committee, was shot in the back. Fifty-eight slugs entered his body. On March 26 the homes of Senator Deneen and Judge Swanson, Deneen candidate for state's attorney, were bombed — "pineappled," gangsters term it — five minutes apart. The infernal machine missed Judge Swanson by barely two seconds. These occurrences were followed by threats of personal violence to Judge Swanson, to members of his family and to leaders in the opposition to Crowe. Bombing threats led to the cancellation of several Deneen meetings. The terrorism culminated in the killing of a Deneen precinct captain on election day.

These terrorist tactics jarred the public apathy and galvanized the entire Deneen forces. The bombings marked the turning point of public opinion toward Judge Swanson. They drama-tized his candidacy and the conditions which he pledged himself to remedy.

Crowe tried to explain away the bombings by saying they were perpetrated by his opponents to create sympathy for their cause.

The Chicago Church Federation, through its political action commission, proclaimed a day of prayer for Chicago and Chicagoans.

The steady growth of sentiment for Swanson was perceptible day by day as the campaign wore on. The opposition successfully punctured several of Crowe's manufactured endorsements.

Crowe claimed the endorsement of the Chicago Crime Commission. This claim was based on complimentary statements in the commission's reports concerning the way Crowe had co-operated with the commission. He also cited a letter of approval sent him seven years before by Frank J. Loesch, a leader of the Chicago Bar, who is now president of the Crime Commission. Mr. Loesch's letter commended Crowe for a specific act.

"I hoped to stimulate him in the performance of his official duties," says Mr. Loesch. "I did not give him a clean bill of health for the rest of his life."

The Crime Commission adopted and widely circulated this flat repudiation:

The Chicago Crime Commission, believing that State's Attorney Crowe is inefficient and unworthy of his great responsibility to maintain law and order in Cook County, and that his alliances are such as to destroy public confidence in his integrity, recommends to the citizens that he be defeated for renomination.

The commission's records show that with the largest staff of any state's attorney his batting average of successful prosecutions between 1921 and 1926 was less than 37 per cent. Of 24,139 defendants tried, 15,331 went free. Coroner's juries declared 1,793 murders were committed. Of this number, 1,154 were prosecuted; 732 were acquitted; 425 were punished and 33 hanged.

Crowe also claimed the endorsement of 4,757 members of the Cook County Bar. Preferential polls conducted by the Chicago Bar Association and the Chicago *Daily News* showed that lawyers favored Swanson over Crowe in the ratio of 5 to 1.

An impromptu committee of business men challenged Crowe to appear at a public meeting in the Auditorium to answer questions concerning his failure to prosecute cases of vote frauds; his deliberate efforts to block such prosecutions; why he had a law passed preventing judges from appointing special prosecutors; his failure to secure a larger number of convictions in criminal cases. A check for $1,000 was posted for payment to charity if Crowe appeared.

Crowe disregarded this challenge and declined to submit himself to any questioning in a public place. At a City Club forum he literally "ran out," leaving his eyeglasses behind in his hasty exit, when questions began to pop after his set speech.

ELECTION DAY

On election day several hundred men and women, members of civic organizations, volunteered for service as watchers at the polls. The committee of business men hired several hundred men to prevent fraud in the "river wards," Crowe-Thompson strongholds. All watchers were deputized as officers of the county by Judge Edmund K. Jarecki, the officer who in Illinois has charge of the election machinery.

Election day dawned crisp and clear. Approximately 75 per cent of the registered vote was polled. The tabulated returns showed practically the entire Deneen ticket victorious. Emmerson won out over Small by 390,000; Glenn defeated Smith by 225,000; Swanson defeated Crowe by 190,000. The 31 bond issues failed to carry by a two-to-one vote. And even "Big Bill" failed of election as republican committeeman in his home ward.

WHERE ZONING FAILS

BY R. D. MacLAURIN

Commissioner of Trade Waste, City of Cleveland

Zoning for industrial uses segregates nuisances in the interest of residential property. But zoning does not abate dust, fumes, odors, noxious gases or offensive wastes, and therefore fails to accomplish its avowed purpose to better public health and welfare.   ::   ::

"For the purpose of promoting health, safety, morals, or the general welfare of the community, the legislative body of cities and incorporated villages is hereby empowered to regulate and restrict the height, number of stories, and size of buildings and other structures, the percentage of lot that may be occupied, the size of yards, courts, and other open spaces, the density of population, and the location and use of buildings, structures, and land for trade, industry, residence, or other purposes."

Thus reads Section 1 of "A Standard State Zoning Enabling Act," as published by the Advisory Committee on Zoning of the department of commerce, under which municipalities may adopt zoning regulations.

The police power enabling zoning is, therefore, derived from the legislature on the grounds that zoning improves health, safety, morals, or general welfare. With the general idea of zoning the writer agrees. As applied to industries, however, the benefits to health, safety, morals, or general welfare are not conspicuously apparent. The creation and recognition of nuisance areas is not conducive to the welfare of industry itself. In short, the object sought, namely, the betterment of health and general welfare, is not realized to any appreciable extent by the present method of zoning industries. Segregation of industry is merely the first step toward the betterment of welfare conditions, and it is only a short one.

SEGREGATION DOES NOT CONTROL NUISANCES

General welfare certainly includes the welfare of industrial as well as residential districts, but zoning seems to divide these interests in a community. Residential interests are set up against industrial interests, or vice versa. There are no scientific grounds for such differentiation of interests in so far as health or general welfare is concerned. There is only one interest. Such interest may be realized by adopting scientific regulations for the control of nuisance.

Zoning of industries into groups is based on the alleged degree of nuisance produced. In other words, unrestricted industrial zones are established in which alleged nuisances may be created. It is, therefore, difficult to determine to what extent industrial zoning improves health or general welfare.

Industrial zoning seems to be based on the following theories:

Firstly, that industries are nuisances *per se*.

Secondly, that industries are segregated for the purpose of protecting residential property.

Thirdly, that industries cannot be conducted successfully without creating nuisance of greater or less degree.

Fourthly, that the abatement of nuisance means that industry is imperilled and in danger of being closed down.

Aerial nuisances are caused by the pollution of the atmosphere by dusts, fumes, odors and noxious gases. Nearly all such nuisances can be successfully controlled by applying scientific methods already known to the various arts. In other words, if the best practical means known for preventing nuisance were generally applied, very little nuisance would obtain in industrial centers. Progressive industries do not want to be classified as nuisances. In fact, the mastery of nuisance is abundant evidence of good business management. Therefore, in cases where nuisance occurs, it is due chiefly to the lack of the proper means to combat it. In industrial zoning, one recognizes a conception of nuisance as applied to certain industries existent twenty-five or more years ago. Conditions that were undoubtedly the cause of just complaint in the past in many industries are not necessarily existent today. Industries cannot be regarded as nuisances *per se* if these industries are not nuisances in fact.

IMPROVEMENT THROUGH ABATEMENT

Zoning also purports to protect residential districts from the ill effects of industries by segregating industry into unrestricted nuisance districts. Such classification cannot benefit a residential district materially as long as nuisance obtains in an industrial district. The only way in which conditions can be improved or residential districts benefited is by abating nuisance. Further, the fact is entirely overlooked that one industry may cause infinite damage to other industries in an industrial district. Many cases can be cited where the manufacture of chemical products would be practically impossible in the presence of well-known atmospheric pollution. It is, therefore, imperative that legislative means should be provided whereby residential and industrial interests shall be mutually protected.

The idea that industry cannot be conducted profitably without creating dusts, fumes, odors, noxious gases, or offensive liquid wastes, is erroneous. Some of the largest and most prosperous industries in America today are conducting business without creating nuisance of any kind. Smoke, fumes, smells, noxious gases, or offensive liquid wastes are not synonymous with progress or sound business principles. The elimination of every form of waste is one of the objects of scientific management, and the idea that it is an advantage for an industry to maintain a public nuisance has no scientific basis in fact. Progressive business firms no longer tolerate nuisance as it is regarded as a stigma on the conduct of business.

Industry is not imperilled or in danger of being closed down if it adopts the best means known to the art for conducting business. There has never been an industry closed down in the history of this country, or its existence imperilled under those circumstances. Such a conception is preposterous, yet it is entertained and nourished in high financial and legal circles. Many instances can be cited in which industries have been induced or compelled to adopt the best practical means

known to the art and have profited immeasurably by so doing. If this were not the history of industrial progress, the chemical engineer and physicist would have no place in industry. These sciences, however, are the cornerstones of industrial progress, and in connection with nuisance, the application of scientific principles will provide the answer for all such problems.

OBJECTIONS TO ZONING

The segregation of industries into groups on the basis of nuisance is subject to the following objections:

(1) There is no scientific basis in fact for classifying industries into groups on the basis of nuisance, as heretofore enacted in zoning ordinances.

(2) Zoning legislation as applied to the segregation of industries does not protect industry nor the public generally.

(3) Zoning legislation does not provide a remedy for abating nuisance, and consequently fails to realize the potential possibilities of zoning by improving industrial and residential conditions, or, in other words, the betterment of health or general welfare.

There is no scientific basis for differentiating between industries as to degree of nuisance. Such an effort to discriminate between nuisances, or degree of nuisance, is futile because adequate standards for such a purpose are not known. Many industries are classified as nuisances in zoning ordinances, which are being conducted by certain manufacturers without creating any nuisance whatever. If an industry can be conducted profitably by one manufacturer without creating nuisance, it is evidence that other manufacturers in the same kind of industry can adopt similar nuisance abatement methods. The mere implication that an industrial district is a nuisance district is injurious to contiguous property and also to the district itself. There are no industries which can be scientifically designated as nuisances *per se*. This implication embodied in zoning ordinances is incorrect and demoralizing. Nuisance is attributable chiefly to the neglect on the part of industry to apply adequate methods for the purpose of controlling the emission of dusts, fumes, odors, noxious gases, or offensive liquid wastes.

Industries are not protected by being segregated into groups. They are still subject to state and municipal laws pertaining to nuisance. It is possible that zoning of industries may create a false sense of security in the minds of manufacturers. Zoning does not provide immunity from the laws of nuisance in cases where the best practical means known to the art are not applied.

COMPEL INDUSTRIES TO ABATE THEIR NUISANCES

Legislation pertaining to the zoning of industry should at least provide means for realizing its constitutional purpose. The alleged purpose of industrial zoning is to promote health, safety, morals, or general welfare. Those are the constitutional grounds empowering municipalities to regulate industry for purposes above designated. Yet regulations contemplating the control of nuisance caused by dusts, fumes, odors, noxious gases, or offensive water-carried wastes, are not incorporated in any zoning legislation yet enacted.

Then how may the constitutional purposes of zoning be realized as applied to industry, and at the same time promote the best interests of residential and other zoned districts? This can be accomplished by a municipality requiring that industries shall secure a permit to conduct business. The permit shall not be issued by a municipality unless the industry or business shall employ the best practical means known to the art for the abatement of dusts, fumes, odors, noxious gases, or water-carried offensive wastes, as determined and approved by the duly appointed authorities of the municipality.

The use of the best practical means in any art is an advantage to industry. That conclusion is axiomatic. Further, the adoption of such best practical means known will abate almost all nuisances and consequently benefit residential interests and other industrial interests. Therefore, a dual purpose mutually advantageous would be realized. That is, the best possible interests of industry and residential districts would thus be served.

THE NEGRO IN CHICAGO POLITICS

BY RALPH JOHNSON BUNCHE

Graduate School, Harvard University

*The story of increasing participation of negroes in Chicago politics
told by a member of the race.*   ::   ::   ::   ::   ::   ::

PROBABLY no racial group in the country (unless it be the Irish) is more manifestly "political" in its everyday life than the American negro. His innate gregarious instinct together with other less natural factors, such as imposed segregation and racial consciousness, have welded him into a more or less homogeneous social unit, within which much of the activity is political. Organizations of every description are legion. They run the entire gamut from shrill sewing circles to high-toned fraternal orders, and into the life of each the negro enters with whole-hearted, wholesome zest. Critical observers often remark of him that he "has too much organization." Be that as it may, he has, apparently, a strong political urge. When this is manifested solely within his own group it is of little significance to the nation at large. But when it begins to find expression through the ballot boxes of towns and cities, as well as state and national elections, it assumes a broader and more vital importance.

The negro electorate of Chicago affords an interesting study in this respect. Any minority group which can and does control a mayoralty election in the nation's second largest municipality must be of more than passing interest to the student of political affairs. It must not be inferred from what is to follow that the Chicago negro in his political aspects is by any means an accurate barometer of the national political position of the American negro. That is not at all true, for the Chicago group is one of the most progressive of the country, economically, politically, and culturally. But it does remain an example of what favorable conditions can do to give a significant position to capable constituencies of the race.

MAYOR THOMPSON'S DEBT TO THE NEGRO

The history of the political development of the negro in Chicago is interwoven with the political career of William Hale Thompson, present Chicago executive. When Mayor Thompson was first elected in the spring of 1915, approximately 55,000 negroes were residents of Chicago. These were concentrated chiefly in the district just south of the "loop," politically designated as the second ward. Many years before, Thompson had been elected alderman from this same ward on the strength of the negro vote. In the municipal election of 1915 he was solidly supported by the same electorate—gaining a majority of more than 10,000 votes over his opponent in the negro district. He was elected, and served for two terms (until 1923), during which time the political influence of the negro population of the city began to assume important proportions. Indeed, in 1919, when Mayor Thompson was reëlected by a plurality of 21,622 votes in a total city vote of

698,920, his poll in the negro wards was 15,569 to his nearest opponent's 3,323. The negro support was consequently sufficiently strong to control the result.

It was during Thompson's first two administrations that the first negro alderman was returned to the city council, and the mayor promptly appointed him floor leader. At the same time there were three negroes appointed as assistant corporation counsels; another to a comparatively lucrative position as attorney for the traction commission; and a number of minor appointments in other city offices were made. This representation in the government of the city served to stimulate the political interest of the negro groups. The ballot was seen as an effective instrument whereby they might to no little extent select those who were to govern them and at the same time win moderate prestige for their race. Negro political leaders with actual political experience were being developed, and the war placed new power in their hands. The exodus from the South greatly augmented their population. The number of negro inhabitants in Chicago jumped startlingly from 44,103 in 1910 to 109,595 in 1920, an increase of 148 per cent, most of which occurred between 1916 and 1919. This increase virtually trebled the number of negro voters, many of whom were of the ignorant, peasant class.

LAST YEAR'S HECTIC CAMPAIGN

Mayor Thompson did not run in the 1923 election but was a candidate for a third term in the spring of 1927. The campaign and election were among the most exciting in Chicago's history. Unfortunately, the racial issue early became predominant. This was due in part to the size of the potential negro vote, which was known to be strongly in support of Thompson; and

in part to the fact that some of the supporters of Mayor Dever's candidacy viciously attacked Thompson as the "negro candidate." The inevitable result was to stampede the negro vote to the Thompson banner more solidly than ever.

A good deal of vilification and scurrilous propaganda was circulated during the hectic campaign. One of the more serious occurrences was an attempt by fraudulent letter to induce large numbers of Thompson's negro supporters to attend a meeting at noon in front of the Thompson headquarters in the heart of the "loop" or business district. The evident purpose of the hoax was to increase the rapidly growing friction between the white and negro groups, perhaps even to the extent of inciting a riot. Only prompt action by negro leaders averted a grave disaster, for all of the ill-feeling engendered by the 1919 riot had not yet been dissipated. Calliopes paraded the streets piping the strains of "Bye, Bye, Blackbird.' One of the many circulars displayed a trainload of negroes headed from Georgia with Thompson as pilot of the train, and the significant legend inscribed below: "This train will start for Chicago, April 6, if Thompson is elected!"

Blue skies and warm sunlight on election day and the extreme intensity of the preëlection campaign brought out a record vote. Thompson surprised political prophets by winning over Dever by a plurality of 82,938 votes. A total of 1,010,582 ballots was cast, of which 10,739 were disqualified. The particular significance of this election to the question under discussion is that by far the major portion of this plurality was gained in the "south side" or negro wards, where Thompson's majorities ran from eight to one to as high as sixteen to one. The second, third and fourth wards, with a negro population respectively of about 98, 95 and 60 per cent,—the "strongholds of the negro vote,"—gave 59,215 votes of the Thompson plurality of 82,938.

NEGRO LEADERS SHARE GENEROUSLY IN APPOINTMENTS

With the Thompson victory and the campaign excitement abated, the color issue was flatly dropped and but scant mention was made of it by the local press, which had featured it so prominently in the preëlection bally-hoo. Interest now centered on the prospective political "house-cleaning" by the new administration. In the new city appointments negro political leaders shared generously. In general the men appointed have been from among the higher levels of the negro race, well trained and capable. One of the first to be designated was that of Bishop A. J. Carey, presiding bishop of the fifth district of the African Methodist Episcopal Church and leader of his race, as a member of the Chicago civil service commission,—a cabinet office. This commission is composed of three members, two Republicans and one Democrat, who supervise the recruiting of more than 30,000 city employees, including the members of the police and fire departments. Another prominent negro, a noted author and lecturer in his group, has been appointed as legal adviser to the city in matters pertaining to state legislation of vital interest to Chicago. Six of the best trained young lawyers of the group hold appointments as assistant corporation counsels. In the city attorney's office the negroes are represented by an assistant city attorney. Two representatives are also found as assistant attorneys for the board of local improvements. In the office of the city prosecutor are five more as assistant city prosecutors.

Another, appointed as a member of the library board, with no salary, has jurisdiction over approximately 3,000 employees.

These men are all entrusted with responsible positions. As an illustration, in the office of the corporation counsel, Attorney P. B. Prescott, as assistant corporation counsel and trial lawyer in property damage litigation, represents the city in suits mounting to millions of dollars yearly. Indeed, in a case now in litigation, a sum of $1,500,000 is involved. There are approximately twenty negro investigators in the various legal departments. Additional appointments in the many city departments, as teachers, clerks, police, et cetera, run into the hundreds.

It is of especial significance to note that many of these appointees are from other than dominantly negro wards. One of the negro assistants in the corporation counsel's office has residence in a ward of which the negro voters number approximately 1,500 out of a total registered vote of 30,000. Another, attorney to the board of local improvements, is likewise from a district in which the negro voters represent only about one-seventh of the resident vote; a third, in the city prosecutor's office, hails from the aristocratic "silk-stocking" sixth ward. Many similar appointments have been made. All of the negro political representation in Chicago is not, however, by appointment. In the two strong negro wards, the second and third, the majority group has elected two of its own members as aldermen. A negro municipal court judge with a salary of $10,000 has also been nominated and elected.

THE NEGRO IN THE STATE GOVERNMENT

The natural result of this stimulated political activity found its expression in an increased interest by negroes in state political affairs. It can, undoubtedly, be not inaccurately stated that Cook county, embracing Chicago and the neighboring towns, has more negroes filling responsible political positions than any other community in the country. The same statement is true of the state of Illinois. Four negroes have been elected to the lower house of the Illinois state legislature and one state senator. State appointments have been numerous. A negro serves as the governor's appointee on the powerful Illinois industrial board, which controls the workmen's compensation awards. Another serves as state commerce commissioner, one of a commission of seven members, controlling all public utilities and state commercial enterprises.

It can scarcely be disputed that the negro is receiving comparatively excellent political representation in Chicago, Cook County, and Illinois today. That the quality of the negro representatives is of the best is a question often disputed. It can, however, be safely stated that the present political representatives, both elective and appointive, of the negro race in Illinois are from among the best and most intelligent members of the group. Their service has been both efficient and capable in their respective offices, as has been that of the negro workers in the other city departments.

The negro confidence, as expressed by his ballot, has often been abused.

Political exploitation of ignorant racial groups of all races is an evil still not unknown to American political practice. Nor have the negro leaders always been able men and true. But even a casual survey of the present situation in Chicago must convey the impression that the negro electorate there is much more intelligent and more capably represented by its own members than at any time in the city's history.

It would seem that the growing activity and influence of the negro electorate portends a new era of negro political development. The twelve millions of negroes in this country, approximating one-tenth of the total population, must inevitably wield a more proportionate and equitable degree of influence in the political affairs —local, state, and national—of the nation. Perhaps not in this generation, nor in the next, but ultimately. Today a large proportion of the negro vote is arbitrarily deprived of the right to exercise the franchise. But such a condition cannot continue indefinitely. It is contrary to every fundamental precept of good government. Even now indications point toward a "letting down of the bars" in respect to negro suffrage in the South; and in the words of Dr. John Hope, president of Morehouse College, Atlanta, Georgia, "the negro can and will exercise his lawful franchise in the South just so soon as he develops capable political leaders."

CONNECTICUT CONSOLIDATES STATE FINANCIAL CONTROL

BY LANE W. LANCASTER

Wesleyan University

The new board of control continues the Connecticut tradition. It has little legal power but may have great influence. :: :: ::

WHAT may eventually come to be regarded as a considerable departure from traditional practice in state financial methods took place in Connecticut at the end of the last session of the legislature when Governor Trumbull approved an act creating a board of finance and control. The act may be said to have been inspired by His Excellency himself, and the ends it is designed to accomplish were set forth by him in an address before the two houses of the legislature. "We should have," he said, "even better facilities than have thus far been provided for the securing, concentrating, analyzing, and interpreting of the facts as to our financial condition and financial needs, as to the opportunities that may exist for improvements in the organization of our work and the functioning of our departments, and as to the results and cost of the work that we are doing and the services that we are rendering to the people. . . . In view of these considerations it seems to me that you would approve a plan whereby we would coördinate the functions of two of our statutory boards, the state board of finance and the board of control, and provide the facilities whereby certain data that we do not now have in usable form . . . can be made available. . . . I have in mind such things as accounting, cost finding and reporting, long-range planning, property control and the like."

A successful business man himself, the governor was recommending to the assembly changes analogous to those which he had found valuable in his own business. The suggestions were variously received and interpreted. To some it appeared that the executive was laying violent hands upon the existing system of institutional control which, though not squaring with the approved theories on such matters, has in practice given good results. Most of the executive functions of the state are in the hands of boards, all of which contain citizen members. Almost all of the institutions receiving state appropriations are managed by boards named by the governor. In such matters as purchases and contracts these latter boards are subject to no central administrative control. The state abandoned the merit system in 1921 and the personnel of the various institutions is chosen by the managing boards. Theoretically this is a bad arrangement. In practice, however, there have been few if any scandals and the state's institutions have been exceptionally well managed. Those who clung to the system of board management were critical of any change which seem to be a step in the direction of centralized control. The opinion of the assembly, however, was that the governor's plan deserved a trial.

THREE BOARDS ABOLISHED

The new act deals only with the organization of the central financial authorities and directly makes no change in the management of individual institutions or departments. It begins by abolishing three previously existing boards which divided among them the financial administration of the state. The first of these was the state board of finance. This board consisted of the state treasurer, comptroller and tax commissioner *ex officio*, and three citizen members appointed by the governor for six-year terms, one retiring every two years. This board, together with the general assembly's joint committee on appropriations, was the budget-making authority of the state. The second board abolished by the new act was the board of control. This was composed of the governor, comptroller, treasurer and attorney-general *ex officio*. This board had power, while the general assembly was not in session, to increase appropriations to any service, where, in their unanimous judgment, an increase was necessary and in case the total of such increases did not exceed $150,000 in any biennium. The third agency abolished was the commission on state institutions. This commission consisted of the governor *ex officio* and five citizen members appointed by the governor for six-year terms. It had general powers of visitation and inspection of institutions under the state or supported in whole or part by state funds. This commission was created in 1925 and does not appear to have been particularly active during its short existence.

THE NEW BOARD

The new board of finance and control consists of the governor, who is *ex officio* chairman, the secretary of state, the treasurer, comptroller, attorney-general and tax commissioner, a commissioner of finance and control and three citizen members appointed

by the governor, with the consent of the senate, for six-year terms. The first four members of the board are at present elective officers serving for two years. The tax commissioner is appointed by the governor for a four-year term. The new commissioner of finance and control will hold office for four years and receive a salary of $9,000. The three citizen members will receive $1,000 a year and expenses.

This is, of course, another board and continues the Connecticut tradition of management of public affairs by boards. But it may be a board with a difference. The distinctive feature is that the state will now have a single financial officer responsible in some sense for financial planning and performance. For the act states that the commissioner shall be the administrative officer of the board, shall give his whole time to the duties of his office and shall receive one of the highest salaries paid in the state service. While the duties of the board would seem to be mainly advisory it is quite possible that the creation of a conspicuous head will in itself go far to consolidate the financial operations of the government. The governor has made a good beginning by appointing to the post of commissioner an able business man who has a record of eight years' service in the two houses of the assembly and who enjoys the confidence of the community.

The powers of the new board are as follows: (1) To keep on file information concerning the state's general accounts and to be equipped to furnish all accounting statements relating to the financial condition of the state as a whole; (2) to inquire into the operation of the budget and the wisdom and economy of expenditures of the various departments, boards and institutions; (3) to examine each department and institution to determine the effectiveness of its policies and management, organization and procedure, and the quality and cost of its service; (4) to devise ways and means for making in advance plans for the future needs of departments and institutions with respect to physical plant; (5) to devise ways and means of establishing and maintaining proper control of state property and equipment and to require the establishment of permanent inventory records; and (6) to prescribe the form of operating reports to be required from the various departments, boards, commissions, institutions, and agencies supported in whole or in part by the state, and to take such action as may be considered necessary to remedy unsatisfactory conditions disclosed by such reports.

DEFECTIVE IN THEORY, MAY WORK IN PRACTICE

By nearly every theoretical test which the books apply the Connecticut plan would probably fail. The members of the new board are in no effective way subject to the control of the governor since their choice is by various means, their terms of different lengths and in some cases the terms overlap. The board would seem to have no mandatory power to establish a uniform accounting system among state agencies and no control over purchases and contracts. Being a board it is presumably not an effective budgetary authority. And, the new commissioner would seem to be the servant rather than the master of the new board.

But if experience counts for anything it would seem that Connecticut practice is not likely to square with the theory. No Democratic governor is likely to come into office and find himself saddled with a board of finance and control of Republican leanings. In fact no Democratic governor is likely soon to come into office at all. As to the internal organization of the board and its relations with the various state agencies and institutions there would seem to be little likelihood of serious difficulties. Reappointment to boards of management is the tradition in Connecticut, and the state is justly proud of the type of service rendered by unpaid officials in such positions. The business of the state is likely in the future to continue to be managed according to tacit understandings among a rather small number of officials accustomed to hold such positions. Under such circumstances any commissioner appointed is likely to be able to exert considerable influence upon the management of affairs and, if filled by men of tact and ability, the office may become one of outstanding importance.

SALARIES OF POLICEMEN AND FIREMEN IN THIRTY-FIVE CITIES, 1928

BY ESTHER CRANDALL

Librarian, Municipal Administration Service

SALARY figures really mean little unless supplemented by certain directly related facts. This is especially true in the departments of police and fire. Are uniforms furnished? What are the hours of duty? Is sick leave with pay provided? Is there a pension system? The answers to all of these must be considered as supplementary factors in considering rates of pay.

In 1923, the Philadelphia Bureau of Municipal Research compiled information on the salaries and employment conditions of police and fire departments in eighteen of the largest cities in the United States. Such facts to be useful must be kept up-to-date. William C. Beyer, director of the Philadelphia Bureau, consented to the use of the 1923 report as a basis for an annual compilation. The original list has been extended to include thirty-five municipalities,—the twenty-three largest, and twelve others selected from the smaller cities. They are listed according to population based on the 1927 estimate of the United States Bureau of the Census. In the few cases, marked with an asterisk, the 1920 population is used since the 1927 estimate was not available. The order of arrangement in the tables presupposes a reasonable growth of population over the 1920 figures.

Only the uniformed force is included. The entire detective force in the police department is excluded, as well as the clerical and special services in both departments. In so far as possible, the facts are stated in the table exactly as they were reported. Policewomen are listed only as to number and salaries. The footnotes at the end of each table explain important variations in individual cities.

Definitions of positions accompanied each questionnaire sent out. Variations in titles, if duties are the same, have been disregarded. For example, it seemed of little importance that a superintendent is called a chief in some cities and in others is given a different title. We have assumed that when a position was listed under the column with the definition of duties attached, those duties were the same or comparable regardless of title. The definitions accompanying questionnaires were as follows:

POLICE DEPARTMENT

Patrolman: Under supervision, during a definite watch, to maintain order or detect violators of law. Patrol an assigned beat or post. Regulate traffic. Apprehend and arrest criminals and assist in their prosecution in the courts. Serve warrants and other police notices. Testify at hearings and in courts.

House sergeant: Under general supervision, to direct police work in a station house.

Street sergeant: Under general supervision, to direct in the field the work of patrolmen. Visit and inspect beats or posts. Report irregularities, accidents or unusual circumstances. Act for lieutenant in his absence.

Lieutenant: Assist in supervision and, in absence of the captain, to act as commanding officer.

Captain: Under general supervision of assistant superintendent, responsible as commanding officer of a police company for the preservation of peace and prevention of crime, and enforcement of laws and orders in an assigned district. Protect life and property. Assign instructions, discipline, and be responsible for the work of subordinates. Responsible for safety of prisoners, their appearance for trial, etc.

Assistant superintendent: Under general supervision, to assist the superintendent in the administration of the police department.

Superintendent: Administrative supervision of the police department and responsible for maintenance of order, prevention of crime, and enforcement of laws. Designate the work of the personnel. Make all reports, maintain general discipline of subordinates.

Surgeon: Under general directions, to perform difficult surgical operations in the service of the police department and perform related work as required.

FIRE DEPARTMENT

Hoseman and ladderman: Under immediate supervision, to attend fires and assist as directed in extinguishing them and in saving lives and property. Perform related work as required, such as taking care of quarters, etc.

Steam or auto engineer: Under supervision, to drive and take care of motor apparatus.

Lieutenant: Under direction of captain, to command a fire-fighting platoon during an assigned shift. To attend fires and lead and work with men as directed. To be responsible for instructions, examination, deportment, efficiency, etc., of a given platoon. To assist captain in maintaining discipline. To be responsible for company records, etc.

Captain: Commanding officer, to be responsible for fire station and for fire-fighting efficiency and operation of a fire company. Responsible for attendance, instructions, examination, discipline and work of the company and maintenance of equipment. Requisitioning and disposal of supplies and properties. Immediate charge of the first platoon.

Battalion chief: Under general direction, to be responsible for fire fighting efficiency in a battalion district. Command the operations of fire companies in the district. Make periodic inspections of records, apparatus, quarters, men and equipment. Instruct personnel.

Deputy chief engineer: Under direction, to assist in supervising the care, maintenance, repair and reconstruction of steam motor and chemical fire engines, water towers, trucks and other fire-fighting apparatus. To aid in instruction and examination of men in the operation of fire apparatus.

Chief engineer: General command of entire fire-fighting service.

Tables I and II deal with police departments, and tables III and IV, with fire departments. Salaries and number of employees in each position are given in tables I and III and conditions of employment for all positions in tables II and IV.

The rates of pay appear by the year, month, week or day as reported by the respective cities. To save space the specific period covered by each rate has not been given but will be obvious from the rate itself.

(1927 estimate) * 1920 census	No.	Rate of pay	No.	Rate of pay	No.	Rate of pay	No.	Rate of pay	No.	Rate of pay
New York 5,970,800	15,853	$1769 to $2500 [1]	1027 [2]	$3000			570	$3500	120	$3850 $4500 [1]
Chicago 3,102,800	4800	$2140 to $2500 [3]	599 [2]	$2900			140	$3200	55	$4000
Philadelphia 2,035,900	4295	$1400 per yr. to $5.50 per day [5]	96	$2050	119	$2100	43	$2400	22	$2600
Detroit 1,334,500	2610 [6]	$2000 to $2520 [6]	155 [2]	$2710			84	$2960	8	$3480
Cleveland 972,500	1200	$1800 to $2419.68 [7]			126	$2613 60	61	$2746 32	19	$3543 36
St. Louis 839,200	1550 [9]	$150 and $180 [9]	3	$216.66	136	$216.66	34	$250	18	$285
Baltimore 819,000 [11]	1350	$31.25 to $36.25 [11]	24	$41 50	151	$41.50 [11]	35	$49 [11]	13	$60 [11]
Boston 793,100	2024 [13]	$1600 to $2000			169	$2300	41	$2500	29	$3500
Los Angeles 576,673	1933	$170, $180, $190, $200			141	$225	32	$250	16	$300
Pittsburgh * 665,500	939	$1800 to $2040 [14a]	46	$2160			47	$2460	6	$3000
San Francisco 576,000	1013 [15]	$2400 and $2580	84 [2]	$2640			35	$3000	16	$3600 1 at $4000 1 at $5000
Buffalo 550,000 [17]	853	$1700 to $2000 [18]	81 [18]	$2000 to $2780 [18]			71	$2240— 1st yr. $2300— 2nd yr.	24	$2540 to $2780
Washington, D. C. 540,000	1188	$1800 to $2100 [19]	53 [2]	$2400			22	$2700	14	$3000
Milwaukee 536,400	817	$1920 to $2040 [21]	22	$2160	54	$2320	7	$2670	'10	$2820
Newark 466,700	1005	$2100 to $2500 [22]	80 [2]	$2600 to $3000			57	$3100 to $3200	10	$3400 to $4000 [22]
Minneapolis 447,700	324	$1800 to $2040 [23]			18	$2160	18	$2280	8	$2400
New Orleans 424,400	377	$125			13	$143.75			16	$187
Cincinnati 412,200	500	$1500 to $1860 [25]			33	$2200	33	$2400	7	$3300
Kansas City, Mo. 383,100	401	$125 to $150 [26]			41	$175 and $200 [26]	2	$200	11	$250
Seattle 375,300	465	$160 to $180 [17]			33	$200	10	$220	8	$250
Indianapolis 374,300	425	$1916.25			33	$2182 50	13	$2382.50	6	$2582.50
Rochester 324,500	375	$2100			22	$2415	8	$2625	8	$2835
Jersey City 321,500	765	$2100 and $2500 [20]	38 [2]	$3000			73	$3200	12	$4100
Akron * 208,435	142	$1800 to $2079 [31]	2	$2257.50	8	$2257.50	5	$2394	4	$2772
Toledo 305,400	334	$2400			18	$2730	6	$2880	6	$3090
Portland * 258,288	302	$160 to $198	6	$208	19	$208	10	$220	6	$250
Columbus, Ohio 291,400	313	$150 to $160			4	$175 to $185	5	$190 to $195	4	$200 to $210
St. Paul 250,100	225	$126.40 to $193.20			16	$158.20	5	$174	5	$200
Syracuse 197,000	300	$1800 to $2040 [34]	12 [2]	$2140			3	$2290	8	$2740
Dayton 180,700	155	$160			15	$190	3	$250	3	$210
Des Moines 148,900	77	$145 and $160	2	$170	2	$170	3	$175	3	$185
Trenton 136,700	175	$1750 to $2200			9	$2450	7	$2600	5	$3400
Fall River 132,600	174	$4.50 and $5.50			1 day 5 night	$2250	11	$2400	6	$2700
Wilmington 126,400	120	$1644 to $1752 [37]	3	$2100	11	$2100	1	$2304	5	$2604
New Bedford 119,539	231	$5.50	9	$6 05	8	$6.05	13	$6.87 ½	7	$8 03
Duluth 114,700	76	$140–$145 $150–$155 $160	7	$175	4	$175	4	$190	3	$190 to $230

Surgeon	Asst. Superintendent	Superintendent	Policewoman		Others
Rate of pay	Rate of pay	Rate of pay	No.	Rate of pay	
1—$6800 23—$4790	$5800	$8000	125	[4]	19 inspectors at $5400 10 deputy inspectors $5000
$3900	$8000 $7500	$10,000	31	[4]	
$1800 to $5000 [5]	$4000	$5500	None		84 sergeants at $2150 8 inspectors at $2700
$4500 [6]	$6000	$7500	35	$1800 to $2220	3 inspectors at $5000 20 inspectors at $4000
$3687.36	$3783.60 and $4416	$6440 16	16 [9]	[4]	
$291.66 and $208.33	$375	$541.66	18	$150	1 inspector at $333.33
1 at $1500 6 at $1000 (part time)	$4000 [11]	$4500 [11]	5	[4]	
	$4000	$7000	8	[4]	1 commissioner at $8000 1 chief inspector at $3800 22 lieut. inspec. at $2500
	$450	$500	19	[4]	2 deputy chiefs at $400
$4500	$3600	$5000	5	$1416	
$2400	$3600	$7200	3	$2400	
$2150 to $3060 [15]	$3300 to $4300 [15]	$5800	5	$1460 to $1700 [15]	2 inspectors 1st yr. $3600—2nd, $3800 [15]
$2150	$3500	$5200		[4]	4 inspectors at $3250
$1060	$3600	$6000		[4]	
$2500 to $4500 [22]	$4200 to $5000 [22]	$5200 to $6000 [22]		[4]	. Commissioner at $4500
	$3600	$5000		[4] [23a]	
$239.56		$416.65		$87.50	
	$3700 to $4000	$6000			
$50 and $200 [25]	$200, $225 and $350 [25]	$416 66			
		$500		[4]	1 inspector at $285
$1500 and $1600 [25]	$3400 and $3600	$4800		$1916 25	
$3600	$3675	$4935		$2100	Director of police at $6500
$4250		$4500		$2200	
$1200	$2940	$4272.50			
	$3390	$4200		$1440, $1500 and $2730	
3—$1000 1—$2000	$312	$400		$186 to $250	30 inspectors at $220
$165 to $195	$210 to $240	$265 to $310		$140 to $160	
$112.50 $122.50 $134 [28]	$269.50	$4000		$134	
$1000	$3140	$4900			
		$333.33		$125 to $180	3 inspectors at $250
		$3220		$145 and $175	2 inspectors at $205
$1100		$4200		[4]	
$2000	$3150	$4000		$5.50	7 inspectors at $2400

Name of city and population (1927 estimate) * 1920 census	Hours on duty per day	Hours on duty per week	Annual clothing allowance	Annual value of uniforms furnished	Reimbursement for clothes ruined on duty	Pension system
New York 5,970,800			None		Allowance if damaged on duty	Yes
Chicago 3,102,800	8	48	None		None	Yes
Philadelphia 2,035,900	8 [5]	56	Purchased by city	[6]	Replaced by city	Yes
Detroit 1,334,500	8	48	None		Upon recommendation of supt.	Yes
Cleveland 972,500	8	48	Material charged to men	Tailor bill— 1927 $28,176.44	None	Yes
St. Louis 839,200	8	56	None		Allowed by board for value [10]	Yes [10]
Baltimore 819,000	8		None [12]		Yes	Yes
Boston 793,100	10 day 7 night	56	[13]	[13]	Yes	Yes
Los Angeles 576,673	8 [14]		None		None	Yes
Pittsburgh * 665,500			None		Replacement	Yes
San Francisco 576,000			None		None	Yes
Buffalo 550,000			None		None	Yes
Washington, D. C. 540,000 [19]				$58.45	Depends on circumstances	Yes
Milwaukee 536,400 [21]			None		None	Yes
Newark 466,700			None		None	Yes
Minneapolis 447,700			None			Yes
New Orleans 424,400			None		Some	Yes
Cincinnati 412,200			None		None	Yes
Kansas City, Mo. 383,100			None		None	No
Seattle 375,300			None		None	Yes (state law)
Indianapolis 374,300			None		None	Yes
Rochester 324,500			None		None	Yes
Jersey City 321,500			None		None	Yes
Akron * 208,435			None		None	Yes
Toledo 305,400			None		Complete	Yes
Portland * 258,288			None		Act of council	Yes [10]
Columbus, Ohio 291,400			None		None	Yes
St. Paul 250,100			None		None	Yes
Syracuse 197,000			None		None	Yes
Dayton 180,700			None		None	Yes
Des Moines 148,900			None		Yes	Yes
Trenton 136,700			None		Damage paid by city	Yes
Fall River, Mass. 132,600			None		Full replacement	Yes (½ pay)

Dues	Relief fund for death, sickness, etc.	Dues	Annual sick leave with pay	Annual vacation with pay	Other leave with pay per year
2% of salary	Part of pension fund		½ salary for sick leave. Full pay if result of duty injury	18 days [1]	
4¼% of salary	Pension fund provides both		No limit	15 days	None
1 day's pay per mo. [5]	Yes	$3.75	Discretion of chief surgeon	14 days	1 day every 3 weeks [5]
1% of salary [6]	$4000 at death or retirement	$5.00 per mo.	No provision	20 days	1 day off in 7
$6 to $15 [7]	None	None	No set rule	12 days	None
5% of salary [10]	Yes [10]	$2 per mo.[10]	No limit	2 days per mo.	None
2% of salary	Non-official assoc.	$3.12 per mo.	Discretion of police commissioner	30 days	None
4% of weekly salary [13]	Voluntary relief assoc.	$10 per yr. [13]	30 days [13]	14 days	1 day in 8 [13]
4% of salary	Yes but not by city	$1 per mo.	12 days [14]	15 days [14]	None
2½% of salary	Yes	$1 per mo. death benefit	None	14 days	24 days
$24	Voluntary and unofficial organization [16a]	$2 per mo.	Discretion of commissioner	2 weeks	52 days (one day in 7)
4% of salary	$20 per yr. for $2,000		6 mos. if injured on duty	14 days	None
2½% of salary	Death benefit	Part of pension system	30 days [20]	20 days	52 days
4½% of salary	Death benefit insurance	[21]	Discretion of chief	15 days	Every 8th day
2% of salary	Private organization		No specified time allowance	14 days [22]	None
1% of salary to $2 per yr.	Yes	$12 per yr.	2—15 day periods [23]	15 days	24 days (2 days per mo.)
2% of salary	Yes [24]			15 days	None
None	Yes	$12 per member	None	15 days	1 day per mo.
	Yes	$2.00 per mo.	½ pay illness; full pay injury	24 days	None
1½% of salary	In pension system and also a private assoc.	1½% of salary 25c per mo.	6 mos. full pay thereafter ½ pay (state law)	15 days	1 day in 8
$15	No	None	None	15 days	None
2% of salary	Private	$16.00 per yr.	6 mo. max.	14 days	1 day per week
2%	Full pay if warranted		Depends on conditions	14 days [30]	Depends on reason
$8.40 [31]	Yes	$6 per yr.	Indefinite	14 days	Every sixth day
None	Yes	$12	6 mos. with pay	12 days	48 days
½%	Yes [10]	$2 per mo.	None	15 days	
City	Yes	$4 per yr. voluntary	6 mos. for duty injury 3 mos. sickness	15 days	None
1% of salary			15 days [33]	15 days	
2% of salary	Yes		Discretion of surgeon	15 days	2 days per mo.
None	Yes	50c per mo.	21 days	12 working days	1 day in 7
1% of salary	Private $1,000 death benefit		Reasonable	15 days	
2% of salary	Yes	$1 per member each death	Half pay indefinite time	14 days [36]	26 days [36]
None	By local police assoc.	$6 per yr.	14 days [39]	14 days	45 days
1% of salary	Yes $500 at death	Members assessed at each death	No limit	7 days	None
City	No		None	14 days	None

Name of city and population (1927 estimate) * 1920 census	Fireman, Hoseman and Ladderman Rate of pay	Steam or Auto Engineer Rate of pay	Lieutenant Rate of pay	Captain Rate of pay
New York 5,970,800	$1769 to $2500 [1]	$2920	$3400	$4000
Chicago 3,102,800	$2140 to $2500 [2]	$2880	$2900	$3200
Philadelphia 2,035,900	$1400 $4.50 per day [3]	$2050	$2150	$2250
Detroit 1,334,500	$2100 [4]	$2700	$2880	$3180
Cleveland 972,500	$2070 to $231 per mo. [5]	$2576.16 and $2724.96 [5]	$2613.60	$2746 32
St. Louis 839,200	$2160	$2280	$2280	$2520
Baltimore 819,000	$1500 to $1700 [7]	$1800 and $1950	$1875	$2000
Boston 793,100	$1600 to $2000	$2100	$2300	$2500
Los Angeles 576,673	$170, $180, $190, $200	$225		$250
Pittsburgh * 665,500	$2040	$2220		$2460
San Francisco 576,000	$2160 to $2400 [10]	$2640	$2670	$2820
Buffalo 550,000	$2250		$2550	$2850
Washington, D. C. 540,000	$1800 to $2100 [11]		$2350	$2500
Milwaukee 536,400	$1920 to $2040 [12]	42 at $2280 43 at $2160	$2280	$2420
Newark 466,700	$2100 to $2500			$3000, $3100 $3200
Minneapolis 447,700	$170	$175	$185	$190
New Orleans 424,400	$125	$143 75	$145	$150
Cincinnati 412,200	$1500 to $1920 [18]	$1950 to $2000	$2150	$2200
Kansas City, Mo. 383,100	$1680 and $1740	$1800	$1860	$2010
Seattle 375,300	$160, $170, $175, $180	$160 to $220	$190 to $200	$210 to $220
Indianapolis 374,300	$1733.50 and $1916.25	$1982.50	$2182.50	$2382.50
Rochester 324,500	$2100		$2400	$2600
Jersey City 321,500	$2100 and $2500 [23]			$3200
Akron * 208,435	$1800 to $2079	$2205		$2394
Toledo 305,400	$2400	$2480 to $2560	$2610	$2730
Portland * 258,288	$160 to $186	$186 and $200	$203, $208	$215, $220
Columbus 291,400	$140, $160		$165, $170	$175, $185
St. Paul 250,100	$136 40 to $153.20	$153.20 $163.40		$153.20 to $173 60
Syracuse 197,000	$1800 to $2040 [28]	[28]	$2200	$2220
Dayton 180,700	$160	$160	$175	$190
Des Moines 148,900	$145 to $160 [30]		$175	$190
Trenton 136,700	$1750 to $2200 [31]		$2500	$2600
Fall River 132,600	$4.50 to $5.50 [32]		$5 91	$6.46

Battalion Chief		Deputy Chief Engineer	Chief Engineer	Others
No.	Rate of pay	Rate of pay	Rate of pay	
86	$4790	$5800	$12,500	
56	$4000	$4500 to $6800 [2]	$8000	1 fire commissioner at $8000
11	$2650	$3500	$5500	
26	$4000	$4240	$7000	
25	$3543.36		$6440.16	
11	$3000	$3600	$5000	
13	$2900	$3800	$5000	
30	$3500	$4000	$5500	1 fire commissioner at $7500
19	$300	$450	$500	3—1st asst. chief at $400 5—2nd asst. chief at $350
14	$3000	$3500	$5000	
21	$4200	$4800	$7200	26 chief operators at $2520
18	$3072	$3786	$5800	
11	$3250	$3500	$5200	55 sergeants at $2200 16 others in uniform
16	$3120	$3600	$6000	
12	$3400, $3700, $4000	$4200, $4600, $5000	$5200, $5600, $6000	
7	$240	$300 and $275	$416.67	
1 [16]	$281.25	$218 75	$416 65	
8	$3000 to $3300	$3700 to $4000	$6000	
11	$2700	1 at $3600 1 at $3050	$4700	3 supts. at $2100, $2400, and $3000
11	$240 to $250	$265, $275, $285	$500	
9	$2582.50	$3000	$4800	2 asst. engineers at $3182.50 1 at $3062.50
8	$3100	$3675	$4935	
7	$4000	$5000	$6000	
		$2923 to $3049	$4350	
10	$3150	$3690 and $3390	$4200	
3	$250	$312 and $275	$400	
5	$190, $195	$210, $240	$265, $310	Supt. of maintenance at $180—$212.50
12 [17]	$154 to $223.10	$3504	$4000	1 chief inspec. at $201.25 1 asst. chief inspec. at $164.80 6 inspectors at $153.20 1 fire marshall at $173 60
9	$2740	$2170	$2740	
4	$250	$200	$4000 per year	
		3—$235 1—$250	$333	
1	$3200	$3400	$4200	
3	$2750	$3080	$3850	
2	$2310		$3300	
3	$2750	$3080	$3850	37 chauffeurs at $5.83 per day Chief inspec. at $46.82

Name of city and population (1927 estimate) * 1920 census	Platoon system	Hours on duty per day	Hours on duty per week	Annual clothing allowance	Annual value of uniforms furnished	Reimbursement for clothes ruined on duty	Pension system
New York 5,970,800	2	9 day 15 night	84 [1]	None		None	Yes, half of pay
Chicago 3,102,800	2	24		None		None	Yes
Philadelphia 2,035,900	2	10 and 14 [3]	72	Uniform purchased	$50	Replace clothing	Yes
Detroit 1,334,500	Yes	24	By week 72 and 96	None		None	Yes (city)
Cleveland 972,500	Yes	24 [5]		Material only paid by men	$27,380 60	None	Yes
St. Louis 839,200	2 [6]	24	84 [6]	None		None	Yes
Baltimore 819,000	2	10 and 14 [7]		None		None	Yes
Boston 793,100 [8]	2 [8]	10 day 14 night		Furnished as needed			Yes
Los Angeles 576,673	2	10 day 14 night [9]	70 day 98 night	None		None	Yes
Pittsburgh * 665,500	2	10 day 14 night	70 day 98 night	None		None	Yes
San Francisco 576,000	2	10	72 day 84 night	None		None	Yes
Buffalo 550,000	2·	14 night 10 day		None		None	Yes
Washington, D. C. 540,000	2	10 and 14 [11]	60 and 84		$58 45		Yes
Milwaukee 536,400	2	24		None		None	Yes
Newark 466,700	2		[13]	None		None	Yes
Minneapolis 447,700	2 [14]	10 day 14 night [14]	70 day 98 night [14]	None			Yes
New Orleans 424,400	2	10 day 14 night [17]		None		None	Yes
Cincinnati 412,200	Yes [18]	24 [18]	One week 96 hrs. Next week 72 hrs.	None		None	Yes
Kansas City, Mo. 383,100	Average 6 men to platoon	12 [20]			84	None	
Seattle 375,300	2	14 night 10 day		None		None	Yes
Indianapolis 374,300	Yes	24	84	None		None	Yes
Rochester 324,500	2 [22]	10 and 14	24	None	Rubber goods only	None	Yes
Jersey City 321,500	2	10 day 14 night		None		None	Yes
Akron * 208,435	Yes [23]	24	96 [24]	None		None	Yes ·
Toledo 305,400	2	48		None		Complete— $1000 in budget	Yes
Portland * 258,288	2	12	84	None		None	Yes
Columbus, Ohio 291,400	Yes	24		None		None	Yes $1000 per yr. after 25 years
St. Paul 250,100	2	10 day [27] 14 night					Yes
Syracuse 197,000	2	10 day 14 night		None			Yes
Dayton 180,700	Yes [11]	24 [29]	72 to 96 alt. weeks [29]	None		None	Yes
Des Moines 148,900	2	24		None			Yes
Trenton 136,700	2	10 day 14 night		None	[31]	None	Yes
Fall River 132,600	2	10 and 14		None		Rubber coats replaced	Yes ½ day at age of 60 after 25 yrs.
Wilmington 126,400	2	10 day 14 night	72	None	$41.70	None	Yes
New Bedford 119,539	2	12 average	84	None	'	None	City
Duluth 114,700	2 [34]	12 [34]	78 average [34] [35]	Yearly	$18 per yr.	Replaced	Private

Dues	Relief fund for death, sickness, etc.	Dues	Annual sick leave with pay	Annual vacation with pay	Other leave with pay per year
	$2000			19 days [1]	None
2½% of salary	Pension includes both		No limit	15 days	None
1 day per mo.	Death only	$1 for each death	Discretion of dept. head	14 days [2]	Off every sixth day [2]
None	$2000 death, disability, retirement	$8 per yr.	If from duty, 1 yr.	2 ten-day periods	
[5]	Private	$5 at each death	No limit	14 days	None
$24	Private		6 mo.	13 days [6]	None
[7]	Yes	$1.75 to $2.75 per month	No more than six mos.	14 days [7]	1 day in 8 [7]
4% of weekly salary	City, sickness Private, death	$2 at each death	½ pay 30 days; duty injury full pay	14 days	24-hr. shift every 5 days 24 hrs. off 6th day
4% of salary per mo.	Private	$2 per mo. $2 each death $2 semi-annually	1 yr. limit, pension thereafter	15 days	3 days per mo. [9]
2½% of yearly salary	Yes	$6 per yr.		14 days	2 days each mo.
City	Private		Duty injury limit 6 mos.	15 days	1 day in 7
4% of salary	$2500 death	$2 per death	6 mos.	14 days	1 day in 8
2½% of salary	Death	In pension system	30 days; additional for injury	20 days	52 days
4¾% of salary	$1500 death benefit	$15 a yr.	Discretion of chief	14 days	
2% of salary	Private	50c per. mo. $1.05 for each death		[13]	None
$18	Yes	In pension fund	Duty, 90 days, may be extended to 1 yr.	15 days	1 day each mo.
1% of salary	Yes	75c per mo.	No limit	15 days	None
$6 per yr.	Private	$10 per yr. $2.10 at each death	None	15 days [18]	None
None	Yes	$15	By special ordinance	15 days	None
1½% of salary	Yes	$2 per quarter	Duty injury 6 mos.	15 days	1 day off in 8
$24	None	None	None	15 days	None
2% of salary	Private	$2.40 at every death	6 mos.	14 days	None
2% of salary	Yes	None		15 days [22]	Depends on reason
			Full pay if duty injury	14 days	None
None	Yes	$6 per yr.	No limit	12 days	
1% of salary	$100 funeral expenses, 3 mos. sickness, ½ pay. Full pay 1 yr. for injury	In pension	3 mos.	21 days	None
City	Yes	Voluntary $4 per yr.	6 mos. injury on duty, 3 mos. other illness	15 days	None
$1 per mo.			15 days. May be extended to 90 days	15 days	
1% of salary			No deduction	15 days	None
None	Yes	50c per mo.	21 days	14 days	None
1% of salary	Yes but not official		Reasonable	15 days	None
2% of salary; city contributes 4% of salaries	Yes	[31]	½ pay for sickness	14 days average	None
None	Private	10c per week	No fixed policy	14 days	None
1% of salary	Yes	50c per mo.	Full pay during sickness	7 days	For reasonable cause
None			None	15 days	None
$4	Same as pension		30 days	14 days	24 days per yr.

[1] Salaries: Patrolman, first 3 years, $1,769; fourth year, $1,920; first half of fifth year, $2,040; second half, $2,100; after 5 years, $2,500. Captains, 100, $4,500; 20 acting captains, $3,850.

Vacation: Patrolman, 18 days; sergeant, 20 days; lieutenant, 22 days: captain, 24 days; inspector, 26 days; deputy chief inspector, 28 days; chief inspector, 30 days.

[2] Includes both house and street sergeants.

[3] First year, $2,140; second year, $2,260; third year, $2,500.

[4] Same as patrolman.

[5] Salaries: Patrolman, first grade, 190 at $4.50 per day; 321 at $5.00 per day; 3,609 at $5.50 per day. Second grade, 175 at $1,400 per year. Surgeon, 12 at $1,800; 2 at $2,200; 1 at $5,000.

Clothing furnished patrolman: Total value, $64.70. Not all furnished each year, but only as needed. Value of clothing furnished increases with increase in rank.

Hours per day: Lieutenant, assistant superintendent and inspector, continuous. Three surgeons 8 hours and subject to call; 12 surgeons, subject to call.

Pension dues: Surgeon, 2% of annual salary.

Extra days with pay: Lieutenant, captain, and inspector, 1 day each week; surgeon, assistant superintendent and superintendent, none.

[6] Number of employees given is allowed in current budget and is slightly higher than the average number actually employed.

Patrolman receives $2,000 for first 6 months, $2,100 for second 6 months, and $2,520 after the first year.

Pension fund: City appropriates balance necessary for current requirements.

Surgeon: Department has 9 medical officers with total budget of $22,970 per year.

[7] Salaries: Patrolman, first year, $1,800; second year, $2,070; third year, $2,200.98; fourth year, $2,419 68.

Pension dues according to salary.

[8] Includes one captain with salary of $3,543.36.

[9] Salaries: Patrolman, 150 probationers, $155 per month; others, regulars, $180; chief surgeon, $291.66; 3 assistant surgeons, $208.33.

[10] Surgeon excepted.

[11] Salaries effective January 1, 1928, for patrolman: first year, $31 25 per week; second year, $33.75; thereafter, $35.25.

Salaries effective January 1, 1929; patrolman, first year, $35 per week; second year, $37.50; thereafter, $40; house and street sergeant, $46.50; lieutenant, $55; captain, $70; assistant superintendent, $4,500 per year; superintendent, $5,000 per year.

Further remuneration from 2½% to 15% of salary, according to years of service.

[11] Department receives bids and lets contract for uniforms for two years. They are then paid for by deductions from the salary of members.

[12] Number of patrolman that are allowed by law. Force clothed and equipped at cost of about $150. Replaced on average of once every 2½ years.

Pension provisions apply if service entered since February 1, 1923. If before that time, unless they choose otherwise, members remain under old non-contributing system.

Volunteer association, after 30 years' dues are waived. . Benefits are $1 per day for sickness, $100 on death of wife and $1,000 to beneficiary on death of member. Sick leave, full pay for duty injury or sickness.

Extra leave: Member may for satisfactory reason absent himself without pay and may have 1 to 3 days with pay upon death in family.

[14] Hours per day and per week: "Or more" added to assistant chief; chief, continuous.

Vacation and sick leave: No specific allowance to chief.

[15a] Salaries: Patrolman, first year, $1,800; second year, $1,920; third year, $2,040.

[15] Includes 129 corporals at $2,580.

[16] Rank of captain.

[16a] Surgeon part time. Death benefit, $2,500.

[17] Salaries: To all except commissioner, deputy chief and inspectors, a bonus of $250 per year is added.

[18] Salaries: Patrolman, first year, $1,700; second year, $2,000. One chief desk lieutenant, first year, $2,540; second year, $2,780 One assistant chief desk lieutenant, first year, $2,240; second year, $2,300. 79 desk lieutenants, first year, $2,000; second year, $2,120. One surgeon, first year, $2,820; third year, $3,060; 1 assistant surgeon, $2,150. One assistant superintendent (day), first year, $3,800; second year, $4,020; third year, $4,300; 1 assistant superintendent (night), first year, $3,300; second year, $3,550; third year, $3,800. Policewoman, first year, $1,460; second year, $1,520; third year, $1,580; fourth year, $1,640; fifth year, $1,700. Others. 1 chief of traffic, first year, $2,360; second year, $2,420; third year, $2,480; 1 chief of park patrolman, first year, $2,240; second year, $2,300.

[19] Salaries: Patrolman, first year, $1,800; second year, $1,900; third year, $2,100.

Policewoman exceptions: 1 has rank of sergeant with salary of $2,400 and 1, of lieutenant, with $2,700.

Surgeon exceptions as follows: irregular hours, no clothing allowance, 3½% of salary for pension, no death benefit, 30 days' vacation, no extra days and no extra sick leave for injuries.

[20] Additional sick leave for duty injuries.

[21] Salaries: Patrolman, first year, $1,920; second year, $1,980; third year, $2,040. Surgeon, part time; superintendent general exception to rules.

Death benefit dues: Up to 32 years, $10 a year; 32 to 40 years, $15 a year; 40 to 46 years, $20 per year.

[22] Salaries: Patrolman, first year, $2,100; second year, $2,200; third year, $2,300; fourth year, $2,400; fifth year, $2,500. Sergeant, first year, $2,600; second year, $2,700; third year, $2,800; fourth year, $2,900; fifth year, $3,000. Captain, first year, $3,400; second year, $3,700; third year, $4,000. Surgeon, first year, $3,500; second year, $4,000; third year, $4,500. Assistant surgeon, first year, $2,500; second year, $3,000; third year, $3,500. Deputy chief, first year, $4,200; second year, $4,600; third year, $5,000. Chief, first year, $5,200; second year, $5,600; third year, $6,000.

Vacation: Sergeant, 16 days; lieutenant, 18 days; captain, 21 days; surgeon and chief, 1 month; deputy chief, 26 days.

[23] Salaries: Patrolman, first year, $1,800; second year, $1,920; third year, $2,040. Sick leave may, with consent of city council, be extended up to 90 days.

[23a] One patrolman at $22.80, rank of lieutenant.

[24] Sickness, one half pay for 30 days; death, one month's pay.

[25] 34 at $1,500; 95 at $1,620; 55 at $1,740; 316 at $1,860.

[26] Salaries: Patrolman, class A at $150; class B at $140; class C. $125. Street sergeant, 2 at $200; others, $175. Surgeon, 1 at $200 and 2 at $50. Assistant superintendent, 3 at $200 and 1 at each of other salaries. Superintendent and 1 assistant superintendent are available at all times. Surgeon is subject to call.

[27] 389 at $180; 15 at $175; 55 at $170; 6 at $160.

[28] Two at $1,600; 1 assistant at $1,500.

[29] Hours: Applies only to patrolman and sergeant; lieutenant and captain, 12 hours per day, 72 hours per week.

[30] Salaries: Patrolman, $2,100 for three years and $2,500 thereafter.

Hours: Captain, surgeon and superintendent, who are callable at all hours.

Vacation: Applies only to patrolman; sergeant and lieutenant, 17 days; captain, 21 days.

Salaries: Patrolman, first year, $1,800; second year, $1,953; third year, $2,016; fourth year, $2,079.

[31] Hours: Secretary, 8 hours per day.

Pension dues: Patrolman, $8.40; sergeant, $9; lieutenant and secretary, $9 60; captain, $10.20; chief, $10.80.

[32] One superintendent at $250 per month; 1 assistant superintendent at $208; 9 operatives at $186.

[33] Surgeon, 3 at $134 per month; 1 at $122.50; 1 at $112.50. Sick leave may be extended to 90 days by department head.

[34] Patrolman: $1,800, $1,860, $1,920, $1,980, $2,040.

[35] Superintendent full time.

[36] Hours on duty: Captain and chief, 8 hours or more per day; surgeon subject to call.

Vacation: Surgeon, none; lieutenant, 16 days; captain, 18 days; chief, 21 days.

Other leave: Surgeon, none; captain and chief, 52 days.

Salaries: Patrolman, first year, $1,644; thereafter, $1,752.

[37] Superintendent of public safety (both police and fire).

[1] Salaries: Fireman, first grade, $2,500; second grade, $1,980; third grade, $1,769; fourth grade $1,769.
Hours per week: Chief excepted.
Vacation: Lieutenant and captain, 23 days; battalion chief, deputy chief, and chief, 30 days.
[2] Salaries: Fireman, probation of 6 months, $2,140; first year, $2,320; second year, $2,440; third year, $2,500.
Deputy chief marshal, 1 at $6,800, 1 at $5,000, 12 at $4,500.
[3] Salaries: Fireman, first grade, 59 at $4.50 per day; 215 at $5 per day; 1,419 at $5.50 per day; second grade, 12 at $1,400.
Hours per day: Battalion chief, deputy chief engineer and chief engineer, continuous.
Vacation: Battalion chief and deputy chief engineer, 21 days; chief engineer, 1 month.
Other days off: Battalion chief and deputy chief engineer, every fourth day; chief engineer, none.
[4] Salaries: Fireman, first 6 months, $2,100 per year; next 9 months, $2,200; maximum, $2,520.
Sick leave: Within discretion of surgeon.
Vacation: No designation, whether for sickness or vacation.
[5] Salaries: Fireman, first year, 24 at $2,070; after first year, 721 at $2,419.68. 45 engineers (steam and auto); 37 assistant engineers.
Hours per day: Chief optional.
Pension dues: Fireman, $6; engineer, $8.40; lieutenant, $7.80; captain, $8.40; assistant marshal, $11.40; fire chief, $15.
[6] Platoon: Battalion chief, assistant chief engineer and chief engineer excepted.
Hours per week: Battalion chief and deputy chief engineer, 112, 48 hours on and 24 off; chief engineer, 168 hours.
Vacation: Battalion chief, deputy chief engineer and chief engineer, 20 days.
[7] Salaries: Fireman: 869 at $1,700; 73 at $1,600; 63 at $1,500. Includes 76 assistant steam and auto engineers.
Platoon: Battalion chief, deputy chief engineer, and chief, single 24 hours.
Pension dues: Appointed prior to January, 1, 1926, no assessment; after January 1, 1926, assessment according to salary.
Vacation: Lieutenant and captain, 16 days; battalion chief, 18 days; deputy chief engineer, 21 days; chief engineer, 31 days.
Extra days: Battalion chief, 1 day in 5; deputy chief engineer, 1 day in 5; chief engineer, 1 day in 7.
[8] Platoon: Chief engineer, continuous; fire commissioner excepted from all information.
[9] Hours per day: Chief engineer and assistant chiefs, continuous service.
Extra days: Chief, none; assistant chiefs, 3 days per month.
[10] First year, $2,160; second year, $2,280; third year, $2,400.
[11] Salaries: Fireman, first year, $1,800; second year, $1,900; thereafter, $2,100.
Platoon: Deputy chief engineer and chief engineer excepted.
[12] First year, $1,920; second year, $1,980; third year, $2,040.
[13] Salaries: Fireman, 113 at $2,100, $2,200, $2,300, $2,400, and 582 at $2,500.
Platoon: 1st platoon on duty first day, 10 hours, second day, 10 hours, third day, 24 hours, fourth day, 14 hours, fifth day, 14 hours, and sixth day, 24 hours, off; second platoon, on first day, 14 hours, second day, 14 hours, fourth day, 10 hours, fifth day, 10 hours, sixth day, 24 hours and off third day, 24 hours.
Vacation: 14 days for first four salary divisions of fireman; 8 days for last four. Captain, 18 days; battalion chief, 21 days; deputy chief engineer, 26 days; chief engineer, 30 days.
[14] Battalion chief and deputy chief engineer, 24 hours off and 24 hours on; chief engineer, no regulation.
[15] Called assistant chief.
[16] Called assistant chief engineer.
[17] Alternate every 3 days.
[18] Salaries: Fireman, 346 at $1,500, $1,620, $1,740, $1,860 range; 45 at $1,920 (fire chauffeurs).
Platoon; hours per day, and vacation: Battalion chief and assistant fire chief not under platoon system, off every fifth day, on duty 31 weeks, 144 hours, 21 weeks; 120 hours with 30 days' vacation. Fire chief off every seventh day, on duty 144 hours with 30 days' vacation. He is not under platoon system.
[19] First class, 175; second class, 55.
[20] Superintendents excepted.
[21] 348 at $1,916.25 and 10 at $1,733.50.
[22] Chief engineer excepted.
[23] Salaries: Fireman, $2,100 per year for first 3 years; $2,500 thereafter.
Vacation: Captain, 17 days; battalion chief, 20 days; deputy chief engineer, 25 days; chief engineer, 30 days.
[24] Chief engineer, 168 hours.
[25] 16 engineers at $2,560 per year; 15 assistant engineers at $2,480. First assistant engineer, $3,690; second assistant engineer, $3,390.
[26] One first assistant, $312 per month; 1 second assistant, $275.
[27] Salaries: Fireman, 15 at $136.40 and 235 at $153.20. Engineer, 3 at $153.20, 39 at $163.40. Captain, 3 at $153.20, 3 at $158.45, 3 at $168.95, 63 at $173.60. Battalion chief, 1 at $154, 1 at $172, 2 at $210, 1 at $217.50, 7 at $223.10.
Hours on duty: Change made every 2 weeks when men on night shift are on 24 hours straight.
[28] Salaries: Fireman and steam and auto engineers, $1,800, $1,860, $1,920, $1,980, $2,040.
[29] Except deputy chief engineer, 8 hours per day, 44 hours per week; chief engineer, full time.
[30] $145 per month first year; $160 thereafter.
[31] Salaries: Fireman, first year, $1,750; second, $1,800; third, $1,900; fourth, $2,000; fifth, $2,100; sixth, $2,200.
Uniforms furnished by city and cost deducted in installments monthly from salary.
Death benefit: Contributed by foreign insurance companies: 2 % of business done in city.
[32] First year, $4.40 per day; thereafter, $5.50.
[33] Salaries: Fireman, first year, $135; second, $145; third, $150; fourth, $155; maximum, $160. Battalion chief, first assistant, $235; second assistant, $210; third, $200; fourth, $195.
[34] Chief engineer excepted.
[35] Battalion chief, 84 hours.

CENTRALIZATION OF NEW YORK CITY GOVERNMENT—CAN IT BE MADE WORKABLE?

BY CHARLES V. POWELL

Engineer in Charge, Queens Topographical Bureau

The author believes that New York City's engineering activities are too extensive and varied to profit from departmental consolidation.

CENTRALIZATION of various New York City departments is in the air. In particular the proposition has been advanced to consolidate all of the engineering activities of the city under one chief engineer. Such is the practice in smaller cities. Would such a system, if applied to New York, effect economies in administration, and be of advantage to the public in obtaining improvements, or would a system that is applicable to a small town break down of its own weight, if adopted by a municipality of such varied activities as New York?

The city engineer of a small town deals with problems quite similar in character to those coming under the jurisdiction of the chief engineers of the various boroughs of New York City, but in addition New York is confronted with various large projects, such as water supply on an unprecedented scale, subways, monumental bridges, and traffic, each requiring a corps of engineers and specialists. Would a consolidation of the engineering departments dealing with such varied projects be of benefit, either to the furtherance of the works, to the economical use of funds, or to the benefit of the citizens in obtaining local improvements; or would such a system be too cumbersome to be of practical use?

WIDE SCOPE OF ENGINEERING ACTIVITIES OF THE CITY

Let us glance over some of the larger activities, that would need to be combined under a centralized engineering department.

The chief engineers of the various boroughs have in the aggregate supervised the paving of 2,550 miles of streets at an expenditure of $530,000,-000; as well as built 2,660 miles of sewers at a cost of $140,000,000. The engineers of the board of water supply, and of the department of water supply, gas and electricity, have designed and constructed thirty-two reservoirs, furnishing 800,400,000 gallons of water daily, through 3,766 miles of pipe, at a total cost of $405,000,000. Engineers of the dock department have built 267 piers and docks, costing $110,000,000. The engineering corps of the department of plant and structures have designed and supervised the construction of fifty bridges, with lengths varying from 40 to 7,400 feet, including approaches at a cost of $130,000,000; they are now working on the plans of the Tri-Borough Bridge, which is estimated to cost $32,000,000, and are about to make borings for the Thirty-eighth Street Tunnel, which, if authorized, will cost about $56,000,000, and will connect Queens, Brooklyn, and the east and west sides of Manhattan.

Engineers in the employ of the city have also built 213 route miles of subways, with 620 miles of tracks, at a cost of $427,000,000; and have seventeen route miles of subways, with sixty-two miles of track, to cost $166,400,000 now under way. In 1926, engineers of the building department passed on and approved of the structural design of buildings to cost $341,000,000.

TOO MUCH WORK FOR ONE MAN

To consolidate all of these engineering activities under one chief engineer would require that Thaddeus Merriman, chief engineer of the board of water supply, with its new projects, estimated to cost $370,000,000; Chief Engineer William W. Brush, of the department of water supply, gas and electricity, who has under his jurisdiction 2,200 men, 32 reservoirs, and 3,766 miles of pipes and aqueducts, reaching from the Catskill Mountains to Suffolk County, L. I.; Chief Engineer Edward A. Byrne, of the department of plant and structures, who has charge of the maintenance of fifty bridges, costing $130,000,000, as well as of the design of the Tri-Borough Bridge, and all other bridges, over navigable waters in the city of New York; Robert Ridgway, chief engineer of the board of transportation, who has been connected with subway work in New York since its inception in 1900, and who is now in charge of work actually under way to cost $166,400,000, and of additional routes planned and approved, at an estimated cost of $416,-600,000 to be constructed during the next eight years, with over 1,500 engineering assistants; that the chief engineers of the various boroughs, who have charge of the construction and maintenance of thousands of

miles of sewers and highways; would all be made subservient to one chief engineer, who would have charge of projects over a far-flung area, larger than the state of Rhode Island, with reservoirs in the Catskill Mountains, and harbor construction works in Jamaica Bay. He would need to be an expert in all branches of engineering, or else to delegate his authority largely to his subordinates, and confine his attention to the legal machinery of his office. Should he attempt to do his full duty, by studying each vast project, whether it be water supply, subways, or whether a certain street should have a box-shaped sewer, or one with an oval outline, he would perforce become an obstructionist in holding back great undertakings, until he could personally find time and opportunity to weigh and consider the numerous features which differentiate a good design from one that is destined to prove inadequate, or so costly as to be impracticable or confiscatory.

To consolidate the engineering departments of the city in this way would also tend to deprive the average citizen of his consultant in the humble, but in the aggregate, vastly important matters of locating his home, and in making such home accessible; and in providing it with services and facilities, such as streets, sewers, pavements, water, and fire and police protection.

To whom would such a citizen go for information and advice in such a centralized organization? Certainly, the chief engineer could not devote time to the study of local conditions in each of the five boroughs of a city of 6,000,000 inhabitants; and at the same time attend to such matters as subways, grade crossing eliminations, water supply, and arterial highways. There would necessarily be a delegation of authority to some petty functionary in most local matters; and in the shifting about of personnel, incidental to the reorganization, it is to be feared that those who are at present in close touch with departmental affairs would either be lost in the shuffle, or else have their authority and prestige so hedged about or curtailed, that their usefulness, in working out plans for the benefit of the average citizen, and in pushing such plans through to the stage of actual construction, would be very much reduced.

A MEASURE OF CONSOLIDATION DESIRABLE

In stating the difficulties in the way of consolidating the engineering departments of the city into a well-knit organization, it does not follow that the principle of centralization should be dropped in its entirety, or that efforts to simplify and coördinate the different departments should be abandoned. There is doubtless overlapping of authority and duplication of work that could be eliminated in many departments, particularly those that have to do with inspection work. For example, the fire prevention bureau and the tenement house department both employ inspectors on building construction, whose work might perhaps be consolidated under one division to the advantage of the city and the benefit of the citizens.

A thorough survey, covering all phases of municipal government in New York City, would doubtless reveal many instances where bureaus could be re-grouped and duplication of activities curtailed.. It is only where the suggestion is made to amalgamate such unrelated departments as those of transportation and water supply; local improvements and bridges between the boroughs; grade crossing eliminations and laying a walk, that centralization can be made to defeat its own object.

CONSOLIDATION ONCE TRIED WITHOUT SUCCESS

At the time of the consolidation of the five boroughs into the greater city of New York, in accordance with the Charter of 1897, when the population was about half of what it is today, the experiment was tried of centralizing all of the engineering work of the city, with the exception of that coming under the jurisdiction of the dock board, under the then newly created board of public improvements; and it resulted in complete failure.

In their report to the Governor, dated December 1, 1900, this thoroughly representative board, after a series of public hearings, at which a large number of citizens appeared and many suggestions were given, spoke as follows:

It is clear that the vast territory comprised within the present City of New York, embracing as it does, districts so essentially different as the crowded east side of Manhattan and the rural districts of Queens and Ridgewood demands some subdivision and some degree of local autonomy. How far and in what respect the powers of administration in the various departments of the city government should be centralized, and how far they should be vested in the city authorities of each borough, are questions which have demanded and received our most careful attention.

The present (1897) Charter centralizes all of the departments which deal with the public works of the city and unites them in a Board of Public Improvements. In this respect, the Commission is satisfied that the scheme of the present (1897) Charter has proved most unsatisfactory in its workings, more especially with regard to Boroughs other than Manhattan.

Accordingly the commission drafted amendments which transformed the charter into its present form by incorporating provisions

(1) Abolishing the centralized board of public improvements and trans-

ferring its functions to the borough presidents, the local boards and the board of estimate and apportionment.

(2) Abolishing the centralized departments of sewers and highways, which had jurisdiction throughout the entire city, and transferring their functions to the presidents of the several boroughs.

(3) Enlarging the powers of the local improvement boards by providing that the resolutions of such boards, if approved by the president of the borough, and the board of estimate and apportionment, shall be all that is necessary in order that proceedings for a local improvement shall be begun.

(4) Decentralizing the department of buildings by establishing a bureau of buildings in the office of each president of a Borough.

The wisdom of this highly competent commission, which drafted amendments to the charter embodying these recommendations, under which the government of New York has functioned since 1902, has been amply vindicated by the results achieved in the growth and prosperity of each of the five boroughs of the city, and in the contentment of the citizens with the large measure of self-government which they have thereby achieved.

COÖPERATION BETWEEN THE FEDERAL AND STATE GOVERNMENTS

BY JAMES D. BARNETT

University of Oregon

The future will increase rather than decrease the scope of federal power. :: :: :: :: :: :: :: :: ::

UNHAPPY experience with the feeble central government under the Articles of Confederation induced an organization in the Union that could "execute itself." [1] "Undoubtedly, it was the purpose of the Constitution to establish a general government independent of that of the state governments—one which could enforce its own laws through its own officers and tribunals, and this purpose was accomplished." [2]

Although the movement toward the substitution of state for local authorities seems to be world-wide, in "dual" governments generally a considerable

dependence of the Union upon the component states has been preserved. In Germany, old and new, in Switzerland, in Canada, to a less extent in Australia, the Union is largely dependent upon the judicial and administrative machinery of the states; and this is peculiarly significant because of the fact that in these countries there is greater legislative centralization than in the United States.

However, so far as independence is essential, a potential independence (guaranteed by the constitution) is not impaired by the maintenance of an *actual* (voluntary) interdependence.[3] So when the constitution was created

[1] Elbridge Gerry (1787), M. Farrand, *Records of the Federal Convention*, vol. 1, p. 474 (1911).

[2] *United States* v. *Jones,* 109 U. S. 513, 27 Law. Ed. 1015, 1017 (1883).

[3] *Cf. United States* v. *Jones,* 109 U. S. 513, 27 Law. Ed. 1015, 1017 (1883).

it was expected that the instrumentalities of the states would be largely used as agencies of the Union. As a matter of fact, from the very first congress the Union has been, to an increasing extent, partially "disfederated" through its use of the states' legislative, judicial, and administrative departments. This has been balanced by a similar use, to a much less extent, of federal agencies by the states. Partnerships also, in distinction from agencies, have been established.

II

LEGISLATION [1]

Various acts of congress have practically effected a redivision of labor between the Union and the states and enlarged the "self-government" of the latter, such as those permitting the taxation of national banks otherwise exempt from state interference, averting the consequences of the "original package" doctrine and subjecting interstate shipments of original packages of liquor to state regulation, and forbidding the shipment of liquor from "wet" to "dry" states. Somewhat different in purpose are the federal statutes applying the state election laws to federal elections, and assimilating process of federal courts to that of the state courts.

On the other hand, confusion within the state is likewise reduced by the states' adoption of federal court procedure, adoption of the Volstead law, or the federal pure food law.

The technical delegation of legislative power, forbidden by constitutional law, is at times clearly averted in this connection by the legislative adoption

of a statute as now existing with no regard to its future amendment. But regard to future action also is necessary in order to avoid the necessity of repetition of adoption, and thus often legislative power is practically delegated by the one legislature to the other or others. However, although the accepted doctrine in regard to the unconstitutionality of the delegation of legislative power has never been expressly repudiated by the courts in this connection, but at times has been clearly stated and strictly applied, more often there have been attempts to avoid a conflict with the doctrine by artificial logic, or the theory has been utterly ignored. Likewise the courts are inclined to cover over the constitutional difficulty involved in a state legislature's adoption of a federal statute (not infrequent) by reference.

In dealing with matters over which congress and the state legislatures have concurrent jurisdiction in the absence of federal legislation the state legislatures are in a way the agents of the Union.[2]

The states act as agents of the Union in legislation to an increasing extent in appropriating the funds and providing for the administration demanded, with varying degrees of specification by congress as a condition of grant of federal money (or service) in activities over which congress has not direct control, or not adequate control, but which it desires to stimulate in the states—agricultural education and experimentation, vocational education, forestry, highways, the militia, etc. This subordination of the states to federal control is technically "voluntary," but non-conforming states are virtually fined for the benefit of the rest; and this is one of the causes for

[1] Cf. J. D. Barnett, "Delegation of Legislative Power by Congress to the States," American Political Science Review, vol. 2, pp. 347–77 (1908); "State Legislation Adopting Federal Standards," Columbia Law Review, vol. 23, pp. 674–8 (1923).

[2] A. N. Holcombe, "States as Agents of the Nation," Southwestern Political Science Quarterly, vol. 1, pp. 316–7 (1921).

a very general acquiescence. This does not apply to cases where the state receives no compensation, but acts merely upon the advice of the general government, as in legislation regarding vital statistics and automobile traffic.

III

JURISDICTION [1]

Although the prevailing opinion in the Constitutional Convention favored the creation of a complete hierarchy of federal courts, there was opinion "that the state tribunals might and ought to be left in all cases to decide in the first instance, the right of appeal to the supreme national tribunal being sufficient to secure the national rights and uniformity of judgments";[2] and opposition to this form of centralization of government has recurred at various periods since—most recently in Senator Norris's proposal to abolish the lower federal courts and vest their jurisdiction in the state courts. A compromise system, suggested at the convention, whereby the Union would "make use of the state tribunals whenever it could be done with safety to the general interest,"[3] has been effected by legislation beginning with the Judiciary Act of 1789.

Such legislation in form purports to confer upon the state courts, to a considerable extent, jurisdiction in cases arising under the federal law, and also "somewhat analogous" quasi-judicial power of a federal character.

As to civil cases, conflict with the principle that the power of the Union may not, except in the few cases specified in the constitution, be delegated to the states, has been avoided by the courts' regarding such legislation as the mere recognition of the principle of private international law, well known when the constitution was established, according to which "the judiciary power of every government looks beyond its own local and municipal laws, and in civil cases lays hold of all subjects of litigation between parties within its jurisdiction, though the causes of dispute are relative to the laws of the most distant part of the globe." [4] But the difficulty of delegation of authority may not be thus met in criminal cases, and hence the state courts have almost invariably refused to assume the delegated authority to execute federal criminal laws. However, some courts have been induced to assume jurisdiction upon the principle that the federal and state governments are "kindred systems . . . and parts of one whole." "The state courts are to give force and effect to a law of congress, as the supreme law of the land." This doctrine is, of course, equally applicable to civil cases, and would, logically, make jurisdiction in both criminal and civil cases compulsory.

Since the beginning of the Union federal statutes have authorized magistrates of the state to act as federal committing magistrates, and higher state courts to naturalize aliens; and other similar powers have thus been conferred upon state courts. The "quasi-ministerial" character of such

---

[1] Cf. "Administration of Federal Laws in State Courts," *Lawyers' Reports Annotated*, vol. 48, pp. 33–41 (1898); J. D. Barnett, "Delegation of Judicial Power to State Courts by Congress," *American Law Review*, vol. 43, pp. 852–68 (1909); C. Warren, "New Light on the History of the Federal Judiciary Act of 1789," *Harvard Law Review*, vol. 37, pp. 49–132 (1923), and "Federal Criminal Laws and the State Courts," *ibid.*, vol. 38, pp. 545–98 (1925); "Power of State Courts to Enforce Federal Statutes," *Yale Law Journal*, vol. 33, pp. 636–42 (1924).

[2] John Rutledge (1787), M. Farrand, *Records of the Federal Convention*, vol. 1, p. 124 (1911).

[3] Roger Sherman (1787), M. Farrand, *Records of the Federal Convention*, vol. 2, p. 46 (1911).

[4] Alexander Hamilton (1788), *Federalist*, Dawson's Ed., no. 82 (1864).

authority has been emphasized by the courts at times in order to avoid the objection to delegation of judicial power, vested in the federal government by the constitution. However, in avoiding this difficulty they come into conflict with the principle of separation of powers of government. But whatever the nature of the power, some kind of power has been thus *subtracted* from the (*granted*) power of the Union and added to the (*inherent*) power of the states. The courts base the validity of such legislation chiefly upon established usage; and, indeed, this is at present the strongest support of all the legislation here discussed affecting the jurisdiction of the state courts.

As to the policy here involved, it was well said long ago: "All the . . . arguments of expediency [of such coöperation to the contrary], such as blending jurisdictions, neglect of state duties, want of responsibility and others of the same description are of little weight." [1]

With the exception of a few cases in which the supremacy of the federal law is interpreted to render the exercise of jurisdiction both lawful and compulsory, the courts have held, either without argument, because, apparently, the matter is too clear for argument, or upon the expressly stated ground of the independent position of the states, that the exercise of jurisdiction is wholly optional with the state authorities.

Congress has never declared the state judges to be federal judges in the exercise of such jurisdiction, and the courts are in confusion as to whether this is the effect of its exercise. But of course federal judges may be appointed as such only in accord with the provisions of the federal constitution.

Apparently federal judges have never

[1] *Ex parte* Rhodes, 2 Wheeler Crim. Cas. 559 (1818).

been appointed as state judges nor state judges as federal judges.

The federal courts act as agencies of the state under authority of the constitution itself when they exercise jurisdiction by reason of the residence of the parties in different states. The United States and the state practically adopt each other's courts when they deny to their respective courts jurisdiction in case of an offense against both that has been already punished by the other; and likewise when an officer of the one government having made an arrest for an offense against both turns his prisoner over to the court of the other.

The lower federal courts are somewhat assimilated to state courts under the established practice whereby the judges are invariably appointed from among the residents of the states they are to serve and owe their appointment largely to the senators or other politicians of the states.

IV

ADMINISTRATION [2]

In the third department of government, administration, there is likewise a constitutional possibility of almost

[2] *Cf.* P. H. Douglas, "Development of a System of Federal Grants in Aid," *Political Science Quarterly,* vol. 35, pp. 255–71, 522–44 (1920); W. L. Wanlass, "United States Department of Agriculture," *Johns Hopkins University Studies in History and Political Science,* vol. 38, no. 1, ch. 3 (1920); A. N. Holcombe, "States as Agents of the Nation," *Southwestern Political Science Quarterly,* vol. 1, pp. 307–27 (1921); B. A. Arneson, "Federal Aid to the States," *American Political Science Review,* vol. 16, pp. 443–54 (1922); A. F. McDonald, "Federal Subsidies to the States" (1922), and "American Subsidy System," *National Municipal Review,* vol. 14, pp. 692–701 (1925); E. W. Allen, "Co-operation with the Federal Government in Scientific Work," *Bulletin of the National Research Council,* vol. 5, part 1, no. 26 (1922); J. H. Wigmore, "President, the Senate, the Constitution, and the Executive

totally independent activity of the Union and the states. However, from the beginning of the Union there has been coöperation, and this has increased, especially in the more recent years.

Under express provision of the constitution the governors of the states perform a federal function in the extradition of fugitives from justice, and local election officers derive their authority over the election of federal officers indirectly from the constitution.

State officers have been endowed with federal functions by act of congress. Since 1789 local peace officers have thus arrested offenders against federal laws and local jailors have kept them in confinement, under orders of magistrates of the state.[1] The Selective Service Act of the Great War was carried out largely by state officers under the president's sweeping (statutory) authority "to utilize the service of any or all departments and any or all officers or agents of the United States and of the several states."[2]

Public service corporations operating a water project under license by the federal power commission must abide by the regulations imposed by the state commission. On the other hand, various federal official inspections are, under state law, accepted as state inspection.

The same principles, both practical and constitutional, apply here as in the delegation of judicial authority to the courts. But the contention that the Selective Service Act was void because of the delegation of federal power to state officials, was held to be "too wanting in merit to require further notice."[3]

Apparently there has been no federal or state legislation expressly designating the administrative officers of the one government as officers of the other. Indeed, such "blanket" appointments would, in some cases, meet constitutional difficulties.

But much coöperation between the Union and the states has been effected by the executive appointment, with or without express authority of law, of state officers as federal officers and federal officers as state officers. Thus the state foresters become federal foresters, the local health authorities federal "epidemicologists," the state employment officers federal employment directors, sheriffs deputy marshals, state prohibition officers federal prohibition officers; and other such appointments are made where the federal and state governments perform corresponding functions. On the other hand, the state governments at times appoint federal officers as state officers. Sometimes the appointment is made in

---

Order of May 8, 1926," *Illinois Law Review*, vol. 21, pp. 142-5 (1926); L. D. White, *Public Administration*, ch. 4 (1926); W. A. Cook, *Federal and State Administration*, chs. 4-5 (1927); *Congressional Record*, vol. 67, part 9, pp. 9922-7, 9944-5, 9982-97, 10103 (1926); part 10, pp. 10997-9 (1926).

[1] Although these peace officers are not considered, technically, to be "agents of the United States," even when acting "solely for the purpose of aiding the United States in the enforcement of its laws," nevertheless in such a case the federal courts will apply the same constitutional guaranties of the fourth and fifth amendments to the prosecution of the prisoners thus brought before them as they will when strictly federal affairs are involved. *Gambino* v. *United States*, 48 Sup. Ct. 137 (1927). Called to my attention by Professor C. W. Tooke.

[2] See especially E. H. Crowder, *Spirit of Selective Service*, ch. 5 (1920); J. H. Wigmore, "President, the Senate, the Constitution, and the Executive Order of May 8, 1926," *Illinois Law*

Review, vol. 21, pp. 144-5 (1926); *Arver* v. *United States*, 245 U. S. 366, 62 Law. Ed. 349 (1918).

[3] *Arver* v. *United States*, 245 U. S. 366, 62 Law. Ed. 349, 358 (1918). See also especially *Harris* v. *Superior Court*, 51 Cal. App. 15, 196 Pac. 895, 900 (1921).

the first instance by joint action of federal and state authorities.

From an early period it has been common for states to prohibit, with much variation as to offices included, state officers from holding federal offices. Doubtless this policy was caused to some extent by a desire "to preserve the state governments free from the influence of the federal government," [1] to separate "the allegiance justly due one [power] by its officers from that due to another power," [2] perhaps "to prevent the employment of federal patronage in a state election." [3] But to some extent at least the motive was the same as that prohibiting the same person from holding two offices under the state—also common. However, in the practical construction of these limitations there has been a tendency to narrow their scope, and at times they seem to have been entirely ignored or forgotten.

There was no restriction on the part of the federal government in this matter until the issue of President Grant's sweeping order of 1873, prohibiting federal officers from holding state offices with certain exceptions. The president here avowed a belief that, "with few exceptions, the holding of two offices by the same person is incompatible with a clear and faithful discharge of the duties of either office; that it frequently gives rise to great inconvenience, and often results in detriment to the public service, and,

moreover, is not in harmony with the genius of the government." [4] But later orders have increased the number of exceptions, and, apparently, no objection whatever was made to the more liberal policy until the issuing of President Coolidge's "order" of 1926: "In order that they may more efficiently function in the enforcement of the national prohibition act, any state, county, or municipal officer may be appointed at a nominal rate of compensation as a prohibition officer of the treasury department to enforce the provisions of the national prohibition act and acts supplemental thereto in states and territories except in those states having constitutional or statutory provision against state officers holding office under the federal government." [5] And it is certain that no objections would have been offered then but for the acrimonious controversy over prohibition. However, the "order" was widely attacked as "unconstitutional," "illegal," "monstrous," "extraordinary." The legal arguments deserve little consideration. The courts have never held federal and state offices to be incompatible as such, and the restrictions

---

[1] Quotation (1791), C. Warren, "New Light on the History of the Federal Judiciary Act of 1789," *Harvard Law Review*, vol. 37, pp. 108–9, note (1923). The restriction "might have been deemed important when it was adopted, before the working of the general and state governments had become fully understood." *State* v. *Fisher*, 28 Vt. 714, 715 (1856).

[2] *People* v. *Leonard*, 73 Cal. 230, 14 Pac. 853, 854 (1887).

[3] *Searcy* v. *Grow*, 15 Cal. 117, 121 (1860).

[4] J. D. Richardson, *Messages and Papers of the Presidents*, vol. 7, pp. 218–9. Note the interpretation of the order, *ibid.*, pp. 219–20.

[5] In *Senate Report*, no. 1048, 69th Congress, 1st Session, p. 1 (1926). See also especially *House Report* no. 1448, 69th Congress, 1st Session; *Opinion of the Attorney General*, Executive Order *in re* Prohibition Officers (1926); *New York Times*, March 25, 1926; *Congressional Record*, vol. 67, part 9, pp. 9922–7, 9944–5, 9982–97, 10103, part 10, pp. 10997–8 (1926); J. Hart, "Some Legal Questions Growing Out of the President's Executive Order for Prohibition Enforcement," *Virginia Law Review*, vol. 13, pp. 86–107 (1926); J. H. Wigmore, "President, the Senate, the Constitution, and the Executive Order of May 8, 1926," *Illinois Law Review*, vol. 21, pp. 142–5 (1926). Statute *requires* that the chief of the bureau of militia shall be a present or former member of the national guard.

noted are additional support to this view. From the standpoint of policy the chief objections were centralization of government in the Union, "compounding into one mass the state and the federal government," confusion by division of the responsibility of officers, imposition of burdens upon state officers. On the contrary, rather than encroachment upon the rights of the states it was declared to be the opposite —as "returning to the states a greater measure of that local self-government which gradually has been curtailed through encroachments of the federal authority"—a "supervised decentralization"; and it was insisted that "a man cannot serve two masters, only where the duty to the one is inconsistent with the duty to the other." But it was admitted that where the policies of the federal government and the state government are not in harmony, such appointments are inexpedient. On the whole, it was well said, the agitation about the "order" was "much ado about nothing."

In some directions coöperation between the two governments has assumed the form of division of labor among the two classes of offices rather than their "amalgamation." Thus the federal prohibition officers have, in the past, given chief attention to the larger liquor traffic, leaving to the state officers the suppression of local violations, with some assistance of federal officers —a practice conducive to discourage the shifting of responsibility from the one administration to the other. So there has been a division of labor between the United States geological survey and the state surveys.

The federal authorities have brought about much (voluntary) coördination among the state governments in the administration of highways, public utilities, health, employment, research, and the like.

Moreover, there is much joint action among federal and state authorities. Joint "raids" are made by federal and state prohibition officers, and by immigration officers and state peace officers; and joint action has long been common between federal and state health officers, etc. A number of annual conferences of the two classes of officers are held, some of very long standing. The permanent arrangement under which joint hearings and joint conferences are held by the interstate commerce commission and state public service commissions in cases affecting both interstate and intrastate commerce is most striking.[1]

There is much assistance given by federal authorities to state authorities —as in matters of education, health, charities, safety in mining, information of state crimes; and state authorities, apparently to a less extent, give similar assistance to federal authorities.

Since 1903 the grants of financial aid to the states, as noted above, have been generally conditional upon the state's acceptance of federal control over the administration engaged in the expenditure of the funds. The states have thus been "bribed" to "share their sovereignty" with the Union. "In every case the statutes virtually declare certain state officials to be agents of the national government to the extent that their relationship with the national officials is defined and established."[2] The control exercised by the national government consists, in general, of inspection, supervision, approval of standards and policies, requirement of reports, approval of appointments (rare). But in most direc-

[1] *Thirty-sixth Annual Report of the Interstate Commerce Commission*, pp. 231-4 (1923); *Thirty-ninth Report*, pp. 1-2, 271-7 (1925).

[2] B. A. Arneson, "Federal Aid to the States," *American Political Science Review*, vol. 16, p. 452 (1922).

tions the initiative has been left to the states, and the general government has not attempted to dominate over them. However, the state militias have very nearly become a part of the regular army, in times of peace as well as when called into service in time of war. Even when there is no obligation on the part of the states to accept federal control on account of receiving aid, there is, generally, national leadership in coöperative undertakings, although in some cases leadership is with the state authorities; and, in at least a very few cases, the federal officers are made the actual subordinates of the state officers.

Some of this administrative coöperation has been effected through express legislative enactment of congress and state legislatures, and some through action of the superior officers of the federal and state departments concerned, but in other cases the relations "are such as have naturally grown out of the circumstances" between subordinates of the two governments. Indeed, the coöperation may consist in the mere imitation of the federal action by the state authorities.

Of course there is no more constitutional power in congress to enforce state administrative coöperation with the federal government than judicial administration. But "in time of war nobody looks very nicely into legal subtleties," and the terms of the Selective Service Act are mandatory.[1] And, it has been urged, the relationship between the two governments is likely to be more harmonious because of the very fact that coöperation is voluntary.[2] Where the policies of the general government and state government are in

conflict, friction has occurred in some cases where coöperation has been attempted, or the state has utterly refused to enter into coöperation, or it has been guilty of downright persecution of federal officers in its attempt to thwart the enforcement of federal laws unpopular in the state.[3] It is futile to urge coöperation under such circumstances.[4]

Some of this coöperation involves a centralization of control in the federal government, and this has been the chief ground of objection to its development. But where this is true, under the circumstances, in most if not in all directions, the absence of such coöperation would have invited a greater degree of centralization of control in the federal government—the more general use by the federal government of its own instrumentalities.[5] And in some cases, as indicated, there is rather created a "decentralized supervision."

There seems to be little possibility, legal or practical, of much decentralization in legislation. On the contrary, changes in economic conditions will probably increase the necessity for much further development of the scope of congressional legislation. Particularly in view of this fact it would seem desirable that the use of the state judicial and administrative authorities as agents of the Union should be extended wherever practicable.[2] There has been, apparently, little fault found with the

[1] See especially *Senate Report*, no. 1048, 69th Congress, 1st Session (1926).

[2] B. A. Arneson, "Federal Aid to the States," *American Political Science Review*, vol. 16, p. 443 (1922).

[3] J. S. Strayhorn, "Immunity of Federal Officers from State Prosecutions," *North Carolina Law Review*, vol. 6, pp. 123–46 (1928).

[4] *Cf.* H. M. Dougherty, "Co-operative Duties of the States," *University of Pennsylvania Law Review*, vol. 71, p. 9 (1922); *Hoxie* v. *New York, Etc. R. Co.*, 82 Conn. 352, 73 Atlantic 754, 760 (1909); *Mondou* v. *New York, Etc. R. Co.*, 223 U. S. 1, 56 Law. Ed. 327, 348 (1912).

[5] *Cf. ex parte* Rhodes, 2 Wheeler Crim. Cas. 559 (1818); W. G. Campbell, *United States Daily*, Oct. 12, 1927.

operation of state courts in federal matters, except, perhaps, in the naturalization of aliens; but that there are strict limitations in the "devolution" of administrative authority appears not only in the unfortunate experience of the Confederation in this direction, but also in the unsatisfactory administration of extradition among the states, abuses in the conduct of elections, failure to coöperate in the enforcement of the Volstead Act, and actual interference with federal officers.   Moreover, it is significant that in spite of the ancient tradition of local self-government, the states are steadily, and necessarily, freeing themselves from dependence upon the localities for the enforcement of the law—not only subjecting the localities to increasing supervision by central authorities, but actually substituting central for local authorities.

[2] Cf. A. N. Holcombe, "States as Agents of the Nation," *Southwestern Political Science Quarterly*, vol. 1, pp. 324–7 (1921); C. Warren, "Federal Criminal Laws and the State Courts," *Harvard Law Review*, vol. 38, pp. 545–98 (1925).

The whole subject is of great importance and deserves very much more consideration than it has so far received.

A LABORATORY COURSE IN BUDGET MAKING

BY RUSSELL FORBES

Director, Municipal Administration Service; Lecturer on Municipal Government, New York University

An experiment in vitalizing the budget.

GLADSTONE said that "budgets are not merely affairs of arithmetic"; but they seem just that to the student after a session in most classrooms. To show the student that the budget is not merely a dull financial document, but is instead a picture of government operations representing the cost of services to be rendered by hundreds of human beings, supplies to be consumed in carrying on scores of public services, and money to be spent for the purchase of public works improvements has long been a most difficult pedagogic task. Governor Al Smith, who is perhaps without a superior in his ability to translate government into the language of the man in the street, in a public address once drew this striking budget metaphor: "What does the average family do," he said, "in planning the expenditures for the year? It decides what will be required for living expenses, and how much will be needed to meet the mortgage on the home or on the automobile, and then computes how much can be spent for needed improvements or luxuries within the range of the family income. Such is the method followed by a government in establishing its annual budget."

THE BUDGET A HUMAN DOCUMENT

Believing that the budget should be presented in the classroom as such a human document, closely related to the everyday life of the taxpayer, the writer undertook to conduct a labora-tory course in budget making this year at New York University in a graduate course on problems of municipal government. The editor of the NATIONAL MUNICIPAL REVIEW has requested a description of the experiment for appraisal by other teachers of this subject and for discussion by other students of municipal administration.

The class is composed of ten graduate students, most of whom are majoring in government and who are consequently familiar with the chief problems of governmental administration. The course began, as most courses do, with classroom discussion of general budget theory. The initial sessions were based on readings discussing the origin and development of the budget idea, and budget methods described in such representative texts as Buck's *Municipal Budgets and Budget Making*, Upson's *The Practice of Municipal Administration*, and Anderson's *American City Government*.

The class was then assigned the task of formulating and adopting the 1928 budget for the hypothetical city of Hometown, N. Y. The following pertinent facts concerning Hometown were furnished by the instructor:

The size, general character and business interests of the population;

The type of government (in this case, strong-mayor);

The 1927 assessed valuation of property;

The 1927 budget;

The 1927 tax rate;

The amount of debt outstanding.

Each member of the class was appointed as the head of an operating department. Three members were also appointed, respectively, as mayor, budget director, and comptroller, and were directed to sources of information regarding the part each would play in the budget-making procedure. Each department head was assigned the task of formulating his departmental estimates of expenditures for 1928, and was allowed two weeks in which to complete it. Each student was directed to the proper chapters in Upson's *The Practice of Municipal Administration* and in Munro's *Municipal Government and Administration* for a study of the functions of his respective department, and to the Census Bureau's report on *Financial Statistics of Cities* for figures on the per capita expenditures made by cities comparable in size to Hometown (50,000 population) for the services rendered by his branch of the government. Each department head was instructed to submit his estimate according to the size, form, and expenditure classification recommended by A. E. Buck in *Municipal Finance*. The 1928 budget of Indianapolis, which closely follows Buck's classification, was made available in the library for study and consultation.

When all departmental estimates had been submitted, the instructor went over them in a private session with the mayor, budget director, and comptroller, and discussed with each in detail his rôle in the formulation of the budget. One two-hour session was then devoted to a budget hearing before the mayor and budget director in which each department head was asked to justify his requests. The class had previously examined the Detroit budget to see the changes made by the budget director, and were aware that their estimates would be subject to challenge and defense. The criticisms made by the mayor and budget director, and the explanations offered by the department heads, showed an intelligent understanding of the problems involved.

Successive sessions were then devoted to a discussion of municipal revenues and debt administration, with assigned readings in Upson's text and in Buck's *Municipal Finance*. The class thus gained an understanding of the sources of the city's income, its requirements for payment for public improvements, and the restriction imposed on its expenditures by the local tax and debt limits. At one session the comptroller reported on the state of the city's finances, presenting his estimates of miscellaneous revenues, the amount required for debt service, and the amount to be derived from a bond issue authorized at a previous referendum.

CLASS BECOMES THE CITY COUNCIL

At the following meeting, the class constituted itself the city council under the chairmanship of the president, previously appointed. The mayor presented the tentative budget and delivered a budget message in explanation thereof. Each member of council was supplied with a copy of the tentative budget, which had been prepared in summary form, with supporting schedules showing expenditures classified, respectively, by departments, and objects; income classified by sources; and showing the amount to be raised by the general property tax.

Here the personality and ability of the mayor injected into the proceedings a verisimilitude which could scarcely be excelled under actual conditions of government. In his budget message, he pointed out that he had "made good" his "campaign promises"; that the 1928 budget and tax rate had been lowered, while the calibre of the administrative heads had been raised through the excellence of his appointments. The budget was subjected to vigorous criticism from the members of the council; it was as vigorously defended by the mayor, who occasionally found recourse to those urbane references which from time immemorial have been good vote-getters, such as "the high intelligence of the good people of Hometown"; "protecting our wives and children from disease and danger"; and "we must not deny our children every educational advantage." The council took particular exception to the proposed budget for the health department, claiming that it had been reduced too greatly over the 1927 appropriation. The tentative budget was referred to the finance committee of council which, at the following session, recommended an increase in the appropriation for the health department. The budget was then adopted by the council, with a small increase over the mayor's estimates, necessitating a slight adjustment in the proposed tax rate. The president of council, a lawyer, then drew up and presented the appropriation and tax rate ordinances, which were duly passed. The signature of the mayor ended the procedure and made the budget effective.

Meanwhile, the class had been assigned to readings on the budget-making procedure of New York City and to an examination of the 1928 budget. The final session was appropriately given over to discussion of New York City's budget and budget-making procedure, which was compared and contrasted with the budgetary procedure of Hometown.

To conduct such a course successfully places a heavy burden on the instructor. Readings must be selected carefully. The budget-making officials must be selected on the basis of their personality and training. The "laboratory" must be made serious, lest the procedure become farcical. The writer believes, however, that it is very much worth while. The best proof is the testimony of several members of the class that this course has vitalized for them a subject which before had seemed abstract and unrelated to life and living, and had translated into substance what previously had been empty words.

RECENT BOOKS REVIEWED

AIRPORTS AND AIRWAYS. By Donald Duke. New York: The Ronald Press Company, 1927. Pp. 178.

This book by a first lieutenant, Air Corps, U. S. A., comprehensively answers the question, "Where·do we go from here after our city has purchased or leased land for the airport?" It is one of a series of volumes in the Ronald Aeronautic Library and deals particularly with the very important matters of cost, operation and maintenance of airports and airways

Among other subjects covered are cost and types of hangars; management of airports; lighting and servicing equipment. There is also information on the special subjects of airship hangars, mooring masts and sea plane landings.

Usually after chambers of commerce and local aeronautical societies have induced municipal officials to acquire airport sites, they calmly sit back and wait for city officials to solve the technical problems of building hangars, installing lights and making leases to private air navigation concerns. At this juncture perplexed city officials, called upon to extract additional revenues from taxpayers for this new public service, may pick up Lieutenant Duke's book and carry on the establishment of the airport in an intelligent manner. Cost data on a number of representative city airports are included.

Without detracting from the excellence of Lieutenant Duke's work, it might be suggested that his discussion on the cost of municipal airports might have been rounded out by a discussion of possible revenues. It may be predicted that as soon as air transportation becomes profitable, commercial concerns will take it over, and there is some danger that cities will give away a large part of their investment in airport facilities.

Possibly some one in the near future will examine to what extent airports may become a self-supporting public utility without discouragement to this civic enterprise.

C. A. CROSSER.

✦

READINGS IN AMERICAN GOVERNMENT. By Finla Goff Crawford, Ph.D. New York: Alfred A. Knopf, 1927. Pp. 800.

The task of preparing a just review of such a collection of readings as that prepared by Professor Crawford is one which could best be done by one who had himself attempted such a work. The field from which "source material" and statements of opinion may be drawn is so vast that a fair critic of the selection made would have to be equipped with the memory of Macaulay. Of this collection, however, which attempts to deal with American government, national, state, and local, it is fair to say that Professor Crawford has succeeded in being useful without being dull and that his material is alive without being superficial. It is a positive relief to learn that the editor did not feel it necessary to reprint either the bombast of Webster or the casuistry of Calhoun to explain to the student the nature of the Constitution. The collection is almost totally free of public documents which are for the most part so badly prepared as to be confusing rather than enlightening to the undergraduate. Nor does the book contain a single page from the *Congressional Record*—a wise omission in the reviewer's opinion in view of the incomprehensible nature of most congressional "debate."

Turning to the question of what the collection *does* contain, it is possible to divide the material into two classes—articles reprinted from the so-called learned journals and articles by journalists and political correspondents. Each class of materials has, of course, very definite limitations. Articles from the learned journals are likely to be careful and informing, but dull and lacking in appeal to immature students. "Stories" by the gentlemen of the press, on the other hand, often succeed in holding the interest by a gripping style which conceals that easy reliance upon half-truths which too often seems the distinctive mark of successful journalism. In this book, however, the extremes of both classes seem to be avoided.

On the other hand, it seems to the reviewer that the selection at several points might have been improved. The readings on the Party seem too few in number in view of the fundamental importance of the subject and drawn too exclusively from what we have called the journalistic type of material. The readings on the Judiciary might have been improved by the inclusion of an actual decision of the Supreme Court or some selection showing clearly how the court voids a statute. It might also have been valuable to present material on the inferior federal courts and the relation between the state and federal judicial systems. The selections on state and local government are particularly well chosen, but one regrets the failure to include material dealing with actual administration.

LANE W. LANCASTER.

Wesleyan University.

✣

URBANIZATION: ITS EFFECTS ON GOVERNMENT AND SOCIETY. By John Giffen Thompson. New York: E. P. Dutton & Co., 1927. Pp. xiii, 683.

READINGS IN URBAN SOCIOLOGY. Edited by Scott E. W. Bedford. New York: D. Appleton & Co., 1927. Pp. xxxiv, 903.

For many generations philosophers and moralists have been in dispute regarding the physical and social consequences of city life. For the most part the verdict has been unfavorable. Although little scientific evidence has yet been assembled, it is encouraging to note the beginnings of a movement, at present chiefly confined to a small group of sociologists, to apply objective tests to the appraisal of urban society as substitutes for the prejudiced generalities of earlier writers.

In his preface, the author of *Urbanization* calls attention to the unsatisfactory character of much of the writing on the subject and implies that this purpose has been to treat it in a comprehensive and scientific manner. With respect to the comprehensiveness of his work there can be no question; but with respect to the application of a new technique to the problem of the city-ward movement he has not been so successful. In 618 pages he discusses the effect of urbanization upon civil and political liberty, economic freedom, democracy in ancient, mediaeval and modern times, forms of government, political activity, public spirit, political purity, efficiency of government, health and physical development, morals, religion and preparedness for war.

For the most part, the city gets the best of the argument, but the evidence is largely based upon the opinions of other writers whose methodology the author rightly criticizes. Some of his material is not relevant and his conclusions, comforting as they may be to one who is an admirer of the modern city, are too often unconvincing. While the cities doubtless deserve credit for leadership in the struggle for democracy, evidence such as that the early advocates of the initiative and referendum were of city origin does not help

us in appraising the influence of the city for human freedom. The author's uncritical acceptance of early statistics relating to population, death rates, morbidity rates and the like, as bases for generalizations as to the present, also weakens his conclusions. The book is rather a digest of opinion about the city mingled with some original interpretation of history in an effort to apportion credit between town and country for contributions to progress.

Mr. Bedford, the editor of *Readings in Urban Sociology*, was formerly associate professor of sociology in the University of Chicago, and this book may be considered as one product of the leadership which the department of sociology in that university is taking in applying the technique of sociology to the problems of the modern city. It consists of more than 600 short excerpts from a variety of materials dealing with the importance of cities in history, their location and growth, city planning, streets and alleys, traffic, civic aesthetics, public health and safety, housing, community and neighborhood and the like.

The book will probably find its greatest use in college classes for which it is primarily designed. For others it will serve as an index to important articles, books and documents. Used in this manner it will be found excellent, but no general reader will be able to plow through the succession of brief snatches from a wide variety of materials. If the average man wishes to know something about urban sociology he had best make a selection of a limited number of the writings of which the book exhibits small samples and read them in their entirety.

H. W. D.

✣

SPECIAL ASSESSMENT PROCEDURE. Kansas City Public Service institute. 1927. Pp. 87.

Considerable public complaint of special assessments in Kansas City prompted the Public Service Institute to investigate special assessment practices in other cities. On the basis of the twenty-three replies received in answer to the Institute's questionnaire, this report aims to summarize special assessment practice in important particulars in twenty-four large cities.

The report emphasizes that Kansas City practices in the matter of special assessments differ from the practices in other cities in important respects. A particularly significant difference in Kansas City is assessing the acquisition costs of parks and playgrounds against a benefit district, instead of following the more general practice of other cities of paying such costs from general funds or bond funds. Kansas City, unlike other cities, also uses special assessments for park and boulevard maintenance. Again in the matter of paving and repaving, none of the cities investigated follow the Kansas City practice of assessing the whole cost on the abutting property. In paying for sewers by special assessments Kansas City varies from the common practice in large cities chiefly in the extent of the assessments. The report points out that considerable injustice has resulted in Kansas City from the area method of distributing assessments for storm sewers. The report likewise condemns the Kansas City practice of paying contractors in tax bills instead of issuing special assessment bonds and paying the contractors in cash. The constitutional limitation which requires a two-thirds vote of the people in order to create indebtedness apparently precludes the adoption of the latter method.

This study is chiefly valuable in that it compiles elementary facts concerning assessment procedure and practice in twenty-four cities. It is a convenient reference report, since the information is classified both by cities and by types of improvement. This report, however, shows plainly the limitations of the questionnaire method of inquiry. It does not penetrate very far into the actualities of special assessment practices and procedure in the several cities considered.

MARTIN L. FAUST.

A STUDY OF ASSESSMENT METHODS AND RESULTS IN COOK COUNTY. Prepared by the Joint Commission on Real Estate Valuation for the Board of County Commissioners of Cook County. 1927. Pp. 62.

This study is the first section of the formal report of the Joint Commission on Real Estate Valuation authorized in 1926 by a resolution of the board of Cook county commissioners. Five members of the board of assessors, three members of the board of review, three members of the board of Cook county commissioners, and fifteen distinguished private citizens comprise the Joint Commission. The purpose of the county board in creating the Joint Commission is set forth as follows: "To study and make recommendations to the County Board on the procedure for obtaining a scientific assessment of real property

in the county, and then to continue as a joint advisory agency in directing and guiding the appraisal work and in the development of procedure for the adoption, interpretation, and effective administration of the complete plan."

In view of recent steady improvements in urban assessment methods, it seems somewhat surprising that Chicago and her surrounding areas cling to archaic methods that are very ill-adapted to modern needs. For example, in determining land assessments outside of the Loop district, the board of assessors divides the city into five districts and assigns to each assessor the task of determining unit valuations in a district. But each assessor, in determining the assessments for his district, depends upon his own sources of information and his knowledge of values in the district. Under such a decentralized arrangement, with no system of standard units or rules and formulae, and without land value maps, it is inevitable that gross inequalities and grave injustices should result. The Joint Commission has included in the report to supplement its own studies the assessment studies by the Institute for Research in Land Economics and Public Utilities at Northwestern University.

The tables showing appraisal variations are particularly significant. They indicate that there is a tremendous amount of discrimination in assessments in favor of or against thousands of property owners. This discrimination, it seems, is not territorial, nor is it particularly in favor of or against certain types of property. It is in effect in favor of or against all types and sizes of improved property in all sections of the city of Chicago. The principal weaknesses of the present method of determining building assessments are, first, that the entire system is entirely dependent upon one man; second, that it is impossible to substantiate the correctness of assessments, since there is a complete lack of information in the office files on income, rents, and operating costs of representative buildings of various types in various localities; third, that the failure to provide sufficient help made it necessary in the 1927 quadrennial assessment to copy from the prior period the large majority of building valuations.

The report concludes with a summary statement of constructive recommendations as to policy and methods in determining assessments. While these suggestions are quite elementary, their acceptance and application would tend to correct the conspicuous shortcomings of present practices. The report has distinctive merit for the admirable succinctness with which it outlines the existing situation in the Chicago assessment procedure. While the report does not outline in detail a more scientific assessment system, it does not seem practicable to do so until there has been at least a partial recogniton of the elementary principles of scientific method.

MARTIN L. FAUST.

✿

Three City Reports.—*City of Lynchburg, Va. Annual Report for the Fiscal Year Ending January 31, 1927. Pp. 117.*—This report maintains the excellency which has characterized previous reports of Lynchburg. First of all, it is attractive. A glance at the cover compels an investigation of the content. The length of 117 pages, unfortunately, will result in much of its value being lost. The illustrative material is well chosen and properly distributed throughout the report. The table of contents, which could have been shortened, will be an aid for ready reference. A clear and complete organization chart at the beginning helps one to a clearer understanding of what follows. The letter of transmittal by the mayor adequately summarizes the accomplishments of the period covered, but the lack of recommendations for the future by either the mayor or manager is a distinct loss to effectiveness. The arrangement of material is excellent and the content is well balanced between activities. The 8″ x 11″ size does not make it as convenient for reading and filing as the conventional size of 6″ x 9″. In spite of shortcomings, however, it stands as one of the best municipal reports issued in months and, in many of the important requisites of report writing, it approaches perfection.

Town of Stratford, Conn. Sixth Annual Report for the fiscal year ending October 9, 1927. By Carlton Day Reed, Town Manager. Pp. 44.—Here is a report that gives a clear and concise account of municipal activities for a city of 18,000. One-half of the 44 pages are devoted to the auditor's report to the town council. This should have been omitted, and in its place a few brief statements included, showing the sources of money collected, what organization unit spent it, and the purpose for which it was spent. The table of contents in the front of the report is commendable, but should have been shortened for such a brief report. The letter of transmittal is well prepared and appropriately touches the high spots of accomplishment. It fails, however, to mention any recommendations for the future. These follow later in the report, but the effect is lessened for many will never find them. The lack of an organization chart, failure to emphasize important facts, scarcity and poor distribution of illustrative material are its chief faults. These are largely offset, however, by the physical makeup, the balance of material aside from the financial statistics, and the thoroughgoing manner and clearness characterizing the general presentation.

C. E. RIDLEY.

✿

Paris Spreads Out.—"Paris s'étend . . . ," by Georges Benoit-Lévy, will prove valuable not only to Parisians, but to anyone studying the more radical aspects of regional planning, for this veteran propagandist has brought under one cover and correlated by application to a typical metropolis many recent but hitherto largely unrelated ideas as to the future distribution of population and its works.

Citing the increasing difficulties of communication and other city services, the mortality of trees and of people, and other metropolitan evils, he favors lineal extensions, as exemplified by "La Ciudad Lineal" outside Madrid, though probably more intensively developed than in that case, as well as isolated garden cities. For the largest of such extensions to Paris the pull of the ocean should be recognized, as it was by Napoleon when he wrote: "Paris, Rouen, Le Havre are but a single city of which the Seine is the great street."

The approach to such regional planning should be both by working down from world or nation planning and by working up from city planning. Paris itself should be limited, and its open spaces, public and private, preserved and enlarged, including a belt around it for agriculture, forests and recreation.

"Must Paris be demolished? We love it too well. Let us simply open the windows on the bountiful nature which surrounds it and give it the air of the fields."

ARTHUR C. COMEY.

JUDICIAL DECISIONS

EDITED BY C. W. TOOKE

Professor of Law, Georgetown University

Special Assessments—Direct Liability of City.
—Referring to the extended discussion of this
question in the April number of the REVIEW,
attention may be called to the recent decision
of the Supreme Court of Iowa in *Ballard-
Hassett Co.* v. *Des Moines*, 218 N. W. 20, which
holds that a recital in the bond that "this bond
is payable only out of the special assessment
fund created by the collection of said special
tax" is a reservation in favor of the city and
protects the city against personal liability on
the bond. This provision now required by
statute is the answer of the Iowa legislature
to the decision of its courts as illustrated in
Hauge v. *Des Moines*.

❧

Municipal Ownership—Proprietary Obligations of City.—In *Vicksburg S. & P. Ry. Co.* v.
City of Monroe, 115 So. 136, recently decided by
the Supreme Court of Louisiana, the city by
ordinance sought to impose the cost of constructing the crossing of its municipally owned street
railway over the tracks of the plaintiff upon the
latter company. The plaintiff constructed the
required crossing and brought suit for the cost
thereof against the city. In holding that the
judgment in favor of the plaintiff should be
affirmed, the court points out that in its operation of the street railway the city acts in its proprietary capacity and the same rules are applicable to it as to a private corporation. It was
therefore its duty to construct the crossing in
question and it is subject to a quasi-contractual
liability for the work done for its benefit. Such
duties imposed upon it in its proprietary capacity it may not shift to others by an attempt to
exercise its governmental powers.

❧

Home Rule—Municipal Affairs—Maintenance of Public Library Held to Be a State
Function.—In *State ex rel. Carpenter* v. *St. Louis*.
2 S. W. (2d) 713, the Supreme Court of Missouri
again had before it the question of the delimitation of authority between the state and its home-
rule cities. Under authority of a statute in operation for the past seven years, a portion of the

municipal tax funds had been turned over to the
library commission of the city for the support of
the public libraries. Owing to the great increase
of general city expenditures and the accumulation of a large reserve in the library fund, the
fiscal officers of the defendant made no provision
for the usual special library tax for 1927, and refused to pay over any of the proceeds of the general tax for such purposes, claiming that there
existed no authority under the statute, as the
establishment and maintenance of libraries is a
purely municipal purpose for which authorization can be given only by the local home-rule
charter.

In sustaining a writ of mandamus to compel
the fiscal officers to turn over the funds authorized by statute to the library board, the court
held that all educational activities of the city are
subject to the general laws of the state and are
not included within those municipal matters
over which the people of the city have exclusive
legislative control. The court went further and
properly construed the permissive form of the
statute as mandatory in effect.

❧

Police Power—Authority of Towns to Establish Building Lines.—An example of a tendency
toward a liberal construction of the police powers
of towns in Massachusetts may be found in the
decision handed down by the Supreme Judicial
Court of Massachusetts, on March 2, in *Slack* v.
Building Inspector of Town of Wellesley, 160
N. E. 285. The statute confers upon towns
"for the prevention of fire and the preservation
of life and morals" the power to pass "by-laws
consistent with law and applicable throughout
the whole or any defined part of its territory"
to "regulate the inspection, materials, construction, alteration, repair, height, area, location and
use of buildings and other structures within its
limits." Under this general delegation, the defendant passed a by-law providing that buildings
of certain designated classes must be placed at
least specified distances from the center line of
adjacent streets. From a dismissal of a petition
for a writ of mandamus to compel the inspector

of buildings to issue a permit for a building to be located nearer the street line than that authorized by the by-law, the petitioner appealed.

In affirming the decision of the lower court, the court held that the by-law has a direct bearing upon the prevention of fire and the preservation of life and morals, and therefore is a valid exercise of the police power. The power given to establish set-back lines by the exercise of the power of eminent domain, as authorized by an earlier statute (c. 462 Statutes of 1893), is held to give an alternative power to towns not inconsistent with the terms of the statute under consideration as amended by Chapter 334 of the Statutes of 1912, which added the words "height, area, location." The constitutionality of the by-law thus construed is sustained by the Supreme Court in Gorieb v. Fox, 274 U. S. 603. The bearing of this decision upon several pending questions of municipal policy is quite obvious.

✸

Franchise Rights—Grants in Perpetuity.— The Circuit Court of Appeals, Eighth Circuit, in Denver v. Denver Traction Corporation, 23 Fed. (2d) 287, has recently construed the franchise of the defendant to be perpetual. The ordinances granting the franchises in question placed no limit of time upon their duration and ran to the grantees and their assigns. While a general power to confer upon public utilities a franchise does not without specific delegation give a municipality power to grant an exclusive franchise, it is now held that a city under the general power to control and regulate the use of its streets may grant to a public utility a franchise in its streets unlimited as to time, and that, if the terms of the franchise show such an intention, a grantee, whose corporate existence is limited, will take a right in perpetuity. (Owensboro v. Cumberland T. T. Co., 230 U. S. 58; Covington v. South Covington St. Ry. Co., 246 U. S. 414.) Subject, therefore, only to the exercise of the police power or forfeiture for nonuser or misuser, the court holds that the street railway franchises granted by the city and county of Denver without express limitation as to duration are perpetual.

The plaintiff in the instant case invoked the inhibition of the state constitution against local or special laws "granting to any corporation, association or individual any special or exclusive privilege, immunity or franchise whatever" and the provision that no law "making any irrevocable grant of special privileges, franchises or immunities shall be passed by the general assembly." The court finds in these constitutional provisions no express prohibition against the granting by a city of easements of this character. In Old Colony Trust Co. v. Omaha, 230 U. S. 100, the Supreme Court of the United States had occasion to construe a similar clause in the constitution of Nebraska, and held that a special privilege in constitutional law is "a right, power, franchise, immunity or privilege granted to, or vested in, a person or a class of persons to the exclusion of others and in derogation of common right." So long, therefore, as no exclusive privilege is granted, the constitutional inhibition does not apply.

✸

Streets and Highways—Condemnation of Public Property Therefor.—In New Orleans v. Orleans Levee District, 115 So. 131, the Supreme Court of Louisiana had before it the question of the liability of the defendant to the city for the destruction of a road made necessary in the construction of a levee. In the extension of the levee about a mile of the boulevard along the river was taken and the right of the city to recover the cost of rebuilding was in question. In the absence of any constitutional restriction, the state may appropriate the streets of a city for other public purposes without compensation; and no right to compensation arises unless directly given by statute. A Louisiana statute of 1920 purported to impose a liability upon the levee districts either to replace roads destroyed or reimburse the municipality for the cost of replacement. The court held, however, that this provision of the statute was in direct conflict with Section 6 of Article 16 of the Constitution of 1921, which limits the liability of the levee districts to the assessed valuation of the property taken, as a highway within a city is not private property subject to assessment for taxation.

That the rule that a municipal corporation has no right to compensation where its public property is taken by the state for another public use has no application in a case where the property is taken by the federal government is affirmed by the Circuit Court of Appeals of the First Circuit in Town of Bedford v. United States, 23 F. (2d) 453. In condemning some four hundred acres of land for a veterans' hospital, a mile and a half of the town highway was cut off. While the court suggested the question whether the power to condemn the highway could exist without an express grant in the federal statute, as that point was not raised by the pleadings and the parties had stipulated the amount of damages in event of liability, the decision was based upon the limitations against federal power imposed by the Fifth Amendment.

The application of the general rule is further illustrated in *State Highway Commission* v. *Elizabeth*, 140 Atl. 335, decided February first by the Supreme Court of New Jersey. The city sought to enjoin the State Highway Commission from condemning certain lands held by it in fee used for public purposes. Vice-Chancellor Berry in an able opinion reviews the relation of the state to the public property of a municipality and, while admitting that the delegation of such an unlimited power to the discretion of a public agency may be dangerous, holds that the legislative control is plenary and that the city should be enjoined from interfering with the action of the commission.

✤

Annexation—Collateral Attack.—It is well settled in the majority of the states of this country where the question has arisen that a municipal corporation may exist *de facto*, not only if erected without compliance with statutory requirements, but even under an unconstitutional statute, the latter being deemed sufficient color of authority to justify an organization and user in good faith. The fundamental requirements, however, are color of authority, an effort in good faith to organize thereunder and a user of the corporate franchises. The principal characteristics of such a corporation are that its acts are valid as to the public and all third persons and that its competency to act or the legality of its existence is not subject to any collateral attack, but may be tested only by *quo warranto* at the instance of the state itself. Even the state may be estopped to question the *de jure* character of the corporation if the legislative authority, whose mandate has been disregarded, has directly or indirectly recognized its existence or acquiesced therein for such a length of time that a judgment of ouster would cause confusion. Especially in jurisdictions where the doctrine of *de facto* municipal corporations under constitutional statutes has not been adopted, the doctrine of estoppel is of necessity freely applied as an alternative rem-

edy. The *de facto* doctrine is applicable not only to incorporation but also to annexation of territory to municipal corporations, the annexation being regarded *pro tanto* as an incorporation. The occasional tendency of the courts to resort to the *de facto* doctrine when not justified by the facts is well illustrated by the case of *Hunt* v. *Atkinson* (300 S. W. 656), decided by the Court of Civil Appeals of Texas last November. The appeal was from a refusal of the lower court to grant a mandamus to the defendant Atkinson, county judge of Harris county, to call an election to determine whether the inhabitants of a portion of the territory of the county should become incorporated under a commission form of government, a petition to that end having been duly filed on May 27, 1925. The territory adjoined the city of Houston, a metropolis of 138,-000 inhabitants, the city council of which by ordinance passed the 31st of May extended the municipal limits so as to include the lands in question. The latter act was given by the county judge as the reason for refusing to call the election. The petitioners set up that they acted under authority of the statute for creating new municipalities and that the act of the council of Dallas was null and void, as the method of annexation it followed, although given by the city's home rule charter, had been superseded by the provisions of a statute applicable to all cities of from 100,000 to 150,000 population, which made such an annexation subject to the approval of the voters of the city.

In sustaining the lower court, the Court of Civil Appeals questioned whether the general statute effected a repeal of the provision of the city charter, but realizing the weakness of this position fell back upon the *de facto* nature of the annexation and held that the petitioners had no standing to attack collaterally its validity, which could be questioned only by the state in *quo warranto* proceedings. As the statutory proceedings, for incorporation had been initiated before the adoption of the ordinance, it is difficult to see how the action of the city council was conclusive to establish the elements of good faith and user essential to a *de facto* character. (*Campbell* v. *Champion*, 138 Atl. 529, reported in this Review, December, 1927, p. 796.)

PUBLIC UTILITIES

EDITED BY JOHN BAUER

Director, American Public Utilities Bureau

The Service Charge Rejected in Boston Gas Rates.—In view of the efforts on the part of many gas companies to institute a "service charge" and the rather intense public opposition to this modification of gas rates, we deem it of interest to publish an opinion by the Massachusetts Department of Public Utilities accompanying an order issued February 28, 1928, which rejected a proposed consumer charge of $1.00 by the Boston Consolidated Gas Company:

This is a petition of gas consumers of the Boston Consolidated Gas Company objecting to a schedule of rates filed by the company on November 18, 1927, the proposed rates establishing a service charge of $1.00 a month, with a commodity rate of 85 cents a thousand cubic feet. It is contended by the company that $1.00 a month constitutes not more than the proportionate cost of each customer to the company of standing ready to serve the customer and that this cost ought to be borne by the customer whether or not he in fact uses any gas. It is asserted that, whereas under the present rates for gas this cost must be absorbed by what is charged for the commodity, a very large part of the customers are being carried by the rest of the customers, and as a result the company is obliged to charge the profitable customers for gas more than they should be charged. This, it is asserted, hampers the company in the development of its business, as it prevents the company from making rates to meet the competition of other fuels in the industrial field which the company could do if all customers paid to the company what it cost to serve them.

That there is a cost to the company of standing ready to serve that can be directly attributable to a customer we recognize. Thus, if the company had never connected a customer who uses little or no gas with its distributing mains, the company would save the interest, maintenance and depreciation charges upon the service pipes from the mains into the customer's premises and upon the meter therein installed. It would also save taxes upon this investment and the cost of reading the meters and keeping the customer's accounts and billing and collecting the amounts due from the customer. These costs, in our opinion, do not exceed, materially, 50 cents a month per customer. To go further involves one in the field of speculation as to what proportion of the distributing cost is due to each customer. We think it obvious that this cost is not substantially the same as to all customers.

For example, a customer served by a main which runs but a short distance from the company's gas holder and which serves a large number of customers does not throw the same burden upon the company as does a customer at a greater distance from the plant who is served by a main which serves a much less number of customers. Thus, a service charge which attempts to allocate to the customers their proportionate burden of the maintenance of the distributing system must of necessity be largely theoretical and may, in its final analysis, be no more equitable than absorbing this cost in the commodity price. We do not intend to assert that a charge to the customers of a proportionate part of the cost of the distributing system or even the manufacturing plant may not at times be justified or be advisable. Practical considerations may even dictate such a method of charging. Moreover, a demand charge may often be justified. What we do think, however, is that there is no such condition confronting the Boston Consolidated Gas Company at the present time as warrants such a radical change in practice as is proposed by the company. It is unnecessary to consider the advisability of allowing a service charge covering these costs of maintenance of the service that can be directly attributed to each customer and to him alone, as the company has indicated to us that unless a service charge of 75 cents be approved it prefers to impose no service charge at all.

✦

The Principle of the Service Charge.—The Massachusetts commission does recognize that there is something substantial in the principle of a service charge. The difference of opinion arises concerning its application in a particular case. No doubt certain costs are dependent directly upon the number of consumers served; if the number is increased, the cost increases substantially in proportion; if decreased, the cost diminishes in proportion. These costs are directly and immediately identified with the consumers as such, without regard to the amount of gas used or to the scope of the property and the organization.

As the commission indicates, these direct and immediate costs are incurred in dealing with the consumers. They include meter reading, commercial billing, collecting, commercial accounting, and commercial supplies and expenses, together with interest or return on the meters. As new consumers are attached, these items of cost increase almost proportionately. Conversely, if the number is decreased, the cost diminishes almost correspondingly.

The Massachusetts commission places these charges at a maximum of 50 cents a month per consumer, while the company asked for a dollar charge. The difference furnished ground for the rejection of the rate proposed by the company, notwithstanding the agreement in principle. The writer has had occasion to analyze consumer service costs, and is now concerned in such a matter before one of the state commissions;— in the particular case, he finds that 30 cents per month would cover the consumer service costs involved. There would be naturally a wide range between companies operating under different circumstances. The important issue is the clear determination as to principle; the items of costs that should be included in the service charge.

In supporting the dollar service charge an effort is made to extend the scope of the costs much beyond the conception set out by the Massachusetts commission and unquestionably justified by the facts. The purpose is to include not only the direct consumer service costs, but also what may be termed "consumer job costs," and especially a substantial proportion of the fixed or non-variable costs incurred because of the physical layout of the property and the scope of operating organization. The only costs which are avowedly excluded from the service charge are those directly identified with the production of gas itself, together with the maintenance, taxes and interest on the gas-producing property.

The principle involved is perhaps best illustrated by the maintenance, taxes and interest on mains, and by general officers' salaries. When a particular line of mains has once been installed, the amount of the investment becomes a fixed sum that no longer varies either according to the number of consumers served or the amount of gas supplied. The same is true of taxes and maintenance. The question is, Shall these costs be absorbed in proportion to the relative amount of gas used, or evenly divided according to the number of consumers? Under the past rates, all of these fixed or non-variable costs have been met on a use basis, absorbed by the direct charge for gas. In the service charge proposed by the companies, a large proportion of these costs is

treated as consumer charges; divided by the number of consumers, and not by the amount of gas used.

The question in any such proposal is, Why should this change be made? What inherent injustice is there in the established practice of paying these costs in proportion to use? What advance in justice is there to shift part or all of these costs on the consumer basis?

Looking at the facts from the standpoint of extremes, it appears plain that if the entire interest, taxes and maintenance of mains were divided on the consumer basis, there would be injustice to the small consumer. The small consumer—say 25 M cu. ft. a month—would be compelled to pay the same amount as the consumer of, say, 100 M cu. ft. per month. No one could defend such a result.

Conversely, however, it is difficult to see any real injustice by continuing the present extreme of requiring all consumers to contribute to these joint and fixed costs in proportion to the relative amount of gas used.

But assume any separation of these costs, partly to be provided for on the consumer basis and partly on the use basis. Any such separation is arbitrary. Suppose 50 per cent were to be apportioned on the consumer and 50 per cent on the use basis: why 50 per cent? Would not the 50 per cent element involve the same incongruity of requiring the small consumer to pay the same amount as the large consumer, without regard to the amount used? Is there any real injustice involved by providing for these charges on the use rather than on the consumer basis to the entire extent?

The same considerations apply to all the relatively fixed or non-variable costs, which are large in their relative magnitude. Take general officers' salaries: what is there unjust in the past practice of requiring consumers to pay in proportion to the amount of gas used? What justice would there be to divide these costs by the number of consumers, without regard to the amount of gas consumed? Why, indeed, is it necessary or reasonable to take in part of these costs and provide for them on the consumer basis? There is a further group of charges about which there can be a misunderstanding as to their character. They are above referred to as consumer "job costs." They include the maintenance and care of all of the company's properties installed on or in connection with the consumer's premises. On their face, these costs would appear to be consumer service costs includible in the service charge. As a matter of fact, however, they have nothing to do with the regular monthly service upon which the service charge is predicated. They represent specific jobs performed for individual consumers, with no regularity and direct connection with the hook-up of individual consumers. This applies to all work on consumers' premises,—removing and resetting meters, and maintenance of services, gas appliances, and meters. One consumer may not have a job done on his premises for a year, another may have had two jobs in a month. Why should costs be divided on a regular monthly consumer basis when there is no direct identification with the current service? If there is to be a refinement of rates in accordance with the character of costs incurred, then these charges should be based upon the direct jobs and each consumer billed according to the actual work done for him. This would not compel the careful householder to pay the bills of the careless.

In principle the service charge is sound, but its application within a properly limited scope does not have the serious importance that has been attached to it in public discussion. While, of course, each consumer should pay the costs directly due to his personal service, actually in most cases these costs are not very great; and if they are absorbed in the general domestic rates on the use rather than the consumer basis, there is no very great injustice involved. As a matter of fact, in every system of refined rates proposed, there are involved much greater disproportions in regard to cost and rates for particular groups of consumers. For example, in any large company there may be found lines of mains which have a small utilization, and other mains with heavy utilization, and yet the cost for maintenance, interest and taxes will be the same for the two mains. Consequently, with the light utilization the cost of serving the particular consumers on that main will be high, while the cost for the highly utilized main will be low. Notwithstanding this obvious fact, there is no active proposal made to meet such inequalities between cost and rates for groups of consumers. A company must take the lean with the fat, it must serve the thinly populated section with the thickly populated region. But in respect to costs, the very fact of density of population affects directly the degree of utilization of mains and other property, and is a determinant of the unit cost of service. And yet, these differences, which are great in the aggregate, are ignored, while the relatively minor costs involved in the consumer service are magnified, and presented as a matter of major and fundamental constitutional rights.

✦

Dr. Wilcox.—The death of Dr. Delos F. Wilcox, on April 4, is a public loss of unusual significance. For the past twenty years he has been a leading figure—through his publications, public addresses and professional activity—in representing and promoting the public interest in the complicated problems of public utility regulation and rate-making. He was a man of unusual mental keenness and ability, with exceptional training in the particular lines to which he devoted his professional life, and was a giant for work and incessant endeavor. His sincerity was unswerving, and his life was constantly dedicated to the public. In his personal relations he was most pleasant and congenial; was generous to the extreme; and was remarkably free of the petty qualities which sometimes characterize men of high professional standing.

He was engaged professionally in many m-i portant public utility cases. In every case, he devoted himself with singular purpose to the public aspects of the issues and facts, without regard to the personal effect upon him professionally and financially. He was so thorough in his work that, as a professional man, he never was compensated according to mete. In several instances he spent large amounts of his own money, to complete investigations which had important public aspects, when the public authorities were unwilling to provide the necessary funds for the purpose. There are few Wilcoxes, indeed; none can be spared.

Dr. Wilcox, in his general mental views, was an advocate of public ownership and operation. On this point there are honest differences of opinion. Dr. Wilcox did not arrive at his position through prejudice and superficial consideration. He understood what was involved as well as anybody could, and was a master of the facts and issues.

Dr. Wilcox devoted himself with unstinted effort and with constant enthusiasm to the public solely because it was the cause in which he believed. He was little actuated by that lure of profit, which, we are sometimes told, is the only motivating force for progress.

GOVERNMENTAL RESEARCH ASSOCIATION NOTES

EDITED BY RUSSELL FORBES

Secretary

Local Self-Government Institute, Bombay Presidency, India.—The Institute has published a *Local Self-Government Yearbook, 1928.* The yearbook contains a directory of officials of the various municipalities in the Bombay Presidency, a list of local self-government institutions of India, proceedings of the conference of the Institute held in July, 1927, vital statistics on several phases of public health work, and various contributed articles on problems of municipal administration. The results of governmental research in the United States and Canada are shown by extended quotations from *Twenty Years of Municipal Research,* published by the Governmental Research Association.

✢

Recent Reports of Research Agencies.— The following reports have been received at the central library of the Association since March 1, 1928:

Buffalo Municipal Research Bureau:
The Police Department: A Memorandum on the organization and work of the uniformed force of the Buffalo police department, with suggestions for increased patrol efficiency.

Municipal Research Bureau of Cleveland:
Industrial Water Supply for Cleveland: analysis of existing and possible supplies.
A Bibliography on Regional Government.

Taxpayers' Research League of Delaware:
Memorandum Concerning the Relative Advantages of Three Proposals for Treating the Surplus in the State Sinking Fund; submitted to the governor, secretary of state, auditor of accounts, and state treasurer.

Detroit Bureau of Governmental Research:
Arguments For and Against the City Manager Plan for Detroit; submitted at the request of the Detroit Board of Commerce.

Ohio Institute:
How Ohio Governments Spend Their Money.

St. Louis Bureau of Municipal Research:
Gasoline Tax Revenue.

✢

Boston Finance Commission.—Since March 1, the commission has made the following reports: Regarding the contract for construction of the new Horace Mann School in the Dearborn district; regarding comparative amount of paving done in the past ten years; regarding revised betterment order for Cambridge Street; and various reports to the governor of the commonwealth in regard to pending legislative matters.

✢

Buffalo Municipal Research Bureau, Inc.— The Bureau's report on its survey of the uniformed force of the police department was released April 6. Two of the local papers printed the report in full, while a summary appeared in the other paper, and all three carried complimentary editorials. The outstanding recommendations of the report were: (1) elimination of six precinct stations and rearrangement of precinct lines, (2) motor patrol for residential precincts, (3) creation of ten police booths or substations on leading roads of egress, and (4) creation of an additional platoon for peak crime hours.

The Bureau is now coöperating with a special investigating committee of council which is delving into the practices and procedures of past administrations with a view to prescribing more businesslike methods.

The survey of the park department, issued in January, 1928, claimed that Buffalo was spending $630,000 more than was necessary for annual park maintenance and operation. The budget for the park department for the fiscal year beginning July 1 has been cut $597,000 below actual expenditures for last year.

✢

Taxpayers' Research League of Delaware.— The League has continued its collection and study of material for the preparation of a state

305

finance code to be prepared in collaboration with a committee of the Delaware Bankers' Association.

It has also continued a study dealing with the cost of establishing, equipping, and operating public rest rooms in the cities and town of Delaware, Pennsylvania, New Jersey, Maryland, and Virginia, to provide information for groups interested in the establishment of public rest rooms in Wilmington and Newark (Del.).

Progress has been made in the study of the coroner's office in New Castle County, and in the League's coöperation with the public affairs committee of the Kiwanis Club to stimulate registration and voting among Kiwanians, their families, and their employees.

The League has prepared two memoranda dealing with the surplus in the state sinking fund, one addressed to the state highway department, and the other to the custodians of the sinking fund. The aim of these memoranda is to secure the absorption of the sinking-fund surplus by the cancellation of approximately $1,404,000 of outstanding state bonds.

In consequence of differences between the state board and the Wilmington board of education concerning the allotment of state school funds, the League has been requested to conduct a fact-finding study of the laws and other factors involved in the allotment of these funds for the purpose of clarifying the issue and bringing about a better understanding of the subject. The city board has approved the study, and has opened all its files and records to the League.

The mayor and town council of Milford have requested the League to make an exhaustive study of the town's fiscal administration. This study, which is now under way, involves a three-year audit of the town's accounts, a determination of the town's bonded and floating indebtedness, and the preparation and installation of a new accounting and budget procedure. Upon invitation of the board of light and water commissioners, which is independent of the town council, the League's study will include the board's fiscal administration, the revision of its accounting system, and an appraisal of the light and water plant.

At the request of the Consumer's League of Delaware, the Research League compiled information dealing with the problem of unemployment in Wilmington, and methods used elsewhere for meeting this problem.

A study has been made of the methods of selecting and compensating tax collectors and treasurers in the incorporated towns in Delaware and a preliminary report has been issued.

The League has made a preliminary study of special taxes on insurance companies and agents in Delaware, which will later be broadened to include all special business and corporation taxes.

✿

Des Moines Bureau of Municipal Research.—At the request of one of the district court judges, the Bureau made a report on the increases in the various accounts of the court fund during the last four years, bringing out particularly the deficits which have resulted in bond issues in 1926 and 1927.

The judges have conferred with the grand jury, urging that body to return indictments only when conclusive evidence pointed to a probability of guilt, in order to cut down the expense of court costs. They are also investigating other court expenses as to the possibility of economies.

• The Bureau is analyzing various types of insurance carried by the local taxing sub-divisions on their properties, as to the aggregate amount of such policies with reference to insurable values, possibility of co-insurance, and a record form which will systematically indicate when policies come due.

The Bureau also made a report on the condition of the county funds at the close of the fiscal year and scrutinized municipal expenditures and revenues collected during the last few months of the city's fiscal year ending March 31, with a view to completing the fiscal year within the income.

✿

Civic Affairs Department, Indianapolis Chamber of Commerce.—The department is presenting a ten-minute discussion of local tax questions by radio to the citizens of Indianapolis each week through the courtesy of station WFBM. The ten-minute period, beginning at 7 p.m. on Wednesday, has been set aside for this purpose for as long as the department desires. Half a dozen such discussions already have been broadcast, and it is expected that they will continue for a number of weeks.

The civic affairs committee, at the request of other civic organizations, has invited all civic organizations in the city each to name a representative for associate membership on the committee. More than thirty representatives have been selected and they will participate in the deliberations of the committee on questions of major civic importance.

❖

National Institute of Public Administration, New York City.—The graduate class in public administration of the School of Citizenship and Public Affairs, Syracuse University, is completing a two months' course of training at the Institute. The members of the class are J. Curtis Jenkins, Sherwood L. Reeder, and Carleton F. Sharpe. Ray Chang of Columbia University, Philip Bramer of the Catholic Charities Organization, New York diocese, and Stanley Church, councilman of New Rochelle, N. Y., are also enrolled as special students.

Dr. Charles A. Beard has returned to this country after several weeks' study of the Yugoslav National Government. Dr. Beard visited Yugoslavia under the auspices of the National Institute of Public Administration and the American-Yugoslav Society.

❖

Taxpayers' Association of New Mexico.— The Association is completing a compilation of governmental expenditures for the year ending June 30, 1927. The purpose of the compilation is to show the actual expenditures for all state, county and local purposes and also the sources of all receipts.

❖

Milwaukee Citizens' Bureau.—The Bureau is continuing to work with the City Charter League in the revision of Milwaukee's Charter of 1874, as amended. The committee is now drafting a comprehensive home rule charter based upon the principles approved by the City Charter League which provides for strengthening the powers of the mayor, consolidating the city's departments, election of aldermen from three districts by proportional representation with the uniform quota of 7,000 votes.

A charter school was conducted by the Citizens' Bureau, League of Women Voters and Federation of Women's Clubs which consisted of seven talks held weekly from February 3 to March 16, inclusive. Milwaukee's conglomeration of laws, known as the city charter, was explained, and the proposed charter was thoroughly examined. In compliance with the demand for another series of talks on the charter, a second charter school is being conducted on six consecutive Wednesdays, March 28 to May 2, inclusive. Several of the speakers for this school

have been selected from those who attended the first charter school.

The Bureau has prepared a speakers' handbook on the proposed charter. The section relating to the subject discussed is distributed after each meeting.

The charter will not be submitted to referendum until April, 1929. This educational work is being done now among the women, because it is anticipated that they will be called upon to do the major work of the campaign.

❖

San Francisco Bureau of Governmental Research.—The Bureau in its capacity as staff agent for the municipal affairs committee of the Chamber of Commerce, coöperated with the executive committee thereof in the consideration, analysis and revision of the order in which projects should be taken up in a proposed "capital development budget" for the city; with the charter section of this committee in the consideration of charter revision plans; with the bridge and highway committee in its consideration of the proposed Golden Gate bridge; with the works and development committee in its consideration of the need for bond issues for sewers and playgrounds; with the executive committee in its consideration of the proposal that the city bear a large part of the cost of Golden Gate Heights improvements, for which the property owners requested the city to meet what were claimed to be excessive assessments.

The Bureau coöperated with the Junior Chamber of Commerce in the consideration by that body of the Cleveland and Indiana plans for the control of local expenditures, and with the program committee of the Junior Chamber in its consideration of various items proposed for inclusion in its program.

With the thought that it might be possible to make employment classification and salary standardization effective at the time of adopting the 1928–29 budget, the finance committee has requested the Bureau to secure information on salaries paid for all kinds of services by the several large cities in the Pacific coast area and by large employers in San Francisco—these data when secured and compiled to serve as a basis for standard salaries to be proposed to the board of supervisors for each class of employment in the city service.

The Bureau's study of traffic and financial factors, estimated as applicable to the proposed Golden Gate bridge, was completed and published as an issue of *The City*, under date of January 25. This involved a mass of detailed work incidental to the compilation of estimates of population, auto registration, vehicular traffic to Marin County, and probable bridge revenues. Many copies of the report were delivered on request to the Down Town Association, the Chamber of Commerce, and the Civic League as a basis for consideration and action on the project by these organizations.

On January 15 the Bureau mailed to members of various civic organizations 10,000 copies of a report enumerating projects officially proposed, totaling approximately $335,000,000, outlining estimates of city revenues for capital expenditure purposes during the next ten years ranging from $172,000,000 (under New York bonding limitation) to $260,700,000 (charter limitation), and recommending the formulation of a "capital expenditure budget" under which projects would be taken up in the order of their relative importance and necessity, and with due relation to the city's ability to finance them. Communications were sent to four of the leading civic organizations offering coöperation of the Bureau in the consideration by each of these organizations of such a capital expenditure program. This has been actively taken up by the Building Owners and Managers' Association and the municipal affairs committee of the Chamber of Commerce.

At the request of the chairman of the supervisors' finance committee, the Bureau has agreed to undertake, as soon as its work on assessment-roll procedure can be completed, a survey of the miscellaneous revenue policies and precedure of the city. The full coöperation of the tax collector has been promised for this work.

The study of assessment-roll procedure has been continued. A study was made of the provisions of the state law controlling assessment procedure. A new real property assessment roll form has been designed which will make possible the posting of all necessary information on one page instead of on a double-page form, as at present. Many conferences were held with representatives of various office-equipment firms, practical demonstrations of the use of office equipment for preparing the roll were made, and estimates of cost of necessary equipment were

secured. A preliminary draft of the proposed report on the real-property roll has been prepared and is now being revised. A start was made on study of the present procedure and requirements for securing assessed values of personal property and writing the personal property roll.

✤

Committee on Municipal Research, Syracuse, N. Y.—Orin F. Nolting of the School of Citizenship and Public Affairs, Syracuse University, has been appointed secretary of the Committee on Municipal Research of the city of Syracuse, succeeding S. Howard Evans, who is now secretary to the mayor.

This committee of citizens was appointed by the mayor to coöperate with the School of Citizenship and Public Affairs in studying methods for increasing the effectiveness of the city government. At the request of the mayor, Charles G. Hanna, the committee is now preparing a ten-year financial program. Other projects to be undertaken include the revision of the entrance examinations for patrolmen and a survey of the department of charities.

✤

Toledo Commission of Publicity and Efficiency.—The commission has released for publication the survey of street cleaning which has been in preparation for some time. It was published in several weekly installments in the *Toledo City Journal* during April. It covers organization, personnel, records, methods and equipment, costs, and financing street cleaning. The report includes considerable comparative data on ten other cities of about Toledo's size.

A study of city tax rates in the six largest Ohio cities for the last ten years has just been completed, and will soon be published. The rates have been adjusted to a 100 per cent basis for comparative purposes. The commission will soon publish a chart showing the per capita cost of government in Toledo for the last fifteen years, and the per capita cost adjusted to the purchasing power of the dollar during those years.

At the request of the city council a study of gas rates in eighteen Ohio cities was made. It was found that Toledo had a low rate to the small consumer and a high rate to the large consumer as compared with other cities.

NOTES AND EVENTS

EDITED BY H. W. DODDS

Queens High in New York City.—A New York borough president's lot is not a happy one. In the brief history of the present charter, three have been removed by the governor of the state under charges, another suddenly sought a more congenial atmosphere in Paris, whence he has not returned, and still another was sent to state's prison. The latest, accused, *inter alia*, of taking one consideration with another, has just abandoned his post. Finding himself confronted with charges so serious that it would cost him $100,000 to prove his innocence, he asked the city to appropriate him this sum, and being refused, it burst his mighty heart and he up and resigned.

Queens borough has fared particularly ill. It has had four borough presidents and all have died unnatural political deaths. The present trouble had been brewing for some time, but in December last it broke, when the taxpayers of Queens were called upon to pay an assessment for some sewer pipe at Tiffany prices. A Republican alderman from Queens, a pugnacious little Irishman named Harvey, championed their cause and filed formal charges with the governor. Borough President Maurice Connolly was accused of (1) gross waste of public funds by exorbitant payments to contractors, (2) unlawful price for a patented type of sewer pipe, (3) fraudulent disregard of engineers' statements, and (4) employment of incompetent engineers. He promptly made the customary protestation of innocence and he and his counsel, the famous and fancy-priced family and criminal lawyer, Max Steuer, proclaimed their eagerness for a full and speedy investigation. This policy has never been formally abandoned, but Mr. Steuer has proved a doughty legal Fabius. Governor Al Smith, and there were rumors that he found the task not unpleasant, promptly appointed an eminent supreme court justice to conduct the investigation. It was commonly believed that Justice Scudder would step from the pudgy carcass of Connolly to the governorship. A former United States district attorney and prominent Republican, Emory Buckner was appointed as prosecutor.

The first snag came when Justice Scudder proposed to hold some secret preliminary hearings to which Connolly would not be invited. This furnished occasion for writs and injunctions and appeals, challenging Scudder's right to hold hearings and finally his right to act in the case at all. After the lapse of three months, the Court of Appeals ruled that a supreme court justice could not sit in such an inquiry, and Scudder was forced to retire.

The Governor now appointed an equally distinguished lawyer, Clarance Shearn, to take up the work. The investigation was proceeding apace, when Connolly sought the city's financial assistance in proving his costly innocence. At first, Mayor Walker looked with favor upon the suggestion, but when the question finally came before the board of estimate, Connolly was flatly denied any public money. His resignation again jerked the inquiry to an abrupt halt. The only way in which it could be resumed was for a grand jury to take it up. Mr. Buckner has been appointed special district attorney, and the investigation is again under way.

Connolly has not been alone in his difficultes. The principal person in the piece, is one Jack Phillips, millionaire pipe and sewer man, who has enjoyed ill health since the whole business began, and is now confined in a hospital at Miami Beach, where he enjoys the society of a United States marshal, for the federal government finding, to its amazement, that he had paid no income tax for the last six or eight years, has brought suit for a million and three hundred thousand dollars for back taxes and penalties.

Needless to say, the revelations thus far have been scanty. A fire occurred in the office of a prominent contracting company, another was burglarized. Zorn, the "cement King" also reports a burglary. Important records have vanished, witnesses have disappeared, and in all, there is little of a positive nature to relate. Connolly has many friends who have doubtless shared his good fortunes and are involved in his fate. Alderman Harvey is certain of this and, in conjunction with a former Republican candidate for the borough presidency, has filed charges with his party's state committee against a local county committeeman whom he accuses of sabotaging the inquiry. Harvey has vigorously insisted that he has had more opposition from his Republican friends and superiors than from even the Democrats.

Connolly came into office fifteen years ago when Governor Dix ejected Gresser. He has been the boss of Queens ever since, although his leadership has often been challenged, at times seriously. He has built up a sturdy political machine of his own, which at times has been in open conflict with Tammany Hall. He supported Hylan against Walker in 1925 and Hearst against Smith in 1922.

Queens has grown. Upwards of one hundred million dollars have been spent yearly in public improvements. Nearly fifty miles of sewer have been laid. The demand for more improvements has been constant and insistent. Connolly has carried these demands to the board of estimate and fought relentlessly for appropriations, which has made him both popular and powerful.

It is much too soon to predict the outcome. The Meyer Committee, a legislative fishing expedition in 1921, tried to prove that Phillips was Connnolly's bagman, but without success. Surrender of his office does not mean that Connolly will surrender Queens. The election of B. M. Patten by the aldermen, to Connolly's place, does not prove that the latter will not continue to dominate the borough. It is, however, a fight between him and Tammany. There are those who think there's a new Tammany, but others think it's the same mangy old beast.

EPEXIGETICUS.

✣

Chicago Government Planning Association.— Last summer on the initiative of the Chicago Forum Council a meeting of representatives of several Chicago civic organizations and three of the largest universities in the city was called to discuss the existing conditions, shortcomings and the needs of local government in Chicago and the metropolitan area. These representatives organized themselves into the Chicago Institute of Local Politics. Six sessions of the Institute were held in October and November and another in January. Problems of government were thoroughly surveyed and discussed. E. O. Griffenhagen of the City Club of Chicago, former Corporation Counsel Francis X. Busch, Professors A. R. Hatton, Leonard D. White and Jerome G. Kerwin led the discussions at the various meetings of the representatives of the civic organizations.

The most obvious and pressing needs for reform in local government were finally grouped under five headings by the Findings Committee of the Institute composed of Professor J. G. Kerwin, chairman, J. L. Jacobs, Professor Leonard D. White, E. O. Griffenhagen, George C. Sikes, Francis X. Busch, Professor A. R. Hatton, and Harold L. Ickes. These needs are stated as follows:

(1) Home rule;
(2) Unification of governmental units;
(3) Simplification of the structure of government;
(4) Better operation of the merit system;
(5) Improvement in the local election procedure.

The members of the Institute decided to concentrate present efforts toward securing home rule for the cities of Illinois. Plans for coöperating with the Illinois Municipal League were adopted. On the subject of unification, the Findings Committee recommended the abolition of the several park areas now existing within the city of Chicago and their unification under one head. It was recommended that a plan of unification for the government of the metropolitan area—a district extending sixty miles in a semicircle from the loop—be considered in the immediate future.

Although the report does not recommend by name the adoption of the city manager form of government, most of the members of the Institute favor its adoption. The report under the heading of structure recommends the separation of politics from administration, the centralization of authority and responsibility, and a simplification of governmental organization. The report also recommends the non-partisan election of judges and a consideration of the adoption of some method of central counting of ballots, and an improved registration system.

One of the most important steps taken by the Institute was the drawing up of a plan for the Creation of a Chicago Government Planning Association which is to be composed of representatives of Chicago's leading civic organizations and of those citizens who desire to promote better government in the Chicago region. A permanent Planning Commission composed of thirty-six members is to be chosen by the Association. This Association through its permanent commission will draw up a Chicago Government Plan to guide civic organizations in their efforts for improving local government. The constitution of the Government Planning Association is now under consideration by the civic organizations of Chicago.

✦

Mayor Landes Defeated for Reëlection.—On March 13 Seattle voters, by a majority of 19,000 in a total vote of 99,000 declined to return Mayor Bertha K. Landes to the chair. Her successful opponent was Mayor-elect Edwards, a dark horse running his first race in the political arena.

The victory of the new mayor by the greatest majority ever given a mayoralty candidate in Seattle comes as a surprise when one considers that every newspaper and many of the leading organizations came out for Mayor Landes. When the votes were in it was found that she had carried only 56 of the city's 295 precincts, nor were her majorities decisive in her own precincts in the university district. Although two years ago Mrs. Landes elected mayor by a very large vote, the fickle public seems now to have concluded that the office can be satisfactorily filled only by a man.

The contest between the two candidates had much of the flavor of an old-fashioned political campaign. Deprived of the support of the newspapers, the mayor-elect on the day before election came out with his own four-page paper. This strategic move seems to have had a great effect on the people. In it he tore into the incumbent's record, answering in strenuous fashion questions she had put to him.

Among the plans of the new mayor is the promotion of the industrial expansion of Seattle. Industrially Tacoma is growing over Seattle, and Edwards has pledged himself to bring new industries and a larger payroll to the city.

GRANVYL G. HULSE.

✦

Death of Dr. Wilcox.—The death of Delos F. Wilcox on April 4 at the age of fifty-five, leaves a wound hard to heal in the liberal ranks and in the hearts of his many friends. He combined an infectious, whole-souled geniality with keen, scholarly, intellectual ability and indefatigable zeal. Successively a critical student of city government and an authority on public utilities, he stood for the traditional American democratic ideal in its more lovely forms, and championed vigorously the doctrine of municipal self-help in public services—public ownership both as

an economic benefit and as an aid to political well-being.

Born on a Michigan farm and trained at the University of Michigan, he took his Ph.D. in administrative law at Columbia, engaged in civic secretarial work in Grand Rapids, Cleveland and Detroit, and was called to New York in the early days of the Public Service Commission to be Chief of the Bureau of Franchises. After a brief period of private practice as a public utility expert he became Deputy Commissioner of Water Supply, Gas and Electricity in 1914 under Mayor Mitchel, after whose administration he resumed practice as a consultant, serving many cities throughout the land and acting as adviser to the Federal Electric Railways Commission appointed by President Wilson. In 1922 he moved from New York to Grand Rapids, Mich.

He was a writer of distinction, on matters of government and utilities, his larger works in the latter field being Municipal Franchises (2 volumes, 1910 and 1911), The Electric Railway Problem (1921), and his two-volume revision of Whitten's Valuation of Public Service Corporations just published.

H. M. OLMSTED.

✦

Progress towards City Manager Adoptions.—A definite proposal that San Francisco adopt the city manager form of government has been submitted to the board of supervisors of that city by William H. Nanry, director of the San Francisco Bureau of Governmental Research.

Due to the activity of Gadsden, Ala., the state legislature in 1927 passed an optional city manager charter bill applicable to cities of 10,000 to 15,000 population. On March 20 the people of Gadsden adopted the plan, effective October first. This is the first municipality in Alabama to accept manager government. The act is also applicable to Florence and Tuscaloosa.

New Rochelle, N. Y., has begun a determined drive for a city manager charter. In March the city council adopted a unanimous resolution establishing a commission to draft a new charter for submission to the voters. A majority of the members of the commission are committed to the manager system. Edward A. Seidman is chairman of the committee. A prominent member is Ernest S. Bradford, who is well known to RE-VIEW readers as author of the book *Commission Government in American Cities*. Mr. Bradford favors the manager form for New Rochelle.

Under an optional act passed by the recent

session of the Kentucky legislature, second class cities of the state are authorized to adopt the city manager form of government. Lexington will probably be the first city to avail itself of the new privilege.

Readers desiring a concise statement of the arguments for and against the manager plan will be interested in Report No. 99 of the Detroit Bureau of Governmental Research. It is entitled "Arguments For and Against the City Manager Plan for Detroit," and was submitted at the request of the Detroit Board of Commerce.

Two additional Wisconsin cities, namely, Beloit and Stevens Point, have adopted the city manager plan. This makes six cities in Wisconsin that are operating or soon will be operating under the manager plan.

✦

Cleveland Charter Election.—The result of the Cleveland election upon abandoning the City Manager-P. R. charter will be known before this number of the REVIEW appears in print. During the campaign the Citizens' League pointed out certain defects in the Davis charter. Irrespective of the undesirability of destroying the present city manager government, the alternative proposal contains unwise features which would vitiate any charter. For example, the Citizens' League points out, the Davis document would practically disfranchise one-half the voters

by giving double representation to the down-town, populous wards. Furthermore, it would give the mayor practically dictatorial authority over administration. Contracts could be made without competitive bids and could be altered by the heads of departments after improvements had been started. Other defects include the omission of all provisions for an outside audit of the city's accounts, failure to guarantee to citizens the right to appear before council, neglect to prohibit council members from personally interfering in appointments in the administrative departments and failure to require administrative officers to resign their posts upon becoming candidates for office. The League also called attention to the defective recall provisions in the Davis draft.

Early in April the city council voted that its investigation into fraudulent signatures on Davis petitions cease and that a transcript of all evidence before the council committee be transmitted to the county prosecutor for appropriate action. The prosecutor has announced that he will begin the investigation and present to the grand jury any evidence of fraud or perjury which he may find. This move was interpreted by some as an effort to pass the buck from the council to the prosecutor. Until the time of going to press no results of the prosecutor's investigation have been announced.

STATEMENT OF THE OWNERSHIP, MANAGEMENT, CIRCULATION, ETC.,
Required by the Act of Congress of August 24, 1912,
Of NATIONAL MUNICIPAL REVIEW, published monthly at Concord, New Hampshire, for April 1, 1928.
STATE OF NEW YORK, COUNTY OF NEW YORK, SS.
Before me, a notary public, in and for the State and county aforesaid, personally appeared H. W. Dodds, who, having been duly sworn according to law, deposes and says that he is the editor of the NATIONAL MUNICIPAL REVIEW and that the following is, to the best of his knowledge and belief, a true statement of the ownership, management (and if a daily paper, the circulation), etc., of the aforesaid publication for the date shown in the above caption, required by the Act of August 24, 1912, embodied in section 411, Postal Laws and Regulations, printed on the reverse of this form, to wit:
1. That the names and addresses of the publisher, editor, managing editor, and business managers are:
Publisher, National Municipal League, 261 Broadway, New York.
Editor, H. W. Dodds, 261 Broadway, New York.
Managing Editor, None
Business Managers, None.
2. That the owner is: The National Municipal Review is published by the National Municipal League, a voluntary association incorporated, 1923. The officers of the National Municipal League are Richard S. Childs, President; Carl H. Pforzheimer, Treasurer; H. W. Dodds, Secretary.
3. That the known bondholders, mortgagees, and other security holders owning or holding 1 per cent or more of total amount of bonds, mortgages, or other securities are: None.
4. That the two paragraphs next above, giving the names of the owners, stockholders, and security holders, if any, contain not only the list of stockholders and security holders as they appear upon the books of the company but also, in cases where the stockholder or security holder appears upon the books of the company as trustee or in any other fiduciary relation, the name of the person or corporation for whom such trustee is acting, is given; also that the said two paragraphs contain statements embracing affiant's full knowledge and belief as to the circumstances and conditions under which stockholders and security holders who do not appear upon the books of the company as trustees, hold stock and securities in a capacity other than that of a bona fide owner; and this affiant has no reason to believe that any other person, association, or corporation has any interest direct or indirect in the said stock, bonds, or other securities than as so stated by him.

                                                                        H. W. DODDS,
                                                                             Editor.

Sworn to and subscribed before me this 21st day of April 1928.
[SEAL.]
                                                                   MICHAEL GILLER,
                                                                        Notary Public.
                                             My commission expires, March 30, 1930.

NATIONAL
MUNICIPAL REVIEW

PUBLISHED MONTHLY BY THE

National Municipal League

VOL. XVII, No. 6   JUNE, 1928   TOTAL No. 144

CONTENTS

EDITORIAL COMMENT.............................*H. W. Dodds* 313

OUR AMERICAN MAYORS:
    X. MAYOR OSCAR F. HOLCOMBE OF HOUSTON ...*Frank M. Stewart* . 317

TAX RELIEF FOR ELECTRIC STREET RAILWAYS........*M. C. Waltersdorf.* 321

VOTELESS WASHINGTON EXPRESSES ITSELF.........*George C. Havenner* 326

THE BONDED DEBT OF 213 CITIES AS AT JANUARY 1,
    1928..*C. E. Rightor*..... 328

ELECTRICITY IN GREAT BRITAIN—A STUDY IN ADMIN-
    ISTRATION — A SUPPLEMENT.................*Orren C. Hormell..* 363

DEPARTMENTS

  I. Recent Books Reviewed.. 340
 II. Judicial Decisions.....................................*Edited by C. W. Tooke* 344
III. Public Utilities...*Edited by John Bauer* 348
IV. Governmental Research Association Notes.................*Edited by Russell Forbes* 352
 V. Notes and Events.....................................*Edited by H. W. Dodds* 357

THE LEAGUE'S BUSINESS

A New Secretary for the National Municipal League.—Acting under the power conferred upon it by the council at its meeting of February 3 the executive committee has accepted the resignation of the present secretary to take effect July 1 and has named in his stead Russell Forbes, at present director of the Municipal Administration Service. The writer will continue the editorship of the NATIONAL MUNICIPAL REVIEW. The administration of the League will be in the hands of Mr. Forbes who will also give supervisory attention to the Municipal Administration Service which he has so successfully started on its way.

Since the report of the Survey Committee of 1918, it has been recognized that the League performs two distinct types of work. One relates to the strictly executive duties such as organizing and directing the working committees, planning and conducting the annual convention, carrying on a wide correspondence and in general looking after the educational and propaganda activities. The task of maintaining a voluntary association such as the League, dependent upon dues and contributions, is in itself properly a full time job. On the other hand there is the function of editing the NATIONAL MUNICIPAL REVIEW and the League's Monograph Series. Since the REVIEW became a monthly magazine its demands upon the time of the editor have been very heavy. If it is to expand in influence it is indispensable that more effort be devoted to it.

If the present secretary and editor, who will soon be solely editor, may be permitted a personal word it is his deep feeling of appreciation for the opportunity to act in the combined capacity for a little more than eight years. For him they have been fertile years of growth. They have been happy years illuminated by repeated evidences of the fidelity of the League members to its cause. To such friends of the League, who have so freely contributed their labor and money, must be credited the consistent expansion in budget and work which has taken place. For the opportunity of their friendship the retiring secretary will always be grateful. He has felt for the past two or three years, however, that further growth involved the division of labor above outlined. His continuance as editor will be on a part-time basis but will not involve any severance of his interest in or contact with League matters.

Mr. Forbes, who takes up the executive work, is exceptionally well fitted for it. Following some experience in chamber of commerce work after graduation from college, he completed the course of the Training School for Public Service of the National Institute of Public Administration. He then became associated with the National Association of Purchasing Agents in charge of the field of government purchasing, resigning in 1926 to become director of the Municipal Administration Service. For two years he has been a lecturer in municipal government at New York University and his book on governmental purchasing will appear in the fall.

H. W. DODDS.

NATIONAL
MUNICIPAL REVIEW

Vol. XVII, No. 6   JUNE, 1928   Total No. 144

EDITORIAL COMMENT

A traffic semaphore operated by the sound waves emitted by an automobile horn approaching street intersections has been pronounced a success by the head of the Baltimore traffic police, according to a recent number of the *Nation's Traffic.*

✤

The second attack launched by Harry L. Davis against the city manager-proportional representation charter of Cleveland was defeated in the election of April 24 by a vote of 44,122 to 40,890. To the Cleveland League of Women Voters must go much of the credit for the victory. A longer account of the campaign will be found in the Notes and Events Department of this issue.

✤

C. E. Ridley reviews in this issue three more city reports. It is his plan to continue this practice, considering briefly each month a few of the better reports. At the end of the year they will all be rated in a longer treatment after the manner of his article in the March Review. Mr. Ridley will be glad to rate confidentially, in accordance with the scale used in the March article, any report submitted to him.

✤

Readers who became interested in the personality of Mayor Lawrence C. Hodgson, through the article by George N. Briggs in the April Review, will be pleased or disappointed, as the case may be, to learn that last month he was reëlected mayor of St. Paul for the fourth term. He obtained the largest plurality ever given a St. Paul mayoralty candidate, defeating two other candidates and obtaining a majority of all votes cast.

✤

It is with the deepest regret that we announce the sudden death of Dr. D. F. Garland from pneumonia. At the time of his death Dr. Garland was president of the Dayton Foundation and of the Dayton Research Association, of which he was one of the founders. As much as any other single person he was responsible for the adoption of the city manager plan in Dayton. For several years he had been serving as director of welfare for the National Cash Register Co. at Dayton. He was a former officer of the League. His death marks the passing of a valiant citizen who was, heart and soul, an ardent supporter of the municipal research movement as a method of municipal progress.

✤

Fred H. Locke, city manager of Grand Rapids, reports a gratifying decrease in fire losses in his city for the past five years. In 1923 and 1924 the losses exceeded a million dollars. In

1925 they dropped to $815,000 and in 1926 to $312,000. In 1927 they reached the low level of $290,000.

Since 1924 the city has conducted a continuous fire prevention campaign. In this the local Safety Council, the Association of Commerce, and many business institutions and organizations throughout the city have coöperated. The firemen inspect every home in the city twice a year and many business houses are visited for inspection twice each week. Particular emphasis has been placed upon the education of the school children in fire prevention activities in the home.

❋

Per capita expenditures for health and charities increased from three dollars in 1916 to $5.79 in 1926, in cities of 30,000 population or over, according to a bulletin of the census bureau. Although the per capita cost has increased, the per cent of total payments for expenses of general departments on account of health and charities decreased from 16.1 in 1916 to 14.8 in 1926. Wide variation exists between the larger and the smaller cities with respect to expenditures for these services. In cities of 500,000 and over, the per capita payments for health, sanitation, charities and hospitals in 1926 totaled $7.65; but for cities of 30,000 to 50,000 the average was but $3.42.

❋

City Manager Sherrill of Cincinnati has devised a yellow card with the following friendly greeting to be attached to automobiles bearing out of town licenses:

WELCOME STRANGERS:

The City of Cincinnati cordially invites you to enjoy its hospitality. This card placed in the corner of your windshield will insure you exceptional courtesy from all city officials and from the public. .

The card also carries a brief summary of traffic rules and a small street map of the city. The card does not of course extend to the stranger the privilege of violating traffic regulations. It does mean, however, that he will receive unusual courtesy if at any time he ignorantly violates a traffic ordinance. In a majority of cases he will not be cited if the offense does not appear to have been willful.

❋

Wichita, Kan., has undertaken an experiment which has rarely been attempted in the United States, but which has become the customary practice abroad. It has appointed O. W. Wilson of Los Angeles to the position of chief of police. Mr. Wilson, who is twenty-eight years old, is a graduate of the University of California where he specialized in sociology, economics and criminology. For four years he was a member of the police force of Berkeley where he served under Chief Vollmer, who is recognized as one of the most able police executives in the United States. Indeed Mr. Wilson walked a beat while he was still a student at the university.

In past years Wichita has enjoyed a succession of police chiefs. All were men who had come up from the ranks, possessing, generally, very little education and with nothing other than their experience to recommend them to the job. It will be interesting to note how a young college man trained specifically for police work will compare with the usual type of chiefs of police.

❋

New York Faces 7-Cent Fare The subway fare controversy now taking place between the City of New York and the Interborough Rapid Transit raises a new legal problem in which other municipalities will be interested. On May 2 a federal statutory court declared that the contract between the city (which built the subways) and the company by which the fare was never to exceed five cents was invalid so far as the rate of fare was concerned. By an act of 1907 the legislature created a public service commission with power to fix reasonable rates, and in the absence of specific legislation to the contrary, the 1913 contract between the city and the I.R.T. is qualified by the rate. making power of the state commission. At this writing the Supreme Court is listening to arguments to decide whether the order for the seven-cent fare is to go into effect at once or is to wait further consideration by the courts. A full discussion of the present situation will be found in the Public Utilities Department of this issue. The B. M. T. lines are not involved. To them the 5-cent fare appears satisfactory and they will continue at the old rate.

✱

A New Offense Interference with
Against Public radio receiving sets,
Welfare it would seem, is
.about to be added to the catalog of crimes and misdemeanors. At least the Iowa League of Municipalities has received many requests for information as to an ordinance prohibiting such interference, and has accordingly drafted a model ordinance which was recently published in *American Municipalities*. By the terms of the ordinance it becomes unlawful to operate any electrical or other apparatus that "causes reasonably preventable electrical interference with any other electrical apparatus including radio receiving sets. . . ." Specifically is it forbidden to use any violet ray machine, x-ray machine, electrical vibrator or other apparatus or instrument causing electrical interference with radio receiving sets between the hours of 6 and 11 o'clock P. M. An exception is made in the case

of x-ray pictures necessary for physical examinations in emergency cases. The Iowa League believes that the power to adopt such an ordinance accrues under the general police power and the welfare clause embodied in section 5714 of the State Code.

According to newspaper reports similar ordinances have been adopted in a number of municipalities. Whether they will be sustained by the courts is open to question.

✱

More About Special On page 196 of the
Assessments in REVIEW for April we
Washington referred to the practice in Washington by which property owners have been able to escape entirely the payment of special assessments against their property. The trick has been to let the county take the property for general taxes, which wipes out the assessment lien, and later to buy it back free of the improvement obligation. Several years ago the supreme court of Washington held that when a county sells land bid in at a tax sale it sells it free from the obligation to pay special assessments standing against it.

Professor Tooke points out in his department of Judicial Decisions in this issue that in the case of *City of Tacoma* v. *Fletcher Realty Company*, the supreme court of Washington on March 5 ruled that under the statute of the state the private purchaser at a foreclosure sale for general taxes takes the property free from the lien for special assessments. It is no longer necessary for the county to be a party to a conspiracy to evade the payment of special assessments inasmuch as such evasion can now be accomplished directly.

Professor Tooke raises the question whether such practices do not impair the obligation of contracts. "The power of the state," he writes, "to take away rights of the bond holder by the exercise of the paramount power of taxation raises the question of a conflict between two primary governmental principles."

✦

Do Cities Need Two Mayors? The social graces of New York's present mayor are known from coast to coast. People like him but many believe that he doesn't attend to business. Yet if reëlection is the test of a mayor's success perhaps the animated and debonair Jimmie is more sagacious than his critics. In this case the following are words of wisdom. We clip them from the *New York World:*

It was never more evident than it is today that what New York needs is two mayors, a working mayor and a playing mayor, a day mayor and a night mayor, a competent mayor and a charming mayor, a cerebrating mayor and a celebrating mayor, a mayor for responsibilities and a mayor for repartee, a mayor to stay home and a mayor to go abroad, a back-office mayor and a front-office mayor, a wise mayor and a witty one, a just man and a jester; in brief, somebody to govern the city and our Jimmie to entertain us. New York obviously cannot get along without our Jimmie, and yet in all truth it does need a mayor. We propose, therefore, quite seriously, that the charter of New York be amended, that we create the post of honorary mayor and elect Jimmie for life, and that we then create the post of acting mayor or city manager and elect somebody who can do the job.

✦

Is the Small Electric Plant Doomed? Almost every day witnesses a small electric plant absorbed by a large system on grounds of economy and expected advantages to consumers. Disappointment by the latter, however, is also frequent. Why?

The answer depends upon circumstances. But the reasons are likely to be twofold: First, the price paid for the local property is usually excessive; there is competitive bidding among utility groups, and the purchase price is often beyond the "fair value" of the property. In the second place, when a property has been acquired, overeagerness to make all possible profit from the purchase is apt to take control of the new management. Changes are likely to be emphasized; reconstruction of the plant will be necessary, to be followed by a revaluation upon "reproduction cost" basis.

When the cycle of adjustment after purchase has been completed, the consumer is likely to find his rates increased although the consolidation promised greater efficiency of operation. Any decrease is usually long delayed. The economies are absorbed to support the excessive purchase price, the management expense, the new investment, and the revaluation on a high basis. Under such circumstances, the consumers are better off under an independent property at low production efficiency.

The Maryland commission has taken an affirmative position in respect to such consolidations by refusing recently to approve the purchase of a property because it appeared detrimental to the public. In such cases this is a proper position for all commissions. Normally, their attitude is passive. They permit consolidations which are obviously unsound and are certain to nullify any benefits to the consumers, except possibly after a long time.

All proposed consolidations should be carefully scanned as to price, prospective operation, and the effect upon the consumers. Every community should be assured that it will share in the anticipated economies before the local property is passed over to outside control.

J. B.

OUR AMERICAN MAYORS

X. MAYOR OSCAR F. HOLCOMBE OF HOUSTON

BY FRANK M. STEWART

University of Texas

First elected at the age of thirty-two and thrice reëlected, Mayor Holcombe represents a type too rare in municipal politics. :: ::

HOUSTON has been called "the city that fooled the geographers," for, though inland, it is a port. A deep water ship channel connects it with the Gulf and eighteen railroads join it with the interior. The city is the second largest cotton export market in the United States and the largest inland cotton market in the world. Every decennial census since 1860 has found the population nearly doubled. In 1920 Houston had a population of 138,276, and according to an unofficial estimate it now has about 250,000 inhabitants.

Since 1905 Houston has had commission government, being the second city in the United States to adopt that form of government. Its type of commission government differs from the ordinary form in respect to the powers that are given to the mayor. Altogether, his position is much like that of the mayor in the strong mayor-council type of municipal government. He appoints, subject to confirmation by the council, the heads of administrative departments, and has the power to remove them with or without the concurrence of the council. He has the veto power over the acts of the council, and has also the item veto of appropriation acts. He prepares and submits to the council the annual budget. His salary is $7,500 a year as contrasted with the alderman's salary of $3,600 a year. By the charter he is designated

MAYOR HOLCOMBE

as the "chief executive and administrative officer of the city." The charter of Houston makes provision for the initiative, referendum and recall, the merit system, and the preferential ballot in primary elections.

Under commission government Houston has fared well. The dominant political party is Democratic: hence the results of the primary are decisive. There have been no bosses and no

317

conspicuous machines. The mayors have been respectable, conservative citizens. Under the administrations of Mayor Ben Campbell, 1913–1917, an extensive program of improvements was undertaken. Because of the war, the improvement program was stopped, the resources of the city being diverted to needed war work. The two years following the war saw the city slowly recovering from the depression in building. At the beginning of 1921 Houston was ready for an era of tremendous expansion and was looking for a leader who could plan and direct a comprehensive building program.

THE MAYOR, A YOUNG UNKNOWN

Into this situation came Oscar F. Holcombe, at that time almost unknown to Houston. He was a young man, only thirty-two years old, whose previous years had been spent in strenuous and successful efforts to "get on" in the world, with no thought of political ambitions. He was a self-made man. When he was three years old, the family had moved from Alabama to San Antonio, Texas, in search of health for the father, a lawyer. The move was only partly successful, for after eight years of invalidism, when Holcombe was eleven years old, the father died, leaving an impoverished family. Young Oscar, who had already been working out of school hours for four years, now had to set to work even harder to help support his mother and younger brother by selling newspapers, acting as cash-boy in vacation periods, and filling such other jobs as he could get. In 1904, at the age of fifteen, he decided to quit school and go to Houston, where he could receive better pay. Here he lost no time climbing the ladder of success. At fifteen he was a floor-sweeper in a planing mill; at twenty, he was assistant manager. All the while he was

studying English and mathematics at night and giving extra hours to the mill work. When he decided to enter the race for mayor, he estimated that his income was about $30,000 a year, so that he had been remarkably successful in a short period of time and in spite of great handicaps.

It is hard to say what did influence Holcombe in his decision to enter the race for mayor, because he made his decision independently. Perhaps the fact that overcrowded school buildings were a problem then, had something to do with his decision, for he had specialized in the construction of school buildings. Perhaps it was the fact that, as a natural builder, he saw the great possibilities ahead for Houston and wished to have his part in the development. At any rate, he himself made the decision. He belonged to not a single club or organization of any sort except the Baptist church. There was no considerable group of supporters except possibly those in the ranks of union labor, for, while he himself never carried a union card, he had always employed union labor in his construction work. He succeeded in "selling" his cause to only one of the three daily papers of the city, the Houston *Press*.

In contrast, his four opponents were men of more established connections. One had been county commissioner and was in addition supported by the Ku Klux Klan; another had been in the business office of a newspaper and had the support of that newspaper; a third was the head of a chain of bakeries; and the fourth had been public service commissioner and head of the legal department under the outgoing administration. All were respected citizens and capable men.

Holcombe's campaign promises were: a business administration, reorganization of the city departments, paving, new school buildings, and the like. His opponents claimed that he promised too much, that he was too young and inexperienced, and that he was merely a newspaper candidate, while he accused his opponents of first promising nothing and then later getting their ideas from him. The campaign was conducted rather quietly, for Holcombe was not the speaker then that he is now. Personal solicitation took the place of speeches to some extent. For instance, he and his campaign workers would get up at four o'clock in the morning to ride with the workmen on their way to work, and in the afternoon they would mingle with them as they returned home. He tried, as he has always tried, to wage a clean campaign free from personalities and based on principles and the fitness of the candidates. He made speeches occasionally, but not often. Nevertheless, his campaign was sufficiently effective and far-reaching, for in the primary of February 9, 1921, he was nominated by a small majority.

Mayor Holcombe prides himself on never having failed to keep a campaign promise. Apparently, the people of Houston feel that he has kept his promises, for he is now serving his fourth two-year term as mayor. At any rate, Houston has grown tremendously during the period, almost doubling in population and building at a phenomenal rate. Much credit, no doubt, is due Holcombe for the proper steering of the building and development. He has realized the value of a city plan and of city planning in general. His have been business administrations, with regard for efficiency and the merit principle, though in the rapid expansion that has come he has not been without the accusation of extravagance.

K. K. K. ANTAGONISTIC

Although in all of his campaigns except the first, Holcombe has had the support of every newspaper in the city, of the president of every bank, of the president of the Open Shop Association, of the president of the Labor Temple, and of the business agent of every labor organization, yet his primaries have not been "walk-offs." He has had his enemies, and there have been serious charges against him. In the campaign of 1922, the Ku Klux Klan, which had control of the Harris County government, strongly opposed him. He had himself been a member of the Klan before his first campaign, but had withdrawn his membership almost immediately. The Klan had offered not to oppose him if he would remove three Catholics in responsible city positions. He refused, and the result was a dramatic campaign. The Klan charged Holcombe with gambling, naming the place and the date. Holcombe's answer was to demand a trial before the deacons of his church. They announced, after a hearing, that the charges were untrue. Opposition speakers insinuated a "whitewash." Then Holcombe requested the Baptist Pastors' Conference of the city to hear the evidence, and the mayor met his accusers face to face before a committee of fifteen ministers. The trial lasted one day and, at the conclusion, the pastors gave out a statement that the evidence failed utterly to sustain the charges.

Still another effort was made by the Klan to discredit the administration. The chief of police was a Klansman. There were rumors that he was helping the opposition by claiming that the mayor had hindered him in the performance of his duty in enforcing the laws. Called into the mayor's office, he emphatically denied that he had been so hindered. Two days later, just as the mayor was preparing to make a speech before a large group, the chief handed the mayor his resignation and gave out a statement that the mayor had not coöperated with him in the performance of his duty as chief of police and that the city was infested with crooks and bootleggers. When the mayor confronted him with a dictaphone record of his prior conversation in his office, he failed to press his charges.

At the close of a campaign of slander and vilification Holcombe was renominated over his Klan opponent by over 1,200 majority, carrying every ward except one.

The campaign of 1924 was not remarkable, the Klan having disintegrated after its defeat in 1922, and there being no conspicuous issues. There was a Klan candidate and one other, but Holcombe was reëlected on his record, defeating his two opponents by a four to one vote.

1926 CAMPAIGN RICH IN CHARGES

In 1926, however, the campaign developed considerable bitterness. Holcombe was charged with letting contracts for public works, notably the city auditorium, without competitive bidding; with allowing city employees to circulate pledge cards while on duty and making them sign cards pledging their votes for him; with waste by overpayment on public buildings; with loss of the gas company's bond; with "white graft" in the form of real estate speculations in which he was able to profit very greatly because of inside knowledge and power; with forming a huge and dangerous political machine; and with traveling excessively at the city's expense. As a rule, Holcombe has ignored the charges of his opponents, taking notice of them only when absolutely necessary and relying on his record to speak for him. However, in this campaign he felt obliged to answer the charges in regard to "white graft" and traveling. He made a statement listing all of his real estate transactions since the date of his becoming mayor, and thereafter ignored the charge. His supporters insisted that he had done nothing legally wrong in his real estate dealings, but regretted that he had allowed himself to be put in a vulnerable position. In answer to the charge of excessive traveling, he said that he had traveled on the city's money only when on business for the city, and that the city had profited as much by his travels as he, his trip to England, for instance, having secured for Houston the convention of the Associated Advertising Clubs of the World. In this campaign the mayor asked his supporters to vote only first choices or "single-shots" under the preferential ballot, alleging that two of his opponents had formed a combination to defeat him on second and third choice votes. The results of the primary gave Holcombe a majority of over 2,600 on first choice votes over his three opponents.

MAYOR'S ENTHUSIASM HELPS CITY'S GROWTH

The major accomplishments of Mayor Holcombe's administrations have been in material construction; his public improvement program has come nearer to keeping pace with the needs of the city, say his friends, than that of any other administration in recent times. Under his administrations the city has experienced its greatest growth. Holcombe does not claim the credit for this, but his friends contend that he has put enthusiasm into the administration of a growing city as no other mayor has done. Space will not permit enumeration of the individual items in the record. Aside from the more usual though by no means unimportant improvements such as paving, sewers, park sites, drainage, traffic signal systems, motorized fire departments, and the like, certain changes have been especially marked. One of these is the creation of a port district. Financial support of the port had for many years been a burden borne by the city alone. Mayor Holcombe originated and had created by the legislature in 1921 the Navigation District, which includes all of Harris County. Under this plan the financial responsibility, including the issuance of bonds, is distributed upon an equalized basis. Another marked change is the large number of public buildings that have been built, among them an auditorium, a new main library building, and several branch libraries. Land has been acquired on which to build a farmers' market to cost $350,000. The site for a civic center has been secured, and plans for a new city hall to cost over $1,000,000 are being drawn. Within the administration there have been changes also. New municipal offices created include that of city manager, who has charge of city purchasing, the municipal store, the city market house, and the auditorium; that of public service commissioner as a separate office; and the restoration of the department of architecture. A city planning commission was appointed in 1922.

These facts indicate the principal characteristic of the mayor—a builder. He seems to have the faculty of getting big things done in a big way. Personally, he is a fine-looking, mild-mannered, likeable executive, a hard worker, with excellent grasp of administrative method and detail and an ability to manage people and situations. He has been able to inspire coöperation from the heads of his departments, and his relations with the council have, with few exceptions, been entirely harmonious. In campaigns he is a clear and effective speaker, though by no means a crusader or an orator, emphasizing principles and issues and ignoring personalities. His patience, calmness, and poise when under fire have attracted commendation. That he has made mistakes even his strongest supporters admit. He himself admits them. But he has been elected four times, and he has the support of all the newspapers and of both capital and labor. Houston wants and needs a builder, and in Oscar Holcombe it seems to have found the man.

TAX RELIEF FOR ELECTRIC STREET RAILWAYS

BY M. C. WALTERSDORF

Washington and Jefferson College

Street railways, writes the author, should be relieved of all unjust taxes which in any case are ultimately borne by the rider.   ::   ::   ::

THE same basis of taxation of real and personal property is applied to public utilities as to other industries, except that special kinds of property owned by these companies may actually be assessed at unusually high rates, because such property cannot readily escape taxation. Some other types of property which do not require extensive special investment can be transferred from one taxing jurisdiction to another. Street railways and other utilities render a service that is essential to the public, and such service cannot be suspended without the approval of the public authorities. Such approval is rarely, if ever, granted because of excessive taxation.

Ordinarily street railways and other utilities are also subject to business licenses, income taxes, capital stock taxes, and imposts similar to the business corporations. Occasionally electric railways are also required to pay special taxes on cars, poles, wires, and mileage of tracks. Frequently a franchise tax is also imposed, either in addition to or in place of some of the taxes already mentioned. Under this tax the franchise may be given a designated value taxable at the prevailing rate for personal property, or its value may be fixed by a process of capitalization of the net earnings; or of net income in excess of certain assumed rates. Under regulation the profits derived from such franchises are limited to those generally obtainable in other business with similar risks. The opportunity, therefore, to carry on the business which the franchise authorizes has no special value and should not be taxed.

SPECIAL ELECTRIC RAILWAY TAXES

In addition to these special taxes electric railways are usually subject to other imposts and burdens of a still more specialized character. They include payment for and maintenance of paving in connection with railway trackage, removal of snow, street cleaning and sprinkling, contributions toward the maintenance of traffic officers, and street lighting. Free transportation may also be required for policemen, firemen, and sometimes for other city employees not in uniform. Occasionally, too, mail carriers are carried free of charge. The extent of these special taxes usually varies with the respective trading abilities of the railways and municipal officers who conduct the

franchise negotiations. At times municipal officers go to the extreme in embodying special requirements in franchises covering electric railways. This has been particularly typical of the street paving requirements.

STREET PAVING

The matter of paving requirements is primarily important and involves such a peculiar misunderstanding on the part of the public that further consideration is justifiable. Since horses ceased to supply the motive power for urban transportation, and regulation came into effect, paving charges often have imposed an unjust burden on this type of transportation. Usually city officials refuse to take the steps necessary to relieve these utilities from the requirements of the long-time franchises granted them years ago when the horses, propelling the cars, actually used the streets, thus causing more rapid wear and tear. Apparently the general public has not yet fully grasped the significance of regulation, and still adheres to the old idea that the street railway business is inherently profitable, and that any burden imposed upon this industry which tends to reduce general taxation is to that extent a relief to all citizens.

In some cases these paving requirements have been continued on the theory that the franchise right granted by the municipality enabled the company to earn large returns, and that the city merely relieved itself of certain expenses in return for the privilege granted the railway company. Under regulation no such value is given franchise rights. Carriers are limited to a fair return, but are permitted to capitalize the cost of paving, to earn a fair return thereon, and to set aside out of gross revenues, an amount sufficient for maintenance and ultimately for replacing the pavement. Under this practice the electric railways are allowed to include an expense in their charge for service which otherwise would be borne by the adjacent property owners or by the municipality itself. The property owners not only are likely to benefit from such paving but also the "jitneys" which freely use the streets and in turn deprive the railway companies of revenue.

Public officials naturally hesitate to espouse the claims of a local railway company for relief even when such relief would benefit its customers. Eventually, no doubt, there will be a general public recognition of the conditions surrounding the service furnished by these utilities. When that time comes the leaders who have persistently adhered to obsolete issues will be compelled to give way to the more progressive and farsighted leaders who perceive the real interests of the public. The electric railways recognize the need of popular education pertaining to the economic issues of their business. Recently they have resorted to a widespread program of education and enlightenment through the medium of newspapers and articles, particularly with respect to the paving situation.

ANALYSIS OF RAILWAY TAXES

In 1920 the President of the United States appointed the Federal Electric Railways Commission for the purpose of investigating and reporting on the condition of the electric railways. This commission held extensive hearings and examined witnesses representing the industries, the public, and other interested parties. It was the consensus of opinion of nearly all the witnesses examined that franchise taxes, paving costs, and other similar charges were unjust burdens imposed upon car riders and should be abolished. The commission itself concluded that . . . "special assessments for sprin-

kling, paving, and for the construction and maintenance of bridges which are used by the public for highway purposes," should be eliminated.[1]

A special committee of the American Electric Railway Association was also appointed to investigate electric railway taxation and report to the Association. The data which this committee obtained covering the year 1922 show that the electric railways of the United States pay approximately $100,000,000 in taxes, or about 10 per cent of their total revenue.[2] About two-thirds of the taxes paid by electric railways are derived from property and income and are similar to those paid by other corporations, while the remaining one-third are franchise, earning, and other taxes of a special nature. It, therefore, appears that special taxes comprise a rather large proportion of the total combined taxes paid by electric railways, and are in excess of those paid by the ordinary business corporation. The taxes levied upon the resources of the electric railways in recent unfavorable years have been burdensome. In 1922 these companies in New York State paid 45 per cent of their net income in taxes.[3] In Virginia the tax amounted to nearly 40 per cent.[4] The electric railways have been subjected to more extensive special taxes than any of the other classes of public utilities.

SHIFTING OF UTILITY TAXES

Apparently the public does not appreciate the fact that public utilities merely serve as collectors of taxes. Special or discriminatory taxes levied upon electric railways or other utilities are shifted to the customers of the

[1] Proc., Vol. III, Sec. I, II, IX, p. 2263.

[2] Proc. Am. Elec. Ry. Assn., 1923, p. 200.

[3] Davenport F. M., "The Taxation Problem," *Aera*, March, 1923, p. 911.

[4] Forward, A., "Taxation in Virginia," *Aera*, March, 1923, p. 920.

service. Utility taxes are not paid by
the utility owners, but rather by the
patrons. The car rider of moderate
means helps to pay for the paving of
streets which his more prosperous
neighbor uses with his automobile.
The rapid increase in the number of
automobiles has further led to such
traffic congestion of the streets as to
slow down the transportation speed,
thus tending to increase the cost of
electric railway service which the .car
riders must support. The patron of
the traction company not only pays for
the cost of his transportation, but he is
required to contribute an additional
sum to pave and keep in repair portions
of the streets which are largely used by
those who generally employ other
means of conveyance. Students of
this subject do not contend that electric
railways should be relieved of the entire
cost of street paving, because certain of
the costs are peculiar to street railway
construction, and are properly chargeable to these companies as are also
certain of the maintenance expenses.
In too many instances, however, a disproportionate part of the total paving
expense is placed upon the company
which, consequently, is shifted to the
patron of the railway service.

Frequently it is assumed that car
riders actually do not pay for this
expense, and, therefore, the burden
should not be transferred to the tax
payers. This contention is based on
the idea that such charges are really
paid by the stockholders because of
their willingness to accept a lower rate
of return. Perhaps in some particular
city an electric railway is unable to
charge a fare high enough to cover the
full cost of the service, including paving
charges. Under such circumstances it
would appear that the stockholders and
not the car riders pay for the burden.
However, as a rule when a public
utility earns an inadequate return

through no fault of its own, it naturally
tries to increase its return in every
practicable way. It will perhaps furnish only a minimum amount of service,
it may fail properly to maintain its
equipment, and it also may neglect to
make the necessary extensions and
improvement of its system which the
community growth demands, and
which a more liberal return would
permit. Obviously the car rider does
not escape. The burden imposed upon
him by such an expense has merely
been changed from an excessive fare to
inadequate and unreliable service.

TAX EXEMPTION

Some students of the problem · of
taxation maintain that public utilities
should be exempt from all taxation
because any taxes imposed upon them
are ultimately shifted to their customers. Such a view obviously is not
consistent with modern methods of
utility operation, which assume that all
the necessary cost of rendering the
utility service, but no more, should be
paid by those using it. If all the
utilities, including street railways, were
tax-exempt, this loss of revenue would
necessitate the imposition of a heavier
tax burden upon other taxable property
or agents; and non-users of the utility
service would be burdened with a
charge that should be properly met by
the utility patrons.

Street railways contend that they
should not be required to pay greater
taxes on property which, although
located on the public streets, causes no
more obstruction than other property
or traffic. Free or reduced service,
cleaning, sprinkling, and paving of
streets, and any other such special
service imposes upon these utilities a
tax which is shifted to the users of the
transportation service. Costs of this
character which benefit the public in
general should largely be covered by

general taxation, while those costs which are of a character properly assignable to the electric railway service should not be borne by the taxpayers in general, but rather by those who benefit directly from the service. Street railways should pay all equitable taxes levied upon their property, but should be relieved of such burdens as add nothing to their service and which benefit the public and other agencies of transportation. Since the patron of the utility service in all cases pays the burden, he should be required only to pay for that cost which in equity is directly assignable to the service which he uses.

RELIEF GRANTED THE RAILWAYS

Taxes derived from motor vehicles pay approximately 15 per cent of the construction costs of highways, or about 25 per cent of the current upkeep of the highways, not including construction costs or interest on such accumulated costs. It is assumed that 95 per cent of the present wear and tear of public highways is caused by motor vehicle traffic. The balance of the cost of highway maintenance is provided for through general taxation, to which the electric railways and other utilities contribute. This contribution of the electric railways is in addition to the upkeep of their own trackage.

To offset this burden upon the railways and other utilities, various states since 1921 have increased the taxes upon gasoline used by motor vehicles. A few states have also undertaken to impose more adequately the burden of highway upkeep upon the users thereof through levying high license fees. In some cases these fees for heavy trucks exceed $500 per annum. It was felt that these agencies should not be allowed to operate upon the public highways untrammeled and untaxed in utter disregard of the fundamental construction costs and depreciation for which the public and the street railways are taxed. When the burdens of highway cost and maintenance are fully imposed upon highway users through such taxes and fees, the rates for highway transportation must be increased materially. This will be necessary when these charges are added to the more direct operating expenses. As the charges which are thus imposed upon other carriers of passengers and merchandise are properly increased, the electric railways will be able to compete on a more equitable basis.

VOTELESS WASHINGTON EXPRESSES ITSELF

BY DR. GEORGE C. HAVENNER

Washington, D. C.

The effective work of spontaneous voters' associations in a district in which no one can vote, told by the President of the Anacostia Citizens' Association, an officer of the Federation of Citizens' Associations, and a former member of the Citizens' Advisory Council. :: :: ::

AT the election held in November, 1800, the citizens of the District of Columbia were entitled to vote and cast their ballot for the president and vice-president of the United States. This was the last time that any citizen of the District participated in a national election. However, from 1800 until 1874 some form of local suffrage existed in the District of Columbia. But in 1874 congress abolished all forms of municipal suffrage in the District, thus leaving to its citizens *petition* as the only method of making their wishes known, both to the municipal heads of the District government and to the congress of the United States.

APPEARANCE OF CITIZENS' ASSOCIATIONS

A few years after the abolition of municipal suffrage, or about 1880, the first citizens' association came into being in southeast Washington. Two years later, in 1882, the Anacostia Citizens' Association was organized, and thenceforward citizens' associations were organized throughout the District. The purpose of these earlier associations was to work for community betterment. There was no unity of action between the several associations, each rivaling with the other to see which one could secure the greatest amount of municipal betterments, such

as sewer, water, street lighting, and street paving for the particular territory embraced within its boundaries. City-wide problems were seldom ever considered by these early associations. This condition of affairs continued until about twenty years ago, when the Federation of Citizens' Associations was organized.

THE FEDERATION OF CITIZENS' ASSOCIATIONS

The purpose of the federation was to unify the action of its several constituent bodies and to discuss city-wide problems. I do not know how many bodies were affiliated with it at the time of its organization, but today we have 56 separate citizens' associations, with a membership of about 40,000. Each constituent body is entitled to elect two delegates to the federation. The term of all delegates is one year, but a delegate may be elected year after year for any number of years.

No association of a political, sectarian or purely social nature is eligible for membership in the federation.

In addition to our own federation there is a colored federation known as the Federation of Civic Associations. There are affiliated with this federation some 20 separate bodies with a membership of about 10,000, making the total membership of organized citizenry in the District of Columbia

about 50,000, representing about 40,-
000 homes. The purpose of the colored federation is the same as that of
the white, namely, to coördinate the
work of its several constituent bodies
and to work for city-wide improvements.

ORGANIZATION OF THE CITIZENS' ADVISORY COUNCIL

In 1924 the commissioners of the
District of Columbia suggested to the
Federation of Citizens' Associations
the organization of an advisory council
to which they might refer matters affecting the District of Columbia in
order to get the citizens' viewpoint on
pending legislative matters and other
questions. As a result of this suggestion a Citizens' Advisory Council
was formed consisting of eight elected
members, the president of the Federation of Citizens' Associations becoming
the chairman ex officio of the council.
The council as now constituted consists of nine members, seven white and
two colored.

Each association affiliated with the
two federations has the privilege of
nominating a candidate for election to
the Citizens' Advisory Council. A
candidate for the council need not be
a delegate to either one of the federations. The candidates nominated by
the several constituent bodies of the
two federations are elected by the
delegates to the federations. The
white federation elects six members to
the council, and the colored federation
two members to the council.

Since the creation of the council it
has annually advised with the District
commissioners relative to the budget.
In fact, it has each year made up and
submitted to them a budget of its own.
Two of these budgets went into great
detail covering every item of appropriation, while one recommended totals
only for major divisions of the budget.

Each year the commissioners have
furnished the council with a copy of
the detailed estimates submitted to
them by the various departmental
heads of the municipal government in
order to assist the council in its study
of the budget.

The commissioners have also submitted to the council other matters
for its consideration and advice.

Shortly after the council was organized both the House and Senate
committees on the District of Columbia sent to the council all bills introduced in congress affecting the National Capital for its consideration
and recommendations. This was followed during the last session of congress, and the chairmen of these two
committees are this year again sending
to the council all bills for its study and
recommendation.

In connection with the estimates
for appropriations for the municipal
government of the District of Columbia, members of the Citizens' Advisory Council have each year appeared before the bureau of the budget
and the appropriations committees of
congress.

The council has also submitted with
its budgetary recommendations to the
Commissioners suggestions relative to
legislation that it deemed of importance to the National Capital.

The *Evening Star* in an editorial
under the heading "The Citizens'
Association" in its issue of December
28, 1927, made the following comment
upon the work of the citizens' associations, using as a basis for its editorial
a report by Dr. Edward T. Devine,
professor of social economy at the
American University, upon the results of an inquiry made by the seminar in social economy:

Washington is fortunate in having a battery
of eighty federated citizens' associations to concentrate the fire of its more than half a million

citizens upon public needs, which arouse and promote civic spirit, which give voice to the largest unit of disenfrachised people anywhere in the world. This is the concentrated verdict of noted students of sociology rendered to the American Sociological Society after a carefully directed, intensive and systematic study of the peculiar situation in the National Capital.

The mere fact of citizens discussing together any common need—for instance, sewers, better bus or car service, or the taking off of a sharp corner that makes driving difficult or dangerous—does help to make people think as citizens, and may have the effect of stimulating civic pride, Dr. Edward T. Devine, professor of social economy at the American University, said in making his report to the national society on the results of an inquiry made by the seminar in social economy. Then he emphasized that the Washington plan is clearly superior to any which concentrate on influencing voters and limits its efforts to the brief period of a campaign. The Washington

associations were found to be free from this seasonal periodicity, often sustaining their interest throughout the year.

The seminar refutes the objection frequently raised against citizens' associations in the National Capital by those who question whether the associations are really seeking any ends not clearly recognized also by the District commissioners, the board of education and other official District bodies, and behind them the Federal congress itself, sitting as a local municipal legislature or working through its committees and subcommittees on District affairs. It points out that central authorities, unhampered by local demands, unenlightened by local petitions and protests, might, indeed, from a purely technical point of view, devise and carry forward a more symmetrical and comprehensive program, but they would be working in the dark. They would be without the very stuff in raw material from which a sound program can be made.

THE BONDED DEBT OF 213 CITIES

AS AT JANUARY 1, 1928

BY C. E. RIGHTOR

Chief Accountant, Detroit Bureau of Governmental Research, Inc.

For the first time, special assessment debt against property benefited has been included in Mr. Rightor's annual survey.   ::   ::   ::

THE tabulation presents the total gross bonded indebtedness as at January 1, 1928, of 213 cities in the United States and Canada, and this total is classified as to general public improvements, schools, and utilities; the sinking fund total, and a similar classification reported in percentages only; the net bonded debt; the net bonded debt excluding self-supporting indebtedness, total and per capita; and gross special assessment debt.

The presentation is similar to that of former years. The cities are arranged according to the population estimates of the census bureau as at July 1, 1927. Temporary loans, made largely in an-

ticipation of either a tax levy or bond issue, are omitted as heretofore.

The primary purpose of the table is to indicate the total amount of debt outstanding as a liability of the property of the city. Such indebtedness will include, therefore, bonds issued by the city, and also, because of diversity in municipal organization, in numerous instances bonds issued by the school board having independent fiscal powers. In some states, the county issues school bonds. Frequently also it will be noted that there is an independent board having authority over a large metropolitan district which includes the city, such as sewer, park, forest or other district. Where the boundaries of the city and other districts are coterminous, or nearly so, the debt is included, the notes giving an indication of deviations from this general condition.

It is agreed that a complete presentation of what is sought by this tabulation would require that the city's portion of county debt be included. In the reports of the census bureau, which are more extensive, for fifteen of the cities in groups I and II a portion of the county debt is included with that of the city. This debt is here included only in cases of city-county consolidation, as it would be difficult to ascertain the amount in most cases. Furthermore, the amount of such indebtedness is relatively small. Similarly, a portion of state debt might in theory be included, but no attempt is made to compile it.

Inasmuch as municipally owned and operated utilities ordinarily pay their own way at least to the extent of their debt service, it is desirable to indicate the net debt charges which must be met from the general tax levy, and for this reason there is shown a separate column entitled "net debt excluding self-supporting." The per capita debt reported, accordingly, is for only such portion of the total debt as must be retired ultimately by direct property taxation. It is recognized that even here difficulties arise, as some cities having self-supporting utilities have provided that the utility indebtedness shall be retired from general taxation, and in such cases the utility debt has not been deducted to arrive at the net debt used as a basis for computing the per capita indebtedness.

SPECIAL ASSESSMENT DEBT

The procedure of former years has been deviated from in the case of special assessment debt, which heretofore has been omitted except as to the city's portion. This was on the ground that special assessments are not a city-wide tax, but rather are usually levied against only a limited portion of the city's total valuation. Because special assessments are being utilized more and more to finance certain kinds of governmental functions, however, it seems desirable to indicate the extent of such practice in the several cities. In some instances, special assessment bonds have the faith and credit of the city behind them. The total of such debt is not, however, included in the computing net per capita debt, owing to varying circumstances attending the use of assessments, and to incomplete reports this year.

On the other hand, the aggregate debt burden upon the taxable property of the city is believed to be more accurately reflected when this form of debt is considered. It may be noted, for example, that California cities utilize this means of financing street paving, sewers, water mains, street lighting, storm drains, parks, bridges, etc., whereas many other cities pay for such improvements from taxes or bonds. Los Angeles spends possibly $20,000,000 annually for such local improvements. Kansas City, Mo., also uses special assessments extensively, but as they are not legal obligations of the city, accurate estimate of the total outstanding at any time cannot be made.

A tabulation so condensed naturally has but limited use. In making comparisons full consideration should be given to the detailed facts respecting any city. While but a single purpose is in mind in compiling these data, numerous conditions make the problem a complicated one. State laws commonly set up independent provisions with respect to the kind of debt that shall be included in preparing debt limitation statements of cities. Varying areas of the political subdivisions having power to incur debt, and certain difficulties of classification, are also encountered. It is not always possible to obtain a separation of the sinking fund by purposes, but this is set up in all cases when reported. Attempt is made to present such figures for each city as will result in the most nearly uniform total possible for comparisons.

A statistical summary does not analyze the bonds by purposes or term, thus indicating the wisdom or necessity of issue, nor does it gauge the adequacy of provision for their amortization. It may be noted that the amount of sinking fund as compared with the gross debt is usually relatively small. This may be construed as due to the fact that cities are more and more availing themselves of the issuance of serial bonds, as in the Massachusetts cities. Some notable exceptions, however, are those of the larger cities. Philadelphia, for example, recently decided not to adopt the serial as against the sinking fund type of bonds. In general, serial bonds are growing in popularity over term bonds. Possibly most fortunate are those cities which have adopted a pay-as-you-go plan, as, for example, Chicago, Boston, and Lansing have done in building schools.

RANGE IN NET DEBT

Analysis of the figures of net non self-supporting debt shows that the city having the lowest debt, excluding Washington, which has no debt, is Moline, with a per capita debt of $8.19. The highest per capita city is Asheville, $200.58. For the Canadian cities, the range is between Winnipeg, with a per capita debt of $64.34, and Edmonton, $283.88.

TREND OF INDEBTEDNESS

Comparison of the gross debt of the cities for 1928 and 1927 shows a gradual increase. Of eleven comparable cities in Group I, omitting New York City, Pittsburgh, and Washington, the net increase in gross debt was $121,788,-125, or a per capita increase of $9.40. Of these eleven, nine cities had an increase, and two a slight reduction. Nine of the eleven cities in Group II, omitting New Orleans and Seattle, which did not report, had a net increase of $27,997,132, or $8.34 per capita. Only one city of this group, Minneapolis, reported a slight reduction. It was impossible to extend this comparison to the net debt excluding self-supporting, owing to changes within the bonds so included in several of these cities.

The *Bond Buyer* reports sales of state and municipal bonds during 1927 amounting to nearly $1,500,000,000. Inasmuch as maturities are not occurring at this rate, the net debt of our cities is definitely upward. It must be pointed out that this is a natural condition, due to the increase in population of our cities, and to the consequent demands for such physical facilities as sewers, schools, water supply and other public services. The cost of such facilities cannot be reasonably met from current taxation and departmental revenues. For this reason, it seems illogical to compare the trend of local debt with the downward trend of Federal debt, and infer that the former should also be gradually reduced.

It is not the purpose of this commentary to argue in favor of bond issues versus a current financing policy for any city, but it is deemed worth while to indicate the wisdom of bonding and the consequent benefits derived. In a recent publication of the Northern Trust Company of Chicago appeared the following:

From time to time questions have been raised regarding the supposed tendency on the part of municipalities toward a heavy increase in their indebtedness. Taxpayers, particularly, are interested in the answer to these questions. Municipal expenditures, wisely made on the part of officials, return to the inhabitants of the municipality benefits which in many instances are several times their cost. In the voting of municipal bonds taxpayers are authorizing a benefit not only for their neighbors but for themselves. In so doing, the happiness and progress of the nation is increased.

The unusual growth of modern American municipalities during the past few decades has necessitated an extension of the scope of their endeavors. The fact that municipalities are doing more today than ever before for their inhabitants should offset the general alarm as to increasing debt, inasmuch as the wealth of the people has shown an increase proportionately much greater than municipal expenditures.

That this condition is recognized by the cities themselves is evidenced from certain data compiled by the *Bond Buyer*, which reports that during 1927 authorizations by the taxpayers totaled $560,714,514. This compares with $606,933,170 so approved in 1926. In December, for example, voters of 98 municipalities in 28 states approved $68,526,625, and rejected about $25,-000,000. Among the authorizations might be noted that of an improvement program for Dallas totaling $23,900,-000, which was approved in December. On the other hand, the electorate of Chicago, in April of this year, voted down by a two to one vote thirty-one issues for over $70,000,000. It will be recalled that a year ago Chicago voters approved thirteen separate proposals, totaling $21,390,000, by a five to one vote. These are but instances of the enduring ability of the voters to discriminate in marking their ballots.

Another indication that debt incurrence is not unreasonable is indicated in the current prices of bonds. Municipal bonds are next in price to government bonds, with a higher price than any other form of security. This high level was consistently maintained during 1927. The maturity of certain Liberty Loans has had somewhat to do with the demand for municipals, owing to the slightly greater yield of the latter. Purchasers of municipal bonds may not in fairness be charged with tax-dodging, however, because the acceptance of a lower yield on municipal bonds really means an ultimate advantage to the borrowing community. If only net return were considered investors naturally would place their money in high grade industrial public utility, railroad, and even foreign bonds.

NEW YORK LAW AMENDMENT

Many cities throughout the country were greatly interested in the proposed legislation in New York which would remove restrictions upon available funds in that state for investment in municipal securities. As was noted last year, interim legislation was enacted permitting the issuance of bonds for a limited time. The 1928 session of the New York legislature finally enacted four bills, which received the signature of the governor, greatly widening the field of investment for such funds. These laws included primarily one relating to the bonds of cities. The former 7 per cent of assessed valuation restriction was removed, and cities and school districts in excess of 150,000 population, with an assessed real property valuation in excess of $200,000,000, and with no tax limit provision in their statutes or local charters, were placed in a class on which there is no restriction as to the amount of bonds which may be issued and continue to remain legal investment in New York State. For cities over 10,000 population, the new limit is 12 per cent of the real property valuation for taxation purposes, and for counties, 5 per cent.

The other laws enacted permit limited investment of funds in certain public utilities, as electric, gas and telephone companies, railroads, etc.

COMPARISON WITH ASSESSED VALUATION

It is of interest to know the relation of total gross or net debt to the assessed valuation of any city. This information may be obtained by reference to the assessed valuations reported by the cities in the comparative tax rate data published in the December, 1927, REVIEW.

Requests for data were sent to 286 cities in the United States and 19 cities in Canada. The cordial coöperation of the public officials which has made possible the compilation is appreciated, especially in this era of questionnaires. It is hoped that the results will justify their coöperation for future compilations.

BONDED DEBT OF 213 CITIES AS AT JANUARY 1, 1928

Compiled by the Detroit Bureau of Governmental Research, Inc.

From Data Furnished by Members of the Governmental Research Association, City Officials, and Chambers of Commerce

City	Census July 1, 1927	General improvement bonds	Public school bonds	Public utility bonds	Total gross bonded debt	Sinking fund Total	Sinking fund General improvement (per cent)	Sinking fund Public school (per cent)	Sinking fund Public utility (per cent)	Net general bonded debt Total	Net general bonded debt Excluding self-supporting	Total gross special assessment debt	Per capita net general debt excluding self-supporting and special assessment
Group I													
Population 500,000 and over													
2. Chicago, Ill.[1]	3,102,800	210,000,150	N.	7,610,500	217,610,650					217,610,650	217,610,650	N.	$70.13
3. Philadelphia, Pa.[2]	2,035,900	433,159,600	$50,861,000		483,020,600	$101,543,543	85	15	27	381,477,056	351,477,056[a]	$30,848,417	172.63
4. Detroit, Mich.[3]	1,334,560	99,515,266	62,376,350	72,897,114	234,788,730	23,129,628	28	35	65	211,659,102	160,205,028	45,081,200[a]	120.05
5. Los Angeles, Calif.[4]	1,280,000	48,401,088	62,617,765	103,635,250	214,654,103	23,583,698	77	33	10	202,070,505	128,960,135	18,725,447	99.19
6. Cleveland, Ohio[5]	984,500	85,271,894	28,263,000	34,487,500	148,212,304	23,836,934	78	6	16	124,385,370	91,998,226	N.	93.45
7. St. Louis, Mo.	839,200	40,787,000	2,219,000	11,053,000	54,059,000	12,164,926	93	2	5	41,894,074	32,783,307	....	39.06
8. Baltimore, Md.[6]	819,000	112,036,281	21,289,192	26,791,370	160,116,843	35,395,350	62	17	21	124,221,493	99,285,253		121.22
9. Boston, Mass.[7]	793,100	77,076,601	13,230,800	51,521,700	141,829,101	45,602,658				96,226,443	54,112,513	530,000	68.23
11. San Francisco, Calif[8]	576,000	18,681,600	16,675,000	46,494,000	82,050,600					82,050,600	51,485,722	4,817,254	89.38
12. Buffalo, N.Y.	550,000	39,326,082	28,286,000	16,827,364	84,439,446	6,618,855	43	..	57	77,820,591	64,762,756		117.73
13. Washington, D.C.	540,000	No bonded	No bonded debt.									N.	
14. Milwaukee, Wis.[9]	536,400	34,331,350	8,645,750	90,000	43,067,100	3,211,800	79	20	1	39,855,500	39,780,300	N.	74.16
Group II													
Population 300,000 to 500,000													
15. Newark, N.J.	466,700	42,432,000	18,463,200	18,140,000	70,035,200	$13,947,904	60	23	17	$65,087,396	$40,306,264	$7,350,000	$105.77
16. Minneapolis, Minn.[10]	447,700	21,648,810	22,241,862	4,996,000	48,886,672	4,831,362	62	7	31	44,035,310	44,035,310	13,688,037	98.40
18. Cincinnati, Ohio[11]	412,200	56,600,662	13,314,500	42,894,230	112,809,412	36,013,695	31	52	17	74,795,717	74,151,845	2,467,312	124.04
19. Kansas City, Mo.[12]	383,100	19,007,355	21,774,500	13,120,000	53,901,855	10,139,104	40	60	64	43,762,751	32,392,865		84.55
21. Indianapolis, Ind.[13]	374,300	14,027,750	10,682,000	N.	25,909,550	957,310	25	11	..	24,352,240	24,352,240	8,582,238	65.06
22. Rochester, N.Y.	324,500	21,268,500	10,245,720	11,918,000	43,432,220	5,314,157	75	7	18	38,118,063	29,600,759	10,250,000	91.22
23. Jersey City, N.J.[14]	321,500	18,711,833	13,276,500	10,656,755	51,645,088	22,742,924	81	9	10	28,902,164	13,495,594	2,353,532	41.97
24. Louisville, Ky.[15]	320,100	16,864,500	6,466,400	1,079,000	24,399,900	3,694,085	82	..	..	20,505,815	19,821,833	N.	61.92
25. Toledo, Ohio	305,400	24,874,200	12,958,000	1,790,000	39,622,300	7,186,042	..	18	..	32,436,258	30,646,258	2,283,375	100.34
Group III													
Population 100,000 to 300,000													
26. Columbus, Ohio[16]	291,400	19,556,200	11,471,500	9,541,000	40,568,700	$16,158,095	78	..	22	$24,410,605	$16,781,605[a]	$11,798,375	$57.59
27. Denver, Colo.[17]	289,800	14,373,600	10,227,000	21,573,600	46,174,200	407,199	86	..	14	45,767,002	10,637,959	18,502,900	36.71
28. Portland, Ore.[18]	282,380	16,414,246	8,500,602	17,635,000	42,549,848	5,461,629	49	14	51	37,088,219	22,240,752	6,642,739	78.76
29. Providence, R.I.	280,800	15,693,000	6,700,000	17,913,000	40,306,000	13,927,828	50	..	36	26,378,172	13,414,734	N.	47.81
30. Oakland, Calif.[19]	267,300	4,640,882	14,972,183	12,951,000	32,564,065		..	..	..	23,364,065	23,364,065		83.67
31. St. Paul, Minn.[20]	250,100	12,344,000	9,546,000	7,704,000	30,594,000	3,141,512	68	..	32	27,452,488	20,755,438	7,990,000	83.99
32. Atlanta, Ga.	249,000	6,593,000	4,175,000	3,544,000	14,312,000	2,600,001	64	9	27	11,711,999	8,358,721	2,807,000	35.58
33. Akron, Ohio	220,000	22,386,318	7,404,663	10,362,000	40,132,981	2,063,735	40	16	44	38,069,246	28,605,257	8,542,880	130.02
34. Omaha, Neb.[21]	219,200	13,640,380	10,830,750	11,392,000	35,863,130	5,323,697	13	17	70	30,539,433	22,372,112	7,514,837	104.34
35. Birmingham, Ala.	217,500	7,274,500	8,822,000	127,000	16,223,500	1,052,332	..	..	..	15,171,168	15,171,168	4,006,500	69.75

BONDED DEBT OF 213 CITIES AS AT JANUARY 1, 1928—Continued

City	Census July 1, 1927	General improvement bonds	Public school bonds	Public utility bonds	Total gross bonded debt	Sinking fund Total	General improvement (per cent)	Public school (per cent)	Public utility (per cent)	Net general bonded debt Total	Excluding self-supporting	Total gross special assessment debt	Per capita net general debt excluding self-supporting and special assessment
GROUP III—Continued Population 100,000 to 300,000													
36. Dallas, Texas	211,600	$8,978,500	$7,005,850	$8,608,000	$22,595,350	$2,579,106	68		32	$20,016,244	$14,252,430	N.	$67.36
39. Worcester, Mass.	195,500	5,202,000	993,000	5,856,800	12,051,800	3,571,082	49		51	8,480,738	4,445,960	N.	22.74
40. Richmond, Va.[32]	191,900	23,464,185	4,380,395	7,213,550	35,058,130	8,422,947	67	13	20	26,635,183	21,104,804		110.03
41. New Haven, Conn.	184,900	10,637,000	806,000	N.	11,443,000	1,091,215				10,351,785	10,351,785	$1,511,638	55.98
42. Dayton, Ohio.	180,700	10,659,303	7,186,000	4,487,000	22,332,303	3,044,707	83	17		19,287,596	15,322,270	N.	84.79
43. Norfolk, Va.[33]	179,200	19,270,333	3,306,108	15,855,058	38,431,500	5,728,159	84	16		32,703,341	18,731,838		104.53
46. Hartford, Conn.	168,300	6,078,481	9,672,500	4,860,000	20,610,981	3,089,013	59	24		17,521,968	13,270,518	N.	78.85
48. Fort Worth, Texas	163,600	11,315,000	5,683,500	5,496,000	21,694,500	1,695,000	51		41	20,199,500	15,393,639	6,041,900	94.09
49. Grand Rapids, Mich.	161,900	5,705,000	5,385,000	3,923,000	15,013,000	1,518,139	51		49	13,494,861	10,316,355	N.	63.72
50. Bridgeport, Conn.	153,000	9,779,000	4,139,000	N.	13,918,000		13		87	13,918,000	13,815,354	N.	90.97
52. Des Moines, Iowa	148,900	5,678,899	8,191,500	5,200,000	19,070,399	427,639	13			18,642,860	11,385,003	2,651,546	92.78
53. Springfield, Mass.	147,440	8,528,500	5,138,400	5,667,000	14,840,940	162,897		25	35	14,678,003	11,385,003		77.24
54. Paterson, N.J.	145,500	3,394,500	3,019,400	5,536,896	14,197,500	5,497,069	40		37	14,673,603	11,360,572	4,804,990	48.00
56. Oklahoma City, Okla.	143,530	9,032,884	8,423,774	3,153,500	13,982,534	2,478,300	63		63	14,980,572	13,978,338	836,067	92.21
57. Flint, Mich.	142,700	6,686,500	8,432,000	1,940,000	19,272,000	830,881	21	11	5	13,978,338	14,856,389	2,008,607	104.11
58. Miami, Fla.	140,000	16,501,000	7,813,628	3,794,000	28,254,628	1,736,100	74	21		17,441,119	22,649,478	2,141,500	161.78
59. Jacksonville, Fla.[34]	138,900	8,923,000	5,398,000	996,000	16,126,000	2,007,460	85	15		24,498,528	12,218,540	705,000	87.97
60. Nashville, Tenn.[34]	137,800	9,579,000	1,960,000	3,794,000	15,433,000	459,065			12	14,118,540	14,973,935	1,113,162	108.66
61. Trenton, N.J.[35]	136,700	8,419,570	5,738,514		15,154,085	3,181,981	63		12	14,973,935	11,375,690	3,063,000	83.22
63. Salt Lake City, Utah[q]	135,700	3,091,500	4,151,750	2,823,700	5,915,200				7	11,972,104	5,915,200*		43.59
64. Camden, N.J.	133,100	8,485,255	2,941,000	1,312,000	13,949,005	2,836,375	76		7	5,915,200	10,010,690	1,874,835	75.21
65. Fall River, Mass.	132,600	7,219,500	1,216,000	1,216,000	11,376,300	2,059,333	51		42	11,112,630	8,970,161		52.93
66. Wilmington, Del.[37]	126,400	6,079,500	1,085,000	3,714,000	10,878,500	463,029	72		28	9,316,967	6,701,471	2,847,700	92.98
67. Erie, Pa.	125,000	4,220,000	4,026,000	230,000	8,476,000	607,014	87		13	10,415,471	7,888,986		62.95
68. Cambridge, Mass.	123,900	1,634,300	654,750	951,000	9,230,050	3,219,219	78		22	7,888,986	6,910,831	1,428,000	44.08
69. Albany, N.Y.[38]	119,800	8,960,000	4,632,210	3,391,000	18,145,815	1,786,816	94		6	6,910,831	13,185,924	3,222,120	110.34
70. New Bedford, Mass.	118,800	9,151,347	2,745,000	2,745,000	20,145,827	775,365				12,249,635	10,984,635		92.28
71. Yonkers, N.Y.	117,500	3,678,575	2,730,500	6,653,000	12,997,876	1,626,703	10	8	82	20,145,827	17,415,327	694,000	146.59
72. Kansas City, Kan.[36]	115,300	3,972,691	2,666,500	10,284,534	18,682,225	1,002,600				11,571,173	6,087,989		51.81
73. San Diego, Calif.	114,700	4,570,000	2,625,000	3,360,000	12,255,000		22	66	12	15,879,625	5,595,091	4,640,050	48.52
74. Duluth, Minn.[39]	114,500	1,353,000	4,225,000	1,136,000	10,321,400	915,918	92			12,255,000	8,995,000		77.55
75. Reading, Pa.	114,000	2,755,000	6,430,400		5,700,850	488,810	32	8	12	9,405,482	8,376,007	2,750,004	73.15
77. Elizabeth, N.J.	113,300	7,723,440	4,347,350	1,509,637	6,280,077	3,264,903	97	56	3	5,212,040	5,212,040	1,438,157	45.72
78. Canton, Ohio.	109,000	3,063,000	7,047,000	1,750,000	7,177,000	1,985,851	96		4	5,191,149	1,505,537	1,589,000	101.55
80. Spokane, Wash.[30]	107,800	8,533,500	2,364,000	3,121,000	11,654,000	1,462,713	20	8		10,191,787	3,760,315	1,584,838	94.50
81. Tampa, Fla.[41]	107,200	4,490,541	2,585,000	6,758,995	13,834,536	2,106,348			60	1,728,188	1,119,973		46.05
82. Tacoma, Wash.[31]	104,300	3,897,630	1,730,643	5,342,000	6,939,620	718,321		20	4	1,721,309	5,050,138		50.67
83. Lynn, Mass.	104,200	7,373,635	6,903,278	5,293,278	13,603,278		8	88		19,252,729	5,310,676		134.09
84. Long Beach, Calif.[28]	103,100	594,500	4,942,000	149,000	4,785,500	409,549				4,785,500	13,972,729		44.97
85. Fort Wayne, Ind.[28]										4,636,500			
87. Somerville, Mass.	101,600	524,000	1,787,000	N.	2,311,000					2,311,000	2,311,000	N.	22.74

BONDED DEBT OF 213 CITIES AS AT JANUARY 1, 1928—Continued

City	Census July 1, 1927	General improvement bonds	Public school bonds	Public utility bonds	Total gross bonded debt	Sinking fund Total	General improvement (per cent)	Public school (per cent)	Public utility (per cent)	Net general bonded debt Total	Net general bonded debt Excluding self-supporting	Total gross special assessment debt	Per capita net general debt excluding self-supporting and special assessment
Group IV Population 50,000 to 100,000													
88. Savannah, Ga.[40]	99,700	$4,837,000	$3,547,000	$240,000	$5,077,000	$202,000		72	3	$4,875,000	$4,635,000*	$367,996	$46.49
89. Allentown, Pa.	97,000	2,303,700	2,588,000	75,000	5,925,700	496,223	25		3	5,429,477	5,370,690	246,500	55.37
90. Evansville, Ind.	96,600	1,930,300	1,697,500	N.	4,516,300	113,434	100	21		4,402,866	4,402,866		45.58
91. Wichita, Kans.	96,100	3,840,724	1,694,500	N.	4,538,224	126,842	79		100	5,411,382	5,411,382	3,605,385	56.31
93. Lawrence, Kans.	93,500	3,035,000	1,465,983	240,000	4,899,500	31,734	50	49	1	4,957,766	4,729,400		50.58
94. Bayonne, N. J.	93,100	3,160,381	N.	4,482,751	12,307,115	2,253,785	100			9,953,330	5,476,615	842,717	50.58
95.	90,900	2,383,000	2,030,166	N.	3,320,000	69,884	44		25	3,250,146	3,250,146	400,600	35.76
97. Wilkes-Barre, Pa.	85,700	83,700	N.	134,000	9,388,000	576,509		56		8,811,491	8,811,491	422,600	102.82
98. Harrisburg, Pa.	84,890	3,163,534	2,565,400	1,050,000	5,328,000	138,639	75			5,189,361	5,055,361		59.61
100. Manchester, N. H.	84,200	1,000,000	N.	1,050,000	4,615,000	240,278			25	4,374,722	3,384,992	N.	40.20
101. South Bend, Ind.	83,500	285,000	592,000	N.	877,000					877,000	877,000	N.	10.50
102. Peoria, Ill.	81,700	3,035,400	4,945,000	1,316,626	9,297,026	2,913,573	59	41	21	6,383,453	5,066,827	1,188,268	62.02
103. Highland Park, Mich.	80,900	575,900	1,732,500	325,000	2,633,400	231,500	35	44	10	2,401,900	2,401,900	804,890	29.69
104. Rockford, Ill.	78,000	3,607,950	2,491,000	2,933,500	8,932,450	373,227	21	69		8,559,223	5,664,223	3,499,850	72.62
107. Shreveport, La.	77,500	1,888,000	2,020,000	N.	3,908,000					3,908,000	3,908,000	5,750,000	50.42
108. Little Rock, Ark.	77,100	5,924,506	2,398,000	N.	11,231,000	215,048			99	11,015,952	8,107,458	4,998,000	105.16
110. Winston-Salem, N. C.	75,600	803,000	N.	2,908,494	5,612,600	506,381	1	18	59	5,304,239	798,000	1,280,085	10.56
111. Lansing, Mich.[33]	75,000	4,928,000	543,000	5,009,600	9,418,000	624,910	23			8,793,090	5,213,983	2,281,000	69.52
112. Charleston, S. C.[34]	74,600	5,383,500	4,587,000	3,947,000	3,622,040				22	10,280,500	10,280,500	2,380,312	137.81
113. Sacramento, Calif.	74,500	3,239,000	1,964,000	3,342,240	7,059,250	737,997	57	21		7,758,003	4,630,264		62.23
114. Saginaw, Mich.	73,000	3,448,250	3,150,000	N.	9,181,500	219,493	100			6,839,847	6,749,847	N.	91.34
115. Binghamton, N. Y.	73,000	4,922,500	4,259,000	90,000	9,777,200	1,192,520	48	52		9,517,198	7,988,980		109.44
117. Johnstown, Pa.	72,900	7,218,700	N.	N.	2,973,000	260,002	100			9,517,198	9,517,198	301,922	130.55
118. Chattanooga, Tenn.	72,700	1,378,000	1,595,000	N.	7,149,000	72,766	100			2,900,234	2,900,234		39.89
119. Terre Haute, Ind.	72,300	3,055,000	1,825,000	N.	12,231,356	1,234,669	52	48	27	3,655,331	3,655,331	390,200	50.56
120. Chester, Pa.	71,200	2,006,000	3,402,000	N.	4,890,000	506,504	46	27	2	6,642,496	5,037,846	207,242	70.76
125. New Britain, Conn.[35]	71,000	8,279,721	3,697,635	1,741,000	12,231,356	3,108,882	80	18		9,122,474	8,827,419		124.33
126. Hoboken, N. J.[a]	70,800	4,447,561	3,338,750	354,000	9,917,461	1,445,116	65	35		8,472,345	6,341,195	1,989,919	89.56
127. Passaic, N. J.[36]	69,900	544,213	4,601,000	2,131,150	5,345,213	120,199	38		62	5,225,014	5,099,778	159,106	72.96
128. Lincoln, Neb.[37]	69,400	509,502	2,482,250	300,000	2,991,752					2,991,752	2,991,752	50,000	43.11
129. Berkeley, Calif.[f]	68,660	1,701,400	40,000	N.	3,741,400	352,263	66	24	34	3,359,137	3,359,137	N.	21.69
130. Wheeling, W. Va.	67,000	824,689	2,070,000	2,000,000	3,341,689	873,420	76			2,368,269	1,489,137		30.17
133. Altoona, Pa.	66,600	5,113,650	5,553,129	347,000	12,949,900					12,368,269	10,686,779	N.	160.16
135. Niagara Falls, N. Y.	65,500	2,091,000	2,298,000	1,983,130	5,649,900	587,338			100	5,649,900	4,359,000		66.75
138. Quincy, Mass.	64,500	1,857,500	693,500	1,821,000	4,008,900	658,376				3,421,562	2,550,300		39.06
139. Brockton, Mass.	63,500	2,857,781	2,353,500	1,458,500	5,191,281	1,449,568	20	27	53	4,532,905	4,532,905		70.79
140. Union City, N. J.	63,300	3,096,500	2,418,245	N.	7,002,745	709,063				5,553,177	4,832,737	2,500	76.35
141. East Orange, N. J.	63,300	4,770,000	2,650,000	1,488,000	7,420,000					6,710,963	6,710,963	N.	106.19
142. Roanoke, Va.	62,200	662,500	4,165,000	N.	4,827,500					4,827,500	4,827,500		77.61
143. Fresno, Calif.	62,200	3,307,000	N.	161,000	8,293,299	1,276,852	68			7,016,447	6,855,447	1,110,037	110.22
145. Topeka, Kans.	61,900	1,826,273	928,000	660,000	3,414,273	233,125	68	16	16	3,181,148	2,557,575	1,795,795	41.32

City	Census July 1, 1927	General improvement bonds	Public school bonds	Public utility bonds	Total gross bonded debt	Sinking fund Total	Sinking fund General improvement (per cent)	Sinking fund Public school (per cent)	Sinking fund Public utility (per cent)	Net general bonded debt Total	Net general bonded debt Excluding self-supporting	Total gross special assessment debt	Per capita net general debt excluding self-supporting and special assessment
GROUP IV—Continued *Population 50,000 to 100,000*													
147. Portsmouth, Va.	60,700	5,104,300	920,000	3,150,000	9,174,300	1,101,360	33		67	8,072,940	5,658,021		$93.21
148. Pasadena, Calif.[a]	60,500	5,046,891	5,117,000	2,247,459	12,411,350	843,361	45	35	20	11,567,989	9,490,709	$11,641,000	156.87
149. Holyoke, Mass.[d]	60,400	2,359,000		2,399,000	4,758,000					2,359,000	2,359,000	N.	39.06
152. Wichita Falls, Texas	58,000	2,676,000	1,962,000	940,000	5,578,000	223,131	16	57	27	5,345,869	4,473,916	N.	77.14
153. Lancaster, Pa.	57,700	1,625,000	1,990,000		3,615,000	322,653		100		3,292,347	3,292,347	N.	57.06
154. Augusta, Ga.	57,300	3,036,500	20,000	499,000	3,555,500	429,355	88		12	3,126,545	2,926,545	N.	52.07
156. Newton, Mass.	56,600	2,283,500	2,283,000		5,575,480	941,234	100			4,634,246	4,237,929	3,352,100	76.03
158. Oak Park, Ill.	55,600	364,750	1,024,000	160,000	1,548,750					1,545,750	1,388,750	1,225,100	24.98
159. Kalamazoo, Mich.	55,300	101,250	2,499,000	68,250	2,668,500	38,484	29	71		2,630,016	2,561,766		48.32
160. Kenosha, Wis.	54,600	258,000	2,527,000	321,000	3,106,000					3,106,000	2,785,000		51.01
161. Beaumont, Texas[ae]	54,400	3,627,000	1,081,038	1,972,250	6,680,288					6,680,288	4,708,038*	1,086,800	86.54
162. Pontiac, Mich.	54,200	1,897,250	2,437,375	3,114,000	5,860,125	583,581	57	14	29	5,276,264	3,821,466	990,000	70.51
163. Atlantic City, N. J.	54,200	8,667,000	4,986,000		16,767,000	3,546,257	92		8	13,220,643	11,134,588		205.44
165. Cedar Rapids, Iowa	52,900	1,729,000	1,466,000	346,000	3,581,500	52,391	100			3,529,109	3,183,109		58.84
168. Malden, Mass.	51,700	1,769,500	1,191,700	48,000	2,968,700	251,781	100			2,716,919	2,691,155	373,181	50.87
171. Newport News, Va.	51,600	2,477,000	940,000	3,271,000	6,688,000	658,966	18	70	12	6,029,034	2,758,034		53.35
172. New Castle, Pa.	51,000	1,045,000		N.	1,045,000	16,905	32	68		1,025,095	1,028,065		19.92
174. Springfield, Mo.	51,000	804,000	614,500	N.	1,508,500	126,709	66		34	1,381,791	1,381,791		26.99
175. Greensboro, N. C.	50,300	3,333,370	1,005,000	2,571,630	6,932,000	335,907		100		6,595,093	4,138,046	6,798,000	82.27
GROUP V *Population 30,000 to 50,000*													
179. Stockton, Calif.	49,800	3,119,400	1,436,000	N.	4,555,400					4,555,400	4,555,400	N.	$91.47
180. Elmira, N. Y.	49,500	1,595,500	610,000	1,090,000	3,295,500					3,295,500	2,205,500	N.	44.55
181. York, Pa.	49,400	1,419,000	873,000		2,292,000	442,975	85	15		1,849,025	1,849,025		37.43
182. Haverhill, Mass.	49,230	1,234,500	393,000	171,000	1,798,000	152,467	95	5		1,645,533	1,474,532		29.95
183. Bay City, Mich.	49,100	1,035,365	2,025,000	2,163,000	4,482,500	764,595	44	48	8	3,717,905	1,873,720	$157,000	38.08
184. East Chicago, Ind.	49,100	724,000	1,301,000	1,956,000	4,292,365	158,179	16	84		4,134,186	2,178,186	1,665,953	44.36
185. Perth Amboy, N. J.	49,000	1,072,400	1,642,000	2,992,000	5,358,500	833,625	30	31	39	4,524,375	2,021,553		41.17
186. Pittsfield, Mass.	49,000	1,938,240	389,000		2,174,400					2,174,400	1,416,400	N.	28.84
187. Chelsea, Mass.	48,900	1,059,540	243,540	738,000	2,186,540	179,768	58	42		2,706,972	2,706,972	N.	55.24
188. Madison, Wis.	48,700	2,141,000	2,130,500	648,000	4,919,500	380,015	100			4,533,453	4,801,485		79.74
189. Lima, Ohio	48,500	3,979,443	1,052,102	1,031,800	6,063,345	415,885	100			5,647,460	4,615,660	1,533,440	94.77
190. St. Petersburg, Fla.[d]	47,300	6,705,600		4,294,000	10,999,600	567,737	100			10,431,863	6,137,583*	14,195,000	126.55
193. New Rochelle, N. Y.	46,100	4,181,997	3,961,676		8,143,673	297,740	100			7,845,933	7,845,933	752,421	165.88
196. Battle Creek, Mich.	45,900	1,283,000	760,000	N.	2,043,000					2,043,000	2,043,000		44.32
198. Muncie, Ind.	45,700	446,678	1,067,000	N.	1,513,678					1,513,678	1,513,678		33.05
199. Durham, N. C.	45,700	5,599,037	1,457,130	3,700,333	10,756,500	757,604	45	20	35	9,998,896*	9,998,896*		218.70
200. Waco, Texas	45,500	2,031,000	1,230,100	807,000	4,068,100	921,446				3,146,654	2,659,000		58.18
201. Muskegon, Mich.	45,700	1,368,500	2,050,000	481,000	3,899,500					3,389,500	3,418,500	1,091,450	75.13
202. Jamestown, N. Y.	45,100	1,530,567	2,037,500	1,114,000	4,682,367	61,675			100	4,620,692	3,568,367	543,482	79.12

City	Census July 1, 1927	General improvement bonds	Public school bonds	Public utility bonds	Total gross bonded debt	Sinking fund				Net general bonded debt		Total gross special assessment debt	Per capita net general debt excluding self-supporting and special assessment
						Total	General improvement (per cent)	Public school (per cent)	Public utility (per cent)	Total	Excluding self-supporting		
Group V—Continued **Population $0,000 to 60,000**													
205. Fitchburg, Mass.	44,700	$1,755,700	$497,000	$592,700	$2,845,400	$517,221				$2,845,400	$2,252,700	N.	$ 50.40
207. rão, llo	44,000	1,670,000	1,614,725	624,000	3,908,725	7,973	99	1		3,391,504	2,767,504	$949,076	62.90
208. Pueblo, Colo.	43,900	1,173,000	712,000	1,489,000	3,374,000	121,623	96	100		3,366,027	1,877,027	1,862,300	42.76
209. Hin, Ohio	43,700	1,596,283		1,544,300	3,140,583	400,595	100		4	3,019,360	1,524,660	745,107	34.89
212. Everett, Mass.	42,900	1,548,300	582,000	110,000	2,238,300					1,837,704	1,727,704	N.	40.37
213. Salem, Mass.	42,900	1,067,500	806,000	432,000	2,305,500	707,832	80	20		2,305,500	1,873,500	N.	43.67
214. Stamford, Conn.	42,100	2,738,000	2,943,000	3,139,000	7,744,500	497,333	33	65		7,247,167	4,871,168	N.	113.81
215. Phoenix, Ariz.	41,900	1,815,300	2,790,000	354,500	7,744,500	51,442		22	78	7,247,168	4,108,177*	602,900	97.58
216. Dubuque, Iowa	41,000	1,842,413	1,316,000	N.	3,262,913					3,211,471	2,896,971	1,099,100	69.14
219. Joliet, Ill.	41,500	373,500	1,880,000	N.	2,253,500					2,253,500	2,253,500	944,000	54.30
220. W Nw Brk, N. J.	40,900	1,423,494	2,738,833	N.	4,162,327	844,986	100			4,037,228	3,317,341	50,000	81.11
223. New Brunswick, N. J.	39,900	1,549,000	1,673,000	917,000	4,139,000	101,772	100			4,037,228	3,120,228	11,675	78.20
224. Superior, Wis.	39,600	843,000	1,306,000	N.	2,151,000	168,782	100	48	2	1,982,217	1,982,217	1,574,058	50.65
226. East Cleveland, Ohio	39,400	2,121,000	2,519,000	61,500	4,701,500	897,562	50		2	3,803,938	3,803,938	95,652	96.35
227. Kokomo, Ind.	39,100	195,300		N.	195,300	25,021				170,279	170,279		2.45
228. ?in, Texas	38,800	917,500	1,050,000	1,078,000	3,045,500	81,556			36	2,963,944	1,885,943	N.	48.61
229. Lynchburg, Va.	38,600	2,046,897	1,079,088	1,753,000	4,879,985	115,790	64	100		1,763,175	1,410,175	1,154,869	62.44
232. Danville, Ill.	38,700	363,845	900,000	N.	1,055,345					1,055,345	1,085,345		27.63
234. Hazleton, Pa.	37,500	1,653,500	1,773,115	500,000	3,426,615	141,594				3,285,021	3,285,021	N.	57.60
235. Petersburg, Va.	37,100	3,309,000		1,371,000	2,880,500	1,256,060	38			3,352,940	2,852,940	823,500	76.90
238. Cranston, R. I.	36,600	1,170,000	1,710,000	435,000	4,483,900	379,447	100	62		379,447			68.33
240. Clifton, N. J.	36,500	1,873,500	1,634,000	3,058,000	4,483,900	122,619				1,123,000	688,000	348,500	110.01
241. Lewiston, Me.	36,100	803,000	110,000	295,000	5,144,000	225,000	100			5,144,000	2,086,000		19.06
243. ?do Springs, Colo.	36,000	906,000	1,180,000	N.	233,000	223,100	48	5	47	1,875,000	1,580,000		57.94
246. Amsterdam, N. Y.	36,000	368,000	1,435,100	878,500	2,728,550					233,000	233,000	986,047	44.01
247. Norristown, Pa.	35,800	233,000	796,550	233,000	1,268,443	49,396			100	2,728,550	1,850,650		6.51
248. Poughkeepsie, N. Y.	35,800	1,053,500	81,000	247,225	2,300,305					1,219,047	1,033,444		51.68
249. Auburn, N. Y.	35,700	954,443	1,155,320	50,000	346,000	8,370				1,200,305	1,953,080		29.00
250. Revere, Mass.	35,200	797,760	281,000	N.	3,994,990	216,104	72	28		337,000	287,630	1,134,200	53.49
251. ?aM, Ill.	35,100	15,000	2,370,150	2,663,896	9,207,756	1,399,053	49	47	4	3,778,886	3,778,886	121,743	8.19
253. Irvington, N. J.	34,600	1,624,860	5,101,000	N.	21,161,050	2,564	100	53	1	7,808,703	5,196,116	608,888	109.22
257. Montclair, N. J.	33,700	1,430,650	741,000	1,137,000	3,320,435	127,174		46		2,158,486	2,158,486	270,658	154.19
258. Marion, Ohio	33,400	1,382,935	700,000	974,000	3,843,154	1,973,867	40	32	28	3,093,261	1,956,872	387,762	64.62
259. Watertown, N. Y.	33,400	1,614,154	1,255,000	120,698	302,545					1,869,287	1,443,487	196,000	58.59
262. Muskogee, Okla.	32,900	181,847		252,000	302,545	63,409				302,545	302,545	280,950	43.87
263. Steubenville, Ohio	32,500	1,081,375	1,478,145	159,466	2,814,520		100			2,751,111	2,499,111		9.28
264. Mansfield, Ohio	32,500	239,389	593,445	N.	992,300	828,500	60	37	3	832,534	832,534		76.90
266. Alameda, Calif.	32,100	1,347,000	2,201,025	3,264,903	6,812,928	193,718		37		5,984,428	2,748,405	477,000	25.70
267. Kearney, N. J.	32,100	3,565,316	3,047,000	5,532,000	12,144,316	139,269	49	51		11,960,598	6,418,598	1,991,384	85.62
269. Asheville, N. C.	32,000	736,862	1,230,000	206,000	2,172,862					2,033,593	1,827,593		200.58
271. Middletown, Ohio	31,900												57.29

BONDED DEBT OF 213 CITIES AS AT JANUARY 1, 1928—*Concluded*

City	Census July 1, 1927	General improvement bonds	Public school bonds	Public utility bonds	Total gross bonded debt	Sinking fund Total	Sinking fund General improvement (per cent)	Sinking fund Public school (per cent)	Sinking fund Public utility (per cent)	Net general bonded debt Total	Net general bonded debt Excluding self-supporting	Total gross special assessment debt	Per capita net general debt excluding self-supporting and special assessment
GROUP V—*Continued*													
Population 30,000 to 50,000													
272. Sioux Falls, S. D.	31,200	$1,140,000	$1,382,000	$415,000	$2,937,000	$813,629	22	59	19	$2,123,370	$1,864,715	N.	$59.77
275. Richmond, Ind.	31,000	181,500	679,400	N.	860,900	8,207	100			852,693	852,693	345,621*	27.51
276. Clarksburg, W. Va.	30,900	422,100	138,000	382,900	943,000	70,222	50		50	872,778	524,800	250,000*	16.98
277. Great Falls, Mont.	30,900	639,000		434,000	1,073,000	349,480	24		76	723,520	555,344	528,775	17.97
278. Norwood, Ohio	30,800	2,431,041	1,162,000	301,137	3,894,178	1,028,035	100			2,866,143	2,565,006	124,096	83.28
280. Bloomington, Ill.	30,700	305,000	100,000	49,000	454,000	76,000	50		50	378,000	267,000		11.95
281. Newark, Ohio	30,450	907,930	343,000	491,000	1,736,930	162,100	99	1		1,574,830	1,324,830	325,339	43.51
282. Zanesville, Ohio	30,450	808,831	960,120	609,500	2,378,471	147,461	8	92		2,231,010	1,624,510	246,279	53.25
286. Nashua, N. H.	30,000	1,316,500	762,500	N.	2,079,000	251,456				1,827,544	1,827,544		60.92
CANADIAN CITIES													
1. Montreal, Que.[42]	942,875	$102,303,446	$29,992,243	$34,756,485	$167,052,174	$17,474,348	82	18	41	$149,577,826	$114,821,341	$20,692,036	$121.77
2. Toronto, Ont.[43]	569,899	48,496,185	25,455,795	94,315,157	168,267,087	27,023,043	41	18	49	141,244,044	58,054,171	10,834,667	101.86
3. Winnipeg, Man.[44]	202,377	9,957,552	9,225,000	27,924,639	47,107,091	13,355,925	32	19	10	33,751,166	13,021,115	13,853,654	64.34
4. Vancouver, B. C.[45]	142,150	22,598,924	5,891,900	6,439,351	34,930,175	8,134,910	75	15	38	26,795,265	21,204,362	3,570,122	149.17
5. Hamilton, Ont.[46]	127,447	10,801,971	4,182,108	6,590,185	21,574,264	4,916,520	47	15	30	16,657,744	11,908,111	2,200,982	93.41
6. Quebec, Que.[47]	126,000	13,625,246	4,504,000	5,069,750	23,498,996	1,711,824	55	35	30	21,787,172*	21,787,172*		172.91
7. Ottawa, Ont.	120,799	9,611,508	3,981,119	4,830,910	18,326,537	4,525,173	52	18	58	13,801,364	13,301,812	5,328,583	110.12
9. Edmonton, Alb.[48]	67,063	19,168,603	3,923,343	11,960,436	35,052,332	9,599,500	38	4		25,452,832	19,043,736	4,414,729	283.88
11. Windsor, Ont.[49]	65,893	5,038,781	3,411,476	3,487,261	11,937,518	138,396	92	61		11,799,122	8,311,860		124.25
13. St. John's, N. B.	52,000	1,838,584	1,655,500	4,258,816	7,772,900	3,502,340	59	8	30	4,270,560	2,807,612		53.99
16. Regina, Sask.[50]	37,329	6,661,753	1,951,796	5,096,871	13,700,420	4,627,248	59	11		9,073,172	5,388,316		144.34
17. Saskatoon, Sask.[51]	33,000	3,967,931	2,092,223	3,404,839	9,484,993	2,704,051	50	8	42	6,780,942	4,508,917	1,753,382	136.63

NOTES.—The cities are arranged in order of population, according to the 1927 (July 1) estimates by the Bureau of the Census, with exceptions noted by that Bureau. Population of Canadian cities is as estimated for 1927 when available. Missing numbers are of cities not furnishing data.

* Estimated. N.—none.

1 *Chicago.* General bonds include $76,480,850 sanitary district bonds, 92¼ per cent of total debt of the district based upon proportion of taxable values within the city. Debt does not include county or forest preserve district (co-extensive with county) bonds, $31,871,000. Ninety-one per cent of the taxable values of the county are within the city. Utility bonds include water, $500,500, and street lighting, $7,110,000; do not include water certificates, $10,300,000, with a sinking fund of $2,100,000, payable from water works income. Special assessment debt not furnished.

2 *Philadelphia.* Includes city and county; general and utility debt not separated. Special assessment bonds are not issued.

3 *Detroit.* Utility bonds include street railway, $22,965,000, and lighting, $15,787,000; in addition to the debt, there is a street railway purchase contract for $11,580,000.

4 *Los Angeles.* Census is local estimate; general bonds include flood control (county), $12,324,250; utility bonds include light and power, $39,405,000, and harbor, $20,342,500; school bonds are issued by the county; school sinking fund includes flood control. Special assessment debt is estimated, except municipal improvement district bonds, $9,119,350, and 1915 district improvement bonds, $961,850; these improvements are installed under state improvement acts and the liens are not obligations of the city.

5 *Cleveland.* Utility bonds include light and power, $7,388,000.

6 *Baltimore.* General bonds include Western Maryland Railroad, $1,875,000.

7 *Boston.* Utility bonds include rapid transit, $50,393,700; gross debt does not include county debt, which is paid by Boston; special assessment bonds are not kept separately.

8 *San Francisco.* General bonds include 1915 Exposition, $2,300,000; utility bonds include street railway, $3,694,000. Special assessment bonds are not issued.

9 *Milwaukee.* Debt does not include metropolitan sewerage commission, $18,345,000, 83 per cent of which is paid by the city. Special assessment bonds are not issued.

10 *Minneapolis.* Utility bonds include light and power, $50,000, river terminal, $510,000, and market, $25,000; sinking fund not separated by purposes.

11 *Cincinnati.* Utility bonds include rapid transit, $6,100,000, and Cincinnati Southern Railway, $21,833,000; rental revenues of the latter yield $1,100,000 to pay interest on general debt.

12 *Kansas City.* Special assessments, in form of tax bills issued against the property assessed and improvement certificates which are not obligations of the city, are not reported because current control of amount is not kept by city.

13 *Indianapolis.* General bonds include park district, $3,130,000, and sanitary district, $3,655,500.

14 *Jersey City.* Utility bonds include dock, $251,000.

15 *Louisville.* The sinking fund owns also the entire capital stock of the Louisville Water Company, worth at least $25,000,000 (par value, $1,275,100).

16 *Columbus.* Utility bonds include light and power, $1,912,000.

17 *Denver.* General bonds include city's portion of Moffat Tunnel; special assessment bonds include city's assessment for Moffat Tunnel, $9,020,000.

18 *Portland.* General bonds include docks, $19,855,000, and city's portion (94.4 per cent) of port, $4,374,496; school bonds are 97.68 per cent of total, based upon city's portion of assessed valuation utility bonds include $150,000 city's share (92.15 per cent) of county debt, $7,816,250, is not included.

19 *Oakland.* Utility bonds include city's portion (60 per cent) of water district, canal and harbor, $2,751,000.

20 *St. Paul.* Special assessment debt is a permanent improvement revolving fund.

21 *Omaha.* Utility bonds include gas, $4,500,000.

22 *Richmond.* Utility bonds include light and power, $300,000, and gas, $3,607,550.

23 *Norfolk.* Utility bonds include port terminals, $6,423,948; general sinking fund includes school.

24 *Jacksonville.* Utility bonds include light and power, $350,000.

25 *Nashville.* Utility bonds include light and power, $328,000.

26 *Trenton.* Utility bonds include dock, $100,000.

27 *Wilmington.* Utility bonds include harbor, $2,300,000.

28 *Kansas City, Kans.* Utility bonds include light and power, $2,991,000.

29 *Duluth.* Utility bonds include gas, $1,110,500.

30 *Spokane.* Utility bonds include crematory, $70,000.

31 *Tacoma.* Utility bonds include light and power, $3,696,000, and street railway, $348,000.

32 *Long Beach.* Utility bonds include gas, $3,950,000.

33 *Lansing.* Utility bonds include light and power, $2,500,000, and mortgage bonds for same, $659,600.

34 *Charleston.* Utility bonds include light and power, $451,000.

35 *New Britain.* Utility bonds include subways for wires, $231,150.

36 *Passaic.* Utility bonds include light and power, $200,000.

37 *Lincoln.* Utility bonds include light and power, $350,000.

38 *Berkeley.* Debt of East Bay utility district, $17,000,000, of which Berkeley is 16 per cent, is not reported.

39 *Pasadena.* Utility bonds include light and power, $922,750.

40 *Beaumont.* Utility bonds include wharfs, $1,107,750.

41 *Salt Lake City, Tampa, Savannah, Holyoke, New Castle, St. Petersburg, Hamilton, Kokomo, Norristown, Steubenville.* School debt not reported.

42 *Montreal.* Utility bonds include underground conduits, $3,330,000; school debt includes Roman Catholic, $21,748,243, and Protestant school boards, debt charges for both administered by city treasurer.

43 *Toronto.* Utility bonds include light and power, $26,014,663, street railway, $39,728,567, housing, $667,000, abattoir, $374,000, exhibition, $3,153,197, radials, $3,487,000, and ferries, $186,000; school debt includes separate (Roman Catholic) school board, $2,940,000, paid from taxes of supporters; special assessment debt reported is portion paid by ratepayers, city's share of local improvement bonds, $6,339,910, included with general debt.

44 *Winnipeg.* Utility bonds include light and power, $17,327,000, housing, $2,650,000, and steam heating system, $1,050,000.

45 *Vancouver.* The Greater Vancouver water district pays debt service on $3,659,001 of water bonds reported.

46 *Quebec.* School debt includes Roman Catholic, $4,624,000, and Protestant, $180,000.

47 *Edmonton.* Utility bonds include light and power, $3,556,400, street railway, $3,048,800, and telephone, $2,331,010.

48 *Windsor.* Utility debt includes light and power, $1,261,369, and housing, $1,331,203.

49 *St. John's.* Utility bonds include water and sewerage, $3,260,710, light and power, $687,020, market, $70,000, and housing, $18,492; general and utility sinking fund not separated.

50 *Regina.* Utility debt includes light and power, $1,831,427, and street railway, $1,470,918.

51 *Saskatoon.* Utility debt includes light and power, $1,375,947, and street railway, $900,036.

RECENT BOOKS REVIEWED

GOVERNMENT AND BUSINESS—a study in the economic aspects of government and the public aspects of business. By Earl Willis Crecraft, Ph.D. New York: World Book Company. 1928. Pp. 508.

The publisher's announcement of this book contains the following statement by Dr. Charles A. Beard:

This book is a path-breaking work—the first attempt, as far as I know, to link up political science and business, to show how business affects government, to outline the business functions of government, and to indicate the points of political control over economic operations—all within the compass of a single volume. It will stir up discussion and make students of political science take a broader view of their field.

Dr. Beard is altogether too modest; for those who are familiar with his writings will recall that he has been a trail-maker himself in emphasizing the economic aspects of government, and no doubt the author found some of his inspiration in the writings of Dr. Beard.

Dr. Crecraft has, however, shown with remarkable clearness, and in a very comprehensive way, the numerous contacts and relationships of government and business.

The book consists of thirty-six chapters, an excellent bibliography and an index.

The author holds that it is entirely normal for business to engage in political activity; and for government to be responsive to the influences brought to bear on it by business forces.

In all of the departments of government, great industries are likely to be active. They keep in close touch with lawmaking, whether it be in congress, the state legislature or the city council; they establish contacts with executive and administrative departments in local, state and national governments; they take part openly or *sub rosa* in election campaigns to promote their interests. As a matter of fact, business pays a large part of the campaign expenses of political parties, and political history gives ample evidence that some of the contributions do not represent the individual's patriotic interest in his party.

The author shows the many ways in which government promotes the production, distribution and exchange of goods, and how it protects consumers as well.

The advocates of the doctrine of *laissez faire*, if there really are any, will probably be surprised at the array of facts which the author has marshalled to show that after all one of the chief objects or purposes of government has been the promotion of the economic (business) welfare of the citizens of the state, both at home and abroad.

The publishers recommend the book as a textbook, but for what courses is not stated. To the reviewer it does not appear to be suited for a textbook, but it should be stimulating to those who have covered the fields of economics and political science.

FRANK E. HORACK.
State University of Iowa.

✻

THE INCOME AND STANDARD OF LIVING OF UN-SKILLED LABORERS IN CHICAGO. By Leila Houghteling. Chicago: University of Chicago Press. 1927. Pp. xvii, 224.

"The Income and Standard of Living of Unskilled Laborers in Chicago" is number eight of a series of social science studies directed by the local community research committee of the University of Chicago, and is aimed at the question of whether the Chicago Standard Budget used by certain relief agencies sets too high a standard for dependent families supported by such agencies. In pursuit of this objective the income and expenditures of 437 families are recorded and analyzed. The result is a faithful, detailed piece of research in which the methods employed are explained in detail and from which much can be gleaned regarding methodology.

The difficulties with a study of this kind, however, are many. First, any statement of what constitutes a minimum standard, whether it be the Chicago standard budget or any other, is subject to the limitations implied in its assumptions relative to the amounts of food and clothing materials, and the minimums in housing such as space, windows, running water, lights, bathrooms, and fixtures. And a statistical study, in the nature of things, cannot verify the standard set. Therefore, the study does not answer the problem it proposes as to whether or not "the Chicago Standard Budget sets too high a standard for

340

dependent families who are being supported by relief agencies." Furthermore, it is but a commonplace to affirm that one cannot lay down a commodity standard and then pretend that a single translation in money terms is good either for a period of time or at the same time in different places.

If the purpose of the study were to find out whether or not the standard set translated into money terms could be met by unskilled workers in Chicago, the survey affords only a partial answer, the chief limitations being (1) the survey includes but 437 cases of workers employed steadily for a year and, therefore, is not representative of the unskilled in Chicago; and (2) it was found impossible to secure a clear understanding of what constituted the difference between a skilled and an unskilled worker. In light of these facts, one is forced to conclude that what we have is a picture of these 437 workers. Further generalization is not justified.

At times it is a question whether or not social workers in setting standards and in testing their shortcomings do not forget the very thing that they so often charge other people with forgetting, namely: the worker is a human being.

The reviewer believes that the process of checking and rechecking formulated standards is worth while for, in the long run, general concepts may be evolved upon which more common agreement can be secured. But for the present any budget standard should be used only for the most general sort of guidance. The income of the particular family and the direction of expenditure should be treated as a case.

WILLARD E. ATKINS.
New York University.

✱

COUNTY GOVERNMENT IN VIRGINIA, Report prepared by New York Bureau of Municipal Research, January, 1927. Published at Richmond, 1928.

This is a "Report on a Survey Made to the Governor and His Committee on Consolidation and Simplification." It is a paper-covered pamphlet of one hundred closely printed pages.

There are one hundred counties in Virginia, and the investigators selected twelve of them for purposes of intensive study, intending to select twelve that would be representative of the varying conditions to be found in the state. However, they have not presented a study of each of the twelve counties separately, but have divided

their report into thirteen chapters, each dealing with a particular problem of county government, i.e., The Fee System, County Indebtedness, Public Welfare, County Highway Administration, etc.

The work apparently has been very well done. The investigators went to the bottom of their problems and have dealt with them most thoroughly. The treatment is clear and concise. If one masters the contents of this pamphlet, he might feel that he had a pretty complete knowledge of county government in Virginia. The investigators were not content merely to describe local government, but sought to discover by means of intimate contact just how the various functions are actually administered in practice. The report is based on a very intelligent first-hand study, and is most illuminating.

It is obvious, however, that the investigators went forth in the spirit of the crusaders. There is no doubt that they were convinced before they ever started that county government in Virginia was exceedingly bad, and was much in need of radical reform. Every page of the report breathes dismay at the alleged shocking conditions. There is no denying that undesirable conditions are convincingly disclosed. But it is rare that careful students exhibit such unbounded confidence in their own criticisms and their own recommendations concerning reform. This report fairly bristles with unqualified assertions that this or that ought to be done, and that certain reforms will bring immediate relief. Indeed the report turns out to be a vigorous plea for the abolition of existing forms of county government in Virginia and the establishment of the county manager scheme. Supervisors, sheriff and prosecutor, to say nothing of others, are brusquely swept into the discard as elective officers, and the new and virtually untried county manager is boldly set up to drag the Virginia counties out of a morass of bad government. Elaborate charts are utilized to show conditions "before, and after."

The county is treated throughout as an area of state administration, rather than as an area for local self-government. No doubt this treatment is in keeping with the tendency of the times. Institutions of local self-government have been decaying rapidly in the past few decades.

On the whole the report is a valuable contribution to our knowledge of the actual workings of county government. One does not need to acquiesce in the proposals for sweeping reform, when expressing admiration for the work that has been done. County government in Virginia has been opened up to public inspection by skillful hands; and public authorities in Virginia, and elsewhere, can profit much by a careful study of this excellent report.

KIRK H. PORTER.

State University of Iowa.

✸

TAXATION: An Introductory Study. By Helen M. Rocca. Department of Efficiency in Government, National League of Women Voters, Washington, D. C. 1927. Pp. 43.

The aim of this study is to present an introduction to the subject of taxation. The writer in plain and simple language emphasizes the importance of a knowledge of the fundamental facts about taxation, defines the technical terms used in discussing the more elementary problems of taxation, and describes the kinds of taxes in use by the local, state, and federal governments. For a brief summary of our exceedingly complex tax situation, this study is admirably executed. It is obvious, however, that within the brief compass of forty-three pages, one cannot penetrate into the subject very deeply. In addition to defining terms, the pamphlet discusses very briefly the causes of increase in public expenditures, the relation of governmental costs to national income and wealth and per capita incomes, the salient features of the state and federal revenue systems. A concluding section considers proposals for new kinds of taxes. The writer does not discuss the equity or justice of the taxation system, expressing no opinions on the relative merits of the different taxes. The subject of tax administration receives mention only in an incidental way. Both students and laymen who desire an easy approach to the intricacies and complexities of our taxation problem will find Miss Rocca's brochure of great assistance.

M. L. FAUST.

✸

Three City Reports.—*Two Rivers, Wisconsin. Second Annual Report for the Year 1927. By Richard Biehl, City Manager. Pp. 45.*—This attractive little report is characterized by its clear charts and well-selected pictures. Their distribution throughout the report, however, could have been improved upon. The letter of trans-

mittal gives a brief résumé of work done, but places too much emphasis upon physical improvements with no mention of the social phases of government. No mention is made of the work contemplated for the future. Taxpayers are likely to be more interested in what they can look forward to than an account of accomplishments, many of which they have already observed. Furthermore, a proper distribution of space between the different activities is wanting. For example, three pages are devoted to a new bridge, while the health department is disposed of in two-thirds of one page. Too little care was used in the arrangement. The letter of transmittal is on page 9 and the organization chart on page 40. Both should be in the front of the report. This carelessness in arranging such good material is all that prevents this report from being among the very best of the year.

Ironwood, Michigan. Annual Report for the Fiscal Year Ending February 28, 1927. By W. M. Rich, City Manager, Pp. 80.—The favorable features of this report are its size, attractive cover, the clear organization chart, and a proper balance of space between the various activities. It lacks impressiveness mainly because it contains long paragraphs of fine print and several consecutive pages of reading material unbroken by picture, chart, or table. On the other hand, there are several well-chosen pictures and a few charts which are none too clear, because they attempt to portray too much. A chart must be simple to attract the interest of the casual reader. The last 21 pages are taken up with a detailed audit of the year's financial transactions. Other more interesting financial statistics are graphically presented in the report proper. The reviewer can see no good reason for including a detailed audit of a city's accounts in a public report intended for general reading.

Dayton, Ohio. Annual Report for the Year 1926. Pp. 48.—This is the second municipal report reviewed in these columns the past year that has been under 50 pages in length, and this one feature alone deserves special commendation. Other good features include a brief summary of the year's work at the beginning of the report, and the use of a good grade of paper and a type easily read. Its appearance is made attractive by a few pictures which, by the way, are poorly distributed among irrelevant reading material. The letter of transmittal deals at length with physical improvements contemplated for the future, but not a word for other activities quite as important but perhaps less obvious. The complete lack of charts and comparative data is disappointing, and the brevity with which the city's finances are treated is unsatisfactory. Except as to the distribution of pictures, the general arrangement of the material is satisfactory. With a little more care, this already good report could have been greatly improved.

C. E. RIDLEY.

✦

"Untersuchung von Wohnungs-grundrissen." —With characteristic German thoroughness, Alexander Klein, of Berlin, demonstrates new methods of measuring the worth of small house plans in the January, 1928, issue of *Staedtebau*, the monthly edited by Dr. Werner Hegemann.

1. An orderly scheme for shortening the lines of habitual movement between rooms and avoiding their crossing one another.

2. Concentration of the floor-areas required for such movements, leaving the maximum proportion of total area for use.

3. Direct access with the minimum of turns between the usable portions of rooms most intimately related in customary use.

4. Preservation of wall-surfaces from being haphazardly broken up by doors, windows and

large furniture, or by spotty shading from unequal natural lighting.

All of these and numerous other minor considerations result in psychologically important benefits to the members of the household through the restful sense of order, simplicity, lack of confusion in carrying on the principal activities of the house, cooking and eating, sleeping and washing, work and recreation.

ARTHUR C. COMEY.

Two Important Yearbooks.—The fifth annual edition of the *Municipal Index* published by the *American City Magazine*, came off the press in March. It reports the progress in the various lines of municipal government during the year 1927. Many valuable bibliographies and lists of municipal and state officials are also included.

The March issue of *Public Management* (pp. 207) comprises the Fourteenth Yearbook of the City Managers' Association. One hundred and twenty pages are devoted to the Proceedings of the Dubuque convention held in September, 1927. Persons studying the practical operation of manager government should not fail to examine these proceedings in which the various branches of municipal administration are discussed in a practical manner by the managers themselves. The cost of the fourteenth yearbook is $1.00, and it may be secured from the National Municipal League or from the City Managers' Association.

JUDICIAL DECISIONS

EDITED BY C. W. TOOKE

Professor of Law, Georgetown University

City Plan—Control of Regulation of Plats in Outlying Districts.—The Supreme Court of Ohio in *Prudential Co-op Realty Co.* v. *Youngstown*, 160 N. E. 695, decided March 7, 1928, upholds the constitutionality of the provision of the general code requiring plats of land within three miles of the city limits to have the written approval of the city planning commission as a condition precedent to the right of the owner of the land to record his plat in the recorder's office of the county where such municipality is located. The opinion of the court reviews at length the delegation of extra-mural powers to cities by the state legislature and sustains its exercise in the instant case. Ohio thus follows the District of Columbia and Michigan in giving its judicial approval to the method of protecting the city plan in outlying districts by the simple means of control over the privilege of dedication of lands for streets and highways. An extended note on the recent decision of the Supreme Court of Michigan on this point was published in the March issue of the REVIEW.

✤

Zoning—Location of Auxiliary Buildings.—In *Sundeen* v. *Rodgers*, 141 Atl. 142, decided by the Supreme Court of New Hampshire, March 6, the question was raised as to the validity of the provision of the zoning ordinance of the city of Manchester requiring that in residential districts auxiliary buildings may be erected only on the rear half of the lot. The court in affirming the dismissal of the bill and approving of the order of the board of adjustment in denying the petitioner a permit to erect such a building elsewhere on his lot, upholds the regulation as distinctly within the zoning powers of the city. It is noteworthy that in this case, as in several others arising in other states since the decision of the Supreme Court in *Village of Euclid* v. *Ambler Realty Company* (272 U. S. 365), the court decides the question upon the general principles of zoning, rather than upon the authority of the many cases upholding a similar exercise of the police power which were decided long before any zoning laws were enacted.

Police Power—Exercise Subject to Admiralty Law.—The paramount force of admiralty jurisdiction over the municipal law of any state is illustrated in the case of *In re Highland Navigation Corporation*, 24 Fed. (2d) 582, recently decided by the District Court of the Southern District of New York. This was a proceeding for the limitation of the liability of the owners of two ships which were destroyed by fire while moored at their piers in the harbor of New York. An ordinance of the city provides that in case any wrecked vessel is abandoned for ten days, and upon notice the owner fails to move it, the commissioner shall cause the vessel to be removed and may recover the expense thereof from the owner. The court held that under the admiralty law the owner had a right to limit its liability to the extent of the provisions of the federal statute under which the proceeding was brought. It was also strongly intimated by the court that the right of the owner of a wrecked vessel to abandon it without any personal liability whatsoever was absolute under the maritime law and also under the federal statutes. State and municipal regulations must necessarily be subject to the rules of admiralty. A common application of this principle is the imposition of liability upon a city to respond in damages for negligence in operation of a fire patrol boat when the action is brought in admiralty. (*Workman* v. *New York*, 179 U. S. 552.)

✤

Public Purposes—Power to Expend Money for Patriotic Celebrations.—The Supreme Court of Pennsylvania in *Sambor* v. *Hadley, City Controller* (140 Atl. 347), passed upon the validity of the Statute of April 6, 1927, empowering the city of Philadelphia to appropriate money to pay for services previously rendered and materials previously furnished for the public exhibition celebrating the sesqui-centennial anniversary of the signing of the Declaration of Independence. The question was raised by a taxpayer's action to restrain the city officers from expending additional funds of the $5,000,000 appropriation voted in 1928 under authorization of the statute,

344

some four-fifths of which had already been paid out of the city treasury. The court upheld the constitutionality of the act upon numerous precedents, and further ruled that the petitioner in any event was barred by his laches in raising the question at this late date. The decision of the court in holding that irregularities in complying with the strict limitations placed upon the exercise of the delegated power is quite at variance with the ruling of the New York Court of Appeals in *Schiefflin* v. *Hylan* (226 N. Y. 254, 1923), in which case, however, the action was brought before the expenditures had been incurred by the city authorities.

✦

Legislative Control over Wages on Municipal Works.—By dismissing a writ of certiorari in the case of *Campbell* v. *City of New York* (155 N. E. 668, reported in the June, 1927, number of the REVIEW), the Supreme Court of the United States has in effect affirmed the decision of the New York Court of Appeals, thus limiting the application of *Connolly* v. *General Construction Company* (269 U. S. 148) to actions to enforce a criminal penalty. In the latter case the Court held that the standard "the prevailing rate of wages in the locality where the work is performed" was too indefinite to define responsibility for criminal action. In *Campbell* v. *New York*, the Court of Appeals held that, notwithstanding the decision in the *Connolly* v. *General Construction Company* case, the statutory provision prohibiting the state or any city from entering into a contract for public work unless such a clause was incorporated in the contract was valid, and that Campbell, as a taxpayer, might maintain his action to enjoin the letting of a public contract without such a provision. The action of the Court, therefore, leaves the decision in *Atkin* v. *Kansas* (191 U. S. 207) in full force, except that the standard prescribed may not be made the basis of criminal liability.

✦

Special Assessments—Direct Liability of City on Bonds Issued.—The Supreme Court of the United States on April 9 affirmed the decision of the Circuit Court of Appeals, ninth circuit, in the case of *Moore* v. *City of Nampa* (18 Fed. (2d) 860) reported in the April issue of the REVIEW. In the unanimous opinion of the Court, Mr. Justice Butler points out that the bonds in question under the statutes of Idaho were made solely a claim against the special assessments to be collected and declared that no holder should have any claim against the city. They were not negotiable (*U. S. Mortgage Co.* v. *Sperry*, 138 U. S. 313) and the holder, therefore, took them subject to all legal and equitable defenses available against the original purchaser. The false certificate by the mayor and treasurer, stating that at the time of the original sale of the bonds no suit was threatened or pending in respect to the validity of the bonds, was issued without authority and could not be binding on the city. The city council was the governing body of the city and the statement was not made or authorized by it. As the action was in tort based upon negligence or misrepresentation, no cause of action was made out in the complaint. The opinion of the Supreme Court is reported in 48 Court Reporter at page 340.

✦

Police Power—Regulation of Oil Wells within City Limits—The courts of Kansas for many years have taken the leadership in recognizing the factual changes in municipal life and in readily adapting the common law principles to the new conditions. They have taken advanced ground in extending the doctrine of implied powers of municipalities to cover with legal sanction the efforts of the local governing bodies to extend their functions to meet the rapidly developing social needs, without waiting for the express authorization by legislative power of the state.[1]

It is not surprising, therefore, to find the legislature of Kansas delegating to municipalities the most extensive of its police powers. In *Marrs* v. *City of Oxford*, 24 Fed. (2d) 541, the validity of an ordinance regulating the operation of oil and gas wells within the city limits was before the federal district court. The action was in equity to enjoin the enforcement of the ordinance which required that a permit must be secured to drill for oil and gas, that only one permit should be granted in a given block and that the person securing such permit should allocate to the other land owners in the block a proportion of the oil and gas thus produced, based upon their proportionate holdings. The first question necessarily involved was the power of the state so to regulate the industry, which was sustained upon authority of the numerous decisions of the Supreme Court on the extent of the police power. The second question of the delegation of this power to the municipality was upheld under the express provisions of section 12-106, R. S. Kan-

[1] Wichita v. Clapp, 263 Pac. 12, reported in the April issue of this REVIEW, Vol. XVII, p. 238.

sas, 1923, which confer upon cities of the third class the power to "grant permits or make contracts with persons or corporations to mine coal, oil or gas within the limits of said city, under such restrictions as shall protect public and private property and insure proper remuneration for such grants." The third question whether the ordinance offended in the method of its exercise was resolved in its favor upon the ground that the classification was upon a reasonable basis. (*Lindsay* v. *Carbonic Gas Co.*, 220 U. S. 61.)

It may be noted that the refusal to grant an injunction against criminal prosecution under this ordinance was affirmed by the Supreme Court of Kansas last December in *Ramsey* v. *Oxford*, 261 Pac. 572. It may also be of interest to compare the decision with that of the Supreme Court of California in *Pacific Palisades Ass'n* v. *Huntington Beach* (1925), 196 Cal. 211, 213 Pac. 538, in which it was held that a zoning ordinance which forbade the erection or operation of any oil or gas wells in certain restricted districts was unconstitutional and void.

✤

Civil Service—Construction of the Constitution of Ohio.—By a decision handed down by the Supreme Court of Ohio, in *Hile* v. *City of Cleveland*, 160 N. E. 621, the cause of civil service has been dealt a severe blow. The state constitution provides that:

Appointments and promotions in the civil service of the state, the several counties, and cities, shall be made according to merit and fitness, to be ascertained, as far as practicable, by competitive examinations. Laws shall be passed providing for the enforcement of this provision.

Section 96 of the Cleveland city charter reads:

No person shall be appointed or employed in the classified service of the city under any title, not appropriate to the duties to be performed and no person shall be transferred to, or be assigned to perform any duties of, a position subject to competitive tests unless he shall have been appointed to the position from which the transfer is made as a result of open competitive test equivalent to that required for the position to be filled, or unless he shall have served with fidelity for at least two years immediately preceding in a similar position under the city.

The court in holding that it is not practical to subject employees of the city who have held their positions for two years to a civil service examination as prerequisite to appointment to the classified service, says that this rule is in accord with the letter and spirit of the constitutional provision, but fails to explain in what way it is not practical for men whose qualifications are supe-

rior because of previous service to submit themselves to such examinations. The constitutional exception evidently was inserted to apply only to instances in which an examination would not be feasible to determine the ability of candidates or those in which an emergency would require summary action. The decision is a remarkable example of constitutional construction, comparable with the decision of the same court last year in *State* v. *City of Fremont* (157 N. E. 318), which practically nullified the initiative and referendum clause of the Ohio constitution.

✤

Special Assessment Liens—Effect of Sale of Lands for State and County Taxes.—In *City of Tacoma* v. *Fletcher Realty Co.*, decided by the Supreme Court of Washington, March 5 (264 Pac. 997), the question involved was whether the purchaser at a county tax foreclosure sale, where the city has been regularly served, takes title subject to local special assessments. The court by a vote of three to two held that, under the statutes of the state, the lien given for special assessments is subject to that for general taxes and that the purchaser at a foreclosure sale for general taxes takes the property free from the lien for special assessments.

The law of special assessment liens is in great confusion, being often subject to vague statutes which have not yet received final interpretation by the courts. General tax liens are paramount to all other liens, judgments and claims, a principle that is laid down by statute in many states,[1] and therefore in some jurisdictions are held superior to those imposed by special assessment laws, unless the statute expressly provides otherwise.[2]

The question whether the purchaser at a general tax sale takes title free from all liens, subject only to the right of redemption, depends upon the existing statutes. In some states the statutes are so construed that the title of a purchaser at a tax sale is not only superior to other earlier tax liens, but free and clear of all prior public liens.[3]

[1] In re Salzberg, 206 N. Y. S. 837, 240 N. Y. 651.
Fleckenstein v. Baxter, 114 Mo. 493, 21 S. W. 852.
Stevenson v. Henkle, 100 Va. 501, 42 S. E. 692.

[2] Bennett v. Denver, 197 Pac. 768 (Colo. 1921).
White v. Thomas, 91 Minn. 395, 98 N. W. 101.
Hollenbeck v Seattle, 136 Wash. 508, 240 Pac. 916.
Turley v. St. Francis Road Dist., 287 S. W. 196 (Ark. 1926).

[3] Abbot v. Frost, 185 Mass. 398, 70 N. E. 478.
First Nat. Bank. v. Hendricks, 134 Ind. 361, 33 N. E. 110.
Verdery v. Dotterey, 69 Ga. 194.
Robbins v. Barron, 32 Mich. 36.
State v. Camp, 79 Minn. 343, 82 N. W. 645.

Other cases hold that the tax sale does not cut off existing liens for other taxes nor prior vested rights, whether acquired by mortgage, dower, homestead or contract.[1] It is, therefore, necessary in any given case to examine the existing statutes and all the decisions construing them to determine the value of any special assessment lien regularly adopted under statutory authority.

In *Maryland Realty Company v. Tacoma* (121 Wash. 230, 209 Pac. 1), decided in 1922, the Supreme Court of Washington had held that when the county sold land which it had bid in at a tax sale, it sold it free from the lien of special assessments. The instant case holds that when a private individual buys land at a county tax sale, all proceedings being regular and the municipality having been made a party, the land is purchased free from the lien of special assessments. It can readily be seen that special assessment bonds, if made subject to the limitations imposed in the case of *Moore v. Nampa* (48 S. Ct. R. 340) and under statutes similar to those in the

state of Washington, are without any adequate security; the purchaser in fact is not making an investment but a speculation. The effect must inevitably be to make special assessment too costly to be a practical method of financing public improvement.

The instant case was in tort and no question of the impairment of the contractual obligation was involved. The laws existing at the time municipal bonds are issued enter into and become a part of the contract protected under the federal constitution. The power of the state to take away remedies of the bondholder by the exercise of the paramount power of taxation raises the question of the adjustment of a conflict between two primary governmental principles. In the only cases where this question has been directly raised, the courts have held that the subsequent statute providing for the cutting off of the special assessment lien by foreclosure of a general tax lien was void as violating the contract clause of the federal constitution.[2]

---

[1] { Becham v. Gurney, 91 Iowa 621, 60 N. W. 187.
Gulf States v. Parker, 60 Fed. 974.
Bouton v. Lord, 10 Ohio St. 453. }

[2] { Moore v. Otis, 275 Fed. 747 (C. C. A., Okla., 1921).
Nelson v. Pitts, 126 Okla. 191, 259 Pac. 533.
Turley v. St. Francis Road District, 287 S. W. 196 (Ark. 1926). }

PUBLIC UTILITIES

EDITED BY JOHN BAUER
Director, American Public Utilities Bureau

New York City Loses First Court Decision on Subway Fares.—The subway fare controversy between the City of New York and the Interborough Rapid Transit Company reached the first definitive point on May 2, when the federal statutory court handed down its decision on the fundamental legal aspects of the case.

It will be recalled that the chief issue is the 5-cent fare fixed by "Contract No. 3" between the city and the Interborough Company. This contract was entered into in 1913, and provided not only for the construction of a number of new subway lines, but also for the operation of all the subway lines, including those that had been constructed under two earlier contracts. It fixed the terms at which the properties were constructed and operated; the relative capital contribution by the city and the company; the pooling of the revenues from all of the properties; the order of priority for the various purposes for which the revenues might be used; and the rate of fare at five cents, and no more.

The company has been operating New York City subways since October 1904, at a fixed five-cent fare. In 1907 more properties were added, and then followed the new subways constructed under the 1913 contract. Up to 1917, when the great increase in operating costs took place, the subway profits to the company were large, and had enabled it to pay dividends up to 20 per cent per annum. Following the great increase in operating costs and the opening up of new subways, the earnings dropped; but the company has realized substantial surpluses every year, with the exception of 1920. During the past fiscal year the surplus as reported from subway operation, above all fixed charges, amounted to over $6,000,000.

The financial returns from subway operation had been steadily improving, and the company would have been in a first-class financial condition, except for losses under its lease of the elevated properties from the Manhattan Railway Company. The city was not a party to this lease, and the operation is in every respect distinct from the subways. Early in February of this year, to the surprise of everyone, the company filed a new rate schedule, under which seven cents would be charged on all its lines. A petition was simultaneously filed with the Transit Commission seeking authorization to put the new schedule into effect at five days' notice. Later, the commission issued an order declaring the new schedule illegal. The company, even prior to the decision by the commission, had applied to the federal court to enjoin the commission from interfering with the charging of the 7-cent fare. Practically at the same time—a very few hours later—the city and the commission applied to a state court for an injunction to restrain the company from charging more than the rate fixed by the contract.

The first issue, therefore, was the conflict of jurisdiction between state and federal courts. This was argued before the federal court, which took and retained jurisdiction over the matter. Then followed the arguments before the federal court as to whether or not it was a matter in which equitable relief could be granted to the company. The city and the commission argued that the company was bound by the 5-cent fare under its contract, and that, therefore, the court was without power to grant relief to the company, even if such relief were needed. Facts, however, were also presented by the city to show that no relief was justified, even if there were no contract. The company, on the other hand, contended that the rate of five cents was not irrevocably fixed by contract; that the commission had denied the company its day in court; and that therefore it was a proper matter for the court to decide.

The court agreed practically throughout with the company's contentions. The substance of the decision is that the 5-cent fare fixed by Contract No. 3 came within the reserved power of the state and was subject to the state's policy of rate regulation. Since the contract was signed in 1913, it was held that the enactment of the Public Service Commission Law in 1907, providing for a comprehensive system of rate-making, had the effect of limiting the city's contractual rights in fixing fares. The chief issue was whether the city had authority granted by the legislature to fix a 5-cent fare by contract. The court did not deny that the legislature might explicitly grant the city the right to enter into such an agreement; and if such express provisions were made, the rate of fare would be binding, notwithstanding the financial results of operation. Such a grant, however, would have to be explicit, and not merely to be inferred. Since the state in 1907 did institute a general system of rate-making and vested such power in a commission, it must be assumed that the city did not have the right to fix a fare by contract unless there were express and direct legislative authorization for the purpose. The court could see no such authorization, either in the Rapid Transit Act or other statutory provisions.

Here we have the heart of the entire problem. There can be no doubt, we believe, that when Contract No. 3 was entered into in 1913, both parties unquestionably assumed that the 5-cent fare was as much a part of the agreement as were any of the other reciprocal rights and obligations. The city was obligated to finance the construction program, and it has a total of nearly $175,-000,000 invested in the properties. Under the contract, it took a deferred position on the greater part of this investment, in order that the company might equip the subways and furnish certain contributions to construction. There were many complicated financial provisions, and the company received substantial compensation or advantages for the obligations that it assumed. Among these obligations was the operation of the property at a 5-cent fare for the duration of the contract, which expires in 1967.

The contract had been thoroughly studied by many lawyers, both on the public and company side, and there was never a hint that the 5-cent fare might be legally defective. The Court of Appeals—the highest tribunal in the state—had passed upon the contract, and decided that it represented a valid city purpose. There can be no doubt that the city did invest its millions of dollars expecting that the company would furnish the service provided for, and that the fare would be five cents.

The statutory court—a federal body—has thus reached a decision which was certainly contrary to the generally assumed state of the law, either when the contract was entered into or up to the present time. It has, therefore, in reality undertaken to construe the statutes and the law of the state of New York. From a broad, public standpoint, the question might be asked, why should the federal court set aside the terms of a contract, when to accomplish that result certain statutes of a state required special construction in the light of other laws of that state? Why not let the state courts construe the state laws relating to special and technical state policies?

This case stands unique among the various cases that have come either before state or federal courts involving rights fixed by franchise or contract. It is true that the Court of Appeals of the state of New York had declared that rates fixed by franchise subsequently to 1907 would be ineffective because of the Public Service Commission law enacted during that year. But that related only to an ordinary franchise grant, in which a fare condition was placed. It did not apply to an extended and financially complicated contract, in which the city and the company were financial partners, and wherein the rights and duties of each were specifically stated. Nor did it apply to a case where a comprehensive statutory authority was granted, as was the case with the Rapid Transit Act applying to subway construction and operation.

If such an important provision in Contract No. 3 can be nullified, it is hard to conceive how any municipality could today enter into any kind of agreement with a utility company with assurance that the clear and explicit terms would not be set aside by the federal courts. The issue, therefore, affects not only the city of New York, but municipalities and public bodies everywhere. What rights of contract do they have? Can they do anything on their own responsibility without the overshadowing power of the federal courts to set aside terms designed for the protection of the public and along lines of policy determined by local authority?

There may be a question of policy whether or not the 5-cent fare in New York is a wise arrangement. There certainly is always a question of expediency in fixing a rigid fare for an extensive period. But this was settled by the 1913 contract, whether wise or otherwise. The company assumed definite responsibilities, and certainly derived proportional advantages. There was a contract which everybody thought was a contract. To a lay mind, it would seem that the legal grounds for setting aside the 5-cent fare should have been explicit; not the other way, as found by the court in this case.

There is a second angle: the court approved the 7-cent fare pending the investigation by the master and the final determination of the adequacy of the 5-cent fare. In discussing the financial set-up as to valuation and return, the court uncritically accepted the company's figures; and thus authorized an increase in fare under circumstances extremely difficult to justify from a responsible public standpoint. There is no clear reason why, in any case, the increase should not be kept in abeyance until the many questions of fact are thoroughly determined through regular judicial procedure.

The legal question as to the contractual basis of the 5-cent fare will go promptly to the Supreme Court of the United States. A reversal is, of course, not impossible. The Supreme Court is much more impressed by public rights and public aspects of utilities than many of the lower federal courts. Unfortunately, we have here a matter that does not depend directly and expressly upon the law, which is plain to all. The decision rests upon fundamental and personal points of view, which involve individual slants of policy, and not the pure substance of legal and constitutional determination.

If the company is sustained by the Supreme Court, then the final matter will be to determine whether in fact the 5-cent fare, under the particular conditions in New York, is unreasonable and confiscatory. If this becomes a question of real inquiry, there are substantial grounds for believing that the city will be finally sustained. But this involves complicated questions of fact, which will be presented in this department as they arise.

❖

Public Utility Propaganda on Grand Scale.—The federal trade commission has made a thorough job investigating the propaganda conducted by the National Electric Light Association through its own organization directly and through various subsidiary and affiliated groups ramifying throughout the country, including practically the entire electric industry as well as other utilities.

The disclosures that have been made cannot be said to be altogether startling to the comparatively few people who have been following intelligently developments during the past five or ten years. The fact, of course, has been plain that the chief function of the National Electric Light Association has been to mould public opinion; to form favorable impressions among people of influence, to guide chambers of commerce, public organizations, women's clubs, colleges and universities, editors of newspapers, and the public schools,—also to sway public officials and legislative bodies.

A summary of the results to date were presented for the press by Basil Manley, under date of May 10. Mr. Manley states that the evidence thus far developed by the attorneys for the federal trade commission shows: (1) Payment of subsidies by the National Electric Light Association to leading colleges and universities; (2 censorship of textbooks used in schools and colleges for the purpose of eliminating material which is considered even remotely injurious to public utility corporations; (3) subsidizing and otherwise cultivating underpaid professors of economics in high schools and colleges so as to promote a friendly and uncritical attitude on their part toward the industry; (4) preparation and distribution in public schools of textbooks and pamphlets prepared at the expense of the utility associations to present public service corporations in the most favorable light and prevent more drastic regulation or public ownership.

The concrete details are a bit raw, but they have been amusing because of the naïveté of the propagandists and their inevitable futility. The work has been clever, far too clever, for its own ultimate success. It was clever to prepare "primers" for the public schools, to distribute "Aladdin Lamps" among school children, and to let Harvard prepare a textbook. But the very light of the "lamps" has flashed back and revealed the propagandists in ridiculous behavior.

In the further interest of light, the commission should bring out also the number of former public utility commissioners who have been brought into the utility organizations, the judges, lawyers, engineers, and other technical men. It should reveal the constant tempting of important persons, and, conversely, the open and veiled intimidation of people on the public side and the creation of an effective blacklist in the field of regulation. There are also the financial practices, including the judicious sprinkling of stock among influential persons, and the control exercised by the large holding company groups over costs, valuation and rates. The country might well be informed completely of the brilliant efforts of the leaders of the industry. Little wonder that there was bitter opposition to the proposed senate investigation.

It is easy, however, to overstate and exaggerate. While it is well to bring out the glaring absurdities that have been perpetrated upon the public, we must not conclude that all public utility managements have been rotten. The ordinary manager is a high-grade man, and he does have a proper conception of his public duties. Perhaps the chief effect of the disclosures is to give the decent element in utilities a chance to survive and to furnish the service that the utilities are intended to provide. The "clever" fringe has had vastly too much influence in proportion to its numbers and ultimate power. Fundamental decency obtains in the general run of public utility people and interests just as in other walks of life.

✦

League of Women Voters to Study Public Utility Regulation.—One of the pre-convention programs of the League of Women Voters in its recent Chicago meetings was devoted to a discussion of public utility regulation. The editor of this department presented the economic background of regulation, described the existing policies and methods, and pointed out the changes needed to make regulation effective.

S. Ferguson, president of the Hartford Electric Light Co., spoke on the problems of the public utility manager, and described efforts made by the companies to meet their public responsibilities in a constructive way. Donald Richberg, who is one of the few first-class lawyers consistently on the public side of utility controversies, spoke of the more dismal side of regulation; how the work is frustrated by the kind of things that have been revealed in recent months by the federal trade commission.

In its formal meetings the League voted to place public utility regulation upon its study program for next year. Its ultimate purpose is to formulate a program which may be placed before the legislatures of the various states to put regulation upon a more satisfactory basis. This is an encouraging movement, which indicates that the pendulum is swinging from apathy to a

healthy interest in this important field of public service.

✦

Indiana Public Service Commission Limits Rate Case Expense.—The common course in a rate case is for the company to spare no efforts as to lawyers, engineers, accountants and other experts to present the facts fully from its own standpoint. The cost is then included in operating expense and charged to the consumers. On the public side, however, there is usually parsimonious regard for its several expenses; only the minimum effort is made in preparing the facts and analysis. The commission usually does little or nothing except to hear both sides. Consumers therefore pay for the elaborate and costly preparation of the company, also the skimpy preparation of their own side, and finally pay the high rates sought by the company.

The Indiana Public Service Commission has instituted a new régime in regard to these matters. For one thing, it makes its own investigation in rate cases, and then actually performs the function originally intended for the commissions. Further, it recently adopted a policy of inquiring into legal fees and other rate case expense incurred by the companies, and of preventing the inclusion of excessive costs in the charges to the consumers. This rule followed the disclosure of a case wherein the appearance for a single day before the commission resulted in a legal fee of $2,000 for one firm, $750 for another, and $350 for a third, in addition to $6,250 for valuation expense. The property was that of a small company.

Here is another ray of light indicating that regulation is taking a turn toward the better representation of the public interest. While, of course, a company should be allowed to include in operating expense the reasonable costs of a rate case procedure, the abuses have been flagrant, and the Indiana commission is to be congratulated for stepping in the right direction. Its lead may well be followed by other commissions.

GOVERNMENTAL RESEARCH ASSOCIATION NOTES

EDITED BY RUSSELL FORBES
Secretary

Recent Reports of Research Agencies.—The following reports have been received at the central library of the Association since April 1, 1928:

Boston Finance Commission:
Letter to the Mayor and City Council Regarding Amount of Paving in the Past Ten Years.
Salary Increases for Officials of City Council.
Letter to the Mayor Regarding Metropolitan Water System.

Chicago Bureau of Public Efficiency:
The Bond Issues to be Voted upon April 10, 1928.

Dayton Research Association:
A Study of the Practices in Feeding Prisoners in Montgomery County Jail.

Bureau of Governmental Research, Kansas City, Kansas, Chamber of Commerce:
Municipal Budget Procedure.
A Memorandum to the Safety Council; Considerations Which Should Govern the Installation of Traffic Signal Lights.

New York State Bureau of Municipal Information:
Delinquent Village Tax Collections, Report No. 820.

Ohio Institute:
Ohio Governments and Where They Get Their Money.

San Francisco Bureau of Governmental Research:
A City Manager for San Francisco.

St. Louis Bureau of Municipal Research:
Gasoline Tax Revenue.

St. Paul Bureau of Municipal Research:
Memorandum re Bureau of Municipal Equipment.
Memorandum re Recommendations of Committee of Schools.
Memorandum re the Functions and Organization of the Department of Public Works.
The Bus Amendment to Be Voted on May 1.

A Few Typical Statements Issued by the St. Paul Bureau of Municipal Research during 1927.

✤

Boston Finance Commission.—The commission has issued the following since May 1: report to the city council recommending that salary increases for officials of the city council, and that the creation of certain unnecessary positions in city departments, be denied; and to the mayor regarding the burden arising from proposed extension of the metropolitan water system.

✤

Citizens' Research Institute of Canada.—The study of the cost of government in Canada for 1926 has been completed. This covers the field of dominion government, nine provincial governments, and seventeen of the larger Canadian cities. Information is published on a per capita basis for comparative purposes and a final report shows the combined cost of government in the seventeen respective cities.

At the request of the township of East York, a suburban district of Toronto with a population of about 25,000, a further supplementary survey of the municipality was conducted, analyzing its financial condition and outlining a suggested program of capital works which might be undertaken during the year. This is the third report of this type made by the Institute for this particular municipality.

The director has completed his work in Winnipeg, Manitoba, where he acted as chairman of its commission on civic salaries. The positions and salaries in the civic service, classified and standardized by this report, numbered in all 1,857, and a large number of recommendations were made bearing thereon.

✤

Cincinnati Bureau of Municipal Research.—Following through an earlier report on police administration prepared by Bruce Smith of the New York Bureau, D. C. Stone of the Cincinnati Bureau has completed a report on the police record system. This system is designed to furnish complete information on police activities from the complaint of crime to final disposition in the courts. The Bureau is now coöperating with the police department in the initial steps of installation.

Philip H. Cornick of the New York Bureau has studied the Cincinnati special assessment situation and proposed many changes in procedure and policy of spreading assessments. Several of these proposals have been adopted. A complete report is in course of preparation.

The findings of the study of felony cases were presented at a public meeting sponsored by the Cincinnatus Association. At this meeting, which was exceptionally well attended, over 100 slides were thrown on the screen. These slides showed the causes of crime and the community facilities for coping with crime. The results of the Bureau survey are now being put in pamphlet form.

This survey, on which J. L. Jacobs has been acting as consultant, is practically completed. The recommendations will discuss the office procedure with special consideration of the relative merits of the photostat as compared with hand or machine recording.

The county commissioners of Hamilton County have formally requested the Bureau to make a preliminary survey of all county departments as the basis for subsequent determination of special surveys to be more intensively followed through later.

Similarly, the board of education has requested the Bureau to undertake a preliminary survey which will afford a basis of recommendation as to the specific surveys to be undertaken.

✻

Cleveland Municipal Research Bureau.—Leyton E. Carter resigned the directorship of the Cleveland Municipal Research Bureau to become director of the Cleveland Foundation on May 1.

The Foundation is a community trust, in fact the first of its kind set up in this country. It is charged with the responsibility of distributing the income of funds held in trust for civic, educational and philanthropic purposes. The idea has been widely copied, there now being 63 such trusts in various American cities.

✻

Taxpayers' Research League of Delaware.—The League has made an analysis of the costs of operation in the Richardson Park school district. A preliminary study, for the Social Service Club of Wilmington, has been made of the conditions bearing on the possible organization of a community chest for the city.

The director of the League has conferred with the state sinking fund commission on the League's proposal for eliminating the surplus in the state sinking fund, and a schedule has been prepared showing how all outstanding state highway bonds (which are redeemable before maturity) might be profitably called and canceled on the equal-payment serial plan.

For the Delaware Association of Insurance Agents, a study has been made of the operation of the state insurance commissioner's office.

Work has been continued on the proposed state finance code, on the study of the fiscal administration of the town of Milford, on the accounting system of the Delaware Industrial School for Girls, and the League's coöperative effort with the Kiwanis Club for the stimulation of registration and voting.

The League has open a position on its staff for a specialist in finance, preferably one who has worked in state finance. The work of this staff member will cover methods of accounting, auditing, budgeting, assessments and financial control, and policies relating to bond issues, sinking-fund administration, and taxation. Correspondence from available candidates is invited.

✻

Des Moines Bureau of Municipal Research.—The Bureau closely scrutinized the 1928 city budget which was prepared during the first week in April. As it appeared that the budget requests were considerably in excess of possible revenues, the Bureau sent a communication to the city council suggesting that the budget be based on the 1927 expenditures. This suggestion was eventually adopted.

The Bureau compiled a report of the janitorial supplies used by every city department and suggested that bid prices be obtained on the year's supply rather than on small purchases as needed as has been done in past years.

✻

Civic Affairs Department, Indianapolis Chamber of Commerce.—The department has led a successful effort for obtaining a new city council composed of leading citizens of Indianapolis. Early in the month of April, it became apparent that most of the seven indicted members of the council desired to plead guilty to misfeasance charges and to resign from office.

The prosecuting attorney asked the aid of the

civic affairs committee, both in advising him as to his course of procedure, and if vacancies occurred, by nominating persons to fill the vacancies.

The civic affairs department invited the Indianapolis Board of Trade and the City Manager League to join in its consideration of the problem, and these organizations almost unanimously approved the plan of accepting pleas of guilty providing strong men were obtained to fill the vacancies.

Nominations were made, and seven new members were eventually elected entirely from the list of nominations made by this committee. Such outstanding citizens as Meredith Nicholson, noted Hoosier author; Edward W. Harris, prominent business executive; John F. White, social reform leader; and Hermon P. Lieber, prominent business and social welfare leader, were drafted for places on the council.

These seven members, with two members of the old council who were in no way connected with the criminal charges against the other councilmen, now comprise the city council of Indianapolis, and the step which has been led by the civic affairs committee has gone far to restore public confidence in the city government of Indianapolis. Indianapolis now has both a mayor and a council who are friendly to the city manager form of government and who will aid in the transfer from the present form to the city manager form at the end of 1929, as voted by Indianapolis 5 to 1 last May.

The civic affairs department conducted a Get-Out-The-Vote campaign for the primary election of May 8.

✢

Kansas City Public Service Institute.—The city bond proposals totaling $18,500,000 and the county bond proposals totaling $12,500,000 have been studied quite extensively. At the request of the city manager the probable tax rates necessary for interest and retirement charges on the proposed city bonds, if voted, were calculated. Tax rates were also calculated on the county bonds. Further study of these proposals is being made with the view to presenting statements to the public giving all possible information.

The report on the survey of county welfare activities has been completed and will be distributed within a very short time. This study has been under way for over a year. Recommendations vary from comprehensive ones such as that for reorganization of welfare work to minor ones affecting merely one activity or one institution. It is expected that this report will form the basis for large improvements in economy and efficiency of welfare operation, as well as for provisions for welfare needs which are not now taken care of.

Further study was made of the adaptability of the photostat method of recording documents in the office of the recorder of deeds. A report on this will be issued soon, and efforts to secure the adoption of the photostat method will be continued.

Some preliminary studies were made of the method of assessing property for taxation in Jackson County. This is a subject in which the Chamber of Commerce is interested and which it will probably ask the Institute to study and report on. The purpose of the study will be to determine the methods used in assessing property, the equality of assessments as now made, and the advisability of establishing a uniform system of assessments such as is used in some other cities.

Some attention has been devoted to the proposed reorganization plan for the state government. During 1926 and 1927, when plans were being drafted and presented to the state legislature, the Institute gave some attention to this subject. A new plan is to be presented to the next legislature. Consideration of various objections to specific parts of the plan last year and consideration of proposals in general has been asked of the Institute by the Associated Industries of Missouri, which is the principal organization active for the reorganization, and by the State League of Women Voters which has given much attention to the subject.

✢

Philadelphia Bureau of Municipal Research.— The Philadelphia Conference on Government held its second annual series of meetings on March 15, 16, and 17. Mr. Beyer devoted a large amount of time to the work of the program committee and presided over a round-table discussion on "Economies in Administration." At this meeting Mr. Shenton presented the possibilities of improving the efficiency and reducing the cost of recording deeds in Philadelphia; Mr. Howland discussed the relation of metering and of reducing wastes in the distribution system to the cost of supplying Philadelphia with water; and Mr. Patterson made a statement of possible economies in the city's borrowing practices. Mr.

Howland and Mr. Beatty served as members of the sub-committee on water supply of the committee of engineers appointed to work out a program of public improvements for the city, and Mr. Howland read a paper at one of the meetings on the possibilities of obtaining water from sources other than the present.

About a year ago the Philadelphia Bureau reported at some length its part in the campaign for the adoption of serial bonds in Philadelphia. It was thought that the story would be of interest to those who concerned themselves with the methods by which municipal research goes over the goal line. At the close of the story the Chamber of Commerce had approved a recommendation of straight serial bonds made by its committee on taxation and public expenditure, on which the Bureau is represented, and the mayor had appointed a committee to study the subject.

Since then the ball has unquestionably moved forward, but as yet is not over the line. This spring the proposal of new bond issues raised the serial-bond question. As the committee appointed by the previous mayor had not reported, the new mayor appointed a new committee, made up, however, of the same persons. The Bureau had the opportunity of furnishing this committee with a large amount of material and made numerous suggestions to it. The report of the mayor's committee, like that of the Chamber of Commerce, favored straight serial bonds. There followed a public meeting called by the mayor to which the Bureau received a special invitation, and at which the Bureau expressed its approval of the report of the mayor's committee. A few days later council's finance committee considered the question of making the pending loans payable serially. Mr. Beyer and Mr. Patterson held forth before this committee for over an hour answering questions put by the councilmen. Amendments to the loan ordinance which would make the loan serial had been drawn by the Bureau and were put at the disposal of the finance committee. The amendments had previously been submitted by the Bureau to a leading firm of Philadelphia bond attorneys, and had been approved by them. In the end the finance committee turned down the serial-bond proposal. Both the Chamber of Commerce and the mayor's committee had recommended straight serial bonds, but the councilmen apparently did not feel like incurring the heavier burden of such bonds in the earlier years of the loans even though this increased burden would be much more than offset by the savings in the later years.

When the loan ordinances came before council, the Bureau submitted a letter, accompanied by a number of tables showing, among other things, that practically all the benefits of the straight serial plan could be realized under an equal-annual-burden plan, except that the savings would be smaller, and that the debt charges under equal-annual-burden plan would be less than the charges under the present sinking-fund plan. However, it was too late to make any change in council's plans.

The attitude of public officials toward serial bonds and the evidences of a better understanding of the question encourage the Bureau to believe that considerable progress toward serial bonds has been made.

❀

Rochester Bureau of Municipal Research.— Raymond P. VanZandt, accountant of the Bureau, is on a six months' leave of absence to manage an industrial survey for the new industries bureau of the Chamber of Commerce.

The Bureau is devoting the major portion of its time to work on a new municipal code required by charter to become effective prior to January 1, 1929.

❀

Toledo Commission of Publicity and Efficiency. —The commission published on May 5 the annual report of the division of health. The report shows that 1927 was a banner health year for Toledo. The infant mortality rate was 62 per thousand, the lowest in the city's history. The death rate was also low—11.92 per thousand. Practically the only unfavorable item was the epidemic of rabies that prevailed during the year, 833 persons reported bitten, with two deaths. The city council passed an ordinance in April creating the position of full-time health officer, which was recommended by the commission over a year ago.

The street cleaning report, published in four installments of the *Toledo City Journal* during April and May, has resulted in the city's adopting five out of the twelve recommendations made. Toledo was found to have an extremely high unit cost for street cleaning—$3.30 per thousand square yards cleaned in 1926 as compared with an average of $.50 for seven other large cities. The commission recommended that flushers be purchased, and unnecessary employes be discharged in order to reduce costs.

Toledo uses special assessments to finance street cleaning. Due to interest charges and overhead assessing costs, this method of finance was found to have added an average of $30,000 per year to the total cost of street cleaning. The method was found to be inequitable, since it is impossible to determine the benefit received. It was therefore recommended that the city abandon special assessments for street cleaning.

A survey of the number of billboards in the city, together with the fees paid, revealed the fact that there are nearly 1,700 large 10' x 25' boards in the city which resulted in a revenue of approximately $1,000 in 1927.

At the request of the city council, the commission has collected information regarding ordinances of other cities regulating fake fire sales, going-out-of-business sales, etc. The council now has under consideration an ordinance presented by the Better Business Bureau for their regulation.

Another study undertaken by the commission at the request of council was the regulation of radio interference by ordinance. The data compiled so far shows only two cities which have this kind of ordinances—Zanesville, Ohio, and Fairfield, Iowa.

✢

Toronto Bureau of Municipal Research.—The study of municipal police service with relation to Toronto has been completed, and the city council has granted an increase to 100 men, instead of 300 requested by the then chief of police. Additional mechanical equipment also has been, or will be secured.

In line with recommendations made by the Bureau several years ago, that an advisory town planning committee be appointed by the city council to assist not only in drawing up a plan for the city and the order in which suggested improvements should be made, but also the method and possibility of financing suggested improvements, the Bureau recently issued two bulletins dealing with town planning in relation to Toronto. The question of the best method of dealing with town planning here is now under consideration by the department heads, having been referred to them for a report by the board of control.

The Bureau completed a study of the component elements which went to make up the city's tax rates for the years 1927 and 1928, and issued a report giving comparative figures in connection therewith for the two years under consideration.

Following considerable agitation for a change in the municipal election date in Toronto from the present New Year's Day to (probably) the first Monday in December, and following a request of the Mayor to attend a conference to consider this question, material was gathered from about thirty Canadian cities, and has been prepared for such use. Advantages of the plan appear to be that it would remove the subject of civic elections from the Christmas period and make it possible for the citizens to take greater interest in the subjects under discussion. It is also alleged that it would make it easier for housewives to attend the polls. In the majority of instances where the change has been made in Canadian cities it seemed to have had little effect in increasing the percentage of those who voted. Points against the change appear to be: (1) that since the fiscal year ends December 31, it would make it possible either for defeated candidates to conduct business for two or three weeks or might make it difficult to carry on business since defeated candidates would not attend council or committee meetings; (2) that it might make it more difficult for employees to vote unless extra time were allowed off by employers; (3) that schools could not be used for polling booths as at present unless they were closed to the children. If these were not used, other booths would have to be provided.

NOTES AND EVENTS

EDITED BY H. W. DODDS

Cleveland Women Voters Save Proportional Representation-Council Manager Plan.—For the second time within six months the present proportional representation-council manager charter of Cleveland has been upheld by the voters. In both cases the margin was scant, the results on April 24 being 44,122 in favor of retaining the charter to 40,890 in favor of abandoning it for the mayor form.

Immediately after the defeat on November 11 last of the Davis charter amendment proposing a return to the mayor-council form of government and the substitution of the ward system for proportional representation, Harry L. Davis pledged himself to continue the fight against the present council-manager charter. On December 2 the Davis headquarters announced that their rejected charter would be re-submitted in April with only a few minor revisions.

DAVIS SPRINGS A SURPRISE

For over a month thereafter inactivity seemed to be the policy of the Davis group until the sudden appearance on January 12 of a substantially altered Davis charter amendment. By revising the amendment to meet some of the most severely criticized items in his former proposal, Mr. Davis was successful in confusing the opposition. Unlike the former amendment which would have ousted the city manager from office six days after adoption, the new charter would not go into effect until January 1, 1930, thus allowing the present manager administration two years of grace. The clause in the rejected charter providing that all contracts in excess of $1,000 should be let by a board of control composed of the mayor and his department heads was revised to prohibit the awarding of such contracts "except upon either the approval of the council or upon competitive bidding." The third important change was the raising of the minimum wage for city labor on public works from $2.50 to $4.50 per day.

PARTIES SHIFT TO NEUTRAL POLICY

The first effect of this new proposal was to change the position of the Republican party organization from active opposition to the Davis charter to a policy of neutrality. Mr. Maurice Maschke, Republican party leader, explained the change in front, declaring that his previous objections to the Davis amendment had now been removed. But his decision was also influenced, no doubt, by his preoccupation with the Hoover-Willis fight in the Ohio primaries and by his desire to keep his party lines, in which there was no little Davis support, intact for the state and national elections in November.

WOMEN VOTERS TAKE CHARGE

The defection of both the Republican and Democratic party organizations from the ranks of the anti-Davis forces left the defense of the council-manager charter entirely with the independent groups of voters. During February and March there was a noticeable absence of activity among those opposing the Davis amendment. The local League of Women Voters attempted with little success to unite men's and women's organizations in defense of the present charter. Finally realizing that its organization was the only one in a position to provide effective and united opposition, the local League of Women Voters assumed complete responsibility. The Citizens League assisted in the campaign by presenting in two issues of its bulletin *Greater Cleveland*, lucid and well directed criticisms of the Davis Plan.

Unlike the three weeks of intense campaigning in the fall, this campaign lasted only a week and lacked both the publicity and the interest that made the November election so dramatic. As part of its tactics the League of Women Voters made little effort to hold many meetings of a general nature. The speakers for the Davis charter held a number of meetings, but found themselves frequently talking to dozens of voters where last fall hundreds had turned out. It was all old stuff to Clevelanders. A possible contributing factor to this lack of interest was the decision of the League of Women Voters to keep the campaign free from personalities and to concentrate on the problem of getting out the voters opposed to the Davis amendment.

There are some other phases of the campaign that deserve mention. The leaders of the Cleveland Federation of Labor added to the dramatic quality of the fall campaign by actively campaigning for the Davis charter. They took no such part in the April contest, due to a reconciliation with City Manager A. R. Hopkins. The labor leaders had been at odds with the manager over the question of overtime pay as provided for in the Sulzmann salary ordinance, but differences were adjusted in a series of conferences after the fall election, forcing Davis to carry on in the spring campaign without the official support of labor. City Manager Hopkins also took no active part in this campaign—even the newspapers desisted from their vigorous attack on Davis and his past record. Naturally, then, the campaign meetings of the Davis forces often fell flat with the element of personal conflict eliminated.

Evidence of fraudulent signatures in the Davis petitions uncovered by the Citizens League was another feature of the spring campaign. This resulted in an inconclusive investigation by the judiciary committee of the city council. The council turned over its findings to County Prosecutor E. C. Stanton, who at the present writing has secured the indictment of four petition signers. One case came to trial, but was dismissed by the court, while the other three were nolled. There is some ground for believing that little will be accomplished despite the numerous and unquestioned evidences of fraud.

By the defeat of his second charter amendment Harry L. Davis has lost much of his influence as a disturbing factor in the Republican party organization and as a foe of the manager plan. The defeat leaves Maurice Maschke, Republican leader, in complete control of the local party organization. It is possible that the next attempt to amend the present charter will seek to eliminate proportional representation and will have the support of Mr. Maschke and the Republican organization. A counter to this attempt may be the submission of an amendment making the present proportional representation system similar to the Cincinnati plan. City Manager W. R. Hopkins' position in relation to the party organizations has been strengthened since they can claim no credit for the recent victory. In a sense the result is a victory for Hopkins.

After all, the outstanding event of this campaign was the effective, organized support of the council-manager charter by the women voters of Cleveland. The local branch of the League of Women Voters successfully substituted for the two party organizations that had organized the defense in the fall election, and deserves the lion's share of the credit for the victory. Twenty-five of the thirty-three wards were organized with ward leaders and precinct captains, who directed an intensive house to house canvass. Precinct workers got out the stay-at-homes on election day while challengers and watchers were appointed in many of the precincts with the coöperation of the Democratic party. This entrance of the League of Women Voters into local politics may mean that hereafter attacks on the council-manager plan will meet with the same concerted and effective opposition in Cleveland as has been the case in Cincinnati.

R. O. Huus and A. H. Gross.
Western Reserve University.

✣

Newport C. M. Charter Again Meets Defeat by State Politicians.—In the spring of 1926, the representative council for the city of Newport authorized the appointment of a commission to study various forms of municipal government and to report back such a form as they deemed suitable for the city. This commission, after a thorough study and with the aid of Professor Edwin A. Cottrell and other eminent authorities, drafted a charter embodying the general principles of the council-manager form of municipal government.

The representative council approved the recommendation of the commission and voted to refer the question of the adoption of the charter to the electorate of Newport. The proposition appeared on the local ballot in November, 1926—"Shall the City of Newport adopt the Council-Manager form of Charter providing for a council of five (5) members elected from the City at large, without regard to ward lines and without party designation as recommended by the Commission on Charter Revision in its report received by the Representative Council on September 27, 1926?" —and was approved by the large vote of 5,020 in favor of the adoption to 1,865 opposed. This proposition received the largest percentage vote for any proposition ever submitted to the voters of this state.

In January, 1927, a new council of twenty-five went into office, created by virtue of a charter (political in type, embodying party designation, party caucus, ward lines and without a centralization of authority or responsibility with an annual budget of $1,500,000) forced upon Newport by the legislature without opportunity for referendum. This council, being hostile to the proposed council-manager charter, refused to submit it to the legislature for enactment into law.

The Volunteer Citizens Committee, a group of citizens who had sponsored the proposed charter from the time it was referred to the council, then took the initiative and caused a bill, incorporating the proposed charter, to be introduced in both branches of the legislature. This bill, by political manoeuvring, was referred to the corporations committee—in which there were no Newport members—when it properly should have been referred to the judiciary committee. The corporations committee gave a public hearing which was attended by numerous Newport citizens, many of whom spoke in favor of the passage of the charter bill. The opposition was mainly from those identified with the political machine in Newport. At this hearing, the members of the corporations committee raised no question concerning the phraseology or structure of the proposed charter.

In February, 1928, the Volunteer Citizens Committee again caused the proposed charter to be introduced in both branches of the legislature. The bill was again referred to the corporations committee, despite the requests of the Volunteer Citizens Committee that it be sent to the judiciary committee. The politicians then began to bestir themselves, and numerous letters appeared in the local press attacking various provisions of the proposed charter. It was strongly suspected that these attacks were made at the suggestion of the leaders of the state Republican organization in Providence.

A public hearing was held in the State House, Providence, in March, which was attended by more than 450 Newport citizens of which number, at least 400 favored the charter. At this hearing, the finance commissioner of Rhode Island, not a resident of Newport, not elected by the citizens of Newport, who is not a member of the legislature and whose duties pertain merely to the finances of the state, expressed at length his opposition to the charter. This gentleman, by virtue of his office, had absolutely no voice in the matter, but spoke as the recognized boss of the Re-

publican machine in Rhode Island. It was very clear that the politicians of the state had decided to deny to the people of Newport the form of government which they had so clearly approved sixteen months before the hearing.

During the closing days of the legislature, the politicians, both in Providence and Newport, attempted to create the impression that the proposed charter was not a council-manager charter and that it was unconstitutional in its terms. Various amendments were suggested by the opponents of the charter which would have nullified some of its most desirable features.

The outcome was as everyone had expected it would be. The politicians were in control in the legislature. In the house of representatives, the bill was reported for passage, but, on the motion of a member of the corporations committee, seconded by the chairman of the same committee, further consideration of the bill was indefinitely postponed. In the senate, the bill died in committee.

To all those who have followed the agitation, it is very apparent that the council-manager form of government is extremely distasteful to the politicians of the state and that they are prepared to use every political manoeuvre to prevent the establishment of such a form of government in any part of Rhode Island.

The Volunteer Citizens Committee are, naturally, disappointed that the wishes of the majority of the citizens of Newport have been disregarded, but the committee are prepared to carry on the fight for better government in Newport.

HORACE P. BECK.

✦

Has Zoning Failed?—An Answer to Dr. R. D. MacLaurin.—

To the Editor of the NATIONAL MUNICIPAL REVIEW:

Such articles as "Where Zoning Fails," by R. D. MacLaurin, in the NATIONAL MUNICIPAL REVIEW for May, are liable to become a barrier to the progress of zoning. Mr. MacLaurin overlooks a very important point. The police power resides in the state legislature, and is delegated by that body to others only under definite regulations and for definite purposes. Thus, for zoning, the police power is delegated "to regulate and restrict the height, number of stories, and size of buildings and other structures, the percentage of lot that may be occupied, the size of yards, courts, and other open spaces, the density of population, and the location and use of buildings, structures, and land for trade, industry, residence, or other purposes." The legislation goes on to define the method, and set up an expert body to prepare and administer the local ordinance adopted for this particular purpose. When the police power is delegated for the regulation of building construction or plumbing, it is done in the same way, and a separate body of experts provided. Factory inspection and regulation is usually delegated to a department of the state government.

If Mr. MacLaurin had read the paper on "Zoning and Health" by Mr. George C. Whipple, he would know that segregation of industry to separate districts is not based altogether on the question of "nuisance." This paper points out that there are "three primary phases of life, namely, work, recreation, and sleep. . . . Adequate provision for work, sleep and recreation . . . is essential to health. The necessary conditions are not the same for all three, . . ." It would evidently be unreasonable to require industry to maintain a condition that would be appropriate to either sleep or recreation.

The segregation of industry or business, that is, grouping industries of like nature, or business of like nature, together produces a gain in efficiency, and thus promotes the general welfare.

Smoke, noise, noxious odors, and fumes, are not the only things which make industries objectionable. The garment trades in New York City could not be classed as objectionable from any of these reasons, yet they ruined one high-class shopping district in lower Fifth Avenue, and came near ruining another on upper Fifth Avenue, until checked by the merchants' own efforts, and later by the zoning resolution.

Zoning is not based on the assumption that industries are nuisances, of themselves, but that they are nuisances when in the wrong place. Industries, especially of a heavy nature, attract a different kind of street traffic from either business or residential districts, and require a different kind of pavement. The mixing of different kinds of traffic produces confusion, increases the danger, and decreases the capacity of the streets. Mr. MacLaurin says, "The idea that industry cannot be conducted profitably without creating dusts, fumes, odors, noxious gases, or offensive liquid wastes, is erroneous"; and further, "Industry is not imperilled or in danger of being closed down if it adopts the best means known to the art for conducting business. There has never been an industry closed down in the history

of this country, or its existence imperilled under those circumstances." Yet, in Pittsburgh, after a smoke abatement ordinance was enforced, several metallurgical industries abandoned all their works inside the city limits.

Zoning is a method of meeting conditions that exist, in accordance with present laws. Certain industries at the present day are objectionable. Zoning merely says to people who want to erect dwellings near these industries, "You do this at your own risk." When any one wishes to build new industrial works, it forces them to build in a location that will not injure residences or business. But zoning is flexible. As soon as any industry eliminates its present objectionable features (which, by the way, are not limited to smoke, dust, odors, noise or vibration), it will be given a wider choice of location, if that is necessary and in the interest of the public welfare. The improvement of industry will have to be undertaken by a different group of experts, operating under different laws, and is not a part of zoning.

CHARLES HERRICK,
City Planning Engineer.

✸

The Regional Planning Federation of the Philadelphia Tri-State District, after three years of preliminary work, is now undertaking to raise a fund of a half million dollars to carry forward the program on an adequate basis. This money is being raised not only in Philadelphia but in the communities throughout the region. The purpose of the Federation in seeking wide spread support for its work lies primarily in its desire to make the regional plan thoroughly *regional* in character, in order that when the plan is completed the 357 separate governmental units in the area may feel that it is their plan.

While the Federation is employing a group of planning engineers and expects to have the benefit of consulting advice from such authorities as Thomas Adams, George B. Ford, Morris Knowles and John Nolen, the plan itself will be developed with the constant coöperation of the engineers, architects and civic leaders of the Region, and will in fact be a program developed jointly by the participating interests.

The preparation of the Master Plan will occupy approximately three years. Coincident with this preparation will be a program of education to be carried forward, which will keep the people of the Region in touch with the problems and progress of the plan.

HOWARD STRONG.

Progress of Regional Government in Cleveland.—Work of the Regional Government Committee of Greater Cleveland and its subcommittees is proceeding satisfactorily. The Fact Finding and Policy Committee, an important subcommittee, has been holding an interesting series of public hearings. At these, county officials and those of various municipalities have been invited to express their views upon the need for some form of regional or metropolitan government. It is significant to note that so far no official has advocated that the community should proceed indefinitely under the existing governmental arrangements. To be sure, divergence of opinion has developed as to what changes should be made or how they should be made.

The Research Committee, a subcommittee of the Fact Finding and Policy Committee, has undertaken a systematic study of the governmental problems involved with the view to presenting a definite plan for making possible the realization of metropolitan government of some practicable and feasible character.

Two other subcommittees have been appointed, one on state coöperation and the other on publicity and education. These committees will soon have important work to do.

✸

English Consultant to Visit U. S.—Municipal researchers and others interested in public administration will be interested in a visit which Arthur Collins, F.S.A.A., will pay the United States this autumn. Mr. Collins has established himself as the leader of the new profession of municipal consultants and counsellors. A considerable part of his practice involves his appearance as witness before Parliamentary committees having in hand special and local legislation conferring new powers upon municipalities. During his visit to this country he will be available for speeches and conferences which may be arranged through the Nomad Lecture Bureau, 150 Lafayette Street, New York.

✸

Death of Sir Ebenezer Howard.—Sir Ebenezer Howard, father of the town planning and garden city movement, died on April 30 at Welwyn Garden City, England, at the age of 78. His loss will be severely felt by the ever-increasing circle of those actively interested in city and country development.

ELECTRICITY IN GREAT BRITAIN—
A STUDY IN ADMINISTRATION

ORREN C. HORMELL

De Alva Stanwood Alexander Professor of Government,
Bowdoin College

NATIONAL MUNICIPAL REVIEW
June, 1928. Vol. XVII, No. 6

NATIONAL MUNICIPAL LEAGUE
261 Broadway, New York, N. Y.

PREFACE

THIS study of British Electricity is limited to the administrative aspects of the subject. Economic and technical phases of the industry are of necessity neglected except when they are essential for an understanding of the administrative side.

The study is primarily the outgrowth of an investigation of public utilities administration in Great Britain undertaken by the writer during the spring and summer of 1927. The writer desires to express his deep gratitude for the generous assistance received from many sources in securing the data necessary for the preparation of this article.

To the following the writer is especially indebted: Sir Harry Haward, Electricity Commissioner; Mr. J. R. Brooke, C.B., Permanent Secretary to the Minister of Transport; Mr. M. L. Gwyer, C.B., Procurator-General and Solicitor to the Treasury; Mr. I. G. Gibbon, C.B.E., D.Sc., Ass't Sec., Minister of Health; Mr. L. Hill, Sec., National Association of Local Government Officers; Mr. Arthur Collins, Financial Adviser to Public Authorities; Prof. G. D. H. Cole, University College, Oxford; W. A. Robson, Ph.D., Lecturer, London School of Economics, and Editor of the *Local Government News;* Prof. J. J. Clarke, M.A., F.S.S., University of Liverpool; Mr. J. W. Beauchamp, M.I.E.E., Director and Secretary of the British Electrical Development Association ("E. D. A."); Mr. Hugh Quigley, Research Expert for the British Electrical and Allied Manufacturers' Association ("Beama."); Mr. A. F. Harrison, F.C.I.S., Sec., City of London Electric Lighting Company, Ltd.; Mr. J. A. Gamon, American Consul, London; the Staff of the *Journal of Public Administration;* officers of the Fabian Society; and members of electricity departments of the cities of Manchester, Birmingham, Liverpool, Glasgow, and Edinburgh.

ELECTRICITY IN GREAT BRITAIN—A STUDY IN ADMINISTRATION

BY ORREN C. HORMELL

De Alva Stanwood Alexander Professor of Government, Bowdoin College

THE year 1926 undoubtedly will go down in the history of industry as a landmark in the development of electricity in Great Britain; for the Electricity (Supply) Act, 1926, marks by far the most important and epoch-making legislation to date in the field of light and power in Great Britain. Competent British authorities consider that that act was "undoubtedly the most important" among the measures passed by Parliament in 1926.[1]

The Baldwin Government, in the presence of the industrial crisis following the World War, was convinced that it was unwise longer to depend upon the traditional English policy of "muddling through"; that further temporizing or haphazard drifting in the electricity field would be industrially disastrous; and that the future development of the generation and transmission of electricity should be boldly determined and courageously undertaken. Parliament, therefore, broke with the past and attempted to recast the whole system of generating and transmitting electricity.[2]

The ground was prepared for the reforms contained in the act by the reports of several select committees which appeared during the decade ending in 1926,[3] and by the work of the Electricity Commission created in 1919. The act was founded primarily upon the report of a select committee presided over by the Rt. Hon. Lord Weir of Eastwood, 1926.[4]

The main purpose of the act was "to secure the eventual concentration of generation in a limited number of well placed interconnected stations operated under unified control," [5] to the end that British industries, householders, and agriculturalists might have a cheap, abundant, and efficient supply of electrical energy. Such a supply of electricity would be fostered, it was believed, by mass production in the highly efficient large generating stations.[6]

The means adopted in the act for the realization of the above named ends are:

First, creating power zones approximately co-terminous with the

[1] The Municipal Year Book for 1927, p. 19.

[2] W. S. Kennedy, *The New Electricity Act,* p. 9.

[3] Important among such committees were: Coal Conservation Sub-Committee of the Reconstruction Committee; Electrical Trade Committee, appointed by the Board of Trade; and the Electrical Supply Committee, appointed by the Board of Trade (cited in this article as Williamson Report, 1918).

[4] The committee was appointed January, 1926, to review the national problem of the supply of electrical energy and to present a report on the broad lines of policy which should be adopted to ensure its most efficient and effective development. (See Weir Report, 1926, p. 3.) The members of the committee were: Lord Weir, chairman, a leading British industrialist, and also president of the Confederation of Employers' Organizations; Lord Forres, a director of the Balfour, Williamson & Co., merchants; and Sir S. Hardman Lever, a director of the Daily Mail Trust, Ltd., Sunday Herald, Ltd., etc.; with Sir John Snell of the Central Electricity Commission as technical adviser.

[5] Sir Harry E. Haward, *Local Authorities under the Electricity (Supply) Acts,* in Public Administration (Jan. 1928), Vol. VI, p. 42.

[6] Parliamentary Debates, H. of C., 1926, vol. 193, p. 1694.

several great industrial districts, within which zones electrical generation and transmission may be thoroughly coordinated and unified.

Second, interconnecting the power zones throughout Great Britain as rapidly as it is economically practicable, to the end that eventually the whole of Great Britain may become a network of transmission lines ("gridiron") into which power may be poured from all available sources. Such interconnection, it is predicted, would produce a marked saving in fuel consumption, and a noteworthy reduction in capital expenditures which would result from an improved load factor, and from a reduction in the amount of necessary reserve plant.

Third, regulating prices both to the distributor and to the consumer.

Fourth, standardizing frequency in order that the economical flow of electric energy throughout the nationwide network of transmission lines might be brought about.

Fifth, creating a state agency to supervise and regulate the generation and transmission of electricity, and to coöperate with existing agencies in putting into effect the reorganization of the electricity industry.

The supply of electrical energy was conceived to be a national duty to be realized through state coöperation and state regulation. The agency created for this purpose by the act is the "Central Electricity Board." The Central Electricity Board possesses the essential characteristics of a board of directors of a limited company (private corporation in the U. S. A.) rather than those of a bureau of the government, since it is responsible for its acts to the courts rather than to the ministry. Its .chief functions are to carry into effect .the "schemes" prepared by the electricity commissioners. The electricity commissioners decide

upon the territory to be included in a given "scheme," and choose the generating stations which are to be the "selected" stations for generation in the district covered by the "scheme"; then the board provides for the building of transmission lines to connect selected stations one with another and with the distributing "undertakers." [7]

When the "scheme" is perfected the board purchases, at the cost of generation, the electrical energy generated by each of the "selected" stations. The board may also purchase "by agreement" surplus electricity from any available source,— such available source at present being especially water power and waste heat plants. The electricity thus pooled and poured into the network of transmission lines is then re-sold in bulk to the several distributing agencies in the district to be distributed by them to the consumers.

It is planned to complete the transition from the old system to the new by 1940. The board is authorized to borrow, on the issue of. stock to the public, not more than £33,500,000 for putting the plan into effect. A large portion of that sum will of necessity be used for building the high-tension main transmission lines, and for transforming equipment in order to secure standardization of frequency. The National Treasury is authorized to guarantee the interest and principal of such loans, but it is the intention ultimately to pay off the loans from the profits of .the industry. [8]

The act was sponsored in the main by three groups or classes of interests:

First, by the technical engineers

[7] The term "undertaker" is used in British law to connote a body having statutory authority to engage in the industry. The term includes both public and private bodies.

[8] Electricity (Supply) Act, 1926 (16–17 Geo. 5, Chap. 51), Secs. 26–29.

under such able leaders as Sir John Snell. Their interest was in the scientific development of the industry as a whole, and they were generally free from local, parochial and individual interests which dominated many municipalities, private distributing companies, and power companies.

Second, by the industrialists, or the great manufacturers, who considered cheap and abundant power an important factor in reducing the cost of production, a factor of overwhelming importance in consideration of Britain's dependence upon world markets. They believed that the capacity of the country to maintain its hold on world trade, in the last analysis, depends upon the cost of production. They recognized that electricity furnishes three factors essential to industrial prosperity, namely, "cheap motive power, fuel conservation, and automatic operation."[9]

Third, political or governmental leaders motivated by the desire to restore as fully as possible to British industry and commerce the prosperity and high position in world trade which they enjoyed prior to the World War.

The measure was opposed, first by the ultra-individualistic right wing of the Conservative Party, containing notably many of the leaders of the private light and power companies. Outstanding among such leaders was Mr. George Balfour, M.P., a director on the boards of thirty or more electricity, tramway and manufacturing companies.[10] This group opposed the act on the alleged ground that it was socialistic; that it supported "the Socialist principles of State control and State management" which would not be "reconciled with the happiness

and prosperity of the people," nor with "the fundamental principles of our old constitution."[11] They contended that the solution of the problem could be found rather in giving private enterprise a free hand and in trusting private initiative to remedy the few ills which seemed to afflict the industry.

The act was opposed, also, by the leaders of the Labor Party, who advocated complete nationalization of the industry. They favored a system by which municipal ownership of distribution should be combined with national ownership of generation and transmission. Their point of view was clearly expressed by Mr. C. R. Attlee, Labor's chief spokesman on this question in the House of Commons. "Electricity," he said, "is one of the master keys of the future. We do not want the master key to be left in the hands of people whose main interest is profit. . . . The Government's view does not go our way far enough."[12]

The Baldwin Government, led by the minister of transport, Rt. Hon. Lt.-Col. W. Ashley, and the attorney-general, Rt. Hon. Sir Douglas Hogg, attempted to steer, what they considered to be, a safe course between the individualism of Mr. George Balfour, and the socialism of Major Attlee. While providing for coördination of the industry, at the same time, they attempted to maintain the *status quo* with regard to municipal ownership and private ownership. Both municipal plants and company plants were incorporated into the scheme and in all but exceptional situations even the generating plants were to remain

[9] H. Quigley, *Electrical Power and National Progress*, p. 21.

[10] Garcke, *Manual of Electrical Undertakings*, 1925–1926, p. 1526.

[11] Parliamentary Debates, H. of C., 1926, vol. 193, pp. 1871–1872.

[12] Parliamentary Debates, H. of C. 1926, vol. 193, p. 1442. A comprehensive presentation of Labor's views on the electricity problem is found in D. J. F. Parson's *Electricity* (1926).

privately owned or municipally owned as the case might be when the act was passed.

The government in sponsoring the act followed the principle advocated by the Weir Committee: "We fully realize the apparent drastic nature of our proposal, but we are convinced that in operation it will not involve any hardship to existing interests. We propose not a change of ownership, but the partial subordination of vested interests in generation to that of a new authority for the benefit of all and this only under the proper safeguards and in a manner which will preserve the value of the incentive of private enterprise." [13] The minister of transport likewise announced in the House of Commons that it was the policy of the government in effecting coördinations in generation and transmission to interfere as little as possible with ownership and management.

SITUATION IN THE ELECTRICAL INDUSTRY, 1926

Prior to the enactment of the Electricity (Supply) Act, 1926, electricity was generated and distributed mainly by "authorized undertakers" receiving their powers from the original Electric Lighting Act of 1882, the amending act of 1888, four or five additional public acts,[14] and numerous special acts and orders. There were also many non-statutory concerns generating electricity for their own use, and also supplying it to the public. The earlier laws which laid the foundation for the development of the electrical industry were enacted when the industry was purely local, and when electricity was used for lighting

rather than for power. Such legislation was "influenced by an insufficiently large and comprehensive outlook." [15] Such legislation was declared by the president of the board of trade to have "restricted the proper expansion of the supply industry." He further stated that "the electrical areas are too parochial and entirely discordant from the economic area of electrical supply. The result has been a great growth of small uneconomical stations, with resultant waste of coal and generally higher charges for energy than would have been the case from larger areas and greater concentration of plant in the larger units, and more economically placed power stations." [16] No less authority than the minister of transport declared in the House of Commons, 1926, that "legislation affecting electricity supply has had all the defects of state interference without effective control." [17] Thus by 1926 the whole country had become set off into small electric districts, each with its monopolistic rights and special privileges.

Under such conditions, it was claimed, Great Britain, in 1926, found herself falling behind other great industrial countries in the electrification of industrial equipment; in the application of electricity to agriculture; in the use of labor-saving devices; and in the per capita consumption of electrical energy.

According to evidence presented by the minister of transport only about one-third of Great Britain was "reasonably supplied with electricity"; probably not more than 34 per cent of the industrial equipment used in production had been electrified; only about one tenth of the rural areas was afforded "even the semblance of · a

---

[13] Weir Report, 1926, Sec. 53, p. 13.

[14] Important among these were: The Electric Lighting (Clauses) Act, 1899, Electric Lighting Act, 1909; Electricity (Supply) Act, 1919; and Electricity (Supply) Act, 1922.

[15] Williamson Report, 1918, p. 5.

[16] Ibid., p. 5.

[17] Parliamentary debates, H. of C., 1926, vol. 193, p. 1697.

supply"; while Great Britain was "pathetically behind" in the use of labor-saving devices in the home, in comparison with Canada and the United States, where according to the minister of transport "the house-wife by using labor-saving electrical apparatus has learned to be happy though servantless." [18]

The following table taken from the Weir Report presents graphically the evidence used by the government to show that Great Britain was falling behind other countries in the per capita consumption of electrical energy:

Country	Consumption per head of population Units
California	1,200
Chicago	1,000
Canada	900
North Eastern U. S. A.	800
Switzerland	700
Tasmania	550
U. S. A. as a whole	500
Norway	500
Sweden	500
Great Britain (authorized undertakings)	110
Great Britain (all sources, about)	200 [19]

Special attention was called to Belgium, one of Britain's competitors, a country similar to England in that it had no considerable water power resources. That country, it was pointed out, consumed 230 units of electrical energy per capita.[20]

According to the statistics submitted by the Electricity Commission, there were in Great Britain, March, 1926, 584 stations generating electricity. Out of the above total, 43.8 per cent (or 256 stations) generated less than 1,000,000 units during the year, and

as many as 73.2 per cent (or 428 stations) generated less than 10,000,000 units each.[21] It appears evident, therefore, that a great majority of the generating stations were small, isolated, inefficient and uneconomical. Their load factor, in most instances, was unreasonably low, often no higher than 25 per cent with not more than one fourth of the plant working at full capacity; while reliable statistics indicate that "the combined load factor for the whole of the generating plant of Undertakers in Great Britain taken collectively, was of the order of 30 per cent . . . in 1924-25." [22] The inevitable result was a very high "standby" plant with an unduly heavy capital investment.

CLASSES OF BODIES OWNING AND OPERATING ELECTRICITY UNDERTAKINGS

The bodies engaged in the generation and distribution of electrical energy in 1926 were divided into two main classes: First, the public bodies called "Local Authorities," consisting chiefly of municipalities; and, second, the private companies.

The local authorities, which are granted statutory authority to supply electricity, are the borough or urban district council and the rural district council in England and Wales; while in Scotland they are the town council and the county council.

The importance of the publicly owned and operated electricity undertakings is evidenced by the fact that "approximately two-thirds of the public supply of electricity is in municipal hands." [23]

[18] Parliamentary debates, H. of C., 1926, vol. 193, pp. 1692-1694.

[19] Weir Report, 1926, p. 5.

[20] Parliamentary Debates, H. of C., 1926, vol. 193, p. 1693.

[21] Electricity Commission, Sixth Annual Report, 1926, pp. 7-8.

[22] Electricity Commission, Electricity Supply, 1924-1925, p. xvii.

[23] Sir Harry E. Haward, in Public Administration, Jan. 1928, p. 52. Electricity Commission, Electricity Supply, 1924-1925, p. xxxiii.

An analysis of the statistics presented by the Electricity Commission shows that, for the year ending March 31, 1926, 65 per cent of the electricity generated by statutory or authorized undertakers was furnished by public authorities, and only 35 per cent by private companies.[24]

The predominance of the municipally owned electric undertakings in Great Britain is due largely, first, to the fact that the municipalities entered the field in the early days of electrical development before the private companies had obtained a secure hold upon the industry; and second, to the fact that on the whole municipal ownership and operation had proved successful. It is generally conceded that the electricity departments of the great industrial cities such as Manchester, Liverpool, Birmingham, Glasgow and Edinburgh, have given proof of initiative, enterprise, judgment, and efficient management equal to that found in the best private undertakings.[25]

It is a significant fact also that municipalization of the monopolistic public utilities—water, gas, electricity and tramways—in Great Britain has not been faced with the adverse public opinion which is so pronounced in America. Some of the most conservative communities in Great Britain have developed municipal trading most fully. Bournemouth and Blackpool are examples among many where the councils are not only extremely conservative, but also highly successful in municipal trading. Conservative leaders who fight national socialism "tooth and nail" consider that municipal ownership is not socialism at all,—merely "good business." Birmingham, a leader in municipal trading among the great

[24] Electricity Commission, *Sixth Annual Report*, 1926, p. 7.

[25] E. D. Simon, Ex-Lord Mayor of Manchester, *City Council from Within*, pp. 13; 173.

English municipalities, owes to a great extent the successful inauguration of this policy to the great Conservative leader, Joseph Chamberlain. A monument erected to his memory by a Conservative city government gave him credit and praise for the beginnings of municipal trading, as follows: ". . . mainly by whose ability and devotion the gas and water undertakings were acquired for the Town, to the great and lasting benefit of the inhabitants."[26] It is interesting to note that the latest experiment in municipal trading, the establishing of a municipal bank in Birmingham, was launched with the approval of the Rt. Hon. Neville Chamberlain, M.P., of Birmingham, minister of health in the present Conservative Government.

Successful municipalization of the electricity industry has been and still is conditioned upon the existence, at the head of the industry, of the trained, permanent expert. Fortunately for the English municipalities it seems never to have occurred to the Englishman that administrative officials should not be permanent. For example, the notable development of electricity at Bristol and in the area around the mouth of the Severn is credited largely to Mr. H. Faraday Proctor, "who has been in charge of the Bristol Electrical Department for thirty-four years."[27] This example is typical, rather than exceptional.

HANDICAPS OF MUNICIPAL
UNDERTAKINGS   -

The municipalities, while developing in many instances electric generating and distributing plants fully capable of meeting the local needs, have been incapable of meeting the national demands for generation and interconnec-

[26] Inscription on Joseph Chamberlain's Monument—Public Square, Birmingham.

[27] *Municipal Journal*, Jan. 28, 1927, p. 119.

tion. Experience seems to "prove that a municipal or Local Government area is not necessarily, and in fact is rarely, the most economical area of electrical supply."[28] Although in a few instances, as in the case of Birmingham, the municipality has been given authority to supply electricity to adjacent territory, in the main the provisional or special order granting authority to supply electricity has limited the area to that of one local authority. In the picturesque words of Bernard Shaw the power of the local authority, "like that of the witch who cannot cross running water, stops at a boundary which dates probably from the Heptarchy."[29]

Municipalities in Great Britain, as in the U. S. A., are corporations of limited and enumerated powers and can do only what is expressly granted by law. Jealousy among municipalities, and especially the fear on the part of the small municipality that the extension of the electricity supply authority of a large neighboring municipality might be the opening wedge of a movement to annex the smaller, has in many cases blocked the economic expansion of a successful municipal undertaking. Moreover, the statutory right of some 71 small local authorities, not electricity undertakers themselves, to purchase the electricity undertaking in their area which forms a portion of the distribution area of a larger local authority has been an inevitable handicap to the expansion of municipal electricity undertakings.[30]

The practice in many municipalities of making a charge for electricity high enough to act as a material relief to the local rate payers (local tax payers) has diminished rather than increased

the possible benefit to industry of the municipalization of electricity. Prior to the Act of 1926 the local authorities could contribute to the "relief of the rates" any surplus up to 5 per cent on the aggregate capital expenditure. Statistics show that in 1925–26, no less than 107 undertakings contributed sums to the relief of local rates aggregating to £760,267, while only 17 undertakings made a demand on the rates which amounted all told to £18,236.[31] The net contribution, 1925–26, of the municipal electricity undertakings thus was £742,031. Public electricity authorities, furthermore (along with private companies), have been assessed for local rates (taxes) to a degree which it is claimed has "unjustly interfered with the supply of cheap power and enhanced its cost."[32]

Municipalities by 1926 found that the purchase clause of the Act of 1888 acted as a severe check upon the further purchase of private plants operating within their territory. The Act of 1888 provided that the local authority may, "after the expiration of a period of 42 years, or such shorter period as is specified in their behalf under the provisional order or the special act . . . and within six months after the expiration of every subsequent period of ten years, . . . require such Undertakers to sell and thereupon such Undertakers shall sell to them their undertaking . . . upon terms of paying the *then value* of all lands, buildings, works, materials, and plant of such Undertakers suitable to and used by them for the purpose of their undertaking within such jurisdiction. Such value to be in case of difference determined by arbitration . . . but without any addition in respect to com-

[28] Williamson Report, 1918, p. 5.

[29] Bernard Shaw, *The Common Sense of Municipal Trading*, p. 64.

[30] Weir Report, 1926, p. 14.

[31] Sir Harry E. Haward, *Local Authorities under the Electricity (Supply) Acts*, in Public Administration, Vol. VI, Jan. 1928, pp. 46–47.

[32] Williamson Report, 1918, p. 15.

pulsory purchase, or good will, or of any profits which may or might have been made from the undertaking before, or any similar consideration."

The "then value" in actual practice became the reproduction value at the time of purchase. Hence the great increase in the cost of material, etc., subsequent to the war, so enhanced the value of the undertaking that many municipalities have deemed it inexpedient to purchase the private undertaking, which they would have purchased under pre-war conditions.

The municipalities were further handicapped in their development of a cheap and abundant power by many minor limitations placed upon them by legislation. Among these may be mentioned the law and policy which favored underground cables, rather than overhead lines.[33]

It has been pointed out recently that "the right of veto exercisable by Borough, Urban and Rural District Councils in England and Wales, and by County Councils and Police Commissioners in Scotland, on the erection of overhead wires, is another factor which has greatly militated against expansion and development, and has raised the cost of the electricity supplied." [34]

Public electricity authorities have experienced great difficulties in securing privileges for "way-leaves" on private property, as well as in public streets, and for authority to break up streets. They have also often experienced aggravating delays and unnecessary expenses in securing authority to make an extension to the existing area of supply.[35] The extension of supply areas into smaller adjoining municipalities was further made difficult by

the difference in pressure and frequencies which made the linking up and interchange of power exceedingly difficult and costly. Furthermore, most of the acts giving to local authorities the right to supply electricity denied to them the right to sell electrical apparatus.[36]

PRIVATE ELECTRICITY UNDERTAKINGS (COMPANIES)

The private statutory electricity companies may be divided into two main classes: First, the distributing companies who receive their authority from the electric lighting acts of 1882 and 1888 and from special orders. These companies are generally given authority to supply electricity for all purposes, and are limited in their authority and in the extent of the area of supply, very much in the same manner as are the public or municipal undertakers. They are subject, however, to purchase by public authorities after a period of 42 years. They have not been as a rule so closely limited with regard to area as have been the municipal or public undertakers. Usually the electric lighting companies have been given authority both to generate and to distribute electricity. The generating stations owned by these companies, in most instances, have been small and inefficient, especially when compared with the stations of the larger municipalities and of the big power companies. These small companies also, for the most part, have been unable to raise the capital necessary for laying high tension cables.

The companies believe that their normal development has been retarded to a certain degree by the purchase clause of the law of 1882 as amended by the Act of 1888.[37] The uncertainty

[33] Advisory Committee on Domestic Supply of Electricity, and Methods of Charge, 1927.

[34] Williamson Report, 1918, p. 6.

[35] Ibid., p. 11.

[36] Weir Report, 1926, p. 21.

[37] See above, p. 369.

of the tenure, and the lack of an agreement between the company and the municipality with regard to the exercise of the purchase privilege has proved, it is claimed, a great handicap to these companies during the last part of the 42-year period, which many companies have now entered. In many instances the municipality is neither willing nor able to enter into an agreement to purchase the utility, nor is it willing to agree to waive its purchase privilege. Hence it is claimed "that so long as the length of tenure and the terms of purchase remain uncertain, as at present, it is practically impossible for many of the small companies to face large capital outlays or to contemplate extensions of the existing area of supply, or to proceed on a proper basis with the development of a cheap supply for general domestic use." [38]

The companies, along with the municipalities, have been greatly handicapped by the refusal of many local authorities to permit overhead wires. They have, furthermore, found the rapid increase in local rates (municipal taxes) a heavy burden during the last two decades. For example, local rates imposed upon the Newcastle-upon-Tyne Electric Supply Co., Ltd., it is claimed by that company, have increased 516 per cent since 1914, while the capital expenditure has increased only 156 per cent.[39]

POWER COMPANIES

The second class of private companies, and by far the more important, consists of the electric power companies. These are companies, dating from about 1900, which have been vested by Parliamentary acts with special power of supply over large areas.

These areas are often as large as a county, and extend over the most important industrial districts in Great Britain, for example the industrial district centering around Newcastle-upon-Tyne, the Clyde Valley district, and the Lancashire district. The main function of these power companies is the generation of electricity on a large scale. The electricity is supplied in bulk to the several undertakers, both private and public, having statutory powers of distribution in the area of the power company. In the second place it is supplied directly to the great industrial companies especially for power purposes; in fact these power companies depend almost exclusively on the industrial power load.[40]

The power companies were in the main limited by the following provisions: (1) "That the company should only supply to authorised undertakers, or to persons requiring a supply for power, and should not supply for lighting purposes to any parties other than authorised undertakers, except that electricity supplied to any person for power might be used by such person for lighting any premises on any part of which the power should be utilized; but, in cases where a supply for power should be given to any person within the area of supply of any authorised distributors, the electricity used by that person for lighting purposes in any year should not, except with the consent in writing of the authorised distributors, exceed the amount of electricity used by such person for power."

(2) "That the company should not supply electricity (except to authorised undertakers or to any railway, tramway, or water company, or proprietors or trustees of any canal or navigation for power) in any area which at the date of the passing of the act authoris-

---

[38] Advisory Committee on Domestic Supply of Electricity, and Methods of Charge, 1927, p. 21.

[39] Newcastle-upon-Tyne Electric Supply Co., Ltd., *Report of Proceedings*, 27 March, 1927, p. 6.

[40] H. Quigley, *Electrical Power and National Progress*, p. 127.

ing the company to supply should form part of the area of supply of any authorised distributors, without the consent of those distributors in the case of each intended customer." [41]

The power companies have held a highly advantageous position in the industry: First, because their powers were perpetual in tenure, not being subject to the purchase clause of the Act of 1888. Second, they were protected against loss from unprofitable extensions by a binding contract relative to a minimum period of supply, and a minimum return on the actual investment incurred in the extension. For example, authorized undertakers before receiving a supply in bulk were required to agree to continue the supply for a period of at least seven years and pay annually for the supply an amount equalling not less than 20 per cent "on the outlay incurred by the company in making provision for the supply." [42]

Third: Through stock ownership and interlocking directorates, many of the large power companies have been able to control within certain large industrial areas not only the supply of power in bulk but also the distributing side of the industry as well.

For example, the Newcastle-upon-Tyne Electric Supply Co., Ltd., one of the largest and most successful British power companies, through ownership of the stock of a large number of distributing companies controls and actually operates the distribution as well as the generation of electricity "throughout an area of over 1,400 square miles embracing practically the whole of the industrial area of the north-east coast." [43]

[41] F. N. Keen, *The Law Relating to Public Service Undertakings*, pp. 253–254.

[42] *Ibid.*, p. 255.

[43] Garcke, *Manual of Electrical Undertakings*, Vol. XXIX, 1925–26, p. 679.

The concentration of control, however, is not confined to districts; it is becoming national (in some instances international) in extent. This centralizing tendency in the private electricity field is being advanced not only by the ownership of stock but also (and especially) by the creation of interlocking directorates. Two examples will suffice to illustrate the point: Sir Hugo Hirst, Bart., sometimes referred to as the "Samuel Insull of British Electricity," is the managing director of the General Electric Co., Ltd. In addition, he holds the following positions in other companies:

Chairman of The Frinton-on-Sea and District Electric Light and Power Co., Ltd.; Electricity Co. of Macclesfield; Steel Conduit Co., Ltd.; General Electric de France, Ltd.; General Electric Co. of India, Ltd.; General Electric Co. of China, Ltd.; Anglo-Argentine General Electric Co., Ltd.; Leamington Glass Works. Vice-Chairman of Pirelli-General Cable Works, Ltd. Director of Aron Electricity Meter, Ltd.; British General Electric Co. (South Africa), Ltd.; Madeira Electric Lighting Co. (1909), Ltd.; Travancore Minerals Co., Ltd.; Société de Produites Chemiques des Terres Rares. [44]

The second example is that of Mr. George Balfour, M.P., who is an officer and director in even more of the British Electricity Companies than is Sir Hugo Hirst. His official positions in the industry are as follows:

Director of Argentine Light and Power Co., Ltd.; Argentine Tramways and Power Co., Ltd.; Arbroath Electric Light and Power Co., Ltd.; Balfour, Beatty, & Co., Ltd. (Chairman); Dumbarton Burgh and County Tramways Co., Ltd. (Chairman); Dundee, Broughty Ferry, and District Trayways Co., Ltd. (Chairman); Dunfermline and District Tramway Co. (Managing); Edinburgh and London Trust, Ltd.; Falkirk and District Tramways Co.; Hydro-Electric Development Co., Ltd.; Scottish Power Co., Ltd.; Scottish Central Electric Power Co.; Fife Tramways, Light and Power Co. (Managing); Fife Electric Power Co.; Lancashire Electric Light and Power Co., Ltd.; Lancashire Electric Power Co.; Llandudno and Colwyn Bay Electric

[44] *Ibid.*, p. 1628.

Railway, Ltd.; Metropolitan Electric Supply Co., Ltd.; Mansfield and District Tramways, Ltd.; Mansfield and District Light Railways Co.; Midland Electric Light and Power Co., Ltd.; Nottinghamshire and Derbyshire Tramways Co.; Midland Counties Electric Supply Co., Ltd. (Chairman); United Electric Tramways of Montevideo, Ltd.; Wemyss and District Tramways Co. (Chairman); Galashiels and District Electric Supply Co., Ltd.; Brentford Electric Supply Co., Ltd.; Cordoba (Argentine) Electric Tramways Construction Co., Ltd.; Uxbridge and District Electric Supply Co., Ltd.; London United Tramways, Ltd.; Power Securities Corporation, Ltd. (Chairman); Grampian Electricity Supply Co. (Chairman); Chesham Electric Light and Power Co., Ltd.[45]

The international aspect of the situation is strikingly illustrated by the position of the electrical manufacturing firm, the British Thomson Houston Co., Ltd., the controlling shares of which are held by the International General Electric Co. of New York. The British Thomson Houston Co., Ltd., is one of the three largest holders of the ordinary shares (common stock) of the Power Security Corporation, the chairman of which is Mr. George Balfour, M.P.[46]

It is apparent that centralization of financial control is taking place in British private electrical industry even though the British have not yet adopted American type of holding companies.

A Step Toward Reorganization, 1919

A step toward the creation of a national system of electricity supply was taken through the enactment of the Electricity (Supply) Act of 1919. The basis of the act was the Williamson Report of 1918. Had Parliament courageously followed the recommendations of that committee the reorganization of the electricity industry would have dated from 1919 instead of

1926. The opposition of the private electricity companies, especially in the House of Lords, emasculated the bill to the extent that it proved to be practically innocuous. The act did, however, make some "important changes in the procedure and administrative arrangements for the control of the electricity supply." [47]

The administrative provisions of the act created, first, a new administrative body termed "Electricity Commissioners," to consist of five members to be appointed by the minister of transport with the concurrence of the board of trade. Most of the powers of regulation previously exercised by several departments of government over the electricity industry were vested in the Electricity Commission. The commission was made by the act solely responsible to the minister of transport.[48]

The commissioners were authorized to define provisional electricity districts on the basis "most conducive to the efficiency and economy of supply and to the convenience of administration." The existing undertakers, both public and private, and large consumers and other interested parties were authorized to suggest a scheme of reorganization for the district. If no scheme acceptable to the commission was submitted then the commissioners themselves might formulate one.

Under such a scheme a joint electricity authority might be created which would be representative of authorized undertakers, local authorities, large consumers of electricity and others interested within the district. The joint electricity authority was entrusted with the duty of providing or securing "a cheap and abundant

[45] Garcke, *Manual of Electrical Undertakings*, Vol. XXIX, 1925–26, p. 1526.

[46] Stock Exchange Year Book, 1927, p. 1225.

[47] F. N. Keen, *The Law Relating to Public Service Undertakings*, p. 256.

[48] Electricity (Supply) Act, 1919 (9–10 Geo. 5, Chap. 100), Sec. 39.

supply of electricity within their district." Under the direction of the Electricity Commission, and in conformity to the detail provisions contained in the scheme, the joint electricity authority was given the power to construct generating stations, main transmission lines and other works, and to acquire the undertakings or parts of undertakings of authorized undertakers in the district.[49] Generating stations might also be acquired with the consent of the electricity commissioners, and furthermore, no new generating stations could be erected by other authorities without the approval of the commission.

The purchase clause of the Act of 1888 was extended to the joint electricity authority, but made subject to the discretion of the Electricity Commission. It is interesting to note that the power companies were still protected against compulsory purchase. The act made it somewhat less difficult to procure "way-leaves" and authority to run overhead wires.

In electricity districts where conditions did not seem to justify the creation of a joint electrical authority, advisory boards could be created to act as intermediaries between the Electricity Commission and the several undertakers, and to function as a central consulting committee with regard to developments within the district.

The law failed to accomplish the efficient reorganization of the industry as proposed in the Williamson Report, largely because voluntary rather than compulsory coördination was depended upon. No existing undertakings, generating stations or main transmission lines could be purchased or brought into the scheme without the consent of the owners, and no existing monop-

oly could be encroached upon by extending the area of supply into the territory of an existing authority without its consent.

Refusal to enter voluntarily into the scheme on the part of many municipalities and many private companies acted as an unsurmountable barrier to the proposed reorganization by the new commission.

By 1926 fifteen districts had been provisionally, and only seven finally, determined. Of the seven districts finally determined upon, four were placed under advisory boards rather than joint electricity authorities. One of the three remaining districts has been handed over to a power company, the North Wales Power and Traction Co., Ltd., which acts as the electricity authority for the North Wales District. In the second remaining district, the Edinburgh District, the scheme placed the industry under the joint control of the Municipality of Edinburgh and the Lothian Electric Power Co., Ltd. The remaining scheme, the London Scheme, as authorized by a special act of 1925, provided for a joint electricity authority, consisting of 14 representatives of local authorities electricity undertakings, 4 of company undertakings, 10 of local authorities, 2 of railways, and 2 of the workers in the industry.

The failure to set up joint electricity authorities with adequate powers is vividly stated in the Lord Weir Report as follows:

Under the Act of 1919 it was contemplated that Joint Electricity Authorities would be set up as executive bodies in each electricity area, and that they would acquire the generating stations and construct the area gridiron leaving local distribution to authorized undertakers. This scheme has been realized only to a very slight extent. At the moment there is one Joint Electricity Authority in being [in actual operation] and that Authority has handed its executive

[49] Electricity (Supply) Act, 1919 (9–10 Geo. 5, Chap. 100), Sec. 8.

duties over to a Power Company.[50] (The North Wales Power and Traction Co.)

Although the powers of the Electricity Commission proved to be inadequate to produce effective results, the commission justified its existence by collecting and publishing full and informing statistics on the electricity industry, and by providing expert information and advice to the Weir Committee in 1926.

Seven years unsatisfactory application of the law of 1919 supported by the information provided by the Electricity Commission, and by the convincing arguments contained in the Weir Report prepared the way for the somewhat revolutionary changes adopted by the Electricity (Supply) Act of 1926.

ELECTRICITY ADMINISTRATION
SUBSEQUENT TO THE ACT OF 1926

The new system of electricity administration, brought into being by the Electricity (Supply) Act of 1926, was vested primarily in two bodies whose functions were limited solely to the field of electricity.

These bodies are: First, the Central Electricity Board, created by the Act of 1926; and second, the Electricity Commission, created by the Act of 1919. These primary administrative bodies are aided by, responsible to, or dependent upon the action of, several other governmental agencies among which are the ministry of transport, the treasury, special boards of arbitration, the minister of labor, and Houses of Parliament.

The Central Electricity Board consists of eight members appointed by the minister of transport. Their tenure of office is for a period of not less than five years nor more than ten, but there is nothing to prevent a member from being reappointed for another term.

[50] Weir Report, 1926, p. 16.

The appointment by the minister is to be made after consulting with such interests as "local government, electricity, commerce, industry, transport, agriculture, and labour." [51] No member of the House of Commons may be appointed, and the chairman and any other full-time member of the board are required to own no securities of any company in any way connected with the electricity industry.[52]

The board began its official career March 1, 1927, with the following personnel: Chairman, Sir Andrew Duncan, vice-president of the Ship Building Employers' Federation; Frank Hodges, secretary, International Miners' Federation; Sir James Lithgow, president of the National Confederation of Employers' Organizations; William Walker, alderman, City of Manchester, vice-chairman, Manchester Electricity Department, and chairman, National Joint Board for the Electricity Supply Industry; Sir John Watson, chairman, London and Home Counties Joint Electricity Authority; W. K. Whigham, director, Bank of England, and member, Trade Facilities Advisory Committee; Brevet-Colonel, The Hon. Vernon Willey, director, Lloyds Bank, Ltd., and ex-president of the Federation of British Industries.[53]

It appears that manufacturers, private electricity companies, public electricity authorities including both municipalities and joint electricity authorities, labor, commerce, and banking interests are represented on the board. As was expected, the financial and industrial interests predominate. The appointments were made with the understanding that administrative ability, business acumen and knowledge of commercial needs rather than knowl-

[51] Electricity (Supply) Act, 1926 (16–17 Geo. V, Chap. 51), Sec. 1.

[52] *Ibid.*, Sec. 3.

[53] *Municipal Journal*, Feb. 11, 1927, p. 205.

edge of the technical side of the electricity industry were needed. Members of the board are expected "to weigh questions of expediency which experts are apt to ignore and to reconcile the interests of all parties within the industry." [54]

The Electricity Commission, rather than the Central Electricity Board, is the body to be depended upon for advice and control in technical matters.

PREPARATION OF ELECTRICITY SCHEMES

The initial steps in the reorganization of the electricity industry are entrusted to the electricity commissioners. The commissioners select the area to which an electricity scheme is to be applied, and prepare the details of the scheme. The proposals for the scheme presented by the commissioners relate to the following matters:

1. The areas to which the scheme relates.

2. What generating stations have been chosen to be the "selected stations" at which electricity shall be generated for the purposes of the board. These stations may include both the selected stations from among existing stations, and new stations to be erected. The commission may not, however, select any stations nor authorize the acquisition of main transmission lines belonging to any railway company, canal, inland navigation, dock or harbor undertakers, or private (non-statutory) generating stations without the consent of the owners thereof.

3. Provisions for main transmission lines to interconnect the selected stations one with another and with the systems of authorized undertakers.

4. Provisions for the standardization of frequency. It is not required by the law to install a general standardiza-

[54] London Weekly Times, Jan. 27, 1927, p. 91.

tion of frequency, but only such standardization as is essential to carrying out the interconnection within the proposed scheme.

5. Such supplemental and incidental matters as appear necessary or expedient for any of the purposes of the scheme, especially such as relate to temporary arrangements to be in effect during the carrying out of the scheme.[55]

ADOPTION OF ELECTRICITY SCHEMES

The scheme as prepared by the Electricity Commission is submitted to the Central Electricity Board for their consideration. The board before finally adopting the scheme must publish it, and give consideration to any representations made by any authorized undertakers or other interested persons. After due consideration they may adopt the scheme with or without modification, and for the whole or only a part of the specified area as they see fit.

The scheme as adopted and published by the board does not go into effect in its entirety until opportunity has been given for complaints, on the part of authorized undertakers upon whom obligations have been imposed, to be referred to the arbitration of a barrister. Such complaints may be made by authorized undertakers who consider that the carrying out of the obligation would be prejudicial to them. The arbitrator is a barrister qualified for judicial office (of not less than ten years standing at the Bar) selected by the minister of transport from a panel of barristers nominated by the Lord Chancellor, and the Lord President of the Court of Sessions.[56]

The arbitrator, if he deems it expedient, may call in the aid of technical

[55] Electricity (Supply) Act 1926 (16–17 Geo. 5, Chap. 51), Sec. 4.

[56] Ibid., Sec. 4, Sub-sec. 3.

assessors. If satisfied as to the justice of the complaint the arbitrator may order the scheme to be amended to meet the objections, or he may order pecuniary compensation to be made. Provided that he may not grant any relief other than pecuniary compensation in any case where the Central Electricity Board certifies "that the grant of such relief would conflict with the basic principles of the scheme or prejudicially affect its efficiency."[57]

Schemes also may be altered or modified from time to time through the same procedure as is used in preparing and adopting the original scheme, with the proviso, however, that no station which has been once selected may be dropped without the consent of the owners.

THE OPERATION OF THE SCHEME

The steps so far described are merely preliminary to the actual working of the scheme. The function of operating the scheme when finally adopted is vested primarily in the Central Electricity Board.

The actual working of the schemes may be conveniently considered under three headings: (1) Generation; (2) Transmission and Interconnection; and (3) Standardization.

Generation of Electric Energy. Electric energy, according to the plan, is to be generated as efficiently as possible in a few large stations. It is intended ultimately (by 1940 if possible) to reduce the number of generating stations in Great Britain from about 600 to 50 or 60. The methods of supply are adopted and extensions and alterations of the stations are made according to the requirements of the board. The board also determines the quantity of energy to be generated by

each selected station and the rate of output.

All of the energy which is thus generated is sold by the owners to the board, which in turn re-sells it to the "authorized undertakers" who have the statutory authority to distribute energy to the ultimate consumers.

In case the owner of a selected station refuses to operate the station under the direction of the board, or refuses to carry out the alteration and extension required by the board, the station may be purchased from the owners.[58] The price to be paid for the station is arrived at by an auditor appointed by the electricity commissioners. The auditor is required to certify the sum which has been "the amount of expenses properly incurred on and incidental to the provision of the generating station . . . less depreciation on a scale fixed by Special Order."[59]

It is interesting to observe that the "then value" or reproduction cost theory of the earlier laws and practice was abandoned in 1926 for that theory, which in the U. S. A. is termed the "prudent investment" (or Massachusetts) theory of valuation. The general adoption of the principle was advocated by the Weir Committee with regard to the future purchasing of private undertakings by public authorities, as follows: "The purchase clause should be simple in character and based upon the capital properly expended less such depreciation as the Commissioners may allow."[60]

It should be noted, however, that the board is not to acquire the station for itself until it has given full opportunity of purchase to the authorized undertakers in the district, first opportunity

---

[57] Electricity Commission, *Memorandum on the Provisions of the Act (Electricity Supply Act), 1926,* p. 4.

[58] Electricity (Supply) Act, 1926 (16–17 Geo. 5, Chap. 51), Sec. 5, Sub-sec. 2.

[59] *Ibid.,* First Schedule.

[60] Weir Report, 1926, Sec. 77, p. 18.

to be given to a joint electricity authority if such there be in the district. The private owners are further protected against an unfair forcible purchase by the proviso that if the owners of the generation station or the board are dissatisfied with the sum certified by the auditor the case may be referred for arbitration to a barrister;[61] and by the further proviso that the order of the minister for completing the transfer of such a station "shall not come into force until it has been laid before each House of Parliament not less than thirty days on which that House has sat, and if either House of Parliament before the expiration of that period presents an address to his Majesty [vetoes the proposal] no further proceedings shall be taken thereon." [62]

In case the board acquires the generating station, the board is further forbidden to operate the station "unless it satisfies the Electricity Commissioners that it is unable to enter into an agreement with any authorized undertakers or other company or person to operate it on reasonable terms," first opportunity again to be given to a joint electricity authority.[63]

The erection of new stations may be required by the scheme formulated by the electricity commissioners. It is still possible under the Act of 1919 for any authorized undertaker to apply to the electricity commissioners for permission to erect such a station. But the logic of the new plan seems to demand that the great majority of such new stations shall be erected under the direction of the board. The board is denied the authority, however, to erect or operate a new station unless and until the commissioners are satisfied

that no other body may be found with whom satisfactory arrangements to perform the service may be made.[64]

Non-Selected Stations. That the non-selected generating stations should be closed down whenever it is economically expedient and as soon as practicable was the obvious intention of the framers of the act. An incentive for the voluntary closing down of inefficient stations, it was believed, would arise from the economic advantage of the availability of cheap energy to be obtained from the board.[65]

Economic forces, however, were not alone depended upon. The act provided that uneconomical stations may be closed down by order of the Electricity Commission upon application of the board under certain specified conditions. The board must first present satisfactory evidence that a supply from the board can be given to the owners of the station at a cost "below the then prevailing cost . . . of generating electricity at the station." Furthermore, the board is required to supply to the owners of the station, for a period of not less than seven years, electrical energy up to the requirements of the owners consequent to the closing down of the station.[66]

Price of Electricity Bought and Sold by the Board. The board is authorized to pay, to the owners of selected stations for the electricity generated, a price based upon the "cost of production." The cost of production includes sums spent for materials consumed, pensions, insurance of persons and property, repairs and maintenance, rents, rates and taxes (excluding profits taxes), management, and interest on money properly expended for capital purposes. The interest allowed to

[61] Electricity (Supply) Act, 1926 (16–17 Geo. 5, Chap. 51), Sec. 5, Sub-sec. 2, and First Schedule.

[62] *Ibid.*, Sec. 5, Sub-sec. 2.

[63] *Ibid.*, Sub-sec. 3.

[64] *Ibid.*, Sec. 6, Sub-secs. 1–3.

[65] Weir Report, 1926, Sec. 46, p. 12.

[66] Electricity (Supply) Act, 1926 (16–17 Geo. 5, Chap. 51), Sec. 14.

public authorities owning a selected station is to be the "average rate payable on money raised by the authority for the purpose"; while that allowed to companies is to be "the average rate of dividends and interest paid by the company on the share and loan capital during the preceding year; so, however, that the rate shall in no case be less than five nor more than six and a half per cent per annum." [67] If any question arises over the cost of production it is determined by an auditor appointed by the minister of transport. Other questions in dispute over prices are referred to the electricity commissioners. [68]

On the resale of electricity the board is not permitted to make a profit. The tariff (or price) is to be fixed by the board and approved by the Electricity Commission so that over a given term of years the income of the board shall balance its expenditures with such margin of safety as the commission shall allow. The price must include the cost of production (as· explained above) "adjusted according to the load factor and the power factor . . . together with a proper proportion of the Board's expenses." An alternate method of fixing the price is by an order of the Electricity Commission setting forth in detail the manner of fixing the price, subject, however, to the veto of either House of Parliament. [69]

The owners of a selected station are given the first claim on the electricity to be sold by the board up to the amount generated by the station if the requirements of their "undertaking" demand it.

They are given a further advantage by a provision that the cost of electricity taken from the board in any one

year shall not exceed "the cost which, in the opinion of the Electricity Commissioners, the undertakers would have incurred in themselves generating the electricity." [70]

Transmission and Interconnection. Both the Williamson and Weir Reports emphasized the need for the establishment of a comprehensive network of transmission mains as an essential part of any effective reorganization of the electricity industry. The Weir Report considered interconnection to be the "first essential towards bringing about subsequent and far reaching improvement in our present system." [71]

Likewise, Parliament, in recasting the operation of the electricity industry made interconnection by means of main transmission lines an essential part of the plan. The electricity commissioners are required by the act to include in the "scheme" submitted to the board a provision for main transmission lines which not only connect up the several selected generating stations and interconnect them with the authorized undertakings within the specified area, but also furnish connections between the several great electric areas under the jurisdiction of the board. Thus is made possible the gradual unification of the industry throughout a greater portion of the nation. [72]

After the adoption of the scheme, the Electricity Board is authorized to "construct and lay down the main transmission lines required for the interconnection." [73] This includes the laying of cables, the erection of overhead lines and the providing of the transforming apparatus in order that the energy produced by the station may

---

[67] Electricity (Supply) Act, 1926 (16–17 Geo. 5, Chap. 51), Sec. 14, Second Schedule.

[68] *Ibid.*, Sec. 7, Sub-sec. 6.

[69] *Ibid.*, Secs. 7 and 11.

[70] *Ibid.*, Sec. 13.

[71] Weir Report, 1926, p. 19.

[72] Electricity (Supply) Act, 1926 (16–17 Geo. 5, Chap. 51), Sec. 4, Sub-sec. 1.

[73] *Ibid.*, Sec. 8, Sub-sec. 1.

be fed into the systems of the several authorized undertakers in the area.

In case the board is authorized to take over existing lines the procedure for acquiring them is fundamentally the same as that for acquiring generating stations.[74] The cost of alterations and replacements necessitated by the installation of the interconnection is charged to the board.[75]

Standardization of Frequency. Electricity experts generally agree that standardization of frequency was necessary in order that interconnection might be made effective. The act provides not only for such standardization as is essential for carrying out the interconnection proposed in a given scheme but also for such standardization as the board, with the approval of the electricity commissioners, may deem expedient.[76]

The board, with the approval of the Electricity Commission, is given full power to require the owners, both public and private, to make the necessary alterations in frequency to effect the required standardization. The owners are to be reimbursed by the board for all expenses properly incurred in carrying out the requirements, and the board, if required to do so, must advance, free of interest, the capital necessary for making the alterations. If an agreement cannot be reached relative to the sum necessary for the work the decision is made by the Electricity Commission or, at the option of the owners, by an arbitrator.[77] It was estimated by the Weir Committee that the alterations effecting standardization would require a net expenditure of about £8,000,000.[78]

[74] Electricity (Supply) Act, 1926 (16–17 Geo. 5, Chap. 51), First Schedule.
[75] *Ibid.*, Sec. 8, Sub-sec. 3.
[76] *Ibid.*, Sec. 4, Sub-sec. 1; Sec. 9.
[77] *Ibid.*, Sec. 9, Sub-sec. 1.
[78] Weir Report, 1926, Sec. 91, p. 19.

REGULATION OF CHARGES TO THE CONSUMER

The ultimate purpose of the reorganization of the electricity industry in 1926 was to make available to the consumers (domestic and industrial) an abundant and cheap supply of electric energy. If the economies created by governmental action were to be merely a gift to the distributors of electricity then the reforms would be mainly futile. Without legislation on that point, the interests of the distributors might have led to a reduction in the cost to the consumer. The economic advantages to the distributing companies probably would have caused a portion of the savings to percolate through to the consumers.

Too much, it is feared, has been left to economic forces. The machinery for readjusting prices to the consumer was not thoroughly overhauled and brought down to date in 1926. The provisions of the act do something for the consumer, but it is questionable if they do enough. The "provisions are hardly stringent enough to bring about a reduction of price in the absence of a will in that direction on the part of the distributor."[79]

Methods of Price Regulation. The earlier method of price regulation (and the one still in use) is that of fixing a schedule of maximum rates in the special act or order giving authority to the undertaker. Actual experience clearly indicates that "fixed maxima are of next to no use in preventing extortion. Either the management, free from direct or indirect competition, is unenterprising and provides services at a cost which, even if originally legitimate, becomes in time higher than it should be; or, if it is enterprising and progressive in consequence of competi-

[79] W. S. Kennedy, *The New Electricity Act*, p. 63.

tion or ability of management it develops business by reducing rates, or in the alternative maintains rates which have become extortionate."[80]

The minister of transport has the authority "to make an Order varying the prices or methods of charge" at any time after the expiration of seven years from the commencement of the special order which established the maximum price. The revision of the price is made only upon the application of a public authority not itself an authorized undertaker, or by the company interested,[81] or by "twenty or more consumers."[82]

By the Act of 1926, the minister of transport has the power to revise the maximum and standard prices charged by a power company where the company takes a supply from the board. The minister is directed to take into account "any reduction in the cost of electricity attributable to this Act."[83]

The most promising provision for regulation of prices in the interest of the consumer is found in the provision for a sliding scale of dividends and charges imposed upon distributing companies taking a supply from the board. When the board, as is intended, ultimately becomes almost the sole source of supply, then the sliding scale will have almost universal application. This is the most effective "assurance given in the Act that the reduction in generating costs caused by intercon-

nection, centralization and coöperation will be passed on to the individual consumer by the companies."[84]

The details of the sliding scale plan for dividends and charges are drawn up by the electricity commissioners and promulgated by them in a special order which requires the approval of each House of Parliament.[85] The sliding scale was adopted for the London Companies by the provisions of a Special Act of Parliament, 1925.[86]

In case the distributing authority is a municipality or other public authority the law limits narrowly the amount of the net surplus which may be applied "in aid of local rates," and provides that the major portion of the surplus shall go to reducing charges, and toward paying off capital loans.[87]

A great deal of thought is being given to "methods of charge." The whole tendency of the industry, public and private, is to encourage the adoption of a "two-part tariff," one part relating to "fixed or service charge, and the other a charge for the quantity of electricity contained in the supply." Such a method is considered "a first essential to the wide use of electricity in the home."[88]

The installation of some such method was made possible by provisions of the Act of 1926 permitting the electricity commissioners, at their discretion, to promulgate a special order subject to the approval of the minister of trans-

[80] Sir H. N. Bunbury, K.C.B., *The Economic Regulation of Public Utility Services*, in Public Administration, Vol. IV, No. 3, (July 1926) p. 212.

[81] Electric Lighting (Clauses) Act 1899, Sec. 32, Sub-sec. 2.

[82] Sir Harry E. Haward, *Local Authorities under the Electricity (Supply) Acts*, in Public Administration, Vol. VI (Jan. 1928), p. 52.

[83] Electricity (Supply) Act, 1926 (16–17 Geo. 5, Chap. 51), Sec. 31, Sub-sec. 1.

[84] W. S. Kennedy, *New Electricity Act*, p. 62.

[85] Electricity (Supply) Act, 1926, Sec. 32, Sub-sec. 1; Electricity (Supply) Act, 1919, Sec. 26.

[86] London Electricity (No. 1) Act, 1925 (15–16 Geo. 5, Chap. 62), Third Schedule.

[87] Electricity (Supply) Act, 1926 (16–17 Geo. 5, Chap. 51), Fifth Schedule.

[88] Advisory Committee on Domestic Supplies of Electricity and Methods of Charge, Report 1927, p. 16.

port setting up an optional method of charges.[89]

REGULATION OF PUBLIC ELECTRICITY AUTHORITIES

Local authorities receive powers to generate and distribute electrical energy in a specified area mainly from special orders issued by the electricity commissioners. Such powers cannot be given up or transferred except upon an order from the electricity commissioners. Uniformity in the details of such orders is usually secured by the incorporation in the order of the clauses in the Electric Lighting (Clauses) Act of 1899. The order usually contains a schedule of maximum prices to be charged for electric energy. Orders called "Fringe Orders" in certain instances give local authorities powers to supply energy to surrounding areas.

The local authorities are granted general powers to borrow on the security of local rates the capital needed for the electricity undertaking, but all such loans are subject to the approval of the electricity commissioners. Furthermore, the maximum period for the repayment of such loans varies from sixty years for land to seven years for domestic apparatus.

They are limited by acts of Parliament (Act of 1899, and Act of 1926) with regard to the use to be made of the surplus revenue. The law provides that the amount that may be applied in aid of local rates in any year shall not exceed one-and-a-half per cent of the outstanding debt on the undertaking; and after March 31, 1930, "no sum shall be paid in aid of the local rates unless the reserve fund amounts to more than one-twentieth of the aggregate capital expenditure on the undertaking."[90]

A local authority is required to report to the electricity commissioners a statement of its accounts on a form prescribed by the commissioners, but such accounts are audited by appointees of the authority itself, rather than by auditors appointed by and responsible to the electricity commissioners.

The consent of the minister of transport is required for the erection of overhead lines by any electricity undertaker. On the other hand the local authorities have no longer the right of absolute veto on the erection of such lines.[91]

The right of a local authority to purchase the undertaking of a private supply company was materially modified in 1919 by the provision that made such purchase subject to the consent of the electricity commissioners.

REGULATION OF PRIVATE ELECTRICITY COMPANIES

Private electricity authorities, including both power companies and distributing companies, receive their powers from Parliamentary acts and special orders. Such acts and orders among other things define their areas of supply, their rights to use streets for cables or wires, and the maximum charges for sale of energy. The private distributing companies are subject in the main to the same general laws as are the public authorities.

The private companies, furthermore, are subject to an audit of their accounts by an auditor appointed by the minister of transport.[92]

The most important change in the regulation of private electric companies effected in recent years has to do with the right to purchase the private under-

[89] Electricity (Supply) Act 1926 (16–17 Geo. 5, Chap. 51), Sec. 42.

[90] *Ibid.*, Fifth Schedule.

[91] Public Administration, Vol. VI (Jan. 1928), p. 53.

[92] Electric Lighting Act, 1909, Sec. Sec. 20, as amended by the Electricity (Supply) Act of 1926.

takings. The purchase clause of the Act of 1888 was slightly modified in 1919 by the provision that the purchase of a private company's holdings by a local authority, except in the district of a joint electricity authority, was conditioned upon the consent of the electricity commissioners.[93] The Act of 1922 further modified the purchase clause by providing that the power of purchase might be suspended for such period and on such conditions as the company and the local authority agreed upon, subject to the approval of the electricity commissioners. Such agreement is to be given effect by an order of the commissioners.[94]

A more important modification of the policy with regard to the purchase of private undertakings was contained in the Act of 1926. The modification applies to companies formed after the Act of 1926 goes into effect and whose area extends over the districts of two or more local authorities. The company's undertaking may be purchased by a joint electricity authority, or a joint committee of local authorities concerned. The company is given a tenure of 50 years. Notice of purchase may be given six months after the expiration of each subsequent ten-year period. The most important part of the provision relates to the principle of fixing the value. The price shall be "a sum equal to the *capital properly expended* for the provision of the land, buildings, works, material and plant . . . in use or available and suitable for use at the time of the purchase for the purposes of their undertaking less depreciation according to a scale as may be determined by special order."[95]

The purchase clause of the Act of 1888 was further modified in 1926 by the provision permitting local authorities and private companies, with the approval of the electricity commissioners, any time within ten years before the date of purchase next occurring or within ten years of any subsequent date of purchase, to contract to amend, vary or alter the terms of purchase.[96]

The act does not fully comply with the recommendation of the Weir Committee that the purchase clause be done away with entirely, but it does remove the occasion for much of the uncertainty facing a company during the last years of its specified term; and under the conditions produced by the new act probably few occasions will arise where it will seem expedient or advisable for a single municipality to purchase the plant of a private company.

PROVISIONS RELATING TO LABOR

Compensation is guaranteed to regularly employed officers and employees of electricity undertakers, who, in consequence of the changes in the electricity industry brought about by the act, have been deprived of employment or suffered diminution in salary, and who have not been given "equivalent employment under like conditions." The guarantee extends over a period of five years from the date when a generating' station has been closed or a main transmission line has been acquired.

The persons affected are required to prove to a referee appointed by the minister of labor that their loss of employment or diminution in salary has

[93] Electricity (Supply) Act, 1919, Sec. 13.

[94] Electricity (Supply) Act, 1922, Sec. 14.

[95] Electricity (Supply) Act 1926 (16–17 Geo. 5, Chap. 51), Sec. 29, Sub-sec. 1 (a).

[96] *Ibid.*, Sec. 41.

NOTE.—The administration of the electricity industry in the administrative county of London was specifically dealt with in the London Electricity (No. 1) Act, 1925; and in the London Electricity (No. 2) Act, 1925. Tenure of the private owners was extended to 1971. Space does not permit a statement of the complicated financial details of the settlement.

not been on grounds of misconduct, incapacity or superannuation, and otherwise comes under the provisions of the law granting the compensation. The amount of the compensation is to be determined by a referee or board of referees, and is to be paid by the owners of the station or main transmission line.[97]

The problem of fixing wage schedules and settling disputes relating to hours and conditions of service is handled almost entirely in the electricity industry by the so-called "Whiteley Councils." These councils are composed of: first, the Joint Industrial Council for the Electricity Supply Industry (so-called National Council); and, second, District Councils, for the several great industrial districts. For example, District Council No. 1 has jurisdiction within the North-East Coast Area. It is composed of twenty-eight members. Fourteen are selected by employers, eight representing "company undertakers," and six "municipal undertakers"; and fourteen, by the trade unions in the several branches of the industry.[98]

The plan, it appears, has been remarkably successful in settling wage disputes, strikes, and lock outs, and in creating more uniform standards of wages and conditions of service in both the privately and the publically owned plants.

INITIAL STEPS IN REORGANIZATION, 1927

Much of the work involved in preparing the first scheme under the Act of 1926 had been completed by the Electricity Commission prior to the final passage of the act, December, 1926.

[97] Electricity (Supply) Act 1926 (16-17, Geo. 5, Chap. 51), Fourth Schedule.

[98] District Council (No. 1) North-East Coast Area Electricity Supply Industry, *Constitution*, revised and reprinted 1927.

The first scheme published in May, 1927, was termed the "Central Scotland Electricity Scheme, 1927," and was applied to the district covering practically the whole of the Scottish industrial, shipbuilding, and coal field area, which extends diagonally across Scotland from sea to sea. The total area covered by the scheme is approximately 5,000 square miles in extent.

The scheme provides for the selection of ten generating stations from among the thirty-six existing stations. Four of these ten, however, in the opinion of the Electricity Commission, should be shut down in time and two new stations should be constructed.

The commissioners stated the factors which were taken into account in selecting the generating stations as follows:

1. The cost of coal delivered to the station.
2. Abundance of water for condensing purposes.
3. Technical characteristics of the station, such as type and size of the plant units, steam pressure, etc.
4. Proximity to load.
5. The possibilities of the site for the further expansion of the station.

Four of the stations selected were owned by public authorities, and six were company owned.

The commissioners determined upon a voltage of 132,000 volts for "the overhead primary transmission lines throughout the United Kingdom," as well as for the Scotland scheme. They also adopted for the Central Scotland area the standard frequency of 50 cycles per second.

The scheme provided for the complete interconnection of the stations by means of a primary transmission system and transforming stations to be procured at an estimated cost of £2,204,-034.[99]

Before the close of 1927 an "Electricity Scheme" was also prepared and published for South-East England which included the county of London and the whole or part of twelve adjacent counties. The principles governing the details of the scheme were much the same as those adopted for the first "scheme" described above.[100]

The commission announced its intention of completing in the near future electricity schemes for at least three other great industrial districts. According to the estimate of the commission the transmission systems for the schemes adopted by the Central Electricity Board will be in the course of construction during the period up to 1933-34.[101]

Concluding Observations

Americans interested in the solution of their own difficult public utilities problems may watch with interest the outcome of the British experiment. The British are attempting to direct the development of a major industry, during the next few decades, on the principle of coöperation between governmental agencies and private capital. They are attempting to bring about, systematically, cheap generation and complete interconnection through the control by, and partial operation of, a national agency, while they are leaving the distribution of electric energy in the hands of the existing local public authorities and private companies. They are protecting the *status quo* (1926) with regard to public ownership and private ownership; although it is be-

lieved that the incentive for the purchase of the private enterprises by local authorities has been greatly weakened if not entirely removed.

It is of special interest to American observers that the British have seemingly adopted for the future the "prudent investment theory of valuation" and discarded the "reproduction cost less depreciation" theory.

The success of the experiment depends largely upon the soundness of judgment in technical matters exercised by the electricity commission; and upon the practical business acumen possessed by the Central Electricity Board, combined with the willingness of Parliament to give the plan a fair test. For nothing, it seems, is more blighting to industry than the uncertainty caused by continuous legislative tinkering.

Much depends also upon the enlightened, progressive, and energetic management of the distributing authorities. The local managers must be willing to pass on to the consumers a major portion of the reduced cost resulting from efficient generation and transmission. They must also encourage the wider use of electricity by the adoption of favorable terms for wiring houses and of more satisfactory methods of charging for current. Favorable results may also be expected from the educational program of such propagandist organizations as the British Electrical Development Association and the British Electrical and Allied Manufacturers' Association.

If this experiment in the field of electricity, launched with such confidence in 1926, proves successful, it will provide further evidence that there is a workable medium between the *laissez-faire* system of unregulated private industry on the one extreme, and the complete nationalization on the other.

[99] Electricity Commission, *Central Scotland Electricity Scheme, 1927, Supplementary Particulars*, pp. 3-8.

[100] *London Weekly Times*, Oct. 13, 1927, p. 423.

[101] Electricity Commission, *Central Scotland Electricity Scheme, 1927, Supplementary Particulars*, p. 3.

NATIONAL MUNICIPAL REVIEW

PUBLISHED MONTHLY BY THE

National Municipal League

| Vol. XVII, No. 7 | JULY, 1928 | Total No. 145 |

CONTENTS

EDITORIAL COMMENT..........................*H. W. Dodds* 387

THE FRENCH PARLIAMENTARY ELECTIONS AND THE
NEW ELECTORAL LAW......................*James K. Pollock, Jr.* 389

PLANNING PLAY AREAS IN PRIVATE SUBDIVISIONS ....*C. C. Hieatt*........ 391

STANDARDS OF FINANCIAL ADMINISTRATION DEFENDED *Lent D. Upson and
C. E. Rightor*..... 393

PROPORTIONAL REPRESENTATION IN GERMAN CITIES.*Roger H. Wells*..... 397

THE RELATION OF BUILDING-HEIGHT TO STREET
TRAFFIC..................................*Herbert D. Simpson.* 405

DEPARTMENTS

I. Recent Books Reviewed 419

II. Judicial Decisions ....*Edited by C. W. Tooke* 423

III. Public Utilities ....*Edited by John Bauer* 426

IV. Governmental Research Association Notes ....*Edited by Russell Forbes* 429

V. Notes and Events ....*Edited by H. W. Dodds* 435

TENTATIVE PROGRAM

ANNUAL MEETING OF NATIONAL MUNICIPAL LEAGUE, GOVERNMENTAL RESEARCH ASSOCIATION, AND NATIONAL ASSOCIATION OF CIVIC SECRETARIES

CINCINNATI, OHIO, OCTOBER 15, 16 AND 17, 1928

October 15—Sessions conducted by Governmental Research Association

10:00 A.M. A Fact Basis for Community Action
Three-Minute Reports from the Bureaus

12:30 P.M. Address of Welcome: The Hon. Murray Seasongood, Mayor of Cincinnati
Address: Colonel C. O. Sherill, City Manager of Cincinnati
Report of Chairman of Governmental Research Association

2:00 P.M. Simultaneous Round Table Sessions
1. Subject: Special Assessments
2. Subject: Financial Statistics of Cities

7:00 P.M. Dinner

October 15—Sessions conducted by National Association of Civic Secretaries
Program to be announced later

October 16—Sessions of National Municipal League jointly with Governmental Research Association and National Association of Civic Secretaries

10:00 A.M. Simultaneous Round Table Sessions.
1. Subject: The Negro and Public Affairs
2. Subject: Measurement Standards in Government

2:00 P.M. General Session: The City's Responsibility in Housing

7:00 P.M. Dinner. Speakers to be announced

October 17—Sessions of National Municipal League jointly with Governmental Research Association and National Association of Civic Secretaries

10:00 A.M. Simultaneous Round Table Sessions
1. Subject: P. R. and Democracy in Elections
2. Subject: Selling the Work of Government to the Public

12:30 P.M. Luncheon. Short business session. Round Table reports
Address by Arthur Collins, English expert in municipal administration and finance

2:00 P.M. Sightseeing

NATIONAL
MUNICIPAL REVIEW

VOL. XVII, No. 7   JULY, 1928   TOTAL No. 145

EDITORIAL COMMENT

On June 30 the editor of the REVIEW sailed for Nicaragua, where he will remain until about January first, assisting in the supervised election for president of that country. During his absence the REVIEW will be in charge of Russell Forbes, the new secretary of the League. As announced in the June issue, Mr. Forbes will continue to devote a part of his time to the directorship of the Municipal Administration Service.

On July first Welles A. Gray became assistant director of the Municipal Administration Service. Mr. Gray received his B.A. degree from the University of Minnesota in 1923 and his M.A. in 1924. During this time he was on the staff of the League of Minnesota Municipalities. Mr. Gray comes to us from the University of Kansas, where he has been teaching municipal government and acting as secretary of the Municipal Reference Bureau.

❦

The following topics have been selected by the Prize Committee, Professor Edwin A. Cottrell, Chairman, as the subjects on which Baldwin Prize essays may be submitted in 1929:

Regional Planning Commissions.
Special Assessments Versus General Taxation for Street Improvements.
Racial Influences on Policies of Municipal Governments.
Objective Examinations in the Civil Service.

The Baldwin Prize of $100 is offered each year by the National Municipal League for the best essay on some phase of municipal government by an undergraduate student in an American college. Manuscripts must be in the hands of the secretary of the League by May 15, 1929. For further particulars address the secretary.

❦

The Meaning of the Recent Cleveland Charter Crisis. —All who are observing the operation of the city manager plan in the United States should read *Greater Cleveland* for May 3, published by the Cleveland Citizens League. The whole number is devoted to an appraisal of the present charter and the work of Manager Hopkins and the city council. Believing that the 73,000 votes cast against the charter last November, and the 40,000 adverse ballots in April indicate dissatisfaction with the present government which cannot be ignored, the bulletin proceeds to reveal some reasons for unrest.

It finds a serious and widespread lack of confidence in the city council, which is at present neither representative nor efficient. The revival of the secret caucus of the majority prior to

387

each council meeting is an important contributing cause to the low prestige in which the council is held. Furthermore, in violation of the fundamentals of city manager government, council members have been active in urging appointments and special favors for constituents and generally meddling in administration. Devotion to politics rather than to business has congested the calendar with important unfinished business. And finally, there is an absence of the right kind of council leadership. During the four years under the manager charter the majority floor leader has dominated and controlled, not by ability and strength of argument, but by fear and silent threats. Councilmen, who as individuals would seek the improvement of the city government, are as a group subservient to the dominating political leaders.

But not all the fault lies with the council; the manager, too, is to blame for the failure of the new charter to work out in every detail as the framers intended. True, the manager must formulate policies for the approval of the council; but it is not his prerogative to attempt political coercion of the council. When he has presented a clear statement of the facts and the arguments in favor of his recommendations his policy function is ended. On several occasions, the bulletin asserts, the manager has been a leading advocate of debatable issues at elections, which has exposed him to political criticism and has resulted in too little attention to administrative detail. The manager should remember that first and last he is an administrator and not a prophet. Moreover, the present manager's conception of his relation to the council has enabled him to withhold knowledge of big plans for public improvements which he was contemplat-

ing, until such plans were well matured and could only be approved or rejected by the council. This has led to a lack of friendly coöperation between manager and council. Another cause of distrust has been the manager's failure to keep the public informed regarding the administration of municipal affairs. During his four years of office no annual report in printed form has been made.

We have recounted the above at some length in the thought that other cities under the manager plan may be falling into the same trap as Cleveland. Manager Hopkins is known throughout the country as a man of integrity, energy and vision. To many, however, he appears as an excellent type of mayor, of which any city would be proud, rather than as the type of manager which is bound to survive. The Cleveland Citizens' League respects the manager; but it has little admiration for the council and wisely directs attention to its shortcomings. In charter campaigns too much emphasis is placed as a rule upon the position of the manager. It is forgotten that what is being considered is *council-manager* government and not *manager* government. Few plans concentrate so much power and responsibility in the council as does this one. Unless, therefore, the council be of a truly representative type the plan will be a disappointment. Proportional representation has supplied Cincinnati with a council of high calibre; it has not been so successful in Cleveland. The progressive deterioration in the calibre of men chosen for city councils at successive municipal elections following the adoption of a new charter has raised misgivings in the minds of some as to the ultimate fate of the manager plan.

THE FRENCH PARLIAMENTARY ELECTIONS AND THE NEW ELECTORAL LAW

BY JAMES K. POLLOCK, JR.

University of Michigan

France has restored the single member system with the second ballot for Parliamentary elections, after two experiences with a bogus form of proportional representation. :: :: :: :: :: :: ::

Scrutin uninominal being very freely translated means "town pump politics." *Ballottage*, the corollary and accompanist of *scrutin uninominal* in France, means "let the politicians decide!" These two weapons in the hands of astute leaders ought to enable them to produce a chamber of deputies to their liking. And such appears to have been the result of the Parliamentary elections held in France in April of this year. Out of an unmistakably clear current of opinion toward M. Poincaré there has emerged a new legislature about which keen political observers are hesitant to prophesy. All sections of the press agree that the elections were a great personal triumph for Premier Poincaré, but what will occur when the party groupings in the Chamber are made, no one can say.

But aside from the general results of the election, how did the new electoral law operate? The law of July 12, 1927, reëstablishing *scrutin uninominal* was pushed through the Chamber despite the known opposition of Premier Poincaré. But rather than have his financial measures jeopardized, he permitted it to become law. The Socialists who favored a real system of P. R. decided in April, 1927, that they preferred a reëstablishment of *scrutin arrondissement* to the *scrutin unique* of 1919, and following much discussion and alteration in the Commission of the Chamber, and several tumultuous

meetings of the Chamber, the law was finally voted by 320 votes to 234. Just how the table of electoral circumscriptions was actually arranged is still a dark secret, and an examination of these circumscriptions will disclose many mathematical inequalities.

GRAVE INEQUALITIES IN DISTRICTS

For instance, the population of the circumscriptions varies from 22,000 to 133,000. Excluding the colonies, there are no less than eighty-six circumscriptions with a population of less than 50,000, and thirty-four circumscriptions with a population above 100,000. In the department of the Seine where there are 59 deputies there are four circumscriptions with a population from 30,000 to 50,000; eighteen with a population from 50,000 to 70,000; twenty-nine with a population from 70,000 to 100,000; and eight with a population from 100,000 to 133,000; It may be mere chance that five of the eight largest districts are Communist strongholds, and that the smallest district elected a Republican of the Left, a sitting member, on the first day. But one is suspicious. The sixth *arrondissement* with 100,000 people has two deputies; the tenth circumscription of Saint Denis with 133,000 people has one deputy. And so on *ad infinitum*. On a mathematical and political basis, therefore, the law is distinctly unfair, even more so than the law which was in effect from 1889 to 1919.

PLETHORA OF CANDIDATES—WAS THERE A REAL ELECTION?

Furthermore, there appeared such a plethora of candidates that the first day of balloting resulted in filling but 187 out of the 612 seats to be filled. There thus remained for the *ballottage* a week later 425 contests—truly the fulfillment of the politician's dream. In the week between the two elections the arrangements and bargainings which took place resulted in the restoration in a general way of the *cartel des gauches;* the maintenance of all the Communists candidates; and the general agreement among the parties of the center and right to avoid a splitting up of their vote. The voters were thus given a rather clear choice on the second day between a Communist, a Radical or Socialist, and a Moderate. The results indicate that the right swing of the first day's voting was successfully counteracted by the successes of the Left parties on the second day.

The Frenchman's fondness for the *ballottage* was well rewarded, but now that the results are known, were the people able clearly to express their opinions, and did the election really decide anything which could not have been decided without an election? The government intimated unofficially what the results would be, and although they overestimated the ability of the cartellists, their early estimates were surprisingly accurate. One wonders how the French people, confronted with 3,687 candidates on the first day of voting, and with 1,273 on the second day; with the whole result of the election turning on the deals made in the week between the two days of voting— a matter over which they had no control—how the French nation could possibly express its opinion clearly.

As the *Journal Des Debats* observed: "The cartellists have deliberately preferred the famous 'broken mirror' which hinders the appearance of great political tendencies."

ELECTION ADMINISTRATION NOT IMPROVED

So far as the law of 1927 is concerned, nothing was done to improve the mechanical side of the election. In the counting, tabulation, and canvassing of the votes there is a laxness which greatly surprises an American. There is also much inefficiency. It takes an inordinate length of time to count the ballots and, although one is not aware of any fraud being committed, to anyone disposed to irregularity, great opportunities still exist. Strangely enough, the Frenchman does not seem to worry about the possibilities of inaccuracy or fraud. Candidates do not seem to be nervous about turning their political fates over to sixteen or twenty men chosen at random from among those present in the voting room. So for the Frenchman, perhaps, the system is all right, but who can know whether it is all right, when some of the papers and paraphernalia of voting can be and are destroyed? Surely the French system is inferior to the splendid English practice, and to the accuracy and efficiency of the modern voting machine.

In one respect at least the new law brings an improvement. According to Article 9 an organization is set up to take care of the printing and distribution of the ballots for the candidates. The candidates may or may not take advantage of the opportunity thus afforded to pool the costs of printing the ballots, but in any event the organization now exists. The next logical step would be for the state to defray the cost of the ballots as has been done in many other countries.

The campaign was not very active nor very interesting. The *affiches electorales*, as in the past, provided much amusement and not a little good publicity for the candidates. Each candidate is given, at public expense, billboards on which he can place his electoral posters. Some candidates who are poor write their own posters; others who are financed by parties or groups indulge in colored posters and printed appeals of all sorts. One anarchist candidate put up a poster in which he exhorted the people not to vote, and especially not for him! Many attractive titles appeared: "The hand in the pocket," "Campaign of lies," "Down with war." As useful as the posters may be, however, the most effective work is done in the cafés where one can buy one's friend a drink and talk leisurely about his troubles and how they can be ameliorated.

Briefly, the various parties and groups fared as follows: The Communists gained about 175,000 votes but lost thirteen seats; the Socialists remained exactly the same; the Radicals and Radical Socialists lost about thirty seats; while the Left Republicans gained about ten seats and the U. R. D. or Marin Group gained about thirty seats. The balance of power in the Chamber is thus shifted slightly rightward. The elections now being over, the playground has shifted from the country to the Palais Bourbon, where for the next four years one must look for the decisions of the French nation.

PLANNING PLAY AREAS IN PRIVATE SUBDIVISIONS

THE REALTOR'S MOTIVE AND THE CITY'S RESPONSIBILITY

BY C. C. HIEATT

Excerpt of an address before the National Recreation Congress at Memphis. ::   ::   ::   ::   ::   ::   ::   ::   ::   ::

A MAN who is in the subdivision business and who is going to develop a certain tract of land for home purposes is doing it as a business proposition. If he is going to carry on his business, he must see his way clear to pay the cost of his land, the cost of the improvements and all of the utilities that have to be put in, and still reap a fair profit. We can expect that he make only those expenditures which he can recover in some way from the sale of that land. Wide-awake realtors of America today appreciate the fact that they can add to the value of their subdivisions by devoting or setting aside parts for public use. It is being done continually.

SOME EXAMPLES

It was my privilege the other day to be in Boston and to see a plat of a subdivision there, planned by Olmsted Brothers, which provides for the following facilities for the people who buy in this subdivision. I want you to remember them, because I think the list pretty nearly runs the whole gamut of recreational activities. There are golf courses, a riding academy, bridle paths, a polo field, ten tennis courts, a yacht harbor, casino, swimming pool, piers out into the bay, croquet grounds and places for quoits. I may have overlooked several other things. It goes without saying that the promoter of this subdivision is going to capitalize on all these things and is going to charge for the remaining land an added price that will cover the part that he is setting aside for public use.

I want also to cite to you another case, not only because I was personally interested, but because it happened here in Memphis, and shows what can be done along this line.

A few years ago some associates and I acquired a tract of land out here in Memphis. It belonged to Mr. Saunders, the originator of the Piggly-Wiggly stores, who had started the erection thereon of a very handsome residence. He spent some $300,000 or $400,000 on the erection of what was called here a "pink palace," and then he failed. We bought the land from the receiver in bankruptcy for the purpose of developing a subdivision. The practical question which confronted us was what to do with that pile of granite, of beautiful architecture, half-completed—all of the exterior, but none of the interior. We either had to tear the building down and utilize the land, or find some purpose to which the building could be devoted which would not injure the rest of the property. We could not turn it into an asylum for insane people, for example, because that would have depreciated the value of the adjoining land.

We hit upon the idea to induce the city of Memphis to accept the house and some land around it. In the center of the property Mr. Saunders had developed an artificial lake of some size. From each end ran a stream, so we laid out a plan that would include the lake in a park and provide room for playgrounds and recreation. We tied on to this another area of

land around the "pink palace" and we submitted it to the city along with the palace, offering to give it to them if they would devote the palace to public use as a library or natural history museum or art gallery or something of that kind. They accepted it. Mayor Paine made the statement that we gave the city $400,000 worth of property, because the building and land actually cost that.

GIFT TO CITY MAKES.PROFIT TO OWNERS

I would not stand here and ask you to believe that we were foolish enough to give away $400,000 worth of property. We didn't give them anything. I think we got back, or we will get back, more than this in the increased value of our property, and eventually we shall be indebted to the city of Memphis for taking the property.

When the property was placed on the market, the highest priced lots were those around the park area and lake. They were the first to be sold, proving it is good business to do such things. Frankly, if we had not succeeded in getting the park commission of Memphis to take over the park area, we should have been put to it to know what to do with it.

THE CITY'S DUTY

I know you will appreciate the fact that a subdivider who has any regard for the future value of his property will hesitate before opening up an uncontrolled and unsupervised playground in the heart of it. There must be supervision, or it will turn out to be a nuisance and depreciate values. So the point I want to make is that the subdivider who expects to do anything of this kind ought to do it in coöperation with the recreation man, or with some expert in recreation, just as engineers are employed to make layouts and devise sewer systems or water systems. The best possible advice should be sought as to where the playground and recreation centers should be located and how they ought to be set up.

If you expect realtors to make gifts of land to the public, you must see that the city in which such land is situated has shown wisdom in accepting the property and will undertake to super-vise it, because the developer cannot obligate himself to supervise indefinitely.

While I think you can count on realtors throughout America, particularly those who subdivide, to respond cordially and willingly to this program of giving their lands, it must be done in a way that will not deteriorate values, but will tend to enhance values. Only thus can they afford to set aside these spaces for playgrounds and recreation.

"STANDARDS OF FINANCIAL ADMINISTRATION" DEFENDED

BY LENT D. UPSON AND C. E. RIGHTOR

Detroit Bureau of Governmental Research, Inc.

We all covet success, and most of us aspire to efficiency and economy in our practical undertakings, but few of us can agree on the criteria which measure success or efficiency. In the supplement to our February number, Messrs. Upson and Rightor, although aware that few would agree with them, undertook the courageous task of sponsoring certain standards of measurement of a city's financial administration. In the following letter to the editor they make reply to Francis Oakey's critical review which appeared in the "American City" for May.   ::

To the Editor of THE NATIONAL MUNICI-PAL REVIEW:

IN the May issue of the *American City*, Mr. Francis Oakey is severely critical of our *Standards of Financial Administration*. In his opinion the pamphlet "includes a large number of principles or proposals which are unsound, omits principles which are essential, contains unsound conclusions or assumptions, and in some cases, inaccurate statements."

Ordinarily, contention between authors and their reviewers is an effort that might better be applied to more useful purposes. However, since the condemnation by Mr. Oakey is so sweeping, and since these standards were sponsored and published by the National Municipal League, some com-ment on the criticism is due to you, and may be of interest to your readers.

We advanced fifty-three standards in the fields of budgeting, revenues, debt, treasury, accounting, and pur-chasing,—confining the statement of each standard and the accompanying discussion to an average of 150 words. This enforced brevity prompted us to say: "Public finance covers a wide scope of community endeavor, and obviously the criteria of correct prac-tices must be expanded in minute de-tail if the numerous ramifications of the subject were to be explored to final conclusions." This explanation is our only rebuttal to certain of Mr. Oakey's criticisms that imply failure to cover the subject completely.

We have endeavored a dispassionate

analysis of Mr. Oakey's criticisms and conclude that he considers four of our fifty-three principles unsound, *i.e.*, activity classification of the budget, pay-as-you-go, maximum interest rates on deposits (in part), and consolidation of storage yards. Two others he thinks unimportant, *i.e.*, appointment rather than election of the treasurer and consolidation of treasurer's funds. He enumerates eight additional standards that he thinks should be included, *i.e.*, preparation of a program of financing, execution of this program in coördination with the expenditure program, consideration of surplus or deficit, determination that expendi-

tures come within the purport of appropriations, safeguards over cash and securities, establishment of complete records of cash and debt transactions, prescription of methods of accounting, and preparation of financial statements. All of these we insist we have included either by direct statement or unavoidable inference in the standards given. The charges of unsound conclusions or assumptions, totaling eleven, are leveled at our discussion of principles which he largely accepts. Finally, he assumes four inaccurate statements.

Our analysis of Mr. Oakey's review and our rejoinders are as follows:

CRITICISM	REPLY
1. "The writers have confined their attention to the expenditure program and have disregarded the program of financing."	1. We defined budget procedure as that "by which the estimated income is correlated with estimated expenses and the latter authorized. . . ." "The estimated costs of this program should be balanced with available or expected income. . . ." "The value of budgeting current income and outgo has been discussed."
2. "No reference is made to a surplus or deficit which may exist at the beginning of the fiscal year. . . ."	2. Does a budget that balances expenditures with "available or expected income" require especial consideration of surplus or deficit?
3. Disagreement is taken with the use of the activity as an appropriation unit.	3. A matter of opinion. We do not urge the activity as the final unit of appropriation. We do think that the budget should be stated in terms of principal activities for each department.
4. "The article appears to sanction the maintenance of the more important funds, referring to various kinds of special funds. The reviewer believes that, with a few exceptions, all special funds, consisting of city revenue set aside for special purposes, should be abolished. The exceptions are sinking funds and special assessment funds."	4. We stated that such funds are created by law—"sometimes with very little reason back of such legislation." We added that the maintenance of more important funds is justifiable, enumerating bond funds, special assessment funds, trust funds to meet the cost of pensions, gifts for specific purposes, etc.
5. It is stated that we have emphasized the control of expenditures and failed to give place to control over revenues.	5. We have said that the budget "should be balanced with available or expected income." We should have repeated this provision, and added "currently, as well as at appropriation time."
6. "No reference is made to the necessity of determining whether the expenditure comes within the scope and purpose of the appropriations to which it is proposed to charge it."	6. "Procedure should be established to insure the funds being spent in accordance with the wishes of the appropriating authorities" and "no order from a department and upon a vendor is valid unless it is approved by the city controller, . . . (who) . . . charges the amount

CRITICISM

REPLY

*against the appropriation of the department.
. . ."*

7. "It is proposed to charge the amounts of purchase orders against appropriation accounts and to correct the accounts when the actual amounts are known. These entries involve a large amount of labor, which is unnecessary, since control can be maintained by means of an encumbrance file."

7. The encumbrance is the important thing; how it is accomplished is a detail. Our experience supports the use of the ledger in preference to the file.

8. "It is also proposed that quarterly allotments be submitted to the controller for approval. To the reviewer it seems that approval of allotments is an important executive function having to do with the general direction of the expenditure program and involving questions of policy. These functions properly belong to the chief executive, assisted by a budget director, rather than to the controller. . . ."

8. Right. The allotments should be reviewed by the chief executive. In actual practice we believe the estimates should be examined by some one with time and interest to devote to financial details,—preferably the controller in all except those very few cities which have or can have budget directors.

9. The reviewer disagrees with the proposal for pay-as-you-go "wherever and to whatever extent possible."

9. A matter of opinion. We venture to predict that large cities at least will come more and more to the acceptance of this principle.

10. Exception is taken to the proposal: "Periodically, depositaries should be selected upon the basis of highest interest rates bid."

10. Right. We should have said "highest rate consistent with safety." If the city stands in no likelihood of collecting either its interest or principal, highest rate would be mere sophistry.

11. Two standards for the treasurer's office—appointment rather than election of treasurer, and consolidation of treasurer's funds "are relatively unimportant."

11. The first, possibly; surely not the latter.

12. "No reference is made to those main principles which are of the utmost importance, namely:

(a) "The establishment of safeguards consisting of controls over (1) cash balances; (2) securities held as investments; (3) unissued and cancelled bonds of the city; (4) paid coupons; (5) the collection of revenue, including interest on investments; (6) disbursements.

(b) "The establishment of complete records of cash receipts and disbursements, and of transactions in city debt."

12. We assume the treasurer to be a custodial officer. As such, his transactions will be under the complete control of the controller, for which we provide. "Such control contemplates a complete, accurate, and current record of the several general classes of financial transactions,—current, capital, special, trust, etc. This includes adequate records of general departments including quasi-independent boards, etc., utilities, bonded debt and debt margins, tax limits, special assessments, pension funds, etc."

13. That "defalcations can occur only by actually absconding with funds in the treasurer's possession," is an inaccurate statement. Many kinds of defalcation can occur, even when the most effective accounting control is established (as enumerated).

13. We believe an adequate accounting and financial control will preclude such possibilities.

14. ". . . the duties of the controller are described as twofold, namely: first, record keeping, and second, auditing. In this definition two of the controller's most important duties are omitted, namely, (1) prescribing the methods of

14. We continue to hold that the controller stands in a dual relationship to the government. In his first position he is auditor, must use discretion in authenticating the acts of his coworkers, and should in no wise be responsible to

accounting; and (2) preparing the statements of financial condition and financial operations."

them; in his second position he is a record keeper, and should be responsible to those who make final use of the records. Prescription of accounts and preparation of records are only incident to these two divergent capacities. "A corollary of such records (kept by the controller) is a report to the public setting forth this information in concise and understandable form."

15. "It is not the function of auditing to pass upon the wisdom of expenditure nor to determine policy."

15. We insist that to audit properly, the auditor must be a free agent, using his discretion as to whether the expenditure is in accordance with law, whether consistent with the order or contract, whether prices are in accordance with the market, etc.

16. There is general criticism of the discussion following our standards that accounts should be centralized in the controller's office; that municipal accounting should be maintained on an accrual basis, and that controlled inventories of the city's supplies, materials, equipment and real estate should be maintained.

16. Perhaps our discussion of these points is poorly arranged. However, the purpose of these standards—complete control records and information—seems clear.

17. "The writers propose that payrolls be checked by the civil service authorities. This would mean unnecessary duplication of labor, since payrolls must be checked in the controller's office on the basis of advices of employment, etc."

17. We think our proposal will stand careful analysis. It is also a requirement of the *Model Charter* of the National Municipal League.

18. "It is stated that the existence of a properly prepared operating statement and balance sheet is in itself a criterion of a sound accounting procedure. In the opinion of the reviewer, this is an unsound conclusion, since many balance sheets and operating statements are recalled which were unsound in form and content, misleading in terminology, and based on an unsound accounting procedure."

18. We think that they are criteria,—if "properly prepared."

19. Exception is taken to our definition of a cash audit as differing from an operation audit.

19. We accept the correction, although the definition has nothing whatever to do with the obvious intent of the text.

20. "The reviewer is not familiar with an operation audit."

20. It is believed high time that our cities provide an organization and procedure—which latter, for convenience, we term an "operation audit"—to weigh against the cost of public services the value of each to the community.

21. ". . . a proposal that all orders be entered upon appropriation ledgers as encumbrances and be paid promptly when the invoice is presented. It does not appear that this proposition has a relation to centralized purchasing, since the proposal could be put into effect whether centralized purchasing existed or not."

21. We did not say that it did have any relation to centralized purchasing. We said that such procedure was a test of efficient centralized purchasing. And we still believe it is.

22. Exception is taken to our proposal that

22. The practicability of this proposal can

centralized storehouses and storage yards should be under the control of the purchasing authority.

We will readily concede that any standards of financial administration suggested by ourselves or by others would probably fall short of what someone else would consider a perfect statement. Mr. Oakey has disagreed with a few of our standards, has suggested that certain of them might be amplified, and that perhaps certain others might be added. These suggestions we appreciate, though we do not agree with all of them. Beyond this, we feel that his review indicates a failure to understand what we

only be determined empirically.

thought was a reasonably clear statement, and an unwillingness to allow for limitations on space.

However, in the difficult and contentious task of setting up standards for evaluating the numerous activities of city government, discussion and disagreement is expected. Out of it all may come a gradual clarifying of principles that will be generally accepted.

Very truly yours,
LENT D. UPSON.
C. E. RIGHTOR.

PROPORTIONAL REPRESENTATION IN GERMAN CITIES

BY ROGER H. WELLS

Bryn Mawr College

An account of the law and the practice of P. R. in German municipal government, 1919–1928. :: :: :: :: :: :: ::

AMONG the current proposals for American municipal reform, proportional representation occupies an important place. However, in spite of the example set by Cleveland, Cincinnati, and several smaller cities, the subject is one which still remains largely in the discussion stage. This situation is in striking contrast to that found in Germany where proportional representation is the rule and not the exception. The following article gives a brief survey of the present status and working of the *Verhältniswahl* in German cities.

By the Weimar constitution of 1919, proportional representation is made mandatory not only for the federal and state legislatures but also for town and city councils as well.[1] This constitu-

[1] *Reichsverfassung*, Art. 17.

tional requirement is scarcely to be regarded as an innovation for it but marked the logical outcome of a movement which extended almost as far back as the days of Andrae and Hare. In fact, the writings of Considérant, Andrae, Hare and Mill in other countries were soon paralleled by those of a number of German publicists beginning with Burnitz and Varrentrapp in 1863.[2] Notwithstanding this literature, proportional representation did not arouse

[2] For a brief account of these writers and of the historical development of proportional representation in Germany, see Ernst Cahn, *Das Verhältniswahlsystem in den modernen Kulturstaaten* (Berlin, 1909), pp. 34–46. See also the standard American work by C. G. Hoag and G. H. Hallett, *Proportional Representation* (New York, 1926), pp. 162–181.

any considerable interest in Germany until the closing decade of the nineteenth century. At that time, the question passed from the theoretical to the practical stage and was incorporated in the platforms of a number of political parties, beginning with the Socialists in 1891.[1] Strong agitation also developed in several German states such as Baden and Württemberg, but it was not until 1901 that the first positive results were secured. Between that date and the outbreak of the World War, proportional representation was authorized for the choice of some of the members of the Hamburg and Württemberg state legislatures, for municipal elections in Baden, Bavaria, Oldenburg, and Württemberg, and for a wide variety of public and semi-public bodies such as industrial and commercial courts, chambers of commerce, social insurance committees, etc.[2] Moreover, as a part of the wartime movement for electoral reform, a federal law was passed in August,

1918, providing that the members of the Reichstag from the great cities and industrial territory should be chosen by proportional representation. Finally, the Weimar constitutional convention was itself selected by the Verhältniswahl, and, with the adoption of a definitive federal constitution by that body, the present fundamental rule came into operation.

Having spoken briefly of the historical development of proportional representation in Germany, one may now inquire as to the existing legal provisions on the subject. Article 17 of the Reichsverfassung, after stipulating that the Volksvertretung or Landtag of each state shall be directly elected "according to the principles of proportional representation," contains the following sentence: "The principles governing the election of (state) representatives also apply to municipal elections." There are three points to be noted with reference to the wording of this sentence. In the first place, it applies only to Ortsgemeinden, a term which includes both cities (Städte) and towns (Landgemeinden) but which does not include other local authorities such as counties (Kreise), provinces, ad hoc districts (Zweckverbände), etc.[3] As a matter of fact, state law has often made proportional representation applicable to the higher local units as well, while for Prussian counties and provinces, there is a constitutional provision to this effect.[4] In the second place, the federal requirement pertains only to the Gemeindevertretung, i.e., to the popularly elected town or city council.[5] This excludes for example, the Magistrat in Prussian cities, a body which is chosen by the council but which exer-

---

[1] See the Erfurt program of 1891 in Felix Salomon, ed., Die deutschen Parteiprogramme (3d cd., Berlin, 1924), ii, p. 127. Proportional representation was also favored in the 1895 program of the South German Volkspartei and in the 1910 union program of the Fortschrittliche Volkspartei. See Salomon, op. cit., ii, pp. 98, 102. The municipal program (1899) of the National Socialists advocated the optional introduction of proportional representtaion. See Cahn, op. cit., p. 36, n. 2.

[2] See the table given in Hoag and Hallett, op. cit., pp. 282–283. The detailed legal provisions governing municipal proportional representation may be found in the following works: Ernst Walz, Das badische Gemeinderecht (Heidelberg, 1914); K. Weber and K. A. v. Sutner, Bayerische Gemeindeordnung (10th cd., Munich, 1913); and Hugo Lindemann, Die württembergische Gemeindeordnung (Stuttgart, 1912). In Baden, Bavaria, and Württemberg, proportional representation was mandatory for municipal elections; but in Oldenburg, its use was optional. See Handwörterbuch fur Kommunalwissenschaften (6 vols., Jena, 1918–1927), ii, p. 314.

[3] See the commentary by Gerhard Anschütz, Die Verfassung des Deutschen Reichs (5th ed., Berlin, 1926), p. 89.

[4] Prussian Constitution of 1920, Art. 74.

[5] Anschütz, loc. cit.

cises legislative power as well as serving as the collegial exec tive. Here again, state law, local ordinance, and political practice have gone far beyond the letter of the federal constitution. In many states, where executive offices, especially unpaid offices, are to be filled by election of the council, or where council committees or mixed administrative committees (*Verwaltungsausschüsse*) are to be formed, proportional representation is either required or permitted. Finally, it will be noted that the federal mandate does not require any special type of proportional representation for conciliar elections, but only that such elections shall be according to the principles of the *Verhältniswahl*. Hence, it would be entirely permissable to use the Hare system of the single transferable vote as is done in Cleveland. But as a matter of fact, the list system is universally followed, thus conforming to the prevailing practice in continental Europe.

Now a list system is one which admits of many variations in detail. The question may, therefore, be raised as to the extent to which such variations are recognized in the municipal government acts (*Gemeinde* and *Städteordnungen*) of the several states. Here one is immediately impressed by the striking similarity which prevails as between state and state. Everywhere candidates for the office of councilman are nominated in party or group lists signed by a certain number of qualified voters, the number of which varies from five to seventy depending upon the state, and, in some instances, varying within a given state according to the population of the city. These tickets or *Wahlvorschläge* must be filed with designated municipal officials not later than a specified date, ranging from ten days to four weeks before the election.[1] The election laws and regu-

[1] It should be noted that councilmen are elected

lations fully recognize that nominations will be made by parties or political groups, but no attempt is made to control the methods by which a given party makes up its own list of candidates. All such matters remain within the jurisdiction of party rule and practice.[2]

On election day, the voter must vote for one party and only for that party. He may not alter the official order of the candidates' names as determined by the nominating petition, nor may he strike out or write in names. In

from the city as a whole and not from separate wards or districts. Hence, the nominating lists of the parties are city-wide tickets. To this rule, there are a few exceptions. For instance, the central city council of Berlin is chosen from fifteen districts but with a provision whereby members-at-large may be elected by the surplus votes from the several districts. Under certain conditions, Württemberg permits a city council to determine if its members shall be elected from districts. See *Gemeindeordnung* of 1906, Art. 11–13.

The election laws likewise prescribe various other details such as the filing of declarations of acceptance on the part of the persons nominated, the inclusion of information with reference to the occupation and address of candidates and petition signers, the prohibition of the nomination of the same candidate on different party lists, the official examination of the legal qualifications of candidates and petitioners, etc. In most states, municipal by-elections are not authorized to fill vacancies. When a seat in the council becomes vacant, the next candidate on the party list automatically succeeds to the place. These and other provisions are in large measure patterned after the federal and state election laws, the texts of which may be found in Walter Jellinek, *Die deutschen Landtagswahlgesetze* (Berlin, 1926).

[2] The extra-legal phases on the nominating process will be dealt with in a subsequent article on parties and partisanship in German cities. The law, however, indirectly recognizes the rôle which the party committees play in the nominating process by the various powers which it vests in the signers of a nominating petition who are in fact usually the party committeemen and party leaders.

fact, the ballots normally do not show the full list of nominees of a given group.[1] The voter sees only the name of the party or an equivalent *Kennwort*, the serial number of the ticket, together with the names of the first three or four candidates (*Spitzkandidaten*). Such is the system of "bound lists" (*gebundenen Listen*), a system which prevails in almost all German municipal elections. It contrasts with the "free list" plan whereby the elector has discretion as to the individual persons for whom he votes, voting for names on different tickets (*panachage*) or writing in "wild" names, *i.e.*, persons who have not been nominated. The free list system prevailed in the municipal elections of Bavaria and Württemberg before the Revolution, and it still exists for those cities of Württemberg which have less than fifty thousand inhabitants. But for all Bavarian cities and for the larger municipalities of Württemberg, the voter is now bound to the party ticket, but may, under certain circumstances, cumulate his votes within the list which he supports.[2]

After the casting and counting of the ballots, the next important question

relates to the division of the seats among the respective parties. In most of the states, the apportionment is made according to the d'Hondt quota method, the quota being determined in the following manner.[3] The number of valid ballots received by each party is successively divided by the integers one, two, three, four, etc. One seat is then assigned to each of the highest resulting quotients until all the places are filled, the last quotient for which an assignment is made being the d'Hondt quota.

The exact procedure will be made clearer by the following illustration. Assume that there are twelve councilmen to be elected, and that there are four party tickets in the field receiving respectively 3,219, 720, 558, and 2,901 votes. Thus, Ticket A receives five seats, Ticket B, one seat, Ticket C, one seat, and Ticket D, five seats. The quota in this particular illustration is the twelfth highest number or 558. Dividing this quota into the number of votes received by each list gives the same

---

[1] The "Australian" or official ballot is steadily supplanting the privately prepared party ballot although the official envelopes still continue to be used in most of the states having the official ballot.

[2] In Bavarian cities with under twenty thousand and in Württemberg cities with over fifty thousand inhabitants, the voter has as many votes to cast as there are councilmen to be elected. He may cumulate his votes giving not more than three to any one candidate, but all such preferences must be expressed within the regularly filed list of nominees of one party. With the great increase in the size of the electorate since the war and with the resulting development of more highly organized party machinery, the bound list form of proportional representation has almost everywhere replaced the earlier free list types.

[3] For a good explanation of the d'Hondt method and of other methods of determining quotas, see Hoag and Hallett, *op. cit.*, pp. 412 ff. The states which do not use the d'Hondt method in the election of municipal councilmen are Anhalt (simple quota), Mecklenburg-Strelitz (quota method determined by local statute) and Saxony (simple quota). In the city of Berlin, the d'Hondt method is used in the choice of the members of the twenty borough councils (*Bezirksversammlungen*), and for those members of the central council chosen by the transfer of surplus votes from the fifteen electoral districts. The simple quota (*i.e.*, the total number of valid ballots cast in the entire city of Berlin divided by 225, the total number of members to be elected to the central council) is used to determine how many central council members are chosen from each of the fifteen electoral districts. Nowhere in German municipal elections is the uniform or automatic quota employed as is the case in the election of the *Reichstag* and of several state legislatures.

Divided by	Ticket A	Ticket B	Ticket C	Ticket D
1.	3,219	720	558	2,901
2.	1,609	360	279	1,450
3.	1,073	240	186	967
4.	804	180	139	725
5.	643	144	111	580
6.	536	120	93	483

Quotients arranged in numerical order from high to low	1st seat 3,219 (A) 2nd " 2,901 (D) 3rd " 1,609 (A) 4th " 1,450 (D) 5th " 1,073 (A) 6th " 967 (D)	7th seat 804 (A) 8th " 725 (D) 9th " 720 (B) 10th " 643 (A) 11th " 580 (D) 12th " 558 (C)

results in distribution of seats,—five, one, one, five. Under the d'Hondt method, if a ticket has fewer candidates than seats to which it is entitled, the seats in question are given to the lists having the next highest numbers. If all the seats but one have been assigned and there is a tie as between the remaining high numbers, the decision is made by lot.

The distribution of seats is also affected by *Listenverbindung* or combination of lists, a practice which is authorized by law in nine states.[1] The legal requirement necessary for a combination of lists is that nominators of the tickets concerned shall file a written declaration that they have agreed to combine their lists. This declaration affects only the counting of the ballots; as before, each voter continues to vote for his own party ticket. But when the ballots are counted, the combined lists are treated as a single list in determining the first

[1] Bavaria, Bremen, Brunswick, Hesse, Mecklenburg-Strelitz, Saxony, Schaumburg-Lippe, Thuringia, and Württemberg. In Berlin, *Listenverbindung* may be used only for the city-wide tickets and not for the district nominating lists for the central council. However, for the Berlin borough councilmen (*Bezirksverordneten*), the combination of lists is permissible. For a general discussion of *Listenverbindung*, see Hoag and Hallett, *op. cit.*, pp. 424–426.

assignment of seats. The seats won by a given combination are then subdivided among the lists within it in proportion to their votes. The advantages of *Listenverbindung* are twofold. In the first place, the parties concerned may thereby win a larger number of seats than would happen if each ticket stood alone. Four or five small groups singly might each fail to secure a seat, but, when combined, there are likely to be two or three seats to be divided among the members of the combination. In the second place, since one party seldom attains a clear majority of the council members, and since blocs or coalitions must usually be formed in any case after the election, the practice of *Listenverbindung* may assist the formation of such blocs. Thus, both in the elections and in the actual work of the council, a "Bürger" bloc composed of the Middle and Right parties may oppose the Socialists and Communists.

Having spoken of the law of proportional representation in German cities, one may now inquire as to the practice of the same. The effects of the *Verhältniswahl* may be examined from three points of view,—that of the voter, the political party, and the actual conduct of municipal government.[2]

[2] The following paragraphs are based largely

From the standpoint of the voter, the bound list system used in most German cities has the great advantage of simplicity. The elector's task is limited to placing a cross or mark in the party circle. Consequently, the number of invalid ballots is small, usually under one per cent except when city and state or federal elections are held on the same day but under different rules. At such times, the proportion of spoiled ballots may reach almost three per cent.

As to whether proportional representation increases the voter's interest in the suffrage and thereby lessens non-voting, the answer is less clear. According to the theory of the *Verhält-niswahl*, every valid ballot will count unless cast for a group too small to achieve the quota. It is, therefore, to the advantage of each party to make a vigorous effort to "get out the vote." But such campaigns do not always produce the desired results, for the voting record in German municipal elections varies from 44 per cent (Mannheim, Baden, 1926) to 92.5 per cent (Schmölln, Thuringia, 1925).[1] True, the general

upon interviews with public and party officials and persons in private life, and upon the personal observations of the writer. At the present time, there is much dissatisfaction with proportional representation in Germany, either with the principle of the system or with the methods by which it is carried out. For a brief but trenchant criticism, see Otto Koellreutter, *Die politischen Parteien im modernen Staate* (Breslau, 1926), pp. 67–71.

[1] The writer selected at random twenty-four municipal elections and found that the average vote was 71 per cent, the two cities named above being the minimum and maximum. The elections chosen were from six different years between 1919 and 1928 and involved cities in four states whose populations varied from a few thousand to more than six hundred thousand. Some large cities had good voting records and some did not; the same was true of the small municipalities. Where federal and city elections were held together, the municipal vote tended to be somewhat larger than was the case otherwise.

average is better than that of American cities but, nevertheless, Germany has its problem of non-voting and there are numerous complaints of *Wahlmüdigkeit*, especially in the less important county and provincial elections where the vote sometimes falls to 25 per cent. And this happens with, or in spite of, proportional representation. What is the explanation?[2] It is claimed that there are too many elections,[3] that the novelty of voting is wearing off and that the bitter experiences of the postwar years have left many people apathetic or disgusted with things political, and, finally, that there are large numbers of voters who object to the bound list system.

This last point merits further examination. It is argued that, in local elections, the voter cares more for the personality of the candidate than for the party or political program involved.[4] Yet his choice must be registered for or against the party as a whole, and there is no one candidate whom he may especially support as his own personal and local representative. The tickets are nominated from the city as a whole by a party process over which the average municipal voter has little or no control. Except for the *Spitzkandidaten*, even the names of the party nominees are not known to him; but on election day, he must support the party slate in its entirety. Such is the case against the bound list system. On the other hand, the free list plan with its greater complexity, its increased opportunity for spoiled ballots, and its encouragement of party "*Zersplitterung*," has its practical difficul-

[2] On this point, see Karl Menne, "Bekämpfung der Wahlmüdigkeit," *Zeitschrift für Kommunalwirtschaft*, xvi (Feb. 10, 1926), pp. 136–137.

[3] Judged by American standards, German elections are not numerous.

[4] *Kommunale Umschau*, (Feb. 5, 1925), pp. 8–10; and Menne, *loc. cir.*

ties. In spite of these objections, however, the writer believes that the free list type of proportional representation should be used in the smaller German municipalities (those with under fifty thousand inhabitants) as is now the case in Württemberg. For the larger cities, bound lists should continue to be employed, but some concession should be made to the need for local and personal representation. This could take the form of the district system now used in Berlin, or single-member constituencies might be introduced with provision for the transfer of surplus votes to city-wide tickets.[1]

From the standpoint of the parties and the politicians, proportional representation appears in a more favorable light. The bound list system is naturally preferred to the free, since it gives the party machine greater control over the electoral process. The chief complaint which the great parties have against the present form of the *Verhältniswahl* is that the nominating process is made too easy. As a result, numerous small groups and "*Splitter-*

parteien" enter the election, groups which are too weak to achieve any great measure of success themselves and which only weaken the major parties. Thus in Hagen, Westphalia, there were fourteen tickets filed for the 1924 election of the municipal council. How to avoid this multiplication of *Splitterparteien* is indeed a question. So far as *Landtag* elections are concerned, attempts have been made in several states to increase the number of signatures required for the nominating petitions of new parties, and to make the validity of the nomination contingent upon the depositing of a certain sum of money which is to be forfeited to the state if the party fails to win at least one seat. But laws of this sort have recently been declared unconstitutional by the federal supreme court, and just what steps will now be taken is not yet clear.[2] Thus far, no similar legislation has been enacted to penalize new parties and groups in municipal elections, and, in the opinion of the writer, such action is not desirable. National party politics already play a large enough part in city affairs and, therefore, the spontaneous formation of purely local groups for local problems, a thing that is possible under the present laws, should not be hindered. Moreover, as long as the bound list system prevails, dissatisfied municipal voters should not be denied the right to put forward their own ticket of candidates.

---

[1] The single-member constituency plan would, of course, have to be "according to the principles of proportional representation." To secure this result, it would first be necessary to ascertain the total number of votes cast in the entire city and then find the quota necessary to elect one councilman. To be elected from a district, a candidate must have received a plurality of the votes in that district which should at least equal the quota as determined above. All surplus and unused votes would then go to the city-wide tickets as is now done in Berlin.

These suggested reforms will, of course, not accomplish everything. For example, it is claimed that the free list plan would *ipso facto* lessen nonvoting. (See Menne, *loc. cit.*) In reply, it may be pointed out that most Württemberg cities now operate under the free list system and still there is complaint of *Wahlmüdigkeit*. At the 1925 municipal election in Tübingen, the university ward polled only a 41 per cent vote. (See *Kommunale Umschau*, i, pp. 422–423.)

[2] Among the laws held unconstitutional was that of Hamburg described in the writer's article, "The Hamburg Election," NATIONAL MUNICIPAL REVIEW, January, 1928, pp. 16–17. The decision of the federal *Staatsgerichtshof* was handed down on December 17, 1927, in consequence of which a new election of the Hamburg legislature was held on February 19. In the previous article, it was stated that forfeit fees were required only in Hamburg and Saxony. To these states should have been added Hesse, Mecklenburg-Schwerin and Mecklenburg-Strelitz.

Apart from the ease with which nominations are made, the party leaders are in general satisfied with the existing form of proportional representation. They emphatically deny that too little attention is paid to the personality and qualification of the candidates nominated and to the principle of local representation. "A great party cannot afford to put up poor nominees. Besides, with *gebundenen Listen*, it is possible to make up a 'balanced ticket' so that all elements in the party and also local districts will be adequately represented. The free list plan is apt to destroy all such carefully arranged balance." There is force in these arguments, but they do not tell the whole story. Candidates A, B, and C at the top of the party ticket are doubtless able men, but it is by no means certain that Candidate X, whose name stands tenth on the list, is qualified to be a councilman. And when it comes to the party substitutes or *Erstazmänner* who automatically succeed to office when vacancies occur, the lack of qualifications is even more apparent.

The effect of proportional representation upon the actual conduct of municipal government is more difficult to appraise. That city government is far more politicized now than before the Revolution is generally admitted, but it can hardly be said that the *Verhältniswahl* is a major cause of this situation. Fundamentally, the change resulted from the introduction of universal suffrage in place of the old restricted electorate with its three-class system of voting, etc. Formerly, municipal government was a thing of the privileged classes; now the full force of democratic ideas released by the Revolution beats upon it. Proportional representation does, of course, emphasize the party point of view, but it is doubtful if it makes the cities more political than they would be under a plurality or majority system of election. On the contrary, by lessening the chances of having the municipality wholly controlled by one party, by Communists or Socialists or Catholics or Nationalists, each with its own class or confessional attitude, proportional representation probably works in the direction of moderating party excesses. But it does mean that the work of the council must be carried on by more or less unstable blocs and coalitions and that the atmosphere of the council proceedings is distinctly political, sometimes even positively belligerent. This, however, has not seriously impaired the efficiency of the administration for two reasons: first, because a great deal of the work of the council is done through committees or by the *Magistrat* where such an organ exists; and second, the permanent executive officials, the real power under the old régime, still hold their place in the new.

One can, therefore, say that German cities since the Revolution have not succumbed to the "spoils system," although the writer has found a number of cases which have a distinctly "spoils" flavor. When the council elects the paid and unpaid executive officers, due regard is paid to the party affiliations of the candidates and to the distribution of the positions among the dominant parties in the council.[1] Where men are equally well qualified from a technical point of view, party membership will be the deciding factor. As between a good candidate who is "right" politically and a superior candidate without such a recommendation, it is not unusual for the former to be

[1] It makes little difference in practice whether or not proportional representation is formally prescribed by law for the selection of the paid and unpaid executive officers. The spirit of proportionality is there in any case and may be carried out through gentlemen's agreements between the parties making up the majority coalition.

preferred. But this practice does not lead to the "spoils system," because it is not good politics for a party to suggest incompetents for the important municipal administrative positions, and because, when once appointed, the holders of such positions enjoy security of tenure and are protected against arbitrary removal. True, the *Bürgermeister* or *Baurat* or *Schulrat* may find himself made the subject of a *Misstrauensvotum* (vote of want of confidence) by the council, but this vote is without legal effect and can do no more than make the official more sensitive to conciliar opinion and less insistent upon carrying out his own preconceived ideas of what is good for the city. Thus municipal bureaucracy persists, but it can be and is tempered by political winds.

In conclusion, one may speak briefly of the present outlook for proportional representation in German cities. Notwithstanding the various defects and shortcomings already mentioned, there is little doubt that the *Verhältniswahl* is and will rightly continue to be a permanent feature of municipal government. There are few indications that the present multi-party system in Germany is passing away,[1] and, so long as it remains, some form of proportional representation is very desirable. The practical question, then, is one of improving the existing system or of finding another to take its place.

[1] See Ernst Jäckh, *The New Germany* (London, 1927), pp. 46–49.

THE RELATION OF BUILDING HEIGHT TO STREET TRAFFIC

BY HERBERT D. SIMPSON, PH.D.

Associate Professor of Economics at Northwestern University

A mathematical study that anyone can understand. It is a new viewpoint and will arouse discussion. The editor invites comment.   ::

"Thus far," said President Coolidge, in a public address a year or two ago, "the victories have all been on the side of the skyscrapers, the elevators and the ever-increasing congestion of population,"[1] implying that by common consent the skyscrapers and elevators are the important factors in this ever-increasing congestion. And the pictorial advertisement of a large electric company in a current periodical carries the headline: "Only electric cars will clear the streets as fast as skyscrapers fill them. Transportation in large cities . . . is a race between the street car and the skyscraper."

[1] NATIONAL MUNICIPAL REVIEW, July, 1926, p. 398.

A MATHEMATICAL APPROACH

Without attempting for the moment to appraise the element of truth in the advertisement, it may be pointed out that the much-harassed street car is also racing against the birth rate, against immigration, the drift to the city, and many other pursuers more aggressive even than the skyscrapers. And the President, likewise, in his statement quoted above, could with equal accuracy have exactly reversed the order of the terms and spoken of increasing congestion, elevators and skyscrapers; for this has been the order, historically and causally, at least as frequently as the other. The possibility of stating the same thing in exactly opposite sequence suggests the difficulty of looking impartially at both sides of the question of building height.

And the difficulty appears to increase when we attempt to consider the effect of building height on one particular form of congestion, that of street traffic, particularly pedestrian traffic; for here there have been two opposite schools of opinion. The one group holds that if twice the amount of building and of business is concentrated on a given area, we must expect to have approximately twice as many people on the streets and sidewalks, in the process of going to and from these buildings. The other group holds that since high buildings involve the location of large numbers of offices and businesses on interior halls and corridors, the patrons of these establishments do much of their traveling on the interior of the building instead of on the sidewalks; and that, therefore, tall buildings must have the effect of reducing sidewalk pedestrian traffic. Between these two extremes are varying shades of opinion, based in the main upon varying attitudes toward the question of skyscraper buildings in general rather than upon any demonstrated facts in connection therewith.

Now, if it were a question of politics or philosophy, one would expect such conflicting opinions and would be prepared to accord perhaps equal rationality to all of them. But in a problem involving concrete and measurable elements of space and number, such diversity of opinion is strange, and the apparent willingness to allow the discussion to continue merely on a basis of opinion stranger still. The present paper, therefore, while not undertaking to solve the problem by any means, will attempt to apply some concrete mathematics at one particular point, where a little plane geometry should go further than any amount of opinion.

THE PROBLEM

But throughout the following analysis it will be necessary to keep in mind, in the first place, that we are discussing the effect of one factor only, namely, differences in building height, independent of the effects of changes in population, transportation facilities, direction of growth, and all of the numerous other factors that influence street traffic. All of these factors will be left out of consideration, not because they are unimportant—for if the reasoning in this study is sound, they are by far the most important factors— but because we shall be making sufficient progress for the time being if we can demonstrate clearly the results due solely to differences in height.

In the second place, in discussing changes in the amount of traffic, we are speaking of *total traffic*, such as would be reflected in traffic counts for twenty-four hours or other period. And by average amount of traffic under the different conditions discussed, we mean the result that would be obtained for a given street or section by making traffic counts at various points, for twenty-four hours or other period, and taking the average of the counts reported. The result would indicate the average number of pedestrians or vehicles traversing the streets and sidewalks of the district in a given time.

Changes in this average amount of traffic, it is true, will not necessarily throw much light on problems of maximum density of traffic at particular times and places, such as at transportation terminals, at the exits of office buildings at five o'clock in the afternoon, or at the theater entrances and exits in the evening,—except as these maximums must necessarily have some relation to the total number of people frequenting a given area. Indeed, the peak load that pours out of an office building at five o'clock in the afternoon must have a very close relation to the average amount of business transacted in the building throughout the day—and this amount of business, in turn, must be pretty closely related to the average number of people patronizing the occupants of the building throughout the day or month or entire year. And so sufficiently complete traffic data in representative cities and districts would probably show a fairly definite relationship between the averages and the peaks of traffic. But be this as it may, our analysis here will be concerned solely with *total* traffic and *average* traffic for blocks, streets, and areas.

In the third place, we must necessarily speak only of comparative amounts of traffic under one condition or another, since there can be no absolute figures under any condition. There is no specific amount of traffic on streets with five-story buildings; so that in calculating the effect of increases in height to ten or twenty stories, we can only say that the traffic would be increased so much, in comparison with whatever it might have been with a five-story height.
· If these limitations on our treatment are somewhat more rigid than are commonly imposed on discussions of the subject, we trust that some compensation will be found in the greater precision of results which we shall hope to attain.

MAIN STREET

We shall first discuss the problem in relation to pedestrian traffic; and in order to get at the factors involved, let us start with a simple situation, namely, Main Street itself. If we had a "pure type" of Main Street city, where all the business was located on one street and all the traffic to and from this business traversed this one street, we trust that no one would be guilty of supposing that the building height could have any *effect* on pedestrian traffic, one way or the other. And this for the following simple reason:

Suppose Main Street is confronting the problem of a daily entrance and exit of ten shoppers (which may represent ten hundred or ten thousand or any other number), who will patronize ten different establishments; that the problem is whether to have these ten establishments built in the form of five two-story buildings, with one establishment on each floor, or to limit the height and have the establishments spread out over ten one-story buildings. If the former alternative is adopted, namely, a two-story height, the pedestrian traffic will be as indicated in Figure 1. We are distributing the patronage equally among the ten establishments, are pouring the shopping public in at one end of the street in the morning and out at the same end in the evening, and are assuming that each person goes to one establishment and back each day. One may make any variations he wishes in number and distribution of patrons, in points of entry and exit, may pour the shoppers in from both ends of the street and a crossroad, if he wishes, and *provided only that he makes the corresponding assumptions in both of the situations below*, he will arrive at the same result, graphically shown in Figure 1.

A total pedestrian traffic of fifty, divided by five frontages equals an average of ten pedestrians passing any one frontage, or other unit, per day.

But if it be decided that an average pedestrian traffic of ten is too great,

FIGURE 1

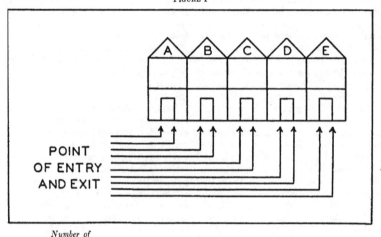

Number of pedestrians	Destination	Traffic count (That is, the number of times one pedestrian passes one building in going to and returning from his destination.)
2	A	2 *
2	B	6
2	C	10
2	D	14
2	E	18
	Total	50

* It should be noted, for purposes of arithmetic accuracy, that the pedestrian who goes to building A only passes *half* of one frontage in going and half again in returning, or *one* frontage on his round trip; the pedestrian who goes to building B, likewise counts 1½ frontages each way, or 3 frontages on his round trip; and so on.

and the height is limited to one story, with the result that the same amount of building and business is spread out over ten frontages in the form of one-story buildings, the traffic will be as in Figure 2.

A total pedestrian traffic of 100 divided by ten frontages equals an average of ten pedestrians passing any one frontage, or any one point, per day. In short, the traffic on a two-story street has not been reduced one iota, or one pedestrian, by reducing the buildings to one story.

And it would be a one-story type of reasoning which could arrive at any other result. For if we took a ten-story building and laid it on its side along the street, the effect on pedestrian traffic would be that persons bound for the various floors, instead of taking the elevator, would walk along the sidewalk from the first to the tenth or other floor and back again,

FIGURE 2

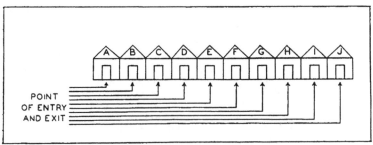

Number of Pedestrians	Destination	Traffic Count (Round Trips)
1	A	1
1	B	3
1	C	5
1	D	7
1	E	9
1	F	11
1	G	13
1	H	15
1	I ˙	17
1	J	19
		Total 100

passing all the intermediate floors in going and coming and adding one to the traffic count each time a pedestrian passed one floor. So that, while the sidewalk over which the traffic is distributed is ten times as long as before, the number of buildings each pedestrian must pass, or the distance he must travel, in getting to and from any point is also ten times as great as before, leaving the number of pedestrians *passing any one point in a given time* exactly the same as before. In this Main Street situation, those who hold that in skyscraper buildings vertical elevator traffic merely replaces horizontal sidewalk traffic are essentially right.

CITY BLOCKS

But this simple solution breaks down in the ordinary situation where

we are dealing with square or rectangular blocks instead of a single linear dimension. For example: Suppose we have a square block with ten one-story buildings on each side, or 40 buildings in all, and that the town or district is confronting a quadrupled amount of business and building accommodations. The alternatives are to build four times as high on the same area (that is, 40 four-story buildings) or to limit the height to one story and spread the town over four times the area (that is, 160 one-story buildings), or any intermediate combinations of height and area. But for purposes of illustration, we shall take the two extreme alternatives.

If height limitation is resorted to, and the 160 establishments are spread in the form of 160 one-story buildings over four square blocks, with ten buildings per block front, and if we suppose the 160 patrons distributed evenly among these establishments and making a daily trip to and from each one, the traffic will be as illustrated in Figure 3. In the illustration, however, instead of counting the pedestrian trips to each separate building and back, we shall count by blocks; assuming, by the law of averages, that all pedestrians going to points in any one block front will average a trip to *the middle* of the block and back. The figures on the graph indicate the average length of trip (measured in number of buildings or frontages passed) of pedestrians going to points in each block. We are here, as in the previous illustration, pouring the traffic all in at one point; but this is only to avoid complicating the graph and the simple calculation which it illustrates. If the reader enjoys "figuring," he may pour the traffic in from all points of the compass and assume any number and distribution of patrons, and provided only that he makes the corresponding assumptions in both situations, he will get the same results.

A total traffic of 6,400 divided by 160 buildings equals forty pedestrians passing any one building, or other point, per day.

If the other alternative were adopted and, instead of one-story buildings spread over four blocks, the *same amount* of building accommodation and of business were concentrated in the form of four-story buildings occupying one square block, would the density of pedestrian traffic remain unchanged or would it be quadrupled? Assuming the same number, distribution and daily habits of patrons as above, that is, the same conditions as above except that we have buildings four times as high, occupying one-fourth as much area, the traffic would be as in Figure 4.

A total traffic of 3,200 divided by forty buildings equals eighty pedestrians passing any one building, or other point, per day. In short, the traffic has neither remained unchanged nor been quadrupled; but has been multiplied by *two* only. And, if the reader will note that two is the square root of four, and will recall the proposition of plane geometry that similar surfaces vary as the squares of their like dimensions, he will realize that no other result could be expected. .

Indeed, for the mathematical reader, it is needless to go further with this article. And we may lay this proposition of geometry on the table without fear of its being trumped by any amount of expert opinion or any number of traffic counts. If, however, the application of the theorem is not clear, a simple mathematical analysis will make it so; such an analysis will involve four separate steps.

MATHEMATICAL ANALYSIS

The first is ·the assumption that, *with a given amount of building accommodation, any difference in height will be reflected in an opposite, and approximately equal, difference in area occupied.* This means merely that a given quantity of building accommodations in the form of twenty-story buildings will occupy approximately half the area that they would if spread out in the form of ten-story buildings— an assumption that would fit the actual situation probably ninety times out of a hundred, since the purpose of erecting tall buildings is ordinarily to get a larger amount of building on a smaller area. With the aid of this commonplace relationship, we may convert *height* variations into *area* variations and speak thereafter in terms of the relations of areas.

The second step is the application, to these area relations, of the theorem

FIGURE 3

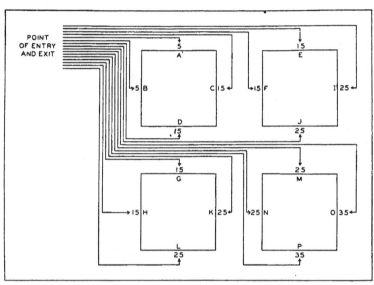

Number of pedestrians	Going to block indicated	Average length of trip	Total traffic created (That is, the number of times one pedestrian passes one frontage.)
10	A	5	50
10	B	5	50
10	C	15	150
10	D	15	150
10	E	15	150
10	F	15	150
10	G	15	150
10	H	15	150
10	I	25	250
10	J	25	250
10	K	25	250
10	L	25	250
10	M	25	250
10	N	25	250
10	O	35	350
10	P	35	350
160			3,200
		Multiply by 2 for round trip	2
		Total	6,400

FIGURE 4

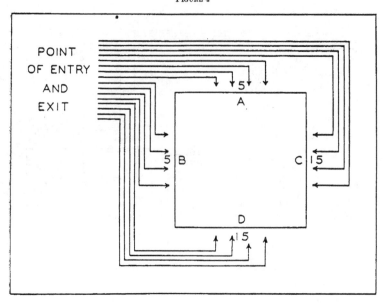

Number of pedestrians	Going to block indicated	Average length of trip	Total traffic created
40	A	5	200
40	B	5	200
40	C	15	600
40	D	15	600
160			1,600
	Multiply by 2 for round trip		2
			3,200

that areas of similar shape will vary as the squares of their like dimensions; or since it is the *dimensions* that we shall be primarily concerned with, we may turn the theorem around and say that *like dimensions of similar areas will vary as the square roots of the areas.*

The third step consists in noting the commonplace fact that the bounding streets and sidewalks of square blocks, or any blocks of uniform shape are the "like dimensions of similar areas."

The total length of sidewalk will not conform to the theorem, because, with the interior, intersecting streets of any area larger than a single block, each segment of the area has its own equal complement of streets and sidewalks. One square block has four linear blocks of sidewalk; two square blocks have eight linear blocks of sidewalk, etc. But the point is, that a pedestrian does not walk around all the blocks in a given area before starting for his destination; if he did, our analysis would break down; and to the extent that any pedestrian circumnavigates a superfluous number of blocks in steering a homeward course, the mathematical precision of our results will be impaired. But ordinarily the pedestrian takes the shortest route available under a given configuration of streets, and therein traces in each trip one or more dimensions of some definite area.

The length of any one trip, as compared with a corresponding trip to a corresponding point on a larger or smaller area, will vary as the square roots of these areas. So that the pedestrian is here confronted with the dis-covery that a trip over a territory twice as large as another is not twice as long as a corresponding trip over the smaller area, but only as much longer as the square root of the one area is greater than the square root of the other. We have found it so difficult to convince pedestrians of the soundness of this diagnosis, that we may be pardoned for resorting to illustrations.

In Figure 5, from A to B (the diagonally opposite points of a square block) is two linear blocks; but from A to C (the diagonally opposite points of an area of four square blocks) is not four times as far but only *twice* as

FIGURE 5

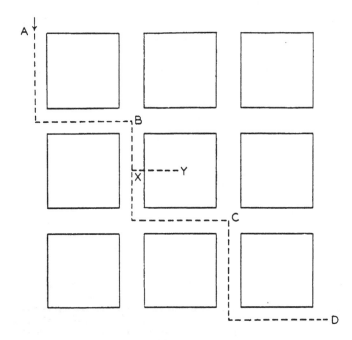

far, namely, four linear blocks. AB is to $\overline{AC}$, as $\sqrt{\text{one square block}}$ is to $\sqrt{\text{four square blocks}}$. Likewise, from A to D (the diagonally opposite points of an area of nine square blocks) is not nine times as far as AB, but only *three* times as far, namely, six linear blocks,—and three is the square root of nine.

Or from A to B, looking at B as the central point of a four-block area, is two linear blocks. Y marks the central point of the nine-block area. On this particular configuration Y cannot be reached by street; but if the pedestrian, after walking around from A to B and down to X, will climb the fence there and cross the lawn to Y, he will have walked exactly three linear blocks. Now 2 is to 3, as $\sqrt{4}$ is to $\sqrt{9}$!

If one walks around a single square block, he walks four linear blocks. But he may walk around an area twice as large, namely, four square blocks, and he will have walked only twice as far, that is eight linear blocks. Or he may walk around an area nine times as large, namely, nine square blocks, and he will have walked only three times as far, namely, twelve linear blocks, because the square root of nine is three.

Or, to get away from the square configuration, let us suppose that a boulevard is cut diagonally through our nine-block area above, and that we are dealing with the triangular area ADC, as in Figure 6.

From A to B (the hypothenuse of a triangular area containing one-half of one square block) is 1.4 linear blocks; but from A to C (the hypothenuse of a triangular area containing $4\frac{1}{2}$ square blocks) is 4.2 linear blocks, or only *three* times the distance from A to B. The areas are as $\frac{1}{2}$ to $4\frac{1}{2}$, and their square roots .7+ to 2.1+, or as 1 to 3. And so, go where he will, the pedestrian

cannot escape this relationship, as long as he travels along the *like dimensions* of *similar areas*.

Having (a) converted height relations into area relations, (b) applied the geometric theorem that like dimensions of similar areas vary as the square roots of the areas, and (c) noted that pedestrian trips must necessarily constitute like dimensions of similar areas, we have but one more step to take, namely, (d) to convert these relationships into their net effects on traffic. With the aid of the first three steps, the fourth becomes easy.

If the building height is multiplied by four and the area reduced to one-fourth of what it would otherwise be, with the number of patrons remaining unchanged, obviously there must be four times as many people going to and from the given area as before. And if, of this increased number of pedestrians, each one travels just as far and is on the streets just as long as before, it is evident that the density of pedestrian traffic on this smaller area must be four times what it was before, or what it would be with the lower building height. But to just whatever extent the average pedestrian trip is shortened, and each pedestrian spends less time on the street, to this extent the density of traffic will fall short of being quadrupled. Now it is just *this extent* which the analysis above enables us to compute. The average length of trip is reduced by a factor equal to the square root of the factor of increased height.

But if the amount of traffic is multiplied by four (on account of the decreased area), and divided by the square root of four (on account of the shortened average trip), the net result is to increase the amount of traffic by the other factor of four, which necessarily is also the square root of four. This amounts merely to saying that if

FIGURE 6

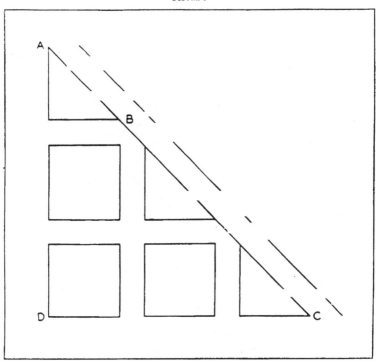

a thing is multiplied by ten and then divided by five, the net result is to multiply it by two, since the factors of ten are five and two. So if a thing is multiplied by four, and then divided by the square root of four, the net result is to multiply it by the square root of four.

All this may be condensed into a simple formula, in which a will equal amount of traffic with a given building height, b equals the factor of increase in building height, and x equals the amount of traffic with the increased building height.

$$\text{Thus, } x = \frac{ab}{\sqrt{b}} = a\sqrt{b}.$$

The portion of this traffic *attributable* to the increased height will then, of course, be x minus the original traffic, or $a\sqrt{b} - a$.

Or we may say the same thing in a different form by comparing directly the square roots of two different heights. If c and d represent two different building heights, the traffic *attributable to the height factor* will vary as $\sqrt{c} : \sqrt{d}$. As between a given amount of building accommodation and business in the form of one-story buildings or four-story buildings, the traffic will vary as $\sqrt{1} : \sqrt{4}$, that is, will be twice as great in the second case. As between one-story and nine-story building heights, traffic will vary as $\sqrt{1} : \sqrt{9}$, that is, will be three times as great in the second case. As between five-story and fifty-story building heights, traffic will vary as $\sqrt{5} : \sqrt{50}$, that is, will be 3.1 times as great in the second case.

THE COMMON SENSE EXPLANATION

Having illustrated the results of differences in building height by the hypothetical pedestrian counts at the beginning of this paper, and then analyzed the mathematical process that makes these results inevitable, perhaps it will be helpful now to drop both hypothesis and mathematics and get at the common sense of the whole thing. For after all that is all it is.

In the Main Street situation, we found that increases in building height had *no* effect on amount of traffic; while in the case of square, rectangular, or other regularly-shaped blocks, an increase in height was reflected in an increase in amount of traffic equal to the square root of the factor of increased height. Why should the lay-out of streets have anything to do with the relation of building height to traffic? For the reason that, with a given number of pedestrians to be provided for, the density of traffic they create will depend upon two things: the *area* over which they are spread and the *average length* of the trips they make.[1]

Now, if ten one-story buildings are pyramided into one ten-story building, the change in area occupied and area of sidewalks "abutted" will be the same, regardless of the configuration

of streets in the neighborhoods. But the other determinant, average length of trip, will by no means be the same, as has been demonstrated above—and therein lies the difference. The pyramiding of buildings on Main Street offsets the reduced area by an *equal* reduction in length of pedestrian trips. The pyramiding of buildings in an area of rectangular blocks offsets the reduced area by *less than an equal* reduction in length of trips, and therefore leaves a net increase in the amount of traffic per unit of sidewalk.

And the reason for this is likewise simple. The elongation of buildings along a single street imposes the maximum traveling distances on pedestrians and therefore affords the widest range for reduction of distance through a more economical arrangement. The spreading of buildings over a square area imposes the minimum increase in traveling distances, since a square represents the maximum area per perimeter that is attainable by any practicable configuration,[2] and therefore affords the minimum range for any further economizing of distances.

QUALIFICATION FOR THROUGH-TRAFFIC

We have spoken of the square root of any factor of increased building height as representing the maximum increase in amount of traffic attributable to the increased height. Thus far, however, we have been speaking of traffic as if it consisted entirely of the traffic that is concerned with getting to and from points located in the area under consideration. But the through traffic, that portion of the traffic representing pedestrians and vehicles merely passing through the district from one section of the city to another,

---

[1] We are, of course, assuming the same pedestrian "velocity" in both cases, which is a safe assumption wherever adequate street and sidewalk width is provided. With inadequate width the slowing up of the rate of movement will aggravate the difficulties in either case.

[2] A circle would embrace a larger area within a given perimeter, were it not for the necessity of having intersecting, spoke-wise streets.

from transportation terminals to destinations beyond the district in question and back again, and, in the case of vehicular traffic, the truck, bus, and tourist traffic merely passing through the city or district,—this portion of the total traffic can scarcely be affected, except in the most indirect ways, by differences in the height of buildings along the route of travel. Occasionally a tall sky line may attract through traffic, but at least as often will detour it, so that for practical purposes we may eliminate this portion of the traffic from the problem.

This means that to the extent that total traffic is made up of through traffic, the maximum effect of increased building height must fall short even of the square root of the factor of increased height. If we make this correction in the formula above (p. 391), letting e represent the amount of through traffic, the formula becomes: $X = (a-e) \sqrt{b} + e$.

If a represents a traffic count of 5,000, of which 1,000 is through-traffic, and the increase in height under consideration is an increase from 10 stories to 20 stories, the result would be:

$$X = (5,000-1,000) \times \sqrt{2} + 1,000$$
$$= 4,000 \times 1.4 + 1,000$$
$$= 5,600 + 1,000$$
$$= 6,600.$$

That is, the difference in traffic attributable to difference in building height is 1,600.

VEHICULAR TRAFFIC

Throughout the discussion above, we have been speaking chiefly in terms of pedestrian traffic, in order to avoid complicating the analysis. But if an imaginary line be drawn down the center of each street, so as to compute separately the traffic moving each way and to allocate more closely the traffic assignable to each side of the street,

then everything that has been said of sidewalks and pedestrian traffic will be equally applicable to streets and vehicular traffic—with two practical qualifications. The first is that almost invariably a larger portion of vehicular than of pedestrian traffic will consist of through traffic. The second is that as traffic difficulties increase, vehicular transportation tends to be abandoned and walking substituted for short distances or for portions of a longer trip; that is, a certain amount of vehicular traffic is converted into pedestrian traffic. The tendency of the second factor is to *add* something to the total effect of building height on pedestrian traffic. The tendency of both factors is to *subtract* something from the total effect of building height on vehicular traffic.

IMPLICATIONS

If we have wearied the reader with the tediousness of the analysis above, it is because the implications that follow from this analysis are too important to be allowed to rest on anything short of demonstration.

If the analysis is sound, it means that the *maximum* possible effect of increased building height [1] on pedestrian and vehicular traffic is *something less* than the square root of the factor of increased height; that the *minimum* effect may be zero; and that under ordinary conditions, the effects will range somewhere between this maximum and minimum.

[1] We are obliged, in order to avoid the repetition of a lengthy formula each time, to speak of "increased building height" rather than of "differences in building height"; but the reader will keep in mind that we are speaking all the time not of the effects of historical increases in building height, with all the concomitants of changes in population, business, transportation facilities, etc., but of the provision of a given amount of building accommodation in the form of buildings of one height or another.

If the alternatives confronting a particular city are to have a small area occupied by skyscrapers, on the one hand, or to have the business section spread out in narrow, elongated form along a lake shore, river front, or other topographical determinant, on the other hand, the conditions are tending toward the Main Street situation in our illustration; and the effect of difference in building height will tend toward the minimum. But if, in another city, the alternatives are to have a smaller area occupied by skyscraper buildings, on the one hand, or to have the business section spread over a larger but roughly similar area, on the other hand, the conditions are tending toward the similar areas of our illustration; and the effect of differences in building height will tend toward the maximum.

In more concrete form, it means this: suppose that in a city or district under consideration, a fifty-foot street width between curbs, with ten-foot sidewalks on both sides, is taking care of the pedestrian and vehicular traffic at the present time, with approximately a ten-story building height. It may be felt that to permit an increase in height to twenty or thirty stories would put an impossible burden upon the present streets and sidewalks or necessitate an impracticable amount of street widening. Yet the adoption of a policy of limitation to the present height (on these grounds alone) would bring about an extremely uneconomical utilization of area, for this reason. If

20 per cent of the traffic is assumed to be through traffic, an increase of building height from ten stories to thirty stories should, at the maximum, increase the traffic by 58 per cent, or say 60 per cent. Sixty per cent of the entire width of street and sidewalk is forty-two feet, or twenty-one feet on each side of the street. Widening the street forty-two feet (or setting the building line for new buildings back twenty-one feet on each side of the street) will provide the necessary sidewalk and highway space for twenty additional stories on both sides of the street. Every addition of nine inches to the street, between curbs, and 3.6 inches to the sidewalk on one side of the street will provide for an additional story on that side of the street.

There are many grounds for the limitation of building height other than the relation of building height to traffic, —including considerations of light and air, aesthetic results, transportation facilities, and forecasts of the amount and direction of a city's growth. Many of these things are matters of taste, judgment, or opinion, and some of them matters of one's individual philosophy with regard to the objectives of urban life. But in so far as limitations of height are concerned with the relations of height to traffic, many mistakes in the utilization of urban areas will be avoided if some such factual basis as the one we have analyzed can be substituted for the guesswork and opinions that have too frequently shaped these policies in the past.

RECENT BOOKS REVIEWED

FEDERAL AID. A Study of the American Subsidy System. By Austin F. Macdonald. New York: Thomas Y. Crowell Co., 1928. Pp. xii, 285.

The hysteria about state and local expenditures, taxes, and debt which seemed to have such a serious effect upon the thinking of many persons in high national offices in the post-war period is probably subsiding. The bogy of "state and local extravagance" which brought on this state of mind has been found to contain very little substance. Like a gas-filled balloon, it needed only to be punctured by pins of fact and logic to be deflated. Readers of the REVIEW are already familiar with some of the studies which have made some of the fatal punctures. To this list must now be added the present volume by Dr. Macdonald.

The official theory ran about as follows: (1) The national government under a budget system is reducing debts and taxes and is becoming a model of economy and efficiency. (2) But state and local debts, taxes, and expenditures are rising. (3) Therefore the latter are wasteful and extravagant and are seriously hampering business. (4) Therefore, also, the national government should use every possible means to force retrenchment upon state and local units. Harangues and exhortations not having produced the desired result, two specific national measures have been proposed.

First came the drive for abolishing the tax-exemption privilege enjoyed since the beginning of our national history by state and municipal bonds. This proposed change was explained and supported as a means of improving the administration of the national income tax by reducing tax-dodging, and as a means of discouraging state and local borrowing. A constitutional amendment to end tax-exemption was proposed but failed to pass Congress. Since that time it has been found that the "facts" used by its proponents had been greatly exaggerated. Now the proposal lies interred in the graveyard of amendments not passed.

Next came the attack upon federal aid to the states. In a presidential utterance of a few years ago it was said that "The reduction of federal aid payments to the states is more important than tax reduction or United States adherence to the World Court." The argument that federal aid laws are bad because they invade the sovereignty of the states has been exposed in all its speciousness by the Supreme Court. Somewhat more substantial arguments are to be found, of course, as any reader of the book under review will find. Be this as it may, however, Congress has done precious little in recent years to decrease and a little something to increase federal aid payments to the states. Maternity and infant hygiene work may be cut off, but agricultural research work and other activities will require increasing contributions.

Dr. Macdonald's work is a concise, straight-forward account of the system of federal aid as it exists today. Beginning with a brief statement of the general features of the system and a short chapter on its evolution, he proceeds to the discussion in separate chapters of federal aid for forest fire prevention, agricultural extension work, highways, the national guard, vocational education, vocational rehabilitation, and hygiene of maternity and infancy. The data used by the author include beside the laws, the reports of departments, and other published materials, a wealth of facts obtained by him during a journey as a research fellow of the Social Science Research Council, in the course of which he visited half the states and had over one thousand interviews with officials and other interested persons. It is these facts which give his work qualities of thoroughness, insight, and reality which are all too rare in discussions of public questions. The volume is, in fact, a good workmanlike job.

We are tempted to spend some time in discussing his excellent last chapter on the future of federal aid, in which he states a series of conclusions almost entirely favorable to the system. The case which he makes out as the result of his careful study is a devastating answer to the critics of the system. That the system could be improved he admits and points out, but despite its present faults in detail it is a system worthy of extension to new activities under careful safeguards. In general the system of federal aid "makes possible the establishment of a national minimum of efficiency and economy without the sacrifice of state autonomy."

WILLIAM ANDERSON
University of Minnesota.

THE ORGANIZATION AND ADMINISTRATION OF PLAYGROUNDS AND RECREATION. By Jay B. Nash. New York: A. A. Barnes & Co., 1927. Pp. 547.

The first four chapters of this book contain a brief survey of the history and present-day development of play activities plus a more detailed discussion of playground objectives. Play is related to character, leisure, democracy, liberty and life, happiness and education. The net result is to deprive the term recreation of any real meaning in and of itself. If Mr. Nash had cast overboard his theoretical background and written critically on the meaning of recreation from his own intimate and first-hand experience one might have expected an original, realistic and exact interpretation. Indeed such an interpretation is suggested but not amplified in other chapters.

The major portion of the book is devoted to organization, administration and activity programs for municipal playground systems. The author has given much thought to the details of organization and the workable relationships that should exist between the city, the public school system and private and commercial agencies. Excellent organization charts and concrete comparative material of current types of recreation organizations are provided. The treatment is neither doctrinaire nor lacking in perspective. The author knows full well that no ready-made plan for conducting recreation activities can be made to fit each and every city. This gives point to his suggestions for coördinating such activities through coöperation. There are equally suggestive and specific discussions relating to the kinds and care of equipment and supplies, office routine and publicity. These chapters are replete with usable information for persons interested in the actual operation of playground systems. Of like caliber are the special chapters on golf, municipal camps, swimming pools, community centers and industrial recreation.

In addition the author devotes considerable space to the nature of recreation activities and the conduct of games and sports. There is only a single short chapter on "Community Social Arts" covering drama, music, and folk and dramatic dancing. And next to nothing on hand crafts and quiet games. Throughout the book active games and sports of the "big muscle" type are emphasized. The author contends that the public schools are providing opportunities

for handcraft, music and dramatics that recreation departments "cannot hope to duplicate." Obviously then a municipal recreation department should stress active sports—swimming, tennis, golf, skating, ball games, etc. Here is an interesting, not altogether orthodox but, to the reviewer at least, a sound approach to the determination of a municipal recreation program. Surely such emphasis seems sensible enough but too often recreation departments spread their limited personnel and funds to include activities that have no relation to health whatsoever and very little to intelligent training for the use of leisure time.

Although it may be said that the author has covered too much ground with the result that the book is of uneven value, the book itself is packed with valuable ideas and information and the attack on recreation problems refreshingly realistic. It deserves a place on the desk of every playground administrator.

RANDOLPH O. HUUS
Western Reserve University.

✤

AMERICAN CITIZENSHIP AS DISTINGUISHED FROM ALIEN STATUS. By Frederick A. Cleveland, Ph.D., LL.D. New York: The Ronald Press Co., 1927. Pp. 397.

This work falls virtually into two parts although the author divides it into three. The first 218 pages treat principally such topics as how American citizenship is acquired, the legal advantages of citizenship, the legal disadvantages of alienage, the relation of domicile to citizenship, and so on. It is legalistic in character. In the remaining 200 pages, roughly, attempt is made to develop a theory of state answering to what are claimed to be American postulates, though this claim is open to serious challenge.

The technical portion of the volume is, for the most part, fairly describable as a rather well-arranged scrap book of material drawn from earlier textbooks and treatises—the names of Ogg and Beard, Woodburn and Moran, Garner, Borchard, Hart, Meili, Van Dyne, Bouvé constantly appear in the footnotes. Some of the works cited are—or were in their day—authoritative, and it may be conceded that proceeding in this way Dr. Cleveland has brought together in brief compass a good deal of information of one sort and another. At the same time, his reliance on secondary authorities has had the inevitable result that the work is frequently out of date, occasionally self-contradictory, and especially as to points of theoretical interest, unsatisfactory.

On page 24 it is asserted that an "individual may be a citizen or member of nation [the United States] and not of state and *vice versa.*" The notion that a person can be a "citizen of a state" in the sense of this term as it is used in the constitution of the United States runs flatly counter to the reasoning of the court in the Dred Scott and Slaughter-House cases, and raises insuperable difficulties. I believe, too, that there is a definite dictum against the idea in the court's opinion in the Wong Kim Ark case. On page 57 it is stated that naturalization "can be administered by United States courts only." Yet on page 59 it is stated on the authority of Hart that "any federal or state court may receive the proof and issue the certificate." The latter is, of course, the correct view. On page 128 it is asserted that "the several states have a right to make any laws in regard to business which do not interfere with stipulations made by the Federal Government." Yet on page 134 a quotation from a department of labor bulletin which evidently refers to the Supreme Court's decision in *Truax* v. *Raich* asserts a very different principle. On page 135 the treatment suffers from lack of knowledge of such cases as *Heim* v. *McCall;* nor is any awareness shown of recent cases dealing with the legislation of certain western states affecting Japanese rights. On page 158, under the heading of Freedom of Speech and Press, the statement is quoted that "in this country the press is entirely free"—that is, is free to aliens. The source of the quotation is a state department dispatch of June 18, 1869. (See 2 Moore 165.) This rather overlooks such cases as *Turner* v. *Williams* and certainly is little harmonious with what is said further along in the book about the American conception of treason and sedition. (See especially pp. 376–377.) The chapter on Exclusion and Expulsion of Aliens makes no reference to important recent cases.

If the first part of the volume is a scrapbook, the second is a medley. What seems finally to emerge is an effort by the author to emulate Krabbe in giving the perennial Jean Jacques a new coat of paint. We are taught that according to the American conception the "People," the "Nation," is "an impersonation of the idealism of a social-minded population" (p. 241), and that it possesses an attribute called "Sovereignty" which

makes anything it choses to do all right. "What must be impressed upon the minds of citizens of a republic," Dr. Cleveland asserts (p. 313), "is: That in dealing with liberty and authority we are dealing with two aspects of the same thing." In other words, the more authority, the more liberty!—which may be so when both belong to the same fellow. At any rate for other cases this great truth seems to have dawned but slowly on mankind, for on page 319 we learn, on the authority of Professor Burgess, that "the history of government should be written around the attempts of people to reconcile authority with liberty."

A great deal of this part of the book is obviously intended to edify rather than to instruct, though exactly to whom it is addressed is a question. The same question, indeed, arises as to the entire volume.

EDWARD S. CORWIN.

Princeton University.

✱

LOCAL FISCAL PROBLEMS: Finance Department, Chamber of Commerce of the United States, Washington, D. C., 1928. Pp. 24.

FISCAL PROBLEMS OF THE STATES: Finance Department, Chamber of Commerce of the United States, Washington, D. C., 1928. Pp. 47.

The Chamber of Commerce of the United States presents these two factual studies on local and state fiscal problems with the hope that they will encourage and assist regional efforts intended to effect improvements in the laws and practices relating to the raising and spending of the public funds.

These studies are merely summary reviews that do not go beyond a bare statement of some of the major fiscal problems that confront our local and state governments. For example, in the first report, we find a brief discussion of such subjects as assessment difficulties, tax exemption, overlapping jurisdictions, budgets and budgetary procedure, accounting and auditing, and longtime improvement programs. Similarly, in the report on the fiscal problems of the states, one finds an explanation of the more important reforms in state finance that have been given serious consideration during recent years. The main emphasis here is on state budgetary reform and state taxation. The latter is dealt with under three main heads: (1) the relation between federal and state governments, (2) the relation between the states, (3) taxation within the states.

The general method pursued in these reports is to give a factual presentation and to review important reform tendencies. For the most part, the two studies avoid taking sides on controversial policies. Incidentally, however, they renew the recommendation of the Chamber that the federal estate tax be abolished. In view of the Chamber's emphasis on governmental efficiency and the simplification of our taxation machinery, such a recommendation provokes suspicion of the Chamber's motives, since every intelligent and disinterested student of taxation well realizes that the only way to administer inheritance taxes equitably and efficiently is through the federal government. Again, while the Chamber of Commerce experts view with alarm the increasing value of tax-exempt property devoted to civic and philanthropic purposes, they maintain a discreet silence on the matter of tax-exemption privileges enjoyed by manufacturing industries, which in such a state as Pennsylvania, for example, results in great inequities in the distribution of the tax burden. While neither one of these studies contains material of special significance, both are very readable and should prove suggestive to interested laymen.

MARTIN L. FAUST.

❖

Three City Reports.—*Lynchburg, Virginia. Annual Report for the Fiscal Year Ending December 31, 1927. By R. W. B. Hart, City Manager. Pp. 119.*—This last report of the operation of the municipal government of Lynchburg maintains the high standard established by the previous publications of that city. To enumerate all its merits would take too much space. First of all, it is attractive. One cannot look at the cover without opening the report, and then the contents compel a further interest. Other commendable features are table of contents, organization chart, comparative data, balanced content, and general arrangement. To partly offset its many merits, one must mention the lack of emphasis upon important facts, a letter of transmittal which fails to either sum up outstanding accomplishments or offer suggestions for future action, and then finally its length of 119 pages. Report writers must condense their reports, for to expect one to read a public report of such length is to expect the impossible.

City of Berkeley, California. Fourth Annual Report for the Year Ending June 30, 1927. By

John N. Edy, City Manager. Pp. 89.—In this report Mr. Edy has departed from precedent in public report writing. He has done it with the purpose of trying to get the people who pay the bills for public services to take more interest in the reporting of those activities. It is gotten up in the form of a series of news articles, written and illustrated in newspaper style. The first impression is that the stories are extracts from current newspaper articles which might have appeared throughout the year, thus reproducing chronologically a newspaper account of city activities for the period covered. One finds, however, upon investigation, that such is not the case. It is, on the contrary, a deliberate attempt to depart from traditional methods in an effort to get people first of all to take notice of it. In this Mr. Edy has succeeded, for the report became the subject of a half-column editorial in a recent issue of the *New York Times*. Such recognition alone perhaps justifies the experiment. However, this reviewer is of the opinion that a continuation of such a method of reporting would defeat rather than aid the cause of public reporting. In the final analysis, Mr. Edy is deserving of high commendation for daring to do the unconventional. If more experiments were made by other city officials, perhaps we might eventually produce reports that would convey all the essential facts in such a way as to compel public attention.

City of Pontiac, Michigan. Annual Report for the Fiscal Year Ending December 31, 1927. By C. W. Ham, City Manager. Pp. 112.—For several years the annual reports of the city of Pontiac have been among the very best. This last report which was available to the taxpayers within two months after the end of the period covered is also entitled to a high rating. The lack of three essentials of municipal report writing keeps it from being the outstanding report of the year. These are a table of contents, an organization chart of the government, and the common fault of most reports—excessive length. More emphasis upon important facts, a few more charts, a more logical arrangement of material, and a letter of transmittal containing a brief résumé not alone of work done, but work proposed for the future as well would also have added to the interest and value of the report. By and large, however, it has a well-balanced content, and in many other respects is so commendable that to begin to name its good points would carry us beyond the limits of this review.

C. E. RIDLEY.

JUDICIAL DECISIONS

EDITED BY C. W. TOOKE

Professor of Law, Georgetown University

Zoning—Limitation of Power by the Supreme Court.—The decision of the Supreme Court in *Euclid* v. *Ambler Realty Company*, 272 U. S. 365, affirming the power of municipalities under delegated authority to enact and enforce comprehensive zoning ordinances, was taken by many as the last word on the subject and as rendering unnecessary any further discussion of the rights of individuals affected to claim the protection of the Fourteenth Amendment. This view gained currency, despite the express statement of the court that it decided nothing but the constitutionality of comprehensive zoning under the police power. That it is by no means certain that the Supreme Court would not uphold many of the decisions of the state courts apparently adverse to zoning if the rights of the individual upheld therein were brought before it when denied by the state tribunals is made manifest by its pronouncement in the case of *Nectow* v. *City of Cambridge*, 48 S. Ct. R. 447, decided on May 15.

In this case, the zoning ordinance was comprehensive in character, as in the Euclid case, but the restriction of the plaintiff's lands located in a manufacturing neighborhood to residence purposes not only destroyed their commercial value, but failed as a matter of fact to promote the health, safety, convenience and general welfare of the community. The court holds that the invasion of the property of the plaintiff in error was serious and that since it did not bear a substantial relation to the bases of the police power, the action of the zoning authorities comes within the ban of the Fourteenth Amendment and cannot be sustained. This case presages the reversal of the decision in the case of *American Woods Products Co.* v. *Minneapolis*, 21 Fed. (2d) 144, criticised in the December, 1927, issue of the REVIEW. It, also, is a warning to these zoning boards which have felt encouraged to indulge in arbitrary acts since the decision of the Euclid case. It may be further noted that an intensive study of the principles underlying zoning will henceforth be quite as essential as ever to insure an administration of zoning ordinances that will stand the test of judicial review.

Zoning—Comprehensive Ordinance Upheld in Texas.—The courts of Texas, which in 1921 looked with disfavor upon the principle of comprehensive zoning, have recently fallen in line with the majority of other states by a decision of the court of civil appeals of the state in *Wichita Falls* v. *Continental Oil Co.*, 5 S. W. (2d) 561. While not overruling *Spann* v. *City of Dallas*, 111 Texas 350, 235 S. W. 513, the court largely shifts the emphasis of the ground upon which the decision in that case was vested from a disapproval of the principle of zoning to the unreasonable nature of the ordinance therein involved. In apparent apology for the sentiments it published in earlier decisions, the court frankly says:

The power to regulate the conduct and location of business and industrial plants has been, in recent years, more generally conceded by the courts of our country than formerly. The tremendous development of our cities has produced new conditions, and the problem of providing for health and comfort of the populations of such cities becomes more and more complex and difficult. The best thought and the closest investigations of municipal authorities are taxed to the uttermost in the solution of such questions, and in determining the relief required from conditions that now threaten the congested population of such cities. We have learned many things. It may be that we have become overly critical, but, nevertheless, conditions which were borne with Indian stoicism 50 or 75 years ago have become intolerable in the present day because of our increased knowledge of what those conditions threaten. The necessity created by new conditions must be taken into consideration by the courts. Regulations passed by municipal authorities that may have seemed unreasonable under old conditions may now be reasonably necessary under the new conditions that confront us. We cannot dispose of the questions now arising and confronting us every day by the application of rules that have become obsolete under such changed conditions.

✦

Zoning—Effect of General Empowering Statute.—In *Dawley* v. *Collingwood*, 218 N. W. 766, the Supreme Court of Michigan in upholding an injunction against a violation of the zoning ordinance of the city of Lansing, which functions under a home-rule charter, rests its decision upon the principle that the general zoning enabling statute has enlarged the powers of all municipalities of the state to which it applies, including the home-rule cities, and that no charter amendment is necessary to authorize them to pass general zoning ordinances. The enlargement of the powers of home-rule cities by general statute, the court holds, is in no wise an interference with this constitutional independence. The decision is of great importance in its bearing also on the effect of other general enabling acts which may be adopted from time to time. Zoning has been tacitly considered in the home-rule states as a municipal function, upon which the local electorate should pass, and the general statute has been accepted rather as declaring the policy of the state and to some extent thereby determining the extent of the police power where the construction of constitutional limitations was raised. While the principle invoked in this instant case is a very useful one, it is somewhat difficult to reconcile it with the general theory of constitutional home rule. The only precedent cited by the court is the case of *Zimmerman* v. *Bedford*, 134 Va. 787, 115 N. E. 362, which, however, did not involve the home-rule question, but only the effect of a general statute upon the charters of towns, which under the constitution of 1902 were to be amended only by special act.

∗

Dedication—What Constitutes Acceptance.— It is generally laid down that an offer of dedication of lands, or of an easement therein to the public must be accepted by the state or some agency thereof to complete the vesting of the proferred rights in the public. As to what acts will constitute such an acceptance, however, the opinions of the courts differ greatly. Of course a formal acceptance by the appropriate agency, or the exercise of such acts of public ownership as reasonably imply an acceptance would be held final in all jurisdictions. In many jurisdictions, however, use by members of the public is held to be sufficient evidence of acceptance. In New Jersey, the doctrine that the acceptance of the public may result from the acts of individuals is carried to its logical extremity and the act of an owner in filing a plat in the county clerk's office and selling lots with reference thereto constitutes a complete dedication of the streets and squares indicated thereon. In *Long Branch* v. *Toovey*, 140 Atl. 415, the Court of Errors and Appeals reaffirms this doctrine and rejects the contention that acceptance of the public must be

by formal resolution or overt acts indicating possession or ownership, subject to which within a reasonable time, laches or estoppel will supervene to eliminate the public right. The acts of the owner, the court holds, effect a complete and irrevocable dedication, unless the concession be expressly rejected by the lawfully constituted authorities.

Another important decision bearing upon the effect of dedication on the rights of subsequent purchasers is *Menstell* v. *Johnson*, 262 Pac. 853, in which the Supreme Court of Oregon holds that the sale of lots thus platted and recorded with set-back lines indicated thereon establishes easements in gross, enforcible by any and all owners of the remaining lots of the tract, even though there be no express renewal of the covenant in the later deeds. The original covenantee thus becomes a trustee of the restrictive covenant for all subsequent grantees. It can readily be seen that the same doctrine is applicable to protect the city plan under the requirement of a statutory dedication by filing the plat of a subdivision in a recording office, and making the privilege of filing conditional upon the incorporation of set-back lines to conform with stated requirements.

∗

Torts—Proprietary and Governmental Functions.— The Supreme Court of Minnesota in its recent decision in *McLeod* v. *Duluth*, 218 N. W. 892, holds that the flushing of streets is a proprietary function, negligence in the discharge of which will impose liability, although the sprinkling of the streets is still to be considered a governmental function, with consequent immunity from tort liability. The court looks to the primary character of each activity and concludes that while sprinkling is for a local purpose and may be made the basis of special assessments because of the peculiar benefits to the adjoining property, still the paramount purpose is to conserve the public health by laying the dust. On the other hand, the application of water with force to the streets is only incidentally to conserve health and mainly to remove débris so as to render the street more safe for travel. Although highway maintenance is a public function, Minnesota, as most other states, recognizes the duty of a city to keep its streets in a safe condition for travel and impose civil liability for neglect, so that completing the logical circle, the maintenance of streets from the point of view of liability in tort is considered to be proprietary. The decision is to be commended, though the reasoning of the court in drawing its distinction is somewhat difficult to follow.

❋

Torts—Liability for Negligence in Care of Parks.—Texas is the latest state to join the ranks of those jurisdictions which hold municipalities liable for negligence in the care of their public parks. In *City of Waco* v. *Branch*, 5 S. W. (2d) 498, decided April 25, the Commission of Appeals held that the city was liable to the plaintiffs, injuries to whose child were caused by the failure of an attendant properly to manage a flock of sheep belonging to the city as an incident of its park maintenance. The flock stampeded into a line of automobiles, causing an accident from which the child suffered severe injuries. The court for the first time takes the position that in the management of its parks the city acts in a proprietary capacity for the peculiar benefit of its own inhabitants. In the earlier cases, the Texas courts, while recognizing the principle of general tort immunity, has struggled to predicate liability in a particular case either on the attractive nuisance theory or on the finding that revenue was incidentally derived from the apparatus negligently operated (*Wiggins* v. *Fort Worth*, 299 S. W. 468). By taking the advanced position in the instant case, the Texas courts follow the example of accepting the principle of extended liability, which has been adopted within the past two years by West Virginia, Wyoming, Mississippi and Colorado. (See note July 1927, Vol. XVI, No. 7, page 476 of this Review.)

In sharp contrast to the progressive step taken by the Texas courts, may be cited the decision of the Supreme Court of Kansas in *Warren* v. *Topeka*, 265 Pac. 78, handed down on March 10. The plaintiff's child was drowned in a park swimming pool, which was negligently operated by a concessionaire, who charged the children fixed rates for the bathing privilege. The court held that the city was not liable even though deriving a revenue, as the function was governmental, and that the concessionaire was not liable as he was merely an employee of the city, which prescribed the rates and laid down the rules of supervision, which he neglected to follow.

Which part of the decision does most violence to established legal principles as well as to practical justice, it is difficult to say. The court says: "The unfortunate accident is to be most seriously regretted and the fond parents have the sympathy of all who know of the accident, but we must recognize the modern tendency to furnish artificial swimming pools instead of natural swimming holes and to locate them in the most convenient places for use and enjoyment, viz., in parks."

Another recent decision illustrating the far reaching scope of the immunity from liability in tort, where the principle of governmental nature of parks is applied is that of *Dakin* v. *City of Somerville*, 160 N. E. 260, in which the Supreme Judicial Court of Massachusetts holds that roads and boulevards laid out as part of the park system do not come within the definition of ways opened and dedicated to the public use, such as to come within the purview of the general statute imposing liability for negligence in their maintenance.

❋

Municipal Ownership—Contract Rates.—The principle that a municipality in operating a public utility is subject to all the limitations of a private corporation, except so far as extraordinary powers are expressly delegated to it, was applied by the New Jersey Court of Chancery in *Federal Shipbuilding & Dry Dock Co.* v. *City of Bayonne*, 141 Atl. 455. In an action to have its contract with the city for a supply of water construed, the facts showed that the company agreed to advance the city $150,000 for water to be taken and ultimately to take additional water to the value of $350,000, the rates to be the same as for water furnished to other consumers of substantially equal amounts. The payment was made and the money used by the city, which later raised the rates to some large consumers outside the city and attempted to charge the increased rates to the company, although still continuing the older rates in force to other large consumers. The court held that the city was without power to make any rates retroactive, as was also attempted, and that the company under its contract was entitled to as favorable rates as any consumers of equal amounts of water whether within or without the city limits.

PUBLIC UTILITIES

EDITED BY JOHN BAUER

Director, American Public Utilities Bureau

False Notions of Economy.—The federal power commission has issued an order suspending temporarily the issuance of water power licenses, because of inadequate personnel and the failure of Congress to enact remedial legislation. Its present force consists of thirty civilian employees and five officers detailed from the corps of army engineers.

The commission declares that it would require double its present force "to catch up on work already accumulated, and do it within the next five years." The situation is "gradually getting worse," due to the influx of applications for water power licenses, and to research and accounting work that must follow. Hence, the order against new licenses was issued to prevent accumulation of work that would leave the commission almost hopelessly behind.

"The purpose of Congress fully to protect the public interest in the issuance and administration of licenses," continues the statement, "has, because of lack of adequate personnel, been impossible of accomplishment.

"The commission has proceeded with the issuance of licenses in the annual expectation that it would be given the means to exercise adequate supervision over them. This has not been given, and it is a serious question whether the commission ought not to cease the issuance of licenses altogether until it is in a better position to safeguard the public interests."

This niggardly treatment of a body created for the purpose of supervising public utilities in the public interest is by no means confined to the federal power commission. It has been the standing grievance of the interstate commerce commission for a number of years, as has been brought out by various members of the commission, and especially by Commissioner Eastman.

Nor is this "penny-wise-pound-foolish" policy confined to the federal branch of the government alone. This false "economy" program which results in crippling bodies that have an important public function to perform has likewise been adopted by most of the states. The results are deplorable and readily felt whenever questions of importance reach a point where they can no longer be ignored.

In the Public Utilities Report issue of April 5, 1928, this problem is very ably discussed by Hon. J. F. Shaughnessy. As chairman for many years of the Nevada public service commission and former president of the National Association of Railroad and Public Utility Commissioners, Mr. Shaughnessy has had full opportunity to know of conditions, and some of his observations will show what a pass we have reached.

Of the interstate commerce commission, he says:

> Despite this increased burden placed upon the interstate commerce commission, and the increased labors of state commissions in nationwide, district, and group rate cases, attending hearings and arguments at geographical centers and Washington, D. C., including heavy expenses for three thousand mile journeys, twenty thousand to thirty thousand page records, and for printing and filing of briefs, etc., no provision has been made by Congress to take care of these extraordinary expenses or to expedite the work over which it has taken jurisdiction. On the contrary, the federal commission is seriously undernourished in the matter of working appropriations and forces; it is overworked, behind in decisions of great public importance, and *so serious in this deficiency that during recent years numerous able commissioners and department heads of that tribunal have resigned from the service and entered other occupations to the great detriment of the public service.*

He then states that any responsible work touching upon utilities requires special training and experience, a fact fully appreciated by the utility companies. These have recognized the importance of continuance in office of the same personnel, and, therefore, provide ample salaries, long tenure of office, and promotion from the ranks. But—

> Quite the contrary policy has been pursued in the field of state and federal regulation, especially during recent years. Since the establishment of the budget system, under the guise of economy in the expenditure of public funds and reduction in taxes, the budget specialists with nothing other

than a superficial knowledge of the difficulties which beset the commissions, in many cases reduce or restrict their appropriations, and if, perchance, taking the interstate commerce commission as illustrative, a commissioner or a department head should speak before the appropriations committee, about some new matter or one disallowed by the budget director, the orders are to dismiss him, with the result that if he be called upon to give testimony in a meritorious case the usual practice is to have his remarks deleted from the record—a sad commentary to say the least.

Here we have a *clear invasion of the legislative prerogative by the executive branch of the government*, and it is remarkable indeed to think of Congress permitting such an invasion of its Constitutional duty as this clearly appears to be.

He then shows the absurdity of the "economy" idea exercised in this branch of the public service, in the following paragraph:—

In this connection the entire annual expenditure of all state commissions is but slightly over five million dollars per annum, while for the interstate commerce commission it is a little more than seven million dollars, or a total of about thirteen million dollars per annum. Compared with these figures the taxes and license fees annually collected for federal, state, county, and municipal purposes aggregate approximately seven and a half billion dollars, from which it follows, of course, that the cost of regulation is in no sense burdensome and that any reduction therein, resulting from mistaken notions of economy, could have no practical effect whatsoever on taxes, but because of the aforesaid reasons the salaries of commissioners and important department heads have in all too many cases remained at the prewar level, and for the same reasons it is almost impossible to secure an increase, while it is frequently difficult to prevent serious reductions in appropriations for the working support of the commissions, from which it follows, naturally enough, that the turnover in personnel of commission organizations has been very heavy during the past few years, a most unfortunate and in fact an uncalled-for condition. While the increase in cost of living, traveling expenses, and subsistence during recent years has been adequately compensated for in every financial, industrial and utility line of activity, it is regrettable that this cannot be said for the regulating tribunals of the nation, because they have not been accorded adequate increases in salaries and appropriations. *Unless this feature shall be given appropriate attention by Congress and state legislatures, regulation will fail and in lieu thereof the public will insist on some form of direct action.*

The writer has come to a poignant realization of this acute problem long ago in his everyday experience. He has seen again and again, utility rate, service, capitalization and other cases, lightly passed over by commissions, with consequent loss to the public interest, purely because of insufficient or entire absence of the required technical staff to investigate the specific problems. It is time that those who have regulation at heart bring these facts to the attention of the proper authorities with a view of correcting this evil.

✤

Service Charge for Gas Consumers.—Service charges in one form or another are being proposed by gas companies in widely scattered sections of the country.

Last February the Massachusetts commission cancelled the schedules, imposing such a charge, filed by the Boston Consolidated Gas Co. A similar proposal was turned down by the Missouri commission. The Laclede organization has filed schedules involving a consumer charge, which the city of St. Louis is now actively opposing before the Missouri commission. Two similar charges by Brooklyn gas companies, one of which was put into effect last August and now being reviewed, are pending before the New York commission.

Thus, the movement has assumed a national character and seems to be a concerted effort on the part of the gas industry to institute a charge that will increase the bill of the small consumer.

From the investigations the writer has conducted into the costs and rates of several companies, the following conclusions seem to be warranted:

1. There are probably some costs which do not depend upon the amount of gas consumed or upon any consumption, as long as the consumer is attached.

2. These specific consumer costs, insofar as they can be sifted out and segregated, amount to only about 20 cents a month.

3. The difference in these costs between the same class of consumers in different sections of a city served by the same company, is, as a rule, greater than the difference between the various classes of consumers in the same section.

4. The service charges proposed exceed by a substantial margin whatever special costs may be incurred for the consumer as a consumer.

5. The entire question is exaggerated by those who insist upon these new schedules out of all proportion to its real merits. Exact measurement of these costs and consumer charges therefor, would result in an altogether too involved rate schedule. And after all the minute classification has been accomplished, greater discrimination would result than those they attempted to eradicate.

Further Developments in the New York Subway Litigation.—After going to press with our former issue, the Supreme Court of the United States granted a stay to the city against the introduction of a higher fare pending its review of the decision by the statutory court. As the argument at Washington will take place in October, the subway riders are assured of the continuance of the five-cent fare, as fixed by the contract, at least till the latter part of October.

Some profess to see in this granting of a stay by the highest court an indication of its decision next fall in favor of the city. While this temporary stay is favorable to the public, it can hardly be said to imply similar action in the disposition of the questions to be decided next October, or in the final adjudication of the case. The granting of the stay, in our opinion, did not involve a consideration of the questions at issue. All that was necessary at this stage was the application of common sense. At the time the stay was argued, one member of the Court asked counsel for the company how long this alleged confiscation had been going on. Counsel answered that it had been deprived of a fair return ever since the great rise in price level,— for eight to ten years.

Counsel for the city then recited to the Court the earlier attempts made by the company to increase the fare. It is developed that the company had appealed to the board of estimate in 1919 and directly to the New York state legislature in 1922, but abandoned the attempts later.

In view of these facts, the Supreme Court could very well take the view than an ordinary man in the street would under similar circumstances. It could ask, why the haste? If the company could rest on its oars since 1923, during which time the subway earnings have concededly increased in gross and net by leaps and bounds, why should an increase be granted now when the basic questions will be decided within a few months?

Meanwhile the city and the commission have taken further action in the matter both before the Supreme Court and the lower federal court. The latter had barred from appeal to the Supreme Court certain papers bearing upon the question of priority of jurisdiction between the state and federal courts of the fare litigation. The city and the commission, however, obtained an order from the Supreme Court to include these documents and to make this priority question part of the case to be argued next October.

In addition, the commission applied to federal court to modify its injunction insofar as the latter interferes with the regulatory powers of the commission over the Interborough outside of the fare provision. Thus, the commission is enjoined from enforcing the lengthening of platforms and the purchase of 432 additional cars. Both of these projects had been before the commission for a long time. Many hearings were held and testimony taken as to the need of these improvements and the relief they would offer in a comparatively short time.

The Interborough denies that the regulatory powers of the commission have been curtailed by the injunction. The commission may issue whatever order it sees fit. All that the injunction does, according to the company, is to make all commission action reviewable by federal court, if the company refuses to comply with it.

GOVERNMENTAL RESEARCH ASSOCIATION NOTES

EDITED BY RUSSELL FORBES

Secretary

Recent Reports of Research Agencies.—
The following reports have been received at the
central library of the Association since May 1,
1928:

Boston Finance Commission:
Reports and Communications, Volume XXIII.
Buffalo Municipal Research Bureau:
*The Annual Budget; covering the fiscal year
July 1, 1928 to June 30, 1929.*
California Taxpayers' Association:
*Summary and Analysis of the County Budget
Law and Budget Procedure.*
Chicago Bureau of Public Efficiency:
*Tax and Bond Propositions; to be voted upon
June 4.*
Cincinnati Bureau of Municipal Research:
*What Happens to Felony Cases in Cincinnati.
Crime and Criminal Justice.*
Cleveland Municipal Research Bureau:
Annual Report.
Detroit Bureau of Governmental Research:
*Charts of the Detroit Metropolitan Area.
Memorandum re Proposed Crime Commission.
Statistical Records of Detroit.*
Taxpayers' Association of Fall River, Inc.:
The High Cost of Government.
Taxpayers' Association, Minneapolis.
*A Study of Teachers Salaries and Some Facts
Bearing Upon an Increase in Such Salaries
in Minneapolis.*
Philadelphia Bureau of Municipal Research:
*Force Account on Unit-Price Construction
Contracts.*
Schenectady Bureau of Municipal Research,
Inc.:
*Know Your City! (And How It Spends Your
Money).*
St. Louis Bureau of Municipal Research:
Recording Deeds by Photography.
Taxpayers' League of St. Louis County, Inc.:
Annual Review of Activities, June 1, 1928.

✣

Boston Finance Commission.—Since May 1
the commission has conducted investigations on
cases in the overseers of the public welfare

department, checking requests for abatement of
taxes, and checking payments made in the soldiers relief department.

✣

California Taxpayers' Association.—The
California Taxpayers' Association has been
active for the past few weeks conducting conferences in different parts of the state to give
opportunity to the taxpayer to familiarize himself with the best methods of getting information
as to budgets and budget procedure. A new
California law requires California counties to
adopt and operate on a budget plan, and becomes effective for the first time for the 1928
budget.

This act was prepared and sponsored by the
California Taxpayers' Association and requires
each county to prepare a budget of proposed
expenditures for all departments and functions,
showing its complete fiscal program for the year.
Copies of the completed budget are to be furnished taxpayers interested enough to request
them, before the appropriations are made final
and the tax rate determined. They are then
given an opportunity to participate in an open
budget hearing and suggestions are offered for
allowance, reduction or increase of budget
requests.

The act was passed as the result of an insistent demand on the part of the taxpayers
that they be given an opportunity to sit at the
council table when their tax burdens are determined, and to have an understanding of their
county's activities and a voice in determining their
fiscal policy. The budget, when finally adopted,
must be adhered to in the expenditures, except
that provision is made for an emergency fund.

The Association is now in the midst of another
county survey. Rolland A. Vandergrift, director
of research for the Association, reports that
the governmental survey of Santa Barbara
County is approximately one third finished.
The field work of this survey has been divided
into three parts: (1) general governmental
receipts and expenditures and accounting

methods; (2) highways, bridges and other engineering features; (3) educational administration, including receipts and expenditures. The survey is being made at the request of the Santa Barbara County Committee of California Taxpayers' Association. It covers the fiscal year ending June 30, 1927. The analysis will be similar to the previous reports made of Sonoma, Kern and San Diego counties.

✤

Citizens' Research Institute of Canada.—The Institute has prepared and will shortly issue a report giving an outline of the tax structure of Canada.

The preparation of the 1928 edition, first portion (city section), of the *Red Book*, financial statistics of Canadian governments, is being proceeded with. It is expected that it will be ready for publication about the end of June. The complete edition of the *Red Book* contains the latest authoritative financial information for all Canadian urban municipalities with a population of more than four hundred.

✤

Cleveland Municipal Research Bureau.—Alden C. Fensel has been appointed acting director of the Cleveland Municipal Research Bureau.

The Bureau has completed its study of the financial requirements of the city of Cleveland for the next fifteen years and also a functional analysis of governmental expenditures for the past five years.

A follow-up of delinquent tax collections is being made to supplement the original study completed in 1925. An abstract of state loans affecting county government is also being prepared for the Regional Government Committee.

The Bureau has consented to give technical assistance to the civic Fact Finding Committee on the New County Jail and Courts Building.

✤

Taxpayers' Research League of Delaware.—The League has continued the preparation of material for consideration in the drafting of a code for the fiscal administration of the state, counties, and municipalities. This code is to be formulated in coöperation with a committee of the Delaware Bankers' Association. The League is preparing from the official records of the state what is probably the first objective analysis that has ever been made of state appropriations and expenditures. A schedule has also been prepared showing how all outstanding

state highway bonds which are forty-year, sinking-fund bonds, may be retired in twenty years without any increase of the present annual sinking-fund and interest payments from the highway fund.

✤

Des Moines Bureau of Municipal Research.—The Des Moines Bureau of Municipal Research is preparing a statement showing the comparative expenses of each activity and bureau of the city, county, and school departments for 1917 and the last four years. This compilation has proved to be exceedingly difficult, owing to the fact that annual statements of the city and county fail to segregate items and do not in every respect present a clear picture of the expense.

The Bureau is analyzing the printing expense in connection with the city and general elections. It was found that there is little competition in these contracts.

A report is being prepared on the consolidation of several high schools and the closing of an elementary school.

✤

Indianapolis Chamber of Commerce.—An amendment to the Indianapolis school city charter, providing for the election of school commissioners biennially at the time when commissioners are elected for the civil city under the city manager form of government, will be proposed by the Indianapolis Chamber of Commerce civic affairs department as a result of a study made by the education committee of the Chamber of Commerce.

A thorough survey of the present provision in the Indianapolis charter and a study of school board election laws in twenty cities of the United States, including the ten immediately larger and the ten immediately smaller in population, were made by the committee.

As a result of the study the committee concluded that the school board should be elected rather than appointed. Certain provisions of the Indiana constitution led the committee to recommend that the membership on the Indianapolis board be retained at five. Under the present charter, a school board election is held once each four years, three members being elected to take office on the first of January immediately following, and two members to take office two years after their election, all members to hold office for four years.

The most important reform recommended by the education committee would provide that all members take office on the first of January immediately following their election and, therefore, biennial elections are recommended.

The department expects to have the coöperation of other civic agencies in support of this amendment, and it is understood that the school commissioners themselves are not unfriendly to the proposal. The amendment will be submitted to the state legislature next January.

✢

Bureau of Governmental Research, Kansas City, Kansas, Chamber of Commerce.—When it was proposed to issue bonds for the resurfacing of a boulevard and the repaving and repainting of the intercity viaduct, the Bureau engaged Black and Veatch of Kansas City, Missouri, as consulting engineers to report on these projects. In addition, considerable data was gathered from municipalities and private corporations concerning the advantages of mechanical painting (the spray gun method). The use of the sand blast was also recommended for cleaning the viaduct preparatory to repainting.

When it was announced that the county commissioners would shortly request the city to install additional traffic signal lights, the Bureau submitted a memorandum to the safety council recommending that no additional traffic signal lights be installed until the city acquires an adequate fund of engineering data on traffic problems. Traffic counts, a spot map of traffic accidents, and the designation of a traffic engineer to make special studies of traffic problems were recommended.

The Bureau's study shows that the existing system of field collection of the city dog tax by temporary appointees, many of whom work only two weeks, is disadvantageous to the city. It was found that some employees did not collect enough to pay their own salaries. The use of Boy Scouts for this work, more effective field supervision, and the establishment of a municipal dog pound are the main recommendations advanced in the report.

The Bureau's report on municipal budget procedure, which was submitted to the finance commissioner last November, has been published for general distribution.

When it was announced that, due to the maturing of $490,000 worth of bonds during 1929, coupled with a shortage in the sinking fund, there might be an increase in the city tax rate, the Bureau issued a bulletin calling the attention of the taxpayers to the need of retrenchment if the existing rate is to be maintained. The city officials are now at work on a program of retrenchment by which they hope to avoid an increase in the tax rate for city purposes.

✢

Kansas City Public Service Institute.—The principal work and activities of the Kansas City Public Service Institute during recent months have been as follows:

County Reorganization.—In coöperation with county officials a study is being made of the organization of the government of Jackson County for the purpose of preparing a bill providing for reorganization to be presented to the 1929 session of the state legislature. A definite plan of organization has not yet been prepared, but it is expected that a considerable consolidation of departments can be made with a reduction in the number of independent departments and independently elected officials.

School Building Financing.—A proposal to issue five million dollars of school bonds was defeated at a special election on March 27. This is the first time that a school bond proposal has been defeated in Kansas City. Following this the Public Service Institute presented to the board of education a plan for establishing school building finances on the pay-as-you-go basis immediately. Whether this will be adopted has not yet been determined. Previous to the bond election the Institute had submitted a plan for establishing the pay-as-you-go plan after the expenditure of the bond funds. This had been informally approved by the board of education.

Conference on Local Government.—In coöperation with the League of Women Voters and several other civic organizations the Institute aided in the plans for a conference on local government held in Kansas City, May 24 and 25. Problems of local importance were discussed by both local and out-of-town speakers. The principal speaker was Colonel C. O. Sherrill, city manager of Cincinnati, Ohio, who spoke on the city manager plan in Cincinnati. Other subjects discussed were: police administration, county government reorganization, method of electing the school board, and a ten-year financial plan.

National Institute of Public Administration.— Bruce Smith has delivered his report on Rural Police Protection in Illinois to the Illinois Association for Criminal Justice. This will be published -as part of the report of the Association covering all aspects of the administration of criminal justice in that state.

"The National Institute of Public Administration" is the title of a new book by Luther Gulick dealing with the history, achievements, and progress of the National Institute of Public Administration which has absorbed and taken over the work of the Bureau and Training School and is conducting advanced courses in training and research.

✤

The New Bedford Taxpayers' Association.— The New Bedford Taxpayers' Association has been active in trying to improve the budget procedure in New Bedford. The first thing to do was to impress the members of the city government and the people with the importance of the budget and then to improve the departmental estimates so that they would be more complete than had formerly been the custom. The departmental estimates were presented to the mayor on a form suggested by the Taxpayers' Association which was followed in so far as the records of the departments made it possible.

Unfortunately, the budget has been used more or less as a "football," having been passed back and forth between the mayor, common council and board of aldermen. The common council, after a series of hearings with the heads of the departments, made a rather unscientific cut in the budget of $370,000. The board of aldermen recognized that some of the cuts made could not be put in force, because the budget is passed after four months of the fiscal year have gone by and they, therefore, made a reduction in the mayor's budget of $162,000. This was finally passed. The budget being a lump sum budget, however, it was possible for the heads of certain departments to propose savings to meet the budget which would naturally be unpopular, and consequently political pressure has been brought to bear for supplementary budgets so as to bring the total of the budget up to what the mayor originally proposed.

We believe that the whole procedure, however, has been beneficial, as it has brought more popular discussion of the budget and governmental expenditures in general.

The general strike in the cotton mills, which is now in its seventh week, has already increased the expenditures for veterans' aid and the welfare department, so that the net results of departmental savings cannot be foretold. Many of the departments, however, are staying within their budgets, although the big problem of overmanned staffs has not been faced by the administration.

✤

Philadelphia Bureau of Municipal Research.— As part of the study of municipal contracts which the Philadelphia Bureau is making as agent of the Thomas Skelton Harrison Foundation, it has prepared a report entitled "Force Account on Unit-Price Construction Contracts." The attention of the Bureau was attracted early in the study by what seemed a very unusual practice in Philadelphia's department of city transit, that of fixing the force-account percentage by bidding. Information obtained from public officials in other cities and from engineers and contractors confirmed the impression that the practice was unusual and that it was disadvantageous to the city, since it opened the way for an unbalanced bid. In the course of the study specifications from a number of other cities were gathered. The report above mentioned analyzes these specifications with respect both to the method of fixing the percentage and to a number of other practices. The department of city transit, it should be added, recently abandoned the practice of fixing the force-account percentage by bidding and has adopted the usual method, that of fixing the percentage in the specifications.

The report calls attention to the fact that one of the most striking things observed in the specifications from the several cities is the lack of uniformity. This, it is thought, increases the chance that out-of-town contractors will meet with costly surprises in the course of the work and makes it necessary for them to reflect the uncertainty in their bids. It is recommended that city officials in Philadelphia take advantage of every opportunity to promote uniformity of specifications.

Mr. Philip A. Beatty of the Bureau's staff is the author of the report. The report is printed as a publication of the Thomas Skelton Harrison Foundation. Copies of it may be obtained, free of charge, upon request to the Bureau of Municipal Research, 311 South Juniper Street, Philadelphia.

St. Louis Bureau of Municipal Research.—
The St. Louis Bureau recently completed a report on the results of the first three months' experience in recording documents by the photographic method. Through the initiative and coöperation of the recorder, excellent work is being done at a considerable reduction in cost as compared with the hand and typewriter methods.

Approximately ten per cent of the documents submitted for recording are unsuitable for photographing because of unusually wide paper or colored paper and colored inks. As a large proportion of the instruments recorded are prepared by real estate firms and attorneys, the Bureau has enlisted the coöperation of the Real Estate Exchange and the Bar Association, who have informed their members as to the requirements for photographing. It is hoped that in this way the proportion of unsuitable documents can be materially reduced.

The Bureau is now engaged in the collection of the statistical information required to make an actuarial study of the police department. A police pension system of the cash disbursement type has been proposed by the police board. Retirement would be permitted on one-half salary at ages forty-seven to fifty-seven. The Bureau has repeatedly urged the adoption of an actuarial type of system. After presenting the matter to the board of estimate and apportionment that body included in the budget an amount sufficient to employ an actuary. The board employed Mr. George B. Buck, consulting actuary of New York City, and requested the Bureau to supervise the collection of the statistical information.

✳

Schenectady Bureau of Municipal Research.—
We received numerous requests from different organizations for talks concerning our Bureau and its proposed activities. This has given us a good opportunity to place the municipal research idea properly before the people. We have had excellent coöperation from the press in this matter. In all our talks we have endeavored to sell the idea that we are not a "snooping" organization, but are here to help whatever administration is in power to conduct the affairs of the city administration in an economical and efficient manner.

Our first work was to examine hastily the local charter and second-class cities law provisions and construct a diagram of the administra-

tive organization. We are following this with a preliminary survey of all departments in the nature of a diagnosis, in an endeavor to locate the "patient's" principal ailments before prescribing any remedies or recommending any major "operations."

We have made an analysis of the city budget, as well as a study of the trends of departmental appropriations over the past five years. This material has been embodied in the form of a short pamphlet which has been printed as *Know your City—and How It Spends Your Money.*

The administration is planning the erection of a new city hall, and will shortly have tentative plans prepared. It has been our thought that an open competition should be held for the selection of the architect. We believe this will be concurred in, but public sentiment seems to prevail for limiting the competition to local architects. We are making a survey of the present and proposed space requirements for the several departments to be housed in the new building and shall suggest to the officials a definite program of procedure to be followed in conducting such a competition, all subject to the approval of the American Institute of Architects.

✳

Municipal League of Seattle.—One of the main objects of activity of the Municipal League of Seattle this year was the clearing up of a large indebtedness, which was a result of a city manager campaign in 1925. The finance committee of the League, under the able leadership of M. H. Van Nuys, received contributions from 119 members, totaling $629, and also increased the current revenue of the League. By their efforts the League indebtedness was reduced by more than half.

In addition to this financial campaign, the League has continued its regular program of investigation of municipal problems. In November and December, Seattle's municipally-owned Skagit power development, where total expenditure and investment is expected to reach from seventy-five millions of dollars to ninety millions of dollars, was investigated, and recommendations made by the committee and adopted by the League, that a Skagit Engineering Commission be created, composed of competent and disinterested engineers, to study the situation and to decide the controversy which is raging in political circles, as to the advisability of building the Diablo or Haning Rock Dam as a next step in the development of the project.

During the spring election, the candidates' investigating committee of the League examined the qualifications of the candidates for the city council and mayor, making a report which received very great publicity through the newspapers of the city. All councilmen elected had received the League's endorsement. Mrs. Landis, however, whom the League found well qualified for reëlection as mayor, was defeated.

The bridge and harbor improvement bonds, which were the subject of a League report and recommended by the League, received popular approval at the spring election.

In late May, the street railway committee of the League recommended an extensive re-routing plan which would loop all street cars in the north central business district and save the city from three hundred thousand dollars to five hundred thousand dollars per year, according to estimates of experts. This report, although opposed by property interests affected, and also because of the widespread change recommended, was strongly resisted, but received the League's approval.

✤

Toledo Commission of Publicity and Efficiency.—A supplement to the *Toledo City Journal*, published May 12, contained the financial report of the city for 1927, showing the distribution of sources of revenue and the percentage of expenditures for various functions.

The city council passed on June 4 the mayor's transit ordinance which gives promise of solving what has been Toledo's most vexing problem for over a quarter of a century. The ordinance was carefully considered by the Commission of Publicity and Efficiency and its passage recommended. Many concessions were granted to the city in return for the prohibition of competition within a quarter-mile of street car and bus lines of the Community Traction Company.

As a result of the survey of the billboard situation which was published in the *Toledo City Journal* of June 9, the commissioner of inspection is taking steps to enforce all billboard ordinances. All boards which are not claimed and have not paid annual inspection fees by July 1, 1928, will be torn down.

The Commission prepared for the Charter Commission pension provisions for the new city charter. This proposal abolishes the two separate fire and police pension boards and sets up a single board, and makes provisions for a contributory, actuarial pension system, with the council having the final authority in raising pension rates. At present the pension boards, consisting of five city employees and the safety director, may raise their own pension without the city council's approval.

NOTES AND EVENTS

EDITED BY H. W. DODDS

Build Subways to Decentralize, Regional Plan Advises.—The carrying out of a billion dollar subway construction program in the next fifteen years will not solve the problem of subway congestion in New York City, unless there is accomplished at the same time a spreading out of the industry and commerce now largely concentrated in lower Manhattan—this is the conclusion of an exhaustive report of the Regional Plan of New York and Its Environs on "Transit and Transportation," the first section of which has been published.

The report shows that the subways have never been able to keep pace with the demand for their use; that the building of new subways to feed the present system of city growth merely creates new congested districts, increases the riding habits of the public, and makes for more crowding of all rapid transit facilities. Instead of trying to bring more millions of workers to and from Manhattan daily, the Regional Plan says, we should bring the place of work closer to the home of the worker.

The report presents the findings and conclusions of a large corps of experts in the fields of economic research, engineering and community planning, who have for six years conducted an intensive study of the situation in New York City and its 400 neighboring cities and villages, preliminary to the drafting of a plan for the future development of this city, and the suburbs linked with it economically.

Close to three million persons enter Manhattan south of 59th Street on a typical business day, the Regional Plan reports, and approximately two million of these use the subways and elevated trains. Of this vast army approximately 1,392,000 persons come into lower Manhattan daily from north of 59th Street; approximately 1,120,000 come from Brooklyn, Queens and other portions of Long Island; 39,000 come from Staten Island; and approximately 316,000 come from New Jersey.

The report analyzes the plans contemplated or in process of execution for increasing the rapid transit facilities of Northern New Jersey, Westchester County and Long Island, and then adds:

It will be seen that the purpose of all these plans is the concentration of suburban rapid transit in the congested portions of lower Manhattan, where unquestionably the majority of the travelers now desire to go. But in so doing it would seem wise to arrange in such manner that this evil will be minimized and means afforded for the future gradual dispersion of such traffic among a multiplicity of subcenters.

As an indication of the tendency of a large part of the population to live as close as possible to subway stations, the Regional Plan's report cites the fact that 90 per cent of the population living within a half mile of subway or elevated stations are concentrated within a quarter mile of these stations. Numerous maps in the report show how closely the population follows new subways.

New York City has been a pioneer in constructing rapid transit lines through virgin and undeveloped territory, and has proved that population will follow such transportation lines promptly and intensively. There is, therefore, a great responsibility upon the shoulders of the rapid transit planners. They can do much toward directing the lines of future growth, which may lead either to increased congestion and time of travel or to dispersion of business and industry and freedom of movement, in accordance with the amount of farsightedness applied to the plans.

The danger of putting such a network of rapid transit lines through the outlying parts of New York City and through the Metropolitan sections of New Jersey as will encourage universal intensive development in those areas should be avoided. While a homogeneous business district is advantageous, residential areas should possess variety and provide for both open and close developments.

❋

Housing for the Small Wage Earner in Michigan.—The Michigan Housing Association has been organized to provide tolerable houses for workers earning less than $1,800 a year who are now compelled to live wherever they can find the cheapest accommodations, irrespective of quality or sanitation. Realizing that any plan for the solution of this problem must function without charity or philanthropy and without the permanent and continuous expenditure of public money, the Association nevertheless, believes that unrelated private efforts will not meet the situation. It has, therefore, proposed for discussion a plan of public credits and mass construction as a means of satisfying the housing needs of the lower income group. The plan involves the following four steps:

(1) Elimination of the present costs of financing by providing capital through public credits;

(2) Purchase of land in parcels of not less than two hundred acres, thus reducing the cost of the land;

(3) Purchase of construction materials in large quantities sufficient for not less than a thousand homes;

(4) Building programs on a mass scale of not less than one thousand homes per undertaking.

Under the plan, regional home loans commissions will be organized to administer the financing, and housing corporations will purchase the land and build the houses. Officers of both bodies will be appointed by the public authorities.

As indicated above, the plan is at present merely a proposal for discussion. It was presented in detail by Dr. S. James Herman at a recent meeting of the Michigan Academy of Science.

❀

The National Committee on Municipal Standards recently created by the National Municipal League, the Governmental Research Association, and the International City Managers' Association, the personnel of which was announced in these columns in the April issue, held its first meeting on May 21. A leaflet is now being prepared setting forth the organization of the committee, its purpose, the scope of the work to be undertaken and the general method of procedure. A copy will soon be mailed to all members of the three sponsoring organizations, inviting their coöperation in this important undertaking. Col. H. M. Waite was elected chairman of the committee, Dr. C. A. Beard, vice chairman, and C. E. Ridley secretary, with headquarters at 261 Broadway, New York City.

A Subcommittee of the Duluth Charter Commission has reported in favor of amending the municipal charter to provide for the council-manager form of government recommending that, in many important respects, the draft of the necessary amendments follow closely the appropriate sections of the Model Charter of the National Municipal League. The common council is to consist of fifteen members with overlapping terms, one member from each of the eleven districts to be formed, and four members at large. The mayor is to be the official head of the city and to preside at meetings of the council. He is to receive a salary four times as large as that of the councilmen. The council is to be the legislative body of the city government but is to be prohibited from interfering in the city manager's administration of the city's business. The report follows the standard provisions appearing in the League's Model Charter, and if incorporated in amendments to the Duluth charter will provide the city an excellent basis for sound administration.

❀

Non-voting in London.—At the last election for the London County Council only 38 per cent of the electors voted, and some Englishmen are lamenting the small number of citizens who turn out at the polls. Obviously the slacker voter is an internationalist. According to a writer in the London Nation and Athenaeum, the dull monotony of triennial elections is one cause of the voters' indifference.

❀

The Toledo Charter Commission is considering the "fixed quota" plan of proportional representation. Under it, one councilman would be chosen for every seven thousand votes cast. Although it has been occasionally discussed, none of the American cities using the Hare plan of proportional representation has adopted the fixed quota.

❀

Wayne Heydecker has resigned as the secretary of the Westchester County Planning Federation. Upon his resignation he was immediately promoted to vice president. Wells F. Wise of White Plains was appointed to succeed Mr. Heydecker as secretary.

A MODEL MUNICIPAL BUDGET LAW

SUBMITTED BY

THE COMMITTEE ON A MODEL MUNICIPAL BUDGET
LAW OF THE NATIONAL MUNICIPAL LEAGUE

CARL H. PFORZHEIMER, *Chairman*
C. E. RIGHTOR, *Secretary*

Supplement to the
NATIONAL MUNICIPAL REVIEW
July, 1928. Vol. XVII, No. 7

PUBLISHED BY

NATIONAL MUNICIPAL LEAGUE
261 Broadway, New York, N. Y.

THE COMMITTEE ON A MODEL MUNICIPAL BUDGET LAW

OF THE

NATIONAL MUNICIPAL LEAGUE

CARL H. PFORZHEIMER, *Chairman*,
Carl H. Pforzheimer & Company, New York.

C. E. RIGHTOR, *Secretary*,
Detroit Bureau of Governmental Research.

A. E. BUCK,
National Institute of Public Administration, New York.

WALTER R. DARBY,
New Jersey Commissioner of Municipal Accounts.

ARTHUR J. EDWARDS,
Smith, Graham and Rockwell, New York.

MARK GRAVES,
State Tax Commissioner, Albany, New York.

LUTHER GULICK,
National Institute of Public Administration, New York.

CLYDE L. KING,
University of Pennsylvania.

GEORGE M. LINK,
Minneapolis Board of Estimate and Taxation.

ARTHUR N. PIERSON,
State Senator, New Jersey.

D. V. RAYMOND,
Caldwell and Raymond, New York.

H. P. SEIDEMANN,
Institute for Government Research, Washington, D. C.

L. D. UPSON,
Detroit Bureau of Governmental Research.

TABLE OF CONTENTS

PAGE

INTRODUCTION... 437

MODEL BUDGET LAW... 439

ENTITLEMENT OF ACT... 439

APPLICATION.. 439

FISCAL YEAR.. 439

NATURE AND SCOPE OF THE BUDGET............................. 439

THE BUDGET DOCUMENT.. 440

PREPARATION OF THE BUDGET.................................. 441

BUDGET HEARINGS.. 442

ADOPTION OF THE BUDGET AND ENACTMENT OF THE BUDGET BILLS..... 442

FAILURE TO MAKE APPROPRIATIONS: AMOUNTS DEEMED APPROPRIATED.. 442

FORM OF THE APPROPRIATIONS................................. 443

ALLOTMENTS... 443

WHEN CONTRACTS AND EXPENDITURES ARE PROHIBITED............. 444

TRANSFER OF APPROPRIATIONS................................. 444

ADDITIONAL APPROPRIATIONS AND TEMPORARY LOANS.............. 444

STATE SUPERVISION.. 445

CONSTRUCTION OF ACT.. 445

FORMER LAWS SUPERSEDED..................................... 445

INTRODUCTION

GOVERNMENT today more than ever before needs careful planning. This is true no less for the smallest school district and drain district than for the largest city or county. Such planning involves consideration of the services to be performed, their cost, and the means of financing them. Indeed, such financial planning has always been necessary to assure citizens and taxpayers stability and economy in the conduct of governmental services performed in their behalf. But it has not always obtained, and "government by deficit" has been commonplace among many political units.

With the increasing cost of government, due to more extensive demands of the citizens and constant expansion of public activities to meet these demands, the need has been emphasized and intensified for planning. A real plan is realized in the budget. And because the budget is universal in its application, involving both the field of activities and the citizens' contribution for their cost, it is one of the foremost problems in government.

In the United States, the first definite budget work was begun in New York City in 1906, in the department of public health. Since that day, the budget idea has spread to most cities and states, until, in 1921, the federal government adopted a law instituting budgetary procedure.

The reason for the model budget law for local governments is that it is felt that each state may desire that all its political subdivisions should definitely recognize certain financial responsibilities and be required to outline their plans in a manner which will be of the widest possible information and interest to those receiving the benefits of such

service and paying the cost. Upon the latter, depends the ultimate success of government.

The law is drafted in the hope that state legislatures will find it completely suggestive as to the elements of a sound and adequate budgetary procedure. It definitely recognizes and provides for three phases of the budget,—the preparation, adoption, and execution. It is believed that, in event there are constitutional or other inhibitions which would make impossible the acceptance of any of these steps, the remaining sections can be adopted.

The Model Municipal Budget Law is a companion to the Model Bond Law, which was promulgated by the National Municipal League in February, 1927, to outline sound practices relative to borrowing by governments for permanent improvements. The committee on the budget law comprises the same chairman, Mr. Pforzheimer, with some changes in membership. The final draft is the result of several sessions of the committee as well as extensive correspondence upon every phase of the subject.

The regulation of temporary loans, while usually identified with current financing, is omitted in the budget law with the thought that it requires separate consideration.

The chief features of the model law are:

1. All undertakings and financial transactions of every local government shall be included in the budget for the fiscal year.

2. The budget document comprises three parts: First, a message and summary, with comparisons with the past and current year, prepared by the budget-making

authority; second, detailed estimates of expenditures and revenues with pertinent financial
and other data, such as bonded
and authorized debt, debt limits
and margin, etc.; and third,
drafts of the appropriation,
revenue and borrowing measures.

3. The total proposed expenditures
shall not exceed the estimated
means of financing them.

4. Departmental estimates shall go to
a budget authority to permit
preparation of a coordinated
plan of public services, which is
then submitted to the appropriating authority for revision
and adoption, these steps being
according to a definite time
schedule.

5. The budget shall be adopted at
least ten days prior to the beginning of the fiscal year.

6. Public hearings shall be arranged
before final action by the appropriating body.

7. An appropriation ordinance shall
be enacted to make the budget
operative.

8. Appropriations for operation and
maintenance are made in lump
sum, and a plan of quarterly
allotments provided to assure
the maximum of economy in the
execution of the budget.

9. Transfers by the appropriating
body are permitted within funds
during the last two months of
the year, if approved by the
budget-making authority.

10. Temporary loans for emergencies
are possible when properly
approved.

11. State supervision is provided, to
assure that debt service and
deficits are adequately provided
for.

C. E. RIGHTOR, *Secretary.*
July, 1928.

MODEL MUNICIPAL BUDGET LAW

PREPARED BY NATIONAL MUNICIPAL LEAGUE COMMITTEE ON MODEL
BUDGET LAW ·

CARL H. PFORZHEIMER, *Chairman*

C. E. RIGHTER, *Secretary*

Section 1. Entitlement of act. This act shall be known and may be cited as "The Local Government Budget Act of ......"

Section 2. Application. This act shall apply to all subdivisions of the state which have power to appropriate money or levy taxes, including [1]......

...... heretofore or hereafter created. For the purpose of this act, any such subdivision shall hereinafter be designated and referred to by the term "local government."

Section 3. Fiscal year. The fiscal year shall begin on the ...... day of .... and end on the ...... day of ....[2] Such year shall constitute the budget year of the local government.

Section 4. Nature and scope of the budget. The budget for any local government shall present a complete financial plan for the ensuing budget year. It shall set forth all proposed expenditures for the administration, operation, and maintenance of all offices, departments, boards, commissions, and institutions, including publicly owned and operated utilities and enterprises; the actual or estimated operating deficits from prior years; all interest and debt redemption charges during the budget year; expenditures for capital projects to be undertaken and/or executed during the budget year, including expenditures for local improvements which may be paid for in whole or in part by special assessments.[3] In addition thereto, the

---

[1] Here should be inserted the several kinds of subdivisions of the state, such as cities, counties, parishes, school districts, townships, boroughs, villages, and special and metropolitan sewer, park, road and other districts, etc. Each state has its own designation of its local governmental units.

The committee proposes that the budget law should be applicable to every subdivision of the state, and has outlined the essentials of a budget for the largest city as well as the smallest school or other district. It is appreciated, however, that states may care to limit its application, initially at least, to only those subdivisions having a considerable population, say cities of the first and second class, to counties and other units having a definite minimum population, etc.

[2] The fiscal year commonly begins on January 1, or July 1; for school districts it is sometimes provided that the fiscal year varies from that of other subdivisions. If uniform within the state, the fiscal year will facilitate the central control and uniform reporting by the state, and also the compilation of the federal statistics.

The fiscal year should be in accord with the tax

---

levying and collecting period. Taxes are levied for a definite time, usually a year, and the basis for the levy fixed a few months or weeks prior to the first date of payment. The fiscal year should begin with the first date of payment, or a short time before or after this date. Thus, the expenditures for the year will be concurrent with the major source of revenue to finance them. This condition simplifies the financial procedure, and, therefore, the budgetary procedure.

[3] It is the sense of the committee that the budget should present a complete plan of all the expenditures of the local government, of every nature,—such as current, capital, debt, local improvement, and special or trust. It is agreed, however, that this complete expenditure statement may not be feasible in all cases, but it should be outlined so far as possible. If it is deemed impossible, for example, to include all

budget shall set forth the anticipated income and other means of financing the proposed expenditures for the fiscal year.[4]

Section 5. The budget document. The budget document, setting forth the financial plan of the local government for the ensuing budget year, shall embrace three parts, the nature and contents of which shall be as follows:

Part I shall consist of a budget message prepared by the chief executive or other budget-making authority which shall outline the fiscal policy of the local government for the budget year, describing in connection therewith the important features of the budget plan; it shall also embrace a general budget summary setting forth the aggregate figures of the budget in such manner as to show the balanced relations between the total proposed expenditures and the total anticipated income and other means of financing the budget for the ensuing fiscal year, contrasted with the corresponding figures for the last completed fiscal year and the year in progress.[5] The

general budget summary shall be supported by explanatory schedules or statements, classifying the expenditures contained thereon by organization units, objects, and funds, and the income by organization units, sources, and funds.

Part II shall embrace the detailed budget estimates both of expenditures and revenues as provided for in section 6 of this act; it shall also include statements of the bonded indebtedness of the local government, showing the debt redemption requirements, the debt authorized and unissued, the condition of the sinking funds, and the borrowing capacity; in addition thereto, it shall contain any statements relative to the financial plan which the chief executive, or other budget-making authority, may deem desirable or which may be required by the legislative or other appropriating body.

Part III shall embrace complete drafts of the budget bills, that is bills required to give legal sanction to the financial plan when adopted by the legislative or other appropriating body. These bills should include an appropriation bill, authorizing by spending agencies and by funds all expenditures of the local government for the budget year, and such other bills as may be required to provide the income necessary to finance the budget.

---

special assessments, such as the projects initiated by the property owners, at least the portion of all special assessment work to be paid by the city should be included.

With the full operation of such a comprehensive budget, the consolidated report of the financial transactions of all kinds for any year would be definitely related to, and be comparable with, the budget plan for that year.

[4] The income side of the budget would include, in general, all those means of financing the classes of expenditures indicated in footnote 3, namely, taxes, special assessments, borrowings (long-term, exclusive of temporary), revenues of publicly owned and operated utilities and enterprises, moneys received from other governmental units, surpluses, and miscellaneous revenues.

[5] The form of the general budget summary should be such as to show the character of expenditures and the method of financing; that is, the expenditures should be divided as between current expenses, acquisition of properties, and

---

debt redemption, while the means of financing should be shown as surplus, revenues, borrowings for permanent improvements, and sales of properties (capital assets). It is desirable in many jurisdictions, on account of local legislation relative to funds, to show both expenditures and means of financing in parallel columns according to funds, or when the funds are too numerous, according to classes of funds, such as, general fund, special expense funds, loan funds, sinking funds, and trust funds. This information relative to funds may be shown either on the general budget summary or on the supporting schedules, preferably on the latter.

Section 6. Preparation of the budget.
At least sixty (60) days prior to the beginning of the fiscal year, all departments, offices, boards, and other spending agencies of each local government shall prepare and submit to the budget-making authority thereof estimates of their expenditure requirements and their estimated revenues for the forthcoming budget year, compared with the corresponding figures of the last completed fiscal year and the estimated figures of the year in progress. The expenditure estimates shall be classified to set forth the data by funds, organization units, character, and objects of expenditure; the organization units may be subclassified by functions and activities at the discretion of the budget-making authority.[6] The revenue estimates shall be classified so as to show the receipts by funds, organization units, and sources of income.[7]

The budget-making authority shall review the estimates, altering, revising, increasing or decreasing the items of said estimates as it shall deem necessary

in view of the needs of the various spending agencies and the probable income of the local government. Such authority shall then prepare a budget in the form required by the provisions of section 5 of this act, and it shall transmit this budget to the appropriating body of the local government at least thirty (30) days before the beginning of the fiscal year.

For the purpose of this act, the budget-making authority in cities having the mayor-council form of government shall be the mayor, in those having the commission-manager form of government shall be the manager, and in those having the commission form of government shall be the commissioner of finance; provided, however, that such authority in any of said cities may be the agency which shall by law or by charter be empowered to formulate the budget. The budget-making authority of any city government shall have the power to appoint or designate, in its discretion, an official, to be known as the budget officer or the budget director to supervise or perform the work of preparing the budget.[8] In each county, having an executive or administrative head of the government, said head shall be the budget-making authority; in each county, without an executive or administrative head, the board of commissioners (or supervisors) shall designate or appoint an officer as the budget-making authority or, in lieu thereof, one of its committees to act in the same capacity.[9] In each school district,

[6] The character classification makes a distinction between expenditures for current operating expenses and those for the acquisition of property. The classification by objects distinguishes the various services and things purchased by the local government.

Some members of the committee believe that the itemization of estimates should be by subfunctions or activities, as well as by departments or other strictly organization units, in order that the budget may be considered in terms of services to be undertaken; also that the expenditure estimates for each activity should be expressed, so far as possible, in terms of units of service to be performed, with the unit cost of same. Development of this idea, they believe, constitutes a most important feature of budget preparation.

[7] It is highly desirable that the budget information be prepared according to a uniform classification of accounts, both for revenues and for expenditures, as prescribed by the budget-making authority. A few states have already adopted such a classification for the use of the local governments within their jurisdictions.

[8] It is desirable that the larger local governments have such officers. Several cities now have budget directors, who not only assist in preparing and in executing the budget, but make investigations and recommendations in connection therewith. The importance of the budget-director of the national government is becoming universally recognized.

[9] If the board of commissioners (or supervisors)

having a board of education with independent fiscal powers, said board shall designate its chief administrative officer as the budget-making authority. In each village, township, or other district, with independent fiscal powers, the appropriating body shall designate some officer of the government to be the budget-making authority.[10] In every local government, the appropriating body shall be the council, commission, board of supervisors, or other board or body designated by law or by charter to perform the legislative or tax levying functions of the government.

Section 7. Budget hearings. Final action shall not be taken on the proposed budget in any local government until at least one public hearing has been held thereon after ten days' notice. It shall be the duty of the appropriating body to arrange for and hold such hearing. The budget, when submitted by the budget-making authority to the appropriating body, shall be published, advertised, or otherwise made available for public inspection at least ten (10) days prior to the date set for the hearing.

Section 8. Adoption of the budget and enactment of the budget bills. The appropriating body shall consider the budget as submitted to it by the budget-making authority of such government. Such body may revise, alter, increase, or decrease the items contained in the budget; provided, however, that when it shall increase the total proposed expenditures of the

---

designates an officer, he should be either the auditor or the clerk; if it designates one of its committees, then this committee should have the assistance of some officer, as the auditor or the clerk, in the preparation of the budget. In the large counties, a special budget officer may be appointed by the board to perform this function.

[10] It is desirable that this person should be the financial officer; however, one or more members of the legislative or appropriating body may serve in the capacity of budget-making authority.

budget, it shall also increase the total anticipated income, so that the total means of financing the budget shall, at least, equal in amount the aggregate proposed expenditures.

At least ten (10) days before the beginning of the fiscal year, the appropriating body shall adopt the budget and shall finally enact the appropriation bill and such other bills as may be required to make the budget legally effective. The several amounts specified in the appropriation bill as finally enacted shall be and become appropriated in the amounts and for the several departments, offices, boards, and other spending agencies of the local government for the fiscal year to which the budget applies. The income of the local government as estimated in the budget and as provided for by the tax-levying ordinance and other revenue and borrowing acts or ordinances, shall be and become applicable in the amounts and according to the funds specified in the budget for the purpose of meeting the expenditures authorized by the appropriation act or ordinance.

Within ten (10) days after final action has been taken on the budget bills by the appropriating body, it shall make public, by publication or otherwise, a summary statement which shall be in the form of the general budget summary provided for in section 5 of this act. Said statement shall show, in addition to the figures set forth in the general budget summary, the changes made by the appropriating body in the course of its review, revision and adoption of the budget. The appropriating body shall also make public, by publication or otherwise, at this time, the tax rate necessary or estimated to be necessary to finance the budget as adopted.

Section 9. Failure to make appropriations: amounts deemed appropriated. If at the termination of any fiscal year, the appropriations necessary for the support of the local government for the ensuing fiscal year shall not have been made, the several amounts appropriated in the last appropriation act or ordinance for the objects and purposes therein specified, so far as the same shall relate to the operation and maintenance expenses shall be deemed to be reappropriated for the several objects and purposes specified in said last appropriation ordinance; and until the appropriating body shall act in such behalf the treasurer or chief financial officer shall make the payments necessary for the support of the local government on the basis of the appropriations of the preceding fiscal year.

Section 10. **Form of the appropriations.** The appropriation bill, provided for in section 5 of this act, shall be drawn in such form as to authorize only lump sum appropriations to meet the expenditure needs of the various spending agencies of the local government. For the operation and maintenance expenses of each department, office, board, or other spending agency, there shall be a single appropriation, which shall be allotted as provided for in section 11 of this act before becoming available for expenditure. Appropriations for the acquisition of property shall be in such detail under each spending agency as the budget-making authority shall determine; provided, however, that such appropriations shall not be segregated into greater detail than the major classes, or projects, for which they are expendable.

Section 11. **Allotments.** Immediately before the beginning of the fiscal year, the budget-making authority of the local government shall require the head of each spending agency to submit a work program for the budget year, which program shall include all appropriations for operation and maintenance expenditures and for the acquisition of property, and it shall show the requested allotments of said appropriations for such spending agency by quarters for the entire year.[11] The budget-making authority shall review the requested allotments in the light of the work program of the spending agency concerned, and such authority shall, if it deems necessary, revise, alter or change such allotments before approving the same. The aggregate of such allotments shall not exceed the total appropriations available to said spending agency for the budget year. The budget-making authority shall transmit a copy of the approved allotments to the head of the spending agency concerned and also a copy to the controller, or other chief financial officer, of the local government. The controller, or other chief financial officer, shall authorize all expenditures to be made from the appropriations on the basis of such allotments, and not otherwise.

The head of any spending agency of the government, whenever he shall deem it necessary by reason of changed conditions, may revise the work program of his agency at the beginning of any quarter during the budget year and submit such revised program to the budget-making authority with his request for a revision of the allotments for the remaining quarters of the budget year. If, upon a reëxamination of the work program, the budget-making authority shall decide to grant the

[11] The proposed expenditures for the acquisition of property, such as land, buildings, new construction, and major equipment, should be set up in the work program separately from those for the operation and maintenance expenses of the spending agency. The appropriations for properties should be allotted by projects according to the quarterly periods of the budget year.

Several city managers require allotments by months, but it is thought that the quarterly basis is sufficient for purposes of administrative control.

request for a revision of the allotments, the same procedure, so far as it relates to review, approval, and control, shall be followed as in making the original allotments.

In order to provide funds for possible emergencies arising during the budget year in the operation and maintenance expenditures of the various spending agencies of the local government, the budget-making authority may require the head of each spending agency, in making the original allotments, to set aside at least 5 per cent of the total amount appropriated as a reserve. At any time during the budget year, this reserve, or any portion of it, may be returned to the appropriation to which it belongs and be added to any one or more of the allotments, provided the budget-making authority shall deem such action necessary, and shall notify the controller, or other chief financial officer, of such action; any unused portion thereof shall remain at the end of the budget period as an unexpended balance of appropriation.[12]

Section 12. When contracts and expenditures are prohibited. No officer, department, board, commission or other expending agency shall, during a fiscal year, expend or contract to be expended any money or incur any liability, or enter into any contract which, by its terms, involves the expenditure of money for any of the purposes for which provision is made in the appropriation ordinance in excess of the amounts appropriated in said ordinance, for such officer, department, board, commission or other expending

agency, or purpose, for such fiscal year. Any contract, verbal or written, made in violation of this section shall be null and void as to the local government, and no moneys belonging thereto shall be paid thereon; provided, however, that nothing herein contained shall prevent the making of contracts for governmental services for a period exceeding one year, but any contract so made shall be executory only for the amounts agreed to be paid for such services to be rendered in succeeding fiscal years.

Section 13. Transfer of appropriations. The appropriating body of any local government shall have the power to authorize the transfer within the same fund of any unencumbered appropriation balance or any portion thereof from one spending agency under its jurisdiction to another; provided, that such action shall be taken only on the recommendation of the budget-making authority, and only during the last two months of the fiscal year.

Section 14. Additional appropriations and temporary loans. The appropriating body may, during a fiscal year, make additional appropriations or increase existing appropriations to meet emergencies such as epidemics, floods, fires or other catastrophies, the funds therefor to be provided from unappropriated revenues, if any, or from temporary loans. Such temporary loans, when made, shall be approved by a two-thirds' vote of the legislative or appropriating body of the local government.

Such temporary loans shall be repaid at an annual rate equivalent to not less than two mills upon the assessed valuation of real property.[13]

[12] It is the opinion of the committee that very small local governments, spending, say, twenty thousand dollars or less each year, may get along without the allotment system. But for larger local governments, the majority of the committee feel that the allotment system should not be optional, if the most modern and effective method of budgetary control is to be followed.

[13] The tax levy of two mills herein provided is based upon the assumption that the legal basis of assessment of real property is 100 per cent of true or full cash value; for those states that have a legal basis of valuation other than 100 per

Section 15. State supervision. The budget-making authority shall, on or before the time of transmitting the budget to the appropriating body of the local government, transmit a copy thereof to the state officer (auditor, controller, or other officer charged with the supervision of local finances) who shall have power and whose duty it shall be to review the same with respect to the sufficiency of the appropriations for the payment of sinking fund requirements, payment of principal and interest on public debt, and payment of any deficit or overexpenditure from the preceding fiscal year or years. In the event that such state officer shall deem appropriations for any or all of said purposes to be insufficient, he shall certify to the appropriating body of the local government the amount whereby he deems it necessary to increase the appropriations for such purposes and it shall be the duty of said appropriating body to make such increases of appropriations, together with corresponding increases of revenues as required by section 8 of this act.[14]

Section 16. Construction of act. If any portion of this act shall be declared unconstitutional, the remainder shall remain in force, and the portion declared unconstitutional shall be exscinded.

Section 17. Former laws superseded. All acts and parts of acts, general or special, to the extent that they relate to the subject matter of this act, are superseded by this act; provided, however, that acts and proceedings heretofore done or taken by any local government or the voters thereof, or any board of officers thereof, pursuant to acts or parts of acts superseded by this act shall have the same force and effect as if done and taken pursuant to this act, and only subsequent proceedings shall be taken as provided in this act.

---

cent of true and full cash value, a reasonably prompt repayment of such loans would dictate a readjustment of the two-mill levy accordingly.

This section does not include provision for temporary loans in anticipation of revenues from taxation or for other purposes other than emergencies. It is believed that there should be definite regulations in other sections of the state laws governing the incurrence, evidences of, and payment of such temporary loans. It is the sense of the committee that this problem requires legislative consideration independent of budgetary procedure.

[14] The Model Bond Law submitted by the Committee of Municipal Borrowings of the National Municipal League contains in section 22 a provision for filing with the state auditor annually complete statements as to outstanding bonds, sinking funds, etc., and additional information prior to each separate bond issue. In states where similar functions are performed by some other state officer, the title of such officer should be inserted. In states where complete information of the nature just mentioned is not required to be filed with some state officer, this section may be omitted.

NATIONAL MUNICIPAL REVIEW

PUBLISHED MONTHLY BY THE

National Municipal League

VOL. XVII, No. 8   AUGUST, 1928   TOTAL No. 146

CONTENTS

EDITORIAL COMMENT...........................*Russell Forbes*...... 447

THE DEMOCRATIC PARTY IN CONNECTICUT..........*Lane W. Lancaster*.. 451

A MILLION SMALL HOUSES FOR GREAT BRITAIN......*Harlean James*..... 456

GRAND RAPIDS PROVES THAT FIRE PREVENTION PAYS *Fred H. Locke*...... 460

DEPRECIATION IN COMMERCIAL AND MUNICIPAL
ACCOUNTING..............................*Adrian M. Landman* 462

LONG TERM BUDGETING AND THE CITY PLAN.......*George B. Ford*..... 465

MINNEAPOLIS LOSES THROUGH ANTIQUE STREET
MAINTENANCE METHODS.....................*H. J. Miller*....... 469

PARTISANSHIP AND PARTIES IN GERMAN MUNICIPAL
GOVERNMENT..............................*Roger H. Wells*..... 473

DEPARTMENTS

I. Recent Books Reviewed.. 482

II. Governmental Research Association Notes................*Edited by Russell Forbes* 487

III. Notes and Events.....................................*Edited by Russell Forbes* 489

AUDITOR'S REPORT

NATIONAL MUNICIPAL LEAGUE

BALANCE SHEET AS AT MARCH 31, 1928

ASSETS

Cash in banks and on hand:	
Treasurer's account..	$2,255.02
Secretary's account..	272.17
Petty cash and stamps...	30.62
	2,557.81
United States Third Liberty Loan 4¼% Bonds.........................	600.00
Interest accrued on United States Third Liberty Loan 4¼% Bonds...	25.50
Furniture and fixtures, less depreciation...................................	596.00
	$3,779.31

LIABILITIES

Accounts payable and accrued salary...		$3,860.48
Portland Prize Fund...		600.00
		$4,460.00
Deficit:		
Balance as at March 31, 1927...	$223.00	
Add excess of expenditure over income for the year ended March 31, 1928.......	458.17	681.17
		$3,779.31

Contingent liabilities—None.

REVENUE ACCOUNT

FOR THE YEAR ENDED MARCH 31, 1928

Revenue—Dues:		
Annual..		$6,032.07
Sustaining..		3,280.50
Contributing..		725.00
		$10,037.57
Contributions...	$18,330.00	
Subscriptions to the REVIEW..	2,482.19	
Sale of REVIEW and other publications..	3,246.73	
Royalties...	102.98	
Services..	258.26	
Advertising...	455.70	
Baldwin Prize...	100.00	
Interest on Liberty Bonds—Portland prize...	25.50	
Interest on bank balances..	60.78	
		$35,099.71
Expenditure:		
Printing REVIEW...		$7,908.84
Salaries—officers...	$10,292.00	
Salaries—clerks...	6,920.11	
		17,212.11
Postage, telephone and telegraph...		2,072.92
Printing and stationery..		3,512.19
Traveling...		983.06
Rent..		1,995.60
Auditing..		200.00
Sundry supplies, books, etc..		591.83
Press clippings...		140.85
Royalties...		73.21
Prizes:		
Baldwin...	$100.00	
Portland..	25.00	
		125.00
Expenses of Meetings (net)...		220.27
Bank charges..		1.10
Miscellaneous expenses...		72.40
Refund on sales of REVIEW and periodicals..		39.54
Depreciation of furniture and fixtures..		66.21
Committee on Government of Metropolitan Areas:		
Stenographic Service...	$282.00	
Expenses..	60.75	
		342.75
		$35,557.88
Balance, being excess of expenditure over income..................................		$458.17

PEAT, MARWICK, MITCHELL & Co., *Auditors.*

40 Exchange Place, New York, May 26, 1928.

NATIONAL
MUNICIPAL REVIEW

VOL. XVII, No. 8   AUGUST, 1928   TOTAL No. 146

EDITORIAL COMMENT

Baldwin Prize Awards The committee on award of the annual Baldwin Prize, consisting of Professor O. C. Hormell of Bowdoin College, Professor George C. Kerwin of the University of Chicago, and Professor Lane W. Lancaster of Wesleyan University, has unanimously granted the first prize to Thomas Arnold McGovern of Harvard College, Class of 1929. The names, addresses, and titles of the three contestants having the highest rank are as follows:

First—Thomas Arnold McGovern, Harvard College 1929, for essay on "Extra Territorial Powers of City Planning Commissions." Address: 27 Moyston Street, Schenectady, New York.

Second—Haig Gregory Abdian, Harvard College, for essay on "Methods of Measuring the Effectiveness of Municipal Government." Address: 19 Menotomy Road, Arlington, Massachusetts.

Third—Krynp Nagelkirk, University of Michigan, for essay on "Extra Territorial Powers of City Planning Commissions." Address: Moline, Michigan.

*

City Government Without General Tax Levy The city of Pawhuska, Oklahoma, has for over two years been operating without a general

tax levy for current administration. A tax is levied on general property for retirement of bonded indebtedness as required by state law in Oklahoma; the current operating costs of the city, however, are financed largely from the revenues of municipally owned and operated utilities. The city of Pawhuska operates its own gas, water and electric light systems, a municipal hospital, and a cemetery, all of which are revenue-producing. This method of finance has not been made possible through neglect of public improvements, since the city bears the reputation of being one of the best paved small towns in the state. However, this system seems to be an indirect form of taxation, for in the long run the taxpayer pays, whether in the form of public utilities charges or through general property taxes.

*

San Francisco Finally Adopts Hetch Hetchy Water Supply Project In May the voters of San Francisco finally approved the Hetch Hetchy water supply project and the plan to purchase the Spring Valley water distribution system. This plan had been submitted to referendum on several previous occasions, but until the recent election had failed to obtain the necessary two-thirds majority. Its final victory ended a long and bitter controversy in San Francisco. Newspaper and popular support for the project was secured through a radical change in the plan of financing the project. According to the present plan the project will be financed largely by the pay-as-you-go method. The administration of the system is also to be taken out of local politics and will be placed in the hands of a public utilities commission.

The Hetch Hetchy project will not be completed for four or five years. Its total cost will approximate one hundred and fifty million dollars. A fuller report will be presented in a later issue of the REVIEW.

*

Virginia Revises   On June 19 the vot-
State Constitution   ers of Virginia ap-
proved by an overwhelming majority the proposed amendments to the constitution of that state as a further step in Governor Byrd's program for reorganization of the state government. Elected two and a half years ago on a platform pledged to state reorganization, Governor Byrd has been conspicuously successful in securing popular approval of his reforms. The New York Bureau of Municipal Research surveyed the state government and submitted a report recommending radical revisions. The General Assembly of Virginia enacted laws carrying out most of the recommendations of the survey. It was found, however, that a thoroughgoing reorganization was impossible without constitutional changes.

The state legislative enactments permitted the Governor to appoint the heads of all the state's twelve departments except three—the commissioner of agriculture, the superintendent of public instruction, and the state treasurer. By the constitutional amendments ratified in June these three offices will be appointive rather than

elective until 1932, after which the General Assembly will have power to provide by law for any method of selection it may choose. The state attorney general is, however, still an elective official. The provision for a short ballot was the chief center of controversy in the campaign preceding the recent referendum.

An early issue of the REVIEW will contain an article appraising the results of the referendum more in detail.

*

A Career in   Antioch College at
Public Service   Yellow Springs, Ohio,
is making a praiseworthy effort to train college graduates for some worthwhile careers. In a recent bulletin, Arthur E. Morgan, president, has given a thought-provoking discussion of the value of a career in the public service and of the importance of careful preparation and training for it. His comments are reprinted in full below. The Editor would welcome expressions of opinion on this subject in which all our readers are interested.

"How should I as a young man seek a career as a public executive? I should avoid an elective office, for the public is uninformed and capricious, politicians often control votes, my choice of locations would be restricted by the requirement of previous legal residence, and my chief ability would have to be that of getting elected. I should, instead, seek a field where good work would create opportunity, where I could achieve recognized professional standing, and where I should be most free from arbitrary chance or political fate.

"I should not want to be simply a routine administrator, but should want a part in defining and executing public policies. If I had the native ability I should want in time to contribute to the theory and practice of government. My job should be my laboratory, as well as my day's work.

"I believe that the new profession of city manager furnishes such opportunities. Let me describe the practical steps I might take toward a career in that field.

TRAINING

"My college program, in addition to a general liberal education such as that required at Antioch for all professional preparation, would combine engineering, business, economics, and government. In my part-time work under the Antioch program I should undertake to become acquainted with the spirit and attitude of labor; I should want experience on public and private construction, and later with administrative methods in business and industry. As part of my extra-curricular activities at college I should desire some share in the college government, which at Antioch includes both students and faculty, to try my hand there at leadership and at the development of government methods.

"In my senior college year I should make a study of city managers, and should persuade one of the best to employ me, preferably as a personal assistant. There I should work, possibly changing positions to get the outlook of more than one man, until I could find or make an opportunity to become manager of a small municipality.

RESEARCH

"During my college course, and throughout my life, I should make a study of government. I should collect the charters of all cities operating under the city manager plan, and typical charters under other plans. I should analyze every one, classify the different methods by which various functions are exercised, and try to learn which methods were best in practice.

"I should study European municipal government, especially in North Europe, thoroughly acquainting myself with the more significant methods. Upon college graduation, if possible, and occasionally thereafter, I should visit Europe, first establishing acquaintances by correspondence, to study municipal government. I should try to get behind the scenes in many cities at home and abroad to see what forces actually control. At all times I should strive to live close to the realities of government and of human nature. I should study the theory of municipal government and of government in general, and, especially by reading cases and decisions, acquaint myself with municipal law.

PUBLICITY

"My program should include consistent publicity, in accord with sound ethical standards. In that publicity I should endeavor to make my best possible contribution to my chosen profession and to the theory and practice of government, and I should expect it to help provide me with opportunities commensurate with my ability. To prepare to do exceptionally good work, and then to lack opportunity, is elemental waste.

"From my college days I should work at building an ideal municipal charter. In time I should write a book on municipal government, to serve as a handbook and guide to municipal officers. I should discuss developments of municipal government in lectures and magazine articles. These would include technical contributions to my profession as well as efforts to promote popular understanding of government.

"I should perhaps present the well-managed municipality as a type of government applicable to counties and states. In my own state I might secure legislation making possible county government on the same plan.

PROGRESS

"If I were wise I should unequivocally maintain independence and integrity as my chief practical assets. I should seek opportunity to draft the charter of a small city, and to be manager under it. After perhaps five years I should move, in one or two steps, to a carefully selected city large enough to serve as a type for American municipal government, and there I should settle down to do my life work.

"I should continually search for promising young men and women as assistants and understudies. My whole organization would go to school to me, that every one might master the theory and practice of municipal government and of his own job. My whole city would go to school to me, too.

"Sometime after fifty, I might prefer to teach municipal government in a university, or be adviser to municipalities. Then, possessing independence, maturity, and experience, I should not avoid elective office as city director or commissioner.

"And sometimes I should go fishing.

APOLOGIA

"An idle dream? Yet, I have done most of these things in a comparable field. As chief engineer of reclamation, drainage, and flood-control districts, which are municipalities created for special purposes, I have found these steps practical and necessary. Serving as executive in practical charge, I have studied the water-control laws of America and Europe, have developed approximately ideal codes, have had them enacted into law in several states, and have operated under them.

"I have found the obstacles to straightforward, effective administration not to be insurmountable. I am of the opinion from my own experience that primitive political methods can be changed, and that well-planned careers, such as I have described, can be effective."

✱

The Relation of Building Height to Street Traffic The article by Professor Herbert D. Simpson in the July number on this subject stimulated the New York *Times* to editorial comment on June 11. While commending Professor Simpson for his fearlessness in entering this battleground, the *Times* predicts that he will be subject to great criticism from both proponents and opponents of the modern skyscraper. "A man of daring," says the *Times*, "is Herbert D. Simpson, Associate Professor of Economics at Northwestern University. Is there any more cruel contest than that waged between the friends and foes of the skyscraper? Yet down between the opposing hosts rides this fearless professor, seeking to impose peace by the strong arm of mathematics. 'Why so hot, my friends?' he says in effect, to Messrs. Curran, Corbett, Adams and all the other warriors who do battle over our congested streets. 'I have a simple little formula that will resolve all your disputations.' He begins his article on 'The Relation of Building Height to Street Traffic' in the NATIONAL MUNICIPAL REVIEW with the premise that in the 'pure type of Main Street city,' with all the business located on one street and all the traffic to and from this business traversing that one street, 'no one would be guilty of supposing that the building height could have any effect on pedestrian traffic one way or the other.'

"However that may be, the situation becomes much more complicated in the ordinary American city laid out in rectangular blocks. It is this problem that Mr. Simpson seeks to analyze. He presents a number of charts on which typical pedestrians are tracked to their lairs, and a number of equations showing that what that typical pedestrian does when he walks around the corner is not nearly so simple as he thinks. The professor comes finally to the conclusion that if a equals the amount of traffic with a given building height, b the factor of increase in building height, and x the amount of traffic with the increased building height, then x equals a multiplied by the square root of b. In other words, pedestrian traffic will vary not in proportion to the two different heights, but in proportion to their square roots. Much the same reasoning would apply to vehicular traffic. If Mr. Simpson is correct, traffic congestion resulting from a nine-story building will never be more than three times as great as traffic congestion caused by a one-story building.

"With the most pacific intentions in the world, Mr. Simpson may find himself in the proverbial position of the bystander who interferes in a dog fight. Both sides may turn and rend him. Will the defenders of the skyscraper concede that it has as much effect on congestion? Will its critics agree that the effect is not greater? Even if they accept the mathematics of the theoretical case, they may argue that as a practical matter there comes a point where the evil effects of congestion increase in geometrical progression. Mr. Simpson suggests wider streets. What if you have already stretched them to the limit? It is to be feared that he has brought to the controversy not peace but a sword."

THE DEMOCRATIC PARTY IN CONNECTICUT

BY LANE W. LANCASTER

Wesleyan University

The party is down but not quite out. Is there any hope for it?

SOME time ago the writer in the course of a conversation with a member of the Democratic State Central Committee of Connecticut asked why it was that the party remained strong in numbers when there was so little sustenance to reward its loyalty. "Well, you see, Professor," he said (he is the very prototype of the county chairman of political literature), "you know some folks are just dyed-in-the-wool Methodists; it's just the same way with Connecticut Democrats." This answer, though a platitude perhaps, is a real answer. The continued existence of the Democratic party in the state can certainly not be explained on any easy theory to the effect that men belong to parties for what they or their friends get out of it. In Connecticut, if they are Democrats they get little or nothing out of it.

DEMOCRATIC PARTY ELIMINATED FROM STATE AFFAIRS

Since 1888 the Democratic party has controlled the executive department of the state government for but six years —1893–1895 and 1911–1915. In the legislative session of 1891 it had a majority in the state senate, and in 1893 its membership in that body was equal to that of the Republicans. But —owing largely to the rotten borough system—it has only once come close to having a majority in the lower house, and even when it elected Simeon E. Baldwin governor in 1910 and 1912 he had to deal with a legislature which

was safely Republican. The Progressive program was not a sufficiently divisive force to weaken the normal Republican strength, drawn as it is very largely from the smaller communities, some of which are six and seven to one Republican. From 1895 to 1909 there were no Democrats from Connecticut in the national house of representatives, and never more than one of the five seats has been held by a Democrat except in the epochal year 1912, when the whole Connecticut delegation was Democratic. And the last Democratic United States senator from the state retired in 1879!

So far as the control of appointive offices is concerned the situation is no more satisfactory. Judicial posts are almost entirely in the hands of the Republicans. One of the five supreme court justices is a Democrat and two of the thirteen superior court judges. All of the judges of the six common pleas courts are Republicans. The judges and assistant judges of the fifty-four city, town, and borough courts are appointed by the general assembly, and are in nearly all cases Republicans. As to the staffs of these various tribunals, almost the same thing may be said. The eight state's attorneys are appointed by the superior court. Seven are at present Republicans. Such officials as coroners, clerks, public defenders, probation officers and messengers, though theoretically selected without reference to political affiliation, are nevertheless usually supporters of

451

the dominant party. One hundred and fifteen probate judges are elected by the people in special probate districts created by special act of the legislature. Since these districts in many cases coincide with town lines, the probate bench reflects pretty accurately the party complexion of the legislature.

County government is of relatively little importance in Connecticut, but every little bit helps in maintaining a party organization. The administration of the few purely county functions (weights and measures, maintenance of the county jail, etc.) is in the hands of the county commissioners in each county. The commissioners, three in number, are appointed by the legislature, on recommendation of the senators and representatives from each of the eight counties in the state. Since 271 of the 297 members of the present legislature are Republicans and since this is about the normal situation in late years, it is not hard to see that a Democratic county commissioner is a rare, if not extinct, mammal. The eight sheriffs are elected by the voters in the various counties and all are at present Republicans. Deputy sheriffs number one hundred and sixteen and are appointed by the sheriffs who name also the jailers and deputy jailers. In addition to these, clerks of the superior court are listed as county officers as are court stenographers, county treasurers, medical examiners and county health officers.

In the administrative branch of the state government, Republicans naturally have a preferred position. Little if any provision is made in the law for minority representation on state boards and commissions, and while some of these are bi-partisan in their composition this is not the rule, at least in the case of the more important ones. Democrats are to be found in considerable numbers on the various boards administering locally the different state institutions, but as such institutions are traditionally administered in a non-partisan way, membership on such boards can scarcely be counted as a substantial asset to either party.

Not much sustenance for Democrats in this!

SOME COMFORT FROM CONTROL OF CITY GOVERNMENTS

From the point of view of the minority party the bright spots in the picture are in the larger towns and cities. In some of these the Democrats occasionally have a chance to capture the administration, and where they are not in a position to win elections they are in too large a minority to be neglected entirely in the distribution of "plums." In some of these communities there would seem to be a tacit understanding by which the minority party gets a share of the good things of public life. Occasionally, even, in the case of elective offices, the minority candidate if popular is endorsed by the majority caucus. From the point of view of the party's welfare, however, it would be better if the victors made a clean sweep of the offices. The morale of the Democrats is undoubtedly weakened by the willingness of their leaders to enter into agreements for these crumbs of patronage. This seems to have been in the mind of a prominent leader when he wrote that "except in rare instances when a Democrat is appointed to office he ceases to be of any value to the Democratic party."

The offices of justice of the peace and constable are also probably of some slight importance in holding the party together. The number of these functionaries varies with the population, but there are hundreds in the whole state divided between the two parties.

Nomination, which is made by the town committee (theoretically by the party caucus), is equivalent to election and it is probably true that a judicious distribution of these petty distinctions with regard to racial origin and social status has some effect in keeping the rank and file in line. So far as the really important town and city offices are concerned, about nine-tenths are now in the hands of the Republicans. At the present time, however, the city governments of Norwich, Waterbury, Middletown, Danbury, Derby and Ansonia are Democratic, while Hartford and New Haven have large Democratic minorities and occasionally get enough votes to elect an administration.

CAUSES OF DEMOCRATS' ECLIPSE

On the whole the picture is not a pleasant one for Democrats. Nor, it must be confessed, a hopeful one. There was a time when the Democracy was at least a respectable minority. Its present low estate may be ascribed to a number of causes. In the minds of many of the older leaders the party has not yet recovered from the effects of the Bryan candidacy in 1896. They speak ruefully of the "Bryan blight." Prior to the early nineties the party does not seem to have lain under the cloud of suspicion with which it is now looked upon by the prosperous and conventionally respectable classes. Democrats seem to have been entirely "respectable" before 1896, but the Bryan view of the monetary question not only split the party at the time but drove from it many of the men who, under conditions as they exist in Connecticut, were well fitted to be popular leaders. Some of the staunchest Republican magnates in Connecticut towns today are the sons and grandsons of men who were Democratic mayors and legislators in pre-Bryan days. In some cases even those who retained the political allegiance of their fathers have formed connections with manufacturing and commercial interests devoted to the Republican doctrine of the tariff, and find themselves prevented from taking an active part in Democratic politics.

In the second place, the party suffers from the fact that it is not "respectable" in the conventional sense of that term. The feudal magnates who have ruled Connecticut society in church and state since the days of the Wolcotts, the Dwights, the Ellsworths and the Trumbulls, are today Republican almost to a man. This group which, it must be confessed, is animated by a high sense of its obligation to the public as members of a ruling caste, and has contributed not a little to the admitted excellence of state administration, sets the pace politically for the gentry. These latter, though not considered as entitled as of right to patents in this modern peerage, form strong centers of influence in nearly every community—an influence which is almost always Republican. On the other hand, the Democratic party, rightly or wrongly, is looked upon by the "respectable" classes as the party of turbulence and disorder. The presence in its ranks of large numbers of voters of foreign extraction, chiefly Irish, Polish and Italian, exposes it to much criticism from the "better element" which its conduct in recent years has done little to disarm.[1] The party has no press and the few so-called independent newspapers in the state are seldom in a position to take a critical attitude

[1] Among the thirty-five male members of the State Central Committee the following names occur: McKone, Barrett, Conroy, Nolan, Kennedy, Mangan, Keyes, Keegan (2), FitzGerald, Maloney, Gallagher, Crary, Lawlor, Kelly, Cornell, Dunigan, McNulty, Connery, Walsh, Murphy, Driscoll, Sullivan, Fagan.

towards Republicans in office. Democratic administrations in such cities as Hartford, New Haven and Waterbury have been freely charged with extravagance and financial mismanagement in the country press. And to the Connecticut Yankee of the small town, making his living by truck gardening, wood-cutting and dairying, extravagance comes close to being at the head of human iniquities.

POOR STRATEGY OF MINORITY

The strategy of the Democratic organization is also largely to blame for the present plight of the party. There are no direct primaries in Connecticut and nominations are still conducted under party rules with some slight regulation by law. The direction of the party in the state at large is in the hands of the state central committee, composed of one man and one woman from each of the thirty-five state senatorial districts. The activity of the committee is confined largely to the conduct of the state campaign although it usually takes a hand in elections in large cities. It interferes little in local affairs although occasionally it furnishes speakers and money (if any is available) to a town committee where it seems that a Democratic victory might be of strategic importance. In local affairs the party is largely controlled by the town chairmen who are chosen by the town committees.

It cannot be denied that the party is weakened by the fact that its official leaders, both in the state at large and in some of the towns, do not in all cases have the confidence of the rank and file. There are, for example, many who believe that the State Central Committee is managed by the New Haven members in their own interests with a view to securing the spoils of office in the metropolis. Moreover, there are charges of unnatural alliances

for personal gain between the state leaders and the Republican state boss. Such charges cannot, of course, be easily proved, but the fact that they are widely believed is as important in its effect on party solidarity as if they were demonstrated.

In order for Democrats to win in any large way it is necessary always, not only to get out the full party strength, but also to attract the independent voters and win over Republicans. These rather obvious facts have been persistently neglected. No serious attempt seems to have been made in recent years, either by the choice of candidates or in the party platforms to give the voter any reason to think seriously of the claims of the party. There are many able men in the party, but they are too rarely called upon to seek office. Among the "better element" the impression is widely current that the party is made up of "boodlers," "rough-necks" and spoilsmen, and that the occasional able and upright candidate is on the ticket mainly for window-dressing. This sort of thing is, of course, an old trick of all parties, but it is an incredibly foolish one in the minority party in Connecticut—where, for purposes of winning elections, at least, candidates and principles must both be, as it was urged of Caesar's wife, beyond reproach. In the last state convention it was only with the greatest difficulty that the committee on resolutions was prevented from adopting a "wringing wet" platform. And this in a state where the dominant party, after almost forty years of uninterrupted power, holds all the important offices, controls the press, and is officially dry!

In state affairs the party in spite of its small numerical strength might play the rôle of critic respectably under intelligent and public-spirited leadership. During the last campaign the party candidates charged the Republican officeholders with extravagance, but the figures produced to substantiate the charge were totally inadequate. The Republicans countered with figures showing that the state was out of debt and living within its current income by following a pay-as-you-go policy. To an amateur politician with no axe to grind it seemed possible to find weaknesses in the pay-as-you-go plan, given the time and money necessary to make a thorough investigation of state administration. But money is not forthcoming for such "theoretical" purposes which, apparently, if indeed they ever occur to the party leaders, are not considered as "practical politics." Some slight attempt was also made in the last campaign to make the state's policy towards the power interests an issue, but since no Democrat was discovered who knew anything about the subject, this came to nothing. In the 1927 session of the legislature the minority attempted to secure an investigation of the whole question, but naturally without success. It is believed in some quarters that the Republican state boss, who is personally interested in the electrical industry, is making use of his political position to alienate the water power resources of the state. This is quite possibly true, but it requires something more than lung-power to substantiate it.

THE FUTURE

In spite of its shortcomings, however, the party hangs together and, where it can pool its strength as in state-wide elections, it has in recent years cast from 30 to 45 per cent of the total vote. It may even have a future. But if it does, certain changes seem to be necessary. First of all, party enthusiasm and party harmony demand some change in the directing committee of the party. The members complained against may be more sinned against than sinning, but many ordinary Democrats don't believe it. Moreover, in one way or another the party must go out of its way to be "respectable." No matter how economic and industrial changes may increase the numbers of those who lean towards its policies, it will for long have to contend against the deep-seated conservatism of the "back country" voter, who has obediently taken his cue for so long from the squirearchy. Such changes at the top of the Democratic organization as would restore party confidence in its leadership and encourage a less sharply adverse public attitude towards the party would do much to improve its position. Moreover a more conciliatory and less purely obstructionist attitude of Democrats in office would help in this direction. Too often the minority in the legislature has been prone to drag partisanship in where it obviously did not belong, and to oppose measures for no apparent reason except to "let people know we're on the job." Finally, though funds are not plentiful a comparatively slight sum set aside for research would place the party in a position to be an effective opposition. As one who belongs to the so-called "better element" and who has also been "on the inside" far enough to see some of the wheels go around, the writer feels that it is only by some such settled policy that what the convention orators sonorously (and erroneously, no doubt) call "the party of Jefferson," can become other than what it is now—a political Lazarus under the table of the Republican Dives.

A MILLION SMALL HOUSES FOR GREAT BRITAIN

BY HARLEAN JAMES

Executive Secretary, American Civic Association

A million new houses erected under government subsidy have brought heavy financial burdens to taxpayers but may be cheap protection against social revolution. :: :: :: :: :: :: ::

IN 1895 Dr. Albert Shaw in a substantial volume entitled "Municipal Government in Great Britain" outlined the causes which led to the increase in urban population, already in evidence at that time and, in both England and America, showing new gains at each successive census. He refused to be pessimistic over the apparently threatening outlook. Naturally the end is not yet. Much remains to be accomplished. But no one can deny that, as Dr. Shaw predicted, *collective effort* to provide adequate living and working conditions for all the people in the cities of England and the United States *has met* with encouraging success. Slums still exist, but they are distinct anachronisms. Urban death rates *have* fallen. Longevity *has* increased. Municipal officials on both sides of the Atlantic seek to provide more and better schools, larger and more scientifically laid-out open spaces, better means of circulation, adequate water, sewage, gas, electric light and power utilities and generally to increase the comfort of city living. With certain deplorable reservations homes are increasingly convenient and sanitary. But in 1928 as in 1895 the United States has much to learn from English cities. Not necessarily by slavish copy, but assuredly by understanding of actual accomplishment and application of policies to fit existing conditions, may American cities profit by worthy English examples.

REALIZATIONS OF TODAY

In England as in America the radius for residential sections attached by bonds of transportation to urban centers of employment has constantly widened. In England as in America, too, the satellite industrial cities are distributing the population over vast metropolitan regions. But England has the proud distinction of having invented the self-contained Garden City. The official housing and town planning schemes of the last decade, under various forms of national and local governmental subsidy, have been realized on a scale unprecedented in the history of any country, and they bear the distinct impress of the garden-city movement in street layout and in actual cultivation of gardens.

HOUSING AND TOWN PLANNING

Housing and town planning in Great Britain are of special interest to citizens of the United States because of the tremendous program undertaken immediately after the war. While the emergency undoubtedly made it possible to pass legislation which otherwise might not have been undertaken it must be realized at the outset that:

1. The accumulation of congestion and overcrowding in British cities before the war constituted a recognized

problem in itself. The cessation of building during the five years of the war only intensified the need for housing.

2. The long and successful experience of British cities in ownership and operation of public utilities made government housing acceptable to the people and to the public authorities.

3. The menace of unemployment and social disintegration made government subsidies justifiable investments in citizenship and civic stability.

4. The accustomed centralized authority of the ministry of health (formerly local government Board) provided a machinery for parliamentary action which would apply uniformly to all local communities of any class.

5. The long series of laws affecting housing, public health and town planning enacted during the half century before the war paved the way for the laws of the last decade.

As early as 1843 the Chadwick Report on the Sanitary Conditions of the Laboring Classes of Great Britain led to voluntary efforts to improve housing conditions and in 1851 the Shaftsbury Act authorized local authorities to provide lodging houses for the working classes. Various legislation which, according to Colonel Freemantle, "gradually accustomed the State to apply its powers in aid of housing where private enterprise could not compete," culminated in the Housing of the Working Classes Act of 1890 which was designed to clear insanitary areas. In the forty years preceding the war, over ten million dollars had been expended by the local authorities in London alone to clear about a hundred acres which had housed nearly fifty thousand persons. But in 1911 London still had nearly 25,000 admittedly insanitary houses.

Perhaps the most far-reaching constructive measure before the war was the Housing and Town Planning Act of 1890 under which power was given to the London County Council, to the boroughs, urban and district councils, subject to the approval of the local government board, to make town plans for all of their areas not yet built upon and to join with neighboring authorities for joint plans. English town planning has been characterized by the control of unoccupied areas which gives direction to future growth. It is under the provisions of the Act of 1909 that the present ministry of health is authorized to prescribe general rules and regulations for the planning of all local communities.

After the war this act was supplemented by the Housing and Town Planning Act of 1919 which made it compulsory for every urban authority of a population over 20,000 to submit a scheme to the board by the first of January 1926, a date extended by the Housing Act of 1923 to January 1, 1929. Under this act, as soon as the local authority has defined the area to be planned, every building or development must conform to the authority's requirements if they are to be protected against uncompensated demolition or other interference with the scheme. A preliminary statement covering width and direction of roads, building lines, open spaces, rules controling height and bulk of buildings and *character* or *use* zoning. The scheme is approved, modified or disapproved only after a public local inquiry or hearings.

The local authorities are given great freedom, but pressure is exerted to make them act and advice is given them to keep them in line with approved town planning practice. The *character* zoning of England is somewhat similar to the *use* zoning of the United States but its administration is quite different from the American machinery.

PLANS FOR THREE MILLION ACRES

Up to March 1928, planning schemes for 3,225,830 acres of land had been inaugurated. While plans for only 37,453 acres had progressed through all stages and received final approval, it must be remembered that intelligent and detailed planning is a technical, laborious and lengthy process. There is no reason to suppose that the entire area exceeding three million acres now being planned will not ultimately reach the stage of being approved by the Ministry of Health.

A MILLION HOUSES

From the time of the Public Health Act of 1895 a movement was begun which was continued in the Housing Acts of 1890 and 1909 by which local authorities were given definite powers of inspection, of demanding improvement, of declaring a building unfit for habitation and closing it. Moreover the local rate payers might complain to the central authority and the ministry was given power to force action on negligent local authorities. From the time of the Local Government Act of 1888, the tendency has been to delegate increasing authority to local officials but to depend on the central authority to lay down general principles for guidance and, if necessary, to enforce vigorous action, in case of neglect by the local authorities.

Before the close of the war an earnest effort was made to stimulate housing but it was not until the Housing Law of 1919, followed by the laws of 1923 and 1924, that building on a large scale was undertaken. Under the Addison Acts of 1919, local authorities were bidden to make every possible use of all existing buildings and in the meantime the government undertook to meet from the treasury the deficit in housing schemes, the grants to be paid over a period usually of sixty years on houses and eighty years on land. The local authorities were limited by the law in their liability.

Over two hundred thousand houses were actually built under the two Addison Acts. The objective had been five hundred thousand houses in five years. The money was spent by the local authorities, but with the pressure for speed and no responsibility for the total cost, there was little incentive for economy on their part, and with the untrammeled working of the law of supply and demand on materials and labor, costs mounted to the breaking point. It was estimated in 1927 that the annual cost to the government would run about seven million pounds or about forty-one pounds per house. The local cost to the rates would come to about five pounds per house. The tenant, therefore, according to Colonel Freemantle, is dependent on public charity at the rate of forty-six pounds a year.

By the Housing Acts of 1923 and 1924 the central authority granted *fixed sums* and paid them over to the local authorities so that there was an incentive for economy. Greater responsibility and consequently greater freedom of action fell on the local authorities. Baths were required in the houses. Rents could be determined by them. Houses might be sold by them, with the minister's consent. The minister might contribute up to half the estimated average annual loss toward slum clearances.

The net result on March 1, 1928, as shown in the April issue of *Garden Cities and Town Planning*, was that 789,580 houses under the three principal acts have actually been completed in addition to 230,690 subsidized houses built by private enterprise, making a total of 1,020,270 completed houses.

DECREASING COSTS

The average costs steadily decreased. By May of 1927 the cost for some 6,000 non-parlor houses was 396 pounds and for over 1,000 parlor houses 475 pounds. By February of 1928 these costs had decreased to 356 pounds for 3,600 non-parlor houses and 430 pounds for 750 parlor houses.

JUSTIFICATION

If industry and agriculture could have been reorganized promptly on a productive basis, with well-paid, self-respecting employees housed in sanitary quarters built by private enterprise, providing a decent standard of living, no doubt the solution of the whole problem would have been placed on a sounder basis. But it must be remembered that the disorganized industrial situation, the demoralizing unemployment, and the hopeless housing congestion which followed the war were responsible for a vicious circle of discouragement, discontent and incipient revolution on the part of the unfortunate victims of forces far beyond easy understanding and control.

In spite of the enormous burden on the central and local governments for more than two generations to come, the benefit of these houses, in the employment which they furnished, in the living conditions which they provided, and in the hopeful psychology that *something was being done to mitigate the sad lot of the unfortunate*, are incalculable. Great Britain was facing a crisis. In the decade since the war she has produced attractive, sanitary houses, with access to light and air, surrounded by gardens in suburbs and subdivisions laid out in many cases on modern city planning principles. She has set up and operated planning regulations and control which in the coming century may save to the local authorities sums of money which will offset the enormous cost of housing subsidies.

If Great Britain's housing program, which has been so severely attacked in the United States by those who saw only the financial burden on the central government and the local rate payers extending over more than half a century, did in fact, as many believe, prevent industrial and possibly political turmoil, the price may not be excessive. At any rate no one who has seen the slums of Manchester and Glasgow can regret that, by any means, at any cost, Great Britain has managed in the scant ten years since the close of the war, to plan, lay out, build and people over a million small houses which probably accommodate three or four million of the least fortunate of her citizens.

After all, the expenditure may be considered in the light of a long-range, sure-fire investment in good citizenship which promises dynamic returns to the industrial and political stability of England.

GRAND RAPIDS PROVES THAT FIRE PREVENTION PAYS

BY FRED H. LOCKE
City Manager

Through united community activity Grand Rapids wins the prize for the best work in fire prevention. Fire losses were reduced to $1.72 per capita. :: :: :: :: :: :: :: :: :: ::

AN effective fire prevention campaign will pay any city a larger dividend in the preservation of lives and property values than almost any other activity in which a city can engage.

In Grand Rapids, the fire division of the department of public safety is performing the dual function of fire extinguishment and fire prevention. Her citizens were justly proud when in 1927 she was awarded first honors of cities from 100,000 to 500,000 population for the best record in fire prevention work during the year in a contest conducted by the National Chamber of Commerce. We accept this honor with gratitude and while we hope to be equally fortunate another year, we are glad to set forth the methods used to accomplish this result for whatever benefit other cities may be able to gain from our experience.

For several years, our firemen had been making thousands of inspections of residences and business houses annually. We had been participating in National Fire Prevention Week by conducting special parades and by talks in schools and before civic bodies. But in spite of this, our annual fire loss had gradually climbed until it had reached the staggering figure of $9.18 per capita.

A plan originating with the assistant fire marshal, Fred Higgins, who heads the fire prevention work for the division, was then proposed for an all year around fire prevention campaign. The local Safety Council was asked to sponsor this campaign, which they gladly did. It involved the coöperation of the various public utilities and the large business organizations of the city. These were divided into groups such as furniture manufacturers, metal workers, coal dealers, milk dealers, bankers, and so on, until we had a group for each two weeks in the year. These groups, at their own expense, put messages into the pay envelopes of all their employees, placed selected posters in conspicuous places and upon their trucks and wagons, and displayed fire prevention messages.

The public utility companies put messages on their bills to the consumers. The street railway carried large posters on their street cars. Milk dealers placed messages on the bottle caps. During the shopping season, the insurance agencies arranged with many merchants to place fire prevention messages in every package leaving their stores. The local newspapers gave freely of their space, and prior to the Christmas season, published notices to be careful with Christmas trees and refrain from using candles.

SCHOOL CHILDREN AND BOY SCOUTS HELP

The school children were supplied with pamphlets showing fire loss experiences and were requested by the teacher to take the pamphlet home to their parents to read, and report to the teacher that this was done, and also to report the location of the fire alarm box nearest to their homes.

A large board was equipped with a fire alarm box and all the appliances electrically connected so that when the box was pulled, it showed how the fire alarm office was notified of a fire and its location. This board was taken by two firemen into every school room and the children were taught how to pull a box.

The sidewalks were stenciled at street corners with the words "Prevent Fire." Nearly all the large factories had these two words stenciled on the walls in front of work benches, posts, and stairways, and any other place where such a sign could be used to act as a constant reminder to all in the building. This plan was put into effect in November, 1924, and has been carried on with a few minor changes since that date.

The local Boy Scout organization has been interested in fire prevention and they have organized into what we term "The Block Plan." We have twelve fire districts with a fire station in each. These boys are assigned to districts according to their troop locations and are instructed in their duties by the officers and men at their respective fire stations. The boy is taken by a fireman and introduced to a few of the people living in the block. He is then expected to make the acquaintance of the other residents of the block. He fills out a card showing the number of houses, number of families, number of children, number of automobiles, and such other information as the card calls for. The scout does not make inspections of the dwellings but if he finds piles of rubbish or other unsatisfactory conditions, he reports to his district station and a fireman investigates the condition and insists upon its correction.

The various fire stations are now conducting meetings within their districts which the people of the neighborhood are invited to attend. Talks upon the various causes of fires in the home are given by the firemen. The meetings are made interesting with music, songs and motion pictures showing fire and street accident scenes.

During the month of April, 1928, these meetings had a total attendance of over 10,000. The official records show that the firemen made 85,000 inspections during the year 1927. They have made speeches before luncheon clubs and factory meetings, and over the radio. Fire drills are conducted by our firemen in all our schools every two weeks. Bulletin boards similar to the accompanying illustration are prepared and posted from time to time in the lobby of the City Hall.

GRATIFYING RESULTS

The fire prevention activities as outlined above have resulted in a marked reduction in our fire loss, as is illustrated by the following figures:

Year	Fire Loss	Per Capita
1923	$1,172,676.00	$7.66
1924	1,077,318.00	6.91
1925	815,888.00	4.98
1926	312,825.00	1.89
1927	290,830.00	1.72

We have received excellent coöperation from every local organization and firm that has been approached. The board of education encourages fire prevention programs in the schools. Such coöperation is not only desirable but necessary to successful fire prevention activity.

The activities and efforts outlined above are the basis for the reduction of our fire loss from $7.66 per capita five years ago to $1.72 in 1927. We are continuing our program and hope that the present year may show a still further reduction.

DEPRECIATION IN COMMERCIAL AND MUNICIPAL ACCOUNTING

BY ADRIAN M. LANDMAN

Of Landman Associates, New York

Many municipalities operating under laws requiring the retirement of indebtedness have a sounder financial structure than large numbers of commercial companies which meticulously set up theoretical depreciation. :: :: :: :: :: :: :: :: ::

DEPRECIATION may arise from a number of causes and an exact definition can hardly be applied to it. In dealing with an example in its simplest form, however, we have before us the general scheme of depreciation and the logical result of its proper application.

Let us assume that a company's money, whether earned, raised by sale of stock or borrowed is invested in equipment usable for twenty years. Theoretically, we will say, the equipment will last twenty years upon a "straight line" depreciation basis. One-twentieth of the original cost of the equipment (ignoring scrap value) will be charged to expense of operations each year and a like amount credited to a depreciation reserve. If an amount of cash or securities corresponding to the depreciation reserve was set aside and made available for reinvestment at the life expiration of the equipment, an ideal cycle of depreciation operations would be complete, as the amount set aside would just equal the cost of the property. The last step, however, which is the culmination and an important corollary of depreciation is very generally neglected, especially by financially weak companies. The depreciation reserve, as accumulated, should be offset by an equal amount in assets, cash or its equivalent, inventories or fixed assets. The reserve is ordinarily offset not by cash or securities but by increases in physical assets such as materials, machinery and so on. The result is that when the original equipment must be replaced there is a so-called "depreciation reserve" but no cash with which to finance the new, replacement equipment. The company must then raise more money by the sale of stock or by borrowing on the strength of assets added or liabilities decreased to offset the "depreciation reserve," to finance replacements. Depreciation and long term borrowing are inextricably interwoven, as depreciable assets are made up of items having years of service. The steps to which depreciation accounting should be directed are: (1) The periodical writing off of depreciation as a current expense; (2) The concomitant building up of a reserve, and (3) (a) the setting aside of a particular fund during the wasting life of the asset sufficient to buy replacements or (b) to retire the indebtedness incurred by the purchase of the assets affected.

In commercial companies the first and second steps are, of course, essential from an executive standpoint, but such companies have generally lost sight of the third step which is not considered important in business where money has been raised by the sale of stock or upon indebtedness secured by the total assets of the company. This step is receiving increased attention by bankers and bond houses and should eventually receive the attention and importance it deserves.

In commercial practice the specific replacement fund is essential when bonds or notes are issued to purchase some particular, depreciable property, which is the primary security for the loan, such as equipment trust certificates issued for the purchase of rolling stock. When money has been borrowed to purchase such equipment, the setting aside a specific sum as a sinking fund to retire the evidences of indebtedness or the serial retirement of these evidences of indebtedness has the result of earmarking and applying cash to offset the shrinking value of the assets securing the debt.

This may appear more plainly if we continue our illustration. Twenty-year bonds are issued and sold to buy equipment. Each year one-twentieth of the value of the equipment purchased is charged to expense as depreciation and a like amount is credited to the "depreciation reserve." At the same time cash to the amount of one-twentieth of the equipment bonds issued for the purchase of the equipment is taken out of the general cash and either placed in a sinking fund or used to retire one-twentieth of the bonds. At the end of twenty years the equipment is worn out, the original amount as set up in the assets is taken off the books and the same is done with the "depreciation reserve." The bonds have been paid off, either in twenty installments or through the sinking fund. The cycle is complete and the company is back where it started. If the procedure outlined in the above example is followed, a co-ordination of depreciation and financing is presented in a theoretically ideal condition.

If a company is sound, well supplied with cash and constantly growing, little or no harm comes from the failure

to set aside specific funds for replacement or bond retirement, but in weak companies, those in which business is failing or even standing still, the results are disastrous. These disastrous results are tragically illustrated in the present financial difficulties encountered by street railway companies throughout the country. Far too often the practice in the past has been to carry equipment on the books long after it has been scrapped, refund the bonds issued in the equipment's purchase, and depend upon increased income to meet charges on new bonds issued to buy replacement equipment.

MUNICIPALITIES IGNORE DEPRECIATION

Commercial accountants are considerably exercised and shocked to find that municipalities take little heed to what they consider to be one of the foundation stones of accounting—depreciation.

Why has depreciation in its accepted accounting sense received comparatively little attention in general municipal accounting?

In common practice little was generally known and even less attention paid to depreciation during the years prior to the federal income tax laws. When executives learned that depreciation could be charged off as expense and thereby reduce the amount of income tax, it was welcomed with open arms.

The reason for depreciation is unaffected but its popularity is founded upon a distinct pecuniary incentive, which influences the controlling business group and compels their serious attention to this branch of accounting.

We must always keep in mind that commercial business is conducted for financial profit, while general municipal activities are conducted not for profit but for service, which cannot be reduced to accounting dollars and cents.

In commercial companies depreciation, if properly handled results in, (1) The proper charge of depreciation as expense and the resultant showing of decreased net earning over a given period; (2) The remaining value of assets after deduction of the depreciation reserve, which should give the estimated, true value of property assets. We have stated the incentive that exists for (1) but (2) is incidental and we frequently encounter efforts to negative the showing made of decreased assets on account of an application of depreciation accounting. The incentive in (2) comes from outside, from the lenders. Banks and loaning institutions were quick to appreciate their need for an accurate statement of depreciated assets and insisted upon their set up.

Now let us take the case of a municipality. No incentive exists for a reduction of net income, as there is no income tax to pay and no distribution to be made to stockholders. In fact every incentive exists to keep down the showing of current expense. There is no pressure from the lenders of money to the municipality, as the borrowing power of a municipality is based upon its assessed valuations and taxing power and not upon the tangible assets owned. Therefore, with municipalities the impelling motive for showing depreciation does not exist. Municipal accounting approaches, as nearly as possible, a cash basis and cuts to a minimum all journalized entries. The matter of importance to a municipality is not what its depreciable property is worth in money but the quantity, the state of repair and the amount of service it is in position to render. The matter of its money value is secondary.   .

It has been pointed out that commercial firms have not given sufficient attention in the past to reducing bonded indebtedness through the use of sinking funds or serial retirements. The point here made is that, if indebtedness incurred for depreciable property is retired during the life or at the end of life of the property, the financial structure, so far as the assets are concerned, is sound.

Municipalities were long wedded to the plan of bonding for improvements and making no provision for the retirement of bonds. Expansion of population, increase of wealth and the resulting increased valuations of taxable property were counted upon to bear the additional burden of interest charges on current improvement bonds and also on the refunded bonds inherited from the past administrations; in the same manner that increased business in commercial companies is depended upon to carry on a similar policy.

Undoubtedly this plan would still be in high favor had not the various states enacted laws compelling municipalities to retire their indebtedness within specified periods of time. By compulsion of law, municipalities have arrived at the resultant third step or corollary to depreciation, which, by retirement restrictions, places each purchase of depreciable property by improvement bonds upon a sound financial basis whether depreciation is specifically taken into account upon the books or not.

To sum up. Depreciation and its proper record in accounts have always been of prime importance to commercial business but have been neglected until an immediate pecuniary incentive existed. In municipal accounting depreciation is only of secondary importance and the incentive for its recognition and use has been lacking. On the other hand amortization of indebtedness incurred in the purchase of depreciable property, which has even more of a salutary and steadying influence upon the financial structure, is imposed by law upon municipalities with the result that municipal bonds, largely by reason of this salutary legal requirement, are assuming a financial rating of the highest order. Commercial companies have neglected proper amortization of indebtedness and spe-cial earmarked funds through absence of compulsion. As a result many municipalities have a sounder financial structure without showing depreciation in their accounts than have large numbers of commercial companies which meticulously set up theoretical depreciation upon their accounts.

LONG TERM BUDGETING AND THE CITY PLAN

BY GEORGE B. FORD
Technical Advisory Corporation, New York

Capital budgets have become an integral element in the execution of city plans. This article is part of an address delivered before the 1928 National Conference on City Planning. :: :: :: :: ::

It is stated by Mr. C. E. Rightor of the Detroit Bureau of Governmental Research in his most interesting pamphlet entitled, *The Preparation of a Long Term Financial Program*,[1] that probably the first long term plan for any governmental unit was that of the Minneapolis Board of Education which was announced in 1916. In 1919 a five-year civic program was outlined for Newark, N. J., as a result of their comprehensive city plan.

The first comprehensive city plan and budgeted program for a long period of years was that for East Orange, N. J., which was prepared by the city planning commission in 1921. A program of public improvements with their estimated cost was worked out for each five-year period from 1922 to 1972. Then the city's financial condition at each of these five-year periods was estimated and the program adjusted so that the city might always

[1] Published by the Municipal Administration Service, 261 Broadway, New York City, 1927. Price, 25 cents.

pay for the proposed improvements within each of the given periods. While this program has served as a guide and object lesson, it has never been officially adopted.

WHAT CITIES ARE DOING?

The first general program for public improvements to be adopted at the polls was that of St. Louis, where on February 9, 1923, a ten-year bond issue program covering twenty-one separate projects and totaling $87,372,500 was adopted by a two-thirds vote. The ability of the city to finance the undertaking without an increase in the tax rate for 30 years was first determined. At this time a big transportation program is being largely financed by local benefit assessments.

In 1924 San Francisco, with limited financial resources, formulated a ten-year development program. The program, however, was not carried beyond the stage of public hearings.

In 1925 a bond program for certain public improvements was prepared

Kansas City. Out of a total of $26,-610,000 only $2,400,000 was approved by the voters. However, a revised program is being submitted again this year backed up by a more thorough campaign of education.

In the same year in Toledo only $3,000,000 out of a $32,500,000 bond program was approved by popular vote. Toledo is also revising its program and resubmitting it.

Buffalo has a capital budget committee under the new city charter and it is expected that it will present its program this year.

In Los Angeles a five to ten year program of capital improvements is being prepared. The extremely rapid growth of the city, however, makes the problem most difficult. They are preparing their program on the principle that limiting the amount of street improvements to the capacity to pay of the property owners affected merits just as much consideration as the plan for distributing the cost of such improvements over a period of years.

Dayton, Ohio, has recently passed several large bond issues based directly on the findings of the city plan.

In Cincinnati in 1927 a committee was appointed representing the various bond issuing authorities (that is, the city, the county, the schools and other boards) to present a plan of procedure for coördinating the bond proposals of these various authorities and developing a common program. At their request the city planning commission and the Bureau of Municipal Research presented a plan of procedure for the preparation of an improvement program and a plan of financing.[1] This program is particularly interesting because it is the first that is thoroughly

[1] The general principles of procedure in Cincinnati are described on page 16 of Mr. Rightor's pamphlet to which reference has been made.

comprehensive, including schools, county and special boards, assigning priorities to each and determining the full financial effect. A complete program, based on the city plan, was made out for five years and a specific detailed program for 1928 was published in October, 1927. Despite the fact that it called for a total expenditure of $10,-553,000, it only raised the total tax rate 1½ per cent.

Detroit, thanks to the work of Detroit Bureau of Governmental Research, published its ten-year public program for Detroit in June, 1925. The program, which was quite comprehensive, called for a total expenditure of $779,991,477. It was estimated that about $63,528,000 could be financed by special assessments. It was also found that the whole program could be carried out within the New York 7 per cent savings bank law with only a small increase in the tax rate.

In April, 1927, the program was revised as an eight-year program. The ten-year program was reduced by about $89,000,000. On the basis of these findings bond issues were voted for the most desirable public improvements, although under the New York 7 per cent banking law the margin for legal investments in the New York market was only $19,000,000, while the borrowing margin under the Michigan state laws was $233,795,867. Most fortunately the recent change in the New York banking law gives Detroit all of the latitude that it needs.

In December, 1927, Trenton, N. J., completed its comprehensive city and regional plan and long term budgeted program of execution. The program is arranged by five-year periods from the present until 1950. It includes all the capital expenditures that are proved to be necessary or at all desirable. The cost of executing the total program would amount to about $26,000,000 including about $9,000,000 for paving and repaving. The latter must be all paid out of general taxation instead of by local benefit assessments which is the usual custom elsewhere. Even so it was found that the whole program can be financed without increasing the tax rate and with an almost complete liquidation of existing and new bond issues by 1950. In other words, without increasing the tax rate and with no increase in the per capita assessed valuations, it is possible to carry out a complete public improvement program on a most comprehensive scale and at the end of the period find the city almost entirely out of debt.

A FIFTY-YEAR PROGRAM FOR WHITE PLAINS

In February, 1928, White Plains, N. Y., published its comprehensive city plan and budgeted program. The total cost of carrying out the plan over a period of 50 years was estimated at $45,596,970. Of this amount $12,944,087 will be assessed against properties directly benefited. The present population is 29,000. The funded debt on the completion of the program will be about the same as it is today, while the borrowing margin will have increased from the present $5,000,000 to $28,000,000. Meanwhile the tax rate, which was 25.027 in 1927, will increase gradually to nearly 31 and then decrease gradually to about 23. The assessed valuations, at present $106,000,000, will probably increase during the 50 years to $343,000,000, and the population will probably increase to about 73,000.

The report for the village of Bronxville, N. Y., was also published in February, 1928. It was found there that on account of the specialized character of the problem it would be necessary to increase the per capita assessed valuations about 25 per cent,

and the tax rate from 2.445 to 2.772 in 1929 with a reduction to 2.453 or less from 1934 on. Meanwhile the total bonded indebtedness for carrying out the whole program would come well within the legal 10 per cent limit.

Dallas, at the end of 1927, through its Citizens' Advisory Committee, prepared an amended Kessler Plan and a comprehensive budgeted program of public improvements to be consummated in nine years or less. The total bond program for $23,925,000 was adopted by the voters, but at present is tied up in an injunction suit. It is interesting to note that the amount of bonds recommended in the program does not much exceed the amount actually issued during the last nine years without any plan. While the tax rate stays at 2.47, the ratio of assessed valuation to real valuation is to be increased from 50 per cent to 58½ per cent.

Rye, N. Y., has recently published its comprehensive plan and budgeted program from 1929 to 1950. The total expenditure for public improvements throughout the period would amount to a little over $3,000,000 including full allowance for sewers, paving, schools and even such things as garbage incinerators and fire apparatus. Only $700,000 of new bonds would be needed, the balance being paid entirely on the pay-as-you-go principle. Meanwhile at the end of the period the total net balance out of current revenues, after deducting all old and new debt service, as well as current operating and maintenance expenses, would amount to $1,246,900. The assessed valuations would probably double during the 22-year period, and the population would nearly double. Meanwhile the village tax rate of 11.26, exclusive of schools, could remain unchanged and the net borrowing margin would increase from $1,379,000 to $5,270,000. In other words, a complete program for capital expenditures of all sorts can be carried out without increasing the tax rate and without any undue increase on the per capita assessed valuations, and at the same time nearly wipe out the municipal debt.

Mount Kisco, N. Y., is just publishing its comprehensive plan and budgeted program for 1929 to 1950. The total expenditure for public improvements is $2,432,250. This again includes all desirable capital expenditures. Only $300,000 of new bonds will be necessary, the balance being paid on the pay-as-you-go principle, leaving a total net balance from current revenue at the end of the period of $589,250 after all debt service charges are paid. Meanwhile both the new and the existing bonds will be almost entirely liquidated by 1950 and the net borrowing margin, at present only $55,000, will increase to almost the full borrowing capacity in 1950, which would be $1,567,800. The tax rate for both the village and school will remain at the present combined rate of $25.70. Population should increase meanwhile a little over 50 per cent. Again the comprehensive plan and budgeted program could be completely executed without any increase in the tax rate or the assessed valuations per capita and with an almost complete liquidation of existing debt by the end of the period.

Briarcliff Manor, N. Y., and Moorestown, N. J., at the present writing are just completing similar comprehensive plans and long term budgeted programs.

PROCEDURE

Taking the Trenton budgeted city plan as an example, all proposed public improvements and other capital expenditures were first determined scientifically by means of mathematical studies, and then the order of relative urgency was similarly calculated. Next, various items were arranged in three classes. First, those that were vitally necessary; second, those that were also desirable and third, those that were interesting but not essential.

Then, the cost of each item was calculated and checked from various sources, so that a definite budget could be determined for each year and for each five-year period. Five-year periods were used so as to allow for an adjustment of the items at the beginning of each period.

As might be expected, the borrowing capacity of the city and the net margin between current revenue and current expenses rarely permits the immediate financing of all desirable public improvements and capital expenditures. Even if the borrowing margin is ample, debt service charges absorb so much of the current revenue that either administration costs would have to be unwarrantedly reduced or taxes unduly raised. Public improvements and other capital expenditures can and should be postponed until actually needed. It is wasteful to undertake them sooner, except where land is about to be improved with costly structures. Recent experience has certainly proved that a budgeted plan and program can determine scientifically just when each capital expenditure should be undertaken as well as its amount. Guesswork, the bane of all municipal financing, can be largely eliminated. A workmanlike program can be substituted.

In making a program and computation of the necessary and desirable capital expenditures, their dates of undertaking and their costs are not sufficient. It is necessary also to determine how much the city can afford to spend in addition to current administration and maintenance costs plus debt service charges. Debt service charges on existing debts can readily be determined for each year in the future. Municipal operating and maintenance costs tend to increase with population except in the case of the very largest cities. Therefore, a projection of population growth can be used as a factor in determining operating and maintenance costs at any given date in the future. Sewer, paving and repaving costs can be determined in a similar manner as, other things being equal, they tend to increase with the population.

The total revenue of a municipality also tends to increase at least as rapidly as population. In other words, the assessed valuations per capita, on which the revenue is largely based, gradually increase as population increases. Tax rates also tend to increase with the increase of population.

The Statistical Abstract of the United States for 1926 also shows that in 250 typical cities nearly 54 per cent of the total expenses of the city were for current operation and maintenance, 5 per cent for the operation of public services, 31½ per cent for permanent improvements and 9½ per cent for debt service. Now if the operation and mainte-

nance costs are subtracted from current revenue the balance, if any, is available for the financing of public improvements. If the latter can be financed directly on the pay-as-you-go principle out of current revenue the municipality is on a very conservative and strong financial footing. However, this can rarely be done, so financing by bond issues, whether serial or term, becomes imperative. The interest and amortization charges must be calculated on each proposed bond issue to see that the carrying charges can be taken care of out of the current revenue balance. Otherwise the bond issues must be reduced to a point where they can be taken care of, or the revenue from taxation increased correspondingly. The interesting part is that in Trenton, and several of the other municipalities above referred to, it was found that small bond issues in the immediate future would suffice and that all the rest of the improvements could be taken care of as needed on the pay-as-you-go principle. This naturally tends to improve the credit of the municipality, giving it a lower net interest rate on its bond issues.

MINNEAPOLIS LOSES THROUGH ANTIQUE STREET MAINTENANCE METHODS[1]

BY H. J. MILLER

Manager, Minneapolis Taxpayers' Association

THE ward plan of financing and supervising street maintenance in Minneapolis has been attacked locally

[1] On June 18 the people of Minneapolis voted on a charter amendment consolidating the present scattered responsibility for street maintenance. The result was very close and court action and recount may be necessary for final decision. On the face of the returns the proposal seems to have carried.

for years. While the intelligent judgment of the community has expressed itself repeatedly in opposition to the plan, it has weathered every storm since its adoption in 1881.

Two events, one an act of God and the other attributed to His adversary, have so focussed attention on the weaknesses of the plan that hope of overthrowing it has again arisen and taken the form of a proposed charter amendment. The act of God alluded to was a severe snow storm last December which tied up about everything in the city except the street railway system, and the expressions of discontent against our ward system of street supervision. The city council in desperation gathered together such authority as it and the street commissioners possessed, and with a gesture concentrated it in the city engineer.

The other act was the looting of our ward funds by certain ward street commissioners, the complete picture of which awaits the results of a comprehensive audit now in progress. Up to the present, one street commissioner has been found guilty by the civil service commission and discharged. Another has confessed and is confined in the state penitentiary. Another has committed suicide, while still another is awaiting trial on numerous indictments. So much for the background.

INEQUALITIES IN WEALTH AND PERFORMANCE

Minneapolis is divided into thirteen wards, each of which elect two aldermen to the city council which in turn appoints a street commissioner for each ward subject to civil service rules. As our ward lines have not been changed since 1887 when they were presumably based on population, it is not startling to find that they vary in the number of miles of streets per ward from 14.6 miles to 183.7 miles. Each ward raises and expends its own money for street maintenance under a charter limitation of 2½ mills. The taxable property valuation upon which this millage is based varies from $4,714,520 in one ward to $80,972,326 in another ward. A comparison of number of miles of streets per ward with the property valuation of that ward discloses little relationship between the two. As a re-

sult, the ward tax now prevailing varies from 1.4 mills to 2.5 mills, the outlying wards levying the maximum while the older districts have generally a lower rate. If ward lines were eliminated for raising ward funds, a levy of 2.1 mills on the city valuation would produce the same amount as is now produced by five wards with a 2.5 mill rate, two wards with a 2.4 mill rate, three wards with a 2.3 mill rate, one ward with a 1.8 mill rate, one ward with a 1.7 mill rate and one ward with a 1.4 mill rate. Applying the annual tax levy per ward to the number of miles of street in the ward discloses a variance from $252.96 to $2,640.81 per mile. Here again the larger appropriations per mile are in the downtown or older districts where a higher percentage of the streets are paved than in the outlying districts. There are twenty-four pieces of real estate owned by these thirteen wards, including warehouses, gravel pits, tool houses, and oil stations, the original cost of which was $286,271. Each ward maintains and operates its equipment independently. The depreciated inventory value of such equipment for all wards in 1927 was $388,352. In eight of the wards this equipment value and real estate value exceeded the ward fund appropriation for 1928. For the thirteen wards this overhead value of real estate and equipment of $674,623 exceeded the total tax levy for all the wards in 1928 of $660,810. (In addition to this ward levy, however, there was also levied in special assessment for sprinkling, over $400,000, which was handled by this overhead, as well as an additional million dollars which was credited to the ward funds from various sources, principal of which was from doing work on special assessment projects.)

To get a picture of the percentage of the tax levy which is apparently spent for new equipment, the levy for 1927 of $626,589 for all the wards may be compared to the expenditure of approximately $90,000 for new equipment. In one ward last year 62 per cent of its levy was spent for new equipment. Accurate knowledge concerning the probable unnecessary duplication of plant and equipment under this ward system must await more engineering analysis. An indication will be forthcoming perhaps this year from the cost accounting department's analysis of the number of use-hours for each piece of equipment in 1928. If so much of a ward levy is expended for plant that sufficient funds are lacking to put it to a reasonable economic use, such an analysis should reveal the fact. If our cost accounting department had been at work on these expenditures for a sufficient length of time there would probably be many unit cost comparisons that could not be explained away. For example, during hearings on city cindering projects last year, some of those present from North Minneapolis were curious to know why the lineal foot charge for cindering their street was much more than in another ward.

The layman's criticism of this ward system is directed to more apparent faults, however. For instance, as ward lines are the middle of the street it is not uncommon to have one side properly maintained while the other side in another ward awaits the action of a different authority. Likewise, in traveling a street running through several wards, the comment is frequent that you can tell by the condition of the street when you reach each ward.

TRY TO FIND WHO'S RESPONSIBLE!

To locate the legal responsibility for supervising the expenditures under this system a layman's examination of the charter is necessary. In section 7, chapter 3, under "Duties and Power of the City Engineer," it states that "the city engineer shall have supervision and general charge of all work done for the city and of all work done on any street, highway or alley in the city, and may direct the manner of performing such work." Then in section 1, chapter 8, under "Public Highways and Bridges" it states that "the city council shall have the care, supervision and control of all highways, streets, alleys and public ways and grounds within the limits of the city." In the same chapter, Section 6, the council is then directed to appoint a street commissioner for each ward who shall "superintend, subject to the direction of the city engineer or general street commissioner, the grading of streets and laying of sidewalks and to carry into effect all orders of the city council, but no street commissioner shall do any work upon the street except such as is necessary to keep traveled streets and improved sidewalks in repair and passable condition, unless such work is especially ordered by the city council." The street commissioners are also designated as health inspectors and directed to work under the direction of the health commissioner. Then follows the famous clause: "All work done by the street commissioners shall be subject to the approval of the aldermen of their respective ward and the city engineer. The city council may also appoint one general street commissioner for the entire city who shall receive and observe the instructions of the city engineer, superintend and have general charge of the work of the street commissioners of the several wards, and do all other things which the city council may require of him to do." Now guess where the responsibility is for the expenditure of our ward funds! It is like the atmosphere of that old-fashioned game, "Button, button, who's got the Button?" In practice the responsibility is as hard to locate as in theory.

In some wards, because of political prestige or otherwise, the street commissioner dominates. In some wards the aldermen appear frequently to be the superior, while again the city engineer appears to have a measure of authority. Probably a better statement would be that the street commissioners, the city engineer, the general street commissioner (the city council has designated the city engineer as general street commissioner, who in turn has delegated the work to an assistant, who is commonly called the general street commissioner), and the two aldermen all dominate at times to the exclusion of the others. The public's contact is usually with the aldermen in the matter of appealing for street improvements. Rather than pass the buck as might be expected, many aldermen are jealous of this contact because of its political possibilities and do not wish to relinquish it to a central authority.

PAY ROLLS

Is it surprising that this system has resulted in a hodge-podge? The disconnected performance of the work is well illustrated by the method of accounting and checking of pay rolls, which is probably as legal as it is economically criminal.

The general system which pertained prior to the recent disclosures was as follows: A timekeeper or foreman in a ward kept a daily time-book with the names and daily record of hours which each ward employee worked. Once a year these time-books were turned in to the street commissioner. In several instances these records have been destroyed. From this time-book, daily distribution sheets were made out which contained the civil service number under which the employee worked, with the hours that he worked each day allocated to certain units such as flush-ing, machine sweeping, etc. These daily distribution sheets were periodically sent to the city engineer's office for permanent filing. During a recent trial these records, as well as the daily time-books, were reported as destroyed so that no original record of each man's time existed. Every pay roll period the street commissioner then made out a master pay roll, presumably from the time-book or distribution sheets, which roll contained the name, civil service number, civil service rating, with rate per day or hour, and the amount due to the employee for the period covered by the roll. The commissioner took this roll to the city engineer's office where it was supposed to have been checked against the daily distribution sheets for that period. At least one instance has been found where this apparently was not done, as a name appeared on the master pay roll which did not appear on the distribution sheets, nor did the total amount of the roll check with the total of the distribution sheets. The city engineer's office then made three pay rolls from the master roll, one copy going to the civil service commission where the names were checked as to certification by the commission and as to the rate of pay. One copy went to the city treasurer who proceeded to make out the checks, while a third copy went to the city comptroller for the purpose of determining whether the fund against which it was charged would permit such withdrawals.

After the city council approved the roll, the original roll, which was the city comptroller's copy, together with the checks, were handed in a bundle by the city treasurer to the street commissioner, who proceeded to distribute them. Under the law the signatures of the payees were supposed to be placed upon this original roll when they received their checks, which roll finally was returned by the commissioner to the city comptroller for permanent record. Such signatures of payees were quite generally overlooked, the treasurer taking the position that the signatures on the cancelled checks were sufficient protection to the city. The cancelled checks, however, were never checked against actual signatures in the civil service office. In several wards this procedure was modified to the extent that the engineer's office made up the master roll from either the time-books or the daily distribution sheets.

It is apparent from this system that a commissioner could add names to the distribution sheets and the master roll without the knowledge of the foreman or timekeeper and could then take out these checks before he gave the rest to the foremen for distribution. Of course, it would be necessary to use the name and number of a person who was properly certified by the civil service commission or that office would have discovered the discrepancy. It was comparatively simple, however, to find any number of names of certified employes who were not working and for whom checks could be delivered to the commissioner.

The defense of one commissioner tried on an indictment which charged him with proceeding under this system, was that on numerous occasions he did put in names of men who did not work and signed their endorsements to the checks and took the cash and paid other persons that amount who could not be officially put on the roll owing to civil service red tape. While the defense did not produce in court a single person who had been so employed with respect to the checks covered in the indictment, the jury rendered a verdict of not guilty.

As the matter now stands under this verdict a commissioner could continue this system at will with nothing to fear but the probable punishment of discharge from the service by the civil service commission for violating its rules.

Is it any wonder that sentiment is crystallizing to do away with our ward system of street maintenance and put it squarely on the city engineer as a responsibility the same as construction of sewers, pavements, and water mains?

PARTISANSHIP AND PARTIES IN GERMAN MUNICIPAL GOVERNMENT

BY ROGER H. WELLS

Bryn Mawr College

A study of city politics in post-war Germany

"In a session of the Hindenburg city council, the Communists tried to prevent a Nationalist from speaking. A fight started. One councilman was knocked down. The chairman twice had to suspend the sitting."[1] This not unusual incident is quoted because

[1] Berlin *Lokal Anzeiger*, Aug. 18, 1927.

it illustrates something of the tempo of post-war city government in Germany. That German municipal institutions are far more politicized now than they were ten years ago is universally admitted; that this condition is primarily the result of the Revolution of 1918 is also conceded. Democratic ideas and universal suffrage have replaced conservative domination based upon a restricted franchise. The present article does not attempt to deal with all phases of this new political development but is primarily concerned with partisanship and party organization in relation to the structure and functioning of the city council.[1]

At the outset, it should be noted that local politics, both in and out of the city council, are largely shaped along national party lines.[2] The dominant groups are the great national parties and these are usually represented in the average municipal legislature. For example, no less than seventy-five of the eighty-four councilmen in the city of Karlsruhe belong to one or the other of the six major national parties. Ow-

ing to the ease with which nominations are made, purely local groups are by no means uncommon but these do not ordinarily secure any considerable strength in the council. In fact, the councilmen chosen by such groups frequently adhere to one of the major party "fractions" as "guests." On the other hand, just as there are blocs in national and state politics, so also in many cities one finds more or less stable alliances among the parties. These alliances may be only for the election or they may result in the formation of an *Arbeitsgemeinschaft* which functions as a single fraction in the work of the council.[3]

The influence of national parties and partisanship appears also in the organization and procedure of the German municipal legislature. The city councils seem like miniature parliaments for they have taken over much of the parliamentary apparatus and trappings.[4] The *Reichstag* has its organized party fractions and these are reproduced in the party fractions of the council. As in the national and state legislatures, the council members are seated according to parties, the Communists on the extreme left of the chairman, the Nationalist on the right.[5]

[1] The council, by its very nature, is the most politicized of all the municipal organs. But the administration is by no means free from politics and the cry of "spoils system" or "invisible government" is often raised. See Dr. Glässing, "Die Verwaltungsreform," *Zeitschrift für Kommunalwirtschaft*, xvi (1926), pp. 961–980. In spite of these allegations, the professional bureaucracy does not seem to have become unduly politicized during the past decade. Partisan considerations have also sometimes influenced the actions of the central authorities exercising supervision over the cities.

[2] This results from a number of factors: (a) Germany is a highly urbanized country and many national problems are city problems; (b) the difficulties of the post-war years have made it necessary for national legislation—especially in regard to finance—more and more to encroach upon the *Kommunalselbstverwaltung*, thus further preventing a sharp separation of national and local issues; (c) the national parties themselves, *e.g.*, the Social Democratic and Center (Catholic) Parties, cannot fulfill their purposes unless they actively enter the municipal sphere; and (d) the electorate which chooses the city council is the same—except for the residence requirement in local elections—as that which elects the *Reichstag* and the state legislatures, an additional obstacle to organizing separate parties for national and local politics.

[3] In 1927, out of 149 city councils, the People's Party had its own separate fraction in 49, while in the remaining 100, an *Arbeitsgemeinschaft* had been formed with other parties, chiefly with the National People's Party or with the Democrats. See Otto Most, *Gemeindepolitik und Deutsche Volkspartei* (party pamphlet, Berlin, 1928), pp. 7–8. The Center and Socialist Parties are, in general, opposed to such local coalitions, while of course the irreconcilable Communists and National Socialists remain aloof.

[4] For a criticism of this "unhealthy Kommunalparlamentarismus," see von Eynern, "Grossstadt und Selbstverwaltung," *Kommunale Umschau*, i (1925), pp. 325–326.

[5] In the official report of the council proceedings, the party affiliation of each speaker is often indicated together with such notations as "ap-

The *Reichstag* representatives vote together as a party group and so also, but to a lesser degree, the *Stadtverordneten*.[1] That distinctly parliamentary device, the motion of want of confidence, is likewise used in the council chamber against the *Bürgermeister* or other executive officials in spite of the fact that such a motion has no legal effect since these officials have a fixed tenure of office.[2]

Small wonder that the political atmosphere of the council room resembles that of the national and state legislatures. The school question, taxation and finance, socialization, unemployment, the housing problem,—these are the subjects of party motions (*Anträge*) and of heated debates in *Reichstag* and *Stadtverordnetenversammlung* alike. Of less intrinsic importance but equally controversial are various questions of sentiment. Shall the city buildings fly the old imperial flag? Shall "King Street" be changed to "Karl Marx Street" and "Kaiser Wilhelm Square" become "Karl Liebknecht Square"? Shall the council send a telegram to the American ambassador protesting against the execution of Sacco and Vanzetti? Germans who long for the old

plause from the Right," etc. See, for example, the *Sitzungsbericht* in the *Amtsblatt der Stadt Stuttgart*, May 3, 1928, pp. 263 ff.

[1] On strictly party questions and, in practice, on many other matters, the municipal fraction votes as a unit. However, most parties do not go so far as the Communist Party which commands its members always to vote alike on all questions. See *Instruktion für die neugewählten kommunistischen Gemeindevertreter* (issued in 1924 by the Municipal Politics Section of the Central Party Headquarters in Berlin), Art. I, Sec. 7.

[2] *Entscheidung des preussischen Oberverwaltungsgerichts*, Bd. 35, p. 27. However, in Lippe, a successful *Misstrauensvotum* necessitates a new election of the collegial executive (*Stadtrat*) but the paid, professional members of the *Stadtrat* do not thereby lose their positions. See Lippe, *Gemeindeverfassungsgesetz* of 1927, Art. 49-2.

régime speak in disgust of the present municipal council, characterizing it as merely "a forum for the exposition of party dogmas." This characterization is hardly fair. It must be remembered that much of the work is done in committee without undue partisanship. Moreover, on every *Tagesordnung* of the council, there are many items which are discussed and decided without political bias. Finally, the permanent administrative personnel is a steadying force which makes for the smooth working of the governmental machine in spite of the tumult in the council chamber.

Enough has been said to give a picture of the spirit of partisanship in the German municipal legislature. It now remains to speak of the relations between the councilmen and the party organizations with especial reference to the nominating process, the party fraction, and the higher municipal agencies of the parties. The methods by which city councilmen are nominated are comparatively uniform throughout the entire country. So far as the legal requirements are concerned, the act of nomination is very simple.[3] A list of candidates may be placed upon the ballot by a petition signed by a small number of qualified voters, usually ten or twenty. No attempt is made by law to control the manner in which a given party makes up its own list of nominees. All such matters remain within the jurisdiction of party rule and practice, but, even so, the process is in the main similar for all parties. In the larger cities, the candidates are nominated by a city convention of delegates (*Vertrauensleute*) who are themselves directly elected by the party voters; in the smaller, by a primary assembly of

[3] For a discussion of the legal requirements, see the writer's article, "Proportional Representation in German Cities," NATIONAL MUNICIPAL REVIEW, July, 1928.

all party members.[1] In such conventions or assemblies, the local party committee plays an important rôle for it prepares in advance a "slate" of candidates which is usually ratified without change. The preparation of this slate is something of a work of art for all important elements within the party must be represented if a properly balanced ticket is to be secured. To a certain extent, this involves a due selection of nominees according to the wards of the city, a selection made necessary because councilmen are usually elected from the city at large and not from districts. Of much greater importance is the representation of groups within the party. The hardships of the post-war years have so emphasized the conflicting interests of economic groups and classes that no party can afford to neglect this factor. Even the Democratic and the Center Parties, which most vigorously deny that they are "class organizations," still find it necessary to shape their tickets in accordance with the economic groups within the party.[2] Take, for example, the procedure followed by the Ortsverein of the Democratic Party in Nuremberg.[3] This Ortsverein has separately organized under-groups,—for public officials, for workers, for women, for the industrial and commercial interests, etc. Each of these under-groups submits a list of candidates to the city committee and from these names the committee makes up the slate for presentation to the city assembly of the party. The position of a

candidate's name on the ticket (and hence his chances of being elected) are to a considerable extent determined by the political importance of the Untergruppe to which he belongs. Thus, if the first candidate represents the commercial interests, the second may be a public official, the third a worker, the fourth a woman, etc.[4]

The recognition of the party's under-groups appears not only in drawing up the slate but also in filling vacancies in the council. Under proportional representation in German cities, the candidates who are not elected become the Ersatzmänner or party substitutes. Whenever a vacancy occurs, instead of having a special or by-election, the law usually provides that the next Ersatzmann of the party shall automatically succeed to office. In practice, this has given rise to difficulties since the ranking Ersatzmann, while of course belonging to the same party, may yet come from a different under-group within the party. To avoid this objection, the law sometimes permits the order of substitutes' names to be changed by a majority vote of the signers of the nominating petition.[5] In effect, this means by the party committee, since the committee members are in many cases the signers of the petition.

After the nomination, campaign,[6] and election, the councilman does not lose touch with the party to which he belongs. On the contrary, he becomes a member of a more or less specialized party organization de-

---

[1] Even in the large cities, if the party be weak in numbers, the nominations are sometimes made by a city-wide primary assembly.

[2] See the Leitsätze für die Vorbereitung der nächsten Kommunalwahlen published by the Kommunalpolitische Vereinigung of the Center Party (Cologne, 1924).

[3] Information supplied in an interview with the secretary of the Nuremberg Ortsverein.

[4] Although women are the strongest numerical group, the party ticket is seldom headed by a woman.

[5] See, for example, the Prussian Gemeindewahlgesetz of 1923 as amended 1924, Art. 8.

[6] For a discussion of campaign methods, see the writer's article, "The Hamburg Election," NATIONAL MUNICIPAL REVIEW, Jan., 1928, pp. 15–19.

signed primarily for municipal purposes, the basis unit of which is the *Fraktion.* The fraction is composed of the city or town council members of a given party.[1] Like the party fractions in the national and state legislatures, the municipal party fraction is often a formally organized body, having its own officers and by-laws and playing a definite part in the proceedings of the council.[2] In fact, the rôle of the fraction is frequently recognized in the *Geschäftsordnung* or by-laws of the council itself. Thus in Dresden, the presiding officer of the council and the chairmen of the several party fractions constitute the Senior Committee (*Aeltestenrat*) of the council, and the fraction chairmen also possess other special privileges as floor leaders of their parties, especially with reference to debate and the bringing in of motions.[3] In most cities, the general practice is for each fraction to meet regularly before every meeting of the council. For example, in Leipzig,[4] the council sittings occur on Wednesday evenings while the committees of the council meet on Monday nights. After the committee meetings are over, the respective fractions gather in the rooms specially provided for them in the *Rathaus,* discuss the committee deliberations, and decide what attitude is to be taken on the various items of the agenda for the plenary session of

the council on Wednesday. In short, the fraction occupies a key position. Through its members on the committees of the council and on the administrative deputations, it is enabled to keep in close touch with all branches of city government. If the *Bürgermeister* or a department head belongs to the party, he may be invited to appear and advise the fraction in its deliberations.[5] It is also important for the fraction to maintain contacts with the local party committee and with the voters. Where the local party chairman is not himself a member of the council, he may be asked to attend the fraction meetings with full power to vote. In order that the fraction may keep in touch with the party electorate, periodical reports are prepared and published by some fractions, especially those belonging to the Social Democratic Party.[6] Or, in lieu of a printed report, a *Kommunal-Abend* may be held in which members of the fraction report to the voters of the party.[7]

The local fractions of a given party may be combined into special, district, state, and national organizations for municipal work.[8] Here one finds greatest differences between the parties.

---

[1] Or of the party members of the county or provincial legislatures.

[2] See Dr. Rheinhold Heinen, *Die Fraktion in dem Gemeindeparlament,* pamphlet of the *Kommunalpolitische Vereinigung* of the Center Party (Cologne, 1927); and Dr. Leonhardt, "Die kommunale Fraktion, ihre politische Bedeutung und Stellung," *Archiv der Deutschen Volkspartei* (Berlin), March 15, 1924, pp. 79–82.

[3] *Geschäftsordnung der Stadtverordneten zu Dresden,* adopted 1926, *passim.*

[4] Information personally communicated by Dr. Hübler, chairman of the Leipzig city council.

[5] It is also not uncommon for the *Ersatzmänner* to attend the fraction meetings.

[6] See *Berliner Kommunalpolitik, 1921–1925,* the report of the Social Democratic fraction of the Berlin city council; and the *Jahres-Bericht, 1927* of the Nuremberg *Ortsverein* of the Social Democratic Party, especially pp. 15–23, "Tätigkeits-Bericht der Stadtratsfraktion."

[7] The communal evenings are sometimes known as "Beer Evenings" for such gatherings by no means exclude sociability and refreshments. Another device is for the chairman of the fraction to report, not directly to a general assembly of the party but to the *Vertrauensleute* or delegates of the party by whom the councilmen were originally nominated.

[8] See Johannes Stelling, "Kommunalpolitische Organisationen," *Die Gemeinde,* iv (1927), pp. 919–927.

On the one hand, the Economic Party (*Reichspartei des Mittelstandes*) and the National Socialist Party have no special municipal agencies (apart from the local fractions,[1] no separate municipal programs,[1] and no municipal journal intended primarily for town and city councilmen belonging to the party.[2] At the other extreme stand the parties having highly organized municipal agencies, such as the Center and the Social Democratic Parties.

The *Kommunalpolitische Vereinigung*, the national municipal organization of the Center Party, deserves special mention because it is the oldest and most complete of all the parties.[3] The *Vereinigung* was first organized on a national scale in 1917 but there had been various district organizations of Catholic councilmen as far back as

1908, and the Catholic municipal journal, *Kommunalpolitische Blätter*, was founded in 1910.[4] The members of the *Vereinigung* are divided into two classes, regular and special. The regular members are Centrist city and town councilmen, county and provincial deputies, and all other persons holding any unpaid local office (*Ehrenamt*). The special members are those Centrists who are active in municipal affairs as party committeemen, state and national legislators, paid municipal officers, ex-councilmen, or *Ersatzmänner*. At present, the *Vereinigung* has over fourteen thousand members representing some twelve hundred Center Party fractions. The local fractions are grouped into county, province, or state unions, and these intermediate unions closely coöperate with the central organization. The chief organs of the *Vereinigung* are the annual assembly of all members, the executive committee, and the permanent *Sekretariat*. The seat of the organization and of the *Sekretariat* is in Cologne where the *Vereinigung* has its own office building and press. Among the services which the central office renders to individual members, to the local fractions, and to the county, provincial, and state unions may be mentioned the following; furnishing of information on general, technical, and legal questions, maintenance of a clipping bureau and of a library, advice and assistance in filling vacancies in the permanent local administrative services, maintenance of a registry with individual record cards for all members, arranging for lectures, study courses, and public

[1] Of course, the general platform of the party may contain planks dealing with municipal questions. See "Kommunalpolitik der politischen Parteien," *Handwörterbuch der Kommunalwissenschaften* (6 vols., Jena, 1918–1927), iii, pp. 1–35; vi, pp. 783–834.

[2] The party municipal journals are an interesting development of the post-war years, although one of the pioneers in this field, the Catholic *Kommunalpolitische Blätter* has been continuously published since 1910. The articles in these periodicals are primarily to instruct the party fraction members in municipal questions and are by no means always written from a narrow partisan viewpoint. In addition to *Kommunalpolitische Blätter*, the best known are *Die Gemeinde* (Socialist, founded, 1924); *Kommunale Umschau* (People's Party, founded 1925); *Die Selbstverwaltung* (Bavarian People's Party, founded 1922); and *Die Kommune* (Communist, founded 1926). Moreover, there are a number of local, district, and state party municipal journals. The regular party newspapers frequently deal directly with municipal questions or print special municipal supplements.

[3] Space will not permit a description of the municipal organizations of the other parties, especially of the Social Democratic Party which was the first to draw up a well thought out municpial program.

[4] For a brief history of this organization, see J. Nellessen, "*Zehn Jahre Kommunalpolitische Vereinigung*," *Kommunalpolitische Blätter*, xvii (1927), pp. 392–394. The facts given in the above paragraph are largely based upon interviews with Dr. Felix Gerhardus and other officials of the *Kommunalpolitische Vereinigung*.

meetings, issuing instructions with reference to the conduct of municipal elections, and calling meetings of the Centrist representatives before every session of the great local government organizations such as the *Deutscher Städtetag*, the *Reichsstädtebund*, the *Verband der Preussischen Landgemeinden*, etc.[1] In short, the *Kommunalpolitische Vereinigung* aims to school its members in municipal problems, to bring about closer coöperation between Centrist *Kommunalpolitiker*, and to secure a substantially uniform execution of the special municipal program of the Center Party.[2]

From the above description, it may be thought that the *Kommunalpolitische Vereinigung* is a purely voluntary body with no element of party discipline connected with it. Such is not the case. In 1920, the national convention of the Center Party decreed that town, city, county, and provincial representatives must belong to a Center fraction of the local legislature and to the *Kommunalpolitische Vereinigung*.[3] This decree is sometimes difficult to carry out in practice but it at least represents the ideal toward which the party strives. In order to facilitate the formation of Centrist fractions, the *Vereinigung* has drawn up a model constitution (*Satzung*) which such frac-

tions may adopt although they are not compelled to do so. Moreover, before a member of the party can become a recognized Centrist candidate for the municipal council, he must file a written statement with the local party committee agreeing to the following: (a) to be ready to take part in the work of the campaign; (b) to join the Center fraction and the *Kommunalpolitische Vereinigung*; (c) to report to the party electorate concerning his activities as councilman; (d) and to resign his seat if he secedes from the fraction and party.

This last point with reference to the obligation to resign merits further consideration. It involves the question of the party recall or *Rückberufungsrecht*.[4] One effect of proportional representation in Germany has been to lay great emphasis upon the elected legislator as the representative, not of the entire community, but of the party. In other words, the seat belongs to the party. Now if a councilman secedes from the party or is expelled from it, he is usually asked to give up his seat so that the ranking *Ersatzmann* of the party may occupy it. Otherwise, the party loses the seat to the detriment of its "proportional representation." Consequently, in party rule and practice, there is a general recognition of the "moral obligation" to resign under such circumstances. Some parties demand no written pledge from the candidates; others follow the example of the Center Party in that regard, while the Communist Party goes so far

[1] The same procedure is also followed by other parties. The delegates to the *Städtetag* or *Reichstädtebund* meet in party groups before the session opens to discuss what attitude they will take in regard to questions that are to come before such gatherings.

[2] For the text of this program, see Franz Hütte, *Das Kommunalprogramm der Zentrumspartei*, pamphlet of the *Kommunalpolitische Vereinigung* (2nd ed., Cologne, 1927).

[3] Nellessen, *op. cit.*, p. 393. Central party control over local representatives is likewise found in varying degrees in other parties. On paper, the Communist Party has a high degree of central control. See *Instruktion für die neugewählten kommunistischen Gemeindevertreter, op. cit.*

[4] See also the writer's coming article, "The Initiative, Referendum, and Recall in German Cities," to appear this fall in the NATIONAL MUNICIPAL REVIEW. The principle of the party recall has been recognized in the legislation of two American states, Kansas and South Dakota. See Holcombe and Wells, *State Government in the United States* (rev. ed., New York, 1926), p. 141.

as to require its nominees to sign in advance a "blanket resignation" (*Blanko-Mandatsniederlegung*) in which only the date is omitted. This resignation is kept on file by the party leaders who merely have to fill in the date when the resignation is to take effect.[1] But just how to enforce these pledges against stubborn political heretics and schismatics (of which German parties have a great many) is indeed a question.

If a party recall were specifically established by law, the problem of enforcing candidates' pledges would of course be simplified. This has been done in Baden. According to Article 17 of the Baden *Gemeindeordnung* of 1921, "Whoever loses his eligibility for office or withdraws from the party or electoral group on whose ticket he was elected, thereby loses his office. The council decides such cases." A somewhat similar provision formerly existed in Thuringian municipal law but this feature was not retained in the *Gemeindeordnung* of 1926.[2] However, in most German states, the party recall is illegal. Thus in Prussia, it is provided that "councilmen are not bound by any kind of instructions or orders of the voters."[3] The Prussian *Oberverwaltungsgericht* has held that a councilman cannot be removed from office if he refuses to resign in accordance with a pre-election agreement. Such a *Rückberufungsrecht* or party recall is unlawful because it violates the article just quoted.[4] A similar decision is that of the *Obergericht* of the Free City of Dan-

zig ruling that blank resignations are illegal and that a political party has no legal means of compelling one of its members in the city council to resign his seat.[5] The matter has not been judicially decided in all states but most of the municipal government acts follow the wording of the Prussian *Städteordnung* and therefore would seem to invalidate any party recall.

In general, then, there is a moral but not a legal obligation to resign. Even so, is it permissible for a councilman voluntarily to give up his seat when he secedes from or is expelled from the party? It is a general principle of German municipal law that the qualified citizen must be willing to serve in the office of councilman or in other unpaid local office. If, without proper cause, he refuses to serve or resigns before his term is over, he may be fined, have his taxes increased or be deprived of his rights as a *Bürger* for a period of years. The municipal government acts (*Städteordnungen, Gemeindeordnungen*, etc.) usually enumerate the specific reasons which are acceptable as grounds for refusal to serve or for resignation,— *e.g.*, sickness, old age, previous long service in office, etc. In addition, one commonly finds a general clause covering "other special circumstances which according to the opinion of the council establish a valid excuse."[6] Since the

[5] See *Kommunalpolitische Blätter*, xvii (1926), p. 403.

[6] Prussia, *Städteordnung für die sechs östlichen Provinzen*, Art. 74. See also Bavaria, *Gemeindeordnung* of 1927, Art. 112; Bremen, *Städteordnung* of 1922, Art. 19; Mecklenburg-Schwerin, *Städteordnung* of 1919, Arts. 12, 14, 16; Mecklenburg-Strelitz, *Städteordnung* of 1919 as amended 1923, Art. 14; Thuringia, *Gemeinde-und Kreisordnung* of 1926, Art. 18. The Saxon law is more specific on this point. "A person may refuse or resign the office of councilman if he is no longer able to share the political and economic opinions of the other members of the party ticket, their permission having been obtained." (Saxony,

---

[1] See *Kommunalpolitische Blätter*, xii (1921), pp. 117–118.

[2] See Thuringia, *Gemeinde-und Kreisordnung* of 1922, Art. 45, and Paul Kiess, *Handbuch des Kommunalen Rechts der Gemeinden, Stadt und Landkreise Thüringens* (Jena, 1922), p. 62.

[3] Prussia, *Städteordnung für die sechs östlichen Provinzen*, Art. 35.

[4] See the note on the Sorau case in *Zeitschrift für Kommunalwirtschaft* xii (1922), p. vi.

council itself possesses the right to judge and punish refusal to serve (subject to appeal to the higher authorities), it is obvious that, under this clause, a councilman may be permitted to resign for political reasons without penalty. He may not, however, be forced to resign against his will.

The present scope of partisanship and parties in German municipal government has now been discussed. National partisanship would seem to be a more or less permanent feature of present city politics, but it is unlikely

that the spirit of partisanship will be carried to extremes. On the contrary, as time goes on and conditions become more settled, it is probable that the extremist elements of the Right and Left will play a less conspicuous and disturbing part. Party spirit will be less bitter but, and this is especially important, the national parties will develop more and more highly specialized organizations for municipal work. The municipal organizations of the Center and the Social Democratic Parties show what can be done along this line. The example set by these parties is one which the other parties are trying more and more to follow in the post-war years.

Gemeindeordnung of 1923 as amended 1925, Art. 25.) A similar provision is found in Lippe, *Gemeindeverfassungsgesetz* of 1927, Art. 19.

RECENT BOOKS REVIEWED

PRIMARY ELECTIONS. By Charles E. Merriam and Louise Overacker. Chicago: The University of Chicago Press, 1928. Pp. 442.

Primary Elections comes as a new edition of the work first published twenty years ago. But it is something more than a mere revision; the overhauling process has been so complete that for all practical purposes the result is a new book. All the chapters, except the first three, have been rewritten and brought up to date. Two new chapters on "Presidential Primaries" and "Analysis of Primary Forces" have broadened the general outlines of the subject. In his "Summary and Conclusions," Mr. Merriam does more than recapitulate previous chapters; he subordinates his inquiry to the general problems of political parties and American democracy, offering valuable suggestions for reform and prophesying the probable future development of nominating methods.

The foundation of the book is laid in minute statistical studies which reveal its scientific character. The first five chapters are detailed chronologies of primary legislation and regulation, the convention system and direct primaries. Together with the appendices on primary laws, cases, and bibliography, they constitute an excellent reference source. Necessarily technical and special, they will probably not have so wide an appeal as the last seven more general, yet scholarly, chapters. The translation of statistics into words may hold some subtle charm for the political "scientist," but the chief significance of the book seems to be that the underlying problem for which it seeks new light and offers possible solutions, is sufficiently earthy to attract the layman, and to have that influence on practical politics for which its authors undoubtedly hope.

The question is how best to secure nominations to important political offices in a democracy. "Party nominating systems . . . are only a part of the larger political problem and are dependent upon the general course of other events. The nominating system is a phase of the American party system; this is in turn a phase of the larger problem of modern democracy. And democracy is a phase of the political order now existing, and this in turn of the economic and social order of the present day and

the Western World,"—this is the broad conception which Mr. Merriam has of primary elections. Tracing nominating methods through personal presentation, caucus, regulated convention, and direct primary—the gradual legalization of political parties—is to show the evolution of our efforts to adapt politics to changing social and economic conditions. The primary is a mechanism of control, not a panacea; it is only one step in a series of experiments. We are really testing the assumption made by democracy that the electorate can formulate social policies and choose wise leaders. Faced with criticism of the primary system, Mr. Merriam defends it against a return to the old convention. He suggests that we go forward first to a party conference and next to the short ballot.

Primary Elections must rank as an outstanding contribution to political science, in method as well as content. Here the problem is the focus of attention, while the disinterested researchers employ as tools the historical, comparative, statistical, and analytical methods, even suggesting the psychological method in treating such a primary force as leadership. Professor Merriam's personal experience with primaries, as well as Dr. Overacker's careful research, have gone to make up a book which deals competently with an important phase of our developing democracy and evolving constitution.

EILENE MARIE GALLOWAY.

Swarthmore College.

❋

PIEDPOUDRE COURTS; A STUDY OF THE SMALL CLAIM LITIGANT IN THE PITTSBURGH DISTRICT. By Gustav L. Schramm, LL.B., Ph.D. Published by the Pittsburgh Legal Aid Society, 1928. Pp. 219.

In Allegheny County, Pa., there may be at one time 391 magistrates competent to try civil causes involving not more than $300. Of these, 242 are country justices of the peace and 46 are aldermen, that being the designation in the city of Pittsburgh. The 288 justices and aldermen are elected, and obtain their compensation only through fees. The jurisdiction of each extends to the entire county. In 99 per cent of 2,000 cases which were studied, the plaintiffs prevailed.

Provision is made for appeals to two excellent courts, in which the cases, if heard at all, must be tried *de novo*. But the expense of retrial is considerable and, in the cases involving less than $75, either appellant or appellee often throws up the sponge.

Working on the investigation for three years, the author, who is assistant professor of political science in the University of Pittsburgh and attorney for the Legal Aid Society, has clearly presented an all but intolerable situation, devoting 219 pages to his text and appendices. The study is a model of thoroughness, and probably will be the starting point for a sweeping reform. But the legal right to fatten on the misfortunes of the poor will not be surrendered without a struggle.

Here is presented a dramatic contrast between the practical genius of a people who lead the world in scrapping inefficient machinery and business organization, and their political genius, which has run to seed along doctrinnaire lines of eighteenth-century thought. So keen in business that they put the entire world under tribute, and so stupid in fundamental political administration that they submit to pilfering from a small army of picaroon politicians, their degradation of justice cannot be offset by thousands of prize essays on the constitution.

HERBERT HARLEY.

Chicago.

✣

THE DISTRICT OF COLUMBIA, ITS GOVERNMENT AND ADMINISTRATION. By Laurence F. Schmeckebeier. The Institute for Government Research, Studies in Administration. Baltimore: Johns Hopkins Press, 1928. Pp. xx, 943.

This comprehensive survey of the organization and operation of the government and administration of the District of Columbia is, like the service monographs of the Institute of Government Research, almost wholly a descriptive account, and makes no attempt to consider matters of administrative procedure, nor to present criticism of the existing system or proposals for improvement. It is planned, however, to issue another volume dealing with the latter problems in the light of other studies in public administration.

A brief examination of the study soon shows the complexity of the existing machinery, arising from the failure to establish a definite policy as to the relations between the local government of the District and those matters which are managed as part of the general administrative system of the national government. The government of the District is far from an integrated whole, but is distributed between Congress, the commissioners of the District, a number of boards and other agencies dealing only with District affairs, a larger number of organs of the national administration, and several national agencies which have contractual relations with the District government.

The District commissioners have the most numerous functions, combining many of the usual municipal activities with some matters, such as insurance supervision, usually under state control. But the Board of Education and the District courts are independent agencies, and a number of other local services are substantially autonomous. More than a score of national agencies, scattered through five of the major departments and independent services, deal with a variety of matters. Thus the control of parks and playgrounds is divided between the National Capital Park and Planning Commission, the Rock Creek-Potomac Parkway Commission, the director of public buildings and public parks, the department of playgrounds under the District commissioners, the Smithsonian Institution and the Architect of the Capitol.

In some respects the situation resembles that in the territory of Alaska; and in both cases there is need for working out a simpler and more definite distribution of authority.

The last chapter, on "Citizens' Associations," deals briefly with a significant group of unofficial organizations, about which further information would be welcome.

JOHN A. FAIRLIE.

University of Illinois.

✣

A SYSTEM OF CLASSIFICATION FOR POLITICAL SCIENCE COLLECTIONS. By William Anderson and Sophia Hall Glidden. Minneapolis: University of Minnesota Press, 1928. Pp. 188.

Almost every special library feels a need for a classification especially adapted to its collection. In 1922 when the Special Libraries Association made a study of methods used in such libraries, it was found that of one hundred and ten replying, seventy-eight librarians indicated that they would welcome a library classification which developed their particular subject further than any existing classification system had done.

That each library was trying to solve the difficulty is evidenced by the fact that ninety libraries reported that they used a combination of several classifications, or used an adaptation, or an expansion, or a special classification for their subject. In most cases, these special library classifications as used by individual libraries are never printed. Therefore the Bureau for Research in Government of the University of Minnesota is to be complimented that the classification under review has been made available in print. Mrs. Sophia Hall Glidden is the one to whom credit should be given for it; it was evolved during her work as librarian of the Municipal Reference Bureau and it has been put to the test of actual use for six years in that library and also in the Bureau for Research in Government library.

This classification covers the subjects of politics, government, and administration, national, state and local. Letters, not numbers, have been chosen to connote the classes. The field of political science has been divided into twenty-one main divisions and each has been assigned a letter arbitrarily.

An alphabetically arranged subject index has been very carefully prepared. It seems to be absolutely complete for all subjects included in the classification and cross-references have been generously supplied. It is intended primarily as a finding list, but it is expected that it may also serve the librarian as a list of subject-headings. The technique of the cataloguer is shown in the fullness with which the "see" and "see also" references have been included in the right-hand column of the subject index for the use of the librarian.

The reviewer knows of only two other classifications in printed form planned exclusively for municipal government material; one is *The Classification Scheme of the Library for Municipal Research at Harvard University*, by Joseph Wright, published in 1917; the other is *Tentative Classification for Subject Files*, issued by the American City Bureau in 1919. In both of these schemes the connotation is letters of the alphabet; in one arbitrarily assigned to the subject, and in the other the first letter of the subject is used. Both use digits following the letters, and one uses decimals like Dewey. The Minnesota classification is more carefully worked out and is more complete than these earlier schemes, and the subject index assures its more consistent application.

It is my opinion that this classification is a good one. I tried to apply it to current civic material being received, and in every case it was easy to assign a number from this system. It is unfortunate that the system has no mnemonic features; the letters are arbitrarily assigned to the classes and, though the subdivisions and subheads are logically made, still the numbers are not given in such a way as to memorize easily. Since the classification has such a splendid finding list I suppose we need not expect mnemonic features as well. It gives all evidences of being a splendid scheme well laid out in its basic principles and well tried out by six years of actual use.

REBECCA B. RANKIN.

Municipal Reference Library,
New York City.

✳

CONSOLIDATING STATE ADMINISTRATION IN OHIO. By the State Committee of the Citizens League of Cleveland, 1928. Pp. 28.

This recent report is addressed to the members of the Joint Legislative Committee on Economy in Public Service, which is now making a survey of the administrative organization and employment conditions of the Ohio state government. The report deals entirely with the state organization under the administrative code of 1921, which has been the subject of considerable criticism. The committee finds that the code organization "has been administered almost entirely since its adoption by a governor who was openly opposed to the principle which it sought to establish, and it has had the silent opposition of a large and sincere group of socially-minded citizens who were wedded to the plan of organization and administration of state welfare activities existing prior to the adoption of the administrative code."

The report goes on to point out the increasing cost of state government, the inadequacy of the old plan of administrative organization to meet the new requirements as shown by the experience of more than a dozen states, and the need for a simplified, direct, and responsible type of state administration. The committee does not claim that the present organization of Ohio is perfect; in fact, it points to several defects that should be remedied. It proposes, however, that these be remedied by further consolidation along present lines. It admits the present need for continuity in administration and suggests that the solution lies in giving the governor a longer term of office, in appointing advisory boards for each department and important division or institution as now provided in the code, and in requiring all heads of divisions and other officers below the directors to be appointed on merit and retained in the service during good behavior. On this point the committee says:

The enormous increase in the state's business requires that the governor be elected for a longer period—four years—which would enable him to get a grasp of the problems and work out the right solution. The appointment of advisory boards with power to consult and advise, but not to execute, would aid greatly in stabilizing administrative policies. When to these two stabilizing influences is added the principle of a trained and permanent service, whereby all officers below that of department heads are chosen solely on the basis of merit, then all of the continuity which is desired will be assured without the loss of the more important principle of executive authority and responsibility.

The report is well planned and carefully written. Although it covers only twenty-eight mimeographed pages, the subject is thoroughly and convincingly treated.

A. E. Buck.

❈

Fiscal Problems of City School Administration: A report by the Special Joint Committee on Taxation and Retrenchment, State of New York. Legislative Document (1928), No. 66 Pp. 130.

This report to the New York state legislature, made after state-wide hearings and comprehensive studies, touches the high and sore spots in the conflict of interest between municipal and school authorities in many of the cities in New York State. The report is of interest in that its authors are convinced that since the previous study in 1919 there are fewer points of friction, and the intensity of disagreement is reduced. In brief, "there seems to be less friction than formerly in those cities where the administration has definite control over the educational budget, and also in those municipalities where there is complete separation. There still exists an unsatisfactory condition in those municipalities where the educational authorities have complete, or practically complete, control of the budget and the city authorities are held responsible for the tax rate."

The committee finds "that since 1919 . . . there has been a noticeable improvement in the business management of city schools." To fur-

ther this, the committee suggests that the boards of education be granted specific authority to create the position of business superintendent to be responsible directly to the board if it so desires. Obviously, this is a recommendation to supersede the present law granting priority in authority to the superintendent of schools with dual control, despite the conceded progress now being made under the existing system of unit control.

The second major recommendation in the report is that the mayor of each city be authorized to sit in the board of education at times when the budget is being discussed. This suggestion raises the question of what the mayor's position would be when called upon in many cities to review the budget of the schools in the making of which he had had a responsible part.

In the chapter covering the place of education in local government, there are interesting historical facts, references to current foreign practice, and recognition of the principle that, so far as administrative reorganization of the schools is concerned, cities should be dealt with individually "in recognition of their several conditions and traditions."

In addition to the supporting data for the recommendation for administrative changes in the schools, there are cost data, references to measuring education, and various appendices.

In this interesting document, which merits the attention of any school official or responsible city head, there is a significant sentence which is well worth remembering: "As we analyze the situation it appears that the difficulty with our city-school relations is that we have permitted a vicious separation of power from responsibility in the local administration and financing of schools."

H. E. Akerly.

Rochester, N. Y.

❈

Three City Reports.—*Staunton, Virginia. Annual Report for the Year Ending March 31, 1928. By Willard F. Day, City Manager. Pp. 62.*—In less than four weeks after the end of the period covered, this report was in the hands of the taxpayers of Staunton. As far as the writer knows, this establishes a record for promptness—a basic essential of reporting. Nor did the quality of the report suffer by reason of this speed in publication. In spite of the absence of three important features, this volume must be classed among the outstanding reports of the year. It is too long, has no table of contents, and lacks an organization chart. The latter would have served a useful purpose in helping the reader to understand more easily the operation of the governmental machinery and the resulting product as expressed in the various activities and services. The poor arrangement of material near the front of the report also detracts from the many good qualities. To name the headings of a few subjects in order of appearance will illustrate,—collections, annexation, city planning, street widening, zoning and building inspection, office of the city manager, building inspections, new high school culvert, etc. The preparation of a clear and simple organization and function chart at the beginning would doubtless have helped in arranging the material in a more logical order.

The last twenty-one pages of the report contain the budget with comparative figures for the previous year, and the city treasurer's report covering the period of the report. This attempt to correlate activities and services with costs is highly commendable, and is indicative of the many other favorable characteristics of this excellent report.

Austin, Texas. Annual Report for the Fiscal Year Ending December 31, 1927. By Adam R. Johnson, City Manager. Pp. 183.—One hundred and eighty-three pages of a public report would under ordinary circumstances condemn the document without further evidence. This report, however, disposes of all the municipal activities in thirty-eight pages, while the remaining pages are taken up by a detailed financial report. These financial tables are doubtless as interesting to a taxpayer as any 145 pages of statistics could be, but it is presuming altogether too much attention by the readers. If only a budget summary

had been placed in the report and a few short statements setting forth briefly and clearly where the revenue came from, what unit of the organization spent it, and the service or activity for which it was spent, the result would have added materially both to the value and to the interest of the report.

A well-prepared table of contents in the front of the report helps the reader to find what he wants in a minimum of time. Among the last ten reports reviewed, this is the second one containing a table of contents. If report writers would draw up an outline before they begin the arrangement of their manuscript, it would aid in the preparation and organization of material and serve later as a basis for a table of contents. This report is made attractive by a neat cover, good paper, clear type, and a few well-chosen pictures.

Westerville, Ohio. Annual Report for the Year 1927. By L. G. Whitney, City Manager. Pp. 37.—This report of municipal activities was available to the taxpayers of Westerville, eleven weeks after the end of the period covered, a record not many reports equal; and yet the report should have been available in but half the time. Its main feature is a few well chosen pictures and charts well distributed throughout the relevant text. The charts portraying the past and present financial condition of the town are especially clear and simple. The defects include an utter lack of emphasis upon important facts, no organization chart or table of contents, and no clear-cut recommendations or other evidence of plans for the future.

While this last report is not up to the high standard set by the 1926 report of Westerville, it nevertheless is far superior to many municipal reports emanating from much larger cities.

C. E. RIDLEY.

GOVERNMENTAL RESEARCH ASSOCIATION NOTES

EDITED BY RUSSELL FORBES

Secretary

Recent Reports of Research Agencies.—The following reports have been received at the central library of the Association since June 1, 1928:

Boston Finance Commission:
  A Study of the Cost of School Lands for the Last Ten Years.
Kansas City Public Service Institute:
  "*Charities and Corrections*," *Jackson County, Missouri.*
Schenectady Bureau of Municipal Research, Inc.:
  Report on a Long Term Financial Program for Schenectady, N. Y.
  Report on Preliminary Survey of the Department of Public Instruction.
  Report on Preliminary Survey of the Department of Assessment and Taxation.

❋

Boston Finance Commission.—The commission has recently issued the following reports: to the mayor regarding commissions paid on certain property purchased by the trustees of the White Fund for the city; to the school committee regarding proposed taking of land for a junior high school in the Charlestown district; and to the school committee recommending that serious consideration be given to the sites on Union Street and Chestnut Hill Avenue for the Brighton Intermediate School.

❋

Citizens' Research Institute of Canada.—The first portion (city section) of the Institute's *Red Book*, Financial Statistics—Canadian Governments, has been issued. The Institute has issued a report on *The Present Tax Structure in Canada*. No attempt was made to show every existing source of revenue tapped by the various governments in Canada. Only the more important sources, which might be termed "taxes," were given. This report has aroused very considerable interest and was reproduced by the press in various parts of the Dominion.

The Institute also issued an open letter regarding the non-allowance of local improvement taxation as a deduction in arriving at income for the purposes of the dominion income tax.

A study of automobile accident fatalities has been started. This study will cover fatal motor accidents not only on the American continent but also in the larger European cities.

❋

Taxpayers' Research League of Delaware.—The League has made progress on the preparation of material for use in drafting a finance code for the state and its subdivisions, which is to be prepared jointly with a committee of the Delaware Bankers' Association. Work has been continued on the objective analysis of the state appropriations and expenditures. J. Ernest Solway, of the Delaware bar, has been retained as a special staff member to compile all existing constitutional provisions and all laws relating to the fiscal administrative affairs of the state and its subdivisions.

The audit and analysis of the accounts and the accounting and budget procedure of the town of Milford has been completed. The League is now engaged in preparing its report and in designing a new accounting and budget procedure.

Having ended a year's work installing and supervising the operation of a new accounting and budget procedure for the Delaware Industrial School for Girls, the League is now analyzing the year's records and preparing a report on the results.

❋

Civic Affairs Department, Indianapolis Chamber of Commerce.—The department has started its annual study of the Indianapolis municipal budget for 1929. A special budget subcommittee has been appointed to advise the staff on matters of policy. It is considering requests of the civil city for increases in street thoroughfare, track elevation and street resurfacing tax levies, as well as requests for large increases in the number of policemen and firemen.

The department is completing a draft of a proposed amendment to the law governing election of school boards in Indianapolis. The amendment will provide for a biennial election with three members elected at large in one election and two members elected at large in the next election, the election to be held at the same time as the election of civil city commissioners under the commission-manager charter which Indianapolis has voted to adopt in 1930. The department is also considering teacher tenure and teacher pension acts with a view to suggesting improvements in these laws.

The department has been successful in obtaining an appropriation for housing improvements at Fort Benjamin Harrison.

✢

National Institute of Public Administration.— Bruce Smith, who is the director of the study on uniform crime records which is being carried out under the auspices of the International Association of Chiefs of Police, attended the meeting of the Association at Colorado Springs, June 25 to 28.

Harry Freeman, director of the Buffalo Bureau, Joseph F. Base, director of the Schenectady Bureau, and Alden Fensel, acting director of the Cleveland Bureau, visited the Institute during the month of June.

Professor Theo Suranyi-Unger of the faculty of law, Miskola, Hungary, is doing some research at the Institute in connection with his study of the social and economic history of New York.

✢

Pittsburgh Bureau of Governmental Research.—Frank L. Olson, associate director of the Bureau, passed away at the Pittsburgh Hospital on June 18. In the death of Mr. Olson, the municipal research movement has lost one of its most capable workers. He was associated with the movement from its very beginning, and has made a great contribution to the advancement of municipal administration.

✢

Schenectady Bureau of Municipal Research.— *Long Term Financial Program.*—The city officials have concurred in our suggestion that a

long term financial program be prepared to cover the city's capital expenditures for the next five or ten years. The mayor, in a special message to the council, recommended that such a schedule of capital accounts be made and that a special committee composed of citizens and city officials be appointed to prepare such a program, as announced elsewhere in this issue. The council concurred in the mayor's suggestion and in a resolution authorized the appointment of a citizen advisory commission and also suggested that the Bureau be called upon to assist in the work. The mayor accordingly appointed a committee of seven, composed of four city officials and three civilians, including the managing director of the Bureau.

The Bureau staff, anticipating the foregoing procedure, has been at work compiling data with reference to the city's income and expense. The first section of the long term financial program study covering this phase of city finance has been prepared and is ready for submission to the city advisory commission at its first meeting.

Civil Service Study.—A. H. Hall, instructor in political science at Union College, has joined the staff of the Bureau for the summer months and is engaged in a special study of the local civil service department. The work is being done in coöperation with the civil service secretary and with the approval of the civil service commission. This work embraces the customary classification of the civil service personnel, including the preparation of job specifications covering the various classes.

A merit system and certain salary standardizations, with lines of promotion to encourage longer tenure of service, will also be suggested.

New Building Code.—The chairman of the council committee on laws and ordinances has requested the Bureau to lend its assistance in preparing a new building code for the city. The Bureau is engaged in making a review of the proposed code which was submitted to the council several years ago. Indications are that this document will need complete revision, due to the fact that it has already become obsolete since its original proposal for adoption.

Charities Administration.—The local League of Women Voters has requested the Bureau to make a study of the administration of charities in the city and county. An outline for the approach to this problem has been prepared and the actual field work on this survey will be commenced shortly.

NOTES AND EVENTS

EDITED BY RUSSELL FORBES

Proposed Consolidation of St. Louis City and County.—A new effort was recently made to effect a merger of St. Louis County with the City of St. Louis, by placing the issue before the voters of the entire state.

The initiative method of effecting the merger was proposed to Mayor Miller by a delegation of county and city residents. The Mayor announced that he would appoint a committee of about two hundred citizens who would endeavor to put the issue to a state-wide vote.

Although the suggestion was made to the Mayor early in April, the Mayor had failed to announce appointment of the proposed committee prior to July 5. The initiative petitions would have to be presented to the secretary of state by July 7 to assure inclusion in the ballot for the November election. As no action has been taken to obtain the necessary signatures on initiative petitions, it is therefore impossible to place the issue before the voters of the state in 1928.

C. W. ATKINS.

St. Louis Bureau of Municipal Research.

✿

Twenty-first Annual Conference of the National Tax Association.—The executive committee of the National Tax Association have decided upon Seattle, Washington, as the place for the twenty-first annual conference of that Association. It will be held in the week of August 27, 1928, with headquarters at the Hotel Olympic.

✿

Summary of Pension Systems.—The Department of Labor has issued the results of a recent survey summarizing the pension systems in nine large American cities. Those covered are Baltimore, Boston, Chicago, Detroit, Minneapolis, New York, Philadelphia, Pittsburgh and San Francisco.

✿

According to the division of building and housing of the Department of Commerce, zoned municipalities in the United States now number 583 with a population of more than 31,000,000.

The Next Annual Meeting of the Assembly of Civil Service Commissions will be held in Denver, September 4 to 7. Charles P. Messick is chairman of the program committee.

✿

First Annual Northwest Fire School.—The University of Minnesota, the League of Minnesota Municipalities and the Minnesota Department of Insurance will sponsor a fire school to be held in Minneapolis, August 13 to 17. An elaborate program has been prepared which will consist of addresses by leading authorities on fire fighting methods for large and small cities. The program will also provide for demonstrations of methods in such phases of fire fighting as laying stairway lines, the proper use of high ladders, and handling emergencies such as burst hose. Harvey Walker, acting executive secretary of the League of Minnesota Municipalities, is serving as director of this fire school, which will be an annual event in the Northwest.

✿

Fourth International Congress of Cities, March, 1929.—The fourth International Congress of Cities will be held in Seville, Spain, March 19–23, 1929. This congress of cities had been called for October 5 to 9, 1928, but owing to the postponement of the opening of the Spanish-American Exposition in Seville to March 15, 1929 the congress was postponed.

The American Municipal Association, which holds an active membership in the International Federation of Local Government Associations (Union Internationale des Villes et Pouvoirs Locaux) which sponsors the international congress of cities, will promote a tour of American city officials to European cities, including in the itinerary the fourth international congress, in March, 1929.

✿

Schenectady Mayor Appoints Commission on Long-Term Financial Program.—During the latter part of June Mayor Fagal of Schenectady appointed a capital accounts commission. The commission is composed of Joseph F. Base, director of the Bureau of Municipal Research; Ira D. LeFevre, general auditor of the General Electric Company; James C. McDonald, well-known real estate dealer; and the following ex-officio members: James A. Horne, president of the common council; Leon G. Dibble, comptroller; Frank R. Lanagan, city engineer; and Walker H. Mishler, commissioner of public works. It will be the function of the commission to study the financial needs of Schenectady's municipal government for the next ten years and to prepare a ten-year budget based on estimated requirements in public works improvements and for current operation. This action is the outgrowth of a recommendation of the Schenectady Bureau of Municipal Research. It has been praised editorially by Schenectady newspapers as one of the most forward-looking events in the history of that city.

Annual Meeting of Colorado Municipal League.—The Colorado Municipal League held its annual convention at Sterling, Colorado, June 14, 15 and 16. Sixty delegates, representing twenty cities, were in attendance.

Minneapolis Charter Changes Defeated.—On June 19 two proposed changes in the charter of Minneapolis were defeated at referendum. One proposal would have centralized the administration of public works as a substitute for the present administration by wards. The other proposal would have brought about a redistricting of the wards of the city for the election of aldermen. The vote on each proposal was close; both proposals failed to secure the necessary three-fifths majority. The sponsors of the charter change have, however, appealed to court for a recount of the ballots.

Institute of Public Affairs, University of Virginia.—The annual Institute of Public Affairs at the University of Virginia will be held on August 5 to 18. In addition to the daily popular addresses by noted authorities, the Institute will have the following round tables, each in charge of a well-known specialist in the particular field: The agricultural problem, women in public affairs, our Latin-American relations, municipal management, county and state government, political parties, the tax problem, the press, economic and industrial development of the South, and arbitration of commercial disputes. The results of the meeting will be summarized in a later issue.

Birmingham's New City Commission.—Three years ago the present writer somewhat caustically handled the former commissioners of Birmingham in these columns.[1] This old commission virtually reached an impasse by reason of antagonisms resulting from mutual incomprehensibility.

In 1923, when I moved to the city, it was the most poorly paved, sewered, and lighted municipality of a quarter of a million that I had seen. The carcasses of dogs and cats were left on the streets to be run over till worn out by passing vehicles. There were but three grade separations, two of them viaducts, and one a tunnel under one of the stations. Later another viaduct was completed.

The old commission, however, made some real improvements, despite its bickerings and unprofessional workmanship. Two elaborate high schools, one of them for colored children, a municipal auditorium and a municipal market were constructed, and traffic lights were installed.

Birmingham's experience with commission government is amusing. Passing from the old mayor and council type to a commission charter by special law, the system was later modified to a five-commissioner scheme, and then, four years ago, the legislature reversed itself and gave the city another three-commissioner charter. The members are paid better than the former commissioners. Three men, well seasoned in county and municipal administration, and not of the ordinary politician type, were elected. These commissioners, J. N. ("Jimmie") Jones, president, W. E. Dixon, and J. H. Taylor, have worked in harmony and if things go wrong squabbling cannot be held accountable.

When this commission entered office there was an operating deficit of $213,000. Two years later they announced a surplus of $201,000. Birmingham bonds are now sold at from 4.15 per cent to 4.25 per cent interest. Current bills are paid promptly each month and discounted.

The lighting system has been more than doubled. The city is operating two golf courses. Thoroughfares connecting the city with the suburbs have been extended. After thirty years of wrangling and many court battles with the rail-

[1] National Municipal Review, Vol. XIV, pp. 661–663.

roads, a compromise has been effected and a four million dollar bond issue for track elevation has been submitted to referendum and passed by a large majority. The city and the roads share the expense fifty-fifty.

The extension of paving and sewage facilities has been really remarkable. When Commissioner Dixon and City Engineer A. J. Hawkins entered the former commission in 1922, Birmingham had but 136 miles of paved streets. In six years they have laid 197 miles of new pavement.

HARRISON A. TREXLER.
Birmingham-Southern College.

✤

Sacramento Creates Traffic and Safety Commission.—The city of Sacramento, California, has established by ordinance a commission on traffic and safety consisting of nine citizens to be appointed by the city council, with the mayor, city manager, city attorney and superintendent of traffic serving as ex-officio members. This commission is charged with the responsibility of investigating the traffic problem in Sacramento and with recommending rules and regulations for its control. The commission is further vested with authority to formulate and carry out a program of public education on accident prevention. The commission is responsible to the city council and is required to report annually to that body.

✤

Traffic Regulation a Hazardous Occupation.—That the regulation of traffic is fraught with dangers to policemen is strikingly shown by a recent report of the chief deputy of the motor vehicle department of San Francisco, who stated that of the 247 traffic police on duty in that city, 91 were killed or crippled during the last fourteen months.

✤

New York City Relaxes Zoning Regulations.—Edward M. Bassett, zoning expert, has shown in a recent report that the New York City Board of Estimate and Apportionment during 1927 adopted more relaxing changes than strengthening changes in the zoning ordinance. This is the first year since 1920 that the action of the Board has resulted in a preponderance of changes which lessened the zoning requirements. The action of the Board is rather inconsistent with its announced policy during 1927 of seeking through every available means to prevent further street congestion by lessening the number and extent of skyscraper districts. Many of the changes authorized by the Board permitted the erection of high buildings; at the same time the Mayor's Committee on Plan and Survey was recommending that skyscraper districts be reduced or restricted to the minimum.

✤

Albion, Michigan, Abolishes City Manager Government.—Albion, Michigan, a town of 8,000 population, has reverted to the commission form of government after operating under city manager charter since 1918. This action was taken by referendum in which the commission plan won by thirty-three votes. Albion is thus the seventh city to discard a city manager charter after its adoption.

✤

The Fifth World Motor Transport Congress will meet in Rome, September 25 to 29. The Congress will meet under the patronage of the King of Italy, and His Excellency Benito Mussolini will serve as honorary president. Official reports on the regulation of traffic will be given by representatives of Great Britain, Germany, France and the United States.

✤

Cincinnati Moves Towards County Manager Government.—One of the issues to be settled at the primary election in August in Cincinnati will be indirectly the question of county manager government. A contest is involved between the regular organization of the Republican party and a group known as the Citizens' Committee, headed by Captain Victor Heintz. The Citizens' Committee has pledged itself to two specific reforms. The first is the promise that, if placed in control of the Republican party in Hamilton County, it will not inject partisan issues into municipal elections in cities which have a charter calling for nonpartisan elections. This amounts to a pledge of support to the present charter and city manager government in Cincinnati.

The second reform promised by the Citizens' Committee is to secure legislation permitting the county manager form of government in Hamilton County. Although a bonafide county manager plan cannot be adopted without legislative consent, existing statutes can be employed to bring about unified control and management of county affairs. The Citizens' Committee has promised if successful in the primaries, to have the Board of County Commissioners employ a county clerk and engineer and to centralize in their hands the administrative and financial affairs of the county government.

✷

Pan-American Congress of Municipalities Planned.—The sixth international conference of American states which met in Havana early this year recommended that the Pan-American Union should sponsor several conferences of a special or technical nature. The Union in a recent report has announced its plan to call a Pan-American Congress of Municipalities. The object of the congress is stated in the report of the Union as follows: "The Sixth International Conference of American States also recommended that a Pan-American Congress of Municipalities be held at Havana in 1931, and that through the Pan-American Union a preparatory meeting take place in Boston, Mass., in 1930, in connection with the celebration of the three hundredth anniversary of the founding of that city. The governing board has already appointed a committee composed of the Minister of Costa Rica, the Minister of Haiti and the Chargé d'Affaires of Uruguay to study this subject in detail.

"Taking into consideration the growing interest in city improvement and municipal questions in general, which is being developed in the great urban centres of America at the present time, an interest which has been promoted in recent years by the series of Pan-American congresses on architecture, this conference promises to be one of the most profitable ever convened."

New York City Committee on Plan and Survey Issues Report.—The city committee on plan and survey, appointed by Mayor Walker nearly two years ago to formulate plans for the improvement of the city government, submitted its report on June 5. This report will be reviewed in this magazine in a later issue. The principal recommendations of the committee were as follows:

Creation of a permanent official city planning commission to work out a comprehensive plan for the future growth of New York.

Appointment of a special committee to investigate the necessity for a complete reorganization of the city government.

New sources of city revenue, including a gasoline tax, to meet the cost of the new subway system and other public improvements.

Spread of industries throughout the city to induce a more even distribution of population and to relieve the overcrowded tenement districts.

Elimination of the slums, improved housing conditions, and extension of the zoning regulations to provide more light and air for dwellings.

More parks in the outlying sections, especially Queens and Staten Island; more playgrounds in the congested districts.

Relief of traffic congestion by cutting new streets through downtown Manhattan, and establishing express highways and a great loop highway around all centres of congestion.

Better control of pedestrian traffic, more night deliveries of goods, and closer regulation of interurban buses and trucks.

A complete system of airports in different parts of the city.

Additional tunnels and bridges.

More efficient use of waterfront space. especially by industries needing both rail and water facilities.

Garbage incinerators in different parts of the city, to obviate dumping of refuse at sea and littering beaches.

NATIONAL
MUNICIPAL REVIEW

PUBLISHED MONTHLY BY THE

National Municipal League

Vol. XVII, No. 9   SEPTEMBER, 1928   Total No. 147

CONTENTS

EDITORIAL COMMENT...........................*Russell Forbes*..... 493
CIVIC IDEALS OF LONG AGO.....................*Carl S. Knopf*..... 495
GOING AFTER THE TAX DOLLAR...................*Welles A. Gray*.... 497
TRAFFIC RELIEF THROUGH BY-PASS HIGHWAYS......*William Beard*.... 499
DOES ZONING PROTECT ONLY THE AESTHETIC SENSE?.*R. D. MacLaurin*.. 504
THE LONDON REGION............................*Harlean James*.... 508
COUNTY CONSOLIDATION IN TENNESSEE............*J. W. Manning*... 511
OUR AMERICAN MAYORS:
    XI. FRANK HAGUE, MAYOR-BOSS OF JERSEY
    CITY......................................*E. E. Smith*...... 514
THE TAX SITUATION IN CHICAGO.................*Herbert D. Simpson* 522
FITZ-ELWYNE'S ASSIZE OF BUILDINGS—
    A SUPPLEMENT.............................*C. W. Tooke*...... 555

DEPARTMENTS

  I. Recent Books Reviewed 534
  II. Judicial Decisions...*Edited by C. W. Tooke* 538
  III. Public Utilities..*Edited by John Bauer* 542
  IV. Governmental Research Association Notes..................*Edited by Russell Forbes* 546
  V. Notes and Events.......................................*Edited by Russell Forbes* 550

THE LEAGUE'S BUSINESS

New Pamphlets on Municipal Administration.—The Municipal Administration Service, operated jointly by the National Municipal League and the Governmental Research Association, has issued a pamphlet on *The Enforcement of Real Estate Tax Liens*, by Carl H. Chatters, city auditor of Flint, Michigan. This pamphlet is described by Welles A. Gray in an article in this issue.

Another valuable addition to the pamphlet series issued by the Service will be *The Valuation of Urban Land and Buildings: A Working Manual for City Assessors*, which is now in press.

✦

Supplement to June Issue Meets with Favor Abroad.—One of our English friends writes that he has read with interest-and profit the supplement to the June REVIEW, entitled *Electricity in Great Britain—A Study in Administration*, and expresses the opinion that it provides a better statement of the present situation in Great Britain than any other available publication.

✦

Municipal Exhibit to be Convention Feature.—One of the features of the next annual meeting of the League, to be held in Cincinnati on October 16 and 17 in conjunction with the conventions of the Governmental Research Association and the National Association of Civic Secretaries, will be an exhibit illustrating the activities of the city administration. Included in the exhibit will be a relief map of the city to show the development of the city plan.

In compliance with the request of the city manager, Colonel C. O. Sherrill, the City Council has appropriated two thousand dollars to defray the expense of preparing the exhibit. In his letter to the Council requesting the appropriation, the City Manager explained the purposes of the exhibit as follows:

"In the first instance, I am suggesting that the city stage a 'City Hall Week,' from September 24 to October 2, inclusive, to acquaint the taxpayers and public with the manner in which the city government is organized and conducted and the purposes for which its funds are expended.

"Secondly, it is proposed that a part of the exhibits to be set up in the City Hall shall be transferred to Music Hall from October 3 to 14 in the Greater Cincinnati Industrial Exposition for the information of out-of-town visitors and others who cannot visit the City Hall.

"And finally, arrangements will be made to have much of this material available for the inspection of delegates attending the joint convention of the National Municipal League, the Governmental Research Association, and the National Association of Civic Secretaries, who will be guests of Cincinnati from October 15 to 17.

"The proposed 'City Hall Week' will provide an opportunity for taxpayers and school children to visit the City Hall and study the operations of city government at first hand. They can also view the rehabilitation of the building, which will be complete by that time. Departments located outside of the City Hall will also be asked to establish exhibits in the building for the occasion. An exhibit of this kind held in the municipal building will be distinctively a *municipal* one and will receive more attention and interest than is the case when city exhibits are mingled with commercial or industrial exhibits. Furthermore, it will develop a substantial increase in interest and pride in their work on the part of the employees of the city."

NATIONAL
MUNICIPAL REVIEW

VOL. XVII, NO. 9 SEPTEMBER, 1928 TOTAL NO. 147

EDITORIAL COMMENT

We welcome to our columns, as a contributor to this issue, William Beard, son of Dr. Charles A. Beard. We hope that his article on "Traffic Relief Through By-Pass Highways" may prove to be the forerunner of many articles written in the style of his illustrious father.

*

The Tax Situation in Chicago

Readers of the REVIEW will be interested in the discussion of the tax situation in Chicago by Professor Herbert D. Simpson of Northwestern University, which begins in this issue. This article describes a scientific attempt to iron out the inequalities of the present assessment system which varies from uniformity by as much as forty per cent. Professor Simpson's discussion, although referring particularly to Chicago, is applicable to the comparable situation in many large American cities at the present time. It justifies careful reading. The subject will be further discussed in our October issue.

*

Doctor Beard on the "Power Trust"

In the midst of his working, writing and philosophizing at his Connecticut farm, Dr. Charles A. Beard has found time to furnish us with the following comments on the "Power Trust":

Not in many a year have we had an investigation in Washington as important as the inquiry into the so-called "power trust," which is being conducted under the auspices of the Federal Trade Commission. In comparison, the various senatorial investigations that have "rocked the country" sink into trivial insignificance. The latter have merely involved temporary scandals, the reprehensible conduct of public officers and private individuals. The Federal Trade Commission inquiry, on the other hand, touches a fundamental, growing, continuous interest—the gas and electrical industry. It has revealed that industry closely organized, and possessing a well equipped publicity system for the purpose of "educating the people" with respect to utility matters in general and in particular with reference to the horrible wickedness and inefficiency of public ownership.

The inquiry has revealed many things, according to the recently published preliminary report. It shows utility concerns hiring professors to carry on campaigns of agitation against municipal ownership, ostensibly under high university authority, subsidizing newspapers under the guise of advertising, deluging the public school with biased propaganda, assailing municipal ownership advocates as Bolsheviks and resorting to back-stairs tactics to discredit them, and granting money to universities and research institutions with an eye to "proper" results. In short, the propaganda of the utility interests stands fully revealed in all its nakedness, and a powerful light is thrown on the nature of the "public opinion" made by newspapers, distinguished speakers, and controlled school books. Much of the testimony has been printed in the *United States Daily*, but we are informed that the complete record will be published by the Commission, it is to be hoped, with the entertaining "exhibits," such as cancelled checks and undercover letters. While it would be unfair to prejudge the final outcome, it is clear that the utility interests will do well to clean house before a wrathful public does something that may be uneconomical.

✦

A Reviewer Reviewed   The June issue contained a review by Professor Kirk H. Porter of the report of the New York Bureau of Municipal Research on *County Government in Virginia*. In view of the interest of our readers in the problems of county government reform, we append a letter from Mr. Frank Bane, state commissioner of public welfare of Virginia, commenting upon Mr. Porter's criticism of the Bureau's report:

"*To the Editor:*

"There is much food for thought in the comprehensive study made by the New York Bureau. This report and the review of it by Kirk H. Porter in the NATIONAL MUNICIPAL REVIEW of June, 1928, are stimulating reading.

"The reasons for Dr. Porter's praise of the survey seem evident. As he says, 'The work apparently has been very well done. The investigators went to the bottom of their problems and have dealt with them most thoroughly.' The report is based on a very intelligent first-hand study, and is most illuminating,' and 'public authorities in Virginia, and elsewhere, can profit much by a careful study of this excellent report.'

"But why stop at recommending it to public authorities? If the counties are spending about \$28,000,000 annually, in a state with a total population of only between 2,000,000 and 3,000,000 persons, why should not business men read it and what it says about the unbusinesslike ways in which we are governed? Why should not the general body of taxpayers be interested in it?

"The bureau suggests furthering both economy—to the tune of millions—and efficiency by replacing methods devised in the ox-cart age by others better suited to this year of grace of the automobile and the airplane.

"Dr. Porter says, 'There is no denying that undesirable conditions are convincingly disclosed.' Yet he seems to shrink from a program of reform. He apparently hesitates to endorse the recommendations of the bureau and he makes none of his own. The boldness of the bureau seemingly almost shocks him. He says regarding the investigators: 'There is no doubt that they were convinced before they ever started that county government in Virginia was exceedingly bad.' It is difficult to see this. If the survey brought to light unsatisfactory conditions, why suppose the investigators were preconvinced that they were going to find these? The report impressed the present reader as made in a very fair-minded spirit. Moreover, although it was published in the state and widely noticed in the Virginia papers, it has not brought out in Virginia accusations of undue bias against existing methods.

"The Virginia public apparently agrees with the report that the machinery of county government is cumbersome and out-of-date. The fee system in place of salaries is open to grave objections. A set-up of thirty or forty officials is not suited to small counties with a population as low as 4,000 to 10,000 persons in thirty-three out of the total of one hundred counties. Laxity in incurring and handling heavy county indebtedness is a serious matter. There is need for full coördination between state and county governments.

"Dr. Porter comments on the investigators' confidence in their own criticisms and recommendations. It is hard to see why after a most thoroughgoing study, the bureau should not have confidence in its findings and should make halfhearted rather than forceful recommendations.

"The newness of the county manager plan also seems to Dr. Porter an objection. He forgets that the manager form of government is quite in accord with political philosophy in Virginia. In fact, city manager government originated in Virginia, and is now in operation in all but two cities.

"On one point Dr. Porter is definitely in error. He says, 'Supervisors . . . are brusquely swept into the discard as elective officers.' This is incorrect. Both plans of organization proposed by the bureau, the manager plan and the elective administrator plan, retain the board of supervisors as elected by the voters of the county.

"Dr. Porter's comment: 'The county is treated throughout as an area of state administration rather than as an area for local self-government,' also seems mistaken, for I note that on page 13 the investigators recommend that 'the supervisors should have more extensive powers conferred on them to pass local legislation. This would be better for the counties and would relieve the General Assembly of a great deal of local and special legislation.'

"After reading the report and Dr. Porter's evaluation, and then re-reading the report, I still feel that not only has the bureau rendered an extremely valuable service to the state, which Dr. Porter evidently believes himself, but also that the work has been done in an exceptionally large-minded way, and that the courage and incisiveness of the investigators add to its value."

FRANK BANE,
Commissioner of Public Welfare, Virginia.

CIVIC IDEALS OF LONG AGO [1]

BY CARL S. KNOPF

University of Southern California

*Many ancient standards of good citizenship are applicable to modern
life.* :: :: :: :: :: :: :: :: :: ::

DRAGGING a mummy into a City
Club luncheon makes us one with the
Egyptian of long ago. It is said that
at the height of the festivities, a
mummy was brought into the banquet
hall as a gentle reminder that "tempus
fugits." However dead the modern
archaeologist-mummy may be, he cannot be dry in discussing ancient civic
ideals. There are too many surprises,
too many startling parallels, too many
pre-views of the passing show.

Any abiding civic structure must be
based upon loyalty and responsibility.
As early as 3400 B.C., the Sumerians,
in the oldest known law code, provided
that a young man who cut loose from
his family and civic responsibility lost
status and rights. On the other hand,
a parent who attempted to cast off a
son had to make a financial settlement.
Sumeria insisted that both the rising
generation and the one responsible for
it must shoulder the task of social
adjustment and mutual understanding,
for the promotion of civic peace and
happiness.

Five thousand years ago this code
made a man responsible for all items of
property under his care—a law which
might now curtail many an item of
petty graft in high places. It would
even be appreciated by honest landlords today when the repair bills
come in.

A PIONEER CIVIC REFORMER

About 2800 B.C., Urukagina took up
the torch of civic reform. In his con-

temporaries he generated more heat
than light, but that was to be expected.
Urukagina emerged from the masses,
and his program was death to special
privilege and vested interests. He
controlled the hours of labor and
forced contractors to provide water and
rest periods. He made the morticians
reduce their charges for the city's poor.
He started a tax reduction program
which cut off the overhead and left
plenty for civic needs.

In that day all men were superstitious, and no undertaking would be
initiated without consulting the omens.
The priests were charging extortionate rates. Urukagina assumed that a
priest is a minister, a public servant,
and therefore ordered that divination
be practised without charge in the case
of the poor. Of course, he never
thought of a county hospital, county
poor farm, city charities, or similar
modern attempts to alleviate misfortune; but his basic idea was the same.

Having no pedigree, and being a bit
too radical for his day, the higher-ups
"got" him. Where Urukagina ruled
there now lie heaps of sand, but his
principles still live in the hearts of good
Americans throughout our land who
are striving to make their cities happier
and more beautiful.

THE HAMMURABI CODE

The Hammurabi Code, about 2000
B.C., is the second oldest known code,
and has been preserved almost complete. An English translation, easily
procured in any city library, will
stimulate the thinking of any in-

[1] Address delivered before Los Angeles City
Club.

telligent business man who spends an evening with it. A few points of interest are as follows:

First, every man must be a producer. The government called to account a man who left part of his field uncultivated.

Second, when a man made a deposit at a bank, due notation must be made, just as in the pass-book today. If the bank were robbed, it stood the loss rather than the depositor. So it is today, though covered by insurance.

Third, insurance was operative in a simple way. If a house were robbed and the burglar not caught, the loss was declared and the city repaid the home owner. One imagines the police force had to function or the town go bankrupt! It was a form of municipal burglary insurance, on the same principle as modern workmen's compensation.

This same code gives us the first minimum wage laws, the first regulation of freight rates, the first contractors' liability, the first graduated scale of physicians' fees, and the first laws against malpractice. Its ideas are so ultra-modern as to approach radicalism; but it is the radicalism of progress, not that of destruction.

THE PENALTY FOR WIFELY INCOMPETENCE

The average citizen can chuckle appreciation over one law: "If a woman be not economical, gads about and belittles her husband, they shall throw that woman into the river!" So was dampened the ardor of a nagging busybody! Parenthetically be it said that this may be an idea rather than an ideal, at least so far as the technique is concerned.

. ANCIENT ACCOUNTING PRACTICES

From legislative ideals it is but a step to business practices. Before us lies a little lump of clay, stone-hard, about an inch square, half an inch thick, covered on both sides with wedge-shaped indentions, the typical cuneiform writing of Babylon. This is a receipt for taxes paid. It says that one fat sheep and one unfattened sheep were delivered by A-Lul-Lul, a slave, as the official payment for Mr. Du-U, the military officer. The document is dated by the fall of a city, 2333 B.C.

Next to this receipt lies another, recording a payment of grain on account. Credit and installment payments were a recognized practice in 2338 B.C. Incidentally, the document is signed "per A-Da-Ga, the scribe." Many a bookkeeper today signs receipts that the president of the corporation never sees. It is all in the day's work and makes intricate organization possible, thus stimulating great business enterprises.

Another tablet, about two inches square, bears the imprint of the private seal of the big boss. He probably could not write his own name, or maybe like modern signatures no one could read it if he did. A scribe acted as stenographer and wrote the document, which was then signed. The ancient business office echoed to the dulcet voice of the manager saying, "Miss Ishtar, take this one."

Visible filing is not new. A document involving certain amounts, or numbers of animals, was often annotated on the side, and when laid in the archives this notation was visible. The business of a day or month might be added up in a short time. Income tax returns held no terrors for the systematic Babylonian business man.

Centuries ago great minds dreamed of an orderly world. In it men would do business on a basis of honesty, good faith and mutual trust. In it the less fortunate would never be legal prey of the more fortunate. Wages, transportation, banking, industry were all subject to the civic idealism of these men of vision. So they are today, and every municipality worthy the name is moving toward its goal to the extent that it too builds up the sense of loyalty and responsibility without which citizenship is but an empty shell.

GOING AFTER THE MUNICIPAL TAX DOLLAR

BY WELLES A. GRAY

Assistant Director, Municipal Administration Service

A recent nation-wide study of the methods of enforcing real estate tax liens.   ::   ::   ::   ::   ::   ::   ::   ::   ::

THE importance of the sale of tax liens as a means for enforcing the payment of taxes on real property cannot be overemphasized. This is the only satisfactory method that has been found thus far; yet a search through the published works on municipal finance will disclose but comparatively little material discussing this important subject. In recent years public and private agencies in a few cities and states, such as Baltimore, Philadelphia, New Jersey, and Ohio, have made investigations along this line with interesting results. Past investigations, however, have dealt with the problem chiefly as it exists in one city or state, and it has remained for Mr. Carl H. Chatters, city auditor of Flint, Michigan, to survey the subject along general lines, tie together what has already been done, and make constructive recommendations of a general nature, applicable widely throughout the country.

In his pamphlet, *The Enforcement of Real Estate Tax Liens,* just published by the Municipal Administration Service,[1] Mr. Chatters discloses the results

[1] Carl H. Chatters, *The Enforcement of Real Estate Tax Liens.* Municipal Administration Service, 261 Broadway, New York City. 35 cents.

of a study of the sale of real estate tax liens in forty-two governmental units. This study shows conclusively the need for a revision of the state and municipal tax sale laws in most parts of the country. He points out that "the present methods of enforcing real estate tax liens are generally inefficient, unfair and lacking in uniformity. They fail to promote the payment of taxes, either before or after delinquency. The best interests of the municipality, the taxpayer, and the tax title purchaser are not harmonized."

PROTECTING THE INTERESTS OF ALL PARTIES

Mr. Chatters considers this problem from the point of view of the city, the buyer of tax titles, and the taxpayer. In formulating laws on this subject in the past, legislators have treated it in a rather haphazard fashion. Their chief consideration has been the collection of taxes; but even there the means used have been in many cases either too harsh, or not severe enough. This phase of the subject is, of course, of primary importance. It is essential to the welfare of the city that its taxes be collected, and, obviously, adequate means for accomplishing this should be provided.

In providing such means, however, the interests of the tax title purchaser should not be overlooked. He is an essential factor in the present system; yet he must often take a gambler's chance. The law in certain jurisdictions does not adequately protect the titles that are purchased. While in most jurisdictions tax deeds are generally *prima facie* evidence of the facts they state, in one or two instances the burden of proof still rests upon the shoulders of the title purchaser. Furthermore, in some jurisdictions an attempt is made to make the tax deed evidence of regular conveyance of the property. This seems hardly fair to the taxpayer, and has been held in some instances to deprive the property owner of his title without due process of law.

Two classes of taxpayers, it is pointed out, should receive protection,—the worthy poor and those who have allowed their taxes to become delinquent through ignorance or misinformation. He recommends that the first group be protected through city or county exoneration, and that the second group be protected through adequate notices of the dates on which taxes are due, dates of delinquency, and dates of proposed sale.

THE PROBLEM OF TAX DELINQUENCY

Some interesting facts about delinquencies throughout the country are revealed by this study. Cities imposing moderately severe initial penalties seem to have, in the main, the lowest percentages of delinquency. Furthermore, the promptness with which liens are sold seems also to be a factor of some importance, for in cities where action is taken soon after delinquency the percentage of unpaid taxes is relatively low. In Detroit, tax sales are held during the year for which they are levied. During the fiscal year beginning July 1, 1926, the tax levy there amounted to $71,381,645.62, of which $66,853,425.55 was collected. Tax sales were held in June, 1927, and netted $3,585,256.87. As a result, only $879,960.20 or one and two-tenths per cent of the levy remained deliuquent. Des Moines, in 1927, levied taxes amounting to $7,568,016.27, and after tax sales held in December, 1927, less than one per cent of the taxes remained unpaid.

The experiences of New York City and the state of Ohio form an interesting contrast here. In New York taxes remain delinquent for three years before liens are sold. In 1925, for example, the total levy of New York City was $328,374,984, and the deliuquent taxes amounted to $37,794,822, or something over ten per cent. In Ohio, taxes are delinquent four years before action is taken. In that state in 1925 the levy was $261,444,876.11, and the unpaid taxes amounted to $26,447,288.90, a delinquency exceeding ten per cent. While undoubtedly the time of the tax sales was not the sole factor in these four cases, it seems from the facts to have been partially responsible for the percentage of uncollected taxes.

SUMMARY OF RECOMMENDATIONS

In addition to the recommendations mentioned above, Mr. Chatters makes, among others, the following:

"Tax procedure should be based upon a carefully-planned calendar with the shortest duration of time consistent with the public good between the date of levy and the final disposition of the lien." (A suggested tax calendar which is adaptable to the fiscal year of any city is included in the pamphlet.)

"Taxes should be payable in two installments with a high rate of penalty added at delinquency.

"Tax certificates should be sold late in the fiscal year for which the taxes are levied.

"Competition at the sales should be based upon bidding down the interest rate.

"The purchaser of a tax certificate should enforce his lien by foreclosure proceedings following the general practice for mortgage foreclosures.

"The tax certificate may be foreclosed one year after sale and must be foreclosed within three years or become invalid.

"All administrative acts relating to tax procedure should be mandatory."

In addition to tables on tax delinquencies and methods of selling tax liens in various parts of the United States, there have been included in the pamphlet valuable appendices, among which should be mentioned the laws or ordinances on this subject in force in California, Detroit, New Jersey, North Carolina, and Rochester, New York, and the ordinance of Flint, Michigan, for the protection of the worthy poor.

TRAFFIC RELIEF THROUGH BY-PASS HIGHWAYS

BY WILLIAM BEARD

National Institute of Public Administration

A discussion of the economic factors and potential savings involved in the construction of by-pass highways. :: :: :: :: ::

"SAY, Jack, is this right for Philadelphia?"

"Sorry, old timer, but you are headed wrong. Go back to the railroad station, take your first right past the library, then your left down Myrtle Avenue and ask someone down there how to get out of the city."

After one has failed to find the railroad station, has been caught up in a maze of one-way streets, has returned to the same spot several times in succession, has severely denounced the traffic lights, and the "no left" signs, one appreciates the need for a direct route through the large modern city.

Besides suffering such inconveniences, motorists in a hurry to reach home after a long journey are likely to be a menace to others on account of their fast driving. Speedy through-traffic is responsible for a long list of city accidents. If such traffic can be removed from the main streets, then travel will be so much the safer for all. The problem concerns the local resident as well as the interurban tourist. Inhabitants of cities located on main trunk lines find streets crowded enough with their own vehicles without having the jam augmented by outsiders who have no local business to transact. The mutual interference caused by the mingling of local and non-stop traffic is detrimental to the interests of both parties in the rapid execution of their tasks.

THE GENESIS OF THE THROUGH-TRAFFIC PROBLEM

Before the problem of the horseless vehicle demanded attention, a town was the focus of a radiating "fan" of short roads. Citizens in the region around a new settlement naturally made it a center of their trading activity. Journeys from town to town were too infrequent to warrant extensive planning for such traffic through construction of by-pass highways. With the coming of the motor age, however, the city, besides developing greater local trade, became a funnel through which non-stop traffic poured with ever increasing rapidity. To make matters worse the engineer of the motor age, in building hard roads, followed the old patterns inherited from the era of stagecoach and oxcart. The veritable flood of through-traffic of the present day hurries in and out of every nook and cranny of the metropolis in its effort to thread its way past the impeding city. This flood demands attention of a new sort; it cannot be handled by pre-motor methods.

THE MAGNITUDE OF THE THROUGH-TRAFFIC PROBLEM

While it is difficult to determine the magnitude of the through-traffic problem for the country as a whole, a study of one great transportation system leading to New York and its environs may serve as illustration.

The New York *Times* of June 24, 1928, summarizes a study made by the bureau of agricultural economics of the United States Department of Agriculture in coöperation with the New York Food Marketing Research Council on the subject of truck delivery of peaches, peppers, canteloupes, tomatoes, and apples into New York City:

It was found that in the period of investigation the five products reported were shipped by motor truck to New York from points as distant as Virginia, Maryland, and Delaware, as well as from the near-by sections of New Jersey, Pennsylvania, Long Island and Connecticut.

Thirty per cent of all peaches arriving at New York during the period reported came by motor truck. Twenty-five per cent of the tomatoes, 20 per cent of the apples and 9 per cent of the peppers also arrived in this way. Taking a single week during the height of the season, the truck receipts of peaches were 58 per cent of all peach receipts, apples 78 per cent, tomatoes 52 per cent and peppers 16 per cent.

Further changes and developments are sug-

gested by the opinion of the reporters that the produce-trucking movement will be still greater within a few years.

THREE POSSIBLE SOLUTIONS

Three remedies have been employed to relieve the congestion caused by through-traffic confined to radial roads and checker-board street layouts:

1. The selection of suitable routes following existing streets and the marking of the same to guide through-traffic.

2. The construction of routes on a level with existing streets but partially isolated from local traffic.

3. The construction of giant elevated or depressed highways running through cities like great railway viaducts and eliminating grade crossings.

While method 1 saves time for motorists, it is at best only a partial remedy. While it guides the traffic, it does not relieve the congestion.

The second method, illustrated by Figure 1, is being employed to isolate local from through-traffic. In this arrangement, the express lanes are separated from the local lanes by artificial "islands." Local loading, unloading or parking may take place on the side lanes unmolested by the rapid express traffic. The local cars are turned into the express lanes only at widely separated intervals, thereby eliminating many intersections. Over or under passes permit local motors to pass across the express routes at intervals. Taken all in all, however, the plan is still inconvenient in comparison with the third method. While planting of shrubs on the islands will give residents on the local roads considerable privacy, there still remain numerous barriers to cross-traffic.

The third method affords the most satisfactory solution. In Figure 2, the reader will observe how an elevated structure, connected by ramps with cross-streets, gives the minimum inter-

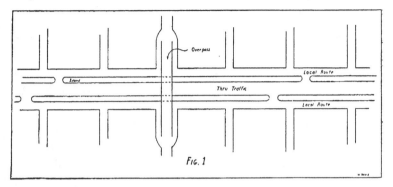

FIG. 1

ference to through-traffic. Ramps are placed only at the intersection of the structure with important highways, the minor roads passing under the structure in tunnels not provided with ramps. To prevent accidents, heavy rails guard the sides of the elevated highway.

For dense traffic, method 3 is the most convenient. It is certainly no experiment since railroads have been following for years the same practice to eliminate grade crossings as a measure both of safety and of speed. By the removal of tracks from the streets, trains can run at reasonable rates through the city without danger from local traffic. Automobile travel has now reached the stage where railway-like construction is becoming a similar necessity.

THE ECONOMIC FACTORS INVOLVED

Obviously an elevated or submerged through-route costs a large sum of money and involves at once the question of economy. The problem cannot be solved by theory alone. Each case must be taken up on its own merits and Mr. F. Lavis, engineer of the New Jersey State Highway Department, has given us an excellent illustration of the correct approach to the subject.

In an article on "Recent Developments in the Construction of Streets and Roads for Heavy Traffic," which appeared in *Engineers and Engineering* for May, 1928, Mr. Lavis describes a new route of thirteen miles between the Jersey City plaza of the Holland Tunnels and Elizabeth, N. J., a project costing over $30,000,000. For eight miles from the tunnels ramps are employed for grade crossing elimination.

Unlike roads evolved from trails or constructed to benefit adjacent land, the new route has been planned more nearly like a railway with a given volume of passengers and freight to be moved from point to point along the lines of least resistance.

The economic factors of traffic movement have been dealt with in detail in their relation to this project. The first question which arises is: What effect will a lengthening of the road have on the cost of operation? Is it economical to detour far around a city? Taking an average composition of 50 per cent heavy trucks, 25 per cent medium weight trucks, and 25 per cent private cars, the cost of operation due to items affected by distance is about 12 cents per mile. With an estimated load of 20,000,000 cars a year, the savings due to a reduction of one mile in highway length would be $2,400,000 a year. Obviously a circuitous route would be inadvisable.

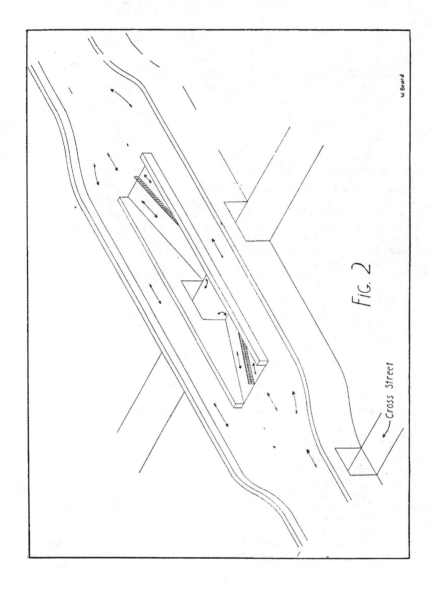

Fig. 2

Besides the question of length, the waste of money from delays at street intersections and the savings accruing from their elimination in the new route must be considered. The cost of operation per minute of the average vehicle of the class using the highway is 2.2 cents. The delays entailed at the intersection of the main highway with an ordinary first-class road should approximate 7,000,000 car-minutes a year, which, at 2.2 cents a minute, involves a loss of $154,000 per annum. This is a sum representing 5 per cent interest on $3,000,000.

In addition to the losses from the delay of cars actually using the highway, there is a further loss resulting from the exclusion of other cars caused by the reduction in the effective capacity of the roadway from interference at intersections. If the elimination of grade crossings, while raising the cost of a highway, will increase the capacity faster than the cost, then the elimination of grade crossings is justified. An estimate of the loss of capacity of the through-route due to crossing delays indicates a reduction of 12 per cent in the traffic flow at times of maximum demand.

If the costs of delays and reduction of capacity are combined, they will be found to equal 5 per cent interest on over $6,000,000. However, the total saving due to the elimination of eight miles of crossings is not as large as the product of the saving per crossing times the number of crossings.

Mr. Lavis concludes with a discussion of the money losses involved, showing that the difficulty of assigning true values to motor vehicle losses, such as the above, is large. Pleasure drivers may not consider it a loss to arrive home a half hour late, while if a truck reaches its destination a half hour after closing time the loss may be large. Exact figures are impossible, but enough calculable factors enter the situation to permit the formation of a fairly satisfactory balance sheet for the three governments involved,—city, state, and national,—which may fairly be called upon to meet the costs.

THE NEED FOR PLANNING

In many cases urban communities are not yet prepared to build such expensive routes as that just described for New Jersey. Localities must, however, plan for the years ahead. Accordingly a study of their problems should be made to determine what thoroughfares will be needed for handling the traffic flood headed toward them. Certain routes should be designed for commercial or express use, with directness and convenience as the first object, scenic value being subordinate. Others may be planned for aesthetic ends and more leisurely use by pleasure motorists. When topography and the extent of the far-flung suburbs permit, routes entirely avoiding the city are to be recommended, especially when they serve not only to make driving more agreeable but also as short-cuts.

The era of house to house roads for through-traffic is doomed. In its place, time is ushering in the application of engineering technique to highway data making possible the construction of wisely planned and economical through-routes.

DOES ZONING PROTECT ONLY THE AESTHETIC SENSE?

BY R. D. MacLAURIN

Commissioner of Trade Waste, City of Cleveland

The author of "Where Zoning Fails" replies to Mr. Herrick's letter in our June issue.   ::   ::   ::   ::   ::   ::   ::   ::

ZONING is now unmasked by Charles Herrick, city planning engineer of New York City, in the June issue of NATIONAL MUNICIPAL REVIEW, wherein he states that "certain industries at the present day are objectionable. Zoning merely states to people who want to erect dwellings near these industries, 'you do this at your own risk.'" Precisely, zoning is a deception. Zoning has been heralded throughout the land as the benevolent protector of the home owner, and now it is revealed by an advocate of the accepted method of zoning that the home owner has no legal rights whatever as regards property or health protection from trade waste nuisances under zoning legislation. Nor does zoning protect the best interests of industry. This point will be argued later. In view of this inextricable legal muddle created by zoning, it is imperative that such legislation should be amended by providing therein a sound, legal and scientific basis which would protect the property and health rights of each and every member of the community.

The writer wishes to make clear again that the special phase of zoning under discussion pertains to trade waste nuisances such as fumes, smoke, smells, dusts, noxious gases, and offensive water-carried wastes. It is recognized that there are other forms of nuisance than those enumerated, but with these the writer is not concerned.

If the present method of zoning industries is constitutional, which the writer does not admit, it simply means that a subterranean effort has been made under the guise of the police power to legalize public nuisances by the subtle scheme of creating unrestricted nuisance districts and others of so-called more or less degree of nuisance. Assuming that this is a valid exercise of police power, the corollary is obvious and is exactly as stated by Mr. Herrick, that the legal rights of home owners have been abrogated. This places the home owner who seeks redress from public nuisance in the embarrassing position of having to prove the unconstitutionality of this particular application of zoning legislation. The presumption of legality is usually in favor of the legislation as interpreted by the lower courts. Why, therefore, should this intolerable legal and financial burden be placed on individuals when it is the undoubted duty of a municipal corporation to protect the property and health rights of its citizens against public nuisance?

ZONING SAFEGUARDS THE AESTHETIC

The accepted view of zoning is an architectural plan of dealing with municipal problems which offend the sight of the fastidious. The results obtained by the zoning method have some aesthetic merit. Yet in analyz-

504

ing this subject purely from an aesthetic point of view, zoning fails to protect the beauty of public buildings and parks against pirates of the air which cause disfigurement. Obviously the solution of trade waste nuisances must be dealt with more comprehensively than by mere exclusion, which is superficial and has no scientific basis. Further, trade waste nuisances offend the senses of smell and taste. Why should zoning discriminate between the senses? One would infer from the prevailing zoning idea that human beings were devoid of all senses except that of sight, and it may be added, defective sight. If the benefits of zoning for residential districts are confined to the exclusion of a garage, a laundry, an apartment block, or other structures, then it should be apparent to anyone living in an industrial city that such legislation is not only almost futile but a dangerous menace, as it challenges the common law protection which residents now enjoy.

In a recent nuisance case in Ohio, a Court of Appeals rendered a similar opinion to that stated by Mr. Herrick. In substance, it was that a residential district had no right to encroach on an industrial district. If such opinions are sound law, why should residents in an industrial city be in favor of zoning? Under those circumstances the alleged protection by zoning to the home owner is a delusion. The plain fact is that zoning as applied to industry hopelessly fails, for it attempts to protect the manufacturing interests against residential districts, jeopardizes the common law rights of residents, and places upon them the burden of proving the unconstitutionality of this application of zoning legislation. The writer feels indebted to Mr. Herrick for the additional citation to substantiate his argument and claim, made in a previous article, that zoning legislation in

its application to trade wastes does not protect the public generally.

ZONING AND THE MANUFACTURER

Although zoning claims to protect the manufacturer, it can only be legally effective providing such legislation is constitutional. Can zoning make an unlawful act lawful? The writer contends that a manufacturer can only be protected against prosecution for nuisance by actual abatement. Such abatement is invariably profitable for the manufacturer. Innumerable instances may be cited. Frequently the abatement of nuisance results in the improvement of chemical and mechanical processes with a resulting betterment of the product manufactured. There are exceptional instances where the value of the product recovered does not pay a dividend on the equipment investment directly. Yet the breathing atmosphere is so much improved within the works that the earning capacity of workmen is greatly increased, their health protected, group insurance rates diminished, and depreciation of mechanical equipment materially lessened. When these factors are taken into consideration, nuisance abatement is a paying proposition. Further, atmospheric pollution outside the works is prevented, which is a direct benefit to the manufacturer in that it is infinitely better business to avoid the necessity of complaint by one's neighbors than to give cause for it.

"Zoning is based on the assumption that industries are nuisances when in the wrong place." This is an armchair conception of nuisance and wholly at variance with the facts. The writer can cite hundreds of instances in many cities where industries were originally located miles away from inhabitants, yet in a few years the whole territory was developed. Exactly the same conditions would obtain if zoning were adopted before the city existed. Dust, acid fumes, and metallurgical smoke nuisances may and do pollute the atmosphere for many miles over a city and are seldom what might be called local. When a nuisance is local it is just as damaging under zoning as without, for many industries seriously damage the property of neighboring industries in addition to residences. It is legally immaterial as far as damage is concerned whether the property is residential or industrial.

"AEROSOLS" ARE PUBLIC NUISANCES

Hundreds of tons of dusts and fumes are emitted into the atmosphere daily in industrial centers. These dusts and fumes do not disperse vertically in the atmosphere, so how can such effects be local? Owing to the physical and chemical properties of "aerosols," the particles are widely dispersed and finally become invisible. Yet these invisible particles remain in the air for long periods of time and are the particles most detrimental to health. Further, these invisible particles are responsible for the formation of fogs and mists which shut off the sunlight. Zoning makes elaborate provisions in building design so as to provide light yet pays no attention to fundamental causes obstructing the reception of light. In manufacturing centers industrial "aerosols" are responsible for a loss of 30 to 40 per cent of the beneficial rays of the sun. Further, these vast "aerosols" which at times blanket a whole city destroy public parks, public and private property, and drive residents to seek refuge outside the city limits. The ultimate economic result of such atmospheric pollution is that the public treasury is depleted of much-needed tax money because of the depreciation in property values. If industries are nuisances only when in the wrong place, what legal status has a manufacturer whose property is being damaged by another manufacturer in an unrestricted zoned area? The writer would like to hear from Mr. Herrick on this point.

Pure air for breathing purposes is a natural right of every citizen. This inalienable right is intimately related to the preservation of health and comfort. No one expects to have mountain air for breathing purposes in an industrial city; but residents have a right to demand that industry shall use the best practical means known to the art for the abatement of dusts, fumes, and noxious gases, irrespective of location. Further, in cases where a practical solution of a problem is not known to a particular art, citizens have a right to demand that every effort shall be exerted on the part of industry and a municipal corporation to determine a satisfactory method to solve the problem. Moreover, in the absence of zoning under the common law, the courts have ordered in the past that the best practical means shall be applied to prevent nuisance.

NEEDED EXTENSIONS OF ZONING LAWS

Mr. Herrick suggests that "other laws" will have to be employed to deal with trade waste nuisances. As zoning presumes to supersede the common law of nuisance and pervert the police power now employed, what laws have you? In the past, nuisance has been dealt with under the police power by commissioners of health. Then zoning presents itself and alleges to be ordained with the same purpose, draws a few maps setting up boundaries where nuisance industries are now located, and says "this is an unrestricted district." The nuisance is now abated. All of which is very simple indeed. Then the residents are saluted: "If you wish to continue living in this district, 'you do so at your own risk.'" Further, a city council, under the police power, heretofore enacted special ordinances dealing with the abatement of trade waste nuisances. By zoning under the same police power and on the same grounds the same city council creates unrestricted nuisance districts. By one legislative act an attempt is made to legalize nuisance, and by another legislative act to declare that an industry located in a legalized district is a public nuisance. It would appear, therefore, that zoning has exhausted all the possibilities of legal gymnastics.

The time to prevent nuisance is before it occurs. Zoning allocates industries to certain specified districts. Obviously the processes to be conducted are inseparable from the buildings. Yet zoning makes no provision for the control of processes. The present procedure is as follows: A manufacturer applies to a city building department for a permit to erect buildings for manufacturing purposes. Great care is exercised regarding every phase of the construction. Every nail and bolt must be in a specified place. When all details are complied with, a building permit is granted the manufacturer. However, the manufacturer does not receive a permit to conduct business. Here is where zoners turn "thumbs down."

For instance, if a permit were granted to build a cement plant, the manufacturer would merely have a permit to construct the plant and would not have a permit to conduct the process. If the manufacturer failed to provide adequate facilities for dust and fume collection, and said dust and fumes polluted the atmosphere for miles throughout a city, the writer submits

that the building permit, insofar as protecting the manufacturer against nuisance is concerned, would be of no avail irrespective of locality. Then how may the interest of the manufacturer and the public interest be protected?

SUGGESTED ADDITIONS TO THE BUILDING CODE

As the zoning law becomes part of the building code, the latter should be amended as follows:

A permit shall be required for the conduct of each and every business or manufacturing operation which results in or is attended by the emission of dust, fumes, odors, noxious gases, or offensive water-carried wastes, and no such business or manufacturing operation shall be permitted to be carried on unless the permit hereby required shall have been first obtained. A permit shall be issued provided each and every business or manufacturing operation shall be so conducted and shall employ the best practical means known to the art for the abatement and elimination of dust, fumes, odors, noxious gases, or offensive water-carried wastes, and such conditions of the business or manufacturing operation must be evidenced by the written approval of the commissioner of health.

When adequate means for the abatement or elimination of dust, fumes, odors, noxious gases, or offensive water-carried wastes, are not known to the art, it shall be the duty of manufacturers conducting such operations to investigate and provide ways and means for abatement in co-operation with the authorized officials of a munic-ipal corporation, and for the conduct of each and every such business or manufacturing operation; a temporary permit may be issued.

A permit issued by a municipal corporation on the above terms would be a legal permit for a manufacturer to conduct business. It would result in the protection of industries individually and collectively, and the public interest generally.

THE LONDON REGION

BY HARLEAN JAMES

Executive Secretary, American Civic Association

The administration of the London Region is centralized in the London County Council. :: :: :: :: :: :: :: ::

GREATER LONDON is not an enterprising metropolitan center which has pushed its way out into the rural regions. It is a nest of old towns and villages which have spread until the fringes of population overlap each other. Many of these old communities still preserve their ancient characteristics. Others have been transformed through changes in use. As in other large cities, residential areas have been displaced by the outward push of business. The city of London is hardly more than a square mile in extent and, while it accommodates like the loop district of Chicago an enormous day population, its night population has grown less at each succeeding census since the eighties.

From this square mile, the site of an ancient city and market place, the scene of centuries of struggle between the government and the governed, the birthplace of legal, social and economic institutions which dominate the English-speaking dominions of the world, there has grown the modern metropolis of London; but the old city still preserves many of its time-honored rights and traditions. The lord mayor is the ceremonial representative of all London as well as of the city. The companies which have developed from the old guilds still exercise a potent influence on the development of the town. The city has a long history of achievement in education, public health and philanthropy.

ADMINISTRATION CENTRALIZED IN THE
LONDON COUNTY COUNCIL

In 1888 Parliament set up elected county councils throughout England, and London was included under the law. The Metropolitan Board of Works, which had been created as a result of an act of Parliament in 1855, was superseded by the London County Council. The council inherited from the Metropolitan Board of Works authority over the main drainage, traffic, execution of street improvements, construction of bridges, tramways, fire brigade, housing of the poor, supervising and laying out of streets and construction of buildings, and provision and maintenance of parks and open spaces. The council also inherited from the justices certain administrative powers. In 1903 the council took over powers of the London School Board and was given additional powers relating to education.

The metropolitan borough councils have charge of paving and other street improvements, local drainage, collection of refuse and other matters of purely local import. The police are controlled by the home secretary through the commissioner of police of the metropolis or by the city corporation.

The London County Council administers an area of 116.9 square miles which in 1921 had a population of 4,483,249. The area over which the

508

police have jurisdiction is much larger, extending over 692.9 square miles and containing a population of 7,476,168. The water area is about five times as large as the county area, but smaller than the police area.

In the seventy years between 1851 and 1921 the population of the area now administered by the London County Council increased from 2,363-341 to 4,483,249 and the assessed value of property quadrupled, increasing from twelve million odd pounds to forty-eight million odd pounds. But in spite of this great increase in population, the death rate has steadily decreased from 23.7 per thousand in 1851 to 20.5 in 1881 and 15 in 1911, with further decreases in later years. This is the result of modern public health control.

THE COUNCIL'S PERSONNEL

Greater London is divided into sixty-one constituencies. Sixty of these return to the council two members each and the city of London four, making a total of 124 councillors who in turn choose 20 aldermen, giving a total membership on the London County Council of 144. In 1923 the number of voters was 1,887,898, representing a broad extension of the suffrage.

ADMINISTRATIVE METHODS

The business of the council is transacted through its committees and by means of administrative departments. With 3,000 employes in the sixteen departments, 20,000 teachers, 2,000 in the uniformed fire brigade and special staffs of public undertakings, the total staff of the council comes to about 50,000.

The council claims credit for the clearing of fifty acres of slums and is in process of clearing an additional thirty-four acres. It has erected 18,000 tenements with accommodations for 120,000 persons, and is continuing this work. It supplements the work of the metropolitan borough councils in providing residential treatment for tuberculosis. It maintains 1,000 public elementary schools for 700,000 boys and girls, and maintains or helps to maintain sixty-seven secondary schools for 31,000 boys and girls, 300 technical and evening schools for 250,000 pupils, and gives assistance to the University of London.

The council operates tramways aggregating 160 miles on which 700,000,-000 passengers are carried annually. Twelve million pounds have been expended for widening streets. Ten bridges have been built over the Thames and a free ferry established at Woolwich.

The council administers 120 parks and open spaces in and near London aggregating eight square miles, a little less than seven per cent of the total area. A curious reflection of metropolitan life is shown in the statistical lists of permits issued during a recent year for 7,000 petroleum stations, 820 employment agencies, 800 massage establishments, 800 practicing midwives, 85,000 shops inspected under the shops acts, 200,000 motor cars and 135,000 driving licenses. The council is reponsible for verifying and inspecting over 2,000,000 weights and measures, and for testing the gas used and the meters through which it is supplied. In all, the annual budget of the council is in excess of 26,000,000 pounds.

The area under the jurisdiction of the council forms a drainage basin, traversed by the Thames and many small tributaries, most of which have disappeared under ground. No city in the world possesses more intimate charm or more architectural aspiration than London. The famous Thames embankment makes the river a part of the artistry of the scene, dominated on one side by the stately houses of Parliament and magnificent Westminster Abbey and on the other by the modern buildings of the London County Council. The quaint courts sequestered in the old city are ever a delight to visitors from the New World.

THE RESULTS OF GOOD PLANNING

The town planning acts have exercised a powerful influence over the growth of London. In the schemes of the county of London, it is the rule for every house to have its own garden, and in most cases a garden front and back. The number of houses to the acre is limited to about twelve, whereas it was not uncommon to find forty per acre in the older schemes.

A very real effort is being made to preserve the individual character and the natural features of the villages which are being overtaken by the tide of population flowing out from the heart of London; but it is realized that the once-lovely rural roads in the vicinity of London are suffering from some of the same invasions which are ruining the rural roads of the United States, and that the open country is being pushed farther and farther away from the great mass of the people living in the inner suburbs. Before it

is too late, it is urged by Mr. Forrest, the architect of the London County Council, that a ring of park land should be acquired within easy traveling distance of the center of London. In this ring should be included such unspoiled rural oases as the Regent Canal and the Wandle River.

Twelve joint town-planning committees have been recently established in the region just outside of the county of London, and an effort is being made to work out, through a major committee advocated by Mr. George Pepler, the realization of the dreams of the town planners "that the planning problems of the capital city of the Empire and its environs might be dealt with over a field sufficiently large to make a fruitful solution possible."

Arterial and by-pass roads are being opened up and proposed for further relief of the traffic congestion occasioned by the increase of the population still attached to the city by economic or social contacts.

London has never adopted the American skyscraper. Its business buildings are low, solid, and dignified. Looking down the vista of Regent Street, with its new buildings, the pedestrian may see the sky and thank Providence and good planning.

COUNTY CONSOLIDATION IN TENNESSEE

BY J. W. MANNING

Vanderbilt University

*The successful consolidation of two counties gives impetus to the plan
to merge the ninety-five counties of Tennessee into eleven new units.*

BECAUSE county government costs the people of Tennessee not less than $20,000,000 per year, efforts are being made and suggestions are being offered to reduce this item by reducing the number of counties. The annual cost of county government is nineteen times the cost of state government; therefore it is not difficult to see why tax rates in some countries are as high as $4.00 on $100 of assessed valuation, while the state rate is only twenty cents. Granting that the cost of local government must, of necessity, be higher than the cost of state government, is there any valid reason for such a marked difference?

Certainly one of the best ways to reduce this enormous cost of county administration is to reduce the number of counties. To abolish the county is a plan which will receive little encouragement; but practical politicians, as well as political theorists, are coming to demand a reduction in the number of counties, and possibly a reorganization of the county's administration.[1] It is altogether logical that such a movement should arise in Tennessee. This state has inherited the English county in as pure form as any commonwealth which can trace its institutional origins directly or indirectly from the mother country; yet the state government of Tennessee today is a notable example of what can be done in state administrative reorganization.

The governor of Tennessee, Henry H. Horton, looking toward a reduction of state taxes, recently named a state tax commission, composed of some of the best known and ablest men of the state. The chairman of that commission is T. R. Preston, president of the Hamilton National Bank of Chattanooga, president of the American Bankers' Association, and one of the best informed men in the nation on the subject of taxation. Mr. Preston thinks that the state's interest could best be served by reducing the number of counties, thus eliminating a great deal of the overhead cost. The number of counties in the state might be reduced by the natural process of absorption of a small county by a large county or by the more artificial method of consolidation of all the counties into a smaller number of local units. Both methods have been suggested for Tennessee, and the process of absorption has actually begun.

TWO COUNTIES MERGED IN 1919

In 1919 two counties consolidated; in 1927 the county courts of two counties agreed to a consolidation, and a measure requesting permission to consolidate will be presented to the next legislature; two state officers have

---

[1] In section 9 of the New York *Times*, March 11, 1926, there appeared an article by J. C. Young outlining a similar plan for the state of New York, suggested by Governor Smith. His plan is to recast the sixty odd counties of New York into thirty-seven units, grouped into regions of common interest, thereby reducing the cost of local government and centralizing administration so that local government will be more satisfactorily carried out.

suggested a plan for redistricting the state, reducing the number of counties from ninety-five to less than fifty. This shows that some attempt is being made to explore that "dark continent of American politics," and to bring the county to the same level of reform as state and city government.

In 1919 Hamilton County, with Chattanooga as the county seat, absorbed James County. The act of the legislature provided for a referendum to be voted on only by the people of James County, the unit both in area and population. The vote which resulted was a ten to one victory for annexation.

THE RESULTS OF CONSOLIDATION

This experiment of the absorption of a small county by a larger county has proved successful. The people who live in what was once James County now pay about one half the tax they paid before the absorption. Prior to 1919 James County had less than two miles of paved highway; now it has between forty and fifty miles. Schools which previously operated between three and four months in the year are now in session eight and nine months, and the one-time James County court house is being used as a public school building. Before the consolidation James County had practically no hope of securing manufacturing plants; but now several plants have been established and others are expected to begin operation in that part of Hamilton County which was once James County because of lower taxation. It is also noteworthy that while expenditures have increased, due to more improved highways and longer school sessions, taxes have been lowered. This emphasizes the fact that the often useless overhead expense of a governmental unit is a larger item than educational and highway improvement.

In such consolidations as that of James and Hamilton Counties, one might conclude that the large county profits most, but this experiment has proved quite the contrary. *Farm and Fireside* recently sent a staff writer to Chattanooga to investigate conditions in the new Hamilton County, and he concluded that the people to be most benefited by a consolidation of a large and small county are the people of the smaller unit.

Meigs County, which adjoins James County, has looked upon this successful experiment with a great deal of interest. In 1927 there was a formal joint meeting of the courts of Hamilton and Meigs County, and it was unanimously agreed between the two that Meigs would petition the next legislature to pass an act abolishing that county and annexing most of it to Hamilton. This desire on the part of Meigs County can easily be understood when we recall that the tax rate now is about $4.00 on the hundred, while in Hamilton it is $1.40.

STATE-WIDE CONSOLIDATION PROPOSED

The chief reason for the absorption of James by Hamilton and the proposed absorption of Meigs by Hamilton is tax reduction, which can be brought about by the abolition of a number of useless and duplicate offices and the centralization of control. With this same idea in mind, A. P. Childress, state tax superintendent of Tennessee, in answer to the request for suggestions as to means of reducing taxes from Chairman Preston of the state tax commission, proposed that the ninety-five counties of the state be consolidated into eleven units, each to be grouped around a town of some importance near the geographical center.

According to this scheme ninety-five counties would be recast into eleven. Eighty-six county seats would be abolished outright, nine would be retained and made the county seats of the same number of new counties, while two new county seats would be created—Johnson City in George Washington County, and Dickson in Sam Houston County.

THE POTENTIAL BENEFITS

Whether we reduce the number of counties from ninety-five to eleven or from ninety-five to fifty, it is certain that a great deal of the inexcusable waste of the taxpayers' money could be avoided, as in James County, and the larger counties administered at a very little, if any, greater cost than any one of the present number with its long roll of unnecessary magistrates and elected officials. After all is there any reason for supporting out of taxation, or otherwise, a set of petty officers for a district as small as 250 square miles, with a population of 3,000, when it is possible to devise a government of the same number of offices, and one just as good and just as responsible to public control, which will care for a section ten times as large?

Under the present alignment of counties each of the ninety-five units supports on the average twenty officers, to say nothing of minor employees on the payroll, at an average cost of some $200,000. For the total number of counties this means 1900 chief officers and an annual expenditure for that item alone of $19,000,000. Even though the present plan of organization be retained, the cost of the eleven units, based on the same estimate, would certainly not be over $2,200,000. This saving to the taxpayer in itself would be worth the experiment.

OBJECTIONS TO BE OVERCOME

Knowing the rural political mind as we do, it is not difficult to anticipate objections to the plan of county consolidation, especially in the rural sections. Before any such plan is accepted, public opinion must be changed. But the secret of educating rural public opinion is ordinarily to be found very close to the purse strings of the rural dweller. If the average man can be shown that it costs him less to be radical than conservative, he will quickly change his views. A potential reduction from $19,000,000 to $2,-200,000 in the annual cost of local government certainly speaks for itself.

Mr. Childress believes that a great deal of opposition will come from the sentimental attachment to present county names, even though many of them mean little to the great majority of people living in the area whose name they cherish. For example, we doubt if there are fifty persons in Davidson County who know why or for whom their county is called Davidson. Mr. Childress proposes to overcome this sentimental objection by naming his new units for some hero or historical personality well known to the majority of Tennesseans. The eleven suggested county names are: George Washington, John Sevier, Robert E. Lee, Andrew Johnson, Benjamin Franklin, Andrew Jackson, James K. Polk, Sam Houston, David Crockett, James Madison, and Bedford Forrest.

On the practical side some objections are to be met. When Mr. Childress announced his plan he anticipated the objection that trade would be drawn from the present centers to the new county seats; and he answered it by stating that such trade transference is already taking place by reason of the good roads system. Possibly the greatest stumbling block in the way of reform is the opposition of present county office holders, many of whom would revert to private life upon the adoption of this plan. Some opposition might be allayed by permitting the office holders to serve out their terms before the introduction of the new plan. This group now dominates the whole county organization, and would work to defeat a plan of county consolidation. But we must hope that there are enough intelligent people to disregard the dictates of a political group when they are convinced that it is to their own financial interests to do so.

OUR AMERICAN MAYORS

XI. FRANK HAGUE: MAYOR-BOSS OF JERSEY CITY

BY E. E. SMITH

Barnard College, Columbia University

After fifteen years of complete subservience, will Jersey City throw off the yoke of the Hague machine?   ::   ::   ::   ::   ::

It is not often that a mayor is boss. Still less often is a boss mayor. Jersey City has both in the person of Frank Hague. A life-long politician, on the public payroll since he was of age, Frank Hague learned the game from ward politics up. By adroitness and leadership he has built up one of the strongest machines the state has ever seen.

To understand how he secured and maintains his power it is necessary to know something of Jersey politics. The state is neither preponderantly Democratic nor Republican. In national elections, like other industrial states, New Jersey tends to go Republican. But its large urban population has recently put the Democrats in a position to dispute the governorship. This latter strength is partly balanced in off years by the firm grasp the Republicans have had on the state senate. The senate is made up of one member from each of the state's twenty-one counties, three of which have a total population in excess of the combined populations of the other eighteen. The rural Republican counties are thus able to exert an influence out of proportion to their population. The senate must confirm the governor's appointments, and when the governor and the senate are of opposite political faiths some *modus operandi* must be developed. This the Republican boss, Edge, and the Democratic boss, Hague, have succeeded in devising.

THE INTER-PARTY WORKING AGREEMENT

United States Senator Edge, former governor and state senator of New Jersey, is the leader of the powerful Atlantic County Republican machine, which thrives in an area that includes Atlantic City; from this nucleus Edge has matured the strong state-wide machine which he controls today.

Mayor Hague is the Democratic state boss because he is boss of Hudson County, which contains more than half the Democrats of the state; he is boss of the county because he is boss of Jersey City, which contains more than half of Hudson's County's population.

A gentlemanly reciprocity, by which neither machine will violently attack

the other, has worked to the great personal and political advantages of both
bosses for more than a decade. Hague
has been allowed to run things in his
county undisturbed by any state action
except one or two sham legislative
probes which resulted in nothing.
Edge has been secure in his enjoyment
of federal and state patronage.

The most recent indication of collusion was the spectacle of Hague Democrats in Hudson County voting for the
Republican gubernatorial candidate,
Senator Larson, in the recent state
primary. "Hagueism" had been made
an issue by one of the leading Republican aspirants for governor, ex-Judge
Carey of Jersey City, and it is not unusual, when the issue between popular
rights and corrupt machine-ruled government is clearly drawn, to find the
two bosses of opposite parties fighting
on the same side. To quote the press:

The state-wide primary registered a victory
for professional politicians and as a result, New
Jersey has two machine tickets from which to
choose a governor and a United States Senator
at the general election next November.

The two men, by virtue of their state
leadership, are also powerful factors in
their national parties. Senator Edge
is not only a strong voice in the counsels
of the Republican party, but had even
been mentioned as a possible presidential or vice-presidential nominee.
Mayor Hague is vice-chairman of the
Democratic national committee and is
manager of Governor Smith's campaign
in several eastern states.

THE MAYOR'S RISE TO POWER

Frank Hague was born fifty-two
years ago in the old "horseshoe" district of Jersey City. His parents were
poor, ignorant folk, and Frank's education came to an end in grammar
school. He held numerous jobs of no
consequence and is reputed to have
been a member of various gangs of none

too savory reputation. Ward politics
early attracted him. His first political job was that of constable in the
county court house at three dollars per
day. Later he became custodian (a
polite term for janitor) of the city hall.
He was by this time the boss of the
second ward, having wrested the leadership from another. In 1911 he sought
a place on the street and water board,
and was nominated and elected.

Wide World Photos
MAYOR HAGUE

By this time the old boss, Bob Davis,
who had held sway for many years, was
dead, and Hague was gradually building up a large personal following by
skillful distribution of patronage. He
used his influence as head of the street
and water board to secure jobs for
followers and favors for big corporations which were large consumers of
water. A break occurred between
Hague and the Democratic mayor,
Wittpenn, and the former became
active in the movement for commission

government which was sweeping New Jersey during Governor Wilson's reform administration.

The movement was successful, and in 1913 Hague became a candidate for city commissioner. There were ninety-two candidates in all, from which ten were chosen in the elimination primary; five of the ten chosen were the Wittpenn candidates and the other five were independents, including Frank Hague and Mark M. Fagan, a former Republican mayor with an invisible record. The people, in a spirit of reform, were urged to vote against the Wittpenn candidates and to elect the five independents. The independent ticket was swept in and with it Frank Hague and A. Harry Moore, a machine Democrat whom Hague later made governor of the state.

On the organization of the commission Mark Fagan was chosen mayor and Hague secured for himself the strategic position of director of public safety. He was already boss of the second ward and this new post offered him an excellent opportunity to extend his sphere of influence. He instituted a notorious delinquency trial system; many demotions, promotions and changes took place until at length the city commission sought to curb his power by requiring that all of his appointments be confirmed by it. But notwithstanding this check, Hague had accomplished his designs when in 1917 with A. Harry Moore he was able to choose and elect his own city commission ticket. One Michael Fagan was found to oppose Mayor Fagan and the ancient political trick of running candidates with the same name for the same office was again employed. The political element represented by Mark A. Fagan was eliminated from the city commission and Hague was chosen mayor.

As mayor he quickly adopted the policy of stifling an opposition in both parties by placing the leaders of the opposition on the city or county payroll. By creating an untold number of jobs he perfected a strong political machine which has produced increasing majorities at each election until the Republican party in the city is practically extinct.

A CHARACTER SKETCH

At this point one naturally pauses to ask what sort of a man Hague is; what are his personality, his good qualities, his capacity for leadership, and his bad qualities.

Mayor Hague is a tall, slim man of fifty-two. He dresses with excessive care. It is said that at a New Year's reception at the City Hall one can pick out the members of the Hague machine by their clothes, for they all dress like Hague. Hague has outgrown his own crowd; he is not a "good mixer." Both he and his wife are suspected of social ambitions. His speech is curious. He pronounces words correctly and uses them accurately — in his ambitious youth he took lessons in public speaking. At grammar he is somewhat less apt—the plural form of verbs scarcely exists for him. His excessive profanity arouses resentment, but he has never been known to smoke or drink. What impresses one most, perhaps, is his alert, intense countenance conveying the impression of an iron will. He fully appreciates the political utility of fear and bullies his following into obedience.

In the coal strike of 1922 Jersey City suffered, though as a railroad center there was plenty of fuel in the yards. Hague stationed a policeman at every ferry and every road leading out of the city, and turned back every load of coal that was being taken beyond the city limits. A big coal company in New York City telephoned and asked by what right he did it. "By the right of the night stick," he replied. When he was looking for a home for the Mothers' Institute, the former clubhouse of Bob Davis's machine of which he was once a humble member was for sale at auction. Hague warned everybody that he wanted it for the city and bid it in for $300. There was no competition. Today the property is worth $100,000.

HIS POLITICAL METHODS

There are two ways of looking at this "benevolent despotism." We may commend the humanitarian motives of the mayor, but we must not lose sight of his political shrewdness in "catering to the people." It is good politics to build a Mothers' Institute, a hospital, or a baby clinic.

Hague, as we have seen, does not differ greatly from the typical boss; but the Hague machine, unlike the more celebrated Tammany across the river, is a one-man organization. If Olvany were to die Tammany would live on, but if Frank Hague were to die his machine might speedily crumble. Why? Because Hague has never tolerated in the organization any one who is superior to him in any way or who can stand alone. He has demanded submission and subservience to the dominant Hague will and has trained none to take his place.

In order to understand what the Hague machine is like and how it functions, it is necessary to know something of the socio-political makeup of Jersey City. Jersey City is the county seat and center of Hudson County and because of its location is one of the key cities of the United States. It is an industrial city and has a large industrial population, two thirds of which is of foreign extraction. The Irish group, constituting about 23 per cent of the total population, is politically domi-

nant and the influence of the church tends to unify its activities. Hague is Irish, as are three other members of the city commission, and in the distribution of patronage and spoils the Irish have received the lion's share. The Italian and Polish groups, numbering about 35 per cent of the population, can be most completely delivered by their leaders on election day.

These groups have been organized into clubs and their leaders have been kept in line by favors, jobs, and threats. One of the mayor's chief lieutenants is an Italian, Michael Scatuorchio, who holds the garbage contract. The following bit of satire, from the pen of a brilliant young dentist, appeared recently in his column in the *Jersey Journal* of Jersey City:

The time draws near for Mike Scat's summer outing; this is an annual event in Jersey City for the Gaekwar of garbage. This year he expects to lead 10,000 Italian-Americans at $6.00 a head. A little multiplication and the amount becomes $60,000. Under a broiling sun Mike parades the poor lads out of the village and past the city hall where they are reviewed by our debonair mayor. As Mike passes Frank, he winks. Hankus returns the greeting with another wink. They understand each other perfectly; $60,000. In cold cash. On a hot day. The simple-minded folk who parade behind Mike really do not know what it's all about. Most of them have been in America only a few years. Many of them speak very little English. But Mike has driven home to them the importance of Hankus, the first; and that next to the sovereign ruler comes Scat, the first. The poor lads are soaked $6.00, given a hat, a cane, a footload of corns and bunions, a ride on a scow and a Sea Girt meal (one sandwich with microscope, a slice of cake and all the water you can drink). Most of them lose a day's pay which they cannot afford. Every Italian-American city or county job-holder has to hand over for twenty-five or thirty tickets each; whether sold or not they have to pay for them. Every Italian-American Democratic Club has to take 300 to 500 tickets. If they refuse, Mike will tell Frank and Frank will tell the detectives, and the club is raided.

There are in Jersey City twelve wards and two hundred and forty election precincts; each ward has a responsible leader or ward boss appointed by the organization for valuable services rendered and for ability to deliver votes. Each precinct contains a certain number of qualified voters and it is the job of the committeeman to get these voters out on the primary and election day and to see that they vote "right." To quote Plunkitt of Tammany Hall, "there's only one way to hold a district; you must study human nature and act according." To do this entails large expenditures for the bosses' benefactions; the turkeys at Christmas, the police court fines, the loans that are never repaid, and all sorts of kindly attention to the poor are costly. Where does the money come from? The main source of supply, the "working capital of the business," is graft.

In Jersey City, as in other cities, the chief sources of graft are the sale of privilege and protection, favoritism in law enforcement, payroll and bid padding, and the awarding of public contracts. This system is in practice throughout Hudson County. The New York *Herald-Tribune* for July 13, 1928 says:

Juggling of city contracts by Mayor Frank Hague's Democratic machine for the financial benefit of political favorites was revealed before the New Jersey legislative investigation committee, sitting in the city hall, Jersey City, yesterday, in the reluctant testimony of a half dozen witnesses who were beneficiaries of Hague's favoritism in Hoboken.

It was developed that James J. McFeely, a brother of Bernard N. McFeely, city commissioner of Hoboken and Democratic boss, received a contract to remove garbage and ashes for $486,-260 and that the price was almost 300 per cent higher than the amount the city paid for the same work in the previous five years. It was also developed that bids at a lower price were rejected in the face of a decision obtained by one contractor

from the Supreme Court and that the cash bond required for the fulfillment of the contract was boosted to $25,000 so that McFeely, who obtained the money from a sister, alone would have a chance to get the job.

In addition to these customary methods of graft the Hague machine has worked out several new and more subtle methods. Great publicity has been given of late to the "three per cent" which the "payroll boys" have to hand over to the party organization. This refers to the annual fee or "dues," amounting to from three per cent to five per cent of the salary of every city and county employee which, it is alleged, the machine demands for party expenses. It has been repeatedly charged that the property of certain wealthy Hague supporters has been greatly under-assessed while that of citizens hostile to the machine has been subject to exorbitant taxation.

THE MACHINE DOMINATES THE COURTS

The administration of justice throughout the state is in the hands of the machine, due to Hague's ability to dictate the appointments of all judges and prosecutors through his control of the executive branch of the state government. It is significant that the three Common-Pleas judges in Hudson County are Democrats, notwithstanding the fact that they were confirmed by a Republican legislature having in the senate three Democrats and eighteen Republicans.

From time to time the press, both state and local, has called attention to the evils of a system, known as "Brandleism." It takes its name from T. M. Brandle, who is said to be one of Hague's chief retainers, and who by controlling numerous labor unions, has come to be recognized as leader of union labor in Hudson County. He has been accused by the press of "throttling trade, dominating industry, and peonizing labor for the benefit of the machine," by calling strikes on certain contractors who refuse to fall in line, and by granting favors to those on the "inside." He owns a large bonding company which is also highly profitable, for unless the building bond insurance business is given to him he can cause building operations to be stopped. He is said to have the power of the machine behind him.

THE CONTROL OF ELECTIONS

The control of election machinery is a factor which must not be overlooked, because it helped to put the machine in power and because ballot box stuffing and other frauds have been charged recently in both municipal and county primaries. Prior to the New Jersey primary in May, 1928, it was disclosed by investigators that thirty-four persons had registered from vacant lots, saloons, boat houses, and rooming houses where they had never lived, or were not living at the time. Assistant prosecutor John Drewen asked that the thirty-four fraudulently registered names be striken from the voting list. When the evidence on all the cases had been submitted, a Democratic member of the county board of elections declared that the thirty-four names be placed on the challenge list, rather than be striken from the voting list. The two Democratic members of the board voted to place the names on the challenge list while the two Republican members who had favored striking the names from the voting list, voted against it. The names were allowed to stand.

CASE COMMITTEE INVESTIGATES

Immediately after this primary, in which it is alleged that 25,000 votes were illegally cast in Republican ballot boxes by Democrats, an inquiry was called for. The Republican state senate, already aroused by alleged illegalities in the granting of bank charters, appointed a committee headed by Senator Clarence Case of Somerset to investigate the government of Hudson County and the primary. As this article goes to the press the Case Committee reports the following items to Attorney General Katzenbach and his vote-investigating grand jury:

The sworn story of a Democratic housewife who said she had voted as a Republican in the last primary "as a favor" to William McGovern, Democratic boss of her district, who had sent her a turkey for Christmas.

The story of an Italian voter, who could neither read nor write English, that two election officials had gone into a booth with him and given him a Republican ticket when he had intended to vote Democratic.

The testimony of four witnesses that they did not sign a Democratic nominating petition on which their names appeared, and the testimony of the two candidates whom the petition designated that they did not know they were on the ticket.

A list of 117 voters with a record which the committee's attorney said showed *prima facie* evidence of violation of the election law.

THE RESULTS OF HAGUE RULE

What has the Hague administration done for Jersey City in fifteen years rule? Is the city prosperous? Are her citizens contented? What is the trend of public opinion?

Today Jersey City has the largest per capita net debt of any city in the country. In 1917 the net debt of the city was $26,000,000; in ten years it had risen to $76,000,000. The per capita net debt has risen during this period from $85 to $241. This state of affairs is due primarily to the rapidly increasing cost of municipal and county government. The policy of putting political opponents and partisans on the payroll has increased the cost of local government so that it is now 30 per cent higher than the average for cities in the United States having 300,000 to 500,000 population. In 1922 the per capita cost of local government in Jersey City was $54, and four years later it had jumped to $76. Bond issues for public improvements have been made from time to time, but the extravagence with which money is spent is notorious. Jersey City in the last five years has provided less permanent improvements out of taxation than any other city of its size. This despite its heavy budget. On the average, other cities of its class have put aside $13 per capita per annum for permanent improvements or for the reduction of permanent improvement obligations. Jersey City has been able to put aside only $2 per capita per annum. The failure of the city to collect a high percentage of the taxes levied has caused the city's net liability on account of tax revenue bonds to increase at an average rate of $1,800,000 per year for the last eight years. It is significant that, despite the great amount of taxes not collected and in arrears, Jersey City has actually collected more taxes per capita than the average for cities of her size. In other words, the tax levy in Jersey City is so heavy that, regardless of the failure to collect an unusually large amount of it, the city still does collect a little more than other cities which are not so deficient in their collections.

The Fusion League of Hudson County recently charged that the city government is "honeycombed with job-holders and sinecures who are on the payroll of the city and who do no necessary work for the city whatsoever," in a resolution demanding that Mayor Hague drop from the city payroll the above-mentioned office-holders. The resolution declared that large sums of money could be released for municipal improvements and that taxes could be reduced if the changes were made.

During the fifteen years of Hague's dictatorship the electorate has been reduced to a state of subservience and demoralization, and the civic spirit of the community has been crushed. Today city, as well as county employees, dare not speak their minds for fear of losing their jobs; business men and corporations have been silenced by the power of the machine to "ruin" them; taxpayers dare not dictate the use of their own money lest they be driven from the city by exorbitant assessments. In one case a man who acted as chairman of a taxpayers' meeting to protest against the tax rate, found, when he received his tax bill, that his nonconformity had cost him $5,000.

A REACTION IS NOW SETTING IN

Throughout this period the community has been without the leadership of the press, for it, too, has been a victim of the fear mania; however, after fifteen years of repression a natural reaction has set in. The *Jersey Journal*, Jersey City's only daily and the leading newspaper in Hudson County, has taken a definite stand against the Hague machine. Several times a week this paper publishes a column written by Dr. Francis L. Golden, who by his satirical observations on Jersey City politics has done more, perhaps, than any other single factor to arouse the inhabitants of this "Hague-ruled Moscow." It is said that "Czar" Hague threatened the newspaper with destruction when it refused to discontinue the column by "F. L. G." The editor of the *Jersey Journal* says:

Every week we receive on an average of one hundred and fifty letters from indignant citizens, complaining of one thing or another. Taxation complaints, construction complaints, school complaints, criticism of streets, criticism of officials are in the pile, and the only interpretation we can put on this mountain of mail is that our citizenry are up in arms over the municipal management.

One citizen writes as follows: "It seems to me that Hague and his henchmen have a misconstrued conception of the word 'democracy,' under whose banner they 'labor.'"

Mayor Hague's lack of discretion in flaunting his wealth before the tax-oppressed city has further incensed the population. The people are asking how it is that the man, who not so very long ago was janitor in the city hall, can own a $300,000 mansion at Deal, N. J., and one of the most costly apartment houses in Jersey City on a salary of $8,000 a year as city commissioner. The *Jersey Journal's* satirist has humorously summed up the situation as follows:

While dwelling on François, I am reminded that he came up from Palm Beach a month ago in a private car. Such luxury entails the expenditure of $5,000. Frank only draws $8,000 a year salary, and you can't go around the country paying $5,000 for a short ride in a private car on that salary. The Pullman Frank rode in was the "National," so suggestive of his ambitions. But if François did pay out $5,000 for the journey, it isn't exactly sportsmanlike, not with all the unemployment around here nor with all the city and country boys who have to cough up the annual tribute and who, at this minute, could use any part of five thousand.

This rising tide of resentment has not failed to alarm the mayor, and in an effort to check it he has laid himself open to further criticism and ridicule. James Burkitt, self-styled "Jefferso-nian Democrat" who has been waging an independent campaign against the machine, has been bombarded on several occasions by rotten eggs when he attempted to speak on the expense of local government. The police made no attempt to intervene, and it has been rumored that one of the attacks was led by an ex-convict from the Rahway Reformatory and that it was made with the full knowledge of the machine. "Jeff's" latest act has been the organization of the "Non-Partisan Rentpayers' and Taxpayer's League of Jersey City." Aside from the efforts of the "Jeffersonian Democrats," a serious movement is being promoted by a group of disinterested citizens to defeat the machine at the next municipal election in May, 1929, when a new city commission is to be chosen.

We have traced the political career of Frank Hague from the "Horseshoe" to the city hall. From his position as boss of the second ward he has risen to greater heights of power than Bob Davis or any of his other predecessors who have dominated the Democratic organization of Hudson County. But unlike them Hague is a mayor-boss. The present question is whether a mayor-boss has a better chance for survival in practical politics than any other kind of a boss. From the facts that have been presented in this article it seems safe to predict that political history is about to repeat itself in Jersey City and that Frank Hague, the city's mayor-boss, is headed for a fall.

THE TAX SITUATION IN CHICAGO[1]

BY HERBERT D. SIMPSON, PH.D.

Associate Professor of Economics, Institute for Research in Land Economics and Public Utilities,
Northwestern University

*A graphic description of a scientific attempt to unravel the inequalities
of Chicago assessments, which formerly deviated from uniformity on
an average of 40 per cent.*   ::   ::   ::   ::   ::   ::   ::

WHEN the Illinois legislature met in special session on June 18 and in five days passed two important bills with reference to the tax situation in Chicago, it occasioned some astonishment, even to those fairly familiar with the situation in that city. And when the State Tax Commission a month later, under the authorization of one of these statutes, issued an order requiring a complete reassessment of real estate in Chicago and Cook County, it precipitated a situation of extreme concern to taxpayers in Chicago and of some interest to students of municipal taxation in general. It will be the purpose of this paper to present a brief account of the events that led up to the action of the legislature and State Tax Commission, and particularly of the facts upon which this action was to a large extent based.

COMPLEXITY OF THE PROBLEM

In fairness to the taxing authorities, it may be said at the outset that the problems of financing a city like Chicago are extremely complex and have been made more so by the rapid growth of the city during the past decade. Chicago now embraces an area of 209 square miles and a population of over 3,000,000 people. This is more people than are scattered today all over the broad areas of Montana, Idaho, Wyoming, Utah, Nevada, New

Mexico and Arizona combined — two tiers of western States and a sweep of territory that stretches from Canada to Mexico. The population of Chicago, in short, is greater than that presided over by seven governors and seven state legislatures elsewhere, and represented by fourteen senators at Washington. These three millions of people are, generally speaking, in comfortable circumstances, being possessed of some twelve to fifteen billions of wealth, which again is sufficient to duplicate that of the seven states enumerated above and still leave enough to buy up the United States Steel Corporation and the state of Delaware.

PUBLIC EXPENDITURES IN CHICAGO

In consequence of its rapid growth in population and wealth, the city of Chicago is spending in governmental activities around $260,000,000 a year, which is as much as the entire federal government was spending forty years ago. In the expenditure of these funds a variety of governmental bodies participate, including, besides the state legislature and the Cook County board of commissioners, the city council, the board of education, the sanitary district, the forest preserve district, certain "townships" within the city which still retain the power to levy taxes, sixteen park boards, and certain other special bodies, which bring the total to more than a score of different legislative bodies that levy taxes on

[1] The discussion of this subject will be continued by the same author in our next issue.

522

property in Chicago—not to mention some four hundred other taxing bodies in the county, whose expenditures affect, directly or indirectly, property holders in Chicago.

It will thus be seen that the expenditure of public money in Chicago is not only a large business but a very heterogeneous one, carried on by a surprising variety of agencies, with a confusing division of responsibility, and with apparently no coördination among spending bodies or purposes of expenditure. Any private business of comparable size that would attempt to conduct its financial affairs through such an organization would certainly go bankrupt; and the only reason the city of Chicago has not gone into receivership is that its citizens have managed their private business better than their public and have accumulated sufficient surpluses in the one account to offset deficits in the other. In short, wealth has increased so rapidly during the past decade that, in spite of wasteful and extravagant expenditures, the government has remained solvent.

SYSTEM OF ASSESSMENT

Of all taxes collected to provide for these expenditures, the general property tax still constitutes more than 90 per cent. The system of assessment on which these property taxes are based consists briefly of the following elements:

1. A county board of assessors, composed of five members, elected for terms of six years, which assesses real estate and personal property in Chicago and has general supervision over assessments throughout the remainder of the county.

2. Township assessors, for townships of the county outside of Chicago, elected by each township, who make the original assessments in these townships but are legally under the supervision of the county board of assessors.

3. A county board of review, composed of three members, elected for six-year terms, which reviews and equalizes the assessments made by the board of assessors and by the local township assessors outside of Chicago.

4. The state tax commission, composed of five members, appointed by the governor of the state, which has broad general powers of supervision over local assessors and boards of review but has hitherto made negligible use of these powers.

The state has a uniformity requirement in its constitution and, in the case of real estate, a quadrennial system of assessment.

This general system of taxation and assessment has come down, in varying portions, from constitutional and legislative enactments of 1898 and 1848, portions of it, in fact, from 1818, when Fort Dearborn still guarded the lake shore against British invasion and when Wacker Drive was nothing but a muskrat track through the weeds along the Chicago River. By the time any system of taxation has been in operation for a century more or less, it would seem to be appropriate to undertake some accurate appraisal of its results; and this the writer, in conjunction with the staff of the Institute for Research in Land Economics, attempted to do for Chicago in the summer of 1926.

SURVEY OF RESULTS

In January, 1927, the board of commissioners of Cook County, in which Chicago is situated, created a Joint Commission on Real Estate Valuation, composed of government officials and representatives of business and civic organizations, with George O. Fairweather, business manager of the University of Chicago, as chairman. This commission, finding our study of assessments in Chicago already under way, undertook to finance the work in order to make possible a much larger and more comprehensive survey. The results of this survey are summarized in the following pages.

The first objective was to ascertain the actual results of the present system of taxation, as reflected in the assessment of property, and to do this in such a way as to demonstrate the facts, whatever they might prove to be, beyond doubt or question. For this purpose the study was concentrated for the time being upon real estate assessment, and a comparison made of assessed valuations and actual sales values.

In order to test fairly the working of the quadrennial feature itself, a period was selected exactly in the middle of the past quadrennium, which proved to be from November 1, 1924 to July 1, 1925. All real estate transfers in Chicago during this period—more than 7,000 in all—were analyzed. After eliminations for incomplete or erroneous data, foreclosures, trades, transfers between members of a family, and transfers which represented only parts of a larger transaction—wherever these facts could be ascertained—the number of transfers came down to 6,445, and on these transfers the results are based.

A number of variations from the usual methods of comparing sales values and assessments were devised for special application to conditions in Chicago, and a large amount of collateral information about real estate values, methods of financing real estate purchases, and the cost of such financing was secured. Space will prevent discussion of these matters here; but, in brief, it may be said that in the determination of actual sales values, the revenue stamps required at that time were used as initial clues, supplemented by correspondence and interviews with buyers, sellers, and dealers, by reference to the Sanborne

insurance maps and the records of building permits for checks upon the improvements at the time of transfer and of assessment, and by physical inspection of a large number of properties. In consequence of these various eliminations, checks, and corrections, it is believed that the sales data herein presented represent as high a degree of accuracy as it is practically possible to attain and one that will make them thoroughly representative of the period covered.

After ascertaining the sales values of properties, the assessments standing against these properties were traced in detail from the quadrennial reassessment of 1923 through the 1927 quadrennial assessment, with a record of all changes made in the intervening years, either by the board of assessors or by the board of review. This affords a complete five-year record of assessments in Chicago.

THE FACTS

Out of some seventy-five tabulations and more than a hundred charts, only a half-dozen typical charts can be shown here. These will have reference chiefly to the assessments of 1926 and 1927, the former representing conditions at the end of one quadrennium, after four years of equalization by the board of review, the latter representing the new quadrennial assessment.

THE ASSESSMENT OF 1923

In order to get a perspective on the situation, we will begin with the quadrennial assessment of 1923, as made by the board of assessors, illustrated in Chart 1. In this and the following charts, vertical distances represent the percentage of assessed to sales value; the base line represents the total number of properties, in the form of percentage from 0 to 100 per cent. The curve is technically a "more than" curve, indicating, for example, that approximately 4 per cent of all properties are assessed at over 70 per cent of their value, 8 per cent of properties at over 60 per cent, and so forth. Its "more than" aspect is less important, however, than the fact that it has proved effective before popular audiences, as a simple device for illustrat-

properties in 1923, namely, 35.4 per cent. We are designating this the "level of uniformity" for that year, because this is the rate of assessment (and this is the *only rate*), at which all properties could have been assessed uniformly and still have yielded exactly the same aggregate assessment and revenue. If all properties had been

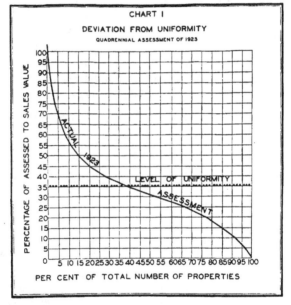

ing the difference between a uniform assessment and the actual assessment. For this purpose, the curve is thought of as representing simply the assessment of the individual properties, in terms of sales value, and arranged in order from highest to lowest.

The dotted horizontal line indicates the average rate of assessment[1] of all

[1] Prior to 1927, the statutes required the assessment of property, for purposes of taxation, at 50 per cent of its full value. Throughout the present paper, however, all figures have been converted into full value equivalent.

assessed uniformly at this level, the assessment of 1923 would have been represented by the straight horizontal line across the chart. How far the actual assessment fell short of uniformity is indicated by the curve, showing assessments ranging from a fraction of 1 per cent of true value to over 100 per cent.

But it is possible to apply more precise measurements to the quality of assessment than merely this range and general distribution. If a horizontal line at any level (in this case, at a

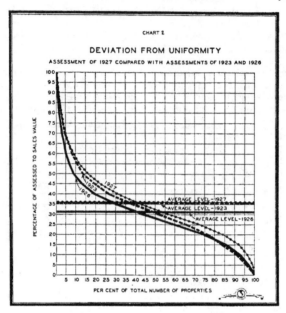

CHART 2

DEVIATION FROM UNIFORMITY

ASSESSMENT OF 1927 COMPARED WITH ASSESSMENTS OF 1923 AND 1926

PERCENTAGE OF ASSESSED TO SALES VALUE

PER CENT OF TOTAL NUMBER OF PROPERTIES

level of 35.4 per cent) represents 100 per cent of equality, the degree of equality attained by an assessment may be measured by the deviation of the actual curve from the horizontal line. *The curve for 1923 has an average percentage deviation of 40 from the level of uniformity.*

Just what a deviation of 40 per cent means depends on what one has in mind. In astronomy a deviation of one or two per cent in the motions of some of the heavenly bodies would upset the equilibrium of the solar system; in matters of ordinary human conduct, on the other hand, we get along with much wider deviations from rectitude. But if one will think for a moment what an average error of 40 per cent would be in accounting; what 40 per cent off specifications would mean in machinery and construction; or how 40 per cent off size would look

in hats, collars, shoes, and ordinary articles of wear, he will comprehend readily what an assessment with an average deviation of 40 per cent means. If one's proper size is 7½ in hats, 15 in collars, 8 in shoes, and a trouser length of 32, an average deviation of 40 per cent would fit him out in either a No. 10½ hat hanging around his ears, or a No. 4½ sitting on the peak of his head; a No. 21 collar resting on his shoulders, or a No. 9 collar strangling his Adam's apple; a pugnacious No. 11 on one foot and a dainty No. 5 on the other; a 19-inch trouser creeping up one leg and a 13-inch train of empty trouser leg dangling from the other. Yet the people of Chicago would be better off today parading down Michigan Boulevard in this deviated garb than parading back and forth to the county building and paying taxes on property *that is on the*

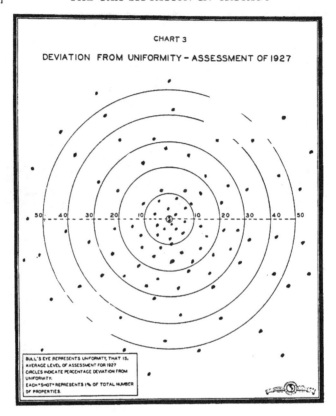

CHART 3

DEVIATION FROM UNIFORMITY – ASSESSMENT OF 1927

BULL'S EYE REPRESENTS UNIFORMITY, THAT IS,
AVERAGE LEVEL OF ASSESSMENT FOR 1927
CIRCLES INDICATE PERCENTAGE DEVIATION FROM
UNIFORMITY.
EACH "SHOT" REPRESENTS 1% OF TOTAL NUMBER
OF PROPERTIES.

average either 40 per cent over-assessed or 40 per cent under-assessed!

THE ASSESSMENTS OF 1926 AND 1927

In Chart .2 the curve for 1923 is carried forward and compared with the assessments of 1926 and 1927.

The curve for 1926 represents the assessment standing at the end of the quadrennium, after four years of equalization by the board of review. The average level has dropped from 35.4 to 31.3; but it requires mathematical measurement to determine whether the assessment, as fixed by the board of review at the end of the quadrennium, is any more nearly uniform than that made by the board of assessors at the beginning. Measured in this way, its percentage deviation from uniformity has been reduced during the four years from 40 to 37.7.

The new quadrennial assessment of 1927 contains food for thought. In view of the general protest it has aroused, one would suppose there had been a violent increase in assessments. The actual increase over the last quadrennial assessment is scarcely detectible (an increase of 1.4 per cent); and even

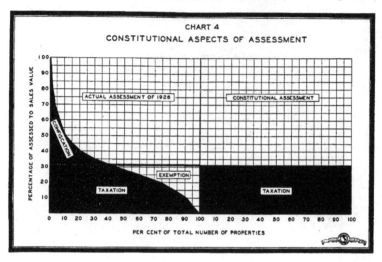

CHART 4
CONSTITUTIONAL ASPECTS OF ASSESSMENT

the increase from the reduced assessment of 1926 is only 14.7 per cent. Taxpayers were prepared for some increase in the assessment of 1927, on account of the general increase in property values since 1923, if for no other reason; and if that increase had been distributed with any semblance of equality, the majority of property holders would merely have breathed a sigh of relief that the increase was less than most of them had anticipated. In concrete form, the *average* result over the entire five-year period was merely that a property which, in 1923, was assessed at $35,400, was assessed at $31,300 in 1926, and at $35,900 in 1927; not something to become greatly excited about. But the extreme inequalities of the reassessment, in conjunction with circumstances to be described later, brought forth a storm of protest.

Chart 3 is self-explanatory, but we may relate the parable. The bull's-eye is equality. The concentric circles measure percentage deviation from equality, the bullet marks above the

dotted horizontal lines representing over-assessment and those below the line under-assessment. Each rifle shot represents 1 per cent of the total number of properties. The rifle company is the Cook County board of review—and the target tells the story, with one qualification. The shots outside of the outer circle are not located to scale, for the simple reason that if they were, many of them would have missed this page entirely.

If one is inclined to smile at the target, he will not smile at Chart 4. Here the right half indicates how the assessment of 1926 would have looked, if all properties had been assessed equally at the actual average rate for that year, namely, 31 per cent. The left half represents the assessment as it *was* made. The curve differs from those on previous charts in the fact that here it represents *value* not *individual properties*, indicating, for example, that approximately 10 per cent of the *total value* of real estate in Chicago is assessed at 55 per cent or

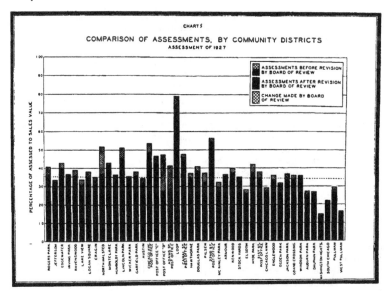

CHART 5

COMPARISON OF ASSESSMENTS, BY COMMUNITY DISTRICTS
ASSESSMENT OF 1927

over, that another 10 per cent of total value is assessed at 42 to 55 per cent, and so forth. This makes it possible to represent aggregate values and assessments in the form of definite areas, drawn to scale on the chart. The quadrangle on the right and the triangle on the left are exactly equal in area and represent an exactly equal amount in dollars and cents.

A FORM OF CONFISCATION

And if the distribution of assessments in terms of value enables us to visualize certain relationships in the form of definite areas, the constitution of Illinois makes it possible to designate these areas with equal precision. That portion of taxes which is collected from property assessed with some approach to uniformity is *taxation* in a constitutional sense. In a state having a uniformity requirement, that portion of taxes which is collected from a stratum of over-assessed property is not taxation but *confiscation*. In Chicago, this amounts to slightly over $30,000,000, in cold dollars and cents, collected from citizens every year by a process which, if the constitution is anything more than a scrap of paper, is outright confiscation.

And it is a particularly vicious form of confiscation, since the taxes collected in this way do not go to increase the revenue of the government, but merely to replace payments that should have been made by other property holders. On the chart, the area from which this $30,000,000 of taxes should have come is designated "Exemption," and is exactly equal to the area labeled "Confiscation." The result, therefore, is precisely the same thing as taking $30,000,000 from one group of citizens and distributing it gratuitously among another group. This, at its best, is a poor type of socialism, and at its worst is organized crime. Which of the two is represented by the present assessment administration in Chicago, we are not in a position to say; but a further analysis of the facts will afford some materials for judgment.

TERRITORIAL DISTRIBUTION OF INEQUALITIES

After measuring the general range and distribution of assessments, an attempt was next made to learn how these inequalities were distributed territorially throughout the city. For this purpose, the city was divided into fifty community districts. These are not wards or political subdivisions but are popularly known as neighborhood districts, which Chicago people will have no difficulty in recognizing. The average rate of assessment within each district was computed, and the result is shown in Chart 5, with the exception of districts for which less than twelve transfers were available, and for which it was felt, therefore, that an average might not be sufficiently representative.

In Chart 5, the districts are arranged as nearly as possible in geographical order, from north to south. The reader will not miss the general resemblance to the city's sky line itself.

But perhaps the most significant thing in the chart is the light it throws upon the work of the board of review. The entire height of the bars represents the initial assessment, as made by the board of assessors; the solid portions, the final assessment after equalization by the board of review. The cross-hatched sections, therefore, measure accurately the result, in each district, of changes deliberately made by the board of review. If anyone can discover here a semblance to any process of equalization, it is beyond the range of mathematics or statistics.

The result is the assessment map of Chicago shown below. A great deal has been said in recent years about tax maps issued for the convenience and information of property holders, such as those issued in Detroit, Minneapolis, and other cities. The map herewith is offered as a contribution to tax geography.

It will be noted that, in contrast with the situation in many other cities, the areas of heaviest assessment are concentrated in the down-town sections, the areas of lighter assessment ranging throughout the outlying portions of the city.

In other words, if the various levels of assessment in Chicago were represented by a relief map, we should have the down-town business section situated upon a distinct peak, surrounded by a broad and irregular plateau of considerable altitude; this plateau falling away to irregular foothills in the northern and western portions of the city, and dropping abruptly to a plain or marsh in the vicinity of Lake Calumet. One of the incidental features of such a map would be a conspicuous depression in the very heart of the plateau, in the neighborhood of the Adams Street post office, for which local gossip affords various explanations.

INEQUALITIES AMONG CLASSES OF PROPERTY

After tracing the territorial distribution of inequalities, all properties were classified under ten general types, in order to determine whether the assessment tended to favor or penalize any particular classes of property. The assessment for 1926 has been selected, because the results of four years of equalization must presumably represent more or less deliberate policy. These results are shown in Chart 6.

The chart appears to confirm the implication of the map above that, in general, business property is assessed at higher rates than residential, vacant,

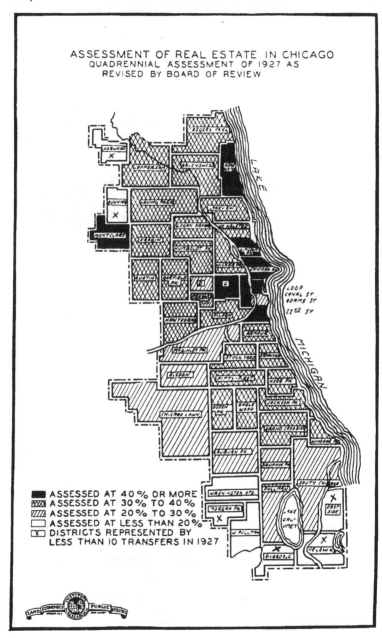

ASSESSMENT OF REAL ESTATE IN CHICAGO
QUADRENNIAL ASSESSMENT OF 1927 AS
REVISED BY BOARD OF REVIEW

■ ASSESSED AT 40% OR MORE
▨ ASSESSED AT 30% TO 40%
▧ ASSESSED AT 20% TO 30%
☐ ASSESSED AT LESS THAN 20%
⊠ DISTRICTS REPRESENTED BY
LESS THAN 10 TRANSFERS IN 1927

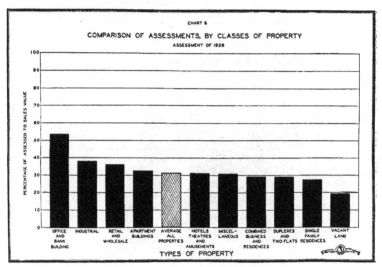

CHART 6

COMPARISON OF ASSESSMENTS, BY CLASSES OF PROPERTY

ASSESSMENT OF 1926

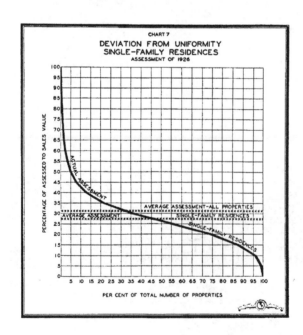

CHART 7

DEVIATION FROM UNIFORMITY
SINGLE—FAMILY RESIDENCES

ASSESSMENT OF 1926

or other classes of property. Vacant land is assessed at 19.7 per cent; all improved property shows an average assessment of 32.4 per cent.

On the chart, the differences in height of this series of bars may perhaps not appear striking; but in terms of dollars and cents to the taxpayer they mean such things as the following. The tax rate in Chicago averages approximately 5 per cent on assessed valuation. This means that the owner of a vacant lot in Chicago in 1927 paid (on the 1926 assessment) a rate of around ten mills on the true value of his property. If he built a home on his lot, his tax rate went up to fourteen mills. If he put up an apartment building, providing homes for a large number of people, his tax rate went still higher, to sixteen mills. If he put up a large office building, representing probably the maximum utilization of the land, his rate went up to 26.7 mills. This is exactly the opposite of the single tax, if that affords consolation to anyone.

Single-family residences are assessed at an average rate of 27.7 per cent. If this lower assessment indicated a concession to home-owners as a class, in the interest of promoting home-ownership, something could be said in its favor, even though it does violate the constitution and statutes and ignores the fact that dwellers in flats and apartments must, on the whole, represent a poorer economic class than home-owners, in a city like Chicago, and are therefore entitled to at least as low a tax rate. In order to determine whether it was the policy of the assessing bodies to favor home-owners as a class, the individual assessments of the 1,327 homes included among our properties were traced, with the surprising results indicated in Chart 7.

Twenty per cent of these homes are assessed at rates ranging from 40 to 100 per cent of value, in an assessment which has a general average of only 31 per cent. On another 20 per cent of homes, assessments range from 23 per cent down to 5 per cent of actual value. Among home-owners themselves, therefore, there appears to be as great a degree of discrimination as exists elsewhere.

RECENT BOOKS REVIEWED

A UNIFORM CLASSIFICATION OF MAJOR OF-
FENSES. By the Committee on Uniform
Crime Records of the International Associa-
tion of Chiefs of Police. Published by the
Committee, 261 Broadway, New York City,
1928. Pp. 55.

Any one who undertook to tabulate statistics
of crime for the United States as a whole would
find himself very much in the position of the
person who set out to discover how many people
take sugar in their coffee for breakfast. Various
methods were open to him. He could choose a
small area and, by going from house to house, ask
people. He could consult the sugar manufacturers. He could ask the local grocer. When
he was through, he would know very little.

So, with respect to crime. We have few
valuable criminal statistics for the country as a
whole. It *is* possible to know how many people
actually enter prisons each year, but this is very
different from the number of persons arrested,
the number of complaints made to police departments, and the number of crimes committed.
It is different, also, from the number of people
tried and the number found guilty—many are
merely fined or placed on probation. In other
words, we do not know the volume of crime, the
cost of crime, the drift of crime, and various
other things about crime.

If it were possible for every police jurisdiction
to report complaints and arrests to a central
authority, and to use uniform crime classifications or schedules for this purpose, we should be
in a much stronger position in the matter of
criminal statistics than we are now.

We should not be at the mercy of every
journalist's warm paragraph about a "crime
wave," or wondering whether Chicago is three
times as bad as New York—or only twice as bad.

Such is the object of the classifications printed
in this booklet. The method of the committee
has been to examine the penal statutes of thirty
states. It has then prepared, for each of these, a
schedule which, when filled out in accordance
with local law and practice, will enable any
police department to make a return to a central
agency, and this return can *then be used with
similar returns from other jurisdictions for the
tabulation of comparable, nation-wide statistics.*
The committee is to be congratulated on having

taken so novel—and somewhat laborious—a
step. If such schedules should come to be
universally used, it would be fine; and there is no
reason why, in the course of time, they should
not be. The committee has justified the faith
reposed in it.

At present, these schedules are limited to
thirty states and to four major offenses— feloni-
ous homicide, rape, robbery and burglary. It is
planned to extend them to other states and to
other crimes. Meanwhile, the committee wants
criticism; these schedules it regards as tentative.
The tasks ahead of it include persuading people
that such schedules are desirable, and overcom-
ing the inertia of police departments. But all
will come. Some day the United States will not
have to say to Europe: "How interesting that
you have statistics of crime! We have none!"

WINTHROP D. LANE.

✠

A SYLLABUS IN AMERICAN NATIONAL GOVERN-
MENT; A SYLLABUS IN AMERICAN STATE GOV-
ERNMENT; A SYLLABUS IN AMERICAN MU-
NICIPAL GOVERNMENT. By Russell H. Ewing.
New York: The General Press, 145 East 32nd
St., 1928.

The author has prepared mimeographed outlines for the three basic courses in American
government. The outline in national government is based primarily on Charles A. Beard's
American Government and Politics; in the field
of state government John M. Mathews' *American State Government* furnished the basis; for
municipal government, Thomas H. Reed's *Municipal Government in the United States* was used.
In each instance many other sources were employed, including all the major texts in the
fields. The syllabi could probably be used in
connection with any text, though their greatest
usefulness would be with those which furnish the
primary source. In each syllabus, the chapter
headings follow the chapters in the respective
text.

Each chapter outlines the material on the subject with which it deals. The student is thus
furnished with a guide to the material in the
texts. At the end of each chapter are a series of
suggestive questions dealing with the material
involved. These have been carefully chosen

with a view to directness and economy of time of both student and teacher.

These are unquestionably usable syllabi. They are clear, inclusive and to the point.

HARRY A. BARTH.
University of Oklahoma.

✽

STATE GOVERNMENT. By Frank G. Bates and Oliver P. Field. New York: Harper and Brothers, 1928. Pp. xii, 584.

According to the prefatory statement of the authors, this book has been written "to serve as a textbook in a survey course in state government offered to undergraduates in colleges and universities." In the selection and treatment of the material which is incorporated in the book, the authors have been governed by "the experience gained in the classroom through several years' teaching of the subject." Although no radical departures from the traditional methods of presentation have been attempted, there are several variations "both in topical arrangement and in emphasis from the models set by previous writers in this field." The most notable of these departures are in the treatment of the relations subsisting and developing between the federal government and the states, of the relations between the states themselves, and of the origin, content and significance of the constitutions of the states. Moreover, a rather unusual, but not excessive, amount of space is devoted to the treatment of the legislative functions and powers and to the subject of finance. Very few footnotes are used, and the bibliographies which appear at the conclusion of the respective chapters list only the more outstanding general treatises on the subject under consideration. There is an appendix of eighty-nine pages containing the constitution of Vermont of 1771, the constitution of Indiana of 1851, the constitution of Arizona of 1910, and the constitution of the United States, selected to illustrate the developing types of constitutions. The volume is equipped with a brief but adequate and usable index, and the development of each chapter is neatly shown by appropriate marginal entries.

In general, the authors have wisely chosen to treat government and governmental agencies as active and developing rather than as passive, fixed and final processes. In addition to an introductory chapter on the nature, purposes and types of government, the nature of political relations and the development of a terminology, the main part of the treatise is concerned with a description and discussion of federal and state relations, inter-state relations, constitutions, parties, suffrage and elections, the legislature, finance, the governor, the administrative system and services, the judiciary, the law and its application, and local governments other than those of cities.

Any person who is at all familiar with the complex structure of the government of any modern state must realize the inherent and insuperable difficulties of preparing a treatise of this kind. If a complete description of the various governmental agencies were attempted, the treatise would assume unmanageable and encyclopedic proportions, and if a general description only is presented, the author would become involved in the risk of producing a work which would be not only unsatisfactory but which might be entirely incomprehensible. The authors of this book seem to have encountered this dilemma with as great a degree of success as any writer can reasonably hope to attain. A narrative of facts sufficiently comprehensive to constitute an adequate and tangible survey of the field of state government is set forth and the discussion which accompanies the narrative is at all times pertinent, illuminating and provocative. The style is dignified, expressive and lively; and the criticisms advanced for and against existing governmental agencies and institutions are of such a character as to stimulate and assure clarity of thought without producing rancor.

The book as a whole must be regarded as a first-class piece of work, the material for which has been well selected, well organized and proportioned, set forth in a pleasing and readable style, and it constitutes a scholarly and authoritative treatise on state government acceptable alike to college students and to general readers.

CHARLES KETTLEBOROUGH.
Indiana Legislative Bureau.

✽

THE NATIONAL INSTITUTE OF PUBLIC ADMINISTRATION: AN EXPERIMENT IN DEMOCRACY. By Luther Gulick. Published by the Institute, 261 Broadway, New York City, 1928. Pp. 106.

In the great changes which have occurred in American government during the first quarter of the twentieth century, no single factor has had a greater influence than that unique American movement known as governmental research.

Created originally as a local institution, the New York Bureau of Municipal Research has established an example of method for the solution of governmental problems which, as gradually applied to other sections of the country, has resulted in new standards of technique, based upon exact information of comparative experience, and a new conception of governmental problems. The significance of this development and the important leadership continuously exercised by the original New York group has not been widely recognized. There is now available, however, an interesting account of this great influence in American democracy told by one who has observed its growth from the beginning, and who has had an important part in directing its accomplishments.

The National Institute of Public Administration, by Luther Gulick, is timely, and deserves a wide circulation. Although it contains an accurate detailed account of great value to the public official and student, there is ever present an underlying philosophy, and a well-told narrative which should appeal to the average citizen who would spend an enjoyable hour in obtaining a better understanding of our democratic institution. Mr. Gulick has written a splendid book on a splendid subject.

Samuel C. May.

University of California.

❋

Nominating Methods, with Special Reference to the Direct Primary. By Helen M. Rocca, Department of Efficiency in Government, National League of Women Voters. Washington, D. C., 1927. Pp. 60.

A Supplement to Nominating Methods. By Helen M. Rocca, Department of Efficiency in Government, National League of Women Voters. Washington, D. C., 1928. Pp. 20.

A Brief Digest of Laws Relating to Absentee Voting and Registration. By Helen M. Rocca, Department of Efficiency in Government, National League of Women Voters. Washington, D. C., 1928. Pp. 98.

These are useful pamphlets and represent a commendable activity of the National League of Women Voters. The first contains a brief history of nominating methods in the United States and an excellent summary of the leading features of the direct primary laws in the several states. This summary is arranged under the significant headings into which primary legislation may be divided, such as parties entitled to nominate by a direct primary, who may be candidates, how candidates qualify for a position on the primary ballot, open and closed primaries, tests of party affiliation in the closed primary states, etc. The requirements of the laws of the different states are grouped under these headings. The material is clearly and succinctly presented in very readable form. Fourteen pages are then devoted to an examination of the important charges against the direct primary and answers to the charges are given. Possible future developments in nominations are briefly discussed. The dates of the direct primary elections and presidential primaries are listed in a table. References to general and special writings upon the primary conclude the pamphlet. The statements are accurate and the discussion fair and enlightening. It is a high-class piece of work, creditable to the author and to the League.

The *Supplement* contains the amendments of primary laws enacted by the legislatures of the states during the 1927 sessions.

The third pamphlet treats the absent voting legislation of the different states in ample detail, and maintains the high standard of accuracy and clearness which characterizes the other two. Equally satisfactory summaries of the state laws upon other subjects would doubtless be welcome in many quarters.

Ralph S. Boots.

University of Pittsburgh.

❋

Three City Reports.—*Oberlin, Ohio, Annual Report for the Year 1927. By D. F. Herrick, Village Manager. Pp. 30.*—This report is a good example of how the activities of a small city can be reported in a clear, brief, and simple manner. The material is divided into nine parts. This is clearly stated in the front of the report and is adhered to as the following subjects are dealt with in turn: finance; streets, roads, parks, and bridges; sewers and sewage plant; public dumping ground; fire; police; water works; improvements needed; and comparisons and conclusions. A few clear tables on current finances, bond statement, and a sinking fund investment record occupy the last eight pages. The report was distributed within thirty days after the end of the period covered. May this be emulated by other cities! Of the twenty criteria upon which the reviewer attempts to grade reports coming to his attention, this report reaches the perfect score on nine, viz.: promptness, size, paper and type, organization chart, letter of transmittal, length, balanced content, comparative data, and absence of propaganda.

The weak points are a lack of emphasis upon important facts, inadequate use of illustrative material, and no table of contents. Other small cities might well copy the technique developed herein with the few exceptions noted.

Fort Worth, Texas. Annual Report for the Year Ending September 30, 1927. By O. E. Carr, City Manager. Pp. 32.—Mr. Carr is using the rather unique title *The Progress of Fort Worth* for his annual reports. This he does perhaps to avoid the odium of the usual title, "annual report." The reviewer is inclined to believe that a municipal report should be called such, and the contents be made sufficiently attractive and useful that readers will pay less attention to titles and more to the content.

This report either equals or surpasses the previous reports of Fort Worth on practically all twenty criteria except promptness and balanced content. The report was two months later than the 1926 issue, and the content does not indicate so good a balance of activities. Of over twenty-five "high lights of civic progress" enumerated, fully four-fifths deal with public works activities. This is not an unusual occurrence in report writing, and it is probably done in the belief that people are more interested in physical improvements than in other activities of their government. This may be a sound assumption; but a continuation of such policy will not help the cause of good reporting nor aid in creating a popular demand for more intelligent appraisal of the various services. The notable improvements over the previous report are the use of a larger number of charts and more comparative data. An especially good feature of the Fort Worth reports, which is not a common practice, is the placing of names of department heads with the report of their respective departments and the names of members of the council, boards, and commissions in the front of the report. Inasmuch as the members of library boards, city planning commissions, and the like, seldom receive any other reward for their faithful service, it would seem that such a recognition is justifiable.

The absence of an organization chart robs the reader of a reliable guide and the reason for omitting a letter of transmittal is difficult to understand, even though the report covers activities not immediately under the supervision of the city manager. The city manager is, theoretically at least, the administrative head of the city government and the report is an accounting of the administrative services of the city. It would seem, therefore, that a letter of transmittal above his signature should introduce the report. Certainly it should not be issued anonymously.

Kenosha, Wisconsin. Sixth Annual Report, for the Year Ending December 31, 1927. By C. M. Osborn, City Manager. Pp. 55.—For many reasons this report is highly commendable. In the first place it starts out with a clear and simple chart of the organization with which the report deals. This feature furnishes at the outset a proper perspective of the governmental machine as a whole. In other words, the chart serves as a frame within which the reader visualizes a picture of action and accomplishment as he proceeds through the pages of the report. Other favorable features are the distribution of illustrative material throughout the report which is always kept within the relevant text, and a letter of transmittal followed by a page showing respectively, accomplishments during 1927, and proposed activities for 1928.

Eighteen of the twenty-one accomplishments and fifteen of the seventeen proposed activities pertain to physical improvements. The inclusion of a page of interesting facts about the city and a table of comparative statistics marking the progress of Kenosha during the past six years add greatly to the interest of the report without leaving so much as a hint of propagandizing. The fact that more than four months expired after the end of the period covered before the appearance of the report will detract from the interest and freshness of its contents; but such a delay, however, is the rule rather than the exception. A constant improvement in promptness, however, is apparent and soon report writers will fully appreciate the news value of prompt reporting.

C. E. RIDLEY.

JUDICIAL DECISIONS

EDITED BY C. W. TOOKE

Professor of Law, New York University

Home Rule—Municipal Ownership—Conflicting Decisions in Ohio.—In *Board of Education v. Columbus*, 160 N. E. 902, decided April 8 by the Supreme Court of Ohio, the court held that the state legislature may not limit the power of the city to acquire and operate public utilities for the benefit of its inhabitants and that a statute prohibiting it from making a charge for water furnished school buildings or other public buildings is unconstitutional and void. This decision apparently overrules an earlier decision of the same court (*East Cleveland* v. *Board of Education*, 112 Ohio St., 607, 148 N. E. 350). The Ohio Supreme Court, however, does not seem to accept such a conclusion, and in effect holds that the same statute may be adjudged constitutional in one district and unconstitutional in another, a most ridiculous position as the court itself confesses This result is reached, says Chief Justice Marshall in his opinion, by the application of the provision of the state constitution (Art. IV sec. 2) which provides that "no law shall be held to be unconstitutional and void by the Supreme Court without the concurrence of all but one of the judges, except in affirmance of a judgment of the court of appeals declaring a law unconstitutional and void."

In the East Cleveland case, the lower court upheld the statute, which decision under the constitutional provision was affirmed by the Supreme Court by a vote of two to five. The court of appeals in the Columbus district refused to follow the decision in the East Cleveland case, and the supreme court itself, evidently not appreciating the force of the constitutional provision, refused to apply the doctrine of *stare decisis* in upholding its own minority decision. The effect therefore is to hold the statute constitutional in the Columbus district, and absolutely uncertain in districts where no decision has been rendered. The members of the supreme court, having thus abrogated their own powers, are now appealing to the electorate to repeal the provision of the constitution, which they find so unworkable.

Zoning—Power to Enact Temporary Zoning Ordinance.—Outside of the recent decisions relating to procedure of zoning authorities and the rights of applicants for permits, which are especially numerous in New Jersey as the courts are endeavoring to work out the effect of the new constitutional amendment, perhaps the most important case which has been decided is that of *Fowler* v. *Obier, Building Inspector of Louisville et al.*, 7 S. W. (2d) 219, in which the Kentucky Court of Appeals affirmed the plenary power of first-class cities to enact comprehensive zoning ordinances.

The plaintiff sought a reversal of the decision of the board of public safety which had supported the building inspector in his refusal to grant a permit for the erection of a gas and oil service station in a block where less than twenty-five per cent of the abutting property was used for business purposes, which was the criterion of a residence district under the temporary ordinance. The legislature of Kentucky in 1922 had adopted a general enabling act, but, for reasons that do not appear, had repealed it in 1924. In 1927 the city of Louisville enacted an ordinance to create a city planning commission to make plans and surveys in order to enable the city council to zone the city. A supplementary ordinance was passed, prohibiting for two years the erection of any buildings for business or industrial purposes without the approval of the board of safety in a temporary residence district, and it was this ordinance that was attacked as beyond the power of the city to enact.

In deciding that the statute giving the general council of the city the "power to pass for the government of the city any ordinance not in conflict with the Constitution of the United States, the Constitution of Kentucky and the statutes thereof" conferred upon the city for local purposes all the unexercised police power of the state, the court held that the city had acted within its clear scope of its delegated authority. The temporary ordinance was adjudged reasonable and necessary to maintain the status quo pending the drafting and enactment of the permanent zoning code. In so holding, the court follows the decision of the Supreme Court of California in *Miller* v. *Board of Public Works*, 195 Cal. 477, 234 Pac. 381, in which that court said:

"It is a matter of common knowledge that a zoning plan of the extent contemplated in the instant case cannot be made in a day; therefore we may take judicial notice of the fact that it will take much time to work out the details of such a plan and that obviously it would be destructive of the plan if, during the period of its incubation, parties seeking to evade the operation thereof should be permitted to enter upon a course of construction which might progress so far as to defeat in whole or in part the ultimate execution of the plan."

✱

Torts—Liability for Negligence in Care of School Property.—Two recent cases of interest involving the question of the recovery of damages by pupils injured through negligence in the care of school property have recently been decided by the courts of California and New York. While the general rule is that neither a city or a school district of itself is to be held liable in tort, upon the ground that the function discharged is purely governmental and that the subordinate body acts merely as an agency of the state in maintaining and managing the schools and the school property and therefore enjoys the immunity of the state from suits, liability may be imposed by statute. Such is the case in California, where counties, municipalities and school districts are alike made liable for injuries to persons and property resulting from the dangerous or defective condition of the buildings, grounds, etc., committed to their care, caused either by their active negligence or their failure to repair after reasonable notice. In *Huff* v. *Compton City Grammar School District*, 267 Pac. 918, the action was brought by a child of nine years, who was burned by contact with a trash incinerator maintained on the school playgrounds. The court, in affirming a judgment for the plaintiff, states, that the dangerous character of the situation was such as to demand its immediate remedy, a condition that was known to the officers of the district who had full power to abate it.

In *Lessin* v. *Board of Education of City of New York*, 161 N. E. 160, an eight-year-old boy fell into an elevator shaft near the sidewalk on the school grounds, the platform giving way when he ran upon it in playing a game of tag. Its defective condition was known to the employees of the board, who had taken no precaution to guard its approach. While no statute exists in New York imposing liability upon municipalities for negligence in the management of school property, the courts of the state in the well-known case of *Herman* v. *Board of Education* established the principle of liability upon the theory that the board was not only an agency of the state, but in reality an agent which should be held responsible, notwithstanding the immunity of its principal. This salutary principle was followed in the instant case, and the board which is charged with non-delegable corporate duties held liable to an individual injured through its failure properly to discharge them.

The extension of the doctrine of the Lessin case to the other governmental duties which the state imposes upon municipalities would largely wipe out the immunity from liability in tort now granted by the courts and firmly entrenched by judicial precedent. Dr. Borchard of Yale, as a result of his recent extensive study of the question of governmental liability in tort, recommends that public governmental corporations as well as the state itself should be subjected to liability in every case in which at present the active agent in the tortious act is today liable. Applying his recommendation in the instant case, the city itself would be held directly liable in place of its agent, the board of education. Admitting the desirability of such a change, the problem of the effective legislation required to bring it about may well command the attention of students of our social and political institutions.

✱

Municipal Ownership—Power to Dispose of Plants.—In view of the concerted plan of the public utility interests in certain states to induce municipalities to go out of the business of supplying gas, electricity or water to their inhabitants and to substitute private ownership and operation, as the evidence before the Federal Trade Commission in its present investigation points out, the question of the power of cities to dispose of such plants is being frequently raised. That a municipally owned water or lighting plant is charged with a public interest, so that in the absence of an express legislative authorization, it cannot be sold under a general power to dispose of property is generally established, the only exception being for that part of the plant that has become useless through obsolescence (*Haron Water Works Co.* v. *Huron*, 7 S. D. 9, 62 N. W. 675).

In *South Texas Public Service Co.* v. *Jalin*, 7 S. W. (2d) 942, finally decided by the Court of Civil Appeals of Texas on June 13, 1928, the court affirmed a decree against the city of New Braunfels and the appellant company, canceling a contract between the city and the service company, an ordinance ratifying it and a bill of sale, whereby the former attempted to sell to the latter its electric street lighting system. The electric system had been built with proceeds of bonds issued for extensions to the waterworks system, and was operated in conjunction therewith for the purpose of lighting the streets. The defendant company furnished the inhabitants with electric service under an existing franchise, and the contract of sale included a provision for the supply of street lighting for a term of years at a stipulated rate. The statutes of Texas (Act 1112 R. S. 1925) expressly provided that "no such light or water system shall ever be sold until such sale is authorized by a majority vote of the qualified electors of such city or town." The contention of the appellants was that this clause applied only to such municipal plants as furnished service to the inhabitants and under the terms of the statute could be mortgaged. The court disposed of the case by holding that the clause covered municipal plants not operated for revenue. It would seem that it might quite as well have admitted the appellant's contention and placed its decision upon the lack of an express legislative authorization to dispose of the property, which the city held charged with a public trust for the benefit of its inhabitants.

A similar question was raised in the case of *Curry* v. *Highland Park*, 219 N. W. 745 (June 4, 1928), in which the Supreme Court of Michigan held that the city in the absence of express statutory authority could not dispose of its garbage plant which was located some distance outside the city limits. The court, however, instead of resting its decision upon the lack of power to dispose of property charged with a public trust without express legislative authorization, limited the application of this principal to property used to discharge a governmental as distinguished from a proprietary function, which was determination of the case as the disposal of garbage is held to be a governmental function in Michigan. While the court came to the correct conclusion, it is submitted that the agreement in the opinion would narrow the application of the principle much further than the court would go were the question of the disposal of property

held in a proprietary capacity but charged with a public trust directly in issue.

That the delegated power to dispose of municipal property must be exercised in the mode laid down by the legislature is illustrated in *Russell* v. *Bell*, 6 S. W. (2d) 236, decided May 1, 1928. In this case the Court of Appeals of Kentucky reversed the lower courts on an appeal sustaining a demurrer to a taxpayer's action to recover for the city either the property itself or the difference between the sale price and the actual value of a municipal lighting plant sold by virtue of a resolution, instead of an ordinance as required by the statute granting the power of disposal. While holding that in absence of allegations of fraud the members of the board of aldermen would not be personally liable, they were held to be necessary parties to the suit.

Where, however, the state as in Georgia confers full power upon the city to dispose of any of its public utility plants, subject only to a referendum upon the timely protest of ninety per cent of the qualified voters, but expressly disclaims modifying existing powers of cities to sell, the Supreme Court in *Byrd* v. *City of Alena*, 143 S. E. 767, sustained a sale of the municipal electric light plant, though the referendum held it was void. The Georgia statute is probably the most liberal to be found, and the disclaimer of modification of outstanding powers renders the acquisition of municipal utilities by private interests extremely easy to accomplish.

✳

Definition—The Municipal Concept.—The content of the term "municipal corporation" has been one of the serious questions confronting the various commentators who have essayed the task of collecting and digesting the mass of law relating to local governmental agencies. An exhaustive treatise on this subject, such as the monumental work of Judge Dillon or more recently the encyclopædic compendium of Judge McQuillan, must necessarily include the consideration, not only of those corporate agencies to which the state has committed the exercise of a portion of its legislative power for local purposes, but also of those other so-called quasi-municipal corporations which are created by the state to aid in the administration of purely governmental powers within defined territorial limits, such as school districts, road districts, reclamation and irrigation districts and in the majority of our states, counties and towns. As a practical matter, the question arises whether the term should be limited to the first class of agencies, the prime characteristic of which is the delegated power of local self-government, as exemplified in cities and villages and the New England town or be extended to cover the ever increasing number of local corporate agencies which have been multiplied to take care of the rapid extension of governmental functions. The question is complicated by the fact that in many of our state constitutions certain provisions, as those imposing limitations upon local indebtedness or special legislation, employ the term either expressly or by necessary intendment to include both classes (*State* vs. *Leffingwell*, 54 Mo. 458; *In re Dowlan*, 36 Minn. 430), and by the further fact that certain generic terms as town or county are frequently applied to local organizations with full powers of local self-government (*State* vs. *Glennon*, 3 R. I. 276; *In re Holmes*, 187 Cal. 640).

Judge Dillon after a thorough examination of the authorities formulated the following lucid definition; "the incorporation, by the authority of the government, of the inhabitants of a particular place or district, authorizing them in their corporate capacity to exercise subordinate specified powers of legislation and regulation with respect to their local and internal concern." He thus recognized and emphasized the delegated power of local self-government as the distinctive purpose and distinguishing feature of a municipal corporation proper. McQuillan in his latest edition adopts the following phraseology: "A municipal corporation proper may be described in outline to be a legal institution, or body politic and corporate, established by public law, or sovereign power, evidenced by a charter, with defined limits and population, a corporate name, and a seal, though a seal is not essential, and perpetual succession primarily to regulate the local or internal affairs of the territory or district incorporated by officers selected by the corporation, and secondarily to share in the civil government of the state in the particular locality."

This somewhat unnecessarily complex definition, elaborated through some fifty pages of text and notes, may hardly be regarded as an improvement upon the more simple and accurate statement of Judge Dillon. The emphasis in his commentary upon the value of the distinction set forth in *Hamilton County* vs. *Mighels* (7 Ohio St. 109) that municipal corporations in contrast to quasi-municipal corporations are based upon the free consent of the inhabitants, a doctrine that has had a marked historical effect upon the theory of corporate liability, may well be perversive of correct and clear analysis, while his inclusion of the requirement of a charter, which left unexplained would imply a formal charter, adds little or nothing to the delimitation attempted. The inclusion also of elements that inhere in all corporations, private as well as public, seems unfortunate.

Both authorities, however, agree in confining the term municipal corporations to those corporate governmental agencies to which for local purposes has been delegated a part of the state's sovereign legislative powers. With this as the primal test, the student may readily determine from the presence or absence of such powers the nature of the corporation, whether called a city of a county, a town or a district. The extent of these delegated legislative powers as set forth in the state constitution, the general statutes and the local charter determines the status of the corporation and serves as the criterion by which the courts can measure the intention of the legislature to vest it with powers incidental to and implied from those expressly granted either in general or specific terms. With this concept in mind, it matters little in determining the scope of implied powers to what extent the state has delegated to the municipal corporation the administration of general governmental duties, which for convenience it has for the most part committed to other local corporate agencies, as counties and towns, which may be appropriately designated as quasi-municipal corporations.

PUBLIC UTILITIES

EDITED BY JOHN BAUER

Director, American Public Utilities Bureau

Utility Consolidation and the Public Interest. —The Consolidated Gas Company of New York filed a petition with the Public Service Commission of the state of New York for permission to acquire the capital stock of the Brooklyn Edison Company, and to pay for such stock— each share $100 par value—one share of its own $5 preferred stock of no par value, and one share of common stock of no par value (the latter to be split into two shares each). The purchase had been ratified by the stockholders of both corporations and needed only the approval of the Commission to become effective.

The purchase is a transaction of unusual magnitude, and involves public interests of far-reaching significance. As to magnitude, the Consolidated Gas Company is already a half-billion dollar corporation. As of December 31, 1927, it had reported assets of $521,242,000, which included direct gas properties, $98,-852,000, and investments in "affiliated companies," $387,821,000. The Brooklyn Edison Company as of the same date, reported total assets of $171,747,000, which consisted altogether of electric plant and equipment, together with working capital and miscellaneous assets.

Through this acquisition, the Consolidated system will control practically the entire electric field in the city of New York. It also controls the entire gas field, except the Brooklyn Union Gas Company, with which it is said to have close affiliations, and which is expected to come under direct control at a later date. It thus represents the largest single control in any city of the country.

The merger, popularly so-called, had been a matter of rumor for more than two years. That it would be approved without serious inquiry by the Public Service Commission had been generally assumed. The petition was presented at the threshold of the summer vacation period. This fact was expected to limit the available time for discussion; so important a matter could not be postponed until after Labor Day; nor could the Commission be expected to give up its vacation to continue drawn-out hearings. This pro-gram of casual expedition was temporarily frustrated by the appearance of the City of New York, and by the Public Committee on Power for the state of New York.

The City of New York took the ground that the purchase price represented by the Brooklyn Edison stock was unjustified. This was based on the market price of the stock during June and July of this year, at an average figure of $250 per share. The actual investment in property represented by the stock is under $100 per share. The high market price was reached during the past year as the result of the rumors of the proposed merger and the effort to buy up the stock. The city objected to the recognition of this market price as the basis of the merger. Its position was predicated formally upon the law regulating the issuance of public utility securities, and practically upon the probability that such a value would be urged subsequently to justify a higher valuation for rate-making.

The city recognized that economies might be effected through the merger, but it pointed out also that there might be public disadvantages through the loss of "system" competition and through the possibility of larger overheads and outside control. It urged, therefore, that prior to the approval of the merger, the Commission should insist upon a reduction in rates from seven cents to five cents per kilowatt hour as the maximum for domestic and commercial uses. This would assure the public at once a proper share in the benefits of the merger, and appeared feasible even under present earnings of the companies concerned.

The Committee on Power appeared to urge upon the Commission the necessity of considering the public aspects of the proposed purchase and the need of bringing out all the available facts as to economies of operation, the relation with outside companies, the effect upon state regulation, and, particularly, the relation to future water power development in the state. It did not outright oppose the merger, but it desired to have the basis of the merger safeguarded in the interest of the public.

The Committee consists of well-known people,

542

and was organized about two years ago primarily to support Governor Smith's water power program. It has continued in existence; its experts have been studying public utility regulation, especially electric light and power, from a broad public standpoint. The Committee's representative was met by the Commission's ruling that he would not be permitted to participate in the hearings. He argued that the proposal is not just a private arrangement between individual stockholders; that it involved the public interest at large; that any substantial and known public group should have a hearing, to present such facts and views as might be helpful to the Commission; that the privilege of being heard should not be controlled by narrow technical rules. He was permitted to file a brief, but was denied the right to cross-examine witnesses or to present evidence.

The refusal to admit the Committee to full participation in the hearings aroused much public discussion. It promptly became not only an important local, but a national issue, because of the prominence of several members of the Committee and because of the relations of some of them to Governor Smith and his water-power program; also because Commissioner Van Namee, closely affiliated with Governor Smith's campaign management, had joined in the ruling of the Commission.

The hearings were closed with striking promptitude; only two meetings were held. The city had requested two weeks' adjournment to complete its study of the facts and prepare for cross examination; but, instead, was given four days to file a memorandum. It filed a day late, and was duly reprimanded; no real opportunity for cross examination had been given. Then the tempest burst. Governor Smith asked the Commission to reopen the case and to hear whatever any public group might have to say for or against the merger. This request was denied, on a strict party vote. Commissioner Van Namee now joined with Commissioner Lunn to vote for a re-hearing, whereas Chairman Prendergast and Commissioner Pooley voted against; the fifth Commissioner, Mr. Brewster, was absent because of illness.

That the merger involves important matters of public policy there is no doubt. That in a narrow legal sense the Committee had no interest in the matter also appears true. But the Commission is not controlled by limited legal procedure; it is free to draw upon information from any source whatever, and may call in the assistance of any group of people it pleases. Naturally, it could not listen without limit to everybody, if hundreds of individuals requested to be heard. It could, however, use discretion. Besides the city, the Committee was the only public group which desired any real participation. Its responsibility was beyond question, and its representative is a well-known member of the bar. There was no good reason why it should not have been granted a full hearing, and why this could not have been granted promptly by all the members of the Commission upon the special request of the governor.

On August 9, the Commission, by unanimous vote of the four commissioners present, approved the petition; Commissioner Brewster was still absent on account of illness. It did, however, expressly limit the statement of capital expenditures on the part of the Consolidated Gas Company to the issue value of the Brooklyn Edison Company in line with the position taken by the city. It has thus minimized the possibility of the market value of the stock at the time of the exchange being subsequently entered as an element of "fair value" for rate-making.

The city's suggestion that rates should be reduced as part of the consolidation program was not followed. The Commission refused to bring rates into the matter; rates can be handled separately later, it held. It referred to past voluntary reductions on the part of the Brooklyn Edison Company, and pointed out that the Commission itself was created for the express purpose of supplying the equivalent of competition; that it can be depended upon to protect the public "from the inertia of monopoly and the evils of competition." The public, however, would have felt more assured of the protection if an immediate reduction had been passed along. The Commission's zeal on behalf of the public has not always been strikingly apparent.

Perhaps the particular case will be duly safeguarded. There is the large city which happily has all along assumed actual responsibility for public utility consumers. But the instance reveals how the vast number of mergers of the country have come about. Usually they are treated as casual matters; mere routine; little or no examination of the purposes and consequences; no positive safeguard of public interests. Here is the reason why usually the public fails to benefit, and why public resentment against holding companies and commissions is rising.

Decision in New Haven Commutation Reaffirmed.—On July 15, 1925, the New York Public Service Cmmoission authorized an increase of about forty-four per cent in commutation rates charged by the New Haven Railroad Company upon intrastate travel to and from New York City. This increase affected New Rochelle, Mount Vernon, Portchester, and other municipalities in Westchester County. Sharp public opposition was aroused, and upon petition by the communities, a re-hearing was granted by the Commission. The higher rates, however, continued; meanwhile rebate slips were given to the commuters. The City of New York had not appeared in the original case, but joined as a party in the re-hearing.

The principal basis for a re-hearing, especially on the part of the cities of New York and Mount Vernon, was to present evidence as to the "differential" cost of carrying commuters and regular passengers. The railroad had presented its entire case upon the assumption that it costs as much to carry a commuter as a regular passenger. It had made a comprehensive study for the month of June, 1924, including all the elements of cost (operating expenses, taxes and return on the property) within the state of New York. It first separated these costs between trains that carried intrastate commuters, and those that did not ("study" trains and "nonstudy" trains), and made the separation principally on the basis of car miles, or car units. The costs thus allocated to the "study" trains were then apportioned between commuters and regular passengers, on the assumption of equal cost per passenger or per passenger mile.

This method of determining the cost of carrying the commuters furnished the chief issue in the re-hearing. There were other issues, but they were of minor character. In its 1925 decision, the Commission accepted the results of the company's allocation, which showed a loss of $127,000 a month from the intrastate commutation business. In the petition for re-hearing, the cities of New York and Mount Vernon contended that the basis of cost apportionment was wrong, that it costs less to carry a commuter than a regular passenger, and that a "differential" should be established on the basis of which the allocations should be made.

After the re-hearing had been granted, the petitioners made a request for certain operating data which, it was claimed, would furnish the basis of the differential for a new cost allocation.

The company refused to supply the data except upon order of the Commission, which did not issue the order as requested, but modified and greatly limited the scope of the facts to be supplied. The municipalities were thus unable to make as comprehensive a study as had been expected. They succeeded in obtaining data only as to a few selected trains. Using the limited figures, their experts computed the cost differentials, and made a reallocation of costs accordingly, taking the basic costs as presented by the company in the original hearings.

The costs were separated into two groups: (1) those that varied in relation to train or car loading; and (2) those that were of a general overhead or nonvariable character. As to the first group, the municipalities attempted to show that it costs about three times as much to carry a regular passenger as a commuter; and as to the second group, six and one-half times as much. Upon this basis they separated all the costs between commuters and regular passengers; with the result that they showed for the month of June, 1924, a profit of $39,000 from the intrastate commutation business, above all operating expenses, taxes and return on property, instead of the loss of $127,000 claimed by the company.

This difference in results is striking; it is due wholly to the basis of apportionment used. If it be assumed that it costs in every respect as much to carry a commuter as a regular passenger, the company is right. If the differentials as claimed by the municipalities are correct, then their computation of a $39,000 profit per month is correct. The municipalities admitted that the extent of data was rather limited; they had sought all the facts, but were denied access to them; they insisted that a complete survey would reveal even greater differential ratios than those used. The differentials are due to the enormous density of traffic on the part of commutation, and the low density on the part of the regular passenger business. This applies not only to the ordinary train costs, but especially to the overhead or nonvariable costs. The greater the volume of business, the less the cost per passenger or per passenger mile

In its decision handed down August 1, 1928— three years after the first decision—the Commission refused to alter its original position. Whether the municipalities will attempt to have the decision reviewed by the courts, has as yet not been determined. The Westchester commuters are thus required to pay an increase of forty-four per cent in rates, which are much higher than those charged by any of the railroads entering the city of New York.

This decision has important bearing not only in the New York district, but throughout the country where commutation business exists to any considerable extent. If the company's theory of "equal cost" is to be accepted, as validated by the Commission, then, undoubtedly, the commutation rates throughout the New York-Metropolitan district should be increased; and the railroad companies will doubtless move speedily for higher rates. Upon the same theory, probably all commutation rates throughout the country are too low, and sharp increases would be justified. If the theory is followed to a logical conclusion, the commutation rates should be placed upon the same level as ordinary passenger rates. It leaves no sound basis for the long existing difference in rates between the two classes of passengers.

What is theory, and what is fact? The municipalities attempted to show as a fact that in respect to all cost elements the amount chargeable to a regular passenger is materially greater than can be properly allocated to a commuter. This applies to all train costs, because of the much greater loading of commuter trains, and because of the inferior service. It applies particularly to other costs (the non-variables) because of the enormous commuter density during the period of the commutation traffic as compared with the regular business. The Commission accepted the company's theoretical view of equal cost, and disregarded the great differences in density and conditions of service as having any bearing upon the relative cost allocation.

A special point involved the allocation of all costs connected with the Grand Central Terminal. This is a monumental structure which required a huge investment, and demands a large annual expenditure for operation, maintenance and return on the investment. In the company's analysis, all these costs were equally divided per passenger between commuters and others; and this received the approval of the Commission. The fact was disregarded that the terminal was constructed primarily for the use of the general passenger traffic for the entire New Haven, as well as the New York Central Railroad, and not for the needs of the commuters. The latter have little occasion to use the ter-

minal, and would be as well served without it; yet under the decision, they are required to pay just as much per passenger as the through Pullman traffic which is dependent upon the station facilities.

The Commission apparently did not consider seriously the questions of cost apportionment presented by the municipalities at the re-hearing. It limited itself strictly to "new evidence," and plainly did not regard the reallocation and the data bearing upon apportionment as constituting "new evidence." It thus restricted its judgment by technicalities and arbitrary limitations imposed by itself. There was no reason, in the first place, why it should not have complied with the request of the municipalities for all the basic facts which were deemed necessary for the cost study along the lines proposed. If in the earlier hearings the proper basis of apportionment was not sufficiently presented, then why not require the company to furnish all the facts necessary to make the desired allocations? Why limit the data to a few trains, when all the essential facts could have been readily obtained, covering the entire traffic for a reasonable period of time?

This decision is glaringly inconsistent with another, made five months earlier, in the Long Island commutation case. The Long Island Railroad Company had sought the approval of a twenty per cent increase in commutation rates, and, apart from mere differences in technical computations, it based its case upon the same theory as the New Haven; it assumed that it costs just as much to carry a commuter as a regular passenger. The Commission here, however, rejected the equal cost theory; it decided that the company had not proved its case, and denied the proposed increase.

If the equal cost theory was untenable in the Long Island case, why is it acceptable in the New Haven case? If the Long Island failed to prove its case, so did the New Haven. If the latter is justly entitled to an increase in rates, so is the Long Island. The technical limitation of the re-hearing to "new evidence," when the latter was circumscribed by the Commission itself, cannot obviate the fact that the fundamental principles adopted in the two cases by the Commission are utterly irreconcilable, and that the underlying theory of the latest decision will justify increases in all commutation rates to the point of extinction of the commutation business.

WHO ARE THE PROPAGANDISTS?

The Federal Trade Commission has continued to rout out the public utility propagandists. Even during the summer recess it has continued its special investigations; covering not only scope and methods of publicity, but also financial practices, and inter-company relations. The hearings revealed the practices of the propagandists, their far-flung organization, and their cynical methods.

We shall not repeat here any of the details, but wish to present reflections which, we believe, are close to reality. From the outset, we wondered to what extent the utilities were directly involved in the sinister activities, and whether they were thoroughly conscious of the anti-public practices. As we followed the investigation, and considered our experience and contacts during the past fifteen years, we have rather come to the conclusion that the utilities have been grossly imposed upon by a comparatively small group of self-seekers, who in no sense represent the regular managements, either in their public relations or financial politics.

Who are the propagandists? They range from the Paul Clapps to the Sheridans; renegade public employes and newspaper men; hardly a one of them who had grown up with the utilities in the actual construction, operation, or finance. They grafted themselves upon a few powerful personalities, and through their cleverness have been able to involve the whole industry in public perversions and seditious activities.

We doubt whether the rank and file of utility men have known what was going on. They have been so busy with their daily problems of plant extension and finance, the furnishing of service and the building up of proper public relations immediately on the ground, that they did not realize what activities were being carried on by these few outsiders; were hardly aware of their existence.

We hope that the financial practices will also be thoroughly gone into by the Federal Trade Commission; and we confidently believe that the great majority of actual managers and financial officers have had no share in the pernicious policies that have been fostered. The company pyramiding and the various holding company evils, we feel certain, have been mostly perpetrated by outside speculators who have left the local officials to face the ruffled public and to bear the consequent attacks upon private management. There are instances aplenty; let the Commission spread them on the record. The preposterous valuations contended for and unhappily approved in far too many instances by commissions and courts, have had their technical and legal support principally in outside talent,—engineers and lawyers bent upon the immediate object and irresponsible as to ultimate consequences to the industry. They have furnished the major support of reproduction cost, high overheads and going values, and the elimination of depreciation.

All this is, of course, unfortunate for the utilities themselves, considered from a long-run standpoint. The holding companies, as such, have undoubtedly their place; they are excellent devices by which to effect economies in the public interest, i.e., if they are not exploited by financial and professional freebooters. If private ownership and operation has stood the test of experience, it needs no hidden propaganda for support. It can be safely left alone; actual management must stand or fall upon its own record.

The industry needs, above everything else, to free itself of the incubus of the outside publicity, financial, and professional parasites. It needs to establish self-determination; let the policies be determined by the people who are responsible for running the business and for getting along day by day with the public. If these groups resume control and dictate the policies, there will be little danger to private ownership and operation. If the prevailing outside domination is continued, private ownership and operation cannot be preserved even by hidden and high-powered propaganda,—but can be thus destroyed more quickly.

GOVERNMENTAL RESEARCH ASSOCIATION NOTES

EDITED BY RUSSELL FORBES

Secretary

Recent Reports of Research Agencies.—The following reports have been received at the central library of the Association since July 1, 1928:

Detroit Bureau of Governmental Research:
The Cost of Government, City of Detroit 1928–1929.
The Teachers' Retirement Fund.

Fall River, Mass. Taxpayers' Association:
Increased Operating Expenditures in 1928.

Bureau of Governmental Research, Kansas City, Kansas, Chamber of Commerce:
The Collection of the City Dog Tax; a memorandum submitted to the commissioner of finance and revenue.

Bureau of Research, Newark, N. J. Chamber of Commerce:
Inter-Municipal Coöperation in the Newark Metropolitan District.

Research and Information Department, Ohio Chamber of Commerce:
Summary of Constitutional Provisions on Taxation of Various States of the Union.
Compulsory Automobile Liability Insurance.

Philadelphia Bureau of Municipal Research:
Universal Metering in Other Cities.

Schenectady Bureau of Municipal Research:
Report on Suggested Program of Architectural Competition for City Hall Building.

St. Paul Bureau of Municipal Research:
Supplementary Report on the Improvement of the Saint Paul Airport.
Tabulation Showing Debt Charges of City and County through 1937.
Memorandum re Repavement of Business Streets.
The Charter Amendment Empowering the City to Own and Operate Bus Lines.

✢

The Annals of Collective Economy.—The 1928 edition of the *Annals of Collective Economy* will contain several articles on governmental and economic problems of the United States. Included in these will be a discussion of the Governmental Research Association and the work of its member organizations. The *Annals* is edited by Edgar Milhaud, professor of political economy at the University of Geneva. The regular subscription price is $5 per year, but any member of the Association may secure it for a special rate of $3.

✢

Local Self-Government Institute, Bombay Presidency, India.—The Institute is conducting this month an exhibition of governmental activities. The exhibits will be arranged in five divisions to demonstrate: the ideal of local self-government; culture of the community; health of the community; wealth of the community; and administration of the local governments. It is planned to make the exhibition an annual event in the future. Methods in vogue in western countries and the degree of their utility in solving Indian problems will be shown.

✢

Boston Finance Commission.—During July the Commission issued reports on the method of checking bills practiced by the school department; the cost of land taken for school purposes during years 1917–1927, inclusive; and the use of back taxes and reimbursement money received from the Boston Elevated Railway Company to reduce the tax rate for 1928.

✢

Buffalo Municipal Research Bureau, Inc.—During the summer months, the Bureau has been giving attention to three major projects: (1) a survey of the water bureau, (2) assisting the civil service commission in a comprehensive salary standardization study, and (3) assisting the comptroller in accounting revision work.

✢

California Taxpayers' Association. The Los Angeles city and county public recreation survey unit of the California public recreation survey, conducted by California Taxpayers' Association for the past eight months, will be brought to a close in approximately thirty days. This survey is unique in that it deals with the coördination of organization and administration of parks, parkways, playgrounds, beaches and all other publicly-owned recreational facilities.

In coöperation with the various departments of government, formulae are being developed to measure the recreational functions of government and the waste in connection with lands, buildings, equipment, maintenance, programs, etc. From these data the present and future public recreation needs are being measured as a basis of recommendations for providing adequate and economic recreation. The Los Angeles park, playground and public school departments have coöperated in making numerous special audits and research studies to provide this survey with a comprehensive basis for analysis of cost and efficiency of recreation as a whole. In addition to these data and the direct measure of the recreational needs of Los Angeles city and county, more than 500 returned questionnaires from all states and the leading cities of the country provide a counter check for the various problems on which opinions have differed.

✸

Des Moines Bureau of Municipal Research.—
A report to the county supervisors revealed unmistakable evidence of "time padding" by precinct officials in the June county primary election. As a result the county supervisors agreed to make a closer check of "time claims" of election judges and clerks at the coming November election and to place officials supervising the preparation of election on a mileage allowance instead of $10 per day as heretofore allowed. Numerous claims for over twenty hours' work in the polling places on primary election day were filed, although voting machines are used here.

The bureau is coöperating with the League of Iowa Municipalities in preparing legislation enabling cities to spend money for airports and to supervise air traffic.

Publicity reports were prepared analyzing the bonded debt of the local subdivisions and garbage collection and disposal. This city, after spending $60,000 in 1918 for an incinerator plant, discontinued its operation and the plant has remained idle for a number of years.

✸

Detroit Bureau of Governmental Research.—
Progress is being made in the work of the Committee on Uniform Crime Records of the International Association of Chiefs of Police, and the advisory committee, of which Dr. Lent D. Upson is chairman. A digest of the criminal statutes of some thirty states has been completed, covering the definition of major offenses. With the completion of this digest for all states, material will be at hand for the preparation of uniform definitions of crime to be used by police departments in reporting. This will constitute the second report of the committee. The first will deal with the procedure of recording complaints, and the third with methods of record keeping. Coöperation from the Bureau of the Census, Bureau of Criminal Identification of the Department of Justice, and International Association of City Managers seems assured.

The Bureau memorandum outlining the possible purposes of a crime commission was utilized by the Detroit Board of Commerce in organizing a local commission. The commission is duly incorporated and will be actively at work in the fall.

The report of the sub-committee of the committee on state and local taxation of the Chamber of Commerce of the United States, of which Director Upson is chairman, has been submitted and reviewed. This report deals primarily with capital expenditures and their relation to taxation.

The report on the status of the teachers' retirement fund has been distributed. This report shows that, upon a full reserve basis, there is a deficit of $8,700,000 in the fund. Realizing the futility of raising this sum by taxation, the Bureau recommended a reserve for those now on the retirement list and a reserve of the amount that might be withdrawn in cases of resignation.

At the request of the budget director, the Bureau is undertaking a study of the five pension systems supported wholly or in part by the city, and one additional proposed system for the employees of the Library. It is believed that all of these funds should be brought up to a full reserve basis, rather than continuing upon a cash basis, and that the benefits, contributions, etc., for each fund should be uniform.

Following the refusal of the voters last fall to approve a proposal to place the county's capital improvements upon a pay-as-you-go basis, the Bureau is coöperating with the county officials in the preparation of a ten-year improvement program which it is hoped will overcome the objections of the prior proposal, and enable construction work to be financed by a ten-year tax levy for capital purposes.

The board of assessors recently gave assurance that the assessment manual, which was drafted over two years ago by the Bureau accountant and the chief engineer of the board of assessors, will be published within a few weeks. This manual sets forth in some detail the procedure followed in assessing real and personal property in Detroit.

In this connection, the Bureau is giving some consideration to a procedure which would permit the mechanical preparation of all assessment rolls, tax bills, etc., in the county through one central office. A trip of inspection was taken to Chicago, where Cook County has had such installation in effect for about five years.

The city council recently set up by ordinance a board of condemnation commissioners which is empowered to investigate all proposed condemnation proceedings and to report recommendations thereon to the council. Some work has been done with the chairman of this board, Mr. Thomas M. Corcoran, relative to the extent of use of special assessments.

Considerable detail work was done for the governmental committee of the Board of Commerce in outlining memoranda to the mayor and to the common council upon the budget for the year beginning July 1. The budget as finally approved totals $142,262,342, and the Bureau has published a number of *Public Business* which gives an analysis of the same.

The Bureau has also analyzed the city's bonded debt as at June 30, which totals $249,-000,000. This analysis will be published as an early number of *Public Business*.

At the request of Mayor Tenerowicz, of the City of Hamtramck, the Bureau spent some time reviewing the budget of that city, with the result that the mayor was able to reduce the tax rate $1 for the year. Some other detailed studies were made, including the proposed installation of an appropriation ledger, the clerical department of the justice courts, and the city's bonded debt.

Attempt to improve the street sanitation procedure has continued unabated. Incident to moving the water board into a new $2,000,000 building, the Bureau has been making a study of the organization and business procedure of that department. Engineer Place has prepared a number of charts indicating the metropolitan areas of the greater Detroit. He has also made a study of proposed airport sites, at the request of certain councilmen.

The Bureau also made a study of the financial procedure of the village of Halfway, and Harrington Place, the Bureau engineer, made a study of the Buffalo water department, for the Buffalo Bureau of Municipal Research.

❋

Civic Affairs Department, Indianapolis Chamber of Commerce.—The department has submitted a comparison of the number of policemen and firemen in twenty-eight cities, including Indianapolis, to the mayor, the board of public safety and the city council of Indianapolis for their use in consideration of requests for large increases in personnel of the two departments.

The department has made a study of the city sinking fund needs for twelve years and has set up a program which would spread the burden over the period without undue burden in any single year. The program was adopted by the mayor and city controller and the tax levy proposed for the first year was recommended to the city council for adoption by these officials.

❋

Taxpayers' Association of New Mexico.—The Association, which has been mainly responsible for the initiation and continued operation of the budget systems for state and local governments in New Mexico, was represented at the hearings on local budgets before the state tax commission during the month of August. The director of the Association has attended the budget hearings in many of the counties, cities, towns, and villages and assisted in the preparation of the estimates which will be passed upon by the state commission.

A complete report of expenditures under the budget was made for the first half year ending December 31, 1927. Early in the second half of the year statements were sent to members of the boards of county commissioners, with comments and suggestions as to the necessity of restricting expenditures both within the budget estimates and within the actual cash receipts available for the year.

❋

Schenectady Bureau of Municipal Research.—*Capital Budget Commission.*—The mayor's special commission appointed to study the financial structure of the city government, together with the preparation of a long-term financial program, has held several meetings, and considerable progress has been made along two fundamental requirements; namely, that of contacting the heads of the various city departments and also various civic organizations. Budget request forms, calling for the anticipated expenditures for each of the next five years, have been sent to all department and bureau heads. Schedules of major improvements have also been requested from the various departments, so that the commission might get first-hand information as to the vital needs of the city with regard to its capital outlays, as well as its anticipated expenditures for current operation.

Civil Service Study.—Fred Telford, director of the Bureau of Public Personnel Administration, Washington, D. C., visited the Bureau on August 3, in connection with the survey of the local civil service department. Mr. Telford also addressed a joint meeting of the capital budget commission and civil service commission on the subject of "Job Classification and Salary Standardization."

City Hall Plan Competition.—The directors of the Bureau have submitted a communication to the mayor indicating that the Bureau is in favor of holding an open competition among local and non-resident architects for the purpose of securing the best possible design for the proposed new city hall building. A report outlining the proposed plan of competition in detail has been prepared, subject to the approval of the American Institute of Architects, and will be submitted to the mayor soon, as the Bureau's suggestion of the manner in which the proposed architectural competition should be held.

❧

Toledo Commission of Publicity and Efficiency. —The secretary of the Commission spent most of the month of July in editing, arranging, and indexing Toledo's proposed City Manager-P. R. charter. It was approved by the charter commission on July 30 and will be submitted to the electorate on November 6. A brief discussion of the main provisions in the charter

will be found elsewhere in this issue of the REVIEW.

At the request of the mayor, the Commission, in coöperation with the building inspector, will draw up a new building code for Toledo, to replace the 22-year-old code now in effect. This work will be completed by January 1, 1929.

A summary of municipal radio legislation was printed in the *Toledo City Journal* of July 14. Eight cities were found to have ordinances dealing with local radio interference.

The recent Toledo Port Survey, made by Griffenhagen and Associates, will be printed in the near future as a supplement to the *Toledo City Journal*.

❧

Toronto Bureau of Municipal Research.— The analysis of the city's budget for the year 1928 has been completed. Three reports bearing on the subject have been drafted. The first, dealing with the amount of taxation and the assessment on which taxation in Toronto is based, with a comparison over a period of years, has already been issued. The second, dealing with the expenditures from the standpoint of activities performed, and the third from the standpoint of things purchased, will be published later in the year. These also give comparisons with last year.

❧

Utah Taxpayers' Association.—The manager of the research department is now engaged in analyzing the audits of the various taxing units, by calling in the organized taxpayers of that group, giving them a complete picture of the manner in which their local affairs are being conducted, and then urging the local group as the constituent voters of that district to call upon public officials to press the reforms called for in the audits.

While Utah has only twenty-nine counties, it has 211 taxing units, all of which are visited during the year with the above-named program.

NOTES AND EVENTS

EDITED BY RUSSELL FORBES

The Sixth Commonwealth Conference at the State University of Iowa.—Under the auspices of the State University of Iowa the Sixth Commonwealth Conference was held at Iowa City on July 9-11, 1928. Benj. F. Shambaugh, chairman of the conference, presided at all the sessions. The purpose of this meeting was to stimulate a creative interest in commonwealth problems through the discussion of current political issues. Representatives were present from at least twenty-five states and from more than forty colleges and universities. Nor were the delegates confined to representatives of the academic group. Representatives of commercial enterprises, Congressmen, members of the state legislature, editors, and men and women of public affairs throughout the state and nation were present.

The theme of the conference was "The Political Issues of 1928." The outstanding aspects of these issues were presented at five round table sessions. The first of these round table discussions, dealing with the question of agricultural relief, centered around a consideration of the McNary-Haugen Bill and aroused a spirited debate on the merits of that measure. The discussion was opened by F. H. Knight of the University of Chicago and Ivan L. Pollock of the State University of Iowa. Almost alone, H. M. Havner, former attorney general of Iowa, assailed the measure as being economically unsound. The measure was supported by Henry A. Wallace, editor of *Wallace's Farmer*, Congressman L. J. Dickinson, and Harvey Ingham, editor of *The Des Moines Register*.

At the second round table, dealing with the subject of government and business, the Boulder Dam project, Muscle Shoals, public utilities, and similar subjects were considered. The discussion was led by William B. Munro and participated in largely by representatives of the academic group.

The round table on the federal government and the states was of a practical nature. It centered around a consideration of injunctions in labor disputes and was led by Martin J. Wade, judge of United States District Court—a man of wide experience in dealing with the legal aspects of labor disputes.

Much interest was manifested in a discussion of the Eighteenth Amendment. Arguments were presented both for the repeal of the law and for its support and vigorous enforcement. Discussion was opened by H. L. McCracken, president of Pennsylvania State College. The appeal for modification was led by Stuart Lewis of the New Jersey Law School.

Under the topic of foreign relations consideration was given to Latin-American affairs, the Philippines, Nicaragua, cancellation of war debts, and renunciation of war. This discussion was led by I. J. Cox of Northwestern University, and J. Ralston Hayden of the University of Michigan.

Aside from the round table discussions, the Conference sponsored a number of public addresses at which the political issues of 1928 and the presidential candidates were discussed. The subject of government and business was presented in a brief address by William B. Munro. Kirk H. Porter addressed the conference on the subject of political platforms. Francis W. Coker, Thomas H. Reed, William B. Munro, and A. R. Hatton discussed the personalities and characteristics of Herbert Hoover and Alfred E. Smith.

An outstanding feature of the Sixth Commonwealth Conference was the distribution of a one-hundred-page program-pamphlet in which twenty-two topics were briefly and concisely defined. These programs were distributed throughout the country in advance of the meeting of the Conference.

Each round table was attended by approximately five hundred persons. Over one hundred persons participated in the discussions.

J. A. SWISHER.

State Historical Society of Iowa.

✲

Convention of the American Legislators' Association.—The American Legislators' Association, organized in 1925, held its third annual conference on July 23, 1928, at Seattle, Washington. This Association is independent of, although closely allied with, the National Conference of Commissioners on Uniform State Laws, which held its meetings July 17 to 23, at the same place.

Only one formal meeting was held, at which the speakers were Mr. Gurney E. Newlin, Los Angeles attorney, member of the Conference on Uniform State Laws, and recently elected president of the American Bar Association; and Hon. F. Dumont Smith, of Hutchinson, Kansas. William Draper Lewis, director of the American Law Institute, and Dean Roscoe Pound of Harvard Law School, who had originally expected to be present as speakers, were unable to be in Seattle for the conference.

The attendance was small but earnest. Mr. Newlin advocated increasing the salaries and lengthening the term of office of state legislators as a means of attracting a higher type of incumbent. Mr. Smith's theme was the compilation of the statutes of Kansas into the code of 1923. He explained that there had been no revision of these statutes since 1868; that the governor had appointed United States Senator Chestor I. Long as a commissioner to codify the laws; that Senator Long was succeeded by the speaker, who completed the work; that he and Senator Long eliminated obsolete and redundant statutory passages and combined and codified others, thereby reducing 4800 pages to 1600 pages of laws; and that the Kansas legislature adopted their work without change.

The Association has as members about 200 legislators, who are about equally distributed among the various sections of the country. A definite outline of its functions has been formulated, and by the annual conferences and by correspondence the project has been clearly defined. Its aim is not to formulate model or uniform state laws, but rather to act as a clearing house of information relating to matters of concern in the field of state legislation; to organize a council made up of five members of each branch of each state legislature; to organize a committee of legislators (aided by advisory boards composed of eminent specialists throughout the country) to consider special problems—such as legislative efficiency, public health, and taxation; to recommend simultaneous consideration of uniform laws proposed by the National Conference of Commissioners on Uniform State Laws and other reputable national organizations; to study and recommend measures for raising the standard and efficiency of state and national

legislatures; to send periodical information to each of the 7,500 state legislators who are in office, concerning current publications and concerning occurrences of legislative significance.

The American Legislators' Associations has great promise; it marks the beginning of converting the business of law-making into a science and a new profession.

M. H. VAN NUYS.

Seattle, Washington.

✦

Michigan Housing Association Completes Its First Task.—Detroit is the first and only city in the United States to complete a housing census which will give an index of congestion for each of the 580 zones into which Detroit has been divided for school census purposes by the board of education. The value of this index is of unusual social significance.

Various national economic bodies including the American Association of University Women, American Home Economics Association, National Housing Association, General Federation of Women's Clubs, American Civic Association and American Federation of Labor are making strenuous efforts to have similar findings obtained on a national scale. Mr. Wm. E. Steuart, chief of the U. S. Census Bureau, has naturally been hesitant in considering this large additional expenditure until some city has made such a study. Detroit should feel justly proud that it has been the one to point the way by undertaking this progressive step.

The subject was originally broached to the Michigan Housing Association by Dr. Edith Elmer Wood, chairman of the Housing Section of the American Association of University Women. The Michigan Housing Association immediately agreed to undertake this effort and was ably assisted by the local branch of the Association of University Women through its recent president, Dr. Mary Thompson Stevens.

It is highly important that the Detroit survey be carried a step further in order to show the total number of families living in one, two, three, four or more rooms. This index will serve as a basis for other important sociological studies. Studies of this character have been made in other cities but were limited to small units such as one block or a series of blocks. Detailed studies of these findings will be undertaken and reported from time to time. It is confidently hoped that since Detroit has shown the way, the U. S. Census Bureau will find it possible to include the same questions and tabulate the same findings in the national census of 1930.

✤

Professor Tooke at New York University Law School.—Professor C. W. Tooke, editor of our section on Judicial Decisions, and for several years professor of law in Georgetown University, has joined the staff of the law school at New York University. Mr. Tooke will fill the chair of professor of municipal corporations, but will continue to contribute monthly to the NATIONAL MUNICIPAL REVIEW.

✤

Death of George C. Sikes.—We regret to announce the death of George C. Sikes in Chicago on July 20. The immediate cause of his death was uraemic poisoning, resulting from heart disease which developed in November, 1925. The biographical data recorded below were contributed by Charles K. Mohler, consulting engineer of Chicago.

He is survived by his wife, Madeleine Wallin Sikes; a son, Alfred Wallin Sikes; a daughter, Mrs. Eleanor Sikes Peters; and a sister, Harriet Sikes of Rugby, North Dakota.

Mr. Sikes was born near Dodge Center, Minn., June 4, 1868. In 1892 he was graduated from the University of Minnesota with the degree of B.S. In 1894 he took his master's degree from the University of Chicago.

He learned the printer's trade while attending the university, earning the greater part of his expenses by this means and was for a time president of the Minneapolis Typographical Union. He was an editorial writer on the *Chicago Record*, 1895–1900; secretary of the Chicago Street Railway Commission, 1900–2; assistant secretary of the Municipal Voters' League, 1903–5 and secretary from 1906–8; with the Chicago Harbor Commission as expert investigator from May, 1908, to February, 1909, and in like capacity for John M. Ewen, Chicago Harbor Commissioner, in the summer and fall of 1909; and secretary and special investigator of the Chicago Bureau of Public Efficiency from August, 1910, to October 1, 1923. During this time he assisted in the preparation of a series of reports issued by the Bureau, especially those on *Unification of Local Governments in Chicago* and on the *City Manager Plan for Chicago*. On November 1, 1923, he was appointed secretary of the board of trustees of the Policeman's Annuity and Benefit

Fund of Chicago and served in that capacity for about two years.

Among these various other activities, he prepared, in 1917, a report on *City and County Consolidation for Los Angeles* for the Taxpayers' Association of California. He was a frequent contributor to the columns of the *Outlook* and for many years was a writer of editorials and special articles for the *Chicago Daily News*. He investigated and prepared data and articles on the subject of postal savings banks for the late Victor F. Lawson. These articles were a material aid in bringing about the establishment of the present postal savings system. At various times he took charge of certain courses in political science for Professor Charles E. Merriam during the latter's absence from the University of Chicago. The fifty-ward system and nonpartisan election of aldermen in Chicago were due almost wholly to his initiative and efforts.

His last work was as secretary of the Chicago Pension Commission for which he investigated the various pension systems of the city of Chicago with the purpose of bringing about uniform administration, placing the funds on an actuarial basis and securing them on a safe and sound foundation.

His civic interests included membership in the National Municipal League, the Illinois League of Municipalities, the Liberal Club, the City Club, and the Public Ownership League. He was a member of the Council of the National Municipal League in 1918 and 1919.

The mere recital of the activities in which Mr. Sikes was engaged gives no indication of his sterling qualities and worth as a citizen, friend and companion. His work for civic advancement was almost invaluable. It may be truthfully said of George C. Sikes that he labored unselfishly and untiringly in the public interest. The world is better for his having lived and labored.

✤

Why the High Cost of Municipal Government? —In the May issue of the *Michigan Municipal Review*, Roy F. Goodspeed contributes a four-page article on the above subject that comes nearer to answering the question than any recent treatment of this important subject. By the use of a table on the changing value of the municipal dollar, he shows that the cost of government in dollars has increased since 1916 because commodities and personal services have likewise increased. For instance, from a large number of items in the table we learn that in 1916 policemen were paid $1,260 each per year, and cement was $1.60 per barrel; while four years later the police service cost cities $2,160, while cement had jumped in price to $4.25. The per capita tax over the same period increased from $20.08 to $31.49.

He next compared, by the use of a chart, the per capita tax with labor and commodity prices by index numbers for each year from 1909 to 1926. This serves as a means of comparing what was paid for municipal government with other essentials such as food and clothing.

This much has been done many times by writers dealing with the same subject, but the uniqueness of Mr. Goodspeed's treatment manifests itself in the next step when he interprets the per capita tax in terms of earning power. After all, is not the meat in the kernel the time that each of us must work to pay the cost of government? He is merely applying the method prevalent but a few years ago when property owners in rural sections worked out their road tax by contributing their team and wagon for an allotted period of time. The farmer is not concerned as much in the dollars he receives for his load of wheat as he is in the suits of clothes, plows and harrows, which that load of wheat will purchase.

In substance, this study shows that while municipal services have increased during the last two decades and while old services are on the whole being better administered, the hours that a common laborer would have to work to earn his per capita tax has decreased from 110 in 1915 to 80 in 1926. The corresponding figures for one of the skilled trades—carpentry—are 30.2, and 31.8. This article is both interesting and significant.   C. E. RIDLEY

✤

Toledo's Charter Ready for November Election.—Toledo's city manager-P. R. charter was finally approved by the charter commission on July 30. It has one distinctly new feature in American city charters. The number of votes necessary to elect a councilman, instead of the size of council, is fixed. The quota for election is 7,000 votes, provided, however, that no less than seven councilmen shall be elected. There is also a proviso that if, at any election, more than nine are elected, the quota shall be increased by 1,000 votes at the next election until again the election of more than nine results,

etc. Thus, in the long run, automatic adjustment is provided to keep the size of the council between seven and nine.

The only elective officials are the members of council. The council selects the city manager by a majority vote and may fix his salary. It also appoints three commissions—publicity and efficiency, civil service, and city plan commission. The city manager appoints the six directors of the single-headed departments and the two boards who head the departments of health and port development. These two boards have practically the complete control of their departments, with the exception of financing, which is under the control of council. Three other boards and commissions—University of Toledo, sinking fund, and zoölogical commission—are appointed by the city manager.

The salary of council is fixed at $2,000, and the mayor will receive $3,000. Council will choose the mayor from its own number, and he will have no vote. His powers are merely honorary and social.

Candidates for council will be nominated by a petition of from 700 to 1,000 signatures, and no person may sign more than one petition. No candidate may get petition papers with room for more than 1,000 names. This was provided in order that one group might not get the signatures of so great a number of people that it would be impossible for independents to get the required number of signatures. Candidates have only thirty days in which to get their petitions filled out.

Votes are to be counted at a central counting place instead of at the various precincts in the city. Every candidate is entitled to have one representative present at the counting.

Council is given power to establish a system of permanent registration.

Toledo's present charter was used to a great extent in drawing up the new charter. Fully half of its provisions were incorporated in the new draft. This could be very easily done, for Toledo has today probably one of the best strong-mayor charters in the United States. All appointive power is lodged solely in the mayor, and he has complete control over all departments, boards, and commissions in the city government.

The new charter, to become effective, must receive a majority vote at the coming November election. If passed it will go into effect on January 1, 1930.

FITZ-ELWYNE'S
ASSIZE OF BUILDINGS

I RICHARD I (1189)

(THE PIONEER BUILDING ORDINANCE)

INTRODUCTION

BY

C. W. TOOKE

Professor of Law, New York University

Supplement to the

NATIONAL MUNICIPAL REVIEW

September, 1928. Vol. XVII, No. 9

PUBLISHED BY

NATIONAL MUNICIPAL LEAGUE
261 Broadway, New York, N. Y.

INTRODUCTION

FITZ-ELWYNE'S ASSIZE is noteworthy not only as the earliest English building act but also as an example of municipal legislation at a period when the powers of English cities were quite indefinite and rested largely if not solely upon custom. The text herein is based upon that of the *Liber Albus* or White Book of the City of London, compiled in 1419, by John Carpenter, the clerk of the city under the mayoralty of Richard Whitington. The translation from the original Latin and Anglo-Norman is by Henry Thomas Riley, M.A., and is reproduced with his notes from the edition of the *Liber Albus* published by him in 1861.

The *Liber Albus* itself is a storehouse of information on the activities of the mediaeval city. The ancient ordinances that were included as still in force at the time of its publication include many relating to the maintenance and use of the streets, the regulation of public callings, rules of the market, local assessments and taxes and the conduct of the public officers. We may note how analogous to modern problems are those raised by the following ordinances: "that no cart serving the city shall be shod with iron" (p. 634); . . . "that no waterman carrying persons from Billyngsgate to Gravesende, or back again to Billyngsgate, shall take more than two pence for one person" (p. 209); . . . "that no carter within the liberties shall drive his cart more quickly when it is unloaded, than when it is loaded; for the avoiding of divers perils and grievances, under pain of paying forty pence into the Chambers, and of having his body committed to prison at the will of the Mayor" (p. 389); . . . "that Servants in the hostels of good folks shall not take more

than they were wont" (p. 587); . . . "that Officers shall not be Brewers or Bakers, nor shall Keep carts for hire" (p. 591); . . . "that the Barbers shall not work or keep their shops open on Sundays" (p. 621); . . . "that no hoards, or palings, or other enclosure, shall be made before any tenement in the high streets or lanes in the City, or in the suburbs thereof, before that the same shall have been viewed by the Mayor and Aldermen. And if they shall see that such works are prejudicial, the same shall be in no manner allowed; and in the same manner let it be done as to steps which persons shall wish to make to cellars, the entrances to which extend out into the high streets and lanes; and let those which are made be forthwith viewed and rectified" (p. 409).

In contrast to the legislative activities of the great metropolis in the fourteenth and fifteenth centuries one may profitably compare those of a small English borough of the same period as set forth in the *Beverly Town Documents*, Volume 14 of the Selden Society publications. Here will be found a prototype of the New England town, a rural community with delegated powers of local self-government, adopting in the general meeting of all the burgesses ordinances relating to the public ways, the confinement of animals, the regulation of markets and fairs, and the exclusion of obnoxious businesses such as brick yards, but for the most part unconcerned with many of the special problems of urban life.

It may be asked in what way these ancient ordinances are of more than antiquarian interest. Obviously under our constitutional system they cannot be regarded as precedents upon the question of the existence of similar implied powers in American cities. They are in fact rather evidence of customs and possibly have some bearing upon the state of the common law at the time they were in force. But the historical analogy one may draw between ancient and modern practice is of itself of value to the student of municipal institutions. For example, one may compare with profit the provisions of Fitz-Elwyne's Assize with the rules and regulations for the erection of buildings in the city of Washington promulgated by the President in 1791 and with the act of congress of January 12, 1809, providing a procedure for the admeasurement of conflicting claims of neighboring lot owners. Though it may not be worth while to delve too far into medieval lore, the student should find some inspiration in noting that questions similar to those we now have before us today confronted the cities of England in the days when the King's courts were little more than a name.

C. W. TOOKE.

FITZ-ELWYNE'S ASSIZE OF BUILDINGS, RICHARD I

IN the year of our Lord 1189, in the first year, namely, of the reign of the illustrious King Richard, Henry Fitz-Elwyne (who was the first Mayor of London) being then Mayor, it was, by the more discreet men of the City (thus) provided and ordained, for the allaying of the contentions that at times arise between neighbors in the City touching boundaries made, or to be made, between their lands, and other things; to the end that, according to the provisions then made and ordained, such contentions might be allayed.

THAT TWELVE ALDERMEN SHALL BE AT THE HUSTINGS

The said provision and Ordinance was called an "Assize." To prosecute which Assize, and carry the same into effect, twelve men were elected, Aldermen[1] of the City, in full Hustings; and were sworn, that they would attend faithfully to carry out the same, and at the summons of the Mayor to appear, unless by reasonable cause prevented. It was necessary, however, that the greater part of the twelve men aforesaid should be present with the Mayor in carrying out the matters aforesaid.

THAT HE WHO DEMANDS THE ASSIZE, MUST DEMAND IT IN FULL HUSTINGS

It should be known, that he who demands the Assize, must demand it in full Hustings; and the Mayor shall assign him a day within the next eight days, for such Assize by the twelve men aforesaid, or the greater part of them, in manner already mentioned, to be determined.

[2] But if a house, stone wall, drain, rain-gutter, or any other edifice shall during the time of petition for the said Assize be built, immediately, at suit of the party petitioning, (the other) shall be forbidden proceeding any further with such building. And if, notwithstanding such prohibition, any carpenters, stonemasons, or other workmen, or even the owner of the said building, shall persist in so building, they shall be sent to prison.

IF THE HUSTINGS BE NOT SITTING, THEN THE ASSIZE SHALL BE GRANTED AT A CONGREGATION OF THE MAYOR AND ALDERMEN

But if the Hustings be not sitting, as at the time of the Fair of Saint Bartholomew,[3] harvest-time, and the Fair held at Winchester, and a person shall deem it necessary to demand such Assize, the same shall be granted unto him gratuitously by the Mayor, some of the citizens being present with such Mayor, and be determined by the twelve jurors aforesaid, in manner already stated, or the greater part of them, and that always in presence of the Mayor.

[1] This word is omitted in the earliest copy of this Assize, that in the *Liber de Antiquis Legibus*. It is, in all probability, erroneous, as it is not likely that the Aldermen, as a body, would undertake such duties.

[2] This passage does not appear in the earliest copy, that in the *Liber de Antiquis Legibus*, preserved at Guildhall.

[3] "Botolph" (*i.e.* Boston, in Lincolnshire) appears in three other copies, including the earliest one.

The provision and Ordinance aforesaid, which has been called an "Assize," is to the following effect:

OF BUILDINGS ERECTED BETWEEN NEIGHBORS

When it happens that two neighbors wish to build between themselves a stone wall, each of them ought to give one foot and a half of his land; and so at their joint cost they shall build a stone wall between them, three feet in thickness and sixteen feet in height. And if they wish, they shall make a rain-gutter between them, at their joint cost, to receive and carry off the water from their houses, in such manner as they may deem most expedient. But if they should [1] (not) wish to so do, either of them may make a gutter by himself, to carry off the water that falls from his house, on to his own land, unless he can carry it into the King's highway.

They may also, if they agree thereupon, raise the said wall, as high as they may please, at their joint cost. And if it shall so happen that one wishes to raise such wall, and the other not, it shall be fully lawful for him who so wishes it, to raise the part on his own foot and a half as much as he may please, and to build upon his part,[2] without damage to the other, at his own cost; and he shall receive the falling water in manner already stated.

And if both shall wish to have arches,[3] such arches must be made on either side, of the depth of one foot only; so that the thickness of the wall lying between such arches may be one foot. But if one shall wish to have an arch, and the other not, then he who shall wish to have the arch shall find freestone, and shall cause it to be cut, and

the arch shall be set at their joint expense.

OF BUILDING STONE WALLS BETWEEN NEIGHBORS

And if any one shall wish to build of stone, according to the Assize, and his neighbor through poverty cannot, or perchance will not, then the latter ought to give unto him who so desires to build by the Assize, three feet of his own land; and the other shall make a wall upon that land, at his own cost, three feet thick and sixteen feet in height; and he who gives the land shall have one clear half of such wall, and may place his timber upon it and build.[4] And they shall make a gutter, to receive and carry off the water falling from their houses, in such manner as is before mentioned as to a wall built between neighbors at their joint expense. But it shall always be lawful for one desiring so to do, to raise his own part at his own cost, without damage to the other. And if they shall wish to have arches, they shall make them on either side, in manner already stated. But nevertheless, he who shall have found the land, shall find the free-stone, and shall have it cut; and the other at his own cost shall set the same.

But this Assize is not to be granted unto any one, so as to cause any doorway, inlet or outlet, or shop, to be narrowed or restricted, to the annoyance of a neighbor.

OF GRANT OF THIS ASSIZE

This Assize is also granted unto him who demands it as to the land of his neighbor, even though such land shall have been built upon,[5] (provided the wall so built is not) of stone.

---

[1] The reading "voluerint," probably, is an error for "noluerint."

[2] I.e., place his joists and rafters upon it

[3] Used as ambries, or cupboards.

[4] Either the joists for flooring, or the wood for the superstructure and roof.

[5] This passage, supplied from the other copies, has been omitted from inadvertence.

OF STONE WALLS AND RAIN-GUTTERS

If any person shall have his own stone wall upon his own land, of the height of sixteen feet, his neighbor ought to make a gutter under the eaves of the house that is situated upon such wall, and to receive in it the water falling from the said house, and lead it on to his own land, unless he can carry it off into the highway; and he shall, notwithstanding, have no interest in the aforesaid wall, when he shall have built (a wall) beside it. And in case he shall not have so built, he still ought always to receive the water falling from the house built on such wall upon his own land, and carry it off without damage of him unto whom the wall belongs.

OF COMMON WALLS OF STONE

Also, no one of those who have a common stone wall built between them, may, or ought to, pull down any portion of his part of such wall, or lessen its thickness, or make arches in it, without the assent and will of the other.

OF NECESSARY-CHAMBERS IN HOUSES

Also, concerning necessary-chambers in the houses of citizens, it is enacted and ordained, that if the pit made in such chamber be lined with stone, the mouth of the said pit shall be distant two and one-half feet from the land of the neighbor, even though they have a common stone wall between them. But if it shall not be lined with stone, it ought to be distant three and one-half feet from the neighbor's land. And as to such pits, the Assize is afforded and granted unto every one who shall demand the same, in reference as well to those of former construction as to new ones, unless the same should happen to have been made before the provision and Ordinance aforesaid, which was enacted in the first year of the reign of King Richard, as already mentioned. Provided always, that by view of such twelve men as are before-mentioned, or the greater part of them, it shall be discussed whether such pits have been reasonably made or not.

[1] In the same manner, proceedings must be taken where disputes arise as to any kinds of pits made for receiving water, whether clean or foul.

OF THE OBSTRUCTION OF THE VIEW FROM WINDOWS

Also, if any person shall have windows looking upon his neighbor's land, although he may have been for a long time in possession of the view from such windows, and even though his predecessors may have been in possession of the windows aforesaid, nevertheless, his neighbor may lawfully obstruct the view from such windows by building opposite to the same, or by placing (anything) there upon his own land, in such manner as may unto him seem most expedient; unless the person who has such windows, can show any writing by reason whereof his neighbor may not obstruct the view from those windows.

OF CORBELS

Also, if any person has corbels in his neighbor's wall, the whole of such wall belonging to his said neighbor, he may not remove the aforesaid corbels, that he may fix them in any other part of the said wall, except with the assent of him to whom such wall belongs; nor may he put more corbels in the wall aforesaid than he had before.

OF IMPEDING THE ERECTION OF BUILDINGS

Be it known, that if a person builds near the tenement of his neighbor, and

---

[1] This passage is wanting in the *Liber de Antiquis Legibus.*

it appears unto such neighbor that such building is unjust and to the injury of his own tenement, it shall be fully lawful for him to impede the erection of such building, pledge and surety being given unto the Sheriff of the City that he will prosecute; and thereupon such building shall cease, until by the twelve men aforesaid, or the greater part of them, it shall be discussed whether such building is unjust or not. And then it (becomes) necessary that he, whose building is so impeded, shall demand the Assize.

THAT THE MAYOR SHALL VISIT THE TENEMENTS WHERE THE ASSIZE IS DEMANDED, WITH THE TWELVE MEN

On the day appointed, and the twelve men aforesaid being duly summoned, the Mayor of the City, with the twelve men aforesaid, ought to visit the tenements of the persons between whom the Assize is demanded, and there, upon view of the twelve men aforesaid, or the greater part of them, after hearing the case of the complainant and the answer of his adversary, to settle the matter.

But either party may, on the day appointed, essoin himself,[1] and have his day at the same place on that day fortnight.

OF DEFAULT ON PART OF THE COMPLAINANT

But if the party complaining shall make default, his adversary shall depart without day,[2] and the sureties of the complainant shall be amerced by the Sheriffs. But if the person against whom the complaint is made makes such default, the Assize shall nevertheless proceed, according to the award of the twelve men aforesaid,

[1] Put in a legal excuse for non-attendance.

[2] *I.e.* absolutely dismissed from future attendance.

or the greater part of them; and the award that shall be given by them ought by the Sheriff to be reported unto him who has so made default, to the end that the award so made may within the forty days next ensuing be carried into effect.

So often as such award shall not within forty days have been carried into effect, and complaint shall have been made thereon unto the Mayor of London, in such case, two men of the Assize, or three, ought by precept of the Mayor proceed to the spot; and if they shall see that so it is, then shall he against whom such proceedings of Assize were taken, be amerced by the Sheriff; and the Sheriff, at the sole cost of such person, is bound to carry judgment into effect.

OF CORBELS AND JOISTS

If a person has a wall built between himself and his neighbor, entirely covered at the summit of such wall with his own roofing and timber, although his neighbor may have in the aforesaid wall corbels or joists for the support of his solar,[3] or even arches or ambries;—in whatever way such neighbor may have the same in such wall, whether by grant of him who owns the wall so covered, or of his ancestor, or even without their knowledge,—he may claim or have no more in the aforesaid wall than he has in possession, without the assent of him who owns the wall so covered; and he ought to receive the water falling from the house built upon such wall, under the eaves of the said house, as before-mentioned in this book, and to carry it off at his own cost.

OF DIFFERENT PROPORTIONS OWNED IN A WALL

If a person owns two parts in a wall, and his neighbor owns only a third

[3] Upper room.

part, still such neighbor may place his roofing on his own part and build, as freely as he who owns the (other) two parts of such wall. And in the same manner ought rain-gutters to be made between them, as already noted in reference to those who have a wall wholly in common between them; provided always that portion be sixteen feet in height.

OF THE ASSIZE

And be it known, that the Assize aforesaid shall not proceed, unless it shall be testified that he against whom the Assize is demanded, has been summoned.

WHERE THE ASSIZE SHALL PROCEED

And if by the Sheriffs the same shall be testified, then upon appearance of him who demands the Assize, and of the twelve men of such Assize, or the greater part of them, the Assize shall proceed, whether the party summoned shall appear or not. Still, however, he may essoin himself upon the day aforesaid, and have his day upon that day fortnight, in manner already stated.

And if it shall be testified by the Sheriffs, that he against whom the Assize is demanded was not in the City upon such day, then the Assize shall stand over, and the Sheriffs shall inform those who dwell in the tenement as to which such Assize is demanded, that he whose tenement it is, must be warned to appear upon that day fortnight; upon which day, whether he shall appear or not, in case he shall not have essoined himself, the Assize shall proceed.

WHERE THE ASSIZE MUST BE DEMANDED AFRESH

And if it shall so happen, by reason of some impediment, that the men of the Assize do not proceed unto the land as to which such Assize is de-

manded, then it will be necessary for such Assize to be demanded afresh, either in the Hustings, or in such other way as is the usage at a different season, as already stated in this book.

But if view is made of the land, the parties pleading being present, and the greater part of the twelve men aforesaid being absent, then, although the Assize will have to stand over, they may continue the proceedings of that day upon the morrow, or upon such day, within the following fortnight, as they may please.

OF THE ANCIENT MANNER OF BUILDING HOUSES

It should be remarked that in ancient times the greater part of the City was built of wood, and the houses were covered with straw, stubble, and the like.

Hence it happened that when a single house had caught fire, the greater part of the City was destroyed through such conflagration; a thing that took place in the first year of the reign of King Stephen, when, by reason of fire that broke out at London Bridge, the church of Saint Paul was burnt; from which spot the conflagration extended, destroying houses and buildings, as far as the church of Saint Clement Danes.

After this, many of the citizens, to the best of their ability to avoid such a peril, built stone houses upon their foundations, covered with thick tiles, and (so) protected against the fury of the flames; whence it has often been the case that, when a fire has broken out in the City, and has destroyed many buildings, upon reaching such houses, it has been unable to do further mischief, and has been there extinguished; so that, through such a house as this the houses of the neighbors have been saved from being burnt.

Hence it is, that in the aforesaid

Ordinance, called the "Assize," it was provided and ordained, in order that the citizens might be encouraged to build with stone, that every one who should have a stone wall upon his own land sixteen feet in height, might possess the same as freely and meritoriously as in manner already stated; it always being the duty, that is to say, of such man's neighbor, to receive upon his own land the water falling from the house built upon such wall, and at his own cost to carry off the same; and if he shall wish to build near the said wall, he is bound to make his own gutter under the eaves of the house for receiving the water therefrom. And this, to the end that such house may remain secure and protected against the violence of fire when it comes, and so, through it, many a house may be saved and preserved unharmed by the violence of the flames.

OF THE BUILDING OF WALLS

If any person shall wish to build the whole of a wall upon his own land, and his neighbor shall demand against him an Assize, it shall be at his election either to join the other in building a wall in common between them, or to build a wall upon his own land, and to have the same as freely and meritoriously, as in manner already stated. His neighbor also may, if he wishes, build another like wall, and of the like height, near unto the wall aforesaid: and in such case, rain-gutters or a gutter shall be made between them in the same manner as already stated in reference to a wall held in common.

THE MANNER OF REGULATING THE ASSIZE

It should be remarked, that when the men of the Assize shall visit the land as to which such Assize is demanded, the parties litigating being present, one of the men aforesaid ought always to ask him against whom the Assize is demanded, if he knows aught by reason whereof such Assize ought to stand over. And if he shall say that he does not, such Assize shall immediately proceed. But if he shall say that he has a deed from him who demands the Assize, or from some ancestor of his, and shall make profert thereof, (benefit of) the same shall immediately be allowed him. But if he shall say that he is not prepared to produce it, but will have such deed at a day and time when etc., then a day shall be given him on that day fortnight; upon which day he may essoin himself, and may have his day at the end of another fortnight. Upon which day, if he shall produce the said deed, (benefit of) the same shall be allowed him; but if upon such day he shall not appear,—or if he shall appear and not produce the deed,—the Assize shall immediately proceed, without further delay.

It should be remarked, that this Assize proceeds in every way, as before stated in this book, both as to pleading and defending, as well against persons under age as against those who are of full age; that so by reason of the tender age of any person the Assize aforesaid shall not be prevented. But forasmuch as such a person has no discretion whereby to know how to plead or defend himself in any plea, it is necessary that his guardian and he should be jointly summoned; that so his guardian may wholly make answer for him, in every way that he would have had to plead if such cause had been his own; and then, whatever shall be done upon award, shall remain firm and established, without reclaim on part of him who was so under age, when he shall have come of age.

Also, if any one shall make a pavement unjustly in the King's highway, to the nuisance of the City and his neighbor, such neighbor may rightfully prevent it, through the Bailiffs of the City; and so it shall remain, until the matter shall have been discussed and determined by the men of the Assize.

It should also be known, that it does not pertain unto the men of the Assize to take cognizance of any case of occupation where a person has had peaceful possession for a year and a day, etc.

OF THE DROPPING OF RAIN WATER, AND OF GUTTERS

[1] And although a person shall have been in possession for a long time, the water that drops from his house,—it not having a wall of stone,—falling upon the vacant land of his neighbor, still such neighbor may build upon the said land, whenever he shall please,

[1] This and the next article are not included in the *Libre de Antiques Legibus*, but are to be found in the later copies.

and may remove the eaves of the said house. And in such case, the person (building) must carry off the water that falls from the said house, without detriment to his neighbor. The same is to be done also as to rain-gutters that discharge themselves upon vacant ground.

OF THE SAME

And if a person's rain-gutter shall discharge itself into the gutter of his neighbor, or shall run through the middle of his tenement, such neighbor may not stop up such gutter; and even if he shall pull down that house, and shall think proper to build it anew, he shall still be bound to receive upon his own land the water falling from such gutter, and carry off the same, as before he used to do; but it must be fully understood by the men of the Assize that the water discharged by such gutter was so received and carried off.

NATIONAL
MUNICIPAL REVIEW

PUBLISHED MONTHLY BY THE

National Municipal League

| VOL. XVII. No. 10 | OCTOBER, 1928 | TOTAL No. 148 |

CONTENTS

EDITORIAL COMMENT........................*Russell Forbes*........ 565

OUR AMERICAN MAYORS:

    XII. "JIMMY" WALKER.................*Joseph McGoldrick* 567

PHILADELPHIA'S FREE LIBRARY...............*Clinton Rogers Woodruff* 578

LABORATORY WORK IN MUNICIPAL GOVERNMENT.*O. Garfield Jones*...... 580

PHILADELPHIA'S STREET RAILWAY PROBLEMS....*Harold Evans*........ 586

THE TAX SITUATION IN CHICAGO..............*Herbert D. Simpson*.... 593

FEDERAL AID TO THE STATES — A SUPPLEMENT ..*Committee on Federal Aid* 619

DEPARTMENTS ·

  I. Recent Books Reviewed... 600

  II. Judicial Decisions.......................................*Edited by C. W. Tooke* 604

  III. Public Utilities..................................... .. ..*Edited by John Bauer* 607

  IV. Governmental Research Association Notes........... .. ..*Edited by Russell Forbes* 611

  V. Municipal Activities Abroad.............................*Edited by W. E. Mosher* 613

  VI. Notes and Events.......................................*Edited by Russell Forbes* 616

THE LEAGUE'S BUSINESS

Nominating Committee Makes Report.—The nominations to fill vacancies expiring in 1928 in the League's officers and council have been made by the nominating committee, consisting of W. P. Lovett, Detroit, *chairman;* W. J. Millard, Philadelphia; T. Glenn Phillips, Detroit; and Lent D. Upson, Detroit.

The nominations of the committee have already been reported to the membership of the League by mail as follows:

For President—Richard S. Childs, New York.

For Vice Presidents—Glenn Frank, Madison, Wisconsin; Carter Glass, Lynchburg, Virginia; Charles Evans Hughes, New York; W. D. Lighthall, Montreal; Meyer Lissner, Los Angeles; A. Lawrence Lowell, Cambridge; C. E. Merriam, Chicago; W. B. Munro, Cambridge; Frank L. Polk, New York; Miss Belle Sherwin, Washington, D. C.; A. Leo Weil, Pittsburgh.

For Council, terms expiring 1931—M. N. Baker, New York; Henry Bentley, Cincinnati; C. A. Dykstra, Los Angeles; J. W. Esterline, Indianapolis; Mrs. George Gellhorn, St. Louis; Chauncey Hamlin, Buffalo; Joseph A. Miller, Pittsburgh; Lawson Purdy, New York; Howard Strong, Philadelphia; Lent D. Upson, Detroit.

✳

Committee Appointed on Teaching of Municipal Government in Colleges and Universities.—The League has appointed a committee on teaching of municipal government in colleges and universities, under the chairmanship of Professor William Anderson of the University of Minnesota. As the first step in its work program, the committee is planning to formulate a statement of the objectives of college and university courses in the field of municipal government. The following have been appointed as the preliminary committee, which may later be increased in number: William Anderson, *chairman;* Charles A. Beard, H. S. Buttenheim, Edwin A. Cottrell, H. W. Dodds, John A. Fairlie, Luther Gulick, A. C. Hanford, O. Garfield Jones, Arthur E. Morgan, W. E. Mosher, W. B. Munro, Thomas H. Reed, C. E. Ridley, and Russell Forbes.

✳

Wide Publicity for Model Municipal Budget Law.—The League's report on the Model Municipal Budget Law, which appeared as a supplement to the July REVIEW, has been reviewed in a number of dailies, weeklies and monthly journals, such as the *New York Herald-Tribune, Detroit News, Bond Buyer, The American City,* and *Michigan Municipal Review.* The entire preface to the law has been published by *The Tax Digest, The Municipality* (League of Wisconsin Municipalities), *Illinois Municipal Review, Colorado Municipalities* and the *Virginia Muncipal Review.*

The *New York Herald-Tribune* quoted from the pamphlet and devoted space to the extent of twenty inches of type matter. The *Detroit News* gave the pamphlet thirteen inches of space and in the headlines stated that "if adopted by the legislature (Michigan) it would save millions annually." In a letter from the editor of *The Tax Digest,* Los Angeles, the following comment was given: "This is a remarkable contribution which the League is making to the science of government." *The Tax Digest* commented on the pamphlet as follows: "In evolving this Model Municipal Budget Law the National Municipal League is doing a great service for the country." *Michigan Municipal Review* made the following comment: "Here is available to cities and states the product of the consultation and coöperation of some of the foremost authorities on municipal finance in the country. It is to be hoped that many cities will find it worth while to incorporate it into their own fiscal systems."

NATIONAL
MUNICIPAL REVIEW

Vol. XVII, No. 10   OCTOBER, 1928   Total No. 148

EDITORIAL COMMENT

Our American Mayors In this issue we print an article on "Jimmy" Walker, New York's mayor-at-large, by Joseph McGoldrick of Columbia University. The article is a fair appraisal of the first three years of Mayor Walker's administration, and is fraught with interesting glimpses of His Honor as a "Prince Charming, who reigns but does not rule." Professor McGoldrick was the author of the article on Mayor Hylan which initiated our series several months ago.

In connection with the article on Mayor Walker, the reader should peruse Professor McGoldrick's excellent discussion of "The New Tammany," which is the leading contribution to the September number of *The American Mercury*.

In November we hope to publish an article on "Big Bill" Thompson of Chicago.

✣

The Tax Situation in Chicago We continue this month the discussion of "The Tax Situation in Chicago," by Professor Herbert D. Simpson of Northwestern University, which began in the September issue. This is one of the best series of articles published in the Review for some time. The series will be concluded next month, with a narrative account of the legislative and judicial struggles which finally

culminated in the court order for a reassessment of all Chicago property. At the conclusion of the series, all will be reprinted and made available for distribution in pamphlet form.

✣

Federal Aid to the States As a supplement to this issue, we offer the report of the League's committee on Federal Aid to the States. The report has been prepared by Professor Austin F. MacDonald of the University of Pennsylvania, chairman of the committee, and the author of a book on the same subject which has been issued recently by Crowell. The report is a worth-while contribution to the literature on the subject of federal aid.

✣

New Department We are resuming this month the department of notes on Municipal Activities Abroad, which were formerly a feature of the Review. This department is edited, as formerly, by Dr. W. E. Mosher, managing director of the School of Citizenship and Public Affairs, Syracuse University.

✣

Laboratory Work in Municipal Government The article by Professor O. Garfield Jones, of Toledo University, on this subject is a timely contribution to the literature of teaching methods in municipal government, and will be read with interest by all students and teachers of the subject, particularly by the newly-appointed League committee on teaching municipal government of which Professor Jones is a member.

The Ohio Woman Voter in April, 1927, published an article by Professor Edward F. Dow, of Western Reserve University, on the subject of "University Training for Citizenship." With reference to Professor Jones' teaching methods at Toledo University, Professor Dow says in part:

The department is constantly experimenting, and we believe, progressing, in an effort to teach not only what should be, but what actually is. In our course on practical politics we adopted this year a method of precinct study used successfully by Professor Jones of Toledo University. One month before election each student chooses an election precinct for special research, preferably the one in which he lives. He is given a series of questions, and instructions as to assembling material in the report. The questions include the drawing of a map of the precinct; following of pre-election activity (rallies, publicity methods, etc.); finding out how the voter is urged to register, vote, and how the voter is influenced; city and county organization (party structure); and names and methods of selection of election officials, ward and precinct leaders.

If the work is done at all, the student is bound to know more of local politics and candidates than ever before. To many it proves a veritable revelation. A precinct leader becomes a living, breathing actuality rather than a textbook myth. Interviews with bosses, clippings from the newspapers, campaign literature, are all worked into the report, often with shrewd analysis or comment. The reports prove fascinating and instructive to the teacher as well as to the student. Political trickery and machinations stand exposed, alongside the legal and ethical endeavors of the parties and their leaders in the locality.

Students derive satisfaction as well as benefit from the personal contacts and political lore unearthed. Ample scope for originality, enterprise and neatness are found in assembling and interpreting material in final form. As a final test of the student's thoroughness, a forecast of the election is required. All the materials are brought together in a loose-leaf notebook and handed in on election day. The best report out of fifty-six handed in on November 2, 1926 was the result of the enterprise, skill and ingenuity of a student at the College for Women.

*.

Convention of the American Municipal Association The American Municipal Association will hold its fifth annual convention in Richmond, Virginia, November 12, 13, and 14. The proceedings of the convention will be summarized in a later issue.

*

Annual Meeting of the Proportional Representation League The Proportional Representation League will hold its annual meeting in Cincinnati on the evening of October 17, the final day of the joint convention of the National Municipal League, Government Research Association, and National Association of Civic Secretaries. The meeting will be preceded by a dinner beginning at 6.30 P.M. at the Hotel Sinton. The following have been invited to deliver short addresses at this meeting: Hon. Murray Seasongood, mayor of Cincinnati; Colonel C. O. Sherrill, city manager of Cincinnati; Henry Bentley, chairman of the Cincinnati city charter committee; Miss Agnes Hilton, president of the Ohio League of Women Voters; Alfred Bettman of Cincinnati; and Dr. A. R. Hatton.

OUR AMERICAN MAYORS

XII. "JIMMY" WALKER

BY JOSEPH McGOLDRICK

Department of Government, Columbia University

The Prince Charming who reigns but does not rule in New York —and how. :: :: :: :: :: :: :: :: ::

"JIMMY" WALKER is one of the accidents of politics. A born politician— he was never born to be a mayor. If for anything, nature intended him for an actor or a sportsman. Some day he may find himself czar of baseball—a job for which his temperament, his affability and his training admirably fit him.

WALKER FANS HYLAN WITH THE BASES FULL

When the batteries were being picked for the 1925 game with the formidable John F. Hylan, the latter was in the height of form. He was the heaviest slugger Hokum had produced. The ease with which he was shut out in that memorable encounter may suggest that he was greatly overrated. But when his name was whispered in the Tammany clubhouse that summer the Braves fairly trembled. To stop Hylan required not steam but speed, and "Jimmy" is nothing if not fast. They needed somebody to fire the imagination of the bleachers and grandstands. And so the elder boxmen, whom Coach Smith longed to put in, were left to warm the benches, and Manager Olvany sent the youngster in.

Jimmy has been hit pretty freely last season and this. Bill Schieffelin and Bill Bullock have scored on him repeatedly. But they have never been able to bunch their hits and drive him from the box. Many a time, perhaps, Coach Smith has wished he could send

him to the showers. He balked badly when Kelby, "the milkman," was on first. He let Connolly steal home. Hedley's subway play caught him napping. And he certainly has kept the Tammany outfield busy chasing long drives. But everything points to his finishing a full nine innings. He is popular with his teammates. He has good press support. And when occasionally he fans one of the Reformers, the stands fairly rock.

All of which means merely that Walker was chosen, against the better judgment of some of the political leaders of the city, because in the hard contest that was anticipated in the primary with Hylan it was thought necessary to have not only the acquiescence but the eager enthusiasm of "the boys," the rank and file of the party workers, upon whom the winning of the primary so frequently depends. Jimmy was "one of the boys." The public knew almost nothing about him except that he looks quite young (which he really isn't, unless you think 47 young) and that he looked quick and keen, which certainly Hylan didn't.

Walker *is* keen—at times remarkably so. In a sense, if another slang phrase may be pardoned, he gets by on his wits. In the state legislature where he was for several years senate leader, and now in the board of estimate, his ability to catch "on the fly" a subject about which he had little or no previous knowledge, adroitly creating his case out of the mouths of his opponents, has been little short of amazing. His lack has been of the soberer qualities of industry and penetration. He hates reports, and he hates quiet. He revels in *vis à vis* controversy.

THE "LATE" MAYOR

He is almost never on time. The nation gasped when he was thirty-five minutes late for an appointment with President Coolidge, but it was nothing unusual for "Jimmy." He prides himself on never answering a letter. While he can read and write it would appear that he seldom if ever does either. He boasts that he never reads a newspaper. At a board of estimate meeting last year, the mayor complained that the park department had no program for spending the million dollars it was asking. An engineer of the department protested that the details were fully set out in his report. Said his honor: "If I spent all my time reading reports I'd have to go without eating or sleeping. I can't be expected to go through filing cases for every bit of information I want. That's why I want my commissioners to come before me here so I can get information clearly and quickly.".

Everything he does is done extemporaneously. This trait has made him tolerant and good-humored. He is never afraid to get into an argument.

THE MAYOR'S ORIGIN AND BACKGROUND

"Jimmy" was born and reared in Greenwich Village back in the days when they pronounced it as it is spelled, and before the Irish had given way to the Bohemians. His father was an old-time Tammany district leader, a big, good-natured man with a heart of gold and teeth to match. When Borough President Ahearn was removed for misfeasance by Governor Hughes,

Walker, Sr., as superintendent of public buildings, was seriously implicated. The son was slight of build—the secret of his perpetual youth. The father was passing rich for his time and place. Many less affluent among "Jimmy's" contemporaries went through college, but he got a job with a music publishing house. His early musical efforts

International Newsreel

MAYOR "JIMMY" WALKER

have been too painfully dinned into the ears of this innocent generation to need mention here. It is said he played professional baseball with a Hoboken team. He was also—perhaps we should say, still is—something of an amateur actor. He was not to be cast for political heavy work, but as an oratorical straight man he found his rôle. Like Hylan he too once worked for the "traction interests," not as motorman but as secretary and treasurer of the New York & Brooklyn R.R.

He gravitated, as many of the political small fry do, to the legislature. And like so many others he stayed there, while harder workers, like Smith, Foley and Wagner, mounted to bigger tasks. In 1912 when he was thirty-two, he gained admission to the bar. By this time he was a leading figure in the legislature—the co-author of the Walker-Donohue Boxing Law, the Sunday baseball and Sunday movies laws and others. The New York Giants made him their counsel as did various theatrical and motion picture groups. So also did Swift and Company and other big industrial concerns. His new status at the bar permitted him to receive lucrative references at the hands of Tammany judges.

His big chance came in 1923, one of the infrequent occasions when the Democrats have controlled the state senate. There were twenty-five Republicans that year and twenty-six Democrats—"the double thirteen." Though from an administrative standpoint his performance left something to be desired, he was clever, almost brilliant on his feet. It was at that session that he earned the right in his party and before the people to be considered for his present post.

WALKER CONTINUES HYLAN'S CABINET

The transition from Hylan to Walker at city hall was simple and smooth. In general Walker took up where Hylan left off. There were one or two conspicuously good appointments, notably those of McLaughlin as police commissioner and of Harris as health commissioner—both since resigned. But these were mere white collars for the dirty Hylan shirt. In general Walker was quite content to don the soiled Hylan vestments, and why not? Hadn't Hylan always worn the livery of Tam-many Hall? Of the twenty-five commissioners, commonly referred to as the mayor's cabinet—though they never function as such—Walker reappointed twenty. The *New York Times* and *New York Herald Tribune* reported quite casually, while Walker was at Miami in December, 1925, that "he expects to find that a tentative 'slate' has been prepared for him by George W. Olvany, leader of Tammany." It is doubtful if the new administration made a one per cent change in the twelve hundred civil-service-free positions which are exempt from the merit system on the theory that they are vital to the policy of an administration. A few of these holdovers he has been forced to retire. A jail delivery at the Tombs cost one commissioner his job and the Tammany sachem who headed the park department had to be dropped; but others, for example his budget director who had been in the health department during the milk scandals and the street cleaning commissioner, he has tenaciously refused to dismiss. It has been suggested that if he was so innocent as not to have known what was going on around him there, he was not a "natural born" budget guardian. If on the other hand, he had known about the graft, as the investigating judge said was highly probable, it may suggest why the annual budget has increased $150,000,000 during his incumbency.

PROBLEMS CONFRONTING THE WALKER ADMINISTRATION

The political skies have been crowded with problems ever since he took office, but our good mayor basks in the sunshine of unconcern. Less than five per cent of the sewage of this city of 6,000,000 inhabitants receives any chemical treatment. The rest pours in its natural state into the rivers, so that the city may be said to be situated on a group of islands surrounded by sewers. But for the rigor of the tides, pestilence would long since have decimated us. The problem cannot long be ignored. The city's garbage is towed to sea and dumped. This is both expensive and extravagant. Much of it washes back and annoys the Jersey beaches, so that the United States War Department may, at any time, revoke the permit under which this practice continues. But the task of locating incinerators or reduction plants is distasteful to one who likes to be liked.

The management of the city's hospitals needs reorganization. The city's thirty hospitals are divided among three wholly independent city departments. There are no figures of comparative costs.

Though the $600,000,000 Catskill water system is only just completed, unless new sources are speedily developed there will again be a water shortage. (The mention of water always gets a wisecrack out of "Jimmy.")

Housing is a crying need. There is not a stick of municipal housing in the city. An abundance of credit has already been claimed for a measly one-block project about to be started. There is nothing more in sight.

All of these and numerous other problems were fully ripe when Hylan was booted out of office. Their neglect was part of "Hylanism." We are now nearing the end of the third year of the Walker administration. A few of these problems are beginning to trickle toward solution. A site was recently designated for a sewage disposal plant and a hospital department was created a few weeks ago. Central Park is also receiving some tardy attention.

THE COMMITTEE ON PLAN AND SURVEY

The city's governmental structure is deplorably ramshackle and archaic.

During the campaign Walker made much of a promise he had given to an independent reformer group to appoint a survey committee. He put them off from week to week for six months before he named this body. Then he announced a committee of 476 persons, which, had it ever mustered in full, would have been one of the most miscellaneous assemblages ever to have gathered in the city. Every political, religious, national, and interest group of any size was comprised in its ample membership, and the whole was abundautly leavened with Tammany trusties to insure its not getting out of hand. For two years the public was urged to be patient while this committee got out its report which was meanwhile promised from month to month. The brain child of this mountainous labor recently placed in the fond mayor's waiting arms,[1] apart from noting that some of the problems here mentioned exist, consists largely of a recommendation that such a committee be appointed to study the city's future needs.[2] As Walker's third year draws rapidly to a close, the possibility of any constructive reform resulting from this effort is ruefully remote.

THE SUBWAY PROBLEM

But the greatest of all is the subway problem and how to preserve the five-cent fare. This was the rock on which the Hylan ship, having weathered eight stormy years, finally foundered. There

[1] The Report of the Committee on Plan and Survey is reviewed in this issue on page 600.

[2] An exception is a report of the sub-committee of budget, finance and revenue headed by Herbert Lehman, banker and Al Smith backer. Mr. Lehman went heavily into his own pockets and employed a group from the Columbia University faculty whose survey and recommendations have also recently been published under the title, Finances and Financial Administration of New York City (Columbia University Press).

is very little else in life that New York-ers take seriously—certainly nothing else in local politics—besides the nickel fare. It is probably the only issue on which any Tammany candidate could be beaten. Al Smith himself could not survive it. The city owns all but the very oldest portion of the subways of the city, an investment of about $380,-000,000. It leases them to two oper-ating companies, the Interborough Rapid Transit Company (the I. R. T.) and the Brooklyn-Manhattan Trans-portation Company (the B. M. T.), which provide the rolling stock and maintain separate systems. The com-panies operate under contracts known as No. 3 and No. 4, signed in 1913, which call for a five-cent fare and pro-vide for recapture of practically all of the lines after twenty years. Neither company has been paying very much to the city since 1918 when the old B. R. T. went bankrupt and the I. R. T. came perilously near to it. The city is, therefore, carrying a $16,000,000 debt item in its tax-budget which amounts, some calculate, to an addition of one cent to the fare.

Real estate and certain business opinion is persuaded that this is a com-plete argument in favor of adding this cent to the fare directly. But such simple arithmetical philosophy over-looks the fact that, apart from other considerations, it may not only be good social policy to promote the dispersion of population which the uniform nickel fare encourages, but it is also not with-out justice to tax central land values thus on the theory of both benefit and cost. The two companies appear to be making money on the present fare. The accumulated preferentials of the B. M. T. are six times those of the I. R. T. The latter will soon be called upon to resume payment to the city. It is earning 8.76 per cent on its own investment, but it is saddled with a

miserably unprofitable investment in the old elevated systems of the city; only by throwing this in with its sub-way accounts is the I. R. T. able to make the poor mouth on which it bases its plea to the courts for a fare increase. Curiously enough if an increase is granted, unless the rate be prohibitive, the revenue will go not to the company but to the city because of the huge arrears in back rent. At a seven-cent fare the stockholders would have twenty years to wait for a dividend.

THE FIGHT FOR THE SEVEN-CENT FARE

Meanwhile, the city, since 1921, has been engaged in building a wholly new and separate subway which it was Hylan's plan and that of certain Tam-many groups to have the city operate at a five-cent fare in competition with "the interests." As the law now stands, however, it would be necessary, after three years of operation at that fare, to fix the rate at a completely self-sustaining one. But since the new system was proving so inordinately costly—$680,000,000—it was early shown that, unless the law could be changed, the fare would then jump to eight cents or perhaps ten. At this juncture Commissioner Delaney ap-peared as *deus ex machina—machina politica*, of course,—and it was decided, at the last minute to be sure, to swallow some $13,000,000 with the tax budget, with a similar or larger sum for this and subsequent years so that the capitaliza-tion, and hence the overhead or debt charges, of the new system might be kept down. Following the customary battle of injunctions and mandamuses, the $13,000,000 was rammed into the budget. The current bills, however, indicate that the subway will vastly exceed the estimates of costs so that all this trouble and ingenuity will have been in vain. Meanwhile the city is being saddled with $40,000,000 in the current year and perhaps $65,000,000 next year to maintain the voracious sacred cow of the nickel fare.

In the last heat of the fare race the city got off to a poor start and finished second best. The wrangling about recapture had continued for nearly a year but the city's legal stars permitted the I. R. T. to get the jump on it with an application to the federal courts for a fare rise, setting aside the contract clauses on the familiar grounds of confiscation. Despite ` the considerable merit of the city's case already suggested, and despite the $90,000 retainer to be paid to Charles L. Craig, Mayor Hylan's ancient sparring partner, the odds are on the city to lose the final purse next autumn.

PROPOSED UNIFICATION OF THE SUBWAY SYSTEMS

It was generally understood during the campaign that Walker favored unification of the subways, old and new, into one well-ordered system on a five-cent fare. Indeed some went so far as to suggest that this was the only course by which that fare could be maintained. Much precious time was lost in getting down to a study of the problem so that the second Untermyer report, proposing a plan, can receive very little attention until the litigation mentioned above is concluded. Political palmistry is a perilous profession, but it would seem that the subway "solons" are going on a very long journey between now and next autumn's election.

THE FIGHT ON THE BUS SYSTEM

Besides subways, Walker made much, during the campaign, of his proposal to give the city a bus transportation system. With a favorable transit commission to grant the necessary authorizations, it seemed that he could surely fulfil this promise. Hylan had failed because he insisted upon municipal operation. Walker would grant franchises and he had confidence his buses would be on the streets in thirty days. The approval of the routes took a prodigious length of time. It was not until the summer of 1927 that he was ready to allot the franchises.

Then a lively and unseemly scramble began. The Equitable Coach Company, newly-organized and favored by the mayor, was rigorously opposed by several rivals including the Fifth Avenue Coach Company, operator of the principal fleet of buses already operating in the city. The board of estimate wrangled interminably over the awards. At length the mayor would brook no further opposition. The matter was placed on the board's calendar and the final showdown loomed. Stewart Browne, president of the United Real Estate Owners' Association and tireless champion of landlords against tenants, was there armed with an injunction, but several policemen kept all strangers away from His Honor. All morning long the air was tense with the impending contest, but the matter was not called because one vote was lacking. During the luncheon recess, the mayor by soft words or hard threats won over the recalcitrant borough president. He was ready now to go through.

Walker is no coward. He resorts to steam-roller tactics with surprising infrequency. The opposition to any proposition is generally sure of a fair and ample hearing. But when the clerk called the fatal number and droned out the title, the wary Browne, who is more than a little deaf, failed to recognize it. So did a dozen or more lobbyists for opposing interests and civic groups. "Jimmy" sensed the situation in a flash. It was too good to miss. "Is there any objection? Call the roll." This particular routine formula is generally reserved for objections from the board itself. A slightly longer form for the public suffices to dispose of fully two-thirds of the several hundred items that usually crowd the board's calendar.

There is some dispute as to what the mayor's *sotto voce* rulings were. But it is a matter of record that the representatives of a score of civic organizations, numerous lawyers and the member of the press (seated within an arm's reach of the board) heard no invitation for a hearing, and that those who had waited through many dreary meetings for several months for an opportunity to be heard, were not heard. When the end of the day was reached, it was apparent that something had been slipped over on Browne—on Browne, the holder with Schieffelin of the standing, running, and long distance records for taxpayers' suits. The interminable delay continues in the courts and before the transit commission, and the mayor's earnest campaign promises about buses —but life in New York is so full!

PARTY ORGANIZATION RESPONSIBLE FOR SCANDALS

The administration has had its full measure of scandal. Whatever his indirect responsibility, any competent observer would agree that his party organization rather than the mayor must be held directly responsible; but the mayor, who makes a great point of party loyalty, has given precious little aid to ferreting out corruption.

The health department milk frauds were waiting on his doorstep when Walker reached the city hall. Certainly the mayor showed no eagerness to adopt the squawking foundling and it perished of inanition. Neither the former head nor the former secretary of the health department was ever publicly questioned concerning the conduct of the office, though Justice Kelby, appointed by the mayor, recommended

ninety-one indictments. Then followed snow removal, sewer, hospital, prison, school building and city marshal corruption. There was "Payroll Jim" McQuade. Let Dr. William H. Allen sum up:

Here was an elected officer, a district leader, a big frog socially, a drawer of $12,000 a year from his city salary alone, solemnly testifying that for two summers six members of his family, middle-aged sisters, a mother of young children, his own housekeeper—and all of them Irish at that—were working through the hottest months at night on unpleasantly hard duties for $5 a day.

Then . . . swore that a woman clerk, who left her self-supporting clerkship for marriage to a husband drawing $4,070 a year from his city salary alone, immediately began working nights full time, kept on working nights full time for four years even while her husband was earning $4,400 and while she reared two babies.

A typically wretched practice is the preying upon pushcart peddlers which still persists. The only result of complaint to the mayor was that the complainant was beaten up by an unknown and uncaught gang of "guerillas." Most recent and perhaps most extensive were the street cleaning irregularities and payroll lootings. When such conflagrations burst out, the commissioner of accounts is alert to lead his brigades, and more care is taken to localize the fire than to seek out the perpetrator or the causes that made its perpetration possible. If the public really gets aroused it may be necessary to drag out some insignificant wretch and cart him off to jail. The commissioner is industrious, but he seems to work on the eminently sound chemical principle that fire cannot live without air.

HOW THE MAYOR TACKLES PROBLEMS

The mayor likes to approach all problems physically. His typical method of attacking the park, hospital or subway problem is to summon one of his limousines and fill another with cameramen so that the tabloid patrons may see their hard-working mayor in action. "Jimmy" was recently de-

mayor passes the gavel to McKee and disappears.

Presently he is on the steps outside the city hall. The battery of "stills"

International Newsreel

ALL IN THE DAY'S WORK

clared to be one of the four most photo-graphed personages in the world.

The mayor is presiding over a busy meeting of the board of estimate. An aide slips up and whispers that the Irish world's champion hockey players, or a young lady with the first sap of the Vermont maple trees, or a delegation from Switzerland with a gift of their national cheese, have arrived. The

advance. His honor smiles, holding up the hockey stick, syrup, or cheese, as the case may be. The stills drop back to reload. The "movies" rattle into place. The mayor swings the stick, tilts can, or otherwise gestures appro-priately. Then a second round of stills; then a parting shot from the movies; and, five minutes having elapsed, the mayor slips unobtrusively into his seat in the board. This is an almost daily occurrence. It may occur twice or even three times in a single day. Of course when Queen Marie, or the Cardinals, or Lindbergh, or some other splendid dignitary arrives, the city business is put completely aside for the pageantry of a Roman triumph.

THE MAYOR REQUIRES MANY VACATIONS

As a fashion plate, he is a close rival of that other celebrated world-traveler and news-reel favorite—the Prince of Wales. Our "Jimmy's" mission in life, like that of the Prince, is to spread good will and to edify the natives. In a little more than two years in office he has had seven vacations (143 days), not to mention short trips. He has been to London, Paris, Berlin and Rome, to Houston, Hollywood and San Francisco, to Bermuda, Palm Beach, and Canada (where his liquor permit cost only one dollar), three times to the Kentucky Derby, and to Chicago for the "Battle of the Century." He tries not to miss a "first night," or a show of any kind. He even went to see the rodeo because he "wanted to see the bull thrown in the open." He is the gayest mayor the city has had since Oakey Hall in the 'forties, Tweed's mayor and author of such plays as *Loyalina* and *Let Me Kiss Him for His Mother.*

"OFF THE RECORD"

"Jimmy" is most at home when he is surrounded by those jolly newspaper boys eager to catch for the waiting world his latest wise-crack. They know how to cajole him. Frequently he is amazed to read in the papers next day the things he has said to them. Recently a two-page interview, profusely illustrated, appeared in Mr. Hearst's *Evening Journal.* The mayor, *inter alia*, explained how he had come to go on the "water wagon" due to the demands of a disordered stomach. He was quoted as having said:

I haven't had a drink since, but how soon I will take one I do not know. Certainly it will not be long, because I feel fine and I believe my stomach is ready for a little more flattery now.

And much more to the same effect.

Reporters sought the mayor promptly and asked him if the interview was authentic. He read it through, line by line, scowling as he read sections aloud. Then after some thought he dictated this statement:

A representative of the *New York Journal* visited me and we talked for a half hour or more on many subjects. I talked very freely. As I read this story now I find in it observations that I cannot remember making and language which I do not remember using. Our discussion was informal and general and no notes were taken. I had no opportunity to see the article before it was printed.

While my viewpoint and attitude on some matters have been correctly presented, in some others, to say the least, the reporter obviously misunderstood me.

When he returned from his most recent tour he was widely quoted as saying:

After traveling 10,000 miles I wasn't in one place where there was any difficulty to see and get liquor. . . . You can get it as easily in the United States as in Mexico, and there is not nearly so much difficulty here as there is in Canada.

BUILDING UP LOCAL PRESS SUPPORT

One of the most interesting tendencies in the present administration has been the emphasis on press support. The movement is by no means local in character. There has been a distinct trend of newspaper men in public jobs. Within the last few years six city hall reporters have stepped into public jobs. Two are with the transit commission; another is an under-secretary to President Coolidge; a fourth has become secretary to the New York city police department; still another is director of the municipal radio station; and the mayor has just appointed one of the group, a former city editor of Mr. Hearst's *New York American*, as his executive secretary. The assistant to the mayor and the second deputy police commissioner arrived by the newspaper route.

Many who are left behind would welcome similar recognition and study to earn it. Since the salaries they pay are wretchedly low the papers, more or less, wink at the practice of accepting retainers from politicians, prominent men and business or utility concerns, for press agent work. A reporter on one of the tabloids has organized an information service which receives a substantial contract from the city and has an extensive clientele among public utilities and city contractors. This same tabloid reporter has just been named Secretary to the Superintendent of Schools at $7,500 per year. Even the *New York Times* published an interview in 1926 in which the writer told of Mayor Walker's getting to his desk at 8.25 A.M. "Seldom does he arrive later than 9.30 and often he is on hand an hour earlier." This at a time when the mayor rarely made it before mid-afternoon. The editorial policies of most of the papers have been more than cordial to the mayor. When they rap him it is done in such a kindly, playful way as not to hurt at all. Mayor Walker has not overlooked the influence of Hearst, Al Smith's inveterate foe. The mayor has reported the Kentucky Derby and similar events for Mr. Hearst's papers. He is a frequent guest at the Hearst home and, like Hylan, he has visited the Hearst ranch at San Simeon and seen "the thousand cattle on the thousand hills." Though the Hearst papers stood by Hylan in the primary against Walker, they have supported the latter steadfastly since. Witness the touching sentiments in-spired by a picture published in the *New York Journal* and captioned thus:

Here is Mayor Walker, of New York, in sunny Florida, showing Babe Ruth how to hold a baseball bat "better," with Jake Ruppert, who owns the baseball team, looking on. Observe the Mayor's extremely youthful, buoyant appearance.

This leading editorial appeared below:

When he was very young, before he knew he would be important in the politics of New York, and later mayor of the biggest city in the world, young Mr. Walker used to write very beautiful poetry and songs.

In one song he asked, "Will You Love Me in December as You Do in May?" He needn't have asked that question, so far as he is concerned, for at forty, which is close to "December," he looks every bit as young as he did "in May," when he wrote the song.

If you have poetry in your soul it keeps you young.

While the mayor was writing poetry, Jake Ruppert was making beer and money. Had he written poetry instead of making beer, Mr. Ruppert would probably look much younger than he does. On the other hand, like Mayor Walker, he would have had a very slim bank account as well as a slim waist. Perhaps Mr. Ruppert would rather look a little older and have a bank account a little fatter, even though more embonpoint must go with it.

Babe Ruth never wrote poetry and never brewed beer, so he looks just so so, about his own age.

The moral of this picture, as you may learn from Mrs. Augusta E. Stetson, who was Mrs. Eddy's representative in Christian Science in New York City, is: "Think young thoughts, happy thoughts, cheerful, healthy thoughts, and your body will stay young and healthy."

The body and the brain are what our thoughts make them. Here you see Mayor Walker, who refuses to allow dull care to roost for one moment on his shoulder, and who wrote poetry when Ruppert was only writing checks. Walker looks to-day about twenty-three years old. That hasn't prevented him from accumulating more wisdom than any politician in New York State with the possible exception of Governor Al Smith.

Governor Smith, like Ruppert, wrote no poetry. Therefore, also, he looks his age. Be cheerful, be gay, keep your mind happy and you'll look almost as young in December as in May, and, what is more important, you'll feel young—as Mayor Walker does.

THE MAYOR'S PALS

Every big political figure in New York must have his rich cronies. Even Hylan nursed the pencil king, Berolzheimer. Walker's ubiquitous chum is Paul Block, proprietor of the *Newark News*, the *Toledo Blade*, and, within the last few months, of the last Republican organ in the city, the *Brooklyn Standard Union*. H. H. Frazee, the theatrical producer, is a frequent host. Jules Mastbaum of the Stanley Film Corporation, until his death, was regarded as one of Walker's closest chums. W. H. Egan, of the Pennsylvania Railroad, frequently accompanies the mayor, as does W. E. Bowman of the Bowman-Biltmore hotels, and "Jimmy" customarily travels in the private car of William H. Woodin of the American Car and Foundry Company. Many of Walker's older political intimates, such as Joseph A. Warren, one-time law partner and legislative colleague, and now police commissioner, are almost estranged from the mayor. But "Jimmy" is everybody's friend.

LOVED, LIKE HYLAN, FOR HIS FAULTS

John F. Hylan and James J. Walker each received pluralities of slightly more than 400,000. Yet the contrast between the sober, plodding, heavy-handed Hylan and the gay and gloriously carefree "Jimmy" is amazing. The glaring incompetence of the one was almost as notorious as the hilarious negligence of the other. Each in his way stands for something essentially true about the people of New York. There are a million Hylans for every thousand Walkers, but every John has a conscious or subconscious longing to be a "Jimmy." New York takes its fun vicariously with "Jimmy." Few New Yorkers ever see a "first night" or get to a night club or know Gloria Swanson. "Jimmy" does. They love him dearly for his very faults.

When the last cheer of the presidential world series has died away and the supreme court proceeds to inspect the slow motion pictures of Walker's weird subway play of last June, it may find that our jolly mayor stole second with the bases full. And when the crowd has to pay seven cents to ride home, will they think he has sloughed the game? Will they still say, "Attaboy, Jimmy," or will it be "Say it ain't so, Jim"?

PHILADELPHIA'S FREE LIBRARY

BY CLINTON ROGERS WOODRUFF

*Philadelphia's new library results in increased use by the reading
public.* :: :: :: :: :: :: :: :: :: ::

AMONG the glories of our modern
municipal democracies public libraries
stand in the very front rank. This is
indicated in many ways. In the first
place they are gloriously housed.
Boston's public library building has
long been famed alike for its exterior
and for its interior, as well as for
its collection. New York's great
library at Fifth Avenue and Forty-
Second Street is another great institution, and a roll call of the cities would
bring forth the fact that the people
want libraries and want them ade-

quately, yes, handsomely housed.
Philadelphia has joined the list with a
monumental structure, the first to be
completed on Philadelphia's Parkway,
which bids fair in time to rival the
Champs d'Elysée. Indeed that great
avenue in Paris has been the inspiration
of those who conceived and planned,
as of those who have helped to carry
out the construction of this boulevard,
connecting Philadelphia's city hall and
Fairmount Park.

Established under a charter granted
in February, 1891, the Philadelphia

THE FREE LIBRARY OF PHILADELPHIA, LOGAN SQUARE

library is governed by a board of trustees, pursuant to ordinances of city council and an act of the state assembly. Its expenses are provided for by annual appropriation by the city council and the income from such trust funds as have been donated, which fortunately are growing at a satisfactory rate. In addition to the

NEW LIBRARY OPENED

On June 2, 1927, the new main library building, facing Logan Circle on a site bounded by nineteenth, twentieth, Vine and Wood Streets, was formally opened with appropriate ceremonies.

The building measures 300 feet in

MAIN READING ROOM (CIRCULATION DEPARTMENT)

main building, the library system includes twenty-nine branches and four deposit stations.

On March 12, 1894, the main library was opened in three rooms in city hall. It was moved to 1217–21 Chestnut Street on February 11, 1895, and on December 1, 1910, it was again removed to Thirteenth and Locust Streets.

length, 200 feet in depth, and is 100 feet high, with a capacity for 1,750,000 volumes. The building is fireproof throughout. Its outer walls are constructed of Indiana limestone with a granite base, and its inner walls of artificial stone. Its floors are of terrazzo and quarry tile, and its stairs and principal halls are of marble. The book stacks and wall shelving are made of steel, and the tables, chairs and all other movable furniture are either of steel or of aluminum.

The total cost of the present site and building, including the furniture, has been $6,300,000, which was well within the appropriation, a fact in which the board of trustees naturally take a proper pride.

INCREASED USE OF NEW LIBRARY

Some idea of the popularity of this new building may be gathered from the figures in the following table.

An analysis of these figures shows how popular the library idea has become because of the appropriate housing among suitable surroundings. As *The Inquirer* has editorially pointed out there is "no doubt that the splendid facilities will make it immensely serviceable to the community and result in a steady increase of patronage. The sole handicap thus far has been in the difference of accessibility between the Locust Street site and that on the Parkway. Hundreds of workers in central offices were in the habit of visiting the library during the day when it was just 'around the corner,' but the habit of taking the beautiful walk up the Parkway to the new institution is already taking hold as a pleasant and healthy diversion during the lunch-hour."

Period	Visitors' main entrance	Recorded use in reading rooms	Readers' cards issued	Volumes borrowed for home use
June, 1927–June, 1928.........	1,990,760	919,597	37,824	859,191
June, 1926–June, 1927.........	....	446,379	16,708	518,845
Increase.................	....	473,218	21,116	340,346

LABORATORY WORK IN MUNICIPAL CITIZENSHIP

BY O. GARFIELD JONES

The University of the City of Toledo

Can the laboratory method be applied to the teaching of government? A forceful argument by one who answers the question in the affirmative.

LIBERAL arts subjects have occasionally been grouped as the sciences, the social sciences, and literature. This by implication classifies political science as neither scientific nor literary. God forbid! Referring to the physical sciences as the "natural" sciences also implies that the social sciences are "un-natural."

Still another classification is that of the "laboratory" and the "non-laboratory" sciences. This is a statement of fact. The chemist, the physicist and the biologist will not teach his subject to beginning college students without the assistance of the laboratory method, whereas the political scientist, the sociologist, and the economist are content just to "tell 'em." This saves time, because the laboratory method is slow, and quite expensive.

Of course the answer is that the laboratory sciences get concrete results; the engineer, the bacteriologist, the physician, and the surgeon are products of their method. On the other hand, the non-laboratory sciences have few results to show.

Recently, the laboratory method has been utilized in the advanced courses of political science, sociology and economics with the result that the graduate specialists in these fields—the municipal researcher, the social worker, and the business statistician—are coming to have some professional standing. But one fundamental distinction still exists: the so-called laboratory sciences demand the use of the laboratory method in beginning college courses, while the so-called non-laboratory sciences do not.

If the laboratory method can be utilized in advanced courses in government, why can it not be utilized in beginning college courses the same as in chemistry or biology? Is there any other reason than the large number of students involved and the lack of sufficient laboratory material?

At the University of the City of Toledo we believe these are the only two valid arguments against laboratory work for beginning college students in government, and we believe that we have been able for the last ten years, in a measure, to solve both the problem of numbers and the problem of adequate laboratory material. The problem of an adequate laboratory has been solved by virtue of our being located in a city of over a quarter million population that has the normal administrative and political organization for its population and area. The problem of numbers we have solved by working out the details of assignment and instruction in a manner not very dissimilar to that of the chemist and the biologist in the early days of their experimentation with the laboratory method.

Two negative statements should be made before attempting to describe our laboratory work in politics and administration. In the first place our laboratory work at Toledo is *not* a "stunt" that is put on occasionally to advertise the department and to stimulate interest. (We have put on stunts and probably will do so again, but we do not call them laboratory work.) Each student has a definite personal assignment to work out at a definite time each year. This has been done every year since 1919 with an average of four sections of thirty students each per year.

In the second place it is *not* the "observation" method. No professor of pharmacy calls it laboratory work when he takes his classes through one of the pharmaceutical factories on an observation tour.

The essence of laboratory work consists in the student's individual contact with, and reaction to the phenomena he is studying. And as a guarantee that such a vital reaction is taking place, a personal assignment must be made for each student and an individual problem worked out in such a way as to reveal, in a measure at least, the student's own reaction in this real situation.

Perhaps biology serves as the best analogy to assist us in the discussion of the laboratory method in government, because biology, like political science, deals with growing organisms, with the evolutionary process, with atrophied and obsolete structure. In the biological laboratory they find it advantageous to study a whole organism rather than fragments of different ones because the part has such an organic relation to the whole that a collection of separate parts of separate organisms can never make a true living organism. In other words, the organism has a personality that is something more than a summation of its parts. It is the interaction of the parts as a unit that makes experience, and it is the effect of this experience on the organism as a whole and as so many parts that makes personality. It is just this effect of experience on the organism and the tendency of today's experience to condition tomorrow's behavior that is so important in political as well as in biological affairs.

THE CITY GOVERNMENT IS THE IDEAL LABORATORY

A city with a simplified charter is as ideal for laboratory work in government as is the starfish for laboratory work in biology. If the city is of some size its government and politics have prestige which is pedagogically quite important. Its organization is relatively simple in contrast with that of the county and the state. Its centralized political and administrative organization greatly facilitate the "setting up" of the laboratory because the personal contact of the instructor with the few "higher-ups" may suffice to keep the entire laboratory going smoothly. And, lastly, most cities have a dramatic history that is readily available to the students, a factor of no little importance in view of the fundamental truth of Professor Seeley's remark about political science without history having no root.

In Toledo we use the municipal government for our administrative laboratory, and the current election for our political laboratory. Whether it be a municipal, state or national election makes no great difference because political behavior in the ward and precinct is essentially the same in each case. For obvious reasons the political laboratory work comes in September, October and November and, therefore, the political chapters in our municipal government text are studied first.

A STUDY OF PRECINCT METHODS

Each student is assigned a separate precinct in which he is to make a study of the election machinery, the political organization and the political methods employed to get voters to register, to get them to vote, and to influence their vote for a particular candidate. This includes a study of the political reporting by the daily press, and detailed observations on political behavior in general in that ward and precinct.

In addition to cataloging the different methods used to get electors to register, to vote, and to vote for a particular candidate, the student must evaluate these methods as to their effectiveness and from other angles. This report, which is frequently quite long, is due on election day. A supplementary report that is due two weeks after election enables the student to check his observations and judgments in the light of the actual election day results. This "post-mortem" in the supplementary report is frequently the best part of the entire exercise.

The average person is quite free with his comments and generalizations before election, but he conveniently forgets his pre-election remarks when the election returns are available to check against his prophetic observations and judgments. On the other hand, the student in this political laboratory work knows that the instructor is checking over his pre-election observations at the very time that he is writing his supplementary report; hence his strong tendency to analyze the reasons for his errors in observation and evaluation.

SURVEY METHODS FOLLOWED BY THE STUDENT

The quantitative check on this laboratory work is the student's own estimate of the vote that each candidate for the most important office will receive in this precinct. (This estimate is on the vote for mayor in the odd numbered years, for president in the national elections, and for governor in the even numbered years when there is no presidential election.) The basis for this estimate is the number of voters registered in the precinct, a definitely ascertainable number. Then the student learns from previous years about what per cent of the registered voters actually voted. This per cent for past years must be raised or lowered in accordance with the amount of local interest in the current election. Accuracy in these two base figures is quite important because errors here are cumulative errors.

When it comes to dividing the vote that will be cast among the two, three or four candidates for the leading office of the election, the student must depend entirely upon his knowledge of the political make-up of the precinct, because the general trend of the vote in the ward, the city, the state or the nation is of little value in this precinct estimate. A particular precinct may be overwhelmingly Republican even though there is a veritable landslide for the Democratic candidate in the county or state as a whole.

Few students attempt a direct poll of the precinct, although those who do conduct such a poll make small errors as a rule. The indirect poll is better for most students. This consists in securing a poll list and then checking each voter's probable political alignment as indicated by the posters in his window or on his automobile, by the campaign button that he wears, by the political temper of the crowd he goes with, by his religious, economic or racial grouping, and by any other ascertainable factors that are thought to be politically significant. Of all the indications the most reliable one is to find out, if possible, what the given voter considers to be the main issue of the election. Few voters resent an inquiry as to issues as they do an inquiry as to personalities, although some students have the unhappy faculty of making an impertinence of all their questions.

The easiest method, next to pure guessing, is that of "cross-checking estimates." The estimate of the precinct worker of one candidate is checked against the estimate of the precinct worker for the opposing candidate. If used intelligently and carried far enough, this method is sufficiently accurate to insure an average error of around 25 per cent. The students are given considerable advice by instruction sheet and by lecture as to how to proceed with this laboratory work.

GRADING THE STUDENT'S REPORT

The estimating of the vote is weighted heavily in the grading. The precinct and the supplementary reports are graded and the two grades are averaged. Then the error of the estimate is calculated from the official returns of the election and the "averaged" grade raised or lowered one entire letter depending on whether the error is large or small. Our grading system is A, B, C, P (passed without points), D (deficient), and F (failed). An "averaged" grade of C with an error of less than 10 per cent is raised to B. An "averaged" grade of C with an error of 65 per cent is lowered to P. An "averaged" grade of D with an error of 65 per cent would compel the student to do the work of the politics laboratory over again the next year.

A student may guess in this work just as he may guess at an "unknown" in a chemistry laboratory; but his chances of "beating the game" are not materially higher in the one laboratory than in the other.

A STUDENT APPRAISES THE LABORATORY WORK

A new instructor in this course who came to Toledo in February of this year and has had, therefore, no experience with the precinct report asked at the final examination for the second semester this spring: "Which feature of the course did you consider most valuable and why?" One of the ablest girl students, a freshman, answered as follows:

I learned more from preparing my precinct report, more that I will never forget, than in any other course in college this year. I am well acquainted with the organization of the Republican party. I know who the influential men are that lead the party. I learned how important the newspaper's influence and good will is. I learned that a city election is the time at which more slander, mud-slinging and disgusting talk is circulated than at any other time. I decided never to run for any office myself because I think too much of the good old name of (her own name). I learned that secret work is the way to discover people's political leanings. I found that meetings in the ward and precinct stir up much trouble but get out the vote. I learned exactly how precinct workers really drag out voters; bother them until they do vote.

These things will all help me to be an effective citizen, for I realize exactly what goes on during an election and how much politicians can pull the wool over citizens' eyes. I have determined to be an intelligent and consistent voter, knowing for whom, what and why I am voting.

LABORATORY WORK IN ADMINISTRATION

The laboratory work in administration comes the second semester. It could, of course, be given either semester. Each student is required to study a separate unit of Toledo's administrative system; for example, the traffic bureau. The procedure can best be illustrated by following the work of a particular student with his individual assignment.

The student assigned to the traffic bureau must hand in at the end of February a bibliography of available material on police administration in general and on traffic problems in particular. This is graded as to form and content and returned with any necessary comments by the instructor as to valuable material not listed.

Then this student must read up on his subject, take notes, and finally write up a "library" report on the purpose and the procedure of police administration with special reference to traffic control and indicate the more important correlations between traffic control and the other phases of municipal administration. The student must also list five or more questions which he will ask the chief of the traffic bureau when he goes to interview that official. This report is due just before Easter vacation.

The library report is graded as to form and content and the questions to be asked are checked by the instructor as being good, poor or impertinent. The instructor may suggest better questions.

If this library report is satisfactory it is returned to the student and he is told whom to interview at the city hall; in this case it would be the inspector of traffic, the sergeant in charge of the traffic bureau and as many subordinates in that bureau as may be necessary to enable the student to write up his final report. This final report covers the organization, the operation and the history of the traffic bureau in Toledo and a comparison of traffic control in Toledo with that in certain other cities.

Obviously the sequence of chapters in the text is ignored in fitting the text to the laboratory work. The study of local political history which we think quite important comes immediately after election. If studied before election it would involve the class in local politics because Toledo's political history since 1900 has centered around non-partisanship in one form or another. And no local election is complete without having one or more candidates share with Andy Gump the distinction of "wearing no man's collar."

Our first divergence from the regular method of teaching municipal government was the laboratory work in the fall of 1919. This departure from orthodoxy, as so frequently happens, led us to examine objectives as well as method. We have now evolved a beginning course in political science that aims to train for "effective municipal citizenship." Limitation of space forbids any detailed description of the other features of the course, some of which we believe to be quite as important and heterodox as the laboratory method.

FUNDAMENTAL ASSUMPTIONS

Perhaps it will suffice to list the seven assumptions on which our present course is based, in what we believe to be their logical sequence:

1. Colleges should give a final, a professional course in citizenship.

2. The psychological age for such a course is the year when the student becomes a voter (or the year preceding).

3. Laboratory work is a necessary part of such a course.

4. This laboratory work should include both politics and administration.

5. The city provides the best laboratory facilities: first, because of their availability; second, because of their extent; third, because most college students live in cities after graduation; fourth, because the rural democracy of the nineteenth century has become the urban democracy of the twentieth century.

6. This professional course in effective municipal citizenship should also include training in the technique for leadership within and through a group.

7. The several (and divergent) phases of the course should be integrated at the end into a composite technique for effective citizenship. (This is attempted at Toledo by the use of the charter convention.)

In yielding to the demands of "orientation" faddists, we political scientists have sold our birthright (special training for citizenship) for a mess of pottage (a chapter in an orientation course). The "Jacobin" orientationalists are still offering us a "mess of pottage" in exchange for our "birthright." Reverting to orthodoxy for a phrase, "What can we do to be saved?"

PHILADELPHIA'S STREET RAILWAY PROBLEMS

BY HAROLD EVANS

MacCoy, Evans, Hutchinson and Lewis, Philadelphia

A discussion of the problems which have arisen under Mitten management of the coördinated street railway system of Philadelphia. The author was a member of the Pennsylvania Public Service Commission in 1925-26 and special counsel for the commission in 1926-27. ::

THE four major transit problems in Philadelphia at the present time are: (1) how to eliminate the underlying companies and leaseholds; (2) what to do with the $200,000,000. valuation; (3) how to control the Philadelphia Rapid Transit Company's operating expenses; (4) what is the best plan of operation of the city-owned high-speed lines.

To understand these problems it is necessary to know a little of the developments that have led up to the present situation.

A COÖRDINATED SYSTEM

There is only one street railway system in Philadelphia. Completely "coördinated" transportation has been the ambition of Thomas E. Mitten who, in 1911, took over the active management of the Philadelphia Rapid Transit Company. With this end in view he has acquired practically all of the intrastate buses and taxicab fleets in Philadelphia as well as the street railways.

The system is composed of upwards of twenty street railway and traction companies, all of which are leased directly or indirectly to the operator, the Philadelphia Rapid Transit Company. By this series of leaseholds, pyramiding guaranteed dividend upon guaranteed dividend, there has resulted "an accumulation of fixed charges probably never paralleled in the history of street railway exploitation."[1] These dividends run as high as 70 per cent on the paid-in capital of certain of the underlying companies and average over 13½ per cent on all of them.

In 1907 the city and the Philadelphia Rapid Transit Company entered into a contract the principal provisions of which were: (1) the company was to call in the unpaid subscriptions to its capital stock amounting to about $9,000,000 and was not to increase. its securities without the consent of the city; (2) its fares (then 5 cents or 6 for 25 cents) were not to be increased without the city's consent; (3) the city was to be represented on the company's board of directors, was to audit its accounts annually, and was given the right to purchase the P. R. T. property in 1957 for the par value of its stock. To furnish a fund for this purpose the P. R. T. was to pay sums ranging from $120,000 to $360,000 per annum into a sinking fund. The city relinquished its right to require the company to repave and repair streets occupied by it and gave up all license fees, accepting in lieu thereof payments ranging from $500,000 to $700,000 per year. It also gave up the rights reserved in most of the franchises to recapture the property at cost and to require the removal of overhead wires, etc. The city,

[1] Report of Hon. C. C. McChord to Pennsylvania Public Service Commission, 1927, p. 14.

however, expressly reserved its right to regulate the operation and management of the company under its police power.

THE BEGINNING OF MITTEN MANAGEMENT

In 1911 Mr. Thomas E. Mitten assumed the management of the company. He inaugurated a new labor policy of coöperation between employers and employes, and under his able leadership conditions improved.

In 1918, however, the situation was still far from satisfactory, and in that year the city and P. R. T. negotiated a contract by which the city agreed to construct certain high speed lines costing upwards of $100,000,000 and to hand them over to the company to operate with its other lines as a unified system. Out of the gross revenue of the entire system the company after the payment of operating expenses, taxes, depreciation, fixed charges and payments due the city under the 1907 agreement was to pay a five per cent dividend on its $30,000,000 stock, and to the city, five per cent on its investment in transit facilities. A supervisory board was created with power to pass upon service, etc. Rates were to be increased if the revenues were insufficient, and decreased if they were too great. The public service commission refused to approve this contract.

In 1920 the P. R. T. sought to increase its revenues by substituting three-cent exchanges for free transfers. The public service commission refused to allow this and prescribed a fare of seven cents (4 tickets for 25 cents) in spite of the provision of the 1907 contract. Then came the valuation case in which the commission in June, 1923 found a value of "substantially upwards of $200,000,000" as of 1919. It approved the existing rates of fare. It was assumed that this fare would "make possible further and continued improvement and extension of transportation service and facilities in Philadelphia."

FARES INCREASED

Thirteen months later, however, the company, faced with an alleged falling off in traffic and an increase of expenses, sought further increase in its rate to eight cents (two tokens for 15 cents) with free transfers substituted for three-cent exchanges outside the central delivery district. The public service commission made a temporary order granting the increase. The company then boosted its dividend rate from six per cent to eight per cent and increased the Mitten management fee from $158,000 to $350,000. The fee was fixed at this amount for three years by written contract. A year later the temporary order approving the eight-cent fare was made permanent by a four to three vote of the commission and the company thereupon, in spite of the three-year contract, increased the Mitten fee to about $1,000,000.[1]

CITY OWNERSHIP, PRIVATE OPERATION

Meanwhile in 1922 the city had completed an elevated railway, extending from the Market Street subway to the northeast and commonly known as the Frankford "L." The city leased it to the P. R. T. for five years at a rental of one per cent of the cost for the first

---

[1] The fee is now fixed at "four per cent of the gross revenue of the system, payable cumulatively after earning the regular dividend to P. R. T. stockholders." It amounts to over $2,000,000. One half of the fee is invested by Mitten management for the employes to compensate for a reduction of wages, and the other half is retained by management (1925 Annual Report). In 1927 the total operating revenue of the system, including buses and taxicabs, was approximately $57,000,000 of which over $48,-000,000 was derived from the P. R. T. Company.

year, and increasing one per cent each year. At the end of five years the city exercised its option to extend the lease to 1957 at five per cent.

In 1925 and 1926 contracts were entered into between the city and the P. R. T. for the construction and operation of a surface car subway under Chestnut Street. By these the city agreed to build the subway, the P. R. T. to pay the interest, and sinking fund and state tax on the city bonds issued for the construction of the subway, so that they would be paid off in fifty years, after which the company was to be given the perpetual right to occupy the subway rent free, subject to the city's right to condemn the system or take over the P. R. T. property in 1957 under the 1907 agreement. The contracts were approved by the public service commission, but the basic agreement was last winter held invalid by the superior court on appeal.[1]

Meanwhile, in 1926 and 1927, there arose a good deal of public dissatisfaction, both with the alleged failure of Mayor Kendrick to protect the public interest in his dealings with the P. R. T. and with the service rendered by the transit company. The newspapers were practically all in a critical attitude. To meet this the public service commission undertook an investigation of the situation and employed Hon. C. C. McChord, formerly a member of the Interstate Commerce Commission, to make a comprehensive survey of the urban transportation facilities of the city.

THE MCCHORD REPORT

In March, 1927 he submitted a report in which he recommended the condemnation of the underlying companies for approximately $136,000,000, turning over to the P. R. T. rent free

[1] Taken by the Northeast Philadelphia Chamber of Commerce and the City Club.

all city-owned transit facilities, including the Broad Street subway now nearing completion at a cost of over $110,000,000, and remitting annual payments made by the P. R. T. to the city of over $1,500,000. He further recommended the creation of a transit conference board of three members, to be appointed respectively by the city, the P. R. T. and the public service commission. In this board was to be vested the city's existing veto power over capital increases of the company. To it the P. R. T. was to pay (1) a special fund of $5,000,000, and (2) its current annual surplus, if any, after the payment of all operating expenses, fixed charges, taxes and dividends on its common stock at eight per cent in addition to its preferred stock dividends. This fund could be drawn upon the company at any time "to make up the amount of its rate of dividend." It was to be invested in P. R. T. securities and used to acquire the property for the city in 1957 under the terms of the 1907 agreement. The board was to audit the company's books but was to have no control over its operating expenses.

Following the submission of the McChord report, a statute was enacted authorizing the condemnation of the underliers.[2]

THE BIBBINS REPORT

In 1927 J. Rowland Bibbins was employed by the city to recommend the course it should follow in the operation of the Broad Street subway. He recommended that, for a trial period ending in 1936, it be operated by the P. R. T. as part of a city-wide fully coördinated system on the basis of an operating fee of three per cent of the net revenues. He estimated these net revenues conservatively at $2,500,-000 during the first full year of opera-

[2] Act of May 3, 1927, P. L. 508.

tion, thereafter increasing from year to year. The proposed agreement specified what were to be allowed as operating expenses, and constituted a board of control to have final decision on all questions of operating expense, maintenance, service standards, etc. Managerial duties, however, were to rest upon the company, the board's powers being supervisory only. It was to be composed of three members,—the director of city transit, a representative of the P. R. T., and a chairman appointed by the mayor.

Mayor Kendrick went out of office at the end of 1927. His successor, Mayor Mackey, abandoned the Chestnut Street subway project and in its stead substituted a surface car subway two blocks further south under Locust Street at an estimated cost of about $40,000,000. An ordinance was passed leasing this subway to the P. R. T. for fifty years at a rental equal to the interest, sinking fund and state tax on the city bonds issued for its construction. Just prior to its passage, this ordinance was amended so as to provide that the subway should be constructed by the P. R. T. for the city at the "actual cost thereof." An injunction, however, has just been issued in a taxpayers' suit, prohibiting the letting of any such contract without competitive bidding as required by law.[1]

In the meantime the city and the P. R. T. were unable to come to terms on an agreement for the operation of the North Broad Street subway, a four-track, high speed line extending north about six miles from city hall, ready for operation on September 1,

[1] This injunction was issued July 13, 1928, by Hon. Harry S. McDevitt, president judge of the Court of Common Pleas No. 1. An exception to the decree is now pending. The suit was backed by the Northeast Philadelphia Chamber of Commerce.

1928, as a two-track line. They therefore joined in an application to the public service commission for a statement of the terms and conditions which it would approve for such an agreement running for not more than two years. The commission in turn has appointed Hon. C. C. McChord to investigate and report to it.

Finding that the Bibbins report was likely to be ignored by the city, the Northeast Philadelphia Chamber of Commerce retained Mr. Bibbins to give the public the benefit of his extensive investigation of the Broad Street subway a year ago. The city, not to be outdone, has now retained Messrs. Ford, Bacon and Davis. There are, therefore, three different transit experts working on the problem, and if a satisfactory solution is not reached it will probably not be due to a dearth of expert advice.

In order to start operation of the subway on September 1, the city has leased it for three months to the P. R. T., which agrees to operate it at the present rate of fare, but without exchange or transfer privileges in the central delivery district such as exist on the surface lines. The company is to pay the city a rental of $200,000 per month and is to render full reports and accounts of operation, keeping operating costs and revenue of the subway distinct from the rest of the system. The lack of adequate feeder lines and the company's refusal to give exchange privileges in the central delivery district will greatly depress the earnings of the subway and render the trial period practically valueless in determining its earning capacity.

Mayor Mackey has also filed with the public service commission a petition for a valuation of the underlying companies for purposes of possible condemnation under the act of 1927. The companies have taken the position that this statute is unconstitutional, and the city has notified them that unless a prompt conclusion can be reached it will drop the proceedings. The public service commission, on the other hand, seems anxious to carry out Mr. McChord's recommendation of condemnation.

THE FOUR MAIN PROBLEMS

With this sketch of the facts we can turn to the four great problems which must be solved before the transit situation in Philadelphia is satisfactory:

1. The underlying companies and leaseholds;

2. The $200,000,000 valuation;

3. The control of the P. R. T. operating expenses; and

4. The operation of city-owned high speed lines.

1. *The Underliers*

It is obvious that so long as the system is burdened with 900 year leases, carrying fixed charges in the shape of guaranteed dividends of over $7,000,-000 on paid-in capital of less than $54,-000,000, a satisfactory solution is impossible.

Three possible methods of dealing with this problem have been suggested:

(a) The first is a plan of *laissez faire*. Those who advocate it believe that the value of the underliers will rapidly decrease and that they can later be acquired much more cheaply than now. In this connection it is worthy of note that the average market value of their stocks held by the public fell from over $158,000,000 in 1907 to less than $96,-000,000 in 1927, a decrease of over $62,-000,000. With the increase in buses and high speed lines the surface lines will become less and less valuable. The security values, however, depend largely on the leases, and as long as they continue in force the rentals must be paid by the P. R. T. even where the

tracks of the underliers have entirely disappeared. The adoption of this plan would require ultimately putting the system through a receivership in order to wipe out the pyramid of leases which lie at the heart of the trouble.

(b) The second suggestion is that the city and the P. R. T. agree to modify the contract of 1907 so far as it waives the right of the city to recapture the underliers on the basis of original cost, which right was reserved by the city in the ordinance of July 7, 1857. The paid-in capital of the underliers amounts to about $54,000,000 and their funded debts to about $33,500,-000. The sum of these two, or $87,-500,000, would seem to mark the maximum limit of original cost and probably far exceeds it. If the underliers could be acquired on any such basis it would be to the interest of the P. R. T. as well as of the city and the public.

(c) The third plan is condemnation under the act of May 3, 1927. This is the plan suggested by Mr. McChord and now being followed by the city, which has filed an application with the public service commission to determine the value of the properties of the underliers. Mr. McChord estimated such value at $136,000,000, which represents the annual rentals capitalized on a seven per cent basis and exceeds by several million dollars the 1927 market value of the company's stocks and bonds held by the public. This legitimates and perpetuates what Mr. McChord has designated as "an accumulation of fixed charges never paralleled in the history of street railway exploitation." Furthermore, the companies are holding out for a still higher price, and have raised the question of the constitutionality of the condemnation. It is interesting to note that, in the somewhat analogous situation in New York City, Samuel Untermyer in his report as special counsel to the transit commission suggests the passage of similar condemnation legislation.

2. The $200,000,000 Valuation

The second obstacle to a satisfactory solution of the transit problems of Philadelphia is the $200,000,000 valuation of the system. This valuation was made as of 1919 when prices were on a very high level. It has been sustained by the Superior Court and must be accepted until a re-valuation is made at lower price levels. Under the practice of the Pennsylvania Public Service Commission the company is entitled to a return of seven per cent of this amount, or $14,000,000 per year.

Comparisons with other systems are difficult because of differences in conditions. When, however, a valuation is quite out of line with those of a number of other cities it is fair to inquire why this should be. Eliminating all high speed lines from the $200,000,000 valuation leaves at least $145,000,000 as the value of 651 miles of the P. R. T. surface lines. This gives a valuation of over $220,000 per mile of track.

This may be compared with other cities as shown in the table below.

The weighted average value of these ten systems is $128,000 per mile of track as compared with $220,000 per mile of track for the Philadelphia sur-

face system. If the Philadelphia surface system were valued on the same basis as Chicago its value would be decreased by $47,000,000 and the allowed "fair return" to under $11,000,000 per year. This would make possible a substantial reduction in fare, larger payments to the city, or further improvements in the service.

3. Control of P. R. T. Operating Expenses

One of the ablest street railway operators in this country is quoted as saying that there was a time when the "big money" was in building street railways, later it was in owning them, now it is in operating them.

In the regulation of railroads and utilities throughout the country one of the most difficult problems today is the proper control of operating expenses. Commissions for the most part have been loath to exercise such control as being an interference with the managerial discretion of the companies.[1] It is

[1] A typical instance of this attitude is found in the report of the Pennsylvania Public Service Commission *in re* Philadelphia Rapid Transit Company, P. U. R., 1926, B. 385, where in refusing to reduce an operating allowance the commission states (p. 406): "It is in the activities covered by the general and miscellaneous accounts that the very heart and essence of

City	Valuation	Miles of track	Approximate Value per mile of track
Chicago..............	$159,113,000	1063	$150,000
Pittsburgh.............	62,500,000	600	104,000
St. Louis..............	51,781,000	460	112,500
Baltimore.............	75,000,000*	400	187,500
Atlanta...............	20,000,000	210	96,000
Rochester, N. Y.........	19,316,000	167	115,000
Indianapolis, Ind........	15,000,000	153	98,000
Norfolk, Va............	8,100,000	99	82,000
Syracuse, N. Y..........	8,920,000	97	92,000
Scranton, Pa...........	9,000,000	92	98,000

* Includes $5,000,000 for easements.

obvious, however, that if expenses are increased with every increase of revenue we are confronted with the prospect of ever higher rates. With the railroads the problem has been accentuated by the recapture clause of the Transportation Act of 1920, and the Interstate Commerce Commission in recapture cases is scanning the operating expenses of the carriers with great care.

A study of the accounts of the Philadelphia Rapid Transit Company shows very large increases in expenses during the last ten or twelve years, especially for such items as general and miscellaneous expenses which include the salaries of officers and office clerks. In 1916 these totaled $1,309,289. In 1926 they had mounted to $5,750,023, an increase of over 300 per cent, and in 1927 they were $5,674,500. Eliminating relief department expenses, pensions, valuation expenses, injuries and damages, the figures are as follows:

1916	1926	1927
$615,137	$3,236,971	$3,468,233

Reducing these to a basis of car miles and passengers carried the figures are:

	1916	1926	1927
Per 100 car miles...	$ .74	$3.61	$4.03
Per 1,000 revenue passengers carried	1.21	4.75	5.33
Per 1,000 total passengers carried...	.97	3.47	3.85

management is found. Except in a clear case of bad management no regulatory commission would be warranted in interfering in this vital matter." In dissenting from this view the minority states (p. 477): "It is the duty of a regulatory commission to allow such operating expenses only as are reasonably necessary to the efficient management of the utility. It would be idle to give a commission power to fix valuations where every dollar of difference in amount means practically seven cents and to tie its hands in dealing with operating expenses where every dollar of difference means one hundred cents in the result."

The salaries and expenses of general officers increased as follows:

1916	1926	1927
$49,531.37	$1,176,610	$1,259,450

There has, therefore, been an increase in this item of over 2,400 per cent in eleven years.

Comparing general and miscellaneous expenses of the Chicago surface lines for the year 1926 on the same basis, it appears that they totaled $1.69 per 1,000 revenue passengers as compared with $4.75 in Philadelphia. In the same year these expenses on the Interborough subway and elevated lines in New York City amounted to $1.58 per 1,000 revenue passengers and on the B. M. T., to $1.28 per 1,000 revenue passengers.

4. Operation of City-Owned High Speed Lines

The city of Philadelphia has so far expended or authorized the expenditure of about $139,000,000 in high speed transit lines. Of these the Frankford elevated is now leased to the P. R. T. until 1957 at a rental of five per cent of the amount of city bonds issued for its construction. Negotiations are now pending for the lease or operation of the Broad Street subway which, when completed, will cost about $110,000,000. A three months' lease to the P. R. T. has just been made on the basis of a rental of $200,000 per month. It will doubtless be followed by another short-term lease or operating agreement. If adequate control of the operating expenses is established, the problem is merely to find a fair division of the burden of the construction of high speed lines between the taxpayer and the car rider.

Unfortunately Philadelphia is without power to assess benefits from high speed transit construction against the property owners affected. If this could be done the problem would largely be solved, as a very large part of the cost of a subway could be collected from property owners whose land values have been swollen by its construction. They are the ones primarily benefited and should bear a large part of the cost. At present, however, either the taxpayers at large or the car riders must foot the bill.

On the whole it appears that a short-term operating agreement with an operating fee based on a percentage of net revenue and adequate city control over operating expense is the most satisfactory method of dealing with city-owned property, but whether this form or a lease is adopted it is essential in the public interest that (1) there should be frequent opportunities for revision of the agreement and recapture by the city, and (2) the city should provide for adequate control of the operating expenses of the company.

THE TAX SITUATION IN CHICAGO [1]

BY HERBERT D. SIMPSON, PH.D.

Associate Professor of Economics, Institute for Research in Land Economics and Public Utilities, Northwestern University

The second of three articles describing the inequalities of the present assessment methods in Chicago.   ::   ::   ::   ::   ::   ::

IN a previous article, the inequalities of assessment in Chicago—inequalities among districts, classes of property, and among individual property holders—were analyzed in detail. These inequalities are attributable in part to the board of assessors and in part to the board of review.

ALLOCATING RESPONSIBILITY

Indeed, one of the worst features of the present system in Chicago is the fact that with two independent boards, with five members on one and three on the other, and all acting independently of each other, so many avenues are afforded for shifting responsibility from one board to the other and from one individual to another that, in the past, taxpayers have been entirely unable to place definite responsibility

[1] Continued from the September number. The third and last article will appear in November.

upon any one. One of the most important problems for the taxpayer, therefore, is to measure the quality of the work done by *each* of the boards and to determine the degree of responsibility assignable to each; and this we will attempt to do in the following pages.

In the first place, the initial assessment, as made by the board of assessors in 1923, has been compared with the final assessment of 1926, after four years of equalization by the board of review. The result is indicated in Chart 8.

FAILURE OF THE BOARD OF REVIEW

To one unfamiliar with the facts it will probably seem utterly impossible that the chart could have been intended to represent any process of equalization. Changes made by the board of review should have consisted of *reductions* in the upper ranges and

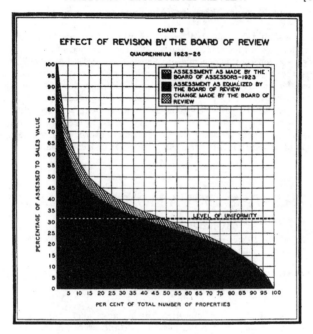

CHART 8

EFFECT OF REVISION BY THE BOARD OF REVIEW

QUADRENNIUM 1923–26

ASSESSMENT AS MADE BY THE BOARD OF ASSESSORS–1923
ASSESSMENT AS EQUALIZED BY THE BOARD OF REVIEW
CHANGE MADE BY THE BOARD OF REVIEW

LEVEL OF UNIFORMITY

PERCENTAGE OF ASSESSED TO SALES VALUE

PER CENT OF TOTAL NUMBER OF PROPERTIES

increases in the lower ranges of assessment, bringing one end *down* and the other end *up* toward the level of uniformity. As a matter of fact, the changes have all been in one direction,[1] constituting a thin stratum of reduction spread over the entire assessment, without perceptibly changing the form of the assessment. It is like trying to level a steep hillside by starting at the top and "stripping" ten feet all the way to the bottom.

Measured mathematically, the degree of equality has been slightly improved—the deviation from uniformity has been reduced from an average of 40 per cent in 1923 to an average of 37.7 per cent in 1926. At that rate of equalization, a uniform assessment would be attained in sixty-nine years, provided the process were not interrupted by subsequent quadrennial reassessments. Measured in another way, this means that with the efficiency of the present board of review, it would require *seventeen* such boards of review, with their complement of secretaries, clerks, and staffs, to secure an equitable assessment for Chicago.

RESULTS OF REVISION BY BOARD OF REVIEW

There are more than a million parcels of real estate in Chicago, however, and it was felt that possibly the character of the assessment as a whole might

[1] This does not mean that there were not single cases in which assessments were increased by the board of review. There were such scattered cases. The chart is plotted in groups of 5 per cent of total number of properties and shows the net result of revision by the board of review within each such group.

represent to a large extent only the results of accident, ignorance, and the necessary inexactness of a wholesale handling of such an enormous number of assessments. For this reason, a more precise test of the deliberate policy of the board of review has been made by taking only those cases in which complaints have been made to the board of review and have been acted upon by them, and in which the assessments have been deliberately revised by the board of review. These revisions should represent the deliberate and intentional policy of the board. These cases constituted 2,046 properties out of our total of 6,445. The results are represented in Chart 9.

These properties, as originally assessed by the board of assessors, show an average deviation from uniformity of 37.9 per cent; after equalization by the board of review, they are 35 per cent away from uniformity. Thirty-one per cent of these properties were already below the average level of assessment established by the board of review, before they came before that board, and had no ground whatever for asking any further reduction. They secured very much the same general amount of reduction as the other 69 per cent of properties, which were originally assessed all the way from the average up to over 100 per cent.

Similar measurements of the work of the board of review have been applied to the 1927 assessment, and the results are shown in Charts 10 and 11. The original assessment, as made by the board of assessors, shows a deviation

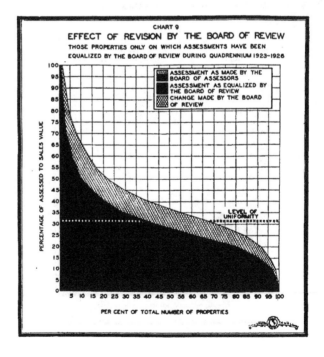

CHART 9
EFFECT OF REVISION BY THE BOARD OF REVIEW
THOSE PROPERTIES ONLY ON WHICH ASSESSMENTS HAVE BEEN
EQUALIZED BY THE BOARD OF REVIEW DURING QUADRENNIUM 1923-1926

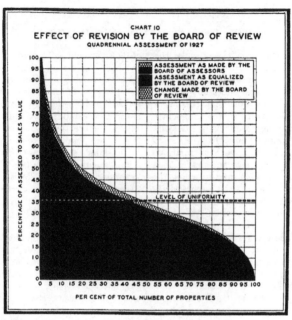

CHART 10

EFFECT OF REVISION BY THE BOARD OF REVIEW
QUADRENNIAL ASSESSMENT OF 1927

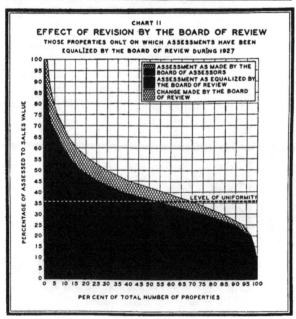

CHART 11

EFFECT OF REVISION BY THE BOARD OF REVIEW
THOSE PROPERTIES ONLY ON WHICH ASSESSMENTS HAVE BEEN
EQUALIZED BY THE BOARD OF REVIEW DURING 1927

of 35.8 per cent from uniformity; after equalization by the board of review it is 36.5 per cent away from uniformity. In other words, it was a more equitable assessment before equalization by the board of review than afterwards.

In order to make all possible allowance for accident, ignorance, and the haste with which the quadrennial assessment had to be made, we have again segregated those cases only in which the board of review definitely acted and deliberately changed the assessments from the figures established by the board of assessors. The results of this deliberate revision by the board of review are shown in Chart 11.

Forty per cent of these properties were already below the average level of assessment established by the board of assessors, when they came before the board of review—29 per cent of them were below the still *lower* level established by the board of review—and had no ground for any reduction whatever.

On what grounds the board of review accorded these particular properties further substantial reductions, can only be conjectured. It clearly was not, as the board of review has frequently stated, in order to protect the small home-owners; for the unhappy fate of the small home-owner at the hands of the board of review is indicated by the figures in the table below.

The largest homes have not only been accorded three times as large a reduction as the small homes, but have enjoyed a final assessment of only 28 per cent of value, compared with an average assessment of 33½ per cent for the smallest homes in the city.

THE PROCESS OF EQUALIZATION

These results are astonishing enough; but the procedure by which they are reached will probably be still more astonishing to people outside of Chicago. The process of review and equalization in Cook County, so far as the procedure is public, is carried out in the form of "hearings." These "hearings" are held in a large room, arranged in general to resemble a court room, with a seating capacity of 150 and standing room for another 150. At one end of this room is a raised platform, or medieval dais, surmounted by three pulpits or altar-shaped desks, behind each of which sits a member of the board of review—still further protected by a heavy railing that runs from one of these pulpit-like desks to another, across the front of the platform. By accident or otherwise, this railing does not run straight across

ASSESSMENT OF SINGLE-FAMILY RESIDENCES

Sales value	Average value per home	Average rate of assessment before equalization by board of review	Average rate of assessment after equalization by board of review	Reductions granted to each class by board of review
Less than $15,000...................	$11,434	34.9%	33.5%	1.4%
$15,000 and less than $25,000........	17,576	36.3	33.4	2.9
$25,000 and less than $35,000........	28,550	33.5	30.9	2.6
$35,000 and less than $50,000........	38,788	33.8	32.5	1.3
$50,000 and over...................	77,752	32.7	28.0	4.7
All homes.........................	....	34.9	32.6	2.3

the room, however, because at the left side of each pulpit both dais and railing are indented sufficiently to make a corner or pocket, just large enough to hold an average-sized taxpayer. Into this pocket the complaining taxpayer is ushered by the clerk, who calls his name and then conducts him to the member of the board of review whom he has asked to see or to whom, in the language of the clerk, he is "next." From this pocket he sends his complaint upward to the member of the board of review, peering down from three feet above.

Each member of the board does his own "equalizing" in the cases he "hears," unmolested by other members of the board or by other complaining taxpayers who may be present. In fact, no one else hears what goes on at the "hearing," because of the general noisiness of the room and of the distance at which spectators sit from the several hearings going on at the front of the room.

It should be noted also that the board of assessors, the very officials whose work is being reviewed, are not represented at these hearings and have no opportunity to defend their own assessments or to present information bearing upon the properties in question. There is apparently no consultation of files or records, no ascertainment of facts, and indeed, so far as can be learned, no reference to any established level of assessment as a standard of what the complaining taxpayers' assessment *ought* to be.

Under such a system, complaints will naturally be numerous. Last year they were reported to number something over 100,000. Before the end of the year, the board simply suspended hearings, making its revisions without the formality of hearings, and many taxpayers were unable to secure consideration of their cases at all. Most students of taxation outside of Chicago will be surprised to learn that such a system of review still exists in any large city in the United States. Under this system the board of review must inevitably produce chaotic results, even when composed of entirely honest and conscientious citizens, and unmitigated favoritism and corruption when composed of any other kind.

RESULTS THAT CANNOT BE MEASURED STATISTICALLY

And there are results which are not susceptible of statistical measurement but which may be even more important than those represented by the bars and curves in the earlier portions of this article. One of these is the fact that a system such as has been described must necessarily become the mere adjunct of whatever political organization is in power.

This is not peculiar to Chicago. It is almost the inevitable result of any system of taxation in which assessments are made arbitrarily, without reference to any scientific or systematic standards of valuation, and without review by any impartial body. But in Chicago it is avowed with an openness and frankness that is little short of amazing. Precinct captains and ward committeemen openly boast of their ability to "take care" of their constituents. The representatives of political organizations in general throughout the city appear to take it as a matter of course that a part of their regular duties is to make the necessary adjustments in the assessment of property. The result is, that in addition to a regularly constituted board of assessors and board of review, Chicago has an extra-constitutional, ex-officio board of revision, consisting of the representatives of party organizations throughout the city, who are engaged every day of the year, without regard to constitutional requirements or quadrennial limitations, in the business of revising assessments to suit the exigencies of party organization.

THE PROFESSIONAL TAX-FIXER FLOURISHES

Another result has been the growth of a whole class of professional tax-fixers, whose methods and activities are too varied to be discussed in the space of this article and probably too well known to require discussion.

A third result has been the general belief, on the part of business men particularly, that the powers of taxation are arbitrarily used to compel contributions to political organizations, to stifle opposition and criticism, and to suppress freedom of speech and of the press. How well founded this belief is, we shall not attempt here to say; for the time being, one illustration will suffice. When the Teachers' Federation of Chicago a year ago proposed to make an investigation of the tax system, Mr. J. L. Coath, president of the board of education, declared, as quoted in the *Chicago Tribune* and the press generally, that any teacher who contributed a dime to that investigation would be considered unfit to continue in the service of the public schools. It is not necessary here to express any judgment as to the need of such an investigation, or the ability of the Teachers' Federation to make it, or the amount of money that might properly be contributed to it. But under republican government, taxation is a subject of concern to all citizens and one on which it is proper to seek any information that can be secured. When responsible representatives of

the city government are obliged to resort to such arbitrary suppression, even the inequalities of taxation sink into insignificance in comparison with the blatant insolence of such methods of intimidation.

DECLINE IN CIVIC MORALITY

And more important than all these is the general decline in political and civic morality, in consequence of the conditions we have described. In Chicago it appears to be taken for granted that of course the tax system is corrupt; that the tax machinery is used for political and other purposes; that taxes are "fixed" by various ulterior methods; and the average citizen of Chicago appears to have nothing but a cynical contempt for the system, its officials and everything connected with taxation.

The writer was introduced some time ago to a typical, successful business man of Chicago. Learning that we were undertaking a study of the tax situation, he pondered for a moment and then said very deliberately: "I hope you will do nothing to disturb the rascals who are protecting me." When a representative citizen comes to have that feeling toward the government of his city, it bodes ill for his city. And if that city were some main street village of a few thousand people, perhaps the rest of us should not need to worry about it. But when it is the second greatest city in the New World, a city of three million people and more than twelve billions of wealth, the trade and financial center for half of the United States, the situation becomes a matter of concern to every one interested in the continuance of democratic government in this country.

RECENT BOOKS REVIEWED

REPORT OF THE CITY COMMITTEE ON PLAN AND SURVEY. New York: 1928. Pp. 218.

When Mayor Walker of New York in June, 1926, addressed the five hundred and seven members of his newly appointed City Committee on Plan and Survey, he invited them to "sift their information into a central body which, from a broad survey, may pick and choose what in all human probability are the best remedies" for the costly lack of some scientific and coördinated method for the improvement of the city and its government.

When the committee reported in June, 1928, its chief and, in fact, its only concrete recommendations were for the appointment of additional committees to study the subject, particularly a permanent planning board. The report was essentially a frank confession that the task was too much for a committee constituted as it was.

Such an apparently meager result was expected from the first by those who knew something of the vastness and complexity of the task assigned to this committee and who realized that the experts in various branches of municipal administration were carefully seeded upon a thick layer of Tammanyites through whom no very drastic recommendations could be expected to penetrate.

There are cynics who assert the committee was never intended to do more than silence criticism of the Walker administration by putting the critics at work upon the preparation of the report. If this was true, the committee was a great success.

Others believe that this was the method taken by the real heads of the "new Tammany" to give a course of education in the need for city planning to their lesser "braves." If in this way the principles of city planning have been sold to the real governing body in New York City, then again the committee was a success.

Much conscientious labor was unquestionably performed by many members of the executive committee and of the various subcommittees; and the best survey of the problems of present-day New York together with suggested remedies for them is contained in their reports. One of the most thorough of these reports is that from the Subcommittee on Finance, Budget and Revenue. This report, as published in a separate volume, contains the best recent exposition of the very complicated financial system of the city, but curiously enough for such a scientifically prepared document, *as published*, it accepts the dangerously unsound subway financing policy of the present administration as good dogma, and never mentions the sleeping liability of $200,000,000 which the city has incurred through its unsound pension policies for employees. The discussions in other subcommittee reports vary from the definite, opposite and easily attainable (as, for example, in regard to amending the zoning resolution), to the fantastic dreams of eight or nine-tiered "multiple highways" which are clearly out of the realm of the practical.

The report of the whole committee was submitted in June, 1928, just as the summer season was beginning, so that nothing could be expected from its recommendations until the autumn. Then will come, in the action taken upon the recommendation for the establishment of a permanent city planning board—a body with real powers and, moreover, powers taken from the borough presidents in large degree—the real test as to whether Tammany was only playing a little game with the reformers and thinkers and best citizens or whether it is sincerely interested in the city planning which New York so badly needs.

GEORGE H. McCAFFREY.

❋

REGIONAL SURVEY OF NEW YORK AND ITS ENVIRONS: VOLUME III—HIGHWAY TRAFFIC. By Harold M. Lewis, in consultation with Ernest P. Goodrich. New York: Regional Plan of New York and its Environs, 1927. Pp. 172.

This document, revised from its first edition published in 1925, now comprises one of the twelve volumes by which the work of the Committee of the Regional Plan of New York and its Environs is presented to the public for permanent record. It frankly "does not enter into the discussion of proposals for relieving traffic congestion, but contains a statement and analysis of certain facts and tendencies of growth that had to be investigated before any plan was made," with the addition of a summary of proposals heretofore made by public authorities.

In comparatively brief space the salient facts

600

are amassed, and many of them analyzed so as to develop their deeper significance by graphic charts. A useful feature of the report is the four-page summary of the outstanding facts revealed by the investigation, of which the following are a few samples:

"Curves showing the relation between population and registration (of automobiles) have been following a quite definite law and can be extended with a reasonable degree of accuracy."

"By the year 1965 the total registration in the Region may reach 6,720,000 vehicles; of this total 2,260,000, or nearly four times the 1926 city registration, might be within the present limits of New York City."

"It is estimated that there were 1,870 fatalities which resulted from motor vehicle accidents in New York and its environs in 1925, representing an estimated financial loss of approximately $7,480,000."

"The financial losses to the community resulting from traffic congestion are estimated at $500,000 per day on Manhattan Island and $1,-000,000 per day in the entire region."

"Traffic on Manhattan avenues crossing 48th Street will reach a point of saturation by about the year 1930—even if the present proposals for increasing the roadway capacity in these avenues are carried out."

Taken alone, it might be thought that by the scientific application of such facts the answer to the traffic problem of the New York metropolitan region, one hundred miles in diameter, would automatically be found; but in his introduction Thomas Adams forcefully warns that expedients designed solely to relieve traffic are apt to be doomed to failure because they do not regard the other functions of the street; and reference is made to discussion in other volumes of the survey of such phases as the relation of highways to zoning and the cause and extent of congestion in suburban areas.

ARTHUR C. COMEY.

✶

PUBLICITY FOR SOCIAL WORK. By Mary Swain Routzahn and Evart G. Routzahn. New York: Department of Surveys and Exhibits, Russell Sage Foundation, 1928.

"Publicity for Social Work" is a handbook for social workers who have to handle publicity for their organizations. To anyone who is familiar with the haphazard publicity in which many organizations indulge, the need for such a book would not have to be demonstrated. Let us hope that this carefully prepared volume, the first in the field, will not fall on barren ground.

Mr. and Mrs. Routzahn set themselves a difficult task. They found an almost virgin field in which to work out a technique. To quote from their introduction, "It soon became apparent, however, that in the majority of cases the choice of a method was determined by economy, imitation, or habit, rather than by deliberate judgment." They go on to say, "Except in rare instances we had no means of determining in any given case the relation between the methods used and the results achieved."

The book is divided into six parts with many pertinent illustrations. Again the authors' difficulty in finding good illustrative material shows a crying need for technical skill. To quote, "Examples of good writing, pleasing design, attractive pictures, and judicious selection of facts and ideas in social publicity to illustrate this book were hard to find. Higher standards need to be achieved in all of these lines before scientific testing is called for."

The newspapers should be grateful to the authors for their careful explanations of when and how publicity through that medium is possible. So often a social work organization will antagonize newspapers by urging on them unsuitable material or by wishing to have something published immediately which has no news value. The book is so painstaking and detailed that the "greenest" social worker with some wit could follow its directions. Besides telling of ways of securing publicity through the newspapers and prepared printed matter, it deals carefully with public speaking, pageants, plays, exhibits, and how to organize and manage a campaign. At the end of their chapters on campaigns there is an apt warning: "Fewer and Better Campaigns might well be a slogan for social workers to follow. When an intensive campaign follows too closely upon the heels of a similar affair the method loses whatever advantages it may have over other forms of publicity."

In their last chapter Mr. and Mrs. Routzahn touch on a number of interesting problems in publicity yet unsolved, such as how to secure persons equipped in social publicity. There are no training schools as yet. No generally accepted ideas as to what should be their duties and their qualifications for the task. Another interesting problem is how to appeal to your public in a popular manner and yet keep abreast with your forward-looking, highly technical organization.

Every organization should own this book. It would be well for heads of organizations to read it with special emphasis on the last chapter. Its fine concept of what publicity in social work connotes is well worth remembering.

GRACE H. CHILDS.
New York City.

❋

AMERICAN GOVERNMENT AND CITIZENSHIP. By Martin and George, New York: Alfred A. Knopf, 1927. Pp. 764, xi.

This book is avowedly a contribution to the experimentation of the period, an attempt at constructive change in the method of presenting an introductory survey of American government.

The most noticeable innovation is the addition of Part III, Foreign Relations of the United States, an extended treatment of 315 pages, covering both foreign policies and diplomatic practice.

The treatment of American Political Theory, Part I, also has new features. The emphasis is upon the *rationale* behind the formation of our political institutions, interwoven with the practice of the Founding Fathers. This involves added historical emphasis, possibly unduly extended. But to this history are harnessed cases and events of later years. For example, the Adams-Hamilton and Jefferson-Madison differences on the theory of federalism are followed at once by the Webster-Hayne debate and Calhoun's theory of nullification. It is an interesting experiment in presentation which deserves careful consideration.

The third innovation, which would be more interesting were it not crowded by the space requirements of the other two, is in Part II, American Government and Politics. According to the preface, the treatment of this section "makes unnecessary the usual divisions into national, state, and local government." "A modest attempt has been made to cut through the rather rigid divisions of government, and to emphasize functions and ideas." Three chapters, The Constitution and the Citizen, Parties and Party Platforms, and The Citizen and His Party, lend themselves readily to this treatment. In the other five, on fundamental laws, the executive, the legislative, the judicial system and the business of government, the governmental divisions are used within the chapters.

Approval or disapproval of the book will turn primarily upon acceptance or rejection of the general plan rather than on the details. To those who desire more material on foreign relations or theory, the treatment may commend itself. To those who feel that these are over-emphasized there will be disappointment over the fifty per cent condensation made necessary in Part II.

The space allotment is roughly: Theory, 17 per cent; American Government, 41 per cent; and Foreign Relations, 42 per cent. Many will not agree that the latter deserves more space than all the remaining phases of American government.

Among the omissions regretted in Part II may be mentioned the following: The method of treatment reserves no space for county or township. The former is mentioned under the judicial system, and both are mentioned under the party system, but that is all. Taxation receives scant consideration; two pages of constitutional discussion under federal, a half page under municipal, and three lines under state government. The mechanics of voting are omitted and the ballot is mentioned solely in a casual reference to the short ballot, which is not explained. Nor is there sufficient space for the *rationale* behind such present-day movements as the reorganization of state administration.

With such definite departure from old methods, involving new allocation of material, the result might be more easily assimilated were the index not so incomplete as to titles and references under titles.

In general, this is a bold grappling with the untried. The triple experiment may handicap it as a text, but there is much of excellent treatment for the general reader.

F. H. GUILD.
University of Kansas.

❋

WATER PURIFICATION. By Joseph W. Ellms. New York: McGraw-Hill Book Company, Inc., 1928. Pp. 594.

Mr. Ellms, in this second edition of his book first published about ten years ago, treats in a comprehensive way the important and intricate processes of the treatment of water for the many uses of modern life.

A first impression made by the book is that its author does not believe the purification of water to be a finished art. Points in the present-day knowledge of water purification where information is insufficient or lacking are indicated. The author is cautious in the discussion of developments which have not yet proved their worth.

Although theories are explained, the author, even at the expense of appearing redundant, stresses practical things. The author describes the various means which may be used to accomplish a purpose but he seems anxious to indicate, wherever possible, a best method. Thus, in the discussion of the handling of chemicals an entire section is given to best practices. Moreover, the author differentiates between acceptable means according to use.

Beginning with an introduction containing a brief history of water-supply development, the book proceeds to a classification of natural waters. Two chapters discuss the relationship of water supply to health and the effect of improvement in water supplies upon health. These are followed by an outline of the objects and methods of water purification. The remaining 28 chapters of the text are devoted to the detailed discussion of water treatment. Costs as well as types of construction and methods and results of operation are given. An appendix presents a discussion by C. N. Miller of the flow of water through rapid-sand filters, and in a second appendix Mr. Miller develops an approximate formula for the capacity of wash-water troughs for rapid-sand filters. Conversion tables and tables of equivalents, coefficients and rates of discharge are also included.

Recent thought in the field of water purification is, in general, adequately presented. There is an excellent account of the part that colloids play in the purification of water. A chapter is given to the effect of the hydrogen-ion concentration of natural waters. It is possible, however, that a reader may not find every development upon which he would like information; for example, sodium aluminate apparently is not considered among the chemicals used in water purification.

The book is simply and clearly written but, of necessity, it is technical. It is not, in its entirety, for the layman. As a book of reference for the water-works man it will be found to contain much information from plants in operation and to be generously illustrated. The student will find frequent references in the text and lists of references at the ends of the chapters.

C. A. HOWLAND.

ELEMENTS OF POLITICAL SCIENCE RESEARCH. By Austin F. Macdonald, Ph.D. New York: Prentice-Hall, Inc., 1928.

This book makes available source material and research methods in the field of political science. It is obvious that such material must be the background of any genuine research in that subject. It discusses the more important sources in the field, and does not attempt a list of all original material. Rather, its aim is to familiarize students with the purposes, methods, and chief sources of research.

The ten chapters are devoted to federal laws, other laws and ordinances, judicial decisions, Congressional and other debates, Congressional documents, executive and other reports, state year books, American and foreign legislative debates, book indices, etc. As to methods, the chapter on "Form" applying to research papers, while elementary and brief, will prove invaluable to beginners. The nature and use of original documents are outlined, and illustrative assignments are given at the end of each chapter.

This is really a handbook intended primarily for students enrolled in the advanced political science courses of our American colleges and universities. To these beginners the book will undoubtedly be of greatest value, although offering suggestions to others. The book is undoubtedly adequate for its purposes, being based upon a number of years' experience at the University of Pennsylvania. We know of no similar publication.

A practical researcher has no basis for adverse criticism of this handbook, when the author concedes its incompleteness, but the reviewer thinks that such an excellent start having been made it is unfortunate that its contents were not expanded beyond the ninety pages. Political science is a large field, including all phases of government, or politics. From the point of view of cost, municipal government is one of the most important of its branches; from the point of view of services rendered the citizen, it is certainly the most intimate. For these reasons, it would be fortunate if the volume were extended to include more specific references to municipal government and evidences of its improved processes during the past twenty years—the texts, the practical reports of research agencies and of the National Municipal League, magazines such as the REVIEW and the *American City*, etc.

C. E. RIGHTOR.

Detroit.

JUDICIAL DECISIONS

EDITED BY C. W. TOOKE

Professor of Law, New York University

Home Rule—Aviation Field Held to be a Public Utility.—In *State ex rel. City of Lincoln v. Johnson, State Auditor*, 220 N. W. 273 (June 27, 1928), the Supreme Court of Nebraska granted an original writ of mandamus to the defendant ordering him to register and certify bonds issued by the relator for the purpose of establishing and equipping a municipal aviation field. In the local referendum the proposal to issue the bonds was carried by a close majority vote and the auditor's refusal to certify the bonds was based upon the terms of a general statute requiring a majority of sixty per cent of the electors voting. The city contended that the provision of its home-rule charter requiring only a majority vote for the issuance of bonds for "public service property" and for "public utilities" was controlling against the provisions of the general statute.

In sustaining the latter contention, the court holds that the establishment of an air-port is peculiarly a municipal function and governed by the terms of the home-rule charter and that an equipped aviation field designed to make aerial transportation of passengers and freight available to its inhabitants is both a "public service property" and a "public utility" within the meaning of the charter which authorizes municipal bonds upon a majority vote. This decision, so far as it relates to air ports as a municipal function, is supported by the decision of the Supreme Court of Kansas in *Wichita v. Clapp*, 263 Pac. 12, reported in the April, 1928, issue of the Review at page 238. One may also compare it with the decision of the Court of Appeals for Cuyahoga County in *State ex rel. Hile v. City of Cleveland*, 26 Ohio App. 158, in which it was held that the requirements of advertising an issue of bonds for an aviation field was controlled by the city charter, as the function was in its nature a local public utility.

✦

Public Buildings—Statutory Liens in Favor of Laborers and Material Men.—In *Boise-Payette Lumber Co. v. Challis School District*, 288 Pac. 26, finally decided by the Supreme Court of Idaho on June 29, 1928, a statute extending the general mechanics lien law to buildings of counties, cities, towns or school districts was held to be unconstitutional. While the state constitution imposes upon the legislature the duty of enacting a general mechanics lien statute, other provisions limiting the power of municipalities to contract debts or to pledge their credit are held to determine the public policy of the state which cannot be varied by legislative act. In the absence of express inclusion, public buildings are held to be exempt from general mechanics lien statutes. The decision in the instant case is supported by a similar ruling in California (*Mayrhofer v. Board of Education*, 89 Cal. 110, 26 Pac. 646).

The only state which has upheld such a statute is Kansas. In *Huttig Millwork Co. v. Randall*, 266 Pac. 106, the Supreme Court considers the effect of the statute, and holds that the foreclosure of such a statutory lien "is only to be regarded in a Pickwickian sense." At the proper time, unless the plaintiff's judgment is satisfied, mandamus will lie to compel payment or the imposition of a tax to raise funds therefor (*City of Frankfort v. Warders*, 119 Kan. 653, 240 Pac. 589). It will therefore be apparent that the remedy is similar to that available to material men or laborers on public works in other states where, as in New York, a lien may be filed against the funds appropriated to pay the contractor (*Italian Mosaic Marble Co. v. Niagara Falls*, 227 N. Y. Sup. 64).

These statutes giving to laborers and material men a qualified lien on public works have an important bearing on the question of their right to recover upon the contractor's bond as sole beneficiaries of the provision that the contractor will pay for work and materials furnished—which prevails in a majority of our states. If other remedies are provided by statute, it may result in the abolition of the valuable security that is now available to the laborer or material man, as they may no longer be properly considered the sole beneficiaries of this clause of the contractor's bond.

Torts—Liability for Pollution of Waters by Sewage.—The highest courts of Missouri and Oklahoma have recently affirmed the liability of municipalities for the pollution of lands and waters by waste of their sewage disposal plants. In *Windle* v. *City of Springfield*, 8 S. W. (2d) 61, the Supreme Court of Missouri held the defendant liable because of the direct invasion of the plaintiff's property by percolating sewage which contaminated his water supply so as to render it unfit for use. The contention of the defense that the injury was due to defective plans and that the function was governmental in character was met by the court's refusal to apply these bases of nonliability, where the operation of the plant resulted in a private nuisance or a direct trespass on private property. In *City of Enid* v. *Brooks*, 269 Pac. 241, the lower riparian owner was given a remedy for the damages caused by sewage pollution of the stream due to faulty operation of the septic tank system. Here again the defendant claimed immunity from liability upon the theory of a governmental function and the judicial nature of the adoption of plans, but the court held that these excuses could not be maintained where the damages were caused by negligent operation. These principles of limitation of immunity were fortunately established at a time when the operation of a sewer plant was looked upon as peculiarly for the convenience of the community and the public governmental character of health as a state function had not been generally recognized. The doctrine of the two instant cases is uniformly followed and almost nullifies any practical importance of the principle of immunity based on the judicial character of the adoption of defective plans (*Johnston* v. *District of Columbia*, 118 U. S. 19).

✤

Streets and Highways—Removal of Encroachments at Suit of Private Citizen.—In *Matter of Green* v. *Miller*, 249 N. Y. 88, the New York Court of Appeals was recently called upon to determine whether a writ of mandamus would lie to require the city officers to remove an encroachment on the street at the suit of a resident taxpayer. The court held that certain structures, as in the instant case a stoop and bay window, which do not interfere with the use of the street are not nuisances *per se* when supported by long usage and especially when erected and maintained under a revocable license; and therefore a taxpayer who was only intended as one of the public might not have the benefit of a writ of mandamus in an action against the city authorities alone. So many actions of this kind have been sustained of late years, that both the Supreme Court and the Appellate Division had decided that the petitioner was entitled to the relief asked for. The extreme cases where such relief is granted, however, are those wherein the property owner is also made a party defendant and the petitioner as an abutting owner on the street avers and proves special damages. Such cases as *Carlan Bros.* v. *Halle Bros.*, 155 N. E. 398, are predicted upon the peculiar rights of the adjacent abutting owner, whose light, air, view or access may have been interfered with. (See note, NATIONAL MUNICIPAL REVIEW, June, 1927.) Of these encroachments which under a license from the city the court refuses to regard as public nuisances, it enumerates cellar ways, iron platforms, news stands, vaults and areaways, awnings, bay windows, show windows, stoops and porticos—all of which have become familiar by long usage as necessary or convenient to the enjoyment of the abutting property. The permit so to use the street, however, is revocable at the instance of the city authorities and can never ripen into a right. For a recent case illustrating the right of the adjacent owner to abate such an encroachment, the reader may be referred to *Denman* v. *Mattson*, 268 Pac. 1045, decided by the Supreme Court of Washington last July.

✤

Streets and Highways—Dedication; Adverse Possession.—The question of the effect of nonaction by the municipal authorities on the dedication of lands, where a street is laid out upon a map filed in a public office and lots are sold in reference thereto, seems to raise recurrent doubts in the minds of many city officials. The notion that in all cases there must be an official acceptance, either formal or by public acts, to complete the dedication is often expressed, and the inference is drawn that in the meantime the offer is subject to revocation. Of course this is not true of a statutory dedication, and as a general proposition the filing of a map demarcating streets and selling lots in reference thereto is held to constitute in itself either a complete dedication of the street to the public (*Long Branch* v. *Toorey*, 140 Atl. 415) or is in effect a restrictive covenant in gross running to all purchasers of lots or their successors (*Menstell* v. *Johnson*, 262 Pac. 853).

The Supreme Court of Mississippi, on August 7, finally disposed of an important case involving this precise question. In *City of Ellisville* v.

Webb, 117 So. 836, an action was brought by a lot owner to quiet title to certain lands claimed by the city as part of a street. In 1891 the street had been platted on a map by the owner of the property as eighty feet in width and lots sold by reference thereto. The city did not move to improve the street until about 1905, when the street commissioner, as he testified, found upon the map a projection of about twenty feet into the street area, and thereupon proceeded to improve the remaining sixty feet as a street, the lot owners in the meantime fencing in the twenty-foot projection and holding it down to 1928. The court held that the dedication was complete in 1891, that the failure of the municipality to improve the street did not affect its title, that the city was not bound by the acts of its officers twenty-three years previous in cutting down the extent of the street, and that the lot owner could gain no right against the public by adverse possession although occupying it under a claim of ownership continuously for thirty-three years. The bill was accordingly dismissed, and the strip awarded to the city.

✤

Parks—Capacity of Counties to Administer.— In *Duval County* v. *Bancroft*, 117 So. 799, the Supreme Court of Florida, in a decision handed down July 3, affirms the capacity of counties in that state to take lands dedicated to park purposes as appropriate to the functions of health control, public welfare and convenience exercised by them. Ellis, C. J. and Brown, J. dissented upon the ground that the acts of dedication occurred in 1907 and that the statutory

power of counties to acquire lands for park purposes was not granted until 1925. While recognizing that the lack of power to acquire by purchase or condemnation would not necessarily preclude an implied power to take by gift, the dissenting justices held that it was strong evidence that, prior to such grant, the administration of parks was not such a county purpose as would enable the county to act as trustee for the public. It seems apparent, however, that the purpose was not only public and for the benefit of the inhabitants of the county, but its administration was so related to the general functions of the county that the position of the majority of the court should be approved.

✤

Zoning—Exemption of Municipal Property.— The Supreme Court of Ohio in *Cincinnati* v. *Wegehoft*, 162 N. E. 389, reversing the Court of Appeals, holds that city property may be exempted from the application of zoning restrictions. The petitioner sought an injunction to restrain the erection of a fire engine house in a residential section, though permitted by the zoning ordinance. That the power to enact reasonable zoning ordinances may determine the classes of buildings permissible, when, as in this case, they are not nuisances *per se* and are designed to protect the property of the district and the safety of its people, would seem too clear to be disputed. Indeed, without the express exemption of an ordinance, where the question has been raised, the courts have held that zoning restrictions are not to be applied to municipal buildings.

PUBLIC UTILITIES

EDITED BY JOHN BAUER

Director, American Public Utilities Bureau

Oklahoma to Regulate Holding Companies.— A bill to be introduced at the next session of the Oklahoma legislature will seek to place the American Telephone & Telegraph Company, and other telephone holding companies, under the control of the state. In Oklahoma, as in virtually all states, holding companies escape practically all form of state regulation. Only the operating companies, strictly so considered, have been brought under control. The line of demarcation between operating and holding company is often narrow. Holding companies frequently form vital functions of operation. Because of the particular form of organization, however, they escape state control, and, to a considerable extent, defeat the purposes of regulation.

The object of the Oklahoma bill is to meet this situation. It provides also for a state-wide investigation of various aspects of the telephone business, so as to determine to what extent further regulation is necessary in the interest of the public. It is designed particularly to reach the vital intercompany relationships, such as the percentage of gross revenue collected by the American Telephone & Telegraph Company from each of its operating subsidiaries, the toll charges, the methods of financing, and contracts with the operating companies for instruments, maintenance, and various managerial services. All these relations result in imposing charges to the controlled companies, which have to be included in the rates. But the commissions are unable to examine the actual costs incurred to see whether the charges are excessive.

The Oklahoma bill points in the right direction. It should be extended to include all public utilities. No doubt, in many instances, the ultimate burden upon the consumer is increased materially by holding company arrangements which escape the scrutiny of state regulation through roundabout devices. The ultimate owners of the properties succeed in acquiring larger returns, in one form or another, than would be approved by the commissions under ordinary standards of rate making. To what extent the holding companies do impose unwarranted charges upon operating companies, is a question of fact that ought to be authoritatively determined. There is widespread opinion that this has reached the point of greatest abuse. This view is probably exaggerated, but it is based upon enough concrete indications to give it substance. The proposed Oklahoma course of a state-wide inquiry might well be adopted in all the states, to find out what the facts are, and what legislation is necessary to meet the situation.

❋

Example of Holding Company Influences in St. Louis.— The subject of holding companies and their relation to operating companies is probably the most important topic of public interest in the utility field at the present time. It concerns the control of the operating companies, the cost of service, and local regulation. It involves especially the relations of the utilities to the public.

We have stated in these columns repeatedly that the holding company furnishes an excellent device for effective economic organization of utilities which in their nature have a more extensive field than a single community. We have pointed out, however, that it lends itself to misuse, and may become primarily an agency for exploitation rather than for carrying out useful economic purposes. Striking illustrations could be produced from all parts of the country, and, it is hoped, many will be brought out in detail by the Federal Trade Commission in its investigation under the Walsh resolution.

We feel that the abuses perpetrated through the holding companies have been responsible, more than any other circumstance, for the mounting criticism against the utilities and the commissions. The holding companies have involved, to a large extent, non-resident control which in many instances has been ruthless toward reasonable public rights. They have imposed excessive costs upon communities, and have supported financial policies which have no reasonable justification. Not all holding companies have been guilty, but some have succeeded in forcing their lack of public spirit upon the management of the industry.

607

An interesting case illustrating what has happened in numerous instances in all parts of the country appears in the Laclede Gas Light Company, serving the city of St. Louis, Mo. This company has a long history of excellent service and satisfactory relations with the community. It had been built up over many years as a local concern, controlled dominantly by St. Louis people. The management understood the public character of the service, and accepted its responsibility to the people at large. It had a real goodwill among its patrons. It was progressive and efficient; it had the motive of public service, and was contented with a reasonable return. The stockholders had always been satisfied with moderate dividends; and there had never been any serious disputes over rates. The public attitude was responsive to the spirit of the management.

All this was changed rapidly about five years ago. Outside interests obtained stock control by paying much more than the local owners had ever considered the stock worth. After the purchase an outside management fee was imposed upon the company, and an outside chairman of the board was installed with a salary for which no evident services were rendered. The company moved for a valuation of its property to be made by the Public Service Commission. It employed the well-known tactics for obtaining maximum valuations, claiming high reproduction costs, large overheads, no depreciation, and huge going value. The Commission fixed a valuation of $45,600,000. Prior to the new control, the company had been satisfied with a return on about $25,000,000.

Naturally, the efforts of the new control aroused public opposition, and the goodwill built up over many years was rapidly dissipated. During the past year, the company has tried to get a rate adjustment which would enable it to earn a seven to eight per cent return upon the valuation fixed by the commission. Besides a general increase in rates, it has sought to impose the so-called "initial charge," which involves a large and unjustified service charge. The City of St. Louis appeared in strenuous opposition to the increased and revised schedule of rates. At the hearings, the antagonism between the public and the utility stood out clearly. Goodwill had disappeared; the public was antagonistic to the company, wholly on account of the outside control introduced and the unwarranted practices imposed upon the public.

In the hearings, evidence was presented that large salaries were imposed, and that outside management fees amounted to about $200,000 a year, although little or no service was rendered. Moreover, it was shown that the company was able to get a supply of gas by piping it some distance across the Mississippi River, from Illinois, where it was a by-product. This gas could be purchased at about 32 cents per thousand cubic feet, and the cost of transmission to the city of St. Louis probably amounted to 5 cents more. The cost of manufacturing gas in St. Louis was about 50 cents. The new source of supply, therefore, made it possible to effect material economy and thus convey an advantage to the consumers.

What did the company do? Instead of proceeding directly to obtain the cheapest gas possible for the public, and reduce its rates accordingly, a special company was organized, under the control of the same holding company. This subsidiary constructed the pipe lines and entered into contracts for the purchase of the by-product gas in Illinois. It transmitted the gas to St. Louis and delivered it to the Laclede Gas Light Company at 50 cents per thousand cubic feet, which was about equal to the cost of manufacturing the local gas. Through this intercompany device, the outside management kept for itself the profit between the low price gas and the old level of cost of production: The consumers were thus deprived of any benefit from the availability of a cheap source of supply. The policy of the new management has been reprehensible throughout. Under strict legal terms, it may not have violated any law, and it may consider itself righteous and abused. It has, however, been blind to its public responsibility, and has turned goodwill into distrust in a city of over 800,000 population.

We have briefly presented what happened in St. Louis. A similar course has been followed in a goodly number of instances, to our own knowledge. Here is the chief reason for public hostility to the utilities. The writer knows that the actual managers in St. Louis have felt humiliated, but have been practically unable to do otherwise than as directed by the outside interests. It is the holding company abuses that are a danger to the industry, so far as the public is concerned. This, we believe, does not involve all holding companies, but includes enough so as to constitute the chief public problem in the entire field of utilities in their relation to the public.

Logansport Telephone Case.—Another instance that typifies what has been going on in many smaller communities appears in the Logansport Telephone case before the Indiana Public Service Commission. The Logansport Home Telephone Company had been a purely local concern. It was organized in 1901 by local men who were eager to obtain for the business and professional interests in Logansport the benefit of modern telephone service. The whole property was built by local money, the stock was held by local people, the directors were Logansport business and professional men, and the management was built up wholly through local personnel.

The company had some serious vicissitudes: one a severe flood; another a bad sleet storm. The losses were taken by the local people, and the growth of the property paralleled the development of the community, with a steady improvement of the service as conditions warranted. The lines were extended to neighboring towns, so that the greater part of Cass County was served by the same concern. The company had no financial difficulties. It was able to make the needed extensions and improvements mostly out of earnings, and obtained steadily what was considered a fair return to the owners. The manager was a local man; all the employees were local people; there was goodwill throughout.

About three years ago the stock was purchased by outside financial interests. The group has been commonly assumed to be acting in behalf of a large holding company; but proof to that effect has never been furnished. A much higher price was paid for the stock than any of the local holders had ever expected; naturally the sales were made. Soon after the purchase, new salaries were imposed and overheads were increased; and a year ago the company appealed to the Public Service Commission for a large increase in rates.

In connection with the proposed increase in rates, the new management brought in outside valuation engineers and hired three groups of attorneys to represent its interests before the Commission. The valuation claimed for the property was based upon unit prices that were shown to be excessive, overheads that involved duplications and pyramiding, and going value that had no foundation in reality. The total valuation claimed was nearly three times the amount of the fair, actual investment made and maintained in the properties. The city of Logansport actively opposed the new rates and brought into the rec-

ord the practices of the new control. The old goodwill has disappeared, and has been replaced by enmity. The proposed rates were denied by the Commission, and the practices of the company severely condemned. The Commission, however, did allow a moderate increase in rates, based upon its own valuation of the properties. The Company, in its new disregard of the public, is appealing to the courts.

Similar instances have occurred throughout Indiana, Ohio, Illinois and rural communities throughout the country. In most instances there had been goodwill because the management had been local and had due regard for its public obligations. This condition usually changed with the new control, which acquired the property for the purpose of making as much money as possible, without regard to local feelings and reactions. This course has destroyed the goodwill that had existed, and has raised antagonism to the companies.

Undoubtedly, the local telephone properties could be more efficiently operated as part of a large system. Greater economies of operation would be possible, and improved service would be available; there would be attainable also a fair and liberal return to the people bringing about the readjustment; and the customers might be rewarded with lower rates. The difficulty has been that the interested groups have not been contented with reasonable profits for themselves. They have not considered the public nature of the business, have disregarded local conditions, have established wider ranges of monopoly, and have sought to the utmost to capitalize the monopolies for their own advantage. Here, let us repeat, is the reason for the growing antagonism to the utilities. If, as we assume, only a small proportion of all the utility people are involved, it is important that the small number be curbed in the interest of the utilities at large.

*

A $522,000,000 Utility Merger.—Last month we had an account of the so-called Consolidated Gas-Brooklyn Edison merger, through which the Consolidated Gas Company of New York acquired the capital stock of the Brooklyn Edison Company, and thus obtained control of practically the entire electric industry in the city of New York. In the meanwhile, the New York Public Service Commission has rejected a petition for rehearing presented by the City of New York and the Public Committee on Power.

The point of our article was the lack of consideration given to such an important development from the public standpoint. The movement of consolidations and the extension of holding companies is going on apace,—all without serious or adequate public consideration and control. As we are writing, we have before us a press statement reporting the control of the American Light & Traction Company purchased by the United Light & Power Company, bringing under a single management public utility properties with assets in excess of $522,000,000 at the close of 1927. Rumors of this particular merger have been circulated for some time. The final transaction, however, was clothed in extreme secrecy. It is said to involve the Koppers interests, linked with United Gas Improvement and other Mellon interests. It reaches into the city of New York, and includes the control of the Brooklyn Borough Gas Company. It is said to have a substantial interest also in Brooklyn Union Gas Company, which serves the greater part of Brooklyn and Queens in the city of New York.

The new system ramifies through wide sections of the country. It includes not only New York, New Jersey and Pennsylvania, but also Indiana, Illinois, Tennessee, Nebraska, Iowa, Ohio, Kansas, Missouri, Texas, Minnesota, Wisconsin, Michigan, and probably other states. The two large holding company groups are thus brought together under a single control, which in one way or another affects the destiny of communities in a large number of states. All this is accomplished as a private transaction, without any immediate public participation. While, perhaps, no substantial public injury will be perpetrated through this consolidation of managements, there is plainly a condition that cannot continue indefinitely, where large public affairs are consummated without public voice.

GOVERNMENTAL RESEARCH ASSOCIATION NOTES

EDITED BY RUSSELL FORBES

Secretary

California Taxpayers' Association.—After a year's work and study on the costs of government and expenditures for the city of San Diego, the tax experts of the California Taxpayers' Association have completed their survey.

The report numbers sixty pages and contains eight charts and two large maps. Numerous tables, scattered throughout the booklet, aid in carrying home the study of San Diego's expenditures in the past and the proposed expenditures for the future.

The survey is divided into two principal parts. First, the receipts and expenditures of the city from 1917 to 1926, inclusive, are examined, and, on the basis of these past expenditures, a financial program to the year 1936 is projected. The second part of the survey deals with the engineering features of the city government and contains an exhaustive study of the costs of operation of the water department and of the harbor department, together with a projected program for each of these departments to the year 1936.

A study of the school system has not been included in this survey because it was thoroughly studied in the San Diego county report, which the Association made public last May.

The intent of this research survey is to present the facts of government to the citizens of San Diego. After reading the report any San Diego citizen should know how his government is conducted, what its sources of income are, how its income is derived, and how it is expended.

The report makes a complete study of the various factors of San Diego's city government from 1917 to 1926. Eight factors of government were considered,—organization of the city government, population, assessed valuation, bonded indebtedness, receipts, disbursements, budgetary control and water consumption.

❦

Municipal Research Bureau of Cleveland.— The Bureau has issued a report on *Paving Work and Paving Costs in the City of Cleveland with an Analysis of Concrete Tests.*

The study of the financial requirements of the city of Cleveland, with an analysis of operating costs and capital improvement expenditures, has been completed and is ready for release.

The Bureau aided a citizens' committee in a study of a new jail and criminal courts building. The committee determined to place the building adjacent to the police headquarters' building, believing that this location would expedite the administration of criminal justice.

Aid is also being given to a citizens' committee which is studying regional government.

The staff has been augmented by J. Curtis Jenkins who was graduated last spring from the School of Citizenship and Public Affairs of Syracuse University.

❦

Milwaukee Citizens' Bureau.—The Citizens' Bureau has requested the common council, school board and county board of supervisors to appoint jointly a committee of citizens to formulate a ten-year public improvement program. The need of the most careful long-term planning was established by comparing the overwhelmingly long list of proposed projects with the limited financial ability of these governmental units. The possibility of new sources of revenue was reviewed in a statement of the present method of financing the construction of sewers. This indicated that while the city is eighty-two years old, one-third of the entire mileage of sewers in the city had been built during the last seven years. Only ten per cent of the cost was paid for by the owners of the property made salable by these improvements.

The financing of the expansion of the water system was cited as another illustration of the possibility of increasing the city's revenue. One-half of the city's investment in the water system has been paid in the last seven years out of the revenue resulting from the 1921 water rates increase, ostensibly made for the purpose of building a filtration plant. It is proposed that the citizens' ten-year improvement committee study the possibility of special assessments for water and sewer expansion.

The proposed strong-mayor proportional representation charter prepared by the City Charter League, to which the Citizens' Bureau acted as consultants, has been printed and distributed for criticism and comment. Preparations are being made for a strenuous campaign in anticipation of the April, 1929, referendum.

A study of the possibility of improving by-path streets to relieve traffic congestion instead of street widenings by setting back curbs or establishing building set-back lines, is being studied by the Citizens' Bureau.

✦

National Institute of Public Administration.—The report of the Subcommittee on Finances and Financial Administration of the New York City Committee on Plan and Survey was recently published by the Columbia University Press. This is the most comprehensive report on the finances of the city issued in recent years. Herbert H. Lehman was chairman of the subcommittee with Lindsay Rogers, Howard Lee McBain, and Robert Murray Haig as consultants. Luther Gulick formulated the research program for the report. Contributors to the different chapters were as follows:

Chapter I, "The Fiscal Structure," Joseph McGoldrick, of the department of government, Columbia University; Chapter II, "Expenditures," McGoldrick, Luther Gulick, and A. E. Buck; Chapter III, "Salaries," R. O. Beckman, examiner, Civil Service Commission, Cincinnati, Ohio, and Luther Gulick; Chapter IV, "Purchasing," Russell Forbes, secretary, National Municipal League; Chapter V, "Revenues," Luther Gulick and R. O. Beckman; Chapter VI, "Taxes and Assessments," Joseph McGoldrick and Luther Gulick; Chapter VII, "Debt" (in part), Paul Studensky, lecturer on public finance, New York University; and Chapter VIII, "Subway Finance," John Dickinson, assistant professor of politics, Princeton University.

The appendices were prepared by William Watson, Joseph McGoldrick, Ernest Wilvonseder, Robert M. Haig, and Donald H. Davenport.

Bruce Smith, of the National Institute of Public Administration, sailed for Europe on August 30 to study methods of collecting criminal statistics in European countries, in connection with his work for the Committee on Uniform Crime Records of the International Association of Chiefs of Police.

Donald C. Stone, formerly of the Cincinnati Bureau of Municipal Research, has joined Mr. Smith's staff at 261 Broadway, New York, and will be associated with him in the preparation of his report on uniform crime records.

✦

Schenectady Bureau of Municipal Research.—A. H. Hall, instructor in political science at Union College, who has joined the staff on a part-time basis, has completed his examination of the administration of Schenectady's civil service. The report not only covers the organization in general, but includes complete rules and regulations for the administration of the city's employment system, together with job classifications for the classified service and suggested salary standardization. The report will be submitted to the mayor and civil service commission after being reviewed by a special subcommittee of the Bureau directors.

City Hall Plan Competition.—On July 31 the Bureau submitted its report containing a suggested program of the manner of selecting an architect for the new city hall building by limited competition. It is gratifying to the Bureau that on August 15 the board of contract and supply approved the Bureau plan and is proceeding in accordance with its suggestions.

Long-Term Financial Program.—The capital budget commission, recently appointed by Mayor Fagal, is now considering the future financial plan for the city. Much attention has already been given to the income side of the budget for the next five years. The Bureau staff has been spending a large part of its time in compiling material for this important project.

A report covering the problem in a general way has already been submitted to the commission. Additional sections dealing with the city's population growth, physical expansion and bonded indebtedness have also been completed. These will be submitted to the commission shortly. A detailed study of present and possible sources of revenues is also nearing completion. This latter study will complete the investigation of the income side of the anticipated budgets for the future period.

Building Code.—The Bureau is preparing a review of the proposed new building code. This is expected to be completed during the next few weeks and will be submitted to the mayor and to the chairman of the committee on laws and ordinances shortly thereafter.

MUNICIPAL ACTIVITIES ABROAD

EDITED BY W. E. MOSHER

Director, School of Citizenship and Public Affairs, Syracuse University

City and Regional Planning.—(a) Preservation of Rural England.—A Council for the Preservation of Rural England has been recently formed, consisting of representatives of local governmental units. In general its purpose is to make the most of the resources of the countryside in any given region, guarding on the one hand against the destruction of attractive features, and planning on the other for the best possible utilization of natural and other resources from the economic, scenic and related viewpoints.

This council would inspire the members of town and county councils as well as the joint town or regional planning committees to look upon their task of planning for the future in the broadest possible way. The power that may be exercised and that should be exercised by these agencies includes the following: zoning; the reservation of wide areas to be retained either for agriculture or open to public use; construction of roads and highways that will relieve congestion in towns and villages on the one hand, and will destroy attractive views as little as possible on the other; prescribing adequate building lines; control of design and materials used in building, so that eyesores may be avoided, and the like.

When it is considered that forty-five regional planning committees are now in existence in England and Wales and that their functions cover an area of six and a quarter million acres, it seems clear that the ambitious program of preserving the attractiveness of the countryside and even making it more attractive may in considerable measure be realized. —*Local Government News*, November, 1927.

(b) The Place of Color in City Planning.—An organization has been launched recently in Germany whose purpose is to arouse interest in the introduction of color schemes as a part of the city planning program. This organization has its headquarters in Hamburg. It publishes a periodical entitled, "The Colored City" (*Die Farbige Stadt*). Its policy is to coöperate with the established organs of administration not alone of the city, but also of the township, county and the state; further, with associations of artists, architects, contractors, houseowners, and trade unions; finally, with technical and trade schools and academies offering training in the fine arts. Its thesis is that the recognition of color as a necessary unit in the development of a city is defensible from the points of view of art, physiology, psychology, and good business. The program of the union embraces education, research, publicity of all kinds, and the maintenance of an information center. The annual dues are fifty marks a year for organizations, and fifteen marks a year for individuals.

That this is not the dream of fantastic idealists is proved by the progress which has been made by the city of Osnabrück. Through the interest and coöperation of the building and housing bureaus of the city government and of the public at large this city has undergone a transformation that immediately strikes the eye of the visitor. A comprehensive color policy has been laid out and widely adopted. It is based on the belief that every structure needs color and that there is a color appropriate to it in its surroundings. The progress already made is in no way due to compulsion; friendly competition and civic pride have been sufficient incentives. As a consequence Osnabrück bids fair to become a pioneer in the use of color for the purpose of enhancing the beauty and attractiveness of its streets and buildings.—*Zeitschrift für Kommunalwirtschaft*, issues of June 25 and July 25, 1928.

✵

Centralization and Decentralization.—An interesting charter has been drawn up for the suburb of Höchst, a town of 3,000 inhabitants, that was recently incorporated into the city of Frankfurt-on-the-Main. The basic conditions in this charter are the following: (a) that the town of Höchst, shall constitute an electoral district by itself, (b) that in its administration as large a number as possible of the representatives shall have a share, (c) that the greatest possible flexibility will be permitted in carrying on the work of the community of Höchst in so far as this does not interfere with the interests of the rest of the city.

Practically, the administration of the suburb is carried on under the auspices of a special district bureau. The city officials with whom the population of Höchst normally come into contact are under the direction of this bureau. In other words, decentralization has taken place so far as most branches of the administration are concerned. Technical control, however, such as of the building department, fire department, hospital, etc., is centralized in the main offices of the city of Frankfurt. It should be noted that a separate unit of the police department has been set up for Höchst.

At the head of the district bureau is a member of the central administration in Frankfurt, but as it happens he was formerly the highest official in the town of Höchst before it united with Frankfurt. The executive head who works under the official just named was also formerly connected with the local government. A special committee is appointed from the council of Frankfurt and charged with general powers concerning the suburb. It coöperates like any other councilmanic committee with the administration of the town. The majority of its membership consists of those who have been originally nominated by the district council of Höchst.

The district council is a representative body consisting of twenty-five members who are elected at the rate of one for every 2,000 inhabitants. The councilmen of the central body of Frankfurt who are elected from Höchst are also members of this council. In this way, the local council of the smaller unit is kept in touch with the council of the city at large.

The functions of the council are advisory. One special function is that it shall watch over the observance of the agreement made between Frankfurt and Höchst at the time of the latter's incorporation and raise objections to any apparent infringement of rights on the part of the central government.

The chief connection between the council of Höchst and the governing body as well as the administration of Frankfurt, is obviously the official head of the district bureau. He is a member of the central government. He has his seat in the district council. He is responsible for the actual administration of the town. Finally, it is provided that in connection with any transaction affecting the district of Höchst, the district shall have the right to demand the appointment of its councilmen from the central body to any

committees or deputations upon which it is otherwise not represented. Committee members are to have only advisory powers.

It should be noted that no basic concessions have been made to Höchst so far as finance and budget are concerned. The necessity for centralization in this respect is obvious. Finally, it should be mentioned that this arrangement may be terminated at the end of fifteen years. It is considered in Germany to be a very interesting and promising break with the normal tendency toward complete centralization.—*Zeitschrift für Kommunalwirtschaft*, June 25, 1928.

✶

English Local Government.—For one interested in a condensed analysis and criticism of important aspects of the structure and method of local administration in England the July issue of *Public Administration* will be of much value. Those who have been accustomed to think of the efficiency and quality of the English local government as a goal to be hoped for but not attained, will find some solace in the remarks of Mr. E. D. Simon. The pessimistic note that he strikes at the outset reminds one very much of an American critic writing of home affairs. Such phrases as "apathy," "decline of civic spirit," "real risk of degeneration in our local government" sound an alarm with which we are all too familiar on this side of the water. The following sentence also has a familiar sound: "The average person feels that our local government is well and honestly run, that it is an utterly boring subject, and that his sole duty consists in giving a casual vote once a year and otherwise leaving it alone."

We are no less astonished when we read that the English would do well to emulate the city of Chicago with its twelve hundred voluntary associations "concerned in some way with endeavoring to promote better local government"; further, that the English might well follow our example and reduce the number of councilmen; and finally, that they would find it advantageous to found a national municipal research bureau modelled after the New York Bureau of Municipal Research. An American reviewer cannot fail to take satisfaction in the fact that we apparently have something to contribute to a country so long and favorably known in the field of local government.

Turning from the introductory statement, we find that the whole of the July issue is devoted to a series of papers read at a special summer conference of the Institute of Public Administration held in Cambridge at the end of June. The program consisted for the most part of the discussion of three topics, dealing (1) with the effect on administrative organization and methods of the increasing scope and diversity in their work as it concerns the elected counsellor and the staff officials, with emphasis upon the relation of the council and the staff; (2) with the organization of central bodies for promoting the services carried on by local authorities, such as the provision of information and advice concerning the organization and administration of the various offices, and finally, with the subject of centralized purchasing; (3) with the methods of selecting local officials.

The authors of the papers in this issue of *Public Administration* were exceptionally well-qualified to talk upon the subjects assigned to them, so that altogether they constitute a brief and excellent diagnosis of important conditions now obtaining in local government in England.

Emphasis is laid upon the importance of better coördination under a responsible and competent head, preferably the town clerk. Belief in the committee system was subscribed to in various quarters, and whenever the city manager idea was advanced it was scouted as being inapplicable to English conditions. In dealing with the desirable reorganization of the county authority, one of the speakers advanced the idea that there should be thoroughgoing centralization of control within any given county unit excepting the large cities and that a permanent executive should be appointed to serve under the legislative authority of the county. This sounds familiar to some of our ears.

The readers of the REVIEW who have been supporters of the Bureau of Municipal Research in one city or another will be gratified to know that the British spokesman on the topic of central agencies felt keenly the need of a central body for the purpose of disseminating information and giving advice with reference to matters of local administration. Due recognition was given to the central bodies already existing whether in the form of national associations of public officials or of governmental bureaus as in Ministry of Health, the Home Office, and Board of Trade, and the like. A new central agency was advocated that would not alone provide information concerning the various functions of government, but also might well contribute to more general knowledge concerning office technique, accounting, county methods, etc. Specific reference was made to the New York Bureau of Municipal Research as a model for this agency.

One paper was devoted exclusively to the discussion of the possibility of centralized purchasing. It was felt in the main that this is a task of coördination between the departments of the government of any given city. Proposals made on this subject are well known to those who are acquainted with centralized purchasing in this country.

Finally, four papers dealt with examinations for local officials. The underlying belief seemed to be that such examinations are feasible for the whole country. Although we think of England as the mother of the civil service system there was no reference to the adoption on the part of local authorities of the idea of civil service commission. There was agreement in the main that the examining body for the various local units should consist of representatives from the association of councils, that is, the legislative branches from professional organizations of public officials and the National Association of Local Government Officials. In one or two instances it was suggested that universities and technical schools should also find representation upon the examining board.—*Public Administration*, July, 1928.

NOTES AND EVENTS

EDITED BY RUSSELL FORBES

Toledo to Submit Two Charters to Referendum in November.—In last month's issue we reported that the city manager-P. R. charter, devised by the charter commission, is to be submitted to the voters for approval in November. Since that time a minority of the charter commission, who refused to approve the majority report, have formulated an alternative charter. The minority charter was passed by the council on August 23. It differs chiefly from the report of the majority group in providing for election of councilmen by wards instead of by proportional representation.

The alternative charter was vetoed by Mayor Jackson September 1. In his veto message, the mayor scored the action of the minority group, charging in part that

Some of the representatives of the people in this free city of ours were threatened with political oblivion, intimidated and coerced to a point where they were practically forced to vote for the measure against their better judgment. . . . I cannot believe that a councilman is doing justice to his constituents by voting for legislation which was prepared by a dissatisfied, disgruntled minority, shrouded in mystery, and rushed through by political connivery and personal threats.

The passage of this legislation, in my opinion, is a serious indictment of representative government in our community. The whole procedure is disgusting to friends of good government.

On the same day as the mayor's veto message was delivered, the court of common pleas held that the mayor's signature was unnecessary to charter amendments, and issued a writ of mandamus, which ordered the city clerk to certify the minority charter to the board of elections. Unless this decision is reversed in a higher court, both charters will appear on the ballot in November.

❖

Institute of Municipal Administration.— Marking the beginning of a new epoch in the study of municipal problems, an institute of municipal administration, under the division of public administration, was held at the University of Southern California, August 13 to 18, inclusive. The institute represents a concrete expression of the belief held by President R. B. von Kleinsmid of the University, that universities exist for the welfare of the community.

One of the outstanding features was the series of lectures delivered by Dr. Otto Schreiber of Germany. Dr. Schreiber holds the chair of law governing aeronautics at Koenigsberg University, Germany. Other features were the lectures delivered by the following national authorities on the subjects given: William B. Munro of Harvard University, "General Problems of Municipal Government"; Miller McClintock of Harvard University, "Street Traffic Control"; Abel Wolman, chief engineer, State Department of Health, Maryland, "Sanitary Engineering"; Ira Hiscock, associate professor of health, Yale University, "Public Health"; Francis H. Hiller, field representative, National Probation Association, "Juvenile Dependency and Delinquency"; Charles M. Spofford, civil engineering, Massachusetts Institute of Technology, "Bridge Engineering"; John N. Edy, president, International City Managers' Association, "City Clerkship Administration"; Tipton R. Snavely, professor of economics, University of Virginia, "Taxation and Assessment"; Edwin A. Cottrell, Stanford University, "Budgets and Accounts."

The institute was very ably handled by Professor Emery E. Olson of the University, as director, with the assistance of a group of public-minded citizens. The institute brought together some 600 public officials and interested citizens. The interest taken by public officials is indicated by the fact that 467 registered for the different courses offered by the institute. A very high standard has been set for all similar future gatherings.

ROY MALCOM.
University of Southern California.

❖

Institute of Public Affairs, University of Virginia.—The second session of the institute of public affairs was held at the University of Virginia, August 6 to 18. It was well attended and its program was interesting and varied. Round tables occupied the early part of each morning, followed by an open forum participated in by the whole institute. Evening lectures in the McIntire amphitheatre completed the day's round of activities. Among the round tables of most interest to the readers of the REVIEW were those on: "Taxation," led by Mark Graves; "County Government," led by Kirk Porter; "Political Parties," led by A. R. Hatton; and "Municipal Management," led by Thomas H. Reed. Among those who participated in these round tables were Professor E. W. Crecraft of Akron, Walter Millard, Leyton Carter, and several members of the staff of the Cleveland Bureau of Municipal Research. The high spots in the round table on Municipal Management were the discussion of personnel administration opened by Fred Telford of the Bureau of Public Personnel Administration, and the discussion of municipal accounting and reporting.

The chief excitement at the institute arose in connection with some of the open forums. The first of them, conducted by Professor Hatton, related to the question as to whether any real difference of principle now divided the Republican from the Democratic party. It provoked several fiery bursts of oratory. The open forum on the press brought out an incidental attack on Governor Smith's religion which caused another succession of super-heated speeches. Less irritating and dramatic, but perhaps of more constructive importance, were the discussions of regional government and the county manager plan. The first of these was lead by Professor Reed, and included papers on the Pittsburgh and Cleveland proposals for solving the metropolitan problem, by Joseph T. Miller, and Leyton Carter, respectively. Professor Porter decried the necessity of a county manager and was supported by his senior colleague at Iowa, Professor Shambaugh. Walter Millard very effectively presented the merits of the manager plan.

The most significant contribution of the institute this year as last was the mingling of Northern and Southern points of view. Most persons who live either North or South fail to realize the extent of difference in attitude of the two sections, or when they do catch a glimpse of the opinions prevalent in the other section they react against them with violent prejudice. No Northerner could fail to be edified by the exposition of the reasons underlying the "solid South" as expressed by Mrs. Sarah Lee Fane, the brilliant and beautiful representative of Norfolk in the Virginia legislature. Professor William E. Dodd of Chicago University, Virginian by birth, approached the same subject in an interpretive

address of extraordinary merit. We of the Northern delegation can only hope that we gave something worth while in return. A note of broad and sympathetic nationalism was struck in the address of W. R. Lounsbery of New York which left a lasting impression on his audience. It is good for men and women of both sections to mix and talk things over frankly even at the expense of having to listen to a lot of nerve-roughening disagreements on prohibition, religion and party candidates.

If I may be pardoned a personal word, I liked it so much I am going back for more at the first opportunity.

THOMAS H. REED.

University of Michigan.

♣

Reading Appoints Supervisor of Public Machinery.—The city of Reading, Pennsylvania, has recently established the office of supervisor of public machinery. The supervisor "shall have the care, management, direction, control and administration of the maintenance and repair of all motor vehicles, fire apparatus, pumps, and other machinery of every kind and description belonging to or used by any of the departments, bureaus, boards and other agencies of the city. All such departments, bureaus, boards and agencies shall obtain all repairs and replacement parts for machinery through the supervisor of public machinery, and not by direct contract with private parties, nor by having said repairing done under their own supervision. It shall be unlawful for the city controller to countersign, or the city treasurer to pay, any warrants or checks for repairs to, or replacement parts for machinery, except upon certificate of the supervisor of public machinery, that such parts or repairs have been obtained by his authority and under his supervision."

The supervisor is given authority to organize and manage a municipal machine shop in which all repairs to public machinery are to be made. All necessary equipment and repairs are to be procured through the office of the city purchasing agent.

A few other cities have centralized the custody and maintenance of motor equipment, but Reading is believed to be the pioneer in centralizing the control of all public machinery in the hands of one official.

♣

New Jersey Adopts Uniform Traffic Law.— On September 1 a uniform traffic law became effective throughout the state of New Jersey. The law represents three years' study by the State Traffic Commission and was adopted by the New Jersey legislature at its 1928 session after introduction by Assemblyman Russell Wise of Passaic County.

The new law enforces uniform traffic regulations in all municipalities and counties of New Jersey. Municipalities are given three years in which to change their local traffic signals in compliance with the law. Center traffic signals, whether automatic or controlled by police, are abolished. The new uniform traffic rules, as summarized in the New York *World* on August 30, are as follows:

No jay walking.

Persons are not to throw from any motor car while in motion, any goods, bundles or merchandise.

Coasting down hill with clutch out or gears in neutral is prohibited.

Pedestrians are prohibited from crossing a street against a stop signal and can use only the designated crosswalk when the signal or officers give them the right of way.

At intersections where traffic is controlled, pedestrians have the right of way over all traffic.

It is unlawful for any person to solicit or stop motor vehicles in the roadway for the purpose of asking for rides.

Forty miles an hour in open country where traffic is not controlled; ten miles an hour while passing a school; fifteen miles an hour on curves and on grades when the driver's view is obstructed within a distance of 100 feet; twenty miles an hour in business districts where traffic is under control and in all residential districts; fifteen miles an hour in business districts where traffic is not controlled.

A three-color system of traffic lights is to be used. The colors are red, amber and green. The latter will be the signal to proceed. Amber will be used as a caution sign for the exclusive use of pedestrians.

Various colors and dimensions for traffic signs have been provided in the law. Stop signs are to be all yellow with red letters and with the word "stop" painted in the center. Slow and caution signs are to have a yellow background with black lettering; direction, information, restriction, one-way and detour signs, white background with black lettering. Corners and edges of all signs are to be rounded slightly for safety.

✢

Fifteenth Annual Convention of the International City Managers' Association.—The International City Managers' Association met in annual convention at the Kenilworth Inn, Asheville, N. C., on September 17-20. On the opening day the forenoon session was given over to the address of welcome by the mayor of Asheville, N. C., and the annual reports of the president and secretary of the association. The afternoon session consisted of reports of association committees.

On the evening of Sept. 19, Louis Brownlow, consultant to the City Housing Corporation of New York City, addressed the annual banquet of the association on "The Human Element in City Administration."

At the various sessions during the convention, round table meetings were held on the following subjects:

Development of airports.

Training for the profession of public management.

Given a community expending a certain sum of money for the operation of its administrative services—How can a reduction of the expenses of operating those services be effected without impairing the cost of the services?

A short course for the new men in the profession under the leadership of the elder members of the profession.

Should not the towns and cities unite in concerted effort to procure their just proportion of the proceeds of the gasoline tax?

Fundamentals of public service.

Problems of the city manager in the large city.

Problems of the city manager in the small city.

A discussion of the practical application of city planning and zoning, its inception and growth, and whether actual results are measuring up to expectations.

Municipal insurance, group insurance and pensions.

Street traffic control.

A feature of the convention was an address by Arthur Collins, secretary of the Institute of British Municipal Treasurers and Accountants, on the subject of "British City Accounting and Taxation." The international interest in the city manager plan was further shown by an address by Dr. Leonard D. White, of the University of Chicago, on "English Opinion of the City Manager Plan." An address was also given on "Centralized Purchasing in Cities" by Russell Forbes, secretary of the National Municipal League.

The proceedings of the convention will be published in the annual yearbook of the City Managers' Association.

FEDERAL AID TO THE STATES

Report of the
COMMITTEE ON FEDERAL AID TO THE STATES
OF THE NATIONAL MUNICIPAL LEAGUE

Prepared by
Austin F. Macdonald, University of Pennsylvania, *Chairman*

Supplement to the
National Municipal Review
October, 1928.   Vol. XVII, No. 10

PUBLISHED BY
NATIONAL MUNICIPAL LEAGUE
261 Broadway, New York, N. Y.

FOREWORD

The committee on Federal Aid to the States was appointed by the National Municipal League in 1927. The personnel, as shown below, is representative of the various groups interested in this important subject.

The preparation of the committee's report was intrusted to the chairman, Professor Austin F. Macdonald of the University of Pennsylvania, who made an exhaustive study of all phases of the system of federal aid and who is today an outstanding authority on the subject. Although the report was prepared by the chairman, the other committee members have given advice and suggestions for certain minor corrections which are incorporated in this final draft.

Part I of the report summarizes the origin, development, and present extent of federal aid to the states. Part II concisely discusses the federal-aid laws and appraises the manner in which they are administered. Part III is a critical estimate of the federal-aid system, with recommendations by the committee for needed improvements in administration by the federal and state governments.

The personnel of the committee which sponsors this report is as follows:

AUSTIN F. MACDONALD, *Chairman,*
    University of Pennsylvania

H. J. BAKER,
    State Director of Agricultural Extension Work,
    Rutgers College, New Brunswick, New Jersey

MRS. LA RUE BROWN,
    National League of Women Voters

PAUL H. DOUGLAS,
    University of Chicago

THOMAS H. MACDONALD,
    Chief, Bureau of Public Roads, U. S. Department of
    Agriculture

JOHN N. MACKALL,
    Chairman, State Road Commission, Maryland

JOHN K. NORTON,
    Director of Research, National Education Association

S. H. THOMPSON,
    President, American Farm Bureau Federation

JAMES T. YOUNG
    University of Pennsylvania

TABLE OF CONTENTS

	PAGE
PART I—INTRODUCTION.	619
Provisions of the Weeks Act	619
Growth of Federal Subsidy	621
States Rights and Federal Aid	622
Constitutionality of Federal Aid	624
Results of Federal Aid	626
PART II—THE SUBSIDY SYSTEM	627
Forest Fire Prevention	627
Agricultural Extension Work	631
Highways	635
The National Guard	637
Vocational Education	640
Vocational Rehabilitation	644
Hygiene of Maternity and Infancy	647
PART III—CONCLUSIONS	651
Summary of Conclusions	651
Recommended Changes in Federal Subsidy Systems	658

PART I

INTRODUCTION

THE history of the present federal aid policy dates from 1911. In that year Congress passed a statute, popularly known as the Weeks Act, which contained an appropriation of two hundred thousand dollars "to enable the Secretary of Agriculture to cooperate with any State or group of States, when requested to do so, in protection from fire of the forested watersheds of navigable streams." [1]

There was nothing new or unusual about the payment of federal funds to the states. For more than a century Congress had been busily engaged in granting to the states millions of acres of federal domain and millions of dollars of federal money.[2] Nor was it surprising that the act should specify the purpose for which the subsidy was to be used. Nearly all the earlier grants carried with them the stipulation that they must be used for schools or roads, or for some other definite purpose.[3] In fact, when Congress authorized federal subsidies to the states for the establishment of state agricultural colleges and agricultural experiment stations, it even went so far as to require annual reports from the colleges and stations established under the several acts.[4]

PROVISIONS OF THE WEEKS ACT

But the Weeks Act was unique in that it provided for federal inspection

of state activities, and made continuance of federal aid dependent upon federal approval of state plans. In other words, it purchased for the federal government a measure of control over matters which had commonly been regarded as affairs of purely state concern ever since the adoption of the federal Constitution. Earlier subsidy laws had directed in general terms that the grants be used for highways or for schools, but they had made no attempt to specify the kinds of highways or the types of schools. Still more significant, they had established no medium through which the federal government could learn whether the states were keeping faith. Under their provisions some states might choose to squander their allotments,[5] while other states might use their portions with honesty and foresight; but in any event federal funds would continue to descend, with almost divine beneficence, upon the just and the unjust alike.

The Act of 1911 set up a new standard. The federal grant for fire protection, though expended by state officials, must be spent by them subject to federal approval. Their fire prevention plans must be satisfactory to the

[5] Many states did squander their allotments. In 1919 the state treasurer of Wisconsin declared: "If the State of Wisconsin had not practically given away its valuable school lands years ago, we would not have to raise any school taxes for generations to come. In years gone by, the State sold hundreds of thousands of acres of fine timber lands for a mere song. Had that timber been preserved . . . it would now maintain the schools of the State for generations to come without raising one cent for school purposes by taxation." (Keith and Bagley, *op. cit.*, pp. 55–61.) Instances of this sort might be multiplied *ad nauseam.*

[1] 36 Stat. L. 961.

[2] *Cf.* Orfield, M. N., *Federal Land Grants to the States*, and Keith and Bagley, *The Nation and the Schools.*

[3] An act of Congress of 1802 granted land to Ohio for the use of schools. *Cf.* 2 Stat. L. 173.

[4] 12 Stat. L. 503; 14 Stat. L. 208; 24 Stat. L. 440; 25 Stat. L. 176; 26 Stat. L. 417; 34 Stat. L. 63, 1256, 1281.

federal Forest Service. Equally significant, every allotment received from the federal treasury must be matched dollar for dollar by state funds. And even the manner of spending these state appropriations must meet the approval of federal officials. The Weeks Law thus contained in embryonic form the essential features of the present subsidy system—all details of administration in state hands, subject to federal approval, and state matching of federal funds.

FEATURES OF THE SUBSIDY SYSTEM

It was not long before the principles of the 1911 law were embodied in other statutes. In 1914 Congress passed an act providing for a subsidy of several million dollars to stimulate agricultural extension work, and during the following seven years six other federal aid measures were enacted into law.[1] All these acts contain certain features in common—features which have now become characteristic of the American subsidy system. They provide for the payment of money from the federal treasury to the states. This money is apportioned, generally speaking, on the basis of population.[2]

Three important conditions are attached to every one of these newer federal aid laws. The first condition imposed is that a state, before receiving federal funds, must formally accept the federal offer. Acceptance implies that it will do its share to make the work a success. It involves the establishment of a coöperating state agency. If federal bureaus are to coöperate with

[1] One of them, the Chamberlin-Kahn Act, providing for the control of venereal disease, was essentially a war-time measure, and work under it has since been discontinued.

[2] The forest fire prevention subsidy is an exception. Population is only one of three bases used in determining the apportionment of funds for highway construction.

state governments, they must have state agencies with which to do their coöperating.

The second stipulation is that a dollar of state funds must be appropriated for every dollar of federal funds received. The appropriation of state money is a *prima facie* evidence of good faith; it is concrete evidence that the state is interested in the work, and is willing to do something more than spend the federal allotment. As a matter of fact, most states do considerably better than match the federal subsidy; frequently the state appropriation is two or three times as large as the federal grant.

The third condition is by far the most important. It is that state plans must be approved by federal officials, and that state and federal money alike must be spent under federal supervision. The initiative remains in state hands. State officials prepare their budgets, formulate their policies, outline their plans. State officials choose their subordinates, direct the actual work, spend the money. But state budgets, policies and plans must be approved by the federal government. State standards must be acceptable to federal officials. State activity must produce results.

ACCEPTANCE OPTIONAL WITH STATES

There is no suggestion of compulsion in all this. A state must establish a board of vocational education, a highway department, or the like, only if it wishes to secure its share of the federal grant. Its plans must conform to federal standards only if it desires to obtain federal money. It is entirely free to refuse the federal offer, and to carry on its own program without federal inspections or federal advice. Or it may make no provision whatever for vocational education or highway construction, as it sees fit. But in order to become eligible for the federal allotment, it must formulate satisfactory plans, and must execute them in a satisfactory manner.

The federal offer is in no sense a club. It is an inducement intended to secure a reasonable measure of uniformity and reasonable minimum standards without taking from the states the control of their own affairs. In fact, it is so powerful an inducement that scarcely a state can resist it. All the states accept the federal subsidy for vocational education, for highways, for agricultural extension work. Only one refuses its National Guard allotment. Forty have adopted approved programs of civilian rehabilitation, and forty-five are coöperating with the federal government in child hygiene work. The number of states qualifying for the forest fire prevention subsidy is limited, of course, by the number of states having forests and forest fire problems. Without attempting coercion in any way the federal government has found a means of inducing virtually all the states to pay respectful attention to its suggestions.

In 1912, the first year of coöperation with the states under the Weeks Law, the total amount of federal funds paid to the state governments was a trifle more than eight million dollars. Most of this money—ninety-nine per cent of it, in fact—went for purposes over which the federal government exercised virtually no control. State agricultural colleges and agricultural experiment stations were large beneficiaries. Large sums were paid to the states from the sale of federal lands within their borders. The state militia organizations were supported in considerable part with federal money. And these grants were made without any real attempt to insure their proper use. The states were left to their own devices.

IMPROVED STANDARDS OF ADMINISTRATION

But the Weeks Law established an important precedent. It pointed the way to improved standards and more satisfactory results. Congress began to realize the possibilities inherent in a system of federal aid. Since federal money was to be paid to the states, the federal government might well ask something in return. It might require the states to establish proper standards, and it might demand the right to satisfy itself that these standards were maintained.

THE GROWTH OF FEDERAL SUBSIDY

Since 1915 federal subsidies to the states have grown by leaps and bounds. In 1915 the total of federal payments was ten million dollars; by 1920 it was nearly thirty-six millions. The next year it mounted to ninety million dollars, an increase of one hundred and fifty per cent within a period of twelve months. The 1927 federal-aid payments amounted to one hundred and thirty-six million dollars. Compared with the eight millions of 1912, the 1927 total seems large indeed. But far more significant than the amount is the fact that ninety-five per cent is given to the states with definite conditions attached. Ninety-five per cent is paid to the states only after state work has met the approval of federal inspectors.

The chart on the following page shows the growth of federal aid, year by year, since 1912.

The largest subsidy is for highway construction. Nearly sixty per cent of all federal aid is for this purpose. Twenty-three per cent is for arming and equipping the National Guard. No other subsidy takes as much as five per cent of the total. The table on the following page shows the distribution of federal aid for the fiscal year ending June 30, 1927.

FEDERAL AID PAYMENTS TO THE STATES, 1912–27 [1]

1912	$8,149,478.21
1913	7,752,961.01
1914	10,533,660.78
1915	10,352,211.79
1916	12,645,489.02
1917	15,625,056.55
1918	22,805,680.12
1919	22,104,992.13
1920	35,923,706.48
1921	90,437,848.13
1922	128,366,639.95
1923	111,727,193.28
1924	128,067,312.27
1925	147,351,393.22
1926	141,614,101.05
1927	136,659,786.47

[1] This chart is taken from Macdonald, Austin F., *Federal Aid*, p. 7, Crowell, 1928.

FEDERAL AID PAYMENTS TO THE STATES FOR THE
FISCAL YEAR 1927

Support of agricultural colleges....	$2,400,000.00
Support of Experiment Stations....	2,400,000.00
Coöperative agricultural extension work........................	* 6,875,727.55
Vocational education............	7,184,901.51
Vocational rehabilitation........	880,263.00
Highways.....................	81,371,013.03
National Guard........	31,363,935.31
Forest fire prevention...........	654,101.57
Distribution of nursery stock.....	71,194.61
Forestry extension work	46,241.64
Maternity and infancy hygiene....	899,824.71
State fund under oil leasing act....	2,498,689.58
State fund from sale of public lands	*13,893.96
Total.....................	$136,659,786.47

*1926.

Nor does this table tell the entire story. The states received thousands of acres of federal domain during 1927. They were given a considerable amount of surplus war material to aid their highway departments in road building. They were paid small sums for the elimination of agricultural insect pests, the eradication of plant diseases, and the like, though the exact amount of these grants cannot be determined with accuracy. So one hundred and thirty-six million dollars is a conservative figure.

STATES RIGHTS AND FEDERAL AID

The federal-aid movement, as it has evolved since 1911, is an attempt to combine the need for national standards with the desire for local autonomy. The importance of local self-government is widely recognized in the United States; it has been stressed for more than a century by nearly every president from Jefferson to Coolidge. The right of the states to control their own affairs is traditional. It is a right supported not only by a written constitution but also by an omnipotent public opinion.

Yet time is making increasingly clear the fact that the states cannot be left entirely to their own devices. Their interests are so closely interwoven, their dependence on one another is so great, that today every state has a very vital interest in what every other state is doing. Some years ago Professor Gale Lowrie formulated the principle that governmental power should be as broad as the problems with which it must deal. When this criterion is applied to the field of state government, the limited sphere of state activity becomes apparent. Highway construction cannot remain solely in state hands, for good roads are a matter of national concern. The equipment and training of state troops cannot be entrusted entirely to the states, for those troops may at any time be needed to protect the nation. The great forests are an important part of the nation's wealth, and their protection from fire cannot be left entirely to state forestry departments. It is obvious, however, that we cannot transfer complete control over our highways, our forests, our education, and a dozen other functions to Washington. While it is important to emphasize the nation's interest in Missouri's highways, for example, it is also essential to remember that Missouri has a most vital interest in its own roads. The establishment of national standards is essential, but no less essential is the preservation of state autonomy, so that programs and policies may be varied to meet varying local needs.

The outstanding problem of American administration is to harmonize the conflicting interests of the nation and of the states, to set up a national minimum of performance, and yet to retain control primarily in the forty-eight commonwealths. The subsidy program of the federal government offers a practical solution of that problem. It insures the recognition of local needs by placing responsibility in state hands. State officials formulate their own plans; state officials spend their own money and federal money as well; state officials direct the actual work of road building, child hygiene, or whatever it may be, from start to finish.

FEDERAL ENFORCEMENT OF STANDARDS

But all state plans, all state expenditures, all state work must be approved by the federal government before federal funds are paid to the states. And state programs that make provision for something less than the national minimum are certain to be rejected by the federal authorities. The "national minimum" is a very intangible but very real thing. It applies to every part of the country, but its exact meaning varies from section to section. Highways financed in part with federal funds, for example, must be properly designed. Satisfactory materials must be used in their construction. Those rules hold good whether the road is to be built across the Arizona desert or across a strip of New Jersey farmland. But it does not follow that the same materials must be used in both states. Nor is it at all likely that a highway designed for Arizona's needs will meet the requirements of Jersey's traffic. Obviously the establishment of national standards does not mean the adoption of a policy of deadening uniformity, without regard for local conditions and local practices.

For more than half a century every attempt to impose restrictions upon the use of land or money granted by the federal government to the states has met with bitter opposition. Many states have squandered wantonly the proceeds from the sale of federal lands turned over to them by various acts of Congress, though other states have prudently administered the funds thus obtained. When the famous twenty million dollar surplus of the federal government was distributed among the states in 1837, most of them wasted it on wildcat schemes or spent it for temporary needs.[1] Yet there have always been some persons to defend the privilege of the states to squander or to hoard as they might see fit. Doughty champions of state sovereignty have

[1] Keith and Bagley, *op. cit.*, pp. 55–61.

long contested the right of the federal government to protect its gifts by imposing conditions that would guarantee their proper use.

The first attempt to safeguard a federal subsidy was made in 1857, when Justin S. Morrill, a representative from Vermont, introduced in the House a bill providing that a portion of the public lands be granted to the several states, the proceeds from the sale of these lands to be used for the establishment and maintenance of colleges devoted to agriculture and the mechanic arts. It must be admitted that the effort to protect federal funds was most feeble. In return for lands worth millions of dollars the states were required only to establish agricultural colleges and to make annual reports, through their governors, on the progress of the institutions.

The bill contained no suggestion of federal inspection or supervision. Yet its introduction was the occasion for a veritable storm of protest from the Southern members in both houses of Congress. Senator Mason of Virginia expressed his opinion of the measure in no uncertain terms. "It is using the public lands as a means of controlling the policy of the state legislature," he said. "It is an unconstitutional robbery of the Treasury for the purpose of bribing the states. Suppose the bill was to appropriate eight or ten million dollars from the Treasury, for the purpose of building up agricultural colleges in the states, would honorable senators who patronize this bill vote for the appropriation; and if they would not, why not? If they have the power to do it, and they believe it is expedient to do it, why would they not just as well take the money from the Treasury, to build up agricultural colleges, as to take public lands? . . . It requires no prophet, it requires none particularly conversant with the workings of any

government, more especially this, to see that in a very short time the whole agricultural interests of the country will be taken out of the hands of the states and subjected to the action of Congress."[1]

IS FEDERAL AID CONSTITUTIONAL ?

Just as Senator Mason advanced the argument of unconstitutionality seventy years ago, so today there are some persons in public life who maintain that the present federal-aid policy is a violation of the rights of the states. Speaking before the Pennsylvania State Chamber of Commerce in the fall of 1925, Governor Albert C. Ritchie of Maryland declared: "It simply cannot be argued that the Federal Government has any right to use federal funds as a means of acquiring a control over local state purposes, which under the Constitution is not granted to the Government but is reserved to the states. That, under our present Constitution, is simply indefensible."

The Supreme Court of the United States, however, is not in complete accord with the Governor of Maryland. Its opinion concerning the subsidy policy of the federal government, delivered in 1923, is difficult to reconcile with Governor Ritchie's views of 1925. "If Congress enacted [subsidy legislation] with the ulterior purpose of tempting [the states] to yield," said the Court, "that purpose may be effectively frustrated by the simple expedient of not yielding." Yet Governor Ritchie and others still maintain that from a constitutional standpoint federal aid "is simply indefensible." The question of constitutionality came before the courts in 1922, when one Harriet A. Frothingham, a resident of Massachusetts, brought suit to prevent the

[1] *Congressional Globe*, 35th Congress, 2nd Session, p. 718.

enforcement of the Sheppard-Towner Act. This law provides for federal aid to the states in reducing maternal and infant mortality and in protecting the health of mothers and infants. When the suit reached the Supreme Court it was joined to a separate action by the State of Massachusetts, also contesting the constitutionality of the Sheppard-Towner Act, and the two cases were decided together.

ARGUMENTS AGAINST ITS CONSTITUTIONALITY

Three main points were raised by the attorneys for Massachusetts. These contentions were:

1. Federal aid (specifically, the grant for the protection of maternity and infancy) constitutes "an effective means of inducing the States to yield a portion of their sovereign rights." The effectiveness of the subsidy system as a means of securing a measure of supervision over state activities is evidenced by the fact that every state accepts some federal aid, while most of the states accept every subsidy offered. In theory the states are quite free to reject any or all federal proposals. But in practice no such freedom exists. State legislatures cannot afford to ignore any possible source of revenue, for they are faced with the perplexing problem of preventing an increase in tax rates while they meet the demand for higher standards of service—better schools, better roads, better protection.

2. "The burden of the appropriations provided by this act and similar legislation falls unequally upon the several states, and rests largely upon the industrial states, such as Massachusetts." It is clear that federal revenues are derived chiefly from the wealthier states, from the states best able to bear the burden of federal taxation. New Jersey's per capita tangible wealth is nearly double the per capita tangible wealth of New Mexico.[1] The per capita incomes of the two states are in about the same ratio.[2] It may reasonably be sup-

[1] "Estimated National Wealth," a part of the Census Bureau's *Decennial Report on Wealth, Public Debt, and Taxation, 1922.*

[2] Leven, Maurice, *Income in the Various States,* National Bureau of Economic Research, New York, 1925.

posed, therefore, that New Jersey is contributing *far more per person* than New Mexico to the federal treasury, that fountainhead of all federal aid. But under most of the subsidy laws New Jersey gets back from the federal government *exactly the same amount per person as every other state,* for population is the usual basis of apportionment. In other words, some states are receiving from the federal government less than they pay in, while others are receiving more. In Massachusetts, a wealthy industrial state, federal aid is regarded by many as a losing proposition.

It is quite obvious that the subsidy system results in a transference of wealth from the richer to the poorer states. The constitutional right of the federal government to transfer wealth in this manner was questioned by the State of Massachusetts, and passed upon by the Supreme Court of the United States in the cases under consideration. The wisdom of such a policy is still a properly debatable question, and will be discussed in another section of this report.

3. Federal aid imposes upon Massachusetts, as well as upon other states, the "illegal and unconstitutional option either to yield to the federal government a part of its reserved rights or lose the share which it would otherwise be entitled to receive of the moneys appropriated." Massachusetts officials are sometimes taunted with the fact that although their legislature has seen fit to refuse the federal child hygiene offer, yet it has accepted every other subsidy proffered by the federal government. Their reply is usually that Massachusetts possesses no real choice in the matter. True, it may accept federal money or may refuse it. But in any event it must contribute to federal revenues through the federal taxes laid upon its citizens.

THE U. S. SUPREME COURT DECISION

The Supreme Court dismissed the two cases for want of jurisdiction, pointing out that no justiciable issue was presented. It then proceeded, however, to make a number of highly significant statements which showed clearly the attitude of its members towards the subsidy system. These

[3] *Cf.* pp. 658–660.

statements, though in the nature of *obiter dicta*, are fairly conclusive proof that no subsidy law framed after the fashion of the present statutes will be declared unconstitutional.

Speaking through Mr. Justice Sutherland,[1] the Court first considered the contention of Massachusetts that the Sheppard-Towner Act was "an effective means of inducing the states to yield a portion of their sovereign rights." "Probably it would be sufficient," declared the Court, "to point out that the powers of the States are not invaded, since the statute imposes no obligation, but simply extends an option which the State is free to accept or reject. But we do not rest here. . . . What burden is imposed upon the States, unequally or otherwise? Certainly there is none, unless it be the burden of taxation, and that falls upon their inhabitants, who are within the taxing power of Congress as well as that of the State where they reside. Nor does the statute require the States to do or yield anything. If Congress enacted it with the ulterior purpose of tempting them to yield, that purpose may be effectively frustrated by the simple expedient of not yielding."

The second claim of Massachusetts, that the burden of the appropriations . . . rests largely upon the industrial states, "was obviously a misstatement. No burden was placed upon Massachusetts, since it did not accept the provisions of the act. A tax burden *was* placed upon its citizens by the act, and this is evidently what the state's attorneys had in mind." But as the Supreme Court pointed out, the citizens of Massachusetts are also citizens

[1] 262 U. S. 447.

of the United States. If the burden of federal taxation becomes unduly heavy, it is to the federal government that they must turn for relief, and not to the state. "It cannot be conceded that a State, . . . may institute judicial proceedings to protect citizens of the United States from the operation of the statutes thereof. In that field it is the United States, and not the State, which represents them." The third contention was brushed aside as inconsequential.

THE RESULTS OF FEDERAL AID

With the question of constitutionality thus settled, the effects of federal aid on state activities and state standards of performance may be given serious consideration. Has the subsidy system stimulated state work? Has it raised state standards? Has it occasioned unreasonable federal interference in state affairs? Has it produced a reasonable degree of standardization and uniformity? Has standardization been carried to an unreasonable degree? These are some of the questions that must be answered by any person or group of persons attempting to evaluate federal aid.[2]

First, however, a clear picture is necessary of the subsidy system in actual operation. One must know just how a device works before attempting to judge its merits and defects. Part II of this report is therefore devoted to a description of the more important federal-aid laws and the manner in which they are administered. Part III contains a critical estimate of the system.

[2] These questions are considered in greater detail in Macdonald, Austin F., *Federal Aid.*

PART II

THE SUBSIDY SYSTEM

Forest Fire Prevention

THE Weeks Law of 1911, to which reference has already been made, limited federal coöperation in fire protection work to the forested watersheds of navigable streams. But in 1924 Congress passed a statute, popularly known as the Clarke-McNary Act, which authorized federal aid for the protection from fire of all private or state forest lands.[1] As under other subsidy laws, the initiative rests with the state. It is quite free to ignore the federal offer. But if it desires to secure its share of the federal appropriation its first step is to frame a plan of fire protection. This plan must show the areas to be protected, the headquarters and approximate routes of patrolmen, and all other relevant facts. The actual or proposed organization of the state forestry bureau must be set forth in detail.

With this information at hand the United States Forest Service, which has been charged with the administration of the law, determines whether the state is prepared to make an honest effort to protect its forest lands from fire, and if satisfied it approves the state plan. The Forest Service has no single standard by which it gages the efficiency of state programs. Every plan must be considered in its relation to local needs, local customs, and even local politics. For federal coöperation will not be refused merely because a state's forest rangers are sometimes appointed as a reward for political activity, nor even because its standards are somewhat below the standards of the federal government. The Forest Serv-

[1] 43 Stat. L. 653.

ice believes that the only way to better conditions in any state is to work patiently with its officials and to point out to them the need for improved standards, instead of refusing to coöperate with a state until it has reached a condition of perfection.

FEDERAL SUPERVISION OF EXPENDITURES

Federal funds and the state funds which match them are expended under the direction of the state foresters. In some states, such as Pennsylvania, the state forester is in complete control. He hires the fire fighters and directs their activity. In other parts of the country the duties of the state forester are more of a supervisory nature, a great deal of the actual work of fire protection and fire fighting being left to the town wardens. This is largely true in New England. The great forest states of the Northwest employ a still different plan, based on the activities of the large timber owners.

But in any event the state is the unit of control. The duty of the Forest Service is merely to approve state plans and to make certain that those plans are carried into effect. Seven federal district inspectors are charged with the task of examining state protective systems and auditing state accounts, and each is assigned to a territory comprising several states. These men spend much of their time in the field, eating and sleeping with the state forces. Most of them devote from six to eight weeks yearly to each state under their jurisdictions, and in that period of time they are able to secure reasonably accurate mental pictures of the effectiveness of state fire protection work. In some of the more progressive Eastern states the period of federal inspection is often reduced because of consistently high standards, making more careful scrutiny unnecessary; and in some of the Southern states it is cut short because the federal inspector for this territory has been placed in charge of too many states, and finds it impossible to cover his entire jurisdiction satisfactorily. Steps have already been taken with a view to splitting up the Southern work still further.

FEDERAL STAFF INADEQUATE

As a matter of fact, every federal inspector is underpaid and overworked. Salaries do not seem excessively low when compared with the compensation of state foresters; but they represent a mere fraction of the amounts paid expert foresters by the private lumbering companies. Very few of the best men remain long in governmental employ; if, indeed, they ever enter it. The salaries of the seven federal district inspectors average but thirty-eight hundred dollars a year, and thirty-eight hundred dollars is a pitifully small sum to pay a man who is qualified to inspect state activities and to point out the weakness of state protective systems. The heavy pressure of work also tends to make the job of federal inspector unattractive. Seven men are not enough; the present inspectional staff should be doubled. And yet, considering the poor pay and the long hours, the federal inspectors are men of surprisingly high calibre and unusual faithfulness. It is generally agreed that the Forest Service is getting full return or a little better for the money paid in salaries to the district inspectors. A number of the men, though experienced foresters, were unfamiliar with the technique of fire protection and fire fighting when first they received their appointments;

but with the passing of time this charge can no longer fairly be brought against them.

THE PROBLEMS OF FEDERAL SUPERVISION

Every federal bureau administering a subsidy law is confronted sooner or later with a number of important questions which must be answered decisively. Shall it set up fairly definite standards to which coöperating states must conform? Or shall it study each state plan separately, making no attempt to establish uniform rules? Shall it exercise its right to cut off federal allotments from any state not living up to its agreement? Or shall it merely try to persuade the errant state to return to the straight and narrow path of honest performance, continuing to pay out federal funds in any event? When state politics interfere seriously with state administration, as they have a habit of doing at times, shall the federal bureau try to correct the situation? If so, how? When incompetents are given posts of authority in state affairs, shall the federal bureau which must coöperate with them demand their removal? Or shall it merely ask that state work be satisfactorily performed, leaving it to the state to remedy the situation?

These are vital questions. The success of federal aid depends in large measure on the way they are answered. And no two bureaus administering subsidy laws have answered them in exactly the same way. Some of the federal bureaus set up rather rigid standards, and require the states to conform strictly. Others make no attempt to set up standards, but measure each plan in terms of local needs, and it is in this group that the Forest Service belongs. As already pointed out, it permits the greatest variation among state plans, allowing states with different conditions to submit totally different programs. When a state fails to live up to the plan which its own officials have drafted, the Forest Service has legitimate cause for complaint. Under the law it would be justified in cutting off all further state appropriations.

In practice it does no such thing, however; and neither does any other federal bureau. There have been a few instances in which federal aid has been cut off entirely from a state; Arkansas, for example, some years ago lost its entire allotment from the highway subsidy because of the unsatisfactory manner in which it handled federal funds. But such instances are extremely rare, and it may fairly be said that nothing short of a scandal will bring about the complete withdrawal of federal aid from a state. Portions of a state's allotment are often held back for a time, however, because federal and state officials are unable to agree as to the wisdom or legality of certain state expenditures.

THE EFFECTS OF POLITICS

In some states politics play havoc with virtually every phase of the administration, and state forestry departments have not escaped their share. Frequently their payrolls are padded with the names of men powerful in vote-getting but weak in forestry, while more than one state forester is chosen with little regard for his ability to fill the post. The federal inspectors soon become familiar with the calibre of the state forces. They know quite well that some of the men with whom they must coöperate are woefully ignorant of their jobs. But they continue to coöperate.

The Forest Service is long-suffering, for it knows that more than one state, if told to choose between political appointments and federal aid, would not need two hours to discard federal aid.

And the loss of federal aid would be a most serious matter. It might undo all the good accomplished in years of coöperation. Despite the handicap of state politics, federal inspection and federal guidance have proved a remarkable stimulus to state activity and a wonderful incentive to improved state standards. If the Forest Service cannot determine which men will be appointed by the states, it can at least make sure that the men who are appointed will have a better concept of their duties because of contact with federal officials. The accepted tradition in Washington is that no federal bureau administering a subsidy law will interfere with state personnel. The demand may be made upon a state to better its standards or to use federal and state-matched funds more effectively, but not to appoint or dismiss any given person. The Forest Service comes nearest to violating this tradition, for though it has never directly demanded the resignation of any state official, it has in more than one instance applied pressure that resulted in a state forester's dismissal. This practice is contrary to the generally understood rôle of the federal government, and has not been adopted by any other federal bureau. Even the Forest Service would probably make formal denial of any such activity.

THE GROWTH OF FIRE PROTECTION

Under the stimulus of federal aid state protective programs have expanded at an astonishing rate. Total state expenditures for forest fire protection amounted to but three hundred and fifty thousand dollars in 1912; by 1927 the total state outlay had passed the two million dollar mark. Federal expenditures have also increased rapidly, but have kept well below the state total. In no year have they exceeded thirty-five per cent of the amount spent by the states. During the decade and a half of coöperation under the Weeks and Clarke-McNary Acts the number of acres of state and privately owned forest land adequately protected from fire more than tripled and the number of states accepting the federal offer has mounted from eleven to thirty-three.

The following table will serve to make clear the remarkable progress that has been made:[1]

by the Forest Service in consultation with state officials, and each state has then been given an allotment based on the quantity and quality of its timber, and on the fire hazard. When the basis of apportionment is not definitely fixed in the law itself, which is customary, but instead is left to the discretion of federal administrators, greater flexibility is secured. It is possible to make a

EXPENDITURES FOR FOREST FIRE PREVENTION

Fiscal year	Number of states Coöperating	Area protected (in acres)	Federal expenditures	State expenditures
1912*	11	61,000,000	$53,287.53	$350,000.00
1913	12	68,000,000	53,247.82	380,000.00
1914	17	83,000,000	79,708.27 †	415,000.00
1915	18	95,000,000	69,581.75	505,924.70
1916	20	98,000,000	90,481.28	408,087.08
1917	21	103,000,000	90,580.14	435,328.11
1918	21	104,000,000	98,529.75	565,625.24
1919	22	110,000,000	99,921.38	625,445.54
1920	23	121,000,000	95,107.86	860,919.49
1921	24	149,000,000	119,529.83	1,066,027.47
1922	26	169,000,000	400,000.00	1,757,000.00
1923	26	166,000,000	394,094.64	1,826,685.78
1924	28	170,000,000	396,479.82	1,473,084.96
1925	29	171,000,000	397,646.97	1,844,191.70
1926	32	182,000,000	638,427.59	1,874,893.19 ‡
1927	33	196,000,000	654,101.57	2,009,416.06

* Period March 1, 1911 to June 30, 1912.
† Expenditure partly made from funds of preceding year.
‡ Includes $263,512.58 expended by private agencies.

THE BASIS OF APPORTIONMENT

The Clarke-McNary Law differs from most of the other subsidy statutes in that it does not provide for the allocation of federal funds on the basis of population. Instead, it leaves the matter of apportionment entirely in the hands of the Secretary of Agriculture, who has ruled that federal aid is to be apportioned among the states according to their fire protection needs. The cost of protecting adequately the timber supply of each state has been determined

[1] Table supplied by United States Forest Service.

nice adjustment between a state's need and its allotment and to make special provision for unusual conditions.

On the other hand there is the obvious danger that federal funds will be allocated without regard to need, and in such a manner as to strengthen the hand of federal officials. The Forest Service, however, has apportioned the fire protection subsidy in an honest and intelligent manner. The state foresters are nearly unanimous in the opinion that no attempt is made to strengthen the federal position by juggling federal aid. Some of the states least willing to accept federal advice are receiving large sums of federal money because of the magnificent forests within their borders.

ENCOURAGEMENT TO REFORESTATION

Under the provisions of the Clarke-McNary Law two other small grants are also made to the states; one for the production and distribution of forest-tree seeds and plants, the other for educational work designed to stimulate interest in tree growing. The administration of these subsidies involves no unusual features.

Agricultural Extension Work

In the United States are about three thousand counties which may be classed as predominantly rural. In two-thirds of these counties are men and women known as county agents, paid in part by the counties in which they work, in part by the states whose people they serve, and in part by the federal government. Each is assigned to a single county,[1] and each is expected to carry to the farmers of his county the message of better agriculture. He must show how to grow better crops, how to improve the quality of livestock, how to market crops most effectively, how to keep more accurate farm records and accounts. This he must do informally and interestingly, for he has no school-house, and no truant officers to aid him. The women agents are called home economics agents; their task is to show the housewives how to do more effectively the work of the farm home.

The activities of these agents are known as agricultural extension work.

[1] There are some exceptions. In some states it is customary to join together two or more very poor counties, employing a single agent for the group; while in other states are found a few county agents "at large," who devote their time to counties having no permanent extension work for the purpose of arousing popular enthusiasm.

THE WORK OF THE "COUNTY AGENT"

In the early days of extension work the average county agent used to spend all his time traveling from farm to farm, repeating at each farm the demonstration he had already given several times in the neighborhood. In each case his audience would consist of from two to five people—the farmer and his boys. Some county agents still work in exactly this manner. Most of them have learned, however, that while a great deal of individual attention is necessary, the most effective work is carried on in relatively large groups. If the message can be told to a handful of persons, why not tell it to half a hundred? A tremendous amount of energy can thus be conserved for more productive uses. The only trouble is to get half a hundred persons together to listen to the agent's message. Organization is required to accomplish that. And the most successful agents have been able to interest the leaders in their communities, inducing them to build up organizations that coöperate in spreading the gospel of improved farming methods.

THE "FARM BUREAU" MOVEMENT

Some years ago the United States Department of Agriculture attempted to stimulate the creation of organizations of farmers by sponsoring the "farm bureau" movement. The farm bureau was to be a voluntary association of farmers in each agricultural county, and its purpose was to be purely educational. It was designed to further the county agent movement, and not to embark upon commercial ventures.

But as the farm bureau movement increased in popularity the bureaus in many states lost sight of their original purpose. They undertook marketing enterprises and other commercial activities; as they united to form state federations they engaged actively in lobbying for or against legislative proposals. In short, they were ordinary commercial farmers' associations, competing with other farmers' associations for rural favor. It is not surprising, therefore, that a feeling of hostility to the whole county agent movement developed among the rival farm organizations. As the Farm Bureau has gradually divorced itself from the county agent movement and assumed the character of a commercial association, this hostility to extension work has lessened, and in time it will doubtless disappear altogether. In a few states the bureaus have never lost sight of their original purpose and today they still serve as educational groups developing extension work.

Federal, state, county and private funds are all used in furthering the extension movement, but the proportion from each source varies greatly from state to state. Federal money is allotted to the states on the basis of rural population. In two states, California and Pennsylvania, each county agent's salary is paid entirely from state and federal funds, and the counties are asked to pay only incidental costs, such as traveling expenses and office rent. In Massachusetts, on the other hand, the state pays nothing, and the entire burden of matching the federal grant rests upon the local communities. Most states require the counties to pay incidental expenses and a part of the salary in addition; but it is customary to make some contribution directly from the state treasury. The money raised in the county may come from public sources or from private contributions. The arrangement varies from state to state.

STATE CONTROL OVER COUNTY AGENTS

There are also great differences in the extent of state control over the county agents. It is customary for each county to choose its own agent from a list of suitable persons whose names are submitted by the state director of extension work, but there is no uniformity concerning the method of dismissal. In most states the county officials may dismiss an agent at will. This act does not force the agent from the extension service; instead he is transferred to another county in the hope that he will give satisfaction at a new post. Should he be unable to satisfy the people in any one of a number of counties, he is eventually dropped from extension work. A few states, such as Montana, place a larger measure of control in the hands of the state director, authorizing him to demand charges and a formal hearing before any agent may be dismissed by county authorities. If local politics seem to be involved, the director may even require a formal vote of the people of the county on the question of dismissing the agent.[1]

QUALIFICATIONS OF COUNTY AGENTS

Ninety-five per cent of the county agents are college graduates. Most of those in the remaining five percent group are farmers who have been in the service fifteen years or more, survivors of the time when emphasis was placed on "practical" experience rather than scientific training. But successful farming experience is still an essential part of the equipment of every county agent, a fact which state directors know, but sometimes ignore of necessity.

The salaries paid county agents are so small that men of high calibre are seldom attracted; and if successful experience is to be made a prerequisite in addition to college training, the financial inducement must be made considerably greater. In one state the

---

[1] For a discussion of the part played by politics in extension work, see Macdonald, Austin F., *Federal Aid*, p. 67 *et seq.*

minimum salary is fourteen hundred dollars; other states offer beginners but little more. Throughout the country the average salary paid to county agents is only twenty-seven hundred dollars, and the agents are worth just about that amount. Some states stand out brilliantly from this mediocrity with high salaries and high-grade men. Illinois, for example, has a salary scale ranging from twenty-five hundred dollars to more than five thousand, the average being about thirty-six hundred dollars. As a result it is able to recruit its agents entirely from the ranks of farmers who have had five years or more of successful agricultural experience after graduation from college.

FEDERAL APPROVAL OF EXTENSION PROGRAMS

As under all the more recent subsidy laws, each coöperating state is required to submit for federal approval a detailed program of work. The office of coöperative extension work of the Department of Agriculture passes on state plans and inspects state activities. For inspectional purposes the country has been divided into four sections, each containing about twelve states. Fifteen federal agents, two of them colored men assigned to Southern territory, visit the state agricultural colleges, examine state accounts and other state records, and make flying trips into the field. Eleven specialists in various phases of agriculture are attached to the office of coöperative extension work, and from time to time they also visit the states. The federal agents spend a short while in each state about three times per year, and soon become familiar with the strong and weak points of state administration. They are therefore in a position to insist that faulty state plans be altered and that unsatisfactory state standards be bettered.

But they never do insist, nor do their superiors at Washington. Instead, the office of coöperative extension work resorts to persuasion. It suggests improvements instead of demanding them; it never withdraws federal funds except for obvious failure to comply with the letter of the law. This method may bring results more slowly than direct action, but it brings about a closer understanding with the states than would otherwise be possible.

The first "county agent," serving a single county and paid in part with local funds, was appointed in 1906. The movement spread rapidly, but it was not until 1914 that Congress coördinated the work by passing a statute known as the Smith-Lever Act.[1] The funds appropriated under this law have been supplemented by large additional federal grants for agricultural extension work, but though the federal subsidy has increased rapidly it has failed to keep pace with state and county appropriations.

The table on the following page shows the growth of extension work funds by sources since 1915.

THE RESULTS OF EXTENSION WORK

The purpose of agricultural extension work is to induce the rural men and women of America to adopt better methods of farming and better methods of home management. The only satisfactory test of the effectiveness of this work, therefore, is the number of people who adopt improved farm or home practices because of the direct or indirect effect of the extension service. A number of studies were made recently in different sections of the country by federal representatives, in coöperation with state officials, to determine whether the county agent had been a vital force in the lives of

[1] 38 Stat. L. 372.

GROWTH OF FUNDS FOR COÖPERATIVE AGRICULTURAL EXTENSION WORK, BY SOURCES

Year	U. S. Department of Agriculture		Smith-Lever	
	Farmers' coöperative demonstration work	Other bureaus	Federal	State
1915	$905,782.00	$105,168.40	$474,934.73	$..........
1916	900,389.92	165,172.01	1,077,923.73	597,923.73
1917	958,333.87	185,893.15	1,575,054.38	1,095,054.38
1918	3,900,406.30 *	507,282.95	2,068,066.29	1,588,066.29
1919	5,564,839.70 *	935,373.64	2,538,828.04	2,058,828.04
1920	1,021,091.39	406,020.96	4,464,344.36	3,984,344.36
1921	1,025,083.33	435,046.70	4,974,048.50	4,494,048.50
1922	1,007,263.48	209,540.93	5,510,349.45	5,030,349.45
1923	1,004,729.29	275,532.24	5,820,816.89	5,340,816.29
1924	991,900.82	234,320.98	5,859,605.01	5,379,605.01
1925	962,390.34	228,856.67	5,879,083.89	5,399,083.89
1926	967,166.73	29,377.72 †	5,879,183.10	5,399,183.10

Year	State and college	County	Other	Total
1915	$1,044,270.38	$780,331.79	$286,748.55	$3,597,235.85
1916	872,733.90	973,251.56	276,786.09	4,864,180.94
1917	832,114.16	1,258,296.14	244,873.55	6,149,619.63
1918	881,091.25	1,863,632.29	494,219.38	11,302,764.75
1919	901,828.49	2,291,209.30	370,653.29	14,661,560.50
1920	1,244,465.72	2,865,730.87	672,073.26	14,658,079.92
1921	1,549,897.30	3,293,566.38	1,020,557.61	16,792,248.32
1922	1,497,379.71	2,972,740.71	954,127.91	17,181,751.64
1923	1,712,766.53	3,420,000.81	910,182.35	18,484,845.00
1924	1,696,878.21	3,883,185.02	1,036,529.99	19,082,025.04
1925	1,978,746.89	3,893,814.16	990,395.56	19,332,371.40
1926	2,113,369.94	3,996,614.08	1,036,557.46	19,485,492.81

* Includes emergency funds.
† Until 1926 funds from other bureaus were included under this heading.

rural people; whether his work had actually resulted in the abandonment of old methods and the adoption of new. To obtain this information house to house canvasses were made in eighteen counties of eight states, situated in every section of the country. Nearly seven thousand farms were visited, and from seventy-five per cent of them came the report of improved practices, the average number of changed methods being more than three per farm.[1]

This is an astonishingly fine record,

[1] *Bulletin No. 319*, Georgia State College of Agriculture, 1926; *Extension Circular No. 221*,

and reflects great credit on the men directing the extension movement. But it cannot be taken at quite its face value. Seventy-five per cent represents the proportion of farms affected in *selected* counties rather than in the country as a whole. Federal and state bulletins reporting the survey speak of the counties selected as "typical" counties, but it is an open secret that a number of the counties selected were far above the average. Seventy-five

College of Agriculture, University of Arkansas; *Extension Bulletin No. 50*, New Jersey State College of Agriculture; *Bulletin No. 1384*, United States Department of Agriculture.

per cent is undoubtedly too high. In some parts of the United States the percentage could be placed even higher—eighty or eighty-five; but in other sections a much lower figure would be nearer the truth. Whatever the real average for the nation, however, there can be no doubt that agricultural extension work has been of very great value to the rural population.

Highways

Federal aid for highways was first offered to the states in 1916. The amount appropriated in that year has since been increased many times, and today the annual appropriation is seventy-five million dollars—more than all other forms of federal aid combined. This money is used to stimulate state highway construction and to insure the adoption by the states of proper methods and suitable materials. "Only such durable types of surfaces and kinds of material shall be adopted for the construction and reconstruction of any highway . . . as will adequately meet the existing and probable future traffic needs and conditions thereon." [1]

THE EXTENT OF FEDERAL RESPONSIBILITY

When a road has been built, the financial obligation of the federal government ceases. The state is expected to make needed repairs and to keep it in good condition without the assistance of federal funds. Yet the federal government does not hesitate to insist that highways maintained at state expense must be maintained according to federal standards. "If at any time the Secretary of Agriculture shall find that any road in any state constructed under the provisions of this Act is not being properly maintained he shall give notice of such fact to the highway department of such state and if within four months from the receipt of said notice said road has not been put in a proper condition of maintenance then the Secretary of Agriculture shall thereafter refuse to approve any project for road construction in said state, or the civil subdivision thereof, as the fact may be, whose duty it is to maintain said road, until it has been put in a condition of proper maintenance." [2] This provision has had a most salutary effect upon dilatory state highway departments. It has since been amended so as to permit the Secretary of Agriculture to make suitable arrangements for repairing consistently neglected roads, charging the cost of such repairs against the offending state's allotment.

METHODS OF FEDERAL SUPERVISION

The Bureau of Public Roads, which administers the highway subsidy, keeps in close touch with the state highway departments. It has divided the country into eleven districts for inspectional purposes, and in each division is a federal district engineer, empowered to pass upon all matters except those of the greatest importance, which must be submitted to Washington for approval. There is also a federal engineer assigned to each state, and directly responsible to the engineer in charge of his district. He has one or more trained engineers to help him—as many as six in some states.

Under other subsidy laws the co-operating state agencies must submit each year programs of work for federal approval. But annual programs do not suffice to meet the requirements of the federal road acts. For every section of highway to be built in part with federal funds a vast amount of detailed information must be sent to the Bureau

[1] 42 Stat. L. 212.

[2] Ibid.

of Public Roads. The exact route of the project, the nature of the construction, type of paving, grades, estimated cost—all these data are required. Proposed routes are examined by federal engineers. When bids are considered for highway construction on which federal money is to be spent, representatives of the federal government are usually present. They cannot accept or reject a bid; that matter is in the hands of the state officials. But since they may refuse to permit the expenditure of federal funds, their opinions are certain to receive respectful attention.

STATE MUST TAKE INITIATIVE

Expenditures for every project are originally made by the state. It is then partly reimbursed by the federal government at the end of each month, after federal inspectors have approved the status of the work. Completion of a project does not mark the end of federal inspection, however. Every foot of the seventy-one thousand miles of highways so far built under federal aid [1] is covered twice a year by federal inspectors, and in this way maintenance requirements are enforced.

FEDERAL INSPECTION

The method of inspection used by the Bureau of Public Roads is obviously a very different thing from the system employed by the other bureaus administering subsidy laws. Engineers of the Bureau of Public Roads examine every specification, and visit every project. It would be impossible for the representatives of the Extension Service to visit every county and pass judgment upon the work of every county agent. The subsidy for extension work would soon be eaten up by the excessive cost of administration.

[1] As of June 30, 1928.

Agents of the Federal Board for Vocational Education could not hope to enter the doors of every school receiving federal aid for vocational education. If they did, administrative expenses would soon equal the grant to the states. So they must resort to sampling—visiting "typical" schools, seeing "typical" extension groups, observing "typical" child health demonstrations. And all too often these schools, extension groups, child health demonstrations and the like are just as "typical" as the state director wishes them to be, and no more so.

But the Bureau of Public Roads is in a very different position, and it takes the fullest advantage of its opportunity. For one thing, the very nature of the work makes complete inspection easier. Then, too, the Bureau has a vast amount of money at its command. Every year it devotes a million and a half dollars to inspectional purposes. And then it is spending only two per cent of the annual grant to the states for highway construction!

SELECTION OF A SYSTEM OF MAIN HIGHWAYS

An act passed by Congress in 1921 made a number of important changes in the original plan of federal aid. One of the most significant provisos of this statute was that federal and state-matched funds should be used within each state for the construction of a connected system of main highways limited to seven per cent of the state's total road mileage. Only after a state's entire system of main thoroughfares was complete might it use federal money to build other roads. Shortly after the passage of this act each state highway engineer was asked to designate the roads in his state which ought to be included in the federal system, and the Bureau of Public Roads then coördinated the highways selected—

totalling in length more than one hundred and eighty-seven thousand miles —into a complete federal-aid system. Practically every community in the United States with a population of not less than five thousand is reached directly by this great network of roads.[1]

FEDERAL STAFF UNDERPAID

The Bureau of Public Roads is seriously handicapped by the low salary schedule fixed for federal highway engineers. The federal men are paid considerably less than engineers of equivalent rank in the service of the more progressive states, and as a result some of them transfer their allegiance to state highway departments. The chief of the Bureau of Public Roads, whose duty is to supervise the highway programs of all the states, receives a smaller salary than many a state chief highway engineer. And yet the federal government manages to retain a large number of highly capable men. It is generally agreed that the federal engineers compare favorably with the highway engineers of the leading states. Their faithfulness should be rewarded with substantial salary increases.

THE BASIS OF APPORTIONMENT

Unlike most of the subsidies, which are distributed among the states according to population—total, urban or rural—the federal grant for highways is apportioned on a three-fold basis. The law provides for distribution of federal funds "one-third in the ratio which the area of each state bears to the area of all the states; one-third in the ratio which the population of each state bears to the total population of all the states, are shown by the latest available federal census; one-third in the ratio which the mileage of rural

[1] *Yearbook* of the Department of Agriculture, 1924, p. 103.

delivery routes and star routes in each state bears to the total mileage of rural delivery routes and star routes in all the states."

The National Guard

The first federal subsidy to the states for the support of their militia was made in 1808.[2] No attempt was made, however, to regulate the expenditure of this grant nor to determine whether state troops were armed, equipped and trained with any regard to reasonable standards of efficiency. The result may well be imagined. While the forces of a few commonwealths were properly equipped and well drilled, in the large majority of the states the militia consisted of men hopelessly ignorant of army fundamentals, commanded by totally incompetent officers of their own choosing, strong in infantry but weak in artillery and auxiliary troops.

THE NATIONAL DEFENSE ACT

Until 1886, however, Congress left militia matters entirely in the hands of the states, contenting itself with appropriating each year small sums for the support of the state forces. But in that year Congress stipulated the minimum number of troops which each state must have in order to qualify for its share of the federal subsidy.[3] Other acts gradually increased federal control, and in 1916 the National Defense Act laid a solid foundation for federal supervision of the state military establishments. This statute has been amended more than twenty times, but it still remains the fundamental law regulating the state forces in their relation to the federal government. Under its provisions the number of men ultimately to be enlisted in the state service is fixed at eight hundred for each

[2] 2 Stat. L. 40.   [3] 24 Stat. L. 401.

member of Congress, and the President is authorized to prescribe the unit or units, as to the branch of service, to be maintained in each state. Officers must meet rigid requirements, and must qualify before a board appointed by the Secretary of War. The number and length of drills, the kind of equipment, even the types of courts-martial to be used by the state forces are prescribed in considerable detail.

LANGUAGE OF LAW MANDATORY

Much of the language of the National Defense Act is mandatory. "The organization of the National Guard shall be the same as that of the Regular Army" (Section 60). "No State shall maintain troops . . . other than as authorized" (Section 61). "The discipline . . . of the National Guard shall conform to the system which is now or may hereafter be prescribed for the Regular Army" (Section 91). It must not be concluded, however, that Congress is forcing its attentions upon unwilling commonwealths. The actual meaning of "shall" in the above sentences is "shall, if a state desires to receive federal aid." But since only one state, Nevada, has been willing to forfeit its share of the federal grant, the military establishments of the states have been worked out according to the federal pattern. It is significant that the word "militia" has been dropped entirely. The state troops are now the units of the National Guard, whose members must swear allegiance to the United States, as well as to their respective states, at the time of enlistment.

The National Guard units are inspected each year by officers of the Regular Army, who determine whether they are armed, uniformed, equipped and trained according to federal standards. Failure on the part of any state to meet federal requirements may be punished by cutting off the offending state from further federal allotments; and although such stringent measures are never resorted to, yet the prospect of losing federal funds is sufficient to keep the states fairly well in line. It may be said that at least they do not openly ignore the standards set by the federal government.

DECENTRALIZED ADMINISTRATION

Unfortunately, no single agency is charged with the administration of the federal subsidy to the National Guard. Instead, control is scattered in such a manner as to make harmonious action almost impossible. Matters of general policy are passed upon by the general staff of the regular army. Most of the details of administration are in the hands of the Militia Bureau of the War Department.

The actual work of inspection is carried on by four hundred and seventy-six officers and about six hundred enlisted men of the regular army, who are assigned to duty with the various units of the National Guard. These men are called instructors rather than inspectors, because it is thought best to place as little emphasis as possible on their inspectional duties. They are responsible to the commanders of their respective corps areas instead of to the Militia Bureau, thus diffusing responsibility still further. The Militia Bureau, according to War Department rulings, is "that bureau of the War Department which is charged with the administration of approved . . . policies for the National Guard,"[1] but its control over National Guard matters is seriously restricted. All its recommendations must be approved by the general staff, and are subject to long and irritating delays. Its relations

[1] War Department General Orders, Number 6, issued March 10, 1926.

with the regular army instructors are indirect, and its problems are made still more difficult by inadequate appropriations. Under the circumstances it is surprising how accurate a picture of conditions in each state the Militia Bureau manages to keep constantly before it.

The "instructors" on duty with the several units of the National Guard have opportunity for very little instructing; most of their time is spent traveling from section to section within their jurisdiction, inspecting equipment and training. Only a few days a year are spent with each section, and occasionally it is found necessary to omit some from the list altogether. Most of the units are rated as satisfactory, less than four per cent failing to meet federal requirements in 1926. Those few states whose units fall below the line are formally warned by the Militia Bureau; but the Bureau is forced to depend in large measure on the corps area commanders for information as to whether conditions have been improved.

The only time that officers of the Militia Bureau come into direct contact with the officers and enlisted personnel of the National Guard is during the summer encampments. Then an excellent opportunity is afforded to observe at first hand the results of the year's training. The National Defense Act provides that every state unit receiving federal funds must participate in at least fifteen days of intensive field training each year, and restricted Congressional appropriations make it necessary to limit the period of actual training to the legal minimum.

TRAINING CAMPS

Ninety-six camps are used by the National Guard; some of them are state property, others are owned by the federal government. Though many of the camps are open for but fifteen days during the year, a number are in constant use throughout the entire summer. An excessive amount of time is devoted to parades and reviews, but intensive work is not forgotten. And during the period of each encampment, while the men are learning something of army fundamentals, the representatives of the Militia Bureau are busily engaged in observing the condition of the different units—their arms, their equipment, and their training. Eighty-five per cent of the enlisted men and an even higher percentage of the officers of the National Guard come to the summer camps each year.

The provisions of the National Defense Act relating to the National Guard were given no real opportunity to function until some time after their passage, because all National Guard troops were drafted into the federal service in August, 1917. After the war came the period of reorganization, handicapped by the natural reaction against all military matters and also by the unfriendly attitude of the labor unions. Enrollment increased steadily until the summer of 1924, however, but since that time it has remained practically stationary. Popular interest in the National Guard has not waned, but niggardly Congressional appropriations have forced the Militia Bureau to curtail enlistments. The table on the following page will show the growth of the National Guard since the war.

The National Defense Act fixed the total strength eventually to be attained by the National Guard at eight hundred men for each member of Congress, but the Militia Bureau has been forced by insufficient funds to keep the enlisted strength down to less than half that number. Drills are limited to the minimum prescribed by law, and practically no new units are recognized.

NATIONAL GUARD STRENGTH 1919–1927 *

Year	Officers	Enlisted men	Total
1919	1,198	36,012	37,210
1920	2,073	54,017	56,090
1921	5,843	107,797	113,640
1922	8,744	150,914	159,658
1923	9,675	150,923	160,598
1924	10,996	166,432	177,428
1925	11,595	165,930	177,525
1926	11,435	163,534	174,969
1927	12,192	168,950	181,142

* Report of the Chief of the Militia Bureau, 1926, Appendix B.

Yet the subsidy to the National Guard amounts to thirty million dollars or more a year—a larger sum than for all other forms of federal aid combined, with the single exception of highways. The growth of the National Guard subsidy is shown below:

PAYMENTS TO THE STATES FOR THE NATIONAL
GUARD *

Year	Amount
1912	$4,131,190
1913	3,740,713
1914	6,499,952
1915	4,847,744
1916	6,467,522
1917	8,876,195
1918	11,053,562
1919 †	3,774,772
1920 †	2,943,208
1921	17,691,674
1922	22,373,633
1923	22,357,478
1924	26,591,308
1925	29,754,151
1926	30,179,781
1927	31,363,935

* Figures furnished by the Militia Bureau.
† Reorganization period following the War.

STATES DO NOT CONTRIBUTE FUNDS

The National Defense Act is the only recent subsidy law which does not require the states to match federal funds. Under its provisions the federal government bears about two-thirds of the total cost of maintaining the National Guard, the states being required only to provide armories and to make adequate arrangements for the protection and care of the property they receive. Congress is willing to assume this large obligation because it recognizes the importance to the national government of properly equipped, well organized troops ready at short notice to supplement the regular army.

The National Guard, as its name indicates, is for all practical purposes a national organization. It is already far larger than any body of troops needed by the states to preserve order, and units maintained by some of the states are of no conceivable use to them. Such, for example, are the anti-aircraft and field artillery units. The states are performing a national service in maintaining their militia under national regulations, and their proportionate contribution ought to be less than under other forms of federal aid, in which the local interest is paramount.

Vocational Education

Until very recently Americans have had but one concept of education beyond the "three R's"—that obtained through such traditional subjects as mathematics, foreign languages and pure science. We are rapidly recognizing, however, that classical training is of very little use to the average man —the man who never completed the grammar school, or left high school after a single year. Within the last quarter of a century has come a better understanding of educational needs, an understanding that has found expression in new curricula labelled "vocational education." Today the city boy is given an opportunity to master the trade of his choice, and the country youngster is taught the elements of scientific farming. Home-making has been raised to the dignity of a science, and its principles are taught to the girls of city and country alike.

DEVELOPMENT OF VOCATIONAL EDUCATION

The rapid development of vocational education during the past decade is in large measure the result of the federal aid first offered the states in 1917. The Smith-Hughes Act of that year provided for a comprehensive system of training in the common, wage-earning employments. Three separate grants were made to the states: one to pay the "salaries of teachers, supervisors or directors of agricultural subjects," another for the "salaries of teachers of trade, home economics and industrial subjects," and a third to be used "in preparing teachers, supervisors and directors."[1] No federal funds might be used for buildings or equipment; the expense of these essentials must be borne by the states. Yet the federal government has not hesitated to pass upon the adequacy of buildings and equipment furnished by the states. And since federal funds for salaries must be matched dollar for dollar by the states or local communities, the federal government exercises supervision over the expenditures of sums considerably in excess of the federal grant.

STATE BOARDS OF VOCATIONAL EDUCATION

The Smith-Hughes Act required each state receiving the federal subsidy to designate or create a state board of vocational education. Some states have designated their boards of education as coöperating agencies; others have created new administrative bodies. These boards are responsible for the expenditure of joint state and federal funds. They formulate plans

[1] 39 Stat. L. 929.

showing in detail the types of schools and equipment, the courses of study, the methods of instruction and the qualifications of teachers. These projects, originally submitted at the beginning of each year, but now drawn up to cover five-year periods, must be approved by the federal government. In each instance, therefore, the state takes the initiative and sets its own standards, but there is a federal veto.

FEDERAL SUPERVISING AGENCIES

The federal agency which passes upon state plans is the Federal Board for Vocational Education, created by the Smith-Hughes Act. This board, composed of four ex-officio and three appointive members, meets only occasionally to consider major questions of policy. The actual details of administration are in charge of a salaried director selected under civil service regulations. Responsible to him are the chiefs of the four services—Trade and Industrial Education, Agricultural Education, Home Economics Education, and Commercial Education.

No federal subsidy is given to the states for commercial education, and so the chief of this service and his single agent devote their time to making special studies and investigations and to aiding the states in developing commercial education programs. Since the federal home economics appropriation is limited, this service is compelled to rely on two agents to cover the entire country and to inspect the work being done in the states. The Agricultural Education Service, however, has five agents: one who devotes his entire time to the colored schools, and four regional agents, each responsible for conditions in a region comprising about twelve states. The Trade and Industrial Education Service likewise has five agents: four assigned to different regions and one without specific territory who is a specialist in the problems presented by women in industry.

FEDERAL INSPECTION

The regional agents of the Board representing the Agricultural and Industrial Service visit each state about twice a year. Home economics agents, having a greater territory to cover, make fewer visits. The length of an agent's stay depends in large measure upon local conditions. If a state seems to be making an honest effort to maintain high standards, three or four days may suffice to audit its accounts and to make a cursory examination of the manner in which its program is being carried out.

If, on the other hand, a state consistently fails to maintain the standards set by its own officers and approved by the Federal Board, the federal agent's visits are likely to be more numerous and of longer duration. He may even go out into the field and visit some of the schools receiving federal funds, although ordinarily he does so only at the request of the state director or supervisor. Visiting "typical" schools is at best an unsatisfactory method of determining the condition of a state's vocational school system, because in practice it is necessary to rely on the state director to select the "typical" schools. The schools chosen are likely, therefore, to be just as "typical' as the state director desires them to be, and no more so. Fortunately, the federal agents have other means of learning what is being done in the states. One of the most effective ways of finding out the calibre of state teachers, for example, is to visit the teachers' conferences. A few short informal talks with the teachers about their problems suffice to give the experienced agent a reasonably accurate picture of the state program in actual operation.

FEDERAL STAFF INADEQUATE

The federal agents are capable and well-trained, but their task is stupendous. They are even expected to carry on a certain amount of research work each year in addition to visiting the states assigned to them. It is no reflection upon their ability, therefore, to point out that the inspectional work of the Federal Board for Vocational Education is less thorough than the inspectional work of some of the other bureaus administering federal subsidies, notably the Bureau of Public Roads.

The Home Economics Service especially is handicapped, since it is compelled to struggle along with a totally inadequate allotment. Federal aid for home economics was not contemplated by the men who framed the Smith-Hughes Bill; in fact, the home economics section was inserted as a last-minute amendment, and carried with it no additional appropriation. Instead, the amendment merely provided "that not more than twenty per centum of the money appropriated under this Act for the payment of salaries of teachers of trade, home economics, and industrial subjects, for any year, shall be expended for the salaries of teachers of home economics subjects."[1] Therefore the states may, if they choose, omit home economics entirely from their plans. But under no circumstances may they use more than twenty per cent of their trade and industry allotments to further programs of home economics.

FRICTION BETWEEN FEDERAL TEACHERS AND COUNTY AGENTS

In a number of states considerable friction has developed between the teachers of vocational agriculture operating under the Smith-Hughes Act and the county agents functioning under the provisions of the Smith-Lever Act.

[1] Section 3.

These two laws set up two groups of teachers—county agents and high-school teachers of vocational agriculture—to work with the farming population of the nation. The county agent is, after all, a teacher, though his methods are informal and though he makes use of no classroom. His task is to teach the farmers how to produce better crops, and how to dispose of them more successfully. He works not only with the adults, but with the children, whom he organizes into clubs. Pig clubs, corn clubs, and cotton clubs stimulate a spirit of friendly rivalry while they also serve to impress on juvenile minds the importance of scientific methods in agriculture.

The high school teacher of agriculture does much the same work, and frequently with the same people. He does not limit himself to classroom instruction. Like the county agent, he makes use of practical demonstrations and practical problems for his pupils to solve. He is required to do so. The Smith-Hughes Act stipulates that every state plan approved by the Federal Board "shall provide for directed or supervised practice in agriculture, either on a farm provided by the school or other farm, for at least six months per year." When adult farmers attend the evening classes of the high school teacher, they, too, are given practical problems to work out on their own farms under the teacher's supervision.

Since the same people sometimes receive instruction in agricultural methods from two different agencies of the federal government, it is not surprising that misunderstandings and quarrels occur from time to time. The county agent and the high school teacher do not always teach the same thing. Even if they are able to agree upon a program, they frequently fail to reach any agreement as to how credit for the undertaking is to be divided between them. As a result there are occasional disagreements in nearly every state, and in two or three states the lack of coöperation between teachers and agents is so serious that it interferes to a considerable extent with the work of both. Formal agreements and understandings have been drawn up from time to time, but have been of doubtful value. It is said by some that the Smith-Hughes and Smith-Lever Acts are not to blame for this situation, since under their provisions any high school teacher or any county agent should be able to use his entire working time profitably without interfering in any way with the representative of another agency. Those who take this view contend that there is plenty of opportunity for both county agents and high school teachers of vocational agriculture to serve the farm people of this country without friction. Others who have studied the problem, however, place the blame squarely on the two acts. They assert that while it is quite possible for teachers and agents to work together harmoniously, yet it is also a comparatively simple matter for them to interfere deliberately with one another, and then quote the letter of the law in justification. Conditions will not be materially improved, it is said, until one or both laws have been amended.

FEDERAL AID ACCEPTED BY ALL STATES

The proffered federal subsidy for vocational education was accepted by all forty-eight states within a period of ten months after the organization of the Federal Board. Since that time remarkable progress has been made. Under the stimulus of federal aid the number of vocational schools receiving federal funds has increased four-fold, and the number of teachers and enrolled pupils has grown almost as rapidly.

Below is a table showing the growth

of vocational education since the passage of the Smith-Hughes Act:

GROWTH OF FEDERALLY-AIDED VOCATIONAL EDUCATION *

Year	Number of schools †	Number of pupils	Number of teachers
1918........	1,741	164,186	5,275
1919........	2,039	194,895	6,252
1920........	3,150	265,058	7,669
1921........	3,877	324,247	10,066
1922........	4,964	475,828	12,343
1923........	5,700	536,528	14,458
1924........	6,817	652,594	16,192
1925........	7,430	659,370	17,524
1926........	8,051	753,418	18,717
1927........	8,696	784,986	18,900

* Figures supplied by the Federal Board for Vocational Education.

† In reports of the Federal Board for Vocational Education the term "reimbursement units" is used instead of "schools," because of the difficulty of framing an accurate and unvarying definition of "school."

Though the federal subsidy for vocational education has mounted rapidly, increasing from less than a million dollars in 1918 to more than seven millions in 1927, state outlays have grown at an equally rapid pace. Every year the states have expended for vocational education two dollars or more of their own money for every dollar they received from the federal treasury. The following table shows how federal payments have increased since 1918:

FEDERAL PAYMENTS TO THE STATES FOR VOCATIONAL EDUCATION *

Year	Amount
1918............	$823,386.29
1919............	1,560,008.61
1920............	2,476,502.83
1921............	3,357,494.23
1922............	3,850,118.79
1923............	4,308,885.68
1924.....	4,832,920.16
1925............	5,614,550.14
1926............	6,548,567.92
1927............	7,184,901.51

* Figures supplied by the Federal Board for Vocational Education.

Vocational Rehabilitation

The duties of the Federal Board for Vocational Education were materially increased in 1920, when it was entrusted with the administration of the newly enacted Vocational Rehabilitation Law. This statute, commonly called the Fess-Kenyon Act, provided for an annual subsidy to the states of one million dollars "for the promotion of vocational rehabilitation of persons disabled in industry or otherwise, and their return to civil employment."[1] For a number of years prior to the passage of the federal law the need for training injured workers had been generally recognized, but only twelve states had made any attempt to devise suitable plans.

WORKMEN'S COMPENSATION LAWS INADEQUATE

In many other states workmen's compensation laws had been relied upon to aid those injured in the course of their employment. It is now generally recognized, however, that workmen's compensation laws are not sufficient. A person who has lost his earning power needs something more than the payment of a small cash sum. He needs to have his earning power restored. In some cases, of course, the injury is so serious that restoration of earning power is out of the question. But such is not usually the case. The skilled mechanic who has lost a leg may be unable to practice his trade again, and yet be quite capable, with suitable training, of earning a comfortable living at another trade,—at shoemaking, perhaps. It has been conservatively estimated that each year eighty-four thousand persons are vocationally disabled in the United States who are unable to pay for rehabilita-

[1] 41 Stat. L. 735.

tion, but who could probably be made independent wage earners. [1]

Moreover, the list of persons in need of vocational re-training is not limited to the victims of industrial accidents. There are thousands of persons disabled by disease or by accidents unconnected with industry who could become self-supporting if properly trained. Recognizing this fact, the Fess-Kenyon Act makes federal funds available for "any person who, by reason of a physical defect or infirmity, whether congenital or acquired by accident, injury or disease, is, or may be expected to be, totally or partially incapacitated for remunerative occupation."

METHODS OF FEDERAL SUPERVISION

Procedure is much the same as under the Smith-Hughes Act. Each state accepting the federal offer is required to designate its vocational education board as the agency to administer the rehabilitation work. State plans are drawn up setting forth in detail plans of procedure, and these plans must be approved by the Federal Board for Vocational Education. The actual details of administration are left in the hands of the states, of course, and federal agents audit state accounts and inspect state work in order to make certain that federal funds are being used satisfactorily. Every dollar of federal money must be matched by a dollar from state or local sources.

Vocational rehabilitation is handled by a separate division of the Federal Board for Vocational Education. A chief and five agents comprise its staff. Each agent is a specialist in some phase of rehabilitation, and is expected to work with any state needing his specialized knowledge. A great deal of

[1] Sullivan, O. M., and Snortum, K. O., *Disabled Persons, Their Education and Rehabilitation*, p. 33.

time must be devoted to inspection, however, and for inspectional purposes each agent has been assigned a definite group of states, varying in number from eight to twelve. The organization of the division is therefore partly regional and partly functional. Inspection is quite thorough. The agents of the Rehabilitation Division visit each state only once a year, but that single visit is sufficient to keep them well informed concerning the progress of state work. The number of cases handled is comparatively small, and the federal representatives find time to visit many of the disabled persons receiving training. State programs do not always prove satisfactory in actual operation, but the policy of the Federal Board is to raise standards by persuasion rather than by threats. It suggests better methods, points out how weaknesses may be overcome, but seldom announces that it intends to withdraw federal aid.

DEVELOPMENT OF REHABILITATION
TECHNIQUE

When the Fess-Kenyon Act became law, only a few pioneers were working in the field of vocational rehabilitation. There was no such thing as standardized procedure. A few states had enacted vocational reëducation laws, and the federal government had obtained some experience through its work with disabled war veterans. But the whole movement was in the experimental stage. Recognizing this fact, the Federal Board made no attempt to set up definite standards for state rehabilitation workers corresponding to its standards for vocational teachers under the Smith-Hughes Act. Instead, it approved every state plan that seemed to give reasonable promise of producing satisfactory results. The years since 1920, however, have witnessed a remarkable development in the technique of rehabilitation. The Federal Board is now in a better position to pass intelligently upon the merits of state programs, and many projects which would formerly have met with federal approval are now rejected because they have been tried by other states and found unworkable.

But procedure can never be standardized to the point where a single formula will cover all cases. Rehabilitation is a highly individualized process, totally different in this respect from vocational education. Any two normal boys who wish to become carpenters may be given substantially the same training. But two sightless men who wish to become piano tuners may require very different treatment. One may be a musician; the other may lack even the slightest knowledge of music. One may be intelligent and readily responsive to training; the other may be stupid and quite unresponsive. One may be able to finance himself during a rather extensive training period; the other may have several dependents, and need training that will give him earning power in the shortest possible time. Nor does it follow that a man will make a good piano tuner because he has lost his sight. In some states the tendency is to have but one job for each type of disability, with little regard to aptitude, previous education, individual preference or a host of other relevant factors. The federal agents encourage state administrators to offer each applicant for rehabilitation the widest possible choice of occupations.

DIFFICULTIES OF JUST APPORTIONMENT
OF FUNDS

One of the most important and yet most difficult tasks of the state board administering the Fess-Kenyon Act is to find the disabled persons who need its services. Very few incapacitated

men and women know anything about rehabilitation; they must be singled out and told of their opportunity to receive training that will make them self-supporting.

Names of prospects are secured in a number of different ways. Those states which have workmen's compensation laws must of necessity keep a complete record of all persons disabled through industrial accidents. In many commonwealths the welfare societies, labor organizations, civic and business clubs report all cases coming to their attention. Some of the state rehabilitation boards make a serious effort to secure wide publicity for their work. They distribute pamphlets and posters, and frequently send stories of actual cases to the newspapers. Motion picture films are also used in at least two states. Public health clinics furnish their share of cases. Unfortunately, however, most of the states do not make the fullest use of these various methods of securing names, and as a result thousands of cases never come to their attention.

Vocational rehabilitation is sometimes defined as the process of fitting a disabled person to engage in remunerative employment, but actually the task is far from finished when the course of training has just been completed. There still remains the important and difficult task of placement. A job must be found for the rehabilitated worker, and he must be given a chance to test his newly-developed skill. Not until he has successfully demonstrated his ability to hold his own in competition with normal men and women over a period of several months can rehabilitation be called complete. And not until then is the case marked as closed upon the state's records.

A few years ago the placement of rehabilitated workers was extremely difficult. Most of the employers who agreed to hire them let it be clearly understood that they did so in a spirit of charity and not as a strict business proposition. More recently, however, the attitude of employers has undergone a marked change. Thousands of rehabilitated men and women have proved their ability to do thorough work consistently despite their physical handicaps, and in the light of their success it is not easy to regard the employment of reëducated persons as charity.

THE DEVELOPMENT OF REHABILITATION
WORK

The development of state rehabilitation work under the stimulus of federal funds has been little short of phenomenal. Although twelve states had enacted some sort of legislation concerning vocational reëducation prior to 1920, only half that number had made any serious attempt to put their laws in force. Within a year after the passage of the Fess-Kenyon Act the number of states carrying on rehabilitation programs worthy of the name had risen to thirty-five. Forty states are now cooperating with the federal government. Federal payments to the states were nine times as large in 1927 as in 1921, but every year state outlays kept well ahead of the federal grant. The following table shows the growth of the federal subsidy for rehabilitation:

FEDERAL EXPENDITURES FOR VOCATIONAL
REHABILITATION *

Year	Amount
1921	$93,335.72
1922	318,608.12
1923	525,387.24
1924	551,095.56
1925	519,553.31
1926	578,847.33
1927	880,263.00

* Figures supplied by the Federal Board for Vocational Education.

Hygiene of Maternity and Infancy

In the matter of maternal death rates the United States makes an extremely poor showing. Recently compiled figures of maternal mortality show that among twenty-one leading nations the United States stands at the bottom of the list. With regard to infant deaths our record is much better, but still not entirely satisfactory. [1] Small wonder, therefore, that in recent years the need for teaching mothers how to take better care of themselves and their babies during the crucial months before and after birth has received widespread recognition. In 1921 Congress enacted into law a bill providing for an annual subsidy to the states of $1,240,000 "for the promotion of the welfare and hygiene of maternity and infancy." [2] Three-fourths of the states had already placed upon their statute books laws providing for some form of child hygiene work, but only a few had gone beyond the experimental stage. Most of the state child hygiene bureaus were seriously handicapped by inadequate appropriations. The federal offer stimulated state interest and aided materially in putting the state work upon a sound footing.

THE SHEPPARD-TOWNER ACT

The new federal-aid law, commonly known as the Sheppard-Towner Act, followed closely the lines of its predecessors. It required each state legislature to make formal acceptance of the federal offer, to match federal funds, and to designate or create a state board empowered to coöperate with · the Federal Board of Maternity and Infant Hygiene. This board, set up under the provisions of the act, is composed entirely of ex officio members—the

[1] Figures supplied by Children's Bureau, U. S. Department of Labor.
[2] 42 Stat. L. 224.

Chief of the Children's Bureau of the Department of Labor, the Surgeon General of the Public Health Service of the Treasury Department, and the Commissioner of Education of the Department of the Interior. It meets but three or four times a year.

All the details of administration are in the hands of the Children's Bureau, which has a Division of Maternity and Infancy directed by a physician. Three physicians, two nurses and an auditor comprise the staff of this division. Their headquarters are at Washington, and from there they visit the several states, inspecting state activities and suggesting improvements in state programs. The intention of the Children's Bureau is to send one of its inspectors to every state at least once a year, but this is not always possible. Narrowly restricted Congressional appropriations have prevented the Bureau from securing an adequate number of inspectors, and as a result only four or five days a year are spent in any one state unless exceptional conditions make a longer visit imperative. Frequent changes in state personnel sometimes result in the employment of inexperienced workers, and the burden of training the newcomers frequently falls upon the agents of the Children's Bureau. Under such circumstances a month or even longer may be spent in a single state, with the result that visits to other states must be curtailed.

METHODS OF FEDERAL SUPERVISION

Other federal bureaus administering subsidy laws depend upon their regular field agents to audit state accounts in addition to inspecting state activities. In most cases the agents are not trained auditors, and their examination of state fiscal records is at best perfunctory. The Children's Bureau employs a different plan which might well be adopted more generally. Its agents confine themselves to the task of inspecting state work and making helpful suggestions, leaving the fiscal examination to a trained auditor who visits every state in the course of a year.

This plan has two marked advantages. Not only does it insure a more thorough audit, but it also provides a double check on state activities; for the auditor, though supposed to devote her time entirely to fiscal affairs, is directed to report any matter coming to her attention which seems contrary to federal policy. Aside from the careful audit, federal inspection is not very thorough. This is no reflection upon the agents of the Children's Bureau, who are well trained, dependable workers. The blame must be laid at the door of Congress, whose parsimonious policy has seriously handicapped child hygiene work.

STATES ALLOWED WIDE DISCRETION

The Children's Bureau permits the states a great deal of latitude in framing their plans. No attempt is made to bring about even a semblance of uniformity. Practically every state program submitted for federal approval is accepted in toto unless it contemplates some violation of the law; unless, for example, it provides that federal funds are to be used for the purchase of land or the payment of pensions to mothers, two uses to which the federal subsidy may not be put. The degree of diversity among state plans is not so great as might well be expected, however. Most of the state child hygiene directors are eager to profit by the experience of other states, and to adopt methods which have proved successful elsewhere. Each year the state directors meet in conference initiated by the Children's Bureau, and at these sessions they receive a better understanding of their common problems.[1]

[1] A more complete picture of state work under

"CHILD HEALTH CONFERENCES"

One of the most widely used devices for stimulating local interest, in child health work is the "child health conference." Each conference is a demonstration in some community by state physicians and nurses, who travel from section to section of the state, giving free advice, answering questions, and pointing out by means of talks and motion pictures the importance of safeguarding child health. In many of the states child hygiene nurses are assigned temporarily to the local communities to stimulate interest. Other states follow a somewhat different plan, making use of nurses who direct entire public health programs, devoting only a portion of their time to maternity and infancy work. When the demonstration period is at an end many communities are so impressed with the value of the service that they decide to finance it permanently with local funds.

OPPOSITION OF PRIVATE PRACTITIONERS

During the early stages of the child hygiene movement a great deal of opposition was encountered from private practitioners, who feared that the public doctors and nurses might become serious competitors. Several years have passed since the inception of public programs, but even yet the fear has not been entirely dispelled. The American Medical Association is still conducting an active anti-federal-child-hygiene campaign. The average physician has long since discovered, however, that public child health work is

the Sheppard-Towner Act is given in Macdonald, Austin F., *Federal Aid*, pp. 215-21. See also the reports made to the League of Women Voters by the American Child Health Association and the Maternity Center Association. These reports are reprinted in abridged form in the Congressional Record, 70th Cong., 1st Sess., May 29, 1928.

designed to increase his practice rather than to interfere with it. Doctors and nurses paid in part with Sheppard-Towner funds are scrupulously careful not to prescribe remedies. They do not cure physical defects. Instead they teach the importance of proper hygiene, and when medical treatment becomes necessary they recommend a visit to the family physician.

SUPERVISION OF MIDWIVES

One of the most important phases of maternity work is the regulation and supervision of midwives. A surprisingly large number of children are ushered into the world by midwives; in some states at least half of the births are unattended by physicians. The seriousness of this situation is obvious when it is understood that most of the midwives are ignorant, untrained women, highly superstitious and without the faintest conception of the elementary rules of hygiene. They do not even appreciate the value of cleanliness.

There are, of course, some very competent women among the professional midwives. In Pennsylvania, New York and some other states many of them are graduates of midwifery schools. But in parts of the South conditions are abominable. The midwives are chiefly negroes, who frequently rely upon the semi-savage rites of slavery days. How to fit them to practice their calling is a problem of considerable magnitude. Classes have been formed in many states, and the rudiments of maternal hygiene have been taught to hundreds of women. Laws prohibiting them from practicing cannot be satisfactorily enforced. In fact, such laws are undesirable, for in many sparsely-settled communities there are no physicians, while in other sections are thousands of families too poor to pay for medical attention.

The solution of the problem is not the elimination of the midwife, but stricter regulation and more adequate training.

WISELY ADMINISTERED, BUT BITTERLY OPPOSED

The Sheppard-Towner Act was passed by an overwhelming vote in both houses of Congress. No other federal aid statute received so large a majority, or escaped with so little criticism.[1] No other subsidy law has been administered with so great regard for the opinions and wishes of state officials, or with so sincere a determination to avoid offending local pride. If any error has been made in the administration of the Sheppard-Towner Act, it has been the sacrificing of federal standards in order to retain the good will of the states.

And yet, curiously enough, the opponents of federal aid have singled out this law as the special target for their attacks. Maliciously or through ignorance, they have repeatedly misrepresented it. They have pictured the officials of the Children's Bureau as a conscienceless group of spies, forcing their way into private homes and compelling parents to raise their chil-

dren according to prescribed federal formulas. "The child belongs to the parents!" has frequently been a slogan in the fight against the child hygiene movement. A true statement, surely, but quite irrelevant. Even well informed persons do not know what is being done by the states with the aid of federal funds. In the November, 1923, issue of the *Illinois Law Review* an editorial declared that the Sheppard-Towner Act "provides for the pensioning of and rendering monetary aid to indigent mothers."[2] This statement should be compared with the exact words of the law, which are to the effect that federal and state-matched funds may not be used "for the payment of any maternity or infancy pension, stipend or gratuity."[3] When the foes of the subsidy system decided to attack its constitutionality, they selected the Sheppard-Towner Act as most likely to meet the disfavor of the Supreme Court. The opposition to continuance of federal aid for child hygiene had become so pronounced by 1927 that in the spring of that year its friends in Congress were obliged to accept a two-year extension, until June 30, 1929, with the proviso that after that date the subsidy would be discontinued. Whether a future Congress will reverse this policy and extend the federal grant beyond the 1929 limit is problematic.

[1] *Congress Record*, v. 61, pt. 4, p. 4216 (Senate vote), and v. 61, pt. 8, p. 8037 (House vote). The National Defense Act of 1916 received almost unanimous support from both parties, but it was primarily a measure designed to strengthen the army at a time when war seemed inevitable. Its subsidy feature was of minor importance.

[2] Vol. 18, p. 204.   [3] Section 12.

PART III

CONCLUSIONS

FEDERAL aid is one of the most controversial subjects before the American people at the present time. Although the system has been warmly defended by staunch adherents, it has been attacked with equal vigor by determined opponents. It has been pictured by some as an instrument for accomplishing great ends, and by others as a practice leading to "the gradual breaking down of local self-government in America."[1] Charges have been made and denied of unreasonable federal interference in state affairs, of attempts to secure excessive standardization, of political manipulations destructive of sound administration.

This partisan discussion has tended to obscure rather than to make clear the real facts concerning federal aid. A definite, impartial investigation of the effects of the subsidy system ought, therefore, to possess some value. Such an investigation this committee has attempted to make. Its conclusions are based chiefly upon first-hand material.

SUMMARY OF CONCLUSIONS

The committee desires first to record its belief that federal aid to the states is a sound principle of administration, and ought to be continued. This statement, however, does not imply an unqualified endorsement of every feature of the subsidy system. On the contrary, it seems that certain phases of the system, referred to on other pages of this report,[2] might profitably

be altered. The reasons that have led the committee to accept the principle of federal aid are set forth below:

1. *Federal aid has stimulated state activity.*—Of this fact there can be no doubt. Figures showing the growth of vocational education, agricultural extension work and other functions subsidized with federal money have already been presented in this report. In every instance the granting of federal funds has marked the beginning of a new era of state activity. The number of states engaged in civilian rehabilitation tripled within a year after the passage of the Fess-Kenyon Act. Agricultural extension work was unknown until it was introduced as an experiment by the United States Department of Agriculture. The opinions of the state directors administering the various subsidy laws furnish further evidence. At the present time there are three hundred and six state officials whose duty it is to coöperate with the federal government under the provisions of the seven federal-aid statutes described above. Two hundred and sixty-four of these men and women—state directors of extension work, state foresters, state highway engineers, state adjutants general, and the like—were asked recently if federal funds had stimulated their state programs.[3] Two hundred and forty replied emphatically in the affirmative. "Without federal aid it would have taken fifty years to bring our state work to the point where it is today," said one. "The federal

---

[1] Lowden, Frank O., in his Convocation Address, University of Chicago, June, 1921.

[2] Cf. *infra*, pp. 639–641.

[3] Nearly half of these two hundred and sixty-four state officials were interviewed. The remainder filled out questionnaires.

subsidy has not only increased the amount of available funds; it has awakened widespread state interest," was the comment of another.

These replies are typical. They have been selected practically at random. Of the remaining state directors, one was uncertain what reply to make, so that only twenty-three out of two hundred and sixty-four—not quite nine per cent—questioned the stimulating effect of federal aid upon the activities of their states. Numbered among the ninety-one per cent who answered affirmatively were officials of several of the wealthiest and most progressive states of the Union.

2. *Federal aid has raised state standards.*—The two hundred and sixty-four state directors were also asked: "Has federal supervision in any way affected your state standards?" The affirmative replies outnumbered the negative by more than two to one. One hundred and eighty-one said "Yes, raised them materially," or words to that effect; eighty-one said "no;" two were doubtful. This trend of opinion is highly significant, for state officials, like other men and women, are reasonably certain to claim for themselves all credit to which they are entitled. Had they been solely responsible for improved conditions, few of them would have hesitated to say so.

The fact that seventy per cent of the state directors whose opinions were asked, willingly conceded the value of federal supervision indicates that the supervision has accomplished results in at least seventy per cent of the states. There is no doubt that some of the subsidies in some of the states have done very little to better the high standards already set. In the matter of highways, for example, some of the more progressive states insist upon specifications considerably above the minimum acceptable to the federal government.

Regardless of federal requirements they would not be satisfied with poorly qualified teachers, inadequately trained nurses, or fire protective systems that failed to protect. But for the large majority of the states (more than seventy per cent, in all probability), federal inspection and advice have proved essential.

It is not necessary to place entire dependence upon the opinions of state directors in determining the effect of federal aid on state standards. The record of state progress following the acceptance of federal aid speaks for itself. In more than one state the college-trained high school teacher of vocational argiculture, for example, paid in part from Smith-Hughes funds, is frequently subordinate to a high school principal who never entered the doors of a college. In more than one state graft and corruption are commonplaces in county road construction, while they play but little part in the building of federal aid highways. In more than one state commercial education, unsubsidized by the federal government, is sadly neglected, while industrial and agricultural training, under the stimulus of federal leadership, are constantly developing higher standards. A comparison of state standards in any field just prior to acceptance of federal aid and three years after acceptance is sufficient to show the effect of the subsidy system upon state administration.

3. *Federal aid has been consistently administered without unreasonable federal interference in state affairs.*—One of the charges most frequently made against federal aid is that it results in federal domination of state activities, that it serves as an excuse for federal bureau chiefs to force their plans and their policies upon unwilling state officials. There seemed to be no better way to determine the truth of such a statement than to ask the men and

women who were allegedly the victims of federal interference.

Accordingly the two hundred and sixty-four state directors, whose opinions on other matters have already been quoted, were asked if the federal government had been guilty of unwarranted intrusion in state affairs. Two hundred and forty-five of them—ninety-two per cent—denied emphatically any federal domination. Three of the remaining nineteen replied: "Occasionally, but not as a general rule." Ninety-two per cent is a very high percentage. It approaches unanimity. Federal officials must have administered the subsidy laws with great tact and skill to have given so little offense. "We disagree on many matters," said one state official. "But the federal government is willing to try to see our viewpoint, and its representatives are always patient and sympathetic. Any one who speaks of federal domination simply doesn't know the facts." Substantially the same words were used by the other two hundred and forty-five.

It is interesting to note that the office of Coöperative Extension Work, administering the Smith-Lever Act,

succeeded in escaping entirely the displeasure of the state extension directors. Of the forty-six state directors consulted, not a single one regarded federal supervision in the light of domination. The Federal Board for Vocational Education, in charge of the work under the Smith-Hughes and Fess-Kenyon (Rehabilitation) Acts, and the Children's Bureau, administering the Sheppard-Towner Act, were also given clean bills by state coöperating officials. Four state foresters, however, accused the federal government of undue interference, as compared with twenty-six foresters who approved of the manner of federal supervision. Five state highway engineers thought there was some truth in the charge of federal domination, though thirty-six characterized federal inspection as most reasonable. Ten state adjutants-general complained of federal interference; twenty-seven others scoffed at the notion.

The following table presents the opinions of state directors in convenient form:

The federal bureau receiving the fewest complaints is not necessarily

HAS FEDERAL AID ENCOURAGED FEDERAL INTERFERENCE IN STATE AFFAIRS? *

Class of officials	Number of coöperating states	Number of state directors replying	Number of state directors answering "Yes"	Number of state directors answering "No"	Number of state directors doubtful
State foresters..............	32	30	4	26	..
Extension directors........	48	46	0	46	..
Highway engineers.........	48	41	2	36	3
Adjutants-general.........	47	37	10	27	..
Directors of Vocational education...............	48	35	0	35	..
Directors of Vocational re-education..............	40	35	0	35	..
Child hygiene directors	43	40	0	40	..
	306	264	16	245	3

* Table prepared from information contained in Macdonald, Austin F., *Federal Aid*. This volume contains a complete analysis of the replies of state officials.

entitled to the highest commendation. Every bureau administering a subsidy law has two important tasks. One is to gain and hold the confidence of the states, taking care not to offend local pride. The other is to maintain minimum federal standards in every co-operating state.

To some extent these duties are conflicting. The bureau that places undue emphasis upon standards and shows itself unwilling to wait with some degree of patience for signs of improvement is likely to encounter the wrath of state officials. On the other hand, the bureau that seeks to gain the confidence of the states at any cost may find it necessary to overlook conditions that should be corrected. Somewhere between these two extremes is the much-talked-of happy medium which makes state directors happy without depressing the advocates of higher standards. The Federal Board for Vocational Education and the office of Coöperative Extension Work have erred, if at all, on the side of undue leniency. The Children's Bureau has seemingly placed too great emphasis on the importance of state freedom from federal supervision, though its attitude has doubtless been made necessary, at least in part, by the bitter opposition to the Sheppard-Towner Act. The Bureau of Highways, with a splendid record of careful inspection, has made but few enemies. The Forest Service has likewise escaped excessive criticism, though its supervision of state activities has been very thorough.

Least successful has been the Militia Bureau. More than half of the total number of complaints are registered against the administration of the National Defense Act, while federal inspection of National Guard units has left much to be desired. It is only fair to the Militia Bureau to point out, however, that most of the slipshod inspec-

tion has been directly traceable to its lack of control over the so-called federal "instructors," while most of the criticisms of state adjutants-general have been directed, not against the Militia Bureau, but against the general staff. It is believed that state objections would largely cease and that federal inspection would be greatly improved if the general staff were divested of most of its control over National Guard matters, with a corresponding increase in the authority of the Militia Bureau.

The widespread belief that the federal government interferes with state affairs is due in part to the fact that many state directors protect themselves from the effects of local politics by shifting responsibility to the federal government. Many a state extension director, adjutant general or highway engineer finds that pressure is constantly brought to bear on him to relax standards; to appoint some incompetent whose chief asset is a host of influential friends; or to approve the selection of an improper highway route as a matter of "courtesy" to some politician. But for federal aid, the state director would be forced to stand on his own feet or else bow to political pressure. The subsidy system, however, makes it easy for him to shift responsibility. "I'm sorry, boys," is likely to be his reply, "but if I did what you ask the federal government would never approve our plans." To his friends he freely confesses the value of federal aid as a shield against the onslaughts of the spoilsmen. Federal bureau chiefs can withstand the pressure brought by state politicians much better than can state directors. Washington is a long distance from Jefferson City, Madison or Montgomery. But every instance of this sort gives rise to the belief that the federal government is interfering in matters of purely state concern, and that it is imposing its will upon reluctant state directors. Some of the federal bureau chiefs do not object to appearing in a false light, since the maintenance of high standards is thereby made easier. Others are inclined to resent the unwillingness of many state directors to accept responsibility.

4. *Federal aid has accomplished results without standardizing state activities.*—Any administrative device that attempts to treat the United States as a homogeneous unit, without varying local needs and varying local problems, is foredoomed to failure. This country is so vast that methods well adapted to one section may prove totally unsuitable for another. Recognition of this fact has been in large measure responsible for the successful development of the subsidy system. The federal aid statutes make no attempt to set up uniform procedure. The Federal Highways Act of 1921, for example, provides that "only such durable types of surface and kinds of materials shall be adopted for the construction and reconstruction of any highway . . . as will adequately meet the existing and probable future traffic needs and conditions thereon." [1] But no attempt is made to define "durable;" the exact meaning of that word will of necessity vary widely from state to state. A durable road in Montana would prove short-lived indeed under the pounding of New York's traffic. The Clarke-McNary Law of 1924 authorizes federal coöperation with any state whose "system and practice of forest fire prevention and suppression . . . substantially promotes" the protection of timbered land. [2] But there is nothing to indicate the kind of system that "substantially promotes" fire protection.

So it is with all the federal aid laws. In every case the chief of the federal

[1] 42 Stat. L. 212, section 8.

[2] 43 Stat. L. 653, section 2.

bureau administering the statute is entrusted with the duty of determining whether state plans are adequate, whether they provide for durable roads or properly trained teachers, and whether they substantially promote the interest of the states and of the nation. And it has already been pointed out that the federal bureau chiefs issue no *ex-cathedra* pronouncements for the benefit of the state directors with whom they coöperate. Instead, the fullest recognition of local needs is insured by permitting state officials to formulate their own plans, and minimum federal standards are maintained by means of the federal veto—a veto but seldom used except with regard to minor details.

5. *Federal administration of the subsidy laws has been uninfluenced by partisan politics.*—The chief of every bureau administering federal aid has been chosen without regard to partisan considerations. Every one had years of experience in the federal service or in the service of some state before becoming chief of a bureau. The director of the Federal Board for Vocational Education was for years one of the agents of the Board. The chief of the Forest Service has been connected with the Service for twenty-three years. The chief of the Bureau of Public Roads resigned as highway engineer of the state of Iowa to accept the offer of the federal government. The staffs of all the bureaus are similarly free from political influence. They are chosen under civil service regulations, and while those regulations have not always operated to secure the best-trained, most desirable men and women, they have certainly succeeded in eliminating incompetents selected at the behest of professional politicians.

6. *Federal aid has mitigated some of the most disastrous effects of state politics.*—No one would seriously contend that

partisan politics have been eliminated from state administration of the subsidy laws. While some states have earned an enviable reputation for honest, efficient administration, others have become notorious as the happy hunting grounds of the spoilsmen. In a number of states the rehabilitation service has been seriously crippled as a result of political appointments. Child health work has also suffered, though to a lesser extent. A few years ago conditions became so bad in one Mid-Western state that the Bureau of Public Roads was obliged to withdraw all federal aid for a time—a drastic step taken only four or five times by all the federal bureaus combined since the inception of the modern subsidy system in 1911. Very recently an able state forester, appointed because of the insistent demand of the lumber interests, had scarcely assumed the duties of his office when he received from the governor a list of the persons who were to comprise the personnel of the forestry department. These instances, which might be multiplied *ad nauseam*, are sufficient to indicate that all the state coöperating agencies have not escaped the baneful effects of politics.

The representatives of the federal government are well aware of the extent to which partisan considerations determine the policies of certain states, and a great deal of their time is devoted to the task of improving conditions. They do not threaten to cut off all federal funds if state administration is not instantly withdrawn from the field of politics. Such a threat would be tantamount to an announcement of federal withdrawal from all further coöperative relationships, for no state could thus forcibly be led into the path of righteousness. But they do insist that state plans at least measure up to minimum federal standards of efficiency, and that these plans be carried out sub-

stantially as approved. It is not federal policy to deal in personalities. A federal bureau chief will not demand the resignation of any person in the state service, [1] but he may insist that someone better qualified be assigned to the coöperative work. Or, if his policy is less aggressive, he may accept without complaint the appointment of a group of incompetents, and direct federal agents to teach the newcomers the essentials of their jobs. In more than one instance state employees have received most of their training from agents of the federal government. But whatever the method adopted, the effect of federal influence has been to produce more competent workers in the less progressive states. Federal aid has not eliminated state politics but it has certainly mitigated the evils of partisan administration.

7. *Federal aid has placed no unreasonable burden on any section of the country.* —Some statesmen and publicists argue at great length that the subsidy system is unfair to the wealthy, industrial East because it results in a transference of wealth from the rich Eastern states to the less wealthy states of the South and West. They point out that federal aid is apportioned among the states on the basis of population, [2] while the funds in the federal treasury are presumably drawn from the people of the states on the basis of wealth or income. The inhabitants of a rich state pay to the federal government in income and other taxes *far more per capita* than the people of a poor state, but they receive in return in the form of federal aid *exactly the same amount per capita*.

To the opponents of federal aid this arrangement seems inequitable. They contend that the system should be abol-

[1] Note, however, the remarks concerning the Forest Service on p. 631.

[2] The subsidies for road construction and forest fire prevention are, of course, exceptions.

ished because every state does not receive a return proportionate to its contribution to the federal treasury. "No argument can be made for it," declared Governor Ritchie of Maryland in 1925, speaking before the Pennsylvania State Chamber of Commerce, "except that the states which other states carry want the money." [1] Reduced to its simplest terms, the contention of Governor Ritchie and of others who reason along similar lines is that the basis of federal expenditures should be wealth instead of need. If federal funds are collected in proportion to wealth or income, they ought to be paid out, it is claimed, on the same basis. The fact that some states get back more than they contribute, while others receive less, "reflects the indefensible discriminations of the fifty-fifty system."

This reasoning is unique. It runs counter to generally accepted concepts. In theory at least, if not always in practice, governmental revenue systems are based on the principle of ability to pay, as indicated by wealth or income. The burden of government rests, or ought to rest, upon those best able to bear it. But governmental expenditures are everywhere based on need, and not on wealth. The largest schools are, or ought to be, erected in the districts containing the most children, not necessarily in those sections paying the highest taxes.

The greatest expenditures for poor relief are made in the poorest neighborhoods. The acceptance of this principle is virtually universal. Cities spend their revenues where they are most needed, without regard to where they were raised; and the fiscal system of every city results in a transference of

wealth from the richer to the poorer districts. The states make large expenditures in the rural sections from funds raised chiefly in the cities. Every large municipality is helping the poorer rural districts to bear the cost of government.

What possible objection can there be, then, to extending the principle of need to the expenditure of federal revenues? To go a step further, what other principle could possibly be applied with any suggestion of fairness? Ought federal judges to be assigned chiefly to the wealthy states on the assumption that most of their salaries are paid by these states? Should the Interstate Commerce Commission devote most of its time to the railroads of the East because so large a part of federal revenues is derived from the New England and Middle Atlantic States? The mere suggestion of such an arrangement is enough to indicate the folly of trying to make federal expenditures bear any relation to the wealth of the states.

Need must be the criterion in determining federal outlays. Population may be a very crude measuring-stick —it may serve but roughly to indicate need. But it does so very much more effectively than the wealth of the several states or the amounts of their income taxes. Federal aid cannot fairly be criticised because it draws from the wealthy and gives to those less able to bear their share of the burden. Every sound governmental fiscal system does the same.

The objection may well be raised that some more accurate means of measuring need should be found. Population bears only a slight relation to any state's need for roads, schools, or county agents. But though population is not an ideal basis for distributing federal funds, it has certain obvious advantages. It is uniform, easily de-

[1] "Federal Subsidies to the States," published by the Pennsylvania State Chamber of Commerce, Harrisburg, Pennsylvania. For an analysis of this and other arguments see Macdonald, Austin F., *Federal Aid*.

termined, and not subject to political manipulations. The committee believes, therefore, that no immediate change should be made in the method of apportioning federal subsidies.

RECOMMENDED CHANGES IN FEDERAL SUBSIDY SYSTEM

Although the committee unqualifiedly indorses the principle of federal aid, believing that the subsidy system has proved a highly effective administrative device, it desires nevertheless to call attention to certain features of the system which ought to be changed in the interest of greater efficiency. Defects found in individual laws, and not characteristic of all federal aid, have already been pointed out and need not here be repeated.

The thoroughness of federal supervision varies greatly from bureau to bureau. Some federal bureaus are familiar with every detail of state work; others are ignorant of much that is done by state officials. Some bureaus establish definite standards of performance which must be met by the states before federal funds are paid out. Others make no attempt to set up standards for the guidance of the states. Some bureaus call the states strictly to account when state practices are discovered at variance with accepted standards. Others are long suffering, accepting virtually any state plan and condoning almost any state practice short of an actual violation of the letter of the law. In plain words, some federal bureaus are doing their task of administration—of inspection and supervision—more carefully and more completely than others.

Apparently there is no good reason why all the federal bureaus administering subsidy laws should not adopt the methods of the more successful. Every bureau should become thoroughly familiar with the work of the

states. Every bureau should go beyond the strict letter of the law, encouraging those practices which long experience has shown to be satisfactory and discouraging unsound customs. Whether every bureau should set up definite standards of performance is a debatable question. In some work, such as vocational rehabilitation, it may be impossible to set up rigid standards.

Some federal bureaus keep too loose a hand on the reins. Some condone too much and insist upon too little. The chiefs of these bureaus justify themselves, and with some reason, by emphasizing the need for continued cordial relations with the states. They point out that the withdrawal of federal aid from a state might destroy the work of years. And they are undoubtedly correct when they stress the importance of good feeling between federal and state officials. Without good feeling there can be no real coöperation. The error of the bureaus which adopt a liberal, or lax policy is that they assume such a policy to be essential to continued friendly relations with the states. Other federal bureaus administering subsidy laws do far more to raise state standards, and at the same time they retain the good will and respect of the state officials with whom they work. Other federal bureaus exercise a most careful supervision of state activities, and yet escape the charge of domination.

The committee realizes that it is no easy task to steer a middle course—to raise state standards consistently and rapidly and yet to retain state good will. It admits freely that the severing of friendly state relations in an effort to force state progress would be a tragic error. Yet it believes that some of the federal administering bureaus err on the side of laxity, and that they might well profit from the experience of other federal bureaus which have successfully carried out a firmer policy.

Congressional appropriations to most of the bureaus for administrative purposes are totally inadequate. As a result the federal inspectors are generally underpaid and overworked. Inspection is cursory in many cases simply because funds for more adequate investigations are not available. It is poor policy to give liberally to the states and then to withhold from the federal administering bureaus the money necessary to make certain that federal allotments are not wasted. Congress could make no wiser investment than by increasing the appropriations for the administration of federal aid. It would receive large dividends in the form of more thorough federal inspection and higher state standards of performance.

NATIONAL
MUNICIPAL REVIEW

PUBLISHED MONTHLY BY THE

National Municipal League

VOL. XVII, No. 11   NOVEMBER, 1928   TOTAL No. 149

CONTENTS

EDITORIAL COMMENT...........................*Russell Forbes*   661

OUR AMERICAN MAYORS:

    XIII. WILLIAM HALE THOMPSON OF CHICAGO ...*Edward M. Martin*   663

THE VIRGINIA REORGANIZATION PROGRAM..........*Robert H. Tucker*..   673

A NEW BOOK ON THE APPRAISAL OF URBAN LAND AND

    BUILDINGS. ....*Philip H. Cornick*   680

THE MODEL MUNICIPAL TRAFFIC ORDINANCE.......*C. W. Stark*......   684

THE TAX SITUATION IN CHICAGO.................*Herbert D. Simpson*   690

DEPARTMENTS

  I. Recent Books Reviewed..   696

 II. Judicial Decisions.......................................*Edited by C. W. Tooke*   700

III. Public Utilities...*Edited by John Bauer*   703

IV. Governmental Research Association Notes................*Edited by Russell Forbes*   708

 V. Municipal Activities Abroad.............................*Edited by W. E. Mosher*   712

VI. Notes and Events ....*Edited by Welles A. Gray*   713

LEAGUE'S BUSINESS

Distribution of League Pamphlets.—During the year ending September 30, 1928, a total of 22,457 copies of League pamphlets were distributed. Many of our publications are used in classrooms. For example, in one month of the past year thirty-two colleges and universities from twenty-two different states placed orders for classroom use. The following table shows the distribution of our pamphlets:

Title	Free	Sold	Total
Administration of the Gasoline Tax in United States.........	2	20	22
Administrative Consolidation of State Governments.........	249	730	979
Administrative Reorganization in Illinois...................	6	17	23
Airports as a Factor in City Planning....................	170	384	554
Assessment of Real Estate........................	5	107	112
City Manager Budget...........................	1	4	5
City Planning and Zoning Budget......................	0	6	6
Constitutionality of Proportional Representation...........	1	38	39
Correct Public Policy towards Street Railway Problem......	2	23	25
County, The..............................	0	22	22
County Manager Plan..........................	687	696	1,383
Electric Light and Power as Public Utility................	4	25	29
Electricity in Great Britain.........................	368	18	386
Employment Management in Municipal Civil Service.......	2	29	31
Fitz-Elwyne's Assize of Buildings......................	302	0	302
German Cities since the Revolution of 1918...............	3	17	20
Land Subdivision and the City Plan....................	1	45	46
Law of the City Plan............................	2	57	59
Loose-Leaf Digest of City Manager Charters...............	1	36	37
Merit System in Government.........................	0	47	47
Minor Highway Privileges as a Source of Revenue..........	2	21	23
Model Bond Law..............................	459	121	580
Model City Charter............................	174	823	997
Model Municipal Budget Law....................	1,490	331	1,821
Model Registration System.........................	20	170	190
Model State Constitution.........................	84	907	991
Modern City Planning............................	6	108	114
Municipal Salaries under Changing Price Level.............	2	29	31
National Municipal League Series......................	4	105	109
National Municipal Review.........................	2,494	663	3,157
New Charter Proposals for Norwood, Mass................	7	10	17
Political Integration of Metropolitan Areas...............	0	4	4
President's Removal Power under the Constitution.........	28	83	111
Primer Chart of Typical City Governments...............	26	29	55
Reprints of Review articles.........................	703	36	739
Service at Cost for Street Railways....................	2	17	19
Short Ballot................................	381	88	469
Special Assessments for Public Improvement..............	5	92	97
Standards of Financial Administration..................	220	124	344
State Parks.................................	2	21	23
State Welfare Administration and Consolidated Government..	3	18	21
Story of City Manager Plan........................	2,115	6,220	8,335
Zoning....................................	2	81	83
Totals....................................	10,035	12,422	22,457

NATIONAL
MUNICIPAL REVIEW

Vol. XVII, No. 11   NOVEMBER, 1928   Total No. 149

EDITORIAL COMMENT

Annual Meeting of the League
As this issue goes to press, plans are being perfected for the annual meeting of the League in Cincinnati, October 16 and 17, in conjunction with the meetings of the Governmental Research Association and the National Association of Civic Secretaries. Next month's issue will reprint two of the leading addresses delivered at the convention, and will contain a résumé and an impression of the convention proceedings by Dr. Lent D. Upson, director of the Detroit Bureau of Governmental Research.

✱

The Tax Situation in Chicago
We conclude this month the series of three excellent articles by Dr. Herbert D. Simpson on "The Tax Situation in Chicago." The series of articles on this subject will be reprinted by the author in booklet form. Interested readers may secure copies by addressing Dr. Simpson at the Institute for Research in Land Economics, 337 East Chicago Avenue, Chicago.

✱

Traffic Control
The readers of the article on "A Model Traffic Ordinance" in this issue will be interested in the recent decision of the City of Boston to install traffic lights for pedestrians.

Those familiar with traffic on James F. Mahoney Square, Boston, better known perhaps as the corner of Tremont and Boylston Streets, the busiest spot in all Boston, will recall that for several years the pedestrian has had peculiar privileges on that spot. When the amber and red lights are both showing, all vehicular traffic must stop and the pedestrian is king. The new Boston traffic code, drafted by Dr. Miller McClintock of Harvard University, which went into effect October 8, provides for this system on practically all important corners of the city.

Crossing lines to be established on all intersections where the traffic is not governed by lights will further protect the pedestrian, for vehicular traffic must allow all pedestrians the right to cross on these lines unmolested. Drastic parking regulations are also included in this new code. In the greater part of the downtown area only cars with licensed operators may be parked. This regulation has aroused some protest from those without chauffeurs who have been in the habit of leaving their cars parked on the streets all day unattended, and who now charge that this provision discriminates against them.

✱

British Municipal Expert Visits the United States
Arthur Collins, F. S. A. A., honorary secretary of the Institute of British Municipal Treasurers

and Accountants, and financial adviser to local government authorities in Great Britain, is at present making a tour of the United States to study American city government at first hand.

Mr. Collins is widely known in England as an outstanding expert in municipal administration, and is frequently called in as a consulting authority by local officials desirous of securing expert advice. During his visit he has made a number of public addresses. He talked on "British City Accounting and Taxation" before the convention of the International City Managers' Association, at Asheville, N. C., on September 18, and on "Cities—British and American" at the joint convention of the National Municipal League, the Governmental Research Association, and the National Association of Civic Secretaries, at Cincinnati at the banquet session on the evening of October 16. On October 24, Mr. Collins also delivered a public lecture on "The Achievement of Efficiency in Modern City Government" at the Association of the Bar in New York City.

✣

Resignations of California City Managers   H. C. Bottorff, city manager of Sacramento, submitted his resignation to the city council, to take effect October 15. His resignation was due to petty politics in the council. Upon the death of one of the councilmen, the vacancy thus created was filled by a successor in sympathy with a group previously elected upon a platform of changing the principal heads of the city government. Conditions became such that it was impossible for the manager to make any progress or to carry to completion the program of development adopted about seven years ago.

Mr. Bottorff has been associated with the city government since the adoption of the manager plan in 1921. He served first as assistant manager and comptroller, and one year later became manager. The following quotations from an editorial appearing in *The Sacramento Bee* give an interesting picture of the situation:

"The present masters of the city government last night voted the removal of City Manager H. C. Botorff.

"His forced retirement is not in the interest of good government. It is not in the interest of efficient administration. It is not in the interest of the public service. It is not in the interest of wise and able direction of city affairs. . . .

"'Bud' Bottorff has his faults. He is only human like the rest of us. But he has served the city well and honorably.

"He was single-heartedly devoted to giving the people of Sacramento a dollar's return for every dollar collected. . . .

"Not a taint or suspicion of graft has attached itself to his official work; no one can say but that his one aim and purpose has been to give his best and most honest endeavor to raising the level of government in Sacramento to a higher plane.

"Bottorff goes; but the principles for which he battled will remain. Let us hope that his successor will follow in his footsteps."

Charles E. Ashburner, city manager of Stockton, California, has submitted his resignation, effective on November 30. The council tried to dissuade him from taking this action, and voted six to two to table the resignation. Despite this, however, Mr. Ashburner informed them that he was definitely "through" and that he would leave office November 30 regardless of any action they might take. In his letter of resignation, he attributed his action to internal dissension, and cited as an example the delay for many years of the federal-state-city project to widen and deepen the San Joaquin channel at a cost of about six million dollars. . .

OUR AMERICAN MAYORS

XIII. WILLIAM HALE THOMPSON OF CHICAGO: THE SAGA OF A SOMBRERO

BY EDWARD M. MARTIN
Chicago

The mayoralty in Chicago: the double play in politics—Thompson to Dever to Thompson; King George repulsed; ballyhoo, bluster and bunk; and "America First." :: :: :: :: :: ::

THE name "William Hale Thompson" is probably more widely known than that of any other American mayor. Its owner, now completing his tenth year as chief executive of the second city of the United States, has achieved national reputation and international notoriety by his exploits as a public personage.

THE MAYOR'S ORIGIN AND BACKGROUND

William Hale Thompson was born in Boston in 1869 and was brought to Chicago in early infancy. He received a common school education. His father, William Hale Thompson, was a well-known business man of the city, had extensive property interests, and had served as colonel in the Second Illinois Guard. His maternal grandfather, Stephen F. Hale, had been a Chicago pioneer, had drawn up the city's corporation charter, and was the first chief of its fire department.

William Hale was intended for Yale, but at fourteen went to Wyoming, where he was successively brakeman, cowboy and cattle owner. These early experiences undoubtedly account for the hero stuff and other "Western" touches of his campaigns. Chief of these has been his trusty sombrero, ever-present emblem in all his campaigns.

At twenty-one, with a stake of $30,000 all his own, Thompson returned to Chicago to take charge of his father's estate. Managing the paren-

tal properties and dealing in real estate occupied him for the next few years. With both means and leisure, he devoted himself to the advancement of the "manly sports." He was active in the organization of the Illinois Athletic Club and in the activities of the Sportsmen's Club of America, of which at one time he was director-general. He interested himself in yachting, and also helped to form a championship football team in the Chicago Athletic Association, traveling over the country with this team in the capacity of captain.

"Big Bill's" love of the out-of-doors led him to champion the cause of public playgrounds; he claims to have secured from the council the appropriation for Chicago's first public playground.

HIS START IN POLITICS

It is credibly stated that "Big Bill" was introduced to politics by the late William Kent, political radical and courageous fighter of spoils and corruption. In 1900 Thompson was elected alderman from his home district, then the city's fashionable residence district and now the heart of the "Black Belt," the old Second Ward. Two years later he was chosen a member of the board of commissioners of Cook County. During these early years he seems to have been "one of the boys" who constituted the Republican cohorts.

Later on, Thompson became associated with Fred Lundin, a survivor of the old Lorimer machine. Lundin was a power in Republican councils as early as 1908 when, though defeated, he led the party ticket by 20,000 votes when seeking the office of city clerk. Later he was elected to Congress.

Thompson's money and position and Lundin's political acumen and showmanship proved to be a successful combination. They were termed the "Gallagher and Shean of Chicago politics." Thompson was called the "front" of the team. His commanding physique, always well-tailored, his open countenance, and his genial manner gave him a winning public presence.

Lundin—called the "brains" of the combination—was known as the "fox." He had been an old-time medicine man and had the talents of the showman. Lundin was pictured to the public as wearing an antiquated shiny black frock coat, an enormous black felt hat, a bow tie, and smoked glasses.

ELECTED MAYOR IN 1915

In 1915 Thompson was elected mayor, defeating County Clerk Robert M. Sweitzer, son-in-law of Roger Sullivan, the Democratic boss, by the vote of 398,538 to 251,061. Newspapers referred to the campaign as a "Donnybrook" and "triviality puffed with wind and filled with sound."

In 1919, with the Thompson-Lundin combination still intact, with the backing of a political machine perfected by four years of city hall "pap," Thompson again triumphed over Sweitzer. This time his majority was narrowed to 21,624.

Again, in 1927, after a tactical retirement, "Big Bill" was elected to his third four-year term in the mayor's chair. In the total vote of 1,000,000 ballots, his plurality over William E. Dever, Democrat, and John Dill

Robertson, independent Republican, was 31,691; his majority over Dever, who had the better element backing, was 83,038.

HIS VOTE-GETTING METHODS

What were the issues on which "Big Bill" rode to victory? What are the characteristics of Thompson as a political leader? How did he come back after apparently being politically down and out?

The answer to these questions will be revealed by an analysis of Thompson's acts as occupant of the mayor's chair, as a party leader, and as a conjurer of political slogans.

Early in his first term Thompson established himself in public confidence by entering the dispute between the transit companies and their 14,500 employees. After a fifteen-hour conference in his office the settlement proposed was accepted.

Thompson made a campaign pledge to enforce the Sunday closing law for saloons. Licenses of saloons violating the Sunday-closing order were revoked; later it was disclosed that these licenses were being secretly restored.

When Thompson became mayor, Lundin was made chairman of the committee on patronage. As such he was the czar of Chicago politics. The administration, with Thompson in the lead and Lundin as "the power behind the throne," proceeded systematically to play the game of politics for all it was worth. Chicago has the strong mayor-council type of government. The mayor is also presiding officer of the council, with the veto power.

When the Thompson-Lundin forces took possession of the city hall, the council was marked by a high level of aldermanic initiative and leadership. The level had been raised from the days of the "gray wolves" largely through the systematic and persistent educational work of the Municipal Voters' League.

CONTROL OF THE CIVIL SERVICE THROUGH "TEMPORARY" APPOINTMENTS

The early attempts of the administration to exploit the executive departments met with opposition from the council. The administration misused "sixty-day" appointments for political purposes to get around the civil service law. The council passed an order calling for a list of all "temporary" appointments. Thompson's civil service commission entirely disregarded the order, stating that it "questions the motives" of the council in asking the information! Many henchmen appointed via the "temporary" route held office three, four, five years, and longer. The commission became known popularly as the "wrecking crew."

By 1918 a surplus of four million dollars in the city treasury had faded to a two-million-dollar deficit. Three times the mayor vetoed a council resolution requesting the Chicago Bureau of Public Efficiency to investigate the condition of the city's finances. A local wag said the Bureau was sired by the City Club and damned by the City Hall!

THE "SOLID SIX"

In 1917 the legislature reduced the number of trustees of the board of education from twenty-one to eleven. The mayor nominated a set of trustees including six persons whose unity of action in partisan decisions led the public to dub them "the solid six."[1] The council voted to confirm the appointments. The vote was subject to reconsideration at the following meeting, but ignoring this fact and without

[1] See NATIONAL MUNICIPAL REVIEW, 8: 196–7, March, 1919.

giving the members of the old board an interval in which to dispose of pending matters, the new appointees swooped down on the unsuspecting school board, put policemen on guard, and ousted the experienced employees of the board.

At the next council meeting an alderman moved to reconsider the vote. Mayor Thompson refused to recognize the alderman, meantime allowing routine business to go on. Suddenly an administration leader shouted a motion to adjourn. Contrary to all legal precedent, the mayor refused demands for a roll call and declared the council adjourned. The aldermen organized in a legal way, and reconsidered the vote of confirmation.

Legal proceedings were begun to oust the "solid six" outfit, and for a year Thompson's corporation counsel spent public money to keep the "solid six" in office. The Supreme Court decided that the Thompson appointees had never been confirmed and were not the school board. In the meantime the previous board and continued in office, and for a year the schools were in a state of virtual anarchy.

Toward the end of the second term, Lundin, two of the "solid six," and twenty-four Thompsonites were indicted for alleged corruption in school affairs. Owing to the political hook-up however, these cases never came to trial.

"BIG BILL" AS A "BUILDER"

The alliterative appellation "Big Bill, the Builder" was applied to Thompson by his campaign copy writers for the major public improvements initiated and completed during his administrations. Among these are the Michigan Avenue link bridge, the Twelfth Street widening, and the Ogden Avenue widening and extension.

In putting through these improvements it became necessary to condemn large areas of land. Members of the Thompson organization were appointed as real estate appraisers to undertake this task on a fee basis. The amounts of money so paid out by the city, it has been charged, were several million dollars in excess of amounts properly due. *The Chicago Tribune* filed a taxpayer's suit for the repayment to the city of excess payments, contending that the excess fees found their way into the campaign coffers of the Thompson forces.

The Circuit Court ruling in June, this year, upheld *The Tribune's* contention and ordered Thompson and several associates to repay the money with accrued interest. Thompson has appealed the decision, but pending the final decision has filed a bond covering his personal liability in the transaction.

Mayor Thompson's neutral attitude during the World War brought down on his head widespread condemnation and gave him national notoriety. He is credited with characterizing Chicago as "the sixth German city of the world." He declined officially to invite the French Mission, headed by Marshall Joffre and René Viviani, to visit Chicago. He refused to prevent the holding of anti-war or anti-conscription meetings.

Thompson "broke" with Governor Lowden when the latter sent militia to break up a pacifist meeting which the mayor had authorized. In 1920 Thompson resigned from the Republican National Committee when Lowden's name was considered for President and used the full strength of his forces to thwart Lowden's presidential ambitions in 1928.

In the 1919 campaign Thompson posed as the foe of public utilities and traction companies, of the bankers and rich tax dodgers. During the war with its rising costs he made a slogan out of the five-cent street car fare and threatened action against the street car companies. In spite of his efforts and protests, the Federal Court ordered an advance in the fare to seven cents, an order which still maintains.

"BIG BILL'S" BALLYHOO

An accomplishment of his second term was the "Pageant of Progress," an industrial exhibition held on the city's Municipal Pier. It was backed by the resources of the administration and was a financial success. The plan of holding the pageant was credited to Lundin.

This activity of the administration well exemplifies the type of ballyhoo publicity which is part and parcel of the Thompson technique. The Pageant of Progress was, of course, widely advertised throughout the country, welcoming all to Chicago, "Big Bill" assuring them a welcome and their money's worth.

Another instance of such propaganda was the formation in 1920 of the Chicago Boosters' Publicity Club. Business men contributed one million dollars to erect sign boards throughout the United States to tell of Chicago's greatness. Each sign board bore "Big Bill's" signature. After the 1927 campaign the city was placarded with the slogan, "Throw Away Your Hammer and Get a Horn."

In 1920 the Thompson-Lundin forces captured the offices of state's attorney and county judge. The latter controls the election machinery of the city.

Thompson then reached out for other branches of the government. In the Circuit Court election of 1921, Thompson's forces arbitrarily dropped a number of sitting judges from the slate, replacing them with political favorites. The Chicago Bar Association fought this move on the part of the Thompson forces to control the judicial machinery of the county. The slogan "hands off the courts" was raised, and a victorious fight was carried on by the Bar Association, in coöperation with the Democratic organization. A vote of more than 80 per cent of the electorate was polled and completely overwhelmed the Thompson slate.

The judicial defeat, the school graft indictments, the bankrupt city treasury and a series of personal conflicts within the ranks shattered the Lundin-Thompson political machine. A rift came in the Gallagher-Shean lute.

As the 1923 mayoralty approached, the Thompson chieftains, after counting noses and pledge cards, advised "Big Bill" not to run. "My friends have crucified me," said "Big Bill." "I believed in them. I did everything I could to help them make good to the people and they betrayed me.

"I am happy in one thing. I believe I have given Chicago the best administration it ever had. We have the greatest record of progress any party or faction can point to."

DOWN, BUT NOT OUT

To the public it appeared that "Big Bill" was down, but it was soon apparent to close observers that he was not by any means out. After a period of silence, occasional references appeared in the public prints concerning "Big Bill" and his activities. He was appointed chairman of the Illinois Waterways Commission, and used that position as a means for obtaining frequent mention in connection with the campaign for the Lakes-to-Gulf waterway project.

A radio station with the call letters WHT was established. Many persons gave the call letters a personal interpretation, and the station with its attractive program features undoubtedly helped out "Big Bill's" cause.

Throughout the next three years

"Big Bill" was a conspicuous figure at community meetings, organizations, and balls, being mentioned in the local press as leading the grand march, and so forth. Always the "glad hand artist" and the hail-fellow-well-met type, "Big Bill" in this way established personal contact with thousands upon thousands of the voting public who knew little and cared less concerning his record as mayor.

"Big Bill" was also a frequent patron of a large and popular North Side cabaret, which has since been closed for violation of the prohibition law. He always sat at the same table, located prominently on a balcony, and was accompanied invariably by a retinue.

Thompson's boat trip down the Mississippi River, reported sarcastically by the newspapers as an expedition to hunt the "tree-climbing fish," and his systematic exploitation of the Lake-to-Gulf waterway project, brought "Big Bill" frequent mention in the public press.

While resuscitating his reputation with the general public, Thompson also had to regain his seat on the band wagon, which he had left when he stepped down from the mayor's chair and from which he had been excluded as a political liability. He had broken with Robert E. Crowe, state's attorney and leader of the Republican faction then dominant in Cook County. But early in 1926[1] Thompson had an opportunity to reënter the Crowe camp when the position of sheriff became vacant, and in the scramble for the office George F. Harding, Thompson's friend, was successful, not by virtue of the latter fact, but because of his own wealth, power, and good running qualities. A shift in plans later, how-

[1] See *Chicago Primary of 1926*, by Carroll Hill Wooddy (University of Chicago Press), especially pp. 28–31.

ever, gave Harding the berth of county treasurer, to which he was subsequently elected.

The presence of Harding in the Crowe-Barrett camp gave Thompson an entering wedge. Harding paved the way, and shortly Thompson's entry into the Crowe fellowship was announced. Thompson later told the Reed campaign fund investigating committee that he had been invited by the Crowe faction to join them with the promise that they would support him for mayor in 1927. He agreed, he said, on condition that a stand would be taken against the World Court, for waterways, and against prohibition.

Thompson was eager to align himself with one of the leaders, for he saw the difficulties of making headway by himself. As assets with which to bargain, he had his own personal popularity and the influential support of Harding, the South Side boss. Both he and Harding were millionaires. It was reported that Harding was willing to spend $500,000 to reëlect Thompson as mayor.

POLITICS MAKES STRANGE BEDFELLOWS

Fortunately, political leaders have short memories, for in 1922, Crowe publicly stated:

I quit Thompson because he indicated he did not wish me to live up to my oath of office. . . . The immediate cause of my breach with Mayor Thompson was my efforts to close hell-holes of prostitution and vice.

In 1924 Thompson had frequently declared:

Ladies and gentlemen, any time you'll find that I am in the same political bed with Bobby Crowe, the Barrett brothers, Ed Brundage, who was the cause of killing Governor Small's wife . . . then you'll know that Bill Thompson has turned out to be a crook.

Many doubted the sincerity of the Crowe faction toward Harding and Thompson. It was said that both were likely to be made the subject of trades. Harding and Thompson, nevertheless, used their opportunities and were not ignored when the rewards were passed out.

From that point on, "Big Bill" more and more played a leading part in the affairs of the Crowe faction. At the county convention, Thompson, as chairman of the resolutions committee, presented a platform and advocated its adoption in a rousing "patriotic speech." The setting was well prepared by patriotic pageantry in a parade of ex-service men headed by the statues of Washington and Lincoln and a trio in costume representing "The Spirit of '76."

Thompson devoted his efforts to the World Court issue. In January, 1926, he formally invited Senator William E. Borah to address a mass meeting in Chicago on the subject.

All of Thompson's talent for pageantry was employed to give Borah's visit and the local campaign a national significance. Letters were circulated over his signature inviting the citizens of Chicago to "assist in keeping Old Glory at the masthead," by taking part in an automobile parade to welcome the senator. The parade consisted of 2,160 cars including 200 supplied by ex-service men, and ten bands, mostly paid for by the Crowe candidates in the April primary.

Thompson was temporary chairman of the mass meeting. His appearance on the platform with his campaign sombrero produced a demonstration. From Thompson's standpoint the occasion was a success; it was a typical Thompson demonstration, with a carefully set stage, resulting in a highly successful show.

An incident of the 1926 primary campaign will illustrate Thompson's circus-minded methods. On April 6 he took two fat, caged rats to a packed house in a downtown theatre. He addressed one animal as "Fred" (for Fred Lundin), and the other as "Doc" (for Dr. John Dill Robertson, who now had mayoralty aspirations). He verbally lashed "Fred" and "Doc" for ingratitude. It was soon obvious that Thompson was to be the Crowe candidate for the mayoralty in 1927.

"AMERICA FIRST"

Preparatory to the primary campaign for the mayoralty, the Crowe-Thompson organization was credited with having obtained 500,000 signed cards pledging support to "Big Bill" and "America First." A highly perfected political machine and campaign enthusiasm polled 342,337 votes for Thompson at the primary. William E. Dever, the Democratic candidate to succeed himself, polled 149,453 votes.

The discrepancy was indicative of how the political cat was going to jump. The primary campaign gave Thompson a tremendous head start. It looked as though he would be an easy winner. Thompson capitalized this state of the public mind. His political machine ramified every precinct of the city. He carried forward his campaign with self-assurance, blatancy, and bunk which surpassed all of his previous efforts. For the first time in months the Republicans presented a united front.

Thompson's slogan was "America first." He campaigned against the World Court, notified King George to keep out of Chicago politics, and otherwise fought for issues which had little or no relation to municipal affairs or the office for which he was a candidate.

The story is told that in a meeting of the party chieftains to select a slogan, Thompson evolved the catchword "America first."

"Why 'America first'?" someone inquired. "You can't get up a controversy over that."

"That's just it," Thompson is said to have replied. "It's a good slogan because there's nothing to argue about."

In his campaign speeches Thompson refers to himself in the third person. He has the conversational style of oratory. He takes the audience into his confidence. Thompson made the waterways project realistic by promising that, within three years, boats and barges would be plying regular runs from New Orleans to Chicago. The resulting prosperity, he said, would produce three jobs where one now existed. He would single out workingmen in his audience, promising each of them three jobs with good pay, "if Bill Thompson is elected."

KING GEORGE PUT TO ROUT

His attacks on King George were centered around William McAndrew, the superintendent of schools, whose facial adornments give him a resemblance to His Britannic Majesty.[1] Thompson's attacks on McAndrew, "stool pigeon of the King of England," and King George, whom he threatened with violence did he venture to "stick his snoot" into Chicago's affairs, provoked his audiences to high pitches of enthusiasm.

The Dever forces, after a tardy start, waged a vigorous campaign. They employed ridicule and revelation. Unusually accurate straw votes, taken daily during the campaign, showed Thompson to be the favorite until the last two weeks of the campaign.

Gradually Thompson's percentage dropped. Dever's debunking campaign was having its effect. Towards the end Thompson's angry attacks on King George provoked his audiences to

[1] See NATIONAL MUNICIPAL REVIEW, XVI: 11, pp. 688–695, November, 1927.

smiles and even titters. Close observers believe that had the election occurred two weeks later, Dever's tactics would have been successful.

Undoubtedly, however, the deciding factor in the election was the wet ficient to overcome Thompson's lead in other wards. "Big Bill" rolled up pluralities in many districts by racial and nationalistic appeals. Ninety-five per cent of the Negro vote went to Thompson.

P. & A. Photos

MAYOR THOMPSON IN HIS HOTEL OFFICE

and dry issue. Although theoretically wet, Dever had vigorously suppressed the bootleggers and had ordered rigid law enforcement. This order angered many Democrats. In the election several West Side wards, normally Democratic strongholds, either were lost to Dever or gave him pluralities insuf- Thompson, on the other hand, was "wet as the Atlantic," and promised to fight crime but to ignore prohibition. He stood for liberalism and a wide-open policy.

Soon after the election Thompson and his cohorts celebrated by a triumphant boat trip to New Orleans over the flood-swollen Mississippi. His victory had given "Big Bill" visions of new political fields to conquer. The Senate seat which had slipped from his grasp in 1918 now seemed a certainty; and the presidency was not an impossibility. One of his first acts after returning to Chicago was to call the flood control congress. "Big Bill" was chosen·chairman of the congress, and used this office as a means of further political advancement. He issued a catchily written folder setting forth several national issues as the needs of the hour, and placed "Big Bill" in juxtaposition to Washington and Lincoln. Following the election, Thompson continued his personal headquarters in a hotel across the street from the city hall. The word soon went around that if anyone had business with the mayor he could find him there rather than at the city hall. He maintained that office until after the April, 1928, primary.

In municipal affairs the mayor undertook to carry out some of his campaign promises. One was to oust McAndrew; another was to repeal the water meter ordinance passed during Dever's term at the insistence of the Federal Government.

McANDREW "GETS THE GATE"

Almost six months after Thompson had taken office, a pretext was seized upon for filing charges against McAndrew and he was suspended. A "trial" before the board was dragged out more than six months. The prosecutor in the case was the man who as county judge had controlled the election machinery during the Thompson-Lundin régime. McAndrew was finally dismissed. He appealed to the courts and his case was one of fifty thousand civil cases awaiting hearing when the current season opened.

Thompson discovered that in the Chicago public library system, the trustees of which are appointees of the mayor, are a number of pro-British histories which had been proscribed in the McAndrew proceedings. Thompson ordered one of his appointees on the library board, a theatre manager, to see to it that the library was promptly purged of the seditious volumes.

"Burn the books on the lake front," someone suggested.

The resulting public clamor again brought Mayor Thompson into the international limelight. Perhaps the light was too hot, for the mayor disclaimed any intention of burning public property, and his theatrical trustee decided to take a trip to the north woods.

These are merely a few of the incidents which occurred during the first year of Thompson's third term in office. With his political ambitions still burning brightly, "Big Bill" worked feverishly to put over his ticket in the April primary. The Thompson-Crowe organization officially adopted the slogan "America first" for their faction. The message of "America first" was broadcast throughout the city by billboards and all the paraphernalia of political propaganda. An "America First Foundation" was founded with membership at $10 a head.

THE 1928 PRIMARY

Thompson's interest in the outcome of the 1928 primary election was more than that of partisan faction, for the administration put up for referendum at the same election thirty-three bond issues, aggregating the enormous sum of $80,000,000. Thompson had paved the way for increasing the city's bonded debt by the simple expedient of having the state legislature alter the basis of assessed valuation from 50 per cent to 100 per cent of full fair cash value.

The city was already bonded to the limit allowed by law. At one stroke the Thompson forces thus proposed to double the bonded indebtedness of the city.

Thompson's frequently repeated promises that he would rid Chicago of crime, and that crime was being reduced, have thus far failed to materialize. The political campaign preceding the 1928 primary was unusually bitter and was marked by the bombing [1] of the homes of Senator Deneen, leader of the opposition, and of the Deneen candidate for state's attorney; also the killing of a Deneen ward leader. Efforts were made to explain away the bombs by saying that they had been thrown by Deneen sympathizers to create sympathy for their faction. Thompson forces offered rewards, which were never claimed, aggregating $65,000, for information leading to the arrest of the perpetrators of the bombing.

The effect of the bombings and other acts of violence. coupled undoubtedly with Thompson's inattention to municipal affairs and reckless attitudes in matters of finance, brought defeat not only on the "America First" ticket, but also rejection by overwhelming vote of the entire city bonding program.

A REST IN THE NORTH WOODS

Although the Thompson forces by a bare majority retained control of the county Republican committee, "Big Bill" appears to have lost interest in things political. After the primary, his dreams of grandeur faded. Although he attended the Republican National Convention, he played no important part in those proceedings and has taken no part in the campaign. Following the convention, "Big Bill" hied himself to the north woods, where

[1] See NATIONAL MUNICIPAL REVIEW, XVII: 5, pp. 255–256, May, 1928.

he spent practically the entire summer. In fact, his absence was so prolonged that rumors became current that on account of ill health he would resign. He reappeared, however, early in September, to preside at special meetings of the city council. It was announced that he would spend several weeks during the fall months on a ranch in the Southwest.

Developments during his absence might well have caused him to seek recuperation. Decision was rendered in *The Tribune's* real estate experts' suit, for instance.

CHANGES IN ADMINISTRATIVE PERSONNEL

Thompson's city comptroller resigned when the council appropriated a fund of $700,000 for surveys, etc., preliminary to beginning Chicago's long-talked-of subway. The council acted despite the fact that the necessary funds were not available to meet the appropriation. Apparently advised by his bondsman that he would be personally liable if he approved any of said payments, the comptroller withdrew, saying his business demanded his entire personal attention. He then promptly left for a several months' trip to Europe.

During the summer Thompson's chief of police, a man who was counted upon to run the crooks out within ninety days, handed in his resignation. Since then a complete new leaf has been turned over in that department. In fact, one of the most striking incidents in Thompson's political history is to be found in the reappointment to the force as assistant commissioner of police of the man who less than a year before had been demoted and dismissed from the service by Thompson's civil service commission. This man was one of the most efficient members of the force under Dever's administration.

The department of public works encountered difficulties by exhausting the funds provided for street repairs without tangible results. A taxpayers' suit restrained the city from carrying out a contract with a paving concern for paving repairs at a price more than double that at which the city previously had done the work.

A new régime holds forth in the board of education. Politics has been eschewed. The board recently requested the Chicago Bureau of Public Efficiency to make a full investigation of school finances.

When it became apparent that the estimated revenues would fall far short of the proposed expenditures for the current year, a message was received from the mayor somewhere in the north woods calling upon the various departments to cut their budgets by prescribed amounts.

With more than two years of his term remaining, Chicago sees evidences in recent events of a new deal in municipal affairs and optimistically hopes that Mayor Thompson will aid, or at least permit, civic leaders to work out solutions for many pressing problems relating to the city's metropolitan development.

THE VIRGINIA REORGANIZATION PROGRAM

BY ROBERT H. TUCKER

Professor of Economics and Business Administration, Washington and Lee University

A concise and interesting appraisal of Governor Byrd's reorganization program, by a member of the commission on simplification and economy of 1922–24, and of the special citizens' committee of 1927.   ::

On June 19, 1928, the voters of Virginia ratified amendments to the state constitution which changed the basis of the administrative structure of the state government, introduced the principle of the short ballot and executive appointment of the state administrative heads, and, through the removal of detailed restrictions existing in the fundamental law, opened the way for the reorganization of county government.

The action on the state constitution had been preceded by the adoption of a substantial body of legislation looking to the reform of both state and local administration. This consisted of twenty-five or thirty measures passed at the legislative session of 1926 and designed to strengthen the lines of administrative authority in the conduct of state and local affairs; of the Administrative Reorganization Act of 1927, which abolished more than thirty offices, boards and commissions, and coördinated the state functions under twelve administrative departments; and of several supplementary measures adopted at the legislative session of 1928. The legislation looking to administrative reform is an essential part of a still larger program designed to reconstruct the state tax system, to remodel the state educational system, and to promote the industrial and commercial development of the state.

Virginia has adopted in the past three years a volume of sound, constructive legislation unequaled in any similar period in recent generations, perhaps in all its history. This result has been achieved largely through the able and effective leadership of Governor Harry F. Byrd. It is also a manifestation of the economic, social and political awakening now discernible in all parts of the state.

PRELIMINARY INVESTIGATIONS AND REPORTS

The question of governmental reorganization is not new. This question has been before the general assembly and the people of the state for more than a decade, resulting in the appointment of numerous commissions to investigate one phase or another of state and local government. Two of these in particular—the commission on economy and efficiency of 1916 and the commission on simplification and economy of 1922—directed attention to the need for administrative reform.

The commission on economy and efficiency pointed out the disorganized condition of the state government and the need of constitutional change. Its proposal of a state budget system was carried out in 1918 under the leadership of Governor Westmoreland Davis.

The commission on simplification and economy confined its investigation to the administrative structure of the state government and to the more general features of county government, and submitted a comprehensive report to the general assembly of 1924. Its recommendations included a number of measures looking to the correction of individual administrative defects; a plan of immediate partial consolidation of the state administrative agencies into twelve departments; and amendments to the state constitution designed to prepare the way for the complete reorganization of state and county government.

The report of the commission on simplification appeared too late for full consideration at the 1924 session of the general assembly. Few of the commission's bills—nearly forty in number —passed the stage of committee consideration. The proposals, however, aroused wide interest and discussion. Simplification and economy became an issue in the campaign of 1925, and both candidates for the governorship committed themselves to administrative reform.

GOVERNOR BYRD PROPOSES REORGANIZATION

On February 3, 1926, two days after his inauguration, Governor Byrd pre-

GOVERNOR HARRY F. BYRD

sented a notable message to the general assembly on the subject of simplification of government in Virginia. This message reviewed the existing conditions and urged specifically: (1) amendments to the state constitution providing for the short ballot, the elective state officers to be limited to the governor, the lieutenant-governor and the attorney-general; (2) the appointment of all administrative heads by the governor, who should be made responsible for administrative efficiency; (3) the abolishment of many bureaus, boards and departments and the grouping of the rest into eight or ten departments; (4) an efficiency survey, to be made by an outside agency, free of personal and political considerations. These recommendations were accompanied by a number of other less sweeping proposals affecting both state and local government.

THE LEGISLATIVE PROGRAM OF 1926

The legislative program of the 1926 session of the general assembly was set in this broad framework. It consisted of an imposing array of twenty-five or thirty measures designed to simplify and facilitate administrative procedure, to promote efficiency and economy, and to prepare the way for administrative reorganization. On the side of the state these measures included the reorganization of the state tax department, with extensive reductions in the number of local assessing officers; the consolidation of several state agencies; and resolutions amending the state constitution with a view to the adoption of the short ballot. On the side of local government, they covered such subjects as the preparation of annual budgets, uniform accounting, tax levies, compensation of fee officers, and local bond issues.

The outstanding measures of the session, however, were an act empowering the governor to appoint a commission to propose amendments to the state constitution, and an item in the general appropriation act carrying a grant of $25,000 for an expert survey of state and county government. Fol-

lowing this legislation a committee of distinguished citizens, headed by Judge R. R. Prentis, president of the Supreme Court of Appeals, was appointed to revise the state constitution, and the New York Bureau of Municipal Research was retained to conduct the survey of state and county government.

THE SURVEYS AND REPORTS OF THE NEW YORK BUREAU

The surveys of state and county government, which were made under the direction of A. E. Buck of the New York Bureau's staff, were conducted during the period from May, 1926, to January, 1927. The procedure included a careful analysis of the constitutional and statutory provisions relating to the various governmental functions, then a discussion of the activities of each governmental agency with the official or board in charge, and, finally, a detailed first-hand examination of the various divisions or phases of the work. This was supplemented by staff conferences and by general conferences with the state authorities and others who were in a position to advise as the work progressed. In this way each function, each part, so to speak, of the governmental machine, was carefully inspected and tested, and rejected or placed in its proper position.

The result was two reports—one on the organization and management of state government in Virginia and the other on county government in Virginia—which are models of their kind. Thorough in conception, comprehensive in form and impartial in approach, they constitute a veritable textbook of efficient government as applied to conditions in Virginia. In very few instances, and these relatively minor ones, could the proposals of the authors be seriously questioned. The reports have won to an unusual degree the confidence of the people of the state.

THE PROPOSED PLAN OF STATE GOVERNMENT

The report on state government emphasized the complexity of the state organization, with its ninety-five offices, boards and departments, and outlined a thoroughgoing plan of reorganization, developed along the generally accepted lines of the elimination of elective administrative officers, the consolidation of state functions into a limited number of administrative departments, each responsible to the governor, and the internal organization of these departments on a functional basis. Emphasis was also placed upon scientific financial planning and control.

According to this plan, seventy-five existing offices, boards and other agencies would be abolished and their functions concentrated in the governor's office and eleven state departments, as follows: finance, taxation, industrial relations, corporations, highways, conservation and development, health, public welfare, education, agriculture, and law.

Each department would be headed by a single commissioner, appropriate boards for the exercise of quasi-judicial functions being established within the departments of corporations and industrial relations. Advisory boards are proposed in connection with several other departments. Detailed provision is also made for the internal organization of all the departments, and for the setting up of the appropriate functional divisions.

The most valuable part of the report is the section devoted to financial organization and operation, which it characterizes as "perhaps the worst feature of the Virginia state organization." It was found that the financial functions of the state were scattered among sixteen offices and agencies, involving numerous "special" funds and a hopelessly complicated and wasteful system of accounting. To meet these conditions, it was proposed to combine the financial functions under two groups: those relating to independent audit, to be placed under an auditor of public accounts; those relating to financial administration, to be placed under a department of finance consisting of bureaus of the budget, the treasury, accounts and control, and printing and purchasing. The report also contains carefully prepared sections on accounting procedure, personnel supervision, classification of positions, and stores and equipment control.

In connection with each department and each major recommendation the report presents a conservative estimate of the annual savings to be effected through the proposed reorganization. These estimates reach the impressive total of $1,366,000.

THE PROBLEM OF COUNTY GOVERNMENT

The report on county government is based mainly upon an intensive study of twelve typical counties selected from the one hundred counties of the state. It is characterized by the same thoroughness as the report on state government. Every phase of the county organization is carefully analyzed and appraised.

The conclusion that in many counties the operation of the government is "grossly political, careless, wasteful, and thoroughly inefficient" is not surprising. Little more could be expected of an organization consisting of thirty or forty scattered offices and boards, appointed or elected in various ways, without definite responsibility or controlling head, without for the most part any coördinating authority whatever. The fault is in the system, and any other result would be little short of a miracle.

The remedy proposed for the defects of county government includes the abolition of numerous offices and boards commonly found in the county organization, and the coördination of the rest under the full control of an elective "county administrator" or of "a county manager" appointed by the county board of supervisors.

The plans also include the coördination of state and county authority and the elimination of the present fee system. The problem of the "poor" county would be met by the direct consolidation of counties or by the creation of administrative areas in which certain county functions would be concentrated under one administrative head.

The details of county government have long been embedded in the state constitution. This condition has been removed by the recent amendment empowering the general assembly to establish optional forms of county government, as has long been the case with respect to the cities. The reorganization of county government in Virginia, however, will doubtless prove to be a slow process. The present form of county government, involving the positions of many of the most influential officeholders of the state, is intrenched not only in organized political strength, but in all the personal ties that naturally exist in small communities.

PARTIAL REORGANIZATION OF THE STATE GOVERNMENT

With respect to state government the problem is simpler. Soon after the New York Bureau's report appeared in 1927, it was presented to a citizens' committee of thirty-eight members, headed by William T. Reed, a prominent business man of Richmond. The committee studied the report with a view to adapting its proposals to existing conditions and to making specific recommendations to the governor and the general assembly. These recommendations followed the general plan proposed in the New York Bureau's report, but with important modifications.

On March 16, 1927, the general assembly met in special session to consider the recommendations of the governor and the reports of the Prentis and Reed committees. Constitutional amendments amounting in effect to a complete revision of the state constitution were approved; and the proposals of the Reed Committee were embodied, again with important modifications, in the Administrative Reorganization Act, part of which became effective August 1, 1927, and the rest on March 1, 1928.

The reorganized state government consists of the governor's office, and twelve departments, as follows: finance, taxation, corporations, highways, conservation and development, health, public welfare, education, agriculture, law, labor and industry, workmen's compensation.

The act sets up divisions of the budget, records, military affairs, buildings and grounds in the governor's office, and divisions of the treasury, accounts and control, purchasing and printing, and motor vehicles in the department of finance. As to the internal organization of the other departments the act provides that the details of each department, not requiring legislative action, may be taken up by the governor and the departments concerned in connection with the preparation of the budget.

Under the provisions of the act, about thirty agencies, the majority of these being ex-officio boards, are abolished. The offices of the secretary of state, the second auditor, and the state accountant were the most important offices abolished.

The most important single change has been the reorganization of the state's financial system and the establishment of an advanced system of accounts and control. This action included the abolition of forty-eight "special" funds, the requirement that all the revenues of the state or its departments and institutions shall function through the state treasury, and provision for a complete system of accounting control. Under the new accounting system, which was devised by Francis Oakey of New York City, a daily statement is placed upon the desk of the governor, showing the condition of the state's finances. A quarterly budget has also been established, thus giving the governor closer supervision over the state's activities. The whole procedure affords a marvelous contrast with the older system which for the most part provided for only a two-year control. The new financial system alone would justify the trouble and expense involved in the reorganization.

SOME DETAILS AND ANOMALIES

Some details and anomalies of the reorganization are worthy of special notice. The department of finance is without an administrative head, its four divisions being in effect independent departments. The department of conservation consists of a group of three separate commissions. In place of the proposed department of industrial relations, two departments were created, namely, the department of labor and industry and the department of workmen's compensation. Only a beginning was made toward creating a department of public welfare, and nothing could be done with respect to the department of education on account of existing constitutional restrictions. The assessment of public service corporations for purposes of taxation was left in the hands of the state corpora-tion commission, and the location of other divisions is open to question. Numerous boards and commissions are retained and attached in various ways to the different departments.

It should be recalled, however, that some of the conditions mentioned above have been bound up in the problem of constitutional change. No doubt these defects will be corrected, now that the new constitution has been adopted, opening the way for reorganization in every detail, and providing for the "short ballot," with the governor, the lieutenant-governor and the attorney general as the only elective state officers. The governor's appointments of administrative heads are subject to confirmation by the general assembly.

RESULTS OF THE REORGANIZATION CHANGES

Of the results of the reorganization changes it is perhaps too early to speak. Many of the changes have become effective only in recent months. Already it is estimated that the changes accomplished are resulting in an annual saving of $800,000, much of which is attributable to the reorganized state administration; and already there are evidences of improvement in the daily administration of the various functions of the government. In 1928, for the first time, the budget provides for a reduction of administrative expense, despite the fact that the activities of the state are being constantly enlarged. As an illustration of what may be accomplished when the plan of reorganization is applied to all the departments, may be taken the record of the state tax department, where, through the activities of an able commissioner, tax procedure has been simplified and improved, and more than a million dollars have been added to the revenues of the state, while the costs of administration have been reduced by $85,000 a year.

Of equal importance has been the unity of spirit with which the program has so far been carried out. The proposed constitutional amendments, especially the short ballot proposal, aroused considerable opposition, but the legislative side of the program was carried through almost without dissent. The administrative reorganization act of 1927 passed both houses of the general assembly by a practically unanimous vote.

FURTHER REORGANIZATION NECESSARY

These notable results, however, should not obscure the fact that the reorganization is in progress, and not yet fully accomplished. Apart from the problem of county government there is still much to be done with respect to the state organization, and the next three years promise to be even more crucial in the affairs of the state than the past three years have been. There must be a full recognition of the steps yet to be taken if Virginia is to reach the goal of complete and effective reorganization. These steps may be summarized as follows:

1. The consolidation of the various labor, conservation, and welfare agencies into three well-organized departments.

2. The creation of an administrative head for the department of finance.

3. The internal organization of each of the state departments into appropriate functional divisions, each major division to be headed by a responsible director or chief.

4. An occupational survey in all the departments and a scientific classification of positions.

5. The establishment of a system of personnel supervision, including appointment and promotion by merit and reasonable security of tenure.

6. The correction of certain anomalies of organization, mentioned in a preceding paragraph, and the appointment of the remaining administrative heads, as provided by the amended constitution.

The need of these further reorganization changes is fundamental. Obviously there is no sound reason for not applying, to the agencies concerned with labor and industry, conservation and development, and public welfare, the same principles that have been applied to the other departments and agencies. Besides, the consolidation of these agencies into well-organized departments would not only promote efficiency, but make possible a saving of at least $200,000 a year. Effective internal organization, with a correct adjustment of positions and work, is in many ways more important than overhead administrative organization. Likewise the need for reasonable security of tenure is self-evident. To leave this matter open would not only impede the work of the various departments, but would invite, if not make inevitable, the creation of an extensive political machine.

That the program will be carried to completion at the 1930 session of the general assembly there is little reason to doubt. The restrictions of the state constitution no longer stand in the way. To falter or delay at this time would be fatal. On this point the experience of the American states is clear. The states that have contented themselves with piecemeal reorganization have usually spread the process over a decade or more without achieving substantial results. On the other hand, the states that have effected complete and thorough reorganization have realized at once vast savings in administrative expense, together with the incalculable benefits of increased efficiency and more orderly processes of government. Moreover, Virginia is on the threshold of an unusual industrial and social development. The governmental organization must be still further strengthened if the state is to function as a great business corporation and meet effectively the opportunities and responsibilities of the future.

A NEW BOOK ON THE APPRAISAL OF URBAN LAND AND BUILDINGS

BY PHILIP H. CORNICK
National Institute of Public Administration

A review of a book which blazes new trails for the city assessor.   ::

UNTIL about ten years ago, it was considered fashionable for cities to prepare and publish assessor's manuals for the information and guidance not only of the local assessors but of the property owners as well. A few of these were excellent pamphlets; others were hastily prepared imitations of one or more of the better pamphlets in the field; a few offered deliberate variations in form from their predecessors, frequently on the quite unfounded pretext that their authors had found by careful research a depth curve or a corner rule which fitted local conditions better than any of the rules used elsewhere. At best, the majority of these manuals served no useful purpose beyond providing sets of rules for local distribution which were not readily available in printed form; at worst, they added to the prestige in local political circles of their sometimes incompetent compilers, and strengthened their hold on their jobs. Regardless of the minor variations within them, their line of descent could be traced to the Somers system, the New York City and Newark systems, and the Lindsay-Bernard system of Baltimore. Few contributed anything new that was of great importance, or questioned anything old no matter how unimportant.

John Zangerle of Cleveland was the first man to build up an eclectic system, taking the best wherever he found it, and—when the best in his opinion was not good enough—filling in the gaps with the results of careful and intelligent computations based on painstaking research. Under his guidance, the valuation of urban property for purposes of taxation may be said to have attained its majority, and to have gone out to do its work in the world as a whole, and not simply in the narrow confines of one municipality or in the hands of one firm. His system was designed to work in any city, and the influence of his book has been marked from coast to coast not only among assessors but also among real estate men and appraisers.

In a current publication by the Municipal Administration Service on "The Appraisal of Urban Land and Buildings—A Working Manual for City Assessors," by Cuthbert E. Reeves,[1] it is believed that the work of integration and expansion, initiated by Mr. Zangerle, has been carried a little bit

[1] Published by Municipal Administration Service, 261 Broadway, New York City.

further in one or two important aspects. In his work as adviser to several large cities on complicated problems and in the course of his installations of comprehensive systems for small municipalities, Mr. Reeves has been led not only to a more complete systematization of his methods in certain fields than is to be found in any current work on the subject, but also to the rejection of certain practices whose advocacy is so general that even to question them will appear to be heresy to the more orthodox students of the problem.

VALUATION OF LAND AND BUILDINGS

The publication is divided into two major parts, the first dealing with the valuation of land, the second with that of buildings. The text itself is clear and concise, and should prove easily understandable even by students not versed in the technique of appraisals. It is illustrated, furthermore, by an abundance of enlightening charts and graphs, and is accompanied by voluminous tables.

Mr. Reeves deals with the actual problems of valuation and also with the closely related problems of indexing and record keeping. His first departure from orthodox teachings comes in this latter connection. The block and lot system of indexing, which has become almost sacrosanct in the eyes of those whose familiarity with the subject is based primarily on reading, is rejected as unduly cumbersome. Instead, he would index his material by street names filed alphabetically, and by street numbers filed numerically under each street. Because the author has sacrificed the use of supporting data in the interests of brevity, no reference is made in the text to the fact that the system he recommends is already in use. It may not be amiss to state at this point, therefore, that certain cities

with perfectly good block and lot systems—Newark, New Jersey, for example—are actually using the street number system because it is more convenient and more easily understood by the taxpayers.

A NEW BUILDING RECORD CARD

The building record card which the author has designed embodies not only all the labor-saving devices which have been adopted in the best cards in use today, but is designed to accomplish one very important thing in addition. Even after a building has been completely described on the usual type of card, the work of classification still remains to be done. On the Reeves card, on the other hand, the mere act of describing the physical characteristics of a normal building automatically places it in a definite class, which in turn indicates its unit cost of reproduction new. Only those buildings whose structural characteristics do not conform to any well-defined type will require the analysis and the exercise of individual judgment, which under current methods are necessary in the case of all buildings.

RULES FOR LAND VALUATION

In his section on the rules for the valuation of land, Mr. Reeves has done a thoroughgoing job in a very brief space. He recommends for use as a depth curve the square root rule—a rule which has made its appearance in a number of publications on land valuations since 1909 under the misleading designations of the London rule, or the Harper-Edgar rule. It has been the official rule of the New Jersey state board of taxes and assessment for a number of years past and, in the form of a "square foot unit foot rule," is also the standard in Washington, D. C. It has the following advantages. It has a constant mathematical relationship between depth of lot and percentage of unit value throughout; for unit depths of 100 feet, it can be read off any square root table, or for any depth of standard, it can easily be calculated in the field in the absence of such tables; and for all depths between 50 and 200 feet, it conforms very closely to the average of the leading depth curves in use today.

The Reeves monograph presents the rule worked out at intervals of one foot on the basis of twelve standard depths varying from 100 to 500 feet. Except for the minor variations incidental to the rounding out of decimal fractions, the ratios between the percentages of unit value assigned to any two given depths are identical in all the twelve tables. This fact, in itself, is a distinct advantage in applying the depth curve with a minimum of computations regardless of variations in the normal lot depths in the area which is being studied.

CORNER VALUATIONS

In the valuation of corners, Mr. Reeves adheres to the original Lindsay-Bernard rule, first worked out in Baltimore, and later applied in modified form in Cleveland. He agrees with the originators that it can be applied in its most extreme form only on certain types of business corners; he feels that Mr. Zangerle's experiments in Cleveland in modifying the rule for use in other sections of a city are worthy of closer study; but he concludes this portion of his work by reference to instances which would seem to indicate that Mr. Zangerle's modification has not solved the problem. Altogether, it is probable that this part of Mr. Reeves' manual is the weakest part of his work.

LOTS ABUTTING ON ALLEYS

In the sections dealing with the appraisal of lots which abut on alleys or which run through from street to street, and in those which discuss the problems of irregular lots, the reasoning is incisive and leads to definite recommendations. The old merge point rule for the valuation of lots with double frontage on adjacent streets—a rule which has been accepted without question by practically all writers on the subject since Mr. Somers first formulated it—emerges from the analysis a total wreck. The tentative substitute proposed varies from the original at least in the right direction, but its final form will no doubt depend on a careful analysis of the net rentals in the arcade developments which are increasingly common in all of our larger cities—notably, for example, in the long blocks fronting on Euclid Avenue in Cleveland. This part of Mr. Reeves' work suffers somewhat from his otherwise highly commendable efforts at brevity..

CLASSIFICATION OF BUILDINGS

The outstanding contribution, however, which Mr. Reeves has made is in his classification of buildings. The early classification in Newark, New Jersey, for example, made provision for ten major groups based partly on use and partly on elements of construction. These ten groups were further subdivided into a total of twenty-seven subgroups. The Cambridge classification contains altogether 102 classes based partly on use, partly on type of construction, partly on single factors entering into the type of construction. The inadequacy of this classification is sufficiently indicated by the fact that the maximum and minimum unit values assigned to each class vary from one another in several instances in the ratio of two to one. Mr. Zangerle's classification for use in Cleveland divides one-family residences alone into twelve groups and forty subgroups, based on area covered, number of stories, materials used in outside walls, and detailed specifications for interior finish. Additions and deductions are made for variations from the standard in area covered or in interior details. This classification represented a big improvement over all previous attempts to systematize the comparative valuation of residential buildings.

Mr. Reeves, however, has not only gone into greater detail in analyzing the effect on costs of the frequent variations in those factors on which Mr. Zangerle bases his classification, but he has also worked directly into his basic tables those differences in cost which depend on changes in the shape and size of the ground area covered, the extent of which Mr. Zangerle indicates only approximately in his tables of deductions and additions. Detached, one-family houses alone, in Mr. Reeves' tables, are divided into 137 groups, based on six sets of specifications for structural and interior characteristics, on number of stories, on presence or absence of basements, and on exterior construction. Each of these groups, furthermore, is divided into from twenty to thirty subgroups based on variations in dimensions. The ingenious building classification card to which reference has already been made, and the logical manner in which the voluminous tables are arranged and keyed, make it easy to turn to either the unit cost or the total cost of reproduction new of any building which conforms with reasonable accuracy to the basic normal types. Tables of additions and deductions are provided for the valuation of nonconforming structures. Altogether, the method employed by Mr. Reeves in the preparation of this part of his monograph marks a distinct advance in the attack on the problem of the comparative valuation of structures. The tables should prove useful not only to those charged with the duty of assessing buildings for taxation, but also to architects, contractors, appraisers for mortgage loans and investors.

ALLOWANCES FOR DETERIORATION AND OBSOLESCENCE

Incidentally, the compact paragraphs which deal with the necessity for modifying reproduction costs new by allowances for structural deterioration and economic obsolescence, present in simple and understandable terms the results of the author's wide reading and practical experience. He was wise enough not to attempt to reduce the solution of these phases of the problem to a simple rule, but his clear statement of the nature and causes of both types of depreciation should prove a boon to the officials who are constantly harassed by the necessity for taking them into account.

Altogether, Mr. Reeves' monograph cannot by any stretch of the imagination be classed with the ordinary run of assessment manuals which make their appearance from time to time. On the one hand, it may easily precipitate a merry war among the advocates and opponents of some of the rules and practices it attacks; on the other hand, it has undoubtedly set a new standard for building classifications which will have a profound effect on future publications on that phase of the subject. Most important of all, however, it places within reach of those assessing officials who are caught between the two millstones of involved and voluminous tasks on the one hand, and inadequate appropriations on the other, a compact and complete working manual which should be of distinct service in reducing the routine drudgery of their jobs to a size more commensurate with the amounts available for expenditure.

THE MODEL MUNICIPAL TRAFFIC ORDINANCE

BY C. W. STARK

Secretary, Committee on Municipal Traffic Ordinances and Regulations,
National Conference on Street and Highway Safety

*The model municipal traffic ordinance, if generally adopted, would
reduce confusion and would cut down the number of accidents.* ::

DRIVING from Washington to New York recently, a friend of mine who is thoroughly familiar with and observant of the traffic regulations of Washington first came to grief at Baltimore when he essayed to make a left turn at an officered corner in the manner prescribed in the Washington regulations; namely, pulling into the intersection on the extreme right on the "Go" signal, and waiting for the change of signal. The intersecting streets were narrow, he found it necessary to back to complete the turn, and he was roundly "bawled out" for failing to be in proper position in the center of the street for the turn.

On Broad Street, Philadelphia, he wished to turn left into a narrow one-way street. Realizing this time that there was not room to make the turn according to the Washington method, he attempted to apply the lesson he had learned in Baltimore, and drew up to the center of the intersection. Again he was wrong. This time he should have drawn up to the right-hand curb, stopped before he reached the intersection, and turned when the light was red.

Coming to Fifth Avenue, New York, from a cross street, there was neither traffic officer nor signal light, and it appeared to him that to turn left into the Avenue he must edge slowly across the fast moving streams of southbound traffic. They did not yield, he was soon in trouble, and then he learned

that he was expected to govern his movements by a traffic signal two blocks up the Avenue. When it showed red, traffic on the Avenue stopped, and he had ample opportunity to make the turn.

Making a left turn safely and without interfering seriously with traffic at a busy intersection is often a difficult feat, and it is highly important that motorists know exactly how it is to be done. The model municipal traffic ordinance provides a standard procedure for this, and selects as the standard that which is followed in the greatest number of municipalities and endorsed by the majority of the most experienced traffic engineers—turning on the green or "Go" signal from a point near the center of the intersection.

Making left turns is only one of a number of driving operations on which there is at present diversity of rule, and the committee has sought diligently to point the way to making these rules uniform in every community, just as far as it is possible to do so.

WHY A MODEL ORDINANCE?

The National Conference on Street and Highway Safety was organized in the spring of 1924 to seek ways and means of checking the rapid increase in street and highway accidents, resulting at that time in more than 20,000 fatalities annually, probably 600,000 serious injuries, and more than $600,000,000 estimated property loss. The Conference was organized under the chairmanship of Secretary of Commerce Hoover, and has been participated in by numerous national organizations, groups and individuals interested in the humane and economic aspects of the problem.

During the first year eight committees were organized and made reports. A theme running through these reports was the need for uniformity in traffic laws and regulations, and it was the consensus of opinion that not only should the principle of uniformity be emphasized, but working models should be developed to show the way to exact uniformity.

There was therefore organized early in 1925 a committee on uniformity of laws and regulations, and this committee applied itself, working in collaboration with the National Conference of Commissioners on Uniform State Laws, to the development of a uniform vehicle code for adoption by state legislatures. The draft of the code suggested by that committee in its report, like the reports of the other committees working at the same time, was reviewed, modified and unanimously approved by a general meeting of the conference in March, 1926. The revised code was subsequently endorsed by the American Bar Association.

The committee at that time considered the matter of uniform municipal ordinances, and recognized the importance of such uniformity. It felt, however, that the time was not then ripe to work this out—that for the time being such ordinances could best be developed by state and regional conferences in which the participants would mainly be public officials and others thoroughly familiar with the conditions in their particular states. Several such state conferences were held, and model ordinances were developed. But comparison of them showed that they differed widely both in scope and in manner of presentation, and that their adoption by the municipalities in their respective regions would still leave us far short of the country-wide uniformity so desirable. The National Conference on Street and Highway Safety was therefore urged to take up the problem in the same manner in which it had taken up the state code, and in July, 1927, a committee for the purpose was organized.

Study of the problem indicated that there is not, after all, such a wide difference in municipalities but that many standard provisions could well be applied to those of all sizes; and meanwhile an increasing number of municipalities were stating their desire for a model ordinance and their intention of delaying the revision of their own ordinances until such a model was available. The committee, therefore, took courage from these expressions and developed a tentative draft which was distributed to public officials and citizen groups throughout the land, with an invitation to them to criticize it freely.

The returns from these criticisms were extremely gratifying. Many who responded, including a number of police officials from large cities, stated their willingness to take the ordinance as it stood. A few suggested changes were reviewed at a three-day meeting of the committee last July, and changes were made in the draft. Comments received on the revised draft sent out in August reflect the same enthusiasm, with practically no adverse criticism.

PEDESTRIAN AND MOTORIST

Newspaper comment on the model ordinance indicates that one of the subjects in which the public is most interested is the relation of pedestrian and motorist. Certainly it is one of the most important, with pedestrians contributing two-thirds of the fatalities on our streets and highways. The provisions of the ordinance are not revolutionary, inasmuch as a number of communities have established definite rules for the respective rights and responsibilities of motorists and pedestrians. The ordinance sets forth clearly, however, where and under what circumstances motorists and pedestrians have, and where each must yield, the right of way.

In the absence of police or automatic signals directing him to stop, the pedestrian has the absolute right of way on a crosswalk, and the continuation of the sidewalk lines across an intersection is a crosswalk whether marked or not. At uncontrolled crossings the pedestrian is not to be required to jump, sidestep or sprint to avoid the oncoming motor car. The motorist must slow down, or stop if necessary, to avoid a collision. At controlled intersections the pedestrian who has started on the "Go" signal may continue to the opposite sidewalk or to a safety island, regardless of whether the traffic signal changes, and when he is proceeding legally on a crosswalk he has the right of way over any vehicle making a turn. In return for these concessions, he is required in controlled areas to do all of his crossing at crosswalks, and must yield the right of way to vehicles if he crosses the street elsewhere than on a crosswalk in uncontrolled areas.

Recognizing two schools of thought on the question of whether the pedestrian should absolutely obey traffic signals, the model ordinance offers the alternatives of merely requiring him to yield the right of way to vehicles proceeding lawfully over crosswalks, or requiring him to obey the signals as religiously as the motorist must. Both methods have their staunch advocates,

and probably no single rule will fit all communities.

AUTOMATIC TRAFFIC SIGNALS

Traffic signals, and the number and meaning of signal colors, are in great need of standardization. The committee, recognizing that quite a few cities use two colors only, has concluded nevertheless that the logic as well as the trend is toward three colors, and that the use of only two colors results inevitably in giving the red light a dual meaning and introducing a serious element of danger.

The model ordinance provides, therefore, that red shall unequivocally mean to stop before entering the intersection, and to remain standing until the green appears. Yellow, which will always precede red in the three-color system recommended by the committee, will eliminate the excuse for entering the intersection on the red "because he could not stop," although he may enter and cross the intersection on the yellow if he is so near the intersection when the yellow first appears that he cannot stop. Green will obviously mean permission to go.

The ordinance calls for the so-called "split yellow"—showing yellow after green but not after red. It was felt that there is no need to warn the standing motorist that he is about to receive a green light; that the disadvantages outweigh the advantages, and that such use of yellow encourages "jumping" the lights.

While, as above stated, the committee recommends the three-color system, it recognizes that two colors only are used in a number of cities, and suggests a form of alternate provision defining the meanings of the two colors as nearly as possible in harmony with the meanings in the three-color system.

The committee recommends that none of these colors shall have any other meaning, and that if it is desired to show other indications, such as an interval for pedestrians alone, some other color or colors should be used. The ordinance provides, however, for the use of a green arrow when a turn in a certain direction, that would otherwise be prohibited, may be made.

In its accompanying text the committee outlines what should determine where signals should be installed and discusses different types of signal systems, as well as lengths of cycles, methods of making turns, special signal indications, and location of, and specifications for signals. This discussion is based on a forthcoming report of a committee on street signs, signals and markings of the American Engineering Council, with whose work the committee has been in close touch.

PASSING STREET CARS

Another of the important provisions of the model ordinance has to do with overtaking and passing street cars. The ordinance prohibits overtaking a street car on the left elsewhere than on a one-way street, but recognizes that the relative position of tracks and roadway may be such as to warrant an exception which can be definitely specified.

Street cars loading or unloading passengers may be overtaken only where safety zones are provided, and then only with due caution for the safety of the car riders. The practice prevails in some cities of permitting such passing in the absence of safety zones at what is regarded as a safe distance from the street car. The ordinance does not sanction this practice, as the committee believed that neither the safe distance nor a safe speed in passing is generally observed. The motor vehicle must therefore stop behind the nearest door or running board of the street car and remain standing until the passenger has boarded the street car or reached a place of safety.

Opinion has differed as to whether or not the track alongside a safety zone is part of the zone. The committee holds that it is not, and that in the absence of definite prohibition a motor vehicle may pass the safety zone on the car track. If a community wishes to prohibit this, whether by special enactment or by power delegated to the traffic authority, the committee believes that it should be required to erect a sign directing traffic to the right at each point where that is required.

OVERTAKING OTHER VEHICLES ON THE RIGHT

Whether overtaking and passing other vehicles on the right should be permitted was discussed by the committee at considerable length. Knowing that this is being done frequently in city streets, without evidence that it is directly causing accidents, a number of members of the committee felt that it should be legalized. The prevailing view, however, was that it is essentially a dangerous practice and should not be endorsed. If to legalize it would be merely to remove from otherwise law-abiding drivers the stigma of being law-breakers when overtaking carefully on the right under safe conditions, the proposal to legalize this would possibly have been sustained. But the plan would be more far-reaching. It would necessarily impose upon the operator of a vehicle being overtaken a duty to refrain from doing exactly what he is required to do when he hears a horn behind him on a two-lane open road; namely, swing over to the right as promptly as possible. If overtaking on the right is legalized, the operator overtaken has a heavy responsibility not to swerve to right or left until he sees that it can be done safely; and we have no assurance that the general run of operators will exercise this precaution.

Another factor in bringing the committee to its decision was that the uniform vehicle code prohibits overtaking on the right, and no state has legalized it; and therefore to authorize it in the model ordinance would be to propose a new and questionable departure from existing law. As a result of its action, therefore, the committee merely omits reference to the subject in the ordinance.

It appears, nevertheless, that a rigid interpretation of the prohibition, where there are multiple lanes of traffic definitely established, is virtually unenforceable and unnecessary. The committee points to the desirability of establishing lanes of traffic in wide thoroughfares, in which cases it can be assumed that the vehicles in each lane may proceed in a straight line irrespective of the rate of speed of those in adjoining lanes.

RIGHT OF WAY AT INTERSECTIONS

The right of way rule at intersections, one of the most difficult of rules to frame equitably, and numerous conflicting versions of which beset motorists at the present time, has been written in a new, simple and, it is believed, enforceable form in the model ordinance. The vehicle entering the intersection first is given the right of way. Only when two vehicles enter at the same time is the operator on the left required to yield to the operator on the right. This wording, I believe, will overcome the tendency of motorists on the right, who have not yet reached the intersection, to speed up and dash across the path of the operator proceeding slowly in the intersection. It is pointed out that as a matter of enforcement the courts have generally given the verdict to the operator first in the intersection in such cases, re-

gardless of the exact wording of the provision.

The ordinance makes it clear that the protection of through streets by stop signs does not give traffic on the through streets an unlimited right of way. There has been lack of uniformity in the wording and uncertainty as to the meaning of through-street stop provisions. The ordinance provides that after the operator on a cross street has come to a full stop the usual right of way rule prevails, and he is entitled to a reasonable opportunity to filter into or across the through-street traffic.

STOPPING, LOADING AND PARKING

For what is believed to be the first time the committee has drawn clear-cut distinctions between merely stopping, parking, and standing motor vehicles for loading, and has imposed reasonable limitations on each.

At certain points, as within intersections, on crosswalks and sidewalks and alongside safety zones, stopping, even momentarily, for any purpose whatever is prohibited, except when necessary to avoid conflict with other traffic or in compliance with police or traffic signal directions. The traffic authority is empowered to designate passenger zones at which no vehicle may stop longer than is necessary for the expeditious loading or unloading of passengers; and loading zones at which either passenger vehicles or trucks may stop, but only for expeditious loading or unloading. In no case shall a stop for loading or unloading of materials exceed thirty minutes, and parking for any other purpose in either type of zone is prohibited.

The traffic authority is also authorized and required to designate bus stops, taxicab stands and hackney stands. Other passenger vehicles may stop temporarily in such places while actually loading or unloading passengers, but otherwise they are for the exclusive use of the vehicles for which they are designated, and these vehicles may not stop elsewhere except temporarily while actually loading or unloading passengers.

To these prohibitions against parking, the definition of which excludes vehicles loading or unloading but makes no distinction whether or not the vehicle is occupied, are added optional forms of provisions prohibiting parking in certain places, limiting the parking time in designated places, prohibiting parking between certain hours in designated places and prohibiting all-night parking. The committee recognizes that individual communities may desire to omit any or all of these latter provisions.

OTHER PROVISIONS

The model ordinance contains numerous other provisions, such as those limiting backing, limiting turning around, prohibiting railway trains and street cars from blocking streets, and prohibiting various dangerous practices on the part of drivers, pedestrians and children in the streets; provisions for the designation of through streets, one-way streets and the like, and standard provisions requiring obedience to the police and designating the responsibility for signs, signals, emergency regulations etc.

The ordinance proper is confined to the provisions which either are not ordinarily found in the state law or which need amplification to adapt them to municipal conditions. The committee believes that, except where necessary to meet constitutional or enforcement requirements, the provisions of the state law should not be repeated in the ordinance. It recognizes, however, that in some states it is necessary to repeat many of these provisions, and it therefore presents those which in such cases may well be repeated. These are provisions found in the uniform vehicle code, and it is obvious that in some states having laws not in harmony with the code the provisions, if used in the ordinance, will require modification to bring them into harmony with the state laws, unless it is possible to secure prompt revision of the state law by the legislature to make it in accord with the uniform vehicle code. This would also make possible the desired uniformity as between municipalities in different states.

The committee also suggests a form of supplementary ordinance to create an official traffic commission, one to create a division of traffic engineering and one to control roadway and sidewalk obstructions. The main and supplementary ordinances are accompanied by text matter explaining the purposes of the provisions, and the committee points to the great desirability of organized study of the traffic problems of each community, including sound and continuous technical advice.

THE TAX SITUATION IN CHICAGO

BY HERBERT D. SIMPSON, PH.D.

Associate Professor of Economics, Institute for Research in Land Economics and Public Utilities, Northwestern University

A narrative of the struggle leading up to the order for reassessment of all real estate in Chicago and Cook County.   ::   ::   ::   ::

In previous articles,[1] the general inequalities of assessment in Chicago have been analyzed. Flagrant inequalities have been shown to exist among different classes of property, among different districts in the city, and among individual property holders. Some of the causes of these inequalities have been discussed, particularly the arbitrary process of revision practiced by the board of review; and some of the results of the system have been pointed out, such as the exploitation of the tax machinery by political organizations, the activities of professional "tax fixers," the general attitude of suspicion and contempt on the part of taxpayers for everything connected with the tax system, and other unfortunate conditions, political and moral, that are directly traceable to the machinery and operation of the tax system.

THE JOINT COMMISSION ON REAL ESTATE VALUATION

In the midst of these conditions the Joint Commission on Real Estate Valuation, referred to in a previous article, was created. It was composed of members of the board of review and board of assessors, other government officials, and the representatives of business and civic organizations, including President Scott of Northwestern University and Professor Viner of the University of Chicago. George O. Fairweather, business manager of

[1] NATIONAL MUNICIPAL REVIEW, September and October, 1928.

the University of Chicago, was chosen as chairman. John O. Rees, formerly with the New York Bureau of Municipal Research, was secured as executive secretary of the commission. The official members declined to participate in the meetings or work of the commission, almost from the first, so that it became virtually a citizens' organization.

The commission mapped out as its first undertaking an investigation of the actual facts of the situation, under the direction of the present writer, the results of which have already been indicated. The board of review refused access to the assessment records, an access that was later secured through the courtesy of the board of assessors.

Conferences were arranged with the board of assessors and hearings with the board of review, in the hope of securing the adoption of some improved methods for making the quadrennial assessment of 1927. In this the commission was unsuccessful. The election of the Thompson administration in April, 1927, only strengthened the assurance of the groups in control of the tax machinery, and the assessment was made in the old way—with even more than the usual haste and confusion on account of the increased number of properties. The assessors did not complete their work until the end of October, after which it appears that from 75,000 to 100,000 complaints were filed. The board of review heard some of them; most of them were still unheard by the first of January, when taxes had to be levied upon the assessment.

Meanwhile the survey of assessment methods and results for the quadrennium ending with 1926 had been completed, and a preliminary report of results was issued in June, 1927—after these results had been presented to the board of assessors and an opportunity to present them to the board of review had been requested.[1] These results were included along with other materials in a preliminary report of the joint commission to the board of county commissioners in July.[2]

Wide publicity was given to these results by the daily papers and by trade journals and other publications. All of the daily papers carried vigorous editorial comment upon the situation, and the keenest interest in the facts themselves was manifested by business and civic organizations and by citizens generally.

Under the auspices of the joint commission, conferences and meetings were arranged at which the facts could be presented in a plain businesslike way, with opportunity for frank and open discussion of the conditions and of means for remedying them. In this way the results of the study were presented to the Association of Commerce, to various local chambers of commerce throughout the city, to property-holders' associations and community organizations, to the city and county real estate boards, to the Chicago Bar Association, the Building Owners' and Managers' Association, to

[1] *The Assessment of Real Estate for Taxation in Chicago*, by Herbert D. Simpson, published by the Institute for Research in Land Economics, Northwestern University, Chicago.

[2] *A Study of Assessment Methods and Results in Cook County*, prepared by the joint commission on real estate valuation, for the board of county commissioners of Cook County, July, 1927.

various divisions of the League of Women Voters and the Federation of Women's Clubs, and to scores of teachers' associations, churches, clubs, forums, and other groups. More than a hundred such meetings were held throughout the city during the following year. In this work the Chicago Federation of Civic Agencies was particularly influential in bringing the subject to the attention of its constituent organizations and in providing opportunity for presenting the facts.

Meanwhile the state tax commission, under the chairmanship of William H. Malone, had taken cognizance of the situation at a hearing held in Chicago, November 10, 1927. At this hearing the formal complainant was the Chicago Teachers' Federation—and thereby hangs a tale of considerable interest.

THE TEACHERS' FEDERATION

The Teachers' Federation, since the days of Catherine Goggin in 1900,[3] had been carrying on a persistent, though fruitless, fight against the tax system in Chicago. Their card of entry had been threats by the Board of Education to reduce salaries, the crowding of children in the schoolrooms, and generally inadequate provision for the needs of the public schools —all on the ground of the impossibility of securing adequate revenues through taxation. The teachers asserted that if it were not for the unscrupulous evasion of taxes and the collusion by tax officials in permitting such evasion, there would be an abundance of money to run the public schools without hardship to honest taxpayers. They had concentrated their attacks largely upon two of the more obvious forms of evasion, although unfortunately the ones most difficult to remedy by isolated treatment; namely, the corporate

[3] *State Board of Equalization et al. v. People ex rel. Catherine Goggin et al.*, 191 Ill. 528 (1901).

franchise taxes and the taxes upon intangible property. They had conducted hearings before the board of review, had taken cases before the courts, carrying them sometimes to the supreme court of the state, and had in this way kept up a running fire of attack upon these two elements in the tax system.

Miss Goggin's mantle had fallen upon the shoulders of Miss Margaret Haley, who for many years has been an aggressive leader of the Teachers' Federation and has carried on the fight against flagrant abuses in the tax system. Her criticisms of tax officials and taxpayers have made many enemies; she has commonly been classified as radical, has been charged with attempting to deliver the votes of the Teachers' Federation in accordance with political bargains previously made, and her methods and vocabulary of attack have not always been approved even by those who might not be unsympathetic toward the general objectives of the Teachers' Federation. Her customary reference to the board of review, for example, as "that rat hole" in the county building, is not exactly literary; and yet, in view of the conditions that have been disclosed, the question of precise terminology is perhaps largely an academic one.

In the present situation the Teachers Federation had demanded the employment of a commercial appraisal company for making the quadrennial assessment of 1927. The joint commission had felt that such an appraisal, however meritorious it might be in itself, would be useless if it had to be made over the opposition of the board of assessors and board of review and then left to their mercies afterwards. The commission had, therefore, urged the necessity of developing a leverage outside of Chicago in the form of public opinion throughout the state and of

action through the agencies of the state government. The writer had urged such plan of action almost from the first meeting of the commission; and tax students will understand how readily such a development was to be anticipated in view of previous tax history in New York, Michigan, Wisconsin, California, and other states, which have passed through much the same evolution that Illinois is now passing through.

THE STATE TAX COMMISSION

At the hearing before the state tax commission, referred to above, the Teachers' Federation, the joint commission, and other groups united in laying the situation before the tax commission and in urging the commission to take any possible measures to remove the flagrant inequalities of assessment that had been shown to exist. In particular, the tax commission was urged to direct a publication of assessments, in accordance with the provisions of a statute of 1898, which appears to have been a dead letter in Chicago since 1911.

The tax commission was deeply impressed by the facts disclosed and by the apparent indifference of the board of review and board of assessors to the provisions of the statutes governing assessment; and on January 24, 1928, the commission issued an order directing the publication of assessments in accordance with the statute. The board of review and board of assessors questioned the authority of the commission to issue such order, declaring that publication of assessments would cost half a million dollars, that no funds were available for such expenditure, and that in any case the statute implied publication by legal description of properties rather than by name of owner, street number, or other form, as had been suggested by the tax commission. The commission appeared to be without legal power to enforce its order.

Later hearings were held by the commission in Chicago, at which the evidence of flagrant inequalities of assessment was gone into more fully, and the commission was urged to avail itself of the statute authorizing it to order a reassessment in any district in which it felt that the existing assessment was inequitable. On May 7, 1928, the commission finally ordered a reassessment of all real estate in Chicago and Cook County.

Tax officials immediately questioned the legality of this order, likewise, on the ground that the assessment of 1928 would not be completed until reviewed and acted upon finally by the board of review; and that the tax commission could not order a *reassessment* until the present assessment had been completed. The board of review had not completed its work upon the assessment of the previous year by December 31; and with the increased number of complaints in 1928 there was little likelihood that the board would have its work upon this assessment completed by December 31, 1928. Under present conditions, the same thing seemed likely to recur year after year. In that case, if the tax commission could not order a reassessment in any year until the board of review had completed its work upon the assessment of that year, it looked as if the commission might never be in a position to order a reassessment. On May 29, 1928, the attorney general of the state handed down an opinion, holding the tax commission without authority to order a reassessment until the board of review had completed its work. Under existing statutes, therefore, the tax commission again appeared to be without authority to take any effective measure for remedying conditions in Chicago.

THE LEGISLATIVE JOINT COMMISSION

Meanwhile, a legislative joint commission on taxation had been authorized by the last session of the legislature, before it adjourned in June, 1927, but the governor had taken no steps toward the appointment of the commission. The Illinois Agricultural Association and other groups had for some time been trying to persuade the governor to appoint the commission, which was to be composed of representatives from the senate and house and from business and agricultural groups outside of the legislature. On May 16, 1928, a year after the legislation authorizing it, the governor appointed the members of this commission, with Senator Dailey, of Peoria, as chairman. The day after its appointment the commission came to Chicago; and a week later invited the joint commission on real estate valuation, the Teachers' Federation and other interested groups to present any facts and information bearing upon the Chicago situation.

The commission was apparently much impressed by the facts presented at this hearing and declared itself ready to support any legislation necessary to remedy the situation. Three weeks later the governor issued a call for a special session of the legislature.

THE SPECIAL SESSION

The session convened on June 18. Representatives of the Teachers' Federation, of the joint commission on real estate valuation, and other groups and individuals, were invited to present the facts of the situation before a joint session of the senate and house. Some of the charts included with these articles were shown at Springfield.

The legislature remained in session only five days, but in that time, largely under the leadership of the state tax commission and the legislative joint commission, two important bills bearing upon the Chicago situation were passed. One of these bills authorized the state tax commission to order a reassessment *at any time, regardless of the stage at which the local assessing bodies might be;* the other provided for the publication of quadrennial assessments of real estate, *specifically requiring that this publication should be by name of owner and street number or other form of address.*

THE ORDER FOR REASSESSMENT

The county commissioners of Cook County appropriated ample funds for the publication of assessments, and the publication was promptly begun. Its effects were startling indeed. From the beginning of the publication to the time of writing the newspapers of the city have been carrying, almost daily, photographs of adjoining properties, frequently properties that appear to be exactly similar, which are assessed at totally different figures. In many cases of similar homes, sitting side by side, one has been assessed at five to ten times as much as the other. It has been extremely effective publicity and has stirred up a vast amount of discussion and of criticism.

As a result of all of these conditions, the state tax commission held a conference in Chicago, on July 19, with members of the board of assessors, representatives of the joint commission, Teachers' Federation, real estate boards and various other groups, after which the commission issued a final and specific order for the reassessment of all real estate in Chicago and Cook County.

At the moment of writing, the board of commissioners of Cook County has just appropriated $800,000 for the reassessment, and the board of assessors is engaged in working out its plans and methods for making this assess-

ment. It has asked the coöperation of the joint commission, of the real estate boards, and various other groups, and appears to be making a sincere effort to bring about an assessment that will be as nearly equitable as can be made in the time within which it must be done.

Injunction proceedings, however, have been initiated in the county court, questioning the legality of the Tax Commission's order; and County Treasurer Harding has announced that he would refuse to authorize payments from the county treasury in connection with the reassessment, on the ground of certain statutory technicalities. These questions will presumably be carried immediately to the State Supreme Court, and may delay proceedings sufficiently to make a reassessment for 1928 impossible.

THE ILLINOIS JOINT TAX CONFERENCE

But meanwhile the scope of the movement has broadened, and in April, 1928, there was organized the Illinois joint tax conference, composed of representatives of state-wide business and civic organizations, including among others the Illinois Agricultural Association, the State Bankers' Association, the State Association of Real Estate Boards, the Illinois Federation of Labor, the State Teachers' Association, and the Illinois League of Women Voters. Omar Wright, of Rockford, since that time elected president of the State Bankers' Association, was chosen president of the tax conference. Mr. Fairweather and other members of the joint commission are upon the executive committee of the Illinois joint conference.

The conference has undertaken, as its first task, to ascertain the actual facts of the tax situation throughout the state. On the basis of these facts, it hopes to develop intelligent public interest and discussion and to carry on informal conferences among the groups represented in the conference and other groups not now represented, in an effort to work out a moderate but practical program of relief.

Space prevents any consideration of the various proposals that are being discussed throughout the state. Probably all will agree that the worst features of the present situation are the wasteful and inefficient expenditure of public money, resulting in almost confiscatory rates of taxation in some sections of the state; the disproportionate share of the tax burden that falls upon real estate and tangible property; the unlimited opportunity for arbitrary favoritism, discrimination, and coercion which the present personal property tax places in the hands of tax officials; and the general irresponsibility and inefficiency with which present tax laws are administered. Agreement upon remedies will not be so unanimous; but suffice it to say here,

that the experience of other states affords abundant guidance in taking steps toward elimination at least of the worst features of present taxation in Illinois.

Opinions may easily differ as to which of various alternatives are the most desirable or most available. After all, with conditions in Illinois as they are today, any one of a half dozen alternatives will afford distinct improvement. The one most essential thing in the present situation is to have an impartial agency that will ascertain the actual facts of the situation, disseminate these facts widely throughout the state, and then afford a medium for continuous conference among the various groups most vitally interested, for the purpose of eliminating minor differences and agreeing from time to time upon at least a minimum of practical constructive improvement. Such an agency now seems to be afforded by the recently formed Illinois joint tax conference.

RECENT BOOKS REVIEWED

FORCE ACCOUNT ON UNIT PRICE CONSTRUCTION CONTRACTS. By Philip A. Beatty. Published by the Philadelphia Bureau of Municipal Research as agent of the Thomas Skelton Harrison Foundation, 1928. Pp. 35.

Thomas Skelton Harrison, a Philadelphian, left the residue of his estate for the improvement of governmental conditions in Philadelphia mentioning specially the dissemination of information on municipal affairs. The trustees of the fund engaged the Bureau of Municipal Research to make a study of the preparation, award, and performance of municipal work contracts. The subject assigned was essentially technical and, therefore, the monograph written by Mr. Beatty discusses matters which have an appeal for a very limited group. Technicists and students only may find interest in it. The author has undoubtedly given much study and research to his assignment and presents the various types and details of construction contracts of many cities. A student of municipal affairs who is seeking for data on extra work and the way in which it may be checked will find points of interesting information. The report, while prosaic in part, could be made as attractive as "The Relation of Building Height to Street Traffic," a paper appearing in the NATIONAL MUNICIPAL REVIEW for July, 1928, by non-technical presentation.

If city governments in America were aristocracies, such a report might be of immediate value, but with the political conditions predominant in most cities, reports on municipal subjects must be presented in simple and colloquial narrative in order to attract the general public and gather support for the recommendations. Dissemination means spreading ideas and beliefs broadcast and that result is only accomplished by reducing technical phraseology to simple words.

The Bureau of Municipal Research has no statutory power to carry out its recommendations and such studies as it makes are, therefore, academic. The movement started in Massachusetts to create with definite functions and powers boards of overseeing authority such as the Finance Commissions of Lowell, Massachusetts and Manchester, New Hampshire should be studied and encouraged. Only when recom-

mendations have the force of authority behind them can we say that they are of practical use.

JOHN C. L. DOWLING.
Boston Finance Commission.

❊

GOVERNMENTAL REPORTING IN CHICAGO. By Herman C. Beyle. Chicago: The University of Chicago Press, 1928. Pp. xxiii, 303.

To penetrate the fog enveloping the municipal phase of reporting, Herman C. Beyle took one area, Chicago, and for three years examined the local reports which form a bookshelf "five foot—plus." Under a picture of that shelf (one of many excellent pictures throughout the book), he asks the question which is the major theme of the volume: "How well does this body of reporting meet the demands which may be made upon it by citizens, other officials, and students of government?" The answer is contained in some three hundred pages of the volume entitled *Governmental Reporting in Chicago*. The process of his examination is dissection: the diagnosis is akin to desiccation.

Mr. Beyle characterizes the reporting system of the city as "spotted with good and bad practice" and as presenting "little or no coördination." The reports of the board of education remind him "of the proverbial person who failed to see the forest for the trees." For Cook County, "the system is like the outward appearance of an office building at night, mostly dark and with only here and there a bright spot." Ludicrous examples are not lacking. An Oak Forest institution devotes nineteen pages to a report of the number of pounds of rhubarb, the number of bunches of green onions and boxes of spinach raised during the first week of June! Whereupon the official rendering the report either became aghast at the result or made an important discovery, so often and sadly rediscovered, when he commented that "it is difficult to make a hard and fast distinction between things that are of greatest importance and matters of lesser note."

To present an illuminating example to the contrary, an illustration of an attractive report, where does Mr. Beyle go? We might have suspected it. To none other than to "Big Bill, the

Builder." Not the least ingredient in Mr. Thompson's flair for publicity has been his manipulation of reports. For example, he put out health bulletins and a readable booklet entitled, "Chicago—Eight Years of Progress." I take it that the booklet is damnably inaccurate and damnably attractive. But never mind; it tells all about how the robust antagonist of King George toiled mightily for the masses—and it won votes.

The first and primary service of Mr. Beyle is to portray what is public reporting in a metropolitan area. Here the subject is measured with exactitude by a surprising amount of relevant minutiæ. The job needed to be done. No one previously had combined the skill and perseverance to waylay a large city and record her method of public accountancy. The real tribute to the volume, one rarely warranted for a pioneering attempt, is that the job need not be done again. Now we know what happens when any large or thoughtless city disregards systematic accountancy to its public. The author has painstakingly cut through the jungle to survey and diagram the ground. From there on, he and fellow members of the guild may push forward.

I am far from convinced that the author was required to exhibit all his surveying tools to his readers. I was taken with a nervous apprehension throughout the reading lest some of the material of the excellent charts would break through the thin lines holding them and bodily occupy the pages of discussion.

The author is not content with showing simply what "is." His familiarity with the subject matter urges him to an advance towards what "may be" by way of two sectors. First, should we not define what should constitute the substance of the reports? Mr. Beyle says "yes." Forthwith he proceeds to ennumerate some twelve parts of a report. The list is a useful catalogue of subjects that may go into reports in general; but it is no guide for preparing any individual report. Its use is in suggesting the nature of subjects that are proper for reporting.

Secondly, a comprehensive analysis is made of the use of reportorial devices. Here he succeeds notably. However the contents of individual reports may vary, all reports partake of a like necessity for effective presentation through whatever devices are available. These methods are discussed with the discrimination required to aid a reporter or editor in choosing devices to strengthen his publication. Since the author is intimately familiar with municipal government and survey methods for its study, his analysis achieves a value for application by public agencies that is almost lacking in the general works on statistics, graphs, and allied topics.

A pointed suggestion for future study is reiterated by the author. To what purpose is reporting if its story is not read because we don't know what are the political interests of voters? The main task, he holds, is to explore "the attitudes of the report's recipients" ("Big Bill" never called his voters by that name). The study would become "an analysis of the nature of political interest, with a view to the determination of what are the approaches to reporting to the citizen, and of how reporting (can) direct the citizen's political interest to some avail in the conduct of government."

WYLIE KILPATRICK.
University of Virginia.

✿

CARTER HENRY HARRISON, I, POLITICAL LEADER. By Claudius O. Johnson. Chicago: The University of Chicago Press, 1928. Pp. xii, 306.

Here we have the second of the studies in leadership prepared under the direction of Professor Charles E. Merriam. Dr. Johnson has taken the career of Chicago's famous World's Fair Mayor and subjected it to searching analysis. This book ought to find favorable reception. It is a clear-cut, objective, unimpassioned treatment of a difficult subject. The rollicking, gallant Carter Harrison, friend of the masses, protector of anarchists, and idol of the libertarians, emerges as the equally good friend of business, the loyal patriot and the able administrator.

Dr. Johnson's study is valuable because he has availed himself of the suggestions of psychologists and sociologists without falling prey to their seductive phraseology and facile generalizations. His treatment of his subject is divided into three parts—Background, Traits, Technique. In the first section he inquires into the ancestral record and early environment of the Mayor. The author finds that the illustrious family name of the Harrisons and the Carters, their wealth, prestige, and exceptional social position had a likely influence on the subsequent fortunes of the Mayor. He does not say, however, that Harrison derived this or that specific trait from this or that ancestor. It is enough to know that the ancestral background was propitious to the development of Harrison's gifts. He does not say that Yale graduates, for instance, occupy preferential positions in reference to the Chicago mayoralty, but he does observe that residence abroad equips a potential urban leader with significant attitudes of toleration and respect for the "foreign-born."

Dr. Johnson lists some forty physical characteristics and mental and temperamental traits, most of which meet with approval. The advantage of this method is that it enables the social scientist to single out the traits in potential leaders which it would be desirable to suppress and those which it would pay to encourage. The third section is a discussion of technique—the "traits in action." At this point the followers of Henshawe Ward and the "practical politicians" will raise their eyebrows. Is politics an art that defies minute analysis? Are their too many variables in the conduct of a leader and the environment within which he operates? This reviewer does not believe so; and Dr. Johnson's analysis of the Chicago background reveals an urban environment which it seems might be approximated elsewhere. If we have any misgivings it is whether the libraries and the stockyards of Chicago are deserving of the special notice which is given them. Ought not studies of urban backgrounds to stress the typical rather than the peculiar? But perhaps we should wait until other similar studies have appeared before entering this objection.

The text is fairly free from typographical errors and minor mistakes. On the whole one must applaud Dr. Johnson's selection and presentation of facts and opinions.

ROY V. PEEL.
Washington Square College,
New York University.

∗

CHARITIES AND CORRECTIONS, JACKSON COUNTY, MISSOURI. A survey of the Welfare Activities of the Jackson County Government. Kansas City Public Service Institute, March, 1928. Pp. 203 (mimeographed).

This report embodies the findings and recommendations of the Kansas City Public Service Institute, which for the past year has been engaged in making an exhaustive study of welfare activities in Jackson County. The work was undertaken by Walter Matscheck, director of the Institute, at the request of the County Court of Jackson County, which is the chief agency for administering the county's welfare services.

Mr. Jesse Sealey, of the staff of the Institute, was largely responsible for the investigation and the preparation of the report.

"Charities and Corrections" in Jackson County account for about three-quarters of a million dollars, or one-fourth of all county expenditures. Responsibility for administering the various services represented by this expenditure is divided between the county court and the juvenile court. The county court provides for care of the indigent insane, feebleminded and epileptic, the tuberculous, the aged and infirm, and makes grants in aid to the deaf and blind in state schools and to other dependent and defective persons. The juvenile court is responsible for the care of delinquent and neglected children and for administration or allowances to mothers with dependent children under 16 years of age. As the report points out, this division of responsibility, plus the inevitable invasion of politics, and the increasing administrative burden put upon the county court, which is essentially a legislative body, has resulted in neglect of scientific study of welfare problems and in failure to apply scientific methods of relief. The chief weaknesses of the present system are cited as follows:

1. Lack of strong administrative organization with centralization of administrative authority.
2. Lack of skilled leadership and properly trained personnel, together with poor personnel administration.
3. Lack of social case work and adequate social case investigation.
4. Lack of a scientific accumulation and analysis of information with respect to the social needs and results of the welfare activities of the county.
5. Lack of sufficient coöperation not only among county agencies themselves, but also with private welfare agencies.

To remedy these defects the report proposes that a department of county welfare be established under a director appointed by the county court, and that all administrative authority and responsibility now vested in and assumed by the county court with respect to public welfare activities be reposed in such director of public welfare. Emphasis is placed upon the necessity of employing a director whose training and experience are such as to insure the development of a sound social policy. The report further recommends the establishment within the proposed department of public welfare of a division of statistics and accounts, a division of social case investigation, and a division for each of the county institutions, the heads of these divisions to be chosen by the director of the department and held directly responsible to him. An advisory council or board is also recommended to consist of the judge of the juvenile court, *ex officio*, and four or more other persons selected by the director of county welfare.

These recommendations are well supported by an exhaustive review of the activities of the county court and juvenile court, together with their relations with other official and unofficial agencies, and an analysis of all available data regarding the operation of the various county institutions now under the control of the county court. Much difficulty was experienced in securing the information desired, either "because it had never been kept or because the records could not be found." But the surveyors have nevertheless been able to present a picture which seems, in the light of the reviewer's experience with county welfare administration, to be highly expressive of its most characteristic defects. The wealth of detail in this report regarding the administration and operation of Jackson County institutions is especially illuminating in its bearing on the reasons for the steadily increasing costs of county government, even though adequate unit cost data could not be secured owing to the lack of properly kept records.

C. E. McCOMBS, M.D.

✸

Municipal Reports.—*Brunswick, Georgia. Annual Report for the Year 1927. By E. C. Garvin, City Manager. Pp. 40.*—If municipal reports were appraised on the basis of charts alone this report would stand out in the forefront of any that have yet come to the attention of the reviewer. In the front of the report appears an organization chart, and this is followed by text material and 29 other charts showing graphically almost every type of information from the disposition of police court cases to the accumulated receipts and expenditures by months.

This last chart is quite an innovation in a municipal report and it is drawn in such a clear manner that an administrator can anticipate a complete financial program several months in advance. This one chart together with the implied possibilities it offers as an effective instrument of administration is alone sufficient reason why this report should receive wide distribution.

Other favorable characteristics of this report are its size, length, and attractiveness. The features which are not so commendable are the utter lack of pictures, the omission of table of contents, and the fact that the amount of space accorded the various activities hardly corresponds to their relative importance. However, for anyone not yet aware of the important rôle that chart making can play as a means of serving both the report reader and the administrator, no better evidence is available anywhere.

Cincinnati, Ohio. Annual Report for the Year 1927. By C. O. Sherill, City Manager. Pp. 217.—This report is labeled "Municipal Activities" in place of the usual title, "Municipal Report." While such a title is not a misnomer, still it would seem that report writers might standardize at least on a title. There are two other faults which must be mentioned before passing to an enumeration of the many good features. It contains 217 pages, which is at least four times what one can reasonably expect to be read, and the delay of five months in making the report available to the public will certainly detract from its interest and usefulness.

It would be extremely difficult to pick many more flaws in this report, which excels in many good features. To mention a few—important facts are emphasized, so if one cares only for a general résumé of the work it can be easily and readily attained by a casual reading. This feature could have been used more extensively to good advantage, for there are whole pages without any emphasis being indicated. If there are no important facts worth emphasizing relative to a certain activity, that in itself might be reason enough for eliminating the passage entirely from the report. If some such criteria of importance were applied to report material, much shorter and more interesting reports would probably result. Difficulty enough is encountered in trying to interest the general public even in matters of supreme importance.

In reality this report is so good that small defects are noticeable which in most reports would pass entirely unnoticed.

C. E. RIDLEY.

JUDICIAL DECISIONS

EDITED BY C. W. TOOKE

Professor of Law, New York University

Counties—Legislative Power to Exclude Park Territory from County System.—In *Yellowstone Park Transportation Co.* v. *Gallatin County*, 27 Fed. (2d) 410, the U. S. District Court of Montana had before it the question of the conflict of federal and state laws affecting jurisdiction over a part of Yellowstone Park situated in Montana. The action was in equity to enjoin local taxation, and the case turned upon the construction to be given to the federal act of 1872 creating the park and to a state statute of 1913 excluding the lands in question from any of the counties of the state. The federal act establishing the park withdrew the lands from settlement, occupancy or sale, and set them apart as a pleasure ground "under the exclusive control of the Secretary of the Interior to make and publish such rules and regulations as he may deem necessary and proper." The act of 1889 provided for the statehood of Montana and of certain other territories "as at present described." The specific definition of the boundaries in the act of 1864 creating the territory included the lands in question, which consisted of the strip four miles wide and one hundred miles long on the southern border of the state. These lands from territorial days were included in Gallatin County, but in 1913 the state legislature, in defining anew the county's boundaries, excluded these particular lands and failed to incorporate them within any other county.

In holding that the lands in question must be considered to be a part of Gallatin County and that the statute was invalid, the court points out that when the state was created its entire area was within organized counties which were declared to continue "until otherwise established or changed by law," that the constitution provided that in all cases of the establishment of a new county it should pay a proportion of the liabilities of the county or counties from which it might be formed and that the legislature was expressly given the power to readjust county lines. The county system thus rests upon a constitutional basis and cannot be disorganized by any act of the legislature.

In disposing of the contention that the federal government has exclusive control, the court holds

that this imports only administrative authority to care for the proprietary interests of the United States and does not confer legislative and judicial jurisdiction or political dominion, which it is beyond the power of Congress to vest in the secretary. Such jurisdiction or dominion not having been reserved to the United States in any act of Congress preceding statehood, it follows that the state is vested with sovereignty and jurisdiction over all its area including the national park lands, which cannot be diminished or impaired without its consent.

✱

Special Assessments—Applied to Ornamental Street Lighting.—In *Fisher* v. *Astoria*, 269 Pac. 853, the Supreme Court of Oregon holds that the city under the provisions of the charter prior to 1926 had the power to erect on business streets ornamental poles for lighting and to assess the cost upon the abutting property. The action was in equity to remove the cloud of the tax lien from the plaintiff's property. At the time the improvement was ordered, the charter gave the city the power to grade, pave, curb and otherwise improve the streets, to delimit districts for such improvements and to assess the cost against the property peculiarly benefited. It further specifically stated that "the power and authority to improve a street includes the power and authority to improve the sidewalks and pavements and to determine and provide for everything convenient and necessary for such improvement." The power was also given to light the streets and to furnish the city with gas, electricity or other lights, and for the erection and construction of such work as might be necessary or convenient therefor.

The plaintiff, relying upon the rule that the power to improve does not include the power of special taxation, contended that the erection of ornamental lights was not a street improvement, but could be justified only as an exercise of the power to light, for which no express power of local assessment was given, and that no benefit aside from that to the general public accrued to the owners of the abutting property. The court

700

held, however, that as a matter of fact such an installation conferred special benefits upon the abutting property and that it was incidental to the improvement of the streets.

In 1926, subsequent to the erection of the ornamental lighting system in question, an amendment to the charter expressly delegated the power to assess the cost of such improvements upon the abutting property and conferred the authority to make assessments for the cost of such work already installed. The court holds that such authority cured any defect in the power of the city to make an assessment, retroactive legislation not being forbidden by the state constitution.

The broad construction given by the court to the power to improve streets is sustained by numerous decisions. (See *Murphy* v. *Peoria*, 119 Ill. 509, 9 N. E. 895, and *Thompson* v *Highland Park*, 187 Ill. 265, 58 N. E. 328.)

＊

Special Assessments—Original Jurisdiction of Federal Courts.—The growing tendency of litigants to resort to the federal courts to test the validity of municipal ordinances is no longer confined to public service corporations, but is manifest in the increasing number of cases wherein private persons invoke their jurisdiction by setting up the claim that their rights under the Constitution are being invaded. The readiness of these courts to take jurisdiction is evident in many recent cases, and sometimes the only basis appears to be the assertion of the plaintiff that the given ordinance may deprive him of property rights without due process of law. In *Adam Schumann Associates Inc.* v. *City of New York*, decided in August by the District Court of the Eastern District of New York, the court denied a motion to dismiss the complaint, which set up that the enforcement of a special assessment for sewer construction would deprive the plaintiff of property without due process of law. The assessment in question was graded by zones according to the determination of benefits to the respective areas and the plaintiff's property came in a zone of heavier assessment, which was but two-fifths of the entire district but upon which four-fifths of the cost was imposed. It appeared, therefore, that the evidence in the case might show a proper exercise of the taxing power, as is frankly admitted by the opinion of the district judge. But the court assumes that a *prima facie* case of illegal inequality is made out by the above

facts, so as to bring it within the federal statute conferring original jurisdiction and states that "practically it makes little difference in what court house in Brooklyn the parties present their controversy."

Upon the facts and pleadings as set forth in the opinion, we believe the judgment of the district court will be reversed upon appeal; otherwise, we may look for a further extension of original federal jurisdiction far beyond what seems to have been contemplated by the statute (28 U. S. C., section 41). If the principle of the decision is to stand, it means that the owner of any property subject to special assessment by the front foot rule or by any other method has the right to invoke federal jurisdiction by merely asserting that the assessment may deprive him of property without due process of law.

＊

Traffic Ordinances—Test of Reasonableness. —The control of the courts over the enactment of ordinances is not limited to the question of the power of the municipality to act with reference to the subject matter, but extends to the determination of whether the power so granted is reasonably exercised. While a considerable latitude of discretion is accorded the municipal law-making body so long as the regulations enacted operate uniformly upon all persons similarly situated and are not clearly arbitrary and unreasonable, nevertheless all police legislation is subject to the limitation that it is required by the interests of the public and that the means adopted are reasonably necessary for the accomplishment of the purpose of the enactment and not unduly oppressive upon individuals.

A nice example of the application of the test of reasonableness to the validity of an ordinance is to be found in the case of *Pennjersey Rapid Transit Co.* v. *City of Camden*, 142 Atl. 821, decided by the Supreme Court of New Jersey August 8. The city adopted an ordinance prohibiting the operation of double-decked autobusses, not equipped with pneumatic tires, in and along any street south of Federal Street. The power to pass ordinances regulating traffic was clearly delegated to the city and the ordinance was not discriminatory merely because it might affect the business of only one company (*Morris* v. *Duby*, 274 U. S. 135). But these questions were not pertinent to the decision of the court, which declared the ordinance unreasonable and void upon the ground that the number of decks on an autobus does not present a substantial basis for classification for regulations to conserve the highways; the weight and not the height of vehicles having the only proper relationship to the purpose of the preservation of the surface of the street. For other cases declaring ordinances void for unreasonableness, the reader may be referred to *People* v. *Gibbs*, 186 Mich. 127, 152 N. W. 1053; *Elkhart* v. *Murray*, 165 Ind. 304, 75 N. E. 593; and *McCray* v. *Chicago*, 292 Ill. 60, 126 N. E. 557.

✤

Gasoline Storage—Requirement of Subsurface Tanks Upheld.—The U. S. Circuit Court of Appeals, Eighth Circuit, in *City of Marysville* v. *Standard Oil Co., et al.*, 27 Fed. (2d) 478, reversing the judgment of the district court, upheld an ordinance requiring the storage of gasoline, oil and other inflammable liquids to be in containers buried at least three feet under ground. The ordinance in question was based on a general delegation of the local police power, but the implied power exercised had been upheld by the highest court of Kansas, which finding the federal court accepted as final (*Reinman* v. *Little Rock*, 237 U. S. 171). The ordinance excepted the storage in receptacles of five hundred gallons or less, but permitted only one such container on given premises. It further repealed a prior ordinance of 1914, authorizing large storage tanks above ground, under which the plaintiffs had erected and operated several large tanks for some nine years.

The findings of fact of the master who took evidence in the case were somewhat contradictory; on the one hand that sub-surface storage would lessen the danger from fire or explosion due to lightning or static electricity, and that the base rate for fire insurance would be reduced one-half; on the other hand, that the dangers of leakage and seepage would be so great as to increase the hazard to the other property in the vicinity; upon which was based the conclusion that the ordinance was arbitrary, discriminatory and unreasonable. The circuit court nevertheless thinks that the record presents no evidence of arbitrary or capricious action on the part of the city council, that the city acted in good faith and that the remedy proposed bears a direct relation to the danger sought to be averted. Judge Phillips wrote a vigorous dissenting opinion upholding the views of the master and of the district court.

✤

Regulations of Business—Control over Advertising.—The charter of the city of St. Louis gives it the broadest powers of control over all persons engaged in business, including the licensing of occupations, subject only to the constitutional limitations on the police power. In *St. Louis* v. *Southcombe*, 8 S. W. (2d) 1001, decided by the Supreme Court of Missouri July 25, the defendant appealed from a conviction for violation of an ordinance making it unlawful for any dealer to advertise goods for sale without stating clearly that he is engaged in the business of selling such goods. The defendant, who had advertised and sold furniture without complying with the ordinance, contended that the ordinance was not a regulation of business, but an attempt to legislate upon something separate and apart from business. The court in confirming the conviction bases its decision upon the obvious fact that the statement required would assist the city officials in discovering persons doing business as merchants without a merchant's license and thus promote the morals, peace, government, welfare, trade and commerce of the city.

PUBLIC UTILITIES

EDITED BY JOHN BAUER

Director, American Public Utilities Bureau

The Five Cent Fare Before the Supreme Court. —The question whether a contract is a contract, or when it is and when it is not, was argued before the Supreme Court of the United States October 15, in the New York City five-cent fare case. The progress of this litigation has been followed in this department. Briefly re-stated, the issue is whether the City of New York had the legal right in 1913 to enter into "Rapid Transit Contract No. 3" with the Interborough Rapid Transit Company in the matter of fixing a five-cent fare. This contract provided comprehensively for the construction and operation of a system of subways. It set forth definitely the obligations and rights of each of the parties; it fixed, particularly, the financial responsibility of each, and prescribed the returns to which each is entitled. The properties are owned by the city, and are leased under contract to the Interborough Company. The latter undertook the operation at a fixed five-cent fare, for the duration of the contract, as a part of the financial plan set up in the contract.

The present litigation involves only the five-cent fare, not the other features of the contract. The Interborough now claims that the city did not have the legal right to enter into a *rate* agreement; that the five-cent fare provision is inoperative, and that the Interborough is entitled to have the fare fixed according to ordinary standards of rate making. In its argument for a seven-cent fare, it seeks to have an 8 per cent return upon the reproduction cost of all the properties, including the elevated and subways, notwithstanding the fact that the two properties are operated as distinct systems, and that the subways are owned by the City of New York and are leased at limited returns to the company. It seems rather incredible that the part that furnished one of the chief motives on the part of the city to sign the contract in 1913 should now be set aside as beyond the contractual power of the city, when all the other parts which are advantageous to the company are accepted as valid. To the lay mind, the contract should certainly be considered as a whole. If the rate part is held invalid, then

the entire contract should be dissolved, subject to redetermination.

This is easily the most important case before the Supreme Court in a generation, so far as the rights of municipalities are concerned in dealing with local utilities. The decision will have far-reaching effect, not only among the larger cities in the country, but also upon state and national policy in dealing with the utilities. If the City of New York cannot contract with a company for a fixed rate of fare, certainly other cities which are seeking adequate transportation cannot proceed, through the instrumentality of contracts, to establish long-term policies with complete protection of the public. Likewise, states which have under consideration water-power developments can hardly expect to lease the properties for private operation, by fixing the rates to be charged to consumers. Even the development of Muscle Shoals by the federal government may be affected, if the basis of rates cannot be definitely fixed by contract to protect the consumers.

A decision in favor of the company can hardly do otherwise than to accelerate greatly the establishment of public ownership and operation, especially for power and transportation. So far as the City of New York is concerned, the Company's immediate success is likely to bring about the recapture of the rapid transit lines by the city, and of municipal operation. If, however, the city's contractual right is sustained, there is a strong probability that the inevitable reorganization of transit will be carried out through the medium of a private corporation, under lease from the city, with contractual control over fares.

The same influences are certain to be determinative elsewhere. The larger cities throughout the country must inevitably enter directly the field of transportation, by furnishing financial support. If they cannot protect the public interest by contract, they will hardly have another choice than to proceed, on their own responsibility, with direct public ownership and operation of the properties. This probable development will be quite a different result from the immediate victory desired by the company. Here, as in other phases of private utility management, the effort is centered upon immediate financial advantages, without regard to ultimate consequences upon the company or industry.

*

New Fare Cases.—As was to be expected, the move by the Interborough Company for a higher fare has been followed by a flood of requests from surface companies in New York City seeking like increases. The Transit Commission has been practically swamped with applications and hearings involving higher fares. If the Interborough wins, there will doubtless be a general increase in street railway rates throughout the city. If it loses, the surface lines can hardly charge a seven-cent fare, even if permitted under their franchises and even if the Transit Commission should be compelled under the law to allow higher rates. The surface lines cannot, as a practical matter, charge seven cents or more, when the rapid transit lines are limited to five cents.

The surface lines, which are already seeking an increase in fare, face also this practical difficulty,—whether they would be better off at the higher fare than at the existing five-cent rate. Their traffic consists largely of short-distance riders, who are not greatly dependent upon the service. The expert for one of the companies estimated that the proposed 40 per cent increase in rates would produce a decrease of 30 per cent in traffic. If this is correct, then in that particular case the higher rates would produce slightly less revenues in the aggregate than the existing five-cent fare. The company might possibly effect a slight reduction in operating expenses through the decrease in traffic. On the whole, it would probably be little better off with the 40 per cent increase in rates than under existing conditions.

With this state of facts, there would be no justification for increasing the rates, even if it be assumed that the company is not making a fair return, judged according to ordinary standards of rate making. The same situation obtains with most of the surface lines in the City of New York. It is a practical condition that must receive reasonable treatment. The companies have suffered mostly because they have lost traffic in recent years, while they should have realized great increases with the growth of population and development of business.

This failure to develop is due largely to traffic conditions and to changes in transportation requirements. Whether, under these circumstances, a 40 per cent increase in rates will actually produce any financial relief, or will move faster toward complete economic failure, is a practical question whose answer depends upon the coming course of events.

The same situation prevails in practically all cities where the companies are struggling for higher fares. While the conditions are somewhat different where the riders depend regularly for long trips upon the street railways, yet the chief difficulty in the industry as a whole has been the failure of traffic development. This has been due generally to traffic conditions, street congestion, and the slowing down of street railway operation. The changed conditions require a more effective mode of transportation which can better meet the needs of the communities. Any movement that will result in further diminution of traffic will hardly serve to put the industry permanently upon a sound economic basis.

*

Proposed Limit to the Jurisdiction of the Federal Courts.—The Interborough fare case has actively revived the discussion and movement to limit the jurisdiction of the federal courts in local public utility cases. One of the features of the Interborough case was the precipitate action on the part of the company to reach the federal court before the city authorities could move to the state courts. While, of course, all courts are supposed to be impartial and just, controlled by established principles of law, actually the company had a preference for the federal court because of assumed advantages.

There has been a widespread feeling that public utility companies have obtained distinct advantages in the federal courts; they certainly have gone there, in preference to the state courts, in numerous rate cases during recent years. It does appear that the federal judges, on the average, have had less regard for the actualities of local conditions than the state courts. They appear, indeed, to be responsible to a considerable extent for the decisions which have greatly reduced the effectiveness of state and local regulation.

In view of the rather obviously unreasonable situation that the very important local matter in the Interborough case, which depends wholly upon state law and policy, had been hustled to the federal court to escape state jurisdiction, bills were introduced in the last session of Congress to place a curb upon the jurisdiction of the federal courts to deal with all utility cases which arise through local conditions or out of state commission decisions. The bills provide that the first recourse shall be to the state courts; that companies cannot move directly to the federal courts, and thus avoid state jurisdiction; they would be required to exhaust the possibilities of appeal within the state before they could move to the federal courts. They cannot, of course, be denied the right of ultimate appeal to the Supreme Court of the United States. The bills, we believe, merit the support of all municipal and state authorities interested in proper policies and methods of regulation.

*

Mr. Young on Street Railway Economics.—At a recent meeting of the Electric Railway Association, Mr. Owen D. Young spoke on the conditions of the street railways. The burden of his message was that the companies should be permitted to pay their way, and that private ownership and operation is a self-checking system in respect to its economic justification. Incidentally, he decried also the practice of absorbing street railway losses through electric rates where both services are rendered by the same company.

Mr. Young is, of course, correct in the general proposition that street railways should be permitted to pay their way, if the traffic will permit. He does not, however, seem to comprehend the basic economic difficulties with which the industry is confronted. He does not appear to see that the entire business is struggling against traffic conditions growing constantly more troublesome, and against the inroad of automobile and bus transportation.

As to the point that private ownership and operation furnishes an economic check upon itself, that is mere language which disregards the realities of the industry. Where is there such an immediate check when a company has a monopoly in transportation, when it is freed from competition, and when it can charge all costs to the public through the rates fixed for service? The prompt working of the supposed check has not been obvious to interested observers. The financial policies followed all

too frequently by the companies indicate that the check works—if at all—after a long interval, when the harm of overcapitalization and unsound management has been perpetrated. The difficulties of the present street railways are due, at least in part, to the absence of adequate check in the past to prevent dangerous practices. In other utilities there is no effective check now upon overcapitalization and unjustified policies imposed upon the companies. The economic rebound will come, unfortunately, in the future, and will then strike innocent investors who had no part in establishing present methods.

*

Rate of Return and Fixed Rate Base.—The Massachusetts system of regulation has recognized the fact that effective rate making must be based upon investment. It realized that "fair value" is too indefinite for satisfactory administration and sound financial control. Investment is a definite quantity that can be maintained through the accounts, while "fair value" is fluctuating, and is subject to dispute and litigation.

The Massachusetts Department of Public Utilities has tried to keep to investment as the rate base.[1] But it has not adopted the companion principle, that the rate of return should be limited on the securities issued. The stockholders, after the initial investment has been made, are entitled at present to all the net income that the company makes above operating expenses and taxes at prevailing rates. There is, thus, no limit upon the dividend rate that may be paid.

This failure to place a limit upon the dividend rate, as well as upon the rate base, impairs the effectiveness of regulation for both the consumers and the investors. Unless the commission keeps the rates constantly adjusted to changing costs, and thus maintains the value of the stock constantly at par, it will be periodically confronted with the choice of dealing unfairly either with the consumers or with a group of the investors. The respective rights cannot be harmoniously preserved under prevailing conditions. The situa-

[1] Whether Massachusetts can keep to this measure is now in litigation before the federal court in the Worcester Electric Lighting case. The commission fixed the rates in Worcester, Massachusetts, at five cents per k. w. h., using practically the investment basis. The companies are claiming "fair value" as determined under ordinary rate-making standards.

tion can be more readily illustrated than explained in general terms.

Assume that an electric company had outstanding 50,000 shares of common stock issued at par, involving an actual cash investment of $5,000,000. Assume also that a 7 per cent dividend would keep the stock at par, but that the net return of the company over a period of years has steadily increased, because of growth in business and decrease in costs, so that dividends at 14 per cent have been established, and the market value of the stock is $200 instead of par.

Suppose, now, 25,000 shares of additional stock are issued at $200 per share, making a new cash investment of $5,000,000, fixing a total rate base of $10,000,000. The new investment at $200 per share involves a yield to the new stockholders of only 7 per cent,—the rate needed to keep the stock at par. But to continue this yield to the new investors will require a permanent dividend of 14 per cent upon all the stock (old and new). The old stock, however, had no right to such a return, and the public is compelled to assume this additional burden in the way of unwarranted profits to the old investors.

But suppose the commission were to limit the rate of return to 7 per cent upon the total cash investment of $10,000,000 (old and new), the new investors would be subjected to a reduction from the expected return of $14 to $9.33 per share. The commission thus faces the alternative of granting the old investors a 100 per cent profit, or imposing upon the new investors a 33⅓ per cent loss. The result almost inevitably will be the profit to the old investors, and a larger burden upon the consumers than is warranted by the actual rate base.

The situation just presented is far from academic. It appears in every electric company where (a) net earnings have increased materially in recent years; (b) where the market value of the stock has advanced according to the higher level of earnings; and (c) where additional capital is obtained through the issue of stock on the basis of present market prices.

The only remedy for such a condition is to limit the dividend rate as well as the rate base. If dividend payments in our example had been kept at 7 per cent throughout, then there would not be the conflict of interest between old and new investors, or between investors and the public. Effective regulation requires a definite rate of return, as well as a definite rate base, both subject to exact administrative control.

Financial Investigation under the Walsh Resolution.—We have been reliably informed that, in compliance with the Walsh resolution, the Federal Trade Commission is planning a thorough investigation of financial practices among public utilities. This is expected to cover not only a general inquiry into security issues, operating results, and holding company connections, but will include also the methods by which properties are purchased and profits made through resale or revaluations and rate adjustments obtained before the commissions and courts. It is to extend to management fees, service contracts, construction profits, and all devices by which hidden returns are obtained through the holding company systems. It will reveal the gaps that exist in our present mode of regulation and permit the evasion of effective control.

There appears to be one danger which may interfere with the thorough job contemplated. The funds necessary for the investigation apparently have not yet been made available, and the actual work has been held back. We do not know whether the delay is due to mere technical difficulties of transferring appropriations, or to actual opposition by the budget director and the Treasury Department. It would be a public calamity, indeed, if the promiseful investigation were to be choked off by inadequate funds for the work. We hope most sincerely that the government's zeal for economy will not hit this particular project.

✽

Commissions and Courts as Experts.—It would be a radical but an extremely salutary reform if, in public utility rate making, the commissions and judges were required upon appeal to justify their decisions and findings, through cross-examination on the part of the appellants. We are not actually proposing this reform, but we have often pondered the effectiveness and desirability of such a change in judicial responsibility.

We have in mind a wide range of economic, financial and technical facts, as to which the commissions and courts make easy-going pronouncements and determinations, which they would have great difficulty to justify if they were subjected to cross-examination upon appeal. When a case is heard before a commission or court, the facts are presented in laborious fashion. Experts are offered, and they must qualify as to training and experience before they are permitted to testify on the technical and complicated matters. They give their testimony, and are then subjected to rigid cross-examination by opposing counsel, covering their knowledge, their reliability, and the consistency of their judgments. They are fortunate, indeed, if they are not made to appear ignorant and to contradict themselves as to important phases of their testimony. This procedure is entirely proper if rate making is to depend upon contest between opposing sides.

We do not subscribe to the idea that rate regulation should be based upon a system of litigation. We believe that it ought to be, and can be, based upon a definite system of governmental policy which involves only an effective administrative machinery, without litigation as to basic financial rights and facts on the part of the companies and the consumers. But since the system of litigation exists, the method of cross-examination is fundamentally necessary to preserve the rights of the parties. We have, however, the curious situation that, after the meticulous course pursued as to the experts, the commissions pass upon technical questions without possessing qualifications as to competence, and without showing the bases and reasons for their determinations.

The commissions and the courts in these cases are not concerned with principles of law, but with the sheer determination of technical facts. In the matter of valuation, they must decide upon the correctness of unit quantities, unit prices, the amount of overheads allowed, going value, and the depreciation to be deducted. All these determinations require a technical understanding, which, unfortunately, the majority of the commissioners and judges do not possess. Likewise in fixing rate schedules, there are difficult problems of cost allocation between different territories, between different classes of service, and between functions of operation. This involves no legal principles, but does require intimate acquaintance with cost relationships.

The experts, in all such matters, are subject to rigid qualifications and rigorous cross-examination. But the commissions and judges who make the findings are mostly unqualified to deal with the facts and issues presented, and far too often disregard the fundamental points to be considered in the determination. We have in mind very specific instances where, we believe, the public interests were unintelligently passed by. We feel that much more care should be exercised in appointments of commissioners; they should be the real experts that they are assumed to be under the law, when they are appointed. Unfortunately, moreover, there are few commissions which have any real experts, either as commissioners or on the technical staffs. Mostly the commissions are woefully ill-equipped to perform their duties. There are few commission analysts who are competent to work through complicated valuations and questions of apportionment between territory, service and functions. And yet the commissions must decide such questions of fact, and, unfortunately, base their decisions upon easy-going considerations so far as the public interest is concerned.

We submit that, if upon appeal involving financial and other technical facts, the commissions and judges were subjected to qualifications and cross-examination to justify their findings, there would soon be an improvement in personnel and equipment, and the public would be the beneficiary in better decisions affecting policies and methods of rate making.

GOVERNMENTAL RESEARCH ASSOCIATION NOTES

EDITED BY RUSSELL FORBES
Secretary

Recent Reports of Research Agencies.—The following reports of research agencies have been received at the central library of the Association since August 1, 1928:

Boston Finance Commission:
Letter to the mayor regarding ways and means of reducing the amount of taxes to be assessed on the taxpayers in the current year.
Letter to the city council presenting a comparative analysis of the tax rates of 1927 and 1928.
Letter to the mayor regarding the buying of cots by the schoolhouse commission.

California Taxpayers' Association, Inc.:
Report of San Diego City, California; an investigation of the principal activities of the city's government and an analysis of municipal expenditures for ten years, 1917 to 1926, with projections of a budget program for the period 1928 to 1936.

Cincinnati Bureau of Municipal Research:
Public Purchase of Materials for Public Works to be Furnished to Contractors.
Underground Wiring in New Subdivisions.

Illinois Municipal League:
Wheel Tax Information.

Bureau of Governmental Research, Kansas City, Kansas, Chamber of Commerce:
The Taxpayers' Guide to the Proposed City Budget for 1929.

Bureau of Research, Newark Chamber of Commerce:
Inter-Municipal Coöperation in the Newark Metropolitan District.

St. Paul Bureau of Municipal Research:
Letter to the voters of Saint Paul regarding charter amendment empowering the city to own and operate bus lines.

Schenectady Bureau of Municipal Research, Inc.:
Report on the Administration of the Schenectady Civil Service.

✠

Governmental Research in Hawaii.—The Hawaii Bureau of Governmental Research has recently been organized, with headquarters at No. 1 Schuman Building, Honolulu. The director is O. F. Goddard.

✠

Buffalo Municipal Research Bureau, Inc.— During the past few months the Bureau has been acting as advisor to the comptroller and the New York and Buffalo Audit Company in devising an adequate accounting system for the city which is greatly needed; acting as technical advisor to the council investigating committee; making a complete survey of the administration of the division of water; acting with the council and the civil service commission in a study of duties and salaries of all city employees with a view to equalization and standardization; working with the city treasurer on a more perfect system for collection of arrears, and a number of other shorter studies.

✠

Taxpayers' Research League of Delaware.— The League successfully tried the experiment of staging its annual meeting this year as a dinner event on September 17, with the result that it had a considerably larger attendance than at any previous annual meeting, and succeeded in conveying to those present a much more definite idea of what the League's work is and how it is done. The election of trustees resulted in adding to the board a number of citizens who are preëminent in the state for their civic interest and activity. The officers elected by the new board are: Edward W. Cooch, Esq., president; Charles Warner, Henry Ridgely, Esq., and Louis A. Drexler, vice-presidents; and Haldeman C. Stout, treasurer.

C. Douglass Buck, the Republican candidate for governor, has stated that he believes the League can prove of inestimable worth to the state, and that if chosen governor he would value the League's coöperation and assistance in securing a thorough survey of the business being done by the state with the methods employed, and would regard it a privilege to review such recommendations as the League might believe should come to his attention. He has indicated, as illustrative of the problems he has in mind, the abolition of useless commissions, the insertion of power necessary for active commissions to function efficiently, the closer coördination of state departmental bureaus, and a survey of the state's financing and auditing system.

Dr. Charles M. Wharton, the Democratic candidate for governor, has said that if he is elected governor he would not merely welcome but invite suggestions and recommendations from the League, and suggests the simplification of taxation, the equitable distribution of the tax burden, and the reduction of that burden whenever and wherever possible. He adds that the names of the trustees and officers of the League carry confidence that its work will be well and sanely done.

Arrangements are now being completed to call together at a smoker a considerable gathering of prominent business men to finance the increased staff and budget which the League's program will require during the coming year. The major items on this program are the administrative reorganization of the state and the state finance code on which the League is working in coöperation with the Delaware Bankers' Association.

✣

Des Moines Bureau of Municipal Research.—The Bureau recommended to the street department that it investigate the feasibility of installing a larger gasoline tank and purchasing gas in tank car lots. The report showed that the various departments of the city of Des Moines use about 108,000 gallons of gasoline yearly. This is purchased on three-month contracts on competitive bids, and is distributed to the five city garages by tank wagons. By contrast the waterworks, operated under a separate commission, buys gasoline in tank car lots at several cents a gallon less than the city pays for it and obtains a fine grade of fuel.

Reports on the six months' expenditures of the county and four months' expenditures of the city were made.

The Bureau is investigating the cost of printing and stationery for the city and county. It found that county stationery, which is purchased almost exclusively from one firm, costs considerably more than that bought by the city. County stationery is characterized by numerous different kinds of paper stock and headings purchased in small lots. The purchasing committee of the board of supervisors will take steps to remedy these conditions. While the report contended that there is not sufficient standardization in stationery used by the city of Des Moines, still

jobs are let after quotations are received, with resulting reasonable prices. A commendable feature of the city's practice is a printing record book in which all city record and stationery forms are numbered and indexed, and quotations and final cost prices are entered.

✣

Kansas City Public Service Institute.—The Public Service Institute, at the present time, is engaged principally on the following subjects:

Assessment Procedure Results.—As a first step in endeavoring to determine the efficiency of the assessment system used in Kansas City and Jackson County and of the uniformity of assessments, an analysis of all sales of real estate during 1927 is under way. The sales prices are to be compared with assessed values of the same properties and the results are to be tabulated by districts, types of property, etc. Other studies of assessment procedure are contemplated.

Financial Plan.—Coöperation of city officials in the preparation of a financial and improvement program apparently cannot be secured. The Institute has undertaken, on its own initiative, financial studies which would form the basis for such a program. It is expected that the improvement parts of the program will be worked out in coöperation with other organizations.

Reformatory Survey.—At the request of the Woman's City Club of Kansas City, a financial survey of the state reformatory for boys has just been completed.

Permanent Registration.—The permanent registration bill drafted for the Public Service Institute and the Chamber of Commerce by Dr. Joseph P. Harris in 1926 is being revised preparatory to submission to the legislature which meets in January.

Police Pensions.—A bill to provide a pension system for Kansas City police will undoubtedly be introduced at the next session of the legislature. The Institute is endeavoring to persuade city and police officials to have prepared a plan constructed on an actuarial reserve basis. The city manager has stated that he is going to employ an actuary to make the necessary studies, but unless this is gotten under way soon it is more likely that a cash disbursement system bill will be introduced.

County Government.—A bill providing for reorganization of the government of Jackson County, in which Kansas City is located, has recently been completed by the Institute. This is now in the hands of county officials for study.

The bill does not provide for a county manager, because there probably would be little chance of its passage; whereas, a reorganization bill providing for consolidation of departments, elimination of a number of elective officials, and the installation of a sound budget and financial system will probably receive approval of officials and have a very good chance of adoption. The bill prepared provides for a long step forward in the government of Jackson County.

The latter three items on this list of activities, together with a bill to provide local control of police for Kansas City, will probably constitute the major items on the legislative program of the Institute for this winter.

Plans for the formation of a joint legislative committee, representing a number of the leading civic organizations, are being prepared for the purpose of combining the effort of these organizations on bills of city-wide importance and on which all the organizations are in agreement.

✸

League of Minnesota Municipalities.—Recent bulletins issued include: *Salaries of Village Official in Minnesota; Telephone Rates in Minnesota; Tax Rates, Assessed Valuations, and Local Indebtedness in Minnesota—1928; Minnesota Fire Department Statistics, 1928;* and *Fire Protection and Fire Prevention Ordinances.*

A special committee of the League submitted a brief to the insurance commissioner of the state of Minnesota to protest the application of new rates proposed by the general inspection bureau, the rating agency for fire insurance companies in this state.

Ambrose Fuller, former staff member of the St. Paul Bureau of Municipal Research, and former city manager of White Bear Lake, Minnesota, has recently joined the staff of the League.

Mr. Harvey Walker, staff member of the League from 1925 to 1927, and acting executive secretary 1927–28, has accepted an appointment as assistant professor of political science at Ohio State University.

✸

Bureau for Research in Government, University of Minnesota.—Beginning on October 1, 1928, Mr. Oliver P. Field will succeed William Anderson as director of the Bureau. Mr. Field was formerly assistant professor of political science at the University of Indiana, and is now associate professor of political science at the University of Minnesota. He is the joint author with Professor F. G. Bates of a book on *State Government* published during the past summer by Harper and Brothers.

✸

Taxpayers' Association of New Mexico.—The Taxpayers' Association at the present time is assisting in compiling and analyzing the expenditures of state and local governments for the fiscal year ending June 30, 1928. The results of this work will appear in a future issue of the *New Mexico Tax Bulletin.* The efforts of the Taxpayers' Association are also being directed toward securing legislation that will provide for a general re-appraisement of property for purposes of taxation. Tentative measures are being prepared for submitting to the legislature at its next session early in 1929.

✸

Philadelphia Bureau of Municipal Research.—Gustav Peck, who has been a member of the professional staff and was making a study of methods of assessing real estate in Philadelphia, resigned from the Bureau in August. Mr. Peck has joined the editorial staff of the Encyclopedia of the Social Sciences in New York. He will outline and edit the section of the encyclopedia on "The City."

The Philadelphia Chamber of Commerce has again appointed a committee on taxation and public expenditure, and again Mr. Beyer, director of the Philadelphia Bureau, is a member of the committee. Special attention is to be given by the committee to improving the methods of recording deeds and other instruments in Philadelphia. The Bureau, which has been studying this subject, is coöperating with the committee.

In its study of the office of the recorder of deeds of Philadelphia, the Bureau has succeeded in measuring in words the volume of work transcribed in the five years, 1923–1927. During the last three months results of a comparison of the volume of work done with the cost of transcribing have been given to the public in *Citizens' Business.* It has been found that Philadelphia pays over 15 cents a hundred words for transcribing and comparing, more than four times the cost in Cook County, Illinois, where photography is the main reliance in recording. The Bureau has shown that if Philadelphia could equal the Cook County cost it would save close to $350,000 a year, more than a cent in the tax rate.

Announcement has been made that after the close of 1928 the Bureau will not be a member of the Welfare Federation of Philadelphia. Following is the text of a public statement signed by the president of the Welfare Federation and the president of the Bureau:

The Welfare Federation and the Bureau of Municipal Research of Philadelphia announce that at the end of the calendar year 1928 the Bureau will cease to be a member of the Federation and will finance its needs independently.

The trustees of the Federation have requested the Bureau of Municipal Research to withdraw because of the Federation's new policy of limiting membership to agencies whose major activities and budgets are for charitable purposes or for purposes ameliorating or removing conditions creative of the need for charity, instead of including educational agencies like the Bureau which was done when the Federation was first organized.

The Welfare Federation fully recognizes the complete coöperation which the Bureau has given since it became a member thereof, upon the invitation of the Federation, in 1921. It recognizes that the Bureau merged its financial support with that of the other agencies to make the Federation possible; that most of the Bureau's former contributors are now contributors of the Federation; that officers and trustees of the Bureau have been and are officers and trustees of the Federation, and have assisted in raising the Federation's budget, doing everything in their power to make the Federation a success.

The trustees of the Welfare Federation, realizing their responsibilities for the continuance of the valuable and important work the Bureau is doing, and desiring to be fully helpful in the difficulty with which the Bureau is confronted in reverting to independent financing, gladly join with the trustees of the Bureau of Municipal Research and approve of the appeal that they will presently make to the public-spirited citizens of Philadelphia for a generous support in meeting the Bureau's financial needs.

✣

Schenectady Bureau of Municipal Research.— *Purchasing Methods.*—Members of the staff are soon to commence a study of the city's purchasing methods. The object is to ascertain present procedure and make such recommendations as seem necessary to bring the purchasing system up to the requirements recommended for a centralized purchasing department.

✣

Toledo Commission of Publicity and Efficiency. —The Commission is engaged in making a survey of the progress of city planning in Toledo. It is checking over the zoning changes made by the council since the passage of the zoning ordinance in 1923, to find out how many of the recommendations of the city plan commission were overruled by the city council.

In 1924 and 1925, six city plan reports were made on Toledo by the Harland Bartholemew Company. The subjects were major streets, transit plan, railroad transportation, port study, industrial survey, and recreation. It is the purpose of the Commission of Publicity and Efficiency to find out the progress made in carrying out the recommendations made in these reports in addition to the zoning changes.

MUNICIPAL ACTIVITIES ABROAD

EDITED BY W. E. MOSHER

Director, School of Citizenship and Public Affairs, Syracuse University

Efficiency in Government.—Since the war a movement has gotten under way in Germany that is now practically nation-wide in scope. It is commonly spoken of as bureau reform. Its aim is to bring about up-to-date and businesslike management of public affairs, along the lines of organization and method. How much importance is attached to this movement may be seen in the organization which bears the imposing title, "The German Institute for Efficient Management in Public Administration." In connection with the International Exposition of Office Appliances and Aids this Institute is planning a series of lectures dealing with various features of the management of governmental offices and bureaus. These lectures are to be given by outstanding public officials and university professors. Characteristically enough, the first lecture has as its title "The Problem of Rationalization." It is to be given by a professor of public administration. Other lectures have to do with bureaucratic reform, with technical innovations in office management, and with scientific investigation in the conduct of public business.

The Institute supplies special guides for government officials who are interested in up-to-date office appliances, furniture, bookkeeping and other forms, and similar matters. It is noteworthy that an exposition of this sort should serve as an occasion for stimulating interest among public officials in modern business methods, and technique.—*Reichsverwaltungsblatt und Prüssisches Verwaltungsblatt, September, 1928.*

✠

State and Local Government in Germany.—Those students of German government who wish a somewhat intimate knowledge of the authority and functions of the state, particularly in its relation to its constitutional units, will do well to read the sections dealing with government in the August and September issues of the *Zeit-schrift für Communalwirtschaft,* 1928, and the July, 1927 number. The first describes the state of Thuringia, the second Saxony, and the third, Baden. Although these four-hundred-page publications treat of cultural, economic and social conditions in a very broad way, particular attention is devoted to the administration of the local governmental units and their relations both among one another and to the central agency of government. Competent and official spokesmen have contributed the articles on government.

✠

Education for Public Administration.—The passing of Lord Haldane, one of England's great public servants, gives the editor of the *Monthly Notes of the Institute of Public Administration* occasion to sound his praises for his consistent emphasis on the supreme importance of education in all the higher and more specialized branches of modern state government. He is honored as one who "among all leading statesmen has paid perhaps more attention than any other to the science and theory of public administration." He emphatically urged the necessity for developing coöperation in universities and was a great believer in the academic approach to all vital questions and social movements. It was through his influence that the Institute of Public Administration was organized and in a considerable measure through his influence that it enjoys its present prestige. The awarding of the diploma in administration in the University of London is a specific outgrowth of the movement in which Lord Haldane was so interested. Incidentally it might be noted that the Institute of Public Administration has appointed an advisory committee for the purpose of counselling with students who intend to undertake a professional preparation for administrative work in the government.—*Monthly Notes of the Institute of Public Administration, August–September, 1928.*

NOTES AND EVENTS

EDITED BY WELLES A. GRAY

Assistant Director, Municipal Administration Service

State Administrative Reorganization and the University of Minnesota.—Students of state administrative reorganization will be interested in a recent decision of the Minnesota Supreme Court regarding the application of the state reorganization act of 1925 to the state university. The case involved more than this particular application of the law, for behind this legal controversy were aligned the forces fighting for and against the continuance of the reorganization act itself.

It will be recalled that the act of 1925 created a commission on administration and finance similar to the commission of that name in Massachusetts. This commission consists of three members,—the comptroller, the budget commissioner and the commissioner of purchases—and is popularly known as the "Big Three." The state auditor may approve no warrant drawn upon the state treasurer for an expenditure from an appropriation unless its object has been approved by the commission.

The dispute centered around an attempt of the board of regents of the University of Minnesota to spend $45,000 to provide group insurance for the faculty and employees of the university. The commission refused to approve such expenditure, and a test case was made, to see whether such approval was necessary. It was contended that this requirement in the law did not apply to the university, inasmuch as that organization possessed certain constitutional immunities, which were based upon acts of the territorial legislature in the fifties. The court sustained this contention, holding that the constitution of 1858 "perpetuated" the board of regents as a constitutional corporation with all executive power over the university. Since all executive power over university affairs was put in the hands of the regents by the constitution, none of it may lawfully be exercised or delegated to other authority by the legislature.

The immediate effect of this decision is to free the university from domination by the state executive, but its ultimate effect is likely to be more far-reaching. By the same line of reasoning (and the court hinted as much in its opinion), the application of this act to the expenditures of constitutional officers, such as the attorney general, the secretary of state, the treasurer, and the auditor, may be seriously impaired. It appears likely that the next legislature may be confronted with the task of patching up a sadly battered reorganization act; or, perhaps, of devising a new scheme not subject to constitutional objections.

HARVEY WALKER.

✦

Six Months of the Holland Tunnel.—The New York City Police Department recently issued a summary of the activities of the Holland Tunnel police from November 13, 1927 to August 24, 1928, inclusive. This we reprint in full below:

Stoppages in tunnels due to some defect in mechanism or operation of vehicles concerned..............	4,083
Stoppages on plazas................	274
Fires extinguished in tunnels........	146
Collisions in tunnels and plazas......	231
Disabled vehicles handled..........	1,558
Gas supplied to vehicles in tunnels...	564
Towing chains loaned to tow vehicles from tunnels...................	385
Arrests...........................	160
Summons issued...................	1,213
Persons warned of violations and record card filed...................	4,100
Persons injured (none seriously).....	108
Vehicles passed through tunnels during period....................	6,396,103
Charges and specifications preferred to superintendent against members of force for disciplinary action	51
Admonished in lieu of charges being preferred......................	40
Dismissals.......................	17
Resignations.....................	23
Total police force in tunnel.........	200

✦

Convention of Illinois Municipal League.—The Illinois Municipal League held its fifteenth annual convention at Joliet, September 13 and 14, with an attendance of 304, representing seventy-seven cities and villages, and sixteen park districts. The following officers were elected to serve during the coming year:

President—The Hon. Charles H. Bartlett, Mayor, Evanston

Treasurer—Professor J. A. Fairlie, University of Illinois

General Counsel—R. F. Locke, attorney, Glen Ellyn

Secretary—A. D. McLarty, University of Illinois

Among the more important resolutions adopted were the following:

That a law be passed authorizing the establishment of municipal utility districts for public utility services, including water, gas, light, heat, power, and transportation.

That municipalities of Illinois be granted the power of excess condemnation for purposes of local improvements and city planning.

That home rule for Illinois municipalities be authorized by constitutional grant.

The outstanding speaker at the convention was Arthur Collins, honorary secretary, the Institute of British Municipal Treasurers and Accountants, who discussed general topics of municipal administration, including publicity for municipal affairs, and professional training for public service.

✤

"Anti-Hague" Bills Pass in New Jersey.—Of especial interest to our readers, who will recall E. E. Smith's article on Mayor Hague of Jersey City in the September REVIEW, are five bills passed on October 9 by the New Jersey legislature, three of them over the veto of Governor Harry A. Moore. The three bills passed over Governor Moore's veto are frankly designed to curb the power of the Hague machine in Hudson and Essex counties, and are commonly known as the "anti-Hague" bills. By the five bills, extraordinary and summary powers are granted to the superintendents of elections (which officers exist only in Hudson and Essex counties). County boards of elections are empowered to dismiss election officials without trial, although cause must be shown, and the authority of the Elisor Grand Jury Act is revived. This last law empowers resident Supreme Court Justices to remove from the sheriff and jury commissioner of a county the power of selecting grand juries, and to place it in the hands of two disinterested persons, who may then select the grand jury from any parts of the state they deem fit.

Of particular interest are the bills dealing with the conduct of elections, whose purpose, according to Republican leaders, is to "guarantee as honest an election as is humanly possible" in Hudson and Essex counties. By the authority of these bills the superintendents of elections, and their deputies, will exercise close supervision over the polls; they can make arrests without warrants

for violations of the election laws. A policeman refusing to assist them in this work is liable to punishment for a misdemeanor. Superintendents are empowered to strike from the voting lists the names of all persons found ineligible. It is expected that this will prevent padding of the lists, voting by dead persons and by persons residing on vacant lots, repeating, exchange of voters by parties in the closed primaries, and other similar corrupt practices. The bill granting sweeping powers of dismissal to county boards of elections was one of the two passed for the first time, and therefore not passed over a veto. While aimed at the Hague machine, its effect will be felt throughout the state, inasmuch as all twenty-one counties of New Jersey have such boards. The other bill passed for the first time, along with the reënactment of the other three bills, authorizes superintendents of elections to place their seals upon the ballot boxes immediately after the ballots have been counted, and empowers them to prevent reopening of the boxes except upon the order of the resident Supreme Court Justice.

Whether these bills will guarantee an honest election, or whether the normal Democratic majority of 100,000 in Hudson County will be cut down, remains to be seen.

✤

New England City Managers Organize Association.—City managers of Connecticut, Maine, Massachusetts, and Vermont have organized the New England City Managers' Association, to be composed of city and town managers in those four states. The following officers were elected at the first meeting:

President—C. A. Bingham, city manager, Norwood, Massachusetts, and formerly manager of West Palm Beach, Florida.

Vice-president—James E. Barlowe, city manager, Portland, Maine.

Secretary—Roy M. Wilcomb, city manager, Springfield, Vermont.

This Association will hold quarterly meetings each year, one in each of the states.

✤

The Municipal Light Plant of Kansas City, Kansas.—As a result of a survey of the Kansas City, Kansas, municipal light and power plant, recently made by Burns and McDonnell, nationally-known consulting engineers, this plant is shown to be among the most efficiently operated in the country. The survey was undertaken at the request of the Kansas City, Kansas, Chamber of Commerce, upon the suggestion of its Bureau of Governmental Research, in order to determine the wisdom of a proposed contract for electric power during peak loads, about to be made with the Kansas City Power and Light Company of Kansas City, Missouri. This contract was under consideration by the city commissioners at the time the survey was made. As a result of this survey, the proposed contract was abandoned by the commission.

Of significance to those interested in the results of municipal ownership and operation of public utilities, are the following quotations from this report:

That the municipal plant is strictly competitive is shown by its rates which are among the very lowest in the country, far lower than those of any utility of which we have record. This is all the more remarkable when it is considered that the plant earned a profit in 1927, in addition to setting aside a sinking fund and a six per cent depreciation.

The plant is enjoying an unusually good load factor, 56 per cent. Compare this with the average load factor of 42½ per cent for all the utilities in this country. It shows that the loads have been balanced on the plant so that the evening peak is but slightly higher than the morning peak or the afternoon peak and the low points filled in. This all points to good management on the part of Mr. Donovan (the manager) and his associates.

✢

A Survey of Housing in Detroit.—The Michigan Housing Association, assisted by the Detroit Board of Health, the Detroit Board of Education, and the local branch of the American Association of University Women, has recently completed the housing survey of the entire city of Detroit, which was announced in the September REVIEW. The 588 school census zones of the city were used as a basis for the survey.

As a result of this survey an index of room density or congestion throughout the city has been obtained. In making this survey the generally accepted standard for the United States of one person per room was used; where there was more than one person to a room, conditions were regarded as overcrowded. The term "room" was taken as meaning only bedrooms, living rooms, kitchens, etc. Bathrooms, open sleeping porches, and halls were not included.

Overcrowded conditions were found in 52 of the 588 school zones, and crowded conditions were found in 88 more. The total population of the 52 overcrowded zones is 109,587, distributed

among 97,546 rooms, an average of 1.123 persons per room. In the crowded zones the population totals 174,721, distributed among 183,559 rooms, —.951 persons per room.

In this connection the following comment was made:

While it does not appear that overcrowding exists in these 88 zones, as a whole, considerable portions of them are undoubtedly very much overcrowded. For example, a family home may consist of four rooms—living room, kitchen and two bedrooms. In this case one person per room would mean that four persons would occupy two bedrooms; with an index of two persons per room, eight persons would occupy two bedrooms; and with an index of three persons per room, twelve person would occupy two bedrooms. Hence an average index of congestion for an individual zone or even a group of zones will not portray many dreadful cases of overcrowding in individual homes. Such conditions can be ascertained only by individual house study, which the Association hopes to undertake in the near future.

✢

Informal Conference on the Personnel Problems of the United States Government.—At the invitation of the Institute for Government Research, the first meeting of the informal conference on the personnel problems of the government of the United States was held at the Brookings Institution, Washington, D. C., September 13. The object of the conference is fully covered in the following resolution, adopted unanimously:

That the chair appoint a subcommittee of three to draft recommendations for an adequate system of personnel administration for the national government, preferably including a proposed bill, and that it also prepare an explanation of the reasons which underlie its recommendations.

That when this sub-committee has prepared its recommendations and its explanatory statements, it submit copies of them to the members of this group and to others that may be specially interested.

That at a reasonable time after these recommendations and statements have been received, this group reassemble to consider in detail the recommendations and supporting statement and to modify and perfect them so that if possible they may represent the judgment of the group.

That the subcommittee shall consult freely with the members of this group and with others interested in the subject and that members of this group agree to coöperate so that the best judgment of the group as a whole may be secured.

This meeting was attended by twelve members of organizations most interested in federal personnel questions.

Milwaukee's Citizen City Charter Movement.
—Milwaukee's charter today is a patchquilt
made up of the last complete revision of 1874 as
amended; general, special, and optional acts of
the state legislature; charter amendments
passed by the common council since the grant of
home rule in 1925. We have a volume of 700
pages as last compiled in 1914. No man knows
today, or would attempt to say, what laws do,
and what laws do not, affect the city of Milwaukee.

The local machine for discharging the powers
conferred by this elusive document is of the
"weak-mayor" type; and to accentuate the dispersion of authority, the "weak-mayor" effects a
doubtful coöperation with twenty-five aldermen
drawn from as many wards, each of whom still
enjoys a veto over local improvements.

A citizen movement got up steam in the early
part of 1927 to convey this mass of rust and legal
verbiage to the junk pile—salvaging, however,
such administrative details as had not outlived
their usefulness for reënactment and revision into
an administrative code by the common council.
This administrative code is to be passed by a
majority vote of the council, but can be amended
by a two-thirds vote limitation. It is to contain
an administrative division, financial division, and
personnel division.

The City Charter League was actuated by a
sincere desire to simplify and modernize, to
shorten and clarify, to induce effectiveness where
inertia has before obtained. Its real source of
inspiration and strength lay in the home rule
constitutional amendment of 1924, and the home
rule enabling act of 1925. The result of its
meditations and prayers for the past year is a
short charter of twenty-five pages, containing
only the framework of government, which was
unanimously approved by the drafting committee.

It most nearly resembles the "strong-mayor"
structure. The city council is to be elected from
three districts by proportional representation
with the uniform quota of 7,000 votes. After
each election resulting in the election of more
than 25 councilmen, the quota is to be increased
1,000 votes.

The city treasurer, city attorney, and city controller are removed from the ballot. The mayor
is to appoint the heads of the departments, with
the council's confirmation for indefinite terms—
removable at the pleasure of the mayor. Five
departments are set up in the charter: law, public

works, health, finance, and building and safety
inspection. The board of estimates is abolished
and an executive budget under the mayor is
established. The form of the budget is specified
in detail.

A new department of finance is created, consolidating seven now separate departments. It
will have complete control over the financial affairs of the city including the keeping of accounts,
current auditing, custody and dispersion of
funds, tax assessing, purchasing supplies and real
estate. The council will appoint an independent
auditor for indefinite term who must be a C. P. A.
As things stand, the elected controller audits the
books for which he is responsible.

The other new department is that of building
and safety inspection which consolidates four
separate departments.

A civil service board of five members, appointed by the mayor and council, is provided
with powers and duties to make rules applying to
personnel administration and to hear appeals
from discharge. The council *may* discontinue
the fire and police commission. All administrative duties are taken away from the two civil
service commissions. Civil service provisions
apply to the selection of bureau and division
heads, but they are subject to dismissal by the
directors of departments with the power to appeal to the civil service commissions.

Ex-officio members are removed from the city
planning commission. Five members are to be
appointed by the mayor and council. The model
law prepared by the Hoover committee was
drawn upon for the city planning and zoning provisions. All acts of the council affecting the
city plan must be referred to the city planning
commission for approval. A two-thirds vote of
the council is necessary to over-ride the disapproval of the city planning commission.

For eight years the Socialist and Non-partisan
alignment has been eleven to fourteen, respectively, but at the last election the Socialists
elected only six aldermen. A charter amendment may be passed by a two-thirds vote, and
consequently the Non-partisans have started a
campaign to deprive the Socialist mayor of his
appointive power, to change the zoning law, and
to meddle with the fire and police commission.
That is to say, they are proceeding to exercise to
the full the powers conferred upon the council by
the home rule act, and they seem to have taken
the bit in their teeth prepared to run away with
the works. It is hoped that they will run far and

fast enough to create some public concern in the fate of the new charter at the April, 1929 election.

HAROLD L. HENDERSON.

Citizens' Bureau of Milwaukee.

✺

Civic Education in Cincinnati through the Radio The government of Cincinnati plans, as a part of its program of civic education, to broadcast every Monday evening, over WLW, a series of talks by city officials, describing the organization and work of the city government, and its various departments.

The first of these talks was given by City Manager C. O. Sherrill on the evening of September 17. This talk consisted of a brief discussion of the general character and advantages of the city manager plan, followed by a short description of the city government.

The usefulness of such a program is unquestionable, and in this connection the following quotation from Manager Sherrill's address is pertinent: "Without the constant interest of all classes of citizens, continuance of good government is impossible, and it is to arouse this interest that this series of radio talks . . . will be given. When a city has good government, streets well cared for, traffic running smoothly, fire prevention and protection carefully provided, city markets clean and well administered, transportation by bus and street car adequate, there is a tendency for people to take these things for granted and forget all about the city government which provides them. They go to sleep, forget their duty as citizens and voters, and, before they know it, good government is gone and gangsters are in control, as they are today in many large cities."

✺

A New Municipal Airport for Cincinnati.—Plans have been made public for the construction of Cincinnati's new municipal airport, Lunken Field. These plans were prepared by City Manager C. O. Sherrill and Service Director Robert N. Olin, in consultation with Kruckemeyer and Strong, architects, and it is hoped that the port will be ready for dedication next year. By these plans the city takes over the operation of the present privately-operated Lunken Field.

Elaborate equipment will be provided. This will include a two-story administration building, which will house the offices of the municipal officials in charge of the field, and the offices of the Embry-Riddle Company, the present commerical operators at Lunken field, who are responsible in a large measure for the field's development. The administration building will also house waiting rooms for passengers. In addition there will be other buildings housing a pilots' room, a restaurant, hangars and other necessary quarters. Ample lighting facilities will be provided, which will include two-lamp changing flood lights of 10,000 watts each, a ceiling light, beacon lights, etc.

✺

Beccari Garbage Disposal System Installed in Florida.—The city of Dunedin, Florida, has contracted for the installation of a garbage disposal system of the "Becarri" type. This system is somewhat new in the United States, but has been in general use in Italy and Southern France for some years.

The system operates by natural fermentation carried on in suitable cells or chambers. By this simple process, garbage and other organic refuse can be converted into an odorless, inoffensive humus which has a commercial value.

The plant was contracted for only after careful study and investigation on the part of the city manager, W. L. Douglas, who is taking an active interest in the construction.

STATEMENT OF THE OWNERSHIP, MANAGEMENT, CIRCULATION, ETC.,

Required by the Act of Congress of August 24, 1912,

Of NATIONAL MUNICIPAL REVIEW, published monthly at Concord, New Hampshire, for October 1, 1928.

STATE OF NEW YORK, COUNTY OF NEW YORK, SS.

Before me, a notary public, in and for the State and county aforesaid, personally appeared Russell Forbes, who, having been duly sworn according to law, deposes and says that he is the acting editor of the NATIONAL MUNICIPAL REVIEW and that the following is, to the best of his knowledge and belief, a true statement of the ownership, management etc., of the aforesaid publication for the date shown in the above caption, required by the Act of August 24, 1912, embodied in section 411, Postal Laws and Regulations, to wit:

1. That the names and addresses of the publisher, editor, managing editor, and business managers are:
   Publisher, National Municipal League, 261 Broadway, New York, N. Y.
   Editor, H. W. Dodds, 261 Broadway, New York, N. Y.
   Acting Editor, Russell Forbes, 261 Broadway, New York, N. Y.
   Managing Editor, None.
   Business Managers, None.

2. That the owner is: The National Municipal Review published by the National Municipal League, a voluntary association, incorporated, 1923. The officers of the National Municipal League are Richard S. Childs, President; Carl H. Pforzheimer, Treasurer; Russell Forbes, Secretary.

3. That the known bondholders, mortgagees, and other security holders owning or holding 1 per cent or more of total amount of bonds, mortgages, or other securities are: None.

4. That the two paragraphs next above, giving the names of the owners, stockholders, and security holders, if any, contain not only the list of stockholders and security holders as they appear upon the books of the company but also, in cases where the stockholder or security holder appears upon the books of the company as trustee or in any other fiduciary relation, the name of the person or corporation for whom such trustee is acting, is given; also that the said two paragraphs contain statements embracing affiant's full knowledge and belief as to the circumstances and conditions under which stockholders and security holders who do not appear upon the books of the company as trustees, hold stock and securities in a capacity other than that of a bona fide owner; and this affiant has no reason to believe that any other person, association, or corporation has any interest direct or indirect in the said stock, bonds, or other securities than as so stated by him.

RUSSELL FORBES,
Acting Editor.

Sworn to and subscribed before me this 3rd day of October, 1928.

MAY F. DONOVAN.
Notary Public.

SEAL]

(My commission expires March 30, 1930.)

NATIONAL
MUNICIPAL REVIEW

PUBLISHED MONTHLY BY THE

National Municipal League

VOL. XVII, No. 12   DECEMBER, 1928   TOTAL No. 150

CONTENTS

EDITORIAL COMMENT.............................*Russell Forbes*.... 719

THE 1928 CONVENTION AT CINCINNATI...............*Lent D. Upson*... 721

REPORT ON THE WORK OF THE NATIONAL MUNICIPAL
  LEAGUE.......................................*Russell Forbes*.... 722

THE CITY'S PLACE IN CIVILIZATION.................*Charles A. Beard*.. 726

REGIONAL CREDITS PROPOSED IN LIEU OF MUNICIPAL
  RECOGNITION OF HOUSING AS A PUBLIC UTILITY....*S. James Herman* 732

ECONOMIC FACTORS IN CITY PLANNING..............*William B. Munro* 738

THE PUBLIC PERSONNEL POLICY OF THE MUNICIPALITY
  OF BORDEAUX..................................*Walter R. Sharp*.. 741

COMPARATIVE TAX RATES OF 237 CITIES, 1928........*C. E. Rightor* 751

DEPARTMENTS

  I. Recent Books Reviewed.. 764

 II. Judicial Decisions...*Edited by C. W. Tooke* 769

III. Public Utilities...*Edited by John Bauer* ˙773

 IV. Governmental Research Association Notes...................*Edited by Russell Forbes* 777

  V. Municipal Activities Abroad..............................*Edited by W. E. Mosher* 781

 VI. Notes and Events.......................................*Edited by Welles A. Gray* 785

THE LEAGUE'S BUSINESS

The League's New Officers.—The annual business meeting of the National Municipal League was held in Cincinnati at noon on October 17, at the conclusion of our thirty-fourth annual meeting. The President made a brief report on the past work and future program of the League. At the conclusion of this address by Richard S. Childs, president, Walter J. Millard of the Proportional Representation League read the report of the nominating committee, which had been prepared by William P. Lovett of Detroit as chairman, Lent D. Upson of Detroit, and Mr. Millard.

Richard S. Childs was reëlected as president. All members of the League will be glad to know that the organization will continue to have the benefit of his helpful direction during the ensuing year. The following were reëlected as vice-presidents of the League for 1929: Glenn Frank, Carter Glass, Charles Evans Hughes, W. D. Lighthall, Meyer Lissner, A. Lawrence Lowell, C. E. Merriam, W. B. Munro, Frank L. Polk, Miss Belle Sherwin, and A. Leo Weil. The following were elected as members of the council for a three-year term expiring in 1931: M. N. Baker, Henry Bentley, C. A. Dykstra, J. W. Esterline, Chauncey J. Hamlin, Samuel C. May, Joseph T. Miller, Lawson Purdy, Howard Strong, and Lent D. Upson. Of the council members elected, Messrs. Bentley, Esterline, May, and Miller are new selections. The others were reëlected upon the expiration of their terms of office this year.

✦

The Thirty-fourth Annual Meeting.—Elsewhere in this issue we print a summary of the thirty-fourth annual meeting, by Lent D. Upson, director of the Detroit Bureau of Governmental Research. In this article Dr. Upson gives his impressions of the convention and the convention program as a whole. We are also printing two of the main speeches of the convention in this issue.

As in former years, the Governmental Research Association and the National Association of Civic Secretaries joined with the League in holding joint meetings. These two organizations held separate meetings on October 15 which took the form of round tables at forenoon and afternoon sessions.

On October 16 and 17, joint meetings, sponsored by all three organizations, were conducted. The attendance at all sessions was very good and the interest throughout the convention was marked and well sustained.

The local arrangements for the convention were made by a committee headed by John B. Blandford, Jr., director of the Cincinnati Bureau of Municipal Research. Mr. Blandford and his associates spared no effort in making the meeting a success and in providing for the comfort of the delegates. The offices of City Manager Sherrill and Mayor Seasongood were also continuously at our disposal. These officials and their assistants coöperated to the fullest. Our thanks are also extended to the Women's City Club of Cincinnati, who held a special tea for the ladies on the afternoon of October 16. About 150 delegates registered for the convention. The attendance at the sessions was larger than this number, for many failed to register. It seemed to be the consensus of opinion that the thirty-fourth annual meeting was one of the most successful ever held by the National Municipal League.

NATIONAL
MUNICIPAL REVIEW

VOL. XVII, No. 12   DECEMBER, 1928   TOTAL No. 150

EDITORIAL COMMENT

**Summary
of Reviews of
Municipal Reports** In our next issue we shall publish a summary of the municipal reports which have been reviewed in this magazine during 1928 by Clarence E. Ridley. Dr. Ridley will grade and rate the city reports in accordance with his proposed essentials of a good municipal report, which were published in the NATIONAL MUNICIPAL REVIEW for March, 1928. It is hoped that this rating table will stimulate closer attention to the form and contents of annual reports by city officials.

✿

**Portland
Prize Awarded** The National Municipal League is the custodian of a fund of six hundred dollars, the interest of which is awarded annually as a prize to the undergraduate in Reed College, Portland, Oregon, who submits the best essay on a phase of municipal government. The prize for 1928 has been awarded to Mr. George A. Corwin of Reed College for his essay on "Portland and the Pollution of the Willamette River." The committee of judges who made the awards consisted of Professors T. S. Kerr of the University of Idaho, Jacob Van Ek of the University of Colorado, and Geddes W. Rutherford of Iowa State College.

**Experts Study
Housing Problem** In connection with the annual convention of the National Municipal League, Governmental Research Association, and National Association of Civic Secretaries, a luncheon was held in Cincinnati on October 16, which was attended by over twenty of the leading housing experts of the United States and Canada. Harold S. Buttenheim, editor of *The American City*, took the initiative in the matter and prepared a memorandum as the agenda for the meeting. At the conclusion of the luncheon, Mr. Buttenheim was authorized to appoint a committee, of which he is to be chairman, to consider in the near future ways and means for raising funds to undertake a nation-wide study of the housing problem.

The proceedings of the luncheon are summarized as follows by Robert L. Davison, who acted as secretary:

The special subject discussed at the luncheon was a memorandum prepared by Harold S. Buttenheim, editor of *The American City*, entitled, "Away with the Slums."

There appeared to be general agreement among those present that much good could be accomplished by a well-organized and well-financed crusade to abolish the slums and provide decent and adequate housing for every family in America.

Some difference of opinion was expressed as to how the movement should be headed, and as to whether the best results could be obtained by helping the National Housing Association to occupy its field more thoroughly than its present limited funds and man-power permit. Special emphasis was given to the need for adequate research as to more intelligent land utilization and methods of reducing house-building and financing costs. It was thought by some that propaganda activities might be conducted through the National Housing Association and research work through such a group as the recently organized Research Institute for Economic Housing.

The opinion appeared to be unanimous as to the desirability of all the objectives listed in Mr. Buttenheim's memorandum, with the exception of paragraphs A, B and C of Section 6. Some of those present were strongly in favor of one or more of these three methods of attacking the housing problem, while others opposed one or all of them. Mr. Buttenheim made it clear that he was not committed for or against these ideas, but had listed them as important subjects for discussion and determination as to policy in the proposed campaign.

Among those present, several of whom took part in the discussion, were Miss Mary E. McDowell of Chicago; Charles Livengood, Alfred Bettman, Henry Bentley, Max Senior, Bleecker Marquette and Fred K. Hoechler of Cincinnati; Morris Knowles and John Ihlder of Pittsburgh; Dr. S. James Herman of Detroit; Mayo Fesler and Miss Charlotte Rumbold of Cleveland; Horace L. Brittain of Toronto; Richard S. Childs, Arthur C. Holden, Luther Gulick, Louis Brownlow and Russell Forbes of New York.

We believe that this project is worthy of the moral and financial support of members of the League and all others who are interested in the very important subject of housing. Further reports will be given as the plans of Mr. Buttenheim and his committee are formulated and put into effect.

✳

The Economics of Recreation
William S. Butterworth, president of the United States Chamber of Commerce, delivered an interesting address before the fifteenth annual congress of the Playground and Recreation Association of America, at Atlantic City on October second, on the economic value of recreation. He pointed out that money invested in the creation of parks and playgrounds is really an economic investment because it almost invariably results in increased land values of abutting and contiguous property. On this question he spoke as follows:

It has long been recognized that parks enhance the desirability of nearby land, thus yielding more taxes to the municipality and boosting the sales value of the property to the owner. This is true because people are willing to pay for sunlight, beauty of surroundings, the opportunity to enjoy wholesome exercise, a sense of space, and contact with things of nature. In the *Park Manual* recently published by the Playground and Recreation Association and edited by L. H. Weir, several instances of the increase of property values near park lands are cited:

"In 1916 the Board of Park Commissioners in Essex County, N. J., engaged the services of an expert to make a report as to the actual value in dollars and cents of the county park system. The report was made on four of the Newark parks. The following extract is taken from a summary published in the *Newark Sunday Call:*

"'The property immediately adjoining the four parks named was assessed in 1905 for $4,143,850 and in 1916 for $29,266,000, an increase of $25,122,150 or 606.3 per cent. At the same time property in the same taxing district and perhaps not wholly outside of what may be called the *park influence*, was assessed in 1905 at $36,606,907 and in 1916 at $111,531,725, a gain of $74,924,818 or 204.6 per cent. In plainer words, while the property adjoining the parks has increased more than six times in value, property in the remainder of the same taxing districts has about doubled in value.

"'If the increase in valuations adjoining these parks had been the same as in other property in the same taxing districts, and no more, it would have been $8,453,454, leaving an increase as a result of the parks of $16,668,700. The fortunate owners of this property have been enriched by this large sum beyond what they would have been had the parks not been established.

"'But this is not all. The cost of these four parks was $4,241,540. The increase is enough to pay for them four times. The cost of all the parks in the county was $6,929,625.47—say $7,000,000. The increase of property adjoining these four parks alone, beyond what it would have been if the parks had not been constructed, is sufficient to pay for all the parks in the county 2.4 times, and the increase from the other parks in the county, while not so great in proportion, is undoubtedly much more than their cost. The increased revenue to the county is already sufficient to pay the interest and sinking fund charges on the bonds issued for park construction, and almost the entire cost of the annual maintenance.'"

The city of Montreal is reported by the City Parks Association of Philadelphia to have acquired 164,504 square feet of land, that is about 3⅘ acres, at a cost of $82,252. In the center it laid out a small park and bounded it by streets. The area taken up by the park and the surrounding streets was 82,466 square feet, or 1 9/10 acres. The city then sold the balance of 82,038 square feet for $99,032, reaping a net profit of $16,780.

THE 1928 CONVENTION AT CINCINNATI

BY LENT D. UPSON

Director, Detroit Bureau of Governmental Research

A summary of the joint conventions of the National Municipal League, Governmental Research Association and National Association of Civic Secretaries, at Cincinnati, October 15–17. :: :: ::

EACH successive annual meeting of those sundry civic organizations which first met in 1894 as a "Conference for Good City Government," reaches in some respects a new high level. This year the Cincinnati meeting of October 15, 16 and 17, was notable, first, for an unusual attendance. The rapidly accelerating interest in civic matters was indicated by representation not alone from bureaus of municipal research and voters' leagues, but from chambers of commerce, women's clubs, and kindred groups, as well as by a substantial sprinkling of officials and citizens. Second, the rather unusual papers of Blandford, Gulick, Beard, Story, Collins, and a few others set high standards with which the balance of the program had to compete.

The program of the first day included, as usual, sessions of the Governmental Research Association. In the morning meeting there was an address by John B. Blandford, director of the Cincinnati Bureau of Municipal Research, upon "A Fact Basis for Community Action"; the report of Russell Forbes, secretary-treasurer of the Association; and a rather spirited discussion of future plans.

At the noon luncheon, with Mr. George H. Warrington, chairman of the Cincinnati Bureau, presiding, the formal address of welcome was tendered by Mayor Murray Seasongood, upon whom rather heavy demands were made during the course of the entire convention. Dr. Luther Gulick, chair-

man of the Association, gave a report of the past year's activities, which was followed by what was probably a forecast of future developments, made by Stephen B. Story, city manager of Rochester, N. Y., in an address linking "Municipal Research and the City Manager." During the afternoon simultaneous round table sessions were held on "Special Assessments," led by Philip H. Cornick, and "Financial Statistics of Cities," with C. E. Rightor presiding and Starke Grogan of the Census Bureau in a title rôle.

In the evening, dinner was provided at "The Barn," and incidentally researchers and other professional reformers were put in their places by the special convention number of the NATIONAL MUNICIPAL REVIEW, by the portrayal of the "you-tell-'ems" by Mr. Hoeck, recorder of Hamilton County, and by "Some Reminiscences of Municipal Research" by the writer.

The remaining two days of the program were devoted to round table and general sessions covering: "The Negro and Public Affairs," "Measurement Standards in Government," "What Is the City Government's Responsibility in Housing," "P. R. and Democracy in Elections," and "Selling the Work of Government to the Public." Some criticism was heard of these sessions to the effect that no amount of new and constructive material was offered, the discussions and reports thus being largely a reconsideration of developed material.

On the other hand, the Tuesday evening dinner, with Richard S. Childs, president of the National Municipal League, presiding, was unusually successful both in attendance and quality of program. The Hon. Murray Seasongood spoke on "Some Hindrances to Good City Government." Noteworthy also were the addresses of Charles A. Beard, on "The City's Place in Civilization," and of Arthur Collins, financial advisor to local authorities of England, on comparison of "Cities—British and American."

REPORT ON WORK OF THE NATIONAL MUNICIPAL LEAGUE

For the Year Ending October 1, 1928

BY RUSSELL FORBES

Secretary

This report shows a steady growth in the League's work and accomplishment.

WITH a budget of less than $39,000, the National Muncipal League during the past year carried on the following work:

NATIONAL MUNICIPAL REVIEW

The REVIEW is the outstanding medium for reporting progress in municipal government. Each issue is distributed to our members and a considerable number of copies are sent free to prospective subscribers, calling attention to articles of special interest to them. Committee reports and other technical pamphlets are issued from time to time as supplements. A total of 9,697 copies of these supplements were distributed during the year.

MONOGRAPH SERIES

During the year the League published a monograph on *The President's Removal Power Under the Constitution*, prepared by Professor E. S. Corwin of Princeton University. Manuscripts for two additional monographs are nearly ready for publication. These will be *Public Borrowing* by Paul Studensky, and *The New York Water Power Situation* by A. Blair Knapp of Syracuse University.

COMMITTEE ACTIVITIES

The *Model Charter*, prepared by the committee on Municipal Government, was revised and re-issued during the year, and has been presented to every city considering charter changes. Over 10,000 copies of the *Model Charter* have been distributed since it was first issued.

The report of the committee on Metropolitan Government is now in the final stages of preparation, and will be ready for press in the near future.

The report of the committee on Federal Aid to the States, prepared by the chairman, Austin F. MacDonald, was published as a supplement to the October, 1928, issue of the REVIEW.

The committee on Model Budget Law, under the chairmanship of our treasurer, Mr. Carl H. Pforzheimer, after several years' study, issued its report which was published as *A Model Budget Law* in a supplement to the July, 1928, REVIEW. *The Model Budget Law* has already been widely praised in newspapers and magazines and will unquestionably exert a great influence upon future legislation on the subject.

The preliminary Committee on Teaching Municipal Government in Colleges and Universities, appointed in August, 1928, has already undertaken its work program. A questionnaire has been circulated to all colleges and universities which offer courses in this field as a means for determining the nature of their curricula. The first objective of the committee is the formulation of a set of objectives for such courses.

Plans are now under way for the appointment of committees to formulate, respectively, a model municipal report, and a model administrative code to supplement our *Model Charter*.

Model State Constitution.—A new edition was issued during the year, but the supply was quickly exhausted. The demand for this publication continues from year to year. A total of 7,500 copies have been distributed since it was first issued.

PAMPHLETS DISTRIBUTED

During the year a total of 22,457 copies of League pamphlets were distributed. Many of our publications are used in classrooms. For example, in one month of the past year thirty-two colleges and universities from twenty-two different states placed orders for classroom use. The table on the following page shows the distribution of our pamphlets.

INFORMATION SERVICE

An average of 500 inquiries were received and individually answered each month during the past year.

These inquiries for information and advice come from public officials, chambers of commerce, research agencies, and other interested individuals and groups, and concern such subjects as: municipal government, county government, city planning and zoning, permanent registration, municipal budgets, and public utilities.

ADVISORY SERVICE

The services of the League are in demand for consultation with city and state governments. During the year staff members and outside consultants advised governments on proposed legislation on optional charter laws, and charter drafting, and took part in several charter campaigns. The League has a preëminent prestige in this field, for it is called upon to aid in practically every charter campaign.

SPEAKERS' SERVICE

The League is likewise called upon to furnish speakers for many luncheons, dinners, and during charter campaigns. Such requests are filled by staff members or by recommended outside speakers. Addresses have been delivered by our representatives on a wide range of subjects, including the city manager plan, permanent registration, metropolitan government, the different forms of municipal government, and centralized purchasing.

ANNUAL MEETING

The annual meeting provides the means for interchange of ideas on municipal government and a review of the year's work. The meeting held last year in New York City, in conjunction with the Governmental Research Association and the National Association of Civic Secretaries, was unanimously pronounced the most successful in the League's history. It was attended by 300 delegates.

Title	Free	Sold	Total
Administration of the Gasoline Tax in United States.........	2	20	22
Administrative Consolidation of State Governments..........	249	730	979
Administrative Reorganization in Illinois	6	17	23
Airports as a Factor in City Planning......	170	384	554
Assessment of Real Estate.........	5	107	112
City Manager Budget.....	1	4	5
City Planning and Zoning Budget..........................	0	6	6
Constitutionality of Proportional Representation	1	38	39
Correct Public Policy towards Street Railway Problem.......	2	23	25
County, The.............................	0	22	22
County Manager Plan...............................	687	696	1,383
Electric Light and Power as Public Utility..	4	25	29
Electricity in Great Britain...........................	368	18	386
Employment Management in Municipal Civil Service.	2	29	31
Fitz-Elwyne's Assize of Buildings.........................	302	0	302
German Cities since the Revolution of 1918	3	17	20
Land Subdivision and the City Plan	1	45	46
Law of the City Plan...........................	2	57	59
Loose-Leaf Digest of City Manager Charters.	1	36	37
Merit System in Government...........................	0	47	47
Minor Highway Privileges as a Source of Revenue..........	2	21	23
Model Bond Law...............................	459	121	580
Model City Charter...........	174	823	997
Model Municipal Budget Law.	1,490	331	1,821
Model Registration System....	20	170	190
Model State Constitution....	84	907	991
Modern City Planning..............................	6	108	114
Municipal Salaries under Changing Price Level	2	29	31
National Municipal League Series........................	4	105	109
National Municipal Review.......................	2,494	663	3,157
New Charter Proposals for Norwood, Mass...............	7	10	17
Political Integration of Metropolitan Areas...............	0	4	4
President's Removal Power under the Constitution	28	83	111
Primer Chart of Typical City Governments...............	26	29	55
Reprints of Review articles...........................	703	36	739
Service at Cost for Street Railways....	2	17	19
Short Ballot...........................	381	88	469
Special Assessments for Public Improvement...............	5	92	97
Standards of Financial Administration....................	220	124	344
State Parks............................	2	21	23
State Welfare Administration and Consolidated Government .	3	18	21
Story of City Manager Plan...........................	2,115	6,220	8,335
Zoning...............................	2	81	83
Totals............................	10,035	12,422	22,457

PROMOTION OF THE LEAGUE'S MODEL LAWS

During the year, the League's *Model Charter* has been recommended to, and has been used wholly or in part in the proposed charters in practically every city which has considered the city manager plan, notably: Flint; Toledo; San Francisco; Oakland, California; East Detroit; Salem, Oregon; Breckenridge, Texas; Dallas; and Lincoln, Nebraska.

The *Model Registration System* has already been adopted by the states of Iowa and Wisconsin, and plans are being made for its recommendation to the 1929 legislatures in the various states.

The *Model Bond Law* has been adopted by the state of Minnesota. Both *The Model Bond Law* and *The Model Budget Law* will likewise be presented for consideration to the 1929 session of state legislatures.

MEMBERSHIP

On October 1, 1927, the membership of the League was 2,034; on October 1, 1928, it was 2,223, a gain of 189. During the year 19 members died, and 302 resigned or were dropped for failure to pay dues; but on the other hand, 510 new members were enrolled, which is the largest number of additions in any year since 1921.

MUNICIPAL ADMINISTRATION SERVICE

The League coöperates with the Governmental Research Association in sponsoring and supervising the work of the Municipal Administration Service, which acts as the secretariat and information headquarters for the municipal research agencies of the United States and Canada. During the year the Service published and distributed six technical pamphlets on municipal administration which have been enthusiastically received by public officials. The secretary of the League acts also as director of the Municipal Administration Service and as secretary of the Governmental Research Association, thus coördinating the work of the research bureaus with our research and publication program.

STAFF

The National Municipal League suffered an irreparable loss through the resignation of Harold W. Dodds as secretary, effective July 1, 1928. Mr. Dodds is now in Nicaragua assisting the U. S. State Department in its supervision of the election for president in that country. The selection of Mr. Dodds for this important post comes as a well-deserved tribute to his expert knowledge of election methods and his splendid services in having drafted in 1922, and redrafted in 1927, the law under which the present election is being held. We are glad to report, however, that Mr. Dodds will return on January 1, 1929, to resume his editorship of the NATIONAL MUNICIPAL REVIEW and to assume his new post as professor of politics at Princeton University.

This report, therefore, covers nine months of Mr. Dodds' administration and only three months of the administration of your present secretary.

Miss Howe continues as the capable, hard-working, and loyal assistant secretary. Without her assistance the administration of the League office would indeed be a difficult task. Richard S. Childs, president, Carl H. Pforzheimer, treasurer, and the members of the executive committee have also been untiring in their assistance. To them, and to the equally hard-working and loyal office staff, the secretary is glad to attribute the bulk of the credit for the accomplishments of the past year.

THE CITY'S PLACE IN CIVILIZATION[1]

BY CHARLES A. BEARD

The city has been the fountainhead, and not the enemy, of modern civilization; but the modern city, the product of the machine age, must be studied, controlled and Taylorized. :: :: :: :: ::

AMERICA is above all things "practical." In our vocabulary of contempt there is no more scornful symbol than "high brow." It seems to be generally supposed that the man who deserves celebration in story and song is the busy individual "who can do things," even though he may never inquire why he is so laboriously at work or whether he could possibly be engaged in some more ennobling enterprise. In a sense there is justice in the verdict, for were it not for practical persons, indifferent to theoretical ends, the whole superstructure of civilization might come crashing to earth. But there is danger in the verdict also, for practical persons are often unable to calculate the more distant outcome of their actions and can make a lot of trouble in the world; for example, the statesmen of Europe who precipitated the World War were all practical men, trained specialists, and yet the damage they did and the unforeseen consequences of their realistic decisions are awful to contemplate.

May we not say, therefore, that the most practical person is one who builds successfully for the longest future, illuminating the task of the hour by a vision of its distant relations? Assuming for the moment that this is true, no apology is now offered for wandering far away from budgets, accounts, city manager plans, and statistical measurements for municipal

[1] Address delivered at joint convention of the National Municipal League, Governmental Research Association, and the National Association of Civic Secretaries, Cincinnati, October 16, 1928.

improvements, into speculations respecting the place of the city in the civilizing process.

THE TRADITIONAL STRUGGLE BETWEEN THE CITY AND THE COUNTRY

Antagonism between the town and country, urbanity and rusticity, capitalism and agriculture, marks the long trail away from the beginning of civilization to the latest political campaign. From it have sprung endless conflicts in parliaments and forums, sometimes raging around scaffolds and flooding out on battle fields. Out of it and in respect of it has arisen a vast literature ranging from Aristotle's Politics, written in the fourth century before Christ, through the works of Thomas Jefferson, down to the age of McNary and Haugen. In a thousand subtle ways, not yet explored by the historians, this antagonism has affected our literature, our arts, and our theories of the good life. Is it not traditional that Babylon is the home of wickedness and the countryside the source of virtue?

Certainly no small part of the criticism directed against the urban business man springs from the ancient contempt which the fighting landlord had for the trader who supplied him with luxuries. Spengler's whole book on "The Decline of the West," one of the three or four mighty books of our time, which has made such a furor in recent days, is built around this historic emotion.

Before he began to canvass for votes, Thomas Jefferson was convinced and openly said that "the mobs of the great cities add just so much to the support of pure government as sores do to the strength of the human body. . . . Cultivators of the earth are the most valuable citizens. They are the most vigorous, the most independent, the most virtuous, and they are tied to their country and wedded to its liberties by the most lasting bonds. . . . When we get piled up on one another as in Europe, we shall become as corrupt as in Europe and go to eating one another as they do there." Even some of the statesmen who, in Jefferson's time, advocated protective tariffs to encourage manufacturing admitted the evils of cities, but thought they were offset by the utility of industries for national defence and independence.

URBAN STANDARD OF LIVING IS SUPERIOR

Vigor, love of liberty, and virtue, these are the signs of rural superiority, according to the makers of tradition. No one will deny that there were in Jefferson's day, and still are, some elements of truth in the argument. But it may now be said with safety that sanitation has made our best cities freer from disease and suffering than most of the countryside. We no longer live in the walled and sewerless towns of mediaeval times. Some of the worst conditions of physical decay are in the pure air and under the open sky of the country. Moreover science and the machine have demonstrated that, by the exercise of imagination and intelligence, cities cursed by their slums and ugliness and dirt can be transformed into places of beauty and inspiration. As for virtue, that must be judged in relation to temptation, and from this point of view neither the public nor the private morals of the city suffer by comparison. County, not city, government is the most con-spicuous failure of American democracy.

Whatever our conclusion on this point for the moment, the fact remains, Aristotle or no Aristotle, Jefferson or no Jefferson, that cities overshadow the country from the Elbe to the Pacific. They increase in number, grow in size, and absorb an ever larger proportion of the population of each industrial nation. Every invention adds strength to them, every increase in production draws the sons and daughters of farmers to their homes and factories. If a boy from an Iowa farm becomes President of the United States next March, it will not be on account of his familiarity with the hoe handle; but because he is primarily an engineer and promoter of business enterprise. If he loses the contest, he will lose to a boy from the sidewalks of a great city. America has seen the last log-cabin and hard-cider campaign.

MODERN CITIES THE PRODUCTS OF THE MACHINE AGE

Unlike the urban centers of antiquity, the cities which dominate our social scene are not built on commerce and handicrafts but upon manufacturing, upon machinery and science, with all that implies for esthetics and the good life. Now no one will deny that industry as developed up to our time has been a deadly foe to beauty and the love of beauty—to the finer things of civilization. If anyone has doubts on this score let him compare any American manufacturing town with Oxford or Cambridge in England —especially with those English towns before the advent of the motor bus. Before the inexorable march of the machine in the nineteenth century, art and architecture crumbled into hideous ruins. Mr. Lewis Mumford is right when he exclaims that: "It is hardly an exaggeration to say that from 1830 to 1890, the period when the traditional methods in all the industries were supplanted or at least modified by machine production, there is not a book, a piece of furniture, a pattern in textiles, a cup or saucer of new design, which deserves a place, except as an historical curiosity in a museum of art." For an even more sweeping indictment of the machine-city, we have only to turn to the writings of John Ruskin.

Criticism of the city is by no means confined to its esthetic aspects. The shrewd French observer, M. Siegfried, declares that America "is a materialistic society, organized to produce things rather than people, with output set up as a god." Our material prosperity, he continues, "can only be obtained at a tragic price, no less than the transformation of millions of workmen into automatons. 'Fordism,' which is the essence of American industry, results in the standardization of the workman himself: Artisanship, now out of date, has no place in the New World, but with it have disappeared certain conceptions of mankind which we in Europe consider the very basis of civilization."

It would be denying the noses on our very faces to reject such criticism as wholly unwarranted and unfounded. With no little justification such critics might add that, compared with our capacity to imagine and design, every industrial city in the western world is a disgrace to humanity—in spite of the amazing things already accomplished in public works and city planning. But without attempting to measure the exact degree of damnation that ought to be meted out to our machine-cities, we may properly ask: "What is to be done about it?"

THE MACHINE AGE IS HERE TO STAY

One school of thinkers, believing that no good can come out of the machine, bid us destroy the steam engine and return to handicrafts and agriculture, the balanced and self-sustaining economy of olden times. Doctors of this persuasion point out the beauty of the old crafts, idealize the dignity enjoyed by the independent workman under that system, and in contrast paint a dismal picture of the standardized automaton of the machine shop who spends his days making standardized motions and his nights in the jerrybuilt house of our industrial slums. It is impossible to ignore the appeal that lies in this scheme of thinking or the attractiveness of the ideal society which it outlines for us.

But whatever may be the heart's answer, the head makes a clear-cut reply: "Economically it is impossible to go back to handicrafts, to restore the self-sufficient community.[1] Whether we like it or not, the machine drives relentlessly forward crushing the old order to earth." If a return to the handicraft system is economically impossible, then a return to its arts is equally impossible. Dreamers may try to reproduce the beautiful old squares, churches, guild halls, and towers of mediaeval Europe, but as the best German city planners well say, all such efforts are artistic failures, simply because it is impossible in the modern age to reproduce the spirit of the artists who did the old work. The best of modern Gothic, if technically correct, is lacking in the indefinable aura which softens down the austerity of stone and crowns the noblest conceptions of the middle ages with a glory that commands silence. No, the lesson of the middle ages seems to be

[1] Time does not permit a discussion of the revolution in the factory system now under consideration in Europe. See W. Hellpach, *Gruppenfabrikation*, and Paul Jostock, *Der Ausgang des Kapitalismus*, pp. 240 ff.

that beauty is not a gingerbread decoration added to utility, but is basically an expression of the esthetic sense working through the whole structure of economy from top to bottom.

There is one other lesson in the cities of olden times, not to be ignored; it is that the pictures usually drawn of handicraft and commercial, or pre-machine cities, are false to life or rather leave out of account the mass of the people. Nearly everybody in America knows about the glories of ancient Athens, the temples, public buildings, and sculptures. How many of them ever asked themselves about the homes and streets of the city, about the art and beauty of the countless thousands who slaved, labored and trafficked in that metropolis? Nearly every American has been to Rome by this time and has delivered an oration to his neighbors on the marvels of the Forum, the triumphal arches, and the Pantheon. How many of them ever stopped to inquire: "How did the mass of the people who toiled and moiled around those centers of glory actually live and work?"

Speaking of the masses in Rome, numbering about 300,000 in the age of Cicero, Mr. W. Warde Fowler tells us that we know little. "The upper classes," he explains, "including all writers of memoirs and history, were not interested in them. There was no philanthropist, no devoted inquirer like Mr. Charles Booth, to investigate their condition or try to ameliorate it. The statesman, if he troubled himself about them at all, looked on them as a dangerous element in society, only to be considered as human beings at election time; at all other times merely as animals that had to be fed in order to keep them from becoming an active

peril. The philosopher, even the Stoic . . . though his philosophy nominally took the whole of mankind into its cognizance, believed the masses to be degraded and vicious and made no efforts to redeem them." Cicero, so well known to our boy orators, "when in actual social or political contact with the same masses could only speak of them with contempt or disgust." These multitudes lived in huge tenement houses; and the tenement house, adds Fowler, "must have been simply a rabbit warren." Cicero himself, like many of the best families of Rome, had money invested in slum property and we know from his letters that it was not always in a good state of repair.

So, too, of the idealized mediaeval city. It would be easy from authentic records to draw a far from beautiful picture of the life of the nameless masses who lived in fever-infested hovels under heaven-searching spires and glorious town halls, in the old days before the advent of the machine. Unfortunately for social science, we do not know much about these nameless masses, but we know enough to warn us against any vain imaginations, idealizing the handicraft city. Moreover, living examples can be found today in all parts of China. If anyone wants to see such an object lesson, he can find it there with his own eyes—and nose.

The challenge of the agrarians, I frankly accept. Their right to their economic reward must be freely conceded. The necessity of maintaining a fair balance between agriculture and capitalism is, perhaps, the most important issue of our age, in Europe and America.

But the city is not inherently a menace to civilization, as Jefferson believed. On the contrary it is from the urban centers that the national economy of the future will be controlled, whether we like it or not, and it is the culture of urbanism that promises to dominate the future.

CITIES HAVE NURTURED LITERATURE AND THE ARTS

Indeed, we may well ask: What great book, painting, imaginative work, or invention has ever come from the country? Sir Isaac Newton was the son of a farmer, but he developed his talents at Cambridge. Gibbon was the son of a landed proprietor, but he wrote his immortal work in London and Lausanne. The talents of the old South were exhausted in oratory and politics. Dr. Long, of Georgia, one of the discoverers of anaesthetics, failed to make great achievements because he was without the laboratory and hospital facilities furnished by urban centers. Matthew Maury, one of our great scientists, a son of Virginia, unfolded his powers in Washington where the city furnished equipment for his researches, and a government job the leisure and opportunity. Noble virtues flourish in the country, but creative, inventive, and imaginative talents must have the facilities and stimulus of urbanism, certainly more or less, if they are to develop into great powers.

WE MUST MASTER AND CONTROL THE MACHINE-MADE CITY

What then is our obligation and our mission? If we cannot go back to the pre-machine city or recover the arts of the handicraft age, what roads are open before us? First of all, many things appear to be inevitable, and with the inevitable we must work. Cities will continue to grow; electricity will make it possible to remove many of the worst offenses against the esthetic sense; motor roads, released from the cramping limits of steel rails, will spread in every direction, bringing the city and country closer together; urban centers will expand into urban regions, breaking down for millions the old antithesis between town and country; city planning, having grown into regional planning, will be merged into state and national planning, with technology as its basis. In other words, we are even now in the very midst of transforming the city inherited from the Augustan age of General Grant and Marcus A. Hanna. Only those whose business it is to observe tendencies have any idea of the magnitude of the processes already at work. Moreover, as Mr. Mumford, Le Corbusier, and the new German architects point out, the signs of a new and powerful esthetics, appropriate to the machine age, are already here, promising beauty as well as strength. That is not all; the vision of the new city takes in those masses ignored or scorned by the upper classes of antiquity and the middle ages.

Our first task, then, is not to run from the machine, but to stand fast in its presence, to explore its significance, and to make ourselves master of it. Our second task is to nourish the imagination in the threefold aspects emphasized by Ruskin; associative, penetrative, and regardant or contemplative, and to keep burning his seven lamps of architecture: sacrifice, truth, power, beauty, life, memory, and obedience. Our third task is to encourage bold and imaginative thinking about the potentialities of the city, having faith that there is more hope in exuberant radicalism than in deadly conservatism. If radicals are usually wrong, it must be confessed that the conservatives who suppose things will never change are always wrong. Finally, let us accept the criticism of the European esthetes that ours is a mass civilization, for it is, and let us see what we can do with it, thus offering at least novelty to an old world heavily laden with other experiments.

But in taking this view, we are not merely American. Many of the best city planners of Europe have frankly accepted steel, concrete, and machinery, and are clothing their dreams in new materials. If it is not sacrilege, I must confess that some of the new working-class houses built by the socialist administration of Vienna are to me more beautiful than most of the old Hapsburg piles, borrowed, copied, and gingerbreaded from half a dozen civilizations and expressing no creative sincerity at any point. Furthermore, it is about as thrilling to see working people living decently as to see upper classes living softly. This is merely personal.

THE TAYLORIZED PARIS OF THE FUTURE

There is high authority for the position taken above. It is the authority of an artist no less distinguished and competent than Le Corbusier. His fundamental position is that we must accept the machine and do our best with it. And in his sketch of a plan for Paris, he has had the courage to outline the field of the coming battle between ideas and materials. "The new event," he flatly says, "is the machine which has reconstructed modern society from the ground up. However, we have not yet measured its significance. A revolution opposed to all previous cen-

turies! No revolutionary spirit reigns, but we stand in the presence of revolutionary relations. We will formulate no revolutionary solutions but will adjust ourselves to a revolutionary state of affairs. If this adjustment does not take place soon, the growing sickness now threatening us will shatter social life."

After this preface, Le Corbusier boldly pictures the new Paris—a Paris that will conserve the beauties of the past while eliminating the consumption-ridden areas now spread all around the glories observed by travelers—a Paris that will make use of standardization, steel, and concrete, a Paris Taylorized. Yes, the artist dares to invoke the shades of the American efficiency engineer! Then, without pronouncing any revolutionary formulas relative to private property, he indicates that the rigidities of landlordism will have to yield to the exigencies of productive industries and the requirements of a decent life.

If the task here outlined is staggering in its complexity and beset with oppressive doubts respecting our powers, still it must be admitted that it is as interesting as driving from one gasoline station to the next. Even the contemplation of its possibilities is as worthy of human nature as meditation on the chances of slipping into heaven through the narrow gate of personal perfection.

REGIONAL CREDITS PROPOSED IN LIEU OF MUNICIPAL RECOGNITION OF HOUSING AS A PUBLIC UTILITY [1]

BY S. JAMES HERMAN, A.M., M.D.

Executive Director, Michigan Housing Association

A discussion of the plan being considered by the Michigan Housing Association for using public credits in the financing of housing projects.

To determine the comparative value of one of a series of proposals, it is desirable that we refresh our minds by summarizing briefly the elements which were responsible for establishing such value.

The seriousness of the housing problem is surprisingly unappreciated even by men and women of the finest public spirit and can only be accounted for by the rapid and revolutionary changes in our economic structure. It would thus seem timely to outline a few salient points which would emphasize the urgency of our housing need.

THE HOUSING PROBLEMS

We are overwhelmed by the tremendous toll of crime, the disintegration of the family, and dereliction from home and religous ties, until we are almost panicky in our attempts to stem the onrush of social ills. We forget that social values cannot be legislated into the hearts of the people but that they must come from within— from the environment, and from the home. We all know that practical good citizenship begins in the home. Sound health, and clean morals, a love of honest endeavor, are in large part the result of home training. One of the most powerful influences in Amer-

ica's rise to greatness has been the integrity of the home. Hence, if we are to progress toward higher standards of accomplishment, we must look to the foundation upon which our greatness rests.

THE DECLINE IN HOME OWNERSHIP

Home ownership, the most potent socializing element, shows a definite and progressive reduction for several census periods. The 1920 census gives New York 12.7 %, Boston 18.5%, and Detroit 38.3%.

Another indication of the breaking up of the American home is the trend of construction toward multiple dwellings as compared with the single detached house and the duplex. The *Monthly Labor Review* for June, 1928 [2] analyzes the total housing construction for the important cities of the country. These tables show that, in 1921, construction of multiple dwellings in New York was 44.2% of the total, whereas in 1927 it had increased to 70.9%; in Chicago it had increased from 44.6% to 76.2% and in Philadelphia from 6.7% to 25.5%, during the same period. Taking the total of the 257 identical cities reviewed in these tables, we find that this type of construction had increased from 24.4% in 1921 to 48.3% in 1927, or 100% in the short period of six years.

On the other hand, the latest avail-

[1] Address delivered at Convention of National Municipal League, Governmental Research Association and National Association of Civic Secretaries, Cincinnati, October 16, 1928.

[2] *Monthly Labor Review*, June, 1928, Vol. 26: pp. 1153–62.

732

able statistics show 81.99% of our people belonging to the class earning $150 or less per month and 54.51% earning $100 or less per month.[1]

The purchase of even a small five-room, one-story frame house with modern conveniences, selling at from $6,500 to $7,500, represents a monthly burden of from $85 to $90, including amortization of principal, interest, taxes, insurance, and upkeep. From this fact it can be seen that three-fourths of our people are denied equal opportunity for home ownership. We must concede that there is no hope for social betterment until we have housing betterment—until every self-supporting family can earn and become owner of a home and garden spot in keeping with American ideals and standards.

There seem to be but three ways of meeting this problem, viz.: (1) philanthropy, (2) governmental subsidies or municipal ownership, or (3) public credits.

PHILANTHROPY

Philanthropy, for some unknown psychological reason, will not invest money in sufficient and continuous quantities. This has been amply demonstrated everywhere, with the City Housing Corporation of New York and its splendid efforts in Sunnyside as a noteworthy example. Organized in 1922, it took nearly six years to complete its first project, in spite of the loyal devotion of its president and personnel and its sponsorship by men of high public spirit.

The International Housing and Town Planning Congress, which met in Paris last July, confirms this attitude, as quoted by Mr. George B. Ford: "Private philanthropy should be used wherever available, but it was recognized that private philanthropy alone

[1] *Income in the United States*, National Bureau of Economic Research, 1921, pp. 134–135.

would not solve the problem of low-cost housing." [2]

GOVERNMENTAL SUBSIDIES OR OWNERSHIP

The use of direct subsidies or municipal ownership by recognizing housing as a public utility offers serious objection. While the housing policies of European governments are valuable guides, we must use guarded caution when it comes to their practical application in our country, and we must shape our program to fit public attitude as well as public need. First and foremost, our principal aim should be to build American character and not to foster the development of a generic, indigent class, forever dependent upon some form of government doles.

Objections to this proposal from the standpoint of municipalities, beneficiaries, and the public at large, are:

A. The bond limits of most large cities prohibit major housing undertakings, and even if such limits are legally extended, any substantial increment in debt is bound to have a like effect upon the interest rate.

B. Frequent changes in the administration of municipalities will deleteriously affect efficiency of management.

C. Political preferment cannot be avoided, hence a large percentage of incompetency will inevitably result.

D. The relationship of landlord and tenant is vastly different from that of producer and consumer in the matter of selling water, light, or fire protection. The city must be paternal, sympathetic, even charitable, and at the same time rigidly enforce hygienic, sanitary and health measures, and, above all, collect the rent.[3]

E. A municipal housing project of this character, would, in time, involve a large percentage of

[2] *The American City Magazine*, August, 1928, p. 81.

[3] The same would apply in the case of purchase and sale, with the city as vendor and the tenant as vendee. With the proposed system of public credits such relation to the municipality is avoided.

the population and a class whose vote could be easily influenced in favor of the existing administration and per contra, a large body of voters can unite in forcing its demands upon political aspirants for lower rents and lower standards of restrictions.

F. Municipal construction will cost more and may, in part at least, nullify the savings established by the elimination of the cost of financing, tax remission and lower rate of interest during tenure under land contract or other conveyance.

G. Municipal ownership of so large an undertaking would involve a substantial loss of taxes in addition to a probable operating deficit. The resulting increment in taxes may become burdensome to other home owners as well as to industries.

H. Admitting that we may be forced to adopt municipal ownership in order to provide proper housing for a certain stratum of society, we should first exhaust every other means to provide an opportunity for a self-earned, self-owned home for every self-supporting family and thus boost citizenship to a higher level of aspiration and self-respect.

I. While some may welcome the innovation, others will object to being stigmatized by governmental subvention.

J. The public is not convinced that a municipal utility of this character would function happily or that direct subsidies in any form are economically sound.

K. American tradition insists upon the policy of equal opportunity and constructive helpfulness but not charity.

PUBLIC CREDITS

Public credits seem to be the logical solution to the housing problem of the normal, self-supporting family. Credits, properly applied, are and always have been a sound economic policy. Our entire economic system, whether applied to individuals, corporate entities, or nations, is based upon credits. The principle of public credits is not socialistic or radical. Rather, the housing conditions in the modern industrial centers have so radically altered that families of the lower wage group find it impossible to obtain hous-

ing facilities that will measure up to American standards of living. With this point of view, prominent leaders of state and nation are in complete accord.

ENDORSED BY PROMINENT POLITICAL LEADERS

Mr. Herbert Hoover has been prominent in efforts for housing betterment and his position in relation to farm relief clearly defines his attitude on public credits. In his ·acceptance speech he states:

"With that objection I have little patience. A nation which is spending $90,000,000,000 a year can well afford an expenditure of a few hundred millions for a workable program that will give to one-third of its population their fair share of the nation's prosperity. Nor does this proposal put the government into business except so far as it is called upon to furnish initial capital with which to build up the farmer to the control of his own destinies."

Governor Alfred E. Smith's efforts for better housing in New York, as well as the measures he has sponsored, include tax remissions and subsidies— more advanced than the principle of public credits.

Governor Fred W. Green of Michigan summarizes his acceptance of this principle in unmistakable terms in a public message on February 4, 1928, in which he says:

"No one should shy away from it on the theory that a program of public building is radical. All remedies for new conditions must be radical just as the conditions themselves are radical."

For over two years I battled with this question myself and was finally compelled to admit that there seemed no other way of solving the housing need of the large majority of our people. During the last three years I have had occasion to analyze its various aspects and to discuss them with bankers, manufacturers, business men, sociologists, and economists, and none of them have been able to offer any substitute or any other solution to this paramount question. With the health, welfare, and comfort of three-fourths of our people at stake, we should be willing to re-align our traditional attitudes in order to meet the unprecedented economic change. Nothing should be allowed to interfere with progressive measures leading to this desideratum, for no other effort will do so much toward fostering a deep appreciation of American ideals of government and society.

CONTROLLING PRINCIPLES

Now as to the practicability of the use of public credits, I do not know of any method that offers so many advantages and yet contains so few inherent faults. By making ample capital available through public credits and combining it with mass buying and mass construction, we are building our plan on a firm foundation and along sound economic lines. Duly recognizing the force of American traditions, the intricacies of our political machinery, and the mandates of our economic institutions, a group of controlling principles are hereby submitted as fundamental to any plan involving public credits. They are:

1. No philanthropy.
2. No gift of public money.
3. Cost to purchaser, including all charges and amortization of principal, must approximate one-fourth of income, namely, $25 to $37.50 per month.
4. Non-interference with the economic status of the real estate and building interests. Hence, accrued benefits must be limited to family incomes of $150 per month or less, a class now unable to buy or carry a modern home on a commercial basis.
5. Must be non-partisan, non-sectarian and free from political interference. Hence, neither the state nor its political subdivisions should have any part in either the purchase or the development of the land.
6. Construction must be of face brick, artificial

stone, or concrete, to permit amortization of principal over a long period of years and to reduce annual upkeep to a minimum.

To meet the rigid requirements of these principles, we are forced to take four important steps:

1. Eliminate cost of financing by making ample capital available at reasonable rates of interest through public credits by means of establishing a home loan commission. This item alone constitutes 20 to 25% of the selling price of the average workingman's home, purchased on the deferred payment plan.
2. Purchase raw acreage for cash in parcels of not less than 200 acres, thus reducing the cost of land.
3. Purchase materials in like manner, in quantities for not less than 1,000 homes, thereby lowering their cost.
4. Schedule the building program on a mass basis, in communities of not less than 1,000 homes per undertaking, thus forcing the cost of production to the lowest level.

THE ACCOMPLISHMENT OF THE METROPOLITAN LIFE INSURANCE COMPANY

Of these four advantages, the last three are well established and in common usage by many large concerns. In the field of housing, the most noteworthy achievement is that of the Metropolitan Life Insurance Company, which constructed, during the period of housing shortage in New York, fifty-four apartment buildings, representing the largest capital investment of its kind. Having ample capital and using modern mass buying and production methods, they were able to rent these apartments for less than one-half the commercial rate charged for apartments of a like class, and in addition thereto, to pay six per cent on their investment, caring for all necessary amortization, depreciation, upkeep and other charges, and to show a substantial margin for surplus purposes.

Briefly, the community plan will

take advantage of many essentials not otherwise feasible, viz.: Architectural variation in line and multiform grouping; a broader field for landscape treatment, including parks and playgrounds; and practical lessons in self-government, such as community administration, recreation, entertainment, welfare, etc. By pooling of interests, we may expect an improved spirit of common fellowship and community solidarity, thus forwarding the ideal of Americanization.

HOW PUBLIC CREDITS WILL BE APPLIED

1. *Home Loan Commission.*—To establish a system of public credits on a non-political basis, it was found advisable to have a distinct cleavage between the loan and housing bodies. Thus we will have a home loan commission for financing purposes and housing corporations to buy the land and to develop the communities. The proposed home loan commission is intended to operate on a regional basis, obligating only the regions needing and desiring it. Its powers will be limited to issuing and selling housing bonds, loaning the proceeds only to non-profit housing corporations to the extent of their gross requirements, and charging a rate of interest sufficient to cover operating costs plus one per cent annually for building up an emergency fund. This commission will provide proper method for repayment of said bonds, to be amortized over a period of twenty to thirty years—preferably the latter—in order to reduce annual amortization of principal to a minimum.

This commission is intended to be a legal instrumentality of the district or region it embraces and is to be authorized to pledge the faith and credit of said district. Said commission will be under state control, the governor having authority to appoint five commissioners, not more than three of whom shall be drafted from the party in office, to serve six years, excepting that the initial appointments shall be for terms of two, three, four, five, and six years, respectively. Commissioners shall serve without compensation either for time or for any expense incurred. This provision is likely to attract men of high calibre and public spirit.

2. *Housing Corporations.*—The housing corporations will be organized wherever they are required and wanted and will have exclusive authority to buy land and to build communities. Each will be a distinct corporate entity, the same as any other business corporation and will operate on a non-profit basis. Each housing corporation will be responsible for its own acts, will function under a special charter to be granted by the legislature which will include suitable safeguards, restrictions and limitations. The city or county in which it is located will not be financially responsible for its undertakings, although its members will be appointed by public authority (mayor or board of county supervisors, as its location may indicate), in the same manner and on the same basis as the home loan commission.

As an additional precautionary measure, it may be deemed advisable to provide that members of the home loan commission, as well as members of the housing corporations, shall be selected from a list of nominees to be submitted by various organizations such as engineering societies, real estate boards, chambers of commerce, bar associations, federations of women's clubs, councils of churches, teachers' associations, etc.

Assuming the home loan commission as actually functioning, and a city desiring to undertake a community building project, the mayor will appoint a group of citizens to form a housing corporation, which will borrow its capital requirements from the loan commission, such loan to be secured by a first lien on all property purchased including improvements; and will buy not less than 200 acres of land and proceed with the construction of a community through its executive personnel.

Various safeguards have been carefully considered in connection with the operation of the home loan commission and housing corporations, and include all reasonable provisions relating to the financial, legal and sociological aspects of the proposal.

CONCLUSION

In order to bring a modern cottage in a livable community within the budget limits of families earning $150 or less per month, it is necessary to construct such homes at a cost not exceeding forty per cent of the normal commercial selling price on a deferred payment plan. To prove that this is feasible with ample public credits, a piece of land was selected, a community plan was drafted, a series of attractive bungalows containing four, five and six rooms each was chosen, and all plans and details were submitted for bid to two firms of reputable contractors. These bids were to include ample bond to cover completion of the community within two years. These independent bids proved with fair conclusiveness that these homes could be constructed under these conditions at a cost below 40% of the commercial selling price.

A further check-up was undertaken to allocate the large differential between the total cost of homes constructed on a mass production basis and the commercial selling price of homes built individually. No difficulty was experienced in doing so.[1]

From the foregoing, we are forced to the conclusion that there seems to be but one practical way of meeting this problem and that is by bringing the cost of a home with American standards down to the wage level of the group under consideration.

[1] The author will be glad to furnish a copy of the plan of the model community, and copies of the tables showing the estimated cost of development and the savings to be effected by mass production, to any interested reader who will write him at Buhl Building, Detroit.

ECONOMIC FACTORS IN CITY PLANNING

BY WILLIAM B. MUNRO

Vice-President, National Municipal League

*How the New York regional survey is helping to put city planning on
a safe and sure basis.* :: :: :: :: :: :: ::

THE science of city planning has been
greatly improved during the past dozen
years. It has widened its scope, bettered its technique, and become much
more regardful of the actualities. The
work of the Regional Plan of New York
and Its Environs is giving us an impressive demonstration of this newer and
broader approach, for it rests upon
what ought always to have been a self-
evident proposition; namely, that the
attainment of greater economic efficiency is one of the prime considerations
in city planning and not merely an
incidental one.[1]

In keeping with this idea, the committee has insisted that the underlying
economic factors in urban life and location be mastered before pencils and
alidade are set to work. The economists have been called into camp as an
advance surveying party for the enterprise. To them was committed the
initial job of examining the trends and
tendencies of business in the metropolis
and its environs, "with the object of
throwing light upon the economic
activities best suited to the region and
to the different areas within it."

The present volume incorporates the
results of their study. In due course
the conclusions of the economists will
be considered along with those reached
by the engineer and the architect, the

lawyer and the administrator. The
ultimate plan will thus be based upon
data and conclusions resulting from
several thoroughgoing studies, each
independent but interlocking. This,
of course, is what a city plan ought
always to be, but almost invariably
has not been.

CITY PLANNING OFTEN OVERLOOKS ECONOMIC FACTORS

Community planning in the United
States has been for the most part narrow in scope and unscientific in procedure. Its slogan of "The City
Beautiful" has been an ill-chosen one,
unhappy in its implications. It has
stamped upon the public imagination
the general impression that city planning is a matter of widened streets and
new parkways, civic centers and athletic fields, monumental high schools
and great white ways—all of them promoted with a sublime forgetfulness of
such prosaic incidentals as bond issues,
tax limits, special assessments, and
constitutional limitations. City planning has been too closely associated
with landscape architecture; it has been
altogether too disdainful of grim realities in the fields of law, economics,
finance, and politics. With not altogether felicitous results, it has repeatedly endeavored to solve problems of
urban congestion and reconstruction
without first securing, by the compilation of adequate data, any real grasp
of the complicated economic, social,
and political factors involved. Even
the zoning of a large community has

[1] *Regional Survey of New York and Its Envi-
rons.* Vol. I, *Major Economic Factors in Metro-
politan Growth and Arrangement.* By Robert M.
Haig and Roswell C. McCrea. Issued by the
Regional Plan of New York and Its Environs,
New York, 1927. Pp. 111.

often been dealt with as an enterprise requiring no more apparatus than a block-and-lot plan to be checked off into areas by someone with a penchant for order and symmetry. Thereafter, and quite naturally, the city council has been obliged to spend much of its time shifting land from one zone to another in accordance with business trends which any careful economic survey would have disclosed in advance.

THE HUMAN FACTOR IN CITY PLANNING

City planning must deal with people as well as with things. It must reckon with human interests and idiosyncrasies. The happiness of the individual citizen does not altogether depend on the attractiveness of the physical environment. A city which does not provide free scope and even encouragement for the growth of normal economic activities is not a well-planned city, no matter how strongly its street layout or its zoning scheme may appeal to the artistic imagination. Laws and ordinances need to be straightened, sometimes even more urgently than streets. The financial aspects of planning and replanning cannot be relegated to a postscript, for they are of determining importance. More blue-prints have gone to the waste basket on this score than on any other, and deservedly so. I recall, for example, a street re-planning scheme which was made for a certain Pacific Coast city of about sixty thousand people a half dozen years ago by one of the best known city planners in the United States. As a plan it was a masterpiece in all respects—except that the cost would have exhausted the borrowing power of the city five times over! A greater futility could hardly be imagined.

Too much city planning has been done with the idea that the sky is the limit to what a municipal corporation can borrow and spend. Too much of it, moreover, has gone on the principle that all forms of business ought to go and stay where they are put, not where they want to be. And too much planning has confined itself within the political boundaries of single municipalities without due need to the essential economic and social unity of whole regions round about. Political boundaries are usually the outcome of an accident, or a series of accidents. They have no necessary relation to the problems of transportation, traffic congestion, or airport facilities; all of which treat such boundaries as if they did not exist.

STUDY OF THE CAUSES OF CONGESTION

City planning, fundamentally, is an enterprise designed to reduce the friction of space. Its outstanding purpose should be that of adjusting activities to areas and resources, both of which are limited,—though not with absolute rigidity. The problem is to expand both and make them go farther. To that end, city planning must inevitably undertake a study of what is being crowded, and what causes the crowding, before it passes to the formulation of plans for relief. That, in a word, is the point of approach adopted by the Regional Plan of New York and Its Environs, and the present volume embodies the first installment of the inquiry into causes.

ARE INDUSTRIES PROPERLY LOCATED?

Where do things "belong" in a metropolitan area? Messrs. Haig and McCrea began with the hypothesis that things belong where they have established themselves; or, to put it another way, that in the competitive struggle for urban sites, the different economic activities tend to gravitate (or to be relegated) into those neighborhoods or localities which are really the best places for them when all the influencing factors are taken into account. By observing the actual drift it is reasonable to expect that some light can be thrown on the outlines of a pattern or plan which would be ideal from an economic point of view.

Indeed this is the only way to get city planning upon a scientific basis and keep it there, for the success of the movement depends in the last analysis upon the answer to the question: "Does it pay?" Industries buy "accessibility" just as they buy raw materials and labor. They pay for it in site-costs and high taxes. Often they pay too heavily. If city planning (by improving transportation, relieving traffic congestion, and by intelligent zoning) can increase this accessibility without increasing the cost of it—there is no limit to the success and popularity which it may hope to achieve. But it must deliver in accordance with the pragmatic test.

The region of the metropolis affords an admirable area for the study of these natural trends in business migration, segregation, and distribution. Its magnitude has enabled the study to be conducted on a large scale, thus minimizing the occurrence of the exceptional, and bringing into bold relief some tendencies which do not become explicit in smaller communities where the pressure for space is not so great. The complexity of the New York region, moreover, implies that every economic activity is not only represented, but well represented. Hence the results of the study are too voluminous to be included in a single monograph. The details have been relegated to supplementary volumes,[1] and only the summaries are given in this one. Indeed the main purpose of the present volume is to outline and submit for criticism certain tentative hypotheses concerning the natural and proper assignment of economic activities to urban areas.

The study of location trends and tendencies has covered, in this instance, about a dozen types of business activity; including the tobacco products industry, textile manufacturing, printing, the men's wear and women's garment industry, wholesale markets, retail shopping, and financial institutions. The conclusions, as set forth in the closing pages of the volume, are of great significance. It is believed that, in the absence of control through adverse zoning, a very large number of fabricating industries will cling tenaciously to sites in the center of an urban area, even in so vast a metropolis as New York. But there are other industries, with different characteristics, which inevitably tend to locate or to drift away from the center and will do this wholly irrespective of any impetus from the zoning laws. Others, again, are edging their way outside the metropolitan region altogether. For example, those industries which employ female labor of a relatively unskilled character, with standardized processes and on a large scale, are drawn to the proximity of heavy man-using industries, wherever the latter may happen to be.

STORAGE FACILITIES IN LESS CONGESTED AREAS

The authors call attention to one very significant practice—the tendency to separate storage from other business functions. Already a large part of the stocks sold in the wholesale markets of New York City are stored in New Jersey. This specialization and physical segregation of the largest space-consuming function in many forms of business will probably become more common and more extensive as time goes on. Conclusions regarding

[1] Volumes 1A and 1B of the *Regional Survey*.

future developments in the central shopping region and in the financial district are also set forth and will repay reading.

All in all, the interest and significance of this volume cannot easily be over-estimated. No one who studies it from cover to cover can doubt that the whole city planning movement is being helped to a safer and surer basis by this work. It deserves attention from many quarters—from the student of applied economics, municipal government, business administration, and real estate values. Certainly the man who desires to be posted on industrial New York can find no better textbook than this. The diagrams which are so liberally used throughout the volume add greatly to its usefulness.

THE PUBLIC PERSONNEL POLICY OF THE MUNICIPALITY OF BORDEAUX [1]

BY WALTER R. SHARP
University of Wisconsin

The administration of the civil service of a typical French city, based on the author's first-hand investigation.   ::   ::   ::   ::   ::

WITH a population of a quarter of a million, Bordeaux is the fourth city of France. Before the war, commerce, chiefly in wines, was the essence of its prosperity. But thanks to its splendid situation on the Gironde, only sixty miles from the Atlantic Ocean, it became almost overnight a great port of transshipment during the war—the port which fed, as it were, most of France, Italy, and Switzerland. For four months it also enjoyed the prestige of serving as the provisional seat of the French government; and from 1917 to 1919 it was one of the principal bases for the American Expeditionary Force. Miles and miles of new docks, with the most modern maritime freight facil-

ities, were constructed along the banks of the Gironde just below the city. An important wartime industry sprang up, and the old town famous for its wines and liqueurs took on an animated American aspect that has never entirely disappeared. The city has many spacious parks and gardens, with broad, tree-lined boulevards forming a semicircle around it, the river serving as the curving diameter between Bordeaux proper and La Bastide on the other side. Bordeaux is also blessed with its full share of historic monuments, among which stands its imposing *Grand Théâtre*, the prototype of the more celebrated but less pleasing Paris *Opéra*.

The natural gateway to French colonial Morocco and West Africa, Bordeaux has also been since 1915 the home of the leading French colonial exposition, held each spring in the beautiful *Place des Quinconces*, which looks out toward the point where Lafayette set sail for America a hundred and fifty years ago.

[1] This article is based upon materials gathered and direct observations made during a year's sojourn at Bordeaux, 1920-21, and again during 1927, when the writer was a traveling fellow of the Social Science Research Council studying French public personnel administration. Except where otherwise indicated, the statistical data here presented was obtained directly from the office of the municipal secretary of Bordeaux.

THE GOVERNMENTAL ORGANIZATION

Like all French cities except Paris, Bordeaux is governed by a municipal council elected integrally every four years. This legislative body chooses from its thirty-six members a mayor and twelve "adjoints" for a term identical with its own. It is these thirteen men who form, as it were, the "political" cabinet of amateurs that supervise and coördinate the work of the professional administrative staffs of the city government. Each adjoint, an unpaid, part-time official, is assigned by the mayor to one, or sometimes two or three, of the administrative departments as the political head. At present, these departments are organized as follows:

1. Central secretariat (at the *mairie*).
2. Finance and *octroi*.
3. Municipal police, of which the commissioners are appointed by the Minister of the Interior at Paris.
4. Administrative police (services of sanitary inspection, etc.).
5. Public works (including water supply, street maintenance, parks, tramway, and fire protection).
6. *État civil* (vital statistics).
7. Assistance and public hygiene.

8. Public instruction (the city maintains a few schools of its own).
9. Fine arts and architecture.
10. Municipal *régie* (operation) of gas and electricity.
11. Burials and cemeteries.
12. Tax collection, military and electoral affairs.

THE SIZE AND COST OF THE CIVIL SERVICE

To man these services there was required in 1926 a personnel numbering 3,090 persons, classified broadly in three main divisions: (1) administrative, with 221; (2) technical, including professional, and (3) skilled and manual labor, the last two with a combined personnel of 2,869.[1] A comparison of the size of Bordeaux's civil service with that of three fairly analogous American cities is presented in Table A below.

Since 1900 personnel costs at Bordeaux have grown as seen in Table B.

These figures show that since pre-war days (1913): (1) the total municipal budget has increased five times, (2) the payroll for city employees has increased seven and a half times, and

[1] The number of employees in each department is not rigidly fixed by regulations, but may vary according to the current needs of the department.

TABLE A

City	Population	Total personnel	Ratio	Per cent of budget absorbed by payroll
Bordeaux	253,386 (1926)	3,090	1 to 82	38
Newark	414,524 (1920)	4,847	1 to 86	55
Seattle	315,312 (1920)	6,012	1 to 52	50
Dayton	152,559 (1920)	973	1 to 157	63

TABLE B

Year	Total budget (in francs)	Payroll (in francs)	Per cent of total	Average per capita compensation
1900	12,539,670	3,690,035	25	Data not available
1913	18,191,282	4,708,271	26	2,000 francs (roughly)
1920	54,833,453	15,639,910	28	4,800 francs (roughly)
1927	91,041,474	35,068,658	38	11,350 francs

(3) the per capita salary and wage scale has increased five and a half times.

But since the cost of living in France has risen more than six times during this fourteen-year period, it appears that as a paymaster the city of Bordeaux has not quite kept pace with the level of prices. In contrast with American compensation standards, the Bordeaux average of $200 in 1913 and $454 in 1927 seems pitifully low. While the low average is due in part to the presence on the city's payroll of a considerable number of part-time employees, it corresponds closely to the average pay of members of the French national civil service for the same period.

THE MERIT SYSTEM

The civil service of Bordeaux has since 1914 been regulated by a personnel code nominally enacted by the municipal council, but actually drawn up by an *ad hoc* commission of twelve members on which the staff is represented equally with officialdom.[1] Prior to 1919 the mayor in most French towns was free to make appointments and promotions as he pleased; but a national law passed that year requires all cities of more than 5,000 inhabitants either to adopt, on their own initiative, legal regulations insuring recruitment on a merit basis and removing municipal employees from the demoralizing effects of partisan politics and personal favoritism; or, failing that, to accept "the standard code of civil service regulations (*règlement-type*) prepared by the Council of State."[2] Action in this direction by the city council of

Bordeaux, along with that of Lyons and a few other large French cities, not only antedated this law, but went beyond the minimum requirements of the standard code worked out by the administrative jurists of the high tribunal at Paris. The principal reason for this earlier and more advanced action was the effective pressure brought to bear upon the municipal authorities by the professional associations (*syndicats*) into which over 85 per cent of French municipal employees are organized.[3]

The personnel code now in effect at Bordeaux applies, with a few unimportant exceptions, to "all the functionaires, employees, agents or laborers in the municipal services." As was stated earlier, this personnel is classified under three heads: administrative, technical, and labor. At the top of the administrative hierarchy stands the "*secrétaire de la Ville*," who, somewhat like the English town clerk, is a permanent official advising the mayor, and who acts also as the personnel officer of the city administration. Generally speaking, he supervises the operation of the several municipal services by transmitting to them the mayor's instructions and giving to them certain coördinating directions of his own. Below this municipal secretary come the *chefs de division, ou de service*, who are the real professional heads of the several departments, or lesser divisions, responsible to their respective adjoints for the proper functioning of their services. Under the *chefs de division* are a varying number of bureau chiefs distributed as needed through the different services. Each of these men has charge of a subordinate staff of ac-

---

[1] The "official" side of this commission consists of the mayor, one adjoint, and four municipal councillors. The present code dates from 1922, the earlier one having been superseded that year.

[2] W. B. Munro, *The Government of European Cities* (revised edition, New York, 1927), p. 311.

[3] Their national organization, with about 43,000 members, includes the employees of territorial *départements* as well; but the latter are few in number. The police, however, are organized separately.

countants, clerks, copyists, stenographers, etc., consisting since the war mostly of women. All this staff constitutes the central "secretariat" at the *Hôtel de Ville.*

CLASSIFICATION OF THE CIVIL SERVICE

In the technical and professional class are to be found a great variety of municipal specialists: engineers, architects, inspectors of public works, supervisors of the public weights, the commissioners and inspectors of police, and public health personnel. Included in it also are a small number of educational administrators and teachers who are paid by the city instead of by the central government. The third personnel category, consisting of skilled and unskilled laborers—foremen as well as ordinary artisans—is subdivided into ten wage groups ranging from 11,000 down to 6,000 francs (not counting family allowances and cost of living bonus). This last category, of course, makes up the rank and file of the 3,090 persons on the city's payroll.

EXAMINATIONS

With the exception of ordinary laborers, who are usually subjected merely to qualifying trade tests, recruitment at the base rests upon open competitive examination. To highly specialized and professionalized posts, however, most appointments are made after the examination of official titles and diplomas granted by the properly accredited training schools, of which there is no end in France, due weight also being given to testimonials and records of professional experience. Only occasionally are such candidates subjected to oral interview; and when that procedure is followed, a special board, or jury, is appointed by the municipal secretary for the purpose. For the rest of the technical positions

and all the administrative posts, the regulations require that open competitive examinations be held. To be eligible for these examinations, a candidate must be a French citizen, preferably a resident of Bordeaux, no more than thirty years old, and be able to produce a certificate of physical fitness from the municipal medical commission.

PREFERENCE FOR WAR VETERANS

Under a national law enacted in January, 1923, French municipalities are further required to reserve to pensioned veterans of the World War at least one-half of the vacancies that occur in the lower grades of municipal employment, while three-fourths of the positions for which women are eligible are reserved to widows of ex-service men. As one would expect, these provisions have already operated so as to affect adversely the quality of subordinate personnel, especially office employees, and as time goes on, its consequences will doubtless become more and more disturbing to the administrative efficiency of the city government.

FILLING VACANCIES

When vacancies actually occur, or are about to occur, in any department or special class of work, notice of the time, place, and character of the examination, as well as of the salary attached to the post, is placed upon the official bulletin board at the town hall and sent to the local press. An examining board consisting of the mayor, or more often an adjoint as his alternate, two members of the municipal council, the municipal secretary, and two division chiefs, is appointed to prepare and conduct the tests. While the regulations leave this board free to adapt the examination to the type of position to be filled, the character of the tests ·

employed undergoes little or no change from year to year. General education, always stressed, is given a varying value according as the work is legal, accounting, engineering, or clerical.

NATURE OF TESTS

Candidates for clerkships, for example, take a double test: first, an "elimination" test of (1) writing, (2) spelling, and (3) elementary arithmetic; and second, if this be successfully passed, a "definitive" test consisting of (4) the preparation of a short essay on some non-technical subject, and (5) oral questions on French municipal law and the elements of constitutional and administrative law. While these five distinct tests are all graded on a scale of 20, the grades are given different coefficients, as follows:

Elimination

(1) Writing........................	1
(2) Spelling.......................	3
(3) Arithmetic....................	2
Maximum points...............	120

Definitive (final)

(4) Essay.........................	3
(5) Oral..........................	2
Maximum points...............	100

A candidate must make at least 80 points in the elimination test to be admitted to the final, and a total of 150 points is the minimum passing grade for the entire examination. Additional points (ranging from 5 to 10) are allowed for personal appearance and the possession of certain academic diplomas and certificates.[1]

To those acquainted with recent developments in the recruitment of

[1] Employees already in another branch of the service, as well as their sons, and the sons of retired employees and crippled veterans, are the beneficiaries of a five per cent addition to their final grades.

policemen in American cities, the method used at Bordeaux will seem exceedingly simple, if not primitive. If the candidate is between twenty-two and thirty-five years of age, is at least five feet five inches tall, has a fairly robust physique, has completed his military service, and can produce a certificate of good moral character from his local authorities (he need not be a resident of Bordeaux), all he need do is to pass a simple "dictation" test, which it is assumed will show whether he knows enough to prepare a daily service report. Inspectors of police (non-uniformed) are recruited from the ranks of ordinary policemen (having at least three years of service) by a competitive examination somewhat more exacting in character. It includes (1) a dictation test of thirty lines, (2) the preparation of a report based upon a practical problem, and (3) a two-hour oral test on criminal law and regulations.

Wherever competitive examination is used, the successful candidates are classified in order of merit according to a majority vote of the examining board. The results are immediately announced to the candidates, and the *liste de classement* is posted in the secretariat of the *mairie*. Vacancies are filled as they occur, but in every case a probationary period of a year must be satisfactorily completed before the candidate receives a permanent appointment. Though he may be discharged at any time during the period of probation, it was learned upon inquiry that very few employees fail to receive appointments at the end of that time.

PROMOTIONS

Increases in salary and promotions are likewise carefully regulated by the personnel code, for it was here that the insidious influence of personal favoritism, nepotism, and partisan politics formerly had free rein in French cities. Generally speaking, salary advancements without change of position take place automatically on a seniority basis. A detailed salary classification chart, drawn up by a special bi-partite commission, indicates the number of years, ranging from one to five, that must normally be served in each salary class before the next may be entered. For disciplinary reasons, such salary advances may be postponed a year or more, though instances of postponement are in practice exceedingly rare. On the other hand, where the normal sojourn in a salary class is three years or more, the rate of advancement may be accelerated by one year for those employees who are placed on a special promotion list drawn up annually by the promotion board. The number of names on this list, however, cannot exceed one-half those in the next-to-the-last year of any salary class. In fact, the number advanced in this manner (*au choix*) is usually less than half. For instance, in the administrative division there were granted in 1927 twenty-four increases by seniority and only nineteen by selection.

Properly considered, promotion in the administrative and clerical classes takes place, in theory at least, exclusively by merit. Mention has already been made of the promotion board, which is composed of the mayor, or an adjoint designated by him, as president; two members chosen from and by the municipal council; the municipal secretary and his assistant; and the appropriate division heads. This board meets annually and draws up a list of those apt for promotion after taking into account the service ratings made of his subordinates by each division chief. The rating sheet is a simple qualitative notation, covering the employee's industry, intelligence, attendance and punctuality, and aptitude for advancement, along with any general observations that the political head (adjoint) of the department concerned may care to make. Each member of the promotion board gives a numerical rating of one to ten to each employee, the aggregate of these points determining the order of the names on the *tableau d'avancement* for the year. Practically, there is not much deviation from seniority in the order in which names are placed on this list.

For the grade of bureau chief, an oral interrogation before the promotion board supplements the service rating. The purpose of this oral interview, so it was explained to the writer, is to size up the man's personality and all those subtle qualities that make or break an administrator. The annual list of those apt for promotion to the grade of bureau chief is limited to one-third the number of officers of that rank. A clerk, moreover, must have served the city eight years before his name can appear upon this list, which means in reality from ten to fifteen years. The average number of promotions to the rank of bureau chief is only two or three a year.

In the technical and labor categories, promotion is normally by special examination. Sometimes this is competitive, often it is merely qualifying. Otherwise, the procedure is analogous to that outlined above.

PROMOTION FROM THE RANKS

When one reaches the highest positions in the municipal service, that of *chef de division* and *secrétaire de la ville*, he finds that the mayor and his cabinet are virtually free to select whom they will. They may even go outside the administrative hierarchy and bring in fresh blood. But the "closed system" prevails. The records show that almost all the heads of departments have come up through the ranks. For the staff associations insist upon the opportunity for the humblest employee to work up to the top; and since the war, at any rate, the political directors of the city's affairs have usually found it wise to comply with this view. As a matter of fact, few capable outsiders could be induced today to enter the city service at middle age for a salary that barely reaches 20,000 francs.

Since the war the average age at which appointments to the upper-grade posts have taken place has ranged as follows:

Period	Chef de bureau	Chef de division
1919–1923	49	52
1925–1927	38	48

As will be seen, the tendency is to promote younger men to bureau headships, whose average tenure is around five or six years, never less than three or four. Heads of divisions, however, average ten to fifteen years of service before they retire. It should be further explained that the avenue of promotion is measurably broadened by the ease with which civil servants may, either for personal convenience or for the good of the service, be transferred at any time from one department to another. If this arrangement were actually followed more frequently, it would mean more than it does.

Perhaps the most illuminating way in which to show the paths to administrative advancement would be to present résumés of the careers of three Bordeaux officials, as follows:

1. *Municipal secretary:* entered municipal employment as clerk at 24; bureau chief at 30; assistant division head at 33; division head at 41; in military service four years; assistant municipal secretary at 48; secretary at 49; had served in that position eight years by 1927.

2. *Head of the division of municipal police:* entered as policeman at 22;

bureau chief at 33; assistant division head at 43; division head at 55; had served in that capacity seven years by 1927.

3. *Head of the division of public instruction:* entered as copyist at 21; bureau chief at 37; division head at 44; had served in that capacity one year by 1927.

LOW RATE OF TURNOVER

As one would be led to expect, the operation of such a personnel system as this gives an exceptionally low rate of turnover. Since 1920 the annual replacement of personnel, for all services, has averaged a scant four per cent. Despite the low rate of remuneration, the number of voluntary withdrawals has been negligible; and since dismissals from the service can take place only after a decision to that effect by the disciplinary council provided for in the code, they are even more infrequent. Thus the annual turnover corresponds closely with the number of employees who are retired.

THE RETIREMENT SYSTEM

Since 1898 a comparatively liberal retirement system, based upon joint contributions from employees and city, has been in operation. A compulsory deduction of five per cent is made from the employee's salary annually, in addition to one-twelfth the first year's pay and one-twelfth of each subsequent increase. After twenty-five years of service he is entitled to a retirement annuity equal to one-half his average salary (and allowances) for the last three years, which sum is increased by one-twentieth for each additional year of service. But the total annuity may not exceed three-fourths of this average salary, or, as it was in 1927, 18,000 francs. Retirement may take place either voluntarily or by request at the age of 55; unless there is a special arrangement for retention by the year, it occurs automatically at 60; and at 65 it becomes compulsory for every one. Permanent disability incurred in public employment entitles the civil servant to proportional pension rights after fifteen years' service, while compensation for accidents is applicable at any time after initial entry. In case of death, widows and orphans are similarly provided for. Until the total revenue from the retirement fund investments equals one-fifth the aggregate salaries subject to contributions, the city agrees to appropriate annually 50,000 francs to the fund. The financial administration of the fund is so complicated, however, as to cause one to doubt its actuarial soundness.

MORALE AND EFFICIENCY

Thus far we have been concerned primarily with an analysis of the "anatomy" of the system. For an outsider, a critical appraisal of its "physiology" is more difficult. High morale and efficiency are largely functions of each other. The first depends, as Professor White has so brilliantly shown in his study of municipal employment in Chicago, upon a complex of material and psychological factors. At Bordeaux, as everywhere in France since the war, the morale of the *fonctionnaire* has been so badly shaken by the chronic salary crisis with which all governmental agencies have been struggling that the other merits of personnel policies hardly stand out in normal relief. Not only have salary increases been inadequate, but they have been granted too laggardly, particularly for those who constitute the administrative *élite*. Cost-of-living bonuses have been invoked as makeshifts, but one wonders whether the otherwise admirable plan of granting special allowances for family charges, increasing pro-

gressively as the number of children increases, has not really served as a depressive of *basic* salary schedules. Nor is the Bordeaux scheme of salary classification by administrative determination, though free from the flagrant abuses of the old practice of specific legislative grants, based upon a comprehensive, scientific study of the relation between training, responsibility, and duties involved. Such reclassification studies need to be made in almost all French personnel jurisdictions. Among other things, they would undoubtedly result in an appreciable reduction of subordinate personnel.

FAVORABLE WORKING CONDITIONS

Materially, working conditions are favorable. The eight-hour day is normal for city work, and over-time is compensated by the hour at a relatively liberal rate. The personnel code guarantees an annual vacation ranging from twenty to thirty days in length, and allows full salary for the first six months during illness, with half-pay for a second period of like duration. The city gives to each employee a gratuity of 500 francs at marriage and a similar sum (400 to 600 francs) to help defray the expenses of childbirth in his family. After twenty-five years of zealous service, policemen, firemen, and street cleaners are awarded municipal medals of honor entitling the holder to a special annuity of 100 francs for life.

SOCIAL ACTIVITIES

Although the writer was struck by the negligible effort made by the municipal authorities to stimulate any sort of social life among employee groups, this morale "incentive" would not be so effective in a country where the family and the café mean so much socially. But through their *syndicats* the employees themselves provide a certain outlet for social and welfare activities. It is these organizations, moreover, that are tending to build up a genuine *esprit de corps* among the members of the different administrative staffs. They are permitted to select representatives to collaborate with their chiefs on technical advisory committees that function in each major department. These committees perform valuable service by stimulating joint discussion of working conditions, improvement in office methods, better use of materials, and so on. Futhermore, as we have already seen, the staff enjoys equal representation with high officials on the special commissions that prepare and revise the personnel code and salary schedules. All of this helps to create a sense of corporate loyalty.

POLITICAL ACTIVITIES AMONG THE CIVIL SERVANTS

In one or two respects, however, the professional movement among French municipal employees has produced dubious results. The *syndicat* leaders are often dominated by a radical political complex that brings the employees' unions into temporary conflict with officialdom. The former do not hesitate to use political tactics in trying to defend their professional interests. Their principal instrumentality is the Socialist party. This fact, one fears, has an undesirable effect upon the maintenance of effective discipline inside municipal departments. The disciplinary councils in operation since 1914 almost never dare to inflict the penalty of dismissal, and only seven or eight of the lighter penalties, such as temporary suspension, retarded salary advancement, and demotion, have been invoked annually since 1920.[1]

[1] When brought before a council of discipline, an employee has the right to see his *dossier*

Although the mayor is not legally obliged to follow the opinion of these councils, upon which sit two employees of the same grade as the accused, he almost invariably does so. But for general mediocrity and indifference, an employee apparently cannot be discharged. For dismissal would mean an annoying situation for the responsible official when called upon to justify his action by the interested staff association.

RELATIONSHIP OF OFFICIALS AND CIVIL SERVANTS

Broadly speaking, French officialdom seems to lack a proper understanding of the human bases of efficiency. The writer could discover little intelligent effort on the part of administrative officers to tap the sources of inventiveness latent in the rank and file of their staffs. Subaltern employees are not allowed to publish criticisms of the operation of their respective departments. Not only are staff schools unknown, but the city authorities make comparatively little use of the facilities of the University of Bordeaux in training men for municipal work before and after entry into the city's employ. Certain employees are permitted to attend courses at the faculty of law during working hours, but that is all.

Nor is there any effective attempt to adjust the incoming *fonctionnaire* to his job—nothing, I mean, in the way of "official" vocational guidance. For scores of clerks, therefore, "routineerism" is the inevitable result; not so

(complete record of his career in the public service), which is kept in the office of the municipal secretary, so as to become fully acquainted, in advance of the hearing, with the source and nature of the offense with which he is charged. He may employ a legal defender. The verdict of the disciplinary council is arrived at by secret ballot.

much at Bordeaux as in certain of the services of the central government, but more than there should be. There is developing in France, however, a national movement to "professionalize" the position of municipal secretary. This holds much promise. It may eventually lead, as for American city managers, to the practice of interchanging and promoting officials from city to city.

SUMMARY

In sum, one finds at Bordeaux a comparatively simple, honestly administered personnel system. It is almost entirely free from the abuses of political and personal favoritism. Legally, it contains the basic ingredients of what might become effective personnel management in the best sense. But it is as yet administered with little creative imagination. French officials are sceptical about the feasibility of using psychological tests, and when the writer ventured to suggest that the existing tests ought perhaps to be "tested" as to

their results, he was greeted with amazement.

A final observation should be made. As "personnel officer," the municipal secretary cannot, because of other heavy burdens on his time, fulfill the rôle of a wholly satisfactory personnel agency. And even if enough time were left from his other duties, he lacks adequate authority effectively to supervise and constantly to investigate the operation of recruitment, promotion, and classification methods, with a view to their improvement. He keeps personnel records on file, but that is about all. This, of course, is a general defect in the decentralized type of personnel administration used by the French everywhere.

From this fragmentary picture of the personnel policy of one French town, students of municipal affairs will, it is hoped, appreciate what a rich field for investigation the French city is beginning to offer. It is a field all the more interesting in that it is strikingly different from the Anglo-Saxon both in mechanics and in spirit.

COMPARATIVE TAX RATES OF 237 CITIES, 1928

BY C. E. RIGHTOR
Detroit Bureau of Governmental Research

Mr. Rightor's annual compilation, which speaks for itself.

THE accompanying table presents in summary form a record of the tax rates upon property as levied in 1928, for all cities over 30,000 population in the United States and Canada replying to the questionnaire.

This is the seventh compilation of these data, and is in the same form as in past years, with which it is believed the readers of the REVIEW are acquainted. Essentially, it is endeavored to keep the tabulation simple, primarily to indicate one thing—the tax on assessed property.

Property taxes constitute nearly two-thirds of the revenue receipts of cities over 30,000 population, as is disclosed by the census bureau's *Financial Statistics of Cities*. It is of interest to note that this report shows, for 146 comparable cities, a gradual increase from this source of revenue from 61.4 per cent in 1903 to 65.6 per cent in 1925. ·

Taxpayers, therefore, are naturally interested in knowing how the property taxes in their city compare with those in other cities, and further how the levies by governmental units compare. This information is furnished by the figures here presented for the current year, both in total tax rate per $1,000 assessed valuation, and a subdivision of the total for city, school, county and state purposes.

The bare tax rates would be of little value without certain pertinent data, and for this reason the table reports the population, assessed valuation, percentage of real and personal prop-erty, the date the city's fiscal year begins, and the date that city taxes are levied. Because the legal basis of assessment in some states varies from 100 per cent of true or market value, it becomes necessary to adjust the given rates to a uniform 100 per cent basis for all cities, in order that a correct and direct comparison between cities may be made of the total rate. This is done in the column "Adjusted tax rate."

Further, because it is generally accepted that the legal basis of assessment (predominantly 100 per cent of true cash value) cannot be realized in actual practice, attempt is made to indicate what the actual tax burden would be in each city were full value uniformly used. The result of such readjustment is presented in the last two columns, and manifestly must represent merely the best estimates that can be made.

The cities are listed in order of population, by the five census groups, and the Canadian cities separately. The census bureau population estimates as at July 1, 1928, are taken where available; otherwise, local estimates are used. It is obvious that these estimates do not cover extraordinary conditions, such as the temporary population of a resort city or added population due to annexations, and so per capita comparisons made without specific information respecting each city might be misleading.

The figures present their own case, and are naturally of limited value.

Local conditions require numerous estimates, either of valuation, total or itemized rate, or of other data, and these exceptions are indicated in the footnotes.

A WIDE SPREAD IN RATES

In theory, the tax rate paid by a parcel of property in every city should be easily set down. In practice, however, it is found that the principle of home rule in taxation makes the task a difficult one. Varying units and bases of assessment, different fiscal periods, etc., enter to complicate the problem, as reflection will make evident.

Different principles and practices in taxation, such as separation of sources of state and local revenues, classification of property, etc., result in a wide range in rates. Analysis of the uniform 100 per cent tax rate column—"Adjusted tax rate"—discloses a range in the total rate from $84.50 per $1,000 assessed valuation for Columbia to $14.14 for Lancaster. For the Canadian cities, the range is from $36.66 for Edmonton to $20.50 for Montreal. This column shows an average of the rates for all cities of $33.39. The average for 249 cities reported in the 1927 tabulation was $33.16. This indicates a gradually increasing burden upon property, as was also found last year when compared with 1926.

THE TREND OF PROPERTY TAXES

Comparison of the present table with the figures for 1927 permits a conclusion as to the trend of taxes. Such comparison was possible for 195 cities reporting in both years, and when made shows that the average of the rates —upon the uniform 100 per cent basis— increased $.80 per $1,000 for 1928 over 1927. Of these 195 cities, 117 showed an increase, fifty-seven a decrease, and twenty-one no change. This is exclusive of the Canadian cities, which show, for thirteen comparable cities, seven having an increase totaling $8.43, four a decrease totaling $6.75, and two no change, giving a net increase for the thirteen cities of $1.68, or an average increase of $.13 per $1,000.

RELATIVE TAX BURDEN UNCERTAIN

The only known way of comparing the actual tax burden in these cities is to revise the foregoing adjusted tax rates further upon the basis of assessing practice in applying the 100 per cent value. This revision, as has been stated, must be merely a guess today, owing to the absence of adequate studies of such practice. The range in rates upon such readjusted basis is found to be from $42.53 for Saginaw to $9.60 for Winston-Salem. For the Canadian cities, the range is from $36.66 for Edmonton to $20.50 for Montreal. The average for all cities is $24.07. This compares with $24.02, the average for cities in 1927. Thus, while indications are that the relative tax burden is tending to increase, it is agreed that the detailed figures are too arbitrarily assumed to be of specific interest.

ASSESSING PRACTICES MERIT ATTENTION

The tax rate per se continues to be the main objective of most enquiries, whether from taxpayers or from students. The rate alone, however, is decidedly inadequate as a basis for comparison between cities. As has been repeatedly stated, the comparative real tax burden may be indicated only when the tax rate is expressed as applied to the true cash or market value in all cities. Most assessing officials will assert that such basis, or any gradation permitted by law, is actually enforced. Yet where is the city in which all the property owners will honestly hold that they believe assessments are made upon that basis? Undoubtedly it varies with cities, and no way has been found of measuring the diversified practices.

The only test of the degree to which such adherence is had by the assessing officials would be a check by an impartial and competent person or agency. And the wonder today, with existing tax demands, is that heavy taxpaying groups in every city have not demanded such independent check. Were the results of such study available in each city, an acceptable basis for the last two columns of the table would be at hand, and furnish a much-sought-for but not now available index to the tax problem.

RECENT REAPPRAISALS

The recent reappraisals of Denver and San Francisco were mentioned a year ago. The result of a study in Chicago merits mention at this time. A joint commission on real estate valuation, comprising both official and citizen representatives, made a study jointly with the Institute for Research in Land Economics and Public Utilities at Northwestern University, comparing the taxation appraisals in 1926 with sale prices, for 6,105 parcels, comprising ten different types of property.[1] The percentage of appraised value to sales value was found to be 31.3 per cent, whereas the statutes of that state required at that time that assessments should be fixed at one-half the fair cash value. (Since amended to provide for full value.) For 1927, the ratio was found to be 40 per cent. This was but one disclosure of the assessing methods which are being constructively considered in Chicago and Cook County.[2] Kansas City reports that a similar study is being made there.

When such analysis has been made in all our cities, it may be assumed that assessing methods will be upon a new plane of efficiency and equality. It will then be possible really to compare the property tax burden in our cities. That the importance of this subject is being recognized nationally is evident from the latest publication of the Municipal Administration Service, *The Appraisal of Urban Land and Buildings*, by Mr. C. E. Reeves;[3] and from the series of reports being published by the finance department of the Chamber of Commerce of the United States. This organization has named a committee on state and local taxation and expenditures, one of whose objectives is the improvement in the assessment of property for general taxation.

To comply with requests for tax data upon a per capita basis for each city, as well as upon the unit property value of $1,000, attempt was made to collect this information, but the data were not adequate or uniform enough for tabulation.

Requests for the tax rate data were sent to 286 cities in the United States and 19 cities in Canada. Replies adequate for tabulation were received from 237 cities, to the public officials of which those referring to this tabulation are indebted for their coöperation.

[1] See Simpson, Herbert D., "The Tax Situation in Chicago," NATIONAL MUNICIPAL REVIEW, September, October, and November, 1928.

[1] Reports I and II, Joint Commission on Real Estate Valuation for the Board of County Commissioners, Cook County; July, 1927, and June, 1928.

[2] See Cornick, Philip H., "A New Book on the Appraisal of Urban Land and Buildings," NATIONAL MUNICIPAL REVIEW, November, 1928, pp. 680–683.

COMPARATIVE TAX RATES OF 237 CITIES OVER 30,000 FOR 1928

COMPILED BY THE DETROIT BUREAU OF GOVERNMENTAL RESEARCH, INC.

From Data Furnished by Members of Governmental Research Association, City Officials, and Chambers of Commerce

	Census July 1, 1928	Assessed valuation	Per cent Realty	Per cent Personalty	City fiscal year begins	Date of collection of city tax	City	School	County	State	Total	Legal basis of assessment (per cent)	Adjusted tax rate to uniform 100% basis of assessment	Estimated ratio of assessed value to legal basis (per cent)	Final readjusted tax rate
Group I Population 500,000 and over															
1. New York, N. Y.[1]	6,017,500	$16,153,945,949	98	2	Jan. 1	May 1; Nov. 1	$20.25	$4.61	$.84	$.83	$26.56	100	$26.53	90	$23.88
2. Chicago, Ill.[2]	3,157,400	4,250,437,799	81	19	Jan. 1, '27	Jan. 2, '28	25.00	15.20	5.30	3.00	48.50	100	48.50	40	19.40
3. Philadelphia, Pa.[3]	2,064,200	4,434,559,207	75	25	Jan. 1	Jan. 25	19.50	9.00	....	....	28.50	100	28.50	90	25.65
4. Detroit, Mich.	1,378,900	3,562,213,760	82	18	July 1	July 15; Dec. 1	15.41	6.08	2.87	2.82	27.18	100	27.18	80	21.74
5. Los Angeles, Calif.[4]	1,330,000	1,863,559,210	86	14	July 1	Dec. 1, '28; April 1, '29	18.70	15.60	7.20	.85	41.50	100	41.50	50	20.75
6. Cleveland, Ohio[5]	1,010,300	2,092,159,170	69	31	Jan. 1	Dec. 20, '27; June 20, '28	11.00	9.72	3.43	.85	25.00	100	25.00	80	20.00
7. St. Louis, Mo.	848,100	1,216,005,261	85	15	April 12, '27	Nov. 1, '27	16.10	8.50		1.30	25.90	100	25.90	75	19.43
8. Baltimore, Md.[6]	830,400	1,935,040,570	57	43	Jan. 1	Jan. 1	18.25	5.65		2.56	26.46	100	26.46	80	21.17
9. Boston, Mass.	799,200	1,943,875,500	92	8	Jan. 1	Sept. 15	15.64	9.29	1.77	2.10	28.80	100	28.80	90	25.92
10. Pittsburgh, Pa.[6]	673,500	1,108,842,440	100		Jan. 1	Oct. 15	18.96	11.50	7.38		37.84	100	37.84	85	32.16
11. San Francisco, Calif.[6]	585,300	866,903,099	85	15	July 1	Jan. 7	28.89	10.71	....	....	39.60	100	39.60	38	15.05
12. Buffalo, N. Y.	555,800	1,059,913,105	94	6	July 1	July 1; Dec. 1	16.23	10.08	4.61	1.24	32.16	100	32.16	78	25.08
13. Washington, D. C.[7]	552,000	1,719,654,710	65	35	July 1	Sept. 1; Mar. 1	11.05*	5.95*	....	....	17.00	100	17.00	90	15.30
14. Milwaukee, Wis.	544,200	899,265,122	83	17	Jan. 1	Dec. 15	13.25	10.15	5.21	.55	29.16	100	29.16	65	18.95
Group II Population 300,000 to 500,000															
15. Newark, N. J.[10]	473,600	846,831,123	80	20	Jan. 1	April 15	19.81	8.98	5.20	4.31	38.30	100	38.30	100	38.30
16. Minneapolis, Minn.[11]	455,900	314,304,769	85	15	Jan. 1	Jan. 6; June 1	33.53	20.20	7.51	7.65	73.89	38	28.08	85	23.87
17. New Orleans, La.	429,400	(not reporting)			Jan. 1	Dec. 1									
18. Cincinnati, Ohio	413,700	1,061,008,780	71	29	Jan. 1	June 1	10.36	7.35	6.04	.85	24.60	100	24.60	90	22.14
19. Kansas City, Mo.[12]	391,000	479,072,000	72	28	May 1	June 1	13.75	11.50	4.50	1.40	31.15	100	31.15	55	17.32
20. Seattle, Wash.	388,200	297,521,194	80	20	Jan. 1	Mar. 1	33.57	13.75	13.20	10.50	76.02	50	38.01	60	22.81
21. Indianapolis, Ind.	383,200	666,461,290	65	35	Jan. 1	July 1	10.65	10.30	3.15	2.30	26.40	100	26.40	80	21.12
22. Louisville, Ky.[13]	329,400	435,164,262	80	20	Sept. 1	Jan. 20	15.20	6.80	3.20*	4.20*	29.40*	100	29.40	80	23.52*

City	Population														
23. Rochester, N. Y.	328,200	634,665,209	100		Jan. 1	{Jan. 1 / June 1}	14.91	10.84	5.50	1.16	32.41	100	32.41	75	24.31
24. Jersey City, N. J.	324,700	(not reporting)													
25. Toledo, Ohio	313,200	584,523,250	71	29	Jan. 1	Dec. 1	11.98	9.00	4.08	.85	26.00	100	26.00	80	20.80
26. Portland, Ore.[14]	310,000	342,908,705	85	15	Dec. 1, '27	{Dec. 1 / June 1 / May 6 / Nov. 5}	20.40	18.25	4.75	5.40	48.80	100	48.80	60	29.28
Group III — Population 100,000 to 300,000															
27. Columbus, Ohio	299,000	594,323,150	75	25	Jan. 1	{Dec. 20, '27 / June 20, '28}	8.60	8.36	3.99	.85	21.80	100	21.80	75	16.35
28. Denver, Colo.	294,200	440,118,465	70	30	Jan. 1, '27	Jan. 1	10.46	14.37	4.23	3.84	32.90	100	32.90	80	26.32
29. Providence, R. I.[13]	296,300	630,340,520	61	39	Oct. 1, '27	Oct. 1, '27	16.23	6.14		1.13	23.50	100	23.50	100	23.50
30. Oakland, Calif.[14]	274,100	270,516,831	85	15	July 1	Sept. 5	22.58	22.71	9.24		54.80	100	54.80	80	27.40
31. St. Paul, Minn.[11]	260,000	180,252,056	80	20	Jan. 1	Jan. 1	32.70	15.14	15.54	7.65	71.03	38	71.03	80	21.59
32. Atlanta, Ga.	255,100	390,000,000	74	26	Jan. 1	{May, July & Sept.}	8.40	6.60	11.00	5.00	31.00	100	31.00	70	24.80
33. Akron, Ohio	225,000	366,732,660	69	31	Jan. 1	{Dec. 20, '27 / June 20, '28}	9.93	10.92	3.90	.85	25.60	100	25.60	70	17.92
34. Omaha, Nebr.	222,800	344,564,779	71	29	Jan. 1	May	11.85	13.00	4.44	2.06	31.35	100	31.35	80	18.81
35. Birmingham, Ala.	222,400	222,037,321	82	18	Sept. 1	Oct. 1	11.50	6.50	11.50	6.50	36.00	60	36.00	70	15.12
36. San Antonio, Texas	218,100	228,751,530	75	25	June 1	April 1	18.90	8.30	8.70	6.40	42.20	100	42.20	75	31.65
37. Dallas, Texas	217,800	(not reporting)	100	13	Jan. 1	May	18.04	11.28	5.89	1.52	36.73	100	36.73	66	24.24
38. Syracuse, N. Y.	199,300	313,945,831	87		Dec. 1	Oct. 10	18.81	8.08*	1.22	1.09	29.20	100	29.20	85	24.82
39. Worcester, Mass.	197,600	346,913,700	93	13	Feb. 1	June 1	16.00	7.50			23.50	100	23.50	67	15.75
40. Richmond, Va.[17]	194,400	282,536,680	95	7	Jan. 1	July 1	16.00	6.50	9.80	2.00	34.30	100	34.30	67	22.98
41. Memphis, Tenn.	190,200	257,570,427	95	5	Jan. 1	Jan. 1	13.00	10.00	.33	.67	24.00	100	24.00	100	24.00
42. New Haven, Conn.	187,900	320,888,245	85	15	Jan. 1	Mar. 1					24.00	100	24.00		24.00
43. Dayton, Ohio[13]	184,500	345,676,290	75	25	Jan. 1	{Dec. 1, '27 / June 1, '28}	10.04	9.67	4.44	.85	25.00	100	25.00	70	17.50
44. Norfolk, Va.	184,200	176,549,294	90	10	Jan. 1	July 1	19.40	9.70			29.10	100	29.10	60	17.46
45. Youngstown, Ohio	174,200	(not reporting)	88	12	April 1		11.32	11.27	.25	.71	23.55	100	23.55	80	18.94
46. Hartford, Conn.	172,300	354,810,870													
47. Houston, Texas	171,000	(not reporting)	74	26	Oct. 1, '27	July 1	16.60	9.50	9.00	6.70	41.80	100	41.80	55	22.99
48. Fort Worth, Texas	170,600	164,938,477			April 1										
49. Tulsa, Okla.	170,500	(not reporting)			April 1										
50. Grand Rapids, Mich.	164,200	265,691,000	70	30	July 1	Oct. 1, '27	12.46	13.40	3.25	3.44	32.55	100	32.55	80	26.04
51. Bridgeport, Conn.	160,000	264,217,255	82	20	April 1	April 1	20.73*	7.95*	.24	.78	29.70	100	29.70	80	23.76
52. Miami, Fla.[19]	156,700	317,429,000	97	3	July 1	{Jan. 1 / April 1 / Sept. 1 / Nov. 1}	11.30	6.24	11.40	2.16	31.10	50	31.10	100	15.55
53. Des Moines, Iowa[20]	151,900	188,575,980	87	13	April 1	March	14.69	16.11	6.35	2.25	39.40	100	39.40	75	29.55
54. Springfield, Mass.	149,800	314,151,780	89	11	Dec. 1	{Sept. 1 / Nov. 1}	14.89	9.92	1.31	1.48	27.60	100	27.60	85	23.46
55. Flint, Mich.	148,800	192,015,900	77	23	Mar. 1	{Nov. 1 / Dec. 1}	15.67	16.28	6.40	3.65	42.00	100	42.00	70	29.40
56. Oklahoma City, Okla.	148,000	121,975,196	85	15	July 1	Jan. 1	15.20	18.69	7.50	2.50	43.89	100	43.89	45	19.75
57. Paterson, N. J.	144,900	(not reporting)													
58. Scranton, Pa.[15]	144,700	126,151,235	100		Jan. 3	Jan. 1	18.72	19.00	10.50		48.22	100	48.22	50	24.11
59. Jacksonville, Fla.[19]	140,700	(not reporting)													
60. Nashville, Tenn.	139,000	169,607,122	75	25	Jan. 1	Aug. 1	16.50	3.50	9.00	2.00	31.00	100	31.00	75	23.25

COMPARATIVE TAX RATES OF 237 CITIES OVER 30,000 FOR 1928—Continued

City	Census July 1, 1928	Assessed valuation	Per cent Realty	Per cent Personality	City fiscal year begins	Date of collection of city tax	City	School	County	State	Total	Legal basis of assessment (per cent)	Adjusted tax rate to uniform 100% basis of assessment	Estimated ratio of assessed value to legal basis (per cent)	Final readjusted tax rate
61. Trenton, N. J.	139,000	(not reporting)	65	35	Jan. 1	Sept. 17	11.00	14.80	4.50	2.70	33.00	100	33.00	65	21.45
62. Salt Lake City, Utah	138,000	191,083,238	91	9	Jan. 1	June 1	13.98	8.39	5.03	4.30	31.70	100	31.70	100	31.70
63. Camden, N. J.	135,400	200,234,525	73	27	Jan. 1	Dec. 1	24.62	13.24	1.46	1.48	40.80	100	40.80	85	34.68
64. Fall River, Mass.	134,300	161,682,250	96	4	Jan. 3	Oct. 1	13.20	14.00	7.00		34.20	100	34.20	80	27.36
65. Erie, Pa.	130,000	142,884,556	88	12	July 1	Mar. 1	15.60	3.40	8.00	1.50	28.50	100	28.50	100	28.50
66. Wilmington, Del.[31]	128,500	136,050,650	88		April 1	July 1	19.00	9.42	.88	2.10	31.40	100	31.40	100	31.40
67. Cambridge, Mass.[32]	125,800	188,528,200	100		Jan. 1	Apr. 1	16.34	10.33	4.22	1.06	31.95	100	31.95	87	27.80
68. Yonkers, N. Y.[33]	121,300	301,891,030	100		Jan. 1	Oct. 15	22.75	5.09	5.16		33.60	100	33.60	80	26.88
69. Albany, N. Y.	120,400	208,006,365	70	30	July 1	Oct. 1		26.60	21.40	.99	63.80	100	63.80	40	25.46
70. San Diego, Calif.	119,700	91,936,120	72	28	Jan. 1	Nov. 1	20.80		4.50		29.20	100	29.20	90	23.36
71. New Bedford, Mass.	119,040	201,580,900	81	19	Dec. 1	Jan. 1	12.70	16.00		4.50	35.30	100	35.30	50	17.65
72. Kansas City, Kan.	118,300	137,975,196	80	20	Jan. 1	Jan. 1	11.50	8.59	9.80	6.70	36.50	100	36.50	70	25.55
73. El Paso, Texas	117,800	102,116,970	75	25	Mar. 1	Jan. 1	27.06		3.27		30.17	100	30.17	80	24.14
74. Duluth, Minn.[11]	116,800	81,972,827	73	27	Jan. 1		7.73	32.41		.85	79.40	38	30.17		22.10
75. Canton, Ohio	116,800	230,291,390	73	27	Jan. 1	{ June 20, Dec. 20 }	13.40	9.15	4.82	4.23	31.60	100	31.60	100	31.60
76. Elizabeth, N. J.	116,000	156,517,107	88	12	Jan. 1	June 1	10.00	12.00	4.00		26.00	100	26.00	60	15.60
77. Reading, Pa.	115,400	282,570,000	100		Jan. 1	Mar. 1	17.97	6.00	4.00	1.50	29.47	100	29.47	50	14.74
78. Tampa, Fla.[34]	113,400	278,283,122	89	11	June 1	Oct. 1	25.64		1.36	1.40	28.40	100	28.40	100	28.40
79. Lowell, Mass.[34]	111,000	136,675,260	82	18	Jan. 1	Oct. 15	20.00				28.40	100	28.40	88	24.85
80. Tacoma, Wash.	110,500	(not reporting)	75	25	Jan. 1		14.80	17.60	7.20		39.60	100	39.60	50	19.80
81. Spokane, Wash.	109,100	86,736,161	85	15	July 1	Feb. 5	20.00	13.50	12.51	11.79	57.80	50	28.90		28.40
82. Long Beach, Calif.	108,000	188,634,100	86	4	Jan. 1	{ Oct. 8, Jan. 7 }	17.00		7.20		32.60	100	32.60	70	22.82
83. Lynn, Mass.	105,500	136,977,895	80	20	Jan. 1	Nov. 1	15.92	8.81	1.66	2.01	28.40	100	28.40		
84. Knoxville, Tenn.	105,400	155,415,923	86		Jan. 1	July 1		4.00		2.60	32.60	100	32.60	80	
85. Fort Wayne, Ind.	105,300	(not reporting)	80	8	Oct. 1							100			
86. Utica, N. Y.[3]	104,200	132,939,704	100		Jan. 1	Aug. 9	16.98	9.98	8.04		35.01	100	35.01	69	24.15
87. Somerville, Mass.	102,700	120,172,300	92	8	Jan. 1	Oct. 15	16.90	8.15	1.08	2.27	28.40	100	28.40	80	22.72
88. Waterbury, Conn.	100,000	(not reporting)			Jan. 1							100			
Group IV **Population 50,000 to 100,000**															
89. Savannah, Ga.	99,900	78,300,000	75	25	Jan. 1	{ April, July, Oct., Jan. }	23.00	10.00	12.50	5.00	50.50	100	50.50	50	25.25
90. Hamtramck, Mich.	99,800	120,148,426	67	33	July 1	July 15	12.63	9.50	2.48	2.11	26.71	100	26.71	100	26.71
91. Allentown, Pa.	99,400	93,000,000	100		Jan. 1	Mar. 1	12.49	15.00	4.00		31.40	100	31.40	50	15.70
92. Wichita, Kan.	99,300	135,169,071	76	24	Oct. 15, '27	{ Nov., '27, June, '28 }	10.00	15.90	4.06	2.74	32.70	100	32.70	65	21.26
93. Evansville, Ind.	98,100	132,856,710	70	30	Jan. 1	{ May, Nov. }	10.70	10.00	5.80	2.30	28.80	100	28.80	100	28.80
94. Bayonne, N. J.	95,300	165,992,185	62	38	Jan. 1	June 1	15.30	12.38	7.61	4.40	39.69	100	39.69	80	31.75

No. City	Population	Assessed Valuation			Taxes Due	Taxes Delinquent									
95. Lawrence, Mass.	93,500	129,085,500	75	25	Jan. 1	Oct. 1	14.00	9.30	1.80	1.30	26.40	100	26.40	100	2
96. Schenectady, N. Y.	93,300	193,723,771	100	..	Jan. 1	Feb. 1	13.12	9.87	2.96	1.03	26.98	100	26.98	95	2
97. Wilkes-Barre, Pa.	91,900	106,933,339	95	5	Jan. 1	Aug. 1	16.70	16.00	8.90	..	41.60	100	41.60	75	3
98. Gary, Ind.	89,100	(not reporting)				April 1									2
99. Harrisburg, Pa.	86,900	86,497,430	100	26	Jan. 5	Mr. 1	16.00	18.00	6.00	2.81	40.00	100	40.00	50	2
100. Highland Park, Mich.	86,400	131,539,700	74	33	July 1	July 1	10.40	11.40	2.68	2.30	27.29	100	27.29	80	1
101. South Bend, Ind.	86,100	201,560,420	65	30	Jan. 1	Nov. 5	7.45	10.75	4.10	2.93	24.60	100	24.60	75	3
102. Manchester, N. H.	85,700	113,440,314	70	30	phil 1	April 1	15.25	7.15	2.17	3.00	27.50	100	27.50	100	3
103. Peoria, Ill.	84,500	88,722,802	70	30	Jan. 1	Jan. 1	16.33	13.75	3.97	3.00	37.05	100	37.05	100	2
104. Rockford, Ill.	82,800	96,055,000	72	28	Jan. 1	Mar. 15	17.30	13.80	4.80	..	38.90	100	38.90	60	2
105. Wilm. N. C.	82,100	(not reporting)													2
106. Shreveport, La.	81,300	121,115,580	65	35	Jan. 1	Dec. 6	10.00	9.25	5.75	..	32.50	100	32.50	55	2
107. Sioux City, Iowa	80,000	100,413,884	80	20	April 1	Jan. 1	11.75	16.62	3.88	2.25	34.50	DO	34.50	80	1
108. Winston-Salem, N. C.	80,000	145,000,000	80	40	June 1	Mar. 1	6.00	4.00	6.00	3.17	16.00	DO	16.00	90	2
109. Lansing, Mich	79,600	149,622,815	76	24	My 1	July 15	11.87	9.52	3.78	8.70	28.14	100	28.14	80	1
110. Little Rock, Ark.	79,200	60,393,285	75	24	Jan. 1	Jan. 1	7.42	18.00	8.50	6.35	21.31	50	21.31	60	2
111. Portland, Maine	78,600	115,998,375	73	26	Jan. 1	Sept. 1	16.86	7.37	1.42	6.35	32.00	100	32.00	65	1
112. St. Joseph, Mo.	78,500	81,258,580	73	27	April 15	May 1	12.50	12.25	7.65	1.40	33.80	100	33.80	65	2
113. Charleston, S. C.	75,900	23,102,935	72	28	Jan. 1	May 15	58.00	13.50	27.00	..	98.50	42	41.37	71	2
114. Sacramento, Calif.	75,700	105,706,960	87	13	Jan. 1	July 15	21.15	13.20	21.35	..	55.38	DO	55.38	72	3
115. Saginaw, Mich.	75,600	93,161,915	78	22	July 1	Oct. 15	16.41	14.44	8.26	3.42	42.53	DO	42.53	100	4
116. Binghamton, N. Y.	74,800	119,546,160	100	-	Jan. 1	July 1	15.97	10.22	5.95	..	32.14	100	32.14	75	2
117. Racine, Wis.	74,400	103,050,215	82	18	Jan. 1	Jan. 1	5.00	12.00	3.26	.75	21.01	DO	21.01	78	1
118. Chester, Pa.	74,200	53,307,798	62	38	Jan. 1	May 1	20.30	18.00	6.00	3.00	47.30	DO	47.30	40	1
119. East St. Louis, Ill.	74,000	(not reporting)													1
120. Johnstown, Pa.	73,700	109,088,536	87	13	Oct. 1	Oct. 1	12.09	6.51	10.00	2.00	30.60	100	30.60	60	1
121. Chattanooga, Tenn.	73,560	(not reporting)													2
122. Terre Haute, Ind.	73,500	138,092,800	70	30	Jan. 1	Oct. 1	12.98	5.85	..	1.17	20.00	100	20.00	100	2
123. Pawtucket, R. I.	73,100	(not reporting)													1
124. Springfield, Ohio	73,000	114,086,238	80	20	April 1	July 1	12.55	12.57	.88	..	26.00	100	26.00	80	1
125. New Britain, Conn.	72,900	(not reporting)													1
126. Troy, N. Y.	72,300	101,706,268	83	17	Jan. 1	June 1 / Dec. 1	17.67	12.10	4.80	4.72	39.29	100	39.29	100	3
127. Passaic, N. J.	71,800	(not reporting)													3
128. Cicero, Ill.	71,600	116,855,639	79	21	Sept. 1	Oct. 1 / June 1	7.75	15.00	1.83	2.60	27.18	100	27.18	75	3
129. Lincoln, Nebr.	71,100		93	7	Jan. 1	Dec. 1 / Oct. 21 / Jan. 5	36.60	..	7.54	4.37	48.51	100	48.51	75	2
130. Hoboken, N. J.	71,000	99,169,553	93	7	July 1	July 1	12.00	19.40	15.00	..	46.40	100	46.40	48	2
131. Berkeley, Calif.	71,000	90,111,075	93	7	July 1	Mar. 1	12.00	12.00	7.50	..	29.00	100	29.00	60	1
132. Mobile, Ala.	69,600	(not reporting)				Nov. 1								70	1
133. Altoona, Pa.	69,100	76,044,305	75	25	Jan. 2	Nov. 1	7.50	9.30	7.50	1.40	24.85	100	24.85	80	2
134. Wheeling, W. Va.	68,662	121,234,207	80	20	July 1	Mr. 1	8.65	11.89	5.50	1.30	23.47	100	23.47	100	2
135. Huntington, W. Va.	68,300	126,310,328	91	9	Jan. 1	Oct. 15	6.58	11.33	3.70	..	27.44	100	27.44	70	1
136. Niagara Falls, N. Y.	68,000	137,463,202	88	12	Jan. 1	Nov. 1	9.88	13.00	6.23	2.08	30.00	100	30.00	100	2
137. Bethlehem, Pa.	67,600	72,890,186					12.00	6.55	5.00	..	26.80	100	26.80		2
138. Quincy, Mass.	67,600	135,942,880					17.10		1.01						1
139. Springfield, Ill.	67,200	(not reporting)				Nov. 1 / June 1								80	2
140. Brockton, Mass.	65,300	78,960,825	85	15	Dec. 1	Dec. 1	23.01	9.22	1.56	1.01	34.80	100	34.80	80	2
141. East Orange, N. J.	65,000	116,581,782	93	7	Jan. 1	Dec. 1	16.43	7.68	5.12	4.27	33.50	100	33.50	70	2

COMPARATIVE TAX RATES OF 237 CITIES OVER 30,000 FOR 1928—Continued

	Census July 1, 1928	Assessed valuation	Realty (per cent)	Personalty (per cent)	City fiscal year begins	Date of collection of city tax	City	School	County	State	Total	Legal basis of assessment (per cent)	Adjusted tax rate to uniform 100% basis	Estimated ratio of assessed value to legal basis (per cent)	Final readjusted tax rate
142. Lakewood, Ohio	65,000	144,382,290	89	11	Jan. 1	Dec. 20, June 20	6.54	12.20	3.43	.85	23.10	100	23.10	75	17.33
143. Roanoke, Va.	64,600	66,603,631	86	14	Jan. 1	Nov. 1	16.67	8.33*			25.00	100	25.00	50	12.50
144. Union City, N. J.	64,400	48,870,753	81	19	July 1, '27	Oct. 1, '27; Jan. 1, '28	24.36	14.50	17.50		56.36	100	56.36	50	28.18
145. Fresno, Calif.	64,000	(not reporting)													
146. Jackson, Mich.	63,700	(not reporting)													
147. Montgomery, Ala.	63,100	93,683,306	75	25	Jan. 1, '29	Nov. 1, '28; June 20, 29	14.35	14.25	4.30	2.10	35.00	100	35.00	80	28.00
148. Topeka, Kan.	62,800	(not reporting)													
149. Pasadena, Calif.	62,100	37,046,447	70	30	Jan. 1	Nov. 1	17.22	9.28			26.50	100	26.50	71	18.82
150. Portsmouth, Va.	61,600	78,537,876	65	35	Aug. 1	July 1; Jan. 1	17.02	19.33	11.04	2.90	50.29	100	50.29	75	37.72
151. Pontiac, Mich.	61,500	52,102,108	72	28	Jan. 1	April 15, Aug. 15; Dec. 15	13.75		17.00	5.00	35.75	100	35.75	47	16.80
152. Macon, Ga.	61,200	112,586,760	83	17	Dec. 1	Oct. 15	14.72	5.78	1.31	1.19	23.00	100	23.00	100	23.00
153. Holyoke, Mass.	60,400	(not reporting)			Jan. 1	Mar. 1	5.00	8.00	1.14		14.14	100	14.14	85	12.02
154. Covington, Ky.	59,000	106,000,000	100		April 1	Jan. 1	13.50	19.25	6.13	2.25	41.13	100	41.13	50	20.57
155. Lancaster, Pa.	58,300	54,000,000	80	20	April 1	Oct. 1	21.50	10.00	4.70	7.00	46.50	100	46.50	60	27.72
156. Cedar Rapids, Iowa	58,200	50,366,110	78	22	Jan. 1	April 1	19.50	36.70	4.50	3.00	63.70	100	63.70	50	31.85
157. Wichita Falls, Texas	58,026	46,371,639	85	15											
158. Oak Park, Ill.	57,700	(not reporting)													
159. Newton, Mass.	57,300	40,000,000	82	18	May 1	Apr. 1	22.10	20.00	5.30	3.00	50.40	100	50.40	50	25.20
160. Decatur, Ill.	57,100	53,194,750	68	32	Jan. 1	April, July, Oct.	17.50	12.60	10.00	5.00	45.10	67	30.22	75	22.67
161. Augusta, Ga.	56,700	69,573,230	80	20	Jan. 1	Jan. 1	19.25	16.33	5.14	9.84	50.56	100	50.56	55	27.81
162. Kenosha, Wis.	56,500	79,492,959	75	25	Jan. 1	July 1	11.00	14.66	6.10	2.96	34.72	100	34.72	80	27.78
163. Kalamazoo, Mich.	56,400	59,354,190	79	21	July 1	Oct. 1	14.80	8.20	9.10	6.70	38.80	100	38.80	60	23.28
164. Beaumont, Texas	56,300	(not reporting)													
165. Hammond, Ind.	56,000	(not reporting)													
166. Charleston, W. Va.	55,200	(not reporting)													
167. Atlantic City, N. J.	54,700	316,740,857	95	5	Jan. 1	June 1; Dec. 1; Jan. 1	14.58	3.88	4.42	4.32	27.20	100	27.20	90	24.48
168. Mount Vernon, N. Y.	54,700	141,928,981	100		Jan. 1	July 1	12.55	11.09	3.32	1.20	28.16	100	28.16	85	23.94
169. Malden, Mass.	53,400	70,127,150	86	14	Jan. 1	Oct. 15	13.70	10.47	4.23	1.21	29.70	100	29.70	100	29.70
170. Woonsocket, R. I.	53,400	(not reporting)													
171. Newport News, Va.	53,300	30,492,969	84	16	Jan. 1	Dec. 1	18.50	13.00			31.50	100	31.50	50	15.75
172. St. Petersburg, Fla.	53,300	149,251,760	87	13	July 1	Oct. 1	14.75	3.50	2.50	.90	21.65	100	21.65	75	16.24
173. Medford, Mass.	52,900	75,518,500	90	10	Jan. 1	Oct. 15	16.50	9.00	1.40	2.50	29.40	100	29.40	90	26.46
174. New Castle, Pa.	52,500	56,682,810	93	7	Jan. 1	Mar. 1	11.75	15.30	7.50		34.55	100	34.55	67	23.15
175. Davenport, Iowa	52,469	66,670,020	87	13	April 1	Sept. 1	13.50	27.48	9.57	4.50	55.05	100	55.05	60	33.03

Table (cities numbered 176–221):

			70	30	July 1	Sept. 1	13.70	14.00	5.30	1.30	34.30	100	34.30	70	2½
176. Greensboro, N. C.	51,900	(not reporting)													
177. Springfield, Mo.	51,700	43,412,072													
178. Stockton, Calif.	51,000	(not reporting)													
179. East Chicago, Ind.	50,800	(not reporting)													
180. Columbia, S. C.[27]	50,600	19,500,000	60	40	Jan. 1	Oct. 15	33.00	4.00	46.25	5.25	84.50	100	84.50	25	21
181. Galveston, Texas	50,600	58,960,560	75	25	July 1	Sept. 1	20.30	8.50	11.00	6.70	42.00	100	42.00	63	24
182. Madison, Wis.	50,500	141,800,940	83	17	Jan. 1	Jan. 1	8.45		4.15	.45	21.55	100	21.55	90	11
183. McKeesport, Pa.	50,400	(not reporting)													
184. Perth Amboy, N. J.	50,100	(not reporting)													
185. Elmira, N. Y.	50,000	(not reporting)													
186. Pittsfield, Mass.	50,000	(not reporting)													

Group V
Population 30,000 to 50,000

			70	30	July 1	Sept. 1	13.70	14.00	5.30	1.30	34.30	100	34.30	70	2½
187. York, Pa.	49,900	55,204,486	97	3	Jan. 1	Mar. 1	9.50	15.00	10.00		34.50	100	34.50	60	24
188. Chelsea, Mass.	49,800	56,043,550	86	14	Jan. 1	April 1	27.06	10.25		3.69	41.00	100	41.00	100	41
189. Lima, Ohio	49,700	81,522,430	77	23	Jan. 1	Dec. / June	10.42	9.89	4.04	.85	25.20	100	25.20	80	24
190. Bay City, Mich.	49,600	47,761,432	80	20	Jan. 1	Aug. 1	15.84	18.20	4.68	2.98	41.70	100	41.70	85	
191. Haverhill, Mass.	49,232	68,149,900	84	16	Jan. 1	Sept. 15	19.48	7.76	1.34	1.42	30.00	100	30.00	100	
192. New Rochelle, N. Y.	48,500	167,930,208	100		Jan. 1	April 8	15.11	7.42	3.15	1.02	26.70	100	26.70	90	
193. Lexington, Ky.	48,700	69,397,825	88	14	Jan. 1	Oct. 31	18.05	7.95	5.00	3.00	34.00	100	34.00	80	
194. Evanston, Ill.	47,600	65,370,469	84	16	Jan. 1	Jan. 1	13.60	49.60	13.00	6.50	82.70	100	82.70	35	
195. Durham, N. C.	47,600	82,656,109	60	40	June 1	Oct. 1	11.00	11.50	2.50		25.00	100	25.00	65	
196. Battle Creek, Mich.	47,300	68,100,000	75	25	July 1	July 1	10.00	11.00	4.80	4.00	29.80	100	29.80	75	
197. Aurora, Ill.	47,100	(not reporting)													
198. Muncie, Ind.	46,800	(not reporting)													
199. Columbus, Ga.	46,600	44,216,276	67	33	Jan. 1	Aug. 1	12.00	6.00	8.00	5.00	31.00	100	31.00	67	
200. Waco, Texas	46,600	58,065,290	76	24	Oct. 1	Oct. 1	15.10	8.20	5.90	6.40	35.60	100	35.60	60	
201. Muskegon, Mich.	46,600	(not reporting)													
202. Jamestown, N. Y.[28]	46,000	64,185,854	100		Jan. 1	July 1	12.12	12.23	9.19		33.54	100	33.54	60	
203. Brookline, Mass.	45,700	149,351,500	87	13	Jan. 1	Oct. 15	12.29	4.76	1.19	3.06	21.30	100	21.30	100	
204. San Jose, Calif.	45,500	(not reporting)													
205. Chicopee, Mass.	45,400	(not reporting)													
206. Fitchburg, Mass.	45,200	60,109,875	77	23	Dec. 1	April 1	17.80	8.97	1.46	1.37	29.60	100	29.60	100	
207. Austin, Texas	45,133	48,460,313	70	30	Jan. 1	Dec. 20	11.80	8.00	8.50	6.70	35.00	100	35.00	67	
208. Lorain, Ohio	44,900	83,159,105	73	27	Jan. 1	June 20 / Mar. 1	8.73	9.32	2.70	.85	21.60	100	21.60	85	
209. Pueblo, Colo.	44,200	37,170,300	76	24	Jan. 1	Aug. 1 / Dec. 20 / June 20	26.40	15.09	9.25	3.84	54.58	100	54.58	70	
210. Hamilton, Ohio	44,200	97,315,260	75	25	Jan. 1	Sept. 1	8.60	6.52	3.10	.85	19.07	100	19.07	100	
211. Williamsport, Pa.	44,000	(not reporting)													
212. Stamford, Conn.[29]	43,800	91,721,868	75	25	Jan. 1	Sept. 1	18.94	10.83	.75		30.52	100	30.52	60	
213. Butte, Mont.	43,600	(not reporting)													
214. Everett, Mass.	43,300	(not reporting)													
215. Salem, Mass.	43,000	57,480,300	81	19	Jan. 1	Sept. 1	19.76	8.71	1.65	1.18	31.30	100	31.30	100	
216. Rock Island, Ill.	42,700	24,105,768	75	55	April 1	Mar. 1	13.10	20.00	6.00	3.00	42.10	100	42.10	50	
217. Dubuque, Iowa	42,300	46,868,508	75	25	April 1	Jan. 1	14.93	12.40	7.42	2.25	37.00	100	37.00	70	
218. Council Bluffs, Iowa	42,100	(not reporting)													
219. Phoenix, Ariz.	42,100	55,057,854	70	30	July 1	Oct. 10	15.80	13.80	15.20	7.70	31.50	60	52.50	50	
220. Joliet, Ill.	41,900	1,097,398	80	20	Jan. 1	Jan. 1	14.10	27.50	8.10	3.00	52.70	100	52.70	60	
221. Portsmouth, Ohio	41,200	(not reporting)													

COMPARATIVE TAX RATES OF 237 CITIES OVER 30,000 FOR 1928—Continued

City	Census July 1, 1928	Assessed valuation	Realty %	Personalty %	City fiscal year begins	Date of collection of city tax	City	School	County	State	Total	Legal basis of assessment (per cent)	Adjusted tax rate to uniform 100% basis of assessment	Estimated ratio of assessed value to legal basis (per cent)	Final readjusted tax rate
222. West New York, N. J.	40,900	(not reporting)				{ June 1 / Dec. 1 }	19.70	12.50	9.70	4.30	46.20	100	46.20	80	36.96
223. New Brunswick, N. J.	40,800	42,488,035	91	9	Jan. 1	{ June 1 / Nov. }	10.00	9.45	3.60	2.33	25.38	100	25.38	90	22.84
224. Taunton, Mass.	40,600	(not reporting)	67	33											
225. Kokomo, Ind.	40,400	38,605,295	83	17	Jan. 1	Dec. 15	8.33	13.58	11.88	.61	34.40	100	34.40	70	24.08
226. Quincy, Ill.	39,800	(not reporting)				Dec. 1									
227. Superior, Wis.	39,671	43,608,988	80	20	Jan. 1	{ Dec. 1 / June 1 }	6.55	12.67	3.43	.85	23.50	100	23.50	70	16.45
228. East ———, Ohio	39,400	92,310,160			Jan. 1	June 1	11.00	16.40	4.30	3.50	35.20	100	35.20	60	21.12
229. ———, N. C.	39,100	(not reporting)	73	27	Jan. 1	Sept. 1									
230. ———, Utah	39,100	40,443,120	100		Jan. 1	Feb. 15	19.56	8.38*	9.02		36.96	100	36.96	80	29.57
231. Poughkeepsie, N. Y.[3]	39,100	46,632,750	72	28	Jan. 1	Jan. 1	14.50	13.80	4.00	3.00	35.30	100	35.30	60	21.18
232. Danville, Ill.	38,800	31,298,311	93	7	May 1	Sept. 15	13.50	10.00			23.50	100	23.50	60	14.10
233. ———, Va.	38,600	43,500,000			Jan. 1	July 1	13.50	15.00	7.00		35.50	100	35.50	50	17.75
234. Easton, Pa.	38,400	39,390,166	100		Jan. 1	April 1	13.00	24.00		8.91	45.91	100	45.91	50	22.96
235. ———, Pa.	38,300	29,275,062	93	7	July 1	July 1	18.53	6.47*			25.00	100	25.00	75	18.75
236. Petersburg, Va.	37,800	29,632,500	90	10			16.00	5.50	2.00	7.00	30.50	100	30.50	67	20.44
237. ———, R. I.	37,500	(not reporting)													
238. Waterloo, Iowa	37,100	(not reporting)													
239. Meriden, Conn.	37,100	(not reporting)													
240. Waltham, Mass.	37,100	(not reporting)													
241. Lewiston, Me.	36,500	34,235,990	70	30	Mar. 1	Aug. 21	21.61	11.60	5.12	4.27	42.60	100	42.60	80	34.08
242. Orange, N. J.	36,500	44,066,644	93	7	Jan. 1	{ June 1 / Dec. 1 }	20.63	13.82	6.05	5.90	46.40	100	46.40	80	37.12
243. ———, N. J.[3]	36,200	42,211,250	90	10	Jan. 1	{ June 1 / Dec. 1 }	15.28	19.11	12.04		46.43	100	46.43	60	27.86
244. Amsterdam, N. Y.	36,200	30,905,012	100		Jan. 1	{ Aug. 1 / July 1 }	12.00	19.00	4.00		35.00	100	35.00	33	11.55
245. Norristown, Pa.	36,200	25,107,775	92	8	Jan. 1	July 1	7.00	10.05	3.50	.86	21.40	100	21.40	90	19.26
246. Warren, Ohio	36,100	74,518,780	90	10	Jan. 1	Dec. 20	11.18	10.40	8.43		30.00	100	30.00	80	24.00
247. Green Bay, Wis.[3]	36,100	52,009,335	79	21	Jan. 1	Mar. 21	14.00	15.75	7.95	3.84	41.54	100	41.54	80	33.23
248. ———, Colo.	36,000	41,270,910	83	17	Jan. 1	{ Jan. / July }	11.30	4.25	8.07		23.62	100	23.62	98	23.15
249. Revere, Mass.	36,000	(not reporting)													
250. Elgin, Ill.[3]	35,700	52,246,971	100		July 1	{ July 1 / Mar. 15 }	15.30	20.00	3.00	6.00	44.30	100	44.30	60	26.58
251. Auburn, N. Y.[3]	35,600	24,773,885	70	30	April 1	Jan. 1	15.52	10.57	4.64	.65	31.38	100	31.38	65	20.46
252. Moline, Ill.	35,600	48,484,126	81	19	Jan. 1	{ June 1 / Dec. 1 }	15.15	11.40	7.78	1.50	35.83	100	35.83	100	35.83
253. Sheboygan, Wis.	35,100	71,521,757	87	13	Jan. 1										
254. Irvington, N. J.	34,600	(not reporting)													
255. Anderson, Ind.	34,600	(not reporting)													
256. Cumberland, Md.	34,400	46,000,000	70	30	Apr. 1	July 25	10.00	4.75	9.95	2.56	27.26	100	27.26	65	17.72

City	Population	Assessed valuation													
257. Montclair, N. J.	33,700	102,108,051	93	7	Jan. 1	{June 1 / Dec. 1}	14.60	9.50	7.74	1.66	33.50	100	33.50	90	3
258. Watertown, N. Y.	33,700	44,941,575	100	..	July 1	July 1	15.60	9.80	8.76	1.44	35.60	100	35.60	80	2
259. Marion, Ohio	33,400	49,291,430	64	36	Jan. 1	June 1	9.40	9.07	4.28	.85	23.60	100	23.60	100	2
260. Oshkosh, Wis.[3]	33,200	59,916,285	82	18	Jan. 1	Dec. 1	12.05	8.74	5.71	...	26.50	100	26.50	80	2
261. Muskogee, Okla.	33,200	29,333,582	80	20	July 1	{June 1 / Nov. 1}	15.33	4.87	9.69	2.50	42.33	100	42.33	60	2
262. Port Arthur, Texas	33,000	30,760,500	78	22	April 1	{June 1 / Oct. 1}	18.40	6.50	6.30	6.40	37.60	100	37.60	70	2
263. Steubenville, Ohio	32,600	78,400,000	70	30	Jan. 1	{June 20 / Dec. 21}	4.85	9.25	5.12	.85	20.07	100	20.07	85	1
264. Mansfield, Ohio	32,500	73,009,880	74	26	Jan. 1	{Jan. 20 / Dec. 20}	6.80	8.90	4.85	.85	21.40	100	21.40	00	
265. Plainfield, N. J.	32,500	55,815,627	88	12	Jan. 1	{June 1 / Dec. 1}	17.50	11.40	4.80	4.30	38.00	100	38.00	60	2
266. Alameda, Calif.	32,400	29,139,500	55	15	July 1, '27	Oct. 15, '27	37.58	7.92	8.70	...	54.20	100	54.20	56	3
267. Kearny, N. J.	32,100	72,059,701	82	18	Jan. 1	{June 1 / Dec. 1}	11.45	10.22	8.11	4.67	34.45	100	34.45	70	2
268. Fort Smith, Ark.	32,100	(not reporting)	80	20	Sept. 1	Sept. 1	12.60	3.60	0.90		27.10	100	27.10	75	2
269. Asheville, N. C.	32,000	100,000,000	90	10	June 1	June 1	11.20	7.77	5.23	2.55	26.75	100	26.75	00	2
270. Hagerstown, Md.	32,000	38,550,400	72	28		{June / Dec. / Mar. 1}	4.69	6.73	3.10	.85	15.37	100	15.37	85	2
271. Middletown, Ohio	31,900	75,699,190	75		Jan. 1	{Jan. 1 / July 1}	13.27	15.74	4.01	3.15	36.17	100	36.17	70	2
272. Sioux Falls, S. D.	31,200	44,280,033		25	Jan. 1	Jan. 1	15.26	13.36	1.35	6.24	36.21	100	36.21	67	2
273. Rome, N. Y.	31,100	27,906,029	100	..	Jan. 1	July 1	11.50	11.10	5.80	...	28.40	100	28.40	65	1
274. Raleigh, N. C.	31,000	51,715,748	74	26	June 1	{Sept. 20 / May 1}	12.50	12.20	4.20	2.30	31.20	100	31.20	00	3
275. Richmond, Ind.	31,000	30,495,933	80	20	Jan. 1	Jan. 1	7.60	8.90	6.00	1.30	23.80	100	23.80	00	2
276. Clarksburg, W. Va.	30,900	50,588,378	75	25	July 1	{Oct. 1 / Nov. 30}	34.25	22.50	4.50	4.33	65.58	100	65.58	28	1
277. Great Falls, Mont.	30,900	49,215,445	75	25	July 1	{May 31 / Nov. 30}	8.06	7.19	6.04	.85	22.14	100	22.14	00	1
278. Norwood, Ohio	30,800	72,490,000	85	15*	Jan. 1	{June 1 / Dec. 1}	13.90	15.70	6.85	3.26	39.71	100	39.71	00	3
279. Port Huron, Mich.	30,700	37,972,835	85	15	May 1	Dec. 1	16.95	13.75	3.30	3.00	37.00	100	37.00	60	2
280. Bloomington, Ill.	30,700	28,700,000	74	26	May 1	Mar. 1								60	2
281. Newark, Ohio	30,500	(not reporting)													
282. Zanesville, Ohio	30,400	(not reporting)													
283. La Crosse, Wis.	30,400	(not reporting)													
284. Newburgh, N. Y.[3]	30,400	38,927,376	100	..	Jan. 1	{Mar. 16 / Sept. 15}	24.60	8.80	0.41		33.81	100	33.81	60	2
285. Norwalk, Conn.	30,100	(not reporting)													
286. Nashua, N. H.	30,000	(not reporting)													
Canadian Cities															
1. Montreal, Que.[79]	699,500	836,873,420	100	..	Jan. 1	{May 1 / Oct. 1}	13.50	7.00			20.50	100	20.50	100	2
2. Toronto, Ont.[80]	588,742	926,027,622	100	..	Jan. 1	{May 1 / July 4}	21.90	9.90			31.80	100	31.80	75	2
3. Winnipeg, Man.[31]	202,377	227,862,310	100	07	Jan. 1	{Sept. 4 / June 15}	27.13	3.53			30.66		31.00	100	2
4. Vancouver, B. C.[32]	142,150	232,335,046	100	16	Jan. 1	Aug. 3	14.34	9.84			24.18	78	31.00	100	2
5. Quebec, Que.[33]	133,000	102,928,689	100	30	May 1	Nov. 1	21.30	9.50			30.80	00	30.80	80	2

COMPARATIVE TAX RATES OF 237 CITIES OVER 30,000 FOR 1928—Continued

	Census July 1, 1928	Assessed valuation	Per cent Realty	Per cent Personality	City fiscal year begins	Date of collection of city taxes	Tax rate per $1,000 of assessed valuation — City	School	County	State	Total	Legal basis of assessment (per cent)	Adjusted tax rate to uniform 100% basis of assessment	Estimated ratio of assessed value to legal basis (per cent)	Final readjusted tax rate
6. Hamilton, Ont.	127,447	153,619,250	100	....	Jan. 1	{June 1, Sept. 1	20.90	12.60	....	....	33.50	100	33.50	100	33.50
7. Ottawa, Ont.[34]	122,731	145,838,403	100	....	Jan. 1	{June 18, Nov. 18	20.75	10.95	....	....	31.70	100	31.70	67	21.24
8. Calgary, Alta.[35]	72,500	55,608,939	100	....	Jan. 1	{June, Aug., Oct.	22.30	22.70	....	....	45.00	80*	36.00	100	36.00
9. London, Ont.	68,404	77,824,099	100	....	Jan. 1	{June 18, Aug. 18, Oct. 18	21.40	14.21	....	....	35.61	100	35.61	80	28.49
10. Edmonton, Alta.[36]	67,063	59,766,310	100	....	Jan. 1	{May, July, Oct., Dec.	24.30	22.70	....	....	47.00	78	36.66	100	36.66
11. Windsor, Ont.	66,893	74,458,509	100	....	Jan. 1	June 15	18.60	16.40	....	....	35.00	100	35.00	60	21.00
12. Halifax, N.S.[37]	55,000	54,247,850	100	....	May 1	Oct. 15	23.80	10.80	.90	....	35.50	100	35.50	80	28.40
13. St. John, N. B.	55,000	51,004,300	100	....	Jan. 1	{May 1, Sept. 1	9.40	12.20	8.00	....	29.60	100	29.60	100	29.60
14. Verdun, Que.	47,000	(not reporting)		....		{Jan., Aug., Oct.									
15. Victoria, B. C.[38]	42,000	53,116,291	100	....	Jan. 1	Aug. 15	28.83	12.17	....	....	41.00	74	30.34	100	30.34
16. Regina, Sask.[39]	42,000	40,616,695	100	....	Jan. 1	{June 30, Dec. 31	20.41	18.30	....	1.59	40.30	81	32.64	68	22.19
17. Sou. Vancouver, B. C.[40]	40,000	24,651,239	100	....	Jan. 1	Jan. 1	22.82	27.18	....	....	50.00	65	32.50	75	24.38
18. Three Rivers, Que.	36,500	(not reporting)													
19. Hull, Que.	35,233	(not reporting)													
20. Saskatoon, Sask.	33,000	(not reporting)													

* Estimated.

[1] *New York City.* The assessed valuation is exclusive of $916,384,320 of dwellings exempted from local taxation until 1932 but assessed for state tax. The official computation gives a single rate for city, school and county purposes; the county rate is computed upon the same basis as when it was levied on the boroughs; the rates for city and school are in proportion to appropriations. In addition to the rate given, levies are made on the several boroughs and city at large for local improvements. The estimated ratio of assessed to true value is based upon the state equalization table.

[2] *Chicago.* The figures given are 1927 valuation and 1928 tax levy. The city rate includes sanitary district and south park district rates, the rate given being for the south park district (central business section and greater part of south side). Rates in other parts of the city are slightly higher because of variations in the park rate.

[3] *Philadelphia.* The city rate includes the cost of county government, which is consolidated with the city. The rates given are on city realty, comprising 95 per cent of all realty; suburban realty (4½ per cent of all realty) is taxed at two-thirds, and farm realty (½ per cent) at one-half the rate on city realty,—except that property in independent poor districts (having local poor taxes) is further relieved of such poor taxes. Money at interest and vehicles to hire, comprising the personalty valuation, are taxed at 4 mills. There is no state tax in Pennsylvania on property subject to local taxation.

[4] *Los Angeles.* The population is a local estimate. The city rate includes flood control, 80 cents. There is no state tax on real estate in California.

[5] *Cleveland.* The school rate, for all Ohio cities, includes a state rate for schools of $2.65, collected by the county and distributed to the school districts.

[6] *Baltimore.* There is no county rate. There are several rates applied to different bases of valuation (see 1926 tabulation for details, December, 1926, REVIEW). Personal property of manufacturers is exempt from taxation.

[7] *Pittsburgh and Scranton.* The city rate upon improvements is one-half the rate upon land, the rate shown being the weighted average of the two rates. Machinery is exempt from taxation.

[8] *San Francisco.* The city rate includes the county, which is consolidated with the city. The assessed valuation reported does not include "operative property" taxed by the state only. Of the valuation reported, $88,455,023 unsecured personal property has a rate of $38.

[9] *Washington.* Appropriations for the District of Columbia are made by Congress, a lump sum of $9,000,000 thereof being paid by the federal treasury. Intangible personalty, $495,908,396, included in the valuation reported, is taxed at one-half of one per cent. Banks, trust companies and public service corporations are taxed at various rates on earnings or receipts. There is a single rate for all purposes, the school rate being estimated.

[10] *Newark.* The state rate includes a $2.66 school tax, which is returned to the local schools.

[11] *Minneapolis, St. Paul, Duluth.* The Minnesota statutes provide for five classes of property, assessed at varying bases of true value: real estate (except unplatted) is assessed at 40 per cent; iron ore at 50 per cent; personalty, in three classes, is assessed at 10 per cent, 25 per cent, and 33⅓ per cent, respectively. The average of all is as reported. Money and credits (not included in the valuation reported) are taxed at 3 mills on the dollar. The total rate in Minneapolis varies slightly in various wards due to varying rates for street maintenance.

[12] *Kansas City, Mo.* The valuation given is for city tax purposes; the valuation of real estate used for school, county and state purposes is about one-third larger. The rates shown are adjusted to the city valuation basis. In addition, a $2.50 park and boulevard maintenance tax on land only is levied, equivalent to a tax of 38 cents on the total valuation.

[13] *Louisville.* Of the valuation reported, $23,500,000 stock of banks, trust and life insurance companies is taxed $2 per $1,000 for city and $4 for schools. Unmanufactured agricultural products, $5,000,000, are taxed $1.50 per $1,000 for city purposes.

[14] *Portland.* The school rate includes $2.15 county school levy, and $2.20 state elementary school levy, which are returned to the local school districts.

[15] *Providence.* There is no county government in Rhode Island. In addition to the rate given, $4 per $1,000 is levied on intangible personalty.

[16] *Oakland.* The city rate includes $4.10 water utility district rate.

[17] *Richmond.* The cities of Virginia are autonomous, having no county government.

[18] *Dayton.* The city rate includes $2.07, and the county rate, $.24, flood prevention.

[19] *Miami.* Rates of $24 per $1,000 for school, $47.50 for county and road, and $9 for state, are levied upon separate valuations but are readjusted to the city valuation reported.

[20] *Des Moines.* Taxable values in Iowa are one-quarter of assessed values. Moneys and credits, assessed at $32,001,959, not included in the valuation reported are taxed at 5 mills.

[21] *Wilmington.* The valuation shown includes $2,388,000 public service corporation property which is taxed at $39 for city purposes and $8.50 for school purposes. The state tax is for schools.

[22] *Cambridge.* The state rate includes metropolitan sewer and park rate.

[23] *Albany, Utica, Charleston, Binghamton, New Britain, Niagara Falls, Jamestown, Poughkeepsie, Amsterdam, Green Bay, Auburn, Oshkosh, Newburgh.* The county rate includes state rate, the separation not being reported.

[24] *Tampa.* Rates of $30 per $1,000 for school, $20 for county, and $7.50 for state, are levied upon separate valuations but are readjusted to the city valuation reported.

[25] *Lowell, Hoboken.* The city rate includes schools, the separation not being reported.

[26] *Shreveport.* Valuation along river pays an additional levy of $5 for levee protection.

[27] *Columbia.* The county rate includes schools, the separation not being reported.

[28] *Stamford.* The city rate is the weighted average of the city and town rates on their respective valuations; the school rate is estimated.

[29] *Montreal.* The valuation is for 1927. The school rate reported is the Catholic rate; the Protestant rate is $10, and the neutral rate, $12, the average of all being $9.36.

[30] *Toronto.* Realty valuation includes 10.4 per cent business and 6.6 per cent income. Dwellings up to $4,000 valuation are allowed a certain exemption from general taxation but not school taxation. The school rate given is the public school rate; the separate school rate is $14.25.

[31] *Winnipeg.* Land, valued at $114,859,300, is assessed at 100 per cent; buildings are assessed at 66⅔ per cent; the ratio of rateable assessment to the total valuation is 85.8 per cent.

[32] *Vancouver.* Land, assessed at $128,010,071, is taxed at 100 per cent; improvements, assessed at $104,324,975, are taxed at 50 per cent; the ratio of taxable valuation to the total is 77.5 per cent. The actual tax levy is $34.44, but was reported $30.91 because over 93 per cent was paid before the expiration of a 10 per cent discount period.

[33] *Quebec.* The city rate includes $5 for water paid by $44,504,260 valuation which is exempt from general taxation.

[34] *Ottawa.* The school rate given is the public school rate; the separate school rate is $17.05.

[35] *Calgary.* Land is assessed at 100 per cent, improvements at 50 per cent; in addition to the rate shown there is a $2 levy on land only for provincial purposes.

[36] *Edmonton.* Land, valued at $34,542,170, is assessed at 100 per cent; improvements are assessed at 60 per cent; the ratio of taxable to true valuation is 78 per cent.

[37] *Halifax.* Realty valuation includes 13.5 per cent business, and 4.8 per cent household, assessment.

[38] *Victoria.* Land is assessed at 100 per cent, improvements at 50 per cent, the ratio of taxable to the total valuation being 74 per cent.

[39] *Regina.* Realty valuation includes 15 per cent business and income. Land, valued at $22,506,260, is assessed at 100 per cent; improvements, at 60 per cent. The separate school rate is $5.90 higher than the public school rate reported, on a valuation of $3,046,936.

[40] *South Vancouver.* Land, valued at $11,526,411, is assessed at 100 per cent; improvements, at 50 per cent.

RECENT BOOKS REVIEWED

THE NATIONAL BUDGET SYSTEM. By W. F. Willoughby, Director, Institute for Government Research. Baltimore, Md.: Johns Hopkins Press, 1927. Pp. 343.

It is eminently fitting that one who did pioneer service in arousing the national government to a realization of the imperative need for reform in financial procedure should review the results of the first five years under the national budget and suggest changes for its improvement.

The central purpose of the study appears to be to describe the financial procedure of the national government as it exists today under the Budget and Accounting Act of 1921. The book opens with an historical sketch of the movement for the adoption of a national budget system and a description of the special agencies established and the adjustments made by Congress to facilitate the consideration of the budget proposals. Parts two, three, and four deal with the formulation of the budget, action upon the budget by Congress, and execution of the budget. The author proceeds to the suggestion of modifications which, in his judgment, would tend to improve the budget system. The description is accurate and detailed, the suggestions well-reasoned and thought-provoking.

Dr. Willoughby points out that "the five years that the new budget system has been in operation have been years of retrenchment, when every effort has been made to curtail government activities and reduce expenditures." In a period of expansion of government activities, the assumption of a retrenchment policy by the chief executive in the hope that it would prove politically advantageous might cause a serious breach between the executive and legislative branches. There is no denying that the attempt which has been made to adapt a British custom to the exigencies of the American political system (pp. 140–142, 152–155) has been partially successful, but it is submitted that perfection shall not be claimed for even the basic principles of a new institution so foreign in its conception to our separation of powers, until it has been tried in a fire of more consuming force (p. 286). The picture of an embattled treasury defended by a militant president against the assaults of Congress is repeatedly brought forward (pp. 9, 26, 97, 184). While this may have been a true picture during the five years just past, we may well witness a complete reversal of policy at no far distant date. With the rapid reduction of the public debt and the present tendency of Congress to rely less and less upon direct taxation, we may expect a more vigorous demand for expansion of federal activities. Where does the budget system stand in such a program? There is no denying that Congress has reluctantly relinquished (temporarily) its power to initiate appropriations (pp. 22, 49), but there is no assurance that this will not be resumed. Under the present system it is the president, acting through his Bureau of the Budget, who actually fixes the final amount which may be expended by the various organization units of the government under his control (pp. 175–187), except Congress itself and the judiciary. It is submitted that this may, in the last analysis, well be held to be an unconstitutional delegation of legislative power to the executive. Similar questions are now being raised in the states.

In his suggestions for the improvement of the system the author advocates the withdrawal of the Bureau of the Budget from the Treasury Department and its allocation to the office of the President. He suggests that the Bureau of Efficiency, the General Supply Committee, the Public Building Commission, and the Joint Committee on Printing should be abolished and their duties transferred to the Bureau of the Budget. This recommendation is made on the ground that the Bureau should be recognized as the sole agency of general administration. To be consistent, such a suggestion might also call for a merging of the Civil Service Commission and the Personnel Classification Board with the general administrative agency. If logically carried out, such a plan would probably elevate the Bureau into just such a "super-cabinet" position as was feared by Congress when the budget plan was first broached (pp. 40). It would seem to some that a combination of the General Accounting Office with the Bureau of the Budget, under the comptroller general would probably offer a solution more in harmony with our political traditions—for the purpose of overseeing administration and reporting to Congress upon the manner in which its appropriations have been expended.

The remaining suggestions are equally stimulating. Supplementary budgets for revenue-producing enterprises, the placing of the District of Columbia budget in the hands of the District Commissioners, the improvement of the appropriation system by the abolition of permanent appropriations, changes in the treatment of unexpended balances, the financing of supply services and the revision of appropriation heads and the phraseology of appropriation acts, and the improvement of the accounting and reporting system are all important reforms which would tend to make the budget more intelligible to the public. In a democracy, that should be the chief aim of a budget—not uncompromising economy.

HARVEY WALKER.

Ohio State University.

✦

ZONING CASES IN THE UNITED STATES. By Edward M. Bassett and Frank B. Williams. New York: Regional Plan of New York and its Environs, 1928. Pp. 57.

Someone has said that one half of city planning is salesmanship. Of its branch, zoning, one half is the law. In the field of zoning the conflict is between the individualist and group action for the common good, with the lawyer appearing as the hired assassin or the defender of the fair. The technician helplessly looks on as his perfect creation is pushed about, an ear lopped off or mayhap the torso truncated by these skilled adversaries, with the court as umpire.

In the twelve years since zoning was first adopted in the United States the zoning battle has been waged with over six hundred engagements in the courts of sufficient importance to be cited in this first exhaustive listing of its legal progress. These cases are now classified for speedy reference under forty-two heads according to subject matter, with an equally long index by states and another of all cases arranged alphabetically. Not light reading this, nor with an easily discernible plot, but the progress of civilization itself is hinted at in some of the headings, such as the first one: "Billboards, Zoning of, Valid," with a list of cases in which it has been so held.

The present compilation was made as a part of the Regional Survey of New York and will appear as an appendix to Volume VI of the report, but the immediate value of such a guide to legal precedents was deemed so great that the Committee on the Regional Plan of New York

and its Environs decided on its publication separately in advance. It is a high example of the thoroughness and detail with which city planning must be studied in all its phases in order to serve the community efficiently.

ARTHUR C. COMEY.

✦

TAX RATES, ASSESSED VALUATIONS, AND LOCAL INDEBTEDNESS IN MINNESOTA, 1928. Publication No. 24 of the League of Minnesota Municipalities. Compiled by Francis J. Putnam. Pp. 33.

This bulletin is a compilation of bare facts concerning taxation and indebtedness in the State of Minnesota for the year 1928. The report does not attempt to analyze the material beyond the computation of a few percentages and per capita valuations and yields. The first tabulation in the bulletin presents the tax rates and assessed valuations applying in each of 725 cities, villages, and boroughs in the state. In a second tabulation, the League publishes for the first time reports of the outstanding indebtedness of the various municipal subdivisions in the state. This table shows that city and village bonds are outstanding for fifteen different purposes. The statement also includes the amounts held in sinking funds, the net bonds, the warrants outstanding, and the net debt. It is interesting to note that an appreciable number of cities and villages in Minnesota have no debt. A third tabulation sets forth the assessed valuations in the various counties. Valuations here are given under the following heads: unplatted land, platted land, personal property, money and credits. In addition to giving facts on the amount of money yielded by the various taxes and special assessments, columns in this tabulation also set forth the various purposes for which levies are made in the counties and the amount of the levy in each case. The fourth and last tabulation presents a complete picture of the outstanding indebtedness of the various counties in Minnesota.

MARTIN L. FAUST.

✦

THE AMERICAN PARTY BATTLE. By Charles A. Beard. New York: The Macmillan Co., 1928.

This is a paper-covered volume of 150 pages, and is one of the series known as the "World Today Bookshelf." In this little volume Dr. Beard has told the story of the development of American political parties with a zest and brilliance probably not elsewhere equaled. The first chapter, in which he discusses the nature of American political parties, is a real contribution. The subsequent chapters are largely familiar history, told, to be sure, with some new interpretations and in a most entertaining style. But even those who know this history very well, will find plenty of stimulation in the pages of the first chapter.

In it he considers the various theories which have been advanced to explain the bi-partisan alignment, and he pleasantly demolishes all of them. James Madison, Lord Macaulay, Brander Matthews, and James Bryce are all discarded; and he finds the origin of parties in a multitude of forces that almost defy analysis. In a word, he repudiates the simple idea, cloaked under various theories, that "God made Democrats and Republicans, and that is all there is to it."

In the second chapter Dr. Beard begins with the Federalists and the early Republicans, and presently betrays his thesis in a single sentence: "In fact, there has been no sharp break in the sources of party strength, in policy, or in opinion." The implication is that during all these years the battle has been waged between men of the same type as those who took up the cudgels in 1789. He frequently refers to the "Hamilton-Webster-McKinley-Coolidge Party," and speaking of 1896 declares, "In not a single relation did they depart from the traditions of a hundred years" (p. 111). And speaking of the other party he says, "With a fidelity to promises not always observed in American politics, the Democrats under the leadership of President Wilson passed a series of laws that squared fairly well with the historic principles of the Jefferson-Jackson-Bryan heritage" (p. 118).

The point is very well made again and again, and even the most skeptical of readers could hardly run through the pages of this book without feeling that perhaps the great American party battle has not been quite the sham that so many hostile critics busily tell us that it is today.

KIRK H. PORTER.

State University of Iowa.

✳

JUSTICE AND ADMINISTRATIVE LAW, A STUDY OF THE BRITISH CONSTITUTION. By William A. Robson. London: Macmillan and Co., 1928.

Mr. Robson, who is a barrister of Lincoln's Inn and lecturer in law at the London School of Economics, has presented in this book perhaps the best introductory treatment of a problem on which a number of noteworthy studies have appeared in this country within the past year. As Mr. Robson phrases the problem, "The social legislation of the past fifty years has introduced a new element into the Constitution. . . . Large judicial duties of an important character have been given not to persons holding judicial office, not even to known and ascertainable individuals, but to vast departments of the state, huge administrative organs employing thousands of anonymous civil servants. The vital feature of the whole arrangement is the fact that there is no appeal to the regular courts of law."

This problem is of interest to students of municipal government since the developments to which Mr. Robson refers have taken place in the field of control exercised by local as well as by national authorities. Of especial interest in this connection is his reference to the London Building Tribunal (p. 107), which exercises appellate jurisdiction over decisions of the London County Council regarding such questions as the erection of buildings at the rear of existing edifices, the conversion of private buildings into public ones, and questions of building lines, the laying out of streets and the sanctioning of open spaces for working class dwellings. Our own municipal experience suggests in addition the quasi-judicial powers which have been vested in health boards, building inspectors, licensing commissioners, and, more recently, zoning boards.

Practically all of the administrative tribunals concerning which Mr. Robson writes belong, however, to the central government,—the Railway Rates Tribunal, the Ministry of Health, the national health insurance tribunals, the tribunals for unemployment insurance, the Board of Education, the Board of Trade, the Ministry of Transport. Neither this fact, however, nor the fact that Mr. Robson is exclusively concerned with British experience detracts from the value of his book for American students of municipal government. This is because he approaches the subject from the broad standpoint of the general issues involved. His approach is not exclusively or primarily legalistic. While his study is thoroughly fortified with citations of decided cases and quotations from the language of the courts, his primary interest is in understanding the practical meaning and effect of the substitution of administrative agencies for the courts as organs for making decisions of a judicial nature.

To this end he annihilates at the outset the futile attempts which have been made in judicial opinions and elsewhere to draw a clear line of demarcation between administrative and judicial functions, reaching the conclusion that historically the separation of powers is a legend and that practically "neither the executive nor the judiciary has any immutable right to a particular province." The vital point is that any organ exercising powers that can properly be described as judicial should do so with a judicial attitude and in a judicial spirit.

Mr. Robson's most valuable contribution to the discussion of a much discussed subject undoubtedly consists in that large portion of his book in which he develops his conception of the judicial attitude and the judicial mind. He believes that the superior confidence which in the past has been enjoyed by the law-courts, as contrasted with political organs of administration is due to the fact that judges, in contrast with administrative officials, have been able to do their work and to approach the problems brought before them with an attitude fostered and protected by certain attributes of their office which can be summed up as independence from personal responsibility or political control. "The only subordination which the judge knows is that which he owes to the existing body of legal doctrine enunciated by his brothers on the bench and the legislative enactments of the king in Parliament." There is thus made possible the judicial process, a process consisting "in the application of a body of rules or principles by the technique of a special method of thought, and emphasizing consistency, equality, certainty and impartiality." It is Mr. Robson's thesis that this technique should be applied to all decisions of a judicial character by whatever organ they may be made. Tested by these standards he believes that the newer administrative organs of decision suffer from the absence of proper requirements of publicity in their proceedings, from the frequent absence of any requirement of an oral hearing, and from the poor quality and insufficient amount of the evidence on which decisions are often based. On the contrary he believes that experience has shown no ground for distrusting the impartiality of such tribunals or for believing that they are any more liable to political interference than the independent courts of law.

JOHN DICKINSON.

Princeton University.

MUNICIPAL REPORTS

DAYTON, OHIO. *Annual Report for the Year 1927. By F. O. Eichelberger, City Manager. Pp. 55.*—This report of Dayton for 1927 is similar in many respects to those of previous years. The format is changed from year to year only sufficiently to identify it as a new report. As a result, anyone familiar with municipal reports would recognize the Dayton report even though it be unlabeled. This, it would seem, is a desirable feature, for many cities are attempting too many changes in the physical appearance of their reports from year to year, often with disappointing results.

One feature of this report in particular merits high praise. It is a summary of the year's outstanding accomplishments which follows the letter of transmittal, under the caption "A Year's Work." The characteristic of this summary which distinguishes it from the usual attempt of this kind is the good balance maintained between the various activities. The enumerated items, 55 in all, classified upon a departmental basis, are distributed as follows: public service, 16; health and welfare, 13; safety, 7; finance, 5; buildings, 3; and miscellaneous, 11. Many of the summaries in municipal reports observed by the reviewer are devoted almost exclusively to physical improvements rather than to activities having more of a social or welfare purpose.

This report is in many respects an example of good reporting, but like many other reports, it omits several essentials which would have given it a high rating. It makes no effort to emphasize important facts in the text, is utterly devoid of diagrams and charts, fails to include an organization chart, and omits a table of contents. The financial statistics are unsatisfactory—it being necessary to search the cost data out of the text material. Comparative data is conspicuous by its absence. The chief defect of this report, however, as was true with those of previous years, is the distribution of pictures invariably in irrelevant reading material. Under the department of law is found a picture of "vitrolithic concrete paving" and illustrations with reference to sewers and sewage disposal, while under the department of finance appear pictures of the "water works laboratory," and an "interceptor sewer under construction." Finally, while the above criticisms are based largely on arbitrary standards and appear greatly to outweigh the praise, yet it must be said that reports of Dayton have become favorably known wherever municipal reports are read.

DURHAM, NORTH CAROLINA. *Annual Report for the Fiscal Year Ending May 31, 1928. By R. W. Rigsby, City Manager. Pp. 65.*—The distinctive features of this report are the clearness of the financial tables and the general arrangement of the content. The letter of transmittal is followed by a report of the major departments in the order named which occupy the following spaces:·Finance, 10 pages; Public Works, 5; Public Utilities, 6; Public Safety, 17; Public Welfare, 3; Schools, 8; Recreation Commission, 5; and Planning and Zoning, 3.

One is surprised to find but a slight account of the health work carried on in the city. Mention is made on page 53 that the "County Board of Health exercises close supervision and works in cooperation with the city authorities in the health program," and the financial statement on page 11 indicates that an amount in excess of $28,000 was spent by the Division of Health. It would, therefore, seem that the work which such an expenditure would represent should be reported upon in more detail.

Some of the features omitted from this report which would have added greatly to its usefulness and interest are: emphasis upon important facts, charts and graphs, table of contents and an organization chart. The report further fails to give either a summary of outstanding accomplishments or suggested improvements contemplated for the future. In spite of these defects, however, it is well worth the attention of those interested in report writing.

ROANOKE, VIRGINIA. *Annual Report for the Fiscal Year Ending December 31, 1927. By W. P. Hunter, City Manager. Pp. 65.*—This report opens with a letter of transmittal by the city manager in which he lists the major accomplishments of the year and suggests several improvements for the future. This latter feature is too often overlooked in public reporting. The balance of the report deviates from the usual method in that it contains reports prepared and signed by the various department and bureau heads. The reviewer sees no valid reason why such a plan should not be used so long as the material is harmonized and a proper balance is maintained between the various activities.

The report is mainly one of statistics with very little supplementary reading and utterly void of maps, charts, graphs, and pictures, with the exception of two "tax dollar" charts. The good judgment used in the type of statistics selected as well as in their arrangement, however, makes up in a large part for the lack of graphical presentation.

The report is attractive and has a clear and concise table of contents. The arrangement of material is logical and the space allotted to the various activities indicates a well balanced content. Other features include two charts of the Roanoke Tax Dollar,—one as received and the other as spent.

If it is possible to prepare a municipal report based almost entirely upon statistics, and have the result sufficiently interesting to be read by the citizens, the Roanoke report is a good example.

WESTMONT, QUEBEC. *Annual Report for the Year Ending October 31, 1927. By G. W. Thompson, General Manager. Pp. 47.*—This is essentially a financial report. It includes, however, some statistics on work done and activities performed. For example, the last few pages of the report are given over to statistics dealing with police, fire, health, and road department activities. Fully three-fourths of the report, however, is devoted entirely to the finances of the city, leaving but ten pages in which to account for the work represented by the expenditure of a three million dollar budget, —hardly a proper balance of content.

The feature which really stamps this report as unique, however, is the letter of transmittal in which the general manager epitomizes the year's accomplishments on the first four pages of the report. This letter classifies the data under the following headings: Finance, Pension Fund of Police and Firemen, Roads, Electric Light and Power Department, Police, Fire, and Health Departments, Parks and Playgrounds, Library, and Victoria Hall. This method of presentation makes it possible for one to gain a clear perspective of the work accomplished in a minimum of time and if a knowledge of the cost and method of financing the various activities is desired, it can be found in the pages which follow. While this report fails to meet many of the standards arbitrarily established by the reviewer, still it must be appraised as a very good report.

C. E. RIDLEY.

JUDICIAL DECISIONS

EDITED BY C. W. TOOKE

Professor of Law, New York University

The Falmouth Billboard Decision.—A surprising decision is that which involves the efforts of the town of Falmouth, Mass., to get rid of a billboard, *Inspector of Buildings of Falmouth* v. *General Outdoor Advertising Co., Inc.*, decided by the Supreme Court of Massachusetts on June 8, 1928 (161 N. E. Rep., 899; Mass. 1928 Advance Sheets, 1317).

In 1920 the Massachusetts legislature adopted a billboard act, which was approved on May 27, authorizing the Highway Division of the state Department of Public Works to make rules and regulations to "control and restrict" advertising on public ways or within public view, as the legislature may under the 1916 amendment to the Massachusetts constitution (Art. 50). This act (now Mass. Genl. Stat., Ch. 93, §§ 29–33) also provided that towns might "further regulate and restrict billboards by ordinance or by law not inconsistent with said rules and regulations."

Eight days later, on June 4, at the same session the legislature also adopted a zoning law giving cities and towns the usual broad zoning powers with respect to the location of buildings and limitation of their uses (now Mass. Genl. Stat., Ch. 40, §§ 25–33).

In 1924 (Ch. 237) the legislature amended the above billboard law, extending the power of "further regulation and restriction" to cities (in addition to towns) and making another amendment not now material.

In 1925 (Ch. 116) the above zoning powers were extended to "structures and premises" (in addition to buildings).

Meanwhile the Highway Division had laid down certain regulations governing the erection and maintenance of billboards in the state. Then the town of Falmouth, pursuant to the above zoning powers, plus the right of "further regulation and restriction," undertook to zone a certain billboard off the map, the regulation was claimed to be illegal, and this suit was brought to compel the removal of the board.

Instead of seeking to test the legality of the town regulation by asking whether or not the local regulation was inconsistent with the state regulation, the Supreme Court of Massachusetts,

in an opinion by Judge Braley, held that a billboard is not a "structure," and that billboard sites are not "premises," within the meaning of the zoning act. The reason given is that there was a "well coördinated and complete system for the regulation of billboards by the highway division" already in existence. Hence the zoning law could not have intended to permit the zoning of billboards. And this statement is made in the face of the legislative declaration that the billboard law was *not* intended to be "complete," because that law itself provided for "further regulation and restriction" by cities and towns. Aside from this surprising limitation upon the *zoning* powers of cities and towns through a restricted definition of "structures and premises," the opinion is wholly silent on why Falmouth is not authorized to adopt its regulation under the "further regulation and restriction" clause of the *billboard* act. In other words, whereas the town of Falmouth thought its billboard regulation had two legs to stand on—one the *zoning* law and the other the *billboard* law, the court knocks the former out from under the town regulation, and shuts its eyes to the latter.

Edward M. Bassett, counsel to the Zoning Committee in New York, puts his criticism of the Falmouth opinion in a nutshell when he says:

The regulation by the highway division means the same regulation of like advertising devices throughout the state. Such regulations would constitute a state code of regulation. Zoning never interferes with codes. Zoning is regulation supplemental to and separate from codes, and which is different in different districts.

New York State had a tenement house law before it had a zoning enabling act. If Justice Braley's argument were transferred to this state, Buffalo's zoning ordinance could not affect tenement houses. The zoning of Buffalo, of course, does not supersede the tenement house law. But neither does the existence of the tenement house law exempt future tenement houses from the operation of the zoning law.

Applying this same argument to Massachusetts, one might remark: Likewise in Massachusetts, before the zoning law, there were building laws, and they had to be obeyed; but under them a man could put any kind of a building where he pleased. Then came the zoning law, and a man had to put a certain kind of a building where the zoning law allowed; but he still had to obey the building laws. Why not the same with a billboard? "Because a billboard is not a 'structure' under the zoning law," says the court!

The opinion has caused great surprise, and some dismay, among those interested in billboard regulation and in zoning, both in Massachusetts and elsewhere. It seems so unnecessary and so wrong from every angle that one wonders how soon it must be disavowed by the Massachusetts Supreme Court itself. For an extended criticism of the opinion the reader is referred to an article by the present writer in the *Massachusetts Law Quarterly* for August, 1928. That magazine also gives Judge Braley's opinion in full.

ALBERT S. BARD.

Editor's Comment.—At the time the Falmouth case was reported last June, we did not deem it of sufficient importance to be made the subject of a note. So much adverse criticism on the part of competent supporters of the zoning movement has been aroused by this decision, however, that we requested Mr. Bard to prepare for this REVIEW the statement which appears above.

In answer to the position taken, we deem it only just to the court to point out that the attack upon the decision seems to be based on a failure to bear in mind certain fundamental principles of statutory construction. Billboard restriction and regulation and zoning in Massachusetts were authorized by *separate* constitutional amendments, both adopted at the same time. As appears from the opinion, in exercising these separate powers the legislature at the session of 1920 enacted two separate statutes: one delegating to the Highway Division of the Department of Public Works the power to make rules and regulations concerning billboards and giving subordinate powers of regulation to the towns, subject to the approval of the Division; and the other conferring upon towns the power to pass zoning ordinances, subject to notice to and hearing of property owners and the approval of the Attorney General. It seems plain that the will of the people as expressed in the two amendments was that the two powers be kept distinct and, so far as the effect of the two separate statutes is concerned, the legislature clearly intended to make each delegated power exclusive of the other. It is an elementary rule that where a delegated power is to be exercised in a prescribed manner,

it can be exercised in no other way. Thus the two acts and the delegated powers by every canon of statutory construction applicable thereto were mutually exclusive one of the other. Billboards clearly were not included in the term "structures" in the zoning statute.

But the objection is made that subsequently, in 1924, the billboard act was amended, removing the requirement of approval of a municipal ordinance by the Division. It must be remembered, however, that the power of towns and cities to regulate billboards still remained subject to the restriction that any ordinance adopted should not be inconsistent with the rules and regulations promulgated by the Division. It is difficult to see, therefore, how this amendment could have had the effect of destroying the mutually exclusive character of the delegated powers. Now the fundamental rule, applied uniformly in all the states, even in those where the broadest home-rule powers are given to municipalities, is that in a field of concurrent powers, any statute which covers part of the field to that extent nullifies the existing local power to legislate on the same subject, and if it appears that the intention of the legislature is to cover the entire field, the local power falls in abeyance. This necessary principle has been repeatedly applied to the regulation of traffic in streets and highways. While it does not appear from the opinion how extensively the Division covered the field, we may assume on the authority of Mr. Bassett that it had adopted a code, a complete plan covering the entire field. It may seem unfortunate that the subordinate power to regulate billboards conferred upon towns and cities in Massachusetts should be subject to this principle of construction, but the fault lies not with the court, but with the legislature, which could have made it inapplicable by an express clause to that end. The effect of such legislative exception would, however, probably prove disastrous in destroying uniformity in a matter vitally concerning the property rights of individuals. From any point of view, it seems to the writer especially unfortunate that the shortcomings of the legislative branch should be made the basis of adverse criticism of the courts when they are compelled to apply the established principles of construction to the plain provisions of the statutes.

✤

Legislative Control—Constitutional Limitation Requiring General Laws.—In the absence of constitutional limitation, the control of the state legislature over the incorporation and powers of municipal corporations is plenary. Of the methods adopted to curb the abuse of the power of special legislation, the most common is the constitutional requirement that laws relating to municipal corporations shall be general. In New Jersey the inhibition is against special legislation regulating the internal affairs of municipal corporations, a clause that has given rise to more litigation than any other in the constitution. Beginning with the important decision of *Van Riper* v. *Parsons* (40 N. J. L. 1, 123), in which Beasley, J., wrote one of his great opinions, the courts of New Jersey have worked out the definition of general law with unusual clarity. The decisions point out that the basis of classification must be a substantial distinction, having reference to the subject matter of the proposed legislation, between the objects or places embraced in such legislation and those excluded. The marks of distinction on which the classification is founded must be such in the nature of things as will, in some measurable degree at least, account for or justify the restriction of the legislation in question.

Notwithstanding this plain principle, the legislature of New Jersey is induced time and again to enact statutes that fall within the inhibition. The latest statute to be declared unconstitutional by the Supreme Court of New Jersey is *Board of Tenement House Supervision* v. *Mittleman*, 141. A. 571, which defined tenement houses, to which its provisions applied, as those buildings leased to three separate families, except that in cities bordering on the Atlantic Ocean the test was fixed at more than three independent families. The court finds nothing peculiar to the latter class of cities that would justify such discrimination. The fact that cities on the Atlantic coast are summer resorts is not a basis for according to them special exemptions in the matter of tenement house regulation.

Eminent Domain—Excess Condemnation.—The principle that the exercise of the delegated power of eminent domain is, in the absence of express constitutional authority, limited by the public necessity, is well illustrated in the case of the *Appeal of the Philadelphia Felt Co.*, 143 A. 208, recently decided by the Supreme Court of Pennsylvania. The park commissioners proceeded to condemn a portion of appellant's lands to enlarge Tacony Creek Park. The land bordered on Frankford Creek above a dam which the company had maintained for some forty years to impound water for use in its mill. The company laid as an item of damages interference with its water rights, which the park commissioners by resolution of record disclaimed. Upon this state of facts the board of viewers found that the company's right to maintain its dam and to flood the lands appropriated was not taken in the condemnation proceedings, to which finding the company filed exceptions, which brought up this question on appeal.

Frazer, J., in writing the opinion of the court which dismissed the appeal, points out that the power to condemn must be based on legislative authority, that the discretion of the body acting is strictly limited by the terms of the statute, and that in no event may the legislature authorize the appropriation of more land or of a greater interest in land than the public necessity requires. It approves the following statement of the limitation upon the city's authority taken from the opinion of the court in *Wilson* v. *Scranton City*, 141 Pa. 621, 21 A. 779:

> It was not obliged, nor in strictness was it authorized, to take more than was actually necessary for its purpose. The limit of the public right is the public necessity, and the residue, as it may be called, of the use of the land remains unaffected in the owner. The extent of such residue depends on the nature of the public use, and that may vary all the way from the exclusive occupation for a schoolhouse or public building to the easement of running a gas pipe underneath or a telegraph wire overhead. The city was therefore entitled to show the extent of its actual taking. This, however, could be shown only by corporate action. The city would not be bound by the opinions of experts, even of the city engineer, as to the amount of interest in the land that should be taken. That was within its own discretion, provided, of course, it did not exceed the limits of necessity for its purpose. The plaintiff was entitled to have its intention shown by action binding on the corporation, and put on the record in such form as to give him a cause of action in case the city officials should at any future time attempt to do anything in excess of their privileges actually acquired and paid for.

For a case illustrating the application of these principles to excess condemnation, the reader may be referred to *Pennsylvania Life Ins. Co.* v. *Philadelphia*, 242 Pa. 47, 88 A. 904, 49 L. R. A. (N. S.) 1062, which sets forth the necessity of constitutional amendments to authorize such a proceeding.

Bonds; Necessity of Complying with Prescribed Formalities.—In *Pollard* v. *City of Norwalk*, 142 A. 807, the Supreme Court of Errors of

Connecticut had before it an action brought by a taxpayer seeking a declaratory judgment whether certain bonds which the defendant was about to issue were legal and binding. The statute authorizing the bonds provided that the issue must be approved by a majority of the electors voting at the city and town election of 1927. The warning or notice of the proposed action was published only thirteen days before the election, whereas the charter required fifteen days' notice. In declaring the proposed issue invalid, the court points out the fundamental rule governing the procedure of the New England town meeting that no valid act can be passed without due warning. (*Brooklyn Trust Co.* v. *Hebron*, 51 Conn. 22; *Bloomfield* v. *Charter Oak Bank*, 121 U. S. 121.)

In *Rogers County* v. *Bristow Battery Co.*, 28 Fed. (2d) 195, decided September 10, 1928, the District Court, N. D. Oklahoma, held that the validity of bonds issued by a municipality of that state could not be attacked after the lapse of thirty days from the final act of authentication. The bonds in question had been declared void by the Supreme Court of Oklahoma (*Bristow*

Battery Co. v. *Payne*, 123 Okl. 137) in a tax-payer's action on the ground that they had been issued to refund invalid warrants after the constitutional debt limit had been reached. The federal court holds, however, that in the hands of a bona fide holder for value, the city is estopped to assert that the bonds created an indebtedness in excess of the constitutional limitation. The statutes of Oklahoma provide that before a refunding issue may be authorized, the validity of the warrants must be determined by the state district court and approved by the Attorney General, after which the taxpayer is given thirty days in which to prosecute an appeal. The latter provision is construed by the court to constitute a short statute of limitations, upon the running of which the adjudication of the district court is *res adjudicata*, and not subject to subsequent attack. The laches of the taxpayer in contesting the action is a bar to the attack of a taxpayer after the bonds are in the hands of bona fide holders for value.

The decision of the instant case is an extension of the doctrine of estoppel by recitals developed by the United States Supreme Court.

PUBLIC UTILITIES

EDITED BY JOHN BAUER

Director, American Public Utilities Bureau

O'Fallon Case Before the Supreme Court.— The St. Louis and O'Fallon case will probably be argued before the Supreme Court of the United States during January or February, 1929. It involves the fundamental issues of effective regulation of railroads, in the interest of the public at large, and, we believe, should be regarded with more than passing interest by public-minded citizens and groups. The decision will either bring victory to the long struggle for definite and workable railroad rate regulation, or will render practically useless the ten-year valuation job of the Interstate Commerce Commission, and make the entire system of regulation unworkable because of the difficulties of administration and because of unsound financial basis of control.

We have discussed the case before in this department. We shall present the issues briefly again, with the object of urging municipalities and public-minded groups to join in supporting the Interstate Commerce Commission. We believe that such action is practicable, and is necessary to emphasize the public aspects of the case. The City of New York, through its law department, will present a brief as *amicus curiae* supporting the Commission. Other cities should do likewise. They might join New York, or present a special memorandum prepared for collective signature. In the interest of such common action, we shall prepare a memorandum, and make it available without cost (except voluntary contributions for printing and other necessary expenses) to all public groups which may wish to coöperate in this important matter. We shall disregard the particular facts and special interests, and confine the discussion to the large public aspects involved in the particular case.

The fundamental issue is the basis of valuation that may or must be employed for the purpose of railroad rate-making (unless the decision should rest upon more incidental points, and thus follow the lower federal court). The Supreme Court is likely to decide, once for all, whether the general plan of regulation in the 1920 Transportation Act, as worked out practically by the Interstate Commerce Commission, will be approved and adopted in the administrative processes, or whether the Commission will be forced back permanently to undefined and indefinite methods. The question is, whether the "fair value" upon which the return to a railroad is predicated can be absolutely defined and preserved through regular administrative machinery, or whether it must be based upon reproduction cost or upon such an indeterminable and variable combination of factors, that it can be fixed at any time only through special appraisal and valuation.

Our principal aim in this department has been to point out the utter unworkability of using "fair value" as the rate base for public utility regulation—that is, "fair value" undefined as to specific rights and obligations, and dependent upon variable and uncertain factors. Through long contact with the work of regulation, our view is clear and, we believe, correct, that the only practical basis of rate-making is to define exactly the rights of the investors and the obligations of the consumers, and to base "value" upon exact facts as shown by accounts and scientific records. In this way only an initial and single valuation of any property would be necessary. Thereafter the "fair value" would be shown constantly by the facts under Commission control, without dispute between the public and the companies at any point of rate adjustment. So long, however, as rates are based upon "fair value" which is undefined and constantly variable, every effort at rate adjustment arouses conflict of interest between the investors and the public, resulting in protracted litigation and enormous costs; regulation remains practically an unworkable system.

There is the same problem in railroad as in other public utility regulation. In the case of railroads, however, contructive steps were taken to place regulation upon an exact and workable basis. In 1913 the Federal Valuation Act required the Interstate Commerce Commission to make a valuation of every railroad in the country as of a particular date, to be fixed for each property. After such date the particular company is required to report regularly to the

Commission its retirements and additions to property. This job of railroad valuation was an enormous one, and exceedingly costly. It has, however, been practically completed. If in any case the Commission thus starts with the initial finding as a fixed sum, and then adds the cost of all new property acquired, and deducts all retirements and additional depreciation, it will have a definite rate base that can be promptly determined at any time for rate adjustment or other purposes. The sum will rest upon exact facts not subject to dispute and litigation.

The Interstate Commerce Commission in the St. Louis and O'Fallon case adopted this policy for the determination of "fair value" for the purposes of railway rate administration. It considered the particular case in the light of requirements in dealing with all the railroads. It recognized the necessity of adopting methods which will not break down in administration, which will meet the financial needs of the country at large, and which will be actually fair to both the railroad and the public. It has taken a statesmanlike position, and presented the facts and issues in a clear and forceful manner. Its frankness and directness are certain to carry great weight with the Supreme Court. Its analysis can hardly be improved, but can be supported by public groups.

Opposed to the Commission is the claim of the St. Louis and O'Fallon Railroad Company that it is entitled to have its return based upon the "fair value" of the property as predicated largely upon reproduction cost. The question is thus squarely raised whether, for purposes of future rate control, the "fair value" can be put upon a definite basis so that it can be readily and promptly determined, or whether it must be left undefined and variable, subject to cumbersome redetermination from time to time. From the public standpoint, it must be plain that a definite rate base is essential if the work of regulation is to be carried out in a practical way. The Commission has to deal with hundreds of individual companies and properties, and will have a difficult administrative task even with the most satisfactory methods. If, however, it is required to base all of its orders involving private and public rights upon revaluations and redeterminations, it will be overwhelmed with administrative difficulties—great cost, endless litigation, delay, and deadlock.

There is also a second fundamental issue— financial stability depending on the system of rate-making. If the rate base adopted by the Commission is approved by the Supreme Court, the rights of the investors will be exactly defined and rates will be constantly fixed so as to bring the returns expected by investors. Under such a comprehensive system, there would be no difficulty at any time in obtaining all the new capital needed for enlargement of the railroad plant and service, in the interest of the commerce of the country at large (as required by the 1920 statute). If, however, the "fair value," based largely upon reproduction cost, is made the rate base, then there is introduced financial uncertainty which may interfere seriously with future railway developments. During a period of rising prices, the returns allowed would be greater than necessary to attract capital for required railway enlargements. During falling prices, however, the reduction in "fair value" would make the acquisition of new funds extremely difficult or impossible. Sound financial policy requires the definite system adopted by the Commission; the opposite would inject uncertainty and speculative features into the system of rate-making.

This, briefly, presents the issues. We consider the decision vital not only to railroad regulation, but also to general public utility rate control. If the Interstate Commerce Commission is upheld by the Supreme Court, the decision will not only make railroad regulation immediately effective, but will point the way to the various states to put rate regulation upon a workable and financially sound basis as to all other utilities. If, however, the opposite view should be sustained, we hardly see how regulation can be worked out satisfactorily. These larger matters of public policy must be emphasized before the Court, so that they will not be disregarded in the special details and claims of the particular. We urge all public-spirited groups to join in the much-needed emphasis.

＊

Electric Bond and Share Refuses to Answer.— The Federal Trade Commission struck an early *impasse* in its investigation of the financial transactions and interrelations of the power companies. It had been rumored during the summer that some of the large holding companies would probably refuse access to their accounts and records, and would not disclose their intercorporate transactions or their financial policies and dealings with the public. During the formal hearings in October, this opposition came out in the open, when the representatives of the Electric Bond and Share Company refused to answer questions directed to them by Judge Healy, counsel for the Commission.

The Electric Bond and Share Company controls probably the largest group of holding companies in the public utility field. It had been a subsidiary of the General Electric Company, and is, presumably, now closely associated with that company. It has subsidiaries and close affiliations in all parts of the country. Its relations consist in part of stock control and in part of managerial and financial advisorship. It has carried through the several systems a unification of policy which, doubtless, has resulted in important economies, and probably has redounded to the benefit of the consumers. It has been regarded, among the more progressive groups, as capably managed and not wholly mediaeval as to its public relations.

The position taken by the Electric Bond and Share Company is rather amazing to those who have been at least somewhat acquainted with the policies of that organization. Presumably, its lead will be followed by other groups. What it expects to gain is difficult to comprehend. While the management doubtless feels strongly that many of the matters inquired into by the Commission are strictly private in character and have no public concern, it cannot hope to have this attitude accepted by the Commission or the Senate—or by the American people. There is no real privacy in a public business. All of its activities have a public interest, inasmuch as the service is public. It cannot escape inquiry into any of its dealings which finally affect the service furnished and the price charged to the consumers —or which help to defeat the effectiveness of existing regulation.

The time has come when all artificial distinctions as to private rights affecting public utility control are discarded. It is true that in most of the states only the actual operating companies, or companies directly owning utility property, have been subjected to public control. In regard to such companies, the public right is all-pervasive as to examination of properties and records. It includes, moreover, the power to limit and direct the activities of the company in matters of management. It recognizes no right so private as to place it beyond public inquiry. In regard, to holding companies, however, such scope of public interest has not been so clearly established. Up to the present they have escaped practically all regulation, notwithstanding the fact that they have assumed more and more the actual force of control and management, and have taken over increasingly the functions which constitute the reality of operation. It is this acquisition of control and the absorption of operating functions which have created the public interest in the holding companies. The extent of these vital activities is the subject investigated by the Federal Trade Commission.

While the holding companies may claim that they are not under the jurisdiction of the regulatory commissions, actually they are an integral part of the systems which furnish service. It is the scope of the actuality with which the Federal Trade Commission is now concerned, and it is this that the holding companies do not wish to disclose. If the facts are brought out fully as to the control by holding companies and their operations in management and financing, also as to their use in evading regulation, they are certain to be brought under public control either through state or interstate agency—as they should have been many years ago. Their growth has been laid to the effort to escape regulation. Naturally, they now resist the public inquiry which is certain to restore a large measure of public control.

✢

Future of Cleveland's Municipal Light Plant.—This is the title of a pamphlet recently issued by Mr. Howell Wright, director of public utilities of the city of Cleveland, in response to a resolution passed by the city council January 30, 1928, requesting a report upon the municipal light plant. There is a foreword by Mr. Newton D. Baker, commenting upon conditions leading to the construction of the plant between 1911 and 1914, and upon the changes which have taken place in recent years—the subject of Mr. Wright's report.

The financial condition of the plant is excellent, both from the standpoint of the balance sheet and the income statement. On December 31, 1927, there was a gross plant investment of $13,458,849.82; a net investment, after deduction of depreciation reserve, of $9,225,146.89. Total net assets amounted to $11,638,182.63. Against this sum, there was a bonded indebtedness of $7,388,000; current liabilities, $290,587.08; operating reserves, $69,601.22; and the city's net equity, above all obligations and reserves, $3,889,994.33. As to income account, the year 1927 showed operating revenues of $3,249,460.

Operating expenses reached a total of $2,375,-431.12, leaving an operating income of $874,-028.88. There was also a non-operating income of $127,672.78. The deductions for interest, "taxes" and other charges amounted to $751,-720.94. There was thus a net income of $249,-980.72. This includes $385,750.76 for taxes, which the city was not actually required to pay. Without the inclusion of taxes, the net income, above all operating expenses and other charges, was $635,731.48.

From the present financial standpoint, the municipal plant thus appears in excellent condition. Among the operating expenses was included $648,793.15 for depreciation, on top of the actual expense of $358,806.04 for maintenance. The results speak well of the management, especially since the maximum rates have been fixed at 3 cents per kwh., among the lowest rates in the country.

The difficulties of the plant appear in connection with future requirements. The generating plant has a total rated capacity of 50,000 kw. This consists, however, of three 5,000 kw. units, which are practically obsolete, two 10,000 kw. units installed in 1919 and 1920, and one 15,000 kw. unit installed in 1926. The plant as a whole, therefore, cannot be classed as thoroughly modern. It cannot operate at as low an efficiency for fuel and labor as large modern plants consisting of units ranging from 50,000 kw. upward in individual capacity.

The question before the city is: what shall be done to meet further demands for current? The present plant cannot be readily enlarged; any material expansion will require a new plant, financed with new bond issues. Mr. Wright suggests as an immediate practical measure the installation of interconnections with other electric utilities. This would provide particularly for emergency service, which might be necessary in the case of shutdown of one or more of the present generating units. The plant hardly has sufficient reserve capacity for possible breakdowns. Whether construction of a new plant. with large generating units, may finally be justified, will depend upon developments during the next few years. It would, of course, be futile for the city to adopt an expansion program, if current may be obtained at a lower cost from generating companies. The same problem, however, does not apply to the distribution system. The department can expand its connections and, particularly, increase the street lighting load with present facilities.

The experience of Cleveland will be interesting to all cities which have municipal plants and face additional plant requirements for the future. Will it be more economical for them to construct additional plant, or purchase current from others? This is a vital question whose correct answer depends upon stubborn facts and not upon fixed doctrines.

GOVERNMENTAL RESEARCH ASSOCIATION NOTES

EDITED BY RUSSELL FORBES
Secretary

Recent Reports of Research Agencies.—The following reports have been received at the central library of the Association since October 1, 1928:

Buffalo Municipal Research Bureau, Inc.:
Comment on the Bureau's Work
Detroit Bureau of Governmental Research, Inc.:
Hamtramck Garbage Incinerator
San Francisco Bureau of Governmental Research:
The San Mateo-San Francisco Survey
Schenectady Bureau of Municipal Research, Inc.:
Final Report on the Administration of the Schenectady Civil Service

Correction.—Through the editor's error, two reports were credited in last month's issue to the Cincinnati Bureau of Municipal Research. The reports on *Public Purchase of Materials for Public Work to be Furnished to Contractors* and *Underground Wiring in New Subdivisions* were prepared by the Municipal Reference Bureau of the University of Cincinnati and not by the Cincinnati Bureau of Municipal Research.

✸

California Taxpayers' Association.—At the semi-annual meeting of the board of directors, held in San Francisco on October 19, the California Taxpayers' Association went on record as favoring the passage in the next legislature of an act which will create the county unit system of school administration. The Association also announced itself as in favor of the passage of legislation which will make the photographic recording of documents legal in the state of California. The Association favors changes in the present special assessments and improvements acts of California.

The research department of California Taxpayers' Association has concluded its field work on the studies of the expenditures of Solano and Santa Barbara counties. It is now fast approaching the completion of its study of the costs of the state educational institutions.

✸

Taxpayers' Research League of Delaware.— A group of trustees and friends of the League

sponsored a smoker in October to discuss problems that will come before the next legislature, and to consider the increased financing of the League. The smoker was attended by about sixty persons, including Governor Robinson, the two candidates for governor, two of the state judges, and other prominent business and professional men.

By formal motion, those present unanimously agreed that the work of the League should be continued and broadened and given the fullest financial support.

The governor-elect, C. Douglass Buck, present chief engineer of the state highway department, and son-in-law of United States Senator T. Coleman du Pont, has requested the coöperation of the League in making a thorough survey of the state's financial policies, administrative structure, and business methods.

The League has completed and submitted to the citizens' committee and town officials of Milford its audit and analysis of the town's accounts and accounting system.

✸

Des Moines Bureau of Municipal Research.— The Bureau sent an open letter to the state budget director urging him to reduce materially the budget requests of the state departments and institutions for the next biennium. Copies of this letter were also sent to chambers of commerce throughout the state to enlist their support. The state budget requests for the next biennium of 1929–30 were 32 per cent over the 1927–28 appropriation, or an increase of $9,000,000 for the two years. The general state departments asked for a 10 per cent increase, the board of control which supervises penal and philanthropic institutions, 39 per cent, and the educational institutions, 37 per cent. By contrast with this proposed increase in state taxes, the assessed valuations in the state have actually decreased slightly.

At the request of the county board of supervisors, the Bureau, in coöperation with a chamber of commerce committee, is working on a report to simplify the present longhand method of preparing assessment and tax records, which involves duplication of hundreds of thousands of entries.

The Bureau also called the attention of the city council to the apparent falling off of city tax receipts below the estimates upon which the annual appropriation was based, and suggested retrenchment before the latter months of the year when the situation might become acute.

Upon the suggestion of the county recorder and the Bureau, the supervisors have authorized the installation of photographic recording.

The Bureau transmitted a report to the finance committee of the board of supervisors on the authority of supervisors over county expenditures with the view that the latter assume closer control over the county purse-strings.

The Bureau also prepared publicity reports for newspapers on consolidation of counties, increase of state levies in urban counties as compared to rural counties, and handled publicity for a fire prevention campaign.

✢

Albert Russel Erskine Bureau for Street Traffic Research, Harvard University.—Dr. Miller McClintock, director, at the present time is in the city of New Orleans completing a survey report on street traffic control conditions.

The survey preceding this report has been conducted by an engineering staff during the past twelve months. The report, which is shortly to be issued, will be one of the most comprehensive reports yet prepared by the Erskine Bureau, and will contain many new factors regarding traffic engineering and administration, due to the peculiar characteristics of traffic in New Orleans.

The survey has been conducted by the Erskine Bureau directly for the city planning and zoning commission of New Orleans and under the general supervision of Mr. Paul Habans, Commissioner of Public Safety. It is understood that copies of the report when printed will be available for general distribution.

✢

Civic Affairs Department, Indianapolis Chamber of Commerce.—Study of the budgets of local units of government has been completed by the department. The staff of the department was invited to sit with the finance committee of the city council in consideration of the civil city budget. Many of its recommendations were accepted by the council and much statistical information was provided, aiding the coun-

cil in reducing the proposed 1929 tax rate from $1.15 to $1.10 on each $100 of taxable property.

In addition, information provided by the department was helpful to the executive department and the council in refusing to grant very large increases of personnel in the police and fire departments, requested by the heads of these departments. Instead, plans are under way to effect a change in the present custom of allowing full pay for all absences from duty on account of illness or injury which, it is expected, will materially increase the number of men available for active duty and perhaps permit some saving in salary appropriations. The department of civic affairs has obtained information from the fire and police departments of thirty-one cities as to their practice in this regard and will soon make a report of this study to the board of public safety for its use in preparing a rule suitable for use in the local departments.

This department made a study of the sinking fund requirements of the civil city covering the next twelve years, and its program providing for meeting these requirements without undue burden in any one year was adopted by the mayor and city council.

The department study of the school city budget revealed serious error in computation of expected revenue. The department urged many appropriation reductions. School officials declined to consider the department's recommendations and an appeal was taken to the state board of tax commissioners. The tax board has not finally acted, but has indicated that it will make a number of the appropriation reductions urged by our department.

The department study of the county budget revealed inadequate provision for meeting the appropriations from the general fund.

✢

The Ohio Institute.—A report on state subsidies for special education in Ohio, prepared for the Ohio State Teachers' Association in 1927, has now been published. Copies can be secured from the Association, Chamber of Commerce Building, Columbus, Ohio.

A report on county welfare organization and administration in Ohio has been completed. Suggestions looking toward reorganization are included.

Data are being compiled to show to what extent judges, in sentencing convicted offenders to the state penitentiary, have made use of their power to impose a minimum sentence in excess of that imposed by statute.

✢

Philadelphia Bureau of Municipal Research.— Philip A. Beatty, who is engaged on the study of municipal contracts which the Bureau began in 1926 as agent of the Thomas Skelton Harrison Foundation, has been designated, upon the mayor's invitation, to represent the Bureau at the meetings of a committee on municipal contracts appointed by the mayor in August. In response to requests made by the committee's secretary, the Bureau has furnished the committee with considerable information about contract practices and also about persons whom the committee might consult for expert advice.

It so happened that two of the most important problems with which this committee has to deal are also problems which the Bureau has been studying. One of them is that of force account, the subject of a report published by the Bureau early this year. Another is that of the irresponsible bidder, which has been discussed in *Citizens' Business*, notably Numbers 853 and 855. Copies of the force account report and issues of *Citizens' Business* devoted to the subject of municipal contracts have been furnished to members of the committee. The desirability of standard questionnaires and financial statements for bidders was also made the subject of a letter to the secretary, and copies of these forms were supplied to members of the committee.

✢

St. Louis Bureau of Municipal Research.— During the past two years the Bureau has devoted much time to a study of police pension systems in an endeavor to induce the board of police commissioners to revise their proposed pension plan along sound actuarial lines. The plan proposed by the board and by a citizens' police pension committee was similar to the police pension system in New York City, but failed of passage in the last legislature and was defeated as an initiative proposal at the election on November 6.

Although the system would have applied only to St. Louis policemen, it was necessary that it be submitted to a state-wide vote. The results of the voting are interesting. In St. Louis the proposition failed to carry by a majority of approximately 70,000. In Kansas City it was approved by a majority of approximately 50,000. Throughout the rural districts the vote, on the basis of unofficial returns, seems to be about

evenly divided. Extensive publicity was obtained in support of the proposition and numerous speeches were made at public gatherings and over the radio throughout the entire state. The Bureau and the board of estimate and apportionment submitted statements of facts about the provisions of the proposed system, and its cost to the newspapers and voters of St. Louis.

The board of estimate and apportionment employed Mr. George B. Buck, consulting actuary, to advise them concerning the proposed system. Mr. Buck's report showed that the system would be financially unsound and extremely costly to operate. The local press gave very satisfactory publicity to the Bureau's reports although three of the large dailies favored the plan editorially and a fourth remained somewhat neutral. A few days prior to the election the board of estimate and apportionment mailed a brief statement of the estimated cost of the proposed system to approximately 240,000 registered voters in the city.

✢

Schenectady Bureau of Municipal Research.— *New Building Code.—*The Bureau's review of the present building code and the one proposed for adoption in 1925 has been submitted to the chairman of the common council committee on laws and ordinances, together with recommendations that these codes be set aside and an entirely new document prepared. The Bureau's services have been offered to the city for the purposes of preparing the new code.

The Bureau's recommendations were concurred in by the committee and by the common council which, by resolution, thanked the Bureau for its work in reviewing the code and authorized it to proceed with the preparation of an entirely new set of building regulations.

*Centralized Purchasing.—*The preliminary draft of the report on the survey of the present methods of municipal buying has been completed. At present there are three distinct buying agencies in the city administration and recommendations for their consolidation will be made along lines of recommended model procedure.

*Water Bureau Finances.—*The capital budget commission has submitted to the mayor a report calling attention to certain fiscal conditions existing in the bureau of water. The increasing bonded indebtedness, together with increased costs of operation of the municipal water plant, is causing a serious condition in the present water rental rates which are considerably below the 1913 schedule. The commission's report, prepared by the Bureau, made a number of recommendations providing for temporary relief and calling for a thorough investigation of the entire municipal water plan so that permanent rates can be established on certain data regarding plant costs, operation charges, maintenance charges, extensions to plant and outstanding debt in order that the system may be on a self-sustaining basis.

Budgetary Procedure.—The Bureau issued a bulletin setting forth the details of the contemplated 1929 city budget as approved by the board of estimate and apportionment, and showing how the total amount of the proposed tax levy compared with that of former years and what its effect upon the taxpayer would be. Subsequent action by the common council reduced the net budget total some $53,000. The Bureau thereupon called the council's attention to an item of estimated surplus revenues amounting to around $147,000, which had not been included in the "income side" of the 1929 Budget. After considerable publicity, the city comptroller publicly announced that the tax levy for the next year would be reduced by the amount of estimated surplus revenues. The Bureau is issuing a pamphlet in explanation of the item. At present it appears that the Bureau's suggestion will be carried out and that the city tax rate for next year will actually be less than last year, while in the face of the figures as adopted by the common council the figure was to be considerably raised.

Toledo Commission of Publicity and Efficiency.—During October the Commission published in the *City Journal* two financial studies of the city of Toledo. The first contained an explanation of the proposed $12,400,000 bond issues ($11,450,000 of which was carried) showing the amount by which each issue would raise the tax rate. In connection with this study, the bonded debt of Toledo was shown during the last fifteen years, together with the present comparative per capita debt of eighteen cities in Toledo's population range. The second study was on the expenditures of the city for a fifteen-year period. The apparent per capita expenditures were shown to have increased 113 per cent during this time, but the per capita expenditures adjusted to the purchasing power of the dollar were found to average less during the last fifteen years than in 1913.

The Commission is engaged in checking up on several of its former surveys to see what progress has been made by city officials in carrying out the recommendations. The matter of fire insurance for city-owned property is also to be investigated.

The *Toledo Port Survey* of 1928, made by the Griffenhagen firm of Chicago, was published by the Commission during November. In addition to general recommendations for a port plan, the survey contains a great deal of information on the Great Lakes water traffic.

MUNICIPAL ACTIVITIES ABROAD

EDITED BY W. E. MOSHER

Director, School of Citizenship and Public Affairs, Syracuse University

Reorganization of Local Government.—A royal commission on local government was appointed in England in 1926 for the purpose of considering desirable revisions in the organization and conduct of local government units. It has issued two reports. The first dealt with the administration of poor relief boards and taxation problems. It has caused widespread debate and has been rather vigorously criticized in more liberal circles. The second report has just been issued. It deals with

1. Reorganization of areas.
2. Extension of the local area in charge of certain services.
3. Revision of the powers of stimulus and default.
4. The progress which has been made toward the full-time employment of medical officers of health.
5. The distribution of functions between the local authorities.

On the whole these recommendations look toward coördination of the smaller units and extension of the control of the county authority. For instance, if it is found that a rural district is not maintaining proper standards along sanitary lines it is suggested that the county council take over such administration with the agreement of the district council and possibly with the understanding that the costs shall be charged against the account of the district council. This does not apply to all the functions, but only to such as are laid upon the councils of the county or district by statute. A second important recommendation has to do with the appointment of full-time medical officers of health. Such appointments are to be made on the retirement of present part-time officers. A further proposal looks toward the ultimate re-alignment of smaller units within the county on the basis of population and taxable values.

Evidence will be found in the report of the tendency to make the county the unit of administration in the name of better standards and lower costs. Although such recommendations run counter to the traditional loyalty to local autonomy, they are apparently moving in the direction of both efficiency and economy.—*Municipal Journal*, October 26, 1928.

✤

Toward the Single Tax.—A special committee of the Sheffield City Council has made a report upon the possibility of relieving tenants and manufacturers of some of their tax burdens by means of a rate on the selling value of land. In speaking of the unearned increment, the well-known quotation from Thorold Rogers is cited. This runs: "Every permanent improvement of the soil, every railway and road, every bettering of the general conditions of society raises the land. The landowner sleeps but thrives. He inherits parts of the fruits of industry and appropriates the lion's share of accumulated intelligence." The committee recommends that a large proportion of the rates be paid by the owners of land. It disapproves of the policy of treating site value and building value according to the same system, on the ground that they are entirely different in character. One of the prime purposes of this proposal is that it would impel owners of vacant lots to sell or improve.

The report also includes information from abroad. Among other things it is pointed out that there are in New Zealand 119 boroughs which levy their rates wholly or in part on the value of the site. This tends to reduce the appraisal of workers' houses where the greater part of the value is in the house.

In Durban, South Africa, the rate on land is six pence and on buildings three pence. This results in the reduction of rates on homes. It has led further to extensive subdivisions and the breaking up of large land holdings.

Pittsburgh, Pennsylvania, is also cited as a place where the municipal tax rate on buildings is but half that on land. Under this system a considerable shift of taxes from buildings to land has been brought about to the advantage of home owners.—*Municipal Journal*, October 12, 1928, p. 1587.

✤

Wider Use of Electricity.—The organization of a special national commission endowed with authority to unify the whole system of generating

781

and distributing electricity in England on a national basis has given considerable impetus to the rates of increase of the use of electrical current, particularly for domestic purposes. In an editorial in the *Municipal Journal* it is claimed that the progress in the utilization of electricity for all purposes represents a record which is one of the greater triumphs of recent civilization.

Perhaps the most significant tendency is the construction of so-called all-electric houses. Enough have been established to prove that they are both economical and capable of giving the utmost of satisfaction.

Where such houses are being built it has been found feasible to eliminate in the construction chimneys and other features required by a coal-heating plant with a saving that enables the builder to install most of the desirable electrical devices.

One of the measures that has been conducive to more extensive usage is the adoption of simple two-part tariffs. For instance, instead of paying a certain rate per kilowatt hour for lighting and another for other uses, the consumer pays an annual charge which is determined by the assessed value of the house plus a single penny per unit for all current used.

A summary is given of the total cost per year for electrical energy consumed by a family in a small or medium-sized house in a modern subdivision. This would amount to about $90. This includes the following services: lighting, cooking, iron, vacuum cleaner, washing machine, electric fans, and partial water heating.

The city of Birmingham encourages the adoption of electric facilities by renting motors on an annual basis and in fact any other domestic apparatus that costs $20 or more. Rental terms may be arranged so that at the end of a period of time the apparatus comes into the possession of the renter. Their program also provides for the installation of electrical devices in residences, to be paid for through increases for the cost of current.

Serious consideration is being given to the replacement of coal for domestic purposes on a nation-wide basis. It is pointed out that 64,-700,000 tons of coal were used for such purposes together with that used in gas and electricity works, whereas if the same consumers depended upon gas, coke and electricity, the total consumption might have been reduced to 12,250,000 tons. This, of course, assumes a thoroughly well-organized system of production and transmission in which gas, coke and electricity would be produced by central stations where the distances from the point of consumption made this desirable.

The whole program looking toward the extension of the "electrical era" is naturally based upon the widespread introduction of inducement rates for current. The English are approaching this problem from the point of view of national housekeeping and are obviously aiming at the universal use of electricity as an instrument of service and comfort and one no longer to be classified as a luxury.—*Municipal Journal*, October 5, 1928, pp. 35 ff.

✢

Management of Electrical Industry.—The development of the electrical industry in Germany for the period 1918–1928 is a topic of a comprehensive article by Senior Burgomaster Bracht of Essen. This development is noteworthy because of the rapidity with which a nation-wide network has been built up and the rôle that has been played by the public authorities in coöperation with private entrepreneurs. Although a law for the whole Empire was passed in 1919 under Socialist influence looking toward the nationalization of the electrical industry with central control and operation, this was never carried through. There has, nevertheless, been a rapid nation-wide organization in which city, state, and private agencies have been involved. The most interesting aspect of this movement is the organization of mixed administrative agencies in which representatives of the given locality and of private enterprises coöperate. It was reported in 1914 that seventy-five cities in Germany shared in such combinations. For the most part these companies as well as many of a strictly municipal character are special corporations functioning independently of the local government itself.

In terms of kilowatt hours distributed the expansion that has been made by municipal companies is brought out by the following figures. In 1918 1.6 billion kilowatt hours were distributed by city plants, while in 1926 this figure had risen to 3.1 billions. This was 20 per cent of the total amount distributed in the country.

In spite of this increase, during the same period there was a steady decrease in the amount generated by city plants, for in 1918 81 per cent of the total distributed by them was generated in this way, while in 1926 only 56 per cent was so generated. This indicates that the cities have entered into the larger network of the industry in which production is being carried on in a wholesale way, often at mineheads or in connection with large water resources.

The distribution of the various generating units as between the purely municipal and the mixed forms and those controlled by the state itself is as follows: According to the figures from the statistical bureau there were 630 state and local public plants, 147 under joint public and private control, and 593 private ones, which sold electricity to the public. From the point of view of production the output of the public works amounted to 4.3 billion kilowatt hours, the mixed plants 4.2 billion, and the private 1.5 billion.

Within a five-year period, 1919–1924, there was a steady decrease of the municipal and private supplying agencies, while the mixed and the state works were distinctly on the increase. In this period the public works, carried on under the auspices of the state, had jumped an even 100 per cent.

It is generally assumed that the officials in authoritative positions in the government have no intention of developing a state monopoly, but only the policy that the state shall supplement the other agencies in the exploitation of natural resources for the purpose of producing electricity. It is to be noted that this intercommunal and interstate system has come about in a very natural and entirely voluntary way. The writer of the article urges that further development along this line is to be hoped. He considers it to be the only procedure that is wholesome and in accordance with a sound economical approach to this problem.—*Zeitschrift für Kommunalwirtschaft*, October 10, 1928, pp. 1762 ff.

✢

Municipal Aid for Air Traffic.—Public support for the advancement of airplane traffic is quite in the order of the day in Germany. This applies not alone to the cities but to the state and the central government.

The cities have formed two organizations, one for the purpose of developing air transportation on a regional basis and the other for the purpose of standardizing airports, and rental charges for storage and use of them. It is estimated that the various municipalities have invested upwards of 150,000,000 marks in airports and their equipment. In addition they are contributing in the neighborhood of 5,000,000 marks a year to meet the deficit of the private airplane combine.

Cities contribute to the maintenance of what may be called the internal transportation, while the state aids those lines of traffic within the boundaries of Germany that are of particular importance to them, and the Empire gives subsidies to the part of the service that is engaged in international transportation.

In general the income of the German Hansa which has a practical monopoly is about one-sixth of the cost of operation. This is chargeable to the fact that only about 50 per cent of the seating space is occupied on the average, even in the good flying months. But even if all the space were used during this period the income would cover but one-third of the expenditures. From a financial point of view, therefore, the enterprise is far from profitable. There is such widespread faith, however, in the possibilities of air transportation that the continued support of the public agencies seems to be assured.

There can be no doubt that this infant industry is making steady progress. In 1920 there were but 27 airplanes with cabin accommodations. This number increased to 194 in the space of eight years. The number of kilometers flown in a single year jumped from 480,000 in 1920 to nearly 10,000,000 in 1927; and the number of persons from carried about 4,000 in 1920 to 151,-000 in the latter year. In the same year freight was carried in the aggregate of 2,326,000 kilograms. This does not take into account mail which amounted to 826,000 kilograms. The cost of flying in Germany is nearly one-half the amount per kilometer of the cost in the United States, while postal matter is carried for one-third the cost charged in the United States.

It is definitely anticipated that the time will come when public subsidies can be withdrawn. Meantime there is widespread prediction that the possibilities of air traffic are so great that public support of this sort is fully warranted.—*Zeitschrift für Kommunalwirtschaft*, October 10, 1928, pp. 1843 ff.

✢

Municipal Cleansing.—The importance attached to street cleaning, refuse collection and disposal is indicated by the gradual increase in the prestige assigned to the municipal official responsible for what the English call "cleansing." Several cities have now adopted the title of Director of Public Cleansing, thus raising the status of this position in the hierarchy of municipal officials.

The Ministry of Health has recently published in its annual report a comprehensive statement concerning the methods of refuse collection and the cost of disposal in a number of towns. This has prompted a number of articles in a recent issue of the *Municipal Journal* as to various phases of the whole problem of "cleansing."

Among other things the annual report summarized the costs of 160 local authorities. Comparative data are presented with reference to the annual cost per 1,000 population and also the average cost of disposing of one ton of refuse. The range of costs for the latter was from one pence to twelve shillings four pence per ton. Similar figures for the various types of refuse disposal are also included. Although not conclusive, such data make possible worth-while comparisons and may well lead to a special investigation where wide discrepancies from the average come to light.

A unique method of refuse disposal is recommended by one of the contributors to this symposium. It is the use of trenches that have been excavated by a trenching machine. They are run about five feet deep and fifteen feet wide. Refuse is dumped into the trench to a depth of about four feet and then covered with the soil from the adjacent piles. It is estimated that the cost for disposing of one ton would be one shilling, or about fifteen pounds per one thousand population a year. The writer suggests that according to this system an acre of land would hold the average output of a town of fifty thousand for twelve months. The scheme would require the addition of a small incinerator for the destruction of carcasses and material from infected premises. —*Municipal Journal*, October 26, 1928, p. 1656.

✦

Public Printing.—The Sheffield Corporation has established a printing and stationery department for the purpose of handling the printing and bookbinding requirements of all departments. The costs of the whole establishment amounted to about $100,000. At the end of the period of three and one-half months there was a net profit of $5,500. Trade union wages are paid and the same general quality of materials and character of work maintained. Several other cities are reported as being interested in a similar enterprise.—*Municipal Journal*, October 19, 1928, p. 1618.

NOTES AND EVENTS

EDITED BY WELLES A. GRAY

Assistant Director, Municipal Administration Service

Cleaning up Chicago Politics.—Crime, graft, and corruption in Chicago politics are an old story since the development of the Crowe-Barrett-Thompson machine in the Windy City. The reign of terror reached its height during the primaries, last April, when the houses of Senator Charles S. Deneen and Judge John A. Swanson were bombed, Octavius C. Granady, the candidate opposed to Morris Eller for ward committeeman, was murdered, and thousands of decent citizens were intimidated and frightened from the polls. It will be recalled that, despite all this butchery, the candidates of decency, opposed to further gang rule, emerged victorious from the electoral shambles. The "better element," however, was convinced that this was not enough to purge Chicago, and that punishment of the guilty by due process of law was necessary to make the clean-up really effective. Readers of the REVIEW will further recall that Frank J. Loesch, president of the Chicago Crime Commission, was appointed special assistant attorney-general to take charge of an investigation of the situation. A fund of $150,000 to carry on this work was raised under the leadership of the Chicago Association of Commerce, inasmuch as the board of Cook County commissioners failed to make the necessary appropriation, and five special grand juries have been empanelled. These juries were charged with investigating, mainly, alleged violations of the election laws, and crimes committed during the elections of November, 1926, June, 1927, and April, 1928, the murder of Granady, and the bombing of the homes of Senator Deneen and Judge Swanson.

Thus far, these juries have examined 525 witnesses and have returned 100 indictments. Among the indictments are the following: three men have been charged with the murder of Granady; twenty-seven indictments charge assault with intent to commit murder; twenty-seven charge kidnapping; one charges malfeasance of police officers; nine charge conspiracy; one, perjury; and three, altering of ballots. While prosecutions are yet to be carried on, we are glad to note that the proceedings have reached this stage successfully.

Some of the findings of the grand juries are of especial interest to students of government and politics. The second concluded that the "election laws are inadequate, inefficient, antiquated, and that these various abuses will continue until drastic amendments to the laws are made." The third stated that "in the minds of the members of the jury there is no question that the police department is rotten to the core." According to Mr. Loesch: "Both the first and second grand juries heard the testimony of officers on duty where kidnappings occurred, that they saw no kidnappings or assaults committed, no guns in the hands of the perpetrators of the crimes, and no crimes committed!"

There is much yet to be done, but such progress is an encouraging sign that Chicago is once again about to depose its underworld rulers.

✠

New City Manager Charters.[1]—At the election on November 6, the people of five cities expressed themselves at the polls as desiring city manager governments, while in a sixth city, Toledo, Ohio, the plan was rejected by a heavy majority.

The largest city to adopt the plan was Fall River, Massachusetts, where the vote was 16,009 for, to 14,345 against, the new charter. In Fall River, history repeated itself, for, as in Dayton and in Galveston, better government followed close upon the heels of disaster. Some readers may recall that a devastating fire swept through the heart of that city last February, destroying the business center, and causing a loss of about $8,000,000. This fire, coming as it did, after several years of severe financial depression in the textile industry, left the city well-nigh bankrupt. Property losses, due to both the fire and the depression, caused a reduction in the assessed valuation of property from $188,935,750 to $161,682,250, or 14.5 per cent. Tax levies

[1] The information upon which this note is based was furnished by Howard G. Fishack of the Taxpayers' Association of Fall River, J. O. Garber of the Commission of Publicity and Efficiency of Toledo, Professor James W. Martin of the University of Kentucky, and Walter J. Millard of the Proportional Representation League.

were likewise reduced out of consideration to the taxpayers, but even so the rate was increased from $35.60 to $40.80. Along with this unfortunate condition came bad politics in connection with the rehabilitation of the city. Street widening projects and plans for rebuilding the destroyed area were made political footballs, and very little constructive work was being accomplished by the city government. The result of this situation was agitation for a new government which culminated in the campaign for a city manager charter.

The press opposed the movement from the start, and it, together with the political machines, carried on a campaign of misrepresentation. It was charged, for example, that Waltham, the only city in the commonwealth that had tried the plan, had found it a failure. Although these statements were contradicted by the proponents of the new charter, and by Mayor Henry F. Beal of Waltham and Clarence A. Bingham, both former city managers of Waltham, they were constantly reiterated by the opposition. Likewise the opponents spread among the firemen, policemen, city laborers, and even school-teachers, the old story that the new manager would cut salaries and deprive city employees of civil service rights —despite the fact that the state law providing for city manager government specifically prohibits any action contrary to existing civil service rules and regulations.

The plan had the support of all the civic bodies of the city, with the exception of the local chamber of commerce, which refused to join the movement upon the grounds that the question was "political." In the campaign a leading part was played by the Taxpayers' Association of Fall River, and its director, Howard G. Fishack, was one of the main speakers. It is interesting to note that the total campaign expenses amounted to less than $1,000. The new plan will go into effect January 1, 1929, and the necessary primary and regular elections for new officials will be held in November and December, respectively.

Three cities in Kentucky—Lexington, Covington, and Owensboro—also adopted the city manager plan November 6. In Lexington it was adopted by a favorable vote of more than two to one, 10,050 votes being cast for the plan, and 4,241 against it. The campaign in Lexington was typical of the average campaign for a city manager government. The press, the Board of Commerce, and the bulk of the progressives favored the plan, while the opposition was led by

the old political crowd who had everything to lose, and, perhaps, nothing to gain by the new charter. This crowd was aided by the conservative die-bards to whom any change in any form of government is always undesirable, a group found in every community. The usual campaign tactics were used, and a house to house canvass was made. The political science faculty of the state university took part in the campaign, and provided speakers and newspaper articles. The new plan will take effect in Lexington, January 1, 1932. In Covington, just across the river from Cincinnati, the experience of the latter city evidently had considerable influence, for the plan was adopted there by a vote of more than three to one. In Owensboro it won by a slender majority.

In Portsmouth, Ohio, the plan likewise won by a slim margin, for the unofficial count gives it a plurality of eight votes. At the time of going to press, therefore, the final result is uncertain, for a movement for a recount is already under way.

Perhaps the hottest, and certainly one of the most interesting of these six campaigns, took place in Toledo, Ohio, the only city of the six where a charter providing for P. R. was up for adoption, and the only one to reject the city manager plan.

The Toledo election was complicated by the fact that there were two city manager charters up for adoption or rejection. One, sponsored by ten of the fifteen members of the charter commission, included provisions for a council to be elected by P. R., under a fixed quota system. This was defeated by a vote of 50,483 against to 35,104 in favor. The other charter was proposed by a minority of five members of the charter commission, and differed materially from the first only in that the council was to be composed of eleven members, elected in the usual way, ten by wards and one at large. It was voted down by an even heavier plurality, 57,110 against to 26,717 in favor.

There are three main reasons for the defeat of the city manager plan in Toledo. In the first place, many voters were confused by the minority charter, although the "organization vote" was against both. P. R. seemed to be the chief issue of the campaign, its friends asserting that it would free the council from machine domination, and its enemies declaring that it was "un-American." Second, an intensive campaign was waged against the P. R. charter by a minority member of the commission, Federal Judge John M. Killits, who made only meager efforts in behalf of the minority charter. Third, there was no wave of civic feeling against the present government of Toledo. The feeling of a great many voters seemed to be that things were going along in good fashion at the present time, and therefore they should let well enough alone.

✦

Convention of American Municipal Association.—The American Municipal Association held its fifth annual meeting at Richmond, Virginia, November 12, 13, and 14. The leading features of the first day's program included round tables on editorial policies of league magazines and on selling advertising space. At the dinner that evening an address on "Planning and Building for the Motor Age" was given by Louis Brownlow, municipal consultant to the City Housing Corporation, New York City. This was followed by a round table on a mutual advertising agreement.

Russell Forbes, secretary of the National Municipal League, addressed the meeting at a luncheon, November 13, on "The Work of the National Municipal League, the Governmental Research Association, and the Municipal Administration Service," and that evening an address on "The Objectives of City Government" was delivered by R. W. Rigsby, president, the International City Managers' Association. On November 14 round tables were conducted on schools for municipal officials and on the functions of a state league of municipalities.

✦

Berkeley Adopts Health Examinations for City Employees.—Since July 5 the salaried officers and employees of Berkeley, California, whose salaries are fixed upon a monthly basis, have had their sick leave conditioned upon annual health examinations. The examinations are made at the employees' expense, by physicians of their own selection. Following each examination a report, giving the general condition of the employee's health and making recommendations for such corrective or preventive measures as may be necessary, must be filed with the city health officer. The ordinance which established these examinations provides for a sick leave schedule as follows:

Ten days at full pay for those in the employ of the city for more than six months and less than one year.
Thirty days for those employed more than one year and less than five.
Forty-five days for those employed more than five years and less than ten.

Sixty days for those employed more than ten years and less than fifteen.
Ninety days for those employed more than fifteen years.

Vacation schedules are also established for those employed more than six months by the city, of one day for every month of service. The total vacation, however, must not exceed twelve working days.

✦

Fund for the Study of Public Administration at Yale.—As a result of a gift of $350,000, Yale University has established the Alfred Cowles Foundation for the Study of Government. This fund will make possible at Yale instruction along the lines of practical public administration, similar to that being advocated for other institutions of learning. President James Rowland Angell said, in commenting on the gift:

At present the college offers a considerable group of courses in the field of government, dealing with theoretical and descriptive branches of the subject. Though the work now offered is substantially equivalent in scope to that of other liberal arts colleges, need has long been felt for further development of study along lines which offer the student the largest opportunities for usefulness in the political life of his community. The Cowles Foundation now makes this possible. A part of the income will be used to equip the University with a comprehensive collection of materials relating especially to the practical problems of state and municipal governments, and the activities of political parties and the electorate. Another part of the fund will make possible a series of courses to provide a historical background of government, and to utilize these materials under the direction of a distinguished teacher soon to be added to the faculty. Graduate work will be promoted by offering generous fellowships to selected students of Yale and other universities; and efforts will be made to stimulate intensive study of political problems by undergraduates through honors courses open to students of high rank.

Though designed primarily as cultural studies, the new courses will provide valuable training of a practical nature for men who plan to enter the public services after graduation; and it is hoped that they will interest an increasing number of students in these lines of life work.

The fund is established in memory of Alfred Cowles, one of the former owners of the Chicago *Tribune*, and the money was given by his children.

✦

E. M. Bassett to Aid in Formation of New York City Plan Commission.—Corporation Counsel George P. Nicholson has been requested to appoint Edward M. Bassett a special corporation counsel to assist in preparing the statutory set-up of the proposed city planning commission for New York City, it was announced by Mayor Walker on November 13. The need of a planning commission for New York has long been apparent, and this action by the mayor points to definite steps being taken in the near future. Before the commission can be organized, however, its legal position and its powers must be clearly defined. Furthermore, its relation to such charter officials as the chief engineer of the board of estimate and apportionment, and to the board of estimate itself must be staked out. While much of the necessary legislation can be enacted by the city under its home-rule authority, the legislature at Albany must pass part of it. The result of this situation is that much preparatory legal work must be done, and this is to be placed in charge of Mr. Bassett.

Mr. Bassett, as most readers of the REVIEW already know, has long been recognized as one of the outstanding authorities of the country on the legal side of city planning and zoning. He has enjoyed a long and distinguished career of public service. Among the public offices which he has held are the following: member of the Brooklyn Board of Education, 1899–1901, representative from Brooklyn in the 58th Congress, and member of the New York State Public Service Commission, 1907–1911. He was chairman of the New York City Heights of Buildings Commission, 1913 to 1915, and chairman of the New York City Zoning Commission in 1916 and 1917. In 1922 he was appointed by Secretary Hoover to serve as a member of the advisory committee on zoning, of the Department of Commerce. He has been a member of the legal firm of Bassett, Thompson, and Gilpatric since 1902.

*

Campaign for Permanent Registration in Michigan.—A campaign for permanent registration of voters in Michigan is now under way, under the leadership of the Michigan League of Women Voters, with the Detroit Citizens' League actively coöperating. This campaign will culminate in a drive upon the legislature when it meets at Lansing, January 1, 1929. At the present time all cities in Michigan over 5,000 population are required to make a new registration every four years, in the presidential year, and to check up on all registrations. The check-up system in use in Detroit is quite effective, but in some of the other cities, particularly in places of less than 5,000 where it is not required, it is very weak; and the polling lists of many cities are said

to be encumbered with the names of thousands of people who have either died or moved out of the state. As a result of this situation, the state League of Women Voters, at their last convention, decided upon this campaign for permanent registration and machinery for an accurate check-up at regular intervals, and formed a committee to draft the necessary legislation.

W. P. LOVETT.

Detroit Citizens' League.

*

Results of New Jersey's "Anti-Hague" Bills.— In the November REVIEW we reported the enactment of a series of laws by the New Jersey Legislature which were known popularly as the "anti-Hague" bills, inasmuch as their purpose was frankly admitted by some of the Republican legislators to be the curbing of Mayor Frank Hague's power in Jersey City. The chief feature of these bills was the grant of power to the superintendents of elections in Hudson and Essex Counties to strike from the voting lists the names of such persons as they deemed improperly registered or otherwise not qualified to vote.

No sooner had the bills become law than the names of 28,000 voters were stricken from the lists in Hudson County. Quite naturally a general uproar followed. Inasmuch as the greater number of the voters whose names were thus removed seemed to be Democrats, the local Democratic politicians were loud in their denunciations of this "outrageous attempt on the part of the Republicans to steal the election in Hudson County." While the protests were being carried to the courts John Ferguson, superintendent of elections in Hudson County, and a Republican, restored more than 7,000 names to the lists. The legal battle resulted in a court decision that the judges of the Hudson County court of common pleas could, when appealed to, restore to the lists names that they deemed had been wrongfully removed.

Thereupon the four judges of the court of common pleas, together with two additional judges imported for the occasion, announced that they would sit until midnight every night if necessary, in order to hear appeals. By November 6, more than 1,000 names had been restored to the lists.

It had been predicted that the Essex County list of ineligibles would contain about 20,000 names. Interestingly enough, when it did appear, several days after the Hudson County fracas, it contained only about 2,000, and but little trouble resulted.

INDEX
NATIONAL MUNICIPAL REVIEW
VOLUME XVII, 1928

AUTHORS

Atkins, C. W.	489	Kamm, Leona	59
Aumann, Francis R.	211	Knopf, Carl S.	495
Bard, Albert S.	769	Lancaster, Lane W.	265, 451
Barnett, James D.	283	Landman, Adrian M.	462
Barth, Harry	22	Lien, Arnold J.	139
Beard, Charles A.	726	Locke, Fred H.	460
Beard, William	499	Lovett, W. P.	179, 788
Beck, Horace P.	358		
Bing, Alexander M.	142	MacLaurin, R. D.	257, 504
Boland, F. H.	214	Malcom, Roy	616
Briggs, George N.	203	Manning, J. W.	511
Brownlow, Louis	136	Martin, Edward M.	255, 663
Bunche, Ralph Johnson	261	McGoldrick, Joseph	567
		Merkel, George C.	199
Cornick, Philip H.	680	Miller, H. J.	469
Crandall, Esther	268	Morgan, John T.	27
		Mosher, W. E.	613, 712, 781
Epexigeticus	309	Munro, William B.	80, 738
Evans, Harold	586		
		Nanry, William H.	147
Forbes, Russell	722		
Ford, George B.	465	Olmsted, H. M.	311
Freeman, Harry H.	13	Overstreet, H. A.	135
Goodrich, E. P.	181	Pollock, James K., Jr.	67, 389
Gross, A. H.	357	Powell, Charles V.	280
Gulick, Luther	12		
		Ramsey, Russell	7
Harris, Joseph P.	153	Rankin, R. S.	114
Havenner, George C.	326	Reed, Thomas H.	616
Henderson, Alfred	20	Ridley, Clarence E.	150, 553
Henderson, Harold L.	113, 716	Rightor, C. E.	119, 328, 393, 751
Herman, S. James	732	Robson, William A.	207
Herrick, Charles	359	Rosewater, Victor	77
Hieatt, C. C.	391		
Hinckley, Thomas L.	226	Sharp, Walter R.	741
Horack, Frank E.	236	Simpson, Herbert D.	405, 522, 593, 690
Hormell, Orren C.	363	Sly, John F.	220
Hulse, Granvyl G.	311	Smith, Bruce	33
Huus, Randolph O.	18, 69, 179, 357	Smith, E. E.	514
		Stark, C. W.	684
James, Harlean	456, 508	Stewart, Frank M.	317
Jones, O. Garfield	578		

Stone, Donald C. 157
Strong, Howard 360
Swisher, J. A. 551

Tanzer, Laurence Arnold 9
Telford, Fred 61, 115, 116
Tooke, C. W. 555
Trexler, Harrison A. 490
Tucker, Robert H. 673

Upson, Lent D. 119, 393, 721

Vanderbosch, A. 200
Van Nuys, M. H. 551

Walker, Harvey 713
Waltersdorf, M. C. 321
Wells, Roger H. 15, 397, 473
Wilcox, Delos F. 74
Woodruff, Clinton Rogers 87, 578

TITLES AND SUBJECTS

Accounting, Depreciation in Commercial
and Municipal 462
Administrative Consolidation:
Administrative Reorganization Adopt-
ed in California 220
Centralization of New York City
Government—Can It Be Made
Workable? 280
Connecticut Consolidates State Finan-
cial Control 265
State Administrative Reorganization
and the University of Minnesota . . . 713
Virginia Reorganization Program,
The 673
Virginia Revises State Constitution . . . 448
Advertising, Regulations of Business—
Control over 702
Airports:
Airports as a Factor in City Planning . 181
Home Rule—Aviation Field Held to
Be a Public Utility 604
Municipal Functions—Airports 238
New Municipal Airport for Cincin-
nati, A 717
Air Traffic, Municipal Aid for 783
Appraisal of Urban Land and Buildings,
A New Book on the 680
Appraising Public Reports 150
Assessments:
Detroit Bureau of Governmental
Research 548
Kansas City Public Service Institute 709
New Book on the Appraisal of Urban
Land and Buildings, A 680
Special Assessments—Applied to Or-
namental Street Lighting 700
Special Assessment Bonds Now Gen-
eral Obligations in Iowa 195
Tax Situation in Chicago, The . 522, 593, 690
Assize of Buildings, Fitz-Elwyne's 555

Attack on Cleveland's Council-Manager
Charter 69
Baldwin Prize:
Awards, 1928 447
The following topics have been se-
lected 387
Beccari Garbage Disposal System In-
stalled in Florida 717
Berkeley Adopts Health Examinations
for City Employees 787
Billboards:
Falmouth Billboard Decision, The . . . 769
Zoning—Exclusion of Industrial Signs
in Residence Districts 170
Birmingham's New City Commission . . . 490
Bonds:
Bonded Debt of 213 Cities, The 328
Bonds; Necessity of Complying with
Prescribed Formalities 771
City's Liability on Street Improve-
ment Bonds in Iowa, The 236
Special Assessment Bonds Now Gen-
eral Obligations in Iowa 195
Special Assessments—Direct Liability
of City on Bonds Issued 237, 345
Bordeaux, The Public Personnel Policy
of the Municipality of 741
Boston:
Service Charge Rejected in Boston
Gas Rates, The 302
Traffic Control 661
Budget:
California Taxpayers' Association 429
Detroit Bureau of Governmental
Research 548
Indianapolis Chamber of Commerce . . 778
Laboratory Course in Budget Making,
A 292

Long Term Budgeting and the City
  Plan........................ 465
Model Municipal Budget Law, A.... 437
New Bedford Taxpayers' Association,
  The........................ 432
Schenectady Bureau of Municipal
  Research...................549, 779
Taxpayers' Association of New Mexico 549
Buffalo Adopts a New Charter—Aban-
  dons Commission Government.... 13
Building:
  Fitz-Elwyne's Assize of Buildings.... 555
  Schenectady Bureau of Municipal
    Research...................488, 779
  Building Height to Street Traffic, The
    Relation of.................405, 450
  Building Lines, Authority of Towns to
    Establish................... 299
  Bureaucratic Control Over English
    Municipalities Increased......... 64
Buses:
  Buses and Trolleys in Newark....... 172
  Municipally Owned Bus System Re-
    places Street Cars.............. 199
  Right of Municipalities in Rate Cases,
    The........................ 105
Business Frontage and City Growth.... 197

California:
  Administrative Reorganization
    Adopted in California.......... 220
  California Taxpayers' Association.... 429
Canada, Citizens' Research Institute
  of........................176, 352
Centralized Purchasing:
  As a consequence of centralized pur-
    chasing..................... 133
  Des Moines Bureau of Municipal
    Research.................... 709
  Schenectady Bureau of Municipal
    Research.................... 779
Charters:
  Buffalo Adopts a New Charter—
    Abandons Commission Govern-
    ment....................... 13
  City Charter Movement in Milwau-
    kee........................ 113
  Cleveland Charter Election........ 312
  Defeat of the Westchester County
    Charter, The................. 9
  Meaning of the Recent Cleveland
    Charter Crisis, The............ 387
  Milwaukee's Citizen City Charter
    Movement................... 716

Minneapolis Charter Changes De-
  feated....................... 490
New City Manager Charters........ 785
Newport C. M. Charter Again Meets
  Defeat by State Politicians....... 358
Subcommittee of the Duluth Charter
  Commission, A................. 436
Toledo's Charter Ready for Novem-
  ber Election.................. 554
Toledo to Submit Two Charters to
  Referendum in November........ 616
Chicago:
  Chicago Government Planning Asso-
    ciation..................... 310
  Cleaning Up Chicago Politics....... 785
  Negro in Chicago Politics, The...... 261
  Newly formed Chicago Institute of
    Local Politics, The............. 133
  Our American Mayors:
    XIII. William Hale Thompson of
      Chicago: the Saga of a
      Sombrero............... 663
  Prayers and Pineapples in Chicago
    Politics..................... 255
  Tax Situation in Chicago, The.522, 593, 690
China, Municipal Research Abandoned
  in.......................... 54
Cincinnati:
  Cincinnati Moves Towards County
    Manager Government.......... 491
  Cincinnati's Second Councilmanic
    Election under Its City-Manager–
    Proportional Representation Char-
    ter........................ 59
  Cincinnati Surveys Its Police....... 157
  City Manager Sherrill has recom-
    mended..................... 248
  Civic Education in Cincinnati through
    the Radio................... 717
  How City Manager Personalities
    Figured in Two Elections........ 18
  New Municipal Airport for Cincin-
    nati, A..................... 717
  1928 Convention at Cincinnati, The 721
  Party Responsibility Under National
    Party Emblem................ 198
City-County (see also County):
  Consolidation of the tax assessment.. 1
  Proposed Consolidation of St. Louis
    City and County.............. 489
  Sixteen boroughs in Pennsylvania.... 133
City Manager:
  Albion, Michigan, Abolishes City
    Manager Government.......... 491

Attack on Cleveland's Council-Manager Charter, The 69
Charter commission has been 133
Cincinnati's Second Councilmanic Election under Its City-Manager–Proportional Representation Charter 59
City Manager in Election Campaigns, The 4
Cleveland Charter Election 312
Cleveland Women Voters Save Proportional Representation–Council-Manager Plan 357
Consolidation of the tax assessment . 1
Dublin's Proposed Manager-Council Plan 214
Fifteenth Annual Convention of the International City Managers' Association 618
How City Manager Personalities Figured in Two Elections 18
Meaning of the Recent Cleveland Charter Crisis, The 387
New City Manager Charters 785
New Effort to Repeal Cleveland Charter 179
Newport C. M. Charter Again Meets Defeat by State Politicians 358
On December 6, Tampa, Fla 2
Politics in Circle City, Oklahoma 22
Progress towards City Manager Adoptions 311
Renewed Charter Activity in Newport 180
Resignations of California City Managers 662
Sixteen boroughs in Pennsylvania 133
Stephen B. Story, First City Manager of Rochester 60
Stephen B. Story has begun his term 63
Students of city manager government 63
Subcommittee of the Duluth Charter Commission, A 436
Toledo's Charter Ready for November Election 554
Toledo to Submit Two Charters to Referendum in November 616
Unsuccessful Recall Attempted in Greensboro 114
Wichita to Clean House 248
City Planning:
Airports as a Factor in City Planning .. 181
Business Frontage and City Growth .. 197
City Plan—Control of Regulation of Plats in Outlying Districts 344

Color in City Planning 613
Control of Streets in Outlying Districts under the City Plan, The 167
Economic Factors in City Planning .. 738
E. M. Bassett to Aid in Formation of New York City Plan Commission .. 787
Footnotes and Fieldnotes in Old England 12
Long Term Budgeting and the City Plan 465
Municipal Land Policies and Their Application to City Planning and Housing 226
New York City Committee on Plan and Survey Issues Report 492
New York's First Satellite Town 142
Pennsylvania Association of Planning Commissioners, The 249
Planning Play Areas in Private Subdivisions 391
Relation of Building Height to Street Traffic 405
Royal Commission on London Squares 252
City's Place in Civilization, The 726
Civic Education in Cincinnati through the Radio 717
Civic Ideals of Long Ago 495
Civil Service:
Alameda County Civil Service Commission Defines Its Functions 116
Berkeley Adopts Health Examinations for City Employees 787
Civil Service and Prohibition 252
Civil Service—Construction of the Constitution of Ohio 346
Classification and Compensation Studies 61
Informal Conference on the Personnel Problem of the United States Government 715
N. A. L. G. O. 87
N. A. L. G. O. a Trustee for the Merit System in English Local Government 65
Officers — Compensation — Constitutional Inhibition against Increase of Compensation During Term Held Not to Apply to Municipal Officers 99
Personnel Legislation in 1927 61
Program for Next Meeting of the Assembly of Civil Service Commissions 116

Public Personnel Policy of the Municipality of Bordeaux The........ 741
Retirement Legislation............ 62
Right of a Citizen to Inspect Federal Personnel Records Denied....... 115
St. Louis Bureau of Municipal Research....................... 57
Salaries of Policemen and Firemen in Thirty-Five Cities, 1928........ 268
Schenectady Bureau of Municipal Research...................488, 549
Cleveland:
Attack on Cleveland's Council-Manager Charter, The.............. 69
Citizen Interest in Regional Government......................... 175
Citizens' League of Cleveland, The.. 134
Cleveland Charter Election....... 312
Cleveland Water Supply and Rates.. 173
Cleveland Women Voters Save Proportional Representation–Council-Manager Plan.................. 357
Future of Cleveland's Municipal Light Plant.................. 775
How City Manager Personalities Figured in Two Elections.......... 18
Meaning of the Recent Cleveland Charter Crisis, The............. 387
New Effort to Repeal Cleveland Charter... 179
Problem of the government of...... 1
Progress of Regional Government in Cleveland..................... 361
Color in City Planning. City and Regional Planning................ 613
Commissions and Courts as Experts.... 706
Commission Government:
Birmingham's New City Commission 490
Buffalo Adopts a New Charter—Abandons Commission Government...................... 13
Commonwealth Conference at the State University of Iowa, The Sixth 551
Comparative Tax Rates of 237 Cities, 1928...................... 751
Compensation—Constitutional Inhibition against Increase of Compensation During Term Held Not to Apply to Municipal Officers...... 99
Conciliation Court, Des Moines Tries the.......................... 211
Condemnation of Public Property Therefor, Streets and Highways... 300

Connecticut:
Connecticut Consolidates State Financial Control................. 265
Democratic Party in Connecticut, The 451
Consolidations at Reproduction Cost.. 174
Constitutional Limitations—Basis of Classification of Cities.......... 98
Convening the Special Session—Oklahoma's Predicament............ 751
Coöperation Between the Federal and State Governments.............. 283
County (see also City-County):
Counties—Legislative Power to Exclude Park Territory from County System...................... 700
Parks—Capacity of Counties to Administer..................... 606
County Budget. California Taxpayers' Association................ 429
County Government:
Cincinnati Moves Towards County Manager Government........... 491
County Consolidation in Tennessee.. 511
Defeat of the Westchester-County Charter, The.................. 9
Fee System Receives Setback in Kentucky, The.................... 200
Kansas City Public Service Institute 709
Courts:
Des Moines Tries the Conciliation Court........................ 211
To Reform Philadelphia Magistrates' Courts....................... 248
Crime:
Detroit Bureau of Governmental Research........................ 55
Municipal Program for Combating Crime, A...................... 33
To Study Classification and Reporting of Crimes................... 115
Cryer of Los Angeles, Mayor George E. Our American Mayors.......... 27

Dallas Adopts Long-Term Financial Program...................... 64
Defeat of the Westchester County Charter....................... 9
Democratic Party in Connecticut, The 451
Depreciation in Commercial and Municipal Accounting.............. 462
Des Moines:
Des Moines Bureau of Municipal Research...................... 709

Des Moines Tries the Conciliation
Court........................ 211
Detroit:
Detroit Bureau of Governmental
Research.....................55, 548
Detroit Railways Reported Finan-
cially Successful................ 249
Survey of Housing in Detroit, A.... 715
Does Zoning Protect Only the Aesthetic
Sense?........................ 504
Dublin's Proposed Manager-Council
Plan........:................. 214

Economic Factors in City Planning.... 738
Economy, False Notions of.......... 426
Education:
Civic Education in Cincinnati through
the Radio..................... 717
Education for Public Administration 712
Laboratory Course in Budget Mak-
ing, A....................... 292
Laboratory Work in Municipal Citi-
zenship...................... 580
Efficiency in Government............ 712
Election Campaigns:
"Anti-Hague" Bills Pass in New Jer-
sey.......................... 714
Attack on Cleveland's Council-Man-
ager Charter, The.............. 69
Cincinnati's Second Councilmanic
Election under Its City Manager-
Proportional Representation Char-
ter.......................... 59
City Manager in Election Campaigns,
The.......................... 4
Cleveland Charter Election........ 312
French Parliamentary Elections and
the New Electoral Law, The...... 389
Hamburg Election, The........... 15
How City Manager Personalities Fig-
ured in Two Elections.......... 18
Labor Party Gains in Municipal
Elections in Britain............ 67
Mayor Landes Defeated for Reëlec-
tion......................... 311
Politics in Circle City, Oklahoma... 22
Recent Municipal Elections in Eng-
land, The..................... 207
Results of New Jersey's "Anti-
Hague" Bills.................. 788
Electricity (see Public Utilities):
Eminent Domain:
Eminent Domain—Attempt to Limit
by Contract.................. 46

Eminent Domain—Excess Condem-
nation...................... 771
England (see also Great Britain and
London):
Bureaucratic Control Over English
Municipalities Increased........ 64
Education for Public Administration 712
English Local Government........ 614
Footnotes and Fieldnotes in Old
England..................... 12
Labor Party Gains in Municipal Elec-
tions in Britain............... 67
Municipal Cleansing............. 783
N. A. L. G. O.................. 87
N. A. L. G. O., a Trustee for the Merit
System in English Local Govern-
ment....................... 65
Preservation of Rural England..... 613
Public Printing................. 784
Recent Municipal Elections in Eng-
land, The.................... 207
Reorganization of Local Government 781
Toward the Single Tax........... 781
Wider Use of Electricity.......... 781
Excess Condemnation, Eminent Do-
main....................... 771
Exemption of Municipal Property—
Zoning..................... 606

Fare:
Five Cent Fare Before the Supreme
Court, The................... 703
Further Developments in the New
York Subway Litigation......... 428
New Fare Cases................. 704
New York City Loses First Court De-
cision on Subway Fares......... 348
New York Faces 7-Cent Fare....... 314
New York's Five Cent Fare in Jeop-
ardy....................... 134
San Francisco Municipal Railway,
The....................... 147
Federal Government:
Coöperation Between the Federal and
State Governments............. 283
Federal Aid to the States......... 619
Proposed Limit to the Jurisdiction of
the Federal Courts............ 704
Right of a Citizen to Inspect Federal
Personnel Records Denied....... 115
Special Assessments—Original Juris-
diction of Federal Courts........ 701
Fee System Receives Setback in Ken-
tucky, The................... 200

Finance:
Connecticut Consolidates State Financial Control.................. 265
Dallas Adopts Long-term Financial Program....................... 64
Long-term Budgeting and the City Plan.......................... 465
Milwaukee Citizens' Bureau........ 611
Schenectady Bureau of Municipal Research....................488, 612
Schenectady Mayor Appoints Commission on Long-term Financial Program....................... 489
Standards of Financial Administration............................ 119
"Standards of Financial Administration" Defended................. 393
Firemen in Thirty-Five Cities, 1928, Salaries of Policemen and........ 268
Fire Prevention Pays, Grand Rapids Proves That.................... 460
Fire School, First Annual Northwest.. 489
Fitz-Elwyne's Assize of Buildings..... 555
Footnotes and Fieldnotes in Old England.......................... 12
France:
French Parliamentary Elections and the New Electoral Law, The...... 389
Public Personnel Policy of the Municipality of Bordeaux, The...... 741
Franchise Rights—Grants in Perpetuity......................... 300
Fund for the Study of Public Administration at Yale............... 787

Garbage Disposal System Installed in Florida, Beccari................. 717
Gas (see Public Utilities):
Gasoline:
Gasoline Storage—Requirement of Subsurface Tanks Upheld........ 702
Municipal Functions—Sale of Gasoline........................... 46
Police Power—Restriction Excluding Gasoline Stations from Certain Districts...................... 100
Streets and Highways—Abatement of Gasoline Pumps.............. 100
Germany:
Centralization and Decentralization. 613
Efficiency in Government.......... 712
Hamburg Election, The............ 15
Management of Electrical Industry . 782
Municipal Aid for Air Traffic........ 783

Partisanship and Parties in German Municipal Government.......... 473
Proportional Representation in German Cities.................... 397
State and Local Government in Germany..................... 712
Going after the Municipal Tax Dollar.. 497
Government Costs. Citizens' Research Institute of Canada............. 352
Graft. Queens High in New York City. 309
Grand Rapids Proves That Fire Prevention Pays.................. 460
Grants in Perpetuity, Franchise Rights 300
Great Britain (see also England):
Electricity in Great Britain—A Study in Administration.............. 363
Million Small Houses for Great Britain, A........................ 456
Greensboro, Unsuccessful Recall Attempted in................... 114

Hague, Frank:
"Anti-Hague" Bills Pass in New Jersey...................... 714
Mayor-Boss of Jersey City. Our American Mayors.............. 514
Results of New Jersey's "Anti-Hague" Bills................. 788
Hamburg Election, The............. 15
Health (see Public Health):
Hetch Hetchy Water Supply Project, San Francisco Finally Adopts..... 447
Hodgson of St. Paul, Mayor Laurence C. Our American Mayors........... 203
Holcombe of Houston, Mayor Oscar F. Our American Mayors.......... 317
Holding Company:
Example of Holding Company Influences in St. Louis............. 607
Oklahoma to Regulate Holding Companies....................... 607
Holland Tunnel (see Traffic):
Home Rule:
Bureaucratic Control Over English Municipalities Increased........ 64
Home Rule—Aviation Field Held to Be a Public Utility............. 604
Home Rule—Municipal Affairs—Maintenance of Public Library Held to Be a State Function...... 299
Home Rule—Municipal Ownership—Conflicting Decisions in Ohio...... 538
Home Rule—No Power to Authorize Discharge of Tax Liens.......... 46

Illinois Cities Want More Home Rule 60
Newly formed Chicago Institute of
Local Politics. 133
Housing:
Experts Study Housing Problem 719
Housing for the Small Wage Earner
in Michigan. 435
Michigan Housing Association Com-
pletes Its First Task. 552
Million Small Houses for Great Brit-
ain, A. 456
Municipal Land Policies and Their
Application to City Planning and
Housing. 226
New York's First Satellite Town. 142
Regional Credits Proposed in Lieu of
Municipal Recognition of Housing
as a Public Utility. 732
Survey of Housing in Detroit, A 715
Houston. Our American Mayors: X.
Mayor Oscar F. Holcombe. 317
How City Manager Personalities Fig-
ured in Two Elections. 18
Hydro-Electric Power Policies in On-
tario and Quebec. 102

Implied Powers—City Held without
Power to Lease Rooms in Memo-
rial Building to a Patriotic Society. 101
Indiana Public Service Commission
Limits Rate Case Expense. 351
Influencing Public Opinion. 135
Institute of Municipal Administration. . 616
Institute of Public Affairs, University
of Virginia. 616
Iowa:
City's Liability on Street Improve-
ment.Bonds in Iowa, The. 236
New Offense Against Public Welfare,
A. 315
Progress of Permanent Registration
for Elections, The. 153
Sixth Commonwealth Conference at
the State University of Iowa, The. . 551
Special Assessment Bonds Now Gen-
eral Obligations in Iowa. 195
Is the Slacker Vote a Menace?. 80

Jersey City, Frank Hague: Mayor-
Boss of. Our American Mayors. . 514

Kansas City, Kansas, The Municipal
Light Plant of. 714

Kansas City, Mo.:
Kansas City Public Service Institute
431, 709
Students of city manager government 63
Kentucky. Fee System Receives Set-
back in Kentucky, The. 200

Laboratory Course in Budget Making,
A. 292
Laboratory Work in Municipal Citizen-
ship. 580
Labor Party Gains in Municipal Elec-
tions in Britain. 67
Land Policies and Their Application to
City Planning and Housing, Munic-
ipal. 226
Landes Defeated for Reëlection, Mayor 311
Legislative Control:
Legislative Control — Constitutional
Limitation Requiring General Laws 770
Legislative Control over Wages on
Municipal Works. 345
Library:
Home Rule—Municipal Affairs—
Maintenance of Public Library
Held to Be a State Function. 299
Philadelphia's Free Library. 578
Liens. Public Buildings—Statutory
Liens in Favor of Laborers and
Material Men. 604
Logansport Telephone Case. 609
London:
London Region, The. 508
Royal Commission on London Squares 252
Long Island Commutation Case De-
cided, The. 242
Long-Term Budgeting and the City
Plan. 465

Magistrates' Courts, To Reform Phila-
delphia. 248
Massachusetts: Classification and Com-
pensation Studies. 61
Mayors:
Do Cities Need Two Mayors?. 316
Our American Mayors:
VIII. Mayor George E. Cryer of
Los Angeles. 27
IX. Mayor Laurence C. Hodgson
of St. Paul. 203
X. Mayor Oscar F. Holcombe
of Houston. 317
XI. Frank Hague, Mayor-Boss of
Jersey City. 514

XII. "Jimmy" Walker......... 567
XIII. William Hale Thompson of Chicago: the Saga of a Sombrero 663
Metropolitan Area, The New York.... 63
Metropolitan Government:
Dublin's Proposed Manager-Council Plan......................... 214
Problem of...................... 1
Michigan:
Campaign for Permanent Registration in Michigan................ 788
Control of Streets in Outlying Districts under the City Plan, The... 167
Housing for the Small Wage Earner in Michigan................... 435
Michigan Housing Association Completes Its First Task........... 552
Million Small Houses for Great Britain, A........................... 456
Milwaukee:
City Charter Movement in Milwaukee........................... 113
Milwaukee Citizens' Bureau........ 611
Milwaukee's Citizen City Charter Movement.................... 716
Minneapolis:
Minneapolis Charter Changes Defeated....................... 490
Minneapolis Loses Through Antique Street Maintenance Methods..... 469
Minnesota:
First Annual Northwest Fire School 489
State Administrative Reorganization and the University of Minnesota.. 713
Model Municipal Budget Law, A..... 437
Model Municipal Traffic Ordinance... 684
Municipal Administration, Institute of 616
Municipal Affairs—Maintenance of Public Library Held to Be a State Function, Home Rule.......... 299
Municipal Aid for Air Traffic......... 783
Municipal Airport for Cincinnati, A New...................... 717
Municipal Cleansing............... 783
Municipal Contracts. Philadelphia Bureau of Municipal Research...... 779
Municipal Corporation. Definition— The Municipal Concept.......... 541
Municipal Land Policies and their Application to City Planning and Housing......................... 226

Municipal Ownership:
Ashtabula, Ohio, Retains Municipal Ownership of Electric Light Plant.. 113
City Government Without General Tax Levy..................... 447
Detroit Railways Reported Financially Successful............... 249
Future of Cleveland's Municipal Light Plant................... 775
Home Rule—Municipal Ownership —Conflicting Decisions in Ohio.... 538
Municipal Light Plant of Kansas City, Kansas, The.............. 714
Municipally Owned Bus System Replaces Street Cars.............. 199
Municipal Ownership—Contract Rates........................ 425
Municipal Ownership—Power to Dispose of Plants.................. 539
Municipal Ownership—Proprietary Obligations of City............. 299
New Municipal Airport for Cincinnati, A........................... 717
Philadelphia Plans a City Theatre... 250
Public Printing................. 784
San Francisco Municipal Railway, The......................... 147
San Francisco Proposes a New Plan for Municipal Operation.......... 74
Municipal Program for Combating Crime, A...................... 33
Municipal Reporting. Appraising Public Reports..................... 150
Municipal Theatre. Philadelphia Plans a City Theatre............... 250
Municipal Works, Legislative Control over Wages on................. 345

N. A. L. G. O...................... 87
N. A. L. G. O.. a Trustee for the Merit System in English Local Government 65
National Municipal League:
1928 Convention at Cincinnati, The.. 721
Report on Work of the National Municipal League.............. 722
Thirty-Third Annual Meeting of the National Municipal League....... 7
Negro in Chicago Politics, The........ 261
New Bedford Taxpayers' Association, The......................... 432
New Haven Railroad. Decision in New Haven Commutation Reaffirmed... 544

New Jersey:
"Anti-Hague" Bills Pass in New Jersey............................ 714
New Jersey Adopts Uniform Traffic Laws......................... 617
Results of New Jersey's "Anti-Hague" Bills.......................... 788
New Mexico, Taxpayers' Association of 549
New York City:
Build Subways to Decentralize, Regional Plan Advises............. 435
Centralization of New York City Government—Can It Be Made Workable?..................... 280
Decision in New Haven Commutation Reaffirmed................. 544
E. M. Bassett to Aid in Formation of New York City Plan Commission... 787
Five Cent Fare Before the Supreme Court, The.................... 703
$522,000,000 Utility Merger, A...... 609
Further Developments in the New York Subway Litigation.......... 428
Holland Tunnel—An Engineering Achievement, The.............. 5
Long Island Commutation Case Decided, The..................... 242
New Fare Cases.................. 704
New Transit Complications in New York......................... 171
New York City Board of Health, The. 63
New York City Committee on Plan and Survey Issues Report........ 492
New York City Loses First Court Decision on Subway Fares....... 348
New York City Relaxes Zoning Regulations.................... 491
New York Faces 7-Cent Fare........ 314
New York's First Satellite Town.... 142
New York's Five Cent Fare in Jeopardy......................... 134
New York Law Prohibiting Gas Service Charge Unconstitutional... 51
New York metropolitan area........ 63
New York Rapid Transit "Movies," The........................... 240
Our American Mayors. XII. "Jimmy" Walker....................... 567
Queens High in New York City..... 309
Six Months of the Holland Tunnel.. 713
Utility Consolidation and the Public Interest...................... 542
Non-partisan Elections. The Rochester city council................ 195

Notes on Public Personnel Management 61
Nuisances:
Does Zoning Protect Only the Aesthetic Sense?................... 504
Torts—Liability for Nuisance Existing in Street................... 48
Where Zoning Fails.............. 257

Ontario and Quebec, Hydro-Electric Power Policies in.............. 102
Our American Mayors:
VIII. Mayor George E. Cryer of Los Angeles................. 27
IX. Mayor Laurence C. Hodgson of St. Paul................. 203
X. Mayor Oscar F. Holcombe of Houston................. 317
XI. Frank Hague: Mayor-Boss of Jersey City............... 514
XII. "Jimmy" Walker........... 567
XIII. William Hale Thompson of Chicago: The Saga of a Sombrero................... 663

Parks:
Counties—Legislative Power to Exclude Park Territory from County System..................... 700
Economics of Recreation........... 720
Parks—Capacity of Counties to Administer...................... 606
Royal Commission on London Squares 252
Torts—Liability for Negligence in Care of Parks................. 425
Parliamentary Elections and the New Electoral Law, The French....... 389
Parties:
Democratic Party in Connecticut, The.......................... 451
Partisanship and Parties in German Municipal Government.......... 473
Party Responsibility Under National Party Emblem................. 198
Pay-as-You-Go Plan:
Detroit Bureau of Governmental Research..................... 55
San Francisco Finally Adopts Hetch Hetchy Water Supply Project.... 447
Pensions:
Kansas City Public Service Institute. 709
St. Louis Bureau of Municipal Research....................... 779
Permanent Registration:
Campaign for Permanent Registration in Michigan.................. 788

Kansas City Public Service Institute. 709
Progress of Permanent Registration
  for Elections, The.............. 153
Proposal to Cure Vote-Shirking, A... 77
Philadelphia:
  Philadelphia Bureau of Municipal
    Research...................... 779
  Philadelphia's Free Library........ 578
  Philadelphia Plans a City Theatre... 250
  Philadelphia Rapid Transit and the
    New Subways.................. 241
  Philadelphia's Street Railway Prob-
    lems.......................... 586
  Regional Planning Federation of the
    Philadelphia Tri-State District, The 360
  To Reform Philadelphia Magistrates'
    Courts........................ 248
Police:
  Cincinnati Surveys Its Police....... 157
  Municipal Program for Combating
    Crime, A..................... 33
  Police Power—Authority of Towns to
    Establish Building Lines......... 299
  Police Power—Exercise Subject to
    Admiralty Law................. 344
  Police Power—Limitation of Rates of
    Public Utilities by Contract....... 47
  Police Power—Public Taxicab Stand
    on Railroad Property............ 238
  Police Power—Reasonable Regulation
    of Business or of Social Activities.. 238
  Police Power—Regulation of Oil Wells
    within City Limits.............. 345
  Police Power—Restriction Excluding
    Gasoline Stations from Certain
    Districts...................... 100
  Police Power—Vested Rights of a
    Property Owner in a Street Number 99
  Police Power—Vested Right of a
    Property Owner in a Street Num-
    ber.......................... 170
  Policewoman's Sphere, The......... 136
  St. Louis Bureau of Municipal Re-
    search....................... 779
  Salaries of Policemen and Firemen
    in Thirty-Five Cities, 1928........ 268
  Wichita, Kan., has undertaken an... 314
Politics:
  Cleaning Up Chicago Politics....... 785
  Democratic Party in Connecticut, The 451
  Hamburg Election, The............ 15
  Labor Party Gains in Municipal
    Elections in Britain.............. 67
  Negro in Chicago Politics, The...... 261

Partisanship and Parties in German
  Municipal Government.......... 473
Politics in Circle City, Oklahoma.... 22
Prayers and Pineapples in Chicago
  Politics....................... 255
Power:
  Doctor Beard on the "Power Trust". 493
  Federal Investigation of Electric
    Power...................... 2
  $522,000,000 Utility Merger, A...... 609
  Hydro-Electric Power Policies in
    Ontario and Quebec............ 102
  Utility Consolidation and the Public
    Interest...................... 542
  Who are the Propagandists?........ 546
Prayers and Pineapples in Chicago
  Politics....................... 255
Progress of Permanent Registration for
  Elections..................... 153
Proportional Representation:
  Annual Meeting of the Proportional
    Representation League.......... 566
  Cincinnati's Second Councilmanic
    Election under Its City-Manager-
    Proportional-Representation Charter 59
  City Charter Movement in Mil-
    waukee...................... 113
  Cleveland Women Voters Save Pro-
    portional-Representation–Council-
    Manager Plan................. 357
  French Parliamentary Elections and
    the New Electoral Law, The...... 389
  Proportional Representation in Ger-
    man Cities................... 397
Proposal to Cure Vote-Shirking, A..... 77
Public Buildings—Statutory Liens in
  Favor of Laborers and Material
  Men........................ 604
Public Health:
  Berkeley Adopts Health Examinations
    for City Employees............. 787
  New York City Board of Health, The 63
  Planning Play Areas in Private Sub-
    divisions..................... 391
Public Machinery, Reading Appoints
  Supervisor of.................. 617
Public Opinion, Influencing.......... 135
Public Ownership (see Municipal Own-
  ership):
Public Personnel Policy of the Munici-
  pality of Bordeaux............. 741
Public Purposes—Power to Expend
  Money for Patriotic Celebrations .. 344

Public Utilities (see also Municipal Ownership, Power, and Rates):
Commissions and Courts as Experts.. 706
Consolidations at Reproduction Cost 174
Each Utility on Its Own Feet...... 104
Electric Bond and Share Refuses to Answer....................... 774
Electricity in Great Britain—A Study in Administration.............. 363
Example of Holding Company Influences in St. Louis............. 607
False Notions of Economy........ 426
Financial Investigation under the Walsh Resolution.............. 706
Franchise Rights—Grants in Perpetuity........................ 300
Is the Small Electric Plant Doomed?. 316
League of Women Voters to Study Public Utility Regulation........ 351
Logansport Telephone Case........ 609
Management of Electrical Industry.. 782
Massachusetts Basis—Prudent Investment or What?............. 104
Oklahoma to Regulate Holding Companies....................... 607
Proposed Limit to the Jurisdiction of the Federal Courts.............. 704
Public Utility Propaganda on Grand Scale...................... 350
Regional Credits Proposed in Lieu of Municipal Recognition of Housing as a Public Utility.............. 732
San Francisco Proposes a New Plan for Municipal Operation........ 74
Strikes in Public Utilities.......... 3
Wider Use of Electricity........... 781
Public Welfare:
Conference on Public Welfare Statistics........................ 246
New Offense Against Public Welfare, A............................ 315
Public Works:
Public Works to Check Unemployment......................... 196
Reading Appoints Supervisor of Public Machinery................. 617

Quebec, Hydro-Electric Power Policies in Ontario and.................. 102
Queens Borough. Queens High in New York City.................... 309

Radburn, New York's First Satellite Town........................ 142

Radio:
Civic Education in Cincinnati through the Radio 717
New Offense Against Public Welfare, A............................. 315
Rates:
Appeal of the O'Fallon Case, The... 102
Cleveland Water Supply and Rates.. 173
Decision in New Haven Commutation Reaffirmed.................... 544
Each Utility on Its Own Feet...... 104
Indiana Public Service Commission Limits Rate Case Expense....... 351
Massachusetts Basis—Prudent Investment or What?.............. 104
New York Law Prohibiting Gas Service Charge Unconstitutional...... 51
O'Fallon Case Before the Supreme Court....................... 773
Police Power—Limitation of Rates of Public Utilities by Contract...... 47
Principle of the Service Charge, The. 302
Rate of Return and Fixed Rate Base 705
Right of Municipalities in Rate Cases, The.......................... 105
St. Louis and O'Fallon Recapture Case, The..................... 50
Service Charge for Gas Consumers.. 427
Service Charge Rejected in Boston Gas Rates.................... 302
What is a Proper Service Charge?... 103
What Price Electricity for Our Homes?...................... 240
Reading Appoints Supervisor of Public Machinery.................... 617
Real Estate Tax Liens. Going After the Municipal Tax Dollar........ 497
Recall Attempted in Greensboro, Unsuccessful..................... 114
Recent Municipal Elections in England, The........................... 207
Recreation:
Economics of Recreation, The...... 720
Planning Play Areas in Private Subdivisions...................... 391
Regional Credits Proposed in Lieu of Municipal Recognition of Housing as a Public Utility.............. 732
Regional Government:
Centralization and Decentralization. 613
Citizen Interest in Regional Government........................... 175
London Region, The.............. 508
Problem of the government of...... 1

Progress of Regional Government in
 Cleveland...................... 361
Regional Planning:
 Build Subways to Decentralize, Re-
  gional Plan Advises............. 435
 By-Pass Highways Recommended... 250
 City and Regional Planning........ 613
 New York's First Satellite Town.... 142
 Regional Planning Federation of the
  Philadelphia Tri-State District, The 360
Relation of Building Height to Street
 Traffic........................ 405
Remedies—Waiver of Constitutional
 Defenses....................... 100
Reorganization of Local Government.. 781
Report on Work of the National Munic-
 ipal League.................... 722
Retirement Legislation.............. 62
Rochester, N. Y.:
 As a consequence of centralized pur-
  chasing....................... 133
 Rochester city council by vote...... 195
 Stephen B. Story First City Manager
  of Rochester.................. 60
 Stephen B. Story has begun his term. 63

Sacramento:
 Consolidation of the tax assessment.. 1
 Resignations of California City Mana-
  gers......................... 662
 Sacramento Creates Traffic and
  Safety Commission.............. 491
St. Louis, Mo.:
 Appeal of the O'Fallon Case, The... 102
 Example of Holding Company Influ-
  enees in St. Louis.............. 607
 O'Fallon Case Before the Supreme
  Court........................ 773
 Proposed Consolidation of St. Louis
  City and County............... 489
 St. Louis and O'Fallon Recapture
  Case, The..................... 50
 St. Louis Bureau of Municipal Re-
  search..................57, 178, 779
St. Paul, Mayor Laurence C. Hodgson
 of. Our American Mayors...... 203
Salaries of Policemen and Firemen in
 Thirty-Five Cities, 1928........ 268
San Francisco:
 San Francisco Finally Adopts Hetch
  Hetchy Water Supply Project.... 447
 San Francisco Municipal Railway,
  The.......................... 147

San Francisco Proposes A New Plan
 for Municipal Operation........ 74
Traffic Regulation a Hazardous
 Occupation.................... 491
Schenectady:
 Schenectady Bureau of Municipal Re-
  search...............488, 549, 612, 779
 Schenectady Mayor Appoints Com-
  mission on Long-Term Financial
  Program...................... 489
Seattle. Mayor Landes Defeated for
 Reëlection.................... 311
Service Charge (see Rates):
Sewage, Liability for Pollution of Wa-
 ters by....................... 605
Single Tax, Toward the............. 781
Special Assessments:
 More About Special Assessments in
  Washington:.................. 315
 Special Assessments—Applied to Or-
  namental Street Lighting........ 700
 Special Assessment Bonds Now Gen-
  eral Obligations in Iowa......... 195
 Special Assessments—Direct Liability
  of City...................... 299
 Special Assessments—Direct Liability
  of City on Bonds Issued.......237, 345
 Special Assessment Liens—Effect of
  Sale of Lands for State and County
  Taxes....................... 346
 Special Assessments—Original Juris-
  diction of Federal Courts........ 701
Standards of Financial Administration. 119
"Standards of Financial Administra-
 tion" Defended................ 393
State Constitution:
 Civil Service—Construction of the
  Constitution of Ohio........... 346
 Virginia Revises State Constitution.. 448
State Control of Traffic Supersedes
 Local Regulations, Streets and
 Highways..................... 169
State Government:
 Coöperation Between the Federal and
  State Governments............. 283
 State and Local Government in Ger-
  many........................ 712
State Legislature. Convening the Spe-
 cial Session—Oklahoma's Predica-
 ment........................ 139
State Reorganization:
 Administrative Reorganization Adopt-
  ed in California 220

Connecticut Consolidates State Financial Control.................... 265
State Administrative Reorganization and the University of Minnesota... 713
Virginia Reorganization Program, The 673
Virginia Revises State Constitution.. 448
Streets and Highways (see also Traffic):
Control of Streets in Outlying Districts under the City Plan, The.... 167
Minneapolis Loses Through Antique Street Maintenance Methods..... 469
Streets and Highways—Abatement of Gasoline Pumps............... 100
Streets and Highways—Abutter's Right to Continuance of Sidewalk.. 168
Streets and Highways—Condemnation of Public Property Therefor .. 300
Streets and Highways—Dedication; Adverse Possession.............. 605
Streets and Highways—Establishment of Taxicab Stand........... 101
Streets and Highways—Regulation of Vehicles for Hire............... 47
Streets and Highways—Removal of Encroachments at Suit of Private Citizen....................... 605
Streets and Highways—Rights of Abutting Owners............... 98
Streets and Highways—State Control of Traffic Supersedes Local Regulations....................... 169
Street Improvement Bonds in Iowa, The City's Liability on........... 236
Street Lighting, Special Assessments —Applied to Ornamental........ 700
Torts—Liability for Nuisance Existing in Street................... 48
Street Railways (see also Fare):
Appeal of the O'Fallon Case, The.... 102
Buses and Trolleys in Newark....... 172
Detroit Railways Reported Financially Successful................. 249
Municipally Owned Bus System Replaces Street Cars.............. 199
O'Fallon Case Before the Supreme Court....................... 773
Philadelphia's Street Railway Problems......................... 586
St. Louis and O'Fallon Recapture Case, The.................... 50
Tax Relief for Electric Street Railways......................... 321
Young on Street Railway Economics, Mr........................... 705

Strikes in Public Utilities............ 3
Subsidy. Federal Aid to the States.... 619
Subway (see also Fare):
Build Subways to Decentralize, Regional Plan Advises.............. 435
Supplements:
Airports as a Factor in City Planning 181
Electricity in Great Britain—A Study in Administration............... 363
Federal Aid to the States.......... 619
Fitz-Elwyne's Assize of Buildings... 555
Model Municipal Budget Law, A... 437
Standards of Financial Administration......................... 119

Taxes:
Citizens' Research Institute of Canada........................ 176
City Government Without General Tax Levy.................... 447
Comparative Tax Rates of 237 Cities, 1928....................... 751
Going After the Municipal Tax Dollar 497
St. Louis Bureau of Municipal Research....................... 178
Special Assessment Liens—Effect of Sale of Lands for State and County Taxes..................... 346
Tax Relief for Electric Street Railways......................... 321
Tax Situation in Chicago, The.522, 593, 690
Toward the Single Tax............ 781
Taxicabs—Extent of Control by City Authorities.................... 169
Tennessee, County Consolidation in.. 511
Thompson of Chicago, William Hale. Our American Mayors........... 663
Toledo:
New City Manager Charters....... 785
Toledo's Charter Ready for November Election.................... 554
Toledo to Submit Two Charters to Referendum in November........ 616
Torts:
Torts—Liability for Negligence in Care of Parks................. 425
Torts—Liability for Negligence in Care of School Property.......... 539
Torts—Liability for Nuisance Existing in Street................... 48
Torts—Liability for Pollution of Waters by Sewage 605
Torts—Proprietary and Governmental Functions.................. 424

Traffic (see also Streets and Highways):
By-Pass Highways Recommended... 250
Holland Tunnel—An Engineering
Achievement, The............. 5
Model Municipal Traffic Ordinance,
The.......................... 684
Municipal Aid for Air Traffic....... 783
New Jersey Adopts Uniform Traffic
Law.......................... 617
Relation of Building Height to Street
Traffic, The.................405, 450
Sacramento Creates Traffic and
Safety Commission............. 491
Six Months of the Holland Tunnel... 713
Taxicabs—Extent of Control by City
Authorities.................... 169
Traffic Control................... 661
Traffic Ordinances—Test of Reason-
ableness...................... 701
Traffic Regulation a Hazardous Oc-
cupation...................... 491
Traffic Relief through By-Pass High-
ways 499
Transit:
New Transit Complications in New
York......................... 171
New York's Five Cent Fare in Jeop-
ardy......................... 134
New York Rapid Transit "Movies",
The.......................... 240
Philadelphia Rapid Transit and the
New Subways.................. 241

Unemployment, Public Works to Check 196
United States:
Federal Aid to the States.......... 619
Informal Conference on the Personnel
Problem of the United States
Government................... 715

Virginia:
Institute of Public Affairs, University
of Virginia................... 616
Virginia Institute of Public Affairs,
The.......................... 249
Virginia Reorganization Program, The 673
Virginia Revises State Constitution.. 448
Voting:
Is the Slacker Vote a Menace?....... 80
Professor Munro Challenged on
Slacker Vote................. 179
Proposal to Cure Vote-Shirking, A... 77
Voteless Washington Expresses Itself 326

Walker, "Jimmy"—Our American May-
ors.......................... 567
Washington, D. C.:
More About Special Assessments in
Washington................... 315
Voteless Washington Expresses Itself 326
Water:
Cleveland Water Supply and Rates.. 173
San Francisco Finally Adopts Hetch
Hetchy Water Supply Project..... 447
Schenectady Bureau of Municipal Re-
search........................ 779
Torts—Liability for Pollution of
Waters by Sewage.............. 605
Westchester County Charter, The De-
feat of........................ 9
Where Zoning Fails................. 257
Wichita, Kan.:
Wichita has undertaken.......... 314
Wichita to Clean House........... 248
Wisconsin. The Progress of Permanent
Registration for Elections........ 153

Yale University, Fund for the Study of
Public Administration at........ 787

Zoning:
Business Frontage and City Growth.. 197
Does Zoning Protect Only the Aes-
thetic Sense?.................. 504
Falmouth Billboard Decision, The... 769
Has Zoning Failed?............... 359
New York City Relaxes Zoning Regu-
lations........................ 491
Police Power—Authority of Towns to
Establish Building Lines......... 299
Relation of Business Frontage to
Population.................... 180
Where Zoning Fails................ 257
Zoning—Comprehensive Ordinance
Upheld in Texas................ 423
Zoning—Control over Building on
Manufacturing Property Included
in Residence Districts 238
Zoning—Effect of Application for
Permit Prior to Enactment of Or-
dinance...................... 49
Zoning—Effect of General Empow-
ering Statute.................. 423
Zoning—Exclusion of Industrial Signs
in Residence Districts........... 170
Zoning—Exemption of Municipal-
Property..................... 606

Zoning—Limitation of Power by the
Supreme Court................ 423
Zoning—Location of Auxiliary Build-
ings........................ 344

Zoning—Power to Enact Temporary
Zoning Ordinance.............. 538
Zoning—Regulations Prescribing Min-
imum Height................. 170